Joseph Conrad

THE THREE LIVES

ALSO BY FREDERICK R. KARL

A Reader's Guide to Great Twentieth Century English Novels (*with Marvin Magalaner*) (*1959*)
A Reader's Guide to Joseph Conrad (*1960; revised edition, 1969*)
The Quest, a novel (*1961*)
The Contemporary English Novel (*1962; revised edition, 1972*)
C. P. Snow: The Politics of Conscience (*1963*)
An Age of Fiction: The Nineteenth Century British Novel (*1964; revised edition, 1972; paperback edition: A Reader's Guide to the Nineteenth Century British Novel)*
The Adversary Literature: The English Novel in the Eighteenth Century. A Study in Genre (*1974; paperback edition: A Reader's Guide to the Eighteenth Century English Novel)*

EDITED:
Joseph Conrad: A Collection of Criticism (*1975*)
The Mayor of Casterbridge by Thomas Hardy (*1966*)
The Portable Conrad (*Morton Dauwen Zabel's edition, revised, 1969*)

CO-EDITED:
The Existential Imagination (*1963*)
Short Fiction of the Masters (*1963, 1973*)
The Shape of Fiction (*1967, 1978*)
The Radical Vision (*1970*)
The Naked i: Fictions for the Seventies (*1971*)
The Existential Mind: Documents and Fictions (*1974*)
The Fourth World: The Imprisoned, the Poor, the Sick, the Elderly and Underaged in America (*1976*)

Joseph Conrad
THE THREE LIVES

A BIOGRAPHY

by Frederick R. Karl

FARRAR, STRAUS AND GIROUX
NEW YORK

Published simultaneously in Canada by
McGraw-Hill Ryerson Ltd. Toronto
Printed in the United States of America
DESIGNED BY HERBERT H. JOHNSON

FIRST EDITION, 1979

Library of Congress Cataloging in Publication Data

Karl, Frederick Robert.
Joseph Conrad: the three lives.

Bibliography: p.
Includes index.
1. Conrad, Joseph, 1857-1924—Biography. 2. Novelists, English—20th century—Biography.
PR6005.04Z759 823'.9'12 [B] 78-13515

To the memory of Lionel Trilling

Contents

Illustrations

FOLLOWING PAGE 222

FOLLOWING PAGE 412

FOLLOWING PAGE 722

Foreword

THIS is the first biography of Joseph Conrad in twenty years, and the first to draw upon the entire range of his correspondence of nearly 4,000 letters. As the editor of his collected letters, the author has been able to use the more than 1,500 unpublished pieces of correspondence, including many hundreds hitherto unavailable to Conrad's earlier biographers. While these letters do not provide any sensational divulgations, they do allow documentation and continuity in many areas of Conrad's life that had been shadowy or vague. Although the correspondence does not fill in the earlier years with any greater precision, it does inform every aspect of his writing life; and during the middle years of his career as a novelist, roughly from 1900 to 1915, his letters allow us both an intimacy and a completeness.

A word about naming: my title points out the "three lives" of Joseph Conrad. Two lives have always been clear, as seaman and as writer. But I have added to those a third, his life as a Pole. By concentrating so much of the book on his first sixteen years in Poland, I have assumed that Conrad carried away from this early experience sufficient freight to make those years into a separate existence. This life did not produce anything tangible, but it informed every aspect of his later years, was the matrix for his ideas, his attachments, his memories and nightmares. Conrad was an English writer because he wrote in English; but he was, also, a Polish writer, although he never wrote fiction in that language, and to a lesser extent, he was a French writer, even though he did not do creative work in French. Even if we cite only Conrad's manipulation of his name—he was alternately Conrad, Konrad, Korzeniowski, and a dozen variations—we observe how Poland retrieved him whenever his signature was involved.

By stressing the Polish background to such an extent, I have made this into a psychological study of the development of the man as much as of the development of the writer. The writer, who is our ultimate objective, cannot be understood without a detailed sense of this unusual man and his remarkable background. George Painter's life of Proust has seemed to me a model biography because he interwove the life and works of his subject, and found implicit in everything Proust saw and did the material of his imaginative life. Conrad, in his retrieval of past memories, is a Proustian of sorts. Once he became a writer, his contemporary experiences did not inform his work; on the contrary, his work was embedded in past experience, both the actual events and people and the imagination working on them.

To ignore the psychological development of the man and writer, as Conrad's previous biographers have, is to ignore the ways in which he went from an interesting man to a writer of international repute. At the same time, this is not a psychoanalytical study. That has been done, and done with extraordinary taste and skill, by Dr. Bernard Meyer. For my purposes, such a study is too selective. It omits much of the life and work in order to say something consequential about a few pivotal areas. It intensifies at the expense of breadth. Although all biography must be selective in its details, I have tried to be inclusive, not exclusive. Conrad's "three lives" all carry their own weight, and none can be faulted.

For if we think of Conrad essentially as a novelist and teller of short stories, then we must also see him as one of the people on whom nothing was lost. My aim has been to fit Conrad into Henry James's ironic, mocking, witty sense of human experience: "Experience is never limited, and it is never complete; it is an immense sensibility, a kind of huge spiderweb of the finest silken threads suspended in the chamber of consciousness, and catching every airborne particle in its tissue. It is the very atmosphere of the mind; and when the mind is imaginative—much more when it happens to be that of a man of genius—it takes to itself the faintest hints of life, it converts the very pulses of the air into revelations."

In many ways, Conrad is our representative modern man and artist. An exile, a drifter, a marginal man until well into his thirties, he exemplifies many aspects of the modern sensibility. In *Thus Spake Zarathustra*, Nietzsche speaks of the "last man," that individual who is interested only in survival and whose value system turns the earth itself into something small and trivial. "His race," Nietzsche says, "is as ineradicable as the flea-beetle; the last man lives longest." As a man who himself moved outside nearly all established forms, Conrad rejected that "flea-beetle" philosophy of the last man, so scorned as well by Nietzsche. Conrad found in marginality itself a way of life, a form of existence, and a philosophy that added up to more than survival and well-being. In probing exile, dislocation of time and place, language disorientation, and shifting loyalties, he extended our view of the shadows of existence. Indeed, he suggested that the shadows were to be the main area of existence in the twentieth century. No less than Freud, his exact contemporary, he explored new territory: irrationality, abnormality, nightmare; and he returned from this primitive, discontinuous world not with solutions but with ways of better understanding that savage Congo and primigenial heart of darkness that dwells under the most bland exteriors.

The writing of this biography has been paralleled by my editing of the Letters of Joseph Conrad; so that my indebtedness to several people and organizations is twofold and doubly appreciated. To be inclusive, the list would be too lengthy, but to those not mentioned I am not any the less grateful for past help and graciousness.

The Guggenheim Foundation and the Fulbright Commission permitted me to spend two years abroad on Conrad research. The American Council of Learned Societies, the American Philosophical Society, the City College Fund, and the City University Research Foundation have provided generous grants-in-aid for travel and other expenses. Their support has been deeply gratifying.

There are a few individuals whose aid has been indispensable: Dr. John D. Gordan, late curator of the Berg Collection; the present curator of the Berg, Dr. Lola L. Szladits; Miss Marjorie Wynne, of the Beinecke Rare Book and Manuscript Library at Yale University; Mrs. Katherine Lamb, the younger daughter of Ford Madox Ford; Professor Richard Ludwig, of Princeton University; Hans van Marle, of Amsterdam; Professor Norman Sherry, of the University of Lancaster; Mr. Ashbel G. Brice, former Director of Duke University Press; Dr. Zdzisław Najder, of Warsaw, Poland; Mr. Clive Driver, curator of the Rosenbach Foundation, Philadelphia; Mr. Borys Conrad.

Past and present librarians: Colgate University—Mr. Bruce Brown; University of Texas Humanities Research Center—Mrs. Ann Bowden, Mrs. Mary Hirth, Mrs. June Moll, Mr. David Farmer; University of Virginia Library—Ms. Anne Freudenberg.

To the above, I would add those who offered their time, knowledge, or private collections: the late Mr. Jocelyn Baines, Professor Karl Beckson, the late Professor William Blackburn, Professor Andrzej Busza, Mr. William R. Cagle, M. François Chapon, Professor Morton Cohen, the late Mr. Richard Curle, Mrs. M. L. Danilewicz, the late Mr. Lew David Feldman, Dr. Donald Gallup, Mr. David Garnett, Professor Albert Guerard, Professor Bruce Harkness, Mr. Rupert Hart-Davis, Professor Eloise Knapp Hay, Professor James Hepburn, Mr. K. W. Humphreys, Professor Neill Joy, Mr. Alfred A. Knopf, Professor R. W. B. Lewis, Mr. Kenneth Lohf, Mr. William McCarthy, Dr. Bernard Meyer, Professor Arthur Mizener, Professor Thomas Moser, Signor Ugo Mursia, Professor Dale Randall, Professor Blair Rouse, the late Lord Bertrand Russell, the late M. Jean Schlumberger, Professor David Smith, Professor Robert Stallman, Mr. Frank Swinnerton, Professor Ian Watt, Mr. Herbert West, Mrs. Purd Wright (Lansburgh).

The following have kindly granted permission for the use of quoted material: Withers (for the Conrad Estate), Doubleday (for American rights), Oxford University Press (for translation of the Polish letters into English), the British Library (for letters to Thomas Wise), the Ellen Glasgow Collection, the University of Virginia Library (for letters to Glasgow and Doubleday), Humanities Research Center, the University of Texas at Austin (for various letters and excerpts from the manuscript of *Victory*), Manuscript Division, the New York Public Library (for letters to John Quinn), University of Illinois at Urbana-Champaign (for letters to H. G. Wells), the Houghton Library of Harvard University (for letters to William Rothenstein), the National Library of Ireland, Casement Papers (for letters to Roger Casement), Columbia University Libraries (for letters to Stephen and Cora Crane), the Trustees of the National Library of Scotland (for letters to Blackwood), the University of Birmingham (for letters to John Galsworthy), the Brotherton Collection, the University of Leeds (for various letters), the Philip H. & A. S. W. Rosenbach Foundation (for various letters), The Lilly Library, the Indiana University Library (for various letters), Dartmouth College Library (for letters to R. B. Cunninghame Graham), The Pierpont Morgan Library (for the letter to W. E. Henley), University College London Library (for letters to Arnold Bennett), The George Arents Research Library, Syracuse University (for various letters), Cornell University Library (for letters to Ford Madox Ford), Colgate University Library (for various letters), William R. Perkins Library, Duke University (for letters to Blackwood, David Meldrum, and Francis Warrington Dawson), Henry W. and Albert A. Berg Collection, The New York Public Library, Astor, Lenox and Tilden Foundations (for letters to James Brand Pinker), Yale University Library (for various letters), New York University Libraries (for various letters), Alfred A. Knopf (for letters to him), Bibliothèque Littéraire Jacques Doucet (for letters to André Gide).

F.R.K.

Joseph Conrad

THE THREE LIVES

Note to the reader In some instances, letters show double dates (for example, June 26/July 8, 1878). The first date is according to the Julian calendar, the second the Gregorian, a difference of twelve days. Sometimes the correspondent gives both forms, on other occasions only one, and it is impossible to know which he intended. Thus, both appear.

Source notes are at the end of the book.

Introduction

ON May 25, 1919, Conrad completed the manuscript of his long novel about the Malay straits, *The Rescue*, which he had begun twenty-three years before. He was now sixty-one and a half years old, crippled by several physical ailments, depleted by the war years, aware that his powers were diminishing, tired, and yet an old warrior unable and unwilling to give up the campaign. *The Rescue* was, for him, a form of rescue. It was a manuscript that had trailed him from the earliest days of his writing career, those days of the Malay novels and stories. It had occupied his thoughts on and off throughout his years of achievement, and it was, at this time, a rounding off: twenty-three years, almost the entire span of his writing career, a span as long as he had spent at sea, more than one-third of his life.

He had hopes for the Nobel Prize, in the 1918–19 years, although he was too proud to admit, even to his agent, James Brand Pinker, how he wanted international recognition of that kind. Yet he did write to Pinker, three months earlier:

> I have heard from Jessie [Mrs. Conrad] through Lady Colvin that there is an agitation (the centre of which is the Ath[eneum]. Club) to put my name forward for O.M. [Order of Merit] Kipling's is the other name.
>
> Of course I was not approached. It is the sort of thing one could not refuse. But I feel strongly that K. is the right person, and that the O.M. would not perhaps be an appropriate honour for me who, whatever my deepest feelings may be, can't claim English literature as my inheritance. My mouth however is closed. In such a matter not even a confidential hint could be safely given to a friend; because it could be misinterpreted (in more than one way) to my great disadvantage. My scruple I assure you is very real. I don't know what you will think of it.
>
> There is however another distinction which has been mooted (by the R.S.L. [Royal Society of Literature]) and that is the Nobel Prize. That was in the air last year; and as it is an international thing and less in the nature of an honour than of mere reward, we needn't have any scruples about acceptance if it ever comes in our way. And as it is not at all an im-

> possible development I must tell you of the thought which had occurred to me as to the policy to follow.
>
> I think sincerely that "Rescue" has a particular quality. Novels of adventure will, I suppose, be always written; but it may well be that "Rescue" in its concentrated colouring and tone will remain the swan song of Romance as a literary art. The serial is being extremely well received. I myself have had many pleasant letters and one or two even remarkable.

In 1918, there was no Nobel Prize in literature; in 1919, the prize was won by Carl Spitteler, of Switzerland. In the year of Conrad's death, 1924, another Pole, Władysław Reymont, won the Nobel Prize for Literature.

The Rescue manuscript brought together nearly all the important elements of Conrad's life: the philosophy of the man, the skill of the seaman, the representative work of his literary imagination, and the development of the writer into a figure of international repute. The life had been spectacular and unique, spanning three countries and three languages, Polish, French, and English; including two separate professions, seaman and writer; and demonstrating achievement in everything Conrad touched. He became a master mariner at twenty-eight and missed a Nobel Prize only because of the shortsightedness of the judges, who also ignored Joyce, Lawrence, Woolf, Kafka, and Proust in that same and the succeeding decade.

Conrad's story begins in the most unlikely way. As son of a Polish patriot and political revolutionary, he had been expected to take up the role of the landowning gentry and provide opposition to the Russian invader. Instead, he left Poland for France and a sea career, at sixteen. In France, he was expected to sow his wild oats, in this traditional refuge of Polish emigrés, and then, through some of the social connections provided for him, settle into a business or profession. However, despite the attractions of culture and language, Conrad never found his bearings in France. Instead, he sought bizarre adventures and then, having gone through his patrimony and accumulated debts, he attempted suicide, firing a shot into his chest.

At twenty, somewhat inexplicably, he left Marseilles, joined the British merchant service, and, proceeding to learn English, worked himself up to master mariner by the age of twenty-eight. A sea career seemed his fate—he was adept at it, he had excellent references, and he appeared temperamentally fitted for that mixture of activity and indolence which marks life at sea. Yet not too long after serving a stint as captain, he began desultorily to write his first novel, *Almayer's Folly*, taking over five years to complete it, at the same time pursuing an active sea career. Dimly now, at thirty-two his life almost half over, the outline of his new career appears, although the main thrust would not surface until he was over forty, married, the father of a son, and frantic with self-doubt.

It is an extraordinary sequence of lives, made doubly remarkable because none of its lines appear to flow into each other. There is no way of predicting why Conrad would do a particular thing at a particular time, and even hindsight cannot discover coherence and continuity where there is little. His life becomes like a plotted novel, full of seeming inexplicables that follow each other and only make "ultimate" sense because by the end they satisfy us. In this instance, the life adds up to three countries, three languages, and a literary influence which remains undiminished in the half century since his death.

I

The Polish Years
1857–1874

ANTIGONE:
O city of wealthy men.
I call upon Dirce's spring,
I call upon Thebes' grove in the armored plain,
to be my witnesses, how with no friend's mourning,
by what decree I go to the fresh-made prison-tomb.
Alive to the place of corpses, an alien still,
never at home with the living nor with the dead.

SOPHOCLES, *Antigone*
(TRANSLATED BY ELIZABETH WYCKOFF)

CHAPTER 1

Soundings

IN 1899, when Conrad was writing *Lord Jim* and "Heart of Darkness," a Polish novelist named Eliza Orzeszkowa attacked him for betraying his country for money. The betrayal had taken the shape of Conrad's emigration to England, his writing in the English language, and his supposed affluence. Her words are streaked with anger and contempt:

> And since we talk about books, I must say that the gentleman in English who is writing novels which are widely read and bring good profit almost caused me a nervous attack. When reading about him I felt something slippery and unpleasant, something mounting to my throat. Really! That even creative talents should join the exodus! Till now we have talked only about engineers and operatic singers! But now we should give absolution to a writer!

This "absolved writer" was, however, still a coterie writer, little read, less bought, sinking, even now, ever deeper into debts and obligations, trying desperately to modulate between popularity and serious work. She continued:

> And to take away from one's nation this flower, this heart and to give it to the Anglo-Saxons who are not even lacking in bird's milk, for the only reason that they pay better for it—one cannot even think of it without shame.

Then, with a stroke of genius for innuendo, she finds a Polish novelist with the same surname as Conrad's:

> And what is still worse, this gentleman bears the name of his perhaps very near relative, that Joseph Korzeniowski [Józef Korzeniowski, 1791–1863, no relative of Conrad's] over whose novels I shed as a young girl the first tears of sympathy and felt the first ardors of noble enthusiasms and decisions. Over the novels of Mr. Conrad Korzeniowski [Józef Teodor Konrad Korzeniowski or Joseph Conrad] no Polish girl will shed an altruistic tear or take a noble decision. But on second thought, this causes me only moderate grief, because believing in the superiority of the

> elements of which all creative power is composed, I do not suppose that our writers would ever embrace the profession of a vivandière or a huckster. Besides, we do not starve even if we remain in our place, that we should need to feed on the crumbs from the table of great lords. In this respect we ourselves are *seigneurs* great enough.

Although we have no evidence that Conrad in 1899 knew of this attack, it is very possible that the substance of the argument was brought to his attention. And how it touched on every aspect of his existence—the very basis of his ideology! For Mme Orzeszkowa's attack opened up not only his relationship to Poland and his allegiance to England but his severely divided early years, his feelings about his father, Apollo, and the very nature of his chosen profession, that of writer and novelist. What Conrad had built very carefully, always colored by his own uncertainty, was now the subject of a lethal blast. Demons or Furies were pursuing him from his father's grave. He had been found out.

Mme Orzeszkowa's assault upon Conrad's values was not an isolated instance of nationalism but had been preceded by a lively discussion of the entire problem: of an emigrant writer who "betrays" his native country by seeking another kind of audience. A well-known philosopher, a specialist in Plato, Wincenty Lutosławski, had a month earlier addressed himself to the broad question of talented people who leave their country when their intellectual pursuits cannot be realized. Lutosławski himself had visited Conrad in 1896 and been living in Boston for some time. Such people, he said in 1899, in the Polish weekly *Kraj*, have every right to emigrate so their individual talents can be nourished in the new land. The imagery of the entire discussion is cast in terms of a mother who nourishes her son, in the expectation that one day he will make her proud and carry out her revenge against the Russian oppressor. There is also present an agricultural metaphor, of the kernel of grain that grows in the rich soil of the homeland. Talent is like a huge belly ever being filled by Polish nutrients.

> He who is strong and great [wrote Lutosławski] would not abandon, forget and betray the mother who had nursed him, and returning to his country would bring with him fame and success. Those who stay at home are not necessarily the ablest but the most patient and enduring.

He concluded: "Let us not condemn those who seek an outlet for their forces regardless of the frontiers of their country." The same issue of *Kraj* fed the controversy with a statement (by Tadeusz Zuk-Skarszewski, a well-known journalist) that it was preferable to be a rural schoolteacher in Poland than a Polish Plato (such as Lutosławski) in Boston.

Conrad appeared caught between two writers arguing irreconcilable points: one ostensibly defending his "betrayal" of Poland and the other attacking him for desertion. Either way, the charge was desertion and betrayal.

And when the individual has Conrad's illustrious forebears, he must be not only a coward but a self-seeking, self-righteous figure of avarice. Eliza Orzeskowa, the implacable Fury of Polish nationalism, saw literary achievement as a force for the freeing of the Polish spirit, an element in the development of Polish nationalism, a step in the development of a revived Polish state. While hers was not the romantic nationalism espoused by Apollo Korzeniowski, it was nevertheless an attitude antithetical to Conrad's post-Darwinian pessimism and completely apposite to his shaky ideology based on individual achievement and a chivalric tradition. If there is a state or country in Conrad's work, it is, like Sulaco in *Nostromo*, ravaged with or without progress. Even though change may deceptively appear beneficial, it is often simply the harbinger of eventual destruction.

From Mme Orzeszkowa's more socially realistic point of view, the writer owes his native country both his talent and his dedication. On both counts, Conrad had forsaken Poland. He had, in fact, chosen that most difficult of stances: to become a marginal man so as to liberate himself from the burdens of the past. His work was in English and his subjects ostensibly had little reference to Poland. His tone was that of a skeptic, a writer who rejected Polish romanticism as the idealism of the foolhardy, a man who questioned English democracy for allowing individual slackness and mob rule. In between, where Conrad tried to locate himself, was the quicksand of illusions, belief in self, the existential choice of variety, a sense of professionalism and individual commitment—whether toward seamanship or writing. The stance was a juggling act, and it produced a life of fits and starts, together with a variety of books as apparently dissimilar as *The Nigger of the "Narcissus,"* "Heart of Darkness," *The Secret Agent*, and *Victory*.

Conrad's defender, Lutosławski, was not arguing an aesthetic or a Jamesian-Flaubertian defense of the artist and the artistic process. On the contrary, he was also caught up in nationalistic fervor. He continued the controversy into 1911, twelve years after its initiation, and asserted that Conrad, despite his writing in English and about non-Polish subjects, was deeply involved spiritually in Polish matters. "He started writing in England—to earn his living, and has given the English a number of novels sparkling with Polish spirit and from which Polish influence goes on [in] the race now dominating the world. His novels are not tendentious like Mme Orzeszkowa's."

Using Polish life as a lever, Lutosławski was attempting to pry Conrad from his comfortable base in England. He continued, rather damagingly, that if Conrad had written in Polish he would not have had the success which his novels now enjoyed in England. At that time, and indeed for the last decade, Conrad would have been astonished to learn that he was considered a financial success, for his economic condition was at low ebb and he was bemoaning to both his agent, Pinker, and his friend John Galsworthy his complete lack of a popular audience. Lutosławski then added a paragraph which indicated he had moved closer to Conrad's most vicious attacker: "Let us not envy the English for a second rate writer, who anyway would not have enriched our literature, since he himself avows that profit was the motive of his creative activity." Conrad needed no such defenders.

How much of this was he even aware of? There is, as we have said, no clear proof whether or not he knew of these specific articles in *Kraj*, but to be certain he could not escape the controversy altogether, Mme Orzeszkowa wrote him directly, possibly enclosing a copy of her attack. Conrad attempted to reply generally to the question in *A Personal Record*, but even his eloquent defense cannot deal with the shifting grounds of the verbal assault and its significance for a serious author. For Conrad would himself have agreed with Mme Orzeszkowa that a writer must not emigrate when his country needs him, and yet, at the same time, he could not at all be certain that when he left he was of any use to Poland.

He emigrated to become a seaman, not a writer, and he emigrated just short of his seventeenth birthday, when his commitments were all self-directed and he possessed no ostensible talents. Further, even if Poland needed him, there is the question of the kind of help either the man or the writer Conrad could have given; for he was, after all, concerned with delicate questions of personal morality and individual ethics, not with issues of state or of national purpose. He knew more than most that national purpose is often destructive of individual achievement, that politics and literature rarely mix, and that questions of state reduce difficult aesthetic issues to literal interpretation. Most of all, he recognized that political movements and politicians use the talented individual as long as he fits an image, and then disdain him. The state itself in Conrad's work is dissolute, or corrupt, or morally blind, or machine-like in its inexorable, indifferent movement toward some vague, amoral end. Such a state, with its intense ideological needs, must be an inhospitable host to the kind of sensibility implicit in the making of art.

For Conrad to have been the author Mme Orzeszkowa desired directly, and Lutosławski indirectly, would have meant the loss of all distinctions between himself and a dozen other writers. In *A Personal Record*, Conrad tried a balancing act. Mme Orzeszkowa had spoken of creative talent as being the "very crown of the plant," the "very heart of the heart of the nation." To take this flower, this heart, and to "give it to the Anglo-Saxons who are not even lacking in bird's milk" for the sake of money, this was indeed shameless. Conrad had to respond to so many confusing issues—an assault on his values as well as taunts about his unfitness for financial reward—that he could only be defensive. First, he tried to defend his sea career:

> Having broken away from my origins under a storm of blame from every quarter which had the merest shadow of right to voice an opinion, removed by great distances, and even estranged, in a measure, from them

by the totally unintelligible character of the life which had seduced me so mysteriously from my allegiance, I may safely say that through the blind force of circumstances the sea was to be all my world and the merchant service my only home for a long succession of years.

So far, Conrad was in the position of defending his struggle for survival at sea and with the English language against those who told him he had wasted his efforts. If he had remained a seaman, of course, he would have been anonymous, and he could have "deserted" Poland without publicity or reverberations. But as a writer, as a serious writer, his desertion, so to speak, becomes the act of a traitor, like Razumov's betrayal of Haldin, and all the anguish and effort that had gone into the literary act are suddenly revealed as worthless by those who want a patriot, not literature.

> . . . I think that all ambitions are lawful except those which climb upward on the miseries or credulities of mankind. All intellectual and artistic ambitions are permissible, up to and even beyond the limit of prudent sanity. They can hurt no one. If they are mad, then so much the worse for the artist. . . . Is it such a very sad presumption to believe in the sovereign power of one's art, to try for other means, for other ways of affirming this belief in the deeper appeal of one's work? To try to go deeper is not to be insensible.

Yet it was not until near the end of *A Personal Record* that he revealed his anguish at such misunderstanding of his vigilance over first the sea and then literature:

> It seems that it is for these few bits of paper, headed by the name of a few ships and signed by the names of a few Scots and English shipmasters, that I have faced the astonished indignations, the mockeries and the reproaches of a sort hard to bear for a boy of fifteen; that I have been charged with the want of patriotism, the want of sense, and the want of heart too; that I went through agonies of self-conflict and shed secret tears not a few, and had the beauties of the Furca Pass spoiled for me, and have been called an "incorrigible Don Quixote," in allusion to the book-born madness of the knight. For that spoil!

Conrad says he has been called a romantic, not as a word of praise, but as an attack on his sense of responsibility, indeed, on his manhood, connected as it is to the reading of books. He defends himself: "I will make bold to say that neither at sea nor ashore have I ever lost the sense of responsibility. There is more than one sort of intoxication. Even before the most seductive reveries I have remained mindful of that sobriety of interior life, that asceticism of sentiment, in which alone the naked form of truth, such as one conceives it, such as one feels it, can be rendered without shame."

Now over fifty, Conrad defends his entire life on the basis of his fidelity to the truth as he has seen it. "I have tried to be a sober worker all my life—all my two lives. I did so from taste, no doubt having an instinctive horror of losing my sense of full self-possession but also from artistic conviction."

The words appear easy, fluent, without too much passion. However, they mask a life of incredible commitment to an idea and to an ideal. Near the beginning of his writing career, Conrad had written a passage which he later deleted upon the advice of his good friend and literary adviser Edward Garnett. Originally, the passage was part of Conrad's Preface to *The Nigger of the "Narcissus"*: "For in art alone of all the enterprises of men there is meaning in endeavour disassociated from success and merit—if any merit there be—is not wholly centered in achievement but may be fairly discerned in the aim." The aim, as the aim of all things, is to discover the "truth of life," to focus on "a moment of vision, a sigh, a smile" and then "return to an eternal rest."

Yet to get this far, into the late 1890s, Conrad had already traveled a lifetime. By the time he wrote those words, he was forty, but a very old forty, with a twenty-year career at sea behind him; and, more importantly, with a way of looking at life. Like Odysseus, who lived in exile, cunning and without splendor, Conrad spent many years of his life marginal, lonely, an isolated man. Born into a country that existed only as a geographic shape and not as a sovereign nation; growing up in the household of a father who relived his days as a patriot and had become a religious mystic waiting for diseased lungs to claim his life; spending twenty years on and off French and English ships or in exotic ports of the Far East; writing for the remaining thirty years of his life, all except the last ten without adequate financial resources—Conrad understood and had experienced a kind of life that was unique.

Henry James, in wonderment and admiration, was to write to Conrad: "No one has *known*—for intellectual use—the things you know, and you have, as the artist of the whole matter, an authority that no one has approached. I find you in it all, writing wonderfully, whatever you may say of your difficult medium and your *plume rebelle.* You knock about in the wide waters of expression like the raciest and boldest of privateers." James adds that he thanks the powers who so mysteriously "let you loose with such sensibilities, into such an undiscovered country. . . ."

"Undiscovered country"—that is the province of every major writer: to seek what has been undiscovered and to find the means to quarry it. We can see Conrad's life as becoming something out of which he would construct his work. And we see his work as becoming increasingly the stuff out of which he could arrange and rearrange his memories of his life. Each element curved inward and around in order to join with the other, so that segments are jointless, indistinguishable. Somewhat like Joyce once he entered the years of *Ulysses* and *Finnegans Wake*, he accepted the curvature and cyclical nature of personal history.

Perhaps Conrad's great admiration for the Proust of *Remembrance of Things Past* resulted from the recognition that in some profound region they were "secret sharers"; that Proust and his work were, also, part of a curving, seamless extension of self and creation, part of the circuitry in which the self unfolds in endless projection so as to become one's lifetime work. Of Proust, Conrad wrote: "I admire him rather for disclosing a past like nobody else's, for enlarging, as it were, the general experience of mankind by bringing to it something that has not been recorded before."

Conrad conceived of the world as an extension of his own beliefs. His major weapons—like the third-category philosophers in a Platonic dialogue—were mirrors of reality and reflections of an ideal world. Not unusually, he dictated (to Ford Madox Ford) the essays of *The Mirror of the Sea*—with its dazzling sequences of sun, water, reflected images, mirrors—while he was also writing his greatest novel, *Nostromo*, a narrative caught up in the past. Ford, a psychological necessity for Conrad at this time, was the receptacle of Conrad's memories of the sea, a living, oral tradition for him; simultaneously, he was writing his longest and by far most complicated narrative, his joining of himself with literature. The key image, perhaps, is of Narcissus: that endless gazing into the well of memories, to create an art based on the past, on winding backward and forward, like that clock in *Tristram Shandy* which must be wound every first Sunday of the month or else all life in the Shandy household will apparently stop.

Like Joyce and Proust, Conrad stored his experiences and hovered over the details. And like them, he did not find his reasons for storing until later on in his life, in his middle thirties. There are at least two kinds of writers: those, like the above, who covet knowledge and experience—even the trivia that the less gifted person easily forgets—without knowing that it will all be turned into art; and those who write a daily quota as they experience their material, turning routine details and characters as met into the materials of their fiction, writers such as Lawrence, Hemingway, and even Gide. For the first, the group with which we will be concerned, memory is the salient factor. Living by memory, living on memories, they peer into the well, see their own lovely image, and turn, pen in hand, to inventions that are often no more than remembrances of an unforgettable past.

Long before Conrad was born, in 1857, the stage for his exile and cunning was being prepared. Like Joyce and Proust, once again, Conrad was, consciously or not, all his days and years preparing for what he was to become, and only very slowly becoming what was implicit in his life and experience. Part of the incredible slowness with which he composed his work resulted from this need to dredge; almost literally, he had to dip deep within, far beneath surfaces and explicits, into areas where memory was intermixed with baser elements. Proust utilized what he called the involuntary memory—that which lay beyond the regular, normalizing memory and which was the container of a different order of being. Similarly, Conrad dipped ever deeper. His first major work of length, *Lord Jim,* was almost completely an act of memory. Based on an actual event, the entire novel is structured on various commentators recalling what occurred, or trying to make sense out of what has become for them part of a distant now dim past. *Lord Jim* and its ship, the *Patna,* were not simply paradigms of Conrad's feelings about Poland but models of his way of thinking and expressing himself; expressions of material lying deep within, far below the surface of conscious recall, which could only be brought up by explicit efforts of understanding: by the artwork itself.

The very country into which Conrad was born created divisiveness and was based as much on memory as on contemporary life. And even if he had never left Poland, and had remained with his Uncle Tadeusz Bobrowski in Podolia (the present Ukraine), he would have needed cunning and shrewdness to stay alive and outside Czarist prisons. And it was not only the country into which he was born that required constant artifice, it was the family also. Conrad's immediate family was itself split between idealistic and practical elements, with personal tragedy at its base and gloom, morbidity, and self-destructive obsessions as its routine experience. Any child, talented or otherwise, born into such circumstances required more than intelligence to survive; he needed a resilience and a mastery of the marginal situation that would carry him through childhood and several careers.

For Conrad to have endured the conflicting experiences of his childhood indicated an elasticity that would give him a method for handling future life. In his sixteen years in Poland, he existed rarely in a home of his own, infrequently with those who could focus their attention upon him. Left alone for long periods of time, he developed his ability to stare and meditate creatively. Like a Dickens character or Dickens himself, he was an orphan even before his parents died. The unsettled years in Poland were a marvelous preparation either for a writer of talent or for a person who would cultivate failure and sink deeply into neurosis. Conrad traveled a thin line. Not unlike his idol, Flaubert, he fell into apathy and indifference, into staring and peering, without doing, only to recover with words and phrases which attempted to express, precisely, what he had seen and heard. The method of external narrators Conrad so frequently employed was the literary equivalent of voyeurism, the perfect tool for the small, marginal child always attempting to put together a story whose parts did not quite fit.

No matter how many myths may have gathered around Conrad in his lifetime—some of them perpetuated by his own romanticization of his past and the exotic nature of his early fiction—no myth was more fantastic than the facts of his early years and development. When Józef Teodor Konrad Korzeniowski (coat of arms Nałęcz) was born on December 3, 1857 (new calendar), at Berdyczów or Berdichev* in Podolia, he was already the heir of numerous divisions and intellectual conflicts. His name: *Józef*, after his maternal grandfather; *Teodor*, after his paternal grandfather; *Konrad*, after two heroes in Adam Mickiewicz's poems, *Konrad Wallenrod* (1827) and *Dziady* (1832). There was, additionally, the family coat of arms, with its heraldic name Nałęcz, which indicated upper gentry status.† That, however, was only the beginning, and we will return to it.

The literary background is in itself of interest, for Joseph Conrad was intended by his baptismal names to be a "Konrad," and that meant he was intended as a romantic hero, a chivalrous, traditionally oriented savior of his enslaved people. Like Samson, he was supposed to save his people even if he destroyed himself; a Pole amid the Russians was not unlike a Semite amid the Philistines. To be a Konrad, then, meant a life combining Odysseus, Samson, and the soul of a poet or the "incorrigible Don Quixote." Literature was never alien to either family strain, and that Conrad eventually became a writer was not at all an unusual consequence of his background. Conrad's father, Apollo Korzeniowski, lived, as it were, inside Odysseus' Trojan Horse as it rested within enemy walls; for the Russia that enfolded and enclosed the boundary lines of Poland was nothing if not a huge hollow body that gobbled up and tried to digest whatever came within its grasp. Conrad's description, in "Autocracy and War," is of a Russia spacious, empty, infinite:

> There is an awe-inspiring idea of infinity conveyed in the word *Néant*—and in Russia there is no idea. She is not a *Néant*, she is and has been simply the negation of everything worth living for. She is not an empty void; she is a yawning chasm open between East and West; a bottomless abyss that has swallowed up every hope of mercy, every aspiration towards personal dignity, towards freedom, towards knowledge, every ennobling desire of the heart, every redeeming whisper of con-

---

* Berdichev is 100 miles southwest of Kiev, 275 miles northwest of Odessa.

† Besides signifying gentry status, the Nałęcz coat of arms distinguished this line of Korzeniowskis from all others, the name being quite common. The coat of arms had as its emblem a handkerchief with two corners tied together, standing for faithfulness to country, religion, and God, and, according to some stories of its background, the warlike character of the family. One such story has the king granting this emblem to a warrior who bound his wounds in battle. Although the family can be traced back to the late sixteenth century, it appears more notable in the eighteenth, with a chancellor of the Lithuanian principality and an army chaplain turned warrior whose feats are celebrated by the great poet Mickiewicz.

Conrad's maternal side, the Bobrowskis, likewise belonged to the gentry landowning class, with their interests almost completely agricultural, only Stefan, Conrad's uncle, being politically active. The Bobrowski coat of arms was the emblem of a hawk, which, although it had a warlike suggestion, was probably more attuned to an agricultural background. The respective coats of arms, the Nałęcz one bespeaking military valor and the Bobrowski one indicating land and growth, provide a good indication of the conflicting strains which affected Conrad in early childhood.

science. Those that have peered into that abyss, where the dreams of Panslavism, of universal conquest, mingled with the hate and contempt for Western ideas, drift impotently like shapes of mist, know well that it is bottomless; that there is no ground for anything that could in the remotest degree serve even the lowest interests of mankind.

The idea of a world within emptiness—indeed a world that goes beyond emptiness—recurs in Conrad's works as idea and image. Perhaps derived from Mallarmé's sense of *néant*, which Conrad's phrasing recalls, emptiness denoted an existence within an existence. In *Under Western Eyes*, Razumov—a young student with a persona that disguises only superficially Conrad's attachment to him—sees Russia sympathetically and yet ambiguously. He views her as a "mother," as enfolding and embracing, but also as limitless emptiness. Lacking a family, Razumov—one of many Conradian "orphans"—makes Russia his parents, relatives, friends, and future. "His closest parentage was defined in the statement that he was a Russian." As he looks out over the infinite land, he recognizes that that vast emptiness is all he has—it is both nothing and everything. He has to fill it, as it fills him.*

The image of emptiness which the young Razumov must shape himself to is not unlike the vastness of the sea which the young Conrad attempted to fill with his own person. We can see, indeed, succeeding careers dominated by his sense of Poland swallowed up by a voracious, unappeased Russia, a Russia which, like the mine in Zola's *Germinal*, is a vast digestive apparatus that chews up all those whom it enfolds and then excretes them as waste matter. Having lost his mother, then his father, having assimilated in his childhood and youth the idea of a Poland devoured by Russia, a child victimized by patriotic parents, he chose another emptiness, the sea, a vastitude that could swallow him up. Following that, he focused on still another emptiness, a limitless, open-ended career as a writer, dominated by sheets of white paper whose horizons extended infinitely.

The point is not that Conrad teetered on the edge of destruction in each career he chose—being ignorant when he began of both the craft of the sea and the language of writing—but that he *chose* directions or careers that would force him to relive a teetering, near-disastrous experience. Comparable to his actual suicide attempt in Marseilles was his use of suicidal situations in which he could confront the worst and could wobble existentially while peering into the abyss. Then, and only then, could he apply himself at his highest level of achievement, whether as mate, captain, or novelist.

Later, with his childhood long behind him, his descriptions of his life as a writer are full of the hollowness of his chosen profession and the emptiness of existence. To come to terms with that emptiness, Conrad threw himself

* "He was as lonely in the world as a man swimming in the deep sea. There were no Razumovs belonging to him anywhere."

into unknown spaces which stretched to infinity. To Marguerite Poradowska ("Aunt" Marguerite) in 1894, while struggling with the manuscript of *Almayer's Folly,* he wrote:

> I begrudge each minute I spend away from paper. I do not say from the pen, for I have written very little, but inspiration comes to me while looking at the paper. Then there are flights out of sight; my thought goes wandering through great spaces filled with vague forms. Everything is still chaos, but, slowly, ghosts are transformed into living flesh, floating vapors turn solid, and who knows?—perhaps something will be born from the encounter of indistinct ideas.

Even Conrad's choice of the phrase "indistinct ideas," with its limitless extensions, indicates an identification with spatiality. His sense of dimensions was oceanic.* Life stretched behind and before him to infinity. This was more than the romantic stance of a young man seeking initiation into the unknown. It was, instead, a compulsive, inner-directed response to the kind of childhood he had experienced in Poland, in the home of a father alternately forlorn and passionate, full of thwarted ideas, harking back to the times when his plans were alive, when his wife, Ewa, was alive, but now with ideas, plans, and hopes attached to a dying body. Growing up in that household, in those terms, with a dim memory of his mother, barely alive, then dying, finally dead, the young Conrad had to make choices before choices were made for him.

It all began with naming. Even after he anglicized Konrad, he thought enough of it to keep it as his pen name. He was rarely known as Joseph to his closest English friends; he was "Conrad," so that we see him turning his surname into a Christian name, matching the "Konrad" of the Mickiewicz poems. The "Konrad" of Christian name and surname firmly embedded in him the idea of Poland, of Poland's role in his history as the pawn of larger European powers. It attached him to the ideals of his mother and father, while in practice he abhorred their revolutionary zeal, their idealistic politics, their hopes of amelioration, their sacrifice under the wheels of a gigantic, impersonal machine. The name, and Conrad's subsequent use of it, already posed the conflict. The intense romanticism of his later years—his attach-

* Oceanic, indeed, is Conrad's sense of sorrow, as we read in an earlier letter to Aunt Marguerite, with its *fin de siècle* despair and self-pity: "Life rolls on in bitter waves, like the gloomy and brutal ocean under a sky covered with mournful clouds, and there are some days when to the poor souls embarked on a despairing voyage it seems that not even one ray of sun has ever penetrated that sad veil; that never again will it shine, that it never even existed! We must excuse those eyes which the harsh wind of misfortune has so filled with tears that they refuse to see the blue; we must excuse those lips which have so tasted life's bitterness that they refuse to express words of hope" (March 23-25,1890; ALS, Yale).

ment to exotic places, his chivalric code, his stress upon personal honor and integrity, as well as his frequent flare-ups of violence, temper, and rage—is profoundly attached to his Polish heritage. He was caught by traditions fixed for centuries; he did not need Darwinian biology to understand how the strong sacrificed the weak in order to survive.

Even as he signed his novels and stories Joseph Conrad, he was writing to Polish friends and relatives as Korzeniowski, but with unusual variations. He signed, alternately, Konrad Korzeniowski, Jph Conrad Korzeniowski, J. C. Korzeniowski, K. N[ałęcz]. Korzeniowski, Konrad N. Korzeniowski, simply Konrad, Conrad Korzeniowski, Conrad N. Korzeniowski, Joseph Conrad (Korzeniowski), J. Conrad K., Konrad Korzeniowski (Joseph Conrad); or, on occasion, J. Conrad, Conrad, Joseph Conrad. To non-Polish friends, he signed Jph. Conrad, Joseph Conrad, J. Conrad, Conrad, even Jph Cd.

The significant element in this confusion of realms we note in the Polish correspondence, where Conrad straddled cultures. Most compelling from the point of view of identity was his use of the middle initial "N." for Nałęcz, the particular Korzeniowski family he belonged to. Strangely enough, this usage turns up with his use of Conrad as a surname, not Konrad, never Józef or Teodor. As Conrad, he was English; as Korzeniowski, he was a Pole; as Nałęcz, he was holding on to the memory of his father and his father's family, even as he was indebted to his uncle, a Bobrowski.* The division of allegiances boggles the mind.

Still another dimension came in his signing as "Konrad Korzeniowski (Joseph Conrad)," which occurs in a letter (dated April 25, 1905) to Aleksander Jasieński, not unusually concerned with straightening out his origins and stressing that he is not related to the novelist Józef Korzeniowski. Conrad had to avoid using Józef—*his own name*—because a well-known novelist and dramatist of that name lived from 1797 to 1863. Further, a historian of the same name, to whom Conrad wrote in 1901, lived from 1863 to 1921, almost an exact contemporary of Conrad's. Thus, something usually taken for granted, one's own name, had to be avoided to escape confusion, especially with the novelist who had died in 1863—in so many ways a fateful year for the Korzeniowskis. How appropriately macabre was Mme Orzeszkowa's use of Józef Korzeniowski's name as a way of attacking Joseph Conrad, even to calling them "near relatives."

To avoid confusion, Conrad compounded it, and he never really settled on a name, since his letters to Poles and non-Poles followed no set pattern. The variety of names manifested the variety of selves, the variety of lives, and the variety of stances Conrad had established for himself. Stretched across his

* That uncle, Tadeusz, was christened Wilhelm (after William Tell), Jerzy (after George Washington), Tadeusz (after Tadeusz Kościuszko)—but used only the last name.

entire life, he confronted the irreconcilable divisions of his identity. Language itself became an ingredient of this split, since the writing and pronunciation of his Polish names involved letters, sounds, and accents lying well outside English; and in the instance of "Nałęcz," he needed to write the unusual barred ł, with the Polish sound of "w," and the consonant cluster of "cz," which for the non-Slav is the essence of foreignness. As for the spoken name: "Korzeniowski" pronounced correctly as a Polish name, not anglicized as Kor-zen-i-ow-ski, makes the sound almost unintelligible to the English ear. We can assume that whenever Conrad pronounced it on board ship—first as seaman, then as mate, and even as captain—he sensed a response that drove home his foreignness. Further, whenever an Englishman, particularly an uneducated seaman, pronounced his name, Conrad heard it mangled or, subconsciously, given an edge that indicated he was an outsider, a marginal man—even when no overt antagonism was intended.

These problems in self-naming, which ended only with Conrad's death, are evident in his naming of characters, most apparently with Jim in *Lord Jim.* Jim is never given a surname—and one recalls Conrad's own use of Conrad or Konrad as his full name. Similarly, one thinks of his other characters and how we remember them, not as figures with a Christian name and surname, but with a single designation only: Razumov, Heyst, Verloc, Gould, Nostromo. If we recall Victorian and late-Victorian novelists in English, we note that well-known characters have recognizable Christian names: David Copperfield, Dorothea Brooke, Becky Sharp, Henry Esmond, Tess of the d'Urbervilles. For Conrad, it was otherwise. While it is true that all his characters except Jim have full names, we note how he was caught between English and Russian usage: English usage stressing the Christian name as well as the surname, and Russian, with its lengthy emphasis upon the entire name, as well as nicknames, diminutives, and other variations. Jim himself had good reason to suppress his last name—since he considered himself a criminal on the run—and we see how Conrad would have particular insight into that kind of evasion; for evasion of his name, or disguise of its foreignness, or bearing up to it were all part of his own attitude.* The modern idea of the deracinated individual floating free of background and tradition as an affirmative response to bourgeois commitments was to be unacceptable to Conrad. He used the idea of deracination not to applaud isolation but rather as a source of tensions, conflicts, and self-destructive attitudes.

Conrad apparently was moving toward that vague area, explored by Kafka, where the character is reduced to an initial, K., or a Christian name and a letter for a surname, Joseph K., that region of anonymity, nobodyness.

* Jessie Conrad writes that, in the arrangement for their Polish trip in 1914, Conrad forgot "some important formality as to the date of his naturalization, and he had omitted to put his full name, Korzeniowski" (*Joseph Conrad As I Knew Him*, p. 63).

Although Dostoevsky is prodigal with names, thrusting them upon us at every turn, Conrad preferred a minimal usage. Part of the distance or impersonality we sense in his characters derives from naming difficulties. Conrad was anxious to be accepted in his adopted country and career, and yet he insisted on his strangeness and exoticism; and this modulation of identities carries over into a most significant area in his work, the naming of characters, or, rather, his desire not to name them, to maintain them as "significant nobodies."

Naming difficulties—his own or his characters'—were paradigmatic of the entire life. Conrad's biography begins here, with the marginality thrust upon him even by birth. His names were a career in themselves, part of that dare to achieve or fail. As Józef Teodor Konrad Korzeniowski, he would, like Proteus, always be in a state of defining and redefining himself. A final shape was not his destiny. Like so many of his barely named characters, he would cut himself adrift in order to establish conditions close to failure, which he could then overcome with a maximum of anxiety and psychic energy. Brought close to hysteria and breakdown, that is, close to psychological death, he would dredge up the effort to continue; or else sink into illness and parallel his childhood mode of dealing with the ineffable.

To begin with the father: Apollo Korzeniowski (1820–1869) was a man of incredible complications, conflicts, and divisions. An idealist in political matters, a rebel against Russian rule of Poland, a romantic, foolhardy activist, and yet a poet, translator, playwright, a literary man of some gifts, Apollo established many of the personality rifts that were to characterize Joseph Conrad as he matured. Apollo was himself the product of severe divisions, a Poland which, in 1772, had been partitioned among Russia, Prussia, and Austria, followed by a second partition in 1793, and a third in 1795; so that Poland as a coherent state had ceased to exist and had become a number of territories held together only by language, literature, and sensibility. In this respect, a Polish nation did exist; but it existed in minds, not as geography. For that reason, perhaps, Apollo upon Conrad's birth dedicated a poem to his infant son, "To My Son born in the 85th year of Muscovite Oppression," clearly intended for him to keep the Polish nation in mind when it no longer existed in fact.

As a Korzeniowski, Apollo could trace his family to the early seventeenth century, when his ancestors were considered nobility, what we would deem upper middle class. Apollo's heritage as a member of the generally comfortable, landowning gentry or nobility (the *szlachta*) gave him access to the cultural lords of the country, whose salient values were romantic, chivalric, military, quite class-conscious, although lacking the patronizing, condescending tone of the English aristocracy. Members of the *szlachta* were not titled, but they were clearly aware of their privileged position, and not until much later, well into the nineteenth century, in fact, were their aristocratic values seriously challenged, by the bourgeois, moneyed element. Social and economic changes in Poland had some broad parallels to what was occurring in Victorian England, although Poland's status as a carved-up and occupied country makes further analogies suspect.

For the Korzeniowskis and other members of their class, money-making was shunned; was, indeed, considered a dirty enterprise better left to vulgarians and Jews. Apollo, then, was born into a traditional society, with certain class, caste, and family pretensions, and his attitude toward money and money-making was clearly transmitted to the young Conrad. Later, when Conrad wrote to his friend Cunninghame Graham about "making money," he referred to it in mock-Yiddish terms as the "shent-per-shent" business, clearly attributing the money business to Jewish elements. And to Garnett, Conrad mentioned that his maternal grandfather, also a member of the land-owning gentry, never wrote anything but letters "and a large number of promissory notes dedicated to various Jews."

Apollo's values were chivalric, intensely idealistic, full of youthful optimism, and committed to social amelioration. As a young man, he was not unlike Shelley, and the circles in which he moved had their analogy in the English romantic movement. But Apollo was also a Pole, so that his keen sense of personal honor in turn involved a sharp awareness of national honor. The Korzeniowskis were part of that class whose tone was set by a Don Quixote-like dedication to freedom, Polish ideals, severe Catholicism, patriotic outbursts against the oppressor—whether Russia, Prussia, or Austria—and continued plots and counterplots against the foreign invader, all doomed to failure because of lack of preparation or insufficient organization. Generations of young men like Apollo had thrown themselves under the grinding wheels of the foreign juggernaut, and Conrad's portrait of Haldin, in *Under Western Eyes*, has in it something of his father as a young man.

Many years later, Conrad's maternal uncle Tadeusz Bobrowski, more sober and cautious than the Korzeniowski side, often castigated Conrad for being "the dreamer—in spite of your very practical profession," as seaman—a laxity attributed to Apollo and his line. In fact, when Conrad was thirty-three years old, Bobrowski still scolded the seaman about his paternal heritage:

> . . . You lack endurance, Panie Bracie, in the face of facts—and, I suppose, in the face of people too? This is a trait of character inherited from your Grandfather [Teodor Korzeniowski]—your paternal Uncle [Robert, who died in 1863]—and even your Father: in short the Nałęczs. The former two were always involved in various projects, most diverse in nature, mostly of a practical type—they hatched them in their imagination and were even offended when anyone criticized them—considering their opponents to be "idiots," but the facts most often gave the lie to their dreams, hence bitterness towards those who saw more clearly. Your Father was an idealistic dreamer; he certainly loved people and he certainly

> wished happiness for them—although he usually applied two measures to them:—he was a lenient judge of the poor and the weak of this world—and he was very sharp and pitiless towards the rich and powerful:—hence we have a cleavage.

Bobrowski uses this judgment, which is not wide of the mark, as a way of castigating Conrad (who, we recall, is thirty-three) for letting his imagination run away with him and then becoming disappointed and pessimistic when frustrated in his dreams. In Tadeusz's criticism of Conrad's romanticism and dreaminess, we note a sharp resemblance to Conrad's own later judgment of his Lord Jim. Jim's plans for himself are never commensurate with the reality as experienced; and, consequently, he misses each considerable chance for stability and success while he pursues the butterflies flitting through his imagination. For him, the fantasy life is the more real. In the godlike Stein we note Conrad's placement of Tadeusz and his advice for the young man. What is remarkable as we trace Conrad's earliest beginnings in his Polish background is how clearly he saw his own situation and knew his own mind. When the time came to re-create memories, he had absorbed everything—his uncle's advice as well as his own situation—and could reproduce it in Jim, Razumov, Heyst, Decoud, Nostromo, even in Verloc.*

---

*As a corrective to Bobrowski's criticism of the Korzeniowskis, we must keep in mind that he exaggerated Apollo's faults, or lied about them; he hid from Conrad the conspiratorial activities of his own mother (*a Bobrowska*), and he dissembled about his brother Stefan, who as an underground chief of the Left was as radical as Apollo.

Bobrowski's letters to Conrad, from 1874 to 1893, are a mine of information, and we shall draw upon them; but their tone and attitudes must be taken with a view toward the writer's own temperament. Tadeusz Bobrowski had a certain view of himself and of his society, and he—like so many Conradian characters—also "remade" reality to fit that view. He was industrious, intelligent, rational, somewhat parsimonious, very much a member of his class and yet impatient with that same class's romantic-idealistic tendencies. A positivist and utilitarian of sorts, he wanted an ordered universe, and he felt that his admonitions had been ignored, to the detriment of those who ignored him. There is little question that as a rationalist he held himself intellectually and emotionally superior to those around him. The posthumous publication of his voluminous *Memoirs* in Lwów in 1900 demonstrated his feelings of superiority to the Polish Don Quixotes tilting at windmills and throwing themselves into disaster.

Irresponsibility, capriciousness, imagination, idealism: these were his *bêtes noires*. He tended to see them all in the Korzeniowskis, especially in Apollo, and yet they existed in the Bobrowskis as well, as part of the gentry class itself. What he sullied as Korzeniowski characteristics were really Polish traits, and he failed to see that Conrad's father had a largeness of spirit and a generosity that were more important to him than tidiness and orderliness. Bobrowski felt that Polish survival depended on keeping one's own house in order, the individual saving himself through industry and tending his own garden—and he may have been right—but he failed to accept any alternative view based on sacrifice, altruism, nationalism, something more than self-serving. Since he was himself generous with the young Conrad, we should not be hard on him. He was a mixture of many traits which Conrad later brought together in his solid, sometimes stolid, characters: MacWhirr, Davidson, somewhat in Marlow, and elsewhere. If Apollo Korzeniowski is the ad-

Apollo was born into a political situation in which his class of gentry or noblemen provided the leadership and impetus for rebellion against Russian rule. In both the 1794 and 1830 insurrections, Polish gentry in Podolia attempted to push out the invader, although their methods did not engage the peasants in the struggle and were doomed to failure. Once Conrad was himself in England, he periodically visited members of the Kliszczewski family: the father, Józef, had fought, alongside Apollo's father, in the November Rising of 1830–31.

One of the outgrowths of this futile attempt against Russian imperial power was the development of Polish Messianism, a religious movement that coincided with sharp political agitation. Messianism suggested that Europe had fallen away from the true sense of Christianity, and that Poland alone remained to carry out the mission of reconverting all of Europe back to the true spirit. Messianism, clearly, was an outgrowth of an intense romanticism, in which political setbacks could be transformed into spiritual and chivalric terms. Amusing or not, the spirit of Shelley was not too distant from the Polish outlook. In fact, the great romantic writers of this period—especially Mickiewicz and Słowacki—expressed this view in language and in terms that helped keep the idea of Poland as a nation in mind.

Running parallel to these ideas as the young Apollo became intellectually aware in the 1830s (twenty to twenty-five years before Conrad's birth in 1857) were profound political schisms. Distant as these conflicts now seem, they entered profoundly into Conrad's decision to leave Poland in 1874 and then surfaced insistently in his work thirty years after that. Polish gentry were divided into three seemingly irreconcilable camps, which have striking parallels to political developments in many other countries where there are oppressed and oppressors. There was one group, the so-called Appeasers, that saw Poland as a nation but clearly within the Russian sphere of influence. They favored a national identity, but Poland would accept Russian rule and the Russian language as inevitable. Next was the group that rejected Russia and Russians and looked to the West for leadership, the so-called Whites. They longed for pre-partition Poland (before 1772), were nostalgic about Polish ways, but eschewed any kind of radical reform of Polish society. They insisted on their prerogatives as gentry or nobility and wished to preserve Poland as a feudal society of peasants and nobility. They were, however, anti-Russian, very nationalistic, with a romanticism heavily streaked, however, with rationalism and hardheadedness. The Whites and their attitudes characterized Conrad's maternal side, the Bobrowskis, especially Conrad's Uncle Tadeusz. His mother, Ewa, appears to have been a Bobrowska with strong Korzeniowski or radical leanings. There is some ques-

venturer who throws himself into life only to sink in the destructive element, then Tadeusz Bobrowski is the ship captain who plods ahead on a straight course, irrespective of the storms gathering around him. In touching up his portrait, Conrad was not unkind to his uncle.

tion as to how much these ideas were her own or those of her strong-willed husband. In any event, once they were married, they functioned as a unit, politically and personally.

There was still a third group, the Reds or Radicals. They were reformists who urged not only Polish independence of Russia, Austria, and Prussia but also a radical revision of Polish society, with land reform and the elimination of feudal serfdom. They rejected reliance on the West (they had been betrayed too many times) and placed faith only in their own activities, which involved a form of guerrilla warfare against Russian rule. They were militant, insurrectionist, romantic to the core, incredibly dedicated and brave; chivalric, without being feudal. Apollo, of course, belonged to this group, a group foredoomed by romantic foolhardiness, as Tadeusz Bobrowski well saw. In the 1863 insurrection, two years after Apollo had himself been seized by Russian authorities and, along with Ewa and the young Conrad, sent into exile, his family suffered critical losses. His father, Teodor, fell dead while trying to join Polish guerrilla forces; his brother Robert was killed in battle, and still another brother, Hilary, was exiled, to die ten years later, as Apollo was himself to die only six years afterward.

Conrad's maternal side, the Bobrowskis, even though they sided with the Appeasers and the Whites and opposed the Reds, also suffered grievously. Among the Bobrowski losses were Ewa's brother Kazimierz, who was imprisoned; another brother, Stefan, was murdered in a staged duel. Three other siblings, a sister, Teofila, and two brothers, Michał and Stanisław, had died earlier; so that as the Bobrowskis died off—Ewa herself in 1865—only Uncle Tadeusz and an ill Kazimierz remained from both sides of the family. Like a prophet in Greek tragedy, Tadeusz stood amid the ruins.

Long before Conrad was born in 1857, then, political and religious lines had formed in both families—even before they were themselves joined by the marriage of Apollo and Ewa on May 8, 1856. The irresolvable conflicts we find in Conrad's politics have at least some of their basis in his heritage. With this background, Conrad as a person and writer has almost no relationship to English or American writers of the nineteenth and twentieth centuries. Hemingway growing up in Oak Park, Illinois, may have had his father's suicide in his background, but his political heritage was based on American destiny, a national purpose, in which at least a semblance of democracy and order prevailed. Even Dickens, born into unstable gentility, feeling rejected and demeaned, had some sense of stability in English institutions, undemocratic as many of them were. But Conrad when he was born arrived in an occupied country which was hardly a nation, a land partitioned, its national language relegated to the home, with its patriots imprisoned, exiled, or soon to be killed in the 1863 insurrection and its aftermath. Furthermore, family lines—like those during the American Civil War—were in opposition: the Korzeniowskis, deeply radical, social and political reformists,

Messianic to some extent, romantic, chivalric; the Bobrowskis, some of them patriotic and quixotic, but less romantic, with a surer sense of practical values, more keenly attuned to self-preservation than to radical reform which, they felt, was doomed to failure under Russian military might.

Although we have no precise proof, Conrad may have left Poland before his seventeenth birthday as the sole way to avoid the irreconcilables of his background. He rejected, on one hand, the futility of an individual life which politics and religion could arbitrarily destroy, and, on the other, the romanticism which made patriots throw themselves against barricades manned by machine gunners. At a time when he strongly needed guidance, he noted only two kinds, the defeated (Apollo's way) or acquiescence (Uncle Tadeusz's). He felt no sense of preservation or renewal, or even support. Not that he was necessarily conscious of what he desired; but he was confronted by adult models with very different apperceptions and orders of intelligence from his own. Such lives were devoted almost completely to reliving the tragedies of the past, the death of relatives, of personal hopes, and of Poland; there was little room in which to live. For a young man of sixteen, they faced in the wrong direction.

Later, in his reminiscences, Conrad tried to explain his "desertion"—the forbidden word had by now become both anathema and magnetic. Conrad had to pronounce it, but his explanation is somewhat ingenuous:

> . . . for why should I, the son of a land which such men as these [Conrad's grand-uncle, Mikołaj Bobrowski, who had served under Napoleon and then in the Polish Army] have turned up their ploughshares and bedewed with their blood, undertake the pursuit of fantastic meals of salt junk and hard tack upon the wide seas? On the kindest view it seems an unanswerable question. Alas! I have the conviction that there are men of unstained rectitude who are ready to murmur scornfully the word *desertion* [my italics]. Thus the taste of innocent adventure may be made bitter to the palate.

Conrad attempts to explain his role by saying that no final accounting of human behavior is possible; that the inexplicable enters into every explanation.

> No charge of faithfulness ought to be lightly uttered. The appearances of this perishable life are deceptive like everything that falls under the judgment of our imperfect senses.

Falling back here on a Cartesian separation of man from things, Conrad divides desire and will, mind and body, so that mind plays us funny tricks and deceives us about the nature of reality. There is only the inner voice which one follows, and which, despite appearances to the contrary, "may last through the events of an unrelated existence, following faithfully, too, the traced way of an inexplicable impulse." Conrad asserts that the "intimate alliance of contradictions in human nature" often makes "love itself wear at times the desperate shape of betrayal." Proust could not have said it better. This is indeed an argument rich in potentialities, made all the more fertile by Conrad's own uncertainty whether he actually believed in it.

Conrad moves from this to an intricate discussion of Don Quixote and Sancho Panza, in which he tries to show that despite the Don's charm and exalted view of reality, he was not to be trusted, and that those who opposed him were not themselves wrong. In such matters, who really *knows?* If the Don deceives us, so does life. Don Quixote, Conrad says, had a "very noble, a very unselfish fantasy, fit for nothing except to raise the envy of baser mortals," and yet he, too, had his frailties.

> He wished to meet eye to eye the valorous giant Brandabarbaran, Lord of Arabia, whose armour is made of the skin of a dragon, and whose shield, strapped to his arm, is the gate of a fortified city. O amiable and natural weakness! O blessed simplicity of a gentle heart without guile! Who would not succumb to such a consoling temptation?

Still, it was a form of self-indulgence, "and the ingenious hidalgo of La Mancha was not a good citizen." The priest and barber, who condemned his activities, were "not unreasonable in their strictures." The Don "rides forth, his head encircled by a halo—the patron saint of all lives spoiled or saved by the irresistible grace of imagination. But he was not a good citizen."

From that, Conrad shifts to the summer of 1873, the year before he left Poland, when his tutor, Adam Pulman, called him "an incorrigible, hopeless Don Quixote," adding, " 'That's what you are.' " If we understand Conrad correctly, he is explaining his alleged "desertion" by pointing to the inexplicability of human behavior, and, by inference, to his invulnerability to external criticism. And yet, Conrad never really believed this—he is offering a sophistic argument to maneuver around a point he has been unable to settle. He did believe in absolutes, and by no means threw his lot in with the philosophical relativists, or those who argued for halfway measures because they assumed that every form of behavior has its elements of truth. Rejecting the relativistic implications of Frazer's anthropology as much as he did Nietzsche's form of demonry, Conrad saw human behavior in terms of the individual's commitment to certain absolutes, certain givens, and if these fundamentals are breached, then such acts are self-destructive.

In *Lord Jim,* Conrad probed this very deep-seated belief: the absolutism of commitment as apart from a world which advocates behavioral relativism. He has shifted the Don argument but retained its dimensions. Jim insists on the absolutism of his idea, and he destroys himself in honoring its terms, whereas those outside him argue for forms of compromise, given the nature of an imperfect world. The process underlying the novel does not involve primarily Conrad's desertion of Poland (Polska, the *Patna,* the fatherland) but is an exploration of the fundamentals of human behavior as they had shaped themselves in his experience: that struggle between basics, which he felt were absolute and incontrovertible, and the shifting sense of reality which demands compromise and revocability. Underneath it all were his unresolved feelings about Poland and Polish, his shift to England and English, and his fears that he might fail.

When he left Poland, Conrad could not consciously know he had assimilated the details of his background as images, scenes, attitudes, even characters, which he would project, later, in his fiction. As he observed his father die by slow degrees, he had—comparably to Proust's young Marcel—entered a time sequence that was like a dream or a novel. The irreconcilables of his background became the irreconcilables of his fiction. He understood things which no English writer knew, for he had left a land whose heritage had no parallel elsewhere in Europe. Even France in defeat at Waterloo and after the Vienna Congress had not been betrayed in the same way as Poland. Truly, Poland, like Jesus, had been sacrificed on the cross, a political sacrifice in a power ploy, a rook that served no further function. The Holy Alliance of the major powers (with the exception of England and Turkey) created a patina of religiosity in order to maintain a feudal stability. In attempting to roll back the French Revolution, the Alliance crushed all democratic movements, gave authority to Russian rule over Poland, and ensured decades of insurrection, revolution, and rebellion. At the time England was preparing to pass the first Reform Bill (of 1832), Poland was reeling from the failures of its 1830–31 insurrection against Russian power, a country divided among Russia, Austria, and Prussia.

For a writer, Conrad's preparation was unique. Generally, an author with a strong political background becomes a propagandist for one side or another; he becomes either progressive or reactionary, and his work reflects his ideology. Conrad, as we see him developing in the 1890s, eschewed ideology, hewed to a fierce skepticism and irony, and turned the activist politics of his forebears into larger metaphysical questions of being and becoming. He was interested in values, not movements; in questions of integrity and sincerity, not belief; in attitudes of mind and spirit, not social or political commitments. He was more a Platonist than an Aristotelian, although he was an ideologue of neither camp. Conrad is often, incorrectly, seen as a reactionary or conservative, when in actuality his value system lay almost completely beyond political and social questions. His turn of mind was to conserve, but it was divided equally between conservation and the forces or elements that destroy. Conrad contained large amounts of Apollo-Korzeniowski, Ewa-Bobrowska, Poland-Polish issues; but he was also a man with a cognitive spark of his own, so that background—however compelling and unique—will never explain his acts of imagination.

Part of the reason those Polish critics cited at the beginning could never understand Conrad was that they tried to nullify the individual spark, the processes of imagination, as if all of a writer's behavior were to be attributed to conditioning or to allegiances *made for him*. Several allegiances were indeed made for Conrad, as we shall see, but there were also the ones he insisted upon for himself. He was, like Proteus, constantly reshaping himself, although at great personal cost; in another respect, he was like Antaeus, seeking the right ground on which he could plant himself and gain his ultimate strength. He chose limitless areas for his accomplishment.

To be a non-working member of the gentry, that is, to remain with his Uncle Tadeusz in Podolia, was to accept a fate set for him and to deny the inner spark. Precisely what drove Conrad from Russian Poland will never be disentangled. Whether it was to escape Russian military service or a past littered with his father's failures, or a dim awareness of his fitness for other worlds, leave he did. What he escaped from, however, deserves further detailing. The story is a multilevel one of endless conflict and unceasing struggle for personal and national survival.

The division of Polish political and social thought into Appeasers, Whites, and Reds conveys only one small part of the intellectual and ideological background of Conrad's father. The reality was far more complicated. In one sense, Apollo Korzeniowski provided a marvelous background for a son who could survive the experience of a broken home, a mother dead when he was seven, and a father drifting toward death. For the son who could transform the experience into an art form, the background had intense drama, and, as well, the sense of language and literature, endless words, an outpouring of verbiage. For Apollo was a literary man of some note. Not a great or memorable writer, he was, nevertheless, a published poet, dramatist, and translator.

Like Joyce, who derived from an oral tradition of words and wordplay, Conrad came from a verbal background, in his instance, the written word.* For not only did Apollo write ceaselessly; also, Conrad's maternal uncle, Tadeusz Bobrowski, wrote voluminously, his two-volume *Memoirs* appearing in 1900. Furthermore, after his father's death in 1869, Conrad was cared for by a number of guardians who wrote, were writers, or considered themselves authors. Words were not alien. Words, in fact, were interconnected with political and social activities. When not writing, Conrad's relatives were haranguing.

---

*Even so, an oral tradition derived from the Russian *skaz* may have entered into Conrad's imagination with Marlow and his other first-person narrators. The *skaz* was a free-flowing oral narrative dependent on the style, tone, and mannerisms of the speaker. The Polish equivalent of this was the *gawęda*, also based on an oral narrative. (See note for page 440.)

During his lifetime, Apollo was more famous as a patriot and Polish nationalist than as a writer. After his death, he was more or less forgotten, only to be resurrected in this century as a writer who fitted Marxist patterns of the class struggle and sympathy for the lower classes.* Born in 1820, one of three surviving sons of Teodor Korzeniowski and Julia Dyakiewicz, Apollo before his marriage to Ewa Bobrowska in 1856 wrote a cycle of poems called *Purgatorial Cantos*. The cycle, started just after the 1848 revolution, was a long lament for its failure, full of Apollo's apotheosis of the Polish nation and solidly in the romantic tradition of the 1830s poets, Mickiewicz, Słowacki, and especially Krasiński. In a somewhat similar vein, Apollo wrote another cycle based on a Ukrainian peasants' revolt in 1855. His attack is on his own class, on the gentry-nobility, for failing to recognize the rights of the peasants, all in keeping with his designation as a Red committed not only to the overthrow of Russian imperial power but to a complete reform of Polish social and economic life. Without holding any doctrinaire or consistent views, Apollo was an early Marxist, a Marxist without Marx; more startlingly, a revolutionary Hegelian.

Yet he was also a member of his own class, as Tadeusz Bobrowski recognized in his *Memoirs*. This split between one's social and economic opinions and the prerogatives of one's own class or achievement not only divided Apollo but apparently was part of Conrad's heritage. In his most strongly worded commentary on Poland and Polish fortunes, "Autocracy and War," Conrad attacked the old monarchies not for their prerogatives but for their inability to change:

> The sin of the old European monarchies was not the absolutism inherent in every form of government; it was the inability to alter the forms of their legality, grown narrow and oppressive with the march of time. Every form of legality is bound to degenerate into oppression, and the legality in the forms of monarchical institutions sooner, perhaps, than any other. . . . The revolutions of European States have never been in the nature of absolute protests *en masse* against the monarchical principle; they were the uprising of the people against the oppressive degeneration of legality.

Conrad's statement here is a curious one from this man of forty-eight trying to work through his background and account for his father's position.

* After World War II, Jan Kott, among others, saw him as a Marxist primarily interested in the class struggle and then went on to attack Conrad for lacking any coherent social philosophy. "Conradian fidelity to oneself," he wrote, "is the fidelity of slaves, for the slave is he who obeys the lord when he despises and cares only about his inner rectitude." Kott's attack in 1945 is, of course, reminiscent of Mme Orzeszkowa's in 1899, in which message, not art, and ideology, not craft, are the sole actualities. Of interest to the biographer is the extent to which the careers of Apollo and Conrad intertwined during the latter's lifetime and then even a generation after his death.

How close this argument is to Apollo's own, and yet how subtly it diverges, for the son by removing the label of revolutionary makes the father into an evolutionist or an ameliorist. Conrad reinterpreted his father's principles into those of an insurrectionist fighting against a foreign power, which is something quite different from a revolutionary in opposition to the social order.

Apollo Korzeniowski was no less complicated than his more illustrious son. About the time of his marriage, in 1856, Apollo apparently found poetry less accommodating to his advanced political opinions than drama, and he turned to writing plays. Part of his struggle—as later Conrad's—was to resolve his own standing as a member of the gentry with his radical political and social ideas, which could only injure the status of the gentry. The Poles of the Ukraine were in a sense something special. Unlike the Russian Ukrainians, who were peasants, mainly illiterate, and Greek-Catholic Orthodox, the Poles were "noble" and Roman Catholic. Among the latter, except for the peasants, there were few class distinctions, with the landowner, clerk, and town professional (lawyer, doctor, teacher) all considered part of the same social class. Although the Poles were under Russian rule, they were themselves a kind of ruling class, with a sharp sense of their distinction from the Russian masses. Both Apollo and his son had a distinct feeling for Polish superiority, identified themselves with the West, not with the Slavic race, and suggested on numerous occasions a racial superiority to the Russians and Pan-Slavs.

Apollo's father, Teodor, had himself been a typical nobleman. A resident of the Ukraine, he was a military man, a daredevil, a romantic. He had once felt that Napoleon would bring freedom to Poland after the final partition and had identified himself with the fortunes of the French emperor. He served also in the Polish struggle against Austria, was decorated in the 1809 battle of Raszyn, a Polish victory over Austria, and then joined Napoleon's army until 1812. Fiercely individualistic and yet caught by Slavic fatalism, he later fought in the 1830 uprising, becoming a captain in 1831, and died trying to join the 1863 insurrection in Warsaw.* Typical of the *szlachcic* or

---

* Conrad himself wrote to Edward Garnett describing his paternal grandfather rather ironically, but sympathetically: "My paternal grandfather Theodor N. Korzeniowski served in the cavalry. Decorated with the cross of 'Virtuti Militari' (a plain white enamel with a green wreath of laurel and these words in the centre) something in the nature of V.C. Attained the rank of captain in 1830 [1831] when the Russo-Polish war occurred after which the so-called Polish Army ceased to exist. Two wounds. Retired to a little hereditary estate adjoining the extensive possessions of the family of *Sobânski* (they are in the Almanach de Gotha) [Apollo, not his father, administered that estate] great friends and I fancy distant relations. . . . Wrote a tragedy in 5 Acts, Verse, privately printed, and so extremely dull that no one was ever known to have read it through. I know I couldn't notwithstanding my family pride and the general piety of my disposition" (January 20, 1900; Garnett, pp, 165–66).

country nobleman, he was as strongly devoted to warfare as to his friends and relatives; when not fighting, he retired to the land to farm—paralleled later by Conrad's retirement to a writing career after twenty years at sea.

According to contemporary stories, Teodor was an autocrat at home; apparently his hopes for a more democratic Poland did not extend into his domestic situation. He tyrannized over his three sons and, at the same time, indulged them. A man of little formal education, he felt profound respect for Apollo when he went away to study Oriental languages at St. Petersburg University. When he was not fighting, Teodor administered for the government the village of Korytna. One sees him as a combination of squire in the English tradition and a Dostoevskian father figure, even a Karamazov. In his *Memoirs*, Tadeusz Bobrowski limns with caustic both the type and the man:

> . . . he was a utopian, and a teller of stories of that particular kind which first lie to themselves, get to believe firmly their own lies, and then pass them on to others and quarrel with those who will not believe them. It goes without saying that he considered himself as a great politician and as a first-class patriot, for, without listening to common sense, he was always ready to saddle a horse and to chase the enemy out of the country. . . . For himself he had a great respect, but for his sons he nourished a strong admiration, especially when he spoke of them to others. It was a habit with him (especially when he was angry, which happened very often) to treat them, not as grown-up people, but as small boys, calling them imbeciles, if nothing worse, treatment which they bore with the greatest respect, kissing the father's hands. The eldest of his three sons, Robert, was a gambler and a drunkard, who died in 1863, no longer very young, having contributed not a little to the decline of the family. The youngest, Hilary, was just the same utopian as his father, and not less sarcastic than his brother Apollo, but without the latter's good manners. . . . Only my brother-in-law [Apollo] did not possess that passion for speculating which had dominated his father and his brothers.

The drinking and gambling of two of the sons, the idealism of the third, the self-destructive tendencies of all three, recall the Karamazovs, even to the hatred of the father implicit in their activities. Rather than destroy him, they destroyed themselves. Teodor ran through his wife's dowry and, according to reports, dissipated whatever money he laid his hands on. Although never impoverished, Apollo was not wealthy and had to provide for himself by administering estates, as had his father. Conrad's tradition, then, was heavily landed, in one sense like George Eliot's background, although hers was of course more stable and free from political radicalism.

At twenty, Apollo left local schools and attended Petersburg University, where he may have mixed with Russian radicals, anarchists, and socialists who sympathized with Poland's plight. In *Under Western Eyes*, Conrad "reproduces" this situation, with Razumov and Haldin, and it is easy to see

Haldin as a prototypical Apollo Korzeniowski—the revolutionary young man a replica of the writer's father, who is, in turn, betrayed by a conservative young man, Razumov-Conrad, a "traitor" to the revolutionary role laid out for him. The entire situation has of course been transformed by Conrad's imagination, but we should not lose sight of how sensitively he probed this early material, covering his tracks, but coming very close to deep divisions within him, even to an imaginative re-creation of parricide. While scorning Dostoevsky for his wildness and madness, Conrad approached Dostoevskian themes and Dostoevskian chaos, playing psychologically with the idea of the son turning the father in to the authorities, gaining revenge to some extent for a childhood and heritage he both rejected and found attractive, an Oedipal situation carefully disguised. After Razumov has betrayed Haldin to the Russian authorities, he sees how much more attractive the young man is than the people to whom he has turned him in. Razumov has, truly, cut himself off, from his past and even from his feelings, and is indeed the marginal man Conrad always sensed in himself.

Apollo, unlike his son, had no such misgivings. At Petersburg, where he studied sporadically for four or five years, he worked on Oriental languages and law, but finished nothing and did not appear to gain any education for a future professional life. He evidently mastered several foreign languages, among them French and English, at least to read them, for he later translated from Dickens, de Vigny, Hugo, Shakespeare, and, possibly, Heine. It was somewhat after this time that Apollo started writing the poetry mentioned above and tried to combine several careers: as political radical, estate manager, and literary man. Once we note this combination, we can see that Conrad's own mixture of ordinary seaman, captain, and novelist is not so unusual; he was accustomed to several seemingly conflicting careers, numerous contrasting activities.

Poetry, as we saw, did not sufficiently serve Apollo's purposes, because shortly before his marriage to Ewa Bobrowska, he began his first dramatic work, in 1855, *Comedy* (*Komedia*), a free adaptation of Griboedov's *The Misfortune of Being Clever*. By this time, Apollo had formulated his literary credo—not a consistent one, but one with considerable overtones for the son who was to start writing forty years later. The writer, as part of his romantic stance, takes a position outside of materialistic society; he sees money-making, commerce, industry, and social rank as sources for his irony and vilification. The writer must himself suffer: poetry is a form of personal stress. The poet, like Jesus, is readying himself to be crucified, or else he is undergoing a purgatorial existence.

Such a view of the poet—which was paralleled by Conrad's view of himself as novelist—has its national image in Poland as the sacrificial lamb offered up by the West to placate the Russian wolf. The constant betrayal of Poland by the Western nations because of their fear of Russian might finds its place in Apollo's sense of the poet's mission: to suffer in purgatory until the betrayal of values and debasement of ideals cease. Such a stance, which fitted well with Apollo's sense of himself as poet and revolutionary, also dovetailed with his courtship of Ewa, who returned his ardor but was not permitted to give her hand in marriage.

Evelina or Ewa Bobrowska was born in 1833 (thirteen years Apollo's junior, as Jessie George was to be fifteen years Conrad's junior) into a large family, the fifth of the seven children who survived. We do not know a great deal about her,* and what we do know derives mainly from her brother Tadeusz Bobrowski, who after her and Apollo's death became Conrad's guardian, friend, and benefactor. Tadeusz outlived Ewa by twenty-nine years, three of his other brothers and remaining sister by over two decades. All the members of the family, except for Kazimierz, died in their teens, twenties, or thirties. Conrad's stock was not particularly hardy on either side.

The Bobrowskis, as all commentaries remind us, and as Tadeusz Bobrowski's *Memoirs* insist, were practical people, very much aristocrats in the Polish gentry-nobility sense. Ewa's father, Józef, firmly opposed the marriage of his daughter to Apollo for the latter's lack of practicality, for his laziness, and, probably, for his desire to be a literary man. At the time the couple met, in 1847, at Korytna near Lipowiec (Apollo having already made the acquaintance of Tadeusz in school), Ewa was only fifteen, Apollo twenty-eight. In his *Memoirs*, Tadeusz attempted to see Apollo as Ewa saw him:

> Of all the young men of the neighbourhood there was only one whom I really liked: Apollo Nałęcz Korzeniowski, as he used to sign his full name rather boastfully. . . . In the countryside he had the reputation of being ugly, and of a sarcastic character, as a matter of fact, he was not beautiful, not even nice, but he had very charming expressive eyes, and his sarcastic character was only a matter of verbiage and society conventions, for I could never trace it in what he felt or did. Passionate in his feelings, expansive, and a sincere friend of everybody, but unpractical in his actions and often even helpless, he was easily implacable in speech and writing, but only too indulgent (apparently in compensation, as I told him often)

---

* Writing in 1900, Conrad recalled her family, and her, generally: "There was an extraordinary Sister-Cult in that family from which I profited when left an orphan at the age of ten [eleven]. And my mother certainly was no ordinary woman. Her correspondence with my father and with her brothers which in the year 1890 I have read and afterwards destroyed was a revelation to me; I shall never forget my delight, admiration and unutterable regret at my loss, (before I could appreciate her) which only then I fully understood. One of her brothers Thaddeus [Tadeusz] to whom I stand more in the relation of a son than of a nephew was a man of powerful intelligence and great force of character and possessed an enormous influence in the Three Provinces (Ukraine, Volhynia and Podolia). A most distinguished man" (January 20; Garnett, p. 166).

> in everyday life, for he had a different measure for the little and simple ones and for the great of this world.

He continues, with a certain degree of acerbity:

> In the salons he was very pleasant, his unusual appearance, his originality and his gifts attracted the women—everybody knows how much women are interested in anything out of the ordinary—and on the other hand, he pleased the men by the ease of his conversation and his politeness, by his traditional Polish attention for old people, and his tactfulness towards the young; for, as I said before, he was only violent and sarcastic pen in hand, and ironical only when conversing with women, strictly within the limits of decency.

Surely, what attracted Ewa was that blend of idealism and ardor with a courteous and chivalrous manner, a kind of charm that carries all before it.*

In the eight-year interval before they were finally united, Apollo was introduced into many families as a possible suitor, and his future father-in-law had himself tried to find a fiancée for him. Apollo, however, persisted in his attention to Ewa, and five years after Józef Bobrowski's death in 1850 he followed the young lady to Terekov, where Ewa's mother was staying with her brother, Adolf Pilchowski, and became engaged, with the marriage following in Oratov on May 8, 1856, when Ewa was twenty-three and Apollo thirty-six. Apollo's son was to marry at thirty-eight.

Tadeusz wrote about Ewa glowingly. She was apparently the "Madonna" of the family, the sole surviving girl (after Teofila's death in 1851) in a family of boys, doted upon by Tadeusz and marked for a socially acceptable marriage. Tadeusz describes her as being a young lady of great intellect and sensitivity, caught between her great love for Apollo and her sense of obligation to her father. The situation is typical, like part of an Italian opera or a Russian novel. From Tadeusz's words—"Dissatisfied with herself, she could not give others that inner contentment which she lacked"—we sense her frustration with the role cut out for her as a young woman in a noble family, her disturbing recognition that no matter what she thought or believed, she could not turn it into action. Possibly this dissatisfaction resulted in her loyalty to Apollo both before and after marriage. Because he was so unsuitable in terms of what the ideal suitor was supposed to be, because his views ran so counter to those of the Bobrowskis, and because he seemed so romantic, idealistic, and helpless, she refused to let her father separate them.

---

* Conrad's own description follows his uncle's: "A man of great sensibilities; of exalted and dreamy temperament; with a terrible gift of irony and of gloomy disposition; withal of strong religious feeling degenerating after the loss of his wife into mysticism touched with despair. His aspect was distinguished; his conversation very fascinating; his face in repose sombre lighted all over when he smiled. I remember him well. For the last two years of his life I lived alone with him—but why go on?" (to Garnett, January 20, 1900).

Whatever the precise terms of the relationship, Ewa turns up repeatedly in her son's fiction, the Madonna figure greatly devoted to her husband, the woman whose own "career" is found only in marriage or in commitment to an ideal. We think of Mrs. Gould in *Nostromo*, or of Miss Haldin in *Under Western Eyes,* both lacking the chance to move actively in the world and forced to live vicariously, whether through husband, brother, or fiancé. Clearly, Ewa would have been unable to unite with Apollo until the "other" man in her life, her father, was dead. Duty was duty, roles were roles; and she "blossomed" only within the boundaries defined by the men in her family.

Ewa's defiance of the Bobrowski plans for her brought Apollo a woman he truly worshipped, and we know that after her death in 1865, at the age of thirty-two, he kept her memory alive to the young Conrad. There is no question that Conrad, who was barely old enough to remember her, worshipped at her shrine with his father. Apollo's grief was real; his guilt profound; his sense of failure overwhelming. Conrad grew up in that atmosphere, learned to assimilate loneliness and disappointment, and plotted, apparently, his escape—somewhere, anywhere. At the end of Part I of *Under Western Eyes,* Mikulin asks Razumov, after his betrayal of Haldin, one of the most pertinent questions in all of Conrad's fiction. "Where to?" he asks ironically. The world is everywhere and nowhere, and we can speculate that the young Conrad, in his teens, an orphan at eleven, had asked himself the same or a similar question.

CHAPTER 2

Birth

ONCE married, Apollo became a lease holder in Łuczyniec, where he also became an estate manager, although his real activities were literary and, later, political. After the Bobrowski estate of Oratov was sold, the dowry was paid, and Apollo and Ewa leased Derebczynka Manor in the part of the Ukraine called Podolia, near Berdichev. It was here that Conrad was born, on December 3, 1857. Before this, Apollo had formed a lasting friendship with a neighbor named Stefan Buszczyński, also a writer, and later a guardian of Conrad for a short time. After three years, Apollo because of poor management was forced to give up Derebczynka Manor, having lost the money he had invested in it.

With a wife and an infant son, and having squandered Ewa's dowry, Apollo threw himself into literary activity. With that incredible duplication which we find in history, Conrad, once married (in 1896) and with an infant son (1898), with no money and with many debts, also took up literary activity as a form of salvation. His letters at this time define his anguished situation and somehow echo Apollo's plight, although the father, born to his situation, secure as a member of the gentry, writing in his native tongue, a familiar among familiars, may not have felt—as Conrad did—quite on the edge of a precipice.* These are matters, however, of individual sensibility. The fact is that Conrad, even though in a strange land, and grappling with a strange language, was undergoing a transformational process such as his father also had undergone forty years earlier. Even a mixture of languages, as

*Just three months after his marriage, with *An Outcast of the Islands*, his second novel, recently published, Conrad wrote to Garnett: "Other writers have some starting point. Something to catch hold of . . . at any rate they know something to begin with—while I don't. I have had some impressions, some sensations—in my time:—impressions and sensations of common things. And it's all faded—my very being seems faded and thin like the ghost of a blonde and sentimental woman, haunting romantic ruins pervaded by rats. I am exceedingly miserable. My task appears to me as sensible as lifting the world without that fulcrum which even that conceited ass, Archimedes, admitted to be necessary" (June 19, 1896; Garnett, p. 59).

we shall detail later, was involved; for Apollo entered into a period of translating from English and French, juggling three languages, as Conrad was also to juggle English and French with his native Polish.

We get some sense of Apollo's anguish on the eve of his marriage and fatherhood in a work already cited, his *Comedy* (1855), as important in *his* development as "Youth" and "Heart of Darkness" are in Conrad's. *Comedy* is based on a conflict in a young man, Henryk, between his idealism and revolutionary fervor and his attraction to the materialistic world, which comes in the shape of a rich, upper-middle-class young lady, not unlike Ewa Bobrowska. In the play, Henryk is without money, which was not quite Apollo's situation, but the play dramatizes opposites and Apollo needed polarities: idealism versus money, pennilessness versus idle living, radical politics versus conservative well-being. The girl's family plots to discredit Henryk, but their machinations are discovered, and the drama winds down toward its happy ending, the union of the two young people, when Henryk suddenly rejects her (she has proposed!) and her world for his own.

Although we do not know if Conrad read this particular work of his father's, we can see how its themes work in and out of the novelist's consciousness in his major period of work, from about 1899 to 1904. Although Conrad was a far less diagrammatic writer than his father, his major work—set so deeply in his Polish consciousness—repeats many of these ideas, and turns Henryk's idealism not into foolhardiness but into ironic commentary on a diseased, contaminated society. In Conrad's work, there are no outbursts at the state or at society as such, but there is ironic, near-satirical criticism, all presented from the point of view of the individual as he enters the corruptive potential of society. One thinks of Kurtz, an idealist, a missionary, a man with humanitarian impulses; one can add Jim, also an idealist, a romantic, who attempts to impose his scheme on an intractable reality. One thinks, chiefly, of Nostromo, Decoud, Dr. Monygham. In trying to find more precise sources for these novels and for these characters, we should never forget how deeply rooted their personal problems and outlooks are in Polish sensibility, how Conrad, in some subconscious cyclical way, was replaying Apollo's old themes.

Conrad's distaste for money and for money matters (while, ironically, being forced constantly to think of money) also has its roots in his Polish heritage and in Apollo's work. In the years just after his marriage, Apollo wrote *For the Sake of Money* (*Dia miłego grosza*, 1857–58), once again based on the character Henryk. He is now ten years older and, like Nostromo after he decides to get rich slowly, has been corrupted by the society he still disdains. Full of his own self-hatred, conscious of his compromises with a society he denigrates, aware of the remnants of his former idealism and high promise, Henryk sinks into irony as a defense against self-knowledge. We see Apollo moving closer and closer to a Chekhovian view of society, and we recognize how a novel like *Nostromo*, although mounted on a panoramic scale, has a comparable Chekhovian substructure implicit in it.

Poland itself was moving closer to another confrontation with Russia, one of the periodic insurrections which led at first to Polish hopes of renewal and which resulted, finally, in a show of Russian strength and in Polish decimation. The events now were leading toward the 1863 Warsaw insurrection, and to Apollo's seizure in 1861 as an undesirable radical and his subsequent exile, along with Ewa and the young Conrad, not yet four years old. At this time, in the late 1850s, as Apollo wrote Messianic but seditious works—in which Poland is compared to Jesus being sacrificed on the cross and Russia is the Christ killer—political ferment against the invader was moving toward another showdown.

The 1863 insurrection, in whose early stages Apollo's fortunes were doomed, was an outgrowth of the unsuccessful insurrection of 1830, and that in turn grew out of Polish hopes dashed by the Congress of Vienna. After the Third Partition in 1795, Russia owned about 45 percent of Polish territory, Prussia 23 percent, and Austria 32 percent, with each territory containing its own political, constitutional, and economic regimes. School indoctrination differed, as did language; there was already that mixing of languages which we associate with Apollo as a translator and with Conrad as a novelist. For a short time, in 1805 and 1807, Polish soldiers wrested what was called the Duchy of Warsaw out of the conquered territory, as a result of Napoleon's conquest of Prussia. Poland tied its fortunes to Napoleon and had hoped for its restoration as a nation—the duchy was itself about a fifth of Poland's prepartition territory, with a little more than a third of the population. When Napoleon moved against Russia in 1812, Poland's hopes reached their highest point since the final partition, only to be frustrated completely when Russia destroyed the French Army Corps. Poles, including Conrad's granduncle Mikołaj, fought loyally alongside Napoleon in the 1813–14 campaign, under the leadership of Prince Józef Antoni Poniatowski, who died during Napoleon's retreat from Leipzig.

While these events seem distant, they entered into the consciousness of every Pole—Appeaser, White, or Red—and became wedded to Conrad's life, as if a genetic inheritance. Wherever he went or whatever he did, the events of Central Europe were part of him. Russia occupied the duchy, and Poland was readying itself for what we call now guerrilla warfare. At first, it seemed as though Russia would be favorable to Polish aspirations—for the emperor, Alexander I, had had a long friendship with the eminent Polish noble Prince Adam Jerzy Czartoryski. The Congress of Vienna, however, treated Poland not as a sovereign nation but as a piece of territory to be carved up along with other land masses, apart from national aim, language, or unity of purpose. One of the spoils for the victors, Poland was divided; Cracow and a small surrounding territory only were made a free republic. A vast borderland territory, stretching from Lithuania and Belorussia to the Ukraine, was incorporated into Russia, and a part of central Poland, about one-sixth of the original country, became known as the Congress Kingdom, under the rule of the Russian emperor, who was also the king of Poland. In effect, except for the Cracow area, Poland was under the three powers, with Russia the major enemy by far.

Under Alexander I, certain promises were made—freedom of the press, freedom to practice Roman Catholicism as the state religion, use of the Polish language in the law courts, right of employment in the civil government, and the like. But even this movement toward an opening of certain freedoms could not mitigate the fact that the king of Poland was the emperor of Russia, albeit a relatively lenient emperor. As long as Alexander was alive, Polish patriotic ardor remained quiescent, surfacing only in small-scale periodic outbursts. Large or organized insurrections did not occur, although students and young army officers were preparing themselves for some outbreak against the oppressor. Polish hatred of Russia and things Russian, despite many who wished appeasement, was high, even though the presence of Alexander tamped down potential violence. Nevertheless, the young Apollo was to hear of imprisonment of dissidents, deportation, and exile of students, including the poet Adam Mickiewicz.

After Alexander's death in 1825, Polish hatred centered on the new czar, Nicholas I, including a plot to assassinate him at his coronation in Warsaw in 1829. Meanwhile, in the rest of Europe, 1830 was an ominous year—a revolution in France in July, the revolt of Belgium, the gradual undoing of the artificial peace enforced by the reactionary Congress of Vienna. On November 29, 1830, young Polish army officers at the training school rose up and were swiftly joined by army regiments and large numbers of the civilian population. When Constantine, the imperial lieutenant, failed to take action, the outbreak grew, including Teodor Korzeniowski as well as all of Poland's major political leaders, and Poland raised an army of close to 80,000 men. The outbreak became a war, of Christian Poland against the barbaric Russia, and lasted for eight months, from January to September 1831.

Once Russia decided to fight, the inevitable defeat of Poland was apparent; and yet part of the reason for the defeat was not only Russian force in the field. The Polish elements were themselves divided, not the least over the question whether the insurrection against Russia was also a social and political revolution. Gentry and nobility—the background of Korzeniowskis and Bobrowskis, and ultimately of Conrad—were set against peasant claims. Only the common Russian enemy held the forces together, for they were rent with internal dissensions of their own. Although the insurrection had been part of the Polish Messianic mission, its sense of itself as the savior of the "free world," this same romanticism led to poor organization, inefficient and inept generals, lack of coherent leadership, and considerable privilege for the ruling classes.

The suppression of the insurrection led to a much broader repression of Polish activities. Russia set out to destroy Polish-style education and the Polish language; Poland was, in a real sense, to be effaced. Whatever constitutional guarantees were held out to Poland—a sop as well as good publicity for the Russians—were illusory. The universities of Warsaw and Wilno were closed, and Polish university students—such as Apollo Korzeniowski—were forced to attend St. Petersburg or Kiev. Russian influence, or Russian hopes for extended influence, became all-pervasive. Censorship, restrictions against Roman Catholics, dispersion of Polish soldiers into the Russian Army—one possible reason Conrad left Poland was to avoid service in the Russian military—enforcement of the Russian language in the legal system: all of these followed the 1830–31 defeat. Polish exiles abroad numbered in the thousands.

Yet, inevitably, the Russians, while thinking they had pulled the claws of the "Polish beast," only intensified Polish nationalism. As Russia oppressed her long-time enemy, Poland prepared for another round of insurrections, if not outright war. During the Crimean War, with Russia occupied with England and Turkey, Polish hopes rose again. Apollo was himself stirred to action, now thirty-three and at the middle of a career that had so far gone nowhere, and advocated a revolt, going as far as to suggest to Tadeusz Bobrowski that he, too, should join the conspiratorial forces. Tadeusz, a typical Bobrowski and, therefore, a conciliator, urged that Polish landowners make concessions to the peasants in the form of land grants and thus win them over to Polish nationalism. Tadeusz argued tactics, long-range planning, amelioration, whereas Conrad's father, romantic and idealistic, stressed visible results and had no time or energy for the long pull in which progress is measured at a snail's pace. Tadeusz, however, cautioned the hotheads to sit back and wait for Poland to recover slowly, build anew, and challenge Russia everywhere except on the battlefield. If we look ahead, Contrad was himself to become a subtle blend of both types.*

---

* The biography of every great writer, we must stress, is the story of details, patterns, rhythms, and styles which dovetail, as well as traces, intimations, memories, and glimpses which do *not* blend. The artist can never appear completely clear; that connection between the man who experienced a particular milieu and the same man sitting at his desk before an empty sheet of paper is elusive. The very nature of literary activity where an intense imagination is at work mitigates against comprehension. We can only, like asymptotic lines, approach closer and ever closer, hopefully clarifying. Psychohistorical studies, valuable as they may be, must be aware of the approximation of their tactics, their failure to reveal what we really want to know. To pinpoint Cracow, Poland, Korzeniowskis, Bobrowskis, and the rest is not to explain Conrad. Unlike the connections made physiologically and biologically, true synapsis in biography is unattainable.

The hopes for Polish independence during the Crimean War did not go far, although peasants of Podolia and the Ukraine did rise up. According to his friend Buszczyński, Apollo rushed there to organize the uprising. But, once again, Poland was hardly foremost in the minds of the European powers, and its fortunes became marginal to more important matters in the Treaty of Paris. The peasants themselves had remained unsupported by the nobility, except for extremists like Apollo, with the result that the typical schisms reappeared; divisiveness and foreign indifference settled Poland's fate.

Conrad's comments to Garnett some fifty years later on Poland's role as a loser give us some of the context in which his creative imagination was to work.

> You remember always that I am a Slav (it's your *idée fixe*) but you seem to forget that I am a Pole. You forget that we have been used to go to battle without illusions. It's you Britishers that "go in to win" only. We have been "going in" these last hundred years repeatedly, to be knocked on the head only—as was visible to any calm intellect. But you have been learning your history from Russians no doubt.

The new Russian czar, Alexander II, tried to follow a policy of greater leniency, allowing exiles to return from abroad, lightening rules for the legal system, the University of Warsaw, and the church. Attempts were clearly being made to reach the Polish gentry. An academy of medicine was established, as well as an agricultural society. But the radicals—chiefly the young—rightly saw that Russian relaxation was merely the means for more effective long-range control. Relaxation was a calculated policy that could contribute only to further Polish subservience, and Apollo was in the forefront of those who used public occasions—state ceremonies, awards, burials, and their like—to demonstrate against Russian control.

Increasingly, such public ceremonies became the backdrop for patriotic demonstrations and expressions of loyalty to a divided, Russified Poland. While Apollo was active in clandestine plotting in Zhitomir* in the Ukraine, events were reaching a serious stage in Warsaw, where various underground groups were seeking a focus for their opposition to Russia. Such an event came in the form of the funeral of Mme Sowińska, the widow of a much honored Polish general who, in the 1830 insurrection, had died in the defense of Warsaw. Her funeral became the occasion of a mass demonstration—ideologically the perfect event for Polish radicals, who had never lost sight of the 1830 insurrection, Warsaw now developed into the focal point for radical ac-

* Where he worked as a journalist and secretary of a publishing firm from mid-1859 to May of 1861, when he left for Warsaw.

tivities, and large groups of incendiary youths and patriots moved into the city, each vying with the other to establish its radicalism.

On February 27, 1861—the fateful year that Apollo was to leave the Ukraine for Warsaw and seal the fortunes not only of himself but of Ewa and Conrad—a large demonstration was held as a sign of anti-Russian feeling, and jittery Russian troops charged, killing at least five people. The Polish radicals had their own Peterloo Massacre. Petitions led to certain reforms, satisfying the Whites, but the Reds were unbending. They smelled blood—but it was to be mainly their own.

In May of 1861, Apollo went to Warsaw under cover of founding a new literary monthly on the order of the *Revue des Deux Mondes*, to be called the *Fortnightly* (*Dwutgodnik*), although his real mission was clandestine political work, intended to foment an insurrection against Russia—what was to surface in 1863 as another abortive attempt. Ewa and Conrad* stayed behind in Zhitomir, and Ewa wrote long letters about herself, the child, and local political matters; letters, incidentally, which were later used against Apollo at his trial. We also have the first letter by Conrad, his hand guided by Ewa:

> [May 23, 1861]
>
> Daddy,
>
> I am fine here [in Terechowa], I run about the garden—but I don't like it much when the mosquitoes bite. As soon as the rain stops I will come to you. Olutek has sent me a beautiful little whip. Please Daddy dear lend me a few pennies and buy something for Olutek in Warsaw.
>
> Have you been to see this Bozia [a crucifix or effigy of God], which [sic] Granny?
>
> Konrad.

When Apollo arrived in Warsaw, dressed in peasant costume—a kind of 1860s Tolstoian figure—he provided leadership for the revolutionary cadres and became a marked man for the Russian authorities. Already known as a writer, somewhat older than the students with whom he associated, and fervent in his desire to see the insurrection benefit the peasants as well as the nation, Apollo was in his element. Although the Russian peasants were nominally freed in 1861, by proclamation of Alexander II, nevertheless their economic situation—and that of their Polish counterparts—remained un-

* By then, Conrad had been baptized in the Roman Catholic church in Jitomir (Zhitomir, just north of his birthplace). This event Apollo commemorated in a bitter poem, itself intertwined with Mariolatry and Messianic fervor: "My child, my son, if the enemy calls you a nobleman and a Christian—tell yourself that you are a pagan and that your nobility is rot. . . . My child, my son—tell yourself that you are without land, without love, without Fatherland, without humanity—as long as Poland, our Mother is enslaved." Poland as a "Great Mother," with its implication of Madonna worship, would continue into the years of Apollo's decline; so that the young Conrad came under quite a mixed influence—country, mother, and religious mysticism, all devotedly worshipped by a grieving, ailing, frustrated father.

changed, and their future fate was a passionate issue. As a member of the nobility, Apollo with his fervor for peasant reform hoped to influence the course of the rebellion. We note how much of him reappears in Haldin, in *Under Western Eyes*, while Razumov, the bastard son of a prince, argues for evolution—the attitude of the Whites and Appeasers.

Apollo helped lead the demonstration on August 12, the anniversary of the union of Poland and Lithuania, and tried to impede the vote in the September 23 municipal elections. Despite the incendiary nature of these activities and their goal of rebellion, they were still within the legal framework. Russian tolerance of civil disobedience was surprisingly broad, although Alexander's policy of leniency was, of course, aimed at winning over the gentry to Russia's side. In many ways, he succeeded, since both Appeasers and Whites among Poles suggested a more orderly form of opposition, or no opposition at all.

Apollo had no intention of surrendering his commanding role, nor did he give up his plan for Ewa and Conrad to join him in Warsaw. He found rooms for them at 45 Nowy Świat, a main avenue, and they joined him in the fall, probably in early October. Their arrival in Warsaw coincided with Apollo's efforts to initiate a secret City Committee (formed on October 17), which was later, after he was imprisoned, to become the National Central Committee, the chief insurrectionist group that supplied cadres for Polish opposition to Russia. Only four days later, on October 21, and only a few weeks after the arrival of his wife and son, Apollo was arrested and imprisoned in the citadel.

In a sense, this fate—which was literally to be the doom of Ewa as well as of her husband, and almost of the young child—brought Apollo full circle. All his activities, from his birth as the son of the patriotic Teodor, his ideological association with the 1830s romantic poets, his own early nationalistic, idealistic writings, brought him to this pass. In his imagination, he was not unlike Byron dying at Missolonghi or Shelley throwing himself, in his mind, on the barricades. As his brother-in-law Tadeusz suspected, Apollo sought martyrdom, as a result of both strength and weakness. He needed to soar so as to hide his lack of concentration, his inability to stick. While his courage and fervor were commendable, the waste of human effort and the individual life was deplorable.

When Conrad later explored the most intimate of father-son relationships in his work, in the interplay between Axel and the older Heyst in *Victory*, he noted the ironic ambiguities of the relationship: portraying the father as if he were Apollo *after* his fall, who, having finally seen the futility of all action, cautions silence, cunning, and withdrawal. His advice to Axel is almost Dedalus' to Icarus; and yet it is also an ironic depiction of Apollo, since Conrad moved in and out of his depressing hopelessness without conveying the courage and spirit of the original. By turning the relationship into an ironic and a paradoxical one, Conrad relived the situation, probably in the only way he could handle it and survive its irresolvable conflicts.

Along with Ewa, co-accused at the military tribunal, Apollo was charged with a broad range of crimes. As the Permanent Investigation Commission indicated, he was far more deeply implicated in underground activities than Conrad's early biographer and friend, Gérard Jean-Aubry, revealed. The latter, in fact, played down Apollo's conspiratorial actions, making him into an upstart rather than a serious revolutionary—a softened attitude he possibly gathered from Conrad himself. Jocelyn Baines, in his biography of Conrad, draws up the list of charges:

> 1. organizing a secret committee with the name of "Mierosławski's Reds," which was to oppose the elections to the Warsaw Municipal Council;
> 2. having caused, with others, the disturbances in Miodowa Street and in Wedel's cake and coffee shop;
> 3. being author of the demand that Lithuania be united with Central Poland and of the pamphlet entitled *Narodzie! Baczność!* (Nation! Attention!);
> 4. organizing in Żytomierz [Zhitomir] a requiem mass for those killed during the Warsaw demonstrations in 1861.

That Ewa—although probably not imprisoned with Apollo at this time—stood as co-accused indicates she had changed completely from her Bobrowska upbringing to Apollo's Red nationalism. There is no reason to believe that she did so simply because of loyalty to her husband; she appears to have shared his fervor for causes, although Conrad later seemed to cast her—in the guise of his female characters—in the role of a martyr not to political causes but to an idealistic husband.

Ewa's health had never been robust—and the activities leading up to the family's expulsion from Warsaw on May 8, 1862, were not calculated to improve her condition. Further, Apollo was not treated for scurvy and rheumatism while in prison, and his health began to deteriorate. Matters of poor health, of waning energies, of constant illness—these seem to have become part of Conrad's early memories. Not only did he share his parents' exile, he must have shared in that daily expression of ailments and dispiritedness that marks a life no longer worth living. Psychologically, the effect was profound. Whether induced or otherwise, he entered into a life for himself that duplicated in many essentials the domestic situation of his early years—illness, dependency, morbidity, parent-son (child) relationships contingent upon a son catering to an indisposed, almost dying father. Consider, for example, the following:

During the writing of *Under Western Eyes* in 1908—titled "Razumov" in manuscript—Conrad wrote to John Galsworthy about his protagonist and then about his own son, Borys, now ten years old. He outlines what will be the first version of the novel, one he ultimately discarded, in which after Razumov's betrayal of Haldin, he meets the latter's mother and sister, and marries the sister. They have a child, and when the child resembles the late Haldin, Razumov confesses to her his role in the betrayal. This series of events leads to the death, apparently, of most of the principals. Conrad moves in and out of a family romance—Razumov's wish for a stable family life, his withdrawal from it, his betrayal of some of its elements, then a confessional role to placate his destructive feelings of guilt.

In the same letter, he speaks of the recently published *Secret Agent*, also an ambiguous statement about family life, in which the father figure—here a man idolized by his ill brother-in-law—sacrifices the boy for his political ends. The parallels here are not only striking—from a psychological point of view, they are sensationally revealing. For the scenario of family events depicted in the two novels consists of objective scenes or actings out of deeply personal matters rooted in Conrad's Polish experience. They are in their intensity and recurrence almost archetypal. This becomes even clearer as we continue in the same letter.

Conrad moves to a discussion of his disastrous financial situation and then to a portrait of Borys in his son's "role" in the Conrad-Korzeniowski household. "He has not a very lively time; he plays the part of the devoted son to me coming in several times a day to see whether he can do something for me—for I am very crippled and once anchored before the table can not budge very well." We have, in this sentence alone, Conrad's three lives: the duplication of the Polish experience, his own career as a writer—now fifty, one year older than Apollo at his death—and the sea career implicit in his use of the phrase "anchored before the table." Conrad follows with a veritable litany of illnesses—his gout, fevers, chills, neuralgia; Borys's ailments—rheumatic fever, general fevers; those of John (a two-year-old)—bronchitis, fevers, coughs; and, finally, Jessie's afflictions—damaged knees, crippled condition, chronic heart ailment. The Conrad house, as described in letters of this and other periods, is a hospital. Doctors—Tebb, Hackney, Mackintosh, later Fox and Jones—are principal characters and reappear in Conrad's correspondence almost as often as do writers.

This duplication of the young Conrad's domestic situation while the family was in exile, leading to his mother's death in 1865, and then, in Cracow, to his father's in 1869, is more than coincidental. Conrad's psychological expectations were set during this time. He had discovered a frame of reference in which illness created a number of responses and fulfilled a variety of needs, not the least of which was its utilization as an attention-getting device. His own illnesses at this time, as we shall see, created intense concern, with every guardian, whether male or female, turned into a mother. While the ailments were, in many instances, quite real physically, their other dimension was functional and, ultimately, more significant. When Conrad later found Jessie at term, or nursing a small infant, his own illnesses proliferated; he needed her as nurse as much as did the newly born infant. So, too, Apollo after Ewa's death, through sickness, remained a focus of attention, even though he had failed in his primary aim, to lead successfully the Polish insurrection.

The young Conrad's presence at illness and deathbeds served, however, more than a psychological function and led to more than his later duplication of the atmosphere. Like Proust, whose use of memory involved an infinity of duplications and overlappings, the young Conrad also formed certain resolutions based on memory. Even as he assimilated an "illness syndrome" as a way of surviving his psychic wounds, he also resolved—albeit the form remained subconscious—to create a life for himself diametrically different from his father's. Although we cannot assemble contemporary evidence for this resolution, we have the evidence of Conrad's creative life and the domestic situations he depicted: in most of these, where there are children (daughters as well as sons), the father (and not the mother) is a figure of death, decay, dying. He must be honored, perhaps, but opposed. His advice, even his way of life, is anathema. To survive, one must resolve to be different and, ultimately, to defy him.

Furthermore, the political atmosphere of Conrad's novels, except for his lifelong detestation of Russia, whether the czar's or post-revolutionary, is a denial of Apollo's political exertions. Idealism and romanticism, although sporadically attractive, are destructive. In *Lord Jim,* Conrad's first fully wrought novel, the romanticism of the young man leads from disaster to disaster; it is indeed self-destroying. Conrad's early letters to Cunninghame Graham, the Scots idealist and radical member of the landed gentry, outline a skepticism basic to his opposition to Apollo's activities and ideology. Conrad was apparently addressing the spirit of Apollo.

> You with your ideals of sincerity, courage and truth are strangely out of place in this epoch of material preoccupations. What does it bring? What's the profit? What do we get by it? These questions are at the root of every moral, intellectual or political movement. Into the noblest causes men manage to put something of their baseness; and sometimes when I think of You [the Polish capitalized "you"] here, quietly You seem to be tragic with your courage, with your beliefs and your hopes.

Later, in the same letter:

> Not that I think mankind intrinsically bad. It is only silly and cowardly. Now *You* know that in cowardice is every evil; especially that cruelty so characteristic of our civilisation. But without it mankind would vanish. No matter truly. But will you persuade humanity to throw away sword and shield?

In a related sense, Conrad later saw Apollo's idealism as only a form of ego:

> In a dispassionate view the ardour for reform, improvement, for virtue, for knowledge, and even for beauty is only a vain sticking up for appearances as though one were anxious about the cut of one's clothes in a community of blind men. Life knows us not and we do not know life—we don't know even our own thoughts. Half the words we use have no meaning whatever and of the other half each man understands each word after the fashion of his own folly and conceit.

We note how Conrad feels attracted to idealism and yet has cast it in such ironic terms that in an imperfect world it can only destroy man. This is a devastating rejection of Apollo's life and achievement. Conrad's father was a word man as well as a political activist. Poet, playwright, translator—words were his medium of expression; and even as an activist, he exhorted and pleaded. He was not a dynamiter, or an assassin. Yet even the words of this word man were tainted by ego, and words deceive and undermine sense. They can achieve little. Fated by his unique background, Conrad sought the interstices, to break free.*

The young Conrad's double resolution, as it were, can be paralleled by another father-son relationship that occurred historically only slightly later. Erik Erikson writes about Gandhi, whose career and resolutions were of course quite different from Conrad's, but whose relationship to his father involved duplication of the older man (service to him) with rejection of his way of life (asceticism, celibacy, antimaterialism). Erikson is concerned with how a gifted and imaginative person manages the complexes which constrict other men. As Conrad is about to go into exile with his parents, we must ask why he was not completely shackled as a youth by the contradictory evidence offered by his father's life. That is, confronted at such an early age by illness, futility of activity, lack of mastery, waste, death itself—faced by such seemingly irresolvable conflicts, how did the young child manage to find a course that did not duplicate the futility? Where did the young Conrad gain the resolution to start two successive careers, each of them stretching to in-

---

* In his interpretation of Shakespeare (in an article in the *Biblioteka Warszawska*, 1868, Vol. II), which came in his final years, Apollo summed up his own ideology along with his view of Shakespeare's principles of dramatic art: "Man fires, but God carries the bullet." This is a defeatist view of life, giving man a limited free will, and then resigning the complexity to God's will. It is more the philosophy of a Pole resigned to his fate than it is the basis of Shakespeare's art; but it did allow Apollo an outlet for his morbid irony. We will see later how Conrad moved in and out of this, substituting Darwinian determinism for God's will, offering an implacable nature as the shaper of man's destiny, and then mocking it all because he could not break free of the dreadful, Kierkegaardian implications. Morf (*The Polish Heritage of Joseph Conrad*, pp. 36 ff.) notes Conrad's use of the phrase in "Gaspar Ruiz," "Man discharges the piece, but God carries the bullet"—a Polish version of "L'homme propose, Dieu dispose"; but he misinterprets Conrad's context. While mocking his father's piety, Conrad acquiesced to the force of it, noting the attractiveness of giving in even while defying fate. Such ambiguities became the givens of Conrad's personal philosophy and creative art.

finity, and each incredibly difficult given the nature of his personal equipment at the point of initiation?

Erikson says that Freud is not instructive here because he "primarily described the conscience which inactivates ordinary people, and neglected to ask aloud . . . what permits great men to step out of line." Yet in a patriarchal era, Erikson writes, a son with a sense of his own greatness has an "early corollary . . . that a parent must be redeemed by the superior character of the child." Each time Conrad faced his father's situation, the slow sinking into helplessness, the religious manias, the fervent worship of the dead wife—the Mariolatry of her memory—all of these encounters had a dual function: revulsion and strengthening of his resolution. We teeter here on the edge of experiences which can be destructive in one person—in which the victim feels "cursed" and guilty and which can lead to a "set of dangerous and pathogenic developments in later life"—and which in another person can be supportive of inner resolutions.

At this point, we can only agree with Erikson's estimation of the young Gandhi: "It is, in fact, rather probable that a highly uncommon man experiences filial conflict with such mortal intensity just because he already senses in himself early in childhood some kind of originality that seems to point beyond competition with the personal father." Erikson then states the position with a cogency that fits Conrad's early career as he repeatedly stumbled in seeking the right course for himself:

> Thus he grows up almost with an obligation, beset with guilt, to surpass and to create at all cost. In adolescence this may prolong his identity confusion because he must find the one way in which he (and he alone!) can re-enact the past and create a new future in the right medium at the right moment on a sufficiently large scale.

Such a prolonged crisis,* which can be so dismaying to those near him (as to Conrad's Uncle Tadeusz), is a necessary preparation for him until he senses he is ready; and then, having sorted out what he will accept and what reject, what he is able to assimilate and what he must eschew, he can utilize his past. Conrad's later sea career, first with French ships and then with English, provided that prolonged period of adjustment. He identified with large

---

* In his *Life History and the Historical Moment*, Erikson's refinement of the same point makes it even more applicable to Conrad: ". . . psychosocial factors can prolong the crisis (painfully, but not necessarily unduly) where a person's idiosyncratic gifts demand a prolonged search for a corresponding ideological and occupational setting, or where historical change forces a postponement of adult commitment." And: "It is dependent on the *past* for the resource of strong identifications made in childhood, while it relies on new models encountered in youth, and depends for its conclusion on workable roles offered in young adulthood. In fact, each subsequent state of adulthood must contribute to its preservation and renewal" (p. 19).

elements—Spanish political rightism as well as English nationalism—but he was in reality preparing himself through what Erikson calls a "premature generativity crisis" for his real role, his life's work. Conrad was in his mid-thirties, as was Gandhi, before the new energies were tapped.

Apollo's case before the military tribunal was foredoomed. He refused to admit the charges, and the judges were ready to sentence him as a politically dangerous person regardless of the evidence. The evidence was, nevertheless, overwhelming, having been accumulated over a six-month period by an examining commission which left no doubt about Apollo's anti-Russian activities, some of which, incidentally, were not uncovered. Buszczyński, Apollo's friend and possibly an unreliable reporter of the events, says that the trial proceeded as if the outcome were implied in the indictment. According to him, the judges stopped the reading of the lengthy indictment before the end and requested Apollo's signature. He agreed to sign where the reading had ended, and so he did.

Along with Ewa, Apollo was sentenced to exile in Vologda, a relatively mild Russian area; leniency perhaps resulted from the fact that a former friend and colleague of Stanisław Bobrowski (Apollo's late brother-in-law) in the Grodno Hussars, one Colonel Roznow, was the presiding judge of the tribunal. Apollo could have been sentenced to remote areas of Siberia, where his death would have been guaranteed. As it was, if his health held out, he could still look forward to several years of activity after his return. On May 8, 1862, when the Korzeniowskis left for exile, Apollo was forty-two, Ewa twenty-nine, Conrad four.

Originally, Apollo had asked to be sent to Perm, about 800 miles northwest of Moscow, for he knew the governor there; but the latter, Lashkarev, a former schoolmate, rejected such a compromising situation, and the Korzeniowskis were turned back short of Perm and sent on to Vologda, only 250 miles northwest of Moscow. The chronicle of their exile now becomes a tale of illness, breakdown, and, finally, death. First, Conrad fell ill—almost dying, apparently of pneumonia*—even before the party reached Vologda, and they stopped just outside Moscow. The Korzeniowskis refused to travel any further with the dying child, and Apollo—drawing on his wide circle of acquaintances—sent for Dr. Młodzianowski of the University of Moscow. He treated Conrad successfully, and the party was forced to continue. Apollo in a letter to his cousins, the Zagórskis, points out how indifferent the guards and escorts were to the life or death of the child.

> Naturally I protest against leaving, particularly as the doctor says openly that the child may die if we do so. My passive resistance postpones

* According to Czesław Miłosz, the illness was meningitis, but he gives no source ("Apollo N. Korzeniowski: Joseph Conrad's Father," *Mosaic*, VI/4, 135).

> the departure but causes my guard to refer to the local authorities. The civilized oracle, after hearing the report, pronounces that we have to go at once—as children are born to die.

Under such duress, the exiles departed.

Although Conrad does not appear in later life to have remembered this episode—he was only four and a half, and it may have been beyond his conscious memory—surely this sequence and the next stage of the journey, when Ewa almost died, became part of the routine conversation as he grew older. Almost certainly, after Ewa's death, when Conrad lived alone with his father, their conversations—as they occasionally broke the silence—must have been of such moments of horror, recriminations, memories stained by inferno-like images and scenes. Conrad's lifelong attempt to create order out of chaos, through sheer force of personal effort, first on board ship and then at his writing desk, may have been his way of containing these images of terror and chaos. Whatever the precise motivation, as a novelist of silences he discovered ways of controlling excess.

When we seek analogies in Conrad's fiction, we think of Flora de Barral and her father in *Chance*, a daughter, not a son, with a father so intent on his own destiny he has no interest in her or her existence.* Apollo was far kinder, more considerate, but the silences must have been deafening, as they were between Flora and de Barral. In fact, if we recall child-parent relationships in Conrad's work, we recognize how conversation, lacking continuity or relevance for the child, seems to come out of a vacuum or a desert. We are, here, almost in Dickens country, and perhaps beyond it; for in Conrad there is little belief in human benevolence—the child is truly Isaac without the staying of Abraham's hand. Even without conscious memories of that trek from Warsaw, Conrad reproduced imaginatively the length of days, weeks, and years in tiptoeing silence while parents (and then father alone) were intent on their own destinies.

As they approached Nizhni Novgorod, Ewa was so weakened that Apollo tried to force the escort to halt. Only when a passing officer spotted her condition and notified the local officials was the party allowed to stop; and this when it was discovered she was a Bobrowska, sister of Stanisław. Once again, the gentry status of the Korzeniowskis saved them; had they been peasants or people without connections, they would have perished. Although

---

* In *Chance*, Conrad suggests that Flora has escaped permanent damage because she was too young to understand the disruption and discontinuity of her life with her father: "Even a small child lives, plays and suffers in terms of its conception of its own existence. Imagine, if you can, a fact coming in suddenly with a force capable of shattering that very conception itself. It was only because the girl being still so much of a child, she got over it. Could one conceive of her more mature, while still as ignorant as she was, one must conclude that she would have become an idiot on the spot" (p. 117).

Conrad in later life never distinguished between czarist and Communist Russia, in the former, there remained—even toward Polish insurrectionists—a regard based on class and status that transcended the political situation.

With Ewa ministered to so that she could travel, the party continued to Vologda, which had a typically arctic climate. Apollo spoke of it as having two seasons, a white winter and a green winter, with wind blowing in unremittingly: his description reminds us of Alaskan outposts, without even a brief summer remission. Fortunately, the governor or commandant, a White Ruthenian named Stanisław Chominsky, was humane and considerate, not only to the Korzeniowskis, but to the score of other Polish exiles. We are now on the eve of the 1863 insurrection in Warsaw. The Korzeniowskis were far indeed from these events, deep into ice and snow and frost, forgotten by all but their closest relatives, dead to their former life. How marginal and remote the boy was from a normal childhood! Even Dickens in his blacking factory, his parents in the Marshalsea, could not have imagined such an exile. We note a message from Conrad—his hand probably tracing the letters under guidance—in which he thanks his grandmother: "To my beloved Grandma who helped me send cakes to my poor Daddy in prison—grandson, Pole, Catholic, nobleman—6 July 1863—Konrad." This inscription appears on the back of a photograph of Conrad at the age of five.

We recall that Conrad later used a similar sequence—"American, Catholic and gentleman"—as descriptive adjectives for the character J. M. K. Blunt in *The Arrow of Gold*, a particularly fantastic and disagreeable creature. More important for us, at this time, is the fact of the young Conrad being drilled as to his heritage. He was, no matter what happened to his parents, to remember he was Polish, a Catholic, and a member of the gentry. The three words and traditions went together, and they defined the boy, as well as Apollo and Ewa.

Although no conscious memory trace remained of the early months in exile—later memories did prevail and appear in Conrad's reminiscences—there was the indoctrination which he could not escape. Of the three traditions, he remained a Pole to his dying days, retaining the language and an interest in the country's fortunes.* As for Catholicism, it never became a significant factor in his life, even though suggestions of it remain implicit in his work and he followed the sacraments. His membership in the gentry he never forgot. In his manner, style, and dress, he was very much gentry, even to the sense of noblesse oblige he demonstrated. One reason England appealed to him was that he could find there remnants of gentry status; even in

* Writing in Polish to his namesake, the historian Józef Korzeniowski, he reaffirmed his nationality: "And please let me add, dear Sir (for you may still be hearing this and that said of me) that I have in no way disavowed either my nationality or the name we share

his residences he modestly tried to duplicate the estates of his ancestors.

While the Korzeniowskis were attempting to survive, great events were occurring back in Warsaw: events that would bring both great personal sorrow and, temporarily, raise national hopes for liberation and independence. But, like all Polish attempts, this one too was foredoomed. Apollo's own career of high hopes and idealism dashed by failure and ultimate disaster seemed a paradigm of the Polish situation. One reason why Conrad eschewed politics in later life was his awareness of its destructive powers: first it seduces and then it discards, having in the process distorted truth and thwarted hope. If he glanced backward, he could note only national disaster and personal tragedy.

Teodor Korzeniowski, the warrior epitomized, died en route to join the insurrectionists. Ewa's brother Stefan was killed in a duel, which was more likely murder, since the duel was planned as a way of eliminating him in favor of his right-wing opponent. One brother of Apollo's, Robert, died in battle, and the other one, Hilary, was exiled to Tomsk, to die broken ten years later, his life in disarray. Ewa herself, now far from the battlefield, was to die in two years. The two families were more than decimated; they were virtually wiped out. Tadeusz, who refused to join the insurrection because he felt it was lost before it began, survived, his views of activist politics substantiated at every turn by the outcome of the rebellion.* Besides Tadeusz, only Kazimierz remained of the seven Bobrowski siblings, and he would die in 1886, leaving seven children for Tadeusz to worry about.

In Warsaw, meanwhile, on January 16, 1863, the Central National Committee exhorted the Polish people to rise against their Russian oppressors and

---

for the sake of success. It is widely known that I am a Pole and that Józef Konrad are my two Christian names, the latter being used by me as a surname so that foreign mouths should not distort my real surname—a distortion which I cannot stand. It does not seem to me that I have been unfaithful to my country by having proved to the English that a gentleman from the Ukraine can be as good a sailor as they, and has something to tell them in their own language. I consider such recognition as I have won from this particular point of view, and offer it in silent homage where it is due."

And two and a half years later, to Kazimierz Waliszewski, another historian, he wrote, also in Polish: "I have pricks of conscience at showering my books on you in this way. However, a few pages of each volume will suffice to give you an idea of what I was aiming at and what I managed to achieve. . . . I consider it a great happiness and honour to return to my home country under your guidance (if I may express myself thus). And if you are prepared to take my word for it and say that during the course of all my travels round the world I never, in mind or heart, separated myself from my country, then I may surely be accepted there as a compatriot, in spite of my writing in English."

---

* When, later, Tadeusz wrote to Conrad and suggested that he cleanse himself of the Korzeniowski taint, he slid over the Bobrowski "black sheep." As we saw, Stefan, who was killed in a duel, had been a Red, even an underground chieftain, and Kazimierz was

against Count Aleksander Wielopolski, who stood for a national policy of loyalty to and union with Russia. The insurrection had a dual purpose: to drive out the Russians, of course, and to eliminate the older order as represented by leaders such as Wielopolski. On January 22, the insurrection formally began, following several clashes with Russian troops in the streets of Warsaw. The two main Polish groups, however, were not in agreement. The Whites, representing the upper bourgeoisie and the gentry, cautioned delay and sought concessions from the Russians, planning to use a potential uprising only as a threat. The Reds, an amalgam of intellectuals, students, workers, and poorer bourgeoisie, chose immediate action.

Although the insurrection went on for almost two years in the form of guerrilla warfare throughout the countryside, the uprising except for sporadic outbursts was suppressed. The Polish forces were outmanned and outgunned; Russian forces in the field outnumbered them by more than four to one, and in terms of equipment, the odds were overwhelming. As in most such actions, the Poles initially had the edge of surprise and of movement, but ultimately they had no resources to fall back upon, and their hopes for foreign intervention never had much chance. Other European powers showed little interest in Russian affairs, and the Polish uprising was viewed as an internal disturbance. The idealism of the Polish Reds was lost amid material interests. As Conrad notes later, European powers would connive not to free Poland but to keep it in Russian hands.

> I am speaking of what I know when I say that the original and only formative idea in Europe was the idea of delivering the fate of Poland into the hands of Russian Tsarism. And, let us remember, it was assumed then to be a victorious Tsarism at that. It was an idea talked of openly, entertained seriously, presented as a benevolence, with a curious blindness to its grotesque and ghastly character. It was the idea of delivering the victim with a kindly smile and the confident assurance that "it would be all right" to a perfectly unrepentant assassin who, after sawing furiously at its throat for a hundred years or so, was expected to make friends suddenly and kiss it on both cheeks in the mystic Russian fashion.

When Nostromo in that 1904 novel decides to "grow rich slowly," he has estimated how far his idealism will be appreciated and what the interests of

---

a dreamer and failure. The Bobrowskis had their own ghosts, including an uncle who was an embezzler. Tadeusz, once he became Conrad's guardian, tried to remake his nephew in his own image, and to do that he had to malign the Korzeniowskis and vaunt the Bobrowskis, whatever the truth of the matter. Tadeusz even hid from Conrad Ewa's extensive role in conspiratorial activities, although such knowledge may have been psychologically supportive to the floundering boy. Further, he constantly cautioned sobriety and warned against romanticism, idealism, dreams—what, somewhat ironically, eventually became the basis of Conrad's art.

the material forces are; and he recognizes that their attention to his idealism extends only as far as it will advance their own material interests. At that moment, Conrad has utilized his political insight, into Poland or into any other country which wishes to intrude idealism in a situation where only national or individual interests obtain. The Poles hoped in particular for intervention from Napoleon III, who apparently promised aid—the old Bonaparte connection to Poland had not been completely forgotten. Yet none came, and when Conrad wrote *Nostromo,* he did not forget the petit Napoleon's regime, mocking it as decadent and vacuous.

Within two years, the Warsaw insurrection was suppressed and was followed by executions, seizure of property and confiscation of businesses, deportations, and proliferating exiles.* During this period of suppression, Poland was transformed completely into a Russian province. The one cementing element in Polish life appeared to be the national government, which went underground and acted as a rallying point for further hopes for reform and independence, somewhat like de Gaulle's Free French after Hitler's invasion. If Apollo's health had survived his exile, and if his resolve had not deserted him, he could have been a natural leader in the underground—as a man and as a writer. If nothing else, his pre-insurrection reputation would have provided him with impeccable credentials for a position of leadership. Perhaps only his romanticism and hotheadedness would have inhibited his advance, for the underground after the failure of the rebellion became more realistic, focusing on practical reforms, such as the freeing of the Polish serfs and gaining concessions from the gentry.

Apollo's involvement in what had been his dream was not, however, to come to pass. Far from it. If it had, the nature of the young Conrad's experience would have been different, and there is good reason to believe he may not have desired to leave Poland. England's loss would have been Poland's gain, although Conrad's work in Polish, if he had chosen that route, may have been in a romantic tradition that was also becoming a victim of social and political change. Forgotten, hidden away, marginal to all activity, Apollo was on a different kind of journey.

Meanwhile, self-government in Poland was suppressed, and all educational systems as well as all forms of justice were Russified. The Russian language became compulsory in official relations and, later, even in private institutions. A Russian bureaucracy ruled, and censorship of press, literature, and utterance was the order of the day. The aim was no less than to wipe out all aspects of the former nation. As part of the Russian plan to erase the gentry, who had supplied the revolutionary cadres, trade barriers were eased, increasing Polish industrial expansion, with the concomitant growth

* Prince Kropotkin estimates that "something like 60,000 or 70,000 persons, if not more, were torn out of Poland and transported to different provinces of Russia, to the Urals, to Caucasus, and to Siberia" (*Memoirs of a Revolutionist,* p. 142).

of a Polish middle class. Russian Poland became the chief industrial region for all Russia. With Poles excluded from state service, their energies—like those of the Jews in other countries—went into business, merchandising, and industrialization. A large middle and upper class developed, a bourgeoisie, with values and ideas quite different from those of the gentry. Their aim was to make money and, in the process, remake the ruling class. The falling trees in Chekhov's Cherry Orchard sound the death knell not only for a particular kind of Russian life but for a Polish one as well.

Further, the Russians drove a wedge between the peasants and the nobility in agrarian areas, hoping that through bad feeling they could weaken the power of the gentry. In March 1864, through agrarian reforms promulgated by the Russian government, all peasants, whatever their tenure, became freeholders, on a more generous basis than that obtained by the freed Russian peasants in 1861. While all this was part of a Russian plan to destroy old Poland, it had other, more important, results, in that it led to the development of a more modern nation and, as well, to fierce resentment on Poland's part, with the parallel formation of underground movements to preserve both the language and former institutions. As we see in Conrad, everything connected to modernization, industrialization, business, capitalism, socialism, or science is corruptive of the individual life. Despite his literary modernism, much of Conrad's thinking remained fixed in his early Polish values.

In Vologda, the exiles were sinking. Even if they had returned from this noisome location healthy and ready for renewed action, they would have found Poland transformed; but their fate now was their physical weakness—a fate we see weaving in and out of Conrad's own life. His survival later as a writer, as the survival now of the Korzeniowskis, was tied to his health—freedom from hereditary gout, attacks of nerves, neuralgia and fevers, bouts of desperate anxiety and depression. Ewa in particular, who had tuberculosis, was failing steadily; and through the kindness of Chominsky and another friend of Stanisław Bobrowski, the Korzeniowskis were permitted to move south, to Chernikhov, about 350 miles southwest of Moscow and not too distant from Kiev, in the Ukraine. Ewa and Conrad, in fact, were permitted to visit Tadeusz Bobrowski's estate near Nowofastów, which lay between Berdichev, Conrad's birthplace, and Kiev. This episode is not lost to us, since Conrad's memory begins to pick up these events, although by now, in the autumn of 1863, he was not yet six years old. In *A Personal Record*, he recalls the time when they left Uncle Tadeusz's after their stay, to return to Chernikhov, where Ewa was to die:

> But I remember well the day of our departure back to exile. The elongated *bizarre*, shabby travelling-carriage with four post-horses, standing before the long front of the house with its eight columns, four on each side of the broad flight of stairs. On the steps, groups of servants, a few relations, one or two friends from the nearest neighbourhood, a perfect si-

> lence, on all the faces an air of sober concentration; my grandmother all in black gazing stoically, my uncle giving his arm to my mother down to the carriage in which I had been placed already; at the top of the flight my little cousin in a short skirt of a tartan pattern with a deal of red in it, and like a small princess attended by the women of her own household: the head *gouvernante,* our dear, corpulent Francesca (who had been for thirty years in the service of the B. family), the former nurse, now outdoor attendant, a handsome peasant face wearing a compassionate expression, and the good, ugly Mlle. Durand, the governess, with her black eyebrows meeting over a short thick nose, and a complexion like pale brown paper. Of all the eyes turned towards the carriage, her good-natured eyes only were dropping tears, and it was her sobbing voice alone that broke the silence with an appeal to me: "*N'oublie pas ton français, mon chéri.*" In three months, simply by playing with us, she had taught me not only to speak French but to read it as well. She was indeed an excellent playmate. In the distance, halfway down to the great gates, a light, open trap, harnessed with three horses in Russian fashion, stood drawn up on one side with the police captain of the district sitting in it, the vizor of his flat cap with a red band pulled down over his eyes.

We note how in Conrad's memory this scene has become like a family portrait, with only a very slight movement suggested. It is, in the main, a still life, a posed scene such as one finds in Velázquez, with his royal family scenes held together for the moment of painting and yet ready to disperse or disintegrate in time. Many of Conrad's literary scenes were of this kind—especially in his first two novels—with motion dissipated, static, still, like encapsulated memories caught forever in time and held together only by the past. If they moved, they would, like the dying Ewa, sink into nothingness.

In the same section of *A Personal Record,* Conrad also speaks of his great-uncle Mikołaj (Nicołai) Bobrowski, whom he refers to as Nicholas B. Conrad later in life wrote a short story—"The Warrior's Soul"—partially based on this uncle, who as a member of Napoleon's luckless army retreated from Moscow. Like Conrad's paternal grandfather, Teodor Korzeniowski, Uncle Mikołaj had attached himself to Napoleon's army in the hopes of effecting Polish independence. The great thing in Conrad's memory of this uncle, however, was not the horrors of the retreat but the fact that this "simple-minded Polish gentleman" was forced to eat dog. As Conrad writes: "It has been the fate of that credulous nation to starve for upwards of a hundred years on a diet of false hopes and—well—dog." Conrad calls it, in his heavily ironic treatment, a "poisonous regimen"; but one notes how he combines politics and the political fate of activists. One starves for independence, and the French finally say: "Let them eat dog."

In *A Personal Record,* he turns the intense old man into another still life, recalling the last time he had seen him:

. . . at the time when my mother had a three-months' leave from exile, which she was spending in the house of her brother, and friends and relations were coming from far and near to do her honour. It is inconceivable that Mr. Nicholas B. should not have been of the number. The little child [Ewa] a few months old he had taken up in his arms on the day of his home-coming after years of war and exile was confessing her faith in national salvation by suffering exile in her turn. [And the little boy watching was, in a sense, the last in a line of Korzeniowski-Bobrowska exiles.] I do not know whether he was present on the very day of our departure. I have already admitted that for me he is more especially the man who in his youth had eaten roast dog in the depths of a gloomy forest of snow-loaded pines. My memory cannot place him in any remembered scene. A hooked nose, some sleek white hair, an unrelated evanescent impression of a meagre, slight, rigid figure militarily buttoned up to the throat, is all that now exists on earth of Mr. Nicholas B., only this vague shadow pursued by the memory of his grand-nephew, the last surviving human being, I suppose, of all those he had seen in the course of his taciturn life.*

When Conrad drew on his memories of the old warrior and his wartime exploits in "The Warrior's Soul," he wrote in March 1916, at the very time Polish hopes were high once more that the great Western powers would consider Polish independence as part of the war settlement. But that was another era. Although Conrad carried away those Napoleonic memories of Mr. Nicholas B. when he was less than six, he was to remain fascinated by the era for the rest of his life. Upon his death, he left unfinished the novel *Suspense*, which he considered to be his masterpiece. In its inchoate state, it is impossible to judge what it would have become with completion and extensive revision; but it demonstrates that in Napoleon and his epoch Conrad found the fusion of many elements both sympathetic and repulsive to his own tem-

* Conrad's parallelism to Proust in their utilization of past incident is rarely more apparent than in a comparison of the above description and Proust's of the Baron de Charlus, in volume 7 of *Remembrance of Things Past*. On his way to the Guermantes' party, the narrator stops his cab and notices a man inside another cab, "his eyes fixed, his figure bent." He "was placed rather than seated in the back, and was making, to keep himself upright, the efforts that might have been made by a child who has been told to be good. But his straw hat failed to conceal an indomitable forest of hair which was entirely white, and a white beard, like those which snow forms on the statues of river gods in public gardens, flowed from his chin." Proust continues: "His eyes had not remained unaffected by this total convulsion, this metallurgical transformation of his head, but had, by inverse phenomenon, lost all their brightness. But what was most moving was that one felt that this lost brightness was identical with his moral pride, and that somehow the physical and even the intellectual life of M. de Charlus had survived the eclipse of that aristocratic haughtiness which had in the past seemed indissolubly linked to them" (pp. 123-4, Mayor translation). It is common method that connects Conrad and Proust, not simply that both are depicting the crumbling remnants of an aristocratic hauteur.

perament. The romanticism of the Napoleonic vision could not have escaped him, nor could the tremendous surge of energy that compulsively asserted itself. In that display of ego and will, Conrad found the antipodes of human existence: salvation and destruction, both curiously yoked like reason and the appetites in Plato's equine metaphor.

Such a yoking, which Conrad caught repeatedly in his doubling of major characters—Nostromo and Decoud, Razumov and Haldin, Jim and Marlow, Marlow and Kurtz—was a splitting of the Napoleonic personality into two, sometimes three. For if Napoleon represented energy, drive, and obsessive will leading to destruction, he also demonstrated the desire for reform, the man rising from the people to the purple; and, further, for Conrad, he represented post-revolutionary France, committed not only to plunder and conquest but to Polish independence. Not coincidentally would Conrad leave Poland and go directly to France, perfect his French, read widely in French literature, and sail on French ships. This was, for him, the land of Napoleon, equal parts of romantic fantasy and hope.

None of this, of course, was even in the shape of dreams for the young child. Conrad returned to Chernikhov with Ewa, this time accompanied by his maternal grandmother. Now in 1864 and early 1865, he was present at the decline and impending death of his mother. Although we lack Conrad's response to this drawn-out event, we do have Apollo's words, to his friend Kazimierz Kaszewski, and they indicate that even before Ewa's death she was becoming a mystical, holy figure, that Madonna figure or "Great Mother" whom Apollo continued to worship after her death. He wrote:

> My poor wife has been dying, for several years, from her sickness and from the repeated blows which have been falling on our family. During the last four months she has been cruelly ill, confined to her bed, with barely enough strength to glance at me, to speak with muted voice. The lack of everything here to support body and soul—the lack of doctors and medical facilities have brought her to this condition. . . . I am everything in the house—both master and servant. I do not complain of this as a burden; but how often has it been impossible for me to help the poor, unhappy woman or bring her relief! Our little Konrad is inevitably neglected in the midst of all this.

The final line of the letter indicates the marginality of the child in the household, a not at all curious beginning for a man who cultivated marginality for the remaining sixty years of his life. His choices of seaman and writer immediately placed him outside larger societies. As a seaman, he joined a tightly knit subgroup, with its own rules and discipline and contempt for the man who remains on land. And as writer, he chose the most solitary of professions, especially for someone like himself who became an acolyte before the altar of perfection. Forced into a marginal position in a household that was disintegrating, a mother declining and dying, a father mourning and guilt-stricken, Conrad made his role into a life role: he chose as much as choices were made for him. He began to fall into what Erikson calls a condition of "aggravated vulnerability," which is accompanied by "an expectation of grand individual promise."

Ewa's last days were filled with hours of steady deterioration. On February 28, 1865, Apollo wrote once again to Kaszewski that his wife was so ill he could place his hope only in God—a prescient statement in the light of his activities once Ewa died. Apollo speculates if she knows herself that she is doomed:

> I ask myself, is this courage or does she not know how ill she really is? . . . I cannot read her eyes. Only, sometimes, a stronger pressure of her hand, in mine, or in little Konrad's, testifies to her courage. . . . We pray that God remove the chalice of bitterness from our lips—for we have drunk from it overmuch, more than enough. But we thank Him that our lips jointly drink up that potion. We should not change it for nectar if each of us had to drink separately.

While Apollo's words assess Ewa's condition, they also, somewhat typically, turn the situation to his own reactions: highly religious and mystical, with imagery borrowed from rituals of life and death; overall, a romanticism of his own situation, in which he sees himself as drinking the potion, whether hemlock or nectar, already dedicating himself to the sacred memory of the woman who has elements of the Holy Mother.

Ewa's strength was exhausted and she died on April 18, 1865. Apparently, she would not have lasted to a ripe age even under the best of conditions, but a better climate, a more hopeful future, and a more normal routine of food and rest would surely have prolonged her life beyond its thirty-two years. Like everyone else in the family, Apollo had viewed Ewa as saintly, intelligent, the very soul and spirit of Polish womanhood, and, for that reason, much too good for him. But no matter how the Bobrowskis had opposed Apollo before the marriage, they could not question his devotion. Between her death in 1865 and his own in 1869, when Conrad was eleven and a half, Apollo devoted himself to her memory.

Conrad's critics have written of the oppressiveness of the child's life at this time, as his father sank into mysticism, religiosity, Messianism, and Mariolatry. And there is little doubt that the death of a mother—and a much loved and respected one at that—is traumatic for a child of seven and a half. Nevertheless, we should not lose sight of the fact that Conrad had been developing defenses for this—he had been born into a precipitous situation and he had acclimated himself to the vicissitudes of life. He was not an American suburban youngster suddenly thrown into a stark, unrelentingly tragic situation. He had been conditioned to violent and uncertain moves, and he had lived close to the bone of a solitary existence, although with much kindness from both parents. The neglect—such as it was—did not result from nastiness or hostility, and he was himself building up ways of handling shifting conditions. Accustomed as he was to the proliferation of new situations, he did not come to each one as an overwhelming tragedy.

We should not see the young Conrad, therefore, as a victim of an unrelenting sequence of tragic events, of conditions which foredoomed him. A tremendous future lay open to him, filled with years of glorious achievement. He was registering, recording, storing memories, and learning to deal with experience, even at this age. He was, apparently, a recording machine of sorts; the brain working was inchoate, uncertain, lacking direction, but it *was* the brain of the future storyteller and novelist. The very fact of his vulnerability was significant for the writer-to-be, however veiled and indistinct the nature of his future course might have been. The brain had fixed itself in certain grooves, although Conrad would not consciously suspect what those grooves were for another twenty-five years. Nevertheless, the recording apparatus was functioning, and he was transforming raw data not only into misery but into memories which he would later utilize.

It is essential to stress that Conrad did not stop living in the years under his father's care following Ewa's death. Time ran differently for father and son. Apollo may have stopped living—although he read, wrote, and translated—but whatever the process of the household, the young Conrad was very much alive, preparing his defenses, learning how to respond, watching, waiting, wary, and apparently making his own preparations—much like the young James Joyce—for flight. Conrad did not see himself as Dedalus—that would come later—but he did fancy himself as Proteus, Neptune, Poseidon, even Odysseus. He identified with the sea and with marine creatures as much as Joyce did with the air; but the results would be similar. Joyce's Paris was a later version of Conrad's Marseilles. That both writers, who were exiles in so many aspects, should see France in terms of freedom and escape is not unusual. For Joyce, politics did not matter, but Paris did; for an Irishman oppressed by England, family, and church, France was the land of Voltaire and Rousseau. For the Pole contemplating a breakout from an oppressive society, France was also the natural outlet—a democracy of sorts, a haven for Poles, and one of the rare countries in Europe which had ever cared about Polish fortunes.

Conrad waited. Apollo was himself quite ill (he would die of consumption) and lacking in funds. First Ewa's brother Kazimierz had supported him in exile, and then her other brother, Tadeusz, took over his support. Apollo was deeply devoted to Conrad—an aspect of the latter's childhood which should not be neglected—and often expressed the view that the sole thing keeping him alive was his concern for the child. Of course, this, too, could have had an untoward effect on the child, causing guilt, remorse, a sense of desertion. And surely the young Conrad's patterns of illness, headaches, attacks of nerves, loss of energy and will, were directed toward resolving his situation. But such illnesses have their positive side as well, forcing personal attention, keeping the individual intensely alive to his own welfare, and creating a human counterthrust of sorts to the impersonal vicissitudes of life. For Conrad, illness was not simply succumbing to circumstances; his malfunctions served another purpose, a living one, however disheartening they may have been for those around him.

Certain patterns were becoming set: the recurring illnesses; the marginal, relatively isolated existence; the lack of a daily routine; the shuttling around from one guardian to another both during Apollo's life and after his death; the need to make crucial decisions or choices about oneself, all of which must be internalized until the moment came when they could be acted upon. Conrad, even though only seven, went underground. Like the Brontës in this respect—small children growing up in a household in which only their imagination was free to escape the confines of *their* father—Conrad indulged an imagination already fed by the kind of work his father chose to do in his remaining years.

Apollo retreated into memories, remorse, and guilt; but he also retained beliefs he had set down while still in exile, in a treatise called *Poland and Muscovy*. The piece came from Apollo and Ewa's period in Chernikhov, while she was declining, and Poland's deteriorating fortunes parallel hers. For Apollo, all Russia is a prison, all Russia is barbaric. On the other hand, Poland, trying to endure under terrible circumstances, stands for civilization, humanistic values, enlightenment. One sees him already intermixing the saintly Ewa with the saintliness of the Polish mission against the Lucifer of nations. One is back in the Garden, before the Fall. In another sense, Poland, martyred and neglected, is an outpost of Western civilization, a bastion of faith against a Russia characterized by "barbarism, obscurantism, and dissent."* Apollo not only justified his involvement in the insurrection but

* While this was Apollo's justification of the 1863 insurrection, Tadeusz Bobrowski, a member of the conservative Cracow School, which mocked romanticism in politics, had his own views of the affair. Bobrowski attacked the senselessness of the assault on Russian forces not because he lacked patriotism but because of the hopelessness of the venture. He said the Reds (and he meant Apollo and his own brother Stefan, among others) had been deluded by their own rhetoric and romantic idealism.

> They successfully used falsehood as a tool, some consciously, in order to realize those would-be-lofty ends the attainment of which is permitted to lofty intellects; others served involuntarily, convinced by the repetition of slogans and exaggeratedly optimistic reports that went in two directions: from Paris to Poland and vice versa. Falsehood was used unscrupulously, whether it was offered to a secretary of Napoleon III's cabinet and Prince Plon-Plon or whether it was disseminated through every layer of Polish society right down to the humble alcove of a rustic clerk who was attracted to the revolution by false representations concerning forces that were to come to the rescue from abroad. Without exaggeration it may be stated that the events of 1861–63 were begun in falsehood and that they ended in falsehood.

drew attention to his almost religious mission, the need to educate the West to the role of Poland. This Messianic strain became more pronounced when after Ewa's death Apollo fell into inactivity and remorse.

Writing fifty years later, in 1905, at the time of the Russo-Japanese War, Conrad's characterization of Russia is, indeed, Apollonian:

> And above it all—unaccountably persistent—the decrepit, old, hundred years old, spectre of Russia's might still faces Europe from across the teeming graves of Russian people. This dreaded and strange apparition, bristling with bayonets, armed with chains, hung over with holy images; that something not of this world, partaking of a ravenous ghoul, of a blind Djinn grown up from a cloud, and of the Old Man of the Sea, still faces us with its old stupidity, with its strange mystical arrogance, stamping its shadowy feet upon the gravestone of autocracy, already cracked beyond repair by the torpedoes of Togo and the guns of Oyama, already heaving in the blood-soaked ground with the first stirrings of a resurrection [the revolution of 1905 that followed Russia's defeat].

These were experiences, memories, and feelings Conrad would have to deal with, for he was almost on the eve of writing his Russian (and Dostoevskian) novel *Under Western Eyes.*

More immediate needs were at hand, however. Left with a young child, Apollo realized he knew little or nothing about being a father, although he was kind and considerate, to the extent he remembered Conrad existed. There is something in real life here of a Dickens novel in the making: the child, not necessarily treated unkindly, but neglected, left to himself, almost an appendage to other events or thoughts; Little Dorrit, for example. Apollo once again wrote his friend Kaszewski, this time about the latter's offer to take care of Conrad if Apollo did not return alive, for he had collapsed from tuberculosis and other complications. With that fullness of rhetoric characteristic of his Messianic style, he said:

> Now that she will never return and I too may never come back, and little Conrad will probably have to grow up without me, fulfill your promise. He is all that remains of her on this earth and I want him to be a worthy witness of her to those hearts that will not forget her. . . . Her heart and soul were so set upon this child that I cannot leave him, I cannot separate myself from him, unless I feel certain that he will fulfill her hopes. . . . I have arranged that Conrad should have a little patrimony sufficient for the needs of life and learning. . . . I have made every sacrifice already to secure his future.

Although this was preparation for Conrad's situation after his father's death, there remained the question of what to do while Apollo still lived. He wrote Kaszewski for schoolbooks and manuals with which to instruct the child. He also speaks of Conrad having to take care of his father—a Dickensian touch indeed. "Since the autumn my health has considerably declined and my little one has had to take care of me. We are alone on this earth. . . . He has inherited his talents from his mother's family, but on the practical side he is not to be envied because he takes after me." We note Apollo's assessment of himself as hopelessly inadequate for the demands of life, a sober evaluation not at all accompanied by any effort to make himself more adequate.

This fixity on what one is, this sense that one is set for life, doomed or fated, this awareness of obsidian at the center of one's being—such qualities characterize most of Conrad's literary creations. So antipathetic to his father in certain ways, he assimilated that fixity of purpose which makes growth impossible. There is, in his novels and stories, almost no sense of change in his characters. Usually, they simply become more of what they are, and even after they recognize their dilemmas, they continue to be whatever brought them to the condition, immersed in quicksand which turns their exertions into deeper failure. We recall in *Lord Jim* Stein's injunction to immerse oneself in the destructive element and "by the exertions of your hands and feet in the water make the deep sea keep you up." This injunction, to do so *ewig —usque ad finem*, eternally—up to the end, is a not so curious turnabout in Conrad's thought. For the Latin injunction fitted his experience with Apollo, which is that the individual intensifies his essential being and rides it to his doom.*

Apollo apparently did just this. As we have seen, he was becoming mystical and increasingly drawn to Poland's Messianic mission. Since his attention to Conrad was only half present, the boy had to survive by fitting himself to his father's life. They became like alternately reciprocating and opposing doubles. Not unlike Axel Heyst's father in *Victory*, Conrad's was an intel-

---

* The motto *usque ad finem* occurs on at least four occasions over a period of twenty-two years. We can assume Conrad saw in its three words a mixture of the romanticism and doom that he carried away from the Korzeniowski-Bobrowska mixture of his background. After first seeing it in Tadeusz Bobrowski's cautionary letter of October 28/November 9, 1891, he uses it himself in Chapter 20 of *Lord Jim*, where Stein tells Marlow one must never give up the dream but must follow it to the end, to doom itself. This is the exact opposite of Bobrowski's sense, which conveys a surrender or resignation. Then in a letter to William Rothenstein, on December 17, 1909, Conrad sees his life as "a failure from the worldly point of view" and yet without relief he must go on *usque ad finem*. Finally, to Bertrand Russell (December 22, 1913), Conrad shifts back closer to the "dream," saying that Russell's pages on "A Free Man's Worship" have been like a gift "from the gods" and he will be "unalterably . . . [his] usque ad finem."

As if to complete the cycle: when Tadeusz Bobrowski's *Memoirs* were published in 1900—Conrad received a copy in 1901—his nephew would have seen the phrase numerous times, a true family injunction to both forbearance and endurance.

lectual of sorts, a word-and-language man. The young boy, surrounded by the silencing of the spoken word, entered a literary world of the written language. In addition to his translations from Victor Hugo's *Les Travailleurs de la mer* and Dickens's *Hard Times*, as well as Shakespeare's *The Comedy of Errors*, which he did in exile in Chernikhov, Apollo delved deeply into Shakespeare's dramaturgy, publishing in 1868 a long treatise called *Studies on the Dramatic Element in the Works of Shakespeare.*

He uses Shakespeare's dramatic art as a way of showing that theater and drama are intrinsically social forms, and that the great dramatist draws together the interests of the mass of people; an art devoted only to the bourgeoisie or the privileged upper classes (the *szlachta*) is a corrupt art, not an art at all. "Dramatic art," he writes, "flourishes and gains in stature only when it is closely linked with the taste, the customs, the whole life of the people; when it becomes a nation's festivals, its entertainment, its absolute necessity." We note how Apollo's evaluation of art, as far as it goes, fits into Tolstoy's leveling views in his *What is Art?* Tolstoy condemned Shakespeare for lacking the very ability to reach the masses that Apollo, however, associates with the dramatist, although both were concerned with an art that had a large popular base. Apollo often read to Conrad from Poland's own great epics, Mickiewicz's *Pan Tadeusz*, *Konrad Wallenrod*, and *Grażyna*, works with a strong social and political component for a people hoping for unification.

Apollo then turned to another side of Shakespeare, his ability to understand the human condition, which for the Pole is always "existential." That is, man is ever aware of his own appetites and desires and, at the same time, conscious how frail his condition is, how distant he is from ever fulfilling these desires. Man is caught between the desire and the fruition. This is man's tragic condition, and, of course, Apollo is reading Shakespeare along the lines of his own shattered career. In one sense, Shakespeare is writing about people such as him, careers such as his. In his tragedies, Apollo goes on, Shakespeare pits man's individual destiny against fate, doom, the destiny of the world;* whereas, in his histories, Shakespeare absorbs man in a process that goes beyond him. In his comedies, however, the playwright demonstrates how the individual escapes into illusions. Apollo clearly associated himself with all three of Shakespeare's creative categories: in the tragic role, as an individual caught in a destiny not of his own making; in his historical role, as an individual caught in a collective role, where he becomes part of a larger reality; in his comic role, as an individual evading reality by seeking out illusions.

---

* We note how Schopenhauerean this interpretation of Shakespeare is. Repeatedly, Apollo moves in and out of Schopenhauer's stress on the individual will, the implacable will of the world, the nature of suffering and the role of art, the futility of individual purpose.

This immersion in Shakespeare, which appears to be the most sustained research of Apollo's life, was not lost on the son. In *A Personal Record,* Conrad mentions having first become acquainted with English literature through his father's translation of *Two Gentlemen of Verona* while they were still in exile in Russia. Conrad recalls Apollo finding him with the manuscript of the translation and telling the boy: "Read the page aloud." Conrad had expected his father to show displeasure at his intrusion, but apparently Apollo saw literary effort as a binding, cementing force, allying father and son where other levels of discourse were missing. Conrad writes:

> It was during our exile in Russia, and it must have been less than a year after my mother's death, because I remember myself in the black blouse with a white border of my heavy mourning. We were living together, quite alone, in a small house on the outskirts of the town of T——. That afternoon, instead of going out to play in the large yard which we shared with our landlord, I had lingered in the room in which my father generally wrote. What emboldened me to clamber into his chair I am sure I don't know, but a couple of hours afterwards he discovered me kneeling in it with my elbows on the table and my head held in both hands over the MS. of loose pages. I was greatly confused, expecting to get into trouble. He stood in the doorway looking at me with some surprise, but the only thing he said after a moment of silence was:
>
> "Read the page aloud."
>
> . . . If I do not remember where, how and when I learned to read, I am not likely to forget the process of being trained in the art of reading aloud. My poor father, an admirable reader himself, was the most exacting of masters. I reflect proudly that I must have read that page of "Two Gentlemen of Verona" tolerably well at the age of eight.

Shakespeare's words remained with Conrad for the rest of his life, the one book he has Lord Jim take into Patusan with him. Conrad himself carried a five-shilling one-volume edition of the plays and speaks of reading in Falmouth "at odd moments of the day, to the noisy accompaniment of caulkers' mallets driving oakum into the deck seams of a ship in dry dock." He continues: "Books are an integral part of one's life and my Shakespearean associations are with that first year of our bereavement, the last I spent with my father in exile (he sent me away to Poland to my mother's brother directly he could brace himself up for the separation), and with the year of hard gales, the year in which I came nearest to death at sea, first by water and then by fire."

Shakespeare was associated in Conrad's mind, then, with his three lives: with his family in exile, and after, when he accompanied his father back to Polish soil; then in his sea career, where, like Jim, he hugged his volume of plays; and finally, in his literary career, where Shakespeare reappears in numerous verbal guises throughout Conrad's vocabulary, associations, and rhythms.* Shakespeare and Dickens, possibly also Trollope, were the chief English influences on Conrad as a person and a writer.†

Conrad writes:

> At ten years of age I had read much of Victor Hugo and other romantics. I had read in Polish and in French, history, voyages, novels; I knew "Gil Blas" and "Don Quixote" in abridged editions; I had read in early boyhood Polish poets [Mickiewicz, Słowacki, Krasiński] and some French poets.

He says his first introduction to English fiction was Dickens's *Nicholas Nickleby*. "It is extraordinary how well Mrs. Nickleby could chatter disconnectedly in Polish and the sinister Ralph rage in that language."

This was the pattern while they remained in Chernikhov: the father austere in his sense of personal loss, full of remorse, yet working; the son caught up by familial tragedy and yet finding escape? strength? renewal? in imaginative literature. Left to himself, Conrad began to learn that the world could emanate from one's head; that in the individual, the whole existed. In exile as a Pole, marginal in his own home, he picked up an awareness of how things were arranged; this condition gave him an angle of vision, and if he survived physically, then he would survive with something gained.

As Apollo embraced a mystical relationship with God, the child suffered mysterious maladies whose origins remain uncertain. Apollo wrote to his cousins, the Zagórskis, who would become devoted correspondents of Conrad later on: "I have kept my eyes fixed on the Cross and by that means fortified my fainting soul and reeling brain. The sacred days of agony have passed, and I resume my ordinary life, a little more broken but with breath

---

* Conrad's father translated five Shakespeare plays into Polish: *Two Gentlemen of Verona, The Comedy of Errors, Othello, As You Like It*, and *Much Ado about Nothing.* Conrad himself used as epigraphs quotations from *King John* (in *Nostromo*), *Hamlet* (in *Within the Tides*), and *Henry IV*, Part 2 (in *Tales of Unrest*). We also know he was reading A. C. Bradley's *Shakespearean Tragedy* at the time he wrote *Victory*. (See Adam Gillon, *Conrad and Shakespeare*, pp. 41–53.)

† The importance of Trollope in Conrad's literary development may come as somewhat of a surprise. But in an unpublished letter to A. N. Monkhouse, editor of *The Manchester Guardian*, Conrad revealed that he found Trollope "a writer of remarkable talent for imaginative rendering of the social life of his time, with its activities and interests and incipient thoughts. . . . I was considerably impressed with them [his novels] in the early eighties, when I chanced upon a novel entitled 'Phineas Finn.' . . . I may be wrong however, I have neither the equipment nor the temperament of a literary critic; and, generally, my feelings of repulsion or sympathy are so strong and so 'primitive' that I dare not venture on criticism. But in the case of Trollope my sympathy is not tempestuous. It is quiet and deep, like his view of life around him. I don't mean to say that Trollope was very deep; but I question whether in his time, in a highly organised, if not complex, society, there were any great depths for him to sound."

still in me, still alive. . . . And so, my friends, I am still alive, and still love what is left me, and still love as fervently as ever, though I can no longer give anything to the object of my affections."

One notes Apollo's language—the mention of the cross, his sacred days, his agony—the words of a man caught up by martyrdom. Mixed in with the honest grief and remorse is a keen sense of suffering for itself, and not a little narcissism. The father then remarks about the son: "I shield him from the atmosphere of this place, and he grows up as though in a monastic cell. For the *memento mori* we have the grave of our dear one, and every letter which reaches us is the equivalent of a day of fasting, a hair shirt or a discipline. We shiver with cold, we die of hunger." Conrad was still too young to hate his father for romantic posturing; but he was not too young to assimilate the atmosphere: hatred of Russia, desire to break out, the need to build up inner strength to fight off physical and mental illness.

Physically, the boy began to succumb. Whatever internal changes were occurring to provide defenses and survival, the physical aspect could not lie. But just before his health became a major source of worry, the young Conrad was sent to Nowofastów to spend the summer with Uncle Tadeusz, where he had the companionship of the latter's daughter, Józefa. One year younger than Conrad, Józefa was to die in 1870. Although we have no way of knowing its effect upon Conrad, her death surely drew Tadeusz closer to his nephew; the young boy was, in several ways, becoming a survivor.

During this visit to his uncle's, Conrad met Prince Roman Sanguszko, whom he later wrote about in his story "Prince Roman." Sanguszko was a legendary figure whose fortunes reached back to the 1830–31 insurrection, and he stuck in Conrad's mind along with the "old warrior," his Uncle Nicholas, who had eaten roast dog. The meeting with the prince had its moments of awe, for his own father was connected to this world of fanatical heroism, romantic idealism, and intensely experienced futility. In the story, the young boy who observes Prince Roman is eight, whereas Conrad was closer to ten, but the experiences overlap. Near the beginning of "Prince Roman," Conrad gives us a glimpse into life at Nowofastów in 1867:

> It was the dead of winter. The great lawn in front was as pure and smooth as an alpine snowfield, a white and feathery level sparkling under the sun as if sprinkled with diamond-dust, declining gently to the lake—a long, sinuous piece of frozen water looking bluish and more solid than the earth. A cold brilliant sun glided low above an undulating horizon of great folds of snow in which the villages of Ukrainian peasants remained out of sight, like clusters of boats hidden in the hollows of a running sea.

The boy, alone, wanders into the billiard room, where he hears footsteps but cannot retreat. He sees a spare, very austere, deaf old man. "My uncle addressed me weightily: 'You have shaken hands with Prince Roman S——.

It's something for you to remember when you grow up.' " The boy continues: "But what concerned me most was the failure of the fairy-tale glamour. It was shocking to discover a prince who was deaf, bald, meagre, and so prodigiously old. It never occurred to me that this imposing and disappointing man had been young, rich, beautiful."

Conrad's temporary relief from exile was coming to an end, and his bad health was slowly to invalid him. As in his later life, he was to duplicate the illness around him. A sick father was to become in thirty years a pregnant, crippled wife and ill children, an enervated household. When they broke down, Conrad's own parallel illnesses made it impossible for him to help and, in effect, made him more indisposed than the invalids. His grandmother brought him back to Chernikhov, to Apollo, in the autumn of 1866, and then he was taken to Kiev for a medical examination, followed by a return to Nowofastów for the winter of 1866–67. Apollo noted that the illness was "gravel" in the bladder, and it may have been, although that is a condition rare in children. We would expect physical ailments more directly connected to Conrad's sense of abandonment, isolation, and marginality; that is, attention-getting ailments, something that would create panic and anxiety in those around him. Conjecture has located his illness as possible epilepsy. The chain of evidence for this latter surmise is that Tadeusz's nephew Michaś (youngest son of Kazimierz) suffered from what seemed to be epilepsy, and Tadeusz wrote Conrad, some twenty-five years later:

> The youngest, Michaś, may be suffering from the same illness as you were—anyway he had a similar fit to yours in the autumn. The only difference is that the symptoms appeared much later than in your case and this makes one wonder if he will grow out of it by the age of fourteen, as you did?

Conrad's later headaches and nervous attacks may, of course, have been epileptic in origin; but there is no evidence, and Tadeusz's comments are those of a layman. As a rationalist and positivist of sorts, Tadeusz was always anxious to assign labels. If Conrad had been epileptic, apart from the personal suffering, there would have been an almost cosmic irony; for he would have been connected by disease to his *bête noire*, Dostoevsky, the novelist he appeared to hate most, and to Napoleon himself, whose fortunes he returned to at nearly every stage of his career. At the same time, he would have formed, unconsciously, a link with Flaubert, another epileptic, and perhaps the single most compelling literary influence on Conrad's development as a writer.

Whatever the precise nature of Conrad's affliction—and it may have been nothing more than a variable set of symptoms that were reactions to a variable set of circumstances— it kept him from most of the routines we associate with a nine-year-old boy. He was, in a sense, an invalid in the eyes of those around him, unable to attend school regularly and quite capable of wasting away and dying. If attention was his aim—it was impossible to ignore him—he succeeded in curbing his marginality by creating a special set of conditions. This was an extremely important time for the boy, and those overlapping illnesses and sick routines—whether physical or psychologically induced—were means by which he could keep alive, not simply methods by which he sought death. We compared him before with Gandhi, and we note how Gandhi's terrible fasts were not only ways of approaching death; they were also approaches to a more intensive life, forms of survival in a death situation.

Conrad was slowly defining himself, gaining the kind of intimate knowledge that would later become the materials of the writer. Back in Nowofastów for the winter, he languished, a semiretired young man of ten. Apollo, meanwhile, was dying from tuberculosis. Only a more advantageous climate could prolong (not save) his life, and doctors recommended North Africa (Algiers) and Madeira. But he lacked money for the trip, and even if funds were forthcoming, he had neither the health nor the will for such a journey. Conrad joined his father in Chernikhov, in the fall of 1867, the slowly dying father, the son full of parallel ailments to the older man's tuberculosis. Apollo's health had so deteriorated that he was permitted to change his place of exile to Lwów, in Galicia, then Austrian Poland and far more liberal than Russian Poland. Apollo and Conrad arrived there at the beginning of 1868.

With all schools Germanized, Apollo tutored Conrad at home—apparently in French, mathematics, and Polish literature—but less to convey subject matter than to maintain the purity of the Polish language, which was Apollo's only link now to the fortunes of his country.* The unbending patriot felt trapped in Galicia, even more than in Russian Poland, because the very atmosphere of increased toleration created complacency. There was little urgency in Lwów for Polish independence, and Apollo saw his country sliding slowly into nonexistence under Austria's easygoing supervision. Consequently, regardless of his physical condition, he moved out into the world, mixing with old friends, meeting new ones, making plans for the future, which involved the founding of a new daily, to be called *Kraj* ("The Country" or "Homeland"), in Cracow. *Kraj* was to be leftist, free-thinking, and patriotic. It is striking that despite his own intense religiosity, Apollo

* The Polish language was easily corrupted by the vocabulary of the oppressors—Russian, French, and German—and often what passed for literary Polish was a polyglot language. Bobrowski's prose in his *Memoirs*, for example, is full of corruptions. Apollo, apparently, wanted Conrad to maintain the purity of the language, the written tongue of the great romantic poets. This meant an intense immersion in the peculiarities of Polish structure and modes of phrasing, forms quite different from the French and German penetrating Polish culture.

never considered writing for the Catholic journals, most likely because they were reactionary and pro-Austrian. In addition, he visited the Mniszeks, old friends, on their estate near Przemyśl, traveled to Topolnica, and worried all along about Conrad.

There would appear to be two Apollos at this time: the man we see here through the eyes of his friends, not at all defeated or reconciled to an early death, ready with plans, and even energetic; and the man who comes down to us in Tadeusz Bobrowski's *Memoirs* as a religious mystic, an eagle with clipped wings waiting for the end and embittered by despair and enervation. Conrad himself stressed the morbid side, possibly because of his close association with Tadeusz after Apollo's death—but the older man was by no means unilaterally oppressive in his personal relationships.

In an undated letter (but surely 1868) Apollo wrote Kaszewski, we see this dualism, of activity and physical decline, with the young Conrad in the middle, tugged by each element:

> I have given up Galicia and have limited my efforts to improving my state and caring for Conrad's health. Both wandering exiles, we need each other; he needs me as his miserable guardian and I him as the only power that keeps me alive.

In this letter, Apollo reports that Conrad at eleven does not work because he is "suffering from his old complaint," which we can assume is the "gravel" condition. From Topolnica, the two returned to Lwów in October 1868, and Conrad, because of Apollo's declining health and inability to teach his son, was placed under a tutor from the Gymnasium. Apollo wrote that Conrad was well, although his nerves had been in a very bad state, and reported that the boy was not attending school for the year. He also indicated that his son had no love for study and had "nothing definite in him." Without irony, Apollo says he would like to see Conrad on a more definite path, as if forgetting that he had himself never found any clear direction, or provided any.

At this time, in late 1868 or early 1869, we find Conrad attempting to write, although it is possible that the witnesses to this performance were speaking of a later time, in 1873–74. It is tempting to see these early attempts as the precocity of genius, but if they indeed emanated from a period four or five years later, when Conrad was sixteen, future genius was still veiled. These early writings, which Apollo noted to Buszczyński—"Konradek . . . writes well"—took the form of patriotic plays, in imitation, apparently, of Apollo's own work. Such plays were performed by friends, an indication that the boy did have acquaintances and that there was a focus of energy which, while introspective and imitative to a marked degree, was something peculiarly his. A compensatory process was already in operation: Conrad reacting to his situation with inner defenses not yet visible, surely not even to himself, and with an external manifestation that was socially acceptable.

Conrad also read voraciously, and broadly. Earlier he had read romantic, adventurous stories and novels, by Cooper, Marryat, and others—fact as well as fiction; but now he appeared to be devoting more time to Polish classics, especially Mickiewicz, which kept before him the exploits of Polish heroes, activists, Don Quixote-like characters. Exactly what these heroes and their exploits meant to Conrad we cannot discover; but apparently they represented to him both the heights of adventure and the depths of folly—or perhaps, with his irony, the heights of folly. Surely, they alerted him to an activist life, and yet, at the same time, they certainly exemplified the foolhardiness of the unrequited romantic. When Conrad wrote about this psychological tangle in *Lord Jim*, he saw Jim as a potential Mickiewicz hero, and Stein as the man who recognizes the quixotic excess of such attitudes. That Conrad should use the Bobrowski phrase "*usque ad finem*" in Stein's injunction to Marlow is an apparent connection to Conrad's own way of arranging this early experience.

During this period of his life, or later, he read the fable of the Two Pigeons, which appears as part of the "First Note" of *The Arrow of Gold*, Conrad's 1919 novel. There, the narrator speaks of being "like the pigeon that went away in the fable of the Two Pigeons. If I once start to tell you I would want you to feel that you have been there yourself." In the fable, one of the pigeons, against the wishes and advice of the other, wants to see the world. He goes out, is buffeted severely, opposed by nature and other birds, and finally returns, wounded, ruffled, indeed half dead. The moral is that no distant land holds happiness, for the distant land does not bring what one looks for. The point of this fable for Poles was apparent, especially as emigration tended to draw off some of the most talented. Since this tale appears in *The Arrow of Gold*, which is concerned with Conrad's Marseilles sojourn immediately following his departure from Poland, we can assume that his reading of the fable struck deeply into his imagination even before he had firm thoughts of leaving. Or else, the cautionary fable simply fed his romantic tendencies and he was willing to face destruction for the sake of the experience. Whatever the precise role the tale played in Conrad's life, his experience of it—possibly at eleven or twelve—rather than discouraging him from leaving strengthened his resolve to follow the dream.

While the boy read, and wrote, Apollo was, unquestionably now, dying in slow degrees. Disillusioned by the influence of Austria on the fortunes of Poles in Lwów, Apollo and Conrad, in February 1869, moved to Poselka Street in Cracow. Cracow had a long tradition of being "free" of foreign intruders and was considered the center of Polish culture, or what remained of it. Apollo had numerous plans, one of which was to work on the editorial staff of *Kraj*. But his illness was too far advanced for sustained activity, and within a few months, by early spring, he became bedridden. He died on May 23, 1869, apparently leading his son to believe he had destroyed all his manuscripts. During these last months, Conrad had been attending a day school, returning in the late afternoon to the house in which Apollo was sinking, either lying in bed or else propped up before his wife's portrait, worshipping her spirit and engaging in a mystical homage to lost opportunities and wasted chances.

CHAPTER 3

Surviving

CONRAD left some reminiscences of this period of his life, in an essay called "Poland Revisited," which he wrote in 1915 after a short, near-disastrous trip to Poland at the outbreak of the First World War. He speaks of the winter months of 1868 (meaning, apparently, after the time they had arrived in Cracow, in February 1869), in which he rose early and by eight o'clock, "sleet or shine, I walked up Florian Street." He says he remembers very little of his first school: "I was rather indifferent to school troubles." He adds: "I had a private gnawing worm of my own. This was the time of my father's last illness."

He describes the scene when he returned at seven in the evening: after entering a large house, he prepared his lessons for the next day, his worktable facing a tall white door, through which a "nun in a white coif would squeeze herself . . . glide across the room, and disappear." There were two such nursing nuns, and their voices were rarely heard. The scene Conrad draws is one of hushed, otherworldly experience, death already present in spirit if not in fact. When the nursing nuns did speak, it was "with their lips hardly moving, in a claustral clear whisper." Domestic matters were handled by the elderly housekeeper of a neighbor, a canon of the cathedral. She wore a black dress, "with a cross hanging by a chain on her ample bosom." She, too, kept her voice low, never above a "peacefully murmuring note." Conrad then adds a note of urgency, a matter of his survival amid decline and death:

> I don't know what would have become of me if I had not been a reading boy. My prep finished I would have had nothing to do but sit and watch the awful stillness of the sick room flow out through the closed door and coldly enfold my scared heart. I suppose that in a futile childish way I would have gone crazy. But I was a reading boy. There were many books about, lying on consoles, on tables, and even on the floor, for we had not had time to settle down. I read! What did I not read! Sometimes the elder nun, gliding up and casting a mistrustful look on the open pages, would lay her hand lightly on my head and suggest in a doubtful whisper, "Per-

> haps it is not very good for you to read these books." I would raise my eyes to her face mutely, and with a vague gesture of giving it up she would glide away.

One is struck by the silence: silence of scene, movement, even of word and voice; and how Conrad reduplicated this scene and its import in his later life! A sea career creates such claustral withdrawal, and then the years of writing—in which he selected houses where he could enjoy absolute silence and retreat into a professionally acceptable version of that early experience.

In his first novel, begun twenty years later, in 1889, Conrad creates a dying, broken Almayer, with a daughter, not a son, anxious to survive by breaking away. Conrad may have been writing of Malayans, but his memories are also of Poles, of his father and of his home in those last days. Descriptions in the novel stress silences, emptiness, gaps, waste, and decline. Conrad writes of Almayer contemplating Lingard's old office, and it may have been Apollo's death room in Cracow.

> The desk, the paper, the torn books, and the broken shelves, all under a thick coat of dust. The very dust and bones of a dead and gone business. He looked at all these things, all that was left after so many years of work, of strife, of weariness, of discouragement, conquered so many times. And all for what? He stood thinking mournfully of his past life till he heard distinctly the clear voice of a child speaking amongst all this wreck, ruin, and waste. He started with a great fear in his heart.

Later in the evening, Conrad writes in "Poland Revisited," he would sometimes be allowed to "tip-toe into the sick room to say good-night to the figure prone on the bed, which could not acknowledge my presence but by a slow movement of the eyes, put my lips dutifully to the nerveless hand lying on the coverlet, and tip-toe out again." He would then go to his room at the end of the corridor, and "often, not always, cry myself into a good sound sleep."

The final months with his father penetrated every aspect of his life and thought. With such moments, he did not need Nietzsche, Schopenhauer, Kierkegaard, or even Freud. They were within. Conrad continues:

> I looked forward to what was coming with an incredulous terror. I turned my eyes from it sometimes with success, and yet all the time I had an awful sensation of the inevitable. I had also moments of revolt which stripped off me some of my simple trust in the government of the universe. But when the inevitable entered the sick room and the white door was thrown wide open, I don't think I found a single tear to shed. I have a suspicion that the Canon's housekeeper looked on me as the most callous little wretch on earth.

Perhaps the boy did not cry because all the wounds inflicted were upon him and he was too preoccupied with his own form of escape, evasion, or letting go to focus on that dying creature whose needs and emotional life had so dominated his entire childhood. Up to Apollo's death, there had been nothing of Conrad's that was *his*, except for his chronic illnesses.

Even in death, Apollo dominated. His funeral became an occasion—not unlike those occasions used by Polish nationalists before the 1863 insurrection—for a patriotic outpouring of affection for the man who had martyred himself to the nation's hopeless cause. The young Conrad, aged eleven, walked at the head of the procession, inconsolable according to his grandmother. Conrad described the scene as he recalled it over forty-five years later:

> In the moonlight-flooded silence of the old town [Cracow] of glorious tombs and tragic memories, I could see again the small boy of that day following a hearse; a space kept clear in which I walked alone, conscious of an enormous following, the clumsy swaying of the tall black machine, the chanting of the surpliced clergy at the head, the flames of tapers passing under the low archway of the gate, the rows of bared heads on the pavements with fixed, serious eyes. Half the population had turned out on that fine May afternoon. They had not come to honour a great achievement, or even some splendid failure. The dead and they were victims alike of an unrelenting destiny which cut them off from every path of merit and glory. They had come only to render homage to the ardent fidelity of the man whose life had been a fearless confession in word and deed of a creed which the simplest heart in that crowd could feel and understand.

In the Author's Note to *A Personal Record*, Conrad returned, in 1919, to the funeral and to the man. "That bare-headed mass of work people, youths of the University, women at the window, school-boys on the pavement, could have known nothing positive about him except the fame of his fidelity to the one guiding emotion in their hearts. I had nothing but that knowledge myself; and this great silent demonstration seemed to me the most natural tribute in the world—not to the man but to the Idea."

Conrad then speaks of Apollo's having burned all his manuscripts a fortnight before his death—a practice Conrad later followed with nearly all the letters he received, and which he would have done with his manuscripts except that his wife preserved them. In actuality, Apollo had given his manuscripts to Stefan Buszczyński, as Conrad later discovered on his visit to Poland. ". . . in July of 1914 the Librarian of the University of Cracow calling on me during our short visit to Poland mentioned the existence of a few manuscripts of my father and especially of a series of letters written before and during his exile to his most intimate friend who had sent them to the University for preservation."

Conrad speaks of having had only "a mere glance" at material in which so much of his own past was locked up—a past that was now encapsulated, indeed deriving from a distant land that could have been no more foreign to him than Tibet or the arctic region. Yet he still spoke the language, he identified with the aspirations of the people, and as he gazed, even for mere minutes, at Apollo's manuscripts (poems, translations, letters), he stared into a past he could never shake.* Conrad continues: "I intended to come back the next day and arrange for copies being made of the whole correspondence. But next day there was war."

Conrad then (still forty-five years later) reminisces about his father's reputation, how surprised he was to find that Apollo was recalled by young men of letters, mainly for his translations of Shakespeare, Hugo, Heine, and de Vigny. Apollo as a patriot was also remembered, and Conrad himself burrows back in time, this man of fifty-six reaching back to his twelfth year and beyond that to his early childhood and a dimly remembered room in Warsaw, with an even more dimly recalled mother:

> Where it [a lofty room with a lofty archway at one end] led to remains a mystery; but to this day I cannot get rid of the belief that all this was of enormous proportions, and that the people appearing and disappearing in that immense space were beyond the usual stature of mankind as I got to know it in later life. Amongst them I remember my mother, a more familiar figure than the others, dressed in the black of the national mourning worn in defiance of ferocious police regulations. I have also preserved from that particular time the awe of her mysterious gravity which, indeed, was by no means smileless.

* Nor did he wish to. When his own background or Poland's role in Europe was misunderstood, he became the true son of Apollo. As late as 1922, in some extraordinary passages to George T. Keating, he tries to fix Polish thought and Poland's outlook. His letter is a response to H. L. Mencken's "harping" on his "Sclavonism," which Conrad feels Mencken has completely misinterpreted: "I wonder what meaning he attaches to the word? Does he mean by it primitive natures fashioned by byzantine theological conception of life, with an inclination to perverted mysticism? Then it cannot possibly apply to me. Racially I belong to a group which has historically a political past, with a Western Roman culture derived at first from Italy and then from France; and a rather Southern temperament; an outpost of Westernism with a Roman tradition, situated between Slavo-Tartar Byzantine barbarism on one side and the German tribes on the other; resisting both influences desperately and still remaining true to itself to this very day."

Conrad then turns to his own past: "I went out into the world before I was seventeen, to France and England, and in neither country did I feel myself a stranger for a moment; neither as regards ideas, sentiments, nor institutions. If he means that I have been influenced by so-called Slavonic literature then he is utterly wrong. I suppose he means Russian; but as a matter of fact I never knew Russian. The few novels I have read I have read in translation. Their mentality and emotionalism have been always repugnant to me, hereditarily and individually. Apart from Polish my youth has been fed on French and English literature. . . . I am a child, not of a savage but of a chivalrous tradition, and if my mind took a tinge from anything it was from the French romanticism perhaps. It was fed on ideas, not of revolt but of liberalism of a perfectly disinterested kind, and on severe moral lessons of national misfortune. Of course I broke away early."

Exactly how the young boy handled the death of his father we cannot tell. Certainly, he preserved the memory with respect in later years; but, at the time, he must have felt tremendous awe that his father's funeral cortege had become an occasion for patriot fervor and personal respect. Such an outpouring would, of course, make it even more difficult for the young boy, since the very political ideals which led to the demonstration were those which had destroyed the family—mother, uncles, grandfather, and now father. It could not have been lost upon the young Conrad, especially after he became the ward of his Uncle Tadeusz, that his father's ideas and ideals had brought the family to destruction. So that caught by memories of exaltation, the boy was also caught by a more practical sense, that political activity and patriotism were the devil's work. To break from Poland was to break from ideology itself.

But while the dreaming undoubtedly continued, more practical needs were at hand. The orphan required a home and adult care. Ultimately, he passed into the most reliable of hands, those of his Uncle Tadeusz; but before that occurred, he was served by several guardians, some of them of considerable interest as individuals or as writers. What is unique about Conrad's later childhood is the nature of his education. As other children his age were moving through grade levels at school, he was weaving through homes and individuals that provided, each in its way, a different kind of instruction. And he himself never stopped reading now, as later he never ceased once he went to sea. This personal nature of his education is more important to his later development than whatever lessons he experienced in school, and the former was surely more significant in shaping his skepticism and his sense of irony and scorn. For those qualities, so essential to his literary art, were honed more by associations with intelligent, independent minds than by the pedagogues he encountered in the mainly Germanic schools.*

His first guardian was Stefan Buszczyński, Apollo's kind friend, and himself a writer of considerable energy and some small achievement. As a poet, dramatist, and historian, Buszczyński resembled Apollo in many ways, being as intense an opponent of all foreign domination as was Conrad's father. Unlike Apollo, however, he also opposed socialism and worker organizations, and he often struck the prickly and independent pose of a Polish Tom Paine.

---

* At St. Anne's, for example, the curriculum fitted into the Germanic Gymnasium plan, of Latin, German, and then the native tongue (Polish). As Morf points out, the Latin sequence consisted of Nepos, Caesar, Livius, Ovid, Sallust, and Vergil. The German courses included readings in Goethe, Schiller, Grillparzer, and Klopstock. In Polish, all patriotic writers such as Mickiewicz were ignored. Other subjects in the curriculum included history and geography (presented from the German point of view), as well as mathematics. (See Morf, *The Polish Shades and Ghosts of Joseph Conrad*, pp. 73 ff.)

He stressed more personal concerns and tried to demonstrate that Poland needed greater moral fiber. Such views inevitably brought him into conflict with the Cracow historical school, which, condemning Poland for its shortcomings, interpreted its weakness as administrative, as lacking in central authority. Buszczyński represented those very political forces which Conrad was later to pinpoint as anarchical. Yet to be passed into the hands of this man must have seemed to the boy a continuation of his father's care, although without the hopelessness and religiosity. Buszczyński was a source of energy, kind to the child, and full of his own work and plans.

It was not a poor arrangement, except that it did not last, and in 1870, as the result of a family council, the young Conrad moved on to the guardianship of Teofila Bobrowska and Count Władysław Młniszek. Teofila was his maternal grandmother, and Uncle Tadeusz probably considered her a safer guardian than Stefan Buszczyński, who would have perpetuated the nationalistic ideas of Apollo. Aunt Teofila, however, had her own beliefs, which were romantic and patriotic; she had been very much on Apollo's side when the Bobrowskis originally opposed the marriage. She was by no means a backward, acquiescent woman. On the contrary, Tadeusz recognized her as independent and intelligent. She would, in all, serve well as an interim guardian, especially since Conrad was now the sole reminder of her dead daughter, Ewa. For both maternal grandmother and uncle, Conrad was to fill a gap created by numerous deaths, either from illness or political activity.

With Apollo dead and buried, Aunt Teofila took Conrad for a cure—probably for his excessive nervousness—to Wartenburg in Bohemia, the first of many "cures" that Conrad was to take in his lifetime. Upon his return to Cracow, he was placed, according to Apollo's wishes, in a pension headed by Mr. Ludwik Georgeon, at 330 Florianska Street. This establishment—one thinks of similar ones in Dickens and the Brontës—was run by Mrs. Georgeon and her two daughters,* although Conrad's studies were actually supervised by an old family friend, Dr. Izydor Kopernicki. The boy could not attend a regular Gymnasium or lycée because at this time he had little or no Latin and German, which formed the basis of the curriculum. Kopernicki was an eminent physician, social scientist, well known then and later as an anthropologist, and a man very close to Apollo's political ideas.

Kopernicki, whose ideas and career suggest Stein in *Lord Jim*, left his

---

* Józef Retinger, who came to know Conrad some forty years later, described the pension: "There were three of them: Madame Georgeon, an old Polish lady, who had married a descendant of French emigres settled in Poland, and her two spinster daughters, who at that time were past middle age. I believe the last one died only a few years before the War. They took care of boys of good families at school in Cracow. Refined and perfumed, prim and snobbish, for many years they made their living out of this *pension* in which the fatherless Conrad, as a boy, spent, according to himself, the saddest hours of his life, notwithstanding the evident care of the Georgeon females."

post in the department of anatomy at the University of Kiev and joined the 1863 insurrection. However, unlike Apollo, he got out intact and wisely went into exile in Paris and then Bucharest, returning to Poland only in 1871, when things had quieted down. Like Apollo, Kopernicki retained an interest in literature, along with his multitudinous other activities. Kopernicki, then, was a perfect adult model for Conrad, and it is unfortunate that we do not know more of the relationship, or how the boy felt at that time. Later, in 1881, Kopernicki's name appears in a letter to Conrad from his Uncle Tadeusz, and he continues to show up in Bobrowski's correspondence with Conrad, an indication that the anthropologist and Conrad exchanged letters through the 1880s.

In 1881, Tadeusz, after running through his various ailments as treated by Dr. Kopernicki, relayed a message from the doctor to his nephew:

> Mr. Kopernicki was most solicitous in inquiring about you. I read out your letters to him, having found one waiting for me. He is engaged on a great work which has already brought him European fame: "Comparative studies of human races based on types of skulls." This particular branch of science is called "Craniology." He earnestly requests you to collect during your voyages skulls of natives, writing on each one whose skull it is and the place of origin. When you have collected a dozen or so of such skulls write to me and I will obtain from him information as to the best way of dispatching them to Cracow where there is a special Museum devoted to Craniology. Please do not forget this, and do your best to fulfil the request of this scientist as by doing so you will bring real pleasure both to him and to myself, for he is not only a worthy, wise, and educated man but also most friendly and sympathetic to me personally. [August 3/15, 1881]

Apparently, Conrad responded favorably, for Bobrowski's letter of August 22, 1881, indicates that Dr. Kopernicki will pursue the leads suggested by Conrad. Perhaps his use of skulls as decorations around Kurtz's jungle house in "Heart of Darkness" was related to Dr. Kopernicki's request; but, in any event, Conrad and Kopernicki appear to have remained on cordial epistolary terms almost up to the time of Conrad's Congo trip in 1890.

A pattern begins to emerge: even after Apollo's death, when Conrad had come under the tutelage of Tadeusz, he nevertheless was in touch with many men who shared his father's ideas and idealism. These men were not "brown study" intellectuals; they were fired by ambitions for achieving Polish independence, and they had in some instances jeopardized their physical wellbeing. Apollo's death by no means meant that Conrad was exposed to reactionary or conservative forces; even under the Bobrowskis, he continued to be influenced by conflicting ideas. And from Kopernicki, he would have heard about Paris, travel in general, and exile abroad. Although we have no chain of evidence, it would seem likely that some of Conrad's interest in going into exile, as it were, derived from his exposure to particular men, like Kopernicki, who returned from abroad with tales of emigrés and other ways of life. If nothing else, Kopernicki's presence demonstrated that one could be both a patriotic idealist and a professional success. Not all of Conrad's models were death-oriented.

Even more than the physical presence of these men and their cosmopolitan backgrounds, we note their ideological position and what that would mean to a boy of twelve, thirteen, or fourteen, whose intellectual development was clearly beginning. Conrad was no longer simply a piece of litmus; at fourteen, in 1871, he would be sorting out conflicting ideas and absorbing what would become his own forms of knowledge and imaginative experience. Lasting ideas were shaping; incoherent forms were solidifying into recognizable configurations. From all three men, his father, Buszczyński, and Kopernicki, Conrad found something congenial; they were all of a class, the gentry, and all of agreement as to Poland's future as an independent nation, fiercely anti-Russian and fiercely anti-materialist.*

Their hatred of the "cash nexus" finds its counterpart in English thought with men like Carlyle and Ruskin, and their opposition to Polish positivism was not unlike Carlyle's attacks upon mechanism and technology. Part of Conrad's choice to go to sea was surely based on this reaction to a technological, commercial class which was growing as a result of eased trade barriers after the unsuccessful 1863 insurrection. Polish positivism, in fact, was no stranger to the development of the movement in France and England, having itself been strongly influenced by the ideas of Comte and Spencer. The Polish version, however, had strong political overtones which were particularly odious to men of the Apollo Korzeniowski stamp. For positivism as it developed in Warsaw meant a renunciation of military action against Russia and a consolidation of economic goals. A strong Poland economically and technologically, the argument went, would mean a Poland more capable of standing up to Russia and its other oppressors. The movement renounced idealism, romanticism, Messianism, and all those other shibboleths of the insurrectionists; it eschewed radicalism in favor of rationalism, activism in favor of cultural and economic independence. Its literary aspect was social realism—a Marxist element was not unreasonable—and its enemy in literature was the dreamy, isolated, romantic individual always ready to fight and die for his

* To Cunninghame Graham, as noted above, Conrad speaks of the "shent-per-shent" business: "I am making preparations to receive The Impenitent Thief [Graham's essay] which [sic] all the honours due to his distinguished position. I always thought a lot of that man. He was no philistine anyhow—and no Jew, since he had no eye for the shent-per-shent business the other fellow spotted at once" (January 7, 1898). Conrad's early letters are dotted with contemptuous references to Unwin, Conrad's first publisher and Edward Garnett's employer, as an "Israelite" intent only on profit.

ideals. Its aim was the consolidation of Polish talent for the long run, and to Apollo's crowd it looked like cowardice in the face of Russian pressure.

This side of the ideological struggle, then, would never be distant from Conrad's thought. Philosophically, he remained a "prisoner" of these ideas for the rest of his life, and although he turned such beliefs into imaginative flow, he nevertheless showed an inability to grow as new ideas presented themselves to him. His *imaginative grasp* may have developed ferociously in the period from 1899 to 1904, but his fund of ideas, his fundamental ideology, was set forever in the patterns suggested by these early years.

Of course as Conrad now passed under the influence and tutelage of Tadeusz Bobrowski,* he received a somewhat different tradition, although the dislike of commerce and trade remained. We get some solid idea of Tadeusz's influence from the seventy extant letters (plus one dated in 1869) that he wrote to Conrad from 1876 to 1893, the year before his death. As late as July 18/30, 1891, he rakes over Conrad's defects, although Conrad was by now a master mariner and an English citizen; the roll call of failings is familiar.

Like the Korzeniowskis, he is himself accused of falling between stools: "In your projects you let your imagination run away with you—and you become an optimist; but when you encounter disappointments you fall easily into pessimism—and as you have a lot of pride, you suffer more as the result of disappointments than somebody would who had a more moderate imagination but was endowed with greater endurance in activity and relationships."

---

* Would it be too much to claim for Tadeusz that with the death of his own daughter, Józefa, in 1870, at twelve, he saw himself not as an uncle to the twelve-year-old Conrad but as a mother, indeed a mother hen? His admonitions and cautions, which extended well into Conrad's thirties, indicate more a maternal than an avuncular role. Tadeusz, in a real sense, appropriated Conrad to his own line, attempting to purge the Korzeniowski lineage, hiding from the boy his mother's complicity in Apollo's plots and "remaking" the Bobrowska image in a more attractive light.

Without straining an analogy, we may, with extreme caution, look at another uncle-nephew relationship, that between Beethoven and his brother's son Karl. Beethoven took an intensely motherly attitude toward his nephew, to the extent that he attempted to strain out the father's possible influence. In so doing, Beethoven tried to control every aspect of Karl's life, making the boy into a private possession without any will of his own. Showering Karl with affection, his uncle made the boy feel guilty about any shortcomings, in fact forcing the boy to turn upon himself and attempt suicide.

We must be very careful here, for we have chosen as an analogy an extreme case, in contrast to which Conrad and Tadeusz are only shadowy flickers. But Conrad's suicide attempt, like Karl's at twenty and with a gun, ostensibly over unpaid gambling debts, did in a sense free him from his uncle's reproofs. A serious suicide attempt is so complicated that no explanation can suffice, but for the person who survives it, it becomes a form of rebirth. In Conrad's case, the attempt was a real display of independence—however self-destructive—and it was one way of exorcising his uncle directly, and Poland indirectly, from his past.

All this is extremely tentative, but I mention it here—instead of waiting until later—so as to alert the reader to aggressive behavior in Conrad that we must somehow account for.

This is Tadeusz's case against Conrad. On the other hand, the older man also looked askance at commercialism. True to his own background in the landed gentry, he disliked any pursuit which created class mobility, and of course money-making was one such activity. Commenting on what the newspapers had called a pogrom in an area between Kiev and Odessa where a large Jewish population resided, Tadeusz wrote:

> . . . we all expect to be affected by a financial crisis resulting from the panic and stagnation of trade, mainly among Jews, who as you know hold "nervus rerum"—money—tightly in their hands. I am mentioning this in order to reassure you that I am exposed to no particular danger apart from a general feeling of discomfort about what could befall all of us who live in this country.

Tadeusz denies any pogrom and ascribes the trouble to "thieving," by which he may simply mean matters of trade and business. This parallelism of dislike of Jews and yet reliance on their merchant abilities runs, as we shall see, straight through Conrad's entire career, as he found himself in the hands of one Jew after another and depended heavily on their good will, from Fisher Unwin to Heinemann to James Brand Pinker, his agent and devoted patron.

Tadeusz Bobrowski was himself a man of many sides, not only the forbidding parent figure of his correspondence with Conrad. As well as being a somewhat narrow moralist and positivist, he was a person of considerable intelligence and insight. He has unjustly been described as a right-wing, conservative, even reactionary force, thrusting upon Conrad a rationalistic, legalistic approach to life and its goals. Although some of this is correct—and should not be denied—Tadeusz deeply resented the Nałęcz strain of foolhardiness and self-destruction. In choosing a tepid life, and rejecting a romantic death, he represented elements of balance and sanity. Lacking the poetic soul of Apollo, he leaned toward the scientific view, but without the easy optimism we associate with the technological mind. Tadeusz's long correspondence with the young, and then not so young, Conrad has elements of Polonius's advice to Laertes; but it has many more ingredients—of perception as to Conrad's divisive tendencies, his wastefulness and extravagances, his need for a mothering kind of attention even when he was well past the age that a boy needs a mother.

Before leaving Poland in 1874, for Marseilles, Conrad passed only gradually into Tadeusz's hands. As early as September 1869, the latter was writing to "little Konrad" about the need for education. "It has pleased God to strike you with the greatest misfortune that can assail a child—the loss of its Parents. But in His goodness God has so graciously allowed your very good Grandmother and myself to look after you, your health, your studies and your future destiny." Tadeusz notes the need for a "thorough education," without which his young ward will be "worth nothing in this world." He stresses that Conrad should master the first principles of every subject, which will lead to his becoming a cultivated man. Tadeusz's emphasis here on education implies Conrad's indifference or neglect, and the latter himself admitted he was less than an average able boy. Bobrowski says he recognizes that all beginnings are tiresome for a boy, but he specifically cites the advantages of becoming an engineer or a technician, perhaps having such professions in mind for his nephew. However, he also mentions medicine and law, suggesting that he had, in this area at least, broken with the traditional idea of the idle landed gentry. Tadeusz had apparently entered into the bourgeois spirit of the new classes forming in the later 1860s; money-making, if still somewhat cheapening, should not be left solely to the tradesmen.

The letter, in 1869, indicates that Conrad's uncle was taking over his guardianship, although he was not directly responsible until some time later. Precisely when we do not know, but all his energies were soon directed toward splitting the boy off from his Nałęcz inheritance. Having lacked true direction in his childhood because of the circumstances of his parents, Conrad began to pass into the care of his first stable parental figure. The situation, and its complicated ingredients, cannot be overstressed. For they set up within the young adolescent a dialectic of conflicting feelings and values which he would carry with him into full adulthood and which would spill over into his literary efforts.

During his later lifetime, Conrad was to find such figures of support, not quite as parental as Tadeusz, perhaps, but adult, solid forms that gave him the buttressing he needed at crucial times. At the beginning of his writing career, Edward Garnett provided this support; then John Galsworthy intermittently through his early literary efforts; but James Brand Pinker, Conrad's literary agent, was the real Tadeusz of the middle and later years, guiding Conrad's financial fortunes, supporting him with money as Tadeusz had done, cautioning about extravagance and his inability to work rapidly enough, catching the writer's rage but also his recognition. There is reason to believe that Conrad—no matter what his age—needed to compensate for that early loss of parental figures, for that early lack of clear and stable direction.* If we read Tadeusz's seventy-one-letter correspondence with Conrad (until the latter was thirty-six years old) and, allowing for suitable differences, compare it with the thousand letters Conrad wrote to Pinker from 1899 to 1922, we note the uncanny recurrence of many ideas and themes. We are, we recognize, in the presence of a repeating psychological situation, even as Conrad turned into his fifties.

Conrad dedicated his first novel, *Almayer's Folly* (1895), to "the memory of T.B." It is ironic that Conrad would think of his uncle in this connection, for Almayer—as we have already seen—has so many qualities of Apollo, so

---

* As we shall see, we should not exclude even Ford Madox Ford (Hueffer) from this scheme, although Ford was fifteen years Conrad's junior when they met.

much of his sense of past waste, of lost hopes, of remorse and guilt over his single child, of recognition of a life that lacked both balance and direction. In that novel, begun in 1889, Conrad was writing, among other things, a much disguised autobiography, turning the psychological details of still fresh memories (twenty years after Apollo's death) into a narrative based on more recent experiences in exotic places. But the fundamental data were clearly present, and the dedication to the memory of his Uncle Tadeusz (dead in 1894) recalls Conrad's major concerns.

In keeping with a basic premise of this biography, we shall see Conrad again and again repeating the atmosphere, forms, shapes, even substance of those early years. When Conrad began to write in 1889, he had had a large body of experience as a seaman—including a glimpse of the original of Almayer—but his imagination was working on certain fixed attitudes that would remain set. These, incidentally, are not limitations for a writer of his stamp, but strengths, advantages, giving him an intensity and a focus necessary for this kind of narcissistic vision.

In his *Permanence and Change,* Kenneth Burke combines memory and rebirth in a way that defines a process we shall see in Conrad once he turned to literary effort:

> Once a set of new meanings is firmly established, we can often note in art another kind of regression: the artist is suddenly prompted to review the memories of his youth because they combine at once the qualities of strangeness and intimacy. Probably every man has these periods of rebirth, a new angle of vision whereby so much that he had forgot suddenly becomes useful or relevant, hence grows vivid again in his memory. Rebirth and perspective by incongruity are thus seen to be synonymous, a process of conversion, though such words as conversion and rebirth are usually reserved for only the most spectacular of such reorientations, the religious.

For Conrad, the spectacular "religious" reorientation was his 1890s conversion to art and Pateresque aestheticism, whose manifesto he wrote in both the Preface to *The Nigger of the "Narcissus"* and in the novel itself.

Tadeusz was himself well educated, having studied law at the University of St. Petersburg (which Apollo had attended earlier) and achieved the degree of Master of International Law, with a dissertation based on the legal aspects deriving from one country being occupied by another. His career in government ended before it began, for when his father died in 1850 he became responsible for the administration of the family estates. The point is that before he returned to the traditional gentry role he had acquired some cultivation and considerable education. Also, the family was not itself culturally illiterate, for the older Bobrowski was well read and passed on his literary interests to Tadeusz.

Tadeusz's later voluminous memoirs attest to his literary interests, but even while at the university he indulged bookish tastes, associating with a group known as the Pentarchy, a number of writers who fought against the principles of romantics such as Mickiewicz. The Pentarchy was reactionary in caste, Catholic, very much at ease under czarist influence, and probably much more conservative than Tadeusz. Needless to add, it was anathema to everything Apollo stood for. Eventually, Tadeusz developed along more liberal lines, for he was himself a critic of the aristocracy and of the very class from which he derived.

What is important about him for our purposes is the play of ideas and type of personality he brought to the relationship with Conrad. He was, apparently, a very private man, not at all given to excesses of any kind, whether physical, mental, or imaginative. We have a commentary on Tadeusz from Włodzimierz Spasowicz, who later edited Bobrowski's memoirs. Spasowicz speaks of him as "a solitary man, lonely as a finger, who had lost not only all his brothers and sisters, but also his wife and daughter. . . . Weeks on end, he would stay at home, with a long chibouk [pipe stem] in his hand, surrounded by books and periodicals, always busy doing something."

Bobrowski was sober, ironic, and sardonic. He condescended toward his own class, admired the principles of the French Revolution, and found himself sympathetic to the peasantry. In some of his contradictory feelings, we sense a minor-league Dostoevsky—devoted to the peasants, admirer of revolutionary principles, mocker of the gentry, and yet contemptuous of political movements and their false aura of panacea and ameliorism. His attitudes also recall Tolstoy, particularly his interest in freeing the serfs, along with his suspicion of any movement that would improve their condition. Despite his criticism of the gentry, he was a man of patronage, a devotée of noblesse oblige, and committed to many of the ideas discredited by the French Revolution. Withal, Bobrowski felt that Poland must accumulate material wealth, become self-sufficient, and rejuvenate itself from within, without opposing Russia militarily. We see how many of these conflicting tendencies fitted into the Conradian imagination.

Tadeusz Bobrowski, then, was a cautious patriot, aware of revolutionary fervor, attracted by it, but a rationalist in his approach to life, on guard against political solutions. He was especially careful of the individual human life, which he felt should not be sacrificed to the unknown or thrown to the winds. His later letters to Conrad, even when the latter was in his thirties, indicate his awareness of the importance of the single life, not at all an insignificant matter for the developing or emerging novelist. We can assume that part of Conrad's withdrawal from the full political implications of his novels, or his caution in dealing with such matters, derives from lessons learned from Bobrowski: that the individual who joins movements, thinks politically, or tries rapid reform throws himself under the wheels of the juggernaut. Evolution, not revolution, Razumov warns. Gradualism, for Bobrowski, was the sole hope, but even that modicum of optimism would not be acceptable to Conrad the writer.

The two-volume *Memoirs*, which Bobrowski worked on over a long period of time, coincides with the letters he sent to Conrad, and we note that what he was writing there has its parallels in what he was telling Conrad; so that the latter was the recipient of more than avuncular wisdom in the traditional sense. He became a repository of everything the older man believed about life, literature, philosophy, politics, and society itself, as if Conrad were his own son preparing to move out into the confusing, deceitful world.

In another respect, Bobrowski was a splendid influence on a boy who would become a writer. Twenty years before he wrote the first words of *Almayer's Folly*, Conrad was close to a man familiar not only with all the great Polish authors but with an international array of writers, from Pushkin and Lermontov among Russians, to Byron and Poe, and Schiller among the Germans. If we add these names to Shakespeare, Heine, Dickens, Hugo, and de Vigny, whom Conrad had become familiar with through his father, we note a broad humanistic pattern begun long before the young man would turn actively to literature. That he wrote in English is the cause of astonishment; that he wrote at all no cause for amazement.

In 1870, when Conrad was twelve, his health took a turn for the worse, and Tadeusz arranged for a tutor, the twenty-four-year-old Adam Marek Pulman, a medical student at Jagiellońian University, to take him to the watering spa of Krynica in the Carpathian Mountains. Bobrowski indicates in his "Document"—an accounting of his financial dealings in connection with Conrad and the Korzeniowskis—how he laid out the money from Conrad's patrimony for his trip with Pulman, and how he paid Pulman for "half a year's maintenance for you and for half a year in advance as he needed it."

The sequence until 1874 was becoming set: the companionship of Adam Pulman, the guardianship of Tadeusz Bobrowski, and irregular attendance at school in Cracow because of intermittent illness. The "patterning" is important, for it led in several directions, which Conrad at this time—from the age of twelve to sixteen—could not possibly control. For each element in the pattern, as we shall see, was to tell him something different. The illnesses were uniquely his own voice; whereas his travels with Pulman showed him something else, and Uncle Tadeusz's advice led him on still another path. Yet unable as he was to control the direction of his life, he was apparently lying back, reacting, trying to discover how he could either resolve diverse elements or escape altogether. These were the years when he decided against all adult advice to seek a sea career, which meant leaving Poland, forsaking physically the land that Apollo and his forebears had considered holy land.

Very likely his reading at this time, either in the classical curriculum or on his own, included *The Odyssey*, for the boy saw the Mediterranean as the sea of romance, beckoning him to adventure. Landlocked in Poland, far from the sea, he dreamed of a landlocked body of water which, like the djinn's bottle, contained the adventures of the world enclosed in itself. In *The Mirror of the Sea*, Conrad wrote of the Mediterranean as the stuff out of which a boy's dreams are shaped.

> Happy he who, like Ulysses, has made an adventurous voyage, and there is no such sea for adventurous voyages as the Mediterranean—the inland sea which the ancients looked upon as so vast and so full of wonders. And, indeed, it was terrible and wonderful; for it is we alone who, swayed by the audacity of our minds and the tremors of our hearts, are the sole artisans of all the wonder and romance of the world.

The sea was, for Ulysses and others, "the fury of strange monsters and the wiles of strange women; the highway of heroes and sages, of warriors; pirates, and saints; the workaday sea of Carthaginian merchants and the pleasure lake of the Roman Caesars."

Then, in an unusual phrase, Conrad sees the Mediterranean "as the historical home of that spirit of open defiance against the great waters of the earth." He views the sailor as leaving this sea and issuing "thence to the west and south as a youth leaves the shelter of his parental house, this spirit found the way to the Indies, discovered the coasts of a new continent, and traversed at last the immensity of the great Pacific, rich in groups of islands remote and mysterious like the constellations of the sky." The juxtaposition of the sea, defiance of the oceans, and departure of the youth from his home all seems significant as a later narration of an earlier, still inchoate model slowly forming in the teenager's imagination.

Yet even as Conrad writes this, he fears he has been born too late for what he has imagined:

> The truth must have been that, all unversed in the arts of the wily Greek, the deceiver of gods, the lover of strange women, the evoker of bloodthirsty shades, I yet longed for the beginning of my own obscure Odyssey, which, as was proper for a modern, should unroll its wonders and terrors beyond the Pillars of Hercules. The disdainful ocean did not open wide to swallow up my audacity, though the ship, the ridiculous and ancient *galère* of my folly, the old, weary, disenchanted sugar-wagon, seemed extremely disposed to open out and swallow up as much salt water as she could hold.

This is the older Conrad looking back and comparing his insignificant voyages to the more spectacular ones of Ulysses, but also looking still further back to those "spots of time" in his landlocked youth when adventure was yet to come and he could dream of a voyager's romance in the Mediterranean basin and beyond.

Not so curiously, Conrad identified with Odysseus, the "wily" Greek, as Joyce was to ally himself with Dedalus, the archetypal creator. For Odysseus, unlike Apollo (a moody, emotional Achilles?), was not enmeshed in a tragic destiny; through cunning, he escaped. His lives were infinite, and he would not die in exile but would return to wife and son. No less than Joyce, Conrad evidently saw patterns of exile and return. In *The Arrow of Gold*, Conrad represents his Monsieur George as "Young Ulysses" and then relates a version of his own French adventures after he left Poland, conceiving of them as *his* odyssey. Odysseus was a voyager—"the first historical seaman," Conrad has one of his characters call him—and something of a fighter, but he was practical, never romantic, less a military man than a strategist, very careful to preserve his own skin. The young Conrad's choice was exemplary, and demonstrated symbolically his opposition both to his father and to father figures.

In *A Personal Record*, Conrad speaks of these final years in Poland very circuitously, for he left no proper autobiography. He himself claimed to have attended St. Anne's Gymnasium in Cracow, but his actual attendance there is in doubt, because his name fails to appear on any class rosters or in the records of the school kept in Cracow. Nevertheless, Conrad did assert he attended the school, did inform others of this fact, and it is unlikely he would confuse St. Anne's with any other school in Cracow.*

Whether Conrad actually attended St. Anne's or another gymnasium (St. Jacek's, with less social cachet, has been suggested as an alternate possibility), he did pass an examination for the fourth form. St. Anne's had among its alumni a most distinguished group of literary men, historians, politicians, critics, and dramatists. At the time they attended, the curriculum was a classical one conducted entirely along the German model and in the German language. Cracow (although semi-free) was the responsibility of Austria, and notwithstanding that the Austrian authorities were more relaxed and flexible than the Russians, they nevertheless saw the educational system as a

* When Najder searched among the student entries for the years 1870–72 at St. Anne's Gimnazjum, Conrad's name was not listed. He would have entered in 1870, along with 150 other new students. But these names were entered only for students who began the school year, whereas Conrad, as well as the Taube brothers and Konstantyn Buszczyński, started during the term. Or else, when he began St. Anne's in September 1870, the name listed was simply Józef Korzeniowski, for such a student is entered for the fourth class, on September 17. (See Morf, *The Polish Shades and Ghosts of Joseph Conrad*, pp. 70 ff.) Najder, however, concluded: "Conrad Korzeniowski's name does not figure on the list of St. Anne's *gymnasium*, printed in the *Memorial Book Celebrating the Three Hundredth Anniversary of the Founding of St. Anne's Gymnasium in Cracow* (Cracow, 1888). Nor is it to be found in the records of the school kept in the Voivodship Record Office in Cracow. Moreover there is no trace in the book of the names of the people who are often mentioned as Conrad's school friends (Buszczyński, the Taubes). There existed at the time another *gymnasium* in Cracow: that of St. Jacek. Unfortunately the records of this *gymnasium* were destroyed during the last war" ("Polskie lata Conrada," *Twórczość* [Warsaw], 11, November, 1956, p. 152). See Busza, the Appendix (pp. 244–47), for a good survey of the controversy.

way of indoctrinating Polish youth. This plan, of course, failed since the graduates of St. Anne's, as well as those of other Gymnasiums, proceeded to take up the cudgels for Poland against the occupation.

Even so, the system was itself beginning to undergo changes, the most radical being the shift from German to Polish in the classroom. These changes came about from an 1867 decree approved by the Austrian government, and it moved Poland slightly toward a more nationalistic posture. Apparently, the shift was not felt immediately, for officialdom remained unchanged even if the official language became Polish. By 1870, when and if Conrad attended, textbooks were in Polish, and German teachers were being relieved of duties or retired from service. There still remained, evidently, a censored list of Polish authors, and these in many instances became the most common reading of defiant Polish schoolboys. In later life, Conrad was an implacable foe of censorship and wrote a ferociously ironic piece on the English lord chamberlain's censoring power over plays.

This shift in languages was accompanied by much literary activity among Polish authors, leading to the so-called Young Poland movement. While far too young to be directly affected by these shifts and himself too distant from regular school activities to be part of them, Conrad was nevertheless caught up in a patriotic fervor for which literature could be a service. Even more, however, he was enmeshed in language shifts—he himself having been exposed, before he came to English, to four languages: native Polish, home-learned French, and the Russian and German of the occupier.

Conrad always insisted he did not know either German or Russian*—especially the latter, the language of the hated Dostoevsky—but it is hard to see how he grew up among these language clusters, in which Polish, German, and Russian were intermingled politically, without becoming aware of vocabulary and even grammar. Such awareness of the limits of languages and their cross-fertilization was excellent preparation for a man who would create a distinctive cadence and rhythm in English, as different from the practices of his predecessors as Joyce's and Woolf's were from theirs.

The Young Poland movement would stress Polish revitalization and was, in actuality, a regrouping of 1830 romantic shibboleths, specifically a withdrawal from positivistic ideas. We note that the movement in Poland had

* Writing to Constance Garnett, that Russophile, Conrad responded to her criticism of Miss Haldin's woodenness in *Under Western Eyes:* "But the fact is that I know extremely little of Russians. Practically nothing. In Poland we have nothing to do with them. One knows they are there. And that's disagreeable enough. In exile the contact is even slighter if possible if more unavoidable. I crossed the Russian frontier at the age of ten. Not having been to school then I never knew Russian. I could not tell a Little Russian from a Great Russian to save my life. In the book as you must have seen I am exclusively concerned with ideas."

And then to Edward Garnett, he touches on Dostoevsky: "I don't know what D stands for or reveals, but I do know that he is too Russian for me. It sounds to me like some fierce mouthings from prehistoric ages."

strong affinities to parallel movements in England and France, especially to the latter. It recalls in some ways how the French *symbolistes* reacted to the Parnassians, a vitalist force attempting to move against a reactionary classicism on one hand and a technological naturalism on the other. One marginal issue of the movement is that Władysław Reymont, the novelist, was connected to it in its later development, and it was Reymont who won the Nobel Prize for Literature in 1924, at the very time Conrad had thought of the prize for himself.

All this, of course, moves us ahead of the young Conrad coming to St. Anne's in the autumn of 1870. Whatever his relationship to the school, he could not have failed to be caught up by some of the new fervor, however unshaped and unfocused it still was. Only a year after Apollo's death and Conrad's heading up of the funeral procession, he must have reacted with mixed emotions to these growing outbursts of patriotism, full of feeling for his father's role and yet aware of the personal damage that role had done. Also, now under the wing of Tadeusz Bobrowski, Conrad was becoming more fully conscious of his uncle's opposition to Korzeniowski romanticism. All the rifts and divisions were surfacing and taking hold.

Regularized schoolwork and regular school attendance were not for the twelve-year-old Conrad. Like so many young people of talent and imagination without clear focus, his development was to be late, and in adolescence he saw school more as a hindrance than as an aid. Everything, in fact, ruled against a regular pattern or system; and schoolwork, especially in the Germanic Latin curriculum, demanded a high degree of discipline. For any young man at St. Anne's or elsewhere, the curriculum demanded work in three languages, Latin, German, and Polish, with Russian not obligatory but never too distant. For Conrad, the essential languages were Polish, French, and English, a very different triad.*

Discipline was the last thing Conrad had been prepared for. Uprootedness, transience, death of parents, lack of continuity—these were the conditions of a life of wandering or a life of intense inner activity in which the imagination could follow its own pattern and not that of a system. We recall Sissy Jupe, at the beginning of Dickens's *Hard Times*, being asked in Gradgrind's school to define a horse. We can, to some extent, substitute the young Conrad, caught up by German positivism as Sissy was by English utilitarianism, and reacting in his own tested way: rejecting it through illness, headaches, fevers. Clearly, Conrad had discovered a form of leverage, utilizing

* While Conrad was living in the Georgeon pension, he apparently studied the French language with a Polish refugee named Czapski, since Mr. Georgeon spoke almost no French. Jean-Aubry adds that Czapski spoke almost no Polish, having come from France to Poland solely to take part in the 1863 insurrection. Central to Conrad's language study was the orientation of the tutor, like Apollo a romantic Red, with a background of escape, emigration, French experience.

illness as much as illness claimed him, whether it was the epilepsy alluded to, kidney disturbances, or less drastic fevers. We do know that for reasons of health he revisited Krynica in 1871 and 1872, and went abroad for a much longer time in 1873. Truancy from school gained Conrad the inner time for measuring something in himself not consciously apparent to him and certainly not visible to those around him.

Admittedly, such forms of control are infantile. They are attempts to regulate the environment in small matters and to gain power through the repetition of stubborn acts or moments of defiance. They bypass almost completely the larger issues, where one's defeat or frustration really lies. And yet, infantile as they are, they buy time, they allow for a waiting game, and for the talented or the late developer they may be effective strategies for survival. Apparently, Conrad husbanded these small victories.

In these years, from 1870 to 1874, the boy was by no means neglected. Besides Tadeusz, his maternal grandmother and other members of the family were quite concerned about him. But he was moving toward decisions and areas of thought they could not begin to follow; decisions were being made for him as much as he was trying to make them. How could they understand that he needed distance from school, that school had become a direction away from, not toward, what was shaping in his mind? Just as the chaotic early years had defied the routine stages of growing up, so the school years did not fit whatever patterns he was forming for himself. Like Sissy Jupe, he identified with another area of consciousness, and like her, he found school an indifferent matrix for his hopes, dreams, and ultimate goals.

There would also be a certain unruliness. Tadeusz's later exasperation with Conrad's way of conducting his life even in his twenties and thirties would appear to be based on an earlier discontent with his nephew's attitudes. We can assume that disciplinary problems arose, especially in 1873, when Conrad apparently proved too much of an enigma for his grandmother to handle. Whatever the precise points here—and this period remains undocumented and dim—we can project certain elements of behavior. The irregular attendance at school would suggest not only a lack of interest and direction but a truancy of spirit; also a sense of isolation and marginality, the boy's failure to find where he fitted and what he belonged to, despite being surrounded by parental figures.

Further, there would be the desire to escape that very solicitude, that plethora of parental figures, some of whom were compensating for their own early loss of children. Then he would recognize his place as an orphan—that it was a condition he could turn to his advantage. Equally, he would feel distaste, even contempt, for his contemporaries, accustomed as he was to adult attention and to the confidentiality of adult talk and discussion. Added to that was his inability to catch up in his school studies, even if he wished to—his disadvantage in the curriculum was apparent at this age. And while he felt pride at Apollo's achievement, it was paralleled by his awareness of what such achievement can bring with it, an irresolvable conflict of feeling leading to guilt and remorse. Overall, there were the conflicts of ideology which he must have noted as he became attached to Tadeusz, a man who mixed kindness and generosity with much stern fatherly advice and who was, implacably, set against nearly everything Apollo had stood for.

These conflicts and divisions, with their unresolved behavioral components, were excellent preparation for the later writer, provided he could survive the cutting edge of such divisiveness. Survival, then, was the thing, and Conrad apparently found in illness the way he could manipulate *his* view of his experience, as distinct from the way his life was viewed by Tadeusz and others. This utilization of illness worked well for Conrad later on as well. While it brought anxiety to a peak, it also gained him a respite from problems as they piled up impossibly. Further, it fed his egocentricity. The isolated child never learns to relate to the outside world except through an egocentric pattern; he must always assert himself as a way of proving himself alive—once again, excellent preparation for an introspective writer, if he can survive those early years.

CHAPTER 4

Breaking Away

ONE of the turning points came in 1872, as the result of something completely outside Conrad's hands. Living in Poland, whether Austrian, Russian, or German, he was caught in the materials of a naturalistic novel, the individual being always smaller than the pattern and potentially sacrificial, even in the more tolerant German-speaking part. Tadeusz had tried to obtain Austrian citizenship for Conrad in 1872, and had failed to do so, which meant that he remained liable to service in the military, for as long as twenty-five years as the son of a convict. These were indeed the facts of a naturalistic novel, the son paying the debts of the father simply as a condition of birth.

His uncle's failure to gain Austrian citizenship for Conrad is not easily explained. The municipal council of Cracow at its December 28, 1872, meeting, in homage to the memory of Apollo Korzeniowski and to his services to the Polish cause, conferred the freedom of the city on his son, which also exempted him from taxes. Such an honor would normally bring the recipient Austrian citizenship when he reached his majority. Tadeusz's "Document" of accounts for the years 1873 and 1874 notes applications and sums expended for Conrad's Austrian naturalization. Nothing, however, came of these attempts, and we can only speculate why, and what would have occurred if they had been successful.

The decision was a bureaucratic one—solidifying Conrad's suspicion of all governmental action—and it may be that Austria and Russia agreed not to permit the exchange of citizens, especially those who had not done military service. Or else Conrad's background, despite his having been granted the freedom of the city, was a factor in his not receiving Austrian naturalization. Even so, it is unlikely that such an act would have kept Conrad in Poland. There is no certainty here, but decisions based on internal needs would have preempted whatever external solutions arose. If we are correct in assuming that Conrad's breaking away was a form of survival for him, then Austrian naturalization would not have been for him a key matter; on the other hand, it could have strengthened his uncle's argument for him to stay and made a definite break more difficult.

Conrad's desire to seek some fresh direction was now becoming more insistent. He was proving too troublesome for his grandmother to control, his health was sporadically breaking down, and his future in Cracow—because of Russian requirements—was increasingly unsure. In 1872, he apparently mentioned his plan to go to sea, and he continued to press for it. It was not unlike an Eskimo boy informing his parents that he wanted to become an architect. Conrad's reasons for going to sea may have been very complicated, or very simple; but whatever they were, they derived from a large cluster of experience which the boy was trying to handle and resolve. His schoolwork, in particular, was as ever going badly, and for him, proud, intellectually precocious, hypersensitive, the low ranking he achieved must have rankled far more than it would have to a boy of less exposed sensibility.

In an essay written near the end of his life, "Geography and Some Explorers," Conrad tells of his love of geography as a boy and his disappointment at its neglect in the school.

> Unfortunately, the marks awarded for that subject were almost as few as the hours apportioned to it in the school curriculum by persons of no romantic sense for the real, ignorant of the great possibilities of active life; with no desire for struggle, no notion of the wide spaces of the world—mere bored professors, in fact, who were not only middle-aged but looked to me as if they had never been young. And their geography was very much like themselves, a bloodless thing with a dry skin covering a repulsive armature of uninteresting bones.

Conrad continues:

> I would be ashamed of my warmth in digging up a hatchet which has been buried now for nearly fifty years if those fellows had not tried so often to take my scalp at the yearly examinations. There are things that one does not forget. And besides, the geography which I had discovered for myself was the geography of open spaces and wide horizons built upon men's devoted work in the open air, the geography still militant but already conscious of its approaching end with the death of the last great explorer. The antagonism was radical.

If we assume Conrad's memory and assessment were accurate, this passage provides many clues as to why he needed to break away. Geographically, Poland was suffocating, enclosed by enemies; beyond was the spatiality of dreams and fantasies, an oceanic infinitude. A "militant" geography posits an explorer who pioneers as an act of defiance. He defies the existing world as well as his own powers. And he does so (*usque ad finem*) knowing that it will all end in death, his or that of exploration itself. Mungo Park, the Scottish explorer, was the ideal: the man who died at thirty-five pushing ever deeper into the heart of darkness.

The sixty-six-year-old Conrad goes on to speak of the paper he had written at thirteen, which he considered an "erudite performance." He says he managed to compress his enthusiasm into just two pages, and yet he received no marks.

> I believe the only comment made to my private tutor [Pulman] was that I seemed to have been wasting my time in reading books of travel instead of attending to my studies. I tell you, those fellows were always trying to take my scalp. On another occasion I just saved it by proficiency in map-drawing. It must have been good, I suppose; but all I remember about it is that it was done in a loving spirit.

In order to redirect the young Conrad's priorities, his grandmother and uncle decided, in 1873, to send him to Lwów, to a boarding school for orphans of the 1863 insurrection supervised by a very distant cousin of Conrad's, Antoni Syroczyński, later referred to as Uncle Antoni. Before that move was made, however, Conrad on doctor's advice was sent abroad for reasons of health; and what was to be a six-week tour of Switzerland with Pulman accompanying him became a full summer tour, from May through August. The family took advantage of the trip to ask Pulman to dissuade Conrad from going to sea. Because of an outbreak of cholera in Cracow, they were told to delay their return, but an additional reason for the extended trip may have been Pulman's difficulty in changing Conrad's mind.

In these areas of Conrad's shifts from one guardian to another, excursions with his tutor, outbreaks of illness, irregular attendance at school, below-average performance, movements from one type of residence to another, we hope to sift the slim evidence for clear directions, or even for where to place the stress. The events of Conrad's early years—up to the time of his English sea career at twenty—are more novelistic and impressionistic than they are the facts of a conventional biography. In his life, Conrad was already, as a youth, living out what would become the analogous events of his characters' lives; and the biographer is left with ambiguous motivations and unclear events.

Fortunately, Conrad has himself left a description of this episode with Pulman, leading up to his tutor's pronounced indictment of the boy and his heritage. He writes:

> . . . we had seen Vienna, the Upper Danube, Munich, the Falls of the Rhine, the Lake of Constance—in fact it was a memorable holiday of travel. Of late we had been tramping slowly up the Valley of the Reuss. It was a delightful time. It was much more like a stroll than a tramp. Landing from a Lake of Lucerne steamer in Fluellen, we found ourselves at the end of the second day, with the dusk overtaking our leisurely footsteps, a little way beyond Hospenthal.

We recall that the purpose of the trip was for Pulman to dissuade Conrad from his desire of going to sea, and yet the trip seemed to make travel so attractive that the boy evidently vowed to make it part of his routine life.

He tells in these passages of how he heard the English language for the first time. He speaks of sighting a building, whose existence was the result of the excavations for the St. Gotthard Tunnel. Conrad relates the episode as if from a fairy tale: the deep burrowing of the tunnel resulting in the strange, unexpected building set on the "very roots of the mountains," like the gingerbread house of Hansel and Gretel. "It was clear that no travellers were expected, or perhaps even desired, in this strange hostelry, which in its severe style resembled the house which surmounts the unseaworthy-looking hulls of the toy Noah's Arks, the universal possession of European childhood. However its roof was not hinged and it was not full to the brim of slab-sided and painted animals of wood."

Conrad recalls eating in a long narrow room, his eyes heavy with sleep, on a table that seemed ready to tilt up like a seesaw plank; dinner over, he fell sound asleep in a room smelling of pine boards. The episode is a dream sequence, for when he awakes in the morning, the fairy hotel has been transformed into a bustling accommodation. As the dining room fills, he notes that the place—his Noah's Ark, his gingerbread house—is really a boarding-house for some English engineers who are working on the St. Gotthard Tunnel. ". . . and I could listen to my fill to the sounds of the English language as far as it is used at a breakfast-table by men who do not believe in wasting many words on the mere amenities of life"—Conrad's first spoken English except for what he had overheard at tourist hotels in Zurich and Lucerne.*

* The trip was ambitious, starting in Cracow and ending in Venice and Trieste. From Cracow, the two—apparently in dispute all the way—went to Vienna, then on the Danube to Linz and Passau. After a brief stay in Munich and Schaffhausen, they arrived at Zurich and Lucerne by way of Lake Constance and then, traveling through Andermatt and Hospenthal, came upon the construction of the St. Gotthard Tunnel, just south of Andermatt. When they received word of the outbreak of cholera in Cracow, they continued down to Italy, reaching Milan, where Conrad saw the cathedral by moonlight. Later, recalling the moment, he asked Edward Garnett, "Are you going to Milan? It's 24 years [23] since I saw the Cathedral in moonlight. Tempi passati—I had young eyes then. Don't give all your time to the worship of Boticelli[sic]. Somebody should explode that superstition" (March 29, 1898; Garnett, p. 136).

From Milan—still arguing over Conrad's desire to go to sea—they moved on to Venice, where from "the outer shore of the Lido" Conrad reports his first "glimpse of the sea," and from Venice to Trieste he made his first sea voyage. Jean-Aubry quotes from a letter in which Mme Tekla Wojakowska, née Syroczyńska, a distant cousin of Conrad's, says that Conrad spent two months at the seaside near Odessa in 1866 or 1867. This information of course contradicts Conrad's own statement in *A Personal Record* and has no other support. Nevertheless, Conrad's memory often played him wrong, and his desire to dramatize his experiences, as if fictive, could have led him to place the sight of the sea in Venice as the climax of a trip which featured an entire sequence of epiphanies or great moments.

Yet what is important is not only the boy's first exposure to sustained spoken English but the associations Conrad made between the language, the locale where it was spoken, and the kind of men speaking it: practical, isolated men living in a large hole in the earth, under mountains, digging through earth as later he would himself "furrow" the oceans and seas. As Conrad presents this scene in his autobiographical memoir, this is a "privileged moment," comparable in his life to Proust's association of memory with tea and the madeleine. Had Conrad's exposure to spoken English come in a more prosaic situation or under less romanticized conditions, it is possible he would have rejected it—but it was indeed a turning point, a moment. He had discovered a mode of survival, and would not let go.

That experience became the apex of the tour. Conrad continues his description of their travels, over the Furka Pass toward the Rhone Glacier, with the intention of following the trend of the Häsli Valley, the Jungfrau in the distance, all this splendid scenery interspersed with their running argument over his intention to go to sea. We note the "scenic analogy": arguments over the sea while they tour a landlocked Switzerland, a Kafkaesque suggestion of endless space outward juxtaposed to endless space upward. Conrad then recalls another "unforgettable episode," an "unforgettable Englishman," clad in a knickerbocker suit and with short socks under his laced boots: "his calves exposed to the public gaze and to the tonic air of high altitudes, dazzled the beholder by the splendour of their marble-like condition and their rich tone of young ivory."

This Englishman, whose splendiferous calves symbolized a great nation indeed, was the leader of a caravan. His self-satisfied, even "exalted," look caught the light of the sun and mountains, which "illumined his clean-cut, very red face, his short, silver-white whiskers, his innocently eager and triumphant eyes." In passing, he gave a glance of "kindly curiosity and a friendly gleam of big, sound, shiny teeth towards the man and the boy sitting like dusty tramps by the roadside." Following in his confident wake was the small train, including two ladies, probably his daughters. "My tutor, after pausing for a look and a faint smile, resumed his earnest argument," which was, by now, a futile gesture.

Conrad had somehow spotted the chosen land from the top of the mountain, Moses on Mount Pisgah. He asks in *A Personal Record* if this divine Englishman—confident, healthy, self-satisfied, well-ordered, at peace with himself—was "in the mystical ordering of common events the ambassador of my future, sent out to turn the scale at a critical moment on the top of an Alpine pass, with the peaks of the Bernese Oberland for mute and solemn witnesses." The locale is chance, but the event and the moment are built into the very sense of what Conrad was seeking. That Conrad should become entranced by this fairyland scene, or that he should conceive of it as having derived from a fairyland, is the result of the confluence of many points. If he had not been so exposed in his own right, that is, out of step with himself, he could not have been exalted by the commonplace. Strong calves, and the sense of bursting vitality that they denote, he could only associate with a strong vital England if he had already seen the connection to a declining, decaying home country, or to his own sickliness in that country. Harbingers are as much of the internal world as they are of the external.

Sound, the talk of Englishmen tunneling under Switzerland, and now sight—the viewing of a particular member of that doughty species—combined to provide that outlet the young Conrad had been seeking. Englishmen meant the sea—and the two elements now consolidated. In this same passage in *A Personal Record*, he speaks of the battle he started once he had mentioned the sea, how people wondered what Mr. T.B. "would do now with his worrying nephew and, I dare say, hoped that he would make short work of nonsense." Conrad reports the general astonishment: ". . . it would not have been greater if I had announced the intention of entering a Carthusian monastery. . . . It stirred up a mass of remonstrance, indignation, pitying wonder, bitter irony and downright chaff. I could hardly breathe under its weight, and certainly had no words for an answer." To Bobrowski's credit, he chose not to crush the boy's expectations, simply warning him not to forget the larger issues involved and not to do badly on his yearly examinations. Apparently, he saw it as a desire that would burn itself out. Yet to the older man, the initial decision on Conrad's part must have looked like the worst of the Nałęcz inheritance, even more quixotic than Apollo's romantic tendencies.

Yet how could Conrad—himself named after the romantic hero of Mickiewicz's poem *Konrad Wallenrod*—escape the fate of Don Quixote, in his case fed on romantic, chivalric literature? The courses of the two were destined to cross. Pulman, Conrad's tutor, then inadvertently drew attention to the analogy, calling the fifteen-year-old boy "an incorrigible, hopeless Don Quixote," at the conclusion of their final argument. Conrad comments:

> I was surprised. I was only fifteen and did not know what he meant exactly. But I felt vaguely flattered at the name of the immortal knight turning up in connection with my own folly, as some people would call it to my face. Alas! I don't think there was anything to be proud of. Mine was not the stuff the protectors of forlorn damsels, the redressers of this world's wrongs are made of; and my tutor was the man to know that best. Therein, in his indignation, he was superior to the barber and the priest when he flung at me an honoured name like a reproach.

By this time, Conrad had read, in Polish, an abridged version of the *Don* and perhaps had observed the relationship between the literary figure after whom he had been named and the Cervantes character whose exploits are based on such fictional heroes.

On Conrad's return from three months of travel in August—more insistent than ever on leaving Poland for a sea career—he was sent to the school mentioned above, in Lwów, designed for orphans of Polish patriots. The setting is ironical, for even as the boy was attempting to efface part of the past with his own inner resolve, he was sent to a school whose very existence was a monument and testimony to that very past, the futility of Apollo's ventures and the ineffectiveness of "sick" Poland, as against vital, throbbing England.

Conrad's stay in Lwów was, predictably, not a happy time for him, although there is evidence that he carried on at least a flirtation with Tekla Syroczyńska, Antoni's daughter. She later commented that Conrad "hated the rigours of school" and would one day become a great writer. This latter he expressed in front of his classmates, with a "sarcastic smile on his face and frequent critical remarks on everything," comments which were sure to receive ridicule. The picture we receive of the young Conrad in school or in society is of someone who does not understand the amenities, or, having understood them, has calculated to what extent he will ignore them. The "relationship" with Tekla—whatever its precise definition—could not have been serious, since Conrad was himself too unsettled, at fifteen, to devote his attentions unreservedly. A flirtation, if that, is more likely.

This episode recalls a somewhat earlier one, in 1871, when Conrad lived at the Georgeon boarding school. At that time the establishment had moved from Florianska Street in Cracow to 43 Franciszkanska Street, in the same house as the Taube family, a large group of four brothers and two sisters. Janina Taube, the later Baroness de Brunnow, an occasional correspondent of Conrad's in later years, is often cited as the focus of the boy's attentions—he was barely fourteen at this time. The idea is tempting: to see the young boy reaching out for love and affection in the circles in which he moved; the orphan seeking attachments wherever he could find them. But there is little evidence to support any intense passion, no less a love affair. The puritanical nature of Polish Catholic girls and the chivalric upbringing to which Conrad had been exposed would almost certainly limit him to a minor show of affection, a squeeze of the hand or a lengthy glance. Although one can err seriously by underestimating the ability of young people to achieve their own ends, Conrad does not appear to have been precocious in romantic matters. The chief evidence for his "amours," whatever shape they took, occurs in his own words, in the Author's Note to *Nostromo* and in the canceled opening to *The Arrow of Gold.*

In the Author's Note to *Nostromo* (written in October 1917, thirteen years after the novel), Conrad speaks of having modeled the heroic figure of Antonia Avellanos on "his first love." He then speaks—and the apparent model for this is Janina Taube—of how we ("a band of tallish schoolboys") "used to look up to that girl just out of the schoolroom herself, as the standard-bearer of a faith to which we all were born but which she alone knew how to hold aloft with an unflinching hope!" Then anxious to make this memory more vibrant than the somewhat forbidding and prim Antonia, Conrad writes: "She had perhaps more glow and less serenity in her soul than Antonia, but she was an uncompromising Puritan of patriotism with no taint of the slightest worldliness in her thoughts." Almost fifty years after the event, Conrad sees her as uncompromising, a strict disciplinarian of both life and love: "I was not the only one in love with her; but it was I who had to hear oftenest her scathing criticism of my levities—very much like poor Decoud—or stand the brunt of her austere, unanswerable invective."

We are not certain whether Janina Taube or Tekla Syroczyńska was the original of this "first love," but the passages are themselves so much part of the mythical aspect of romance that one can hardly accept Conrad's version. Aspects of the description seem to fit Conrad's memories of his mother as much as they do either of the girls; in fact, the girls are intermixed with Conrad's view of women, part of which rested profoundly on his mother's idealism and patriotism and some of which derived from the Don's view of Dulcinea. In *A Personal Record,* in the words of his Uncle Nicholas B.—the eater of roast dog—Conrad says of his mother: "Meeting with calm fortitude the cruel trials of a life reflecting all the national and social misfortunes of the community, she realised the highest conceptions of duty as a wife, a mother and a patriot, sharing the exile of her husband and representing nobly the ideal of Polish womanhood." From this description, we can see that Conrad's attitude toward women—no matter what occurred later—was to be attached to the chivalric ideal. If Apollo was the knight (the bookish Don tilting at windmills), then Ewa was, in reality, his Dulcinea. For their son, she was a prototypical woman, the Great Mother who lay behind all femaleness.

In Conrad's view, women are almost always finer and more delicate than men in their demands on life. They provide moral guidance and insight into areas men neglect or fail to see, and their nobility is apparent. Conrad had evidently turned memory of an idealized mother into a handservant of his romantic need. Further, the Antonia of *Nostromo* is based on at least one definite source, Edward B. Eastwick's *Venezuela,* where she is named Antonia Ribera. More likely, Conrad's memory—with all the license allowed the novelist, but not the critic of his own work—allied several different people and several different moments in time to create a composite. Where the precise truth lies, we cannot tell. It is not unusual, however, that two of the literary figures Conrad found closest to his way of thinking were Don Quixote and Odysseus, whose respective women, Dulcinea and Penelope, are idealized and untouchable. The confluence of these two women is surely the Great Mother, of whose presence Conrad had only a dim memory, indeed a Penelope twenty years in the past.

In *Under Western Eyes,* that shadow novel of so much in Conrad's life, perhaps more an autobiography than *A Personal Record,* he has played several reversals on his own "first love," whether his mother or Janina or Tekla. Mrs. Haldin, in the novel, has lost a són, and Razumov lacks a mother; the agent is Miss Haldin, a possible wife for Razumov. But he seeks a family—a mother and a sister—as much as he does a wife; and if he did marry, as the original plan of the novel was to have it, he would have married a family, Victor Haldin's. Haldin, we should add, is more Apollo Korzeniowski than he is Odysseus. Miss Haldin has all the characteristics that Conrad ascribes to his "first loves," and Mrs. Haldin has many of the qualities of Conrad's prototypical women; so that we can see in their juxtaposition in this intimate and revealing novel how Conrad merged one with the other, sister, possible wife, and mother—romantic love and family need.

At the end of the *Nostromo* passage, Conrad describes how at his leave-taking, when as "a shrinking yet defiant sinner" he came to say a final good-bye, "I received a hand-squeeze that made my heart leap and saw a tear that took my breath away." This same "hand-squeeze" reappears in the canceled opening to *The Arrow of Gold.* In the Yale manuscript of this passage, the reference seems to be to Tekla, not Janina, although the romantic memories are applicable to either, or neither. In the novel proper, Conrad speaks of a woman who seems "to have been the writer's childhood's friend. They had parted as children, or very little more than children." The story is itself intended as a narrative for the ears of this woman, who has now communicated with him across the span of years. He answers her that he "chummed with her even more than with your brothers," and he wonders what has become of her. The tale follows, a tale of an Odysseus, of romantic idealism, a great love affair, a duel—a Byronic, even Rafael Sabatini composite of the material that puts in doubt the biographical authenticity of the canceled passages.

In those latter, he speaks of her, this great love, as the "moral centre of a group of young people on the threshold of life," but he resists her influence publicly, while succumbing privately. However, she was not, he assures us, his first love. "That experience had come to him the year before in the late summer of his last school holiday." Their relationship—and this is possibly of more importance than whether it ever really occurred—was based on his pain. She tortured him: ". . . then discovering that she could make him suffer she let herself go to her heart's content. She amused herself again and again by tormenting him privately and publicly with great zest and method and finally 'executed' him in circumstances of peculiar atrocity." He came out of it, Conrad relates, "seamed, scarred, almost flayed."

The masochism of the experience, whether true or not, would appear to be a replay of Pip's relationship with Estella in *Great Expectations*, and as a recollection generates a lot of suspicion. The older Conrad, now sixty, looks back across more than forty-five years to Poland and then forward a few years to France for the setting of the novel, and turns the past into a hard, cruel time. There is too much *Weltschmerz:* "From the nature of things first love can never be a wholly happy experience." It is difficult to accept any of this as fact, for there is no proof of Conrad's great Polish loves, just as there is considerable doubt about his affair with Rita, of *The Arrow,* in his own Marseilles years. The claim for the duel, as we know, proved false, and the claims for those early Byronic romances seem doomed by lack of supporting evidence or psychological plausibility.

Whatever his relationship to Tekla in Lwów—and apparently Conrad was chastised for it by her father—his stay there did not last long. His old ailments returned, headaches as well as attacks of unknown derivation, and in the summer of 1874, a fateful year for him, he traveled to the country accompanied by Pulman. By this time, he was firmly set upon going to sea, and one can speculate that his illnesses were forms of reaction to frustration, disappointment, lack of direction, anxiety, or all combined. Conrad lived to sixty-six, and had the headaches been serious malfunctions they would have killed him long before. Although we cannot ascertain how deeply the other ailments were also psychologically derived, the headaches are a probable indicator Conrad had discovered a painful and disagreeable way of achieving his goals.

As Conrad readied himself to leave Poland, we get some sense of his attitude, not from contemporary accounts, but from something he wrote John Galsworthy forty years later. He had just been invited by the mother-in-law of Józef Retinger, a Polish acquaintance, to visit her house, located sixteen miles from Cracow, over the Russian border. The time was July 1914, just before Austria began to mobilize for war. Conrad says the invitation caused such excitement in his house that if he had not accepted immediately he "would have been torn to pieces." They planned a month to six-week journey, via Hamburg. He writes: "[As] to this Polish journey I depart on it with mixed feelings." The project then sets off a parallel feeling, which suggests his exodus from Poland forty years before. The imagery, incidentally, recalls Lord Jim and *his* moving along into a dream.

> In 1874 I got into a train in Cracow (Vienna Express) on my way to the sea, as a man might get into a dream. And here is the dream going on still. Only now it is peopled mostly by ghosts and the moment of awakening draws near.

Of course, that dream, already verging on nightmare in Conrad's memory, becomes true nightmare when the war breaks out and the Conrads find themselves trapped, possibly subject to Austrian detention until the end of hostilities. But that is ahead of them, although Conrad's memories of the past give him a tool by which he can reckon what the future will bring. If one's dreams are nightmares, one can turn all reality into nightmare.

He left in a dream, not because the memory is distant but because he felt that decisions were being made for him as much as he was himself making them. That hallucinatory experience resulted from a series of events which must have seemed to the teenager a "dream sequence"; for no part of his life had been continuous, and the disconnectedness of his months and years up to sixteen had the non-sequential order of dreams popping into the consciousness and then subsiding. Conrad's was a past of invariable segments, each lasting a few months, or at most a year. Strikingly, perhaps out of some inner necessity, he continued to structure his life in the next twenty years along the same lines. His choice of a sea career was apparently predicated not on peace but on disruption, a life of wandering, voyages, intermittent shore leaves, brief relationships, lack of permanent residence, barely a mailing address. Not until he was close to forty did he have any sense of permanence, and then as a literary man he paradoxically had to seek out the dream material—making himself swim in the destructive element and holding himself up by the exertion of his pen.

It is significant that for the boy foreign countries did not come solely as colors on a map; they became lands with distinctive languages, Russian and German as well as English and French. France had, in addition, traditionally been the haven of Polish emigrés, a second home, just as the French language was a second tongue for educated Poles, whether at home or in exile. The idea of an isolated, landlocked Conrad gives way to someone for whom geography appeared as a destiny.

His reading, not unusually, lay in travel books. Since his temperament—indeed his name—was already romantic, far-off places appealed to his sense of things and fed his romanticism, as much as the latter directed his reading. We must always recall that, when we discuss the teenager, we are focusing on someone in whom the growth into seaman and writer was already potential. Unless we believe that individual choices are really part of the throw of the dice, as Conrad himself came to believe, then we cannot see him as simply *any* teenager casting about for ways of developing himself. The tenacity of the later years and the incredible fortitude in the face of disaster indicate a certitude that began in the early years. Conrad's reading, we can assume with some certainty, was feeding not an idle curiosity but a deeply implanted sense of something which he hoped to discover both in himself and in the reading.

There is a story Conrad told of himself, which may have been apocryphal, except that he told it three times. Staring at a map of the world as a child, he stuck out his finger, finding a spot in the "white heart of Africa," and indicated he would go *there.* In *A Personal Record*, he writes:

> It was in 1868, when nine [ten or eleven] years old or thereabouts, that while looking at a map of Africa of the time and putting my finger on the

> blank space [the Stanley Falls region] then representing the unsolved mystery of that continent, I said to myself with absolute assurance and an amazing audacity which are no longer in my character now: "When I grow up I shall go *there.*"*

This may have been a childish fantasy—only he did go *there*—and he went there as an English sea captain, the only Pole who had risen to captain in the English merchant service.

Conrad's reading was extensive, far more than what we would attribute simply to a normal boy's curiosity. And the crux of the reading was to support his desire to travel. At first, his imagination was stirred by novels about the sea, Hugo's *Les Travailleurs de la mer* and tales by Marryat and Cooper. Readers have shown astonishment that the sophisticated Middle European Conrad, with his roots in the Slavic temperament and consciousness, could have attached such importance to fiction by Marryat and Cooper. But they forget he was not evaluating them by literary standards; he was not using Jamesian or Leavisite criticism to question their literary values and/or moral probity. What Conrad sought, he tells us in an essay called "Tales of the Sea," which he wrote in 1898, was more visceral and personal, a sense of fidelity to fact, fidelity to the experience as it was known. Despite his own romanticism as to place and event—this was the time of *The Nigger of the "Narcissus"*—Conrad insisted on the truth of the experience. Marryat, he says, portrayed people who belonged not to life but to the service. "There is a truth in them, the truth of their time; a headlong, reckless audacity, an intimacy with violence, an unthinking fearlessness, and an exuberance of vitality which only years of war and victories can give." Conrad grants that Mar-

---

* In "Geography and Some Explorers," written almost sixty years after the event, Conrad redescribed the moment: "Once only did that enthusiasm expose me to the derision of my schoolboy chums. One day, putting my finger on a spot in the very middle of the then white heart of Africa, I declared that some day I would go there. My chums' chaffing was perfectly justifiable. I myself was ashamed of having been betrayed into mere vapouring. Nothing was further from my wildest hopes. Yet it is a fact that, about eighteen years [twenty-two] afterwards, a wretched little stern-wheel steamboat I commanded lay moored to the bank of an African river."

And in "Heart of Darkness" itself, Marlow, in a variation of the above, explains his passion for maps and exotic places: " 'Now when I was a little chap I had a passion for maps. I would look for hours at South America, or Africa, or Australia, and lose myself in all the glories of exploration. At that time there were many blank spaces on the earth, and when I saw one that looked particularly inviting on a map . . . I would put my finger on it and say, When I grow up I will go there. The North Pole was one of these places, I remember. . . . Other places were scattered about the Equator. . . . There was one yet—the biggest, the most blank, so to speak—that I had a hankering after. True, by this time it was not a blank space any more. It had got filled since my boyhood with rivers and lakes and names. It had ceased to be a blank space of delightful mystery—a white patch for a boy to dream gloriously over. It had become a place of darkness.' "

rayat—whose *Mr. Midshipman Easy* he has primarily in mind—is crude and sentimental, but his great appeal to young boys is based on the faithfulness of his conception, and he did not lie.

Having always disclaimed any standing or skill as a literary critic, Conrad is responding here to the truth of his own sensations. Although he subsequently modified such extreme subjectivity, we can never lose sight of this fact: that the "truth of sensations" meant far more to him as a young reader than did the shape of the literary idea. Not until later did he become a devotee of Flaubert, Turgenev, and James, or of some of the formalist ideas of the French *symbolistes.* In his crucial period from 1899 to 1904, Conrad of course eschewed these early notions of literature and refined his imagination, so that in his best creative work he is not only an artist of considerable breadth but a critic of great taste and insight.

Conrad also found in Cooper's work—his sea stories, primarily, not the Cooper of the Leatherstocking Tales—an authentic voice. He called the author a man of "true artistic instinct." These comments, coming as they do in 1898, when Conrad had three books to his credit, provide a sense of continuity with those somewhat vague final Polish years. More than twenty-five years after the original reading experiences, he conveys to us what Cooper meant to the boy, not to the adult writer. In his sea tales, Conrad says, the "sea inter-penetrates with life; it is in a subtle way a factor in the problem of existence, and, for all its greatness, it is always in touch with the men who, bound on errands of war or gain, traverse its immense solitudes." The "truth is within him," and that truth, the Conrad of 1898 says, at the time of his own *Nigger of the "Narcissus,"* was the truth of his boyhood, that Polish orphan moving from guardian to guardian, from experience to experience, seeking the nature of his own center in *its* "immense solitudes."*

Still later, in his novel *Chance,* Conrad returned to the boyhood experience of a "psychological wilderness," a meaningful phrase in his own transference of wilderness to sea. The narrator says to Marlow, apropos of Cooper:

> "You are the expert in the psychological wilderness. This is like one of those Redskin stories where the noble savages carry off a girl and the hon-

* Writing to Edward Garnett's ten-year-old son, David, Conrad nostalgically returned to Cooper: "We have sent off three volumes of the 'Leather-Stocking Tales'—one from each of us—with our love to you. You have promised me to read these stories and I would recommend you to begin with the *Last of the Mohicans*—then go on with the *Deerslayer* and end with the *Prairie.* I read them [in Polish] at your age in that order; and I trust that you, of a much later generation, shall find in these pages some at least of the charm which delighted me then and has not evaporated even to this day. . . . I have great confidence in you; and I believe that you shall respond—as I did in my time—to the genuine feeling of the descriptions and the heroic temper of the narrative" (December 22, 1902, Garnett, pp. 185–86).

> est backwoodsman with his incomparable knowledge follows the track and reads the signs of her fate in a footprint here, a broken twig there, a trinket dropped by the way. I have always liked such stories. Go on."

Marlow indicates that *his* tale "is not exactly a story for boys," which helps place Cooper in Conrad's mind as a storyteller for boys. Conrad read Cooper and Marryat first in Polish, later in English, and surely these writers fitted in very well with Mickiewicz and Słowacki, whom he also read before he left Poland. Their stress on the individual's responsibility to his society and nation would not be alien to the ideas of Cooper and Marryat and their protagonists' responsibility to the larger needs of the ship at sea.

Conrad apparently, even when young, never lost touch with himself, and could find the correct coordinates for an understanding of his own experiences. The synthesizing mind we associate with the artist was already measuring life into component elements he could, however dimly, comprehend. The move out to the sea was, we note, an internal compulsion as much as it was socially or politically based. In 1898, he concludes this touching memoir:

> Life is life, and art is art—and truth is hard to find in either. Yet in testimony to the achievement of both these authors it may be said that, in the case of the writer at least, the youthful glamour, the headlong vitality of the one [Marryat] and the profound sympathy, the artistic insight of the other—to which he had surrendered—have withstood the brutal shock of facts and the wear of laborious years. He has never regretted his surrender.

These were the books of fiction. The travel books were an even more essential part of Conrad's education. He writes of Mungo Park, of explorations in the western Sudan, of James Bruce in Abyssinia, but chiefly of Sir Leopold McClintock's *The Voyage of the "Fox" in the Arctic Seas*, a book as compelling in Conrad's day as it is to a contemporary reader. He indicates that he probably read the book in French, when he was ten.

> There could hardly have been imagined a better book for letting in the breath of the stern romance of Polar exploration into the existence of a boy whose knowledge of the poles of the earth had been till then of an abstract formal kind as mere imaginary ends of the imaginary axis upon which the earth turns. The great spirit of the realities of the story sent me off on the romantic explorations of my inner self; to the discovery of the taste for poring over maps; and revealed to me the existence of a latent devotion to geography which interfered with my devotion (such as it was) to my other school-work.

Conrad contrasts stargazing with map-gazing, with the former leading to the borders of the unattainable (such as we find in the early work of H. G. Wells with his Martians and Morlocks), and the latter to the attainable and, therefore, more attuned to Conrad's kind of romantic realism. ". . . map-gazing . . . brings the problems of the great spaces of the earth into stimulating and directing contact with sane curiosity and gives an honest precision to one's imaginative faculty. And the honest maps of the nineteenth century nourished in me a passionate interest in the truth of geographical facts and a desire for precise knowledge which was extended later to other subjects."

The words Conrad uses here in reference to geography—that sense of space connected to detailed knowledge—were an inchoate form of his later literary doctrines, in which he entered into exotic experiences with a precise sense of human character and human event. He always sought the sharp realistic detail that would disturb a purely romantic conception of his material. He feared the deliberately vague and the imprecise. Part of his heritage from symbolism—which interpenetrated both French poetry and fiction during his Marseilles years—was his emphasis on the hard gemlike intensity of the image. As he wrote in his manifesto, his Preface to *The Nigger of the "Narcissus"*:

> And it is only through complete, unswerving devotion to the perfect blending of form and substance; it is only through an unremitting never-discouraged care for the shape and ring of sentences that an approach can be made to plasticity, to colour, and that the light of magic suggestiveness may be brought to play for an evanescent instant over the commonplace surface of words: of the old, old words, worn thin, defaced by ages of careless usage.

In his essay on geography and explorers, Conrad speaks of how his mind fluctuated between polar and tropic regions. He says that he gave up almost every day of his schoolboy life to these men who "worked each according to his temperament to complete the picture of the earth." He adds that not the least reward of geographical discovery is the insight gained into that "special kind of men who devoted the best part of their lives to the exploration of land and sea." These men, not fictional characters, were his "first friends." We recall how the exploits of Lord Jim, and to some extent Tom Lingard's, were modeled on those of Sir James Brooke, Rajah of Sarawak. Repeatedly, Conrad based his fictional characters on real men—explorers, discoverers, pioneers of sorts—whether it was men he read about or those who bounced off him during his extensive travels. That storing up of precise images, as apart from general information, which is so essential to the future novelist was already begun.

After locating the spot in Africa where he would one day go, Conrad indicates that at twelve he could not express his wishes aloud without incurring the chaffing of his friends and chums. "I myself was ashamed of having been betrayed into mere vapouring." Yet hugging the secret, and living as if it did not exist, meant that he was already inhabiting, however incompletely, the world of the novelist; for his imagination was playing with incoherent images and ideas, drawing them together and seeking order. The later stories and tales would provide the direction; now his imagination could only hold some of the images in balance. One thinks of the Brontë children with their Angria and Gondal juvenilia, and how these romantic tales were prefigurations of the novels to come, acts of imagination shaped into tales that were themselves completed only later. Conrad, of course, did not shape his images in this way; but his mind became a repository while he waited. He and his Uncle Tadeusz, good man that he was, were moving on two completely different planes of existence.

This preparation for later life through the experience of travel books and travelers Conrad continued throughout his life. He was not a literary man in our usual American or English sense; that is, he did not gain his fund of ideas and material from either current activities or from other creative writers. He built up a rather different base of information.* As he traveled, he read widely in Malayan history, then African, later South American, and, through it all, French around the time of the Revolution. He preferred journals, memoirs, and histories to works of the imagination. And although he read broadly in the literature of three countries and three languages, his mind found order in that kind of reading that proved continuous with his earliest years of literacy.

Conrad's decision to go to sea was not, as some commentators have suggested, a simple affair. Like all momentous, life-changing decisions, its com-

---

* With some simplification, Gustav Morf, drawing on Jung, speaks of Conrad as the "intuitive type." He says that the "intuitive type possesses in a remarkable degree the faculty of putting himself in the place of others, or rather, of feeling as if he were some third person, of 'identifying himself' with others, as the technical expression is. The consequence is that he adapts himself very easily to whatever appeals to his imagination and that he understands and penetrates and literally 'makes his' the motives and enthusiasms of all sorts of men. . . . Intuitive types have the faculty of viewing things from different angles (always provided it appeals to their imagination), and they can play more than one part. To use the precise language of analytical psychology: they often give up one identification for another. They apprehend reality by means of identifications" (*The Polish Heritage of Joseph Conrad*, pp. 91–92).

The difficulty with this formulation is that, in varying degrees, the "intuitive type" is characteristic of all great artistic types; its notion of identification is intrinsic to creativity. For Conrad, it was perhaps more exaggerated, since his art depended not on current activity but, like Proust's, on memory, recall, "moments." The intuitive artist—and here Conrad fits the type—would eschew conscious perception and judgment and rely chiefly on unconscious memory traces of past and forgotten experiences and judgments. By this method, he would be able to draw on a storehouse of unconscious wisdom—what Yeats called the *spiritus mundi*—which he had accumulated in the past (in unconscious memory). Pastness would become present; memory would nourish art. Nevertheless, it is unwise to try to categorize Conrad as one type or other; since the creative act is so imperfectly understood, one can explain it by almost any system, Jungian, Freudian, mythical, symbolical, or another. It is far better to build on specifics than to systematize.

plications are both broad and profound. There are really two parts to this decision: the first is going away in itself, and the second is to go to sea. Although we lack solid evidence, it would seem from what we do know that Conrad's primary intention was to escape; that is, to rid himself of an array of adult figures, no matter how kind and generous, who had no idea of what and who he was. He barely knew himself. School of the conventional type did not appear fruitful; Conrad's illnesses and irregular attendance demonstrated his abhorrence of the experience, or his contempt for it. Also, as a Russian citizen, by law, and yet under Austrian control in Cracow, he must have felt trapped by a destiny that made no sense to him; snared, indeed, by a destiny that had brought only destruction to those close to him. It was possible to act like a patriot if he felt like one; but it was quite another circumstance to be the son of a patriot without corresponding feelings. Conrad always voiced great sympathy for Poland, retained use of the language, and carried himself like a Polish gentleman; but such actions are a far cry from the romantic-idealistic mold into which his destiny had cast him.

The facts suggest that, if he had chosen to, he could have remained. Although he may have been subject to military service—of up to twenty-five years—and that service in the Russian Army, such an outcome seemed unlikely under Austrian rule. The Austrians had never felt the sense of vengeance of the Russians toward Polish gentry and had not tried to destroy them. Poles were, for the Austrians, Westerners; for the Russians, they were part of the Slavic race and, therefore, cast in the same mold, to be subjugated and humiliated. In this sense, in the semi-free state of Cracow—more traditionally liberal than other parts of Poland—and only nominally under Austrian hegemony, Conrad would not have been inhibited from pursuing any career (except that of revolutionary) he wished. Of course, Tadeusz felt differently, exhorting his nephew to seek foreign citizenship, whether French, English, or, mockingly, even Japanese.*

We are on the verge of a distinctive move in the life of a man of great literary significance. The 1874 decision was the first of several that moved Conrad toward some consciousness of himself; the suicide attempt in 1878 was to be the next. The emerging artist is always creating the conditions so that he can be what he has to be; freeing himself from the past was Conrad's way of gaining the freedom to try whatever was stirring. His decision, however, does not have the relative simplicity we find in Joyce's fleeing Dublin

---

* He wrote to Conrad: "You are right in what you say about Swiss naturalization;—if you could obtain it in the United States I would have nothing against it—if you have the possibility of arranging it there or in one of the more important Southern Republics. Who is the Baron Drużkowicz? The Austrian Consul? And this Japanese consul, who likes you, 'you do not know what for and why'—who may this individual be? Perhaps he could help you to find something in Japan after you get your Master's certificate? Perhaps you will become an Admiral in Japan?"

for Paris, or in Lawrence's departure from Nottingham. These were moves so central to their sensibilities that there could be no other choice. One does not find such direct lines in Conrad's choice—because of his youth, his inexperience, his lack of any definite talent or calling. His decision to depart lacked future definition; it was simply the decision itself. Of course, all three, Joyce, Lawrence, and Conrad, were certain of one thing, that they must escape a destiny which was not theirs and which, in the ultimate sense, they could not identify with.

The choice of the sea was not simple, either. It was the consequence of several factors: Conrad's ill health, for which mountain or sea air was recommended, along with physical activity, as a means of alleviating or eliminating the severe migraines. The lack of alternatives: Conrad's poor performance in school or indifference to the discipline of school made other "land" professions unlikely. Although not so clearly at this time, he was following a different route from other teenagers of his class and background, and school was not the means by which he would achieve whatever was within him. By the summer of 1874, Conrad would have needed, at sixteen, two more years in the Gymnasium, in a curriculum which he found unpleasant, and which perhaps contributed to his headaches and nervousness. Personal reasons: the sea appealed to his own sense of adventurousness and was continuous with the reading he had done. We do not know if the desire for a sea career preceded the main reading of sea literature, or the other way around; but each reinforced the other, which is not unusual when a talented but directionless person is seeking his vocation.

Another reason is that Conrad may not have been the most tractable of teenagers and no one really wanted the innumerable confrontations of personality that must have occurred regularly. A child who does not attend school is, to his elders, a child on the edge of abnormality, essentially unmanageable. Part of the way a young person is regulated in Western society is through school. Without it, the parents or guardians must handle the child's large amount of free time, and this becomes insufferable. School in Cracow did not work for Conrad. His uncle apparently could not handle the situation from a distance, and he had little support from Teofila Bobrowska, who as maternal grandmother would have been unable to countermand her grandson's wishes, he being the sole survivor of his line of the family. The school alternative in Lwów, under Syroczyński, was also untenable, and the Georgeon sisters' boarding school was likewise out of the question. Conrad had, by sixteen, exhausted his options.

There is a further cultural question, one that moves relentlessly outside of any individual life or desire. In Poland in the 1870s, there was a version of our 1960s struggle between the generations. The development of the Young Poland movement was based not only on ideological grounds—that is, not only on a romantic reaction to positivism and scientism—but also on a dissatisfaction with the older generation as a whole and a cultural desire to replace the older values with values of its own. While the young generation did not reject the activism of the older groups, it tried to reach beyond the specifics of a political struggle and attempted to build on a more broadly based cultural movement. Also, it expressed dissatisfaction with aspects of Polish insularity, advocating an understanding of what was occurring in the rest of Europe, in all demonstrating more personal feeling and expression and moving away from the restrictions of ideology.

While Conrad was too young to enter into any of this cultural stir, he would have sympathized with, as part of his own sense of independence and marginality, some of the more general ideas of this slowly growing group of writers. More possibly, when he returned to visit his uncle some sixteen years later, he came into active contact with the ideas of the movement. Certainly, at sixteen, he would have been aware, however vaguely, of the stirring of foreign ideas; and thoughts of France, for a Pole, were themselves never too distant. The essential point is that there was considerable ferment, a certain broadening of the Polish cultural base, and an attempt to free the "Polish idea" from narrow patriotic commitment.

While only a few of the writers involved in the movement built up a reputation outside of Poland—Żeromski and Reymont come to mind—the stir of ideas was exciting, especially since the movement stressed art and artistic values. In some of its aspects, it had affinities to French symbolism and English *fin de siècle* decadence, although its roots were deeply embedded in Polish romantic poetry. When we see literary stirrings in Conrad later, in the 1890s, we observe him moving along lines of development not at all alien to the ideas of the Young Poland movement, as well as those of French naturalism and symbolism.

There were still further elements of ferment, both cultural and political, and while we do not know how Conrad, at sixteen, fitted into them, we can recognize them as part of a general stirring, which in turn would commend itself to a young man trying to escape entropy. In 1866, the Austro-Hungarian empire suffered a severe defeat at Sadowa, a small town in Czechoslovakia, by the Prussian armies. Although this did not seem of major importance for Poland, that country had known for years that any shift in power, as the result of war or other developments, affected Polish fortunes.

Austria's defeat at Sadowa led to even more persecution of Poles by Russian and Prussian authorities as they gained in confidence in this shaping and reshaping of Central Europe; whereas Austria, in defeat, tried to pull closer to Poland. As a consequence, conditions were eased considerably, and the Polish minorities under Austrian authorities were granted concessions. Galicia itself, where Apollo had gone, was made almost autonomous, and the Polish language, as we have seen, began to replace the German of the school system. For Poles, including Conrad's family and guardians, such an easing created further ideological divisions.

With concessions, new ideas began to appear, especially those recommended by a historically oriented group called the Stańczyk Party, which suggested close cooperation with Austria and severe opposition to Russia. This party tried to rally Poles to the support of Austria as a way of fighting Russia. It was deeply conservative and gradualist, eschewing military solutions as suicidal. Through its mouthpiece, the *Polish Review*, the party argued that Polish history was a series of mistakes, not misfortunes, and that her fate had derived from God's punishment. The argument was clearly an attack on romanticism and heroic solutions to the Polish situation. The Stańczyks, then, were deeply antagonistic to what Apollo Korzeniowski had stood for, and yet they also advocated continued implacable opposition to Russia.

Conrad himself felt divided, as his comments indicate, for he sensed some kinship with Austria in later years.* Furthermore, the party, intensely conservative politically, was fanatically Catholic and sided with right-wing Catholic movements in European politics, including the Carlist attempt to regain the throne of Spain. Conrad's pro-Carlist activities in France, however brief and however embroidered, may have been part of this frame of reference; or they may simply have been the desire of a young man to thread his way through danger.

It is impossible to pinpoint how much of this affected the young man, and we must always keep in mind his age, so that we do not overestimate his conscious reaction to cultural and political phenomena. But we can speculate

* At the beginning of World War I, Conrad handed over to Dr. Teodor Kosch, a Cracow lawyer, a document of considerable prescience regarding Poland's relationship to the warring powers: "To support and develop the feeling of sympathy for Austria (which existed already in July and was expressed in some newspapers). To show that England had and has no personal quarrel with Austria, to strive to develop a friendly atmosphere of public opinion, explaining that Austrian policy under the heavy pressure of Russia was the result of hard necessity and not the symptom of an unlawful ambition to increase its territory—*but* emphasizing that after many years of a patient and prudent peace policy Austria has the right to demand a reward for its endeavours in this war."

Conrad continues: "I intend to show that Germany (Prussia), though it cannot be defeated, nevertheless can be subdued to a certain degree and that the only way to this end is to support the demands of Austria as far as they concern Polish territories—precisely to increase the anti-German elements in the setup of this empire to create an equilibrium against Prussian preponderance in Europe. In this respect England cannot count on Russia—first, because Russia will be defeated—and secondly (and chiefly) because Prussia and Russia may come to an understanding in the near future."

These ideas came forty years after Conrad left Poland, but they reflect developments in Galicia in the late 1860s and early 1870s, when he himself, through his uncle, tried to become an Austrian national.

that a young man coming from such an emotionally charged background would be more sensitive than most sixteen-year-old boys to intellectual shifts, especially when every intellectual shift brought with it political change. It is also very possible that the conflict of ideas here—the very irresolute quality of the situation—helped Conrad make up his mind to escape. One thinks once again of Joyce caught between Parnell's ideas for Ireland and the clergy and government responsive to reactionary forces. The way out of a searing conflict which cannot be resolved is to evade it altogether; escape, and renew oneself under different conditions.

For the biographer, Conrad's 1897 novel, *The Nigger of the "Narcissus,"* brings to the surface artistically the various psychological conflicts which apparently dominated his adult as well as his early life. In his first novels *Almayer's Folly* and *An Outcast of the Islands,* although he had drawn on broad subjective elements, Conrad was, in the main, utilizing the "adventure" side of his experience. With *The Nigger,* however, he began that internal descent, that dark journey into the perilous elements of his background and heritage. Using the sea, a crew, and a ship, he dredged the past, harrowed the infernal regions. After *The Nigger,* which is the lighter freight of this dredging operation, he comes to "Heart of Darkness," *Lord Jim,* and then *Nostromo*—that period of work in which he confronted the most dreaded dimensions of his inner life. *The Nigger,* then, is the first longer work in which he must find artistic correlatives for intense and urgent personal experience. The "Narcissus" of the title was not only the name of a ship on which he had sailed in 1884; it was the narcissism of an art that depended on mirror images of personal interiors.

The Nigger displays elements of loyalty and desertion, aspects of staying, marginality, group welfare, male bonding, family loyalty. Through the crew of the *Narcissus* runs an objective re-creation of Conrad's own feelings about Englishmen and foreigners, but especially about psychological isolation and loneliness. In Donkin more literally, but in Wait, the "Nigger," more subtly and imaginatively, Conrad suggested a marginality that was one part of his own mental baggage. To make Wait a black amid a white "society" is for Conrad to use color psychologically, as he would later in "Heart of Darkness." There is the disorder of synesthesia here, the utilization of color schemes to convey the other senses, here gradations of feeling. His subtlety in presenting Wait's destructive influence upon the crew derives from his realization of how close malingering was to his own indolence and reverie, and how accommodating these qualities are to pessimism, depression, and even death.

Donkin and Wait represent the members of the crew who refuse duty—to the ship directly, and indirectly to captain-father, country, fellow man. In figurative terms, the *Narcissus* is a synecdoche for all that engaged Conrad—not only his background in the 1860s and 1870s, but his assimilation of eighteenth- and nineteenth-century philosophy, Rousseau, Hegel, Schopenhauer, and Nietzsche. What Conrad posed in the interplay between individual and crew was a sense of roles and role-playing in which the ship is the universe and the author is seeking divine guidance.

Through Donkin and Wait, Conrad can try out the marginality which will disrupt the ship's company and lead it toward disunity; and yet through Finn and Singleton, he can provide examples of loyalty that lead back toward unity. While these figures may be various personae for Poland and Polish experiences, we can assume they are psychologically more intimate than that: they implicate not Poles but Conrad personally. They are aspects, then, not of national but of individual character; they are ontogenetic, not phylogenetic.

The Nigger, apparently, helps fill in the inner landscape of Conrad as he poised to leap from Poland. Its meaning for him went far beyond its role as a reflection of his sea career soon after it had ended; and if we see its psychological implications, we can better understand the affection he felt for this particular novel. It was his only book which he did not criticize as a partial or total failure.* In *The Nigger,* Conrad gives himself several voices—some speaking for his dutiful side, some for the devil within, some attempting to define a purely objective reality—but all of them continuous with aspects of his life in the early 1870s.†

Although Morf simplifies the term considerably, he points out that Conrad was providing the literary equivalent of the psychological state of "abreaction." That is, he was bringing to consciousness—to mind, words, narrative, print, page—materials which he had repressed, or had certainly been unaware of as lying deep within the sub- and unconscious. And he was doing this not only as recollections of forgotten or repressed memories but as a reliving of the accompanying emotions. In psychiatry, abreaction is a stage of awareness on the part of the analysand of his previously undischarged, or

* Typical is his comment to Cunninghame Graham: "There is a thing of mine coming out in the *New Review.* Being, as you inform me, my 'Prophète en titre' I am afraid you must consider it your sacred duty to read everything over my signature. Now in this special case *please don't.* In Nov[er] I shall send you the book—if you allow me—and then you shall see the whole. I am conceited about that thing and very much in love with it, and I want it to appear before you at its best" (August 9, 1897; ALS, Dartmouth).

† In a letter to an unidentified reviewer of *The Nigger,* Conrad suggested the seamless, continuous universe into which the novel fell: "I wrote this short book regardless of any formulas of art, forgetting all the theories of expression. Formulas and theories are dead things, and I wrote straight from the heart—which is alive. I wanted to give a true impression, to present and [sic] undefaced image. And you, who know amongst what illusions and self-deceptions men struggle, work, fail—you will only smile with indulgence if I confess to you that I also wanted to connect the small world of the ship with that larger world carrying perplexities, fears, affections, rebellions, in a loneliness greater than that of the ship at sea" (December 9, 1897; ALS, Rosenbach).

repressed, emotion and his symptoms; and the consequence is often that the patient can modify his behavior to the degree he understands his emotional reaction. In literary or imaginative terms, Conrad's "understanding" has emerged from beyond his reason or consciousness. The objective material of his sea career is suddenly joined by subjective experiences that reach back into an earlier phase, all of which the imagination must find some way of blending into an artistic form. Conrad's concern for the artistry of *The Nigger*, we can speculate, was attached to his awareness of this blending or merging process taking place, although it may well have been unclear to him why he was so concerned, or so pleased.

However, his addition of the Preface to the last installment of the novel in *The New Review* indicates a deep psychological awareness of something momentous occurring in his art. There was a qualitative change shaping, a deeply significant event in the life of an artist, a time of great moment in culture if that artist is going to say something of humanistic importance. Like the analysand who finds himself poised before a great insight, the artist discovers himself on the crest of something profound, and he must devise the form for the blending and expression of these materials, or else the insight is lost. For Conrad in *The Nigger*, the form was the utilization of several conflicting voices which, inexorably, returned him to those earlier voices—whether Uncle Tadeusz, grandmother Teofila, Adam Pulman, or others; so that, for the first time in his fiction, he came to see the present linked to the past in a continuous flow. Rather than trying to escape those 1870s voices he would transform them.

Conrad's will to leave, to seek a career at sea, dominated the family, and Tadeusz finally relented, since he faced a young man he could no longer control and whose life he had no desire to thwart. Unlike Beethoven with his nephew Karl, Tadeusz knew when to retreat before Conrad's frustration grew unbearable. The whole idea, in actuality, was not so nonsensical as it seemed, for if Conrad went to France, he could, like Laertes, be looked after; unlike Hamlet, he would be entering a haven, not remaining in a corrupt court. Polish emigrés filled parts of France, and the gentry could look after their own. As the son of Apollo Korzeniowski, Conrad had a certain fame that would precede him, and even the most conservative of Polish elements abroad would recognize the patriotism of the father. That part, of course, the son would not escape. As long as he was Konrad Korzeniowski, Apollo was his father.

After a summer in the country with Pulman, Conrad returned to Cracow, and then left for Lwów, where he stayed with the Syroczyńskis. In September, he was joined by Uncle Tadeusz and his maternal grandmother. Tadeusz and Mme Bobrowska accompanied him to Cracow, and probably on October 15, 1874, he boarded a train that would take him, via Vienna,

Zurich, Geneva, and Lyons, to Marseilles, for his second view of the sea.

In his Document, Tadeusz Bobrowski provides the historical record in measured, unemotional terms. This was, after all, a financial report, not a sentimental letter.

> *In September* on my arrival in Cracow and Lvov in order to send you off to the Merchant Marine which you had been continually badgering me about for two years, *I repaid* Mr. Antoni and Mr. Leon Syroczyński the 190 Austrian gulden for your maintenance during the vacation. On your clothing and various other items, I spent 119 gulden. To the solicitor who, unsuccessfully, occupied himself with your naturalization in Austria—80.50 gulden. Your twenty-five days' stay in Cracow cost 43 gulden. Finally, your journey to Marseilles cost 137.75 gulden and as I couldn't afford more than 450 roubles for your maintenance for that half-year, I was obliged to sell for 841 gulden the 1,000 gulden in securities (purchase of which is mentioned above)—so that part of this money would cover the difference between the actual expenses and the sum appointed for your maintenance, as can be seen from the detailed account under the date of 3/15 October 1874.

The phrasing is astringent, and there is a critical tone to the kinds of expenditure necessitated by Conrad's plans. The tone appears to derive from the first lines, in which Tadeusz speaks of Conrad's "badgering me about for two years." The forecast is, apparently, one of impending doom, the kind of disaster that Tadeusz also foresaw in Apollo's fortunes. Right after this passage, Tadeusz indicates he has deposited in the bank in Cracow his nephew's half-yearly allowance, dating from October 3/15, 1874, which appears to establish that Conrad departed on the fifteenth. The Document, however, provides more than an insight into Conrad's financial position until 1890; it gives us a sense of the family attitude toward him on the eve of the departure. While his maternal grandmother would surely have been tolerant and forgiving of this prodigal grandson, his uncle evidently disapproved even after he had given his approval for the venture.

The October 15 departure was momentous. In retrospect, we see it as merely one minuscule event in the life of a man who later achieved distinction, a pinpoint in the long sweep of time, a flickering ash in a bonfire. And yet such decisions when made by an individual are part of the great events in the history of mankind. Conrad did not prove to be a figure larger than life; he was no Luther, Napoleon, Gandhi, or Freud. As a creative person, however, he entered the consciousness more slyly, not by great surges of energy or an electrifying charismatic presence, but by permeating the consciousness and slowly altering its quality. Much of the way we think of Africa, the jungle, and colonialism has been shaped by "Heart of Darkness." Our view of South America and of new political states has been formed by *Nostromo*. Our sense of pre-revolutionary Russia comes from *Under Western Eyes*, as well as from Dostoevsky. And, finally, our knowledge of revolutionaries and their world derives in part from *The Secret Agent*.

In his "Familiar Preface" to *A Personal Record*, itself a very sly form of autobiography, Conrad writes of just those minute mutations of feeling: "Joy and sorrow in this world pass into each other, mingling their forms and their murmurs in the twilight of life as mysterious as an overshadowed ocean, while the dazzling brightness of supreme hopes lies far off, fascinating and still, on the distant edge of the horizon." Yet despite the vagueness and indistinctness of that, Conrad says he would like "to hold the magic wand giving that command over laughter and tears which is declared to be the highest achievement of imaginative literature."

He would like to be a great mover, a Napoleon, but indirectly; and even as a writer, he must make terrible choices. For to be a "great magician one must surrender oneself to occult and irresponsible powers, either outside or within one's breast. We have all heard of simple men selling their souls for love or power to some grotesque devil." Yet he refuses to do that: ". . . anything of the sort is bound to be a fool's bargain." He must, somehow, thread his way between his Faustian desire for a kind of power or domination, without himself "losing even for one moving moment that full possession of myself which is the first condition of good service." The dilemma is clear: man must choose among terrible powers, aware that he wants control and domination and yet hesitant about succumbing to their temptation. As much as Mann, Conrad was to explore these themes. A little after this, he admits that in order to "move others deeply we must deliberately allow ourselves to be carried away beyond the bounds of our normal sensibility—innocently enough, perhaps, and of necessity, like an actor who raises his voice on the stage above the pitch of natural conversation—but still we have to do that."

The danger, he writes, comes in the "writer becoming the victim of his own exaggeration, losing the exact notion of sincerity, and in the end coming to despise truth itself as something too cold, too blunt for his purpose." The conflict is there: to achieve control and mastery over some aspects of human existence through imaginative effort and yet not to do so by climbing "upward on the miseries or credulities of mankind." Conrad says he sanctions all "intellectual and artistic ambitions . . . [as] permissible, up to and even beyond the limit of prudent sanity."

Those feelings of power, control, mastery—however they were restrained by humane considerations—were implicit forces in the sixteen-year-old Conrad. The entire future life was already submerged within, although the shape and intensity of the breakthrough were unknown, no more than indistinct urges and twinges. Yet to suggest they were not there is to argue against the ways in which human experience is formed. By his departure for the unknown and into the unknown, Conrad was entering into the initiatory process by which he would define his mission or focus in life. In *A Personal Record,* he speaks of not condemning "a man for taking care of his own integrity." Conrad questions the limits of morality in the individual's desire to demonstrate his mastery: "Is it such a very mad presumption to believe in the sovereign power of one's art, to try for other means, for other ways of affirming this belief in the deeper appeal of one's work?"

Conrad's departure, then, was an attempt to realize these elements. Erikson speaks of each successive stage of the life cycle as becoming a "potential crisis because of a radical change in perspective." He says: "Crisis is used here in a developmental sense to connote not a threat of catastrophe, but a turning point, a crucial period of increased vulnerability and heightened potential, and therefore the ontogenetic source of generational strength and maladjustment." For Conrad, only by exposing himself to potential disaster, only by making himself vulnerable, could he gain the line of his own development.

His situation was made far more difficult than that of most teenagers by the fact that had he remained in Poland his future identity would be indefinite. As for his personal situation at the control of guardians, we have noted his reactions. More significantly, for his professional orientation or work potential, what could he expect? As a member of the gentry, he was not expected to work with his hands, and as the son of a well-known revolutionary, a career for him in government service—if he had been so inclined—seemed unlikely. Certainly promotion appeared beyond expectations. The professions demanded achievement at school, academic discipline, a measure of self-control well beyond the young man at this time. A business career was socially and traditionally something he was expected to dismiss out of hand, although a merchant bourgeoisie was forming in the 1870s. Yet it would be somewhat like Nostromo when we see him in business clothes running his enterprises, incongruous, even obscene. Consequently, there was not much for Conrad except a gentleman's existence, and for that he did not have much money. He could have handled what estate remained in the family, perhaps, and joined his Uncle Tadeusz in Podolia, but that would have entrusted his future to his uncle's domination, the very thing he needed to escape.

When Conrad left for Marseilles, he left behind a past that was only partially his own, a tradition that was based on false hopes and frequent defeats, a social and political history which would have muffled whatever potential he may have sensed within himself. And yet he carried within a blending of all these elements—that past which was not personally his, those romantic-idealistic social and political traditions, and a sense of ceremony based on the ideals of the gentry. He was to go to France and remain for over three years, but he was never to become a Frenchman. He was then to spend the next forty-seven years on English ships and English soil, but he was to become an Englishman only in name. For even as he strove to find an identity through exposure and potential disaster, he never left off completely being what he was. Like Henry IV, he would seem to be a truant to chivalry, and like Hamlet, he would appear to put on an antic disposition in order to be more of himself.

Part of the fascination Conrad's career poses for the reader and the biographer rests with his attempts to blend elements of his life which remain singular and irresolvable. Related to that is Conrad's reduplication of his father's life, only on a different scale and with different means. For as Conrad left Poland, he was to substitute the sea for his father's immersion in the adventure of political insurrection. He was to substitute commitment to crew and ship for Apollo's devotion to fellow conspirators and country. He was, still later, like Apollo, to become a literary man, although with greater application and success. He was, as we have seen, to marry at thirty-eight, as compared with Apollo's thirty-six, and a woman of twenty-three, the same age as his mother when she married; and he was to have two sons, to Apollo's one. He was to complain, lifelong, of ailments, pains, crippling illnesses, as a parallel to Apollo's own poor health, declining condition, and need for personal attention. The parallels are too obvious to ignore, the implications too clear. Even as it seemed to end, Conrad's Polish life had just begun.

II

The French Interlude
1874–1878

It has been before observed that images, however beautiful, though faithfully copied from nature, and as accurately represented in words, do not of themselves characterize the poet. They become proofs of original genius only as far as they are modified by a predominant passion; or by associated thoughts or images awakened by that passion; or when they have the effect of reducing multitude to unity, or succession to an instant; or lastly, when a human and intellectual life is transferred to them from the poet's own spirit.

COLERIDGE, *Biographia Literaria*

CHAPTER 5

Bearings

BY departing for Marseilles, Conrad was able to pursue in his own way the very adventurousness denied him in Poland as Apollo's son. If he had dreams of Odysseus, or of sailing the Mediterranean like the Phoenicians, then he could only realize such dreams far from those who would compare him to his father and shake their heads or raise their brows.

Conrad's French years, from his arrival in Marseilles until he sailed on an English ship, the *Mavis,* in April 1878, were momentous, an interlude or interim that served several functions. If we assume that all young people go through some kind of initiation, whether from external or internal circumstances, then Conrad experienced his testing period in those three and a half years beginning in October 1874. Since this period almost ended with his suicide attempt in 1878, when he was twenty, these years cannot be dismissed as lighthearted or fun-filled, in which the young man simply sowed his wild oats or exorcised his Polish romanticism. They were a period of desperation as well as a time of high adventure. The suicide attempt locates an extremely grave side of Conrad's inner life, the basis for the morbidity and pessimism that later characterize his literary works. Although the attempt may have been directly motivated by gambling debts, and may have had some of the chivalric in it, it was, as an act of desperation, deeply involved with his entire life style in those French years.

If we agree the suicide attempt was not an afterthought, was not a spur of the moment "solution," then we must note some grave motifs running through those years. If the departure for France in 1874 was an act of freedom, a decision giving the young man the opportunity to develop whatever stirred inchoately within him, then the suicide attempt in the early winter of 1878 can be viewed as a morbid part of that freeing process. There is no reason to believe that those years of adventure in France freed Conrad from the nightmares of the past. He carried with him everywhere, and at all times of his life, that sense of defeat and frustration which had been his heritage and immediate background, the aimless wandering, that early loss of mother, the celebration of a father sunk deep into mysticism and lost chances.

Conrad apparently needed periodic trips to that shrine of defeat, sporadic journeys to that underworld in which he could find the equivalent of all that was death or close to death. The suicide attempt, then, would be—harsh as this may sound—the final stage in his attempt to free himself from the burdens of the past, to liberate himself from that ambiguous Polish twilight experience and the contemptuous words of his uncle. Well deserved as his admonitions may appear to be, Tadeusz's remarks were scornful and corroding. Just months before the suicide attempt in early 1878, he had written Conrad that he had reacted like a true Nałęcz, by which he meant without any thought for the future. Whenever Tadeusz denigrated the Nałęcz strain—which was at every opportunity he could find—Conrad must have felt the conflict. These are tensions one can work through in later years; for a teenager, they are irresolvable.

Tadeusz goes on to say:

> You write that you are looking for employment that would bring you some profit. Mr. Déléstang in his majesty condescends to offer you such employment. Common sense should have made you accept this opportunity as he obviously trusted you in spite of your youth and of your being a foreigner; he showed a preference for you over his countrymen and trusted you; you could, when replying to him, have made him feel the unsuitable tone he used; but accepted it, while laying down your conditions, both as to present remuneration and as to his making your voyage to India free of charge. Had the épicier [philistine] observed that you were tactful and could take advantage of your opportunities, que Vs avez de l'étoffe pour faire un homme de commerce, you would have profited in three ways: you would not have broken with a man who in one way or another might be useful to you; you would have raised yourself higher in his opinion; you would have earned something;—considerations not without importance!! Certainly I cannot expect of you in your 19th year to have the maturity of an old man, but I warn you that some day, perhaps soon, you will regret that conversation.

Tadeusz also mentions Conrad's plan to transfer to the English merchant service and asks if he speaks English. He suggests that Conrad seek Swiss naturalization, not French, since the latter would involve military service. Bobrowski's Document of accounts is also harsh with his nephew, calling his expenditures "extraordinary," accusing him of having "squandered" his money, chiding him for spending money that is not his.

The suicide attempt, then, had significant causes that went to basic needs. With this act, Conrad would either eliminate the problems by eliminating himself, or break clean from the past. He could free himself from Tadeusz and his advice by demonstrating how far he was willing to go; free himself from Poland, to some extent, by attempting the greatest of sins for a Roman Catholic; and allow himself—if he survived—the freedom of movement he wanted. The suicide attempt, coinciding with his desire to leave France and French ships for the English merchant service, was attached to another stage or level of decision, as momentous in its way as his desire to leave Poland.

By attempting to kill himself, he was focusing on some inner thread of existence or direction far too deep for him to recognize except in the need for death and renewal. To bring himself beyond what he must have sensed as a stagnating life, to bring himself to life itself, Conrad had to expose himself to fire. With an extraordinary sense of symbolism, he shot himself in the chest, trying to reach his heart, and missed everything. All he suffered were external wounds, as the bullet went straight through, touching nothing vital. Although he had prepared the circumstances as a hedge against death—he had invited a friend to tea—nevertheless, the act of placing a gun against his breast and pulling the trigger preempted any idea of being saved. It was an act of desperation that set its own terms. To some degree, then, the entire span of French years must be viewed as pointing toward an extraordinary act, the suicide attempt in early 1878, just two months or so before he decided to ship out on an English vessel bound for Lowestoft.

These are, we repeat, areas of speculation, since we cannot document a twenty-year-old's attempt at extinguishing his life. Yet if our ends are indeed implicit in our beginnings, then Conrad's life had its own consistencies; nothing, according to whatever inner plan he was shaping for himself, would be extraneous or outrageous, even an attempt at death. After all, his choice of a sea career meant, in those days, a constant flirting with violent death. Like Hamlet with his uncle—perhaps the archetypal uncle-nephew relationship—there was the alternating attraction and repulsion that went beyond words and deeds, that struck into deeper impulses than even desire for murder, into self-destruction as a form of survival and liberation.

En route to Marseilles, the teenager was passed along to Polish friends and acquaintances, a kind of "old boy" route of emigrés. Conrad himself noted that he stopped for a day at Pfaftikon, on Lake Zurich, in Switzerland, with Mr. Orzechowski, formerly a representative of the Polish government at Constantinople. Once he arrived at Marseilles, he was to be watched over by Wiktor Chodźko, himself a Pole from a good family and now in the French merchant service. What is ironic about Conrad's move toward freedom is how closely he was kept to the source by the network of friends, by the allowance of 2,000 francs (about $450–$500) a year which came from a patrimony deeply embedded in the Polish past, and even by a Pole, Chodźko, who had taken something of his own route.

Not the least of this symbiosis was the fact that Conrad's correspondence at this time was chiefly or wholly in Polish; the only letters we are certain he wrote at this time—to his Uncle Tadeusz—were in that language. Further, during the entire time Conrad pursued his sea career, and even after he began writing in English, he was continuing this Polish correspondence with Tadeusz, and using the language with a correctness and stylistic nicety that impressed even his critical uncle. At every stage of his liberation, he was faced with elements of past history, a kind of dialectic between his internal needs and the external circumstances of his situation.

Chodźko put Conrad into the hands of still another young man, named Baptistin Solary, who would be responsible for finding him sea employment, not at all an easy thing at that time. Conrad's own words in *A Personal Record* indicate Solary had written Uncle Tadeusz he would put "*le jeune homme* in the way of getting a decent ship for his first start if he really wanted a taste of *ce métier de chien.*" Conrad says he was a little taken aback by having his future career characterized as a "dog's business," and he must have wondered at his Odyssean dreams of power and conquest on the Mediterranean cast in that less than exalted description. Nevertheless, he found Solary the perfect "guardian" for a young man like himself:

> This Solary (Baptistin), when I beheld him in the flesh, turned out a quite young man, very good-looking, with a fine black, short beard, a fresh complexion, and soft, merry black eyes. He was as jovial and good-natured as any boy could desire. I was still asleep in my room in a modest hotel near the quays of the old port, after the fatigues of the journey *via* Vienna, Zurich, Lyons, when he burst in, flinging the shutters open to the sun of Provence and chiding me boisterously for lying abed. How pleasantly he startled me by his noisy objurgations to be up and off instantly for a "three years' campaign in the South Seas." O magic words! "*Une campagne de trois ans dans les mers du sud.*"

Solary had himself been at sea until twenty-five, and then discovered he could earn his living on shore by way of several Marseilles bourgeois families to whom he was related. His connections all appeared to be in the business of shipping or piloting: ship brokers, ships' stores, shipwrights, even caulkers and master stevedores. Around him was the entire romance of seamanship. It is clear that Solary perpetuated the colorful aspects of the sea for Conrad; he represented the successful side of it, and he was young enough to seem himself a teenager on the prowl for success, not yet stodgy or lacking in dreams. Conrad writes:

> The very first whole day I ever spent on salt water was by invitation, in a big half-decked pilot-boat, cruising under close reefs on the look-out, in misty, blowing weather, for the sails of ships and the smoke of steamers rising out there, beyond the slim and tall Planier lighthouse cutting the line of the wind-swept horizon with a white perpendicular stroke. They were hospitable souls, these sturdy Provençal seamen. Under the general designation of *le petit ami de Baptistin* I was made the guest of the Corporation of Pilots, and had the freedom of their boats night or day. And

> many a day and a night too did I spend cruising with these rough, kindly men, under whose auspices my intimacy with the sea began. Many a time "the little friend of Baptistin" had the hooded cloak of the Mediterranean sailor thrown over him by their honest hands while dodging at night under the lee of Château d'If on the watch for the lights of ships. Their sea-tanned faces, whiskered or shaved, lean or full, with the intent wrinkled sea-eyes of the pilot-breed, and here and there a thin gold loop at the lobe of a hairy ear, bent over my sea-infancy. The first operation of seamanship I had an opportunity of observing was the boarding of ships at sea, at all times, in all states of the weather. They gave it to me to the full. And I have been invited to sit in more than one tall, dark house of the old town at their hospitable board, had the *bouillabaisse* ladled out into a thick plate by their high-voiced broad-browed wives, talked to their daughters—thick-set girls, with pure profiles, glorious masses of black hair arranged with complicated art, dark eyes, and dazzlingly white teeth.

All the routine duties of these grizzled men—in fact, our first views of the Nostromo prototype—took on the aspect of the golden voyages of Odysseus, Jason, and those other heroic figures who used the sea in order to realize their dreams. Although Conrad is writing these words as a middle-aged man, he evidently has not been untrue to the earlier feelings; he has not let the intervening years of frustrating literary work remove the gloss from that teenage dream. In this and other descriptions, he has remade the reality into something suitable for his dreams, and that is one good reason why we must so mistrust his own presentation of these years in *The Arrow of Gold* and elsewhere. Over all is an aura of his reading and imagination, not of reality. Apparently, he chose to pursue his Don Quixote even so far as to experience the latter's illusions and visions, and then followed the dream as if the illusion were itself the reality. He was already, himself, at the heart of many of his later literary characters. This romanticism of spirit and outlook characterizes these three and a half years of Conrad's life, which—despite the suicide attempt—included some of the happiest times he had experienced and were truly a liberation from the restrictions of the past. He exulted.

Within two months of his arrival in Marseilles, Conrad was on board a ship, as a passenger, on the *Mont Blanc,* which sailed for Martinique on December 11, 1874. The *Mont Blanc* belonged to the shipowning firm of C. Déléstang & Son, whose salon Conrad also visited. Of the three and a half years he passed in and around Marseilles, about half the time, eighteen months, he spent on board ships belonging to that firm. When we speak of Conrad going to sea for twenty years, we must take into account the fact that half or more of his time was spent ashore. He was not the kind of seagoing man who, after a couple of nights on the town, goes from one berth to the next. In that Marseilles period, Conrad sailed on the *Mont Blanc,* as a passenger, from December 11, 1874, to May 23, 1875, a total of five months; once again on the *Mont Blanc*, this time as an apprentice seaman, from June 25, 1875, to December 23, 1875, for six months; and as steward on the *Saint-Antoine*, from July 8, 1876, to February 15, 1877, for seven months. For the remaining twenty-four months of his French stay, he pursued shore activities, although, unfortunately, we have little information and less documentation of his allocation of time.

In *The Arrow of Gold*, Conrad recounts the split in the life of his protagonist, Monsieur George—Conrad was himself known as M. Georges around the Vieux Port: "What Mills [George's friend] had learned represented him as a young gentleman who had arrived furnished with proper credentials and who apparently was doing his best to waste his life in an eccentric fashion, with a bohemian set (one poet, at least, emerged out of it later) on one side, and on the other making friends with the people of the Old Town, pilots, coasters, sailors, workers of all sorts. He pretended rather absurdly to be a seaman himself and was already credited with an ill-defined and vaguely illegal enterprise in the Gulf of Mexico." To this accounting might be added Conrad's movements in the salon of the Délestangs among the "ultras," the respectable Legitimist-Royalist types.

We have the young man moving, in varying degrees, on four parallel levels: with the coasters, pilots, and assorted seamen of the Vieux Port and old parts of Marseilles; among the bohemians of café life; in the Délestang salon, among Carlists, Royalists, and Catholic ultras; and on his own, attending occasional operas and theatrical performances. Yet what about his intellectual development in this period?

From the few documents and literary versions,* we can surmise and speculate. Of great interest would be some sense of Conrad's reading and literary development, for which he had ample time on shore. What contact, if any, did he have with French literary figures at this time, either through reading or through meeting them in Marseilles cafés, restaurants, or even salons? The poet Arthur Rimbaud, for example, spent a few days in Marseilles in June 1875, and his stay overlapped with Conrad's shore leave there before he sailed on June 25 for Martinique. The latter was, apparently, picking up images, sounds, smells, feelings, and those other accouterments of his art. He was also sharpening his command of French, raising the feasibility of his writing in French—when and if he was to decide to write.

Exactly when he met the Délestangs, the shipowners, we do not know. He may have come to know them directly from Baptistin Solary, who was prob-

* For example, *The Arrow of Gold*, the incomplete *The Sisters*, the essay on the *Tremolino* in *Mirror of the Sea*, and a few passages in *A Personal Record*. There are no extant letters. How completely do we trust Conrad's statement to Captain Frederick George Cooper, who wrote an appreciation of Conrad, that "your surmise that Mr George of the A of G is in a sense myself is just"? (January 16, 1921; ALS, private collection).

ably related to Mme Déléstang (her maiden name was Solary). The senior Déléstangs were quite ancient when Conrad met them—he left a memorable description of them in *A Personal Record*—and he moved among their children and even their grandchildren, who would have been about his own age. The Déléstangs, as Conrad depicted them, were precisely the kind of people Apollo Korzeniowski would have mocked; and if we can speculate that Conrad had something of his father's eye, we can see that he also had something of his father's tone:

> Madame Delestang, an imperious, handsome lady in a statuesque style, would carry me off now and then on the front seat of her carriage to the Prado, at the hour of fashionable airing. She belonged to one of the old aristocratic families in the south. In her haughty weariness she used to make me think of Lady Dedlock in Dickens' "Bleak House," a work of the master for which I have such an admiration, or rather such an intense and unreasoning affection, dating from the days of my childhood, that its very weaknesses are more precious to me than the strength of other men's work. I have read it innumerable times, both in Polish and in English; I have read it only the other day, and, by a not very surprising inversion, the Lady Dedlock of the book reminded me strongly of the *belle Madame Delestang.*

Although this description comes many years after the meeting, we note that Conrad has translated the relationship into a literary event, seeking his dimension of reality not only in words but in a literary equivalent to something in his early reading. While not momentous in itself, this method of conveying a real event through literature makes it possible for us to gain some insight into Conrad's mind in Marseilles, which was his need to find correlatives for what was happening, and seeking those correlatives in literature; which, in turn, would appear to indicate a more active storing up, even shaping, of his experience toward a literary end.

Conrad then comes to M. Déléstang, a man well into his seventies, who must have appeared even more ancient to the teenage observer accustomed to people dying far younger:

> Her husband (as I sat facing them both) with his thin bony nose, and a perfectly bloodless, narrow physiognomy clamped together as it were by short formal side-whiskers, had nothing of Sir Leicester Dedlock's "grand air" and courtly solemnity. He belonged to the *haute bourgeoisie* only, and was a banker [not a banker by profession, but perhaps Conrad's banker], with whom a modest credit had been opened for my needs. He was such an ardent—no, such a frozen-up, mummified Royalist that he used in current conversation turns of speech contemporary, I should say, with the good Henri Quatre; and when talking of money matters reckoned not in francs, like the common, godless herd of post-Revolutionary Frenchmen, but in obsolete and forgotten *écus*—*écus* of all money units in the world!—as though Louis Quatorze were still promenading in royal

splendour the gardens of Versailles, and Monsieur de Colbert busy with the direction of maritime affairs.*

The Délestangs, as Conrad recorded the scene in *The Arrow of Gold*, were Royalists hopeful of returning Don Carlos to the Spanish throne and overthrowing the shaky republic. Don Carlos, the Pretender, represented the conservative clergy and opposed both the liberal constitution and centralization. The Carlist war began in the spring of 1872 and was, when Conrad arrived in Marseilles and came to know the Délestangs, already doomed by the accession to the throne of Alfonso XII. Although Don Carlos had set up his court in Navarre on July 16, 1873, his days in Spain were numbered as even clergy rallied to support Alfonso. By March 1876, Carlos had been driven into exile, and his cause became one of those fanatical ventures which return us to Bonnie Prince Charles in 1745 and the novels of Sir Walter Scott. That Conrad should have become involved in such ventures had little to do with belief. In fact, the Délestangs would have been far to the political right even of Bobrowski and the more conservative elements Conrad had known in Poland. The venture itself—hopeless, adventurous, antiestablishment—would have an appeal for its very futility, as a comparable venture has for John Kemp in Conrad and Ford's *Romance.*

The young man evidently moved easily among the Délestangs—although he came to resent M. Délestang's imperious manner; for in his record of those years, he speaks of coming for his money, which was paid out in modern francs, not in Louis Quatorze *écus:*

> The accounts were kept in modern money so that I never had any difficulty in making my wants known to the grave, low-voiced, decorous, Legitimist (I suppose) clerks, sitting in the perpetual gloom of heavily-barred windows behind the sombre, ancient counters, beneath lofty ceilings with heavily-moulded cornices. I always felt on going out as though I had been in the temple of some very dignified but completely temporal religion.

The tone of the passage indicates bemusement, the sense of a lark, the antics of a young man moving in and out of an adventure that is separate from his real life. In *Arrow*, Monsieur George speaks of his conduct "as an act of independent assertion," as though he had separated into two—perhaps already Konrad and Conrad. He continues, in *A Personal Record:*

* In *The Arrow of Gold*, Conrad catches other aspects of the relationship: "He, of course, was just simply a banker, a very distinguished, a very influential, and a very impeccable banker. He persisted also in deferring to my judgment and sense with an over-emphasis called out by his perpetual surprise at my youth. Though he had seen me many times (I even knew his wife) he could never get over my immature age. He himself was born about fifty years old, all complete, with his iron-grey whiskers and his bilious eyes, which he had the habit of frequently closing during a conversation" (pp. 243–4).

And it was generally on these occasions that under the great carriage gateway Lady Ded—I mean Madame Déléstang, catching sight of my raised hat, would beckon me with an amiable imperiousness to the side of the carriage, and suggest with an air of amused nonchalance, "*Venez donc faire un tour avec nous,*" to which the husband would add an encouraging "*C'est ça. Allons, montez, jeune homme.*" He questioned me sometimes, significantly but with perfect tact and delicacy, as to the way I employed my time, and never failed to express the hope that I wrote regularly to my "honoured uncle."

Then, in what must have seemed to the teenager a repetition of so many earlier moments, Mme Déléstang gives him his uncle's very advice, not to throw away his life in idleness. Perhaps Bobrowski had prodded her.

I made no secret of the way I employed my time, and I rather fancy that my artless tales of the pilots and so on entertained Madame Delestang, so far as that ineffable woman could be entertained by the prattle of a youngster very full of his new experience amongst strange men and strange sensations. She expressed no opinions, and talked to me very little; yet her portrait hangs in the gallery of my intimate memories, fixed there by a short and fleeting episode.

The "moment" is a revelation; Conrad sees himself through another's eyes.

One day, after putting me down at the corner of a street, she offered me her hand, and detained me by a slight pressure, for a moment. While the husband sat motionless and looking straight before him, she leaned forward in the carriage to say, with just a shade of warning in her leisurely tone: "*Il faut, cependant, faire attention à ne pas gâter sa vie.*" I had never seen her face so close to mine before. She made my heart beat, and caused me to remain thoughtful for a whole evening. Certainly one must, after all, take care not to spoil one's life. But she did not know—nobody could know—how impossible that danger seemed to me.

Conrad had considerable hindsight and fifteen volumes of literary accomplishment behind him when he wrote that. The contemporary observer may well have come to Mme Déléstang's conclusion, as Bobrowski also had. For without knowledge of Conrad's inner life—and he appeared to have given few glimpses of it in this period—one would see an amiable young man, with excellent manners and a pleasing appearance. We have a photograph of the delicately balanced Konrad-M. George in 1873, and he looks suitably dreamy, with regular features, his hair worn long and swept back from his forehead. His face has the wide cheekbones we associate with the Slavic facial structure, but not the width of bone we note in later photographs or in Epstein's sculpture. In all, he seems a very self-contained young man, carefully gotten out in coat, vest, and bow tie, neat but not completely regular. Apparently, he had no difficulty splitting himself into a gentleman around town, a kind of prodigal son who had vowed never to return, and an adventurer of sorts at the docks of the Vieux Port, among the men who did the dirty work on board ship. He was, indeed, shaping his experiences and reshaping himself to fit his early reading and adolescent dreams in Poland.

While high-strung, he presented a combination of elements not at all neurotic, or chronically ill—as he had been in Poland—but, in fact, quite enviable. He may, of course, have desired this impression, a romantic pose and a disguise. To the observer, there would seem to be no ambition, no drive toward accomplishment. He was living for the moment, a not unusual attitude for a teenager. Although we do not know what was occurring internally, we do know the mind was accumulating details, the eye observing carefully, the imagination gleaning what would later be called upon.

In a passage following the one above, he speaks of how Mme Déléstang's warning rang in his ear even as he went off to his "first love," his romance with the sea and with small boats.

> I tried to understand and tried in vain, not having any notion of life as an enterprise that could be mismanaged. But I left off being thoughtful shortly before midnight, at which hour, haunted by no ghosts of the past and by no visions of the future, I walked down the quay of the *Vieux Port* to join the pilot-boat of my friends. I knew where she would be waiting for her crew, in the little bit of a canal behind the Fort at the entrance of the harbour. The deserted quays looked very white and dry in the moonlight and as if frost-bound in the sharp air of that December night. A prowler or two slunk by noiselessly; a custom-house guard, soldier-like, a sword by his side, paced close under the bowsprits of the long row of ships moored bows on opposite the long, slightly curved, continuous flat wall of the tall houses that seemed to be one immense abandoned building with innumerable windows shuttered closely. Only here and there a small dingy *café* for sailors cast a yellow gleam on the bluish sheen of the flagstone. Passing by, one heard a deep murmur of voices inside—nothing more.

The young man is exultant, tense, as he comments:

> How quiet everything was at the end of the quays on the last night on which I went out for a service cruise as a guest of the Marseilles pilots! Not a footstep, except my own, not a sigh, not a whispering echo of the usual revelry going on in the narrow, unspeakable lanes of the Old Town reached my ear—and suddenly, with a terrific jungling rattle of iron and glass, the omnibus of the Jolliette on its last journey swung round the corner of the dead wall which faces across the paved road the characteristic angular mass of the Fort St. Jean. Three horses trotted abreast with the clatter of hoofs on the granite setts, and the yellow, uproarious machine jolted violently behind them, fantastic, lighted up, perfectly empty and with the driver apparently asleep on his swaying perch above that amazing racket. I flattened myself against the wall and gasped. It was a stunning experience.

How could any adult's counsel go against the experience of that adventure, with mustachioed "volatile southern" types as companions, men of great fury and gentleness? The patron of one particular company of pilots was the brother-in-law of Baptistin Solary, "a broad-shouldered, deep-chested man of forty, with a keen frank glance which always seeks your eyes." It was as if the still younger Conrad had been describing Odysseus, and these pilots were those ancient Greeks and Phoenicians attempting unfathomable seas. "He is worth a dozen of your ordinary Normans or Bretons," Conrad writes, "but then, in the whole immense sweep of the Mediterranean shores, you could not find half a dozen men of his stamp." We have here not only the prototypical Dominic Cervoni, Conrad's companion and leader in desperate ventures, but that Odyssean figure who was one of the forerunners of Nostromo, Captain Fidanza. "For there is such a type in which the volatile southern passion is translated into solid force."

On his last outing with the pilots, Conrad recalled a historic meeting, for on this occasion his "hand touched, for the first time, the side of an English ship." Ashore on an islet, the pilot's telescope picked up a "black speck like an insect posed on the hard edge of the offing." The speck emerged rapidly, a "big, high-class cargo-steamer," with "low, white superstructures, powerfully rigged with three masts," not at all unlike the Flying Dutchman, a ship moving out of the ghostly fog to rendezvous with the observer. "The name—I read it letter by letter on the bow—was *James Westoll.* Not very romantic you will say. . . . What better name could an honourable hard-working ship have? To me the very grouping of the letters is alive with the romantic feeling of her reality as I saw her floating motionless, and borrowing an ideal grace from the austere purity of the light."

The ship is like an apparition, and the hallucinatory meeting has the impact of myth-making. Conrad says he volunteered "to pull bow in the dinghy which shoved off at once to put the pilot on board." The magical moment arrived: "A few strokes brought us alongside, and it was then that, for the first time in my life, I heard myself addressed in English—the speech of my secret choice, of my future, of long friendships, of the deepest affections, of hours of toil and hours of ease, and of solitary hours too, of books read, of thoughts pursued, of remembered emotions—of my very dreams!"

Like the mysterious building near the excavation work for the St. Gotthard Tunnel, where Conrad first heard English spoken, the *James Westoll* becomes an unknowing link in a destiny whose resolution is mastery of the English language. As the dinghy and the *James Westoll* bump slightly, the teenager hears the command "Shove off—push hard"; and "when I bore against the smooth flank of the first English ship I ever touched in my life, I felt it already throbbing under my open palm." Under his touch, the steamship is alive, a vital throbbing organism, and still vibrating in Conrad's imagination as he recalls those events of thirty-five years earlier, when that throb—sexually passionate in its excitement—had conveyed its vitality to the seventeen-year-old. While he follows the ship affectionately with his eyes, she hoists her flag, as regulations demand. There, flickering and streaming out on the flagstaff, is the Red Ensign!

> In the pellucid, colourless atmosphere bathing the drab and grey masses of that southern land, the livid islets, the sea of pale glassy blue under the pale glassy sky of that cold sunrise, it was, as far as the eye could reach, the only spot of ardent colour—flamelike, intense, and presently as minute as the tiny red spark the concentrated reflection of a great fire kindles in the clear heart of a globe of crystal. The Red Ensign—the symbolic, protecting warm bit of bunting flung wide upon the sea, and destined for so many years to be the only roof over my head.

The description, written when Conrad was over fifty, links the experiences of the early 1870s with the reading of the young Conrad back in Poland, and that, in turn, with the romanticism of Apollo Korzeniowski and the Nałęcz desire for adventure. There is, in those phrases of *A Personal Record,* a single line that extends deep into his heritage and surfaces repeatedly in his adult life, beginning first as a choice, later as action, finally as words.

The young man was deeply involved in a consuming passion. And since passion did dominate him, all the ill fortune and turns of fate that might have discouraged someone of less intensity only gave him greater impetus to pursue his particular love. As we follow Conrad's trail as best we can in these murky years, we note, once again, how he has found a substitute for his father's own passion. Apollo's fervor for revolutionary ideas and movements has been transformed into another kind of passion, and no amount of misfortune could turn either father or son aside from his pursuit. Once we begin to pick up Bobrowski's letters to Conrad, in 1876, we can see how the observant uncle has himself sighted this parallelism of activity, and how conscious he is that the son may destroy himself the way his father had, and that the Nałęcz line—like the House of Atreus—will have its revenge on all those unfortunate enough to be born with its blood.

CHAPTER 6

On the Edge

IN the following passage, from *The Mirror of the Sea* (1906), a work of considerable magic and insight, Conrad wrote of perhaps that first voyage he took on the *Mont Blanc,* which left Marseilles on December 11, 1874, bound for Martinique:

> The charm of the Mediterranean dwells in the unforgettable flavour of my early days, and to this hour this sea, upon which the Romans alone ruled without dispute, has kept for me the fascination of youthful romance. The very first Christmas night [1874?] I ever spent away from land was employed in running before a Gulf of Lyons gale, which made the old ship groan in every timber as she skipped before it over the short seas until we brought her to, battered and out of breath, under the lee of Majorca, where the smooth water was torn by fierce cat's-paws under a very stormy sky.
>
> We—or, rather, they, for I had hardly had two glimpses of salt water in my life till then—kept her standing off and on all that day, while I listened for the first time with the curiosity of my tender years to the song of the wind in the ship's rigging. The monotonous and vibrating note was destined to grow into the intimacy of the heart, pass into blood and bone, accompany the thoughts and acts of two full decades, remain to haunt like a reproach the peace of the quiet fireside, and enter into the very texture of respectable dreams dreamed safely under a roof of rafters and tiles. The wind was fair, but that day we ran no more.
>
> The thing (I will not call her a ship twice in the same half-hour) leaked. She leaked fully, generously, overflowingly, all over—like a basket. I took an enthusiastic part in the excitement caused by that last infirmity of noble ships, without concerning myself much with the why or the wherefore.

With his eyes and imagination filled with Odysseus' adventures in the Mediterranean, Conrad was beyond recall. He could obtain adventure, of course, only under sail; for as he remarked later, steam eliminated the struggle with nature, which was the very heart of the bout. Conrad wrote of sailing as a fine art, as something that went beyond utility; and in those words of a later time, we sense something of what he may have felt as he pursued his elusive course in his teens, all the while strengthening those attitudes which he was then to transfer to his conception of writing and literature.

> Now the moral side of an industry, productive or unproductive, the redeeming and ideal aspect of this bread-winning, is the attainment and preservation of the highest possible skill on the part of the craftsmen. Such skill, the skill of technique, is more than honesty; it is something wider, embracing honesty and grace and rule in an elevated and clear sentiment, not altogether utilitarian, which may be called the honour of labour. It is made up of accumulated tradition, kept alive by individual pride, rendered exact by professional opinion, and like the higher arts, it is spurred on and sustained by discriminating praise.

He was clearly moving against the shibboleths of his own era, opposing machinery for having eliminated the skillfulness that real enterprise affords; and in this sense, he was quite loyal to his Polish traditions of the "how" more so than the "why," of the manner more than the achievement. He writes:

> This is why the attainment of proficiency, the pushing of your skill with attention to the most delicate shades of excellence, is a matter of vital concern. Efficiency of a practically flawless kind may be reached naturally in the struggle for bread. But there is something beyond—a higher point, a subtle and unmistakable touch of love and pride beyond mere skill; almost an inspiration which gives to all work that finish which is almost art—which *is* art.

Conrad's first extended voyage, beyond his experiences with the pilots of the Vieux Port, came, then, with his five months' voyage as a passenger on the Déléstang-owned ship, the *Mont Blanc*, under Captain Duteil. He was now seventeen. The *Mont Blanc* was an old vessel, having been built in 1852, a three-masted barque of 394 tons, and not at all a reason for romance except for a teenager prepared to act out his fantasies. The ship reached St. Pierre, Martinique, on February 16, 1875, and remained six weeks, until March 30, returning to Marseilles on May 23. Conrad may have tried to get on another ship, or else decided to stay with the barque, probably the latter, since he knew the crew.

He remained in Marseilles another month and, on June 25, sailed out once again on the *Mont Blanc*, destination St. Pierre, as an apprentice seaman. He arrived at the end of July, spending two months there, but we have no idea of his activities, or in fact of any on these first voyages. Conrad left St. Pierre on September 23 and made stops throughout the Caribbean area—St. Thomas in the then Danish West Indies (later the Virgin Islands), Cap-Haïtien in

Haiti, sailing from there for Le Havre and arriving on December 23.*

The *Mont Blanc* was in no condition to sail after her stormy voyage, and Conrad left the ship at Le Havre, without even bothering to take along his trunk. In a letter of general annoyance with him and his activities, written by Bobrowski on September 27 (old style), 1876, there is a reference to that trunk:

> You always, my dear boy, made me impatient—and still make me impatient by your disorder and the easy way you take things—in which you remind me of the Korzeniowski family—spoiling and wasting everything—and not my dear Sister, your Mother, who was careful about everything. Last year you lost a trunk full of things—and tell me—what else had you to remember and look after if not yourself and your things? Do you need a nanny—and am I cast in that role? Now again, you have lost a family photograph and some Polish books—and you ask me to replace them! Why? So that you should take the first opportunity of losing them again? He who appreciates something looks after it.

To draw the distinction between Bobrowski care and Korzeniowski indifference, Tadeusz reports that a small picture given him by his mother in 1839 is still in the same condition as when he received it. He says he will send on whatever family photographs he has, but if Conrad loses them he does not want to hear about it.

To us the words may seem amusing, coming as they do while Conrad's thoughts were on fantasy, adventure, romance; but they were also wounding and punitive. Tadeusz took every advantage of Conrad's carelessness—and there were sufficient opportunities—to attack his nephew's values and his background. Conrad was already experiencing difficulty with his name and his foreignness, and to have someone from the home country also prick his pride and reveal his flaws was degrading. It must have seemed to him that he

---

* Jean-Aubry reports that Conrad's name appeared on the muster records as "Conrad Korrcuiwski," which is more interesting for the use of "Conrad" than for the casual misspelling of the surname. (Jean-Aubry's transcription probably compounded the error.) Of course, the Christian name may have been recorded incorrectly also, but since naming is so much a part of Conrad's background and development, we can see this as simply another instance of how his foreignness was ever present—in both the spoken and written language.

The voyage back, Jean-Aubry writes, was very stormy, and the ship reached Le Havre badly damaged. According to the captain's report: "As she pitched, the upper bobstay broke and also the jib-boom. It brought the topgallant mast down with it, which broke too at the truck. The jib-boom, hanging by its rigging, became a battering ram crashing against the bows. Impossible to make anything fast." Although Conrad did not call directly on this experience for the storm scenes of *The Nigger* and "Typhoon," he had met the ocean's potential early in his career. If he had wanted to leave the sea for another pursuit, this could have been the deciding experience, early, the danger still crashing around his head, the discomfort of an old ship pitching and losing head on the ocean.

needed an even sharper break, although what shape or form that break would take he could not foresee. His suicide attempt in 1878, whatever its other motivation, afforded that split, enabling him either to seal off the past or deliver himself from it.

In his Document, Bobrowski reports that he has sent 300 rubles to cover Conrad's allowance, using Chodźko as his intermediary. He says he sent, at Conrad's request, another 100 rubles beyond his allowance for the boy's journey from Le Havre to Marseilles, at which time the young seaman stopped off in Paris for a few days. Once he returned to Marseilles, Conrad did not have any ship—the *Mont Blanc* was under repairs, and the other Délestang vessel, the *Saint-Antoine*, had already left for Martinique. As a consequence, from the beginning of 1876 to July 8 of that year, a period of six months, Conrad lay over in Marseilles. Precisely what his activities were we do not know, but his running through his allowance and drawing against his future monies became the subject of Tadeusz's irate notation in his Document. He wrote:

> I learned from Mr. Wiktor Chodźko's letter of 5th April that you had drawn from the Bank in one sum your allowance for the eight months from January till October of that year, and having lent it (or possibly squandered it) you are in need. Subsequently, in May, you wrote to me apologizing but not offering any clear explanation. At last on the 21st May you sent a telegram requesting an order for *700 fr.* which was paid out to you on the 2nd July; again in answer to another telegraphic request I ordered 400 fr. to be paid out to you, and on departing from Marseilles you wrote asking me to pay 165 fr. to a friend of yours—Mr. Bonnard, who had lent you this sum and so I did. Thus in the course of three months you *spent over and above* your allowance 1,265 fr. that is 664 gulden. As it is only fair that everyone should be made to pay for his own follies out of his own pocket and as I lack an extraordinary income for covering the extraordinary expenditure of my nephew, therefore for this purpose *your own 500 gulden* (out of the gift of Miss Korzeniowska) deposited in the Bank of Galicia (see the previous page) were used for this purpose.

Without documentation for Conrad's activities in that six-month period, we must rely on fragments. We do know that he enjoyed café life, that he moved with a circle of bohemian artists and writers—among them the sculptor Frétigny, who becomes Prax in *The Arrow of Gold;* later, he became involved in some gun smuggling for the Carlist cause, and he may have given some of his own money toward the working out of those activities—a possibility, not a probability. Further, he knew the journalist and politician, Clovis Hugues, although the nature of the relationship is unknown. Conrad, apparently, fell into some radical political circles, because in a letter to Edward Lancelot Sanderson, on August 24, 1895, he mentions looking up people he knows or used to know in France, including Pascalis of the *Figaro* and the deputy Jules Guesde, "all acquaintances of my young days." Of the names listed, Guesde's is the most interesting. Born in Paris, Guesde was a radical journalist in the 1870s and later became an organizer and early leader of the Marxist wing of the French labor movement. In 1877, Guesde founded the socialist weekly, *Égalité*, and in 1880 consulted with Marx and Paul Laforgue (Marx's son-in-law) on a socialistic program for French labor. If Conrad did indeed know Guesde in the 1870s, then he was moving in far-left political groups as well as among the reactionary Royalist salons of the Déléstangs.

All this, however, is searching for ghosts. One further possibility: the young man, so much more youthful than his companions, may have compensated for his youth by throwing around whatever money he had. Dominic Cervoni, the Corsican seaman who figures in both the "Tremolino" essay and in *The Arrow of Gold*, speaks of young men who have nothing to do but waste their money. "He stated generally that there were some young gentlemen very clever in inventing new ways of getting rid of their time and their money." As a Polish noble, the young man could have tried to increase his stature in others' eyes by prodigality, picking up checks, buying drinks for the crowd, and other acts based on fantasies rather than on a realistic assessment of his allowance.

On July 8, 1876, Conrad sailed from Marseilles on the *Saint-Antoine*, listed as steward on the muster sheets, although he may have served another function somewhere between crew and officer. The *Saint-Antoine*, a three-masted barque, only six years old, was a step up from the *Mont-Blanc*, more modernized, seaworthy, and comfortable. This was an extremely important trip for Conrad, since it solidified his desire to remain a seaman and provided him with experiences on which his imagination was already beginning to work. The voyage on the *Saint-Antoine*, further, brought him into first touch with Dominic Cervoni, that Corsican sailor and adventurer who was, for the teenager, the embodiment of the Odyssean figure of his imagination. Conrad's fantasy life was reaching a new stage, where it could begin to coincide with his real life, and his dreams from past years could find anchorage in the unfolding of actual events.

For the young Conrad, Dominic Cervoni, now forty-two, was the complete man, confident of his powers and of himself. "Astute and ruthless, he [Dominic] could have rivalled in resource the unfortunate son of Laertes and Anticlea. If he did not pit his craft and audacity against the very gods, it is only because the Olympian gods are dead. Certainly no woman could frighten him. A one-eyed giant would not have had the ghost of a chance against Dominic Cervoni, of Corsica, not Ithaca." Further: ". . . there was nothing in the world sudden enough to take Dominic unawares. . . . From the slow, imperturbable gravity of that broad-chested man you would think he had never smiled in his life. In his eyes lurked a look of perfectly remorseless irony, as though he had been provided with an extremely experienced soul." Unlike Apollo, Dominic is the man who can bring to the practices of unlawful things "much wisdom and audacity."

For looseness, lack of structure and direction, and plain carelessness, Conrad's relationship with his father had been the obverse of John Stuart Mill's with James Mill. Unlike the young Mill, who needed to unfasten the parental noose, Conrad sought to find father substitutes who provided balanced and stable ties.* Dominic was for the young Conrad the man he hoped to become. Further, Conrad could assume a son-father relationship with Dominic without forgoing his own superior birth and background. Consequently, the Corsican led the young apprentice into his initiation with the sea, as the father—now dead for Conrad—would have led him, had he been alive.†

The *Saint-Antoine* was small enough so that any member of the crew would have to double and triple in his roles. Under Captain Escarras, toward whom Conrad felt considerable affection, the ship had a crew of thirteen along with three other officers. The situation was ideal for the eager young man—a small boat, a chance to learn his craft, the presence of an older "father figure" among the crew, and an avuncular captain. In addition to Dominic, Conrad came to know his nephew César, who was virtually the same age, and a young man who was also to become involved in gunrunning, according to the "*Tremolino*" episode. Of course, what happens to César in the Conrad version has no relationship to what actually occurred—rather than being pushed overboard by Dominic to drown, weighted down by a

---

* The comparison with Mill is not fanciful. Like Mill, Conrad to survive had to "remake" himself, both within his father's own image and outside it. Neither young man could break away, for the father had stamped them too firmly, Mill through education, Conrad through Apollo's political reputation. In a suggestive passage, Bruce Mazlish speaks of the nineteenth-century "intrusive parent," who does not ignore the child (usually a son) but thinks of him as a way of achieving a second life of his own. Such a child carries a double burden, since to escape brings with it a heavy freight of guilt, apart from the difficulties of breaking away.

† Nevertheless, when Conrad came to represent Dominic Cervoni in his character portraits and especially as transformed into Nostromo, he noted the incompleteness; that is, his old friend lacked a certain moral sensibility that Conrad found necessary once Dominic became part of a literary portrait. In *Nostromo* itself, the "capataz de cargadores" is really a half figure, completed by Decoud, who in his turn lacks the half provided by Nostromo. The demands of artistry were, for Conrad, one thing, the relationship to the Dominic he recalled another. One reason for the weaknesses of *The Arrow of Gold* lies just here, in Conrad's inability to gain distance on these characters recalled from his youth, his failure to remake them in the round, his utilization of their qualities as if they were part of an essay. All that recollected material is one-dimensional, as though Conrad were back in the "Tremolino" episode of *The Mirror of the Sea* and not immersed in an imaginative re-creation.

money belt (a touch Conrad had used earlier for Decoud in *Nostromo*), César lived to prosper.

The *Saint-Antoine* arrived in St. Pierre, Martinique, on August 18. St. Pierre was an obvious port for the Déléstang-owned ship, since the ruling families were very much Royalist and legitimist. St. Pierre—at least its planter-owners—was more Royalist than the king, so that Conrad's later activities on behalf of Don Carlos, the Spanish Pretender,* were surely strengthened by contacts he made during this visit. There is, in addition, slight evidence that Conrad participated in unlawful or nefarious activities while on this trip, although exact details are impossible to determine. It is clear that Conrad, at eighteen and a half, was moving across a broad spectrum of political belief, meeting people different from those in his immediate Polish background, and entering into their activities, not for ideological reasons, as he makes clear in *Arrow of Gold*, but for purposes of the experience itself. Good training for the novelist, somewhat appalling for the ideologue. We note also that political cynicism which was to develop in Conrad: the fact that it mattered little which side was supplied with arms, since political activity was itself a farce—perhaps a solid and necessary part of Conrad's feeling about his own political heritage, which had made a sad farce of his childhood.

There is no way to trace what the crew of the *Saint-Antoine* was doing in the month after its arrival, until September 19. If Conrad engaged in unlawful activities, this was the period, assuming we accept as accurate what he wrote Richard Curle in 1923: that he had been ashore at Puerto Cabello in Venezuela for twelve hours. "In La Guayra [La Guaira, just north of Caracas] as I went up the hill and had a distant view of Caracas I must have been 2½ to 3 days. It's such a long time ago! And there was a few hours in a few other places on that dreary coast of Ven'la." In *The Arrow of Gold*, Conrad speaks of "lawful and unlawful" experiences on his second West Indies voyage, experiences that "startled me a little and amused me considerably."

These experiences, if Conrad's vague words are credible, would have involved running contraband arms to rebels in Colombia, possibly even to Puerto Cabello. The "rebels" here were rightists fighting the more liberal government. Whatever the precise nature of Conrad's activities, his views of Puerto Cabello and La Guaira in Venezuela and Cartagena in Colombia gave him some sense of the kind of South or Central American republic he would

* Although the Pretender and his cause in Spain seem far removed from Conrad's Poland, apparently politically conservative forces overlap everywhere. The values of the Carlists in Spain and those of the *szlachta* in Poland were not that dissimilar. Both championed traditionalism, provincial rights, aristocratic-chivalric assumptions; both opposed industrialization and technology, or any form of obvious money-making. Both stood for God, country, and king and saw the enemy as those who supported republican, anticlerical government.

capture in *Nostromo.* The shifting battles between liberals and rightists in Colombia become reproduced, with artistic intensity and focus, in the battle sequences of Costaguana, a country torn by strife that is a mixture of farce, ideology, and greed. We do not wish to overstress the South American model, because Costaguana has strong affinities, also, to Conrad's views of Polish politics; but certainly landscape and scene were significant for the young man.

On this venture, Conrad began to accumulate characters who would appear in his novels, that "reality" which is so much the source of his imaginative ventures. As we note the stirrings of the young man's sensibility, and the depositing of image and scene, we also observe how Conrad's imaginative processes were anchored in fact. His background was a steady building process of people, images, events, and scenes, unstructured experiences that would cohere fully twenty years later. As a late starter in fiction—in this respect like George Eliot—Conrad had an extraordinarily long apprenticeship to observation and notation, and the opportunity, fortunate or not, to arrange and rearrange people and objects in his memory long before he used them in his fiction. When he came to the novel, then, he arrived fully armed.

Conrad met, among others, the original for Ricardo of *Victory.* In the Author's Note to that novel, he speaks of Ricardo being a fellow passenger on "an extremely small and extremely dirty little schooner, during a four days' passage between two places in the Gulf of Mexico whose names don't matter." He also probably heard the name of Santiago Pérez, retiring president of Colombia, whose son, Santiago Pérez Triana, became the partial model for Don José Avellanos in *Nostromo.* Settings, as well, reappeared in *Nostromo.* Although Conrad asserted that Costaguana could be any South American republic, geographically Cartagena in Colombia would appear to be the basis for Sulaco, and the islands off its coast would seem to be duplicated by the Isabels in that novel; obviously, such islands were not rare in Conrad's travels. Although we can fix some of his memories here, we should not make these the sole basis in fact for his characters and settings in *Nostromo.* That novel became a mixture of fact, reading, Polish political ideologies, and imaginative thrust apart from any observed materials. Where one strand separates from the others is, as in any artistic work, impossible to determine.*

---

* No specific evidence connects Conrad's Costaguana directly with any South or Central American republic, although a persuasive political and geographical argument can be offered for Colombia, which after Bolivar's death became a battleground of liberals and conservatives. But the argument here is that Costaguana was, as Conrad himself asserted (see page 812 n.), a place of the imagination, although heavily indebted to literary sources and information from Graham. (For an attempt to fix Colombia as the location, see Avrom Fleishman, *Conrad's Politics*, pp. 168 ff.)

We may cautiously advance that Conrad observed the mountain range in Colombia which became the Cordilleras in *Nostromo,* and he may have seen the original of the port of Esmeralda. This view would be intermixed with his reading, with information supplied by his friend Cunninghame Graham, and with observations gleaned from his other travels. From Cartagena, possibly, he brought away a name, Antonio Guzman Blanco, who may have become Guzman Bento, the dictator in *Nostromo,* and possibly a further insight into the senseless struggles between right (the Blanco party) and left (liberals and anticlerics).

The *Saint-Antoine* returned to St. Pierre on September 16, 1876, and then left for St. Thomas, reaching that port in the Danish West Indies on September 27. This aspect of the voyage appears notable less for its contemporary importance than for its future implications; for, once again, Conrad was meeting people and attitudes, as well as scenes, which he was storing up, much like Proust as he summered on the Normandy coast or observed family servants. In a letter addressed to an unknown correspondent, Conrad said that the Heyst of *Victory* dates far back, resulting from "my visual impressions of the man in 1876; a couple of hours in a hotel in St. Thomas (West Indies). There was some talk of him after he left our party; but—all I heard of him might have been written down on a cigarette-paper. Except for these hints he's altogether 'invented.' "

In his Author's Note to *Victory,* Conrad is quick to note that the Heyst he met briefly was "not the whole Heyst of course; he is only the physical and moral foundation of my Heyst laid on the ground of a short acquaintance. . . .The flesh and blood individual who stands behind the infinitely more familiar figure of the book I remember as a mysterious Swede right enough. Whether he was a baron, too, I am not so certain. He himself never laid a claim to that distinction. . . . I will not say where I met him because I fear to give my readers a wrong impression, since a marked incongruity between a man and his surroundings is often a very misleading circumstance."

In the same Note, Conrad pinpoints his meeting with Jones, the effete criminal who thinks that Heyst is of his party: "Mr. Jones (or whatever his name was) did not drift away from me. He turned his back on me and walked out of the room. It was in a little hotel in the Island of St. Thomas in the West Indies (in the year '75 [actually 1876]) where we found him one hot afternoon extended on three chairs, all alone in the loud buzzing of flies to which his immobility and his cadaverous aspect gave a most gruesome significance." Then, mysteriously, Conrad adds: "Mr. Jones's characteristic insolence belongs to another man of a quite different type. I will say nothing as to the origins of his mentality because I don't intend to make any damaging admissions."

These are not, of course, the whole cloth of either Heyst or Jones. Conrad caught only a glimpse, and the impression, like that of a camera eye, stayed with him. Possibly, what made all if it stick was the sheer disorder of impressions and the potential synesthesia of the scene. Here was Conrad, a French-speaking Pole, on a French ship, stopping off at a Danish possession, catching a glimpse of a Swedish baron (or so dreamed up) and an English-speaking "Mr. Jones." To that, later, he adds Lena, whom he saw in an orchestra in the South of France; and Pedro, the primitive, ape-like member of the Jones-Ricardo trio, observed in Haiti on the same voyage.

It was also while he was in Haiti shortly afterward that Conrad received the letter from his uncle, referred to above, in which Tadeusz sarcastically chided him for having lost his trunk and the family photograph. In that letter, dated October 9 (our calendar), in response to Conrad's of September 10, Bobrowski sees himself, relentlessly, as the stern guardian. The tone remains caustic, full of the sense that Conrad has entered into some kind of jumbled existence which eventually he will have to surmount.

> There was no anger [Bobrowski writes] on my part—and indeed it is a moot point whether my silence would be a punishment to you. Apparently, however, from your last letters I see that it could have been so understood. But, of course, I thought nothing of the kind! On the contrary I consider it my duty by advice and reminders to keep you on the right path: that is to say on the path of reason and of duty. Which I do and shall continue to do as often as is necessary. And if I ever had to remain silent "in anger"—which in any case depends on you—then it would most likely be for ever. But that is a possibility which I do not even imagine.

The letter then reverts to money, Conrad's extravagance, an area about which he is, understandably, upset, since he had other financial obligations, primarily to Kazimierz's large family. "You've thrown out my calculations with your requirements, so that my purse will be strained to meet all the obligations I promised, and as I was due to send money to Uncle Kazimierz I gave him priority as he was not guilty of depleting my resources, and was the most in need." Since we do not have any of Conrad's responses, all lost in the 1917 revolution, we cannot determine the tone of his excuses. His suicide attempt in a little over two years, however, becomes more comprehensible if we see it as connected not only to immediate debts but to a whole history of money matters.

In the same letter, Tadeusz mentioned that Conrad would have a long letter awaiting him when he returned to the Délestangs in Marseilles. The letter, immensely long at over 3,000 words, is the familiar mix of financial mishaps and reprimand. It will appear in its place, when Conrad returns to Marseilles, full of scenes, impressions, and personalities he has met in his new life, only to discover all the old ties thrown up to him in the form of his uncle's letter in Polish. Even the language is ironic, the Polish of his childhood and youth pouring in while he had moved into French and was, apparently, learning some basic English phrases and words from his friend Henry Grand, the original of Mills in *The Arrow of Gold.*

Still another form of impression occurred at this general time, and that was the experience of storms at sea, the role of the crew in a bad sea, and the damage that can be done to a ship; the consequent fear, the initiation into the unknown, the confrontation with oneself as the ship flounders and the sea beckons; the terrible moments of solitude as one may die, washed over, forgotten, in a high sea; and the maturation that occurs in the young man who can face the very worst nature offers and not succumb. Exactly where and when such a dramatic initiation for Conrad took place we do not know, but we can pinpoint this part of his career as providing some glimpses of the sea's ferocity.

In *The Mirror of the Sea*, he wrote of the overdue ship: "Details [of the ship], of course, shall follow. And they may unfold a tale of narrow escape, of steady ill-luck, of high winds and heavy weather, of ice, of interminable calms or endless head-gales; a tale of difficulties overcome, of adversity defied by a small knot of men upon the great loneliness of the sea; a tale of resource, of courage—of helplessness, perhaps." As for the missing ship, Conrad says one has never turned up within his memory, although the *Jeddah*, the basis for the *Patna* incident in *Lord Jim*, reported missing, was towed into port. All the terror is there; the moments of hopelessness, of dying in the middle of a great unknown waste, the sea closing over one's head, and of being forgotten for eternity—a Pole sailing on French or English ships, an orphan no different from Melville's Pip, who cannot stand the sound of the terrifying silence.

The *Saint-Antoine*, after fifteen days in St. Thomas, departed for Port-au-Prince, Haiti, and was caught in a series of hurricane-strength storms, not making port until October 26, having doubled its voyage time. In *The Mirror*, Conrad writes of the majestic presence of the east-west winds, especially of the westerly wind. Those of north-south he dismisses as "but small princes in the dynasties that make peace and war upon the sea." They are never assertive on a large stage, and "depend upon local causes." The west wind, however, is ruler of a kingdom.

> The West Wind is too great a king to be a dissembler: he is no calculator plotting deep schemes in a sombre heart; he is too strong for small artifices; there is passion in all his moods, even in the soft mood of his serene days, in the grace of his blue sky whose immense and unfathomable tenderness reflected in the mirror of the sea embraces, possesses, lulls to sleep the ships with white sails. He is all things to all oceans; he is like a poet seated upon a throne—magnificent, simple, barbarous, pensive, generous, impulsive, unfathomable—but when you understand him, always the same.

We receive the impression that while for the average seaman wind and storm were related to survival, Conrad, not at all average, observed natural phenomena as mythical, poetical, romantic elements which—he could not yet know—he would tame by virtue of his art. In effect, the sole way he could control the west wind (and its storms)—itself a poet of sorts—was by becoming a greater poet, a more magnitudinous creator.

From Haiti, where she had taken on a cargo of logwood and sugar, the *Saint-Antoine* departed for Marseilles and after a voyage of about two and a half months arrived in port on February 15, 1877. Conrad had turned nineteen on the voyage home. Awaiting him was a long letter from his Uncle Tadeusz, many aspects of which, we can conjecture, contributed to his suicide attempt the following year. The letter is a rehash of the last twenty-four months, and it begins, not unusually, with words about Conrad's departure from Poland at sixteen, carrying his fortunes up to the point Tadeusz wrote the letter, in October 1876. To start, Bobrowski presents a carefully worked-out chart of monies he has sent to Marseilles since Conrad's arrival there. Financial matters were inextricably wedded in his mind to his nephew's activities—and he could not speak of money, apparently, without raking over the entire past. His raking action must have been, for Conrad, more like a harrowing of hell.

He writes:

> On that day [in October 1876] two years will have passed since the moment when I, with constricted heart, your Grandmother with tears, and both of us with a blessing, let you go free into the world as you wished, but with our advice and help—and by the time you read this letter you will be 19 years old. That is an age at which one is a fully fledged young man, often even earning one's own living and occasionally even supporting a family, in any case an age when one is completely responsible to God, to other people, and to one's self for one's actions.

Tadeusz's tone throughout the correspondence with Conrad maintains the manner of a man who is speaking to a ward still a child. He goes on:

> When we parted I took on myself the duty of supplying you with the means of subsistence until you were able to earn them yourself; means which are modest but sufficient, and which correspond to my resources even though they may be somewhat stretched—but which were fixed voluntarily by me after having secured Mr. Chodźko's opinion. You, for your part, have undertaken to make prudent use of these means for your education, for your personal benefit, and for your future. Let us after these two years go over the past and ask ourselves to what extent each of us has fulfilled his duties; for by answering this question, the recapitulation will enable us to correct any shortcomings that we may find in our conduct and will make each of us think of corrective measures to avoid them in the future.

Then begins the long, torturous accounting of monies, which evidently excited Tadeusz to anger and yet gave him intense pleasure. As a careful man, he could castigate the spender; as a saver, he could impugn the motives of the squanderer. Tucked away in his estate in the Ukraine, he was like Robinson Crusoe on his island, storing provisions against catastrophe and gaining joy as he watched his goods mount. He points out to his prodigal nephew that exceeding the allowance in Conrad's favor "either deprives me of some comforts or forces me to diminish the help I give to your Uncle—my Brother—to whom with his five children I can give barely one and a half times (i.e., 1,000 roubles annually) as much as to yourself." We cannot tell from Bobrowski's letters if Conrad felt conscience-stricken about Kazimierz and his five children.

Tadeusz pressed his attack and recounted how Conrad, on an allowance of 2,000 francs a year, had exceeded it by fr. 1,919: ". . . in short, during 2 years you have by your transgressions used up your *maintenance for the whole third year!!!*" Bobrowski then drives home the shame he expects his nephew to feel profoundly:

> . . . let us jointly consider if such expenditure on your behalf is and was possible, fair and worthy??? As regards possibility, perhaps it seems to you that I can bear such extraordinary expenditure out of love for my "dearly beloved Nephew"? But this is not the case! My income is around 5,000 roubles—I pay 500 roubles in taxes—by giving you 2,000 francs I am giving you approximately 700 roubles and to your Uncle 1,000 roubles yearly; so I give the two of you about one-third of my income. If therefore I were to give you 300 roubles more per year (as two years have used up the third one) I would have to cut down by half my expenditure on underwear, shoes, clothes, and my personal needs—since my budget for all these things is limited to 600 roubles a year for the very good reason that I cannot have more—there is no more to go round, if I am to fulfill my obligations toward my Brother and Nephew. Is it fair that I should repair your thoughtlessness at the expense of my personal comforts or, I should rather say, my essential needs? Would it be proper for me to reduce the help which I give to my Brother and his children, whose right to my heart and help, if not greater (they are six), is certainly not less than yours?

Since Tadeusz is not at all certain what Conrad's answer may be, he comforts himself by adding:

> I am only too sure that the threefold reply to my threefold question could be only: impossible! and unfair! and unworthy! That will be the answer of your heart, but I wish for an answer of your will—not words, which I have had more than once—but deeds, i.e. the strictest adjustment of your expenditure to the allowance that I have allotted you, and if, in your opinion, this does not suffice, earn some money—and you will have it. If, however, you cannot earn it, then content yourself with what you

get from the labour of others—until you are able to supplant it with your own earnings and gratify yourself.

Bobrowski then passes from expenditures alone to his real theme, an attack upon the young man's entire attitude toward life: careless, unthinking, proud—characteristics we recall from Apollo Korzeniowski. He writes:

Apart from the fact of the expenditure itself, I must say frankly that I did not like the tone in which you refer to what has happened. Vous passez condamnation trop complaisante sur les sottises que vous avez faites! Certainly, there is no reason for one to take one's life or to go into a Carthusian monastery because of some folly one has committed—even if that folly causes acute pain to someone very close to you!—but a little more contrition would not be amiss and particularly a more thoughtful mode of behaviour, which would prove that after a temporary imprudence, reflection and common sense have prevailed! But these latter—my dear—in spite of my great wish to, I have not found—unfortunately! Thus, at first you keep a stubborn silence for two whole months, silence which you must know was disquieting to me! Then, you write me a long letter admitting your fault, but you do not say how much you need to repair your stupidities, when the plainest common sense would have made you connect one with the other, and not expose me to uncertainty and disquiet.

Satisfied that he has entered a rewarding vein, Bobrowski presses his point, hoping to reform his nephew's life in one swooping condemnation of it:

What is the conclusion to be drawn from this whole recapitulation of our actions? It is this: that you have committed absurdities—that in view of your youth and because it is the first time, all has to be forgiven you—and I, the victim of these absurdities, forgive you with all my heart, on condition, *that it is for the first and last time!!* And I myself, am I wholly innocent? Certainly, I am guilty, because I met your demands too promptly! I also beat my breast and swear to myself that this will be *the first and last* case of such giving way on my part! And I pledge myself to keep my word!

Tadeusz then cites Conrad's mother and grandmother as the reasons for his forbearance in the face of such sins:

And I ask you to remember this—both for yourself and for me. I would have refused my own son outright after so many warnings, but to you, the child of my Sister, grandson of my Mother, for once, but *only for once*, I forgive you—I save you so that it should not be said that I was too hard on you! May the shades of these two beings dear to us both protect you my dear boy in future from similar transgressions, *for believe me* I shall not give way a second time to any tenderness of heart.

The letter then returns to finances, Tadeusz concluding that Conrad should pay for his extravagances from his own patrimony and not from his allowance. He indicates he does not want his nephew denying himself "food and modest but decent clothing," or at the same time incurring further debts. Then in a warning that foreshadows almost the same words the mature Conrad would receive from his agent, James Brand Pinker, he says: "I ask as well that you should refrain from philanthropy until you are able to practise it at your own expense."

The caustic tone of the last sentence is his only attempt at wit. The remainder of the letter is cautionary: be good, reform, watch yourself, and try not to be a Korzeniowski:

> If you have to stay on land, I ask you and recommend you not to take out of the Bank more than one or at most two months' allowance of 150 fr. and use it so that it suffices. As you hope again to have a free journey —*please do not count on it,* so that what has happened this time should not occur again—don't prematurely spend the money destined for it, and should your hope of a free journey be fulfilled, keep what you need as argent de poche, leaving the rest in the Bank—you will find it there on your return—and you will be able to use it sensibly for lessons, clothing, etc.,—this being your earned savings. In this way only you will give proof of your good sense. If I remember rightly, you were usually back in January and sailed in February to return in July—you will thus spend only one month on land, your health permitting—and in March I shall again send your half-yearly allowance, so that if you make in 1877 two free journeys, you will be able to save enough to spend a couple or more months on land by having lessons in science, and enjoy a slightly more comfortable life,—for only when the means are there is it fair to think of an easier way of existence.

As he nears the end of the letter, Tadeusz mentions that he had wanted to see Conrad, whether in Switzerland or Cracow or even in Marseilles, sometime in later 1877, but his investments, with the fall of sugar prices, have not been doing well, and he does not have the capital for such an adventurous journey. Underlying his words is the sense of self-sacrifice, that while Conrad cavorts around the world, a young man of leisure, he, Tadeusz, is burdened by financial matters and cannot even travel to Western Europe. However, with unforeseen irony, he indicates postponement until 1878, when they can meet; "ironical" in that Tadeusz did see Conrad in early 1878, when, receiving word of his nephew's suicide attempt, he journeyed to Marseilles.

Bobrowski has not finished, however. For he is anxious that Conrad study as well as go to sea. He does not intend his nephew to be a common seaman, no more than riffraff in the eyes of a Polish gentleman.

> Please give me also full details of *your studies.* What have you been working on during the voyage? You praise the present captain [Escarras]. So you have presumably profited from him? Did he give you lessons? If so, in what? What did you work on yourself? and what did you teach yourself? Are you also working on English or other languages? and so on. In short, write about everything regarding your moral and physical being. Did you recover your trunk which you so carelessly left in Havre? Your things and Polish books must have been in it?

Conrad's uncle then inquires about the price of "*une caisse de Liqueurs des Iles,*" that is, forty bottles of a Marseilles liqueur; as well as the price of ten thousand Havana cigars, which he assumes Conrad—as a fancier of cigars in Cracow—probably looked into when he was in Martinique. He suggests some "small business in the two articles." Tadeusz closes this pleasant and open part of the letter with the injunction: "Please answer all my questions—but not from memory but from my letter—as you are, my young man, very absent-minded and you frequently forget what I have asked you." The final piece of advice is to write his Uncle Kazimierz, Stefan Buszczyński, and his former tutor, Adam Pulman, none of whom Conrad communicated with. The letter ends with:

> Well, enough of this my boy, you have had a recapitulation of your wisdom, a lavasse which you deserved—and have advice and warnings for the future! Hoping that it is the first and last time that you cause me so much trouble, you have my embrace and my blessing. May they be effective!!!

Remarkable to us is the split in Conrad's life between the words as received from Tadeusz—evidencing the voice of caution, reason, logic—and what inner voices were telling him, at nineteen. Conrad apparently ignored all this good but harsh advice; not only ignored it, but intensified the very activities and impulses which so disturbed his uncle. The point must be stressed: as Conrad received this and future letters from Tadeusz, he was heading into the most impulsive adventures of his youth, the "*Tremolino*" episode, in which he would help smuggle arms into Spain for use by the Carlists, and then administer his own coup de grace in more ways than one (his attempt at suicide). Each letter from his uncle, then, appeared to fuel Conrad's desire not only to prove the latter wrong but, even more so, to test himself in ways that Tadeusz could not help but disapprove.

Conrad himself remained elusive during this period, between his return to Marseilles in mid-February 1877 and his gunrunning activities toward late fall of the same year. We do know from a letter Bobrowski wrote to Stefan Buszczyński that Conrad intended to sail on the *Saint-Antoine* on March 31, but was prevented by an anal abscess. Tadeusz is pleased to report that both the shipowner and Captain Escarras gave the "most favorable testimonials possible about his application to work and his conduct." The next sentences are curious, since we do not know what Conrad was telling his uncle: "The ship sailed much to the regret of Captain Escarras, who even wrote to me about this, leaving Konrad behind, who, not wishing to sign on under another captain, remained in Marseilles pursuing his theoretical studies and awaiting the return of his chief with whom he was to make a voyage round the world."

The "theoretical studies" Tadeusz alludes to could only be Conrad's application to technical materials leading to mate, although in what merchant marine it is unclear. Back in Marseilles, where his activities cannot be verified for this period, Conrad was without his friend Dominic, who was serving as second mate on the *Saint-Antoine.* Through free spending, he probably advanced his standing in the cafés of the demimonde. Aubry also mentions the Café Bodoul, a more exalted meeting place for Royalists, and we know from Conrad's letters that he attended the theater (Scribe and Sardou) and the opera. Just how intense the cultural aspect was, we cannot tell. Most likely, Conrad was moving lightly through cultural activities, waiting for moments, the nature of which was dim and shadowy, that would turn his drifting life into direction and purpose. The surface may have been light and amusing, as befitting the Second Empire, but underneath was a serious tentativeness that caused worry, even anguish. Very possibly, he was learning some English, from the young Englishman Henry Grand, mentioned in Tadeusz's letter to Stefan Buszczyński, who was also the prototype of the Henry C of the "*Tremolino*" episode. We cannot place these activities precisely, and they may have been scattered, or come at a later, or even earlier, time. The nineteen-year-old Conrad was moving in shadows.

Bobrowski, too, was trying to discover what was occurring. On June 10/22, he wrote to Conrad, in response to the latter's correspondence of May 8, offering local news, which was strongly affected by the Russo-Turkish War of 1877. The letter, however, focuses on finances, which Tadeusz has also noted in his Document—to the effect that Conrad had far overdrawn his account and was halfway into next year's allowance. His uncle points out he is very low, and the rate of exchange very poor, so that he has drawn on Conrad's own money, the 1,000 gulden left him by a distant cousin, Katarzyna Korzeniowska. He adds, characteristically: "This will be the interest which has accumulated during two years. You see now how long it takes to accumulate money and how quickly one can lose it." Tadeusz mentions Conrad's plan (which came to nothing) to go "to India for a whole year" and the difficulties of paying out his allowance under these conditions.

He concludes, Polonius warning Laertes as he departs for Paris:

> So now you see, Panie Bracie, how a man always pays for his faults. If it had not been for your last year's escapade, which swallowed up your

whole allowance for half a year, you could get your whole annual allowance straight away as I could have arranged here for half a year's allowance always to be accumulated in advance. Discuss all this my dear fellow, and inform me how to arrange about this allowance while you are on the voyage to India, and think of it quickly, discuss it and write.

From Bobrowski's next letter, of July 28/August 8, we can deduce several things about Conrad's activities, none of them, however, either precise or enlightening. He was looking for employment but had found nothing; he had objected to M. Déléstang's tone when he asked him for help in finding a position and had broken with the shipowner; and he had indicated to his uncle some intention of joining the English merchant fleet. He was in a period of sharp drift, full of his own importance and sense of his Nałęcz blood, but incapable of finding any formula for dealing with his inner needs. We can sense a great pride, a large amount of indecision, even an awareness of waste; but since all of this must be read back from Tadeusz's letter, we must take into account that we are filtering our information through his disapproving eye. Not only is our information secondhand, it is biased, and therefore Conrad's drift may seem more accentuated from his uncle's letters than it was in actuality. Even after noting this, however, it does seem evident that Conrad's shifting from French to English ships, his break with M. Déléstang over a matter of tone, and his entering, shortly, into gun smuggling for a cause he did not care deeply about are all indicative of a very bored, directionless young man.

We should read his Carlist activities not solely as a desire for adventure but as a consequence of boredom and spiritlessness. When Conrad turned to the subject later in life, he romanticized the episodes with the nostalgia of one whose youth has passed. Old and tired when he wrote *The Arrow of Gold*, he created a fantasy life for Monsieur George in Marseilles, along the way embroidering several marvelous episodes. They were dream materials, wish fulfillments, desires that the young man had fantasized as a result of his reading and episodes that the older man no longer found within his grasp. Not fortuitously, *The Arrow of Gold* was written near the end of World War I, when Conrad's son Borys was at the front lines, an updated Monsieur George(s) and "Young Ulysses" for whom the older man needed to find an equivalent. Although France did relieve his frustrations and provide an outlet for his energies, we should not overstress the young Conrad's happiness at this time in Marseilles. He must have sensed—despite his later denial to the contrary—that as he approached twenty he was wasting his time, and if he ever forgot it, his uncle's words were there by the thousand to remind him.

Conrad possibly roomed in a house, during this period, very near the Vieux Port, on the rue Sainte, No. 18. If his landlady were someone called Mme Fagot (the Mme Tagor mentioned in Bobrowski's Document), then Conrad stayed in this rather sleazy establishment, and Henry Grand, from whom he was taking English lessons, lived a couple of houses away, at No. 22. The somewhat rundown quarters, if Conrad did indeed room there, would not be unusual for a seaman, who might leave suddenly if a ship became available; once Conrad settled in London, he sought out comparable quarters near Victoria Station, accommodations not at all known for quality or tone. Apparently his noble background did not impede his assimilation into the living habits of a seaman ashore.

His uncle's letter was sobering. Not the least of the content was directed, familiarly, at Conrad's background, as if he were a Renaissance prince whose blood was poisoned by some vile intermarriage, a morganatic connection.

> I see from your account of the talk with him [M. Déléstang] that you have la repartie facile et suffisamment acérée in which I recognize your Nałęcz blood—in this tendency to fly into a passion I even detect a drop of Biberstejn blood [Tadeusz's mother was née Biberstejn-Pilchowska; her brothers, reminiscent of Apollo Korzeniowski, lost their estates in the 1830–31 insurrection];—unfortunately, I do not perceive in this whole affair any trace of that prudent common sense of which on the distaff side you have the right to be proud, deriving it from the House of Jastrzembczyk [derived from the Bobrowski coat of arms, "Jastrzembiec"] to which I have the honour to belong.

One more letter from Bobrowski to Conrad in this sequence indicates how the young man was thrashing around for something to support him. All his plans, at least as far as his uncle knew about them, had fallen through, and he was floundering—quite a different picture from that which we obtain in *The Arrow of Gold*, where as "Young Ulysses" and Monsieur George he was moving with élan through society and various capers. Although we cannot "read" Conrad solely through his uncle's letter, since the young man was exaggerating the truth considerably, even misleading the older man, nevertheless we can see a variety of activities which still belie any direction. In Tadeusz's letter of September 2/14, 1877, the final one before his journey to Marseilles to see the wounded Conrad, he touches on a multitude of points. We have noted that the plan for an India or round-the-world voyage with Captain Escarras had become impossible. We also learn that Conrad is in financial difficulties, since he had already drawn on monies for the coming year on the assumption that he would be at sea.

The arrival of this letter, probably in later September, coincides roughly with the beginning of an amazing year in Conrad's life, and with a sequence of events that almost ended it.

CHAPTER 7

"Don Quixote"

WE can pick up a rough sequence, which carries Conrad from October 1877 through late February or early March of 1878, in an urgent Bobrowski letter addressed to Stefan Buszczyński on March 12/24, 1879.* According to the letter, the following information was garnered from both Richard Fecht and Conrad himself:

> Although Konrad had been absolutely certain of accompanying Captain Escarras on his next voyage, the Bureau de l'Inscription forbade him to go on the grounds of his being a 21-year-old alien who was under the obligation of doing his military service in his own country. Then it was discovered that he had never had a permit from his Consul—the ex-Inspector of the Port of Marseilles was summoned who in the register had acknowledged the existence of such a permit—he was severely reprimanded and nearly lost his job—which was undoubtedly very unpleasant for Konrad. The whole affair became far too widely known and all endeavours by the Captain and the shipowner proved fruitless (the shipowner, Mr. Déléstang, himself told me all this) and Konrad was forced to stay behind with no hope of serving on French vessels.

The next stage in this sequence, whose exact dating is impossible to determine, moves us into Conrad's desperate gunrunning activities and even more desperate attempt on his own life. Bobrowski writes:

> However, before all this happened another catastrophe—this time financial—befell him. While still in the possession of the 3,000 fr. sent to him for the voyage, he met his former Captain, Mr. Duteil, who persuaded him to participate in some enterprise on the coasts of Spain—some

* Although Jocelyn Baines first made wide biographical use of this letter, it was published in a Warsaw journal (*Kurier Warszawski*) in summary form as early as 1937 and then in *The New York Times* (as "Conrad Once Sought to Take His Life"), on August 15, 1937, also in a shortened form. The full text of the letter, which is in the Polish Academy of Science Library in Cracow, appeared in Cracow's *Zycie Literackie* on October 6, 1957.

> kind of contraband! He invested 1,000 fr. in it and made over 400 which pleased them greatly so that on the second occasion he put in all he had—and lost the lot. This Mr. Duteil consoled him with a kiss and then went off to Buenos Aires. He, Konrad, was left behind, unable to sign on for a ship—poor as a church mouse and, moreover, heavily in debt—for while speculating he had lived on credit, had ordered the things necessary for his voyage, and so forth. Faced with this situation, he borrows 800 fr. from his friend Mr. Fecht and sets off for Villa Franca where an American squadron was anchored, with the intention of joining the American service. He achieves nothing there and, wishing to improve his finances, tries his luck in Monte Carlo and loses the 800 fr. he had borrowed.

Then the critical part:

> Having managed his affairs so excellently he returns to Marseilles and one fine evening invites his friend the creditor to tea, and before his arrival attempts to take his life with a revolver. (Let this detail remain between us, as I have been telling everyone that he was wounded in a duel. From you I neither wish to nor should keep it a secret.) The bullet goes durch und durch near his heart without damaging any vital organ. Luckily, all his addresses were left on top of his things so that this worthy Mr. Fecht could instantly let me know, and even my brother, who in his turn bombarded me. Well, that is the whole story!

When we try to disentangle the events of this year, we find a mélange of fact and fiction, real events intermixed with romance and fantasy. Conrad apparently constructed his "autobiographical" works in the same way he conceived of his pure fiction, as a blending of real events and people with an imaginative re-creation of such materials. Don Quixote is as much a part of this period as Don Carlos.

We discover several irresolvable contradictions. Although the most compelling involves Conrad's suicide attempt, there are other conflicting elements as well. Not the least are the nature of Conrad's smuggling activities, his involvement with the fellow conspirator Dominic Cervoni and the *Tremolino* itself, his supposed love affair with Rita de Lastaola, or Paula de Somogyi in real life, his near-fatal duel with an American Southerner. Conrad insisted that all these details caught in memory were "literally true" and "fundamentally true," stressing in the Author's Note to *The Arrow of Gold* that all was based solidly on autobiographical fact. These memories may have indeed been "truthful," but not quite in the way Conrad suggested.

The best place to begin is with the lesser document, the "*Tremolino*" episode as described in *The Mirror of the Sea*, the book published in 1906. The story is a great one, as we see the youthful Conrad in the midst of his Odyssey, not devising a horse by which to infiltrate Troy, but bringing in contraband as a way of perpetuating a romantic struggle for the throne of Spain. Even Conrad's attempt to make his activities seem part of the actual struggle for the throne—when, in fact, the Carlist war was over by February 1876—is part of his attachment to romantic, not actual, recollections. Of course, real people were being killed, but for the youth, death was for others, distant indeed from his thoughts of personal immortality.

In the episode, "We four formed . . . a 'syndicate' owning the *Tremolino;* an international and astonishing syndicate." The four were all "ardent Royalists of the snow-white Legitimist complexion." The oldest was the one who "lived by his sword," the Southern American Blunt, "*Américain, Catholique, et gentilhomme,*" as he used to describe himself. Next in age was Henry C, who had broken loose from a bourgeois family in a London suburb. Henry C was bookish: "narrow-chested, tall and short-sighted, he strode along the streets and lanes . . . his white nose and gingery moustache buried in an open book: for he had the habit of reading as he walked." When not reading Virgil, Homer, or Mistral, Henry C "indited sonnets (in French)" for the love of Thérèse, the daughter of Madame Leonore, who kept a small café for sailors. The third partner was Roger P. de la S——, a six-foot-high descendant of sea-roving Northmen, witty and scornful, a writer of a comedy, but caught by a hopeless passion for a beautiful cousin married to a "wealthy hide and tallow merchant."

Conrad then parallels this fantastic group—a strange assortment even among the weird groups that cluster around any Pretender to the throne—with legends from his early reading. "The antique city of Massilia had surely never, since the days of the earliest Phoenicians, known an odder set of shipowners." Also involved was a banking house, probably the Déléstangs', although they were primarily a shipowning firm. Central to the enterprise was the young woman Doña Rita, a Carlist and of Basque blood, with a priest-uncle, a lovely woman with the confidence of highly placed personages, and, we learn, the mistress of the Pretender himself. She was the liaison and dealt directly with the narrator, who was the seagoing member of the syndicate.

Suddenly, without warning, the moment arrives, and they are off. As part of the Mediterranean myth, we meet Dominic Cervoni, the ever-watchful *padrone* of the boat. Accompanying Dominic is his brother's son, César, a young man whom the uncle can only criticize and mock—we should note how Conrad has paralleled here the terms of his own relationship to Uncle Tadeusz. César is lacking in nearly every way—looks, fortitude, will; and he has a nose for ill-gotten money, as well as for betrayal.

After several trips on the *Tremolino* with contraband, one particular mission of importance arises, where they will have to evade the coastal patrol craft. They expect no difficulty, for they are assured that the craft is lying, unsuspicious and unready, at anchor. The *Tremolino* starts out, only to find itself within view of the guardacosta. The balancelle runs for her life, Dominic in charge, hopeful of outracing the patrol boat. They then realize they have been tricked, that the patrol knew their route and was awaiting them, deceived by none other than César, Dominic's nephew. Facing capture, Dominic chooses destruction of the boat, to smash it on the rocks and to escape with the ten thousand francs on board. As the *Tremolino* rushes toward its fate, Monsieur George goes for the money, only to find it has disappeared. The boat crashes in a fury of splintered planks and smashed timbers. "This shipwreck lies upon my soul with the dread and horror of a homicide, with the unforgettable remorse of having crushed a living, faithful heart at a single blow. At one moment the rush and the soaring swing of speed; the next a crash, and death, stillness—a moment of horrible immobility, with the song of the wind changed to a strident wail, and the heavy waters boiling up menacing and sluggish around the corpse."

As the crew recovers from the shock, Dominic pursues his nephew, who has twice deceived them, with the patrol and with the francs. With a sweep of his arms, he throws the traitor overboard, and the nephew sinks like a stone with the money belt around his waist. The false César is no more; in his place is the angry, cunning Odysseus, now even more closely tied to his spiritual heir, Monsieur George:

> Imprisoned in the house of personal illusions thirty centuries in mankind's history seem less to look back upon than thirty years of our own life. And Dominic Cervoni takes his place in my memory by the side of the legendary wanderer on the sea of marvels and terrors, by the side of the fatal and impious adventurer, to whom the evoked shade of the soothsayer predicted a journey inland with an oar on his shoulder, till he met men who had never set eyes on ships and oars.

This is the first version of the supposed "*Tremolino*" episode in his Marseilles years, as Conrad chose to tell it in 1905–6. In *Some Reminiscences* (later retitled *A Personal Record*), which began to appear in Ford's *English Review* in December 1908, Conrad ranged impressionistically over his formative years in Poland and France in a kind of autobiographical memoir. Strikingly enough, he does not enter into this particular episode. Since he felt obliged, perhaps, to stick fairly close to fact, he avoided the romantic implications of this sequence; or else his motives may have been to avoid something he had already related in an earlier book, *The Mirror of the Sea.* Whatever his reason, he stopped short, in his description of his Marseilles years, of any mention of the *Tremolino.*

His next opportunity came with *The Arrow of Gold,* in which the original event, the destruction of the *Tremolino,* becomes a very small matter, while the experiences surrounding that episode form the basis of the novel. We are moved, in *The Arrow,* into an even more romantic involvement than gunrunning, and that is romance itself. Conrad has shifted his material around and placed himself, disguised as Monsieur George, in the center of a great romance, not itself too different from the role of John Kemp in the early novel he wrote in collaboration with Ford Madox Ford, called, appropriately enough, *Romance.* That novel preceded by only a couple of years *The Mirror of the Sea,* and it is very possible that the prolonged and torturous writing of the collaborative effort jogged Conrad's memory so as to produce the *Tremolino* episode.

Whatever the chronology, or the motivation, *The Arrow of Gold* has as its center the passion of Monsieur George, our "Young Ulysses," for Doña Rita, Rita de Lastaola. In exact proportion as she steps to the foreground of the novel, the "*Tremolino*" episode moves to the shadows. Women and war did not mix. Since this is the only other "document" of Conrad's later Marseilles years, we must sift it very carefully; for he has developed a persona in George and altered many of the significant details. The still larger question arises of how much to believe of the story, or, even further, whether to believe any of it. So much fantasy life is here, which we also found in Conrad's early reading, that we can, of necessity, view much of the story as a Cervantean episode, a concoction for the literary Don, a forceful realignment—and blurring—of reading and real life.

In this novel of his later years, Conrad stressed both a passion and an adventure to equal his son's heroic deeds at the front in World War I. He brings back the cast of the *Tremolino* syndicate—Blunt, Dominic Cervoni, and Henry C, now in the more substantial shape of Mills, and the liaison figure Rita, now the object of George's passion. Especially interesting is how closely the tale of their passion parallels the Don's "creation" of Dulcinea. Implicit in both is a fantasy creation of a woman—the mythical Pygmalion—and the idealization of that woman once she is created.

Rita is the stuff of dreams. She was a goat-girl—a girl who tended flocks and was transformed by a wealthy painter, Allègre, into a cosmopolitan woman of great charm and presence, a grande dame. Thus, we have the country and city extremes: the wild, primitive creature tamed into an urban sophisticate. Her last name is itself eponymous, deriving from a pass in the Basque country around Bidassoa—this fact giving her solidity in her former role as a goat-girl. George meets her as a result of their common interest in the Carlist war; it is approaching a crucial stage, and she, as the mistress of the Pretender Don Carlos, has busied herself soliciting support for his cause.

Conrad relates the story through a first-person narrator, the Monsieur George whose adventures so closely parallel Conrad's own chronology. He indicates that this sequence of events follows from his second West Indies voyage, and that it occurs during the height of the second Carlist war against the liberal government of Spain, under Alfonso XII. An interesting sidelight is Alfonso's own youth—although he never appears, Conrad must have known that his adversary, so to speak, in these activities was a monarch of only seventeen (in 1875), at a time when Conrad himself was the same age.* George stresses he has no "political, religious, or romantic reasons" for his involvement. For while all this is transpiring, he makes it clear he is equally involved socially with a bohemian group of artists and sculptors led by "Prax," who was probably the sculptor Frétigny. Like Conrad, George moves in three worlds: the bohemian demimonde, the royalist realm centering on the Café Bodoul, and the salons suitable to a celebrated emigré. Since he was between voyages, he apparently had plenty of time to devote to all three, although *Arrow of Gold* focuses increasingly on Royalist activities. When Uncle Tadeusz worried about his nephew wasting his time on trivialities, he had divined the true state of affairs in Marseilles, no less than Polonius had about Laertes in Paris. The one element not seen by the uncle, however, was the nephew's use of eye and imagination, that storing up of objects, like an animal preparing for a future season.

Blunt, the North Carolinian adventurer, also gains a larger place in *Arrow* than in the "*Tremolino*" episode; necessarily, because toward the end of the novel George is to fight a duel with him over Rita, a duel that shortly afterward, in Conrad's own chronology, became a cover story for his suicide attempt. Blunt, further, has in him something of the fantasy figure, suggesting a Faulknerian character from a defeated South. He is a suave, proficient adventurer, charming, capable, a crack shot, careless of his life, devoted to futile causes, the son of a grand lady whom he honors, a man who idealizes women because he hates and fears them and yet needs their fortune. One Conrad touch, the neurotic component, is Blunt's insomnia: our sole glimpse into his inner life. As Blunt repeats to all who will listen, he "lives by his sword." He becomes Paris to George's "Young Ulysses," although instead of fighting over Troy, they duel over Helen, perhaps the same thing.

The conflict is set: smuggling and gunrunning to aid the Carlist forces in Spain, an operation run out of Marseilles and activated by Doña Rita; a cast of characters led by young George and not so young Blunt, with Dominic Cervoni close by whenever adventure is at hand; and the tension between George and Blunt, which gradually takes over the foreground of the novel to the exclusion of all else. The novel is the obverse of the "*Tremolino*" in *The Mirror of the Sea*, as if additional retrospect had bleached out the adventure and brought into relief the romance. Although the original of Rita is thought to be Paula de Somogyi, a Hungarian actress who became the mistress of Don Carlos, the novel was apparently triggered by something closer to the mature Conrad than his memories of forty years before.

* To heighten the excitement of the smuggling enterprises, Conrad has moved his own 1877–78 activities back to 1875, when the Carlist war was still active and there was as yet some doubt about the Pretender's chances of success in obtaining the throne. By 1877, it was all over, and much of the danger was gone.

Conrad's 1916 meeting with Jane Anderson, then married, but loosely, to the composer and musicologist Deems Taylor, apparently set off his memories of the youthful romance of George and Rita. This is the view of Józef Retinger, and it seems supported by contemporary evidence apart from what Retinger knew from Conrad. While this line of reasoning moves us far from Conrad's French years, it does suggest that his recollections of these early episodes were romantic and fantastic, part of a fabulous tale and at variance with nearly every aspect of his experience except perhaps its broadest lines. These later versions of the Marseilles "odyssey" are aspects of Conrad's imaginative life, to be judged as literature, but not to be taken seriously as autobiography; and to understand Conrad's manipulation of his materials, we must catch the psychological moments, the turn of his mind, the romanticism implicit in the older man's desire to duplicate the magnificent stories he read while his father slowly died a few feet away and his own future loomed problematically before him.

Jane Anderson entered Conrad's life in 1916, through Lord Northcliffe, the press lord who had shown interest in Conrad and his work. Writing about her to Richard Curle, on August 20, 1916, Conrad said: "We made the acquaintance of a new young woman. She comes from Arizona and (strange to say!) she has an European mind. She is seeking to get herself adopted as our big daughter and is succeeding fairly. To put it shortly she's quite yum-yum. But those matters can't interest a man of your austere character. So I hasten away from these pretty frivolities to inform you that we had here Lord Northcliffe for a Sunday afternoon."

In *Joseph Conrad and His Circle,* Jessie Conrad picks up the episode, giving it such a circuitous narrative that she seems, herself, to have entered into its legendary rather than real qualities; her impressionism fits the impressionistic, shadowy nature of the sequence. She says that Anderson came to them shaken by the horrors of the war she had witnessed and spent "a month practically in bed." She showed particular interest in Borys, then at the front, and intended to look the boy up when she next went to Paris on a writing assignment. Jessie says: "And I brought myself up short, when I heard the short, terse tone in which Joseph Conrad replied: 'None of that, you let the boy alone.' " Although Jessie asserts she heard this, Conrad was telling Pinker at the same time that if Borys must "meet a Jane" then better at nineteen than at twenty-four. Jane left and went up to London, carrying Conrad's promise to meet her for lunch, with everyone to get together eventually for a brief vacation in Folkestone. Jessie was to stay there while John Conrad, then ten, recovered from a feverish cold and Conrad was away on assignment with the Admiralty. When Conrad joined Jessie at Folkestone, he apparently expected to see Jane Anderson along with his wife and son. We now pick up Jessie's confused narrative of events.

"He had hardly come within speaking distance when he asked: 'Where is your stable-companion?' " Granting that Conrad's query seems dripping with persiflage, his disappointment was evident, although the depth of it is difficult to determine from Jessie's "great-big-boy-of-a-husband" tone. He speaks of the danger he has been in, flying for the Admiralty, and remarks her lack of concern, no less approval. " 'My flight was every bit as dangerous as any other observer's might have been, and yet you greet me like this. I am disappointed in you, very disappointed.' " Jessie responds: " 'Your flight—of fancy? do you mean. I heard a great deal about that, but she told me she had destroyed the letter, and we will say no more about it, but I don't think I want her to stay with us any longer—at least not at present.' "

Conrad goes into a funk and returns to Jessie's lack of concern about his flying. She says it's the first she's heard of it. Then:

> A light fell on the situation, and almost in a flash I saw that our fair American had been amusing herself at my expense. The seriousness of that deliberate attempt to spoil our long understanding affection had probably never struck her and more than likely would not have troubled her if it had. Something of this I made Joseph Conrad understand before we reached the hotel. I was not present when the first interview took place, but I gathered that it had been more than a little stormy. We stayed two days longer at Folkestone, and when we left our lady friend elected to return to town.

Apparently Conrad had written a rather compromising letter to Jane Anderson, which she said she had burned. Jessie put her hands on it, a "very high flown epistle, without signature or superscription." Conrad seized it and threw it into the fire. So the episode ended.

We can speculate that this brief episode with Jane Anderson, vague and uncertain as it was, very possibly carried over into the fantasy figure of Rita de Lastaola and her relationship to young Monsieur George as Conrad described it in *The Arrow of Gold.* If so, then we cannot begin to accept the *Arrow* story as the basis of Conrad's Marseilles period, and his attempts to convince us of such facts become very suspect. What, then, do we know? Where do fact and fiction separate? Did the youthful Conrad, still a teenager, run guns for the Carlists and have a passionate affair with the worldly Rita, the Pretender's own mistress? It is the contention here that Conrad tried to turn fantasy into fact and that we can find in literature and in certain aspects of his life the so-called truth of these Marseilles episodes.

Although Rita may superficially have been based on Paula de Somogyi, she is more likely a composite of Conrad's chance acquaintances, his reading, and characters he had himself created, not the least of whom would be Seraphina, from the novel *Romance.** John Kemp muses about Seraphina in the terms of romantic literature, which *Romance* tried to imitate:

> I needed that something not wholly of this world, which women's more exalted nature infuses into their passions, into their sorrows, into their joys; as if their adventurous souls had the power to range beyond the orbit of the earth for the gathering of their love, their hate—and their charity.

Although Kemp's love for Seraphina is more purely romantic and less painful or masochistic than George's for Rita, nevertheless, we can read the above passage against this one from *Arrow of Gold:*

> . . . the delicate carnation of that face, which, after the first glance given to the whole person, drew irresistibly your gaze to itself by an indefinable quality of charm beyond all analysis and made you think of remote races, of strange generations, of the faces of women sculptured on immemorial monuments and of those lying unsung in their tombs. While she moved downwards from step to step with slightly lowered eyes there flashed upon me suddenly the recollection of words heard at night, of Allègre's words about her, of there being in her "something of the women of all time."

This is a literary creation, deriving from Conrad's reading and consistent with his other literary portraits. It is, in fact, a portrait in keeping with Conrad's interest in Pater and owes not a little to Pater's famous description of the Mona Lisa. Pater writes:

> Set it for a moment beside one of those white Greek goddesses or beautiful women of antiquity, and how would they be troubled by this beauty, into which the soul with all its maladies has passed! All the thoughts and experience of the world have etched and moulded there, in that which they have of power to refine and make expressive the outward form, the animalism of Greece, the lust of Rome, the mysticism of the middle age with its spiritual ambition and imaginative loves, the return of the Pagan world, the sins of the Borgias.

And then this key passage:

> She is older than the rocks among which she sits; like the vampire, she has been dead many times, and learned the secrets of the grave; and has been a diver in deep seas, and keeps their fallen day about her; and traf-

* Dr. Meyer sees Rita as a combination of female figures in Conrad's life and reading, although he does not view her as based on characters Conrad had created. "Rita is a composite creation derived from a number of sources, and from various epochs in his life—'Aunt' Marguerite [Poradowska, his distant cousin by marriage], Paula de Somogyi, a childhood sweetheart, and last and most important, his dead mother. Surely it was the image of her, sick and wasting away, yet steadfastly maintaining a resolute fidelity to her patriot husband, that in his fiction Conrad transformed into the all-powerful Rita de Lastaola, the indestructible supporter of her 'king.' "

> ficked for strange webs with Eastern merchants, and, as Leda was the mother of Helen of Troy, and, as Saint Anne, the mother of Mary; and all this has been to her but as the sound of lyres and flutes, and lives only in the delicacy with which it has moulded the changing lineaments, and tinged the eyelids and the hands.

In returning to a period of his youth, Conrad, inadvertently or not, reverted to the romantic prose of his first attempts at English, when he was reading, among others, Pater and several *fin de siècle* writers who affected his prose in the 1890s. Compare the above description by Pater with this one of Rita in *Arrow of Gold*, then with others from Conrad's 1890 period. This of Rita contains Conrad's early mannerisms at their worst:

> I only breathed deeply the faint scent of violets, her own particular fragrance enveloping my body, penetrating my very heart with an inconceivable intimacy, bringing me closer to her than the closest embrace, and yet so subtle that I sensed her existence in me only as a great, glowing, indeterminate tenderness, something like the evening light disclosing after the white passion of the day infinite depths in the colours of the sky and an unsuspected soul of peace in the protean forms of life. I had not known such quietness for months; and I detected in myself an immense fatigue, a longing to remain where I was without changing my position to the end of time.

This Mona Lisa is, like Pater's, all women with something of the cruel and ambiguous about them, women for whom men debase themselves. "Like the vampire," Pater remarks, she has learned the grave's secrets; and the comparison is not lost upon Conrad, who sees his Rita as something of a vampire, a "goddess in furs," before whom George is penitential, groveling, and overjoyed at his subservience.* We can see that Rita derives less from experience than from literature, and if we scan Conrad's earliest fiction, *Almayer's Folly* and *An Outcast of the Islands*, we find comparable descriptions of "other Ritas."

* Dr. Meyer draws a close comparison between the masochistic pleasure George gains from Rita in furs and Gregor's pleasure from Wanda, his "Venus in furs," in the Sacher-Masoch novel of that name. Although there is no proof that Conrad actually read this 1870 novel, "the similarities between the two writers are instructive; they reveal Sacher-Masoch's book as a blatant expression of the same sexual fantasies which Conrad expressed in a veiled and restrained manner. A comparison of *Venus in Furs* and *The Arrow of Gold*, for example, offers evidence of the pains that Conrad took to attenuate and censor the perverse sexuality implicit in his novel. Thus, although the heroes of both novels dress their scantily clad lady loves in luxurious furs, M. George performs this service for Rita not because it excites him but because she is shivering with cold. By the same token, through the use of metaphor and other literary devices, Conrad succeeded in partially desexualizing the image of the phallic woman and in dulling the impact of the sado-masochism and other erotic deviations implicit in his fetish-ridden romances" (pp. 315–16). Convincing as Dr. Meyer makes his case, one need look little further than decadent and *fin de siècle* literature to see Conrad's sources for many of his female portraits.

When we return to *The Arrow of Gold,* then, as a reflection of Conrad's Marseilles period, we must be extremely wary. Events and people, as well as entire episodes, are novelistic and may be no more than broad outlines or faint intimations of fact. As a product of the last year of World War I, the novel must not be dissociated from the romance and heroism that Conrad connected to that conflict, embodied in Borys, his "Young Ulysses," and in his friendship with Jane Anderson, a journalist. Here is how the novel presents the facts:

Rita de Lastaola, in *The Arrow,* as in the "*Tremolino,*" is a goat herder until sent to Paris, where she is noticed by a wealthy painter, Henry Allègre, a kind of Svengali to her Trilby. He transforms her into a sophisticated woman of the world, and when he dies, she becomes the mistress of the Pretender, Don Carlos. She lives in Marseilles, acts as liaison for Don Carlos, and meets Monsieur George through Captain Blunt, the North Carolina gentleman who has been courting her, chiefly, we discover, for her fortune. The two sides of the novel come together, with George—Conrad's surrogate here—as the key: the adventurer and the would-be lover of Rita. Rita also has a sister, the puritanical, prim Therese, who is installed in a second house in Marseilles, on the street of the Consuls, a house that serves as a stopping place for Carlist sympathizers.

After the failure of a major mission, and the destruction of the *Tremolino*—here telescoped into a few phrases—George stumbles through the Marseilles streets during carnival time and ends up, accompanied by the sadistic Ortega—a madman obsessed by his childhood images of Rita when she was a goat herder—at the house on the street of the Consuls. After a wild evening of fending off Ortega and his attempts either to love or kill Rita, George and the Pretender's mistress depart for an idyllic cottage in the Maritime Alps and enjoy a love affair of several months. On a short visit to Marseilles, George learns through hearsay that Blunt has been slandering him, and he fights a duel with this crack shot. Predictably, George is wounded, in the chest, is nursed back to health by Rita, and then discovers she has vanished when he no longer needs her services. These are the outlines of a story whose authenticity Conrad insisted upon in letters to friends and in the Author's Note to *The Arrow of Gold.**

* "The present work is not in any sense an attempt to develop a subject lightly touched upon in former years [in the "*Tremolino*"] and is connected with quite another kind of love. What the story of the *Tremolino* in its anecdotic character has in common with the story of 'The Arrow of Gold' is the quality of initiation (through an ordeal which required some resolution to face) into the life of passion. In the few pages at the end of 'The Mirror of the Sea' and in the whole volume of 'The Arrow of Gold,' *that* and no other is the subject offered to the public. The pages and the book form together a complete record; and the only assurance I can give my readers is, that as it stands here with all its imperfections

The title of the book derives from a hairpin worn by Rita, a gold arrow with a jeweled shaft. As an emblem of art, the arrow symbolizes Rita's transformation in the hands of the artist, Henry Allègre, from a peasant girl into a desirable woman of the world, a "belle dame sans merci." It is emblematic, therefore, of the triumph of the artificial and sterile, as well as the cruel, over the natural (goats, a pastoral setting, primitive life). Further, it is a symbol of the attempts of aestheticism to control a world of meanness and jealousy, but at a great cost in human feeling. Conrad's motive, accordingly, was to give both depth and scope to the personal material by treating the world of art through a central symbol of considerable potentiality. The arrow, however, fulfills a more traditional function. In its direct use as Cupid's dart which pierces George's heart, it symbolizes chivalrous love intermixed with sensual, and often abnormal, overtones. The arrow comes with Rita, is, in fact, Rita, and when George finally seizes it, he gains her as well.

Through possession of the arrow, he successfully fulfills his quest, self-mastery and maturity. The erotic suggestiveness of this relationship is obvious, in ways Conrad foresaw and, apparently, in ways he did not consciously plan. The arrow is an evident object of passion, more directly as a male sexual symbol and then, upon possession, as an ambiguous female emblem. George, who literally owns the arrow, finally loses it when he realizes his true mission, and, now free from this diversionary feeling, can return to his first love, the sea. But like Tannhäuser, whom this pattern recalls, George is temporarily unmanned by Rita's demands upon him and by the kind of love she offers. For, apparently subconsciously, Conrad demonstrated an affair of extreme ambiguity, fully in keeping with the literary background of Rita we have already noted.

For her way of dealing with men is to pierce them: her love brings with it only perverse joy. The men in her life are a diverse group, from unbalanced monsters like Ortega, to mama's boys like Blunt, to Allègre, who "makes" her according to his ideal, to George, who kisses her foot and the hem of her fur coat and grovels at her whims. In a sense, except for Allègre, they are all like the goats, men she can herd and lightly whip if they do not stay in line. Even Dominic Cervoni is tamed by her; and George realizes that "henceforth his devotion was not for me alone." A conflict of ambiguous sexual roles is implied. Rita is almost always shaking with cold, is immobilized by male passion, and evidences deep antagonism toward those she attracts.

Some of Conrad's insistence on this strangeness—her "delicately mascu-

---

it is given to them complete" (viii–ix). Richard Curle, Sidney Colvin, Jean-Aubry, and Jessie Conrad, among others, accepted Conrad's tale as authentic autobiographical fact.

line head," its "inspired strength" as a result of her modeling—derives from his desire to create a Mona Lisa, an enigmatic creature, and is consistent with his sense of George's great passion. Her portrait also suggests Conrad's reliance upon the kind of literary description of women that obtained during the later nineteenth century, when his literary tastes were being formed. It is compatible with this argument that Conrad should have patterned Rita on the type of woman who came to dominate fiction and poetry in the post-Victorian era. Our guide here is Mario Praz:

> These are elements [in which the young man falls in love with the woman precisely because she is unattainable] which were destined to become permanent characteristics of the type of Fatal Woman of whom we are speaking. In accordance with this conception of the Fatal Woman, the lover is usually a youth [George], and maintains a passive attitude; he is obscure [George is a marginal sailor], and inferior either in condition or in physical exuberance to the woman [here in socio-economic status], who stands in the same relation to him as do the female spider, the praying mantis & c., to their respective males.

Praz maintains that toward the end of the century, "the perfect incarnation of this type of woman is Herodias." Mallarmé's Herodias loves "virginity's horror," enjoys the terror, like Medusa, that her "locks inspire," senses that her flesh is purposeless, is frozen within, described, in the famous line, as experiencing "Nuit blanche de glaçons et de neige cruelle ['White nights of ice-clots and cruel snow']." Flowing hair-snow-white feet and limbs-ice-cold body and heart: these aspects of Herodias are paradigmatic for Rita. Praz continues:

> It is curious to follow the parabola of the sexes during the nineteenth century: the obsession for the androgyne type towards the end of the century is a clear indication of turbid confusion of function and ideal. The male, who at first tends towards sadism, inclines, at the end of the century, towards masochism.

Further aspects of Rita, either as a real or a fantasy figure, return us to *still another Rita,* the chief female character in Conrad's early uncompleted novel, *The Sisters* (laid aside in 1896). That Rita, like the later one, has several characteristics which curiously double those of the young Conrad, and her presence in both works is not only as a fantasy figure but as someone very close to Conrad's own experience. In *The Sisters,* Rita, like Conrad, is an orphan, marginal to society, taken in tow by a benefactor, shuttled around, lacking any solid base or commitment. Her father has died in a romantic adventure—here as a smuggler, shot by frontier guards; Conrad's father as a revolutionary persecuted by the guardians of Poland's frontiers. Moved around from family to family—from an uncle-priest, to still another uncle, an orange merchant, and then to a benefactor friend, who takes her in for company—she is a pawn, pitied, tossed aside. The overlapping with

Conrad's background is striking: both orphans, romantic history juxtaposed to dreary present, powerlessness, a certain wildness, a potential for the bizarre and exotic.

This Rita of *The Sisters* is then carried along, more than twenty years later, into the Rita de Lastaola of *The Arrow of Gold.* Besides the common name of Rita, both are Basque peasants; both have sisters named Therese or Teresa who are devout and puritanical; both are involved with men named Ortega (the family the first Rita stays with, the name of the second Rita's mad cousin); both Ritas are sent out by strict and holy priests to be cared for by another uncle.

Still further aspects of this literary parallelism help destroy the theory that Conrad's fiction is descriptive of his real activity in Marseilles. In *The Arrow of Gold,* Blunt is addressed as Don Juan (his Christian name is John), and juxtaposed to him is Monsieur George. The juxtaposition is a literary one and carries with it the sense of literary encounters—what occurs when Don Juan meets an aspiring Ulysses? The two ends of the novel are there, between love and adventure, or the uses of love and the uses of adventure. Conrad was conceptualizing in literary terms and using mythological counters as a way of dealing with experience; hardly the procedure of a writer interested in reliving actual events. In the novel, Blunt may be Don Juan, but he is less interested in love than in Rita's fortune; whereas George, who is ostensibly a potential Ulysses, is really interested in Rita as a love object. The confusion of the novel, and the failure of it, is that Conrad caught himself between conflicting demands. Using art to disguise life, he never used it sufficiently, and using life as the basis of art, he was insufficiently honest with himself.

Any attempt to see the love affair, the smuggling and gunrunning, or the duel as an accurate reflection of Conrad's activities must account for several significant factors. For his reminiscences of that earlier time, Conrad was modeling his adventures on youthful fantasies; on both his early reading and later literary development based on symbolism, decadence, and *fin de siècle* elements, with their own view of male-female relationships; on his creations, such as Seraphina in *Romance;* and, finally, not on any particular woman but on a combination of female figures, Jane Anderson, possibly Marguerite Poradowska, also his early childhood "love," herself a kind of fantasy figure.

None of this depreciates Conrad, of course, since, inevitably, each work he created—whether the turgid, overwritten *Arrow of Gold,* or the charming, more effective "*Tremolino*"—must stand on its own literary merit, apart from its biographical truth or falsity. Nevertheless, for the biographer, there is always the additional ingredient of how closely, or not, the work reflects elements in the writer's life, and, therefore, to what extent one can view a particular work as a reflection of the author. The latter kind of speculation becomes especially crucial when we are faced with months and even years in which the documentary evidence is slim or nonexistent. Then the temptation to derive fact from literary material is irresistible—as it was for Jean-Aubry and Jerry Allen, although somewhat less so for Jocelyn Baines.*

---

* Jean-Aubry, who as friend as well as biographer had Conrad's own words in mind, interchanges George and the author as if the *Arrow* were straight autobiography. In *The Sea Dreamer*, a strangely inaccurate updating of his earlier *Life and Letters*, he speaks of Rita and Conrad being "just about the same age." He continues: ". . . after the loss of the *Tremolino* and the utter ruin of Carlist hopes, when Conrad, haggard and beaten [this is Conrad's description of George], abandoned even by Dominic, had returned to Marseilles, Rita no longer had the strength to fight against her infatuation with this young man who was suddenly left without anything" (p. 73). Aubry speaks of the brief affair in the Maritime Alps as occurring in the last two weeks of 1877 and the first two months of 1878. That brings us to the edge of the duel with Blunt, which Aubry retells almost phrase for phrase from *Arrow*. He speaks of her as Rita, locates the duel late in February 1878, and says she nursed the wounded Conrad back to health on the Rue Sylvabelle in Marseilles, and then disappeared from his life. Fortunately, she did not write her memoirs.

Jerry Allen (in *The Sea Years of Joseph Conrad*) carries this intermixture of fact and fiction even further. Appearing to accept *The Arrow* as incontrovertible fact, she even insists on the duel with Blunt in the face of all contrary evidence that it proved an acceptable cover-up for Conrad's suicide attempt. She identifies Rita as Paula de Somogyi, the mistress of Don Carlos, and as definitely the young lady with whom the adventurer Conrad had an affair. According to Allen's account of Rita's background, Don Carlos met a lovely Hungarian actress, barely eighteen years old, changed her name from Pauline Horvath to Paula de Somoggy (Somogyi), and used her as liaison with Carlist forces in the Marseilles region. During her activities on behalf of the Pretender, she met Conrad, through Blunt, and began the year-long relationship that culminated with their idyllic affair and ended with Conrad's duel with Blunt. Allen says that when Paula died in November 1917, Conrad felt free to tell his story and to reveal the former relationship—although she neglects to mention that Conrad had outlined the story to Pinker fully three months before Paula's death.

Baines pokes numerous holes in the Allen edifice, although he fails to see how purely literary the conception of Rita was. Chiefly, Paula's arrival on the Carlist scene did not coincide with Conrad's, and she evidently was not available in Marseilles when Conrad was there. At the point that Conrad reports George's affair with her, the Carlist cause was already lost, having ended in early 1876 with a general amnesty offered by the constitutional government. Carlos was in exile and no longer actively interested in pursuing the throne. Accordingly, the relationship and its circumstances have no basis in fact, even though Conrad may have drawn on Paula for some aspects of Rita, without of course making his literary license into biographical truth.

On the other hand, John Young Mason Key Blunt and Mrs. Ellen Key Blunt did exist, although their exploits did not coincide with what Conrad made of them in *Arrow*. Blunt, however, did fight in the Carlist war, and Mrs. Blunt did move in Parisian circles, appearing to know, among others, Théophile Gautier and his daughter Judith. How much Conrad knew of the Blunts personally is difficult to determine, perhaps Blunt only slightly and his mother not at all. His description of the Southern gentleman in *Arrow* would seem to have been based, in part, on Francis Warrington Dawson, whom Conrad met in 1910 and corresponded with thereafter. Although Dawson was far from being an adventurer, he was a Southern gentleman of the oldest possible school, and his mother—a dignified, doughty widow—embodied several qualities Conrad gave to Mrs. Blunt. All this is speculative, however.

Apart from the fact that dates and places make Conrad's relationship with Rita or Paula de Somogyi impossible, there is a further point that deserves stress. That is, if we see the affair from the vantage point of the principals: why would Rita, well protected by the status and wealth of the Pretender to the Spanish throne, have an affair with an unsettled, understandably awkward young man whose only support came as a sailor? From her point of view, it would make little sense. Further, there is the essential point that Conrad himself would not have been in any shape psychologically to pursue the mistress of the Spanish Pretender. The disparity of position and wealth would make such an alliance virtually impossible; it smacks of Lady Chatterley and Mellors—another fantasy sequence—rather than of the potentialities of Conrad's life at twenty.

Conrad's fictional retelling of this period in his life involved the novelistic license to which he was entitled; his attempts to make fiction and life congruent—in his letters and other comments—were the efforts of the older man to spin a web of youth, to retrieve a part of it. Intermixing females he knew at various stages of his life with a glimpse or view of Paula de Somogyi, he created a "family romance" for himself, now sixty, his youth far behind. It is all very touching, and had *The Arrow of Gold* been a better novel we could have swept past Conrad's own statements concerning truth and actuality. But because *Arrow* strains for its effects, we are tempted to view it as biography, precisely because it fails as art.

We return to the actual Marseilles, not the Marseilles of Conrad's later recreation. The chronology of this period is difficult to determine, mainly because Conrad stated clearly in both the "*Tremolino*" episode and *The Arrow of Gold* that the Carlist war was raging and his gunrunning was essential to its success. Yet the war had peaked in 1875 and was terminated by the winter of 1876, with Carlos departing from Spanish soil on February 28. Thus, Conrad's activities should have fallen in the period before Carlos's departure, either in very early 1876 or late 1875. Yet, as Baines demonstrates, Dominic Cervoni was serving as second mate on the *Saint-Antoine* from mid-June 1875 to October 14, 1877, and therefore unavailable for contraband running on the *Tremolino.*

Two possibilities arise, one of them a matter of dating, the other an act of imagination. In the first, Conrad simply updated the Carlist war so as to add some piquancy and additional romance to his gunrunning, which actually took place once the war was over and the danger had lessened. This fits Bobrowski's understanding of the episode, that Conrad was persuaded by Captain Duteil, himself at sea until April 1877, "to participate in some enterprise on the coasts of Spain—some kind of contraband!" According to this reasoning, which Baines accepts, then the *Tremolino* episode fell late in 1877, when Captain Duteil was available, and had nothing to do with the Carlist war as such but with gunrunning to remnants of the Carlist forces.

The second possibility is speculative, but it is consistent with the fantasy component of Conrad's entire presentation. That is, Conrad's activities, the extent of which we cannot determine, indeed took place during the Carlist war but did not include Dominic Cervoni. Since Dominic was not available until October 1877, Conrad could have compressed several elements and their dating, about which he was notoriously remiss anyway, and turned the facts of his life into literary fodder, all the while insisting on the validity of his inventions. Further, the inclusion of Dominic in the literary version, even when he was absent from the actual event, would have fed Conrad's romantic view of the adventure and provided that necessary father figure for his "Young Ulysses."

If we accept this version on a trial basis—that is, that the "*Tremolino*" episode occurred without Dominic—we cannot date the sequence of events. If, however, we assume it took place during the war, then the "*Tremolino*" could have occurred in late fall of 1877, or in early winter of 1878. A complicating factor is that no record of the *Tremolino* has turned up, and there is the additional possibility that Conrad invented this sequence of events, or else put it together from a variety of sources, none of which occurred in the way he presents it.* When we try to combine the information as potential biographical detail, we find only contradictions: no boat of any kind called the *Tremolino;* problems of place and dating which locate Conrad and the alleged original of Rita many months and miles apart; psychological difficulties attendant upon accepting Paula de Somogyi's liaison with the young impecunious sailor; the chance that Dominic Cervoni was not even involved in these episodes; the possibility that Conrad invented sufficiently at every level so as to make both people and events into composites, none of which serves any biographical function.

Unfortunately, we do not know more, because these events, in whatever shape they actually occurred, preceded Conrad's suicide attempt, which was

* Hans van Marle indicates after careful examination of shipping records "that no craft by the name of *Tremolino* ever came into port, at least legally, during the period under consideration (October 1877–March 1878). Nor was any of the 3,500 ships that entered the harbour in those months under the command of a Dominic Cervoni" ("Young Ulysses Ashore," p. 4). Further investigation revealed that no balancelle, tartane, or felucca fitted Conrad's description, and none, of course, fitted his name. We are speaking here of legal entries, and Conrad may have entered coastal regions either between Marseilles and Toulon or between Toulon and Cap Carmarat. Further, he could have used the name *Tremolino* as a disguise for the real boat on which his smuggling occurred. C. T. Watts suggests that Conrad may have borrowed what he knew of smuggling from the so-called Tourmaline venture of 1897 and altered that name to *Tremolino.* (See Watts, ed., *Joseph Conrad's Letters to Cunninghame Graham,* p. 77.) The variations multiply once we begin to doubt Conrad's version of the facts.

momentous, crucial, and its own kind of ending. We learn of the suicide attempt in Tadeusz Bobrowski's March 1879 letter to Stefan Buszczyński, cited above. CONRAD BLESSÉ ENVOYEZ ARGENT—ARRIVEZ was the terse telegram that brought Uncle Tadeusz from the Kiev Fair to Marseilles, and there he found his nephew with a hole in front where the bullet had entered and a hole in back where it had exited without seriously damaging any vital organs.

In the aftermath of the letter, Tadeusz's attitude appears calm, even complacent, very likely because he saw the incident from a distance and without any compelling sense of the young man or his complexities. Apparently, he never recognized Conrad's desperate act as an attempt to break the connection not only to the present situation but to himself as well. His letter turns, finally, to financial matters, and he swears that if Conrad tries suicide again (we assume he means unsuccessfully) he will not come to his rescue:

> I spent a fortnight in Marseilles, at first investigating the whole affair and then the Individual himself. Apart from the 3,000 fr. which he had lost, I had to pay as much again to settle his debts. Had he been my own son I wouldn't have done it but—I must avow—in the case of my beloved sister's son, I had the weakness to act against the principles I had hitherto held. Nevertheless, I swore that even if I knew that he would shoot himself a second time—there would be no repetition of the same weakness on my part. To some extent also I was influenced by considerations of our national honour, so that it should not be said that one of us had exploited the affection, which Konrad undoubtedly enjoyed, of all those with whom he came into contact. He is lucky with people.

In his Document of accounts, as well as in his next letter to Conrad, Tadeusz mentions the suicide attempt, all rather casually and all intermixed with money matters. Having received a request to meet Conrad's bill of exchange for 1,000 francs ($200), and almost simultaneously getting word from Fecht that his nephew had shot himself, Tadeusz "at the end of February hastened direct from Kiev to Marseilles." The Document continues:

> I found . . . that the 2,000 fr. sent to you via Mr. A.S. had been lost in speculation, as you maintained, the truth of which I saw no need to investigate—and that you had got into debt. I paid your debts for you as follows: *Mr. Al. de Toussaint* (Fecht, Richard) 1,706 fr., *Mr. Bonnard* [a money-lender?] 1,000 fr., *Mrs. Tagor* [Mme Fagot, possibly the landlady of the rue Sainte house where Conrad may have roomed] the housekeeper 233 fr. and the *doctor* 700 fr.—in all 3,009 fr.

These are the externals. We obtain some clues to the internal problems from Tadeusz's letter to Conrad of June 26/July 8, 1878, fully four months after the attempt:

> You were idling for nearly a whole year—you fell into debt, you deliberately shot yourself—and as a result of it all, at the worst time of the year,

> tired out and in spite of the most terrible rate of exchange—I hasten to you, pay, spend about 2,000 roubles, I increase your allowance to meet your needs! All this is apparently not enough for you. And when I make a fresh sacrifice to save you from idleness and to ensure that you could stay on the English ship that you fancied, you leave the ship.

Those events leading up to Conrad's voyage on the English ship, the *Mavis*, are crucial, for they suggest a broad range of emotional problems: the idleness and directionlessness, the indebtedness, the failure to achieve independence, his uncle's personal attacks and criticism of the family background, the awareness of guilt and failure—toward Uncle, Bobrowskis, Korzeniowskis, the loss of original energy and drive. All of these—and we cannot determine their order of precedence—were apparently present, to the degree that the twenty-year-old saw suicide, the attempt or the accomplished fact, as preferable to continuation. It is not a question here of whether Bobrowski is right or not—he is, from the guardian's point of view, correct in his estimation of his nephew. And consciously Conrad evidently agreed, for he felt very close and grateful to Tadeusz.

Subconsciously, however, the young man was touching unexplored territory, and there, far from his uncle's sight, ideas and decisions that only he could work out were shaping themselves. The margin of error was to be enormous. We do know, according to Bobrowski, that Conrad invited his creditor Fecht to tea before shooting himself, and he may have thought of that young man as arriving in time to prevent the act. That is always a consideration: the desperate person hedging or playing for time. Nevertheless, the fact remains that he proceeded to shoot himself in the chest, and that act indicates no last-minute salvation. The idea of putting a gun to one's breast and pulling the trigger suggests a desperation that cannot be allayed by any competing idea. It has the full sense of an ending.*

---

* Conrad's attempt to recoup his debts by means of a final fling at gambling—while possessing its own surface logic—contained elements of severe rebellion against logic and moderation. Although gambling is an extremely complicated phenomenon, and Conrad was not in the strict sense a "gambler," nevertheless his act suggests a certain cast of thought. Many psychologists are convinced that, as Bergler puts it, gambling "activates the *latent rebellion* against logic, intelligence, moderation, morality and renunciation." This sense of disruption is accompanied by feelings of grandeur, in which the individual scoffs "ironically at all the rules of life he has learned from education and experience." The inner components of this outer act would be a sense of unconscious aggression along with an unconscious tendency toward self-punishment. Thus, the suicide attempt at the conclusion of the act of unsuccessful gambling would be a natural development given Conrad's feelings toward his background and toward his uncle in particular.

In a larger sense, Conrad had "gambled" with his life, and his mounting debts were an outward sign of his failure; having tested out fate (his fate) and "lady luck," he had lost. The sole way to expiate his guilt was through the suicidal act. None of this, of course, can

Since Conrad did not seem a suicidal type—that is, he did not try a second time, nor did his uncle really expect succeeding attempts—we must stress his act as a one-time way of drastically cutting himself off from the entire scene. It *is* of interest that he invited Fecht to tea; for Fecht was, in many ways, a substitute for Uncle Tadeusz himself. Fecht was liaison between Bobrowski and Conrad, and handled many aspects of their financial affairs. He was a connection to every phase of Conrad's Marseilles stay, an uncle and a father substitute, and, as well, a young man whose prudence and application contrasted with Conrad's own lack of these qualities. In inviting Fecht, if that is indeed what occurred, Conrad was committing an act against Tadeusz, against his past, and seeking independence both from his uncle's criticism and from his family tie. Conrad's decision shortly after this to sail on English ships was based not only on his inability to obtain a French berth but on a desire to cut himself adrift even further. By leaving France, he took still another step in emancipating himself from the past, from family connections, and from dependency on Polish life.

There existed an apparent dualism in Conrad, which we see developing even here, and it was based on escape and marginality as a form of self-expression *even when* such acts led to self-destruction. Even now, at twenty, Conrad was becoming an actor in his own drama, transforming himself into the creature whose sensibilities would become the foundation of nearly all his major characters some decades later.

Conrad, of course, never resolved this struggle between opposite attractions. *Lord Jim* holds us so compellingly three-quarters of a century later because of its unresolved dualism of behavior. Before that, in *The Nigger of the "Narcissus,"* we meet the struggle, but in more simplistic terms—the absolutism of the elemental Singleton and the captain and the relativism of Wait and Donkin. The issue becomes clear-cut, the confrontation won. By *Lord Jim*, however, Conrad was deeply immersed in role playing at its deepest levels, identifying with the idealist and yet showing that he was a bad citizen; then shifting the terms, seeking the obverse, and finding those who argue relativism less noble than the man who destroys himself for absolutes. Conrad constantly pivots the moral center of *Lord Jim*, as if responding to his own uncle's attacks upon his sobriety, and this pivoting and shifting help explain the magnetism of the novel, its ability to move beyond us in time and space even as we attempt to grasp it.

By this desperate act, Conrad, like Jim later, cut himself off. Whatever his uncle said—and the criticism continued almost unabated—it could not touch

---

be definitive, nor is it intended to be, since we have such sketchy evidence. It is an attempt to find some consistency in an act of Conrad's early life which has no equal later, unless we choose to see his decision to write as itself an act of gambling and the endless sheets of white paper he faced each day as a quotidian equivalent of suicide.

him in the same way. For he had risen from the near-dead, and once that experience had been passed through, what else could affect him? In an ironic way, his *bête noire,* Dostoevsky, had similarly risen from the dead, as the target of a czarist firing squad, and, having risen, was free to imagine whatever worlds he wished.

Tadeusz's letter to Stefan Buszczyński picks up a few further details. After noting that Conrad was recovering rapidly and having investigated the affair to his own satisfaction, Tadeusz is pleased by one thing: that Conrad "is able and eloquent" in his use of the Polish language and "appears to know his profession well." He suggested to the young man that he should return to Galicia, the Austrian portion of Poland, so as to be naturalized, but Conrad refused, on the basis of his profession. His uncle runs through Conrad's good qualities: he does not drink; he does not gamble, except for that one occasion in Monte Carlo; his manners remain good; he is popular with both officers and sailors, to whom he is known as Monsieur Georges; and he seems well versed professionally.

Bobrowski then moves to a more generalized sense of the young man at this time, pointing out that "in his face he rather resembles his Mother and is quite a handsome boy." In his build, he "is more like his Father and is quite robust." Ideologically, in his ideas and discussions, "he is ardent and original." Tadeusz continues: "We Poles, particularly when young, have an innate liking for the French and for the Republic—he, however, does not like them at all and is an imperialist. De gustibus non est disputandum—but several times I couldn't control myself and rebuked him." To be an "imperialist" possibly meant support of the now defunct Second Empire, although this attitude conflicts strongly with Conrad's presentation of that period in *Nostromo,* where the petit Napoleon and his court are detestable. Napoleon's misuse of power and his deception in gaining increasing imperial power found nothing but revulsion in Conrad's later life. Of course, his "imperialism" may have reverted to Napoleon I, whose life and career held a lifelong fascination for Conrad, or else referred to his support of Don Carlos.

In any event, Conrad was "ardent," which meant hot-blooded, romantic, adventurous—the very qualities he was to present so ambiguously in his writing. He was, in a sense, acting out that aspect of his character, giving it full rein as imperialist, gunrunner, supporter of lost causes, romantic Don Quixote-like figure, and as a moody, suicidal, Byronic character to boot. He is, at this time, both Decoud and Nostromo, both the suicide-to-be and the man who arranges and supports causes he does not believe in. Like Nostromo, he sees the workers as rabble, their leaders as self-serving, and yet himself as honorable, a man of integrity; and like Decoud, he sees through it all, to his own distaste for any ideals whatsoever.

Events moved rapidly now. With the aid of Richard Fecht, Conrad obtained a berth on an English ship, the *Mavis,* without going through all the formalities of the French service. Apparently the English asked few questions, and Conrad's lack of the language—except for some words and phrases learned in Marseilles—was no hindrance. As Tadeusz says, his English "had been rather weak," except for what he had learned from Grand. The *Mavis* was a 764-ton steamer, carrying coal out of the Vieux Port bound for Constantinople, sailing on April 24, 1878. It did not have the look of the romantic feluccas of the ancient world, but Constantinople was an exotic port and the voyage through the Mediterranean would have something in it of the travels of the ancient mariners.

Conrad later reminisced about this period, saying that even as he was making preparations for his trip to Marseilles from Poland, he had fixed in his mind that "if a seaman, then an English seaman," his words about England and English ships being formed, "of course, in the Polish language." Whether his resolve was that clear, when still sixteen, we cannot prove. It is very possible, however, that he dimly resolved that a career as a seaman must be an English career, since the seas belonged to England. Whatever he said inwardly, he kept to himself, and he left for Marseilles at sixteen, only to find himself, at twenty, in his element, carrying a cargo of coal to Constantinople. The future writer was to have another fifteen years at sea, all on English ships except for his short stint in the Congo; and we can say, with some certainty, that those dim beginnings—that desire to be both the Don and Odysseus—were now starting to cohere into some semblance of a career.

In *Notes on Life and Letters,* Conrad provides an excellent description of a voyage on English ships, and his description could stand, as well, for his sense of life itself, *his* life, as he stepped onto the *Mavis,* a new culture, a new language, a new experience, and an unknown opening its magnitude before his young eyes, a new planet swimming into his ken.

> In my early days, starting out on a voyage was like being launched into Eternity. I say advisedly Eternity instead of Space, because of the boundless silence which swallowed up one for eighty days—for one hundred days—for even yet more days of an existence without echoes and whispers. Like Eternity itself! For one can't conceive a vocal Eternity. An enormous silence, in which there was nothing to connect one with the Universe but the incessant wheeling about of the sun and other celestial bodies, the alternation of light and shadow, eternally chasing each other over the sky. The time of the earth, though most carefully recorded by the half-hourly bells, did not count in reality.

His life up to this time had been like that, a mixture of inner resolve to emancipate himself for some great task and yet the necessity of placing himself in a subordinate position in order to achieve it. He felt the oceanic quality of the uncertain and the undefined. These men he was to sail with "were a very special kind of men," for "in their collective capacity they can be best defined as men who lived under the command to do well, or perish utterly." To do well or perish utterly—such was that mixture of Don and Odysseus in the young man of twenty who now sailed on English ships, getting ever closer by slow degrees to his final calling.

III

The English Mariner

1878–1889

Nothing! this foam and virgin verse
To designate nought but the cup;
Such, far off, there plunges a troop
Of many sirens upside down.

We are navigating, my diverse
Friends! I already on the poop
You the splendid prow which cuts
The main of thunders and of winters;

A fine inebriety calls me
Without fear of its rolling
To carry, upright, this toast

Solitude, reef, star
To whatever it was that was worth
Our sail's white solicitude.

MALLARMÉ,
"*Salut*"

CHAPTER 8

Sailing on English Ships

CONRAD sailed on the *Mavis* bound for Constantinople. The ship took on linseed at Yeysk on the Sea of Azov, northeast of the Crimea, and returned to Lowestoft on England's east coast on June 18, 1878. Conrad was at sea for eight weeks, learning his duties and assimilating as much English as he could. In the course of his voyage, he had sailed the Mediterranean and the Dardanelles into the Sea of Marmara, gone through the Bosporus into the Black Sea, and moved along the coast of the Crimea. He had gone even further than Odysseus.

Thus began the young man's formal sea career. It was unromantic and exceptionally hard work, unsanitary, unglamorous. This trip was uneventful, but two years later the *Mavis*, without Conrad aboard, sank on a routine voyage from Wales to Bordeaux. In the fifteen years Conrad sailed on English ships, he was involved in several near-wrecks, lived amid men who had been shipwrecked, assimilated their harrowing stories as well as his own hazardous experiences, and read about the famous wrecks or near-wrecks that filled the maritime history of the day. Perhaps we fail to recognize how sheerly dangerous sailoring was, how close to drowning Conrad was, and how the "romance of the sea" was intermixed with the claims of the sea, those ships and crews who went down, marginal to the last.*

* A reliable report on the conditions aboard sailing vessels on the London-Sydney run in the 1880s can be found in Brooking's "Around the World Under Sail in the Eighties," and it presents a scene of little romance. Six apprentices shared a cabin 14 by 6 feet, with six bunks in two tiers; the remaining space left room for only sea chests, no chairs. "There were two portholes, and a door opening on to the main deck. We had no baths, basins or heating. Latrines for crew and apprentices were under the forecastlehead, and there was no privacy." As for food: "Everything was rationed, including water, except the unbiteable ships' biscuits. Salt beef or pork was served four days a week, pea-soup on two days, potatoes one day. The other rations consisted of margarine, marmalade, sugar or molasses, and lime juice (this had to be taken publicly daily). None of these lasted for the whole week, and it was a good thing that our sea-chests held tins of various foodstuffs, jams, milk, etc." Working hours were normally twelve per day, but the crew was on call at any time. "There were no conveniences; none for drying clothes, oilskins; not

About two years after signing on the *Mavis,* Conrad took the first step upward in his profession, sitting for and passing his examination as second mate, the first of three examinations that would make him a captain in the English merchant service. That, however, was later, when his plans were slowly beginning to solidify. Now, as he sailed on the *Mavis* and returned to England, aged twenty, nothing was settled. Positions were not easy to find, even for an ordinary seaman; later, as an officer, they were even more difficult to come upon. England's financial condition was healthy enough for those well-born and able to enter professions or business; but for those who were incidental to England's class system, the romance of the sea created a glut of able-bodied seamen and lower officers. England may have been empress of the waves, but her ships were not large or numerous enough to hold all those young men who wished to avoid farm or factory jobs.

With his Polish name, his foreign looks, his somewhat formal manner, his very uncertain command of English, his marked intellectuality, Conrad did not necessarily inspire confidence that he was the "typical English seaman" capable of enduring hardships and privations. Conrad's lifelong touchiness about the spelling of his Polish name and his heavy accent when speaking English derive from this period. Years after he had stopped going to sea, he wrote to Cunninghame Graham that he would be pleased to meet Frank Harris, but ". . . you know I am shy of my bad English. At any rate prepare him for a 'b——y furriner' who will talk gibberish to him at the rate of 10 knots an hour. If not forewarned the phenomenon might discourage him to the point of kicking me downstairs."

This letter comes twenty years after Conrad had tried to master spoken English, and its somewhat witty, somewhat pained manner demonstrates how difficult, psychologically and emotionally, Conrad's professional career as a seaman must have been. Yet even as he suffered indignities and mockery, actual or imagined, he developed his independence and pursued whatever he felt was correct for himself.

His departure from the *Mavis,* after its arrival back in Lowestoft on June 18, 1878, resulted from a quarrel with Captain Munnings, by no means the last of Conrad's disagreements with captains and other officers. According to

---

even when a big wave washed over the high doorstep and flooded up to the lower bunks. We often had to go to rest wet through, in oilskins and sea boots and all, in a bunk that had been swamped."

Worst of all, however, was the risk. "I believe there is no hazard to equal the reefing of a topsail under the severe weather conditions which make this operation necessary. In most cases the men are already tired, cold and wet through with the work on deck necessary for the operation; they are standing on a swaying footrope about fifty feet up, and are for safety bent double over the yard, while on a dark night their utmost two-handed efforts are required to find the reef points and lash them up with the ship rolling and plunging under them" (*The Annual Dog Watch,* Melbourne, No. 10, 1953).

Bobrowski's letters from this period, Conrad had been bombarding him with messages and requests for money.

He chides Conrad, who had just left the *Mavis* under disagreeable conditions. He says he would not mind sending money if he felt appreciated. "But unfortunately this by no means seems to be the case! Reflect, I pray, if you are still capable of doing it, on what mischief you have done this year [the suicide attempt, the debts, the idling in port]? and answer for yourself if even from your own father you could expect such patience and indulgence as you get from me,—and whether this should not have reached its limit?" Ironically, Conrad's father probably would have understood exactly what his son was undergoing, and indulgent as Tadeusz proved to be, his use of Apollo's name only strikes the contrast between himself and his brother-in-law.

We can garner some information from this letter about Conrad's activities:

> And when I make a fresh sacrifice to save you from idleness and to ensure you could stay on the English ship that you fancied, you leave the ship [the *Mavis*], giving me to understand that you did so because of the impossibility of paying the premium (for which they would certainly have waited, having in hand your 400 fr.)—you travel to London, God knows why, being fully aware that you could not manage by yourself, having nothing and knowing nobody—you then lose half the money you have left and you write to me as if to some school-chum 'send me 500 fr. which you can deduct from the allowance';—from which allowance, pray?—from the one you give yourself? and 'advise me what to do in these difficult circumstances.' "

Bobrowski then laces into Conrad's impracticality, although there is a real possibility his nephew had traveled to London seeking a berth of some sort.

> In other words you treat me like your banker: asking for advice so as to get money—assuming that if I give you advice—which you will or will not follow—I shall also give money for putting my advice into practice! Really, you have exceeded the limits of my patience! What possible advice can I—so far away—give, not knowing the conditions of your profession in general and the local conditions in particular? When you decided on this unfortunate profession, I told you: I don't want and am not going to chase after you to the ends of the world—for I do not intend nor do I wish to spoil all my life because of the fantasies of a hobbledehoy.

Then, as always, the advice given, the lesson pointed, the threats laid out, Bobrowski relents and sends additional money. As a final chastisement, his uncle reminds him that he has lost all trust in the boy: "Try to retrieve it, not by words but by deeds. You will retrieve it by working persistently in your chosen profession, by becoming serious and considerate, by telling the truth." He continues: "If you cannot get a ship, then be a commission agent [clerk] for a time, but do something, earn something, for one cannot be a parasite." Bobrowski tells him he is on the way "to becoming a nuisance" to his family. He must learn what poverty is, so that it will teach him the value of money. The letter ends prophetically: "I now call on you to reflect! Think of your parents, of your grandmother, who sacrificed so much for you—remember my sacrifices, my fatherly indulgence and leniency—reform yourself—work—calculate—be prudent and doggedly pursue your aim and with deeds, not with words—prove that you deserve my blessing."

Within a month of signing off the *Mavis,* Conrad found a new berth, on a coastal vessel, the *Skimmer of the Sea,* which, unromantically, hauled coal between Newcastle and Lowestoft.* Conrad made three round trips, from July 11 to September 23, 1878, earning in all three shillings, with a contemporary buying power of less than $5. He could hardly be expected to indulge himself on that. But the ship did prove a good experience in other ways, for the operation of such a vessel was not arduous. Its very lack of romanticism meant that the crew would not be extended; and Conrad would have found himself with sufficient opportunity for talk and reading, as well as for studying his seamanship manuals. There is little question that his command of English improved by leaps in these three months of coastal sailing, dull though the voyages may have been, especially after he had sailed the waters of Odysseus.

Such voyages were almost literally a dead end, simply a holding action, and more suitable for older men who did not want to be extended. Like any ambitious young man, Conrad used the occasion for what he could gain: sailing experience, knowledge of the ship—its vocabulary and its potentialities, as well as a broader mastery of the English language. In a letter to Cunninghame Graham twenty years later, he mentions those very elements:

> A coaster eh? I've served in a coaster. Also a barque[nc]. "Skimmer of the Seas" [Sea] what a pretty name! But she is gone and took a whole lot of good fellows away with her into the other world. Comme c'est vieux tout ça! In that craft I began to learn English from East Coast chaps each built as though to last for ever, and coloured like a Christmas card. Tan and

* Conrad signed the ship certificate himself, as Conrad Korzeniowski, and thus assured the correct spelling of his name. The only occasions his name was not misspelled occurred when it was in his own hand. At other times it contained many different kinds of error, although Jean-Aubry's listing of variations in *Vie de Conrad* (*The Sea Dreamer*, pp. 288–89) is almost completely untrustworthy. Jean-Aubry compounded the average English mariner's difficulty in spelling Korzeniowski with numerous errors in transcription of his own. For example, on the *Tilkhurst* roster, for 1885–86, Conrad's name is third and listed as Conrad Korzeniowski—clearly so for anyone familiar with his signature. Yet Jean-Aubry has reproduced this signature as Conrad Kokeniokth, an absurdity. If Conrad's biographer could himself make such a hash of the name, even when written, we have insight into the naming difficulties Conrad ran into before he became the unmistakable Joseph Conrad.

> pink—gold hair and blue eyes with that Northern straight-away-there look! Twenty two [twenty] years ago! From Lowestoft to Newcastle and back again. Good school for a seaman. As soon as I can sell my damaged soul for two and six I shall transport my damaged body there and look at the green sea, over the yellow sands. Eheu! Fugaces!

Even as he sailed the North Sea, with its turbulent and decidedly unromantic waters, he read an English newspaper, the *Standard*, and started his lifelong affection for Shakespeare's works in English; he had, of course, read some plays earlier in his father's translations into Polish. Surprisingly enough, he also tried to read Mill's *Political Economy*, perhaps being drawn to Mill as the quintessential English liberal of his day, the man who represented to the foreigner the very best in English political and social thought. In *Notes on Life and Letters*, he looked back affectionately on this period of his life, learning, seeking, trying to find direction, although it is difficult to accept this as an especially pleasant time. From one point of view it was—he was indeed free; from another, however, he was moving toward twenty-one, and his uncle's letters reminded him of duties and responsibilities. Conrad probably had some sense of his capabilities at this stage, but how much we cannot tell. Extant letters from him, in any language, are still several years off. In *Life and Letters*, he left a record of this entire episode, including comments on his *Skimmer* experiences:

> That sea [North Sea] was to me something unforgettable, something much more than a name. It had been for some time the school-room of my trade. On it, I may safely say, I had learned, too, my first words of English. A wild and stormy abode, sometimes, was that confined, shallow-water academy of seamanship from which I launched myself on the wide oceans. My teachers had been the sailors of the Norfolk shore; coast men, with steady eyes, mighty limbs [appropriate to Odysseus], and gentle voice; men of very few words, which at least were never bare of meaning. . . .
>
> That is what years ago the North Sea I could hear growling in the dark all round the ship had been for me. And I fancied that I must have been crying its voice in my ear ever since, for nothing could be more familiar than those short, angry sounds I was listening to with a smile of affectionate recognition.

Conrad kept his balance, and he kept his eyes open—not only for instruction but for a way of advancing his fortunes. Answering a newspaper advertisement of a shipping agent seeking "respectable youths," Conrad wrote what is believed to be his first letter—indeed, his first writing of any kind—in English. In itself a dramatic moment for him, and for his future career, it would be presumptuous to make too much of his mastery of the language at this time, since one can put together the answer to an advertisement from a dictionary, and grammatical correctness and other niceties would not be expected from a young man willing to sail at the lowest levels. This is another way of saying that even if Conrad's abilities in English were small indeed, he would not be very different from uneducated English boys seeking a berth. The average youth who went to sea in the 1880s was not Lord Jim with his half-crown Shakespeare in hand but a rural or an urban type who had escaped early education or had so little that literacy was barely a factor. As Richard Altick says: "How long a youth remained in school was determined largely by his prospects in life, and these in turn were regulated by his social position."

The agent, who may or may not have answered Conrad's letter before the young sailor came up to London, was seeking a crew for the *Duke of Sutherland,* a sailing vessel of over a thousand tons. More momentous for the future writer was his encounter with London, his initial encounter, really, with a modern metropolis, the London of Dickens in particular. Later, in *Notes on Life and Letters,* Conrad tried to capture the buzz of confusion and bewilderment he felt.

> At nineteen [actually almost 21] years of age, after a period of probation and training I had imposed upon myself as ordinary seaman on board a North Sea coaster, I had come up from Lowestoft—my first long railway journey in England—to "sign on" for an Antipodean voyage in a deep-water ship. Straight from a railway carriage I had walked into the great city with something of the feeling of a traveller penetrating into a vast and unexplored wilderness. No explorer could have been more lonely. I did not know a single soul of all these millions that all around me peopled the mysterious distances of the streets. I cannot say I was free from a little youthful awe, but at that age one's feelings are simple. I was elated. I was pursuing a clear aim, I was carrying out a deliberate plan of making out of myself, in the first place, a seaman worthy of the service, good enough to work by the side of the men with whom I was to live; and in the second place, I had to justify my existence to myself, to redeem a tacit moral pledge. Both these aims were to be attained by the same effort. How simple seemed the problem of life then, on that hazy day of early September [after the twenty-third, when he landed at Lowestoft on the *Skimmer*] in the year 1878, when I entered London for the first time.

Entering London as a youth was not unlike encountering Bangkok in "Youth," and not too distant from his exploration of the Mediterranean as a youthful reader. In his pocket was a scrap of paper with the address he was seeking, and before him the streets of the city itself, waiting to be explored on foot, like arctic wastes or ancient cities of gold. He held a small plan of the streets in his hand, and using that, he circumnavigated the city, the address "as if graven in my brain."

> I muttered its words to myself as I walked on, navigating the sea of London by the chart concealed in the palm of my hand; for I had vowed to

> myself not to inquire my way from anyone. Youth is the time of rash pledges. Had I taken a wrong turning I would have been lost; and if faithful to my pledge I might have remained lost for days, for weeks, have left perhaps my bones to be discovered bleaching in some blind alley of the Whitechapel district, as it has happened to lonely travellers lost in the bush. But I walked on to my destination without hesitation or mistake, showing there, for the first time, some of that faculty to absorb and make my own the imaged topography of a chart, which in later years was to help me in regions of intricate navigation to keep the ships entrusted to me off the ground.

The older Conrad conveys the sense of exploration and adventure, but omits the awe, the hesitation, even the fright. The unknown challenged, unquestionably, but Conrad at twenty had come very far for a berth as an ordinary seaman. When he found his destination, was he to give his name as Józef Teodor Konrad Korzeniowski? Even Conrad Korzeniowski, his standard name at this time, would cause difficulty unless he wrote it himself, and even then it could be transcribed incorrectly. While seeking out the essential London, he could become lost in its labyrinths or fail to decipher its codes.

> It was one of those courts [on Fenchurch Street, near the Tower] hidden away from the charted and navigable streets, lost among the thick growth of houses like a dark pool in the depths of a forest, approached by an inconspicuous archway as if by a secret path; a Dickensian nook of London, that wonder city, the growth of which bears no sign of intelligent design, but many traces of freakishly sombre phantasy the Great Master knew so well how to bring out by the magic of his understanding love. And the office I entered was Dickensian too.

Conrad's description of the interview is also pointedly Dickensian. Although Conrad is writing thirty years after the fact, we can observe how Dickens, as well as Shakespeare, has permeated his sense of the English language.

> It was one o'clock in the afternoon, but the day was gloomy. By the light of a single gas-jet depending from the smoked ceiling I saw an elderly man, in a long coat of black broadcloth. He had a grey beard, a big nose, thick lips, and heavy shoulders. His curly white hair and the general character of his head recalled vaguely a burly apostle in the *barocco* style of Italian art. Standing up at a tall, shabby, slanting desk, his silver-rimmed spectacles pushed up high on his forehead, he was eating a mutton-chop, which had been just brought to him from some Dickensian eating-house round the corner.

Conrad then comments on his own command of broken English, and the phrasing suggests that his written English was just as uncertain: "I produced elaborately a series of vocal sounds which must have borne sufficient resemblance to the phonetics of English speech, for his face broke into a smile of comprehension almost at once. 'Oh it's you who wrote a letter to me the other day from Lowestoft about getting a ship.' "

In effect, Conrad had answered a notice looking for young men of means and background to serve as "premium apprentices with a view of being trained as officers." Conrad was of course, of this social class, but he lacked the means to pay a premium, and as he indicates, he wanted a simple berth as an able seaman. The "burly apostle" who now held Conrad's present and future said he was forbidden by an Act of Parliament from helping young men procure ships. The "Act of Parliament" he cited must have sounded to Conrad much like the manifold regulations imposed upon Poland by imperial Russia, and now visited upon him once again, in distant England, the democracy of Mill's "political economy." Yet the agent was flexible, and they circumvented the Act. Conrad gained a berth on the *Duke of Sutherland* as ordinary seaman, the ship a wool clipper that ran between London and Sydney, Australia.

Conrad speaks of walking the streets of London in the year 1878, as "lone as any human being." Each place he was to arrive at, he was to be alone, testing out new directions or lines of thought and behavior that placed him far outside the world of seamen even as he embraced their world physically. His London of those days is a mythical, ahistorical city, almost Byzantine in its winding streets, its ever-present Thames. Conrad was most comfortable in ports, where no one is permanent and life itself seems to be a transitory gift from the historical past. The symbol of a port is a ship which is at home only while goods are put into it or taken from it; and thus a port is always a means to another end, the journey itself.

> London, the London before the war [he writes in 1915, during wartime], flaunting its enormous glare, as of a monstrous conflagration up into the black sky—with its best Venice-like aspect of rainy evenings, the wet asphalted streets lying with the sheen of sleeping water in winding canals, and the great houses of the city towering all dark like empty palaces above the reflected lights of the glistening roadway.

On October 12, 1878, still short of his majority, Conrad embarked on the *Duke of Sutherland*, a trip that would take a little over a year. Although the voyage was uneventful, Conrad was observant, already catching those bizarre or "privileged" moments which he would later incorporate into his fiction as acts of penetrating memory. One of the great moments in Conrad's imaginative life came when a Negro named George White responded to the roll call on board the ship at Gravesend before embarkation. In *The Nigger of the "Narcissus,"* White becomes Wait, and his command "Wait" both announces his presence on board the *Narcissus* and disrupts the crew. " 'Wait!' cried a deep, ringing voice. All stood still. . . . 'Who said "Wait"? What . . .' " We could add "White" to Wait and What, the Beckett-like confusion of sounds in perfect accord with Conrad's own experience as he would pronounce Korzeniowski and hear What? or What did you say? "Then again the sonorous voice said with insistence: 'Wait!' " The voice belongs to the "nigger" of the *Narcissus*, an isolated black on a white ship, and a disruptive force, an evil genius, a marginal creature of great satanic and yet sympathetic attraction.

The transference of White to Wait was not an act of misunderstanding on Conrad's part but an imaginative re-creation of the moment, so that the name becomes itself part of the theme of the novel—for whenever Wait is involved, the crew does indeed wait, halt, hold back, hesitate. Conrad was already turning the problematics of identity into questions of meaning. Jean-Aubry, in his *Life and Letters*, quotes Conrad's own words about the novel in June 1924, just before his death in August. The comments appear authentic.

> The voyage of the *Narcissus* [on which Conrad sailed as second mate from June 3 to October 16, 1884] was performed from Bombay to London in the manner I have described. As a matter of fact, the name of the Nigger of the *Narcissus* was not James Wait, which was the name of another nigger we had on board the *Duke of Sutherland*, and I was inspired with the first scene in the book by an episode in the embarkation of the crew at Gravesend on board the same *Duke of Sutherland*, one of the first ships the crew of which I joined. I have forgotten the name of the real Nigger of the *Narcissus*. As you know, I do not write history, but fiction, and I am therefore entitled to choose as I please what is most suitable in regard to characters and particulars to help me in the general impression I wish to produce.

As Conrad was preparing to leave on the year-long voyage to Australia, he carried with him his uncle's cautions:

> Therefore, Panie Bracie, write to me about your intentions and decisions and later on do not forget about your humble servant but fortify him with letters while he labours for your maintenance, for as I have told you in my last letter, I desire the reformation of the sinner and not the getting him out of my mind, thoughts, heart, and pocket; that would have been the easiest way and my concern is to be able to cherish him, love and, what is most important of all, respect him—which is all now up to you.

The *Duke of Sutherland* passed around the Cape of Good Hope, reaching Sydney on January 31, 1879. Conrad had turned twenty-one during the voyage of over three months. The crew appears to have been unruly, for eighteen new men had to be recruited, the shifting of captains and crews being endemic to a maritime career. Conrad himself stood watch in Sydney, an experience he recollected in *The Mirror of the Sea*. His approach to the memory is typically impressionistic; if he experienced the episode as he later retells it, he was already taking in images and sights as his fiction would reflect them:

The tinkle of more or less untuned cottage pianos floated out of open stern-ports till the gas lamps began to twinkle in the streets, and the ship's night-watchman, coming sleepily on duty after his unsatisfactory day slumbers, hauled down the flags and fastened a lighted lantern at the break of the gangway. The night closed rapidly upon the silent ships with their crews on shore.

Conrad continues:

The night humours of the town descended from the street to the waterside in the still watches of the night: larrikins rushing down in bands to settle some quarrel by a stand-up fight away from the police, in an indistinct ring half hidden by piles of cargo, with the sounds of blows, a groan now and then, the stamping of feet, and the cry of "Time" rising suddenly above the sinister and excited murmurs; night-prowlers, pursued or pursuing, with a stifled shriek followed by a profound silence, or slinking stealthily alongside like ghosts, and addressing me from the quay below in mysterious tones with incomprehensible propositions.

Conrad reports an intellectual discussion "with a person whom I could not see distinctly, a gentleman from England. . . . We touched, in our discourse, upon science, politics, natural history, and operatic singers." The gentleman comments: " 'You seem to be rather intelligent, my man.' " We note Conrad's advance in the speaking of English, if indeed the conversation ran along the lines he mentioned many years later. Along with "intellectual conversation" were the more mundane duties of the night watchman, such as helping the drunken chief mate aboard. Despite upper-class birth and an artist's sensibility, Conrad evidently found such routine duties part of the romance of the sea, or else an inescapable part of the landscape.

The difficulties of shipboard life, both at sea and even in port, must have been stressed in one of Conrad's letters to Tadeusz, for the latter reports to Stefan Buszczyński that Conrad "complains of the uncomfortable conditions on English ships where no one is in the least concerned with the crew's comfort." Bobrowski then offers some highly interesting information about Conrad's future plans:

In spite of all this [failure of his allowance to arrive on time] Konrad's letters are satisfactory—a liking for his profession and hope of a better future shines through them. He expects to be back in England by September and, not wasting much time, to set off in October again on a voyage to Australia—but this time in order to stay there several years—or at least two. *He has it in mind to devote himself to the investigation of trading arrangements on the Archipelago of the Sunda Isles, the beauty and wealth of which he describes with the greatest enthusiasm.* In Sydney he became acquainted with some captain famous for his knowledge of the trade with that Archipelago and for his contacts there and well known both in geographical and trading circles. [Italics mine.]

What is remarkable is that Conrad was contemplating an arrangement—which never developed—not unlike Tom Lingard's in the waters west of the Sunda archipelago, trading arrangements which dominate Conrad's early fiction. Lingard owns his own brig and establishes a number of outposts, in competition with Arab traders who seek to cut into his markets. At twenty-one, Conrad was beginning to move on the periphery of his novelistic material; he was to find in trade in marginal places the tensions that reflected his own imaginative needs. Oblivious to this, Tadeusz continues:

> His prospects would be: naturalization in England and experience of a trade which he considers profitable—and who knows, maybe in time he would try his luck in this branch of activity? Obviously, not having myself any special views on this matter, I do not feel that I can oppose this project. . . . Here I should add—not so much a credit to him as to his gift for languages—that the Polish in Konrad's letters is as good as if he had never left Poland, when in fact, since his departure from Cracow (1874) he has spoken Polish only once—with me in Marseilles.

At this stage of his language development, Conrad was moving on three co-equal fronts: retaining his Polish, apparently fixed forever in his mind; retaining his French—also fixed; and mastering English, in order to bring it up to his use of Polish and French. He would be learning in English at this time a specialized maritime vocabulary, which the Polish language, not based in a seafaring nation, itself lacked. Even his use of French would differ, since his knowledge of French ships was restricted and his experience of English ships was to broaden. Also, his shifting to English involved different thought processes, since Polish is a highly formal language, much more restricted because of its morphology than English.

In addition to the formal aspects of Polish, there was a personal reason: the fact that it was the language of his father and of his past. As he turned to writing, Polish would have meant a duplication of his father's career—writing in the language of his forebears. Thus, even at this early stage, when Conrad was twenty-one, his desire to master English went well beyond the basic needs of advancement and naturalization. It had a strong psychological component, a driving energy of its own. For even as Conrad began to duplicate aspects of his father's career, substituting a sea "fling" for Apollo's revolutionary activities, all the while harboring a literary imagination, he was marking out his own ground. Going from Polish to English, the reverse of Apollo's English to Polish translations, meant he could both reverse Apollo's defeat and set his own course.

The suicide attempt had meant a break, also, with language itself, if by language we mean an entire culture and cast of mind. Conrad's energies were devoted to separating himself geographically and mentally, and a new language is a definitive statement of separation, almost a final divorce. It was a final move as much as had been his substitution of water life for Poland's land mass. That he retained Polish and French for his correspondence is relatively unimportant, since for him letters, received and written, were not the major thrust of his life. He was to save hardly any, discarding them once answered. Although he was himself to write over four thousand letters, the language of his correspondence—while of great significance to the biographer—did not appear crucial to him; he roamed languages as necessary.

He felt also a growing desire to find some direction or guideline for his life. Intermixed with rather vague plans to remain in Australia—which we know about only secondhand—were schemes to sail the Mediterranean and also visit Uncle Tadeusz in Odessa, or at his estate in the Ukraine. What we know of this "floating" through various possibilities derives from a Bobrowski letter awaiting Conrad when he returned on the *Duke of Sutherland* to London (on October 19, 1879):

> As far as the idea of sailing the Mediterranean is concerned I answer as usual—do as you think! as you wish! I have no knowledge of it. I have read more than once that it is only "a great lake," so a sailor enamoured as you are of your profession I suppose might like the ocean better? Besides, as I have mentioned before, I would like to see in you a sailor combined with a salesman, and as the roads around here are better trodden and known, I should have thought that the more distant and less known ones would be more appropriate for you. But you may know more about it and therefore do what you think best. What happened to the captain and the ship that tempted you? Did you come across them? I should like to know. You plan to come to Odessa next year and to see me there. It is difficult to predict what will happen in a year's time—there might be a war—my old self might die [Bobrowski was fifty and was to live for another fifteen years]. However, neither the one nor the other is in our power to prevent but it is our duty to foresee and avoid unnecessary trouble, and therefore I do not wish you to visit Russia until you are naturalized as an English subject; but what you have not written to me about is whether after passing your examination for second mate you will obtain naturalization [not until 1886].

Through it all, with plans moving on several levels, Conrad was studying for his second mate's license, the first step toward a serious career in the English merchant fleet. This step toward a ship's captaincy appears as a constant in Conrad's life, from now until 1886, when he became a master mariner. Whatever else floated through his mind or caught his imagination, the invariable element was his desire to master the tools of his profession and to rise in it.

Conrad's Mediterranean plans materialized when he signed on the *Europa*, a 676-ton steamer that plied Italian, Sicilian, and Greek ports, under Captain Munro. On December 12, 1879, at twenty-two, he sailed from London, as an ordinary seaman, his last berth before he passed his examination for second mate and sailed as a ship's officer. From evidence in Bobrowski's letter to Conrad, the *Europa* provided a stormy time, not because the Mediterranean generated high seas, but because of difficulties Conrad encountered on board. Although we have no firm evidence, apart from Bobrowski's letter quoted below, Conrad had fallen into a familiar pattern—quarreling with people in position of power or command.

More than suggesting an inability to "get along"—which is how his uncle interpreted it—his behavior demonstrated a desire for freedom and a chaffing at authority figures in general. One side of Conrad's psychological makeup, as he revealed in his later written work, was an intense streak of anarchy, a sympathy for the very elements that prove destructive in a world which rewards moderation and limitation. Conrad did more than present anarchic tendencies in characters whom he could destroy; as in Jim, and a host of others, he found the anarchic element attractive and defended it against those characters who represent stodginess and sobriety, although he ultimately sided with the latter. As we seek psychological and emotional factors in Conrad's sea years—those elements which will link his early career with his later and final one—we note an "antiauthority" personality, something which may have developed very young as a form of survival and which remained, through his suicide attempt, as an intense inner need to allow himself to develop according to his own timetable.

Although this analysis is based on Conrad's future career, we can find here, almost twenty years earlier, those rudimentary imaginative elements that would only appear later. Much of what we select as important depends on the kind of artist Conrad became. Of interest to us is Jung's analysis of two basic artistic types, in "Psychology and Literature," for we can find in Jung's distinctions a way of dealing with Conrad and his careers. Jung speaks of the "personalistic" or psychological artist who attempts to describe human destiny and fate in fairly straightforward terms of experience and emotions. This artist's tools are order and discipline. He works almost exclusively with conscious materials, and his stress is on design and reason. A good example would be Gustav Aschenbach in Mann's "Death in Venice" as he pursues his career in Munich prior to his Venetian journey, which makes him the greater artist even as it destroys him.

The second type Jung discusses is the visionary artist. He writes:

> Here everything is reversed. The experience that furnishes the material for artistic expression is no longer familiar. It is something strange that derives its existence from the hinterland of man's mind, as if it had emerged from the abyss of prehuman ages, or from a superhuman world of contrasting light and darkness. It is a primordial experience which surpasses man's understanding and to which in his weakness he may easily succumb. The very enormity of the experience gives it its value and its shattering impact. Sublime, pregnant with meaning, yet chilling the blood with its strangeness, it arises from timeless depths; glamorous, daemonic,

> and grotesque, it bursts asunder our human standards of value and aesthetic form, a terrifying tangle of eternal chaos, a *crimen laesae majestatis humanae.* On the other hand it can be a revelation whose heights and depths are beyond our fathoming, or a vision of beauty which we can never put into words.

Essentially, the second type, the visionary artist, must confront intense anarchic elements in himself. While his exterior behavior may be formal and stable, his interior world is seething with discordant visions. He has, in a sense, become two people—the normal functionary on the surface decrying chaos and the demonic, satanic creature beneath celebrating anarchy. Conrad moved along this scale of values and experiences, becoming the visionary artist, so to speak, in his revelatory moments of the 1899–1904 period, in "Heart of Darkness," *Lord Jim, Nostromo,* then later in parts of *The Secret Agent* and *Under Western Eyes.* In his well-known Preface to *The Nigger of the "Narcissus"* (1897), Conrad was to move between these two basic types of artist: the realistic-naturalistic, on one hand, and the visionary on the other. Although that preface was prophetic of Conrad's future fictional course, it was also the product of hindsight. It was the verbal equivalent of the way in which he had chosen to observe and store away.

He wrote that the "artist descends within himself, and in that lonely region of stress and strife, if he be deserving and fortunate, he finds the terms of his appeal. His appeal is made to our obvious capacities: to that part of our nature which, because of the warlike conditions of existence, is necessarily kept out of sight within the more resisting and hard qualities—like the vulnerable body within a steel armor." The artist appeals to what is, in us, "a gift and not an acquisition."

In these words, Conrad was teasing from himself the visionary aspect which he assimilated from French symbolism and which he opposed to naturalistic determinism and causality. Yet himself the child of Polish defeats, of a doomed father and of doomed causes, he could not completely throw off naturalism. His whole cast of conscious mind—as opposed to the more integrated imagination of the artist—was toward determinism, particularly when he saw that in Schopenhauer, Darwin, and Nietzsche he could find metaphors for his own sense of doom. Still, the visionary aspect—although never complete and never wholehearted—was a way of qualifying the grimness of the universe, a way of giving man a sense of grace, an awareness of what he called in the Preface the "solidarity of dreams, in joy, in sorrow, in aspirations, in illusions, in hope, in fear, which binds men to each other." It was toward this that the early anarchy and discontinuity pointed.

Tadeusz's letter of January 31/February 12, 1880, mentions Conrad's trouble on the *Europa,* which involved a quarrel with Captain Munro and considerable illness with cough and fever.

I was not so much upset by the troubles you had on the *Europa,* though I realize you must have felt them keenly, for these are inseparable from life and getting to know people. They pain you because you feel you did not deserve them and that you are being exploited. I understand this and partly agree with you. But in your position, in which everything you gain must be won by work and endurance, in a profession where the conditions are extremely hard, what has happened was to be foreseen—and was foreseen by me;—and probably now that you have had the first dose of experience they don't surprise although they hurt—and hurt they must! I am much more affected by the news that you "cough and sometimes have fever," for these are symptoms which, if prolonged, may endanger your health and even your life.

Pleading poverty, Bobrowski says he will forward Conrad's 1,200-franc allowance to Marseilles, via Richard Fecht; all this accompanied by chastisement of his nephew for leaving so little money for his needs in London. Bobrowski makes a special plea for Conrad's health—justifiable in the light of the premature death from lung complications of so many of the Korzeniowski clan, as well as the early death of Tadeusz's own wife and daughter.

Back in London at the end of January, after seven months on the *Europa,* Conrad fell into his now familiar drift. Those long periods between berths were apparently terrible times for him. In Marseilles, they had been youthful larks; in London, they took on a different cast. The pressures were growing: questions of career, direction of his energies, sexual needs and desire for companionship, use of his free time, which appeared considerable. The possibilities were almost infinite and, because so numerous, unacceptable. He even thought of returning to service on French ships, and either for that or for purposes of documentation related to his examination for mate secured a testimonial from M. Déléstang, stamped by Alexandre Escarras, a Marseilles shipbroker, on April 26, 1880. We know little of his London whereabouts, although he had rooms with a Mr. William Ward (mentioned in Bobrowski's Document of accounts) at Tollington Park, London N4. It was during his stay with Ward that Conrad met G. F. W. Hope, who turned out to be a lifelong friend, and Adolf Krieger, whose presence weaves in and out of Conrad's life for almost the next twenty years.

He had still not rejected the Australian venture, or even East Indies trading; naturalization remained open—American, English, French. Then in a letter from Bobrowski, we see that Conrad was toying with a Canadian venture, caught up as he was by a general European interest in Canadian railway stocks. His uncle's letter of May 18/30, 1880, ranges over several interesting topics, all of them leading to the inevitable lecture:

Your discomposure because of that madman Captain Munro [of the *Europa*] worries me not less than it does you, although I don't understand English logic, since if the Captain is a madman his certificate and commission should be withdrawn. Until he is judicially proclaimed mad his certificate must remain valid. Well, we won't change the English, so having to deal with them, we must adapt ourselves. I suppose that while I am writing, your *Europa* is in port and you have the testimonial from the present Captain, the previous second mate, and that you have either already passed your examination [passed on June 1, 1880] or are about to sit for it shortly.

Then Tadeusz turns to the real matter, Conrad's desire to change professions.

> You would not be a Nałęcz, dear boy, if you were steady in your enterprises and if you didn't chase after ever new projects. This refers to what you wrote about Mr. Lascalle's proposal [railway investments by a Canadian businessman] that you become his secretary and later make money on the railways! But I would not be myself and your uncle if I did not discourage you from changing professions and did not warn you that such changes make people become "déclassé," who never having warmed a place for themselves nor having built anything for themselves . . . bear a grudge against the whole world for not having succeeded.

Bobrowski then turns to his nineteenth-century homiletics—a page from Samuel Smiles—all of it sound and logical but missing his nephew's unease with himself. While Conrad was waiting for some inner directive, Tadeusz was telling him to keep moving along on an external course of action.

> Work and perseverance are the only values that never fail. In the life of every man a momentary success may occur, but a sensible and moderate man will not misuse it but use it, while a thoughtless and stupid man will either miss it or misuse it. But to expect that success should appear while one is on the threshold of life, and at any time it's needed, without any work or merit, is childish dreaming and a product of our epoch whose only slogan is "enjoyment." . . . It is much more dignified and sensible to devote your life and tie your future to a certain profession, putting into it your work and determination.

Tadeusz then demonstrates a finer sensibility than previously when he admits that "I cannot express my opinion, however firmly I hold it, without knowing the circumstances in which you are situated. As a man of clearly defined position I feel sympathetic to people of the same kind." He finishes with this keen sense of others: ". . . and whatever bed may be your lot, provided that you make it with dignity and diligence, you may be certain of my wholehearted blessing."

CHAPTER 9

The First Test

BOBROWSKI'S encouragement arrived somewhat after Conrad had taken a huge step in his life, the examination, on June 1, that led to his becoming a second mate in the English merchant service. The application for the examination was signed "Konrad d[e] Korzeniowski," and the address given was 6, Dynevor Road, Stoke Newington, London N[orth]. The name is of some interest, on two counts: the "K" in his Christian name indicates a desire to preserve the Polish part of his background; and this is furthered by the use of the aristocratic "de," which also appeared on the roster of the *Skimmer of the Sea.* Both parts suggest a young man caught between nature and nurture. On subsequent applications for first mate and master, Conrad was to change the "K" to "C" and to drop the gentlemanly "de," an indication of his submission to nurture.* An additional point: the use of "de" could indicate a psychological dependency on background, a fear of breaking away until inner coordinates were more certain. All this, however, is speculative.

The moment, nevertheless, was propitious, part of that inner timing which Conrad must have sensed and which was so at odds with his uncle's expectations. Childhood and adolescence, which are not easy under the best of conditions, were intensely difficult for someone of Conrad's background, and for the first time, with his becoming second mate, he achieved some integration. He becomes almost a classic case in terms of Erikson's definition of roles and role-playing: "It [integration] is the accrued experience of the ego's ability to integrate all identifications with the vicissitudes of the libido, with the aptitudes developed out of endowment, and with the opportunities offered in social roles." Whatever the process within the young Conrad, his ego had reached a stage of some assurance, and he moved certainly toward identification between inner need and social goal. We should not underestimate

* Hans van Marle calls our attention to the fact that Conrad, on his application, signed a record of service that was inaccurate, for his testimonial from the Délestangs appeared to indicate fully three years of French service, from December 1874 to February 1877. In actuality, Conrad, having spent a good deal of that time on shore, probably extended his sea time to satisfy a minimum requirement which, in effect, he did not meet.

the difficulty of his undertaking even in a technical sense, with his knowledge of English barely two years old, and the frustration involved in understanding the various regional accents and the sea terms themselves. Conrad left an account of the examination in *A Personal Record*, and even though well known it is worth quoting.

> The first [examiner] of all, tall, spare, with a perfectly white head and moustache, a quiet, kindly manner, and an air of benign intelligence, must, I am forced to conclude, have been unfavourably impressed by something in my appearance. His old thin hands loosely clasped resting on his crossed legs, he began by an elementary question in a mild voice, and went on, went on . . . It lasted for hours, for hours. Had I been a strange microbe with potentialities of deadly mischief to the Merchant Service I could not have been more submitted to a more microscopic examination. Greatly reassured by his apparent benevolence, I had been at first very alert in my answers. But at length the feeling of my brain getting addled crept upon me. And still the passionless process went on, with a sense of untold ages having been spent on mere preliminaries. Then I got frightened. I was not frightened of being plucked; that eventuality did not even present itself to my mind. It was something much more serious, and weird. "This ancient person," I said to myself, terrified, "is so near his grave that he must have lost all notion of time. He is considering this examination in terms of eternity."

Conrad continues in the same tone of self-mockery:

> At last there fell a silence, and that, too, seemed to last for ages, while bending over his desk, the examiner wrote out my pass-slip slowly with a noiseless pen. He extended the scrap of paper to me without a word, inclined his white head gravely to my parting bow. . . . When I got out of the room I felt limply flat, like a squeezed lemon, and the doorkeeper in his glass cage, where I stopped to get my hat and tip him a shilling, said: "Well! I thought you were never coming out." "How long have I been in there?" I asked faintly. He pulled out his watch. "He kept you, sir, just under three hours. I don't think this ever happened with any of the gentlemen before."*

We can speculate that Conrad's foreign appearance and unusually heavy accent when speaking English, plus perhaps his almost unintelligible name, had helped create the extraordinary circumstances.

The arrival of his uncle's letter later that month supported Conrad's own sense of achievement.

---

* Conrad says that it was "only when I got out of the building that I began to walk on air." He repeats some of this scene in *Chance;* there, Powell and Marlow agree that their proudest moments came "when they had passed successfully their first examination and left the seamanship Examiner with the little precious slip of blue paper in their hands" (p. 4).

> It has been a profound pleasure and my first reward to learn that you have received that piece of "ass's hide" upon which so many terrible threats were written by the gentlemen of the Board Office in the event of your failing in the duties of your chosen profession, in the hierarchy of which you have now achieved the first step!! I fully share your satisfaction, which you can say arises from a twofold source. Firstly, Dear Sir, you have proved to our country and your own people that you have not eaten your bread in the world for four years in vain; secondly, that you have succeeded in overcoming the difficulties that arise from the language itself, and from your difficult position as a foreigner without any patronage to support you.

From this, Tadeusz cites the help Conrad received, from Professor Newton, who tutored Conrad, to Baptistin Solary and Richard Fecht, and others—all of which makes him generalize: "Let the pessimists say what they will about the defects of the human race, but I will tell you from my own experience that there are more good than bad people." An ironic comment from Tadeusz, in that Conrad was himself to be one of those "pessimists," an inheritor of the century informed by Schopenhauer and Nietzsche.

Bobrowski also sees the examination as a means to Conrad's independence; the certificate, he assumes, will lead to numerous openings on board ship, a matter in which he was sadly mistaken. Overjoyed as both Conrad and his uncle were, nevertheless the profession suffered from an overabundance of mates and a limited number of berths. Almost three months were to pass before Conrad could find a ship. We can still see Conrad's uncertainties in Bobrowski's remarks, which indicate his nephew was thinking—how seriously?—of becoming an American and going to work for an American politician. In the light of Conrad's later distaste for Americans and his dislike of things American in general, the following is amusing:

> I would not be in favour of changing over from a maritime career to going into the service of an American politician, though even that would not scandalize me if you insist on acting contrary to my view; but always under two conditions: firstly, that you bear in mind our proverb: "you have made your bed and must lie on it," and secondly, that you will never forget what is due to the dignity of the nation and families to which you belong—especially if you choose an American business life. So here are my conditions; I am not to be held responsible for your behaviour;—I am not to blush for your actions;—and as far as the rest is concerned—may God always help you!

In a letter written later the same month (June), Bobrowski even has something good to say of the Nałęcz line—that it engenders a spirit of "initiative and enterprise greater than that which is in my blood." He expects Conrad, as possessing the blood of two such great lines, to be part of a race "which by its endurance and wise enterprise will astound the whole world!"

Evidently, Conrad had asked for money, and Bobrowski turns to that, saying that his income comes at a fixed time and that Conrad will have to wait until October. If he is short, he suggests Fecht as the source of a loan—a situation oddly duplicating Conrad's plight before his suicide attempt. He tells Conrad he will continue his allowance, of about $500 annually, until his nephew is twenty-four. He says, tellingly: ". . . acknowledge the fact—you, a Nałęcz—that economy and calculation are indispensable in every position, especially in yours!"

Meanwhile, back in London, berths were scarce as ever, and Conrad signed on the *Loch Etive*, a fine wool clipper, as third mate, not as second mate, for which he was qualified.* Throughout his career as officer, he was forced to accept berths that were a step or two beneath what he had attained by examination, a severe blow to his pride and to his sense of accomplishment, and which, as much as poor health, may have contributed to his decision to leave the sea for a writing career. There was a point, about eight years hence, when Conrad would begin to hedge on a sea career and start to write sporadically on what became *Almayer's Folly.*

In *The Mirror of the Sea*, in the section called "Cobwebs and Gossamer," Conrad recorded some reminiscences of his voyage on the *Loch Etive*, which he rightly saw as another stage in his development into a seaman and into maturity. It was one of his many initiations. The captain, Stuart, was a man "famous for the quick passages he had been used to make in the old *Tweed*, a ship famous the world over for her speed." Probably, Conrad's love for sailing vessels was formed here, when he saw how the skillful combination of sails and wind could produce a speed and grace that were perfectly in alignment with nature.

The chief mate, William Purdu, was nearly deaf, and Conrad overheard the mate and Stuart in deep conversation about sails and sailing: "To hear *him* [Stuart] make a fuss about too much sail on the ship seemed one of those incredible experiences that take place only in one's dreams." On the iron-clad *Loch Etive*, Stuart tried to duplicate his English-Australian runs on the *Tweed*, a wooden vessel, an impossible attempt and yet an act of artistry not lost on the young third mate. He himself became involved when the second mate fell ill, and he was "promoted to officer of the watch, alone in charge of the deck. Thus the immense leverage of the ship's tall masts became a matter very near my own heart." Conrad adds: "I suppose it was something of a compliment for a young fellow to be trusted, apparently without any supervision, by such a commander as Captain S——."

---

* In *Chance*, Powell runs into similar difficulties, although he does find a second officer's berth.

This was superb training, caught as the seaman was in matters of judgment, moments of profound thought and concentration, a sense even of revelation as the ship raced along in dark waters, with his decisions as to quantity and type of sail the determining factor. There was not only the awareness of craft—of doing things correctly or endangering a sleeping crew—but the sense of command, that one was responsible for the "entire product." With the actual captain asleep or below deck, the young third mate was commander of a 1,287-ton sailing vessel sweeping either toward doom or toward its destination. Conrad was twenty-two and distant indeed from Poland and from Tadeusz's caustic remarks. At the same time, he was learning how to survive on the edge of the abyss, for a sailing vessel caught by wind in its sails at night is always near disaster no matter how steady the captain and crew; the unexpected may lie anywhere, and sails and entire ship can break up. This, too, was psychological preparation for a career in which personal disaster was at Conrad's elbow as he wrote his few hundred words each day against a dwindling financial return.

The *Loch Etive* arrived in Sydney on November 24, 1880. Conrad was to turn twenty-three while in port, after an uneventful journey well behind Captain Stuart's best times in the *Tweed.* On the return journey, also uneventful, Conrad observed two separate incidents which stuck in his mind, two of those revelatory moments out of many which worked upon his imagination. In the first, "Christmas Day at Sea," he speaks of the first whaler he had ever seen, the *Alaska*, fully two years out of New York, and 215 days on the cruising ground.* The *Loch Etive* drops a gift for the whaler over its side.

> I never saw anything so ready and so smart as the way that whaler, rolling desperately all the time, lowered one of her boats. The Southern Ocean went on tossing the two ships like a juggler his gilt balls, and the microscopic white speck of the boat seemed to come into the game instantly, as if shot out from a catapult on the enormous and lonely stage. That Yankee whaler lost not a moment in picking up her Christmas present from the English wool-clipper.

---

* This incident evidently impressed Conrad in several ways; for five years later, he wrote Spiridion Kliszczewski, a new friend, that his soul was "bent upon a whaling venture." Conrad added: "I am brimful with the most exhaustive information upon the subject. I have read, studied, pumped professional men and imbibed knowledge upon whale fishing and sealing for the last four years. I am acquainted with the practical sort of the undertaking in a thorough manner. Moreover I have the assurance of active help from a man brought up in the trade—and although doing well where he is now—ready to return to his former pursuit (of whales). Finally I have a vessel in view, on very advantageous terms" (November 25, 1885). Toward this end, Conrad tried to raise £1,500 and asked Kliszczewski for advice. The latter discouraged Conrad, and nothing came of the plan.

The second episode was more dramatic and more closely connected to the serious aspects of sailing, the rescue of a crew of a Danish brig "homeward bound from the West Indies."

> The most amazing wonder of the deep is its unfathomable cruelty. I felt its dread for the first time in mid-Atlantic one day, many years ago, when we took off the crew of a Danish brig homeward bound from the West Indies. A thin silvery mist softened the calm and majestic splendour of light without shadows—seemed to render the sky less remote and the ocean less immense. It was one of the days, when the night of the sea appears indeed lovable, like the nature of a strong man in moments of quiet intimacy. At sunrise we had made out a black speck to the westward, apparently suspended high up in the void behind a stirring, shimmering veil of silvery blue gauze that seemed at times to stir and float in the breeze which fanned us slowly along. The peace of that enchanting forenoon was so profound, so untroubled, that it seemed that every word pronounced loudly on our deck would penetrate to the very heart of that infinite mystery born from the conjunction of water and sky.

Conrad continues, modulating his words to fit the more violent modulations of the sea:

> On that exquisite day of gentle breathing peace and veiled sunshine perished my romantic love to what men's imagination had proclaimed the most august aspect of Nature. The cynical indifference of the sea to the merits of human suffering and courage, laid bare in this ridiculous, panic-tainted performance extorted from the dire extremity of nine good and honourable seamen, revolted me. I saw the duplicity of the sea's most tender mood. It was so because it could not help itself, but the awed respect of the early days was gone. I felt ready to smile bitterly at its enchanting charm and glare viciously at its furies. In a moment, before we shoved off, I had looked coolly at the life of my choice. Its illusions were gone, but its fascination remained. I had become a seaman at last.

In this period, from Conrad's success in passing his examination for second mate and his voyage and return on the *Loch Etive,* in April 1881, several ship incidents came into the newspapers and the crews' scuttlebutt. Conrad was to pick up information, gossip, and rumors as well as seamanship; and in many ways his indirect, discontinuous method of narrating these incidents in his fiction was true to the manner in which he first heard of them. The first involved the *Jeddah,* a ship carrying Moslem passengers from Singapore to Jeddah, a Red Sea port. Leaving Singapore on July 17, 1880, the *Jeddah* ran into a stormy passage and suffered boiler trouble and serious leaks. On August 8, her crew abandoned her off Cape Guardafui, and when picked up later reported that the ship and all her passengers had gone down. The next day the *Jeddah* was towed into Aden, and the abandonment of the ship created a huge scandal in London and in Eastern waters. Before Conrad sailed on the *Loch Etive*, he may have heard of the *Jeddah* and its fate.* However he did learn of it, the *Jeddah* episode became the basis for the first part of *Lord Jim*, almost twenty years later, where that ship becomes the *Patna*, an old vessel whose bulkheads are ready to give way at any moment.

The second incident involved the *Cutty Sark*, in September 1880, when Conrad was at sea on the London-Sydney run. The *Cutty Sark* episode, which formed the basis of Conrad's "The Secret Sharer," was of more limited scope, more clearly an individual psychological matter than a broad moral drama. The chief mate, named Sydney Smith, ordered a member of the crew, a Negro named John Francis, to perform a particular job. When Francis refused and threatened the mate with a capstan bar, the latter struck the Negro on the head with the bar, a blow which eventually killed him. Smith stayed in his quarters for the remainder of the passage, and then persuaded the captain of the ship, Wallace, to permit him to escape. He was later caught, tried, and sentenced to seven months' imprisonment. The method of "escape" was to have Smith smuggled aboard an American ship, the *Colorado*. Shortly afterward, Captain Wallace committed suicide. That suicide, incidentally, may have called up kinship feelings with Conrad, himself a "suicide" and the future creator of numerous suicides.†

In "The Secret Sharer," Conrad used symbols of transformation to fit the facts of the episode, which he could have heard about on board the *Loch Etive* or read about in the London newspapers when he returned. In any event, he took the basic facts and, through what Freud referred to as the artist's "flexibility of repression," reworked the materials to suit his own childhood and young manhood. By that phrase, Freud implied that the artist, because of his ability to be less repressed than others by culture, more readily has clues to his childhood, as if he had access to the sub- and unconscious. Since the artist can gratify his instinctual needs with a fantasy life, he can embody this fantasy life in his art and then rove back and forth to reality, without losing touch with it.

---

* Norman Sherry indicates that Conrad may have learned of the story directly from London newspapers, which reported the event as early as August 11, 1880, a full week before Conrad's departure on the *Loch Etive*. Among others, the *Daily Chronicle*, the *Globe*, the *Times*, and the *Daily News* all reported the abandonment and the saving of ship and crew intermixed with horror at the cowardice of the men who deserted her. Wrote the *Chronicle*: "We sincerely trust that no Englishman was amongst the boatload of cowards who left the *Jeddah* and her thousand passengers to shift for themselves." (*Conrad's Eastern World*, p. 62). Even if Conrad missed these news reports, his later visits to Singapore would have brought him into contact with the story, which stayed alive as gossip and as a cautionary tale.

† Almost fifteen in all, if we include those who put themselves knowingly into suicidal situations: Jim, Razumov, Heyst, Brierly, Peyrol, Flora de Barral, and Decoud, among others, from every stage of Conrad's writing career.

When Conrad used the *Cutty Sark* episode, as also the *Jeddah* incident, he found coordinates for each in his own background and experience, seeing in both patterns of abandonment and rescue, or attempt at rescue, that had deep accumulated meaning from his own childhood, from his own sense of abandonment and rescue. Through these episodes, he could free, in himself, what may have been repressed beyond conscious recall in another man; and through his art, he could put himself in touch with aspects of his personality that would otherwise have been closed off to him except by means of analysis. In Part VI, on the workings of Conrad's powers of imagination—and his conscious sense of these powers—we can explore how he turned gossip, hearsay, and newspaper accounts into artistic forms that were the objective correlatives of his own childhood experiences, fears, and fantasy life.

When Conrad returned to London, in the latter part of April 1881, he began, as well, to accumulate the sights and sounds of London, the sense of a large "anarchistic" city that becomes the basic motif of *The Secret Agent.* Potential now in his conscious memory as well as in subconscious reaction to his Polish past were *Under Western Eyes, Lord Jim, Nostromo,* "The Secret Sharer," several short stories, and many of the episodes of *The Mirror of the Sea* and *A Personal Record.* Conrad was twenty-three and a half and only five years away from becoming a master mariner. For a boy who had in the eyes of his uncle completed so little, he had accomplished a great deal. He had settled some of the seemingly irresolvable conflicts of his Polish background; he was studying for his chief mate's exam and building up the sea experience necessary for that post; and he was accumulating tales, episodes, and incidents, storing them away in memory. The third of his lives was becoming implicit.

Bobrowski wrote twice in May 1881, expressing delight at Conrad's safe return from the Antipodes and then thrusting between them some of his customary caustic: "I was greatly pleased to be able to give you a surprise by announcing your half-allowance and not the quarterly allowance that you were expecting. Usually young people expect more than they should. This time, however, if I can believe in your assurance (and why should I doubt it?) you have shown a greater maturity for your age than could be expected."

Tadeusz mentions that he expects his nephew to "sit for at least one examination if not two" during the next three years, and the allowance will provide an opportunity for Conrad to remain in London to pursue his studies. He suggests that the latter find something nearer than Australia or Cape Horn and asks if he can possibly spend some weeks with him in Wiesbaden, after September. Tadeusz says he will leave, in the middle of July, for Ischl via Lwow and Vienna, arriving July 26/August 7 for the tenth anniversary of the death of his daughter, Józefa. After four weeks in Marienbad, he would like to go for the "grape cure" to Wiesbaden, where they could possibly meet in October of 1881, their first sight of each other since Conrad's suicide attempt in Marseilles in 1878. Bobrowski cautions Conrad, however, not to waste his time on shore waiting for the two-week meeting and, if necessary, to accept even a distant voyage.

In Bobrowski's next letter, dated May 18/30, 1881, we can follow Conrad's activities as they are reflected in his uncle's remarks. Conrad had evidently indicated that the pressure of work—studying, presumably, for his chief mate's license—precluded a fall meeting in Wiesbaden. "I was very pleased," Tadeusz writes, "that you look with adult determination and common sense at all the difficulties which prevent our meeting, instead of becoming submerged by grief and lamentation, which can lead nowhere except to a loss of energy." In the same letter, Tadeusz indicates that his health is deteriorating—"the machine is run down and needs repairing," a mechanical image in keeping with his own positivistic-naturalistic view of men and events.

Bobrowski's next two letters include some contradictory matters and may even imply some deception on Conrad's part as a way of gaining financial help from his uncle. Conrad evidently wrote that he was planning a long voyage, and Tadeusz confirms that they will not be able to meet. He warns his nephew not to forget his Polish and suggests that he send some contributions to *Wędrowiec* (*The Wanderer*, a Warsaw weekly).

> It would be an exercise in your native tongue—that thread which binds you to your country and countrymen, and finally a tribute to the memory of your father who always wanted to and did serve his country by his pen. Think about this, young man, collect some reminiscences from the voyage to Australia and send them as a sample—the address of *Wędrowiec* is known in Warsaw. Six reports sent from different parts of the world during the year should not take much of your time: they would bring you some benefit and provide you with a pleasant recreation, while giving pleasure to others.

Most important to us is Bobrowski's recognition of Conrad's writing talent in Polish, not at all idle flattery coming from a man who kept a long journal of some distinction and read the best of literature.

Tadeusz's next letter, from Marienbad, is another matter altogether.

> Thank God that you survived, that you are alive and only had a few days in hospital, which this time has provided the necessary refuge, and that you had the uncommon luck to emerge safely from that ill-fated adventure! It is true that I should have preferred it if together with your bones you had saved your belongings, but what has happened has happened and we must both reconcile ourselves to that and patch up your present poverty as well as we can.

Tadeusz goes on to say that he thinks the shipowners of the *Anna Frost*, on which Conrad lost his kit and almost his life, should negotiate for compensation for equipment lost by its officers as well as for the ship. "But perhaps it is not practised in a country where the rich manage well, while no one thinks of the poor." Bobrowski reacted, apparently, precisely as Conrad had planned, and the larger question is whether Conrad really sailed on the *Anna* or *Annie Frost.* First, there is no question that the *Annie Frost* existed and that she was severely damaged in an accident on June 11, 1881. But that was the *Annie,* not the *Anna Frost.* The latter name has not turned up on any registry lists, and Tadeusz was usually extremely accurate with names. Second, Conrad's name did not appear on the crew's list of the *Annie Frost,* and when he signed on the *Palestine,* his next ship, he gave his preceding berth as the *Loch Etive.* Thus, we are left with two alternatives: that Conrad did sail on the *Annie Frost* for that eight-day period bound for Cochin China and did lose his gear and almost his life; or, more likely, that he manufactured the accident as a way of getting hold of sufficient money to tide him over until he found a berth.* Or else he lost his gear in some other way and feared to tell his uncle the truth. Whatever the facts, he gained ten pounds beyond his regular allowance, an extra for a "mariner in distress," his uncle put it.

Bobrowski then turns to what is apparently a speculative deal on Conrad's part, which he says he does not oppose provided the young seaman can speculate with his own money. "Since you are a Nałęcz, beware of risky speculations based only on hope; for your grandfather squandered all his property speculating, and your Uncle, speculating always with other people's money and on credit, got into debt." Exactly what the deal was to be and who the fellow speculator, a man named Sutherland, we cannot determine, and it may well have been nothing.

Tadeusz closes this extremely lengthy letter with a report on Dr. Izydor Kopernicki, the anthropologist and physician who was at one time briefly a guardian of Conrad. As we noted above, Kopernicki was collecting skulls for "comparative studies of human races based on types," an outgrowth of the nineteenth-century interest in craniology and other physical characteristics as ways of comprehending personality and racial types. Conrad was himself to introduce the Lombrosan types in *The Secret Agent,* satirizing the whole method as dehumanizing and mechanical, in a sense subhuman. As we saw, Kopernicki requested that Conrad collect skulls of natives and write on each

* In his original biography, Jean-Aubry mentioned that Conrad "seems to have embarked in a ship, the *Anna Frost,* but of this there is no trace in official records" (I, 65). In his later *Life of Conrad,* Jean-Aubry dropped some of the hesitation, merely qualifying the voyage by saying it was not a very "explicit" episode. There, he called the ship "the *Anna Frost* (or *Forst*) . . ." (p. 91). Baines was the first to suggest that Conrad had manufactured the incident: "It may well be that he had planned to sail in the *Annie Frost* and that this was the prospective long voyage to which Bobrowski had alluded in an earlier letter. The episode had an uncanny sequel: the *Annie Frost* did in fact founder on this voyage, but not until just over a year later, when she was nearing home" (p. 69).

an identification, a particular mission he turned down; instead, he gave Dr. Kopernicki a list of places where he could find correspondents to help him.

By the time Conrad received this letter in late August or early September, he had been out of a berth for almost five months—one more long period when we have little precise knowledge of what he was doing. We do know he was studying for his chief mate's examination, and toward fulfilling the time at sea needed for that application, he accepted a berth on an old barque, the 425-ton *Palestine,* an ill-fated ship if ever there was one. Conrad, however, could sail as second mate, and his career would be stymied if he were to turn down a posting he did not particularly like.

Conrad must have complained bitterly about the *Palestine,* for Bobrowski mentions matters of pride and yet forbearance, his view of Conrad's twin heritage.

> It seems to me that you are not very satisfied with your post: is it because being on a "barque" touches on your honour? Then, of course, £4 a month is disrespectful to your pocket, and, finally, the captain seems to you to be merely a "creature," which gives me a sad picture of his intellect. However, perhaps the last point will enable you to distinguish yourself as a "man conscious of his craft, and useful."*

Conrad's voyage on the *Palestine* imprinted itself upon his imagination, eventually finding itself transformed into "Youth," where it is narrated by Marlow, Conrad's first conscious shaping of memory beyond a third-person narrative. In the Author's Note written in 1917, some thirty-six years after the voyage and nineteen years after he wrote his version of it in "Youth," Conrad called it a "feat of memory . . . a record of experience." He adds, however, that the "experience, in its facts, in its inwardness and in its outward colouring, begins and ends in myself."

The *Palestine*—the ship of fact and not the mythical *Judea* of "Youth"—was to make a routine trip, sailing from London on September 21, 1881, to Newcastle-upon-Tyne for a cargo of coal, and then to Bangkok, with a crew of thirteen under Captain Beard. It was a prosaic ship, itself twenty-three years old, Conrad's own age, on a prosaic voyage, the single exception being that Conrad was sailing for the first time as second mate. This fact, seemingly minor in retrospect, must have created some aura of romanticism.

---

* As part of the younger generation which Bobrowski had so much difficulty in understanding, we must include Conrad's former tutor, Adam Pulman. Apparently, Pulman was a trickster with money and deceived several older people, including Conrad's uncle. Tadeusz writes: "From him [Dr. Kopernicki, in Montreux-Vernet] I heard about Pulman—apparently during his last examinations he tricked a number of people out of money, including Dr. K. out of 200 gulden. He turned a deaf ear to all calls for repayment, ignoring them as he did mine. . . . Write to him to Sambor; perhaps that will move him, for to your Uncle 600 roubles means a lot" (August 30/September 10, 1881).

Conrad, at least in his own eyes, was moving slowly toward a command; and his perceptions, his awareness of detail, his incessant staring into the sea and sail must have taken on a more acute sharpness, a more profound sense of mythical power. Beard himself, a man of fifty-seven, a fatherly, even grandfatherly, figure, was not the type of man calculated to bring out the best in Conrad. There would be a mixture of rebellion, translated into fantasies, and a sense of duty. Conrad would be very aware of his greenness—he called the story "Youth"—in a ship commanded by older men (the first mate, Mahon, was fifty), on which he was a twenty-three-year-old second mate.

In "Youth," he makes himself even younger, twenty, and he speaks of it as a "memorable affair," in this case a spur to his imagination. Marlow emphasizes his uniqueness, saying in "Youth": "It was my first voyage to the East, and my first voyage as second mate; it was my skipper's first command. . . . What induced him to accept me was a wonder. I had come out of a crack Australian clipper, where I had been third officer, and he seemed to have a prejudice against crack clippers as aristocratic and high-toned. . . . Fancy! Second mate for the first time—a really responsible officer! I wouldn't have thrown up my new billet for a fortune."

This is Marlow speaking. The plain facts of the *Palestine* defy romanticism. The captain and first mate were old, the ship was ancient, and the cargo of coal, besides being dirty, was difficult to control. A captain of fifty-seven named Beard and a cargo of shifting coal already seemed destined for trouble. It came only shortly after sailing from London, at Gravesend (later site of the *Nellie* in "Heart of Darkness"), where it was delayed for a week. It left Gravesend—the name itself an ill portent for any venture, whether a voyage to the East or a verbal journey to the Congo—on September 28 and ran into heavy winds and high seas. The short trip up England's east coast took three weeks, so that the *Palestine* had to defer her loading and wait in Newcastle for six weeks. She was already almost two months overdue. On November 29, nine weeks after Conrad had left London, the ship sailed from Newcastle, with just under six hundred tons of coal, for Bangkok, with almost a new crew, the original having fallen ill or deserted.

The Court of Enquiry report indicates that once in the English Channel—a fury at this time of year—"the vessel encountered a succession of heavy gales, losing sail and springing a leak on 24 December 1881." Under these conditions, the crew refused to proceed, and the vessel, already three hundred miles from England, returned to Falmouth on the Cornish peninsula. All but ninety tons of the cargo of coal was removed and stored under cover, and the ship underwent repairs.

As though trapped in some slow-moving nightmare, the *Palestine* remained in Falmouth from January 10, 1882, to September 17, 1882, a total of eight months. In this period, Conrad apparently went up to London, if we accept Marlow's version of the story, where he blew three months' pay on some good food, a "new railway rug," and a complete set of Byron's works. The delay must have been agonizing, for Conrad complained to his uncle, who answered that he understood his nephew's impatience at the limbo-like situation. Tadeusz wrote:

> Your misfortunes of the past year fill me with despair! I purposely refer to the "past year," for I hope and trust that the "malchance" will leave you alone this year. Certainly your success depends to some extent on chance or luck, but your judgement plays an important part as well. This time at least, after the wreck [*Annie Frost*], cool judgement seems to have deserted you when you accepted such a wretched ship as the *Palestine.* I quite understand, my dear boy, that you decided to do so in order to avoid being a burden to me by a long stay in London, also by serving as a second officer to qualify for your examination for a first officer. But, you didn't take into account that if as a result of all the mishaps and accidents that are bound to happen in a situation such as yours you should become sick or injured, I would not abandon you! . . . Both your Captain Beard and you appear to me like desperate men who look for knocks and wounds, while your ship-owner [John Wilson of London, "Wilmer, Wilcox" in "Youth"] is a rascal who risks the lives of 10 good men for the sake of a blackguardly profit.

Bobrowski indicates his financial support for his nephew and suggests that Conrad return to London: ". . . curb your noble ambition and do what reason dictates."

A year in all was to pass before the *Palestine* would leave with her cargo of coal for Bangkok, a lifetime for her second mate. In "Youth," Marlow speaks of the horror of that time. "It seemed as though we had been forgotten by the world, belonged to nobody, would get nowhere; it seemed that, as if bewitched, we would have to live for ever and ever in that inner harbour, a derision and a by-word to generations of long-shore loafers and dishonest boatmen." Successive crews deserted, and the *Palestine* obtained a fresh crew only the day before sailing. Conrad must have read a great deal, and formed plans for his chief mate's exam, his sense of urgency perhaps hastened by his lack of respect for both top officers of the *Palestine.* He could not have been completely downcast or hopeless about his career, for Bobrowski's letter to him for May 14/26, 1882, demonstrates "inexpressible pleasure" at Conrad's energetic letter, "so full of exuberant ideas and the desire to work." Of course, this distant response to Conrad's letter is rather different from the way Marlow presents that dismal time in port.

Another of Conrad's plans may have involved a business venture, for Tadeusz moves rapidly to a discussion of money, pointing out that, for Polish gentry, money-making was a "filthy" business; but that part of their tradition no longer holds. One must move beyond traditions toward realities:

> You have now lived for some years in England and have been taking

> part in the life there and you will have learned to respect money, and it therefore probably surprises you to hear me calling it "filthy." This expression is a survival from the "romantic period" in which I was born and grew up, and to some extent it reflects our national character, a trait of which was supposed to be disinterestedness in money matters. . . . This is because we did not work to get it but worked rather to squander it! Now our esteem for it has increased, mine possibly more than others, for we have come to realize that it is the "nervus rerum" and the basis of both the external and inner independence of both an individual and a whole society.

Although Conrad was stalled in Falmouth, neither sailing nor making money, his position was not quite that of Sisyphus. He could have left the *Palestine* and sought another berth; or he could have given up the sea altogether. Whatever hesitations he felt, and they were surely intense, he made no move to leave, even though he may have used this time to think through alternate careers. We have no evidence for this, but it is quite possible Conrad was arriving at the same conclusion as his uncle when the latter praised his nephew's writing style (in Polish), and Conrad—now reading deeply in English literature—began to harbor the idea of a writing career. In any event, the semi-retired year on the *Palestine*, most of it in the quiet of Falmouth, gave him an unusual amount of time for contemplation.

Conrad had apparently shown interest in Poland's fortunes based on a Pan-Slavic movement, although what benefit he could foresee for Poland in such a Russian-dominated alliance one cannot tell. In any event, he was trying to find some way in which the Polish future could be improved, perhaps in a loose alliance with other Slavic countries which would resist Russian influence—although Conrad, later, insisted that Poland was not a Slavic but a Western nation. We note that his idea, as romantic as Apollo's twenty years earlier, comes from afar (from Falmouth) and is a kind of daydream. Bobrowski's answer, based on Realpolitik, contains a sharp sense of how nations seemingly cooperate with each other so as the better to deceive each other. Since Tadeusz was abroad and thus beyond Russian censorship, he could express himself freely on these extremely sensitive issues of Polish nationalism, in which he reveals himself to be as patriotic as Conrad's father. Sounding like Bismarck, Bobrowski writes:

> What you write about our hopes based on Panslavism is in theory both splendid and feasible, but it meets great difficulty in practice. You don't take into account the significance which actual numbers have in the affairs of this world. Each of the more influential nations starts by relying apparently on the Panslavic ideal and by forgetting about its own interests—but secretly and almost unconsciously relies on some aspect of its existence which will ensure its leadership. You yourself have fallen into the same error, attributing to our country certain positive qualities, which

> are partly but not wholly true. And so Russia does not interpret Panslavism otherwise than as a means of russifying all other nations or even converting them to the Orthodox church. . . . And to our claim that we have a higher culture and a longer history they reply: this was only the life and culture of one class [the gentry] which claimed to be a nation (this contains a grain of truth) and that only she, Russia, will develop the real elements of the people.

Tadeusz's projection of coming events is tinged by his ever-present sense of human duplicity, which makes any romantic assessment fallible; in this respect, as in so many others, he recalls the figure Stein in *Lord Jim:*

> I am certain that eventually out of this chaos some form of federation will emerge, but by that time I shall be long dead and possibly you too. In the meantime, since like pariahs we are deprived of our own political and national rights, we, more than the others, have to preserve our individuality and our own standpoint, till the time comes when Nemesis, as a result of our own efforts, spins out some situation which will give us the right to have a real national existence—and possibly something more.

The use of Nemesis is itself interesting, since Nemesis measured out to mortals both happiness and misery, and brought loss and suffering upon all those who were seemingly blessed with too many gifts of fortune. She was the great evener and moderator, and she remained at Conrad's elbow throughout his mature years, embodied in the Stein or Stein-like figure in nearly every major novel, and if not actually present, then implicit. The point, particularly, of Jim is that he never recognizes the presence of Nemesis, and therefore she can sport with him until his acceptance of death. In "Youth," Marlow speaks of a "stealthy Nemesis" which "lies in wait, pursues, overtakes so many of the conquering race, who are proud of their wisdom, of their knowledge, of their strength."

On September 17, 1882, the *Palestine* moved out of Falmouth harbor for the long, torturous voyage to Bangkok, a difficult trip under the best of conditions with the best of ships. The report of a marine Court of Enquiry, held at the Police Court, in Singapore, on April 2, 1883, catches Conrad's first voyage as second mate:

> The passage was tedious owing to persistent light winds, but nothing unusual occurred until noon of the 11th March, when a strong smell resembling paraffin oil was perceived; at this time the vessel's position was lat. 2 36 S and long. 105 45 E. Banca Strait [also called Bangka Strait, off the coast of Sumatra, in the Java Sea]. Next day smoke was discovered issuing from the coals on the port side of main hatch. Water was thrown over them until the smoke abated, the boats were lowered, water placed in them. On the 13th some coals were thrown overboard, about 4 tons, and more water poured down the hold. On the 14th, the hatches being on but

> not battened down, the decks blew up fore and aft as far as the poop. The boats were then provisioned and the vessel headed for the Sumatra shore. About 3 p.m. the S.S. "Somerset" came alongside in answer to signals and about 6 p.m. she took the vessel in tow. Shortly afterwards the fire rapidly increased and the master of the "Palestine" requested the master of the "Somerset" to tow the barque on shore. This being refused, the tow-rope was slipped and about 11 p.m. the vessel was a mass of fire, and all hands got into the boats, 3 in number. The mate and 4 seamen in one boat, the 2nd mate with three hands in another and the master in the long boat with 3 men. The boats remained by the vessel until 8.30 a.m. on the 15th. She was still above water, but inside appeared a mass of fire. The boats arrived at Mintok [Muntok, on the island of Bangka, off the southeast coast of Sumatra] at 10 p.m. on the 15th, and the master reported the casualty to the harbour master. The officers and crew came on to Singapore in the British steamer "Sissie" arriving on 22nd March.

The court exonerated captain and crew, giving the cause of the fire as spontaneous combustion, the result of an unusually protracted voyage. In hindsight, we see a prosaic voyage, with a bone-breaking ending to it—a crew forced to work day and night to extinguish the fire and then to pump out the same water, all the while fearing the worst; then the destructive explosion, the ship slowly consuming itself, the crew caught between desire for escape and their duty not to abandon ship until the situation became hopeless.

In "Youth," a story that comes the closest of any of his fiction to reproducing earlier experiences, Conrad reshaped this experiential material in crucial ways. We could call attention to the alteration of basic details, to the protraction of the experience in the story as contrasted with the much shorter time the small boats took to arrive at Muntok (not Bangkok). Such differences, however, are themselves negligible. The significant element comes in the shaping of the material through Marlow, an older man himself dealing with several levels of experience and memory. This shaping suggests Conrad had already developed an angle of vision, a mode of observation, long before he turned to writing. For the memory, as he recalled it later in Marlow's words, had already achieved an economy and a form which gave him a start toward its utilization. That is, Conrad could only have used it later if he had previously observed it as something that could be manipulated for purposes beyond itself as a pure and simple experience.

Even as Conrad went through the extremely trying experience on the *Palestine*, we can speculate, he was placing it in some perspective with his reading as a teenager and with his dreams of achieving the exploits of Odysseus and the Don. He was turning the *Palestine* incident into a preconceived romantic ideal, and while it did not exactly fit—for someone else it probably would not have fitted at all—for him it was necessary to reshape what had occurred so as not to lose the potential of the romance fixed in his mind. Marlow, from his initial introduction, treats the episode as a "first." That word reappears throughout—his first command, his first berth as second mate, the skipper's first command. Further, he reduces his age to twenty, from the twenty-four–twenty-five in actuality; and he tunnels the experience twenty-two years back, when it was only sixteen. These are minor changes, but reducing his age creates a more "romantic" distinction; at the same time, he makes Captain Beard and First Mate Mahon appear even older: old men of the sea.

In casting the experience as a recollection, a sequence fixed by time and frozen, as it were, Conrad was trying to approximate the way he had seen it *then*, not now. When he wrote the story, he was forty-one, going on forty-two, the same age as Marlow; while the Conrad on the *Palestine* was twenty-four–twenty-five. Such an artistic reworking of the experience gives a glimpse into the working of his mind both earlier and later. The recasting is no certainty, of course, that Conrad was already observing with the eye of the artist, or even conscious of what he would do with the experience, but it gives some intimation of a sequence very consciously fixed in the observer's memory. Near the end of his narrative, Marlow says: " 'This was the East of the ancient navigators, so old, so mysterious, resplendent and sombre, living and unchanged, full of anger and promise' "—when he says this, we are thrown back into Conrad's Polish years, the years of reading and daydreaming.*

Another aspect, often neglected in discussions of the story proper, is its humorous tone. Once again, the humor indicates the distance of an experience which has already been observed, as if the subject were himself outside the sequence of events which were happening to him: When the smoke on the *Judea* becomes poisonous and thick, the crew begin to pour large amounts of the Indian Ocean into the hold. Marlow comments: " 'We poured salt water as into a barrel without a bottom. It was our fate to pump in that ship, to pump out of her, to pump into her; and after keeping water out of her to save ourselves from being drowned, we frantically poured water into her to save ourselves from being burnt.' " Although there is no way to move back with certainty from Marlow describing this to the observations of the twenty-four-year-old Conrad, nevertheless the story is sufficiently rooted in historical and psychological fact for us to assume, however speculatively, that the youthful seaman had already objectified the experience, which would be the initial step toward his observing it for purposes outside the nature of the event itself.

---

* Strikingly, in "Youth," he remarks: " 'To Bankok! Magic name, blessed name. Mesopotamia [recalling Odysseus] wasn't a patch on it.' "

CHAPTER 10

Moving Toward the *Narcissus*

CONRAD was free of the *Palestine* on April 3, 1883, receiving back wages of $171.12 in Malayan currency for the greater part of his ordeal. He was twenty-five, without a ship, and his "romantic" view of the East had taken place at Muntok—what he later described as "a damned hole without any beach and without any glamour"—and not at Bangkok as originally planned. Now in Singapore, after eight years of sporadic seagoing, his career seemed stalled and lacking in continuity, the pattern for the remainder of his ten years at sea, with almost as much time spent on shore as on board ship. No matter how diligently Conrad applied himself to his sea career, and his achievement was considerable indeed, he did not pursue it with the single-mindedness of a man with nothing else on his mind.

Even now, as he moved toward his license as chief mate, he appeared to hold back, to be following some inner voice unconnected to a maritime career. One can speculate that he was, at this time, wavering, although no other clear alternatives had presented themselves and he may have remained at sea by default. That he was seeking other opportunities we shall see shortly, when he asks his uncle for an advance of money to purchase an interest in a firm of shipping agents, Barr, Moering & Co. Yet even that was not a solid commitment to a business career, for when Bobrowski agreed to lend between £300 and £350, Conrad was pursuing another berth as second mate. In the next two years, he was to intermix plans for his chief's and master's examinations, further business ventures, and even a whaling enterprise.

Of great interest at this stage of his career is the fact that Conrad had been establishing relationships with people in England. As noted, he had already met G. F. W. Hope (in January 1880). He also came to know Adolf Krieger, who was part of the firm of Barr, Moering & Co., shipping agents, and who later helped Conrad obtain his Congo steamer captaincy; as well as a Mr. Ward, with whom he lived in Tollington Park, and to whom Bobrowski forwarded Conrad's allowance. Conrad was also, by 1885, to become acquainted with the Kliszczewskis, and especially with the son, Spiridion. Of the above, Hope and Krieger were to be significant friends, with Conrad and Krieger breaking only in the later 1890s, apparently over Conrad's indebtedness. It is very possible that Conrad lodged with the Kriegers between 1881 and 1885, since the former lived at 6, Dynevor Road, Stoke Newington, and the newly married Krieger also lived in Stoke Newington.

For years, Conrad's movements were little more focused than those of any seaman picking up friends and lodgings as he went along, between voyages. In the middle of this uncertain time, in July and August of 1883, he visited with his uncle at Marienbad and Teplitz in Czechoslovakia, the first time they had met since Conrad's suicide attempt in 1878. This meeting seemed especially advisable from Bobrowski's point of view, since he felt his health deteriorating and did not know when he would be able to see his nephew again. From Conrad's point of view, the meeting was also desirable; despite his uncle's caustic comments, there was undeniably affection between them. And from the nephew's position, Bobrowski was his sole family connection, the kind of father figure he evidently needed throughout his life.

They had originally expected to meet in Cracow, but Tadeusz impressed upon Conrad the need for him to stay in London for his examination (for chief mate) and for naturalization. Apparently, Conrad had been telling his uncle for over a year that the examination was imminent. When they planned to meet in the summer of 1883, the examination was still more than a year in the future. Naturalization was of course urgent. As Tadeusz remarks: "I must admit that I should prefer to see your face a little later, and as that of a free citizen of a free country, rather than earlier and still as that of a citizen of the world." The rest of this May-June letter keeps Conrad informed about his first cousins, Uncle Kazimierz's children, who besides being penniless were seriously ill as well. They remained a financial and emotional burden to Bobrowski for the rest of his life.

Conrad responded frequently in this period; Tadeusz's return letters indicate several received. In his next letter to Conrad (dated June 12/24, 1883), Bobrowski indicates that gastric disorders have forced him to alter his plans, so that instead of meeting in Cracow, they will meet in Marienbad; ". . . and this month spent together will be a rest for you, a cure for me, and a long-awaited pleasure for us both." His letter is full of detailed plans, indicative of his compulsive need to control every aspect of Conrad's journey from England as well as the financial arrangements. He tells Conrad to try to pay for his own journey, rather than forcing him to send money from Odessa to London. He assures his nephew that all expenses will be refunded to him immediately on his arrival. If he needs funds for purposes of naturalization, he should borrow from Krieger—and Tadeusz will cover that also. Apparently,

Conrad began to borrow from Krieger, continued it over a long period of time, and his failure to pay back the loans, or complications arising from his indebtedness, led to a cooling of the friendship.

A few days later, Tadeusz wrote worriedly that Conrad had not responded to his registered letter; the latter, in fact, had written that because of the need to sit for his examination for chief mate on July 4 he had given up plans for naturalization. This leads Bobrowski to repeat all his plans about their meeting in Marienbad, about details of Conrad's trip, and reassurances about reimbursement. He ends his letter with an address to Conrad as "a first Officer of H.M. the Queen of Great Britain which you no doubt are by now."

The examination, however, was still so distant that it is difficult to understand why Conrad continued to refer to it this soon, unless he was using the impending ordeal as a method of controlling his situation vis-à-vis his uncle, or as a way of explaining his inactivity. He was not to sail again until early September, almost six months after he had left the ill-fated *Palestine.* One other possibility occurs: that Conrad was deliberately fudging the date of the examination so that in the event he failed he could disguise the fact. Since there is evidence that he did fail it the first time he sat for it, on November 17, 1884, we can, with hindsight, suggest he feared the result long before then and was simply protecting himself against a declaration of failure. If his uncle could be kept from the actual date through constant postponement, then Conrad could take cover behind that confusion.

The meeting between the two, for a month first at Marienbad and then at Teplitz,* went very well. Conrad apparently carried over from his early days in Poland a real affection for his uncle, as he felt later for even the most distant members of his family. Perhaps because of his loneliness at sea, and those almost endlessly empty, solitary days, he was tenacious about family ties. Even as we see him wandering, the Odysseus of his dreams, he sought, however futilely, more solid roots. His 1880s were characterized by this kind of search, for something firmer than a wandering career; just as the 1870s can be viewed, in retrospect, as the period of his wanderlust—a *Wanderjahrzehnt*—with a desire for nothing more substantial than a ship's timbers beneath his feet.

Bobrowski's letter to Conrad, for August 19/31, 1883, indicates his pleasure at seeing his nephew and then hearing from him as Conrad returned to England by way of Dresden. Tadeusz speaks of his ills and describes his cure, which is to induce sweating so as to prevent "the formation of uric

* On August 14, Conrad, we know, was at Teplitz. An 1883 photograph derives from this period, taken at Marienbad. He was twenty-five (not twenty-six, as Jean-Aubry indicates) and very respectable in appearance, if his photo can be accepted as typical. He is solid, handsome, reliable, with his face hair carefully trimmed, his mouth firm, and his eyes—the most obvious feature—bright and penetrating, yet thoughtful.

acids and salts" that cause swelling at joints and arthritic pains. From his description, we realize that Bobrowski has classic gout, the formation of uric acid at the joints, with severe pain and loss of energy and will. It was a family disease, which Conrad was to suffer from for most of his mature life; attacks would immobilize him for days and weeks at a time, draining his energy and exhausting his desire to go on. Evidently, his attacks of gout were triggered not only by the physiology of the disease but by extreme nervousness and worry, and once he entered his writing career, money worries, in particular, seemed to create the "gout situation," although the precise etiology of the disease was surely more profound.

Bobrowski's letter turns to now-familiar subjects, his nephew's seagoing and naturalization. Conrad had apparently discussed alternate professions and had mentioned that partnership with Adolf Krieger for which Tadeusz had allotted £300–350. This was Conrad's own money, as Bobrowski's Document makes clear. By the time Conrad received this letter, he was preparing to embark on his next ship, as second mate, on the *Riversdale*, a 1,490-ton sailing vessel bound for Madras, India. Conrad embarked on September 10 and left the ship on April 17, 1884, at Madras, apparently after a rift with the captain, L. B. McDonald. On Conrad's certificate of discharge, an important document for a seaman seeking a new berth, Captain McDonald declined to comment on his "Character for conduct," although next to his "Character for ability" he wrote "very good." Since Conrad's record as a seaman is unblemished except for this bad mark, we can speculate that he misbehaved, if he did, because of McDonald's poor seamanship. Jerry Allen reports that McDonald was relieved of his command of the *Riversdale* six weeks later after stranding it, badly damaged, two hundred miles up the coast from Madras. There is reason to believe that the rift between the captain and his second mate was based on professional competence, Conrad refusing to go along, perhaps, with a man whose ability he questioned or doubted. Since he reacted later to writers in terms of their professionalism or lack of it, we can assume that he brought the same expectations to the men under whom he served.*

* Conrad took court action against McDonald, to restore his good name as a seaman. According to Kazimierz Bobrowski's letter (December 8, 1884), Conrad won his case against his ex-captain and "came safely out of the whole affair" (Najder, p. 95). Whether this was true or not, in the inquiry following McDonald's stranding of the *Riversdale*, there was an investigation into the captain's grading of his second mate, Conrad Korzeniowski. Apparently, Conrad had reported McDonald to the doctor as drunk, for which he later apologized by letter, calling his statements baseless. McDonald, in turn, accused Conrad of having been asleep on watch on two or possibly three occasions. According to the evidence, Conrad agreed with this assessment and paid sixty rupees to defray costs for a replacement as second officer. Most likely, Conrad wanted to present an unblemished record and told his uncle he had won the case when, in fact, he had merely settled it.

There are intimations of the *Riversdale* voyage in Conrad's first popular novel, *Chance*, which appeared in 1914. McDonald had taken his wife with him on the *Riversdale*, and Powell, in *Chance*, comments on the mischief that a captain's wife can work on board a ship. Powell's comments are in keeping with his misogyny, but they perhaps reflect Conrad's own sense that professional competence is diluted if there are distractions. Powell says: "In the general opinion a skipper with his wife on board was more difficult to please; but whether to show off his authority before an admiring female, or from loving anxiety for her safety, or simply from irritation at her presence—nobody I ever heard on the subject could tell for certain."

The presence of women on board ship was for Powell, and for Conrad, an anomaly, for the primary appeal of the sea "lies in the suggestion of restless adventure which holds out that deep sensation to those who embrace it." Part of the attraction of the sea was its removal from land problems, from emotional entanglements, and, we can assume, from the conflicting emotions following from the presence of women. Although Conrad never shared Powell's misogyny, nevertheless the all-male crew of a ship creates its own bonding, and the presence of women, those land creatures suggesting marriage and children, can only be something very fearful. One goes to sea to escape the land, as much as one goes to sea for what it offers. Conrad may originally have been like Wordsworth's narrator in "Tintern Abbey," ". . . more like a man / Flying from something that he dreads than one / Who sought the thing he loved. . . ." but he came to view the sea as more than escape: as life itself, pure, untrammeled, pristine.

This time Conrad did not remain long on shore, for he journeyed across India from Madras, on the southeast coast, to Bombay on the west coast, where berths were more available. There, after declining service on a steamer, he saw a ship that was to play an enormous role in his imagination, going well beyond the details of the voyage itself. Sailing into the harbor of this swarming, very realistic coast city was the graceful *Narcissus*, a fateful event for the young sailor now in his mid-twenties. Jean-Aubry probably received the following description from Conrad:

> One evening he was sitting with other officers of the Mercantile Marine on the veranda of the Sailors' Home in Bombay, which overlooks the port, when he saw a lovely ship, with all the graces of a yacht, come sailing into the harbour. She was the *Narcissus*, of 1,300 tons [actually a little more, 1,336], built by a sugar refiner of Greenock nine years before. Her owner had originally intended her for some undertaking in connection with the Brazilian sugar trade. This had not come off, and subsequently he had decided to employ her in the Indian Ocean and the Far East.

The *Narcissus* was so fateful for a variety of reasons. As we shall see, Conrad experienced events and crewmen that profoundly stirred his imagination; to the extent that his 1897 novel, *The Nigger of the "Narcissus,"* was, at least in his own mind, a turning point in his career as a novelist. The very name of the ship, the only ship name he took directly for one of his titles, must have penetrated some area of experience in Conrad that lay beyond self-awareness, in those recesses that were already stirring and moving him toward his next and final career. The ship name, like the title of the later book, apparently fitted into his view of art itself, as something based on mirrors, memories, and reflections, an indirect, not a mimetic art. Conrad always balked at being called a sea novelist—first, because it really was not accurate; and second, and more importantly, because he felt that a "sea novelist" meant a mimetic author, one true to the dictates of realistic detail.

Conrad identified with the conjurers, with the narcissists, with that Don Quixote-like bag of conjuring tricks. After all, for years he had stared into watery depths and he would call one book of reminiscences a *mirror* of the sea. Although Orpheus and the Orphic tradition have much to tell us about the nature of art, Conrad identified more with the tradition associated with Medusa and Perseus as the mythical explanation of art. That is, Perseus could only resist the terrors of Medusa's look without being turned to obsidian if he immunized himself by catching her image *reflected in a mirror.* The mirror suggests a symbolic, imagistic, highly deceptive kind of art, in which reflection, refraction, distortion replace realistic presentation. Also, as Kenneth Burke has commented, the mirror allows the artist "to confront the risk [of immersion in art, of staring at the Medusa], but by the protection of an indirect reflection." The artist becomes medicine man, shaman, magical.

Conrad signed on the *Narcissus* on April 28, 1884, her destination being Dunkirk, France. Shortly before he died, Conrad gave Jean-Aubry some details in which his *Nigger* follows the voyage of the *Narcissus,* remarks which we quoted above. James Wait of the *Nigger* did not sail on the *Narcissus,* but on the *Duke of Sutherland;* and the real "Nigger" of the *Narcissus* was another man altogether. Apparently he was a thirty-five-year-old American black named Joseph Barron, who died at sea on September 24, when the ship was in the North Atlantic, three weeks from port. Conrad then continued, as reported by Jean-Aubry:

> Most of the personages I have portrayed actually belonged to the crew of the real *Narcissus,* including the admirable Singleton (whose real name was Sullivan), Archie, Belfast, and Donkin. I got the two Scandinavians from associations with another ship. All this is now old, but it was quite present before my mind when I wrote this book. I remember, as it had occurred but yesterday, the last occasion I saw the Nigger. That morning I was quarter officer, and about five o'clock I entered the double-bedded cabin where he was lying full length. On the lower bunk, ropes, fids and pieces of cloth had been deposited, so as not to have to take them down into the sail-room if they should be wanted at once. I asked him how he felt, but he hardly made me any answer. A little later a man brought him

> some coffee in a cup provided with a hook to suspend it on the edge of the bunk. At about six o'clock the officer-in-charge came to tell me that he was dead. We had just experienced an awful gale in the vicinity of the Needles, south of the cape, of which I have tried to give an impression in my book. . . .
>
> As to the conclusion of the book, it is taken from other voyages which I made under similar circumstances. It was, in fact, at Dunkirk, where I had to unload part of her cargo, that I left the *Narcissus.**

The departure of the sailing ship from Bombay into the vast expanses of the Arabian Sea and the Indian Ocean has a mythical, supernatural quality, a lonely boat on the edge of a great adventure in the loneliness of distant, mysterious places: a ship of life or a ship of death.

> The *Narcissus* left alone, heading south, seemed to stand resplendent and still upon the restless sea, under the moving sun. Flakes of foam swept past her sides; the water struck her with flashing blows; the land glided away slowly fading; a few birds screamed on motionless wings over the swaying mastheads. But soon the land disappeared, the birds went away; and to the west the pointed sail of an Arab dhow running for Bombay, rose triangular and upright above the sharp edge of the horizon, lingered and vanished like an illusion. Then the ship's wake, long and straight, stretched itself out through a day of immense solitude. The setting sun, burning on the level of the water, flamed crimson below the blackness of heavy rain clouds. The sunset squall, coming up from behind, dissolved itself into the short deluge of a hissing shower. It left the ship glistening from trucks to waterline, and with darkened sails. She ran easily before a fair monsoon, with her decks cleared for the night; and, moving along with her, was heard the sustained and monotonous swishing of the waves, mingled with the low whispers of men mustered aft for the setting of watches; the short plaint of some block aloft; or, now and then, a loud sigh of wind.

Even as Conrad entered into the experience on the *Narcissus* that intensified his attachment to the sea and led to his next step, the taking of his chief mate's examination—even as this occurred, he was moving slowly toward his next career in that *Narcissus* as it gracefully plowed the Indian waters of the subcontinent, a mythical ship racing toward France and England with a second mate who would immortalize her.

Conrad signed off the *Narcissus* on October 27, 1884, at Dunkirk, the ship's destination. Captain Duncan's comments on Conrad's certificate of discharge indicate a high recommendation: "This is to certify that Conrad Korzeniowski has served with me on board the ship Narcissus as second offi-

* There was, Allen and Baines tell us, no Sullivan on the *Narcissus*, but a Daniel Sullivan on the *Tilkhurst*. Archie was Archibald McLean from Scotland, and Belfast was James Craig of Belfast. Donkin cannot be clearly identified.

cer from 28/4/84 to 16/10/84 on a voyage from Bombay to Dunkerque for which I can recommend him to any Ship Master requiring his services as being a good and sober officer and should take him as Chief Officer if he should succeed in passing."

For the next six months, Conrad remained in London, studying for his chief mate's examination and then searching, once again, for a suitable berth. In *A Personal Record*, he left a witty and touching description of his examination, omitting, however, the fact that he had previously sat for it, on November 17, and apparently failed it, "having been found wanting in the subject of 'the Day's Work.' " In his personal memoir, Conrad made it appear that he had passed each of his three examinations on the first try, but that was incorrect with both his chief mate's and master's examinations; thus, he sat at least five times for the three certificates. In *A Personal Record*, Conrad transformed what must have been a harrowing experience, some of it perhaps attached to language as well as to actual seamanship, into a Dickensian description, taking advantage of twenty-five years of hindsight and accumulated wisdom. He wrote, in part:

> But when the time of ordeal came round again [after the ordeal of his second officer's test] the doorkeeper let me into another room, with the now familiar paraphernalia of models of ships and tackle, a board for signals on the wall, a big long table covered with official forms, and having an unrigged mast fixed to the edge. The solitary tenant was unknown to me by sight, though not by reputation, which was simply execrable. Short and sturdy as far as I could judge, clad in an old, brown, morning suit, he sat leaning on his elbow, his hand shading his eyes, and half averted from the chair I was to occupy on the other side of the table. He was motionless, mysterious, remote, enigmatical, with something mournful too in the pose, like that statue of Giuliano (I think) de Medici shading his face on the tomb of Michael Angelo, though, of course, he was far, far from being beautiful.

Conrad then moves into the proceedings, technicalities flying upon technicalities:

> He began by trying to make me talk nonsense. But I had been warned of that fiendish trait, and contradicted him with great assurance. He kept inscrutably silent for a moment, and then, placing me in a ship of a certain size at sea, under certain conditions of weather, season, locality, etc., etc.—all very clear and precise—ordered me to execute a certain manoeuvre. Before I was half through with it he did some material damage to the ship. Directly I had grappled with the difficulty he caused another to present itself, and when that too was met he stuck another ship before me, creating a very dangerous situation. I felt slightly outraged by this ingenuity in piling up trouble upon a man.

Conrad argued that he would have seen the ship before that, but the examiner, imperturbable, says that the weather was thick. The examinee begins to think that a berth on the doomed *Flying Dutchman* would be preferable to his present situation. At this point in the proceedings, the examiner has him so backed up with such little equipment left that Conrad asks for time since "so many accidents have happened that I really can't remember what there's left for me to work with." The examination, like Conrad's later life, came down to a sharp focus of will against adversity, the self against the meagerness of the means. The examiner praises the young man's work thus far, draws him out a little more, and then tells him that if there is nothing more to do, he can always say his prayers. In forty minutes, Conrad "escaped from the room thankfully—passed!" "I walked on air along Tower Hill, where so many good men had lost their heads, because, I suppose, they were not resourceful enough to save them." Now on December 3, 1884, his twenty-seventh birthday precisely, he could call himself a chief mate in the British merchant service.

On April 24, his search for a chief mate's berth unavailing, Conrad embarked at Hull as second mate on the *Tilkhurst,* a sailing ship of 1,527 tons. Whereas his voyage on the *Narcissus* had had overtones of one kind, his signing on the *Tilkhurst* had its own type of significance. For the *Tilkhurst* was to call at Penarth, near Cardiff, Wales, for a cargo of coal, and Conrad was requested by a Polish sailor named Komorowski to repay a small loan to a watchmaker in Cardiff. The watchmaker's name was Józef Kliszczewski, a man who had emigrated to England after the failure of the 1830 Polish insurrection, in which Conrad's paternal grandfather, among other relatives, had participated. The visit to Kliszczewski led to Conrad's friendship with his son, Spiridion, and that, in turn, was followed by his first attempts at letter writing in English, apart from his response to an ad in the *Evening Standard* for a seaman's berth. The letters show that by 1885, when the correspondence began, Conrad had mastered idiomatic English—as far as the demands of letter writing were concerned. Although the English is a little stiff and somewhat indebted to Polish prose styles, it is clearly English and not merely mental translations.

Conrad stayed in Penarth for five days while loading coal, and then on June 10, with much of the *Tilkhurst* crew changed, sailed for Singapore. The master was Captain Blake, an experienced seaman toward whom Conrad felt drawn. In *The Mirror of the Sea,* he left an affectionate account of Blake and his wife. "Well over fifty years of age when I knew him [Conrad writes], short, stout, dignified, perhaps a little pompous, he was a man of a singularly well-informed mind, the least sailor-like in outward aspect, but certainly one of the best seamen whom it has been my good luck to serve under." Conrad was particularly pleased when, at the end of the voyage of the *Tilkhurst,* in Dundee, Blake said that if Conrad ever needed a berth ". . . remember that as long as I have a ship you have a ship, too."

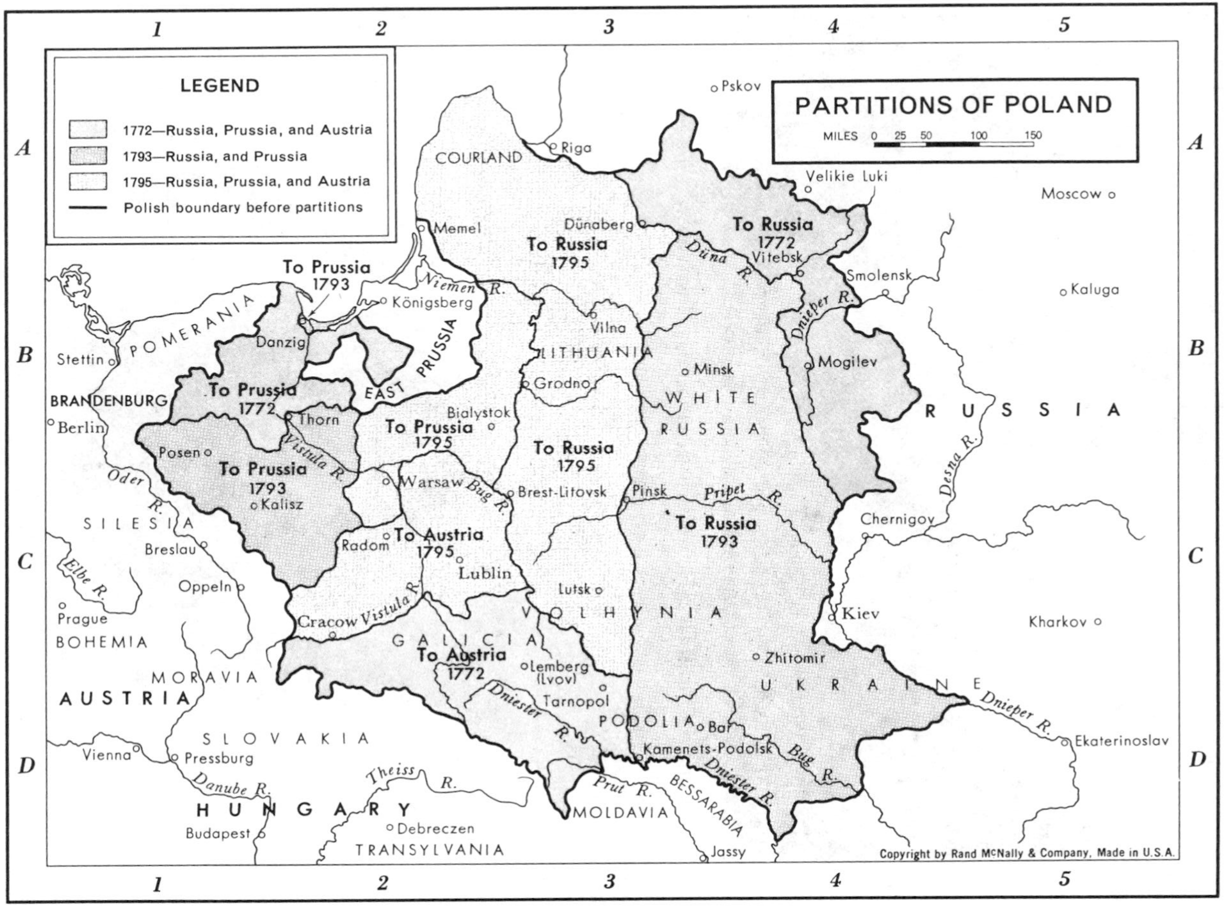

Conrad's Poland

Conrad's birthplace, Derebczynka Manor, near Berdyczów, the Ukraine

Ewa Bobrowska, Conrad's mother

Conrad, at about four

Jail and courtyard in Warsaw, where Apollo Korzeniowski was imprisoned

No. 12 Poselska Street, Cracow, where Apollo died. The inscription reads: In this house about 1869 Józef Konrad Korzeniowski, son of an exile poet, lived. He brought a Polish spirit to English literature which he enriched

Apollo's grave in Rakowicki Cemetery, Cracow. The inscription reads: To the man who loved his homeland, dedicated himself to it, and died for it. His compatriots

Florian Street, Cracow, where Conrad lived at No. 43 in 1869 and 1870

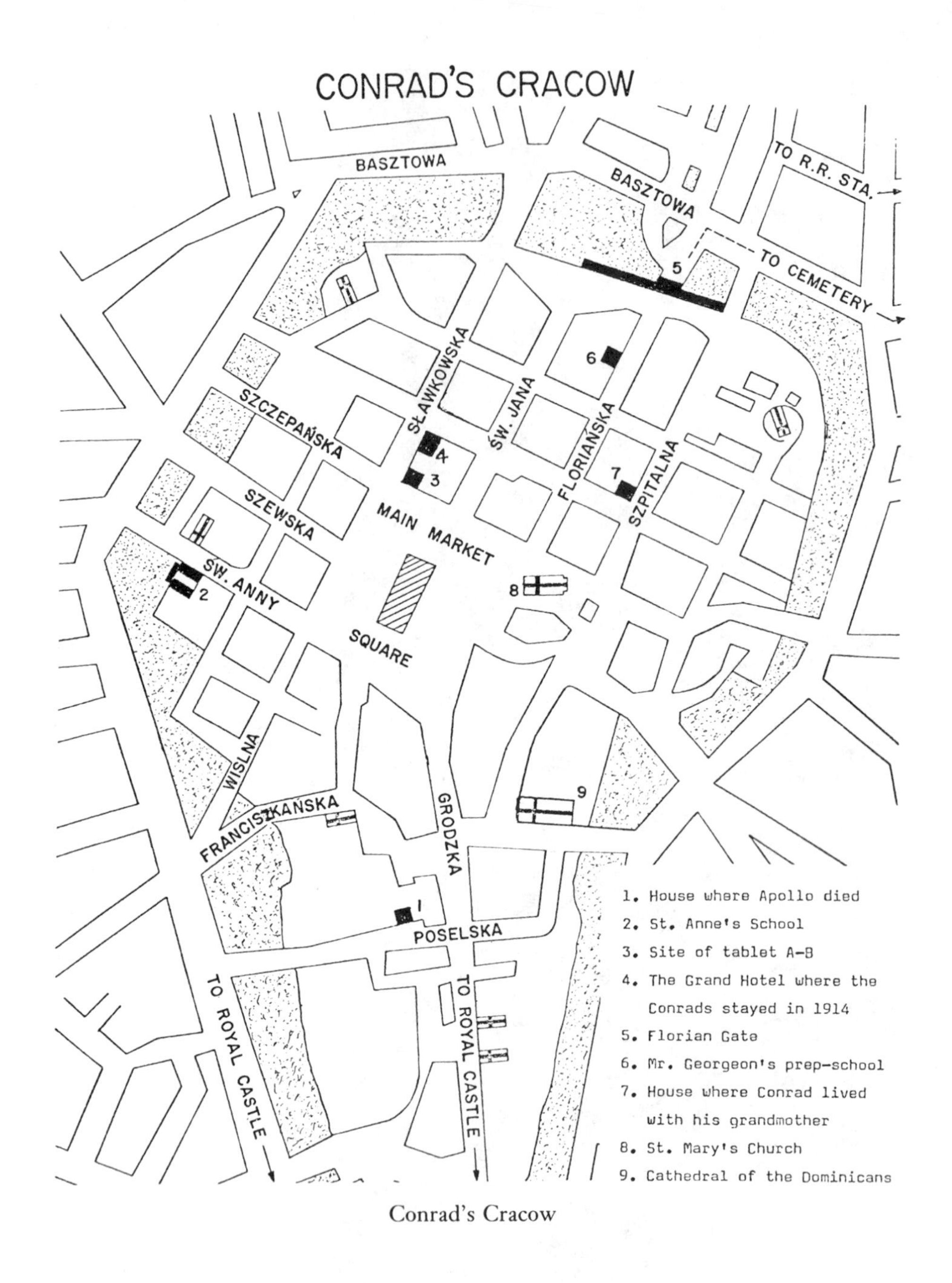

Conrad's Cracow

(*opposite*) Marseilles: the Vieux Port. Conrad lived a few streets away

Conrad in 1873, just before he left Cracow for Marseilles

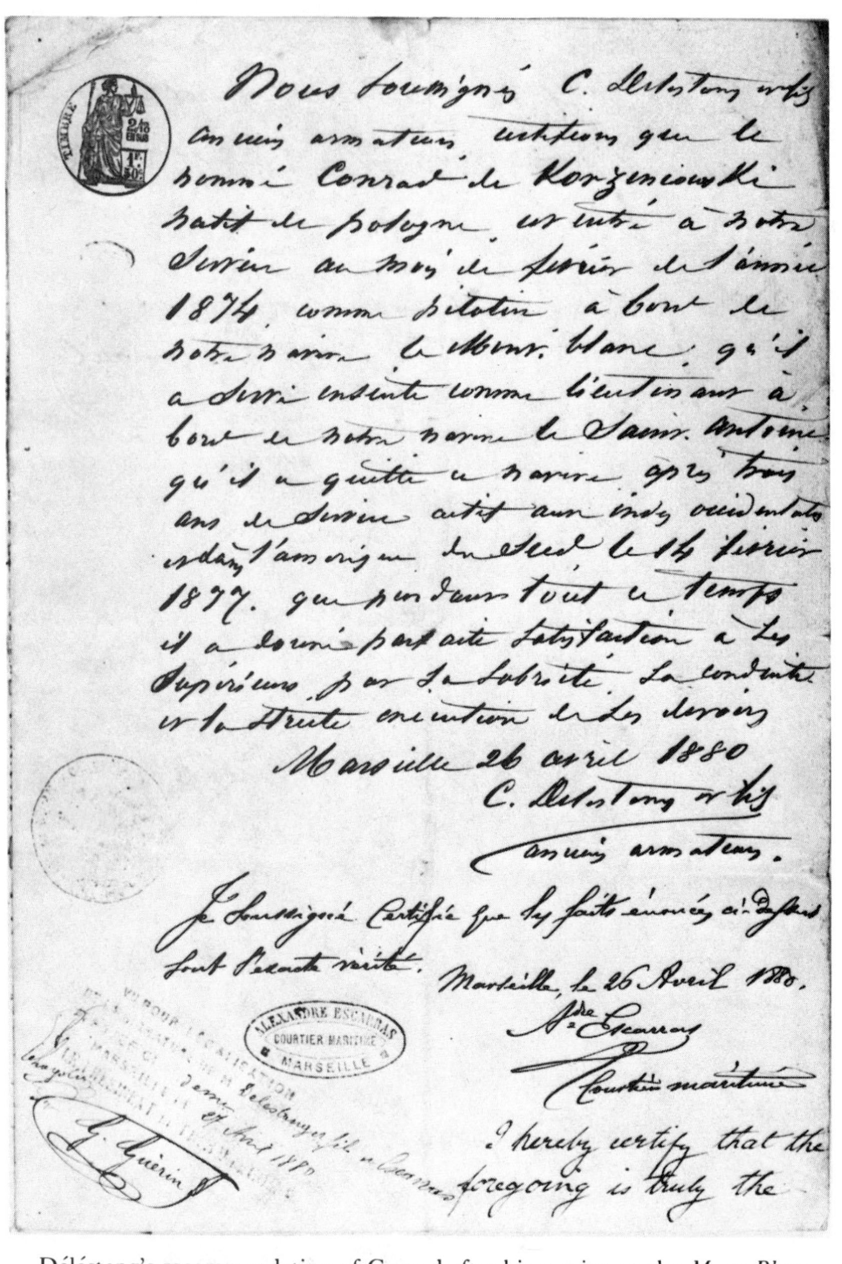
Nous soussignés C. Delestang et fils
anciens armateurs certifions que le
nommé Conrad de Korzeniowski
natif de Pologne est entré à notre
service au mois de février de l'année
1874. comme pilotin à bord de
notre navire le Mont-Blanc. qu'il
a servi ensuite comme lieutenant à
bord de notre navire le Saint-Antoine
qu'il a quitté ce navire après trois
ans de service actif aux Indes occidentales
et dans l'Amérique du Sud le 14 février
1877. que pendant tout ce temps
il a donné parfaite satisfaction à ses
supérieurs par sa sobriété, sa conduite
et la stricte exécution de ses devoirs

Marseille 26 avril 1880
C. Delestang et fils
anciens armateurs.

Je soussigné Certifie que les faits énoncés ci-dessus
sont l'exacte vérité.
Marseille, le 26 Avril 1880.
Ale Escarras
Courtier maritime

ALEXANDRE ESCARRAS
COURTIER MARITIME
MARSEILLE

I hereby certify that the
foregoing is truly the

Déléstang's recommendation of Conrad after his service on the *Mont-Blanc* and the *Saint-Antoine*

(*opposite*) View of St. Pierre, Martinique, where Conrad sailed on the *Mont-Blanc* and the *Saint-Antoine*

Lowestoft Harbour, where Conrad first landed on English soil in 1878

I here certify that the bearer Konrad K[illegible]zenstein served as Third Mate on board the "Loch Etive" of Glasgow on a voyage from London to Sydney & back (21st Aug' 1880 to 23 April 1881) during that time I found him perfectly sober very willing & attentive to his duties,

London 24th April 1881

Wm Stuart
Master "Loch Etive"

Conrad's certificate of discharge from the *Loch Etive*, on which he served as third mate

(*Substitute for* E 1, C 11, *and* C C 5.)

Dis. 1.

CERTIFICATE OF DISCHARGE.

For Seamen discharged before the Superintendent of a Mercantile Marine Office in the United Kingdom, a British Consul, or a Shipping Officer in British possession abroad.

SANCTIONED BY THE BOARD OF TRADE, JANUARY 1869.

No. 11

Name of Ship.	*Offici. Number.*	*Port of Registry.*	*Registd. Tonnage.*
"Riversdale"	29953	Liverpool	1490

Horse Power of Engines (if any.)	*Description of Voyage or Employment.*
—	Foreign

Name of Seaman.	*Age.*	*Place of Birth.*	*No. of R. N. R. Commissn. or Certif.*	*Capacity. If Mate or Engineer No. of Certif. (if any.)*
Conrad Korzeniowski	26	Poland	—	2nd Mate

Date of Engagement.	*Place of Engagement.*	*Date of Discharge.*	*Place of Discharge.*
10th Sept/83	London	17 Apl/84	Madras

I certify that the above particulars are correct, and that the above-named Seaman was discharged accordingly* and that the character described on the other side hereof is a true copy of the Report concerning the said Seaman.

Dated this 17th *day of* April 1884

L. B. McDonald *Master.*

AUTHENTICATED BY

Signature of Supert., Consul, or Shipping Officer.

OR OFFICIAL STAMP.

Signature of Seaman: Conrad Korzeniowski

* *Obliterate these words if they do not apply.*

Note.—*Any person who makes, assists in making or procures to be made any false Certificate or Report of the Service, Qualifications, Conduct or Character of any Seaman, or who forges, assists in forging or procures to be forged, or fraudulently alters, assists in fraudulently altering, or procures to be fraudulently altered, any such Certificate or Report, or who fraudulently makes use of any Certificate or Report, or of any Copy of any Certificate or Report which is forged or altered or does not belong to him, shall for each such offence be deemed guilty of a misdemeanor and may be fined or imprisoned.*

Conrad's certificate of discharge from the *Riversdale*, 1884, on which he served as second mate

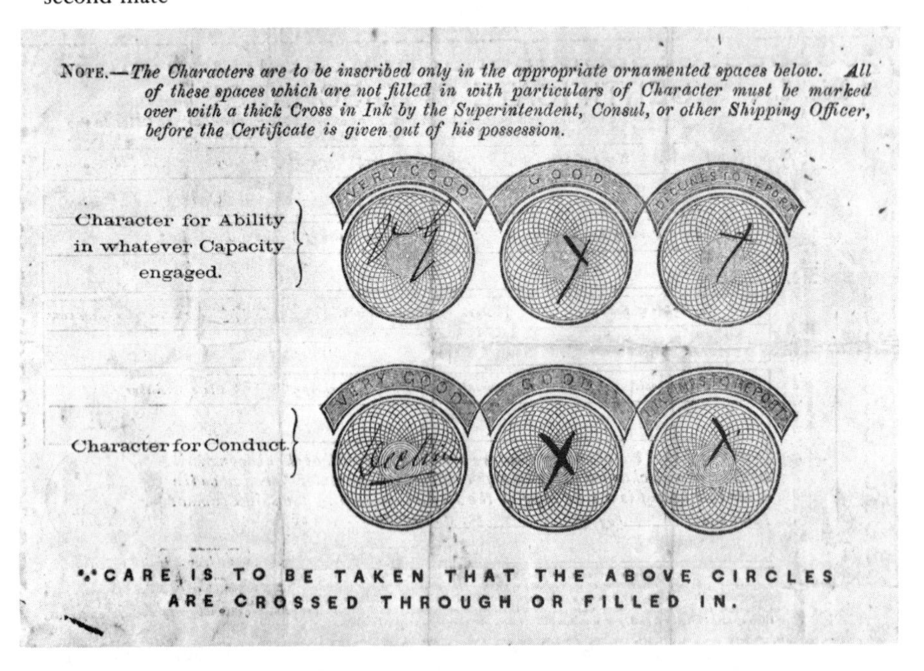

Note.—*The Characters are to be inscribed only in the appropriate ornamented spaces below. All of these spaces which are not filled in with particulars of Character must be marked over with a thick Cross in Ink by the Superintendent, Consul, or other Shipping Officer, before the Certificate is given out of his possession.*

Character for Ability in whatever Capacity engaged.

VERY GOOD — GOOD — DECLINES TO REPORT

Character for Conduct.

VERY GOOD — GOOD — DECLINES TO REPORT

∴ CARE IS TO BE TAKEN THAT THE ABOVE CIRCLES ARE CROSSED THROUGH OR FILLED IN.

Captain McDonald's report on Conrad's performance as second mate on the *Riversdale*, 1884

The harbor at Bombay, where Conrad joined the *Narcissus* as second mate in April 1884

PARTICULARS OF ENGAGEMENT.

Reference No.	SIGNATURES OF CREW.	Year of Birth.	Town or County where born.	If in the Reserve, No. of Commission or R V 2.	Ship in which he last served, and Year of Discharge therefrom.		Date and place of signing this Agreement.		In what Capacity engaged, and if Master, Mate, or Engineer, No. of Certificate.*	Time at which he is to be on board.
					Year.	State Name and Official No., or Port she belonged to.	Date.	Place.		
	1	2	3	4	5	6	7	8	9	10
21	Evan Morgan	1861	Cardiff.		1883	Pilot No 53	1883 1 Nov	Penarth	AB	6 am 2 Nov
22	Thos Matthew	1865	Newport		"	Evelyn bff	Do	Do	OS	Do
23	Edward his x Manning	1847	Waterford		"	Rl Sovereign Lpl	2 Do	Do	AB	5 p.m. Do
24	Charles Dutton		St Ellens			St Ellens Do	2 Nov	Do	AB	
25	David Davis	29	New Quay		83	"Dunkeld"	24/1/84	Cape Town	AB	25/1/84
26	Thomas Rowley	24	Scar'bro			"Forest Grove"	"	"	AB	"
27	Samuel Nichols	24	Bristol			"Jessomene"	"	"	AB	"
28	Henry Powell	21	London			Holefield Packet	"	"	OS	23/1/84

No.	Name	Age	Birthplace		Ship last served in	Date	Place	Capacity	Date joined
29	John. [illegible]	46	Woolwich	83	British America	25/1/84		Cook	[illegible]
30	Conrad Korzeniowski	26	Poland		Riversdale	28 apl/84	Bombay	2 Mate	29 apl/84
31	Joseph x Barrow	35	[illegible]		County of Dumfries	30 Mar	Do	AB	12 May
32	Hamilton Hunt	42	[illegible]		[illegible] Calcutta	16 May/84		1 Mate	[illegible]
33	J. [illegible]	38	London		[illegible]	16 do	Do	AB	19 May 84
34	[illegible]	31	Belfast		Do	16 do	Do	AB	do
35	[illegible]	35	Norway		Do	16 do	Do	AB	do
36	John Williams	[illegible]	Guernsey		County of Cardigan	28 do	Do	AB	[illegible]
37	Arch. [illegible]	23	Scotland		do	[illegible]	Do	AB	[illegible]
38									

Crew list of the *Narcissus;* Conrad is No. 30

Eng. 1.

Executed in Sixteen Pages.

*** …re, Interlineation, or Alteration in this Agreement will be void, unless attested by some Superintendent of a Mercantile Marine Office, Officer of Customs, Consul, or Vice-Consul, to be made with the consent of the persons interested.

SANCTIONED BY BOARD OF TRADE, Nov., 1882, In pursuance of 17 & 18 Vict. c. 104.

AGREEMENT AND ACCOUNT OF CREW.

FOREIGN-GOING SHIP.

The term "Foreign-going Ship" means every Ship employed in trading or going between some place or places in the United Kingdom and some place or places situate beyond the Coasts of the United Kingdom, the Islands of Guernsey, Jersey, Sark, Alderney, and Man, and the Continent of Europe between the River Elbe and Brest inclusive.

Name of Ship.	Official No.	Port of Registry.	Port No. and Date of Register.	Registered Tonnage. Gross.	Net.	Nominal Horse power of Engines (if any).
Narcissus.	76149	Greenock	38/1876	1336	1270	—

REGISTERED MANAGING OWNER. Name.	Address. (State No. of House, Street, and Town.)	No. of Seamen for whom accommodation is certified. (30 & 31 Vict. c. 124.)	Distance in feet and inches between centre of the Disc showing the Maximum load line in salt water and upper edge of lines indicating the position of the Ship's decks above that centre. First Deck, above it. ft. in.	Second Deck, above it. ft. in.
Robert R. Paterson.	City Buildings Greenock.	50	4 – 1½	—

Scale of Provisions to be allowed and served out to the Crew during the Voyage, in addition to the daily issue of Lime and Lemon Juice and Sugar, or other antiscorbutics in any case required by 30th & 31st Vict., c. 124, s. 4.

	Bread lb.	Beef lb.	Pork lb.	Tinned Meat lb.	Soup & Bouilli pint.	Preserved Potatoes lb.	Compressed or Preserved Vegetables lb.	Flour lb.	Peas pint	Rice lb.	Tea oz.	Coffee oz.	Sugar oz.	Molasses oz.	Water qts
Sunday	1	1		1	1	2	1/4	½			1	4	14	8	3
Monday	1		1	Weekly					3		Weekly				Daily
Tuesday	1	1						½							
Wednesday	1		1						3						
Thursday	1	1	1					½							
Friday	1								3						
Saturday	1	1								1/4					

Note.—In any case an equal quantity of Fresh Meat or Fresh Vegetables may, at the option of the Master, be served out in lieu of the Salted or Tinned Meats …

SUBSTITUTES.

AT THE MASTER'S OPTION

NO SPIRITS ALLOWED

The several Persons whose names are hereto subscribed, and whose descriptions are contained on the other side or sides, and of whom ten are engaged as Sailors, hereby agree to serve on board the said Ship, in the several capacities expressed against their respective Names, on a Voyage from [1]

Penarth (Cardiff) to Cape Town and/or any Ports or places within the limits of 75 degrees North and 60 degrees South Latitude the maximum time to be three years trading in any rotation and to end in the United Kingdom or Continent of Europe calling for orders when and where required.

Crew agreement of the *Narcissus*

The *Tilkhurst*, on which Conrad sailed as second mate from April 1885 to June 1886

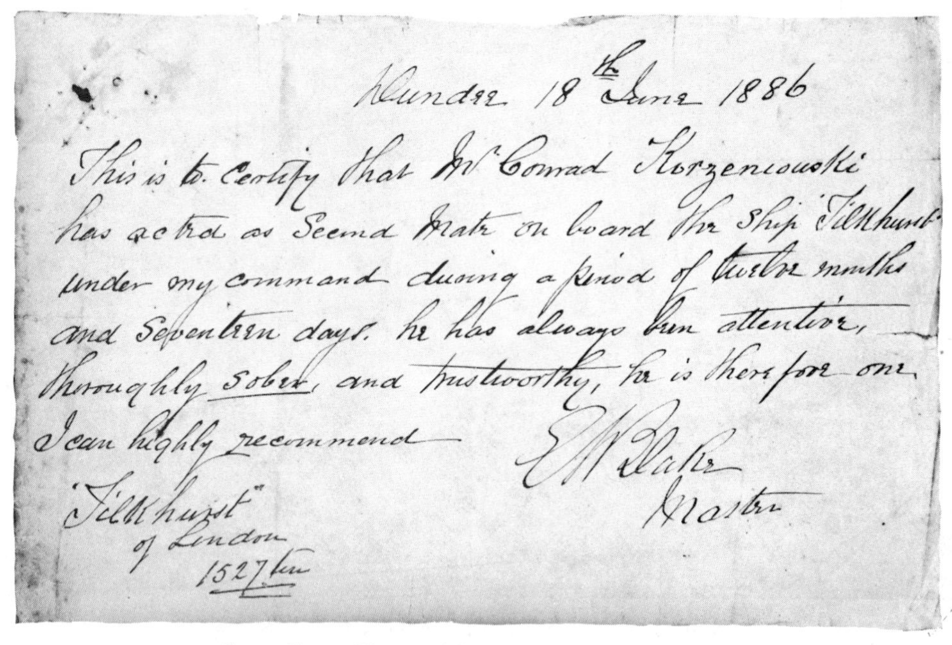

Dundee 18th June 1886

This is to Certify that Mr Conrad Korzeniowski has acted as Second Mate on board the Ship Tilkhurst under my command during a period of twelve months and seventeen days. he has always been attentive, thoroughly sober, and trustworthy, he is therefore one I can highly recommend

E W Blake
Master

"Tilkhurst"
of London
1527 tons

Conrad's certificate of discharge from the *Tilkhurst*

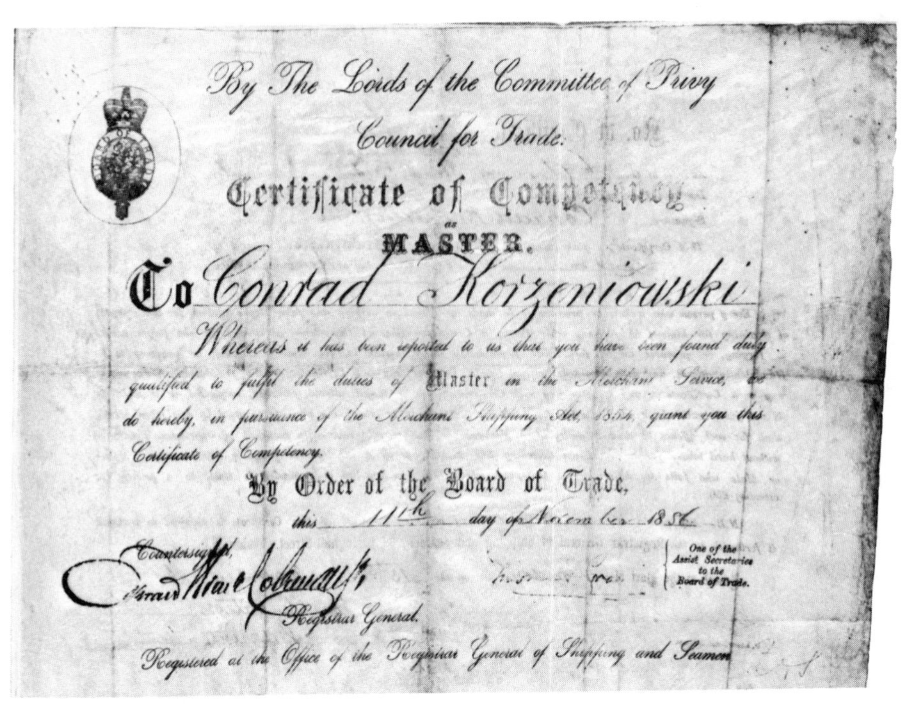

By The Lords of the Committee of Privy Council for Trade.

Certificate of Competency
as
MASTER.

To Conrad Korzeniowski

Whereas it has been reported to us that you have been found duly qualified to fulfil the duties of Master in the Merchant Service, we do hereby, in pursuance of the Merchant Shipping Act, 1854, grant you this Certificate of Competency.

By Order of the Board of Trade,
this 11th day of November 1886

Countersigned,

Registrar General.

One of the Assist. Secretaries to the Board of Trade.

Registered at the Office of the Registrar General of Shipping and Seamen

Conrad's master's certificate, 1886

The *Otago*, which Conrad captained in 1886

Shortly after, Blake became a convalescent and Conrad visited him—"This is the only one of my captains I have ever visited in that way." Apparently, the fatherly Blake, the motherly wife, the solidity of his background—all of these created in the young man a feeling of kinship, the desire to be the son or else to share in that solidity he had never really known. Blake was also extremely competent, and that was equally necessary for the demanding second mate of the *Tilkhurst.*

The ship with its dangerous cargo of coal had an uneventful voyage to Singapore, arriving on September 22, 1885, having been at sea for three and a half months. It remained almost a month in Singapore unloading its cargo, and the long wait in port, added to the long voyage, was more than the crew could bear and it broke out in a riot. During the brawl, one William Cumming was struck on the head, but appeared to recover once the *Tilkhurst* sailed for Calcutta, on October 19. The crew took turns watching over Cumming, since his behavior was erratic and gave indications of brain damage. As it moved between the Malayan and Sumatran coasts, the ship was almost becalmed in the Strait of Malacca. The crew observed and waited, the situation Conrad possibly drew upon for *The Nigger of the "Narcissus,"* but Cumming finally eluded them and jumped overboard, to be lost at sea. On the same voyage, Conrad met the Daniel Sullivan who would be the Singleton of *The Nigger,* a virtually illiterate Irish sailor who became for Conrad the epitome of the devoted, single-minded English seaman.

Once in Calcutta, the *Tilkhurst* remained until January 8, 1886, Conrad turning twenty-eight. During this time, while the ship was in Singapore and then laid over waiting for a cargo of jute in Calcutta, Conrad wrote several letters to Spiridion Kliszczewski. Although Conrad had almost surely written to Hope and Krieger, his friends in London, those letters have never turned up and are presumed lost; so that the letters to Kliszczewski, as noted, are the first extant Conrad letters in English. And except for a letter in Polish to Stefan Buszczyński, dated August 14, 1883, these are the first letters we have from Conrad's hand in any language.*

The second letter, dated October 13, 1885, shows a fluency in the language and a concern for Polish matters. Conrad comments happily on the defeat of the Liberal government in the 1885 elections, finding in this the hope of improved relations with Germany, "the only power with whom an Anti-Russian alliance would be useful, and even possible, for Great Britain." His remarks here about Poland's fortunes suggest the pessimism and anti-romanticism which would dominate his mature political and social outlook, making him appear both reactionary and anarchistic.

* I exclude the letter Conrad "wrote" to his father when he was three and a half since his hand was evidently directed by his mother.

> Events are casting shadows—more or less distorted—shadows deep enough to suggest the lurid light of battlefields somewhere in the near future, but all those portents of great and decisive doings leave me in a state of dispairing [sic] indifference; for, whatever may be the change in the fortunes of living nations, for the dead [i.e., Poland] there is no hope and no salvation. We have passed through the gates where "Lasciate agni [sic] speranza" is written in letters of blood and fire, and now the gate is shut on the light of hope, and nothing remains for us but the darkness of oblivion.

Conrad remarks that personal happiness is difficult to achieve in such times of national misfortune, but when "speaking, writing or thinking in English, the word 'Home' always means for me the hospitable shores of Great Britain." Conrad was moving toward naturalization, although "home" in Great Britain never permitted him to forget his other home, Poland, with his foreign name and desolate political background. He mentions, in the same letter, that he will soon be free of his examination and when at liberty he will visit in Cardiff.

The letter of November 25, 1885, written four days after Conrad arrived on the *Tilkhurst* in Calcutta, is a momentous one. While he lays out intricate plans for a business venture in whaling, more significantly for his later life, he begins to use Conrad as a surname, not as a Christian name. At the end of this long letter, in itself a feat of English, he asks Kliszczewski to address letters to "Mr Conrad. 2[d] mate 'Tilkhurst' Sailors Home. Dundee. To be delivered on arrival. —Write about end May. Say the 20th." Since Conrad in 1886 wrote what we can assume was his first story, "The Black Mate," the change of name has broad implications.

We can see the name change in his sea career, accompanying his naturalization, as a synecdoche of his entire life. To go from Korzeniowski to Conrad was, indeed, a foreshadowing of authorship in English. The naming, to give it its mythical quality, is a kind of incantation to the self, the beginning of a ritualized process; a "naming," literally, and therefore the lending of the self to a chain of developments that may either distort or expand the self.*

Conrad was moving experientially, journeying endlessly outward. The year 1886 was to incorporate the dimensions of a name change: he was to

---

* Kenneth Burke comments on such changes as accompanying changes of identity—Saul becoming Paul, for example. He writes that "such identification by name has a variant in change of clothes, or a change of surrounding in general, a change of 'environmental clothes.' Such investing by environment may sometimes enlist the very heavens, as with the change of identity in 'The Ancient Mariner' where we move from suffering under the aegis of the Sun [Apollo] to release under the aegis of the Moon [imagination]" (*Philosophy of Literary Form*, p. 24).

pass his master's examination, become naturalized as an Englishman, write letters in English and his first short story in any language. By twenty-eight, he had reached a critical point in his life—he felt himself ready to go in more than one direction and had proven to himself, despite his uncle's opposition to his sea career, that he could achieve success in his profession. His letter to Kliszczewski from Calcutta is part of this "new" self, for in it Conrad is brimful of schemes. Saying he takes it for granted that on his return he will pass his last exam, he turns to what is uppermost in his mind at this time, the whaling venture.

The big problem, obviously, is funding of the enterprise. Conrad indicates he needs £1,500, a considerable sum indeed, equivalent in buying power to about $20,000. He jests: "I do not know a man willing and able to advance me that amount of hard cash for the sake of my distinguished appearance, or any other sentimental consideration."* For lack of funds he suggests a plan whereby he would take out a life insurance policy, pay the premium out of "the London business [Barr, Moering] . . ." and borrow, using the policy as security. Even as he requests specific information, he wonders if these plans are "something more than the ravings of an unbusinesslike lunatic."

True to his background, Conrad disclaims any interest in making money and says he simply has the "wish to work for myself. I am sick and tired of sailing about for little money and less consideration. But I love the sea; and if I could just clear my bare living in the way I suggested I should be comparatively happy." In the light of Conrad's later dismissal of Melville's *Moby-Dick* as being full of "portentous mysticism," it is amusing to note his desire to pursue a whaling career; apparently only Melville and not the whale was portentous. He tells his friend he has been carefully nursing these plans for the past four years, but he will follow what Kliszczewski tells him and "go on plodding in the old way" if the response is negative. When they met later, his friend dissuaded him, and nothing further came of the project.

Conrad's next letter to Kliszczewski (dated December 19, 1885), from Calcutta, is a document of considerable importance, since it reveals political

* Conrad knew he could not ask his uncle for the sum. In a letter which he received at Singapore (Bobrowski's, of August 2/14, 1885), he noted that his uncle had paid in his £30 allowance to Barr, Moering, surely not failing to observe the difference between that and the £1,500 he needed. In the same letter, Tadeusz alludes to a liver ailment which was bothering Conrad: "In spite of your assurance that from September through December the climate in India is good, I am not convinced and I would have preferred you to aim in a different direction; for if your first Indian voyage has already affected your liver, the second one could cause serious harm. This possibility is not an enviable one, even if for the price of it you were to become an admiral" (Najder, p. 99). The letter is addressed to Mr. Conrad N. Korzeniowski, the spelling of the Christian name going from Polish to English.

With the death of Kazimierz Bobrowski, in 1886, Tadeusz became responsible for his seven nieces and nephews, a situation that made additional outlays for Conrad unlikely.

and social corners of his mind as he pondered the 1885 General Election from ten thousand miles away. Conrad's extreme reactionaryism becomes plausible only if we understand his opposition to all plans of social improvement. His suspicion of such idealistic schemes, further, can be traced to his roots in Polish politics, the generations of idealism and romanticism, including his father's, leading to greater acts of repression by the conquering country. If we keep in mind that Conrad's political ideas were shaped less by reading and later experience than by his early reaction to Polish events, we can understand how visceral his politics were. He wrote:

> By this time, you, I and the rest of the "right thinking" have been grievously disappointed by the result of the General Election. The newly enfranchised idiots have satisfied the yearnings of Mr. Chamberlain's herd [followers of Joseph Chamberlain, later Liberal-Unionist leader in Commons] by cooking the national goose according to his recipe. The next culinary operation will be a pretty kettle of fish of an international character. Joy reigns in St. Petersburg, no doubt, and profound disgust in Berlin: the International Socialist Association are triumphant, and every disreputable ragamuffin in Europe feels that the day of universal brotherhood, despoliation and disorder is coming apace, and nurses day-dreams of well-plenished pockets amongst the ruin of all that is respectable, venerable and holy. The great British Empire went over the edge, and yet on to the inclined plane of social progress and radical reform. The downward movement is hardly perceptible yet, and the clever men who started it may flatter themselves with the progress; but they will soon find that the fate of the nation is out of their hands now! The Alpine avalanche rolls quicker and quicker as it nears the abyss—its ultimate destination! Where's the man to stop the crashing avalanche?

He continues in this jaded vein, pessimistic, full of Nietzschean disenchantment with mass man and mass politics. God is indeed dead, but, ironically, long live his assassins!

> Where's the man to stop the rush of social-democratic ideas? The opportunity and the day have come and are gone! Believe me: gone for ever! For the sun is set and the last barrier removed. England was the only barrier to the pressure of infernal doctrines born in continental back-slums. Now there is nothing! The destiny of this nation and of all nations is to be accomplished in darkness amidst much weeping and gnashing of teeth, to pass through robbery, equality, anarchy and misery under the iron rule of a militarism despotism! Such is the lesson of common sense logic.

Then Conrad stated what was to be echoed throughout his life: "Socialism must inevitably end in Caesarism." He drives home his Nietzschean disdain for "die grosse Masse": "The whole herd of idiotic humanity are moving in that direction at the bidding of unscrupulous rascals and a few sincere, but dangerous, lunatics. These things must be. It is fatality."* He admits his prejudices:

> I live mostly in the past and the future. The present has, you easily understand, but few charms for me. I look with the serenity of despair and the indifference of contempt upon the passing events. Disestablishment, Land Reform, Universal Brotherhood are but like milestones on the road to ruin. The end will be awful, no doubt! Neither you nor I shall live to see the final crash: although we both may turn in our graves when it comes, for we both feel deeply and sincerely. Still, there is no earthly remedy for those earthly misfortunes, and from above, I fear, we may obtain consolation, but no remedy. "All is vanity."

This extremely strong letter, written when Conrad was twenty-eight, must not be distorted. While it by no means outlines the whole of his politics, it is not to be minimized as simply the ravings of a youthful, unformed mind. Conrad was, after all, twenty-eight, and while his personality may have displayed a certain heedlessness, there is no question that he had tested the truth of his feelings. Although he was to read political economists later (Mill and others) and meet a strong countering force in the socialist Cunninghame Graham, his political reactions remained visceral, not strategic or fully logical. One thing he did believe: no matter what the state did—or how benevolent were its intentions—it must deceive the individual to gain its goals and end in totalitarianism.

We must observe Conrad from the peculiar vantage point he brought to politics: the tortured, desolate background, the ambiguous attitude he had toward his father's achievement or lack of it, the uniqueness of Poland as a pawn caught between uncontrollable historical forces, his need for allegiance

* Yet Conrad's sense of fate was quite different, more in tune with Nietzsche's "*amor fati*" (love of fate): "My formula for greatness in a human being is *amor fati*: that one wants nothing to be different, not forward, not backward, not in all eternity. Not merely bear what is necessary, still less conceal it—all idealism is mendaciousness in the face of what is necessary—but *love* it." Although we have no evidence linking Conrad directly to Nietzsche, they shared a common Middle European outlook, not the least of which was the philosopher's Polish background. Zarathustra declaims the following equation of socialism with Caesarism which Conrad echoed: "You preachers of equality, the tyrannomania of impotence clamors thus out of you for equality: your most secret ambitions to be tyrants thus shroud themselves in words of virtue. Aggrieved conceit, repressed envy—perhaps the conceit and envy of your fathers—erupt from you as a flame and as the frenzy of revenge." Besides their obvious heuristic similarities here, both Nietzsche and Conrad felt that idealism was simply a disguise for individual failure and a consequent worship of power. Nietzsche's Notebooks, especially the part of *The Will to Power* called "European Nihilism," find their echo in Conrad's letters to Marguerite Poradowska and Cunninghame Graham later in the 1890s.

to England and her policies—both the mother and father country for him, his intense desire for roots in a political atmosphere that made rational sense, and his own ironic blend of idealism, romanticism, and pragmatism which he never completely resolved. All of these factors and qualities cannot add up to a fully coherent political rationale.

Even a political rationalist such as John Stuart Mill—the seeming epitome of logic and realism in the political process—was deeply affected by his background, his relationship with his father being the obverse of Conrad's with Apollo. Mill's "liberalism" and sense of individual rights would appear to be a direct reaction to his own subservience and feudal relationship to his father as he grew up, for he was cultivated like a cash crop by a father interested in a fruitful product. Furthermore, Mill's admirable interest in women's rights would be attached to his need to resurrect his own mother from family relationships in which she had become a negligible factor amid strong males. The point is that even a man whose political ideas resulted from deep reading and thought was deeply affected by his background; so that as we pass to Conrad, we can never minimize those early unresolved influences, in which politics or even the idea of it was as closely allied to death as it was to life. For the remainder of his years, no matter how sophisticated he became, Conrad reacted to a certain feeling that political and social change did not necessarily bring happiness or improvement; it brought change.*

Conrad had evidently been trying out these ideas on his uncle over a period of years, because, in 1891, Tadeusz wrote to him, beginning with "My Dear Pessimist." He says that he begins thus because that at least "suggests the aroma which your letters have for some time been bringing me." Of course, some of these letters had been posted after Conrad's Congo expedition, and he had become more despairing, having seen indifference to life and death, destruction, imperialistic motives never dreamed of. His letters apparently took on darker hues, but we can suggest with some certainty that the post-Congo letters were simply a continuation of earlier attitudes.

Although we are jumping ahead more than five years, Bobrowski's letters

---

* Throughout his later career, as we shall see, Conrad set forth various schemes for a "solution" of the European power struggle, all of them intended to contain a ruthless Germany and Russia. Many of his schemes—beginning with his plan (in November 1912) to put Constantinople under international control—were based on the Realpolitik of power blocs with competing interests; later, he repeated this plan with his hope of putting Poland under French and English supervision. From this, one could argue that Conrad had some national and international vision or ideal, or that he held some organic view of the state. But the fiction argues otherwise: that any attempt to impose a holistic view of society or the state is doomed to failure. That is the very point of *Nostromo*, Conrad's most complex political statement. For the son of Apollo Korzeniowski, the sole political idea that can exist begins with the individual. *He* is the state, and while, like Razumov, he may be doomed to failure, that *is* the nature of life, that *is* the political idea.

to Conrad tell us something about the twenty-eight-year-old sailor as he was poised to leap in several directions. Tadeusz attributes Conrad's pessimism to the result of his heritage, an aspect of his being a dreamer, in spite of his very practical profession. Tadeusz then gets into the substance of Conrad's own remarks, which we can now read back filtered through his uncle's commentary:

> My dear lad, whatever you were to say about a good or bad balance of the forces of nature, about good or bad social relationships, about right or wrong social systems, about the boundless stupidity of crowds fighting for a crust of bread—and ending up in nothingness—none of this will be new!! You will never control the forces of nature, for whether blind or governed by Providence, in each case they have their own pre-ordained paths; and you will also never change the roads along which humanity goes, for there exists in social development an historical evolutionary compulsion which is slow but sure, and which is governed by the laws of cause and effect derived from the past and affecting the future.

The older man's social Darwinism and acceptance of the mechanical view of man's development were clearly opposed to Conrad's pessimistic refusal to accept the mechanist's, even Hobbesian, sense of man. Conrad offered, despite his pessimism, a vitalist's sense of change, a view of man's genius and of the individual life triumphing over stodginess and complacency—that is, a dreamer's quixotic feel for things. Yet, as we read back, even as Conrad offered this reading of self and history, he knew it could never be, for society would be dragged down by those Nietzschean mass men, the crowd fighting for a few moments of pleasure. Disdain, cynicism, and idealism are all part of Conrad's pessimism, and lost entirely upon his reasonable uncle.

Bobrowski then unfolds his own carefully nurtured view of man and life, as that of a ". . . modest tiny ant which by its insignificant toil in fulfilling its modest duty secures the life and existence of the whole nest!" One should not be a peacock with a desire for greatness, but an insect pursuing duty. Even these mass men who move in crowds ". . . no longer seem detestable when, as often happens, a more thorough evaluation reveals that they embellish their existence, their work, and often even their shortcomings, by some higher moral idea of a duty accomplished, of a love for their family or country."

As we read his comments, we observe how Conrad himself found such ideas not at all incompatible with his temperament. And yet as an artist he had to struggle against the dullness and homogeneity of this view, its inapplicability to man under the artist's scrutiny. To become an artist meant that he had to split himself into at least two; that while he recognized the validity of Tadeusz's stress on duty and discipline, he could not turn his art into homiletics. More aware than his uncle of the need for tensions held in balance, Conrad sought out the very extremes that so worried the older man, who had settled these conflicts for the sake of life, not art.*

Whatever Conrad's personal feelings about English politics, his return to England from Calcutta was to cement his Englishness: naturalization and a master's certificate. His last letter to Kliszczewski—and unfortunately his last extant letter in any language for nearly four years—came on January 6, 1886, just two days before the *Tilkhurst* was to sail for Dundee, on the Firth of Tay, just north of Edinburgh. Conrad asks him to write directly to Dundee, recalling the insurance scheme to raise money but with little reference to the whaling idea itself. He indicates that he will not come to Cardiff until he passes his examination. The *Tilkhurst* after a five-month voyage arrived in Dundee on June 17, and Conrad went up to London with Captain and Mrs. Blake.

Two months later, on August 19, 1886, Conrad became a naturalized English citizen. Naturalization was, again, a piece of the whole, less significant in itself than as a portent; for with naturalization a whole series of possibilities would open up. Becoming an English citizen meant of course a commitment to the English language, especially for someone such as Conrad who sought parental figures throughout his life. His assumption of citizenship involved assumption of country, parent, and mother tongue. It is inconceivable that he would, given his background and emotional needs, turn away from the language so closely tied to his new mother country. By becoming a citizen of another country—an act of tremendous moment when one is not actually forced to do so—Conrad had already made certain choices, not the least of which were political and linguistic allegiances. When later he said that if he were to be a writer, he could be only an English writer, he was voicing a decision made as early as 1886.

Bobrowski's letters throughout the first half of 1886 express anxiety about Conrad's naturalization and his master's certificate. Reading back, we can assume Conrad had made both seem imminent, especially the master's examination, although it was still a half year off. Writing while his nephew was still at sea (Calcutta or Dundee), Tadeusz cautioned Conrad to consider seriously his "examination for a captaincy" and also his naturalization—"the final steps in your career, which I still insist on; first get your captain's li-

---

* Foreseeing Conrad's criticism, Bobrowski bases his outlook on the fact of having suffered, all men suffer: "Perhaps you will tell me that what I have said is but the words of a man who has always been comfortable in the world, 'qui a eu toujours chaud'; but this is not so—you know this well. I have gone through a lot, I have suffered over my own fate and the fate of my family and my Nation, and perhaps just because of these sufferings and disappointments I have developed in myself this calm outlook on the problem of life, whose motto, I venture to say, was, is, and will be 'usque ad finem.' The devotion to duty interpreted more widely or narrowly according to circumstances and time—this constitutes my practical creed" (Najder, p. 155).

cense and your naturalization, then you can do, Sir, as you please." Part of Bobrowski's insistence was attached to his fear that his brother Kazimierz would die soon and he would be left with the widow and six children to support. The possibility of a meeting between them was out of the question, since there was no money for such matters. Bobrowski then commented on Conrad's plans:

> For your information and that of your partners, in case you decide to embark on business, I would strongly recommend a thorough investigation in London of two possibilities: *trading in wheat-flour*, for here milling has become very popular and eventually wheat will be exported in the form of flour; and *trading in granulated sugar*. . . . You should act more speedily, cheaply, and profitably than these big dealers . . . and you should investigate the position of London, Odessa, Libau, and Królewiec and should be prepared to content yourselves with a smaller profit in order to secure more orders.

Tadeusz's plans for Conrad to become a trader in flour and granulated sugar are amusing, since he completely misread his nephew's state of mind. If Conrad went into business, he sought whales, not granulated sugar. While his uncle thought in terms of small items—grains of flour and sugar—Conrad thought in cosmic terms, whales and whaling. For him great lives contained great events, great objects. His career was based on taming wind and waves, on human ingenuity mastering nature's worst; now he was thinking of taming whales, while his uncle suggested trading goods. Sancho wanted a mere governorship; whereas Quixote wanted the world. They were at opposite ends of the universe from each other, held together only by mutual affection and family ties.

CHAPTER 11

The Master Mariner and the Apprentice Writer

IN his next letter, Tadeusz asked the usual questions:

> (1) How is your health? (2) When is your examination for a master's certificate (for I am not going to give way over this!)? (3) What are you going to do next?—this you may decide as you please. (4) What about your partnership—will you find it advantageous if you leave the Mercantile Marine? (5) Finally—when will you get your naturalization? And don't forget to draw the attention of your partners to the possibility of trading with Russia in sugar and flour.

This letter, like the previous one, was inaccessible to Conrad until after he arrived back in England, on June 17; and yet Bobrowski's tone is insistent, as though he must have an immediate answer. He wrote still another, which was in response to Conrad's, discussing Kazimierz's death on April 20 and his increased burdens. In this, also, he keeps pressing for naturalization and a master's certificate, the latter surely in reference to his nephew's assurance of an imminent examination.

We now begin to enter thickets of deception. In his letter of July 8/20, 1886, Bobrowski refers to Conrad's phrase in his last letter: " 'I decided to try my luck, providing my health is good,' " from which Tadeusz deduces Conrad's health is poor. Evidently Conrad had mentioned taking his examination, for his uncle follows with: ". . . as the examination will be over by the time you answer this letter, let me know how it went." He then turns to flour, sugar, average prices, producers, et al.—all rather ironic in the light of what was occurring.

In actuality, Conrad had taken his master's examination and failed. Documents in the General Register and Record Office of Shipping and Seamen at Cardiff, Wales, indicate Conrad had sat for the examination on July 28, 1886, and failed in the Day's Work and probably in Arithmetic as well. With this fact in mind, we can understand why he skirted the subject in his further letters to his uncle, diverting him with detailed questions about business and his naturalization. For the next four months, until November 10, Conrad had to avoid the painful subject, too ashamed to admit to a failure after his cockiness with Bobrowski and Kliszczewski. Rather than accepting what he had already achieved, he saw failure as part of the character flaws his uncle said he possessed. How else can we explain his deception? Pride? Shame? Embarrassment? Desire for perfection? Protection of self and ego? Surely, all of these entered into Conrad's secrecy as he went about his plans to retake the examination and to keep his uncle uninformed until he had only good news to tell. It was, after all, *his* news, his life, his ability or lack of it. Conrad was already entering into the experience of so many of his protagonists who carry with them great secrets, men who move silently for fear their privileged knowledge will become revealed to a public for whom they feel contempt.

Bobrowski's letters continued to arrive during this four-month period, most of them concerned with farm prices and agricultural products, matters distant indeed from Conrad's mind.* Then on November 10, he passed, a few weeks short of his twenty-ninth birthday, and he must have written his uncle immediately. He had few other people to inform. In *A Personal Record*, he recalls how he felt:

> I walked across the Hill of many beheadings with measured steps. It was a fact, I said to myself, that I was now a British master mariner beyond a doubt. I had an exaggerated sense of that very modest achievement, with which, however, luck, opportunity, or any extraneous influence could have had nothing to do. That fact, satisfactory and obscure in itself, had for me a certain ideal significance. It was an answer to certain outspoken scepticism, and even to some not very kind aspersions. I had vindicated myself from what had been cried upon as a stupid obstinacy or a fantastic caprice. I don't mean to say that a whole country had been convulsed by my desire to go to sea. But for a boy between fifteen and sixteen, sensitive enough, in all conscience, the commotion of his little world had seemed a very considerable thing indeed.

Hearing of the news, Bobrowski was delighted. He immediately wrote to Conrad:

> Long live the "Ordin. Master in the British Merchant Service"!! [in English] May he live long! May he be healthy and may every success at-

* Conrad, nevertheless, continued the business chatter, although how seriously we cannot tell. In any event, Bobrowski is full of strategies to protect his less than practical nephew from coming to financial grief. He is afraid that all will be lost: ". . . and now I ask you to let me know clearly and definitely what is in fact being done with the £350 capital which I put up and sent you to London. Does it remain entirely in the hands of Krieger? Or is it in the business of Barr, Mo[e]ring & Co.? For if, as you say, Krieger is ill and might 'kick the bucket,' who will be responsible for the capital involved and who will look after carrying out the Agreement?"

tend him in every enterprise both on sea and on land! You have really delighted me with the news of the "Red Seal" on your certificate. Not being an Admiral I have no right to give orders to a newly created Master and I leave to his own discretion the solution to the question—whether he is to change his O.M. into E.M. [*Magister Emereti?*—Master Emeritus]??—which depends on your prospects and plans for your future career. As the humble provider of the means for this enterprise I can only rejoice that my groats have not been wasted but have led you to the peak of your chosen profession, in which Mr. Syroczyński, the heir to the virtues of the Romans and the Greeks, drew twelve years ago such an unfavourable horoscope for the young aspirant to Neptune's service. You are, my dear Sir, now 29 years old and have mastered a profession; it is for you to know and understand what you must do further.

He returns to his twin worries: that Conrad make certain his money invested with Krieger is secure in the event of Krieger's sudden death; and that he obtain a release from Russian citizenship from the Embassy before he contemplates any visit to Polish soil. Bobrowski still fears military service or some comparable difficulty from imperial Russia unless his nephew divest himself of his dual citizenship.

This was, indeed, an annus mirabilis for Conrad. Some twenty-two years later, in 1908, he published an inconsequential story called "The Black Mate" in *London Magazine*, a story which in style, content, and accomplishment had little connection to the kind of fiction Conrad was writing at that time and seemed a throwback to some of his lesser fiction of an earlier period. As we sift through the conflicting evidence, it would appear that the story derives from 1886, from some version of "The Black Mate" that Conrad wrote for a competition in the magazine *Tit-Bits*. The competition Conrad entered may have been for the May 1, 1886, number, which advertised: "Special Prize for Sailors. . . . We will give the sum of Twenty Guineas for the best article entitled 'My Experiences as a Sailor.' " The stipulation of an "article" may have been sufficiently broad to include fiction.

In a letter to James Pinker in 1922, Conrad indicated that "The Black Mate" of 1908 was a revised form of the earlier story:

I am surprised at the length of the thing. My feeling about it is that there will be nothing actually disgraceful in its inclusion in my collected editions [in the posthumous *Tales of Hearsay*] (for that is what its publication in book form would ultimately mean) but it would complicate my literary history in a sort of futile way. I don't remember whether I told that I wrote that thing in '86 for a prize competition, started I think by Tit-Bits. It is an extraneous phenomenon. My literary life began privately in 1890 [*Almayer's Folly* was begun in 1889, not 1890] and publicly in 1895 with *Almayer's Folly*, which is regarded generally as my very first piece of writing. However, the history of the "Black Mate," its origins etc.

> etc., need not be proclaimed on housetops, and *Almayer's Folly* may keep its place as my first serious work.

In an edition of "The Black Mate" privately printed in 1922,* in a copy belonging to his friend and biographer Richard Curle, Conrad indicated that while his memories of the story were confused, "I have a notion that it was first written some time in the late eighties and retouched later."

It is difficult to reject Conrad's recollection of this event, even when he wished to keep the lines of his career neat and claim *Almayer* as his first work. Yet Jessie Conrad maintained in at least two places that Conrad's recollection of the story was altogether wrong, asserting that the 1908 "Black Mate" was an original story suggested by herself. "I gave my husband the facts and matter for the tale [she wrote] but he received it in such a manner that my astonishment was great when I saw the 'bones' I had given clothed in the story and heard his unexpected claim that it was his first story." And to R. L. Mégroz, she was equally insistent that "The Black Mate" was not Conrad's first piece of fiction: " 'That is not true. . . . I can remember giving Conrad material for 'The Black Mate.' But on one of his naughty days he said that 'The Black Mate' was his first work, and when I said, 'No, *Almayer's Folly* was the first thing you ever did,' he burst out: 'If I like to say "The Black Mate" was my first work, I shall say so!' "

This conflict of memories should not be crucial in determining the date of the story, for both Conrad and Jessie had difficulty in remembering dates. The argument must be settled not by memory but by the story itself, which is crude and amateurish, and therefore would appear to be quite early, very much a first attempt. "The Black Mate" has a faltering narrative technique, in that the initial narrator is an "I" character who for the sake of orderliness gives way to an omniscient third-person narrator. The "I," possibly an early attempt at Marlow, cannot be present at the ship's events, and therefore, the technique could not be sustained. Such a confusion of narrative means would not be in keeping with the highly sophisticated storyteller of 1908 and would appear to date the story as an early effort.

There are other, perhaps even more compelling, reasons for assuming the story is early. The focus of "The Black Mate" is an older man who dyes his hair so as to be able to obtain a mate's post on board the *Sapphire.* His great secret is his advanced age and his white hair. He must protect that secret or else in the competition for berths he will be rejected. Of some psychological interest is the fact that Conrad himself harbored a great secret in 1886—his failure on his master's examination—and if the story predates that setback,

* Fifty copies were printed for the author, for private distribution only, by the Dunedin Press of Edinburgh. The sole reason for this would be Conrad's desire to sell a limited item to private collectors of his works.

then the failure on his mate's examination, in 1884. Further, the secret of Bunter (the so-called black mate) extends beyond that, for he had command of a ship in the Indian Ocean which was lost and had his certificate suspended for a year. Like Lord Jim of a later time, he was to wander the docks and waters trying to avoid the divulgation of that information.

Bunter's past—the loss of a command—duplicates what happened to Captain McDonald of the *Riversdale*. After Conrad left the ship, in a dispute with the captain, McDonald stranded the ship at Masulipatam, two hundred miles up the coast from Madras. Like Bunter, McDonald suffered the suspension of his master's certificate. Then, also, the captain of the *Sapphire*, Johns, seems based on McDonald, a man whom Conrad disliked intensely. Conrad used Johns's spiritualism—quite a faddish thing in the 1880s—as a way of commenting on his inadequacy as a master. Further, the run of the *Sapphire* to Calcutta and then the return to Dunkirk with a cargo of jute parallels Conrad's voyage from Bombay to Dunkirk on the *Narcissus*.

Sufficient details of fictional technique and abundant evidence of events filtering in and out of Conrad's life in the 1880s make it almost certain that this is an early story, conceived and written before Conrad had developed his craftsmanship, and certainly not the product of 1908, the period of *Under Western Eyes* and "The Secret Sharer."

If we accept this story as an effort of the 1880s, the immediate question is whether Conrad intended to shift careers now rather than in the 1890s. His entrance into the *Tit-Bits* competition, if that is indeed what occurred, indicates a broader prospectus, a diversification of his energies, somewhat akin to the whaling idea or the fleeting plan of serving as secretary to a Canadian businessman. Did it, however, go deeper? Conrad's difference from most other sailors was already explicit in his background and gentry status, his heavy accent in speaking English, his interest in reading, the breadth of his general knowledge, and the introspective turn of his imagination. These very factors isolated him and provided a post of observation, a narrative distance, an objective eye. We note this angle or post even when he retells how he passed his examination for master, for the examiner comments on Conrad's Polish background: " 'Not many of your nationality in our service, I should think. I never remember meeting one either before or after I left the sea. Don't remember ever hearing of one. An inland people, aren't you?' "

Further, we know of Conrad's desire to find berths on sailing vessels, his dislike of steam, his resistance to the very forces that would destroy sailing as a craft. This stress on craft and technique, here with ships, indicates he was interested early in the "how" of a process as much as the "what." Getting a cargo to its destination was his immediate aim as a mate and captain; but how he got it there was the goal of the individual lying under the official duty. In a real sense, Conrad had divided himself into halves, the professional seaman and the craftsman, although he did not consciously see the schism and would not accept it for more than another decade. We can assume, therefore, that his turning to a story contest in a fifth-rate publication was an expression of needs that ran deep within, not a passing fancy, although the story may itself have been amateurish in the light of what the writer was to become. For Conrad to have written anything at this time, in 1886, was remarkable, like the first inchoate stirrings of a talent in any field where craftsmanship and achievement will occur later.

We can assume that with this first piece of fiction behind him, Conrad had gained an even more acute angle of observing. Even if he planned no other writing for the time being, until he started *Almayer* in 1889, the mere fact of his having written anything at all would have alerted him to a way of seeing. Also, he would be reading with a different bias, not simply for the language of the material and its narrative, but for strategies, methods of narration, presentation of character and event, angle of vision or post of observation. He was no longer only an individual seeking the momentary experience; he was looking with an eye toward the permanence of words and paragraphs, even narrative lines.

The master's certificate, like the earlier one for chief mate, did not guarantee Conrad a command, and he was forced to sign on the *Highland Forest* as chief mate, on February 16, 1887.* The *Highland Forest*, a sailing vessel of 1,040 tons, was waiting in Amsterdam for its cargo, now icebound, and was to sail for Semarang (Samarang) in Java. This voyage moved Conrad ever closer to his third life, not only in time, but in the local color and characters of his early material. Conrad was beginning to enter into the chain of events, places, and people who would engage his imagination and turn him, finally, from the sea. Yet, ironically, this voyage that would lead to the heat of the East Indies began in the frozen canals of Amsterdam. If the canals of that city made Conrad think he was in the Inferno of Dante, it was a frozen Inferno and a frozen Conrad who awaited the cargo that would allow him to thaw. In *The Mirror of the Sea*, he catches the frigid wastes of the canal city, using some of the ice imagery, perhaps, of his early reading of Arctic explorers:

---

* There has been speculation that Conrad sailed on still other ships; for example, the *James P. Best* and the *Falconhurst*. We can dismiss the *Best*, but some chain of evidence suggests that Conrad may have served on the *Falconhurst* for five days in December 1886, sailing from Gravesend to Penarth. This short voyage would have come between his service on the *Tilkhurst* and the *Highland Forest*. For an attempt to prove this, see Edmund Bojarski, "Conrad at the Crossroads: From Navigator to Novelist with some New Biographical Mysteries," *The Texas Quarterly* (Winter 1968); also, Gerald Morgan, "Conrad's Unknown Ship," which he kindly sent me in manuscript. The evidence does not seem conclusive that Conrad sailed on the *Falconhurst*, since no certificate of discharge has been discovered.

> I call to mind a winter landscape in Amsterdam—a flat foreground of waste land, with here and there stacks of timber, like the huts of a camp of some very miserable tribe; the long stretch of the Handelskade; cold, stone-faced quays, with the snow-sprinkled ground and the hard, frozen water of the canal, in which were set ships one behind another with their frosty mooring-ropes hanging slack and their decks idle and deserted, because, as the master stevedore . . . informed me, their cargoes were frozen-in up-country on barges and schuyts.

Furious with frustration, as he would be later in the sweltering Congo, he describes how his mind and body hardened with anguish:

> I was, as the French say, biting my fists with impatience for that cargo frozen up-country; with rage at that canal set fast, at the wintry and deserted aspect of all those ships that seemed to decay in grim depression for want of the open water. I was chief mate and very much alone. Directly I had joined I received from my owners instructions to send all the ship's apprentices away on leave together, because in such weather there was nothing for anybody to do, unless to keep up a fire in the cabin stove.

Ice dominated his imagination, as later jungle would.

> Notwithstanding the little iron stove, the ink froze on the swing-table in the cabin, and I found it more convenient to go ashore, stumbling over the Arctic waste land and shivering in glazed tramcars in order to write my evening letter to my owners in a gorgeous café in the centre of town. It was an immense place, lofty and gilt, upholstered in red plush, full of electric lights, and so thoroughly warmed that even the marble tables felt tepid to the touch.

There, amid the noisy crowd, who suffered no cold at all, he would write to the owners in Glasgow a familiar plaint: "There is no cargo, and no prospect of any coming till late spring apparently." And yet "all the time I sat there the necessity of getting back to the ship bore heavily on my already half-congealed spirits—the shivering in glazed tramcars, the stumbling over snow-sprinkled waste ground, the visions of ships frozen in a row, appearing vaguely like corpses of black vessels in a white world, so silent, so lifeless, so soulless they seemed to be."

"The very air," Conrad writes, "seemed as hard and trenchant as steel," but he adds that "it would have taken much more than this to extinguish my sacred fire for the exercise of my craft." He speaks of himself as a young man of twenty-four—in actuality, he was twenty-nine, with a master's certificate—who would not let a "Dutch tenacious winter penetrate into his heart." The orders from the owners would come, almost every morning, for him to go to the charterers and clamor for his cargo; for him to demand that they release this icebound cargo. Then, "like an Arctic explorer setting off on a sledge journey towards the North Pole," he would go ashore and head, shivering, into the very heart of town, a whited sepulchre. Once at the charterers, he would try to obtain some answer from Mr. Hudig, a "big swarthy Netherlander, with black moustaches and a bold glance." However, it "was impossible to threaten a man who, though he possessed the language perfectly, seemed incapable of understanding any phrase pronounced in a tone of remonstrance or discontent." This Hudig Conrad never forgot, for two years later, when he tentatively began his first novel, Hudig surfaces as a Dutch trader; Conrad used the name in both *Almayer* and *An Outcast,* deeply interwoven into the past lives of his chief characters.

As chief mate, Conrad was in charge of loading the cargo when it finally began to arrive. As a result of his inexperience, the shifting cargo made the ship roll excessively. Finally, the captain himself arrived, "obviously not a Hollander, in a black bowler and a short drab overcoat, ridiculously out of tone with the winter aspect of the waste lands, bordered by the brown fronts of houses with their roofs dripping with melting snow." This was Captain John MacWhirr, immortalized by Conrad as the captain (MacWhirr) of the *Nan-Shan* in "Typhoon," who no matter what the weather would not alter his course. "A gale is a gale," he says, "and a full-powered steam-ship has got to face it"; for "How can you tell what a gale is made of till you get it?" MacWhirr of the *Nan-Shan* is thus characterized as a man "who had sailed over the surface oceans as some men go skimming over the years of existence to sink gently into a placid grave, ignorant of life to the last, without ever having been made to see all it may contain of perfidy, of violence, and of terror. There are on sea and land such men thus fortunate—or thus disdained by destiny or by the sea."

In *The Mirror of the Sea,* our sole document for this episode, Conrad tells of the furiously violent voyage, the rolling of the ship so abrupt and heavy that once she began, "you felt that she would never stop, and this hopeless sensation, characterizing the motion of ships whose centre of gravity is brought down too low in loading, made everyone on board weary of keeping on his feet." Eventually, some of the spars let go—"nothing important: spanker booms and such-like"— and the chief mate, Conrad himself, paid the penalty of poor loading procedures. "A piece of one of the minor spars that did carry away flew against the chief mate's back, and sent him sliding on his face for quite a considerable distance along the main deck." A Dutch doctor in Semarang stressed that the resulting spinal condition needed a three-month rest, advice which Conrad heeded; and after signing off the *Highland Forest* on July 1, 1887, he went into the Singapore Hospital.* Although

* Twelve years later, Conrad turned this episode of his life into fiction. In plotting how Lord Jim became chief mate of the *Patna,* Conrad has a spar disable Jim so that he goes into a Sinapore hospital before sailing out on his ill-fated voyage. Conrad's description of Jim perhaps reflects his own morbidity when struck down: "Jim . . . spent many days stretched on his back, dazed, battered, hopeless, and tormented as if at the bottom of an abyss of unrest. He did not care what the end would be, and in his lucid moments over-

Conrad's first berth since gaining his master's certificate was hardly auspicious—and as chief mate at that!—nevertheless in the *Mirror* he left a suitable valedictory of the need for craftsmanship so that man and ship are in accord:

> A ship is not a slave. You must make her easy in a seaway, you must never forget that you owe her the fullest share of your thought, of your skill, of your self-love. If you remember that obligation, naturally and without effort, as if it were an instinctive feeling of your inner life, she will sail, stay, run for you as long as she is able, or, like a sea-bird going to rest upon the angry waves, she will lay out the heaviest gale that ever made you doubt living long enough to see another sunrise.

Conrad wrote to his uncle about his affliction on July 2/14, and Bobrowski, very much worried, answered in agitated terms, perhaps fearful that his nephew would become an invalid. Understandably prone to see disaster everywhere after having lost so many relatives under adverse circumstances, Tadeusz read doom into all matters of illness or debilitation:

> And indeed it looks like that if our mariner, who risks death, is later to be faced with the prospect of rheumatism! This is too early for you, and once you have had trouble in your leg I very much doubt if you will ever quite get rid of it. You did not write to me exactly what the trouble is; is it ordinary rheumatism? or sciatica?—or perhaps paralysis? It could be any of these. . . . I would like to think that it is something slight, but the sad experience I have gone through with persons dear to me continually eggs me on to think the worst. With old age comes doubt!

Bobrowski suggests that Conrad apply to the same shipowners for a berth, all as part of his hope that Conrad can financially as well as physically return to his feet. With his discharge from the *Highland Forest*, Conrad received wages of £16, about $200 in current money. After a little more than six weeks in the hospital, he signed on the *Vidar* as chief mate, for voyages to the Dutch East Indies with frequent returns to Singapore. In terms of Conrad's reaching out toward writing—the beginning of *Almayer's Folly* was less than two years off—this was the most important berth he was to take; for it became the linkage between the seaman and those observations which became too intense for him to ignore. The *Vidar*, a steamer of 300 tons, would bring him deep into the Malay archipelago, where he would catch glimpses of William Charles Olmeijer, the physical model for Almayer, his first major fictional protagonist. Conrad asserted that it was the sight of Olmeijer that triggered his imagination and got him started as a writer of fiction: ". . . if I had not got to know Almayer pretty well it is almost certain there would never have been a line of mine in print."

---

valued his indifference. The danger, when not seen, has the imperfect vagueness of human thought. The fear grows shadowy; and Imagination, the enemy of men, the father of all terrors, unstimulated, sinks to rest in the dulness of exhausted emotion" (p. 11).

Conrad signed on the *Vidar* on August 22, 1887; the steamer, owned by an Arab, sailed under a Dutch flag, since these waters belonged to Holland, and was commanded by Captain Craig, an Englishman. It is doubtful if Conrad once he had settled on English citizenship would have sailed under a foreign national. The *Vidar* carried to Borneo waters the general junk merchandise—crockery ware, pots and pans, etc.—that white traders used to barter for local products such as rattan, beeswax, gutta-percha, cane sugar, and rubber. It is also possible that the *Vidar* sold guns, gunpowder, and other contraband, either for money or goods. The three-week voyages were characterized by frequent stops, and on his return trips to Singapore, the home base, Conrad probably still received medical treatment for his dorsal ailment. The routes or names of places followed by the *Vidar* would become the staples of a significant number of Conrad's works, not only in *Almayer's Folly*, *An Outcast of the Islands*, and *The Rescue*, but also in *Victory*, "Because of the Dollars," "The Planter of Malata," and *Lord Jim.*

The route of the *Vidar* was essentially to steam from Singapore southeast through the Karimata Strait, a broad sea path between Java and Borneo, connecting the South China Sea with the Java Sea—the waters traversed by Tom Lingard's brig in *The Rescue.* Two of the stops would be Banjermasin (Banjarmassim) and Pulu Laut (Pulo Laut) on the south Borneo coast, and then the ship would head into the Macassar Strait to Donggala (Dongala), on the west coast of Celebes. From Donggala, the *Vidar*'s trading pattern would take her across the strait to Coti Berau on the eastern fringe of Borneo, north to Bulungan along the Borneo coast, and then on the return trip follow the same pattern in reverse to Singapore, a run of about three weeks in all.

Although we have the large advantage of hindsight, we can try to see these voyages from the point of view of the seaman Conrad, who was, evidently, seeking alternate modes of experience and livelihood. The voyages were not frenetic, and they fell into patterns, with sufficient repetition of places and people for Conrad to be able to renew his observations, even time for him to shape distinct impressions against imaginative re-creations of them. The pattern of voyages, with their recurring mixture of exotic scenery, expatriate Hollanders, crooked traders, piratical shippers, Arabs, and local tribesmen, was precisely the kind of experience to feed Conrad's imagination, which had early been nurtured on the strange, distant, and bizarre. While these seas were not the Mediterranean, and the events were alien indeed from the exploits of Odysseus, nevertheless it must have seemed to Conrad that he was teetering on the edge of civilization, deep in the beginning of time, where mankind itself may have begun in the Borneo jungles.

In *The Shadow-Line*, written at the time of World War I, Conrad caught the contrasting shades of his narrator's life. He has reached a point of boredom, weariness, and dissatisfaction, and in just such a mood—we can assume it was Conrad's—he throws up his berth.

> It was in an Eastern port. She was an Eastern ship, inasmuch as then she belonged to that port. She traded among dark islands on a blue reef-scarred sea, with the Red Ensign over the taffrail and at her masthead a house-flag, also red, but with a green border and with a white crescent in it. For an Arab owned her, and a Syed at that [Syed Mosin Bin S. Ali Jaffree].

He continues:

> Excellent (and picturesque) Arab owner, about whom one needed not to trouble one's head, a most excellent Scottish ship—for she was that from the keel up—excellent sea-boat, easy to keep clean, most handy in every way, and if it had not been for her internal propulsion, worthy of any man's love, I cherish to this day a profound respect for her memory. As to the kind of trade she was engaged in and the character of my shipmates, I could not have been happier if I had had the life and the men made to my order by a benevolent Enchanter.

Conrad says that suddenly he "left all this. I left it in that, to us, inconsequential manner in which a bird flies away from a comfortable branch. It was as though all unknowing I had heard a whisper or seen something. . . . One day I was perfectly right and the next everything was gone—glamour, flavour, interest, contentment—everything. It was one of those moments, you know. The green sickness of late youth [Conrad was turning thirty] descended on me and carried me off."

From what did this "green sickness" carry him off? What was he seeing and doing on this auspicious series of voyages into Borneo, this naturalized Pole from a revolutionary family now certified as a sea captain? The pattern of his own life up to this time was not any less exotic and bizarre than the scenes of people and events he was observing. Subject and object joined in one who could understand the sensory qualities of the East. Sight-sound-smell-taste-touch: where did one end and the other begin in this crazy mix? As he later wrote in his Preface to *The Nigger of the "Narcissus"*: "All art, therefore, appeals primarily to the senses, and the artistic aim when expressing itself in written words must also make its appeal through the senses, if its high desire is to reach the spring of responsive emotions. It must strenuously aspire to the plasticity of sculpture, to the colour of painting, and to the magic suggestiveness of music—which is the art of arts." Although Conrad may have been persuaded by the Wagnerites and the *symbolistes* of the merging and blending of all the arts, more likely he reached this conclusion many years before when he tried to make sense of the crazy-quilt pattern of Europeans and Borneo natives observed from a ship owned by an Arab, commanded by an Englishman, and recorded for history by a Pole.

What precisely did Conrad observe? Primarily, he sailed into an area that was a curious balance of cutthroat capitalism and loose colonialism—what he was to find in more intensive form in his Congo experience. The Dutch and the English had struggled for hegemony in this East Borneo area, and the Dutch, much to Almayer's chagrin and anger, became the colonial power to reckon with. Several major characters in Conrad's fiction were based on actual figures he met here, or on figures, such as William Lingard, whom he heard about from local gossip and printed sources.

Olmeijer (or Almayer—Conrad spelled it as he heard it) was born in Java in 1848 and thus was thirty-nine when Conrad encountered him in Berau (the Sambir of *Almayer's Folly*). Olmeijer was of Dutch background but clearly oriented toward the English, for when Conrad saw him he was a partner in the English firm of Lingard & Co. Olmeijer was related by marriage to William Lingard (the "Tom Lingard" of *Almayer, An Outcast,* and, more importantly, *The Rescue*). After Lingard married a cousin or niece of Olmeijer, the latter went to work for him at his trading post in Macassar and later in Berau, where he was chief of the trading station. In 1874, Olmeijer married a girl of mixed blood, a Eurasian, whose first name, Johanna, Conrad used for the name of Willems's wife in *An Outcast.* Johanna Marie Cornelia van Lieshout was the daughter of a Dutch naval officer and a Manadonese mother. In *Almayer's Folly,* Conrad apparently invented the background for Almayer's wife, making her into a deserted child who is taken in by Lingard and later married off to Almayer;* he did, however, draw upon the Eurasian background for the composition of Joanna in *An Outcast.*

Involved here is a transposition of people and their derivation, the use of composites, of fragmentary knowledge mixed with incomplete information gained from gossip, hearsay, and some written sources. For someone of Conrad's own "composite" background, the situation seemed quite appropriate; and we can speculate that one reason he found the Borneo area a spur to his imagination was its similarity to Poland. Borneo was an area of contention between Dutch and English imperialists, its people fought over by Arabs, Malays, and various piratical forces. In this respect, Lingard, the "Rajah Laut" or "King of the Sea," was a benevolent dictator, a quasi-local man who set general policy.

In *Almayer's Folly,* Conrad captures the disrupted plans of the individual caught in a country which is the plaything of colonial or imperialist powers,

* Conrad writes: "Almayer had heard of him [Lingard) before he had been three days in Macassar, had heard the stories of his smart business transactions, his loves, and also of his desperate fights with Sulu pirates, together with the romantic tale of some child—a girl—found in a piratical prau by the victorious Lingard, when, after a long contest, he boarded the craft, driving the crew overboard. This girl, it was generally known, Lingard had adopted, was having her educated in some convent in Java, and spoke of her as 'my daughter' [as she well might have been]. He had sworn a mighty oath to marry her to a white man before he went home and to leave her all his money" (p. 7).

a clear throwback to his view of Poland caught among Germany, Austria, and Russia.

> The deliberations conducted in London have a far-reaching importance, and so the decision issued from the fog-veiled offices of the Borneo Company darkened for Almayer the brilliant sunshine of the Tropics, and added another drop of bitterness to the cup of his disenchantments. The claim to that part of the East Coast was abandoned, leaving the Pantai river under the nominal power of Holland.

The Olmeijer whom Conrad saw in Berau had little to do with the defeated, languid, bitter old man whom he describes as Almayer; nor was Olmeijer's wife the *Macbeth*-like witch portrayed as Almayer's wife. Conrad portrayed his fictional character as a man whose life was passing by him as if disconnected to will or want. The living Olmeijer was a bustling trader, a gunrunner (like the young Conrad in Marseilles), a seller of ammunition, as well as a family man—not with the one daughter of Almayer, but with five sons and six daughters born to him during his marriage. The birth of the eleventh child evidently led to Mrs. Olmeijer's death. Thus, whenever Conrad glimpsed the trader, he saw a man of active bearing, hopeful mien, and favorable future.

The Almayer whom Conrad drew from this model was a composite of his own experiences. Much of Apollo and his own background is read forward into Almayer and his situation. The father-son relationship becomes one of father and daughter, whereas the mother is a spectral, divisive figure (a "Bobrowska," as it were), with the foreground a struggle between the father's heritage and the child's "mixed" inheritance. The lost hopes, the dreams of gold, the fantasies of wealth, the bitterness of the political situation, the waiting for death, the acceptance of steady decline, the lapse into false hope—all of these recall Conrad's own memories, however transposed into a new key. They also reflect, beyond his childhood experiences, his Schopenhauerean pessimism, his sense of the individual will beating futilely against the will of the world and seeking temporary gratification in the vale of tears. Intermixed with these remnants of German pessimism is the occasional malevolence of nature, Schopenhauer reductionism linked with Darwinian nature; so that man becomes more frail in one's imagination than in actuality.

In a passage in *A Personal Record*, he details how he started to write *Almayer's Folly*. The impressionistic method is apparent; for Conrad is writing in 1908–09 of a memory that reverts to 1889–91, when he began to write about something he recalled from 1887, and the three times and three places merge with each other as a composite experience. One could add to this tripartite recollection a fourth, that of his father, Apollo, in his pajamas, ill, a figure of decline and deterioration. Conrad writes:

> I had seen him [Olmeijer] for the first time some four years before [more likely two] from the bridge of a steamer moored to a rickety little wharf forty miles up, more or less, a Bornean river. It was very early morning, and a slight mist, an opaline mist as in Bessborough Gardens [where Conrad began *Almayer*] only without the fiery flicks on roof and chimney-pot from the rays of the red London sun, promised to turn presently into a woolly fog. . . . He stepped upon the jetty. He was clad simply in flapping pyjamas of cretonne pattern (enormous flowers with yellow petals on a disagreeable blue ground) and a thin cotton singlet with short sleeves. His arms, bare to the elbow, were crossed on his chest. His black hair looked as if it had not been cut for a very long time and a curly wisp of it strayed across his forehead. I had heard of him at Singapore; I had heard of him on board; I had heard of him early in the morning and late at night; I had heard of him at tiffin and at dinner; I had heard of him in a place called Pulo Laut from a half caste gentleman there, who described himself as the manager of a coal-mine; which sounded civilized and progressive till you heard that the mine could not be worked at present because it was haunted by some particularly atrocious ghosts.

In addition to the old and depleted Almayer whom we meet in *Almayer's Folly*, we also encounter an old Lingard, who is trying to salvage something of the ruins of his fortune with explorations of the interior. The Tom Lingard of Conrad's novel is clearly in decline, although as he appears in later Conrad novels he becomes increasingly younger. The method of observation is curious, tied as I believe it is to Conrad's own background, which created a way of seeing. He had, first, to confront decline and deterioration, as in the old people surrounding him when his mother died and later when he was orphaned. Before he could focus on their earlier lives, when achievement was possible, he had to relate himself to the full extent of their failure. Once he noted the aging process—an old Almayer, an old Lingard, their lives in ruins—he could then work back through them to an earlier time when they were hopeful and full of plans and energy. Conrad's desire to work in reverse, to move backward in time, is attached, I believe, to a psychological need; so that his burrowing method of narrative is, for him, the only way he could approximate the data of his own past. Characters did not grow up to face the future; the future had already been met by them, the future had defeated them, and only then could Conrad conceive of their earlier lives before defeat and decline.

William Lingard, the rough basis for Tom, was an energetic seaman, shipowner, and trader, moving in and out of legal and illegal activities as befitting a man renowned as the "Rajah Laut." Although it is quite possible that Conrad never met him, Lingard caught the young seaman's imagination. Like Dominic Cervoni, Lingard was as close as Conrad was ever to come to the Odysseus of his childhood dreams and reading. Very possibly, his mixture of shrewdness as a trader, daring as a contender with sea pirates for routes and goods, and expertise as a handler of sailing vessels recalled to Conrad those daring adventurers, both real and fictitious, both Polish and Greek, with whom his own childhood was so closely connected. Further, Lingard, we know, was renowned as a storyteller, a spinner of tales, with his favorite resting place Emmerson's Tiffin Room in Singapore. As a teller of tales, there was in William Lingard many of the characteristics we also associate with Marlow, Conrad's own archetypal "artist figure," the narrator of four of his novels and tales.

The character of William Lingard deserves our attention, not only for the biographical data which establish him as central to many of Conrad's early ideas of character, but as a presence who very possibly prodded Conrad's literary imagination far more than did the real figures behind Almayer and Willems. As already suggested, Lingard fitted into Conrad's imagination as a combination of Odysseus, those early Polish romantic heroes, and his own forebears in their struggles against imperial Russia; and yet he was shrewd, did not get trapped, mixed adventure and romance with trade and wealth, and, beyond it all, managed to be a storyteller.

Marlow, who is so clearly a surrogate figure for Conrad the writer, also suggests a former time of adventure and romance, even while presenting a contemporary image of solidity and sobriety. His art is based on a past career that must be sifted through the memory, then balanced with present circumstances; so that even the horrors of the Congo do not come to us raw or as having occurred in the present. This is an art structured on stasis, on immobility, even as it tells of great movement, activity, and emotional turbulence.

In *A Personal Record*, Conrad insists that "the conception of a planned book was entirely outside my mental range when I sat down to write; the ambition of being an author had never turned up amongst these gracious imaginary existences one creates fondly for oneself at times in the stillness and immobility of a day-dream." He says that the necessity which impelled him to write "was a hidden obscure necessity, a completely masked and unaccountable phenomenon." Although there is much to argue with here, nevertheless, he may be correct in a narrow sense. He was, that is, carried along to write by the desire to emulate those storytellers who had captured his imagination, in a sense to pour out what he had known and seen, and to do this in a manner consistent with the prose and manner of whatever art his reading had gained for him.

In another section of *A Personal Record*, Conrad gave clues as to the workings of his mind:

> Only in men's imagination does every truth find an effective and undeniable existence. Imagination, not invention, is the supreme master of art

as of life. An imaginative and exact rendering of authentic memories may serve worthily that spirit of piety towards all things human which sanctions the conceptions of a writer of tales, and the emotions of the man reviewing his own experience.

In these seemingly innocent lines, Conrad suggests memory, imagination, and the man's "own experience" as the key elements in his art. And these elements were precisely those being blended when he came upon the presence of William Lingard in Singapore, whether in the flesh or through local gossip and written sources. None of this should be misunderstood. The old trader alone, without Conrad's early identification with men of Lingard's stamp, would not have prodded his imagination. Further, a Lingard in the flesh may have discouraged Conrad—for the sailor and trader by now was old, in his early sixties; but a Lingard of gossip, storytelling, a mythical Lingard blown up out of proportion to the real man—such was the stuff which could nourish Conrad's imagination.

William Lingard was a Lancashireman, born in 1824. We know that, like Conrad, he broke away, at nineteen, from a traditional landed family in order to pursue a sea career. Lingard's career was mysterious, possibly consciously kept cloaked to hide illegal activities. He apparently owned several ships at one time and traded extensively in the East Borneo areas around the Macassar Strait, in and around Berau, Bulungan, and Macassar. Moreover, Conrad's Tom Lingard is evidently a composite of William Lingard and another Far Eastern trader, Captain John Dill Ross. Some of the past events ascribed to Tom Lingard in *The Rescue* can be traced not to William Lingard but to Ross. The latter, however, was more a businessman than a sailor, and therefore far less romantic to Conrad.

A matter of even greater biographical interest is that William Lingard seems to have adopted protégés, much as Tom Lingard does. Sherry shows that the flesh-and-blood Lingard became the guardian of two children of a merchant named Secretan. This fact, probably known to Conrad, since he makes Tom Lingard's fortunes hang on just these actions, fitted in perfectly with his own experience, having been the ward of several people before Tadeusz Bobrowski became his guardian. The duplication of past experiences, and, therefore, the presence of Bobrowski in Lingard's actions, could not have been lost on Conrad's imagination; reinforced by the fact that guardianship and wardship would become so central to his early novels. Added to this is the creation of the character Stein, in *Lord Jim*, who has strong affinities to aspects of the real Lingard and was himself another "guardian" of sorts, helping Jim to find post after post as he runs from himself.

For the biographer seeking connections between the outward life and the inner imagination, this succession of fatherly or guardian figures in Conrad's early work is indeed relevant to an understanding of how his imagination was organizing the material that his activities churned up. In other respects as well—and chiefly in matters of water routes, mouths, openings, rivers—Conrad was pursuing in his early fiction imaginative re-creations of childhood experiences and postures. Of extreme importance in his first two novels is the river Berau (the Pantai in *Almayer's Folly*), where Captain William Lingard had established a trading post and where Olmeijer and Jim Lingard (a nephew of William) were traders.* As mentioned above, this area and its river enter into three and possibly four Conrad works: *Almayer's Folly*, *An Outcast of the Islands*, the second part of *Lord Jim* (as Patusan), and possibly in *The Rescue* as an Eastern river. Stressed in Conrad's first two novels is the entrance (one or more) to the river, which only Lingard knows of and which is the secret of his success as a trader.

Conrad's founding so much of his early fictional world on secret information, betrayal of confidences, on mouths, entrances, secret routes, on rescues, wards, guardians, protégés surely has artistic implications. Although we cannot be precise in such matters, we can read back through the fiction to the Conrad of 1887–88 and see him as reaching toward some secret activity. The nature of his early material suggests a squirreling away of data, the construction of holes and burrows in his mind where he could secrete details, his imagination as a kind of castle keep or treasure trove. Captain Craig of the *Vidar* told Jean-Aubry in 1924 that when he visited Conrad in his cabin, he would usually find the latter writing. Since Conrad's correspondence with his uncle was little more than one letter a month and his circle of friends quite small—Hope, Krieger, the Kliszczewskis—we can assume that he was keeping a diary or journal (as he was to do in the Congo) or else already working on *Almayer*. It is even possible he was attempting stories, essays, or novels which he later destroyed. Whatever the facts, it seems possible Conrad was already moving toward a parallel activity, at least entertaining an alternate existence based almost completely on innerness. It was as if in his stress on secret routes and disguised openings he had sought out the very opposite of ocean and sea.

Psychologically, his choice of novelistic materials, one is tempted to say, suggests a course back toward the mother he lost so early, in which he plays the double roles his father played as adventurer and writer. The way back to the mother, according to his speculation, could come only when he completed the circuit of his father's existence and himself became a writer. Inner and outer would finally meet in his movement toward a literary career, and he would discover not only his own talents but, because of the nature of his material, the secret routes to the lost one.†

---

* As Sherry points out, when Conrad visited the river Berau, it was in actuality the Pantai. Conrad made no change for fictional purposes. Conrad also referred to the Berau (or Berouw) as the Brow.

† In trying to find ways in which John Stuart Mill reached back to his father, James, and his mother, Harriet, Bruce Mazlish shows how the younger Mill duplicated the childhood situation, what we are suggesting in

Besides the local topography which he reproduced, as well as major figures, Conrad also found names such as Lakamba, Dain Maroola, Babalatchi, and others. Further, he probably saw his "outcast of the islands," Willems, here, in the figure of Carel de Veer, an alcohol-ridden Hollander. In his Note to the *Outcast* many years later, Conrad spoke of the man, a prototypical European who ended up on the slag heaps of a culture he could never penetrate.

> The man who suggested Willems to me was not particularly interesting in himself. My interest was aroused by his dependent position, his strange, dubious status of a mistrusted, disliked, worn-out European living on the reluctant toleration of that Settlement hidden in the heart of the forest-land, up that sombre stream which our ship was the only white men's ship to visit. With his hollow, clean-shaved cheeks, a heavy grey moustache and eyes without any expression whatever, clad always in a spotless sleeping suit much befrogged in front, which left his lean neck wholly uncovered, and with his bare feet in a pair of straw slippers, he wandered silently amongst the houses in daylight, almost as dumb as an animal and apparently much more homeless. . . . The only definite statement I could extract from anybody was that it was he who had "brought the Arabs into the river." . . . I knew that Almayer founded the chronology of all his misfortunes on the date of that fateful advent.

Intermixed with Willems and the local tribesmen is Jim Lingard, the nephew of William Lingard, and as we shall see, himself a person of some consequence in Conrad's fictional treatment of his career. When Jim appeared at Berau, Olmeijer had been head of the trading post for ten years, and the proximity of the two men, one the nephew of William Lingard and the older man related to him by marriage, could only have proven competitive and fractious. This interplay of wards, guardians, benefactors, and protégés must have appealed to Conrad. These overlapping patterns of his life with his early work indicate that he found in the Lingard (William and Tom)–Almayer-Willems relationships a replay of his own past, the reproduction of what he had always known. As though funneled through memory, Conrad noted the old father figure, Lingard, who gave Almayer his start, and then, later, Willems—a descending order which leads to the loss of his secret trade routes. His benefactions end in deception and treachery; his protégés all fail him, as in a sense he has failed them.

In *Lord Jim*, the locale remains much the same, although the cast of characters changes. There, Stein helps Jim, as before that he had himself been

---

Conrad's emphasis on secret paths and openings. Mazlish shows that the names Harriet, John, and Taylor recur at intervals in Mill's life—for example, the "Harriet" of his grandmother and mother, and of the woman he married. Mill's way back was through names, which in turn duplicated careers. Conrad sought a return not only through careers but in the very imagistic shape that career took. Of course, Conrad had his own naming problems, as we have already observed. (See Bruce Mazlish, *James and John Stuart Mill*, pp. 284–85.)

aided by a Scotsman, Alexander M'Neil. Still another protégé appears in the person of Cornelius, whose benefactor Stein had once been. Of further interest is the fact that in each instance of benefaction there is treachery. In the trilogy of *Almayer, Outcast,* and *Rescue,* Willems is the viper; in *Lord Jim,* Cornelius betrays whatever trust was invested in him. For the biographer, Conrad's ordering of these slight and glancing experiences suggests that he shared to a large extent his uncle's evaluation of his own character as a wastrel and prodigal nephew. While none of this is conclusive, we cannot help but be struck by Conrad's insistence on failure, deception, treachery, betrayal of trust. Although these are themes he could have picked up from his own Polish past and reading, nevertheless, his insistence on the motif suggests a more immediate connection to the Conrad of the 1880s and 1890s.

The trips back and forth between Singapore and East Borneo apparently gave Conrad time to recover from his assorted ailments—back, lameness, and liver—and with recovery came the familiar boredom, the urge to move on. Also in his mind might have been the fact that with a master's certificate he was serving as chief mate, a condition that would rankle someone as proud as he and as vain about his gentry status; born to lead, he had, thus far, only served.* Whatever his precise reasons, and we should not discount the disquiet he would be feeling if the decision to begin writing had also taken place, he left the *Vidar* at Singapore, just after his thirtieth birthday, on January 4, 1888. In all, Conrad had spent very few days in Berau. Although he made four journeys in all, the layover was quite short, at most three days; and thus Conrad made his observations for a total of less than two weeks. In nearly all instances when his fiction had some factual basis, the latter is very skimpy, whether the view of South America for *Nostromo* or the experience of East Borneo and its surrounding waters for his early fiction.

Apparently, Conrad read extensively in Malay materials in order to bolster his rather few observations. Even here, we should not overstress his study of the literature, since Conrad's way was to suggest authenticity and then to move into imaginative re-creation. In nearly every use of backgrounding, as we saw with topography, he left his sources far behind. For *Nostromo,* he had written sources underlying every aspect—the names of characters, their careers, the geography, main themes, the critical turning point—and yet he used the material in ways not at all suggested by the sources. So here. His Malayan reading was more than sufficient for him to

* The captain in *The Shadow-Line,* for example, exults over his first command: "I was already the man in command. My sensations could not be like those of any other man on board. In that community I stood, like a king in his country, in a class all by myself. I mean an hereditary king, not a mere elected head of a state. I was brought there to rule by an agency as remote from the people and as inscrutable almost to them as the Grace of God" (p. 62).

gain authentic detail. Among others, he consulted: Wallace's *The Malay Archipelago*, the *Journals* of Rajah James Brooke of Sarawak, McNair's *Perak and the Malays;* as well as several which Norman Sherry has uncovered: Osborn's *My Journal in Malayan Waters*, St. John's *Life in the Forests of the Far East*, Marryat's *Borneo and the Indian Archipelago*, and Belcher's account of the voyage of H.M.S. *Samarang.* As was typical of his way of proceeding, he used names unchanged from his reading, possibly to ensure authenticity but, more probably, to make certain of the correct spelling. Baines shows us how he took from McNair's *Perak and the Malays* the names of Doramin (Doraman in the original), Tamb' Itam, and Tunku Allang, which appear in *Lord Jim;* as well as an entire phrase used in *The Rescue:* "Even a lizard will give a fly time to say its prayers," a Malay proverb which Conrad could have picked up elsewhere.

If we work closely with *Perak and the Malays*, we note that Conrad went even further than names and individual lines; he incorporated into *Lord Jim* parts of scenes and incidents. Although these details are interesting, even more compelling was Conrad's method of working; so that reading, actual figures, and his own background blended into each other in a seamless flow. Sources, his own life, and real people are present even as they are transcended. Lord Jim is himself a good example of this transformation, for the two parts of the novel, the first devoted to the *Patna* incident and the second to Patusan, are really based on two different people. The first, as we have seen, rests on an incident in the life of A. P. Williams; whereas the second, in Patusan, is more clearly founded on Jim Lingard. Although it is doubtful that Jim Lingard's presence in East Borneo influenced Conrad's expansion of *Lord Jim* to a second part—considerations of serialization and placement in *Blackwood's Magazine* appear more important—nevertheless, he did find the young man's presence memorable enough to form the basis of the later character.

When Conrad met or saw him in Berau, Jim Lingard was, at twenty-five, only four years younger than the future writer. His clean-shaven and fresh appearance apparently caught Conrad's eye, seeking as it was someone whose physique would belie the hesitancy and destructive romanticism within. Also, we know that Jim was known as "Tuan Jim," that is, Lord Jim. Although there was nothing especially compelling about this young man, aside from his hopeful, expectant manner and physical solidity, he fitted into Conrad's developing view of mankind, in which the inner drama contradicted whatever face one presented to the world. The East, as later Africa, was a fruitful testing ground for such assumptions about man, as much as his earlier reading in Polish literature had formed his sense of the Don-Sancho split.

Although Conrad could not know it, his career as a mariner was cresting at just the time it would begin to wane. That is, with his first solid command, of the *Otago,* he was already moving into his third and final life, with the beginnings of *Almayer's Folly.* In *The Shadow-Line,* as we have observed, he speaks of the boredom, weariness, and dissatisfaction that come on one, and which led, he says, to his throwing up his previous berth—clearly a reference to Conrad's giving up the *Vidar,* an Eastern ship "in an Eastern port."

If we pick up Conrad's comments in *The Shadow-Line* and fill in with some documents still preserved (in the Keating Collection at Yale), we can follow his movements after he left the *Vidar.* Having given up his berth out of ennui,* he hung around the Sailors' Home in Singapore, in a sense will-less, waiting for something to happen to him, ostensibly awaiting a passage back to England. A Captain Patterson advised Conrad to get after the steward of the Sailors' Home until the latter informed him that the very important Captain Henry Ellis, the marine superintendent, was seeking someone with a captain's certificate for a ready command, the *Otago,* at that time in Bangkok. In *The Shadow-Line,* Conrad disguises some of the names, but retains Captain Ellis; he also uses a memorandum which, in actuality, ordered Conrad to Bangkok to pick up his command.†

In a 1917 (February 27) letter to Sir Sidney Colvin, a close friend, Conrad wrote of the circumstances of March–April 1887 (really 1888), when he moved toward his first command. He points out that Giles in the novel was in reality Captain Patterson, and that the "experience is transposed into spiritual terms," which in art Conrad says is "a perfectly legitimate thing to do, as long as one preserves the exact truth enshrined therein." Conrad worked closely indeed with reality, even confusing the name of the actual chief mate "Born" with "Burns" in the novel, letting "Born" get into the manuscript and "Burns" into his letter, as if the two, one real and one fictional, were indistinguishable once the imagination had worked on them.

For Conrad's experiences on the *Otago,* we will have to follow the broad outline of *The Shadow-Line,* keeping in mind that the novel would inevita-

* Conrad suggests the malaise by using as epigraph for Chapter I of *The Shadow-Line* Baudelaire's "D'autres fois, calme plat, grand mirroir / De mon désespoir." For this great poet of despair, ennui, and malaise, the lines from "La Musique" indicate the sea as itself a great mirror or glass for his despair, a perfect image for the bored Conrad seeking, like Narcissus, some meaning in the reflection.

† Dated January 19, 1888, the memorandum is worded: "This is to inform you that you are required to proceed today in the s.s. *Melita* to Bangkok and you will report your arrival to the British Consul and produce this memorandum which will show that I have engaged you to be Master of the *Otago* in accordance with the Consul's telegram on a voyage from Bangkok to Melbourne. . . ." It is signed by Henry Ellis [Keating Collection]. On the same day, Captain Ellis wrote to the Consul at Bangkok: "The person I have engaged is Mr Conrad Korzeniowski, who holds a certificate of Competency as Master from the Board of Trade. He bears a good character from the several vessels he has sailed out of this Port. I have agreed with him that his wages at £14 per month to count from date of arrival at Bangkok" (London Public Record Office).

bly sharpen situations for dramatic purposes. Conrad went up to Bangkok, where he met the chief mate, Born, and heard about the strange former master, now dead. From Burns (Born), Conrad learns of things which turn the *Otago* and its experiences into something of a Flying Dutchman. The former master (John Snadden) would keep to his cabin, let the ship "loaf at sea for inscrutable reasons," and at times come up on deck only to return below, where he sawed away on his violin for hours on end, often playing all night. Burns feels the ship is haunted by the now-dead master and is embittered by having been passed over for the command. In addition, as if the eeriness had spread to the entire crew, it is infected with a malady which lays everyone low except the captain and the cook, Ransome. This is the ship and situation Conrad inherited as his first command.*

Interestingly, Conrad cast his first command fictionally as a combination of "The Ancient Mariner," with the crew cursed by illness, and the Flying Dutchman, a ship and captain cursed. Although Conrad sidesteps the question of faith, which is central to the Dutchman legend, he does focus on fidelity, which for him was the practical aspect of faith. Ransome, with his heart ailment, has fidelity to an idea, as does the captain, and the two of them, along with a devoted crew, turn the cursed "Dutchman" into a barely functioning ship. When, finally, they sail into Singapore harbor, they have beaten the curse of the dead master, the misfortune of land maladies, and the doom of a calm sea. The captain has passed his initiation.

It is psychologically compelling that Conrad saw himself as part of a curse, an infection, a malady, all of which he, as a kind of sickened king, would have to set right before he could call himself a master mariner. Apparently, he had, in some corner of his mind, accepted the tainted quality of his existence, however he explained it to himself, and saw himself as achiev-

---

* Although we are well warned not to equate novelistic dramatization with the real thing, for which we have little direct evidence, there are two letters in the Keating Collection at Yale which appear to substantiate Conrad's presentation of his first command. One, dated April 5, 1888, is from the firm of Henry Simpson & Sons of Adelaide, the owners of the *Otago:* "Your favours dated Bangkok 2 and 6 February, latter with Postscript dated 7th on the eve of sailing, duly reached me [James Simpson], and have been interesting as detailing the melancholy circumstances under which you took charge of the barque *Otago.*" Simpson goes on to say that he cannot compare them with other documents as he never received any word from the late captain.

In another note, this time from a physician, William Willis, we have corroboration of the crew's condition when Conrad took over the command of the *Otago:* "I think it is not out of place on my part that I should state, although not asked by you to do so, to prevent any misapprehension hereafter, that the crew of the sailing ship *Otago* has suffered severely whilst in Bangkok from tropical diseases, including fever, dysentery and cholera; and I can speak of my own knowledge that you have done all in your power in the trying and responsible position of Master of the Ship to hasten the departure of your vessel from this unhealthy place and at the same time to save the lives of the men under your command" (February 1888).

ing certain goals solely by hurdling successive obstacles. It is perhaps not happenstance that he chose a sea career, with its stages of examinations and trials, each of which was a torture to prepare for and sit for; as if by passing through each stage of *that* world he could set right the inner coordinates of *his* world. The image of the Flying Dutchman is particularly apt for this Pole sailing on English ships, an apparition of sorts, deriving from a tainted background, and seeking fidelity to an idea as a way of balancing out the curse of the sea. The Dutchman has treasures in its hold—that mysterious treasure at the heart of every trial and testing; and those treasures, which Conrad sensed in himself, could be released only through an expiation of sorts.

The *Otago* experience, besides its importance as Conrad's first and sole major command (the only other was a brief stint on a Congo riverboat), generated several pieces of fiction: *The Shadow-Line*, a work of the war years, and the stories "Falk," dating from May 1901, and "A Smile of Fortune," dated August 1910. "Falk," with its mysterious tugboat captain who at one time had indulged in cannibalism and would now like to bite chunks of swelling flesh from a Brünnhilde-like young woman, seems to derive from the time when Conrad was waiting for his cargo in Bangkok. Also, in this story he mentions the name of Schomberg, the hotel keeper who is peripheral in "Falk" itself and *Lord Jim*, but of major importance in *Victory*.

We should note how tenaciously Conrad hung on to his view of people, his sight of Schomberg coming in 1888, mention of him seemingly exhausted in his work of 1899–1901, and then the character resurrected for major purposes in the 1912–14 period. Conrad's imagination worked not only on a tunneling through memory but on a duplicating and overlapping of characters and scenes. This aspect of his method helps to explain the terrible intensity of his presentation, especially in those later years when all essential ingredients came together.

Bangkok to Singapore in the cursed ship took three weeks, more than double the normal sailing time for the eight hundred miles. With a fresh crew on board, the *Otago* continued on to Sydney, Australia, where it arrived in early May. On May 5, Conrad wrote to his uncle from Sydney. The *Otago* loaded up, and on August 7, he took his command to Port Louis in Mauritius. In his essay "Geography and Some Explorers," he left an account of the voyage, a long and tricky one. The trip to Mauritius, which lies off Madagascar (Malagasy Republic), due east of the southeast African coast, encompassed two possible routes: either south around the coast of Australia and then due west across the Indian Ocean, which was the routine way; or north through the Torres Strait between the northern tip of Australia and New Guinea, past Darwin, and then due west to Mauritius. The latter was more dangerous because of the Torres Strait, and it was the route Conrad preferred.

In order to take this route, however, he needed the permission of the owners. Part of Conrad's reason may have been boredom, a desire for a challenge, a wish to test out his mariner's skills. In any event, he wrote the owners and suggested the northern route, expecting to receive "a severe rap on the knuckles" for wasting their time. Their response, to Conrad's surprise, merely pointed out the additional insurance premium for the more dangerous journey, and gave him permission to take the *Otago* on this hazardous route, pointing out that calms prevail in the Arafura Sea. In his essay, Conrad describes the voyage, now a matter of an initiation into the hazards of a treacherous sea.

Anxious to avoid the calms, Conrad left Sydney in a heavy gale, and on the ninth day reached the entrance of the Torres Strait. The strait was named after "the undaunted and reticent Spaniard who, in the seventeenth century, first sailed that way without knowing where he was, without suspecting he had New Guinea on one side of him and the whole solid Australian continent on the other." We note how Conrad was caught up by his early reading, experiencing that sense of adventure in going over routes he had once only imagined as a small boy in Poland. That romance of water and land masses never left him. Although the essay describing the voyage to Mauritius came at the very end of his life, it nevertheless conveys those feelings of awe felt by the captain of the *Otago* fully thirty-five years before as he tested out his prowess.

Aware of the background of the route—James Cook himself had laid it down—Conrad was also aware that his was "very likely the first, and certainly the last, merchant ship that carried a cargo that way." Conrad was to chart the route through the Torres Strait, as if it were necessary for him to follow the procedures of the great navigators before him and to update the past through his own presence. Passing through, Conrad saw wrecks of ships which had failed, especially a large American vessel that "loomed up, a sinister and enormous *memento mori* raised by the refraction of this serene afternoon above the far-away line of the horizon drawn under the sinking sun." As he came to the end, he mused on James Cook and the *Endeavour*, which had been hove-to in 1762, so that its captain could go ashore on a tiny spot of earth for half an hour. "It may be that on this dry crumb of the earth's crust which I was setting by compass he had tasted a moment of perfect peace." This recollection, too, came from Conrad's reading; and the memory juxtaposed to the actual experience in the Torres Strait amid the treacherous waters of the Arafura Sea suggests the quality of a paradise despite the dangers of the unexpected.

Jean-Aubry uncovered an exceptionally interesting passage describing Conrad when he reached Mauritius, a description of him by Paul Langlois, one of the charterers of the *Otago*. We must be cautious, however, for this description was related by letter to Savinien Mérédac, a local Mauritius man of letters, fully *forty-two years* after Langlois saw Conrad. The description, nevertheless, has some compelling touches. Langlois indicates his memory is precise because he saw a good deal of Conrad during the latter's six or seven weeks in Port Louis. He catches Conrad's facial expressions, which he says were unforgettable.

> He had vigorous, extremely mobile features which would change very quickly from gentleness to an excitability bordering on anger; large black eyes which were as a rule melancholy and dreamy, and gentle, too, except in his quite frequent moments of irritation; a determined chin, a well-shaped, handsome mouth, and a thick, well trimmed dark-brown moustache—such was his appearance, certainly agreeable but, above all, strange in its expression and difficult to forget when one had seen it once or twice.

Of particular significance is Langlois's assertion of Conrad's difference from the other skippers in the port. In appearance, Conrad stood out.

> In contrast to his colleagues Captain Korzeniowski was always dressed like a dandy. I can still see him (and just because of this contrast with the other sailors my memory is precise) arriving almost every day in my office dressed in a black or dark coat, a waistcoat, usually of a light colour, and "fancy" trousers, all well cut and of great elegance; he would be wearing a black or grey bowler tilted slightly to one side, would always wear gloves and carried a cane with a gold knob.

With his elegance of dress, he was dubbed "sarcastically 'the Russian Count,' " a title that would have amused the ferociously anti-Russian Pole.

Langlois stresses Conrad's nervousness, an affliction that had existed since childhood:

> As to his character, he had a perfect education, and a varied and interesting fund of conversation when he was in the mood—which was not always. He who was to become famous under the name of Joseph Conrad was often enough very taciturn and irritable. On such days he would have a nervous tic in the shoulder and eyes: anything unexpected, something falling on the floor or the slam of a door, would make him jump. He was what one would call a "neurasthenic"; in those days one spoke of "nerves."

Langlois points out that Conrad rarely appeared in public places, dropping in at Krumpholtz's, the shipping agent's, for only a few minutes each day. As far as socializing with the other captains at the Hotel Oriental, a common meeting place where the latest scuttlebutt was discussed, Conrad abstained from that also; even to taking no discernible walks in the country and eschewing, Langlois says, all contact with fashionable society. This, of course, contradicts Conrad's own presentation of his narrator in "A Smile of Fortune." But Langlois's remarks do indicate a not at all surprising introspective turn, which suggests if not writing then at least reading, accumulating, squirreling. Conrad was, apparently, readying himself for a leap into the heart of darkness: into the actual Congo on the map of Africa and into the "Congo" of a new career on his own inner map.

Even while less gregarious than the other captains, Conrad's stay in Port Louis appears to have been more social than Langlois observed. In fact, we come up against a very interesting situation, where we have some evidence of Conrad's stay (if we can believe Jean-Aubry's account) and a fictional presentation of that period. Although the two appear to be contradictory, each is really the obverse of the other. Much, of course, depends on accepting Jean-Aubry's version: The very day after his arrival in Port Louis Conrad met, at the offices of Blyth Bros., his consignees, the brother of one of their employees, a young merchant-navy officer named Gabriel Renouf, for whom Conrad had done a good turn in Bombay four years earlier. Renouf belonged to one of the best families in Mauritius, and the two, of similar class and manner, became friends, to the extent that Renouf introduced Conrad to his family, three sisters and two brothers. With his command of French and courteous address, Conrad had impressed the family, so that he was invited to come often. He related interesting stories, and he was to these provincial ladies (the very opposite, however, of Circe and Calypso) what Odysseus was to the islanders in Homer's epic. The young women were indeed less than epical, but they were attractive and good listeners. For Conrad, who had wandered in marginal areas for years without family ties, the Renouf residence would seem a home, even a nest.

Jean-Aubry then relates how Conrad's manner began to change, from volubility to coldness and preoccupation, so that the family did not expect to see him again. He did, however, return to this house on the corner of the rue de la Bourdonnais and the rue Saint-Georges. Conrad had apparently been busy with chartering problems, chiefly those connected to freight prices, which were being undercut by competition among the numerous sailing vessels. He had tried to get a better price but had had to accept the low rates that prevailed. Nevertheless, he did astutely think of inserting in the charter contract a clause making the charterer responsible for all tug and pilot charges incurred in entering Melbourne, where his cargo was bound, a practice that Jean-Aubry says became standard. Furthermore, since Conrad had carried out a cargo of fertilizer, he now needed jute matting to cover the dunnage and bottom boards before he could load his cargo of twelve thousand sacks of sugar for the voyage home. With the jute matting unavailable because of a fire, he was forced to wait.

Out of boredom, Jean-Aubry says, Conrad returned to the rue de la Bourdonnais, to the Renouf family, whom he described later in "A Smile" as descendants of the old colonists, "all noble, impoverished," and living a narrow, dull, and dignified life of decay. One thinks of the Faulknerian South or of the Polish *szlachta.* The men never rose very far, since they were not supposed to work too hard, and they took positions in inferior government offices or in low-level business operations. As for the women: they were pretty, "ignorant of the world, kind and agreeable and generally bilingual," in French and English. Apparently, Conrad and the young women in the family carried on a flirtation, since the latter subjected their very courteous guest to a series of queries, part of an "Album of Confidences" or a Confession Album. The questions, which were intended to be frivolous, were in French, and Conrad's answers were in English. The use of both languages is of interest. The French of the queries is to be expected, since this was the language Conrad spoke with all members of the family. In Conrad's English responses, I sense an attempt at wit, a way of demonstrating his inability to take it all seriously enough to answer in kind, even to Eugénie, to whom he later proposed. It does not, in any way, show discomfort or shyness. On the contrary, his replies display an intellectual superiority to the very girls whom he found attractive, a male putdown of female frivolity.

The reader may judge, as the entire sequence follows:

1. Quel est le principal trait de votre caractère? *Laziness.*
2. Par quels moyens cherchez-vous à plaire? *By making myself scarce.*
3. Quel nom fait battre votre coeur? *Ready to beat for any name.*
4. Quel serait votre rêve de bonheur? *Never dream of it; want reality.*
5. Où habite la personne qui occupe votre pensée? *A castle in Spain.*
6. Quelle est la qualité que vous préférez chez la femme? *Beauty.*
7. Que désirez-vous être? *Should like not to be.*
8. Quelle est votre fleur de prédilection? *Violet.*
9. Dans quel pays voudriez-vous vivre? *Do not know. Perhaps Lapland.*
10. Quelle est la couleur des yeux que vous préférez? *Grey.*
11. Quel est le don de la nature dont vous voudriez être doué? *Self-confidence.*
12. Que préférez-vous dans un bal? *Not dancing cannot tell.*
13. Quelle est votre promenade favorite? *Hate all "promenades."*
14. Que préférez vous, les brunes ou les blondes? *Both.*
15. Quelle est votre plus grandes distraction? *Chasing wild geese.*
16. Dîtes l'état présent de votre esprit? *Calm.*
17. Que détestez-vous le plus? *False pretences.*
18. Vous-croyez vous aimé? *Decline to state.*
19. Votre devise? ________
20. Votre nom? J.C.K.

Still, according to Jean-Aubry, Conrad played the gracious sea captain, inviting the family to tea, served in the Jardin des Pamplemousses by the *Flore Mauricienne*, then another time aboard the *Otago*. In the meanwhile, the loading of the *Otago* was almost concluded, and Conrad could relax, although he was being badgered into accepting a small load of potatoes. If we accept Jean-Aubry's version, we are now moving toward the climax, a kind of reverse *Madama Butterfly*. As soon as the *Otago* was ready, Conrad knew he would never see Eugénie again. He continued to appear and disappear, falling into silences, then into bursts of disconnected conversation: Jean-Aubry presents him as a man caught by the panic of love or gusts of infatuation. Then one day, according to Jean-Aubry, Conrad appeared at the office and asked one of the brothers for the hand of Eugénie in marriage; she was then twenty-six. When the women at home heard this, they were not surprised, having recognized the familiar signs; but the brother had to express his regrets to Conrad, for Eugénie was already betrothed to a pharmacist, and her marriage was only two months off.

Jean-Aubry sees Conrad as having planned an attachment, a family and a home, only to have all his "castles in Spain" crumble to nothing. Stricken by sorrow, Conrad remained on board the *Otago* until sailing time two days later, sending to Gabriel Renouf a farewell note to himself and his sisters and indicating his wish never to return to Mauritius. According to Jean-Aubry, it contained the following: "On January 14, at the time when Mademoiselle Eugénie is standing before the altar, I shall be near you in my thoughts." Incidentally, this note has never turned up.

Jean-Aubry's account, which must have come from Conrad himself thirty or more years after the event, suggests soap opera or Puccini. The elegant but lonely Polish mariner forms an attachment far outside the routine limits of civilization, is drawn to a pretty but frivolous young lady, dreams of family and home; this man of thirty, who has never known a stable domestic situation, proposes in the accepted manner through the medium of the girl's brother, finds himself preceded by another, and retreats vowing never to return. The patterning of the material and Jean-Aubry's reading of it is too much a stereotypical "romance" for us to accept it wholly as fact. What Conrad apparently related to Jean-Aubry was as much a fiction as "A Smile of Fortune," and it would be a serious mistake to accept Jean-Aubry's account as biographical fact.

In "A Smile of Fortune," the ship captain (Conrad, we can say) pays several visits to the home of a ship chandler named Alfred Jacobus, who has both a magnificent garden and an illegitimate daughter named Alice. The "garden" in Conrad's handling has something in it of the Garden, but Alice is not quite Eve, although she plays at it, and Conrad refuses to become Adam by succumbing to her wiles. Many of the details from Jean-Aubry's version of Conrad's stay in Port Louis are present: the captain awaits sacks as Conrad had waited for jute matting, the boredom level is similarly high, and the atmosphere is heavy with longueurs. In "A Smile," the captain seems in charge all the way; he flirts with Alice and raises hope in her and in her father that a match might be made. It is because of this flirtation and its ensuing circumstances that the chandler offers the captain a load of potatoes, which the latter subsequently sells at a good profit. Fortune has indeed smiled on him, just as he has attempted to gain a smile from the gloomy

Alice. Having no serious intentions, although tempted by her massively twisted hair and her goddess-like forehead, the captain leaves with his regular cargo and the potatoes.

Both episodes—the one related by Jean-Aubry and Conrad's "fictional" treatment—are mutually compatible.* What is especially compelling about the fictional version is the masochistic element in the captain's attraction to Alice. She is described as "snarling and superb and barely clad . . . with wild wisps of hair hanging down her tense face." Conrad says that "even her indifference was seductive." These are by no means isolated comments. They form the basis of the relationship, with her gloom and seeming indifference stoking the captain's passions. Despite this aspect, however, the captain remains playful, trying to make the morbid young woman smile and toying with her affections. The tone of the story is very much in keeping with the tone of Conrad's answers to the Renouf queries for their album.

The exact nature of what occurred in Port Louis will probably never be unraveled. We must be skeptical of Jean-Aubry's account of Conrad's wounding at Eugénie's hands precisely because Jean-Aubry heightened the romantic drama of the event and was surely following Conrad's own desires in his handling of the episode. Similarly, in "A Smile of Fortune," we must see how the captain enjoys the masochistic-sadistic overtones of the relationship, even while maintaining a playful and debonair attitude toward Alice. In both treatments, we are faced with "fictions"; for Jean-Aubry, in his acceptance of everything as truth, is perpetuating a fiction as much as Conrad, by heightening events himself, was transforming fact.

---

* From a psychoanalytic point of view, Dr. Bernard Meyer feels the two accounts are contradictory. He writes: "It is indeed the incompatibility between these two romances, both allegedly occurring concomitantly during a seven-week interval, which supports the impression that, far from possessing autobiographic validity, 'A Smile of Fortune,' like *The Arrow of Gold*, was a fantasy designed to convert humiliation and defeat into bittersweet success, from which the author might retire with honor." Using this reasoning, that is, finding Conrad humiliated in the real situation and then compensating for it in the fictional one, Dr. Meyer sees "The Planter of Malata," with its humbling of the male character, as coming closer to the truth of Conrad's experience.

The difficulty is in accepting Jean-Aubry's interpretation of the actual event, in which Conrad was rejected. Even if we acquiesce in the facts, Jean-Aubry's analysis of them dramatically heightens Conrad's despair. Note the language of the interpretation as he relates Conrad's reactions: "All the castles in Spain that Captain Korzeniowski had been building for the last month in the solitude of his cabin aboard the *Otago* crumbled to nothing. He had been dreaming of an attachment, a family, a home. Once more, circumstances threw him back into isolation. He was obviously born not to have roots anywhere." This is Jean-Aubry's Conrad: suffering, noble, lost for the love of a woman. This is, also, Jean-Aubry's fantasy life of Conrad, whom he idolized and adored. If we cut through the idolatry, we can perhaps lessen the captain's disappointment and move the actual experience, if indeed it did occur as Jean-Aubry indicates, closer to the experience in the fictional model, although the two differ in details.

The *Otago* left Port Louis on November 22, 1888, for Melbourne, Australia. The potatoes that were forced on the captain in "A Smile" proved to be fortunate indeed—almost a "fortunate fall," if, in fact, he had fallen for Alice. But that episode may have been fictitious, too, fitting well into Conrad's view of fortune and events as lying outside any causal relationships. If the potatoes did indeed exist, the captain enjoyed a windfall when he found that there was a failure of the potato crop in that part of Australia.

Conrad decided during this general time to give up the *Otago*, his first and sole oceangoing command. His motives are dim, for he appeared to be in good standing with the owners. In fact, after Melbourne, he took the *Otago* to Port Minlacowie in southern Australia, loading there a cargo of grain for Adelaide. Here we enter thickets of possibilities. At Adelaide, a letter awaited him, dated April 2, 1889, from the owners, Henry Simpson & Sons, severing his relationship to the *Otago*.

> Referring to your resignation of the command (which we have in another letter formally accepted) of our bark *Otago*, we now have much pleasure in stating that this early severance from our employ is entirely at your own desire, with a view to visiting Europe, and that we entertain a high opinion of your ability in the capacity you now vacate, of your attainments generally, and should be glad to learn of your future success.

In "A Smile," Conrad's captain tells of a long letter he wrote the owners proposing the employment of the *Otago* in the China Seas for the following two years, but his suggestion was rejected and the owners requested that he continue in the sugar trade, which meant a return to Mauritius. With this, the captain resigned his command. Once again, if we accept the Jean-Aubry version as fact, we can say that Conrad resigned his command rather than return to Port Louis, where his proposal had been rejected and he feared ridicule. This is, of course, very possible. But it ignores other aspects of his situation. The first is the correspondence he was receiving from his uncle in the Ukraine, indicating that Tadeusz was not well and wanted to see his nephew again before he died. More importantly, however, Conrad was undergoing a significant internal change, for in 1889 he was to begin to write his first novel. No matter that he tried later, in *A Personal Record*, to seem indifferent to this momentous event, it was for him a major decision, even if at this time he did not consciously see it that way.

This two-year period, from 1888 to 1890, was crucial for Conrad. His internal mechanism was saying something to him and becoming increasingly insistent. He was reaching into the seams of his life, where significant decisions are made, or where the individual works out vital elements as yet invisible to him. He had attained the epitome of his outward claims for success, the logical conclusion of his career as a seaman; the captaincy was, in this sense, an achievement for those back in Poland as well as for himself. He had demonstrated that he could achieve the outward trappings, and he could do it in a difficult area where no other Pole had succeeded. It is very important that we understand his need to have attained a captaincy as a way of rejecting the Korzeniowski strain of failure. Having achieved that, having proven Uncle Tadeusz wrong about his heritage, he was, in a real sense, free to move to other areas. In his case, writing was not so unusual, especially if it could be combined with another career that earned him his keep, the sea.

In this two-year period, then, we have Conrad undergoing three seemingly separate experiences: the captaincy of the *Otago*, and his resignation; the beginning of his writing career, with the first pages of *Almayer's Folly;* and the journey into the Congo, which was to jar his sensibilities and disarm him morally. His life had become a kind of mosaic, of three key brightly colored patterns, surrounded by pieces of lesser brilliance and of secondary importance; as yet an unfinished or unresolved mosaic. In the early summer of 1889 at the age of thirty-one, Conrad returned to London by steamship from Adelaide, knowingly, or not, beginning to throw his life into disarray as a way of gaining greater order.

IV

In Leopold's Congo
1889–1890

. . . and even so didst thou become
A silent *Poet; from the solitude*
Of the vast sea didst bring a watchful heart
Still couchant, an inevitable ear,
And an eye practised like a blind man's touch.

WORDSWORTH,
"*When to the Attractions of the Busy World*"

CHAPTER 12

Embarking

IN the summer and fall of 1889, Conrad was on a threshold. But before he penetrated Leopold's Congo, he returned to Victoria's London. His external life would now seem a patchwork of activities, but, beneath, a cementing element was taking hold. He was also developing intellectually, for the early pages of *Almayer's Folly* indicate an assimilation of many literary traditions. When Conrad returned, he may have first made a short visit to the Kliszczewskis in Cardiff, and then took furnished lodgings in London in Bessborough Gardens, off Vauxhall Bridge. It was here, in September, that he was to begin *Almayer's Folly*, if we are to believe his words in *A Personal Record.* Coinciding with this start was the search for a command, although this particular quest may have reflected his lack of income. Marlow in "Heart of Darkness" comments on his own quest for a command after a period of seagoing, rest, and malaise:

> "I had then, as you remember, just returned to London after a lot of Indian Ocean, Pacific, China Seas— a regular dose of the East—six years or so, and I was loafing about, hindering you fellows in your work and invading your homes, just as though I had got a heavenly mission to civilise you. It was very fine for a time, but after a bit I did get tired of resting. Then I began to look for a ship—I should think the hardest work on earth. But the ships wouldn't even look at me."

Marlow then moves into how he tried to obtain a post as a Congo steamer captain, and thus parallels Conrad's own attempts to find a Congo command. However, he omits a significant parallel activity in Conrad, his cautious beginning on a novel. When we speak of Marlow as a stand-in for aspects of Conrad, we must be circumspect indeed, for Marlow lacks Conrad's imaginative strain as a writer (although he is an effective storyteller) and is, therefore, qualitatively different.

While the malaise and layover in London may have been frustrating to Conrad, the period nevertheless was an open stretch of time into which he had to pour something of himself. The writing was a natural impulse that had found its moment. Conrad always maintained that serious writing was outside his frame of reference, indicating, as we have seen, that a "planned book" was well beyond his mental range. We can believe this, since the materials were latent, embedded, and needed the right time. A counterargument would be that if Conrad had found a command he would never have turned writer. But this ignores the fact that he was internally juggling a number of alternatives, consciously or not. He needed to give himself time, and he used that time to allow other impulses to surface. These energies were apparently operating on parallel lines, not in sequence, and Conrad was crossing circuits of alternating desire and need. "Never had Rubicon," he writes in *A Personal Record,* "been more blindly forded, without invocation to the gods, without fear of men." The fact that he could joke about his writing in mock-epical terms indicates it had become a normal, not an artificial, impulse, and therefore part of his very fiber, a routine event.

Conrad then relates what occurred on that fateful morning when he wrote the initial 200 words of the first page of his first novel. The passage is much quoted, but deserves repeating:

> That morning I got up from my breakfast, pushing the chair back, and rang the bell violently, or perhaps I should say resolutely, or perhaps I should say eagerly, I do not know. But manifestly it must have been a special ring of the bell, a common sound made impressive, like the ringing of a bell for the raising of the curtain upon a new scene. It was an unusual thing for me to do. Generally, I dawdled over my breakfast and I seldom took the trouble to ring the bell for the table to be cleared away; but on that morning for some reason hidden in the general mysteriousness of the event I did not dawdle. And yet I was not in a hurry. I pulled the cord casually, and while the faint tinkling somewhere down in the basement went on, I charged my pipe in the usual way and I looked for the matchbox with glances distraught indeed but exhibiting, I am ready to swear, no signs of a fine frenzy. I was composed enough to perceive after some considerable time the matchbox lying there on the mantelpiece right under my nose. And all this was beautifully and safely usual. Before I had thrown down the match my landlady's daughter appeared with her calm, pale face and an inquisitive look, in the doorway. Of late it was the landlady's daughter who answered my bell. I mention this little fact with pride, because it proves that during the thirty or forty days of my tenancy I had produced a favourable impression.

He continues:

> "Will you please clear away all this at once?" I addressed her in convulsive accents, being at the same time engaged in getting my pipe to draw. This, I admit, was an unusual request. Generally on getting up from breakfast I would sit down in the window with a book and let them clear the table when they liked; but if you think that on that morning I was in the least impatient, you are mistaken. I remember that I was perfectly calm. As a matter of fact I was not at all certain that I wanted to

write, or that I meant to write, or that I had anything to write about. No, I was not impatient. I lounged between the mantelpiece and the window, not even consciously waiting for the table to be cleared. It was ten to one that before my landlady's daughter was done I would pick up a book and sit down with it all the morning in a spirit of enjoyable indolence.

After ranging through the books he has read since five—Dickens, Hugo, Cervantes, Lesage, Trollope, Shakespeare—Conrad returns to the matter at hand, how the usual turned into the unusual.

And I remember, too, the character of the day. It was an autumn day with an opaline atmosphere, a veiled, semi-opaque, lustrous day, with fiery points and flashes of red sunlight on the roofs and windows opposite, while the trees of the square with all their leaves gone were like tracings of an indian ink on a sheet of tissue paper. It was one of those London days that have the charm of mysterious amenity, of fascinating softness. The effect of opaline mist was often repeated at Bessborough Gardens on account of the nearness to the river.

There is no reason why I should remember that effect more on that day than on any other day, except that I stood for a long time looking out of the window after the landlady's daughter was gone with her spoil of cups and saucers. I heard her put the tray down in the passage and finally shut the door; and still I remained smoking with my back to the room. It is very clear that I was in no haste to take the plunge into my writing life, if as plunge this first attempt may be described. My whole being was steeped deep in the indolence of a sailor away from the sea, the scene of never-ending labour and of unceasing duty. For utter surrender to indolence you cannot beat a sailor ashore when that mood is on him, the mood of absolute irresponsibility tasted to the full. It seems to me that I thought of nothing whatever, but this is an impression which is hardly to be believed at this distance of years. What I am certain of is, that I was very far from thinking of writing a story, though it is possible and even likely that I was thinking of the man Almayer.

Although we know what books Conrad had been reading since childhood, his ostensible reading alone cannot explain the language, textures, and tones of the early parts of *Almayer's Folly.* In assessing Conrad's literary background as he went to sea in the 1880s, we should not be too diffident about his accomplishments. Although we lack hard evidence of precisely what he was assimilating, he was literarily conscious and sensitive in three languages. Accordingly, it would not be extraordinary for him to be aware, in all the spare time he had, of literary battles, particularly as they raged in France and especially after he had completed his studies for his master's examination—that is, after 1886.

In the light of Conrad's 1897 Preface to the *Nigger*, with its clear affinities to *symboliste*, Wagnerian, and post-*symboliste* doctrines; in view of his first letters to Marguerite Poradowska in French, with their symbolistic phraseology and their reaching after infinitude; with our knowledge of his early prose with its striving after symbolistic colors, tones, and sensory expression, its reaching after synesthesiacal sensations—if we consider all these, we can see how heavily dependent Conrad was on French sources even as he was consolidating his use of English. In one sense, of course, he was a *symboliste*, embodying in his own self and command of languages almost pure symbolistic doctrines of crossing over, obfuscation, confusion of the senses, desire to clothe the body or emotions in weighted prose.

France in the mid-1880s was, culturally, in a symbolist ferment. In early 1886, the publication of *La Revue Wagnérienne* brought together eight sonnets of homage to the German composer. None of this is incidental to Conrad's development, given the Wagnerian insistence, in his Preface, on the amalgamation of the arts, and his apparent awareness of symbolist influences both in his letters to his Aunt Marguerite and in his own early prose style. The eight contributors of sonnets included Mallarmé and a Polish critic and poet, Teodor de Wyzewa. De Wyzewa is of particular interest, not only for his Polish background, but for his attachment to Mallarmé and Wagner and his attempt to see in the German's theater something applicable to literature and to language. Mallarmé himself contributed to this blending of theater and language in his own sonnet, an extremely difficult and torturous attempt to hail Wagner for getting beyond realistic theater and, at the same time, to criticize him for not being more abstract and mysterious than he was.

We are not really concerned with how much of this Conrad knew firsthand or even understood—since most of it is difficult and devious stuff indeed—but with how far he was influenced by a prevailing sense that words and language, even ways of seeing and noting, were being altered: that language had to undergo a freshening process. As he says in the Preface: ". . . that the light of magic suggestiveness may be brought to play for an evanescent instant over the commonplace surface of words: of the old, old words, thin, defaced by ages of careless usage."

Although Conrad disclaimed any ability to read symbolist poetry—despite his use of lines from Baudelaire's *Les Fleurs du mal* in *The Shadow-Line*—we do know he frequently dissembled, preferring to create an aura of the country boy who stumbled into literature. Although he chose this know-nothing attitude, it is quite possible he was familiar with the broader outlines of Mallarmé himself. In 1886, this annus mirabilis of French symbolism, the time also of Jean Moréas's *symboliste* manifesto, Mallarmé distinguished between two kinds of speech, "immediate" and "essential." The first is the routine order of speech, language that transmits information, reports, describes events, allows for the exchange of thought, and is what we assign to the "scientific" aspect of language for purposes of communication. The second is the "real" or "essential" kind, what pertains to literature in general, to poetry in particular, and especially to symbolistic usage.

Since this second kind turns up as the essential language of Conrad in his early work and in his Preface, Mallarmé's distinction warrants some attention, as does Moréas's manifesto, which Conrad's own later "manifesto" echoes.* Mallarmé saw the second kind of speech as an abstraction or purification of language, away from its function to communicate to its more primary or essential quality as the "idea" of language. The aim, as Wallace Fowlie has put it, is to bring about a trick "whereby something is changed into its absence." As an example, when a poet speaks of flowers, he means an idea of flowers that he does not find in a bunch or a bouquet. If a writer intends language as communication or routine speech, then he has fallen into chance, coincidence, happenstance; if he sees language as a way of abstracting "real" qualities of things, then such language falls outside of chance into patterns or laws detailing sound, sense, suggestivity.

For Mallarmé, the purpose of language was to separate things from their commonplace status in the world of objects, as it was Conrad's, through language, to make the familiar seem unfamiliar, the usual appear unusual. In a real sense, Mallarmé's use of language—and poetry in particular—was for purposes of purification and served a quasi-divine function. Moréas's *Un Manifeste littéraire* (published in the literary supplement of *Le Figaro* on September 18, 1886) suggested a somewhat similar intention:

> Enemy of explanation, of declamation, of false sensibility, of objective description, symbolist poetry tries to clothe the Idea in a palpable form, which, nevertheless, is not an end in itself, but which, while serving to express the Idea, remains subject to it. The Idea in its turn does not let itself be seen without sumptuous trains of exterior analogies; for the essential character of symbolic art consists in never going to the conception of the Idea in itself. Thus in the art, pictures of nature, actions of men, concrete phenomena are not there for their own sake, but as simple appearances destined to represent their esoteric affinities with primordial Ideas.

Moréas asserted that symbolism was a reaction against a type of language that *says* rather than suggests. In practice, symbolism would free literature from the bondage of rhetoric, externals, regular beat in poetry, from the cataloguing of nature and the chance accidents of daily life, liberating the literary arts of all elements of materialism. Literature can, in these terms, attain liberty and authentic speech, becoming, as an English interpreter, Arthur

---

* As does his 1913 letter to Francis Warrington Dawson, in which Conrad's response to Dawson's program for a "sane Art" suggests Mallarmé's distinction between two kinds of speech: "Art for me *is* an end in itself. Conclusions are not for it. And it is superior to science, in so far that it calls on us with authority to behold! to feel! whereas science at best can only tell us—it seems so! And that's all it can do. It talks to us of the Laws of Nature."

Symons, put it, "a kind of religion, with all the duties and the responsibilities of the sacred ritual."

Given Conrad's predilections, he could have acquired many of these ideas—purification of language, the sacred duties and trust of the artist, the need to create a different relationship between creator and created—from *symbolistes* or from Flaubert, with whose work he was apparently familiar in the 1880s. There were several routes by which Conrad could have come to conclusions we associate with symbolism—through reading (possibly), direct contact (unlikely), awareness of a particular literary atmosphere (likely), or the priestly advice of Flaubert. Flaubert is everywhere in Conrad, virtually a divine presence, a guru.

Despite Conrad's occasional disclaimers that he did not know the French novelist's work while he was writing *Almayer's Folly*, we also have his own words that he did. In a letter to Marguerite Poradowska, for April 6, 1892, when he was still in the early stages of his novel, he wrote: "You remind me a little of Flaubert, whose *Madame Bovary* I have just reread with an admiration full of respect." By this time, he had *reread* the novel. In a letter to Robert d'Humières, the French translator of *The Nigger*, Conrad speaks of having memorized whole pages of *Bovary*, a masterpiece, and he recalls that when he was writing *The Nigger* Flaubert's *Salammbô* "was his morning reading." It was for him a book that bordered on a miracle, and as he drank his coffee, he would read a page or two at random. He says that in his handling of his sailors there were pale reflections of Flaubert's treatment of his Mercenaries. More than anything, Conrad learned from Flaubert what the French writer taught future generations of novelists: that, to quote Allen Tate, the "action is not stated from the point of view of the author; it is rendered in terms of situation and scene. To have made this the viable property of the art of fiction was to have virtually made the art of fiction."

Yet once we establish that Conrad felt Flaubert's presence and had definitely read *Madame Bovary* before April 1892, probably even as early as the 1880s, we must distinguish his method from the French novelist's. Although Conrad wrote his two or three hundred words daily with a very careful and conscious search for the correct word and phrase, he never possessed the kind of verbal modulation Flaubert was capable of. Flaubert's sense of language leads to Joyce, not to Conrad, although there is some overlap. To draw the distinction more severely: Flaubert sought to eschew the self and to find the correct modal variety that would purge subjective elements; whereas Conrad sought the correct word and phrase so he could all the better reveal the self. Flaubert threw off subjectivity through his language; Conrad probed more deeply into self through his. Each sought precision of expression, of course, as a key to his method of working, and each was in a sense a literary priest. And yet each was constructing a language for very different ends, Flaubert for effacement, Conrad for greater expression of the ineffable. For the latter, language had to express what he had observed for years in wind and waves and storm, as a man who found himself moved repeatedly by external forces; whereas Flaubert wanted to purge himself of subjective feelings, for whatever reasons, and needed the perfect neutral language. As a consequence, Flaubert worked modalities and tones within neutrality, while exploring burnishment and gloss.

Of great importance to Conrad's development as a writer in English is the kind of French he used in his letters to Marguerite Poradowska. For in these letters, we have almost the sole chartable progression of his verbal ability while he was writing *Almayer.* Although he was using a different language in each medium, we see that the mind was singular, the assumptions similar, and the outcome not at all split. The Conrad of the French letters beginning in 1890 was to be the Conrad of *Almayer,* in 1889–94.

After a few letters of news and family matters, Conrad wrote on March 23–25, 1890, about "life": "La vie roule en flots amers, comme l'ocean sombre et brutal sous un ciel couvert des tristes nuages, et il y a des jours ou il semble au pauvres âmes embarquées pour le désésperant voyage que jamais un rayon de soleil n'a pu penétrer ce voile douleureux; que jamais il ne luira plus, qu'il n'a jamais éxisté!"* Such inflated language has its qualities as contemporary prose. But distinctly Conradian is the use of language as a mirror; or, conversely, a way of seeing so that language serves as a reflector and mirror of life. "Ray" (*rayon*), "sun" (*soleil*), "veil" (*voile*), "shine" (*luira*)—all of these indicate reflection and refraction. Having stared into the sea for so many years, Conrad considered water as a gigantic metaphorical mirror, a source of poetry as well as life. His was an art based as much on Perseus and Medusa as on the sea gods Proteus and Poseidon.

What this suggests so far in the Conrad who was storing images, scenes, characters, and events is that he was conditioned as an observer to viewing in a particular manner. The fact that so much of his work, early and otherwise, is retrospective—cast into flashbacks or on doubling back, based on past within past and on narrators recollecting and tunneling into shadows—indicates an author attempting to find the objective correlative of *what he saw at the moment he saw it.* Working back and through these narrative devices, we can assume that Conrad's imagination fixed elements forever, and all that changed as he developed artistically was the intensity of the vision, not the vision itself. These images of reflections we catch in his letters are the same images and reflections he was to carry over into his work, and both are comparable to his mode of seeing even before he turned to fictional writing.

* Life rolls on in bitter waves, like the gloomy and brutal ocean under a sky covered with mournful clouds, and there are some days when to the poor souls embarked on a despairing voyage it seems that not even one ray of sun has ever penetrated that sad veil; that never again will it shine, that it never even existed!

There is much in Conrad the artist who, while writing ostensibly about a subject, is also speculating about the uses of the imagination. The tradition of this dualism goes back at least as far as Coleridge and Wordsworth and extends beyond Conrad into Proust, Mann, Gide, and others. According to this mode—which fits well indeed into the metaphor of Perseus slaying the reflected image of Medusa—one level of the imaginative act is concerned with imagination itself. That is, the artist is not only re-creating a scene or event, or limning particular characters, but is also demonstrating how the imagination works while performing these acts. Implicit in this method is the artist's use of symbolic language, his avoidance of allegory, and his functioning in dual roles: as external or internal narrator and as conscious artist suggesting how art is created. As Robert Penn Warren writes of "The Rime of the Ancient Mariner," the "Ancient Mariner is written out of and about the belief, that in the poetic act the moral and aesthetic concerns are aspects of the same activity, and that this activity is expressive of the whole mind."

In his novel, from the first paragraphs Conrad writes of Almayer's dissolution, of his life as a "dreary tranquillity of a desert," of the whispers of water, of whiteness, veils, mists; of a wasted imagination, a useless art. In a limited way, Conrad's Almayer is caught between opposing forces, trapped in the conflict of hopes and fears, a man who, having lost his center, waits, held by ennui, in his own Sargasso Sea on the east coast of Borneo. The first page of the novel, in fact, has Almayer absorbed in dreams of wealth and power, in fantasies of gold or a golden era.

From all this, we can deduce that Conrad brought to his material—to his first sight of Olmeijer in Berau—this mode of seeing and noting. It is very important for us to try to understand what and how Conrad saw or else we cannot jump that gap between adventurous seaman and struggling novelist. Unlike most major novelists, Conrad did not enjoy a linear development, from early beginnings as an author and then gradually to a writer of fiction, what we can trace in Dickens, Thackeray, and even the Brontës. Also, Conrad lacked what George Eliot had, that is, George Henry Lewes, who provided critical support until she discovered her own means. Conrad had no one but himself, and his transformation from mariner to writer was an intensely internal decision veiled from the observer and perhaps even from his own consciousness. What is remarkable is that outside of his own reading and the occasional letters of his uncle, he had no literary contacts, no professional guidance, no bookish friend to whom he could speak. His correspondence with Marguerite Poradowska, in the 1890s, was his sole contact with someone of a literary mind or someone cultured along his lines. Unless we leave it all to chance, we must try to understand his transformation by probing into the creative act itself, by attempting to diagnose the ways his imagination performed. We can assume, then, that once he had begun his first novel, however carelessly and indifferently, every external experience was to take on a grave intensity and every memory or recollection was to gain substance by its linkage with his "new life" as a writer. The early pages of *Almayer* may limn the graveyard, but for Conrad they were a rebirth.

Yet this was only half the plunge. Conrad descended into himself for literary materials and was beginning to seek his depth as an artist; but running parallel to this was his descent into another kind of experience, his other half, what Marlow called an exploration of "an immense snake uncoiled, with its head in the sea, its body at rest curving afar over a vast country, and its tail lost in the depths of the land." Conrad was moving toward the Congo.

Those mornings in September in Bessborough Gardens, while he wrote the first pages of *Almayer's Folly*, were to be his calmest for some time, even though they contained the frustrations attendant upon his failure to find employment as a captain. Conrad's activities for this period are dim, a series of tryings-out rather than anything steady. It is difficult to determine if he wanted to go to Africa in particular or if he desired a command simply as part of his lifelong ambition to explore new land and sea areas. Was the journey to the Congo coincidental, a means of financial support, or did he head for Africa out of some desire to go there—an echo of his childhood boast "When I grow up I shall go *there*"—and nowhere else? Although motives are impossible to disentangle, I think we must see Conrad in this 1889–90 period as caught amid conflicting currents; that is, having arrived at certain choices: a maritime career, the beginning of his writing career, the desire to explore "dark" areas—having arrived *there*, Conrad was ready to move in all directions or none.

Before he headed for Africa and the Congo, he did try other positions. For some indeterminate period, he worked for Barr, Moering & Co., in which through Krieger and Hope he had made a small investment. Then he must have been associated with the firm of Walford & Co., with the possible promise of a command to Mexico and the West Indies, a matter which he brought up with Albert Thys (then acting managing director of the Société Anonyme Belge pour le Commerce du Haut-Congo) when he was seeking a Congo command. Evidently, he tried still another tack, looking for a position through Barr, Moering with G. de Baerdemacker, Ghent shipping agents, although nothing came of this. In the letter to Thys outlining this latest attempt, Conrad mentioned that he possessed a commission from the Board of Trade which qualified him to command sailing boats and steamers, obtained by examination in London, 1885. One would have expected Conrad to remember this single most important date in his life as having occurred in 1886; but possibly his secretiveness about his examination addled his memory. In the same letter, he gave Hope as his reference. It was the firm of Baerdemacker that on September 24 wrote to Thys about finding Conrad a Congo post.

From this flurry of job applications, we can speculate that the African venture was by no means inevitable. The fall of 1889 was crowded with aborted efforts. If Conrad had obtained a command to return to the scenes of his young manhood in the Indies, he would have accepted it with alacrity. None of it came about, however. Simply staying alive through work was the primary consideration. In his accounting, Bobrowski indicated having sent Conrad his last money, stating: "*Thus the making of a man out of Mr. Konrad has cost*" 17,454 rubles, or about $9,000, with triple the current purchasing power. In his last two entries, he noted that Conrad had been freed from "subjection of the Russian Empire"—that is, he was no more a Russian national, no longer subject to Russian courts or conscription. Then: "*In June* you returned after three years sailing the Indian Sea and as you had to increase your share in the partnership Barr Möring et Cie, I sent you on the 4th May via Odessa the remainder of the capital intended by me for you"—the sum of four hundred rubles. Thus, at thirty-one, Conrad was finally on his own, his patrimony exhausted. This could help explain his furious activity to find a post, even though the parallel activity of writing had already begun to intrude on his imagination.

Africa, to turn there, had by this time entered the news because of fresh exploits by Stanley. As a still dark and relatively unexplored land mass, the continent would have appealed to what was a constant in Conrad—that desire to seek out and explore, to test frontiers and limitations at the expense of self. The old self had to be renewed constantly through annihilation or flirtation with death; he had to intensify in order to feel alive. Africa was a means to that end, even if Conrad fell into it fortuitously.

Henry Morton Stanley, by 1889, was known throughout the world as having found Dr. Livingstone, in 1871, and then, in 1876–77, as having penetrated the jungles of Africa from Zanzibar to the Lower Congo, in the process tracing the course of the Congo River. Further, Stanley reentered the news when in 1887 he went to Africa once again, this time on still another rescue attempt: to bring back Mehmed Emin Pasha, governor of the Equatorial province of Egypt, who had been cut off by the Mahdi revolt of 1882. Stanley contacted Emin in April 1888 and found the pasha unwilling to evacuate his province. News of Stanley's announcement that he had found Emin began to filter back to Europe, and in the spring and summer of 1889, when Conrad was himself returning to London, Stanley's new exploit was the talk of the city.

Apart from the celebrity aspect of Stanley's work—and commentary on it poured into Europe, from his geographical discoveries to his personal heroism—Stanley was a man after Conrad's own heart. As an illegitimate child, he came from an unsettled background, and even the name Henry Morton Stanley derived from a benefactor, his own being John Rowlands. Further, Stanley, before he fell into his life's work, had been an adventurer, soldiering in the American Civil War, serving as a seaman in the merchant service and in the federal navy, then turning journalist. Himself parentless, struck by wanderlust, and having followed careers paralleling those of Stanley, Conrad could not help but be struck by similarities of temperament and motive. There is even the possibility he was familiar with Stanley's early books, *How I Found Livingstone* (1872) and *Through the Dark Continent* (1878), although this must remain speculative.

Even without direct exposure to Stanley from his books, Conrad could hardly have missed reports in the London *Times* and elsewhere of Stanley's Emin Pasha rescue effort, recalling to the seaman his earlier enthrallment with Mungo Park and other African explorers. Certainly part of Conrad's interest in Africa can be attributed to Stanley's celebrity status, but I think it would be in error to accept Conrad's Congo expedition as a direct result of this publicity. The patterning becomes too neat for someone who resisted patterns. We know that in the thirty-five years before Conrad settled down to writing, he moved in several seemingly skew directions, and it was this very lack of plan that created Uncle Tadeusz's misgivings and placed Conrad under an increasing burden to prove himself capable of mature behavior. For over half his life, he was involved in tryings-out, testing of self, not in establishing clear directions. The Congo journey came in just such an uncertain time, harking back to his Marseilles period, when he entered into gunrunning for the Carlists.* If we continue to see the strain of Apollo Korzeniowski in him, we cannot discount those uncertain elements, those meaningless thrusts and counterthrusts into life which characterize the son as much as they had the father before him.

Still nothing came of his application to Thys for a posting to Africa. Meanwhile, Conrad was planning a visit to Uncle Tadeusz, which would

---

* Dr. Meyer recounts that during Conrad's Marseilles interlude Stanley received considerable publicity. "Conrad's youthful susceptibility to the Stanley mystique [see *Last Essays*, pp. 23 ff.] was undoubtedly rekindled during his Marseilles era when the famed explorer, returning from his second major African expedition, arrived in triumph in that city on January 13, 1878, a few short weeks, incidentally, prior to Conrad's suicidal gesture. Whether Conrad was among the capacity audience that attended a reception in Stanley's honor on January 14, or was part of the crowd that accompanied the celebrated traveler to the railroad station on the following day, is unknown, but he could hardly have missed the colorful and detailed coverage of the stirring occasion in the local press. The *Gazette du Midi* of January 18 devoted several columns to Stanley's visit, describing his appearance, reviewing his heroic career (including his encounter with Livingstone), and recording in detail Stanley's speech before the Société de Géographie de Marseilles. On January 19 *Le Sémaphore de Marseilles* reported that the president of the Société had shown Stanley a number of articles which had belonged to Livingstone, including a pistol given to him by Stanley at the time of their meeting. The same paper noted that Stanley had received three medals of honor during his stay in Marseilles" (p. 96n).

take him out of circulation for a few months at least. As he wrote Thys, on December 27, 1889, "a short visit would not be worth the trouble and expense of leaving." He asked the managing director how much time he could have at his disposal and when Thys would require his services. The latter evidently had nothing to offer, and Conrad was, once again, left in limbo. As a last resort, he decided to attempt pressure from another quarter, an effort that put him in touch with a distant relative, his so-called aunt, Marguerite Poradowska, an extremely important association for Conrad at this time.

In "Heart of Darkness," the misogynist Marlow indicates how low he had fallen and how hopeless his employment opportunities appeared, so that he had to resort to women for help: " 'Then—would you believe it?—I tried the women. I, Charlie Marlow, set the women to work—to get a job. Heavens! Well, you see, the notion drove me. I had an aunt, a dear enthusiastic soul. She wrote: "It will be delightful. I am ready to do anything, anything for you. It is a glorious idea. I know the wife of a very high personage in the Administration, and also a man who has lots of influence with," etc. etc. She was determined to make no end of fuss to get me appointed skipper of a river steamboat, if such was my fancy.' "

Tadeusz probably advised Conrad to try Aleksander Poradowski, a cousin of Conrad's maternal grandmother, then living in Brussels with his wife, Marguerite, whose connections to some Congo colonists might prove useful. This was the "women" to whom Marlow turned, and the tone perhaps indicates how scornful Conrad felt about turning for help to this quarter. Of course, "Aunt" Marguerite in the flesh was to prove something else. Conrad wrote (on January 16, 1890) to cousin Aleksander recalling their previous meeting in Cracow and the kindness shown him there. Conrad's tone, in Polish, takes on a polite deference that seems obsequious, so tentative was he in his demands on the older man's time and perhaps wary because he was returning to Apollo's world. Now, after years of escape from that net of Polish romanticism and political idealism, he was back, with a relative who had lost all in the 1863 insurrection, another exile. Conrad tried to arrange a meeting: "I do not ask whether you will permit me to visit you—for I permit myself not to doubt it [in Brussels, on Conrad's way to the Ukraine]; but I would very much like to be certain that you are in Brussels and that I shall be able to find you there in the course of the next month."

Conrad conveys some of his background, including the "fact" that he spent two years as master of a vessel. The "two years" which he cites is an approximation typically in his favor, what he also claimed about his previous service when he applied for his chief's certificate. The "two years" were in reality fourteen months, which rounds off more closely to one year. Such exaggeration is quite possibly not conscious duplicity but his desire to stretch his accomplishments toward some inner ideal of what he felt he should be achieving. One cannot dismiss Conrad's errors with figures as "just his way" or as "carelessness," not when the errors always went in his favor. To some extent, he saw his own life as material for his fiction, and even as he related his past he was intertwining it with a fictional component: heightening, exaggerating, intensifying. The deception may have lain there.

Conrad added that he would be in Brussels on his return from visiting Tadeusz, if he did go to the Ukraine; if he did not, he would be in Brussels anyway, "in connection with the post in the Congo." Therefore, he wrote, "in any case I shall have the pleasure of seeing you, my dear Uncle, and of making myself known to Aunt Poradowska whom I only know from that portrait of her which you had with you in Cracow." When a return letter informed Conrad that his "Uncle" Poradowski was in poor health, he indicated he would visit Brussels on his way to the Ukraine. He mentions that in the same mail he has received word from Tadeusz to come. "However, those villains in the Russian Consulate do not want to grant me a visa—which means further delay, inconvenience, and visits to the Embassy, perhaps to no avail." But a few days later, on the thirty-first, Conrad could write that he had all the necessary documents and would leave on February 4 or 5 for Brussels, hoping that he would be permitted to remain for twenty-four hours. On February 4, Conrad wrote his first (extant) letter to Aunt Marguerite to indicate he was leaving London at 9 a.m. Wednesday, February 5, and would arrive in Brussels at 5:30 p.m. He arrived as planned, but two days later Aleksander Poradowski died, at fifty-four. This, in turn, set up an interesting situation.

For the next thirty years Conrad was to write to Marguerite Poradowska in French, and for the period from 1890 to 1895, until diverted by Edward Garnett, John Galsworthy, and Cunninghame Graham, she was his most sustained correspondent. Further, beyond whatever literary yield we can gain from his letters to Aunt Marguerite, there is a strong personal undertow, for undoubtedly Conrad found Marguerite, almost ten years his senior, an extremely attractive woman. Conrad's "Tante Margot" was also a person of cultivation. Here was a relationship he could depend upon, as before he had depended upon Tadeusz: a woman of some matronly and motherly bearing who was also attractive, a person of refinement and literary achievement, and a "relative" to boot.

The Poradowski-Poradowska association is extremely interesting on other grounds as well, since it brought Conrad so close to his own beginnings. Aleksander had been involved in the insurrection of 1863 and in many ways seemed cut from materials similar to Apollo's pattern. In seeking out Aleksander, Conrad was reliving a portion of his heritage, and in hanging on to Marguerite he was curving back upon his own past. Until 1895, when his correspondence with Marguerite declined sharply, he was very much in her world of Polish relatives and Polish literary themes.

Aleksander, the first cousin of Conrad's maternal grandmother, had found in the 1863 insurrection a focus for his energies. Before that, as a young man he had tried many different activities, not unlike Apollo, and then fought gallantly in the uprising, only to be taken prisoner by the czar's troops and condemned to death as a traitor to the Russian Officer corps. He escaped, however, through the aid of a fellow Russian officer and went into exile, first to Dresden, then to Paris and Brussels. In the latter city, he met Marguerite Gachet, whose father, a scholar of note associated with the royal Belgian Archives, later become bureau head of the paleography department. He worked chiefly in old manuscripts, compiling numerous editions of Old French texts and undertaking a dictionary of words in the literature of the Middle Ages.

After his death, Marguerite's mother was dismayed at her daughter's interest in Aleksander. We have an almost exact duplication of Apollo's courtship of Ewa Bobrowska: the romantic, idealistic young man with few prospects and no real focus to his life seeking the hand of an attractive, intelligent young lady who was expected to make a more suitable marriage. Marguerite was indeed attractive, and her hand was sought after by many suitors, including Charles Buls, later burgomaster of Brussels, respectability personified. Apparently, Mme Gachet's opposition was intense, and the courtship was broken off until Aleksander could promise financial support for the couple. He left for Galicia, where it was safe for him, obtained possession of a small property in the neighborhood of Lemberg, and then returned to marry Marguerite. The couple lived in Lemberg and surrounding areas for several years before returning to Brussels, in 1884, because of Marguerite's health, or more likely because she found a French-speaking country more congenial.

Her knowledge of Polish customs derives from these years abroad and from her association with Poradowski and, through him, with Conrad's distant relatives. Thus, in a real sense, she had entered into the Korzeniowski-Bobrowski-Poradowski worlds. Before his death, Poradowski helped to found a charitable organization for Polish refugees and thus maintained a lifeline with those compatriots who had fought in Apollo's own causes. With his life nearly half over, Conrad now found himself intertwined in Polish affairs, personally and psychologically. The network extended outward from Poland to Tadeusz in the Ukraine, then to the Poradowskis in Brussels, and on to the correspondence he would have with Marguerite between London (then Africa) and Paris.

After Aleksander's death, Marguerite spent several months in Lublin, Poland, with Poradowski relatives, all of whom were part of Conrad's outer world. She soaked up material for her novels and stories; in her fiction, as we shall see, she kept before Conrad's eyes the roll call of his past. After this, she returned to more familiar places and spent the remaining years of her long life (she outlived Conrad by thirteen years) in Brussels, Lille, and Paris, maintaining an apartment at 84, rue de Passy. For the next five years, Conrad established one of the most intensive friendships and correspondences of his life with this woman, whose fiction he could not have possibly appreciated, but whose lively intelligence and psychological support he needed desperately both during and after his Congo journey. It was to connections supplied by her, possibly Charles Buls and also the geographer A. J. Wauters, that Conrad turned for help in finding a post.

In a somewhat different but related sense, much has been written about Conrad's indifference or even antagonism to his female characters and to his lack of respect for women in general, such views making him into a roughhewn sailor who preferred male bonding to female companionship. Those who hold to that idea, however, must account for his extraordinary friendship with Marguerite Poradowska, in which he reveals his inner self, bares his most frail longings and hopes, exposes himself without shame or embarrassment, and never indicates any sense of male superiority or feminine dependency. He honors Marguerite for what she is, a woman of some talent intent on establishing an independent life after the death of her husband despite numerous marriage proposals from very suitable men. And we cannot explain Conrad's attitudes away by asserting he simply needed someone to listen to him in those trying times when he was alone and fearful of the future. That may have been true, but it does not exclude his acceptance of Marguerite as an equal—not at all as the person Marlow condescends to in "Heart of Darkness" when he brags to his male audience that he has never needed "Women!"

Perhaps most important of all, Marguerite had already authored two books when Conrad met her, *Yaga, esquisse de moeurs ruthènes* (*Yaga: Sketches of Ruthenian Ways*) and *Demoiselle Micia, moeurs galiciennes* (*Miss Micia: Galician Ways*), both of which had appeared in the prestigious *La Revue des Deux Mondes.* Although we do not know how Conrad felt about her slight work—he praised it lavishly in his letters—the relationship to someone who was an authoress and had published her work was of immense significance as he, at a snail's pace, moved along uncertainly on *Almayer's Folly.* She became someone to whom he could reveal his problems of composition, as he did in the next five years, and at one time he felt certain enough of her ability to recommend that they co-author *Almayer's Folly* in French. In still another sense, as Uncle Tadeusz grew older and fell out of Conrad's immediate circle—he was to die in 1894—his nephew had acquired another "adult" figure, a woman of great beauty, charm, and some accomplishment who would be both guardian and the "woman" in his life.

We can observe the complexity of the relationship in his use of the term "aunt" when he referred to her. "Aunt" or "auntie" can be a term of endearment in Polish, by means of which a distant relative is accepted into the immediate family. But it also has a more compelling psychological potential, by means of which Conrad could carry on an apparent flirtation, however serious or frivolous, under the guise of showing respect and obligation toward a member of his family. In a sense, she was less than aunt and more like mother; in still another sense, more like a fiancée who awaited him when he left for the Congo, like Kurtz's fiancée left behind in Brussels. Uncle Tadeusz, whom little escaped, picked up the ambiguous intimations from Conrad's letters and warned him ". . . to give up this game, which will end in nothing visible. A worn-out female, and if she is to join up with somebody, it will be with Buls who would give her a position and love. . . . It would be a stone around your neck for you—and for her as well. If you are wise you will leave this amusement alone and part simply as friends."

Once Conrad met Jessie George, the correspondence with Marguerite fell off dramatically, and then picked up sporadically until four years before Conrad's death in 1924. Also, Conrad's growing friendship with Edward Garnett gave him a "replacement" figure in the literary world. How conscious any of this was we cannot tell, but the pattern of Conrad's dependency cannot be ignored. Dr. Meyer, with his own psychoanalytic purpose in mind, says that Conrad "was addressing her with the accents of love, but the love not of a grown man for a woman but of a hurt and weeping child for a compassionate mother." He quotes at length from a letter in which Conrad described himself as a doll whose back "was broken in two," whose nose was dragging on the ground, and whose arms and legs were flung aside in an attitude of profound despair, a doll which he hopes she will cushion on her lap. But this image of childish dependence is not the dominant note of the correspondence; the dominant chord of dependence does sound, but the dependence is that of a man who is trying out a new career and is using language and literary ideas as a way of finding out how art is created. The difficulty of the psychoanalytic method here is that it neglects the context of Conrad's dependence, which is a literary one; and it ignores a very positive fact, that Conrad was in a learning situation, sitting at the feet of a published, almost established writer, the sole one he knew personally at that time.

It is true enough that the years of isolation and marginality, as well as the illness and enervation he suffered in the Congo, made him dramatize his insufficiency, even turn himself into a broken doll, a torn-up Orpheus. But that is only one of many roles Conrad played with Marguerite, the chief of which was that of a pupil desiring to discover how literature was made, how images were put together, how language could be used expressively. What he needed from her, beyond the flirtation, was what he wished from Flaubert, Maupassant, Turgenev, and others: language and craft, imagery, even a philosophy of existence. For in a letter written only a month before the one in which he posed as a broken doll, he set forth an ironic, even stoic resolution which is quite mature; and in letter after letter he tried to buoy her up, taking the role of older brother to this woman nearly ten years his senior.

Having met his aunt, Conrad departed from Brussels before Aleksander was buried and headed directly for Warsaw, where he intended to see Karol Zagórski, a nephew of Aleksander. The Zagórski family, however, had left Warsaw, and Conrad found them in Lublin, ninety miles to the southeast. Conrad's letter to Marguerite (for February 15–16, 1890) indicates the family's grief when it heard of her husband's death and, more revealingly, demonstrates how closely Conrad identified with these distant relatives, all well beyond any blood relationship. He hurried on from Lublin to his uncle's estate at Kazimierówka, 325 miles southeast, in the present Soviet Ukraine and in what was then called the Government of Kiev. With this, Conrad returned to the area where he was born and where he had spent those very early years preceding dislocation and exile.

For the man of thirty-two, it must have been a strange curving in on experience. In terms of language, he was back in Apollo's mold: he was speaking and listening to Polish, writing in French to his aunt in Brussels, and thinking about *Almayer's Folly* in English. In terms of geography, he was deep into the snow-covered Ukraine, right up against the Russian wolf, corresponding with a Western European, and writing about the steaming jungles and almost impenetrable rivers of East Borneo, with himself on the edge of a Congo appointment. The mixture of tongues, sensations, and topography is important, since Conrad the writer was developing as a blend of many traditions, personally, psychologically, culturally, and aesthetically. His life was, in itself, almost paradigmatic of the synesthesia which was the nub of *symboliste* doctrine.

On February 16, Conrad arrived at Kazimierówka, to begin what was to be a two-month stay. After some ten days of travel in the immediate area, probably to revisit childhood memories, Conrad wrote Marguerite (March 10) of his fear that his recommendation "in the service of the Company of the Congo was not strong enough and that the business will not go through." At the same time he was pressing for this appointment, Bobrowski was attempting to discourage him from undertaking the journey. In the same letter, Conrad commiserates with his aunt over the death of Aleksander and mentions with what pleasure he had read about Henry Merzbach's funeral elegy. Merzbach, like Poradowski and Apollo Korzeniowski, had been involved in the events leading up to the 1863 insurrection, another instance of people and events curving back upon Conrad as he pursued such very different affairs of his own.

In a curious confusion of place and time, Conrad in a letter to Gustaw Sobotkiewicz (March 17/29, 1890), a distant relative, speaks of his former tutor, Adam Pulman, who was reported to have died in the ruins of a flaming Vienna theater, a report that Conrad discounts. He writes: "Probably he is living in Sambir." Sambir or Berau, in actuality, was located in Borneo; Conrad meant Sambor, in Galicia. The juxtaposition of past and present, of location in his fiction and of geography in actuality are all part of his dislocation of language and imagination; for the letter to Sobotkiewicz was composed in Polish at the same time he was writing in French and English. Also, we must not forget that Conrad, despite the happiness of seeing Tadeusz and revisiting old scenes, was in a kind of limbo: sailor without a ship, a writer without a book, a man of thirty-two without any definite financial or psychological support. He was drifting, waiting for a letter from Thys, renewing old memories without having discovered what to do with them or with himself.

Two weeks later, on April 11, he wrote to Thys to thank him for the letter sent to Barr, Moering, and then rerouted to Russia, where it was mislaid or lost. Conrad, therefore, did not know the contents, but assumed it had to do with a Congo post. He tells Thys he will be in Brussels at the end of April and "will present myself without loss of time at the office of the Society of the Upper Congo in order to learn of your decision concerning my affairs." Ironically, since such gaps in information were to become a Conradian motif, he was to hurry back from Kazimierówka to Brussels in order to respond to a letter whose contents he did not know. Although he assumed an offer was being tendered, Thys's letter could as easily have indicated no post at all. Meanwhile, he had heard from Marguerite about her intervention in his affairs and he wrote to thank her for her "kind attention" to his African plans. None of this, however, was proof that he would be offered a definite position, since intervention in the past had proven useless. For another three weeks, he was to remain in limbo.

CHAPTER 13

Journey to the End of the Night

CONRAD planned to leave Tadeusz's on April 18, spend two days in Lublin with relatives, and return to Brussels on the twenty-ninth. He apparently returned, instead, on the twenty-sixth and found that because one of the Congo steamer captains had been killed—a Dane named Johannes Freiesleben (Fresleven in "Heart of Darkness")—his own appointment was firm. He would replace Freiesleben. He was to make himself ready, which involved two rapid trips back and forth between London and Brussels. In "Heart of Darkness," Marlow conveys some sense of the turmoil:

> I flew around like mad to get ready, and before forty-eight hours I was crossing the Channel to show myself to my employers, and sign the contract. In a very few hours I arrived in a city that always makes me think of a whited sepulchre. Prejudice no doubt. I had no difficulty in finding the Company's offices. It was the biggest thing in the town, and everybody I met was full of it. They were going to run an oversea empire, and make no end of coin by trade.

A replacement for a dead man, Conrad never felt more alive than he did in Brussels, if we accept Marlow's narrative as fact.* He visited the company's office (with or without the two Fates in the outer room); had his facility in French tested by the great man himself of "pale plumpness in a frock-coat"—apparently Albert Thys; was ushered back into the waiting room and then taken by a clerk upstairs to see the old doctor, who wonders if Marlow has had any madness in his family; and finally is approved, with the doctor's

* In a letter to Karol Zagórski from Freetown, Sierra Leone, Conrad wrote of his flurry of movement in tones that foreshadow Marlow's: "From London to Brussels, and back again to London! And then again I dashed full tilt to Brussels! If you had only seen all the tin boxes and revolvers, the high boots and the tender farewells; just another handshake and just another pair of trousers!—and if you knew all the bottles of medicine and all the affectionate wishes I took away with me, you would understand in what a typhoon, cyclone, hurricane, earthquake—no!—in what a universal cataclysm, in what a fantastic atmosphere of mixed shopping, business, and affecting scenes, I passed two whole weeks."

ironic farewell advice in his ear: " '*Du calme, du calme. Adieu.*' " Marlow then goes to say goodbye to his aunt, and the die is cast. He says: " 'I was going to take charge of a two-penny river-steamboat with a penny whistle attached.' " His aunt spouts idealistic words about missionary work, and Marlow hints that things are run for profit. Marguerite, if it is she, is made to look like a fool, but Marlow is a misogynist and Conrad was not.

The experience in "Heart of Darkness" is hallucinatory, a journey into the unconscious or to the end of the world: " '. . . a queer feeling came to me that I was an imposter. . . . I felt as though, instead of going to the centre of a continent, I was about to set off for the centre of the earth.' " Going by rail from Brussels to Bordeaux, Conrad boarded the *Ville de Maceio* on May 6, planning on a three-year stay in Central Africa. Destination: Boma, on the southwest coast of Africa, the entry point for the Congo. Conrad's first letter, to Marguerite, dated May 15, comes from Tenerife, the initial port of call. He reports he is "comparatively happy," which for him usually meant freedom from illness. He repeats his uncertainty about the future, expresses some haunting memories, suggests some vague regrets and vague hopes. He speaks of the design of life, a rather hopeless affair as he faces an uncertain future: "A little self-deception, many dreams, a rare flash of happiness, then disillusionment, a little anger and much suffering and then the end. Peace! There is the design, and we must see this tragi-comedy to the end. One must make up his mind to it."

He speaks of his two selves, the other "I" who is with her and who will precede her to Poland. It is the letter of a man who senses he is completely alone in a world of chilling indifference. Conrad never felt more marginal as he headed into the dark, his mind preoccupied with the future while his imagination grappled with Almayer in the past. "And the MS of 'Almayer's Folly,' carried about me as if it were a talisman or a treasure, went *there* [Stanley Falls] too." By the time he left Africa, he had six chapters of the book.

"The screw turns and carries me off to the unknown," he wrote Marguerite, a complicated image of fate intertwined with technology, the twisting, thrusting mechanical screw diminishing his humanity even as it propels him toward the future. He was to write even more ominously to Karol Zagórski a week later about what he felt his future might hold:

> As far as I can make out from my "lettre d'instruction" I am destined to the command of a steamboat, belonging to M. [Alexandre] Delcommune's exploring party, which is being got ready. I like this prospect very much, but I know nothing for certain as everything is supposed to be kept secret. What makes me rather uneasy is the information that 60 per cent. of our Company's employés return to Europe before they have completed even six months' service. Fever and dysentery! There are others who are sent home in a hurry at the end of a year, so that they shouldn't die in the

> Congo. God forbid! It would spoil the statistics which are excellent, you see! In a word, there are only 7 per cent. who can do their three years' service. It's a fact! To tell the truth, they are French! Des nevrosés! (C'est très chic d'être nevrosé—one winks and speaks through the nose.) Yes! But a Polish nobleman, cased in British tar! What a concoction! Nous verrons! In any case I shall console myself by remembering—faithful to our national traditions—that I looked for this trouble myself.

His irony here was a form of prescience.

The last port of call before Boma was Libreville, in Gabon (near Lambaréné, where Schweitzer later built his famous hospital), where Conrad addressed a long letter to Marguerite. Conrad speaks of how impossible it is for him to "get rid of the memory of my charming Aunt," apparently because his recollection of her haunts him. He adds: "You have endowed my life with new interest, new affection; I am very grateful to you for this. Grateful for all the sweetness, for all the bitterness of this priceless gift." He talks of their two paths, she following one, he another. He does not know, he says, where his road leads. "I go along it with my head lowered, cursing the stones." Conrad warns that he may not be able to write for a while, for after his departure from Boma, which occurred on June 13, he would have no opportunity until Leopoldville (Kinshasa). He adds that he is waiting for the inevitable fever.

On June 12, Conrad arrived in Boma. He had reached the Congo. In "Heart of Darkness," he describes the voyage down this stretch of coast, an area no less strange than East Borneo, and even more desolate. "Every day the coast looked the same, as though we had not moved; but we passed various places—trading places—with names like Gran'Bassam, Little Popo; names that seemed to belong to some sordid farce acted in front of a sinister back-cloth." Conrad saw the coastline, as he later would see the Congo region, as part of an hallucination or a nightmare.*

Contrasted with the ghostliness of the *Ville de Maceio*, the Africans "had bone, muscle, a wild vitality, an intense energy of movement, that was as natural and true as the surf along their coast." They belonged, whereas the white man was an intruder. "Once, I remember, we came upon a man-of-war anchored off the coast. There wasn't even a shed there, and she was shelling the bush. . . . Pop, would go one of the six-inch guns; a small flame would

---

* Louis-Ferdinand Céline's version of his African journey, which owed much to Conrad's "Heart of Darkness," stresses the same sense of reflected madness: "It is hard to take a reasonable view of people and things in the tropics because of the aura of colour which envelops them. Things and colours are in a haze. A little sardine tin lying open at noon in the middle of the road throws off so many different reflections that in one's eyes it takes on the importance of an accident. You've got to be careful. It's not only the human beings who are hysterical down in these parts; things get involved in it too" (*Journey to the End of the Night*, p. 124).

dart and vanish, a little white smoke would disappear, a tiny projectile would give a feeble screech—and nothing happened. Nothing could happen." Such things occurred as though in a dream, and our comparison to the unconscious and to dream materials is appropriate, for only a few months after "Heart of Darkness" Freud's *Interpretation of Dreams* appeared.

The actual Congo region that Conrad was about to explore on foot and by steamboat was the ghastly product of a very real world. Conrad's Congo was really Leopold's *domaine*, the virtual private property of the King of the Belgians, from 1865 to 1909. Running parallel to Leopold's predatory acquisition of the Congo were Roger Casement's repeated attempts to expose what Leopold was doing, not an idle point here since Conrad met Casement in the Congo and then exchanged several letters with him in 1903–04. These letters to Casement, which are not generally known, provide a kind of capstone to Conrad's Congo trip. There are, for our purposes, really three Congos: Leopold's, which operated behind intricate disguises and deceptions; Casement's, which was close to the reality; and Conrad's, which fell midway between the other two, as he attempted to penetrate the veil and yet was anxious to retain the hallucinatory quality.

"Heart of Darkness" demonstrates this desire to comprehend the truth, whatever it was, but still to submit oneself to the very anarchy that blurred the truth. While the story exaggerated and distorted much of Conrad's experience, its tensions, we can assume, were his. If Marlow represents the rational part, what Conrad had himself become with maturity, then Kurtz, who had abandoned himself to the jungle, represents the anarchic, chaotic youth. Each demonstrates a form of power.

There was, in a sense, a fourth Congo, that of Henry M. Stanley. In 1876, when Leopold formed the African International Association, a scientific and philanthropic organization, Central Africa was largely unknown. Conrad equates it with Britain under Caesar's legions. In the years 1874–77, Stanley had followed the course of the Congo River, and when Leopold decided to open up the Congo it was natural he would turn to Stanley as his chief agent. Leopold formed two organizations which served as façades for his real business, the Comité d'Études du Haut-Congo (1878) and the Association Internationale du Congo, or A.I.C. (in 1882). Stanley's role was very important and fed into Conrad's initial view of the Congo, for Stanley gave great respectability to Leopold's enterprises, which, apparently unknown to the explorer, were for purposes of exploitation, not missionary work.

Stanley's function was to establish stations along the Congo River all the way to Stanley Falls, deep in the interior of the region. When he signed agreements or treaties with the local chiefs, he did so thinking he was bringing civilization to the bush. For Leopold, however, the activities pointed elsewhere. Through a series of manipulations, he arranged to have the vast region opened up to free trade, and toward that end he had it declared a free state, the so-called Congo Free State, which was announced in 1885, with its seat of government at Boma. The sovereign of this Free State, which was independent of Belgium, was, of course, Leopold.

For Stanley and, shortly afterward, for Casement, the declaration of the Free State would give them, and men like them, the opportunity unburdened by imperialism or colonialism to mold the new nation. Casement, in fact, went out to the Congo to establish a transport system, to administer a vast land area about equal to Western Europe, and to help stamp out the slave-trade system still practiced by the Arabs entrenched in the area. It was, in the terms of the period, a great missionary work, not unlike the ideals we see in Conrad's Kurtz when he first goes out to the Congo. Casement, in particular, took on the job to survey the land for a railway that would link Matadi and Stanley Pool, then an overland journey that took several weeks to negotiate. Conrad writes of walking it, a distance of almost two hundred miles, in "Heart of Darkness," accompanied by the Free State agent Prosper Harou.

When a company was formed to construct a railway, Casement seemed the obvious choice as manager. It was during the spring of 1890 that he met Konrad Korzeniowski (mentioned in Conrad's Diary entry for June 13), and apparently an impression was made on both the Dublin-born adventurer and diplomat and the Ukrainian-born English sea captain. For them to have encountered each other in the Congo was perhaps no more bizarre than for Dante to have met former friends in the Inferno.

Conrad had come to the Congo under the auspices of the Société Anonyme Belge pour le Commerce du Haut-Congo (S.A.B.), formed in 1888, whose acting manager was Albert Thys, a Leopold deputy. Both Casement and Conrad later discovered that Leopold's agents were using African workers as slave labor. The workers had themselves been sold by Arab slave traders or else were simply indentured by the station agents. By virtue of the device known as the *régime domanial,* through which all vacant land was declared state property, only state agents were empowered to collect rubber and ivory. Thus, operating behind his philanthropic enterprises, Leopold penetrated vast sections of the Congo territory, bypassing Belgium altogether.

Under these conditions, local labor operated under slave contracts, and we find the circumstances Marlow observes:

> They were dying slowly—it was very clear. They were not enemies, they were not criminals, they were nothing earthly now—nothing but black shadows of disease and starvation, lying confusedly in the greenish gloom. Brought from all the recesses of the coast in all the legality of time contracts, lost in uncongenial surroundings, fed on unfamiliar food, they sickened, became inefficient, and were then allowed to crawl away and rest. These moribund shapes were free as air—and nearly as thin. I began to distinguish the gleam of eyes under the trees. Then, glancing down, I

saw a face near my hand. The black bones reclined at full length with one shoulder against the tree, and slowly the eyelids rose and the sunken eyes looked up at me, enormous and vacant, a kind of blind, white flicker in the depths of the orbs, which died out slowly. The man seemed young—almost a boy—but you know with them it's hard to tell. I found nothing else to do but to offer him one of my good Swede's ships biscuits I had in my pocket. The fingers closed slowly on it and held—there was no other movement and no other glance. He had tied a bit of white worsted round his neck— Why? Where did he get it? Was it a badge—an ornament—a charm—a propitiatory act? Was there any idea at all connected with it? It looked startling round his black neck, this bit of white thread from beyond the seas.

Marlow's isolation of this particular African makes the general situation even more poignant. Genocide becomes meaningful only if we sense the plight of individuals. The others are described in geometrical, mechanical terms: bundles of acute angles, bodies shaped like triangles, limbs squared off, boxed in, these dark figures approaching the death that would merge them with the very heart of darkness. The scene is of eternal misery and dislocation, as much of the Inferno as of the concentration camp.

Almayer, by this point in Conrad's Congo experience, had reached Chapter 6, nearly half of its length in manuscript. As Conrad wrote in his first novel about Almayer's slow death, in East Borneo, he was assimilating images of the more rapid death of Africans in the Congo. The juxtaposition of early parts of *Almayer* and Conrad's Congo experience should not escape us; nor should his own sense of personal stagnation. Those dying Africans, given a different time and place, were not unlike the Polish exiles—indeed, the Korzeniowskis—he had experienced in his childhood, dying physically or spiritually under the Russian, not Belgian, eye, indifferent deaths in an indifferent universe. These waste-land images were deeply embedded in Conrad's imagination, so that Poland, the Congo, and East Borneo blend with each other: the past life, the present experience, and the future work.

Conrad's actual journey in, however, was less dramatic. Having arrived at Boma, he continued forty miles up to Matadi, where he arrived on June 13, according to his Diary.

Made the acquaintance of Mr. Roger Casement, which I should consider as a great pleasure under any circumstances and now it becomes a positive piece of luck. Thinks, speaks well, most intelligent and very sympathetic.

Feel considerably in doubt about the future. Think just now that my life amongst the people (white) around here cannot be very comfortable. Intend avoid acquaintances as much as possible.

Except for his correspondence with Casement thirteen years later, Conrad forgot about the Irishman until Casement surfaced as an insurrectionist intent on disrupting the English war effort against the Germans. At the time of Casement's trial for treason in the spring of 1916, Conrad wrote to John Quinn, the famous American lawyer and collector:

> I met Casement for the first time in the Congo in 1890. For some three weeks he lived in the same room in the Matadi Station of the Belgian Société du Haut-Congo. He was rather reticent as to the exact character of his connection with it; but the work he was busy about then was recruiting labour. He knew the coast languages well. I went with him several times on short expeditions to hold "palavers" with neighbouring village-chiefs. The object of them was procuring porters for the Company's caravans from Matadi to Leopoldville—or rather to Kinchassa (on Stanley Pool). Then I went up into the interior to take up my command of the stern-wheeler "Roi des Belges" and he, apparently, remained on the coast.*

On the twenty-fourth of June, Conrad attached his movements to those of Gosse, the station chief: On Gosse's return, "intend to start up the river. Have been myself busy packing ivory in casks. Idiotic employment. Health good up to now." On the twenty-eighth, he announces he left Matadi with Prosper Harou "and a caravan of 31 men. Parted with Casement in a very friendly manner." As in "Heart of Darkness," the trip upland of over two hundred miles to Kinshasa, by Stanley Pool, was made miserable by the terrain, the heat, the mosquitoes, lack of drinking water, and Harou's indisposition, which made it necessary for him to be carried. As Conrad wrote wryly to Marguerite, he was traveling on foot: "Not an ass here except your very humble servant. Twenty days of caravan."

---

* The rest of the letter having to do with Casement updates Conrad's relationship. "Next time we met was in 1896 in London, by chance, at a dinner of the Johnson Society. We went away from there together to the Sports Club and talked there till 3 in the morning. I asked him down to Pent Farm (where we lived then) [actually not until October 1898]. He came for the night. Lord Salisbury had taken him up or was going to take him up. Certain Liberal circles were making rather a pet of him; well-connected Irishman, Protestant Home-ruler, of romantic aspect—and so on. In 1911 (I think—but anyhow before the Putumayo atrocities Report) we came upon each other in Surrey St. Strand. He was more gaunt than ever and his eyes still more sunk in his head. There was a strange austerity in his aspect. He told me he was Bsh Consul in Rio de Janeiro on leave home for 3 months. We parted after 5 minutes conversation and I never even heard of him (except the Putumayo Report) till I read the news of him being in Germany. We never talked politics. I didn't think he had really any. A Home-ruler accepting Lord Salisbury's Patronage couldn't be taken very seriously. He was a good companion; but already in Africa I judged that he was a man, properly speaking, of no mind at all. I don't mean stupid. I mean that he was all emotion. By emotional force (Congo report Putumayo—etc) he made his way, and sheer emotionalism has undone him. A creature of sheer temperament—a truly tragic personality: all but the greatness of which he had not a trace. Only vanity. But in the Congo it was not visible yet."

There is no mention in the Diary of what Conrad relates of Matadi in "Heart of Darkness." In the novella, Conrad sees a wasted landscape of industrial junk: a "boiler wallowing in the grass"; "an undersized railway truck" lying on its back, its wheels in the air. Once part of industry, it has now become part of dying nature: "The thing looked as dead as the carcass of some animals" or of the Africans themselves, defunct beasts of burden occupying a human burial ground. Marlow sees more "pieces of decaying machinery," "a stack of rusty nails," a puff of smoke indicating a railway under construction—the human beings working on it indistinguishable from the industrial waste surrounding them.

The metallic waste now becomes human waste, as Marlow hears a clinking, a chain gang of indentured Africans. The scene is Inferno-like, a descent, whether that of Dante, Odysseus, or Aeneas, into the underworld of human existence. A single paragraph, still based on Marlow's view of Matadi, cuts through the detritus of Western civilization; so that the very ribs and joints of the Africans seem to become part of the clinking: *they* clink, deathlike, indifferent, with that unhappy look which signifies death for the primitive life. Behind them comes a member of the "new world," carrying a rifle and wearing a uniform jacket with one button off. Human beings and machines join, in a "grove of death." How prophetic that Conrad should have written this on the threshold of the twentieth century!

Meanwhile, his Diary followed what he thought an explorer's diary or a mariner's chart should be: daily entries giving the terrain, campsites, the condition of the caravan, chance meetings. The Diary, which, except for letters, is our first view of Conrad as a writer, stresses details but contains very little natural description. Such an omission is not unusual, since he was probably fatigued and pressed for time, and prone to emphasizing those details he wished to remember, hoarding impressions, nature, descriptive elements for the manuscript of *Almayer.* Even so, the entry for July 3 contains a kind of shorthand description, the work of a man caught by an impression and hurrying to get it down.

> A few minutes afterwards saw at a camp place the dead body of a Backongo. Shot? Horrid smell.
>
> . . . Another broad flat valley with a deep ravine through the centre. Clay and gravel. Another range parallel to the first-mentioned, with a chain of low foothills running close to it.
>
> . . . General tone of landscape grey-yellowish (dry grass) with reddish patches (soil) and clumps of dark green vegetation scattered sparsely about. Mostly in steep gorges between the high mountains or in ravines cutting the plain.
>
> Noticed Palma Christi —Oil Palm. Very straight, tall and thick trees in some places. Name not known to me. Villages quite invisible. Infer their existence from calbashes [sic] suspended to palm trees for the "Malafu."

> Good many caravans and travellers. No women, unless on the market place.
>
> Bird notes charming. One especially a flute-like note. Another, kind of "boom" ressembling [sic] the very distant baying of a hound. Saw only pigeons and a few green parroquets. Very small and not many. No birds of prey seen by me.

These entries would continue until August 1, when the convoy reached Nselemba, about fifteen miles from Kinshasa (Kinchassa), with a break both in the journey (at Manyanga) and in the Diary from July 8 to July 25. The interesting point, however, is how removed the Diary entries are from the later "Heart of Darkness." In the novella, Conrad encapsulated the entire first part of his Diary into one very long paragraph of about a thousand words. That paragraph is full of description, narrative, and even dramatic action (as the porters balk at carrying the "sixteen-stone" Harou). At the end of the novella paragraph, the convoy on the fifteenth day stumbles into the Central Station; in the Diary, the overland journey takes from June 28 to August 1, with an additional day needed to go from Nselemba to Kinshasa. Further, the Diary entries are a form of awkward, almost discordant shorthand, far removed indeed from art or artifice, little more than jogs to the memory. When we compare the distance Conrad traversed between these entries in 1890 and "Heart of Darkness" less than a decade later, we note the leap and see how clearly he discerned that the Diary entries were insufficient as fiction.

Conrad's immersion in language clusters once again intrigues us. In these Diary entries, in English, Conrad was writing a kind of shorthand, with a phrase and sentence brevity. Yet at the same time he was jotting down his impressions of African phenomena, he was writing in fullness of his Borneo memories, not at all in shorthand but in the roundness of paragraphs and pages. Almost simultaneously, he was writing in French to Marguerite and commenting on her work, which was concerned with Polish scenes; and he was writing in Polish in and around this time to distant relatives or to his uncle. As for speaking, he was using French with Harou and listening to a variety of African dialects among the porters, all the while thinking in English as he planned variations on Almayer.

The Diary, meanwhile, not at all concerned with reflections, catches images directly. On Friday, July 4, Conrad writes:

> Saw another dead body lying by the path in an attitude of meditative repose.
>
> In the evening three women, of whom one albino, passed our camp; horrid chalky white with pink blotches; red eyes, red hair; features very negroid and ugly. Mosquitos. At night when the moon rose heard shouts and drumming in distant villages. Passed a bad night.

In "Heart of Darkness," as Richard Curle notes, this straightforward observation becomes transformed: "A great silence around and above. Perhaps on some quiet night the tremor of far-off drums, sinking, swelling, a tremor vast, faint; a sound weird, appealing, suggestive, and wild—and perhaps with as profound a meaning as the sound of bells in a Christian country."

The Diary describes discomfort, but without any dramatic intent. On July 5: "To-day fell into a muddy puddle—beastly! The fault of the man that carried me. After camp went to a small stream, bathed and washed clothes. Getting jolly well sick of this fun."

The entry for July 8 attempts some description: "The country presents a confused wilderness of hills, landslips on their sides showing red. Fine effect of red hill covered in places by dark green vegetation. ½ hour before beginning the descent got a glimpse of the Congo. Sky clouded." This entry logs the arrival at Manyanga, where the caravan remained until the twenty-fifth. On the twenty-fifth: "H. lame and not in very good form. Myself ditto but not lame." Unlike Marlow, Conrad passed several villages, and, except for the normal discomforts of an African climate and a rough terrain, his trip was considerably different from Marlow's journey. Conrad encountered normal people, saw some elements of civilization, and experienced directly little of the ominousness associated with the story. On the twenty-ninth, he notes meeting a Mr. Louette, who was escorting a sick agent of the company back to Matadi.

At that point, Conrad learned the bad news: "All the steamers disabled—one wrecked." In "Heart of Darkness," Marlow is informed that his steamer is at the bottom of the river. The Diary notes that after crossing the Inkisi River in canoes, the party puts up in a government shimbek. "On the road to-day passed a skeleton tied up to a post. Also white man's grave—no name—heap of stones in the form of a cross." Harou is increasingly indisposed, vomiting and feverish. ". . . put him in hammock and started for Kinfumu. Row with carriers all the way." Conrad indicates he assembled the carriers and "made a speech, which they did not understand. They promise good behaviour." Conrad would himself, later, become far more indisposed than Harou, almost dying from attacks of dysentery and fever, ailments that apparently remained with him in varying degrees for the rest of his life.

On August 1, the party finally arrived at Nselemba, within reach of Kinshasa the next day. "Chief came in with a youth about 13 suffering from gun-shot wound in the head. Bullet entered about an inch above the right eyebrow, and came out a little inside the roots of the hair, fairly in the middle of the brow in a line with the bridge of the nose. Bone not damaged apparently. Gave him a little glycerine to put on the wound made by the bullet on coming out."

On August 2, Conrad's journey to Kinshasa would end, with a total of thirty-six days on the trip, nineteen of them traveling and seventeen at Manyanga. At this point, Conrad and Marlow began to part ways. Each would pass into a different kind of world, Conrad into the actual experience and Marlow into experiences already reshaped by the synthesizing powers of memory and imagination.

What about *Almayer's Folly* during this period? In *A Personal Record*, Conrad says that the novel proceeded "line by line, rather than page by page." And shortly before this observation, he notes that the entire manuscript up to that stage was almost lost in a "specially awkward turn of the Congo," and this on his return home, with six chapters (he mistakenly says seven) of *Almayer.** While in the Congo, Conrad may have completed Chapter 5, which he had begun in the Ukraine while visiting his uncle, and all of Chapter 6. We cannot be certain, however, since he may have done much of this writing before coming to the Congo. We do know he carried six chapters out of the Congo, for Chapter 7, worked on at Champel, has a reference to Geneva on the verso of page 1 of the chapter.

Nothing in the sixth chapter gives us clues as to Conrad's state of mind in the Congo, if indeed he did write that part while fighting illness and climate and trying to gain his command. We would have to speculate that as problems accumulated for him (as for Marlow), the small pile of manuscript he kept with him must have become a form of security, even a source of sanity. Certainly it must have occurred to him that the tangibility of the paper with his writing upon it—with its memories of the *Vidar*, his furnished room in Bessborough Gardens, his nostalgic stay in Kazimierówka—was a kind of anchor amid Congolese experiences. That Conrad stuck so doggedly to the manuscript, despite incredible obstacles of language, career frustrations, and slowness of composition, indicates he was making some kind of resolution that writing had a certain solidity or personal reference which contrasted favorably with his drifting professional career, particularly in the Congo when his future was so little in his own hands and so much in the control of men like Delcommune.

Once at Kinshasa (the Central Station of the novella), Conrad discovered that the *Florida*, the vessel he was to command, was wrecked, but he was

* "I call to mind, for instance, a specially awkward turn of the Congo between Kinchassa and Leopoldsville—more particularly when one had to take it at night in a big canoe with only half the proper number of paddlers. I failed in being the second white man on record drowned at that interesting spot through the upsetting of a canoe. The first was a young Belgian officer, but the accident happened some months before my time, and he, too, I believe, was going home; not perhaps quite so ill as myself—but still he was going home. I got round the turn more or less alive, though I was too sick to care whether I did or not, and, always with 'Almayer's Folly' amongst my diminishing baggage, I arrived at that delectable capital, Boma, where before the departure of the steamer which was to take me home I had the time to wish myself dead over and over again with perfect sincerity" (*A Personal Record*, p. 14).

delayed at most two days, not the three months attributed to Marlow. On either August 3 or 4 (depending on whether one accepts Conrad's second Congo notebook entry or the notation in the *Mouvement géographique* records), he departed on his upriver journey on the *Roi des Belges*, but not as captain. He left as a "supernumerary," to learn the river. In the sole supporting personal document for this period, we have Bobrowski's letter to Conrad, dated October 28/November 9, in which Tadeusz responds to his nephew's letters from various places along the way, including one from Stanley Pool on August 3. Bobrowski writes:

> I see from your last letter that you feel a deep resentment towards the Belgians for exploiting you so mercilessly. In general there is no love in your heart for the Latin races, but this time, you must admit, nothing forced you to put yourself into Belgian hands. You can say to yourself: "Tu l'as voulu, Georges Dandin"; and if you had paid any attention to my opinion on the subject when discussing it with me, you would have certainly detected a lack of enthusiasm in me for this project.

To pinpoint this resentment is difficult, although on it depended Conrad's future in the Congo. Chiefly, it concerned the manager of the station, Camille Delcommune, whose antipathy for Conrad (and Conrad's for him) appears to have been established immediately. It was this mutual dislike which was to wash away Conrad's plans for a permanent position in the Congo, even if his health had held out. In "Heart of Darkness," Marlow's meeting with the manager is auspicious indeed, since the latter, without considering Marlow's condition after his long journey, begins to speak at once of his own problems. We can assume that the hostile relationship was set at first sight, and Conrad from that point forward was not to assume a large role in company affairs.

When Conrad returned to Kinshasa in late September after making the trip to Stanley Falls on board the *Roi des Belges*, he poured out his feelings to Marguerite. After indicating his regret in coming to the Congo and expressing his confidence that she would understand him, he arrives at the nub of the problem, his lack of advancement:

> Everything here is repellent to me. Men and things, but above all men. And I am repellent to them, also. From the manager in Africa who has taken the trouble to tell one and all that I offended him supremely, right down to the lowest mechanic—they all have the gift of irritating my nerves; so that I am not as agreeable to them perhaps as I should be. The manager is a common ivory dealer with base instincts who considers himself to be a merchant when he is only a kind of African shopkeeper. His name is Delcommune. He detests the English, and I am naturally regarded as one of them. I cannot hope for either promotion or salary increases while he is here.

Conrad continues that promises made in Europe, for a command, apparently carry no weight with Delcommune in the bush. He complains of his health—fever on four occasions, an attack of dysentery lasting five days—and says he feels physically debilitated and "not a little demoralized." He indicates homesickness for the sea as a kind of purification of Congolese rot: ". . . the desire to look again on the plains of salt water which so often lulled me. . . . I miss all that. But what I miss even more is having tied myself down for three years." Conrad suggests that either someone will find reason to discharge him or another attack of dysentery will send him "to another world, which would be a final solution to all my distress."

Norman Sherry ascribes Conrad's inability to get along with Camille Delcommune to a series of circumstances, not the least of which was Conrad's extreme slowness in arriving at Kinshasa and Delcommune's own nervousness about a local fire and the damage to the *Florida.* In addition, there was an immediate clash of will between two ambitious young men (Conrad was thirty-two, Delcommune thirty-one) of very different social classes. At sea, class meant little; on land, everything.

Despite this, Conrad and Delcommune left on the *Roi des Belges* to go upriver to Stanley Falls, to relieve the Inner Station and bring back Georges Antoine Klein, the inner-station agent now close to death. The trip, a considerable one of a thousand miles, normally took well over a month because of obstacles in the river and the nature of the waterway itself.

Jean-Aubry's assertion that everything Marlow describes is a direct reflection of Conrad's memories is incorrect on nearly every count. It is unfortunate that Conrad's upriver Diary provides little more than maritime information, but even without such direct evidence, we can piece together quite a different journey from Marlow's in the novella. At every turn of the fiction, Conrad heightened and intensified in order to strengthen his view of Marlow as a man being tested by an irrational and anarchic situation. Conrad's need in the story is not only the description of a journey but the creation of a chaotic, amoral atmosphere which tempts Marlow. If Marlow is all superego, then the challenge must derive from the id.

As the *Roi des Belges* chugged upriver, there was apparently considerable traffic, and numerous opportunities for other vessels to have removed the desperately ill Klein. Also, there were several trading stations along the way, and the Inner Station at Stanley Falls was not nearly so isolated as Marlow indicates. Another key difference, and a crucial one for the biographer, is the fact that Conrad, unlike Marlow, was not the captain of the *Roi des Belges* and, therefore, was not in charge. In the novella, the fact that Marlow is answerable for the upriver operation is essential for an understanding not only of the man but of his relationship to Kurtz and the Inner Station. For if Marlow, the person of account, can waver in his fidelity to purpose, then Conrad can challenge the very nature of the civilizing process.

Conrad was in actuality a supernumerary in someone else's drama. He did indeed share the bridge with Captain Koch—the bridge, we must recall, of a 15-ton stern-wheeler, what Marlow refers to as an "empty Huntley and Palmer biscuit tin" with "a penny whistle attached." As the extra to Captain Koch's chief actor, Conrad was employed in making notes on the upriver journey, as his Diary shows. He was, almost throughout, an observer, not a decision-maker or an active participant. As an observer, he apparently partook of two kinds of experience: those observations, connected to his employment, which had to be accurate and preserved as navigational aids; and, more importantly for the future writer, those observations which were impressions, tones, textures, imaginative configurations, many of which were preserved not only for "Heart of Darkness" but for colors and textures in *Almayer's Folly.*

That novel, and the ensuing *Outcast of the Islands,* have tones and feelings carried over from the Congo experience; and, in many places, Conrad's sense of exotic and foreign places catches indiscriminately the lushness of East Borneo and the jungles of Africa. For fictional purposes, he was storing up memories of one kind, and for purposes of employment he was hewing to a factual journal of observations and aids. We recall Mallarmé's distinction between two types of speech, the first being that which transmits information, the second attributed to the language of literature. Conrad's observations were of these two kinds.

Conrad's journey upriver was far less bizarre than what he created for Marlow. The dealings with the Africans, the use of brass wire as currency, the peculiar food eaten by the workers, the dangers of the journey itself, and the isolation of Marlow—all of these were imaginative reworkings of materials which, in actuality, were more prosaic, with the chief dangers being the climate, the debilitation of illness, the ever-present dysentery.

In "Heart of Darkness," the Inner Station has a totemic value as the lair for a dragon or primitive beast, as the mythical hiding place for Loki or another satanic figure of evil. We are transported into another order of being, a topsy-turvy, synesthesiac reality with the harlequin-like Russian, the screeching of the steam whistle, the extraordinary reputation of the chief inhabitant, and the decorative human heads. Conrad writes:

> A long decaying building on the summit was half buried in the high grass; the large holes in the peaked roof gaped black from afar; the jungle and the woods made a background. There was no enclosure or fence of any kind; but there had been one apparently, for near the house half-a-dozen slim posts remained in a row, roughly trimmed, and with their upper ends ornamented with round carved balls [human skulls]. The rails, or whatever there had been between, had disappeared. Of course the forest surrounded all that. The river-bank was clear, and on the water-side I saw a white man under a hat like a cart-wheel beckoning persistently with his whole arm. Examining the edge of the forest above and below, I

was almost certain I could see movements—human forms gliding here and there.

This is the imaginative re-creation of what was, for Marlow, a descent into the underworld. The actuality was more ordinary, as was Klein, on whom Kurtz was ostensibly modeled.* The Inner Station was quite well organized and its chief threat came not from Klein and his methods but from conflicts between Belgians and Arabs in the collection of ivory. Apparently the Belgians found the Arab method of raiding settlements and the gaining of slaves, later to be sold for ivory, too crude and, as a consequence, had to use military muscle as a form of discouragement. For the novella, Conrad needed to intensify Kurtz's role in order to strengthen his view of the agent as a new type of European demigod, the refined product of the best Europe has to offer, who, when unsupported by his own civilization, descends into the unspeakable.

The upriver trip to Stanley Falls ended on September 1, with Conrad himself brought low by attacks of dysentery and fever. With Captain Koch also ill, the departure of the *Roi des Belges* was delayed until September 6. When it chugged out of Stanley Falls, it was captained by Conrad, both the sick Koch and Klein aboard. Klein was to die, but Koch would recover and retake command of the tub. Conrad's short spell at the wheel of the vessel, with sickness among the crew, a sick or dying passenger (Klein), and an ill

* The name Klein recurs in the manuscript of "Heart of Darkness" (at Yale), and then is altered to Kurtz. Monsieur Small becomes Monsieur Short, a piece of crude satire Conrad could not resist.

Georges Antoine Klein, who was twenty-seven when he died on the downriver journey of the *Roi des Belges*, need not concern us despite Conrad's use of his name, since he was so little a model for Kurtz. He seems to have been an ordinary agent, not at all the remarkable phenomenon we find in his literary counterpart. In some way, he touched Conrad's imagination—perhaps because of his relative youth, his lost hopes, his dreams shattered by illness (dysentery, like Conrad's)—but he was conventional in life and conventional in death. He did not last out the three-year enlistment; health, or lack of it, was his destiny. Norman Sherry posits an agent named Arthur Eugene Constant Hodister as a more likely model for Kurtz; but Conrad never met Hodister and may only have known of him through hearsay.

Possibly, Stanley's expedition to relieve the Emin may have led indirectly to Conrad's sense of Kurtz, although the latter was more a blend of types than an actual person. When Stanley left for Africa, he took with him a Major Edmund Musgrave Barttelot, who was left in the Congo to guard the rear of Stanley's party, while Stanley himself pushed on to meet the Emin. Completely unsuited for such work, Barttelot brutalized the Africans with floggings and executions, until he was himself murdered in July of 1888, fourteen months after Stanley had left him in charge. His savagery may have provided Conrad with some sense of Kurtz's method of dealing with the Africans, especially since Barttelot's *Diary on the Congo* was published in 1890 by Bentley. Although we have no proof that Conrad read it, some of the descriptions in "Heart of Darkness"—especially of men as ghostly, as phantoms—recall Barttelot's own terms. Of course, such descriptive phrases would be a common language for Europeans who tried to "see" the Africans.

officer, became an archetypal situation for him with numerous variations. We find in this not only *The Nigger of the "Narcissus"* but *The Shadow-Line* and elements of several stories. In his September 26 letter to Marguerite, Conrad catches the tangential quality of the experience even for someone as marginal as himself. "Indeed [he writes], while reading your dear letters I have forgotten Africa, the Congo, the black savages and the white slaves (of whom I am one) who inhabit it."*

As the downriver journey began, Conrad was hardly well; if not exactly invalided, he was weakened and dispirited. Survival, physical and professional, took what remaining energy he had. It is difficult to determine how much of the trip was under Conrad, how much under Captain Koch. Possibly Conrad negotiated the entire downriver journey of eighteen days; but Koch may have taken over at some point, perhaps at Bangala, about midway between Stanley Falls and Kinshasa. Although he could not have foreseen it, this was to be the extent of his command experience, in the Congo or elsewhere. Yet when he returned to Kinshasa on the twenty-fourth of September, he was still full of plans for a captaincy and looking forward to the expedition on the river Kassai (Kasai), toward Katanga Province. Writing to Maria Tyszkowa, his cousin, on the twenty-fourth from Kinshasa: "I am busy with all the preparations for a new expedition to the River Kassai. In a few days I shall probably be leaving Kinchasa again for a few months, possibly even for a year or longer." The Kasai expedition was the one Conrad had counted upon when he went to the Congo and the journey he had written to Karol Zagórski about on May 22: "As far as I can make out from my 'lettre d'instruction' I am destined to the command of a steamboat, belonging to M. [Alexandre, Camille's brother] Delcommune's exploring party, which is being got ready."

The experience on the *Roi des Belges*, then, while discouraging, was to be a preliminary, not the main event. The journey on the Kasai would have taken Conrad deep into south-central Africa and been a far greater adventure

* Despite these and similar comments, Conrad—or Marlow—did not see his own role, in the pay of the Belgians, as part of the European rape of Africa. As an Englishman (enjoying the "vast amount of red" on the map of Africa—"real work is done in these parts"), Conrad considered himself outside the frame of reference of what he saw in the Congo. That is, Marlow—and we can assume Conrad—accepted the captaincy as a necessary one, and only balked at the particularities of Belgian methods, the unnecessary and cruel wastage of human life, the "unspeakable" elements of the enterprise; its excesses, but not the thing itself. Throughout both the actual trip and its fictional re-creation, Conrad stressed the extraordinary quality of the experience as it struck him, the individual, not the rightness or wrongness of colonialism. None of this is to suggest, however, that he was not overwhelmed by the waste land he had observed. One of our twentieth-century touchstones of colonialism will always be Conrad's description of the Congo in "Heart of Darkness." But he ordered his material to "make you see," not as a politician. His sense of the Congo has remained long after Roger Casement's reports have been laid away.

than the upriver trip to Stanley Falls, which was well traveled and held few uncertainties. There was in the Kasai expedition sufficient challenge for someone like Conrad, and it would, in a sense, duplicate those early explorations, not the least of them Stanley's, which he had assimilated in his reading since childhood. As an "exploration," it not only had the danger, the illness, the strangeness, but would have afforded him the opportunity to hit upon something unknown—the 1890 equivalent of what he was aiming for in his manuscript of *Almayer's Folly*. In a certain ironic sense, Conrad was trying to reverse the career pattern of his fictional protagonist: as Almayer headed into decline and collapse, Conrad was himself attempting to explore new experiences so as to prove in life what his fiction was telling him otherwise.

Between September 24, when he wrote to Maria Tyszkowa from Kinshasa, and September 26, when he corresponded with Marguerite, Conrad's plans were dashed. Almayer's fortunes were a more predictable bellwether of life than his own hopes. On the twenty-sixth, as we have already noted, Conrad wrote Marguerite that everything in the Congo smelled: "Men and things, but above all men." Delcommune—and here he means Camille, the station manager, not his brother, Alexandre, who was to head the Kasai expedition—had turned against him, and promises made in Europe had no bearing on Congo matters unless in the contract. In this, his last letter for 1890, Conrad had to face another defeat; his sea captain's license meant nothing here, he felt, where he was associated with inferior men with small minds and mean hearts.

Conrad's inability to please Camille Delcommune, whether personally or professionally, doomed him. The decision to keep Conrad in limbo, without a command, was made before Alexandre Delcommune returned. Very possibly, Conrad hoped to persuade the still-absent brother otherwise when he appeared in October, but nothing is known of that. Just after mid-October, the Delcommune Kasai expedition departed from Kinshasa without Conrad. Part of the irony and bitterness which characterize the tone of "Heart of Darkness" surely derives from Conrad's dashed hopes in 1890.

In the novella, Marlow speaks of the Eldorado Exploring Expedition led by the "uncle of our manager"—in actuality, the brother, Alexandre. The unruly band is presented as a bunch of pirates, of "sordid buccaneers." Marlow describes it as "reckless without hardihood, greedy without audacity, and cruel without courage." This was exploration at its worst, the aim being "to tear treasure out of the bowels of the land . . . with no more moral purpose at the back of it than there is in burglars breaking into a safe." We glimpse from this sarcastic passage that Marlow was trying to justify his own participation in the escapade by way of "moral purpose," but this defense becomes almost an afterthought, a means of attacking the Delcommune enterprises rather than a vindication of his own activities.

Living through a recurring pattern, Conrad could not disguise from himself his lackluster prospects. Now at close to thirty-three—surely an auspicious age—and in ill health, his past decisions had really seemed to close down the future. If ever his uncle seemed correct in his estimation of the whole venture—and Tadeusz would rub it in in his letter of October 28/November 9, 1890—it was now. In a real sense, his maritime career had come to nothing, and all he had were those six chapters of *Almayer's Folly*—themselves almost lost en route. This was little enough to show for those thirty-three years. At this point, a writing career may have appeared as the sole possible anchor in a whirlpool of threatening waters, and an ineffectual anchor at that.

Conrad made some attempt to rectify what he felt was a great injustice, and he asked Marguerite to exert whatever influence she could. She did write to Albert Thys, in a letter dated November 29, from Lublin, Poland. She set forward the terms that Conrad conveyed to her, that promises made in good faith in Europe carried no weight in the Congo unless part of the original contract. According to Jean-Aubry, she wrote: "It is sad to think that a man of Captain Korzeniowski's abilities, accustomed to commanding ships, should be reduced to this inferior post and exposed to such deadly diseases." By this time, however, Conrad had decided to break with the entire enterprise. On October 19, he had passed on to Bobrowski his decision to leave, even though it meant breaking a three-year agreement after only four months. His illness with dysentery, however, gave him reason for annuling the contract, although he had contemplated picking a quarrel as another way out. With his sense of honor and propriety, Conrad's insistence on abrogating the contract suggests the depth of his despair.

After the close call with the manuscript of *Almayer's Folly* at Kalina Point, he completed the journey back to Matadi on December 4, a six-week overland from Kinshasa, the extended length of the trip probably dictated by Conrad's illness. On the journey back, he had to be carried—like Harou on the way out—an ironic coda to the fortunes of the hopeful mariner who had gone out to Africa as a riverboat captain.

At Boma, Conrad caught a ship back to England, and, like Marlow, returned to the "sepulchral city," Brussels. The intended of Kurtz's whom Marlow visited was probably based on Marguerite, although Conrad certainly did not pass on "The horror! The horror!", which he had himself experienced. That "horror," while present in the circumstances, was also a matter of feeling, of felt attitudes. For that kind of experience, there were no simple words; he would have to "make you see."

Returned to England in late January of 1891, Conrad was now back at square one, only older. Possibly, his experiences in the Congo turned him into a writer, or at least gave him a sense of the indifference and negligibility of human life which he could shape into his fiction. But it was only one ingredient. What he had experienced as a boy in Poland, as a child in his parents' exile, then in his years as a seaman and later in the waters around Borneo—all of these episodes taken together created what Conrad knew about human depravity, baseness, degradation, and cruelty, as well as the individual's ability to survive such knowledge. The Congo alone did not suggest images of hell; it supported such experiences which Conrad had already accumulated.

We can suggest that the Congo experience showed him how fickle any enterprise could be which was not completely in his own hands. In the sense that he learned not to give himself to uncertain plans, he may have come to the knowledge that a literary career was possible. But even that is too strong a statement, for Conrad continued to search for commands and exotic posts—as a Suez pilot, for example—and continued to push along in his maritime career. Ultimately, the Congo episode, which became so momentous in his later work, may have been no more than the kind of defeat which brought him to the brink of existence, his own rather than that of civilization. At that edge, where he had to stare into the abyss, he saw himself drowning, and the question for him was whether he was worth saving.

V

The Writer
1891–1899

Now the Sirens have a still more fatal weapon than their song, namely their silence. And though admittedly such a thing has never happened, still it is conceivable that someone might possibly have escaped from their singing, but from their silence certainly never.

KAFKA, "*The Silence of the Sirens*"

CHAPTER 14

Limbo

UNCLE Tadeusz certainly felt he was worth saving. With his trenchant view of his nephew's needs and his ability to mix sympathy with fatherly advice, Bobrowski wrote very sharply in late December of 1890, a letter Conrad received as a belated New Year's present. First, he discharges a salvo of his disapproval of the African venture, stressing that one never receives what one expects, that the individual has to cut his expectations or suffer eternal disappointment. ". . . for neither the people nor the circumstances responded to your expectations. This in my view would be only half the evil—although a year lost at whatever time of life is not a good thing—but what worries me most is your health and what will happen to it in the future."

Bobrowski then zeroes in on matters of health, a topic very close to him because of his own run-down condition and the early deaths of members of his family. He warns Conrad not to let his ailments deteriorate and recommends consultation with specialists in tropical diseases and gout—for Russian physicians do not understand the latter. He says that a rest at Kazimierówka would not provide adequate medical attention. Generously, he offers whatever money might be necessary for Conrad to regain his health. "My sole concern is that my beloved nephew should get well as quickly as possible, and when that is achieved he himself will think of further work! I shall wait with the utmost impatience for news of your return and for the opinion of the doctors."

The next three and a half years for Conrad would be particularly trying, for he had reached thirty-three, with a body that was already failing to respond to treatment and a family history of short lives. Consumption, the scourge of the nineteenth century, was as familiar as measles. His life was, in fact, half over, and although he may have had only fleeting intimations of that, he did know with certainty that his early expectations, however defined, whatever their shape, had been frustrated. Up to his completion of the first draft of *Almayer's Folly* in April 1894, he had existed in terms of fits and starts. Whatever he began, he either did not finish or else found too tedious for consistent application. The itch to move on was still there—he did not settle into harness until the turn of the century—but when he did relocate he was still dissatisfied: with his work, with his career as a seaman, most of all with himself.

Characteristic of his attitude was his attempt to present his achievements as a lack of deficiencies; he turned himself into a figure of fun, almost a fool, in order to express indirectly how he felt about fate and fortune. He had been cheated somewhere along the line, and now he must bow to kings and crown as the court fool; no longer Hamlet, he was Polonius or Osric. Writing to Marguerite on his return to London, he expressed his scorn for life by mocking his own hopes:

> If you believe Péchet [Pécher, Antwerp shipping agents] approachable, I inform you I am thirty-two years old [really thirty-three]. Have English Master's certificate for service in sail and steam. Commanded both—but principally sail. Can furnish good references from shipowners and also from London merchants. With all these assets, I burn with the desire of having the honor of commanding one of M. Péchet's steamers. You can also add that judging from the appearance of my nose, I get drunk only once a year, that I don't seem to have any penchant for piracy, and that—according to what you know of me—you do not believe me capable of committing embezzlement. I have never passed within the jurisdiction of the police, and I am capable of looking discreetly upon a pretty face without squinting. It is true I limp, but I am in distinguished company. Timoléon [probably Tamerlane] was lame, and there is even a devil in the same condition, according to my information. If after having understood all that, he refuses to entrust me with a ship, well, then, we will abandon him to his sad fate—and look elsewhere.

Especially disturbing to Conrad, besides his generally poor physical condition, was the lack of continuity in his life. As he reflected, there was, of course, the very real achievement of his maritime career, in which he took great pride to his dying day. But even with that achievement, one post did not lead to another. The depressed conditions of the English economy made berths exceptionally difficult to come by, and as Conrad completed one tour of duty he found it impossible to move on to something comparable or better. The Congo experience, in that respect, was not unusual. In the 1890s, he was to take posts far beneath his competence: as first mate on the *Torrens* and as second mate on the *Adowa,* when he had a master's certificate. The *Adowa* posting was especially humiliating. The high regard he sought in shipping offices simply was not forthcoming.

It was clear he had lost forward movement. And while the manuscript of *Almayer's Folly* was indeed an anchor of sorts, it was frail and yielding: this scribbling in English, page by page, chapter by chapter, a novel set in Borneo, with Malays, when he understood Polish, French, and even English characters far better. For him to write a novel about Malays and an area he had barely glimpsed seemed part of the foolishness; he knew neither the people nor the customs nor the language. And even while he was trying out this novel, he was writing in Polish and French, speaking English and French, corresponding with Marguerite about her work set in Poland.

Conrad was traveling in very treacherous waters, keeping himself afloat only by small amounts and slow degrees. The constant illnesses, the subsequent visits to Champel for hydrotherapy, the crippling conditions, only some of which derived from hereditary gout—all of these indicate a man moving uneasily, while trying to reach neutral ground. Walter Benjamin, writing of Kafka and his metamorphosed character Gregor Samsa, suggests a condition not too different from Conrad's in the early 1890s; the latter was close, in his own eyes, to turning into a bug: "For just as K. lives in the village on Castle Hill, modern man lives in his body; the body slips away from him, is hostile toward him. It may happen that a man wakes up one day and finds himself transformed into vermin. Exile—his exile—has gained control over him."

Conrad was not transformed into vermin, but his exile did in a sense gain control over him. Within the next six months, his letters manifest more than illness: they suggest a change of shape, a new body, limbs deformed by disease. The following ailments accrued after his return from the Congo, through July: legs swollen, rheumatism in left arm and neuralgia in right arm, stomach in bad condition, hands swollen, nerves disturbed, palpitations of the heart, attacks of suffocation, malarial attack, dyspepsia. His body was, quite literally, re-forming itself, and he was becoming a grotesque.

The images of malformation reach their climax when he speaks to Marguerite of having changed into a doll, the Punch of his childhood.* If we take the symbolic doll as the desire of the man, then—whatever the precise motivation—he has tried to metamorphose himself. The exile could no longer gain control without hydrotherapy, and the water cure was as much for his head as it was for his body. Conrad may have later found Freud's theories a jumble, but he was going through the very kind of breakdown that made Freudian analysis of the unconscious such a great creative achievement. Never to meet, never to read each other's work, they were, notwithstanding, reaching toward one another.

---

* "Could I be a Punch? The Punch of my childhood you know—his spine broken in two, his nose on the floor between his feet, his legs and arms rigidly spread in that attitude of profound despair, so pathetically droll, of toys tossed in a corner. . . . This evening I seem to be within a corner, spine cracked, nose in the dust. Would you kindly scrape together the poor devil, put him tenderly in your apron, introduce him to your dolls, let him play at dinners with the others. I see myself at this banquet, nose besmeared with jam, the others watching me, with that air of cold astonishment natural to well-made dolls."

In his own life, now as earlier, Conrad was paying the psychic price for what had become in the nineteenth century a distinct phenomenon and what was to become so familiar in the twentieth: the life of the exile. One thinks of Wagner in Paris, Marx in London, Conrad himself in France and England, Bakunin in Dresden, Zola and Hugo in England, Shaw and Yeats in London, later Joyce in Trieste and Paris, Pound in Italy. Many went into exile for political reasons, others for aesthetic, some to resolve profound personal problems. Conrad's exile—his self-conscious, self-imposed marginality—straddled all, political, aesthetic, and personal. The depth of his exile was, in fact, so great that when he returned from the Congo to resettle in London in 1891, the pieces were becoming greater than the whole: thus, that doll image of disintegration and fragmentation.

As a latter-day Ulysses, Conrad had lost the notes of the Sirens. They surely beckoned him toward some kind of destruction, or some form of salvation, but he was no longer sure he could even hear their voices. One is reminded of Kafka's description of Ulysses, who, when he approached the Sirens, stuffed the crew's ears with wax and had himself chained, like Prometheus, to the mast. All his efforts were expended in evading the allurement of their song; he had heard of it and he knew where the struggle would occur: they were after his very soul. Kafka:

> And when Ulysses approached them the potent songstresses actually did not sing, whether because they thought that this enemy could be vanquished only by their silence, or because the look of bliss on the face of Ulysses, who was thinking of nothing but his wax and his chains, made them forget their singing.

Ulysses, of course, "did not hear their silence; he thought they were singing and that he alone did not hear them." The pact one makes with art is ever illusory. As he yearned for what he was certain did exist, the very sounds he expected were not forthcoming. One's expectations, the only sustaining element in a sea of uncertainties, could no longer be trusted; facing the chaos of his own sensations, Ulysses senses only illusions. If he had not been chained to the mast, he would have fallen. Conrad, our Ulysses, was not heroic, however, and his recovery could not take epical lines; it required hydrotherapy.

His letters to Marguerite for this general period, when not concerned with illness and reshaping, fall into despondency. They make no mention of *Almayer's Folly.* The despair is tantamount to nihilism, which may have been Conrad's defense against the fragmentation of personal and professional aims that he sensed. He speaks of enduring existence, of the inevitability of occurrences, of the hopelessness of any action, and compares himself with Sisyphus rolling the stone uphill. He stresses his inability to think or feel or to touch pen and ink. In a letter of September 15, 1891, he shows gratitude for her sympathy: ". . . but to be honest I don't care a straw for happiness. I hardly know what it is. I am neither more courageous nor more independent than the others; I am perhaps rather indifferent. . . . We are ordinary people who have exactly the happiness we deserve, neither more nor *less.*"

He begins to ramble, becoming almost incoherent in trying to compare ordinary people and convicts, who have, at least, the virtues of their faults. He mocks the Catholic belief in atonement through suffering, saying it leads either to the Inquisition or to bargaining with the Almighty. We can expect no bending, no flexibility, no relenting. "Each act of life is final and fatally produces its consequences despite all the weeping and grinding of teeth, and the sorrow of feeble souls who suffer when fright seizes them at the results of their own actions. As for myself, I will never need to be consoled for any act of my life, and that is because I am strong enough to judge my conscience instead of being a slave to it as the orthodox believers would like to make us."

This line of argument, which suggests Conrad's nihilism of the 1890s, culminates in a paragraph, in French, he wrote to Graham on June 15, 1898. The use of French is itself curious, perhaps a direct linkage to comparable remarks he had made earlier in the decade to Marguerite, or else an indication of his Continental orientation when he spoke of nihilism. The English scene in 1898 was perhaps too hearty—colonialism, imperialism, militarism, et al.—for the feelings he would express. He wrote, in translation:

> There are none converted to ideas of honor, justice, compassion, liberty. There are only those who, without knowing, understanding, or feeling, exist on words, repeat them, shout them—without believing in anything but gain, personal advantage, satisfied vanity. And words vanish, and nothing remains, do you understand? Absolutely nothing, oh foolish man! Nothing. A moment, a wink of the eye and nothing remains—only a drop of mud, cold mud, dead mud launched in black space, turning around an extinguished sun. Nothing. Neither thought nor sound nor soul. Nothing.

These are surely more than post-Darwinian cries of anguish, or the ravings of a Nietzschean figure, a Zarathustra. They are, like Conrad's earlier comments to Marguerite, an attempt to understand himself and to create coherence. The difficulty with a psychoanalytic interpretation of these remarks, as indicating Conrad's "unmanly" dependence on a strong woman or his regression to a helpless infant seeking refuge in motherly love, is that it loses sight of the context. In the context, Conrad's sense of things has an objective truth; things *were* falling apart, not only in himself, but in England and in Europe. The century was closing on a different note from the one sounded forty or fifty years earlier. And Conrad, as a developing artist, as the novelist seeking comprehension of his materials, needed to face fully the consequences of his helplessness. In *his* futility, he was attempting to discover general truths; and therefore, his plaints to Marguerite and, later, to

Graham are not simply calls for help, not the seeking of a mother or father figure, but the way of the artist attempting recognition of his themes so as to master them.

In moving to Conrad the person at this time, we recognize that his mind was working imaginatively, and that each personal factor had its aesthetic counterpart. Every segment of subjective history would find transformation in his work; and every bit of knowledge, personal or literary, was undergoing the reshaping that occurs in the creation of a literary artifact. We have not only *Almayer* in incubation but a career of thirty years; we have implicit now the creative talent that includes everything. That is, if we are to deal with Conrad's internal mechanism at this stage, we must consider not only the six chapters of *Almayer* manuscript at hand but the whole body of work potential in his imagination.

Conrad had already taken on, unconsciously, that quality of the artist in which, as Jung says, he "is nothing but his work, and not a human being." That is, his artistic drives have taken over from his conscious self, although he continues to function as a "human being," marries, works, has children. While many of Conrad's ailments were physically palpable, the sense of anguish, the inability to find wholeness, the malaise that accompanied the illnesses—all indicate he was undergoing intense forms of depression that occur because of irresolvable inner forces. None of this is apparent to the sufferer; at best, he may achieve only glimpses. Certainly in the evidence we have, mainly in the letters to Poradowska, we obtain only those persistent images of fragmentation, reshaping, transformation, bodily change. These are Conrad's glimpses, what he was capable of describing. But what they meant actually, in terms of the conflicts and divisions he was experiencing, was not clear, since he continued to putter along on *Almayer* and sought maritime berths for almost the length of the decade.

Yet the metamorphosis, the final one in his case, was occurring. In that first stage, in Poland, when he recognized he had to break away, he achieved his will in part through illnesses, some of them frightening enough to gain his uncle's approval of a wild scheme. Now, recurring illnesses, some real, some induced, were suggesting comparable images of flight. Instead of his uncle, however, he had Marguerite. At this stage in his career, she was crucial; she provided continuity with the past (family, Poland, politics) and with the future, as a novelist, a woman of culture, and someone with literary connections. In 1891, we can characterize Conrad as having, in Jung's words, caught "sight of the figures that people the night-world—spirits, demons, and gods"; as someone who felt "the secret quickening of human fate by a suprahuman design."

Once back in London, having visited Marguerite in Brussels, Conrad fought his ailments with at least a show of activity. He demonstrated interest, incredibly, in returning to Africa if he could obtain command of one of the steamers run by the Prince Steam Shipping Co. of Antwerp. Marguerite apparently had some connection with Pécher, the agents for Prince, and Conrad mentioned (on February 8) that he might run over to Antwerp with his friend Hope, director of the South African Mercantile Co. Nothing came of this, however, and on February 17 he wrote Marguerite that he had just returned from Scotland, "as always on business," which meant he had sought a command or even a lesser berth.

By the end of the month (the twenty-seventh), he wrote tersely: "Sick in bed in the hospital." From Bobrowski's letter to Conrad, we learn the latter had been admitted to the German Hospital in London, probably through the intercession of his friend Adolf Krieger. The ailments were non-specific: rheumatism, neuralgia, swollen legs, and stomach trouble. On March 30, to Marguerite, Conrad indicated that Mr. Knott of Newcastle, who controlled the Prince Steam Shipping Co., was "making overtures" to him to command a steamer, and he had also received an invitation from his uncle to visit. The letter from Knott and the invitation from Bobrowski, both of them welcome under other circumstances, must have seemed appropriately ironic in the light of Conrad's condition.

In a letter to Maria Tyszkowa (April 15, 1891), he mentioned that for three weeks his hands were so swollen he "only managed with the greatest difficulty" to write a few words to his uncle. The "swollen hands," the very tools necessary for the writer, are like obvious clues awaiting the investigating detective. To find his resolution—not cure—Conrad would have to deal with the swelling of those hands by putting them to almost exclusive use.

A Dr. Ludwig of the German Hospital recommended that Conrad go to Switzerland to attempt a water-mountain cure, which was as much for nerves as for specific ailments. He left London on May 17 for Champel-les-Bains, near Geneva, a hydrotherapeutic establishment which provided a water cure, diet, rest, quiet. Having stopped off in Paris for one day (Marguerite was in Lille), he arrived at Champel on May 21 and remained until June 14, staying at the Hotel-Pension de la Roseraie, which is situated between Geneva and its suburb of Carouge. Just before he left, he wrote Marguerite that he was "still plunged in densest night" and his dreams were "only nightmares."

Once at Champel, he began to write fairly rapidly. In *A Personal Record,* he indicated that Geneva, "or more precisely the hydrotherapic establishment of Champel, is rendered for ever famous by the termination of the eighth chapter in the history of Almayer's decline and fall." Evidence in the manuscript, however, seems to contradict this statement, for while Conrad obviously worked on Chapter 7 here (there are computations and notations on the verso sheets of this chapter) he could not have reached Chapter 8. Probably, in his subsequent renumbering of the manuscript, in which Chapter 7 becomes part of 6, he lost track of exactly what he had achieved at each stage; and then in the much later account in *A Personal Record*, he misremembered. Nevertheless, the stay at Champel indicated that under perfect conditions he could work. The real test, however, would come when he returned to London, where the fairy-tale atmosphere of a hydrotherapeutic establishment would vanish in the demands of a large city. The question was no longer how to live, but, more insistently, how to write.

On his way back to London, he stopped off in Paris to see Marguerite, one of their infrequent meetings despite their numerous plans. In fact, in his letter of June 3, Conrad apparently tried to forestall a meeting—"it seems [he wrote] unwise to bother you." If they were indeed carrying on a flirtation, language—not physical feeling—seemed more their medium. Conrad's plans for the future were as uncertain as ever. Bobrowski's letter of May 25/June 6 sounds exasperated with his nephew's indecision: "You speak so enigmatically about your plans for the future that I can understand nothing: were you referring to your professional plans or to the possibility of visiting me towards the end of your convalescence? State your thoughts, Panie Bracie, with more clarity and lucidity." Conrad's ideas involved, among other things, a command on the Niger River and unspecified business schemes arranged by his friend Hope, none of which even remotely materialized. Meanwhile, he sailed on Hope's yacht and waited for something to break, heading into the second half of 1891 no more established than in the first half. On July 8, he could write to Marguerite: "Truthfully, we are the slaves of fate before birth, and we pay tribute to calamity before having known it."

We do not know what Conrad was saying to his uncle, but we can judge by Bobrowski's responses. As Baines remarks, Conrad must have outlined a large number of schemes for the future, most of them impractical, even foolhardy. Tadeusz lectures his nephew as he had done when the latter was a very young man. He dredges up the Nałęcz "taint," which Conrad had spent the last fifteen years trying to escape and, as if speaking of some doomed Atrean bloodline, attacks Conrad's lack of endurance, his indulgence of himself in fantastic plans, his depression when his wild ideas do not turn out. They may have been the plans of a desperate man, or else of a man indulging his imagination—the public side of the writer. Bobrowski did not know at this time the fact of Conrad's progress on a novel, an omission of considerable importance. This might also have seemed impractical to Tadeusz, another wild scheme; or else it might have indicated, to this man of some literary achievement, that Conrad was moving toward respectability. It is difficult to determine, since Bobrowski could have easily found in Conrad's turn to writing simply another indication of the Apollo taint.

Bobrowski's letter of July 18/30, whose arrival coincided with the misfiring of many of Conrad's plans, raked over the latter's character and then turned to his relationship with Marguerite. Tadeusz feared their seeming flirtation would become something serious. He calls her, unfairly in the light of the facts, "a worn-out female" and warns Conrad to find his amusement elsewhere. In a later letter, he mocks her as being "as romantic as a girl of sixteen." Tadeusz's remarks were made, however, in ignorance of Conrad's interest in writing and in Marguerite as an established writer. Also, we find it difficult to judge since we do not know what tone Conrad used in speaking of his "aunt" to his uncle.

Further, and this is speculative, it does not seem as if an alliance with Marguerite would have been so disastrous for Conrad at this time, and it is very possible that, whether he felt romantically about her or not, he may have measured marriage in terms of its practicality. She had money, social position, a literary reputation; she was not, of course, a blood relation and was liked by the family. She shared many of Conrad's interests and was intelligent as well as handsome. If anything, at this point, she would have made a misalliance had she married Conrad. Unless we lack information available to Tadeusz, a marriage between the two does not augur tragedy.

There is, of course, a still further consideration: that Conrad did contemplate marriage with her and withdrew from the idea because she was excessively formidable and he felt himself too vulnerable professionally, personally, and financially to undertake such a venture. Under such conditions, he would treat her as some sacred figure—he does speak of her as being on a pedestal—so that he could abase himself before her. In these terms, marriage was out of the question psychologically.*

Such an analysis of the relationship, while possibly valid, assumes at least two factors: first, that Conrad's emotional life remained fixed forever, monolithically, and that experience and maturity had no bearing on him psychologically. Yet the very fact that he could move so tenaciously and now, near middle age, turn toward another career, indicates a steady pattern of growth.

---

* Dr. Meyer sees the relationship as such: "Viewed in this light Marguerite Poradowska was a precursor of his statuesque fictional heroines who inspire not so much sensuous longing as awe-filled adoration. Just as Razumov in *Under Western Eyes* confides his love of Nathalie Haldin not to her directly but to his diary, so did Conrad confine his love for his 'beloved Aunt' to the written page." Comparably, just as Rita of *The Arrow of Gold* is a fantasy, not at all founded on the fact of a Conrad affair with Don Carlos's mistress, so, too, he fantasized Marguerite: "Conrad could have attained a physical relationship only with a woman who failed to inspire such worshipful sentiments. For the sensuous women in Conrad's fiction are not the monolithic Rita and her like, but those creatures who spring from a much lower station in the hierarchy of social organization, women like Aïssa, Winnie Verloc, and the simple hired girl, Amy Foster. The girl with whom the Russian student Razumov finds final peace is not the revered Nathalie Haldin but the bedraggled Tekla. In like manner, Conrad could have given little if any consideration to the idea of experiencing erotic excitement with Madame Poradowska, but by the same token he might encounter a much less formidable psychological barrier in seeking the hand of the relatively obscure and undistinguished English girl, Jessie George."

Second, and more significantly, Marguerite was not an outsider. The very fact that she was involved in his family and his own national patterns would reduce the unfamiliarity which is often such an impediment to erotic feelings and to possible satisfaction. Marguerite was sufficiently in the family to remove the difficulties of an exogamous marriage, and yet, not being exactly "family," would not recall the worst of memories and experiences. In these terms, her formidability would become less harsh; that he would worship her might be part of the relationship, indeed be necessary for his artistic development, but it would not in itself preclude an erotic attachment.

Yachting with Hope, with his maritime career stalled and *Almayer* moving very slowly, was fiddling while his health burned out. Conrad's ailments seemed directly correlated with his lack of direction, a throwback to his childhood with Apollo and various guardians. As an interim activity, he took a position with the establishment he had invested in in 1883, Barr, Moering, at the firm's warehouse. However, because of renewed illness with malarial symptoms, his assignment was delayed until August 4. The job at the warehouse, which was located at 95, Upper Thames Street, brought out Conrad's sense of himself as Sisyphus. "There is nothing very cheerful [he wrote Marguerite] in doing disagreeable work. It too much resembles penal servitude, with this difference, that while rolling the stone of Sisyphus, you lack even the consolation of thinking of the pleasure you had in committing the crime. There, convicts have the advantage over your servant." Under such conditions, even a writing career would appear an escape, and in *A Personal Record* Conrad indicates "the events of the ninth [chapter of *Almayer*] are inextricably mixed up with the details of the proper management of a waterside warehouse."

Conrad's spirits were reaching their nadir. His letters become increasingly gloomy, even desperate. His language to Bobrowski was so despairing and pessimistic that his uncle possibly feared a recurrence of Conrad's suicidal impulse. Tadeusz's response of late September or early October discourages his nephew's talk about dying young, saying that such a philosophy "does not even enter the head of anybody young and healthy, and this worries me greatly, my dear lad." Intermixed with letters from Kazimierówka are Conrad's own exchanges with Marguerite, no less morbid. He cautions: "If I let you occasionally glimpse at my sometimes difficult life, it is a weakness of mine which I am very ashamed of—but you should not take me too seriously. I bear quite well the weight of the entire world on my shoulders—as do also the five million miserable souls who make up the population of this city."

These comments are more than *fin de siècle* weariness or *Weltschmerz;* and they are more than the traditionally gloomy "Slavic soul." Having reached a critical stage in his development, Conrad was undergoing an internal upheaval. The mental and emotional disruption he sensed was the equivalent of a patient waiting for a fever to break or to continue and carry him under. With hindsight, we know Conrad turned this period of his life to good use, but for him, experiencing the weeks and months of malaise, there was no foreknowledge. On October 16, he attempted to be witty about existence itself: "I am vegetating. I do not even think—then I do not exist (according to Descartes). But another individual (a learned man) has said: 'Without phosphorus, there is no thought.' From which it seems it is the phosphorus which is absent, while I am always here. But in that case I would exist without thinking, which (according to Descartes) is impossible." Behind the playful analogy is a profound frustration at the whole range of creation, a questioning of man's very purpose and function.

He must have written to Bobrowski along similar lines, because at the end of October or in early November, his uncle replied at great length, trying to place Conrad's pessimism in philosophical perspective. It is a very touching document, parts of which have been cited before, because it demonstrates Tadeusz's attempt to impress the reality principle on someone caught between gloom and romantic-idealistic notions of himself and his role in life. Bobrowski indicates he feels he should begin his letter with "My Dear Pessimist." He continues: "I can't say that I am pleased with your state of mind, and having now recognized it for what it is, it is difficult for me to contemplate your future with equanimity." Of course, he knew nothing of Conrad's writing plans. He heard only of the gloom, the drift, the lack of future opportunities at sea, the failure to find anything but demeaning work.

Tadeusz then moves to his chief theme, how pessimism can be understood and placed in proper perspective. As a Darwinian and positivist of sorts, Bobrowski always argues proportion with his nephew—as Stein was to do with Marlow in regard to Lord Jim. Like a modern Benthamite, he weighs the alternating elements of pessimism and optimism in each man's soul; ultimately, one must achieve the "golden mean," which contains, he says, the "basic truth of life." All morbidity, he feels, has a cause, whether from oversensitivity, fear of death, or a diseased imagination. He advises that one must think of oneself as an ant in the vast cosmos of things—in nature's plan—and in fulfilling its duties, this ant "secures the life and existence of the whole nest!" Since fate is never in one's hands, one must obey the order of nature, with "an understanding of shortcomings of the order of society."

Remarkable about the advice is how perfectly it would suit a man who had decided to devote himself to the sea. That is, despite Bobrowski's opposition to Conrad's maritime plans, his advice on living in accord with nature and obeying nature's dictates fitted the life of the mariner. Such views, or variations upon them, are indeed incorporated into several of Conrad's fictional seamen: Singleton, MacWhirr, among others. And had Conrad not himself been stirred by other conflicts, he could have rested quite easily with this advice, as Tadeusz intended him to.

Such counsel, however, while wholesome for the man, was death to the creative artist, anathema to the imagination. It would lead, if carried further, to the very kind of art that Conrad wished to avoid. If his touchstones were Flaubert, Maupassant, and late-nineteenth-century French practices, then such views could be only the source of mockery. Flaubert had covered this entire ground in *Madame Bovary*, and the ridicule of it could not have been lost upon Conrad. He was grateful for his uncle's time, effort, and concern. But he could not tell the now aging man his advice had little or no application; that he was testing out other ideas altogether and they would not allow him release from demons, fates, or strange destinies.

On November 14, 1891, Conrad announced to Marguerite that he had a post. He had received a letter from an acquaintance (Captain W. H. Cope) who commanded the clipper ship *Torrens* offering him a first mate's berth. Even though the berth was a step beneath what he was qualified for, his mood was elated. He would leave on the twenty-fifth, destination Port Adelaide, South Australia, a journey of about three months.

The *Torrens* was a choice posting for any officer. One of the last of the clippers, it held records for the voyage from Plymouth to Port Adelaide. Her captain, Cope, had replaced a more famous predecessor, H. R. Angel, who had turned the *Torrens* into possibly the most illustrious ship of her class. Under Cope, the *Torrens* was not so successful, but by then sailing was giving way to steam and such records and average times held less interest. The posting itself, however, was tribute to Conrad's reputation as a seaman. Not only had he received a berth, he had obtained a prime one. He wrote his uncle almost immediately, evidently in a more enthusiastic tone, because Bobrowski comments on the "air of satisfaction and energy. . . . An active life [he says], even the most commonplace one, is the best remedy for pessimism."*

* Other aspects of Bobrowski's long letter are of interest, since in many of his remarks he touches Conrad's life at sensitive spots, although missing others altogether. His letter serves as a kind of gloss on a poem whose deeper meanings defy full interpretation. He writes: "If I am not mistaken I imagine that you didn't want to take a position below that of a captain and as none came your way you waited in London becoming more and more embittered, helping your friends who deep inside might have been surprised—or else might have shared your opinion? until at last, bored and tired, you finally decided to accept a less brilliant position, but one which would prevent you from sinking deeper into pessimism. . . . In any case, you couldn't have acted more wisely—that is under the circumstances—for I would also have preferred to know that you had gone as a captain with a £1,000 salary instead of what you have got! One has to submit to necessity, and the moral advantage derived from the present decision will compensate you for the lost chances." He adds that if Conrad were to find in Australia what he had been looking for in London, he

Conrad sailed on November 25, 1891, and arrived in Port Adelaide on February 28, 1892. His memories of the ship in an essay written a year before his death indicate his pride: ". . . the *Torrens* had a fame which attracted the right kind of sailor, and when engaging her crew her chief officer had always a large and promising crowd to pick and choose from . . . for apart from her more brilliant qualities, such as her speed and her celebrated good looks (which by themselves go a long way with a sailor), she was regarded as a 'comfortable ship' in a strictly professional sense, which means that she was known to handle easily and to be a good sea boat in heavy weather." Writing thirty years after having served on the ship, he could jest about it and himself: "The *Torrens* was launched in 1875, only a few months after I had managed, after lots of trouble, to launch myself on the waters of the Mediterranean. Thus we began our careers about the same time. From the professional point of view hers was by far the greater success." "The Wonderful *Torrens,*" Basil Lubbock called her in his book *The Colonial Clippers,* and she proved to be a wonderful ship on Conrad's second voyage.

Meanwhile, the first voyage was still upon him, and magical though the *Torrens* was in both myth and substance, Conrad was nevertheless floundering. *Almayer* remained untouched. His letter to Marguerite from Port Adelaide, a very sober document indeed, is concerned mainly with her problems, her relationship to an autocratic, selfish old aunt who was making unusual demands upon her time and energy. With his own family background firmly in mind, Conrad insists on the individual's right "to arrange his life as he chooses." He adds that "the respect due old age is at bottom only a veiled feeling of deep pity for the miserable ones whom death has forgotten but time has stripped of hope." Conrad was drawing a sharp line between duty to others and duty to oneself, apparently a living matter with him.

On April 7, he was to leave Port Adelaide for Cape Town, South Africa, on the long voyage back to England, which would include a stop at St. Helena. Before departing, however, he wrote a final letter to Marguerite announcing his plans and telling her he has been in a kind of "intellectual torpor which oppresses me." She did not know of his manuscript, and yet his reference, as we know, is clearly to his progress, or lack of it, on that. In this letter, while directing his comments to her work, especially to her ability to "observe and describe," he remarks on his reading of *Madame Bovary.* Apparently, as Conrad was stalled on *Almayer* somewhere in or slightly after Chapter 9, he was attempting to visualize characters and scenes through the

---

should take advantage of it and forget their future meeting.

Tadeusz then goes on to more intimate matters and discusses the fits and possible retardation suffered by Michaś, Kazimierz's son and Conrad's first cousin. From this, he alludes to Conrad's own "fits" in childhood, suggesting a common epilepsy. Convulsions and fits, however—and in Conrad's instance possibly psychosomatically induced—may suit a variety of physical conditions. Since Conrad's later malarial seizures also had epileptic symptoms, claims of epilepsy based on Bobrowski's comments seem misplaced.

eye of Flaubert or his disciple Maupassant. Yet his long stay in Port Adelaide and voyage over apparently produced no further pages of manuscript. He arrived back in England on September 3, after a trip of five months.

On his return, a letter from Uncle Tadeusz told him of poor health and indicated that Conrad had been writing him about "indisposition and weariness," which meant depression and malaise. Bobrowski was concerned at the drift of his nephew, almost thirty-five and apparently living simply from year to year. He then mentions Conrad's cousin Stanisław, Kazimierz's son, who had been imprisoned, and Conrad was suddenly thrown back into the world of those who had stayed behind. Stanisław's case seems suggestive of Razumov's in *Under Western Eyes.* Stanisław had, in fact, been accused of the unauthorized teaching of artisans, which meant he was using Polish—strictly forbidden in Russian Poland—as the language of instruction. Stanisław represented both the heroism and futility of those who struggled, however minimally, against the Polish oppressor. "He is [Bobrowski writes] still under lock and key in the Warsaw citadel," where Apollo Korzeniowski had been imprisoned thirty years before.

In his next letter, also awaiting Conrad's return to London, Bobrowski picks up Stanisław's situation, a hopeless entanglement in the Russian bureaucracy. Bobrowski had generously sent bail, but no one had requested it and the boy remained under lock and key. ". . . in any case this poor boy has spoiled his future, and knowing him, it is difficult to believe him as guilty as he seems. His reputation must have been tarnished by false appearances or friends." In future letters Bobrowski's account of the involved case continues, as Stanisław is passed over to the St. Petersburg court. There, Tadeusz fears, he may be sentenced without a trial, and "he will be sent to Siberia for a period." With Apollo and other quixotic idealists in mind, he adds: "Whichever way it goes he is a lost man—especially as he has studied law—he could never become either a government official, a solicitor, or a notary—not even in Kamchatka!! His whole life has gone off the rails—together with all the hopes and confidences I had placed in him. There is nothing to be done!" Stanisław was finally sent to St. Petersburg, to serve a prison sentence of eighteen months.

It was as if Bobrowski were heuristically parading Conrad's past before him, and we perceive in the uncle's words the justification of his philosophy and his counsel to his nephew. Although we cannot know how Conrad responded, we do have *Under Western Eyes,* which is a more complicated answer than any letter could contain.

Conrad stayed in London, sticking to the *Torrens,* for he needed the wages of £8 a month (about $125 in current purchasing power). Writing to Marguerite, he tried to console her about her own nephew Jean, a flighty young man,* and took the opportunity to justify his own life so far: "One always thinks one's important at twenty. The fact is, however, that one becomes useful only by recognizing the extent of the individual's insignificance within the arrangement of the universe. When the individual well understands that by himself he is nothing and man is worth neither more nor less than the work he accomplishes with honesty of purpose and means, and within the strict limits of his social duties, only then is he the master of his conscience and has the right to call himself a man." Conrad's analogy demonstrates his Darwinian orientation: "Otherwise, he could be more charming than Prince Charming, richer than Midas, wiser than Dr. Faust himself, but the two-clawed, featherless creature is only a contemptible wretch stamping in the mud of all his passions." Bobrowski could not have put it better.

Except for his duties pertaining to the next voyage of the *Torrens*, Conrad seemed to be otherwise inactive, writing letters to his uncle that show him alternately depressed or hopeful, and to Marguerite full of support for her but with himself effaced. He can even jest at his own expense. In a letter of October 19, announcing his departure on the twenty-fifth for Port Adelaide, he is amused at her comparison of him to Hamlet—perhaps a Hamlet of the Steppes:

> You are laughing a little at your nephew in comparing him to the late Hamlet (who was, I believe, mad). Nevertheless, I allow myself to say that apart from his madness he was an altogether estimable person. So I am not offended by the comparison. I do not know where you found any signs of my contempt for mankind. This proves to me that, in generalizing, one can well say that even those who know us the best know us very little. The philosopher who said, "Know thyself," was, I believe, probably befuddled (having supped with Greek ladies—which was a philosophical custom of the day), since I cannot admit him to be stupid.

The second trip on the *Torrens* was auspicious, not for anything it consolidated in the present, but for becoming a focus for several developments in Conrad's future life: his sailing career itself (his final voyage out); his manuscript of *Almayer*, which had its first reader; and his meeting with John Galsworthy and Edward Lancelot Sanderson, who became lifelong friends. In Galsworthy, in particular, he was to find, beyond friendship, someone who could help him financially when he needed such support desperately.

In *A Personal Record*, Conrad writes laconically but affectionately about showing his manuscript to W. H. Jacques, a young and desperately ill Can-

* The absence of parents and the preponderance of nephew-uncle, nephew-aunt relationships is striking. We have, of course, Conrad and Uncle Tadeusz and Conrad and Aunt Marguerite, as well as Stanisław and Tadeusz, now Jean and Marguerite.

tabrigian traveling for his health. The moment was propitious, for Jacques was the first to know of and to read Conrad's work, and there was the possibility, very real at this time, that an adverse reaction could have discouraged Conrad altogether. We recognize how anxious the writer was to show his manuscript to an educated person outside of his own immediate circle of Tadeusz and Marguerite, and Jacques was very possibly the first such person he had encountered.

> "Would it bore you very much reading a MS. in a handwriting like mine?" I asked him one evening on a sudden impulse at the end of a longish conversation whose subject was Gibbon's History. Jacques (that was his name) was sitting in my cabin one stormy dog-watch below, after bringing me a book to read from his own travelling store.
>
> "Not at all," he answered with his courteous intonation and a faint smile. As I pulled a drawer open his suddenly aroused curiosity gave him a watchful expression. I wonder what he expected to see. A poem, maybe. All that's beyond guessing now. He was not a cold, but a calm man, still more subdued by disease—a man of few words and of an unassuming modesty in general intercourse, but with something uncommon in the whole of his person which set him apart from the undistinguished lot of our sixty passengers. His eyes had a thoughtful introspective look. In his attractive, reserved manner, and in a veiled, sympathetic voice, he asked:
>
> "What is this?" "It is a sort of tale," I answered with an effort. "It is not even finished yet. Nevertheless, I would like to know what you think of it." He put the MS. in the breast-pocket of his jacket; I remember perfectly his thin brown fingers folding it lengthwise.

Conrad then returned to his chief concern as first mate, the "sustained booming of the wind, the swish of the water on the decks of the *Torrens,* and the subdued, as if distant, roar of the rising sea. I noted the growing disquiet in the great restlessness of the ocean, and responded professionally to it with the thought that at eight o'clock, in another half-hour or so at the furthest, the top-gallant sails would have to come off the ship."

The turbulent sea, the quietly anxious Conrad, the imperturbable Jacques—as Conrad writes more than fifteen years after the event—suggest all the crazy ingredients of his career, a bizarre meeting of goals achieved with those yet to be attained. He was a master mariner ready to take over as captain of a celebrated ship, and yet as a writer the merest apprentice, awaiting like a schoolboy the approval or disapproval of his first reader. The words came with sufficient encouragement.

> Conrad asked: "Is it worth finishing?" This question expressed exactly the whole of my thoughts.
>
> "Distinctly," he answered in his sedate veiled voice, and then coughed a little.
>
> "Were you interested?" I inquired further, almost in a whisper.
>
> "Very much!"

Exactly then, the ship's roll and pitch intrude:

> In a pause I went on meeting instinctively the heavy rolling of the ship, and Jacques put his feet upon the couch. The curtain of my bed-place swung to and fro as it were a punkah, the bulkhead lamp circled in its gimbals, and now and then the cabin door rattled slightly in the gusts of wind. It was in latitude 40° south, and nearly in the longitude of Greenwich, as far as I can remember, that these quiet rites of Almayer's and Nina's resurrection were taking place. In the prolonged silence it occurred to me that there was a good deal of retrospective writing in the story as far as it went. Was it intelligible in its action, I asked myself, as if already the story-teller were being born into the body of a seaman.

Conrad asks one final question, and receives a laconic reply, sufficient for the moment:

> "Now let me ask you one more thing: Is the story quite clear to you as it stands?" . . . "Yes! Perfectly."

That was all Conrad wanted to hear. He had had his reader and reading. It was enough for him to continue.

On January 30, 1893, he arrived in Port Adelaide once again, having been ill for two weeks on the voyage. He looked to a command, and had the captaincy of the *Torrens* been available, it is quite possible he would have remained with the sea. "I have neither plans nor projects," he wrote Marguerite. His existence continued to worry him. "What causes this discouragement is not my current ill-health . . . but the uncertainty of the future—or, rather, the certainty of the 'uniform gray' awaiting me." There seemed to be no escape—a succession of berths awaiting him, none of them adding up to a career; a manuscript in English, the very language still strange to him; a past history of achievement which had not resolved anything; and the reality of his age, thirty-five in December.

Aging would be particularly terrifying for the man who was unfulfilled and isolated, with the concomitant fear of accomplishing nothing, the horror of dying without anyone having recognized his existence. Conrad peered over the edge of the abyss, and it presented a mirror reflection. If he was becoming increasingly narcissistic, it was a process that occurred with full self-knowledge of what had happened to Narcissus when he observed his reflection. There seemed no ready solution, and all the color appeared to have passed out of Conrad's life. Existence was gray, the future was gray, he was graying.

On the return voyage to England, there were respites from the morose grayness of an uncertain existence. In "Reminiscences of Conrad," which John Galsworthy wrote immediately after the former's death in 1924, we gain some sense of that meeting on the *Torrens:*

> It was in March, 1893, that I first met Conrad on board the English sailing ship *Torrens* in Adelaide harbour. He was superintending the stowage of cargo. Very dark he looked in the burning sunlight, tanned, with a peaked brown beard, almost black hair, and dark brown eyes, over which the lids were deeply folded. He was thin, not tall, his arms very long, his shoulders broad, his head set rather forward. He spoke to me with a strong foreign accent. He seemed to me strange on an English ship. For fifty-six days I sailed in his company.
>
> The chief mate bears the main burden of a sailing ship. All the first night he was fighting a fire in the hold. None of us seventeen passengers knew of it till long after. It was he who had most truck with the tail of that hurricane off the Leeuwin, and later with another storm: a good seaman, watchful of the weather; quick in handling the ship, considerate with the apprentices—we had a long, unhappy Belgian youth among them, who took unhandily to the sea and dreaded going aloft. Conrad compassionately spared him all he could. With the crew he was popular; they were individuals to him, not a mere gang; and long after he would talk of this or that among them. . . .
>
> On that ship he told of life, not literature. On my last evening he asked me at the Cape to his cabin, and I remember feeling that he outweighed for me all the other experiences of that voyage. Fascination was Conrad's great characteristic—the fascination of vivid expressiveness and zest, of his deeply affectionate heart, and his far-ranging, subtle mind. He was extraordinarily perceptive and receptive.

The meeting with Galsworthy, and to a lesser extent with Sanderson, was the first of Conrad's pivotal friendships in the 1890s; after Galsworthy, there would be Edward Garnett and then Ford Madox Ford (Hueffer) in 1898. Galsworthy-Garnett-Ford: each was to play a huge role in Conrad's life, personally and professionally; and this threesome would replace Bobrowski, who was to die in 1894, and Marguerite, whose presence receded after 1895. Conrad found intelligent, educated men for friends; he could try out his ideas and fictional theories on them, and he could expect informed, even imaginative, responses. He would add others: H. G. Wells and, to a lesser extent, Arnold Bennett, W. H. Hudson, George Gissing, and Edmund Gosse. Hovering in the distance, a presence rather than a friend, was the revered, almost deified Henry James, the master. Conrad always felt he was first mate to James's captain, and that reverence, as well as James's own need for distance, never allowed a close relationship. It was balletic, full of intricate steps and mirror images.

Galsworthy and Sanderson were passengers on the *Torrens*, having set out several months before to visit Robert Louis Stevenson in Samoa. To Conrad's thirty-five, Galsworthy was twenty-five and seemingly the very opposite of the seaman. His background was solidly in the English upper middle class: education at Harrow and New College, training in the law, a well-to-do solicitor father, sufficient spending money for travel and "experience," and deep roots extending into Victorian England. He was the embodiment of Conrad's younger fantasies: family, roots, income. And yet he was not entirely like that. He was dissatisfied with the role expected of him—he never practiced law, for example—and he felt the stirrings of a different career in which self-expression would be possible. He was, at least, sufficiently liberated from his traditional background for Conrad and his strange manner to strike him sympathetically.

Writing home on April 23, 1893, Galsworthy mentioned Conrad: "The first mate is a Pole called Conrad and is a capital chap, though queer to look at; he is a man of travel and experience in many parts of the world, and has a fund of yarns on which I draw freely." Conrad did indeed spin yarns about the Congo, Malacca, Borneo, and his Marseilles smuggling; for Galsworthy mentions these with youthful admiration.

"Ted" Sanderson, Galsworthy's companion on the voyage, was the son of the headmaster of the Elstree (Hertfordshire) preparatory school, one of a family of twelve surviving children, part of a turbulent and busy household which Conrad visited several times. On his return to England, Sanderson added an M.A. to his B.A. from King's College, Cambridge, and became assistant master at Elstree, later headmaster. Conrad was to dedicate *An Outcast of the Islands* (1896) to Ted and *The Mirror of the Sea* (1906) to his mother, Katherine Sanderson. This relationship, while pleasant, was not a crucial one for Conrad. Although Sanderson was a poet of sorts, the association had none of the literary overtones of his friendships with writers; and yet it apparently meant something to him. Aspects of Ted surface in Lord Jim, some invisible destructive pattern behind the resolute, heroic young man who wanted to do good for God and country.

Like Jim, Ted was possibly the English boy Conrad wanted to be, the epitome of the English virtues of courage, manliness, and determination to do right. Further, the large, active family created stability, as Conrad saw it, and even *he* was able to work when he visited Elstree. When Sanderson and Conrad met, the difference in age was almost fifteen years, and the friendship took on father-son overtones. But as Conrad began to know Ted and, later, Helen Watson, his wife, he saw that beneath the courageous exterior were a fragility, a moroseness, even an extreme sense of depression. This contrast between exterior rosiness and internal disintegration was an element Conrad would cultivate in his fiction, and Ted may have already embodied such qualities to the novelist's eye.

Gratifying as these acquaintances were on the voyage back (Galsworthy disembarked at Cape Town), they resolved none of Conrad's problems. Only Jacques's reading of the manuscript advanced his fortunes ever so slightly; at least he had had some confirmation of a talent he only suspected. Conrad arrived back in London on July 26, 1893, and found awaiting him letters from Bobrowski that indicated his uncle was ill and wanted to see his nephew for perhaps the last time. But he noted that if Conrad felt he might succeed Captain Cope as master of the *Torrens*, he should forgo the journey to Kazimierówka. The succession did not materialize, however, and Conrad left for the Ukraine at the end of August, for a stay that would last about a month.

It could not have been a very happy stay, for Tadeusz was not well, Conrad himself fell ill, and in addition, there he was back at his beginnings. Nostalgia must have been intermixed with entrapment. Some of the disorientation can be noted in his account of the manuscript of *Almayer* even before he arrived at Kazimierówka:

> And so it happened that I very nearly lost the MS., advanced now to the first words of the ninth chapter, in the Friedrichstrasse railway station (that's in Berlin, you know) on my way to Poland, or more precisely Ukraine. On an early, sleepy morning, changing trains in a hurry, I left my Gladstone bag in a refreshment-room. A worthy and intelligent Kofferträger rescued it. Yet in my anxiety I was not thinking of the MS. but of all the other things that were packed in the bag.

On his journey to Kazimierówka from Berlin, where the manuscript had almost disappeared, Conrad passed through many memories of childhood, including the meeting with a friend of his early years whom he had not seen for over twenty years. That childhood passage, the negligence with the manuscript, the crisis over the lack of direction: all of these threads came together when he arrived at the estate. He fell into Tadeusz's arms and became as ill as he had been in childhood. As he wrote Marguerite: "It's convenient to be ill here (if one must be ill). My uncle cared for me as if I were a little child." His sick uncle, under the circumstances, had to stop playing the admonitory father figure and become the nursing mother. By becoming so sick that he had to be tended like "a little child," Conrad defused his uncle's criticisms, present or forthcoming. Thus, the passage Conrad made back into his childhood, for a final view of his uncle and the region where he grew up, was accompanied by all the childhood symptoms of disorientation, illness, desire for mothering and comforting.

Such regression is quite significant for the writer or artist whose work would be so deeply involved with memory and with transformations of childhood images. If his art had been one of a more realistic kind, or one in which his fiction was contemporaneous with the experiences embodied in his fiction—such as Hemingway's—then the regressive element would have hobbled him aesthetically. But, as in Proust, what might seem to be most debilitating personally could be the very strength of his art; personal weakness could feed aesthetic needs, in that very reversal of elements which is so essential to artistic transmutation. Once again, we must insist on the kind of artist that Conrad was becoming as the basis on which we can observe him personally.

Meanwhile, Marguerite evidently became upset when she thought Conrad had returned to marry Marysieńka Ołdakowska, her niece by marriage. Conrad was himself amused: "It is perfectly true Marysieńka is getting married; but in the name of all the follies, what have I to do with this matrimonial affair! Besides, I can hardly believe you are speaking seriously of the matter in your letter, for it must seem strange to you to see someone hasten suddenly from the depths of Australia, without warning anyone, to the depths of the Ukraine to throw himself into the arms of—the whole idea is very funny." The girl was, in actuality, getting married to the son of Bobrowski's neighbor.

Conrad left Kazimierówka at the end of September and, without stopping, traveled via Amsterdam to London, where he settled at 17, Gillingham Street, near Victoria Station. Since he could not obtain its command, the *Torrens* was long behind him, and he had no prospects. He may have written portions of *Almayer,* although certainty is impossible. In *A Personal Record,* he speaks of working on the manuscript in a furnished apartment in Pimlico Square, where "Almayer (that old acquaintance) came nobly to the rescue. . . . Unknown to my respectable landlady, it was my practice directly after my breakfast to hold animated receptions of Malays, Arabs and half castes." Conrad, in retrospect, apparently confused his beginning of *Almayer,* in Bessborough Gardens, a "Pimlico Square," with the later time, after his return from Kazimierówka in 1893, when he continued work on the novel, from about Chapter 9.

Almayer was, now, virtually the sole source of activity. Close to his thirty-sixth birthday, he wrote to Marguerite:

> I am at present without work, and since my return from Poland [the Ukraine] I have spent my days in disheartening indolence. You who describe things and men, and consequently have raised a corner of the veil, know very well there are moments when the mind slumbers, the months slip away, when hope itself seems dead. I am experiencing one of these periods. It seems to me I have seen nothing, see nothing, and will always see nothing. I would swear there is only the void outside the walls of the room where I am writing these lines.

Under such circumstances, the absence of things, of objects and of life itself, is considerably more palpable than what was present, and only memory provided a lifeline.

Then, as Conrad describes it, "one murky November afternoon," he spoke to Captain Froud, who said he had a berth on a steamship, the *Adowa,* for a second mate who could speak French. For Conrad, who held captain's papers, the step down was more than ironic, and in steam as well, which he disliked. He saw his situation quite clearly: "I had given myself up to the idleness of a haunted man who looks for nothing but words wherein to capture his visions." The impression from this and succeeding passages is that Conrad was more or less hypnotized by his manuscript; that is, in several ways, he had gained the greater reality and intensity, and in order for him to readjust to his present situation he had to wrench himself out of those Malayan memories. "For many years he [Almayer] and the world of his story had been the companions of my imagination without, I hope, impairing my ability to deal with the realities of sea life."

As though surfacing after a long period under water, Conrad listened to Froud's offer: "He explained to me that the ship was chartered by a French company intending to establish a regular monthly line of sailings from Rouen, for the transport of French emigrants to Canada." Since the ship never sailed, it was the perfect berth for a man who wanted to recapture memories. He spent his *Adowa* assignment on *Almayer's Folly*, possibly rewriting and recasting rather than moving forward with the narrative.

On the twenty-ninth of November, Conrad signed on, and on December 4 arrived in Rouen. On the ship anchored in Rouen, he turned thirty-six, a captain with a second mate's berth, a would-be author with a manuscript more than four years old. He was not joyful. He wrote Marguerite that he was to sail on the ninth for La Rochelle and then Halifax, and followed that letter with another on December 18, also from Rouen. As though a descendant of Jonah, he had infected the entire enterprise. ". . . it appears the Franco-Canadian Company has not kept to its agreement with our shipowner, and consequently our sailing has been postponed. Right now there is a trial which will take up, next Friday at Paris, the question of damages; but, in any event, the affair is lost, and we will not be going to Canada. When the trial is over, we will return to England, to load there for India, the Persian Gulf—who knows where else?" In the same letter, he asks Marguerite how he can go about getting a post as a Suez Canal pilot. He suggests she inquire and, implicitly, use whatever influence she has.

Suspecting that nothing would come of the *Adowa*, he wrote her two days later, on the twentieth, that one must get settled into something, and toward that end he was taking steps (unspecified) "to get a position in the pearl fisheries off the Australian coast." He also asked her once again about Suez. In his next letter (on the twenty-fifth), he sent his service record, a document, incidentally, which has never turned up. Conrad was to spend the New Year in Rouen, in all until January 12, 1894. The tenth chapter of *Almayer* owes its existence to this aborted journey on the *Adowa*. "I indulge in the pleasant fancy that the shade of old Flaubert—who imagined himself to be (among other things) a descendant of Vikings—might have hovered with amused interest over the decks of a 2,000-ton steamer called the *Adowa*, on board of which, gripped by the inclement winter alongside a quay in Rouen, the tenth chapter of 'Almayer's Folly' was begun." With that, Conrad was less than three chapters away from the full-length novel in manuscript, a book going forward at the rate of about two to three chapters a year.

Interrupted by the third mate of the *Adowa* while writing the passage " 'It has set at last,' said Nina to her mother . . . ," Conrad moved along several levels of awareness: the quarters on board the ship where he is writing, anchored in a freezing port; the Malayan setting of his novel, hot, ornate, cluttered with vines and jungle; the ever-present mix of languages—French, English, Malayan, Polish; and, finally, the view of a café from the porthole which brought back memories of another sight, where the ship had previously been berthed. In that view, the one in memory, was the café "where the worthy Bovary and his wife, the romantic daughter of old Père Renault, had some refreshment after the memorable performance of an opera which was the tragic story of Lucia di Lammermoor in a setting of light music." There was, in this Proustian moment, the real sense that Almayer had qualities of Emma Bovary and that the Donizetti opera, with its passions and madness, was not an inappropriate backdrop for his own novel of inner rage set in Borneo waters.

On January 7, 1894, we have Conrad's first public mention of his "story of Almayer," although the tone in which he speaks of it indicates prior discussion. As a defensive gesture against the admission, he turns his project into a reward: "If you are a well-behaved little girl [he tells Marguerite], I will let you read my story of Almayer when I've finished it." At that point, Conrad was somewhere in Chapter 10 of the unrevised manuscript, and he would subsequently propose to Marguerite several roles she could possibly play in the production of the novel. Conrad arrived in London on the *Adowa* on January 12, although he was not officially discharged from the ship until the seventeenth. He reveals to his aunt fears he "will be forced to leave on a long voyage shortly," but nothing came of that, or of any other attempts at either a berth or command. Instead, he returned to his Gillingham Street quarters.

His existence now can be traced only through his letters to Marguerite. On February 2, he wrote a lengthy commentary on her novella *Le Mariage du fils Grandsire,* which he praised extravagantly. Since his tastes were forming along such different lines from those Marguerite displayed in her fiction, it would be of great interest to know what Conrad really thought of her novels and sketches. He may, of course, have felt exactly what he was saying to her—"While reading certain passages, I clapped my hands as one applauds at a performance. And how many sympathetic characters you have succeeded in producing!" The comments seem condescending, although it is very possible Conrad lacked a critical vocabulary and was stating as precisely as he could what he honestly felt. His only "critical" piece from this general period is the Author's Note to *Almayer's Folly,* which dates from 1895 (not from the much later time when he wrote his other author's notes for the Collected Edition). This short piece, which reveals very little, nevertheless does seem to suggest a dimension lacking in Marguerite's work. For although Conrad speaks of the need for an "elaboration of detail" in discussing his own work, he also mentions the "blessings of illusions," the colors and tints; and we reach out for intimations of an art that goes well beyond detail and recognizable "sympathetic characters." One does not wish to wrench this early, rudimentary statement into something it is not, but it does appear to forerun the Preface to *The Nigger of the "Narcissus"*; and that document surely implies that Conrad could not have considered Marguerite's realistic work serious fiction.

Whatever his reaction, Conrad was sufficiently impressed by her or her work to offer collaboration at a later stage, and whether he recognized the fact or not, he was, by February of 1894, a writer. He always discounted authorship as a conscious choice, saying that he slid into it, as into *Almayer*, "line by line, rather than page by page." And he was uncomfortable even with the term novelist or author. Still, the orientation was there, as we have seen; and his mind had been working imaginatively, picking up and sorting out, since his Marseilles days, if not before. The image of Apollo dying by slow degrees may have turned the young Conrad against revolutionary politics, but it did not make him reject books or the writing of them.

On February 10, 1894, Tadeusz Bobrowski died. Conrad's announcement to Marguerite was terse: "I have just received a message from Poland. My uncle died on the 11th of this month [more likely the tenth], and it seems everything has died in me, as though he carried off my soul with him" ("Il semble emporter mon ame avec lui"). Now, with Bobrowski in the forefront of his mind, the entire past became present. He had heard previously that he would receive 15,000 rubles in all a year after his uncle's death, and he learned that the latter had also appointed him one of a committee to supervise the publication of his *Memoirs*, which appeared in Lwów in 1900. Thus, his uncle, in life and death, remained with Conrad for the remainder of the decade, at least.

The death of someone so closely associated with oneself as well as with one's past is a profound event in any circumstances, but far more so for Conrad, since he had devoted his energies to escaping that very past which his uncle represented and for whose values often argued. Several commentators have connected Conrad's more rapid completion of *Almayer's Folly* with the death of Bobrowski. Dr. Meyer sees Conrad mastering a painful loss by "advertising a fictional one, thus becoming the active-author rather than the passive recipient of a piece of bad news." Comparably, Guerard's view is that as a "substitute father" Bobrowski, both his criticism and his presence, inhibited his nephew, and as long as he lived Conrad could not do meaningful work.

Conrad, however, did not experience a burst of creative energy when his uncle died. He spent another three months completing the novel, and during this time he had no other meaningful work. There were no intrusions or diversions, his circle of friends was still quite small, his money limited. As he pointed out to Marguerite, he had no work.* With time at his disposal for writing, he did not by any means whip himself into a creative frenzy. The tenth chapter had been begun at Rouen, the eleventh toward early April, and the twelfth and final chapter in mid-April; Almayer's death was announced on the twenty-fourth. Since work on the tenth chapter preceded his uncle's death, Conrad completed two chapters, perhaps part of a third, after Bobrowski died. We are speaking of about 10,000 words, if that, in over two months of enforced idleness, about 1,000 words a week, 150 words a day. All this was first-draft work, and it does not add up to a burst of creativity.

More likely, because of the enforced idleness which preceded his uncle's death, Conrad had reached certain inner decisions, and those decisions were to intensify his commitment to his new profession, to let the drift into authorship take on a more pronounced direction. To stress Conrad's "burst" in terms of any particular event is to lose sight of the preceding context, in which it was becoming increasingly clear that a maritime career was closing down for him. The experience on the *Adowa* could have been as much a factor in his completion of *Almayer* as the death of Bobrowski and, from the point of view of biography, a stronger consideration. On the *Adowa*, every aspect of his maritime career was aborted or mocked: himself a captain serving as second mate (and then only because he spoke French); the ship steam, not sail; the enterprise itself frustrated; and the temporary service monotonous and disagreeable. And all this to cap his disappointment that he had not attained command of the *Torrens!* We find here an almost natural ending to Conrad's maritime career, and we can assume that his depression, moroseness, and physical ailments so meticulously described in his letters to his aunt are a recognition on his part of what was happening to him. What could be more natural—indeed more attached to survival itself?—than for him to have come to an inner decision in the idle period after the failure of the *Adowa* that he needed some kind of shore enterprise?

* "The worst is that in the idleness to which I am condemned at this time I can scarcely forget my suffering [from neuralgia and rheumatism]. Oblivion is a good thing, but difficult to find." He repeats his desire for Suez employment and questions the silence of his potential employers.

CHAPTER 15

Turning to Shore

THERE was the further, and by no means insignificant, point that Conrad was considering marriage, or at least considering the idea of settling down, and for that he needed shore employment. In 1894–95, he was to become involved with two women in addition to Marguerite, if we can consider that relationship an "involvement." They were Jessie George, whom he ultimately married in 1896, and Emilie Briquel, whom he met in 1895 at Champel, near Geneva. Such considerations, even if still dim in early 1894, would help explain his commitment to writing and suggest, further, his speedup in production—if we can call it that—which occurred after the *Adowa* fiasco.

Conrad had clearly discovered something within himself. In a letter to Marguerite (dated March 29 or April 5), written after a brief visit to Brussels, he said: "I begrudge each minute I spend away from paper. I do not say from the pen, for I have written very little, but inspiration comes to me while looking at the paper. Then there are flights out of sight; my thought goes wandering through great spaces filled with vague forms. Everything is still chaos, but, slowly, ghosts are transformed into living flesh, floating vapors turn solid, and who knows?—perhaps something will be born from the encounter of indistinct ideas."

Conrad left to stay for ten days at the Sanderson home in Elstree, and he wrote Marguerite from there (on April 16) that he had completed Chapter 11 and was "beginning Chapter XII in a quarter of an hour." He returned to London on the twentieth and on the twenty-fourth announced the death of M. Kaspar Almayer. He promised, in his letter of the twenty-fourth, to send two chapters when typed, by which he meant 11 and 12, although in actuality he sent only 11.

The completion of the first draft of *Almayer* was the beginning of a crucial year for Conrad, the major pivot for the remainder of his life. For in 1894 he would complete the novel and its revision, submit it to a publisher, experience the surprise of its acceptance, begin a second novel, *An Outcast of the Islands*, and in November of the same year meet Miss Jessie George through their mutual friends, Mr. and Mrs. Hope. He would also begin his long friendship with Edward Garnett.

In his next two letters to his aunt, he speaks of "rewriting the first four chapters" and "retouching my first three chapters," tasks he finds "not only disagreeable but absolutely painful." The early manuscript, as John Gordan demonstrates, was much worked over, and even elements of plotting were altered. The most important, in terms of the completed text, was the addition of Almayer's attachment to his daughter, Nina, which in turn affected the relationship between Almayer and Dain, Nina's suitor. Repeatedly, the manuscript or a comparison of manuscript and later typescript indicates not only changes in word, phrase, and line but a tightening of plot development, character relationships, and matters of motivation and subsequent action. In a sense, the first draft for Conrad was a working sketch, over which he could play like a composer over a score. This method of working, incidentally, was not unique with *Almayer's Folly;* for if we move twenty years ahead to *Victory,* we note a similar revision of passages and the introduction of paragraphs and even entire pages to tighten attachments or strengthen direction.

In all probability, Conrad had had a typescript made which he could show to Marguerite when he was in Brussels. She probably read the first ten chapters, unaltered, and her reaction must have been favorable in the light of Conrad's attempt to draw her into a collaboration of sorts. On May 17, in any event, Conrad announced to his aunt that the "whole manuscript" was in the hands of a "rather distinguished critic, Edmund Gosse." Gosse, at this time, was a Heinemann editor, in charge of its "International Library." The library consisted of English translations of foreigns novels, and as Baines suggests, Conrad may have felt that an English novel by a French-speaking Pole fitted the general idea. Gosse's role in this matter is otherwise a mystery, and it is very possible his was a name Conrad had heard of, so that he sent the manuscript to the man rather than to the firm. They remained friendly in later years, and Gosse played a large role in Conrad's receiving a Civil List pension at a time when he desperately needed funds. Gosse may have suggested that the manuscript be sent to Fisher Unwin, but we have no record of his opinion of Conrad's earliest work.

In a June letter to Marguerite, Conrad indicated he had completed Chapter 12, by which he meant the revision. Shortly after this, on July 4, he submitted the novel to Fisher Unwin. He thought of Unwin, he says, because that firm published a series of "des romans anonymes," by which Conrad meant not "anonymous" but "pseudonymous." The Unwin "Pseudonym Library" was an on-going collection, and in fact, one of its novels was *John Sherman and Dhoya* by Ganconagh, the pseudonym of William Butler Yeats. For *his* pseudonym, Conrad used Kamudi, the Malayan word for "rudder" and pronounced, he tells us, "Kamoudi." In his letter of July 12, he minimizes the importance of the novel and his submission of it to Unwin, saying: "To be frank, I don't sense any interest in the fate of *Almayer's Folly.* It is finished. Besides, it could in any case be only an inconsequential episode in my life."

The attitude was, of course, feigned, as we learn from future letters, and was undoubtedly a defense against an expected rejection. Conrad had, in fact, begun another novel—a story called "Two Vagabonds"—before hearing of the fate of *Almayer;* and this fact alone would contradict his seeming insouciance. Furthermore, the circumstances of the submission of the novel were an almost perfect blend of Conrad's boldness and diffidence when it came to his new calling. Publication by a pseudonymous library would be an apt mating of author and publisher. In terms of naming, his Polish surname had already been transformed and reshaped by numerous captains and mates: mispronounced, misspelled, or abbreviated. The word "Kamudi" written on the typescript was as solid an identification as any—the French- and English-speaking Pole using a Malayan word to identify himself and his novel, writing about a Dutchman who is, in part, Apollo Korzeniowski.

The confusion of realms was already Conrad's heritage; and when he finally changed Kamudi to his own name, he used, for the first time, Joseph Conrad, in itself a pseudonym, even though it remained his name to the world for the next thirty years. Captain Korzeniowski was somewhere behind all this, and behind that was the Józef Teodor Konrad Korzeniowski of his childhood and school days, and behind even that was the family heraldic name, Nałęcz, with its profound connection to the Polish past. Although an English citizen and shortly to marry and raise English children, with "Joseph Conrad" he was deracinated.

He was to inhabit double and triple layers of skin, marginal to the last, far more deeply buried than Mary Ann Evans, who became George Eliot to the world at large and George Eliot Lewes and then Mary Ann Cross to her personal circle. Since there was no way he could escape transformation, there is good reason to believe he sought it out when he chose the Pseudonym Library, finding in these areas, as Kafka later did with his K. and Joseph K., the very kind of thing he knew best.

Yet, we must never forget the mastery which he sensed in himself as he shifted his energies. He may have wavered from month to month, even from day to day, but he sustained himself with a Schopenhauerean pessimism grafted onto a Darwinian survival of the fittest, however gloomy he might present himself. Trying to cheer up Marguerite, who appears to have drifted in and out of depression, he wrote: "Man must drag the ball and chain of his individuality up to the end. It is what one pays for the infernal and divine privilege of thought." As he waited now for Unwin's word, he had virtually nothing else working for him. His desire for a maritime berth was stalled; his career as an author was in limbo. In July 1894, he was moving toward his thirty-seventh birthday.

His letter tentatively dated July 25 indicates mental torture that struck deep. He was swimming in a vast ocean and had lost his strokes; keeping afloat was the best he could hope for. "According to the Arab expression applied to those who have incurred the displeasure of the sovereign, 'I live in the shadow of the sword'; and I ask myself morning and night when it will fall, today, tomorrow, or the day after." And in the same letter: "I no longer have the spirit to do anything. I hardly have any to write to you. It is an effort, a forward rush to finish before the pen falls from my hand in the depression of complete discouragement."

About July 30, he wrote again, struggling with disappointment, having hoped for a response from Unwin by this time, although only three weeks had passed since his submission of the novel. More was, of course, at stake than the acceptance of a manuscript; he had absolutely no back-up position. "I have had no response from Fisher Unwin. . . . Here, in this country where four novels appear every week (and what novels, good heavens!), one must dance attendance for a very long time." He then made a strange proposal to his aunt: "If you have said nothing to the *Revue*, we might perhaps be able to have *Almayer* appear not as a translation but as a collaboration. Haven't I any amount of cheek to speak to you like this, chère Maitre."

Expecting to be rejected in England, Conrad apparently wanted to be translated into French by Mme Poradowska and published in the *Revue des Deux Mondes*. His plan for a "collaboration," however, is not satisfied by the above explanation. Implicit in his remark is his desire to be associated with Mme Poradowska because of her literary successes in France. Thus, if *Almayer's Folly* appeared as a collaboration, it would be published originally in French with the help of her connections and under her name, as Conrad indicates in his August 18 letter from Champel.

The nervousness and fever attendant on his situation threw him back into uncontrollable anxiety, and into the childhood ailments which required nursing, water therapy, rest. For him to go to Champel at this time for hydrotherapy indicates he was desperate, for he had to husband his money and channel his energy. He wrote Marguerite:

> I have requested the return of the manuscript and upon my return to England [from Champel] I will put it at your disposal. I wish to keep my name of "Kamudi." . . . To think of these things is altogether typical of your kind friendship! To have your lovely language to express my poor thoughts is a joy and an honor. . . . The name of "Kamoudi" [sic] in small letters somewhere will be adequate. Let your name appear on the title page—an explanatory note will suffice to say K. has collaborated there.

In the same letter, a kind of "survival letter" in its reach and implications, Conrad indicates he must find a position quickly, for his resources will soon be exhausted. He asks her to intervene with her shipowning friend, Pécher, whose name Conrad chronically misspelled as Péchet, either an indication of disdain for his own role in using influence or a rejection of the very role he was seeking. He mentions he can post 12,000 francs for a command on the first of March 1895, which would be the last of his money from his uncle. He cites some of his reading, Maupassant "with delight," and Anatole France's *Le Lys rouge*, "which means nothing to me." The important news is that he has begun something "very short," no more than twenty to twenty-five pages, called "Two Vagabonds." This was an early draft of *An Outcast of the Islands*, a novel of well over 100,000 words. His idea was reasonably secure even at this early date.

> I want to describe in large terms, without shadows or details, two human strays such as one finds in the lost corners of the world. A white man and a Malay. You see Malays stick to me. I am devoted to Borneo. What bothers me most is my characters are so true. I know them so well they shackle the imagination. The white is a friend of Almayer—the Malay is our old friend Babalatchi before he arrived at the dignity of prime minister and confidential adviser to the Rajah. But I am missing a dramatic climax. My head is empty, and even at the beginning there is some difficulty. I tell only you this. I feel like letting it all drop already. Do you think one can make something interesting without any women?

This suggests that although Conrad had found his main outline he had not yet seen the connection between Willems and Aïssa, nor had he thought of the destructive passion that would become the very heart of the novel and of Willems's corruption.

Conrad's announcement to Marguerite about this new "story" contradicts his later version that Garnett's words encouraged him to "write another." He was writing "another" well before he met Garnett or even suspected that *Almayer* would be accepted. Conrad said he planned to return to England at the end of August, and he actually returned on September 6, bypassing Marguerite in Brussels and going directly to London. If Conrad had been romantically interested in her, he would surely have spent some time in Brussels before going to London from Champel, but he quite clearly had no intention of doing so.

He still had no information about *Almayer*, and he wrote Unwin on September 8:

> I venture now upon the liberty of asking you whether there is the slightest likelihood of the MS. (Malay life, about 64,000 words) being read at some future time. If not, it would be—probably—not worse fate than it deserves, yet, in that case, I am sure you will not take it amiss if I remind you that, however worthless for the purpose of publication, it is

> very dear to me. A ridiculous feeling—no doubt—but not unprecedented I believe. In this instance it is intensified by the accident that I do not possess another copy, either written or typed.

Conrad certainly had the handwritten manuscript and possibly even another typescript. It is, however, the rather witty but defensive tone of the letter that interests us. We must take the depreciating tone for its opposite and venture that Conrad considered his manuscript and work as essential to survival. The acceptance of his book had now begun to take on the same importance as the passing of his master's examination in 1886.

On October 2, two days before hearing of the novel's acceptance, he wrote Marguerite that he could not get hold of the manuscript after having asked twice and that he was "sufficiently busy with negotiations for several ships." These negotiations, which came to nothing, may have been with M. Pécher of Antwerp or with some Liverpool people about serving on a small barque called the *Primera.* On October 3, Conrad received the unexpected news, an acceptance from Unwin, offering terms of £20 for the copyright, equivalent to about $250–300 at present. In his letter of the fourth accepting the terms, Conrad requested the French translation rights for Marguerite, so that he could appear in the *Revue* and "still more have the advantage of being translated by such a competent and charming writer." He notes that his aunt has spoken to M. Ferdinand Brunetière, the well-known literary critic and historian, who was then editor of the *Revue des Deux Mondes.*

In a long introduction to his collection of letters from Conrad, Edward Garnett revealed how chancy the acceptance of the manuscript actually was. As a lowly reader at Unwin's, Garnett had his attention called to *Almayer* by another reader, W. H. Chesson. Garnett was at this time just starting out in the literary world. Himself the son of a distinguished scholar and museum keeper, Richard Garnett, Edward was about to make one of his discoveries, the first in a line that would include Galsworthy, W. H. Hudson, D. H. Lawrence, among many others. He writes:

> My wife recollects that I showed her the manuscript, told her it was the work of a foreigner and asked her opinion of his style. What particularly captivated me in the novel was the figure of Babalatchi, the aged one-eyed statesman and the night scene at the river's edge between Mrs. Almayer and her daughter. The strangeness of the tropical atmosphere, and the poetic "realism" of this romantic narrative excited my curiosity about the author, who I fancied might have Eastern blood in his veins. I was told however that he was a Pole, and this increased my interest since my Nihilist friends, Stepniak and Volkhovsky, had always subtly decried the Poles when one sympathized with their position as "under dogs."

Garnett's insistence that the manuscript was publishable tipped the decision in Conrad's favor, and Unwin followed with his offer. After that, the meeting between author and reader occurred in one of two places, either in the Unwin offices or, later, in November, at the National Liberal Club. Conrad wrote to Marguerite about this auspicious beginning:

> At first the two readers of the firm received me and complimented me effusively (were they, by chance, mocking me?). Then they led me to the presence of the head to speak of business. He told me frankly if I wished to take part in the risk of publication, I would participate in the profits. Otherwise, I get £20 and the French rights. I chose this latter alternative. "We are paying you very little," he told me, "but, remember, dear Sir, that you are unknown and your book will appeal to a very limited public. Then there is the question of taste. Will the public like it? We are risking something also. We will publish you in a good-looking volume at six shillings, and you know whatever we bring out always receives serious critical attention in the literary journals. . . . We will print immediately, so that you can make corrections, and we will send the 'proof sheets' to Mme. Poradowska before Christmas. Write something shorter—same type of thing—for our Pseudonym Library, and if it suits us, we will be very happy to give you a much better check."

If we assume the two readers were Garnett and Chesson, then Conrad and Garnett met at the Unwin offices on October 8. Garnett, however, published a different account, a recollection Conrad had described to Mrs. Gertrude Bone the last Christmas before his death. Unwin had arranged a meeting at the National Liberal Club.

> The first time I saw Edward [Conrad related] I dared not open my mouth. I had gone to meet him to hear what he thought of *Almayer's Folly.* I saw a young man enter the room. That can not be Edward so young as that, I thought. He began to talk. Oh yes! It was Edward. I had no longer doubt. But I was too frightened to speak. But this is what I want to tell you, how he made me go on writing. If he had said to me, "Why not go on writing?" I should have been paralyzed. I could not have done it. But he said to me, "You have written one book. It is very good. Why not *write another?*" Do you see what a difference that made? Another? Yes, I would do that. *I* could do that. Many others I could not. Another I could. That is how Edward made me go on writing. That is what made me an author.

In the Author's Note to *An Outcast of the Islands,* Conrad's account places Garnett's advice at still another meeting, but the message was essentially the same: " 'You have the style, you have the temperament; why not write another?' " Garnett left his own amusing account of that first meeting, in November:

> My memory is of seeing a dark-haired man, short but extremely graceful in his nervous gestures, with brilliant eyes, now narrowed and penetrating, now soft and warm, with a manner alert yet caressing, whose speech was ingratiating, guarded, or brusk turn by turn. I had never seen

> before a man so masculinely keen yet so femininely positive. The conversation between our host [Unwin] and Conrad for some time was halting and jerky. . . . Conrad, extremely polite, grew nervously brusk in his responses, and kept shifting his feet one over the other, so that one became fascinated in watching the flash of his pointed, patent leather shoes. The climax came unexpectedly when in answer to Mr. Unwin's casual but significant reference to "your next book," Conrad threw himself back on the broad leather lounge and in a tone that put a clear cold space between himself and his hearers, said, "I don't expect to write again. It is likely that I shall soon be going to sea."

The meeting, the interview, Conrad's dissembling about not writing again—these have the contradictory quality of myth and legend. Exactly what occurred may never be discovered, but the following seems likely. It is typical Conrad, in keeping with the secretiveness, circuitous narration, and circumlocutory manner of his later fiction. The "two readers" he mentioned in the Unwin office probably did not include Garnett; one reader was Chesson and the other person, reader or not, is unknown. At the November meeting (their first), Garnett did utter those famous words, already quoted, " 'Why not write another?' " but he said them to a man who had already made his own resolution about continuing; Conrad had a second manuscript, however rudimentary, in the making. Further, Conrad probably remarked to Unwin that he did not expect to write again because he did not want the publisher to "own" him. In his October 10 letter to Marguerite, he speaks of being part of the "Slave trade, word of honor," with himself as slave. Further, Unwin was a dominating, possessive type of person, described by Garnett as having a "falcon-like [read "Jewish"] glance," and these physical as well as personal qualities may have turned Conrad against him. This point is, of course, speculative, but later Conrad letters mocking Unwin personally and drawing attention to his Jewishness cannot be discounted when we look back to their first meeting.

Conrad, in fact, had not completely forsaken his search for a maritime post, and continued to mention Marguerite's shipowner friend, M. Pécher. He was, here, at close to thirty-seven years old, at the exact meeting point of careers, subject to severe bouts of neuralgia, nerves, depression, and fever, with hereditary gout not too distant. Any attempt to pin him down, to "buy his soul," or to redirect him from whatever the inner voices were telling him—any of this was certain to enrage him. His position was delicate indeed. And as he turned to writing as a career, it must not have been lost upon him that, like Apollo after the failure of *his* political activities, he was turning to an authorial career. The irony of it was apparent.

Since *Almayer's Folly* was too long for the Pseudonym Library, Unwin decided against publishing it in that series. But Conrad moved into a pseudonym anyway, going, as we have seen, from Konrad Korzeniowski to Joseph

Conrad. Except for a few English friends, he was an unknown man; his passport gave his Polish name, and the Poles and Frenchmen he knew would not have recognized Joseph Conrad. Only Hope, Krieger, his landlady, and a few others could have connected the two; and when he was introduced to Jessie George in November, it was as Konrad Korzeniowski, even though by then he was about to become Joseph Conrad. Like Verloc, who would go by the pseudonym of a delta sign, part of Konrad disappeared from view. To compound the irony, the man who pronounced his name "Joseph Conrad" sounded in speech exactly like someone escaping from "Konrad Korzeniowski." In his later story "Amy Foster," all these undigested elements of name, background, foreign accent, foreignness itself would come together to destroy the Polish intruder cut off from his past.

In a curious sense, Conrad was launched, in that shadowy manner we find so striking in all his activities. Lacking money, exact knowledge of the English language, friends in high places, and ability to work rapidly, he had entered into a profession where there was almost no middle ground. An author either did the hack work of Grub Street or else tried to become a best-selling novelist by writing on popular themes. It was a situation never lost on Conrad, who insisted on the quality of his work and yet raged at his lack of sales and at the popularity of novelists of little worth.

Conrad could, indeed, have been tempted into the following type of career, as Walter Besant described it:

> . . . the kind of life led daily by the modern man of letters—not a great genius, not a popular author: but a good steady man of letters of the kind which formerly had to inhabit the garrets of Grub Street. This man, of whom there are many—or this woman, for many women now belong to the profession—goes into his study every morning as regularly as a barrister goes to chambers. He finds on his desk two or three books waiting for review: a MS sent him for opinion: a book of his own to go on with—possibly a life of some dead-and-gone worthy for a series: an article which he has promised for a magazine: a paper for the *Dictionary of National Biography:* perhaps an unfinished novel to which he must give three hours of absorbed attention. There is never any fear of the work failing as soon as the writer has made himself known as a trustworthy and attentive workman. The literary man has his club: he makes an income by his labour which enables him to live in comfort, and to educate his children properly. Now this man a hundred years ago would have been an object of contempt for his poverty and helplessness: the cause of contempt for Literature itself.

Conrad may have lacked the facility and temperament that would have opened all these possibilities of income, but he could have, at the outset, tried to attain this kind of comfortable existence as an ideal way of life. In the 1890s, the temptations were especially strong, as Besant remarks, with the proliferation of journals, periodicals, reviews, little magazines, and other publications of various personal kinds. The most flamboyant established permanent reputations, such as *The Yellow Book* and *The Savoy*, but there were a myriad of others between *The Yellow Book* and the Yellow Press. The growth of little magazines—the *Quarto*, the *Hobby Horse*, the *Dome*, among others—was so great an author could find one or another to publish his work regardless of quality. To publish, and keep publishing, as it is for academics now, was one way to become known. Arnold Bennett, we recall, got his start by winning a competition in *Tit-Bits*, a fairly obscure journal in which Conrad very possibly published his first story. From there, Bennett went to *The Yellow Book*, moving up to the higher-paying publications as his name became better known.

At the outset, Conrad faced the temptation to publish, although it is questionable, given his temperament and slow method of working, whether he would have succeeded on the "popular route." But as he approached forty and the Malay stories came with a certain ease of composition, the temptation to become known and thus increase his rates was overwhelming.

Conrad expected advance sheets of *Almayer* by mid-November, but still seeking a sea berth, he apparently sent his record to M. Pécher. Very possibly, he hoped to combine a maritime career of sorts with the slow, occasional writing of fiction. On the Continent, he had an excellent example in Pierre Loti, and in fact, Ford was to draw attention to the resemblance. Loti, who was seven years Conrad's senior, during the course of his sea career became a captain in the French navy and also saw service in many of the exotic places Conrad visited. He moved into fiction writing in 1879, at twenty-nine years of age, and worked in both the naval service and authorship until his retirement from the navy in 1910. Conrad very possibly read his *Pêcheur d'Islande* (1886) and knew of Loti either from his period in France or from Marguerite, in whose general literary circles Loti moved. The latter had the admiration of Brunetière, who was Marguerite's editor at the *Revue*, as well as Anatole France and Jules Lemaître, whom Conrad read. Whatever Conrad knew specifically of Loti, whether his work or the man's reputation, there was before him an author who had effectively pursued a parallel maritime career.

A complication in this plan or idea, however dim it was, arose when Conrad met Jessie George through Hope, who was acquainted with the George family. There is some confusion about the actual circumstances of the meeting, since Jessie in *Joseph Conrad As I Knew Him* indicates meeting the Hopes somewhat later: "I remember shortly after we were engaged, his telling me that now his uncle was dead, Mr. and Mrs. Hope, as far as his feelings could go, were the nearest relations he had in the world, and that he wanted to take me to make their acquaintance." In the same book, however, she indicates having met Conrad "early in November 1894" through a "mutual friend" (Hope). The time of the meeting is not in dispute, although Jessie several years afterward was to speak of it as having occurred late in 1893. Most likely, the Hopes were the means by which Conrad and his future wife got together, since Conrad had few other friends at this time and virtually no way of meeting a marriageable young woman.

Just two weeks before he married Jessie, in a March 10, 1896, letter to Karol Zagórski, Conrad gave an amusing account of his feelings:

> I announce solemnly (as the occasion demands) to dear Aunt Gabrynia and to you both that I am getting married. No one can be more surprised at it than myself. However, I am not frightened at all, for as you know, I am accustomed to an adventurous life and to facing terrible dangers. Moreover, I have to avow that my betrothed does not give the impression of being at all dangerous. Jessie is her name; George her surname. She is a small, not at all striking-looking person (to tell the truth alas—rather plain!) who nevertheless is very dear to me. When I met her a year and a half ago she was earning her living in the City as a "Typewriter" in an American business office of the "Caligraph" company. Her father died three years ago. There are nine children in the family. The mother is a very decent woman (and I do not doubt very virtuous as well). However, I must confess that it is all the same to me, as vous comprenez?—I am not marrying the whole family. The wedding will take place on the 24th of this month and we shall leave London immediately so as to conceal from people's eyes our happiness (or our stupidity) amidst the wilderness and beauty of the coast of Brittany where I intend to rent a small house in some fishing village.

This was Conrad's view of it just on the eve of the marriage. In November 1894, when he met Jessie, then twenty-one, the situation was not appreciably different: Conrad alone, his uncle dead, surely lonely, his prospects uncertain—he needed companionship or the sense of a family life. We can speculate that the energies which had carried him forward for twenty years had been dissipated; he had lived off the original capital and now he felt the need for "family" once again, especially if he was to pursue something as uncertain as a writing career.

These questions arise because of the nature of Conrad's choice for a wife. If he had been romantically inclined with Marguerite, there would be ready explanations, but Jessie fell far outside the circle of someone like Konrad Korzeniowski. There were radical differences in age, class, background, status, education, sophistication, and expectation. Their sensibilities could not have been more different if they had derived from two distinct planets. Almost the sole certainty was that Conrad was extremely lonely and sought a relationship that had as little "side" to it as possible. His letter to Zagórski describing his bride-to-be is not demeaning; it is not, either, that of a man marrying someone whom he considers to be an equal. The comments are affectionate and caring, but very much those of a man who recognizes distinctions between himself and his fiancée. Indistinguishable from this view is Conrad's sense that his new career, or his combination of maritime and writing careers, will require a wife with few expectations, simple tastes, and little ego. He also could not escape self-mockery, that of the man of thirty-seven marrying for the first time.

In terms of the type of person Conrad was, and turned out to be as an author, his choice was perfect. Jessie was not an intellectual equal, nor could she be expected to be, but she possessed emotional and psychological qualities which fitted exactly into what he needed; and there is no reason to believe he ever regretted his choice. Jessie was a straightforward, devoted, quite competent young woman, and, her marriage photo shows, a handsome one as well. Conrad's description of her as "rather plain" was self-deprecatory; he was not making a "big match." Her place in a family of nine children without much money had undoubtedly prepared her psychologically for all kinds of familial eventualities; and her former situation, caring for younger children and working as a typist, made her ready to accept whatever emotional and psychological demands Conrad made upon her. She was not to become overly upset by the strangeness he demonstrated, nor was she incapable of dealing with his radical shifts of mood, temperament, and tone. Although not a victim in any obvious sense, she saw her marriage as a series of sacrifices, not demonstrations, of self. She would spend her life arranging his, while he pursued the inner voices—not unlike millions of Victorian marriages.

All this is jumping ahead, however. In November 1894, when we can assume Conrad met Jessie, we have no indication of any serious feeling on his part. On the contrary, he was still "involved" with Marguerite, and he was as yet to meet Emilie Briquel in Champel. Meanwhile, he was still caught in uncertainties, with nothing settled in his professional life. In a letter to Marguerite about the translation of *Almayer* into French, Conrad discouraged her from undertaking the job while her own work languished; and this was either consideration on his part or a gradual withdrawal from involvement with her. The letter is of interest, also, for reaffirming Conrad's interest in Maupassant, especially his *Pierre et Jean:* "It seems nothing, but it is of an intricate mechanism which makes me pull out my hair." The French influence, as we have seen, was particularly strong in Conrad's early work and then diminished somewhat as he began to find his own voice in those distinctive years between 1899 and 1904.

He felt more authoritative about "Two Vagabonds," which he saw more clearly than *Almayer*. After sitting for three days before a blank page, the forerunner of many hours and days contemplating the whiteness of the paper, awaiting a word or phrase, he came upon his idea, and the theme solidified.

> First, the theme is the unrestrained, fierce vanity of an ignorant man who has some success but has neither principles nor any other line of conduct than the satisfaction of his vanity. Also, he is not even faithful to himself. Whence his fall, the man's sudden descent to physical slavery by an absolutely untamed woman. . . . The catastrophe will be brought about by the intrigues of a little Malay state, whose last word is: Poisoning. The dénouement is: suicide, still through vanity.

Although the final version was to demonstrate some divergence from this (from the "suicide," if Conrad meant it literally), nevertheless he followed the plan. Even more, we note how many elements in "Vagabonds" were forerunners of ideas in *Lord Jim*, especially in some of Conrad's descriptive terms, such as "vanity," "fall," "descent," "physical slavery," "suicide, still through vanity." The situations of Willems, the outcast, and Jim, the fallen angel, are of course different; yet Conrad, as early as 1894, experienced intimations not of immortality but of his major materials—and not only of Jim, but of Kurtz, Nostromo, Razumov, even Heyst. All of these future Conradian fixtures, the outposts of his imagination and sensibility, were implicit in his description of Willems. In a sense, the latter was to be the criminal side of the later fallen angel: the petty, trivial man who embodies the same qualities as the man of greater stature, both of whom are brought low through vanity, self-love, narcissism. And yet despite these considerable stirrings, Conrad indicated he was still looking for a maritime berth.

In the continuing series with Marguerite,* Conrad notes a trip to Antwerp to see Pécher, but nothing came of that. On the other front, Unwin has mentioned *Almayer* will not appear until the next year, in February—and actually not until late April. Conrad demonstrated a lack of concern about that, but it is hard to believe he did not want the physical book in hand, something to indicate solidity after years of dealing with the bulk of a ship, the volume of water, the presence of a crew. "If I remain longer on shore, all will be ruined, alas!" he writes. Destroyed, for lack of a physical book and a maritime berth, was his concentration, a clear working pattern. He was still stumbling, although his bitter plaints about inability to work must be somewhat discounted. By early fall of 1895, he was to complete *An Outcast*, over 100,000 words in less than eighteen months.

Yet in this still early stage of the novel, when all of it was already imminent in his imagination, he threatened to burn it. "It is very poor! Too poor!" Marguerite evidently responded in horror, and Conrad followed with characteristic cynicism: "I have burned nothing. One speaks like that, but lacks the courage. There are those who speak like that of suicide. And then there is al-

* His correspondence with her is our chief source of biographical material, for in the entire year of 1894, there are extant only three Conrad letters (two to Unwin, one to Chesson) not to Marguerite.

ways something lacking, sometimes strength, sometimes perseverance, sometimes courage. The courage to succeed or the courage to recognize one's impotence. What remains always ineradicable and cruel is fear of final things. One temporizes with fate, one seeks to deceive desire, one tries to juggle one's life. Men are always cowards. They fear 'nevermore.' I think it is only women who have true courage."

Much of this "philosophizing" must be discounted, however, as the meanderings of a lonely, embittered man who was beginning to feel the impact of a crowded imagination that could not transform itself into fiction rapidly enough. In his December 27 letter to Marguerite, just past his thirty-seventh birthday, he announces he has changed his title to *An Outcast of the Islands.* "And the thing itself has been changed. Everything has been changed except doubt. Everything, except the fear of the ghosts which one evokes and which often refuse to obey the brain that has created them." He indicates he has completed Chapter 8, with four more to go. "Four centuries of agony—four minutes of delight and then the end—an empty head—discouragement and eternal doubt." The completion of eight chapters, in terms of the whole, however, is misleading, because the final draft came to twenty-six chapters, and with revisions those eight chapters were, possibly, no more than a quarter of the book.

In the same letter, he mentions having received sixteen pages of *Almayer* proofs. Despite his disclaimers as he turned toward 1895, he was deeply caught in a writing career: receiving proofs of *Almayer,* with an early spring publication date, and eight chapters of *An Outcast* in hand, with the overall idea reasonably firm. Besides this, he frequently commented on Marguerite's work—*Yaga,* as well as other pieces—and spoke out about literature in general. Further, he was writing the short Preface to *Almayer's Folly.*

He had begun to establish some pattern: desultory work on *Outcast* interspersed with intense application to the novel, long bouts of depression, anxiety over the appearance of *Almayer* (repeatedly postponed), some meetings with Garnett, perhaps some social gatherings with Jessie George present, and occasional forays, either in actuality or imagination, to seek a maritime berth. "My nature is to be miserable, morally beggared, bankrupt of courage," he wrote Marguerite while awaiting his first copies of *Almayer.* He indicates a departure for Newfoundland on business, but like all his other speculatory ventures, nothing came of this. He complains steadily of illness. Yet none of this can be construed as simply appeals for compassion or as neurotic reactions: he was not a well man, and his situation was uncertain and trying. We should not forget that with all his will to succeed, English was a nightmare; he was writing in a language he was uncertain of. In his brief letter to Chesson, the Unwin reader, he stands corrected on his idiomatic use of "aversion," and this suggests his fear that there were idioms, words, meanings he did not know and whose usage he could mangle. Moving into English as a creative language was an exploration, and like most explorations it had the anxiety attendant upon the unknown.

Edward Garnett, meanwhile, was reading *An Outcast.* On March 8, Conrad sent four chapters. He speaks of a "new style" in Chapter 12 (really 5 in the revised chapter headings). "Please say in the margin what you think. One word will do. I am very much in doubt myself about it; but where is the thing, institution or principle which I do not doubt?" The section in question begins: "And now they are back in the courtyard wherefrom, at their appearance, listlessness vanishes, and all the faces become alert and interested once more." The "new style" apparently involved use of the present tense so as to create a more pictorial scene. Conrad did not consistently hold to this style in *An Outcast,* but his "experimentation with tense here does foreshadow the far more profound experimentations of his later novels, when time sequencing became crucial to his narratives. His hesitation here was connected to his anxiety over language itself. As his confidence grew, a period that begins to be apparent in 1899, he could synthesize various elements of technique. Until then, he proceeded with one venture at a time—pruning the rich vocabulary of the *fin de siècle* and decadent period, experimenting gently with time sequencing (flashbacks, involution of scenes, etc.), tilting ever so slightly the straightforward presentation of character and event.

Conrad wrote to Unwin jesting about dying on the firm's office carpet if his novel did not appear soon, a frivolity, as he says, which "disguises very deep feeling." He is, also, anxious about the French translation of *Almayer,* which was now in question, and he indicates he has sent the proof sheets to Paris, to "Th. Bentzon," a colleague of Marguerite's on the *Revue* and herself a woman of considerable interest. Th. Bentzon was the pseudonym (Conrad could be at home here!) of Marie Thérèse (de Solms) Blanc, a prolific journalist, novelist, and author of a pioneering study, *The Condition of Women in the United States* (1895). Conrad hoped she would give the novel an appreciatory reading and perhaps convince Brunetière to publish a translation. Nothing came of this, however, and *Almayer* did not appear in French translation until 1919.

He returned from a week's trip to Brussels on March 15, still looking forward to the publication of *Almayer* and, perhaps more importantly, awaiting word from Edward Garnett about the early chapters of *An Outcast.* Garnett's praise and encouragement cannot be overestimated here. While it is quite probable Conrad would have continued to write—the energy and drive were there—it is also possible that without support his continuity, so essential for a beginning author, would have been upset. "Your appreciation has for me all the subtle and penetrating delight of unexpected good fortune—of some fabulously lucky accident like the finding of a gold nugget in a deserted claim, like the gleam of a big diamond in a handful of blue earth."

So Conrad wrote to the Unwin reader. He even tried out some "theory," which is that "theory is a cold and lying tombstone of departed truth." But since even truth is questionable in this relativistic universe, theory is not to be sneezed at. Conrad's comment contains irony within ironies: sneering at theory when faced with truth, then questioning truth itself, which "is not more immortal than any other delusion," and finally admitting that he has submitted Willems to his own "pet theory," which he stands by, "lamenting and grinning with the spade in my hand." We do not know how Garnett received this Nietzschean outburst, whether he thought his volatile correspondent had suddenly gone mad.

Conrad bombarded Unwin with inquiries about the appearance of *Almayer.* His growing dissatisfaction with Unwin, besides the latter's rather niggardly terms, began here, in the delay of publication. But even had Unwin done everything Conrad desired, there was little chance of satisfying him; the very nature of Conrad's talent and his inability to pick up a sizable audience would predispose him to bickering with his publishers. At the end of March he went to stay with the Sandersons at Elstree and returned to London on April 2. By then, he had, finally, obtained advance copies of *Almayer,* promising Marguerite one of the first copies. Throughout, he moved along on *An Outcast,* as far as Chapter 17, with 20 or 21 expected to conclude it. By the time *Almayer* appeared at the end of April, Conrad had in hand almost a first draft of *An Outcast,* but at the expense of much nervous energy. Although his letters do not yet indicate it, he was building up for an attack of nerves and anxiety—a clear pattern by now. Like Persephone, he surfaced, in order to write, but at the expense of a periodic stay in the underworld of near collapse.

As the publication date for *Almayer* approached—its delay caused by Macmillans in America and copyright law—he began to fall to pieces. On April 30, the day after *Almayer* appeared, he wrote Marguerite: "I am not at all well. I am leaving my bed and setting out for Champel for the water cure, to restore my health. This explains to you my long silence. You know when I'm not well I have attacks of melancholy which paralyze thought and will." He thought of appearing in Polish and told Marguerite to write to Angèle Zagórska, her niece. Nothing came of this, however, although *Almayer* did appear in Polish in 1923 and 1928, translated by Angèle's daughter Aniela.

Just before departing for Champel on May 1, Conrad wrote Garnett in a jocular tone, his jesting manner here contrasting with his deadly earnest one with his aunt. He says he called on Unwin and discovered that William Ernest Henley, then an important critic and editor, could not read "more than 60 pages of the immortal work—after which he 'lays it down.' " Conrad indicates he will commit suicide "by thirst on Henley's doorstep" as revenge for his dislike of *Almayer.* He says he cannot find work but hopes the mountain air will enable him to complete *An Outcast* in "about 3 weeks," if the "lenient gods" are willing. He would, in actuality, complete it on September 16.

We do not know whether Conrad was seeing Jessie George alone or with friends during this time; there are no letters or references until later. When Garnett did meet her, at a future date, he tried to dissuade Conrad from marriage with a woman intellectually beneath him. At Champel, Conrad attempted to carry on a normal life—he was to stay there for a month. He immersed himself in *An Outcast* and began to receive his first reviews of *Almayer* from the English and Scottish journals. Fighting his nervous ailments as his professional life began to shift before him, he found the moment delicate and auspicious. He was edging toward self-discovery.

CHAPTER 16

Toward the Self

THE idea of a Dutchman in Borneo as the subject of his first novel was, of course, the product of Conrad's observations of the land and people; but it was also the fictional re-creation of his own sense of himself, not in any direct relationship, but in his periodic movement on the edges of both familiar and unfamiliar places. Those who might see Conrad as responding in his early work to the "romantic" literature of his day—Stevenson, Haggard, Kipling, Anthony Hope, among others—fail to recognize he was reacting to impulses in himself far more than in his reading.

The early reviews stressed the strangeness of Conrad's exotic scene and characters. Arthur Waugh, in the *Critic*, for example, hoped that Conrad's novel would not lead to "a torrent of Bornean fiction." Yet the point is not the influence of exotic places or literature on Conrad as he wrote his early "trilogy" (*Almayer*, *Outcast*, *Rescue*) but how closely these novels followed psychological impulses in their author. The character of Almayer follows the line of Apollo and of Conrad himself: a fairly realistic view of Apollo in decline, with his dreams of gold, and a projection of Conrad's own fears about himself, all of it imaginatively re-created in a heightened romantic style. In his old Dutchman who relies on memories for sustenance, Conrad attempted no less than the "myth of failure" and the "myth of marginality"—exactly what he was emphasizing in his letters to Marguerite.

As the trilogy moves into the past—with passage after passage caught in flashback*—we find Conrad attempting to discover in technique what he senses as his material. Memory is crucial, since with this book he went from

* Significantly, the novel has barely begun before Conrad flashes Almayer back twenty years: ". . . but his memory lagging behind some twenty years or more in point of time saw a young and slim Almayer" (p. 5). When Conrad started this section, in 1889, the flashback of twenty years would have taken him to 1869, the year of his father's death, the long period of Apollo's malaise and illness, his own time of indecision and uncertainty when he had only youth. The points of reference to Conrad's own memories, while of course never congruent, are testimony to how profoundly his early art was touched by his psychological experience.

Konrad Korzeniowski to Joseph Conrad, a name change that signified a disengagement from the past and from past memories; all of which would have solidified a technique that keeps memory before him. In a letter (already quoted) to his namesake, the historian Józef Korzeniowski, he indicated his touchiness about the name change and charges of "betrayal" of his Polish past:

> And please let me add, dear Sir (for you may still be hearing this and that said of me), that I have in no way disavowed either my nationality or the name we share for the sake of success. It is widely known that I am a Pole and that Józef Konrad are my two Christian names, the latter being used by me as a surname so that foreign mouths should not distort my real surname—a distortion which I cannot stand. It does not seem to me that I have been unfaithful to my country by having proved to the English that a gentleman from the Ukraine can be as good a sailor as they, and has something to tell them in their own language.

Conrad wrote this letter to acknowledge receipt of Tadeusz Bobrowski's *Memoirs* and to thank Korzeniowski, "bearers of the same name and . . . [having] the same family crest." The interconnectedness of Conrad's experiences cannot be lost upon us. Almayer's relationship to a daughter who deserts him—who runs off with "her love," Dain—is, given the context, an artistic re-creation of a youthful Conrad experience, only the first of such "desertions" in his fiction. How carefully he nurtured the break: " 'You wanted me to dream your dreams, to see your own visions—the visions of life amongst the white faces of those who cast me out from their midst in angry contempt. But while you spoke I listened to the voice of my own self.' "

The relationship of Nina—a child who has grown up apart from her parents—to Almayer and his wife is an obvious parallel to Conrad's own former situation. The family triangle is reproduced: the mother and father, the one strong in her weakness, the other weak where he could have been strong, as Conrad puts it. He writes about Almayer: "All passion, regret, grief, hope, or anger—all were gone, erased by the hand of fate, as if after this last stroke, everything was over and there was no need for any record." Even more compelling is the way in which Conrad slides from Nina to Dain and turns the "false Dain" into a mangled, crushed corpse, not unlike his description of himself to Marguerite as a broken doll, "his spine broken in two." The transformation into "two Dains" is significant, the Dain who remains whole and gains Nina, but, also, the Dain whose flesh and bones are smashed.

Perhaps most compelling of all these parallels is the series of benefactions which lie at the core of each of the early novels. As we have seen, Lingard saves Almayer's future wife; he befriends Almayer; and he salvages Willems twice (in *An Outcast*). The novels are cast in terms of help given, resentment at the help, lack of reward for the benefactor, feelings of guilt and helplessness on the part of the recipient. The question arises of the mythical "gift" or "exchange," here transmuted into benefactions which never go beyond the act itself; that is, the benefaction is never reciprocated, and the recipient is never part of a moral, personal transaction. Conrad's way of presenting the transactions is a gloss on his memories, on the way he has fitted himself into his past.

Yet, unquestionably, *Almayer's Folly* clearly manifests the language, the deliberate rhythms, and many of the mannerisms of *fin de siècle* literature. In its formal aspects, it is a prose counterpart of 1890s poetry, of early Yeats and Dowson, of Arthur Symons and the lush siftings of the Pre-Raphaelites, in particular the softness of D. G. Rossetti and the otiosity of William Morris. Conrad's novel, as befitting its background, is one of filmy torpor and fatigue. Its key images are those of languor: a languor of character, prose, and setting. Many of the early reviewers paid tribute to Conrad for his adventurous use of language and recognized the importance of his awareness of words, although in many instances they were undecided whether or not it was advantageous to the theme. In his manner of presentation, the apprentice Conrad (for all his thirty-six years) was not unlike the young Yeats or the young Melville, about whose early work he was enthusiastic. As their vision deepened their verbal style changed, Yeats becoming leaner and harder, Conrad and Melville less embellished and more conservative. Conrad's early enameled prose has many striking similarities to Yeats's "woven" world. The long-drawn-out vowel sounds of the following passage suggest the languorous setting:

> . . . the big open space where the thick-leaved trees put black patches of shadow which seemed to float on a flood of smooth, intense light that rolled up to the houses and down to the stockade and over the river, where it broke and sparkled in thousands of glittering wavelets, like a band woven of azure and gold edged with the brilliant green of the forests guarding both banks of the Pantai.

Those critics who pointed to Conrad as a strikingly new figure working in English did not see the continuity between Conrad's early work and the poetic language of decadence; itself a carryover from the French *symbolistes*, and failed to recognize how significantly he was part of the 1890s milieu. The work of Arthur Symons, a central nineties figure who Jessie Conrad said was the only poet Conrad read with pleasure, is full of "sea moans" and "dark shivering trees," "sicklemoons" and "delicate ivory"—that whole paraphernalia of late-nineteenth-century poets who combined the vivid mannerisms of romanticism with a misunderstood and misused French symbolism. Like Ernest Dowson, that frail figure of washed-out manhood who wrote of pale and faded roses, long-dead leaves, the pallor of ivories, the "dread oblivion of lost things," "languid lashes," and a vast assortment of exhausted objects, Conrad, similarly, wrote of the murmuring river behind the white veil, the soft whisper of eddies washing against the riverbank, and the breathless calm of the breeze. As much as Yeats and Dowson, Conrad learned his literary English at the end of the century, and was only able to make it leaner and more pungent as he developed a more mature style. For him, this would come at the end of the 1890s.

Of parallel importance in Conrad's early work is his use of another type of image: the image of despair. Among Conrad's contemporaries, this imagery had of course gained prominence—in the necropolis of James Thomson's nocturnal imagination, in Dowson's personal laments, in Beardsley's nihilistic sketches, in the pessimism of John Davidson's distorted visions; it would reappear in Housman's *A Shropshire Lad* (1896) and come to fruition in Conrad's own "Heart of Darkness" (1899), in which a personal malaise became objective and gained almost epic proportions. In *Almayer*, this image supports the languor of the jungle, but it is essentially a city image, a civilized image transferred to an exotic setting. In the scene, for example, portraying Almayer's desolation, his exhaustion, his life-come-to-nought, we have a virtual waste land of sterility and dust.

> He went towards the office door and with some difficulty managed to open it. He entered in a cloud of dust that rose under his feet. Books open with torn pages bestrewed the floor; other books lay about grimy and black, looking as if they had never been opened. . . . In the middle of the room the big office desk, with one of its legs broken, careened over like the hull of a stranded ship; most of the drawers had fallen out, disclosing heaps of paper yellow with age and dirt.

The language of desolation joins with the language of exhaustion and retreat to fix the atmosphere of *Almayer's Folly* and give substance to its ghostly characters. Like Ibsen, Conrad was concerned with "ghosts"; only his were the ghosts not of society but of his own background.

Despite this attraction to the language and images of the 1890s, however, Conrad should not be compared with the romancers popular at that time—Stevenson, Haggard, and Anthony Hope. His manipulation of narrative alone, so as to create simultaneity of past and present, was an attempt to impose on the novel form an idea about life and mind alien to the romancers. Further, any serious critical attempt to see the weaknesses in Conrad's early work as embodying the failings of popular romance must weigh more carefully his own awareness of the pitfalls. Writing to Edward Noble, a seaman starting out as an author, Conrad wrote: ". . . do not throw yourself away in fables [or romance]. . . . You have a remarkable gift of expression, the outcome of an artistic feeling for the world around you, and you must not waste the gift in (if I may say so) illegitimate sensation."

He goes on to speak of the psychological intensity of each event: "Remember that death is not the most pathetic—the most poignant thing—and you must treat events only as illustrative of human sensation—as the outward sign of inward feelings—of live feelings—which alone are truly pathetic and interesting." Then displaying his reading in Maupassant and Flaubert, and his sense of *symbolisme*, his rejection of formulas based on naturalism, realism, and romanticism, Conrad wrote: ". . . you must squeeze out of yourself every sensation, every thought, every image—mercilessly, without reserve and without remorse; you must search the darkest corners of your heart, the most remote recesses of your brain;—you must search them for the image, for the glamour, for the right expression."

This is a letter written coterminous with *Almayer* and *Outcast*, and its stress on precision of image and word is a direct blow at the popular romance, in which, except perhaps for Stevenson, the manner of expression is incidental to the sensational effect intended. Unless Flaubert can be considered part of this romantic tradition, then Conrad must himself be judged in the main as separate from that tradition also.

As far as the reviewers were concerned, the author of *Almayer's Folly* had arrived from nowhere with a name unknown to all but those in the Unwin office. In an unsigned piece in *Saturday Review*, H. G. Wells, himself an apprentice novelist, wrote that *Almayer's Folly* is "indeed exceedingly well imagined and well written, and it will certainly secure Mr. Conrad a high place among contemporary story-tellers." Even more enthusiastic was the Sunday *Weekly Sun*, which selected Conrad's novel for its lead book review article. T. P. O'Connor (in whose journal Conrad would publish *Nostromo*) was extravagant in his notice. He wrote that soon the world will know "that a new great writer and a new and splendid region of romance have entered into our literature." Calling Conrad a "writer of genius"—hardly the case with this novel as the sole evidence—O'Connor judiciously selected passages that supported his view of the new author.

While other reviews were more moderate, nearly all gave encouragement. Reviewing may have been hack work, but the modern reader cannot but remark how astute the critics were in their estimation of this new writer. The *Atheneum* critic, the *Daily Chronicle* reviewer, James Ashcroft Noble in the *Academy*, and others in the *Speaker*, the *Guardian*, the *Bookman*, the *Literary News* all praised the effort and the result, while pointing out excesses of language and characterization.

Conrad's stay at Champel, however, went beyond the reading of reviews, writing to his aunt, and working on the manuscript of *An Outcast*. At the La Roseraie pension, he had met the Briquel family, rich bourgeoisie who came originally from Lorraine and were presently living in Lunéville; a family that consisted of the mother, son Paul (aged seventeen), and daughter Emilie, who was twenty. Apparently, Emilie and Conrad spent many hours together, although exactly what occurred between them cannot be untangled.

We do have two sources, however: Conrad's letters to the brother and sister and Emilie's diary, some of whose entries appear to indicate a close attachment to the man almost twice her age. Although we have no proof, we can conjecture that Mme Briquel did not look with favor upon her daughter's preference for an impecunious foreigner, even if he did come more or less from their own class.

At the time of the meeting and during the ensuing relationship, Conrad continued to correspond with his aunt, chiefly about her own work; with Unwin, over reviews of *Almayer;* and even with Charles Buls, Marguerite's long-time admirer. The outward display remained constant, but surely an internal drama was occurring. For in May of 1895, Conrad was at the meeting point of several "courtships"—especially crucial for someone of his temperament, not at all the normal or routine family man. Whatever his precise feelings about Marguerite, something triggered a reaction that led to her suppression or destruction of his letters between the one for June 11 and the next, almost five years later. Without question, the correspondence continued, but no letter from this period has turned up. Whether this was because Conrad became too intimate, in a move to marry Marguerite, or whether he began to discuss other relationships, we do not know. Our suspicion that Conrad had possible romantic motives, a marriage, as we have already noted, that had a good deal to offer both parties, is, of course, attached to the abrupt drop in extant letters. Whatever happened occurred with finality.

Conrad was, very possibly, still seeing Jessie George, although how frequently and under what conditions of intimacy we cannot tell. One suspects that he saw her rather little, on the assumption that his abrupt decision to marry her came on impulse. Further, the vast gulf between them, not only in age and background, but in ideas about life, experience, and art, would appear to argue against a long relationship before marriage; too much exposure might have discouraged both parties. With Conrad, it hardly seems a question of "love conquers all," but of a willful decision that he should marry, and Jessie was available.*

* Although her details are often inconsistent and unreliable, Jessie does indicate that several months "elapsed between our fourth and fifth meetings—months in which I heard little of the strange and courteous gentleman, the author of my inscribed copy of 'Almayer's Folly' " (*Joseph Conrad As I Knew Him*, p. 101). This "fourth meeting" took place either in late April, when Conrad may have had an advance copy of his novel (published on the twenty-ninth) or, more likely, in June upon his return from Champel. Jessie then indicates that Conrad saw a good deal of her in the months before *An Outcast* was completed in mid-November of 1895; in fact, she says, Conrad brought the "bulky package of manuscript from which he suggested I should read him some pages right away. That night was my first experience of his characteristic impatience; and after all these years, I can still feel as I felt that night, trembling with pleased interest, and with my mouth as dry as cinder." But the chronology of Conrad's activities suggests that he spent little time with her prior to

With Emilie, Conrad had the best of both worlds. She was young and, therefore, adoring of this older man with the cosmopolitan manner and the unending supply of exciting stories and adventurous episodes, Desdemona to his Othello. With her, he was truly the mysterious romantic stranger: deeply cultivated and naturally courtly, a writer with a published novel behind him, another almost completed, a family history that made him respectable, a long career at sea that was socially responsible, a fluency in French and a heavily accented English. He apparently disguised his Polish background. She was herself intelligent and sensitive—she began a French translation of *Almayer* which Conrad appeared to admire. Her family wealth meant that Conrad could have written his novels in some leisure, the very kind of support he needed for the type of fiction he would write. Emilie, further, brought the respect Conrad apparently needed from a woman and, at the same time, had the intelligence we associate with Marguerite, although hers was as yet unformed.

Emilie's diary reveals her admiration for Conrad and, at the same time, provides our sole glimpses of him as an active suitor. After an especially pleasant outing on Lake Geneva, where Conrad demonstrated his skill with the boat, they saw each other constantly. She wrote that Conrad would listen to her play the piano and was particularly fond of selections by Schubert, Massenet, and Chopin. They discussed books, and he indicated that he read Pierre Loti, Hugo's poetry, and Daudet, her own favorites. She notes that on May 20 Conrad inscribed a presentation copy of *Almayer's Folly:* "To Miss Emily Briquel—whose charming musical gift and ever-bright presence has cheered for him the dull life of Champel, the book is presented by her most humble, grateful and obedient servant *the Author.*" In her diary ten days later, she noted three types of love—that for family, the kind she will have for her husband, and, finally, "friendship, which is how I love Mr Conrad." She was, of course, twenty, and Conrad was thirty-seven; much of her admiration, even infatuation, can be explained by that.

---

his proposal in January of 1896, and her memory seems to have played her false.

Ford Madox Ford offered another view altogether, in the form of a malicious novel, *The Simple Life Limited*, published in 1911 under the pseudonym of Daniel Chaucer. Conceived of as a satirical view of the Garnett circle, and especially of their Fabian-socialist friends, Ford depicts a Pole named Timeon Brandetski who changes his name to Simon Brandson when he settles in England. Similar to Conrad in several ways, Brandson has traveled in exotic places, proven himself as a colonial administrator, and then turned to a writing career, striking it rich with a book called *Clotted Vapours.* The title would indicate Ford's view of Conrad's prose style. Lazy and half-mad, Brandson hires a typist (Jessie?) for his manuscripts and seduces her; she becomes his mistress and they eventually marry. Ford's version, which came after he and Conrad had fallen out over the former's personal excesses, would account for the sudden marriage between the sophisticated foreigner and the uneducated typist.

Conrad's letters to her and her brother are circumspect and for the most part reveal a paternal flavor. In a July 3 letter, for instance, he lectures Paul, twenty years his junior, that the sole chance of happiness comes from a "task accomplished, in an obstacle overcome—no matter what task, no matter what obstacle." "One must," Conrad continues, "accomplish tasks which are boring, painful and revolting; one must make the world go without paying attention to eternal error, for it is full of truths we must help make triumphant." The relationship with the Briquels, Conrad may have recognized, would always have this paternal undercurrent. They looked to him for advice, and Emilie may have confused awe with love.

Conrad's first long exchange with Emilie came on July 14, a little more than two months after the meeting, in response to her letter. She had been working on a French translation of *Almayer*, and Conrad was appropriately touched by her devotion and by her ability. On her part, it could have been a way of ingratiating herself intellectually with the older man; on his, gratitude at her application and his real desire to see the book in a French translation, even if by a twenty-year-old. "Since you have begun [he writes], it's going to be you—or nobody. Here you are properly captured—caught in a trap. Eh? But, seriously, I am enough of an egoist to want to see you finish this translation although my conscience is crying out to tell you—to persuade you the book is not worth the trouble."

He indicates he is wrestling with Chapter 23 of his new book. "Then comes Chapter XXIV and then—the deluge. The deluge of doubts, remorse, regrets and fear amidst which I shall swim until some charitable critic extends me a helping hand made up of flattery. Otherwise, I shall let myself go to the bottom and will never be heard of again." Except for this outpouring of romantic *Angst*, Conrad never becomes personal, sending regards to her brother and mother and commenting lightly on his work. Unknown to her, however, he was involved in enterprises besides the writing of *An Outcast*. He was yachting with his friend Hope and indulging in several business deals involving Hope's brother-in-law, a man named Rorke.

Conrad clarified his role in this transaction in a long letter to Ted Sanderson (written on August 24, 1895), indicating furious bursts of activity—crossing the Channel "six times (three trips) in a fortnight." After announcing the sale of *An Outcast* to Unwin for 12½ percent royalty and £50, plus half serial and American rights, he gets down to this strange episode:

> First of all I was induced to look up and make use of my old French acquaintances for the sake of a very good fellow called Rorke (of Rorke's Drift) whom I knew some years ago and who is Hope's brother-in-law. That man owned some 150 claims on the Roodeport gold reef for the last 6 or 7 years. Of course he tried many times to sell, but during the period of depression (since 1889) nobody would look at them. Now the boom came a few months ago and a French Syndicate approached Rorke (out there in

> Johannesburg) and actually concluded the sale, paid £500 deposit and induced Rorke to part with documents. Then various hitches occurred. Rorke waited, paying meantime the Statutory licenses,—to keep his title to the claims. For that purpose he parted with every penny he could scrape,—sold his freehold, farms, etc.: and at the end of last June found himself without a penny, with his documents somewhere on the Continent of Europe,—so that he could not sell to anybody else. He wrote a despairing letter to Hope praying to be saved. There was no time to lose. The unsophisticated Rorke was at his last gasp. As the Syndicate was in Paris, I went over there on the 8th and looked up people I know or used to know. I enlisted many influential and sympathetic people for my cause.

Conrad then mentions some of these people—Pascalis of the *Figaro*, the bankers Jullien and Epstein, and, a sensational figure, Guesde, a deputy. He calls them all "acquaintances of my young days." There is no way to determine how well Conrad knew them or in what capacity; but Guesde in particular demonstrates a radical turn for which we have little other evidence in Conrad's Marseilles years. Jules Guesde was born Mathieu Basile in 1845, and when Conrad purportedly knew him in the seventies Guesde was a radical journalist, later becoming an organizer and early leader of the Marxist wing of the French labor movement. When Conrad renewed the acquaintanceship, Guesde was serving in the French chamber of deputies and trying to augment his program of carrying the class struggle to the halls of parliament. He apparently stood for everything Conrad detested.

The letter to Sanderson continues:

> We found out (to my intense satisfaction) that the French Syndicate were all Germans. We sat upon them with an order from the President from the X court and ascertained that they have been trying to sell already to some shady people in London. The documents, reports and plans were also in London. Epstein got very interested and proposed to come back with me. Agreed. He snored ignobly all the way. At 8.30 in Victoria. At 10 in Hope's office. At 3 p.m., same day, the London people (called Thompson) parted with all the papers for the sum of £100! They had no more chance, of course, to float a company than any crossing sweeper. As a matter of fact they are penniless Jews. They tried to bluff and bully,—but collapsed before a firm attitude. Next day Epstein, Hope and I met some people of good standing here and before evening a Memorandum of Association of an Anglo-French Syndicate was signed by which they agreed to buy Rorke's claims for £8000 cash and 25,000 shares. We cabled Rorke the terms and he cabled consent. Meantime power of attorney for Hope arrived from Africa. We concluded the sale. On the 11th Aug. I was on my way back to Paris with Epstein. He snored all the way.

Even in the retelling, Conrad's excitement is evident. He was caught up in a true adventure, a financial deal in which he showed to good advantage. He goes on:

> For two days there was much cabling and rushing about. In my two trips I managed to get rid of £117. On the 14th (evening) I left Paris with a check of the French Syndicate of £4,000 in my pocket. On the 15th the English half was paid up and £8,000 less expenses (some 370 pounds) were cabled through African Banking corporation to the unsophisticated Rorke,—and we all sat down and wiped our perspiring brows.—Epstein (previously unknown to me) is a very straightforward Jew and the French part is in very good hands. The English undertaking is practically floated and shall be put on the market within the next fortnight as Rorke-Roodeport Goldmine. There are two Rhodesia directors on the board and the thing is sound. Of course I do not make anything. My expenses are paid and I shall take 200 shares as acknowledgment of my services. They wanted to give me 1,000 which I declined. Yet I must say I was very smart. Nobody was more surprised than myself!

Following upon this success, Conrad was cabled by a man named Maharg, from Johannesburg, offering him the selling of fifty claims on the black reef next to the so-called Minerva Mine. Conrad says he took the thing up, to gain payment in shares—"for the base purpose of carrying on a wretched and useless existence." He made still another trip to Paris, and then sold the property in London. "It was exciting and interesting work and I had a glimpse into curious depths! Very curious!" If the actual episode was close to Conrad's narration of it, then he was still quite ready for an adventure; and we remark how rapidly his ailments seem to have disappeared as he raced back and forth between London and the Continent.

At the end of August, on the twenty-sixth, he was back in Gillingham Street, writing Emilie Briquel that he had returned from a yachting trip around the Shetland and Orkney Islands on Hope's 23-ton cutter, the *Ildegonde*. He had, in actuality, made only a North Sea cruise to the Dutch coast. He says he is immersed in his book once again, with *An Outcast* drawing to its close. He would complete the first draft on September 16. He also indicates a desire to return to the sea, saying he would like to "buy a ship and command it for a voyage of two to three years." He admits, "Those are just plans." In a further letter to Emilie (on October 1), he mentions "a whale fishery in the South," an enterprise, incidentally, recalling the one he had outlined ten years before to Spiridion Kliszczewski.

The development of the imagination of a major writer is, indeed, a mysterious thing: even while Conrad's imagination was flooding with characters, plots, scenes, endings and beginnings, he was skewing off into other areas. In this October 1 letter to Mlle Briquel, he discloses illness, attendant upon the completion of *Outcast* and Garnett's criticism of the ending, and then reveals his circus of activities, a veritable juggling act.

> Also, according to my idiotic habit of doing many things simultaneously, I became involved in all sorts of affairs (gold mines, coal mines, a

> vessel for whale fishery in the South—one is not such a fool . . . after all!). You can imagine that while I was enjoying the luxury of different kinds of neuralgia in a room with its curtains drawn, the Devil (who is most obliging) interfered in all those magnificent affairs so that having presently emerged into sunshine, I cannot find my way about. It is like a skein which had passed through a kitten's paw. I've missed a number of meetings, people I have trusted committed colossal blunders, my ideas have been badly understood—and now there are only explanations, recriminations, disgust, and desolation. I am being made to take on absolutely impossible commitments and forced to swallow fantastic stories. My hands are full and my head is crammed with figures, facts, theories, heavy truths, and light but poisonous lies.

Conrad's awareness of himself here is appealing, for he says his ability to struggle without thought of victory distinguishes him "from a common adventurer," an insight worthy of the novelist at his best. In his litany of episodes, disastrous or otherwise, he might have mentioned Jessie George, to whom he would propose in less than four months, and Marguerite Poradowska, who was either receding or becoming too important.

Yet even as he wrote so candidly to Emilie on October 1, that relationship was ending. Only two more Conrad letters (on November 14 and December 29) followed, and this episode, except for his announcement to Mme Briquel of his impending marriage, was closed. Emilie's diary does not reveal what occurred—she was herself to become engaged on February 10—and perhaps nothing more than a flirtation, if that, had taken place. Whatever emotional investment Conrad had made in Emilie, he moved rapidly to other things.

On September 17, he announced to Garnett the "death of Mr. Peter Willems late of Rotterdam and Macassar murdered on the 16th inst at 4 p.m." The composition of *An Outcast* indicates Conrad's advancement both in his confidence in English and in his conception of his work; for while *Almayer* required considerable revision, *An Outcast* appears to have been written straight through, with significant revisions coming only on the twenty-fourth chapter, a result of Garnett's criticism. Not that the novel satisfied him. He wrote to Edward Noble on October 28 that he looked upon the book now it was finished "with bitter disappointment," and he told Emilie he expected many "savage reviews." A full twenty-three years later, in his Author's Note to the novel, he admitted that the "story was never very near my heart."

Garnett, in his Introduction to *Letters from Joseph Conrad,* indicated his reservations about the character of Willems, perhaps sensing how close the conception of Willems, outcast, borderline criminal, traitor, was to his own creator. Willems was, in many ways, the first of Conrad's "outcasts," certainly the first of his antagonists to carry the burden of the author's sense of life beyond the respectable pale. A recipient of trust and benefaction, Willems repeatedly betrays his trust, moves to the margins of respectability, and finally in Faustian fashion succumbs to an inner demon: not money, not power, but women. The relationship between Willems's outlaw career and Conrad's inner life may have been in Garnett's mind; for he wrote he was himself "too enthralled by the strange atmosphere and poetic vision, and too intent on encouraging him to criticize Willems till the end was at hand." However, on the delivery of the final installment, "I criticized adversely the psychology of Willems' motives and behaviour just before his death at Aissa's hand; and Conrad agreed, with reservations, to my strictures and set to work to remodel various passages."

In his letter to Garnett for September 24, Conrad responded at great length, and the letter as well as the cast of his remarks gives us considerable insight into his imaginative processes at this confusing time. After indicating his gratitude to Garnett for his care, he says: "You gild the pill richly—but the fact remains that the last chapter is simply abominable. . . . I am glad you like the XXIII chapter [the penultimate]. To tell you the honest truth I like it myself. As to the XXIV I feel convinced that the right course would be to destroy it, to scatter its ashes to the four winds of heaven. . . . [However] I am afraid I can't! I lack the courage to set before myself the task of rewriting the thing. It is not—as you say—a matter of correction here and there—a matter of changed words—or lines—or pages. The whole conception seems to me wrong. I seem to have seen the wrong side of the situation. I was always afraid of it. For months I have been afraid of that chapter—and now it is written—and the foreboding is realised in a dismal failure."

Conrad then, rather surprisingly for this willful man, displays a view of creativity which places him among the visionaries, what Pater in his essay on "Style" called the *soul writers,* those who reach us through "vagrant sympathy" and a "kind of immediate contact." Conrad told Garnett he could not unmake his mistakes. "I shall try—but I shall try without faith, because all my work is produced unconsciously (so to speak) and I cannot meddle to any purpose with what is within myself—I am sure you understand what I mean. —It isn't in me to improve what has got itself written.—" This is, of course, purely romantic theory, with special reference to the *symboliste* poets. This is Rimbaud's poet as a "drunken boat." Once he has plunged into the "Poem of the Sea," Conrad, like Rimbaud, suggests he is a drunken craft tossed by the sea of his imagination, meeting glaciers, silver suns, pearlwaves, coal-like skies, hideous wrecks, giant serpents, all of which control him more than he can control them. The work gets itself written out of this kind of imaginative seizure, and the seizure, whatever shape it takes, is the poem or artwork.

Now, Conrad was to revise this view significantly as he moved along the decade; and it is questionable whether he ever really believed in this kind of "automatic writing." We can speculate that, carried along as he was in a new profession before he had fully committed himself to it, he tended to observe himself as a drunken boat caught up—"getting himself written"—by uncontrollable forces. But as he settled later into writing as a lifetime's work, he moved toward a different set of precepts: the careful, structured author creating dimensions of narrative method and layers of narrators, the craftsman utilizing tone, angle of vision, textures. As we shall see in the 1899–1904 period, when he achieved literary maturity, he responded to what Pater called *mind,* a condition, when the literary artist reaches us, as Pater said, "through static and objective indications of design in his work."

Conrad explains to Garnett that he intended Willems to want to escape from *both* women (Aïssa and his wife); from a personal point of view, Conrad's own underlining is interesting. "That *is* the very idea." He outlines his plan, which was to have Willems react to Aïssa at the end passionately even when his passion is spent: "It's an impulse of thought not of the senses. The senses are done with. Nothing lasts!" He has already withdrawn from the relationship, and his effort to recall passion is a last resort; for only after his passion is gone does he recognize what he has lost and now he regrets what he has given up in pursuing his senses. Yet passion saves nothing, for Aïssa herself, beyond her "woman's affection which is simply the ambition to be an important factor in another's life," is burned out also. Still, they "both long to have a significance in the order of nature or of society." Conrad closes this part of his analysis by saying that they seem typical of mankind "where every individual wishes to assert his power, woman by sentiment, man by achievement of some sort—mostly base."*

Conrad's conception was clearly tragic, his achievement hardly that at all. What Garnett correctly objected to was Conrad's desire to impose a large conception on basically trivial people. His development of Willems contradicts an imposition of largeness, certainly not any universal feeling of wasted passion, desire for power, slippage of grandeur, debasement through the

* It is, of course, tempting to read these comments to Garnett about Willems and Aïssa as a gloss on Conrad's own intimate affairs, especially since so much of the novel does rove in and out of Conrad's past. Yet whatever we say is purely speculative and not backed by biographical evidence. Such conjecture would perhaps view the very intention as based on women as an evil element: the parasitical wife, who turns out to be far less than one bargained for, and the vampirish mistress (a nineties phenomenon), who sucks out one's very soul. In this view, the man is a fly caught in the spider's web: Conrad carrying on simultaneously with three women and resisting the temptations of each, or measuring himself as lover and/or husband. The dangers of such speculation, however, are precisely that one never knows when to stop.

senses, loss of self in the pursuit of a mad sensuality. Aïssa, at the same time, is no Medea, and Conrad was surely striving after a Medea-like figure. Poor Joanna, Willems's wife, is no Clytemnestra. The difficulty lay, originally, in the scale, not in Conrad's intentions, which may have shifted as he worked over the manuscript. His wish to measure passion against reason and spent sensuality against regret for a lost past is a potentially tragic theme. But Willems cringes, Aïssa is undeveloped as a female character, and Joanna is pitiful—scale precludes the intention.

Conrad explained to Garnett that he was too lazy to change his thoughts, words, and imagination, even his dreams. "Laziness is a sacred thing. It's the sign of our limitations beyond which there is nothing worth having." Yet he had a view of things and he could not suppress it, telling Garnett he "wanted to convey the kind of placidity that is caused by extreme surprise." We get the sense he wanted to utilize his own torpor, as he referred to it, and reshape it into a mode of being; so that his inner response to objects was transmuted into his characters, whose basic laziness is then outraged by astonishment, change, need to shift to different values. "That's why they are so quiet. . . . That's why I put in the quiet morning—the immobility of surrounding matter, emphasized only by the flutter of small birds. Then the sense of their position penetrated the hearts—stirs them. —They wake up to the reality. Then comes violence: Joanna's slap in Aïssa's face, Willems' rush, Aïssa's shot—and the end just as he sees the joy of sunshine and of life.—"

Yet we recall Willems as a petty embezzler in Hudig's office; then as an outcast and a betrayer of Lingard's trust. Although he has some of the anonymous background of the tragic or epical hero, he achieves none of the roundness of life; nor does his reversal amount to much. His recognition, such as it is, cannot go beyond his trivial needs. He may think of himself as Paris and Aïssa as Helen, or of the two of them as Jason and Medea, but the scale is more Emma Bovary and Rodolphe. Conrad calls it a "complete failure"; he says he "simply could not express . . . [himself] artistically." Yet even as he stresses failure, he hopes that both he and Garnett are wrong.

For Conrad now, in the fall of 1895, the situation was a death watch. Although he awaited the publication of his novel, which would occur in March, he knew his work was not yet what he was capable of writing. "Talent is a long patience," the French naturalist Buffon wrote, and Conrad had apprenticed himself for only six years, really four of steady work. He sensed his talent would work out at its own pace, and in a letter to Noble he speaks of squeezing out of oneself every thought and every image. The artist searches the "darkest corners" of his heart. The answers, if they came, would not derive from reviewers, but from oneself. Not until "Heart of Darkness" and perhaps *Lord Jim* did Conrad feel he had emptied himself of what he was capable.

None of this suggests that *An Outcast* was a throwaway. In many ways that novel seems continuous with *Almayer*, especially because of the overlapping cast of characters, but such similarities are not the entire story. While the language of both remained lush, Conrad was attempting to find a distinctive rhetoric for himself even within a frame of reference of languor, enervation, depletion, and impotence. Remarkable about both novels is that, as first books, they seem the work of a worn-out, burned-out man. The central characters, whether English, Dutch, or Malay, are aged or aging, impotent, depleted. Old men control all fortunes, and even the younger people—Willems and Aïssa, for example—age rapidly while still young in years. The descriptions themselves have begun to take on a leaner, more functional line, even though purple passages remain. Conrad was capable of both kinds of writing, the ornate, decorative style of the nineties, as in the following passage, and the more trenchant, ironic style which was beginning to emerge. The following suggests how much he still owed to *Almayer* and his *fin de siècle* contemporaries:

> As she [Aïssa] spoke she made a step nearer, then another. Willems did not stir. Pressing against him she stood on tiptoe to look into his eyes, and her own seemed to grow bigger, glistening and tender, appealing and promising. With that look she drew the man's soul away from him through his immobile pupils, and from Willems' features the spark of reason vanished under her gaze and was replaced by an appearance of physical well-being, an ecstasy of the senses which had taken possession of his rigid body; an ecstasy that drove out regrets, hesitation and doubt, and proclaimed its terrible work by an appalling aspect of idiotic beatitude. He never stirred a limb, hardly breathed, but stood in still immobility, absorbing the delight of her close contact by every pore.

Yet here is the leaner look, characterizing Babalatchi, Lakamba's wily old prime minister:

> In his readiness to learn from experience that contempt for early principles so necessary to a true statesman, he equalled the most successful politicians of any age; and he had enough persuasiveness and firmness of purpose to acquire a complete mastery over Lakamba's vacillating mind—where there was nothing stable but an all-pervading discontent.

The ironic undertone foreshadows the language of "Heart of Darkness," *Nostromo*, and *The Secret Agent*.

In this passage, which points backward and forward, an image-making power is struggling to escape from an excess of words:

> He [Willems] struggled with the sense of certain defeat—lost his footing—fell back into the darkness. With a faint cry and an upward throw of his arms he gave up as a tired swimmer gives up: because the swamped

craft is gone from under his feet; because the night is dark and the shore is far—because death is better than strife.

There is, everywhere, an attempt on Conrad's part to work through, by means of images, his Hell-Death motif, which dominates the entire conception. His use of a veil image, for instance, is an attempt to break away from language toward some pictorial conception of scene and event, what he would formalize less than two years later in his Preface to *The Nigger.* Aïssa veils herself against Willems like a mummy in "cheap cotton goods," and she uses her hair as a veil-like network to hide behind or reveal herself. Conrad describes it as a "funeral veil," an image he would later use to good advantage in *Under Western Eyes.*

The Hell-Death motif takes on additional power from Conrad's use of images from nature, a far more insistent presence here than in *Almayer.* For the man who had spent twenty years on and off staring at water and re-creating in his imagination its force and fury, nature is an adversary, not a decoration. It had to be placated, not embraced. Conrad's jungle background, despite its torpor, is a snare, a den of struggle for survival in which man is worn down and subjected to inhuman forces. Towering over Willems and emphasizing his isolation, the trees themselves look "sombre, severe, and malevolently solid, like a giant crowd of pitiless enemies pressing round silently to witness his slow agony." Nature becomes the sole enduring thing, deathless in its omnipotence, and man in his struggles becomes frailer and more ephemeral.*

He had, nevertheless, reached a new level of awareness about *Almayer.* He had begun to see more clearly the dialectic which he would intensify and make more distinctive: the uselessness of struggle against nature—yet the need to continue that struggle even if useless; the torpor and languor that lie at the center of every enterprise—the need to struggle against such depletion; the sense of destiny, fate, even nemesis—the concomitant need to shape one's individual destiny; the marginal, isolated individual working out his life in places that seem discontinuous with what he is—the need to try to shape that discontinuous universe to make it accommodate oneself even when it fails to work at all; and, finally, for the author himself the recognition that only irony can begin to provide a perspective on human folly, need, and potentiality. If individual human life was a whim, and if the universal will was always potentially triumphant, Conrad was now asking, then what was left, where did

* The epigraph to the novel—Calderón's "Man's greatest crime is having been born"—may have come either from *Life Is a Dream* or from Schopenhauer's *The World as Will,* where it is quoted in a passage on suffering. If the latter, then Conrad read the German philosopher in terms of pure determinism; from birth to death, man runs a hopeless course. Conrad's pessimism was not always so inexorable, although, as Galsworthy points out, he read Schopenhauer with sympathy.

one search, and how did one know one was even seeking the right answers?

In the final pages of *An Outcast*, there are startling hints of a "new" Conrad. As Willems dies, the style changes, and Conrad describes the death in a stream-of-consciousness prose, as language itself winds down in the awareness of someone facing death:

> And he saw her [Aïssa] very far off, throwing her arms up, while the revolver, very small, lay on the ground between them. . . . Missed! . . . He would go and pick it up now. Never before did he understand, as in that second, the joy, the triumphant delight of sunshine and of life. His mouth was full of something salt and warm. He tried to cough; spat out. . . . Who shrieks: In the name of God, he dies!—he dies!—Who dies?—Must pick up—Night!—What? . . . Night already.

Following this extraordinary passage is a short section devoted to a chance visitor from Europe: "He was a Roumanian, half naturalist, half orchid-hunter for commercial purposes, who used to declare to everybody, in the first five minutes of acquaintance, his intention of writing a scientific book about tropical countries." Although incomplete, this "half naturalist" prefigures Stein of *Lord Jim* and is, in fact, the first Conrad character, however briefly presented and vague, who is not a part of that lush jungle world of his first two novels, the first not committed to making his fortune in East Borneo.

With *An Outcast* off his desk, Conrad apparently took some of his own advice to Edward Noble to heart. He had told Noble to write and rewrite "from an inward point of view" and to use Edward Garnett as his reader, as Conrad planned to do with his next effort, *The Sisters.* Speaking of Garnett, he said: "He is young but very artistic" and also "a very severe critic." It was, incidentally, that very severity which began to rankle, especially when Garnett was candid about his feelings. Conrad repeated his advice to Noble in a November 2 letter: "Everyone must walk in the light of his own heart's gospel. . . . That's my view of life—a view that rejects all formulas, dogmas and principles of other people's making. These are only a web of illusions. . . . Another man's truth is only a dismal lie to me." Although he was to write *The Sisters* in "other men's" style, Conrad's remarks really skip that effort and look ahead to *The Nigger of the "Narcissus,"* which marked his attempt to free himself of 1890s ideologies and mannerisms.

Awaiting the appearance of *An Outcast,* which was postponed by a fire that burned the American edition and delayed the English, Conrad was apparently heading in several directions. He began *The Sisters* in February or March, and put it aside by the latter month; he began the "Rescuer" (*The Rescue*) at the same time, a novel whose writing and development were to extend almost the entire length of his career; he was seeing Jessie George, whom he was to marry on March 24; and he wrote twice more to Emilie Briquel—not love letters, however. In addition, he was still seeking a distinctive style or manner for himself, which he would discover in *The Nigger*, begun on his extended honeymoon in Brittany. Threading through it all was a half-hearted quest for a command, continuing well past the writing of *The Nigger*. We can say that, two years short of his fortieth birthday, Conrad was moving along at all levels of his life, his imagination beginning to soar over his physical ailments; but challenged by uncertainties at every turn.

The ailments were unabated, apparently running parallel to the energies going into creative work and planning. Writing to Mlle Briquel about his use of an epigraph from Calderón for *An Outcast*, instead of the Hugo quotation suggested by her brother, he speaks of his neuralgia—he could, in fact, have used another trip to Champel. He followed this letter with New Year's greetings to Emilie and her family, announcing the delay of his novel until February, although he had already told Noble it would have a March publication date. So ended 1895 for Conrad: if nothing else, he had proven to himself that without serious interruptions he could create a long novel in eighteen months. When he began *The Sisters*, he evidently hoped to follow approximately the same course.

The incomplete manuscript of *The Sisters*, however, suggests bizarre developments in Conrad's imagination. About 15,000 words were written before, with Garnett's discouraging criticism to face, he put it aside. This fragment of a novel never appeared during Conrad's lifetime, not even as part of the Heinemann or subsequent Collected Edition. It was first published in 1928, in the *Bookman*, along with a lengthy commentary by Ford Madox Ford. By 1928, Ford had already written a study of Conrad—rather more a study of their collaboration—and his comments, in the book-length study and in the commentary on *The Sisters*, have to be sifted for the truth beneath the hyperbole. Ford groups *The Sisters* with "The Return," a story of the following year; but in reality they are quite different in style and execution.

The Sisters is far more interesting than "The Return," for its Slavic artist-protagonist is a real departure for Conrad in both character type and conception. Stephen, the artist-hero of the fragment, is a typical *fin de siècle* disillusioned idealist, showing traces of Pater's Marius, an early counterpart of Conrad's own Martin Decoud and Axel Heyst. Stephen draws back instinctively from personal contacts and seeks salvation in the pursuit of immortal masterpieces. This Alastor-like spirit with the exhausted manner of Huysmans's Des Esseintes suffers from a soul infected by ennui, torpor, and a mysterious longing for completion. In nature he seeks the sources of all inspiration, but with a sigh of "Not here! Not here!" he turns away to the "undesirable security of perfect solitude." The placement of this fragment of work in Conrad's personal life is of considerable interest, for even as he was writing of "perfect solitude" and exquisite withdrawal—echoes of Villiers de l'Isle-Adam's Axel, and foreshadowing his own Axel—he was preparing to marry Jessie George. In still another dimension, the Rita of *The Sisters* looks backward and forward, forward to Rita de Lastaola of *The Arrow of Gold* and backward to that childhood sweetheart, that "early love" referred to above.

The Sisters concerns two characters, Stephen and Rita, along with several subsidiary figures who will recur in *The Arrow of Gold*, Conrad's "autobiographical" novel of 1917. As a Slavic wanderer, Stephen himself recalls unmistakable aspects of Conrad. He is a painter, and the woven texture of Conrad's language, overblown as it is, is an attempt "to paint" the former's vocation. We note the influence of Pater: "The prodigies of chisel and brush transported him at first with the hope of a persuasion, of an unveiled religion of art—and then plunged him into despair by refusing to say the last word."

Stephen is a child of the Russian steppes whose father cannot understand why he should want to paint; we recall Conrad's announcement that he wanted to go to sea. He leaves, nevertheless, with his younger brother taking over the family business while he wanders seeking fulfillment. He intends to seek the origin of all inspiration, nature: ". . . to clothe the august form of the terrible, of the immense and tormenting Idea." In pursuit of this idea, he wanders the face of Western Europe. Conrad's immersion in a *symboliste* ideal, the Mallarmé "absence" and "blankness," was rarely more apparent: "Cold silence, absolute silence, is better than the unfinished melodies of deceived hopes. He resolved to return to the cities, amongst men; not because of what the poet [Baudelaire] said about solitude in a crowd; but from an inward sense of his difference from the majority of mankind." He chooses to live, withdrawn, among the crowd.

Stephen finds the "ideal retreat" on the outskirts of Paris in Passy, which, we recall, was the location of Marguerite Poradowska's house. His studio is situated near an establishment owned by Ortega, an orange merchant. The novel fragment now shifts to Rita. Raised by an uncle who is a devout priest, she has been sent to live with another uncle, the orange merchant outside of Paris. She is in many respects a female counterpart of the young Conrad—an orphan, someone moved around from relative to relative. Her father, a smuggler, was shot by frontier guards, and she is the unwanted product of a past everyone would prefer to forget. She is, like Conrad at that age, untamed, directionless. This Rita, only roughly sketched out here, recurs twenty years later in *The Arrow of Gold.* As we have seen, both Ritas are Basque peasants; both have sisters named Therese or Theresa—intense, fanatical women; both are involved with men named Ortega.

Rita proves to be the joy of her uncle, the orange merchant, a henpecked man of simple tastes; but he has no understanding of her or her needs. The fragment ends suddenly with the placement of Rita on one side of the road, Stephen on the other. Ford indicates Conrad had concocted quite a melodrama. He says the theme was to be incest, not the consummation of the forbidden desire, but the rendering of the emotions "of a shared passion that by its nature must be the most hopeless of all." Ford writes: "Stephen was to have met, fallen in love with and married the elder sister [Theresa]. The younger sister [Rita], failing in the religious vocation that her uncle the priest desired her to have was to come to Paris and to stay with the young people in Stephen's pavilion, the tyrannous power of her aunt being such that she could not live with the orange merchant and his wife. The elder sister proving almost equally domineering, Stephen was to fall before the gentler charm of the younger. And the story was to end with the slaying of both the resulting child and the mother by the fanatic priest." Ford suggests further complications, in that Stephen's brother was to visit Paris and to fall in love with Rita also, thus establishing a rivalry between the two brothers as well as the two sisters. Still further, Conrad intended to transport all the characters first to Spain and then to Russia, "so as to get the last drop of contrast out of opposed race natures."

Surely none of these complications could have been worked out at novella length, so that even if half of what Ford relates is true, the 15,000 words of the fragment would have needed at least another 50–75,000 words for completion, especially with the use of Spanish and Russian backdrops. Of great biographical interest is the kaleidoscopic nature of the materials. With this novel, Conrad was entering profoundly into personal materials in a way only faintly suggested by his first two novels. The histories of the characters, their psychological states, their quest for ideals, the backgrounds of France, Spain, and Russia—all of these cut across and pick up large segments of Conrad's early life. Although the final result, the slaying of mother and child by a priest, recalls Maupassant, it is clear the rest of the material is distinctly Conrad's.

This strange fragment, whose abandonment is usually explained by Garnett's adverse criticism, has such intense psychological overtones we are tempted to speculate about every aspect of it. The rivalry between an older and younger sister, a situation repeated in *Nostromo*, has no clear parallel in Conrad's early background; but it does reflect his romantic attachments of the mid-1890s. If we assume he felt any attraction to Marguerite, abandoning her as he became more serious about Jessie George and flirtatious with Emilie Briquel, we find some semblance of that older and younger "sister" sequence at the time he wrote *The Sisters*. All of this is conjectural, but an incest pattern—if Ford is to be believed—would not be distant from his mind if he were thinking of marrying Aunt Marguerite, or even Emilie or Jessie, the latter two almost young enough to be his daughters.

Even without these parallels, which depend on Ford's projection of the novel, we find what we might call "philosophical incest," a manifestation of Conrad's own feelings, embodied in Stephen, about his abandonment of Poland. There is, in Stephen, considerable guilt, and there would be in Conrad in the mid-1890s a comparable misgiving as he moved inexorably toward an English career, even to the extent of marriage to an English girl, while Poradowskis, Bobrowskis, and Korzeniowskis receded. The March 10 announcement of his marriage, to Karol Zagórski, with his somewhat condescending description of his bride-to-be, seems to place Zagórski as his true family, with Jessie as the outsider.

In the same letter, Conrad dismisses his in-laws—nine children, father dead, mother very decent—but he assures Zagórski he is not marrying the family. It was, as Dr. Meyer suggests, an exogamous marriage, and one that carried over profoundly into his fiction of the nineties, certainly to Almayer and his wife, then to Willems and Aïssa, more personally to Stephen and Rita. *The Sisters*, then, presents both a reordering of earlier "life" situations in Conrad and a "screening" of present possibilities, including the emotions that would be attendant upon his choices.* Not unusually, his next project, once he dropped *The Sisters*, would be a manuscript called "The Rescuer," a manuscript that fitted particular needs at this time. So deeply did it probe into Conrad himself that he found it impossible to resolve its various elements, and not until 1919 did he complete the novel.

---

* Dr. Meyer pursues quite a different kind of argument here, seeing in Conrad's choice of Jessie a distancing from his image of a European mother figure (such as Marguerite). Meyer points out, rightly, that such attempts often fail, since the aim is to find someone different from the mother, not someone necessarily sufficient in herself. He sees the marriage as not having met with "significant success," for Conrad was not "psychologically equipped to enjoy the satisfaction of love, marriage, and family life." I prefer to view Conrad's marriage as really a means toward his major and dominant preoccupation: *to establish the best terms on which he could continue as an author*. The move toward authorship, with the mid-nineties rush of published books and incomplete manuscripts, was as intense in its ways as the decision earlier to go to sea; and Conrad would do whatever was necessary, within responsible limits, to make it possible for the choice to be effected. This is not to assert that Jessie was merely a means to an end; but it does suggest that his priorities made it necessary for his private life to be settled and that the choice of a woman was secondary to the greater pressures within. Those pressures, based on choice of career, would dictate the type of marriage he would ultimately make.

CHAPTER 17

Marriage and Rescue

ON March 23, just one day before the ceremony, Conrad made another decisive choice besides the marriage itself. Writing to Edward Garnett in response to apparent criticism of *The Sisters*, he first fell into a characteristic defensive pose, which is that life is only ironic and mocking.

> When once the truth is grasped that one's own personality is only a ridiculous and aimless masquerade of something hopelessly unknown the attainment of serenity is not very far off. Then there remains nothing but the surrender to one's impulses, the fidelity to passing emotions which is perhaps a nearer approach to truth than any other philosophy of life. And why not? If we are "ever becoming—never being" then I would be a fool if I tried to become this thing rather than that; for I know well that I never will be anything. I would rather grasp the solid satisfaction of my wrongheadedness and shake my fist at the idiotic mystery of Heaven.

Such "philosophizing" was not only Darwinian and Schopenhauerean, it was also the product of Conrad's years at sea, when man's disproportion in terms of waves, sky, and horizon became apparent. For all those years, Conrad had lived within a different scale of reference from that associated with land and urban values. Man was miniaturized when measured against the elements or the scale of the ship—whether crawling on spars, wrestling with huge sails, or being tossed about by wind and waves. He could only achieve size and scale by blending with other men; in the mass, on board ship, a man could gain a more harmonious relationship with nature, although the basic disproportion remained.

After such "trifles," Conrad arrived at his main business—*The Sisters* would be laid aside and he would take up a sea story, "The Rescuer," which he hoped to complete within twelve months. Conrad had already outlined it to Garnett, very possibly in conversations. After calling his friend a "Gentle and Murderous Spirit," he asks him for suggestions about a title, himself offering "The Rescuer. / A Tale of Narrow Waters" as a working title. Beneath the jesting tone, one detects some personal strain, especially since

Garnett had already indicated disapproval of Conrad's impending marriage to Jessie.

Nevertheless, having settled his order of writing and having drawn Garnett into his plans, Conrad proceeded with the marriage. Jessie was twenty-three (having been born on February 22, 1873), whereas Conrad had turned thirty-eight the previous December. Besides the information about her family divulged in Conrad's letter to Zagórski, we know her father was either a warehouseman (cited in her birth certificate) or a bookseller (noted on the marriage certificate), or had shifted from one position to the other. Jessie herself had little formal education and had apparently grown up among privations—small income, huge family. With few expectations, she possessed a quality that would surely have appealed to the hard-pressed Conrad, even though he still had the remainder of his 15,000-ruble legacy from his uncle. Throughout their difficult early years, she appears to have made do with whatever they had, and in many ways was far more economical than Conrad. On the face of it, Conrad had caught a meek and compliant woman. But if we assume that his primary purpose was to settle his private life so as to get to the main matter at hand, then his quirky courtship of Jessie and subsequent marriage make sense.

No letters of Conrad are extant from his period of courtship, if it can indeed be called that, and we must depend for our information on Jessie's confusing and inaccurate autobiographical memoir. She says she and Conrad spent many pleasant times together chaperoned by her thirteen-year-old sister. As noted above, Conrad presented her with an inscribed copy of *Almayer's Folly,* and she was ordered to read aloud from the manuscript of the *Outcast* during its composition, while Conrad reprimanded her for not speaking distinctly. Some months later, she reports, he abruptly proposed: " 'Look here, my dear, we had better get married and out of this. Look at the weather. We will get married at once and get over to France. How soon can you be ready? In a week—a fortnight?' " The proposal, if it did take this shape, probably occurred in late January or early February of 1896, some time before Conrad's letter to Garnett of February 22. Conrad told his fiancée the reason for haste was not overwhelming passion but "the weather, his health, his work." She continues: "He even urged as a further inducement that he would not live long." She faced the prospect of early widowhood and they were not yet even engaged.

The period of engagement, she says, lasted six weeks, although this estimation is suspect and contradictory; all the while, Jessie fought her mother's prejudice against a foreigner as son-in-law. At this time, Conrad carried himself like a Middle European count and spoke English with a very heavy accent; so that to Mrs. George it seemed as if her daughter would be swallowed up either by Europe or by the sea. Her marriage was not an easy one for her lower-middle-class family to accept—the footloose, foreign-looking and -sounding Conrad, his background at sea, the lack of regular income, his new career as an author, fifteen years' difference in age, and a remoteness that could never be bridged.

The marriage ceremony took place on March 24, at the St. George Register Office, in Hanover Square, with Hope and Krieger attending. Conrad gave his name as "Joseph Conrad Korzeniowski," his profession as "Master Mariner," and his father's profession as "Landowner." For some inexplicable reason, Jessie gave her age as twenty-two; she had turned twenty-three on February 22. In terms of inaccuracy about dates, they were well matched.

Shortly afterward, the Conrads left for Lannion, on the Brittany coast, a rough, wind-swept area that was popular with French tourists. Conrad needed a remote, cheap, and fairly obscure place where he could work uninterruptedly. The manuscript in hand was "The Rescuer," and one hates to think of the quality of his early relationship to Jessie as he became increasingly baffled by the unresolved elements of that book. A great deal was at stake: his own development as an author of books that had not sold well; his relationship to a very young wife, who expected him to produce something; and the need to earn an income. Lannion itself proved too large, and the couple sought, preferably, an island where there would be no danger of French tourists during the summer months. On April 7, they took possession of a small house on Ile-Grande, by which time Conrad said he had completed eleven pages of "The Rescuer." He wrote to Garnett that Jessie was a good comrade "and no bother at all." The house was on a rocky and barren island off Lannion, an area noted for its fishing widows.

In this extremely difficult period for Conrad, Garnett was to prove his single lifeline with literary sanity. For all her good and gentle qualities, Jessie could not be consulted on artistic matters, nor could she ever be. That was the choice Conrad had made. Once he had isolated himself, he relied on "his reader" with increasing and overwhelming need. He begins by reporting the quota of "Rescuer" he is writing. On April 13, it is twenty-four pages, but even more important are the indecision and hesitation, as if Conrad needed paternal reassurance, whereas Garnett was the younger man by eleven years, not much older than Jessie, in fact. Conrad wrote:

> I am so afraid of myself, of my likes and dislikes, of my thought and of my expression, that I must fly to you for relief—or condemnation—for anything to kill doubt with. For with doubt I cannot live—at least not for long. Is the thing tolerable? Is the thing readable? Is the damned thing altogether insupportable? Am I mindful enough of your teaching—of your expoundings of the ways of the reader? Am I blessed? Or am I condemned? Or am I totally and utterly a hopeless driveller unworthy even of a curse?

He then attempts to turn his desperate need to jesting: "I am ready to cut, slash, erase, destroy, spit, trample, jump, wipe my feet on that MS at a word from you. . . . I have become one of the damned and the lost." The intensity of the verbs, their violence, and their manifestation of explosive rage indicate the depth of his desperation.

Critics have offered many explanations for Conrad's difficulties with "The Rescuer." While acute and ingenious, none of them, unfortunately, has sufficiently taken into account how deeply Conrad was beginning to wrestle with his talent. "The Rescuer" was so difficult a manuscript because it occurred at almost exactly the time Conrad's literary direction was changing; he was writing a novel in a manner that for the next twenty years he was to forgo. He was returning to a period, of *Almayer* and *Outcast,* which in imaginative terms he had already begun to reject for more intense experimentation. Had "The Rescuer" proven easier to write, it would have been a far worse novel than it actually turned out to be. That is, for Conrad to have created it with ease would have meant he was ready to accept the formulas of romance and melodrama endemic in the nineties.

In mid-April, Garnett fell seriously ill with typhoid fever, a particularly dangerous disease at that time, and Conrad's letter to Constance Garnett, Edward's wife, indicates real concern. Meanwhile, reviews of *An Outcast* were beginning to appear, and they were in the main quite favorable. Unfortunately, one of the first Conrad read was from the *National Observer,* a review sent him by Fisher Unwin. The unsigned notice, which Conrad acknowledged as no doubt being correct, was indeed quite accurate, if harsh. The reviewer suggested that Conrad on the basis of *Almayer* would seem to be shaping up as "the Kipling of the Malay Archipelago," but that *An Outcast* disappointed this expectation. He complained of diffuseness in the narration and contended that the author, after a solid beginning, had lost his grip on the subject. "The story melts away among a desert of words, and the desert alas is dry. Unhappily, his characters, on whom he has evidently expended considerable pains, are not in themselves particularly effective." The reviewer then went on to compare Conrad's novel to an R. L. Stevenson story, "grown miraculously long and miraculously tedious." Such criticism pinning Conrad between Kipling and Stevenson would remain with him a long time, as would his reputation as a sea novelist that resulted from *The Nigger of the "Narcissus."*

Other reviews, in the *Daily News,* the *Daily Chronicle,* the *Scotsman,* the Glasgow *Herald,* the *Illustrated London News,* the *Sketch,* and, most of all, the *Saturday Review* (whose reviewer was H. G. Wells), however, were favorable and supportive. They were not simply puffs but the kind of criticism especially valuable for a young writer. Amid the avalanche of fiction published in the 1890s, including all the derivative Kipling, Anthony Hope, and

Stevenson, the reviewers were still able to thread their way through the factitious to more imaginatively conceived books, even when such novels were still tryings-out.

As we noted, the remarks by Wells in the *Saturday Review* were particularly gratifying. Wells was then beginning to establish himself as a writer of science fiction (*The Time Machine* and *The Island of Dr. Moreau*). He also possessed a critical intelligence and was able to get beneath Conrad's 1890s prose and poses to quarry the real thing. His notice demonstrated reviewing at its best, coming at a time when a talented but flawed book could have sunk into the muck and vanished. Wells wrote:

> Mr. Conrad is wordy; his story is not so much told as seen intermittently through a haze of sentences. His style is like river-mist; for a space things are seen clearly, and then comes a great grey bank of printed matter, page on page, creeping round the reader, swallowing him up. You stumble, you protest, you blunder on, for the drama you saw so cursorily has hold of you; . . . Then suddenly things loom up again, and in a moment become real, intense, swift. . . . It never seems to dawn upon him that, if a sentence fails to carry the full weight and implication it was meant to do, the remedy is not to add a qualifying clause, but to reject it and try another. . . . After all this has been said, one can still apply superlatives to the work with a conscience void of offense. Subject to the qualifications thus disposed of, "An Outcast of the Islands" is, perhaps, the finest piece of fiction that has been published this year, as "Almayer's Folly" was one of the finest that was published in 1895.

Wells noted prophetically: "He writes so as to mask and dishonor the greatness that is in him. Greatness is deliberately written; the present writer has read and reread his two books, and, after putting this review aside for some days to consider the discretion of it, the word still stands. Only greatness could make books of which the detailed workmanship was so copiously bad, so well worth reading, so convincing, and so stimulating."

Wells's review uncannily perceived that Conrad was preparing to move on to another style, and that the writer's excesses and faults were those of an author who had not yet discovered his own greatness. Wells's shrewdness in seeing that the author was still masking his real qualities was an act of perception fully appreciated by Conrad. The review, coming in mid-May, when he was wrestling with the very style Wells had condemned, was especially supportive; we have here one of those significant meetings of a growing talent with its recognition, comparable to Garnett's support earlier with *Almayer*. It was Conrad's good fortune, and ability, which made it possible for him to receive encouragement at every crucial turn of his work; the next would be Henley's appreciation of *The Nigger*, then Blackwood's of "Heart of Darkness" and *Lord Jim*.

Conrad responded to Wells on the eighteenth of May:

> I have tried to tell myself that gratitude has nothing to do there; that you have written all your thought regardless of pain or pleasure for the—more or less—thin-skinned creature behind the book. Such considerations and also the sense of my insignificance should have deterred me from this—say—intrusion. But I own I have been so awed by the evidence that a man of letters had thought it worth his while to give more than a passing thought to my endeavour that I prefer to throw myself upon your indulgence, of which your review of my book is such a signal proof.

He went on to this unknown reviewer, his gratitude apparent in such a difficult period for him—a young wife and a manuscript heading toward an impasse: "I wish to thank you for the guidance of your reproof and for the encouragement of your commendation. You have repeated aloud and distinctly the muttered warnings of my own conscience. I am proud to think that, writing in the twilight of my ignorance, I have yet seen dimly the shortcomings which you point with a hand so fine and yet so friendly."

Wells identified himself in reply in one of those rare instances when Conrad saved his mail. Wells opened by reaffirming his high regard for *An Outcast,* continuing:

> I, for instance, could not more write your "Outcast" than I could fly. But, unlike the huge majority of reviewers, I do happen to have written an (unsuccessful) book or so and to have learnt something from my failures of the method of the art.
>
> If I have indeed put my finger on a weak point in your armour of technique, so that you may be able to strengthen it against your next occasion, I shall have done the best a reviewer can do. You have everything for the making of a splendid novelist except dexterity, and that is attainable by drill.
>
> Looking forward to reading your next book.

Writing to Garnett, Conrad was ecstatic. Wells was the first novelist to recognize his talent, the first to praise him in print: "And who do you think it is? —He lives in Woking. Guess. Can't tell? I will tell you. It is H. G. Wells. May I be cremated alive like a miserable moth if I suspected it! Anyway he descended from his 'Time-Machine' to be kind as he knew how. It explains the review. He dedicates his books to W. Henley—you know."

Conrad wrote Wells a week later in the same ecstatic tone. It was as if the latter's review had justified the entire direction of his life up to this indecisive and difficult time:

> If I praised highly the review before I knew who wrote it—it becomes still more precious now, when the name of my kind appreciator is known. Strangely enough—about five months ago—when turning over the last page of the "Wonderful Visit" in the full impression of the extraordinary charm and suggestive realism of that book, I remember reflecting—with contemptible bitterness—that a mind which could conceive and execute

such work was absolutely beyond my reach. That to a man who could think and write so anything I could do—or attempt to do—would probably never seem worth a second glance. Its [sic] a shameful confession but you know how difficult it is for a common mortal to kick himself free of his own clamorous carcass. However it appears that the feeling (besides being base) was uncalled for. I am immensely surprised. But you can imagine how delighted I must be!

. . . Your book[s] lay hold of me with a grasp that can be felt. I am held by the charm of their expression and of their meaning. I surrender to their suggestion, I am delighted by the cleanness of atmosphere, by the sharp definition—even of things implied—and I am convinced by the logic of your imagination so unbounded and so brilliant. I see all this—but the best I am probably unable to see.

Pardon this uncouth outburst of naïve enthusiasm. I am, alas, forty [38] and enthusiasms are precious to me and to be proud of. I am also very thankful to those who can raise them in my battered brain. I did not intend to bore you really.

Just a few days before, Conrad had indicated to Unwin he had turned out about 9,000 words of a story of Brittany peasant life. This was "The Idiots," to be published in *The Savoy* for October 1896. "The Idiots" is Conrad's first short story as a professional writer (if we exclude "The Black Mate," written when he was a seaman). Although he announced to Unwin that he had 20,000 words of "The Rescuer" in hand, the short story was the first fruit of his growing impasse with that novel. While "The Idiots" is imitative of Maupassant's naturalistic methods at their most simplistic, it is an extraordinary biographical document. Written within two months of Conrad's marriage, "The Idiots" charts a cruel destiny through the experience of a woman, Susan. Having given birth to four idiot children in succession, she stabs her husband in the throat with a pair of scissors when he tries to make love to her. Hearing the dead man's voice, haunted by him and her memories, she leaps into the sea and drowns. The story became part of *Tales of Unrest*, which Unwin published in 1898.

The entire series of stories Conrad wrote beginning at this time and which appeared as "tales of unrest" are of comparable biographical interest. The fact that he conceived of his fiction as materials for "unrest"—especially "The Idiots," "An Outpost of Progress," and "The Return"—indicates how fiercely he had entered into personal conflict. Very possibly, these intense antagonisms and hostilities, as Dr. Meyer suggests, developed from Conrad's problems in adjusting to the needs of a woman and to married life, difficult enough for anyone in the early months and surely more intense for a man who had had only himself to consider until well into his thirties. One can, then, see these stories as continuous with both *Almayer* and *Outcast*, especially the latter with its murder of Willems by Aïssa, another man haunted by a woman and eventually destroyed by her extraordinary needs, which he cannot fulfill. These fictions, as such, display images of impotence, hostility, hatred of the "other," and an uncontrollable desire to break out and away.

Such a view, or reading, however, sees Conrad as the man, not as the creative artist. While the stories may reflect such conflicts within him, they are also the means by which he has surmounted the conflict. For the artist, the very conflict that would destroy, either partially or entirely, the non-artist might become for him the materials by which he could examine and transform his materials. These stories of intense hostility toward women, with rage, hatred, and even murder as the outcome, indicate how deeply Conrad was prepared to enter into certain areas of his imagination. They are reflections of the creative process, manifestations of his creative materials, experiments in matter and tone which had become part of his imagination. With such stories in 1896 and 1897, Conrad was entering the arena of his own developing talent; what he turned up was not only neurosis or neurotic need but everything that was to become the major part of his creative life for the next twenty years. The fact that he may (or may not) have found marriage unbearable is of some passing interest; but, ultimately, it becomes secondary to what he was to make of it in his fiction. Once he had committed himself to authorship, he made the tacit agreement that his personal life was to be subsumed under his art. If nothing else, his Preface to *The Nigger* the next year meant that.

Even while he was describing the morbid sentiments of "The Idiots," he was expressing to Garnett his delight with life: "I swear by all the gods that I haven't had such a smashing day [May 22] since I came here—as today"—as though the creation of the story had, at least temporarily, pacified the inner rage. The long letter expresses his delight in Garnett's recovery, indicates it was Wells who did the *Saturday Review* piece, reveals he has seventy pages of that "most rotten twaddle" of "The Rescuer," and brags he has written 10,000 words of "The Idiots." "I've been living in a kind of trance from which I am only waking up now to a sober existence." Once sober, he announces, he will never write anything worth reading, a touch of masochism that apparently served as a goad.

In late May, Garnett began to express his views of "The Rescuer." On May 26, he gave a most enthusiastic reading of the first chapter, but Conrad sensed beneath Garnett's remarks some reservation, probably his own misgivings. For he seized on a slight criticism of page 1 and responded almost entirely to that aspect.* "The first page *is* bad. Can't I be bad! Can't I! It's perfectly rotten, that paragraph, and when one touches it the putrid particles

* What Garnett said was: "There the *description*, the tone seems to me not up to your level. The *feeling*—though poetical—seems a little *forced*, a little over elaborated . . ." (May 26, 1896). But he had commented on the opening chapter as "most artistic; just what is right for an opening chapter." Garnett continued this favorable criticism through the

stick to the fingers." Conrad kept up a barrage of adverse criticism of the manuscript in letters to Garnett, as if it were necessary to prepare him for the worst before the actual reading. "If you knew how idiotic the whole thing seems to me you would pity me. . . . I feel as if I could go and drown myself—in a cesspool at that—for two pence." or: "Here I have used up 103 pages of manuscript to relate the events of 12 hours. I have done it in pursuance of a plan. But is the plan utterly wrong? Is the writing utter bosh? . . . I doubt the sincerity of my own impressions. Probably no more will be written till I hear from you. If you think I am on a wrong track you shall say so and I may try some other way."

By the following year, Conrad would not lean on Garnett to such a degree; but now he was undergoing the most severe doubts about his direction. He had hoped to be freed from routine concerns by isolating himself with his bride, and he had expected his imagination to flow. What he was learning, instead, was the primary lesson of his creative life: that each word, scene, and page would have to be wrenched out with the greatest difficulty. And that, further, he would have to confront fully those aspects of memory and past he might have wished to forgo. In other words, to be a writer—*his* kind of writer—was far more difficult than he had imagined; and just as he had failed his tests for chief and master, so there was the chance he might fail the test of authorship. He was learning Flaubert's lessons firsthand, that authorship was a priesthood and that eminence came from the agonies of creation. In this, he was alone, and even Garnett would not be able to help him.

Ever familiar were the signs of illness—rheumatism in the extremities, which kept him in bed for two weeks, and a swollen hand which made writing even more difficult. Jessie speaks of his raving in Polish during one of these attacks, when fever led to delirium. The cycle was familiar: the inability to work, the illness accompanying the malaise, the return to Polish as the language of frustration and illness, the childhood regression, the need to be nursed, the regaining of attention, and then the slow recovery toward some sense of achievement. Conrad literally had nothing left to fall back upon except himself, for Jessie reveals that just two weeks before their marriage, he "had, through the failure of some gold-mining company, lost all but a few

---

next month: ". . . all is in your best style—and rather a new style for you—so crisp, so admirably firm and concentrated in the handling and presentation" (June 17). Then reading it twenty-three years later as a serial in *Land and Water*, Garnett found a key flaw, the tone: "Perhaps the strain of reading the story in bits, perhaps a lack of mental agility, or of ability to adjust myself to your own manner; perhaps a slight insistence in *your* commentary on the drama as it goes along, combine to create my uncertainty. . . . Yes it must be something in the self-expression of the characters that worries me, and perhaps conflicts with the solidity & depth, the force and fluidity of the whole spectacle in which the figures are playing their parts. The *tone* of the expression perhaps does not harmonize with the drama" (June 4, 1919).

hundred pounds of his modest capital." This episode is murky, but probably connected to Conrad's ventures in South African stock, when he helped Rorke and then provided some service for Maharg.

"The Rescuer" became that more insistent. And the more insistent it became, the more impossible became the task. Writing to Garnett, his sole anchor in these shifting waters, he thanks him for his approval of the manuscript thus far and then laments his situation:

> Since I sent you that part 1st (on the eleventh of the month) I have written one page. Just one page. I went about thinking and forgetting—sitting down before the blank page to find that I could not put one sentence together. To be able to think and unable to express is a fine torture. I am undergoing it—without patience. I don't see the end of it. . . . Other writers have some starting point. Something to catch hold of. They start from an anecdote—from a newspaper paragraph. . . . They lean on dialect—or on tradition—or on history—or on the prejudice or fad of the hour; they trade upon some tie or some conviction of their time—or upon the absence of these things—which they can abuse or praise. But at any rate they know something to begin with—while I don't. I have had some impressions, some sensations—in my time—impressions and sensations of common things. And it's all faded—my very being seems faded and thin like the ghost of a blonde and sentimental woman, haunting romantic ruins pervaded by rats. I am exceedingly miserable. My task appears to me as sensible as lifting the world without that fulcrum which even that conceited ass, Archimedes, admitted to be necessary.*

The degree of difficulty was surely not created by Conrad's loss of faith in himself but was the consequence of his attempt to grapple with deeper levels of his imagination, all the while working with materials which were antithetical to this more profound artistic sense. As long as Conrad struggled with "Rescuer," he would be, in effect, denying the deeper reaches of his talent, and it was in perfect keeping with his development that he should put the manuscript aside and then take it up again in his later years. The manuscript fitted him like a skin in those years, just as it did in his very early ones; but as he moved toward a deeper expression of his material, it was unsuitable and inappropriate.

---

* This statement is archetypal Conrad and fits quite easily into Razumov's statement to Haldin in *Under Western Eyes,* in which he laments his lack of a starting point: " 'You are a son, a brother, a nephew, a cousin—I don't know what—to no end of people. I am just a man. Here I stand before you. A man with a mind. Did it ever occur to you how a man who had never heard a word of warm affection or praise in his life would think on matters on which you would think first with or against your class, your domestic tradition—your fireside prejudices? . . . Did you ever consider how a man like that would feel? I have no domestic tradition. I have nothing to think against' " (p. 61).

The Conrads in their isolation had Unwin's mother-in-law, Mrs. Brooke, as a visitor, and Conrad received her warmly despite all his difficulties and his dislike of interruptions during his working day. He also notes making the acquaintance of a local poet, possibly the M. le Goffic mentioned by Jessie. There were frequent cruises in the cutter *La Pervenche*, which Conrad had hired from a retired shipmaster, Lebras. Apparently "The Idiots" reflects some of their own life: the stonecutters, their landlady, their sense of their surroundings. Also, the idiots themselves, according to Jessie, were observed while the Conrads were being driven by their friend Frijean from Lannion to Ile-Grande. There were other occasional visitors, but by and large Conrad had perfect conditions for consistent work.

Unwin sent on a notice of both *Almayer* and *Outcast* in the *Indian Magazine and Review*. What is interesting about the review is the fact the reviewer correctly identified the original of Tom Lingard. Conrad was especially pleased by its "level-headed appreciation." By July 22, he was still puttering with "Rescuer" and asking Garnett to send on the first part to Hope to check his seamanship terms. But he could not have been working too seriously on the novel, for he produced the lengthy story "An Outpost of Progress," then called "A Victim of Progress," in the first weeks of July.* He found it relatively easy to write the short stories of this period as a relief from "The Rescuer," although the writing of stories was difficult when he concentrated solely on them. These tales were either based on direct observation—such as "The Idiots"—or on the still-fresh past: "An Outpost," with its memories of the Congo, or "The Lagoon" and "Karain," with their Malay settings. The fifth story, "The Return," became very difficult, but for other reasons, chiefly that Conrad attempted to move away from the kind of thing he could do into areas that required a different kind of talent. Perhaps with "The Return" he hoped to challenge James or even Flaubert; but his own imagination was of such a different blend of elements that the story proved almost as intractable as the novel he had interrupted.

As for the sale of his stories, he pretended indifference as to where they appeared as long as he received payment. "But I must live [he wrote Unwin]. I don't care where I appear since the acceptance of such stories is not based upon their artistic worth. . . . If you knew the wear and tear of my writing you would understand my desire for some return. I writhe in doubt over every line. . . . I perspire in incertitude over every word!" Conrad was moving ever closer to becoming a Grub Street writer with these early stories, superior though his poorest efforts were to the average fiction of the day. His need to secure high payment, however, saw him appear in mag-

* Quite possibly, Conrad began *Lord Jim* or some version of it as early as the summer of 1896, although the evidence for this is necessarily speculative, or at best circumstantial.

azines he did not respect: *The Savoy* and *Cosmopolis*, for example. Only with *The Cornhill* and, of course, *Blackwood's*, did he achieve respectability; but the danger was ever there, and once he no longer appeared in *Blackwood's*, he backslid into some less than prestigious publications.

His description of "An Outpost" foreshadows his feelings about the material for "Heart of Darkness." "All the bitterness, of those days, all my puzzled wonder as to the meaning of all I saw—all my indignation at masquerading philanthropy—have been with me again, while I wrote." This line, vaunting the story, was the one he took with Unwin. His "real life" he displayed to Garnett, calling "Rescuer" ghastly. The further he plunged into the heart of the story, the more he saw its intractability. "Your commendation of part I plunges me simply into despair—because part II *must* be very different in theme if not in treatment and I am afraid this will make the book a strange hybrid, fit only to be stoned." Conrad fears his work may be taken for a Clark Russell puppet show—Russell was a novelist of marine melodramas, the very type of writer he wanted to dissociate himself from. Yet to make the dissociation, he had to skirt the kind of romance his material led toward. "Besides [he writes] I begin to fear that supposing everything conveyed and made acceptable (which seems impossible) supposing that—I begin to fear that I have not enough imagination—not enough power to make anything out of the situation; that I cannot invent an illuminating episode that would set in a clear light the persons and feelings."

He sits before the empty page, having been almost completely stalled for the previous two months, its whiteness or absence of words mocking his aspirations. "When I face that fatal manuscript it seems to me [he tells Garnett] that I have forgotten how to think—worse! how to write. It is as if something in my head had given way to let in a cold grey mist. I knock about blindly in it till I am positively physically sick—and then I give up saying—tomorrow! And tomorrow comes—and brings only the renewed and futile agony. I ask myself whether I am breaking up mentally. I am afraid of it."

Turning to another story, "The Lagoon," which he called "very Malay indeed," he hammered it out of himself with "difficulty but without pleasure." Conrad was heartened by Fisher Unwin's agreement to collect the stories into a volume, although by this time he was disillusioned by the latter's niggardly terms. The two men, author and publisher, could not have been more different and lacking in understanding of the other. Unwin found it almost impossible to handle individuals, and he tended to drive a hard bargain with his authors. On the other hand, Conrad did not sell, and Unwin could not expect much in the way of return except prestige for a well-received author. Conrad, for his part, mocked Unwin's Jewishness, making fun of him to Garnett and Graham, portraying him as the stereotypical Hebrew tight with money and deceptive in business affairs. In *The Inheritors*, Conrad and Ford would portray Unwin as Polehampton, a cultural ignoramus for whom books were simply marketable commodities.

With the stories to be collected in 1898, Conrad at least did not feel he was throwing his work into magazines where it would die. While a volume of stories did not have the weight of a novel, it did keep his name before the public in the only form that mattered, something of book length. Answering Garnett's criticism of "An Outpost," Conrad tried to sidestep the relative tepidity of that story by saying he intended none of the particular stories for him, only the volume itself. He toyed with a title: *Idiots and Other Stories* or *Outpost of Progress and Other Stories.* It would appear as *Tales of Unrest* and be dedicated not to Garnett but to Adolf Krieger.

As Conrad fell more and more into the grip of short stories—he had written three in three months and would write two more ("Karain" and "The Return") the following year—he became increasingly Maupassant's disciple. Writing to Unwin, he expounded almost pure Maupassant. Ostensibly, he was commenting on *A First Fleet Family* by Louis Becke and W. J. Jeffery, but struggling to escape was that clarification of personal aims that would lead, eventually, to the Preface to *The Nigger.* He wrote:

> Everything is possible—but the note of truth is not in the possibility of things but in their inevitableness. Inevitableness is the only certitude; it is the very essence of life—as it is of dreams. A picture of life is saved from failure by the merciless vividness of detail. Like a dream it may be ludicrous or tragic and like a dream pitiless and inevitable; a thing monstrous or sweet from which you cannot escape. Our captivity within the incomprehensible logic of accident is the only fact of the universe. From that reality flows deception and inspiration, error and faith, egoism and sacrifice, love and hate. That truth fearlessly faced becomes an austere and trusted friend, a companion of victory or a giver of peace. While our struggles to escape from it—either through drink or philanthropy; through a theory or through disbelief—make the comedy and the drama of life. To produce a work of art a man must either know or feel that truth—even without knowing it. It must be the basis of every artistic endeavour.

Unwin had pressed Conrad to meet a Frenchman named Ortmans, possibly in connection with some dealings with a French publisher, but nothing came of it, although Ortmans did send Conrad a small check in 1897. This episode, if indeed it was even an episode, remains unclear. Conrad mentions it at about the time he and Jessie were planning to return to England at the end of September.

After a few cramped days spent in the Gillingham Street bachelor quarters, they moved to the first of their many homes within a two-hour train ride of London. From this time on, that is, from October 1896, Conrad remained in a rural setting and would visit London only rarely. They set up in a small house in Stanford-le-Hope, in Essex, near the Thames Estuary and not far from Gravesend, the locale of the *Nellie* in "Heart of Darkness." The location placed them near the Hopes and afforded Conrad the opportunity to sail. It was clearly intended as temporary quarters, for the house was badly constructed and drafty; Conrad referred to it as a "damned jerry-built rabbit hutch." Although visitors came, Galsworthy, among others, the Conrads remained only until the following March, when they picked up to go to Ivy Walls Farm, an Elizabethan farmhouse.

Conrad apparently felt strong enough about his career and work to balk at Unwin's terms. The latter had promised fifty pounds in two installments for his next book, which Conrad found offensive, since the terms had not improved over *An Outcast.* Smith, Elder, another publisher, was interested in his work, and with the rift growing between him and Unwin for financial and personal reasons, he was poised to begin his peregrinations among publishers, which were to last most of his early and middle writing career.

The book he was negotiating for was his collection of stories, which Unwin would indeed publish as *Tales of Unrest.* But Conrad also had something else in mind, the novel which he saw as a turning point in his imagination and in his career. This was *The Nigger of the "Narcissus,"* the volume that was to shift his concern from Malay subjects to a much deeper and more intense concern with life and death, the mythical sea and the transient individual, survival itself, themes which in ensuing years would become his major subject matter. *The Nigger* was begun in June 1896, while Conrad and Jessie were in Brittany—the wrapper of the manuscript notes: "Begun in 1896—June." He probably fitted it in during one of his impasses over "The Rescuer," and very possibly in mid-June, when he had completed Part I of that novel. Jean-Aubry says Conrad had about ten pages of the new novel in hand when he left Brittany.

The new novel, however, was apparently to be only a short story. Conrad first mentions it in an October 19 letter to Unwin, indicating it will contain "25,000 words *at least.*" Begun as a long short story, *The Nigger,* there is good reason to believe, was intended for inclusion in a collection of stories, along with "The Idiots," "An Outpost of Progress," and "The Lagoon," three of the five pieces in *Tales of Unrest.* In a letter six days later to Garnett, Conrad mentions a projected length of 30,000 words—the final version was well over 50,000. He very possibly had in mind something along the order of "Heart of Darkness," although it is hard to see where it could have been cut almost in two.

He told Unwin he would like to place *The Nigger* with Henley, then editor of *The New Review* and a man of great influence among younger writers. To be considered one of Henley's "young men" was, in a sense, to have been recognized. Conrad indicates his admiration: "I would like to try *W. Henley* . . . not so much for my own sake as to have a respectable shrine for the memory of men with whom I have, through many hard years, lived and worked." By the time Conrad wrote this letter, he had possibly thirty or forty pages of manuscript in hand, no more than 10,000 words. It would become his major preoccupation during this period, and he hoped to complete it rapidly so as to peddle it with the three other stories to Smith, Elder.

While planning *The Nigger,* Conrad decided to send on a copy of *An Outcast* to Henry James, with an inscription that was tantamount to a short letter of deference and worship. The novel was sent on October 27, the inscription having been written on the sixteenth. Unfortunately, Conrad did not use the ensuing time to revise what he wrote, for it is an embarrassing document, in poor taste and overbearing in its flattery.

> I address You across a vast space invoking the name of that one of Your children You love the most. I have been intimate with many of them, but it would be an impertinence for me to disclose here the secret of my affection. I am not sure that there is one I love more than the others. Exquisite Shades with live hearts, and clothed in the wonderful garment of your prose, they have stood, consoling, by my side under many skies. They have lived with me, faithful and serene—with the bright serenity of Immortality. And to You thanks are due for such glorious companionship.
>
> I want to thank you for the charm of Your words, the delight of Your sentences, the beauty of Your pages! And, since the book before You has obtained some commendation, (for men have been good to an erring brother) I trust that You will consent, by accepting this copy, to augment the precious burden of my gratitude.

The "children" of the address are, of course, James's books. The gift led to James's sending Conrad an inscribed copy of *The Spoils of Poynton* in February 1897, with the message: "Joseph Conrad, in dreadfully delayed but very grateful acknowledgment of an offering singularly generous and beautiful." The exchange of books and praise was followed by a luncheon meeting and a somewhat chary friendship. Knees bent, head bowed, ceremonial French on his lips, Conrad approached James to acknowledge his master. Many critics have written cogently of the influence of the older writer on Conrad, but I think they overstress the linkage between two writers who are, in their assumptions and execution, really quite different, despite certain overlapping characteristics. Certainly at this early stage of their relationship, there is no clear Jamesian influence. Part of their later commonality can, of course, be attributed to their mutual attitudes toward writing, their sense of themselves as first acolytes and then priests, and their devotion to a French tradition of careful, precise composition. Also, both were moving to stress the "how" and the meaning of an event, rather than the "what" or the working out of events. Both were highly introspective at a time when other more external modes or styles—realism, naturalism, aestheticism—were more common.

For Conrad, who was still trying out his powers, James was a novelist who showed what could be accomplished in fiction, not necessarily a writer who provided any specific guidance. Very possibly, of course, Conrad's development of Marlow as a central narrative figure was influenced by James's "registering consciousness"; but even here Conrad's use of a central consciousness is quite different in weight and implication and seems to have derived from his own personal needs for distance and impersonality rather than from any direct literary influence. Chiefly, Conrad's obeisance before James at this time, in October 1896, was not the deference of the apprentice before the master in any literary sense—surely not Maupassant before Flaubert. Rather, it was Conrad's way, we can speculate, of dissociating himself from the Grub Street practitioners of the novel by linking himself with the most serious of writers: in a sense, the only competitor each was to have in the novel in that pre-World War I era.

Conrad now began to see his short stories in print, three in three months: what would become for him a regular pattern of stories written in the interstices, as it were, of his novels. These stories would earn him the necessary money to continue while he plodded along for a year, even two, on his longer fiction; then the stories would appear in a volume in both England and America, picking up another advance, which would carry him along as he wrote his 300 or so words each day. His dissatisfaction with Unwin's terms, as we see in his comments to Garnett, was connected to his need to glean every possible cent from the volumes of collected stories; for his own inner timetable told him his longer works could be produced only if he subsidized himself with the collections. It was this method of writing which made Conrad's dealings with publishers so precarious. And even when he began to employ Pinker as his agent, he demonstrated considerable dissatisfaction with the latter's deals as having provided insufficient funds for maintaining his lifeline with greatness: the long novels.

With his city connections, Garnett began to offer suggestions to Conrad about the use of an agent, A. P. Watt, in this instance, or a new publisher, Longmans and then Heinemann. It was through Garnett that Conrad was put in touch with Sidney Pawling of Heinemann and, through Pawling, with William Ernest Henley of *The New Review*. Moving away from Unwin was to have enormous implications for Conrad's developing self-confidence and his ability to do his work even when sales were minimal. By November 1, he noted *The Nigger* was growing, but was pleased because he would need at least 55,000 words for a volume of short fiction and *The Nigger* could fill out the book. This pattern, of a work beginning as a story, or novella, and then growing to novel length—even the length of *Lord Jim*—was intrinsic to Conrad's method of working. Since so much of his work began in memory, he started with circumscribed episodes and characters, what he could grasp in memory, and then expanded them as his mind and pen began to find larger worlds in which to place the otherwise enclosed material. The analogy would be of concentric circles that result from a stone thrown into a pond; the inner vibration sets off increasingly broader circles until the smaller inner core becomes the whole, the world, the universe. Staring at the sea had suggested a method and supplied a structure.

For a time, the firm of Smith, Elder considered becoming Conrad's publisher—they judged him, he says, an "hintfant phenomenon"—but nothing came of it. Conrad was very excited, however, by the interest of two Cambridge dons in seeing him, spurred by their praise of *An Outcast.* The two were Walter Headlam, a classicist and poet, and Charles Waldstein (later, Walston), a reader in classical archaeology and then Slade Professor of Fine Art. Conrad was amused, as if he were a kind of archaeological artifact which they wanted to check out. "What do such fellows think and talk about?" he asked Garnett. Conrad's connection with the academy or with dons and professors was always one of bemusement. Like William Faulkner in our time, he put on the air of a country bumpkin who happened to write novels; and unlike his academic admirers, he conceived of the writer not as a man of letters but as a man who came to writing from a life of experience.*

Yet even as he sailed along on *The Nigger* and could report good progress, "The Rescuer" intruded. Reginald Smith, of Smith, Elder, showed interest in that novel, but felt an offer should await its completion. Conrad told the publisher he could finish it within six months (it would take almost another twenty-three years). He hoped for a serial of "The Rescuer," which was another way to earn money while he worked on a long novel, and it was, of course, the favored method of the nineteenth-century novelist. Under the more severe calling of "modernist" fiction, not a little abetted by Flaubert and James, this procedure began to disappear; but Conrad, who disliked serialization and rarely began it until he had his novel well along, found it a necessity, since English and American book sales alone did not provide a livable income.

In mid-November of 1896, as he approached his thirty-ninth birthday, Conrad was the author of two novels and three short stories. He had three other incomplete manuscripts: *The Sisters,* which he had put aside permanently; *The Rescue* ("Rescuer" dropped), whose conflicting elements frustrated its development and completion; and *The Nigger of the "Narcissus,"* which he still considered the fourth block in a volume of stories with the other three he had completed. His sources of income were few, royalties being negligible. He was dependent on magazine sales of the stories, a one-

---

* Very possibly he would have acquiesced to Flaubert's mockery of artists in his *Dictionary of Accepted Ideas:* "ARTISTS. All charlatans. Praise their disinterestedness (*old-fashioned*). Express surprise that they dress like everyone else (*old-fashioned*). They earn huge sums and squander them. Often asked to dine out. Woman artist necessarily a whore. What artists do cannot be called work."

shot earning; on outright sale of his novels, also a one-time sale; on serialization, which he had not yet obtained; on collection of his stories into a single volume, which had not yet occurred; and on foreign rights, which had proven negligible. Financially, he was in desperate shape. Furthermore, in terms of his later dealings, he was getting himself into great difficulty by negotiating with several publishers, so that neither he nor the publisher himself could build up confidence in the other and his copyrights would be scattered. Financial expedience impeded any coherent pattern from developing for many years.

Conrad, at this point in November, feared he would remain in limbo while his work simply piled up. He felt, and rightly so, that he needed to keep himself before the public eye with an annual book. So precarious was his hold on himself and his ability to work, he needed the feel of the magazine or book to give him the sense he existed, however insubstantially, as an author. For a novelist whose work so discouraged popularity, he still required the physical necessity of an audience, as if he were closer to Marie Corelli than to James and Flaubert. Meanwhile, negotiations continued, for serialization of *The Nigger* and *The Rescue*, and for the volume of short stories, which would revert to Unwin. Conrad's chief support during this time was Garnett, for introductions and for advice. Pawling of Heinemann showed definite interest in *The Nigger*, which Conrad was producing with some difficulty. He wrote to Ted Sanderson that the easy, fine days of *Almayer's Folly* were gone. "The more I go on the less confidence in myself I feel. There are days when I suspect myself of inability to put a sentence together; and other days when I am positively incapable to invent anything that could be put into a sentence." The difficulty was, surely, attached to the new mode Conrad sought: a leaner prose style, a more symbolic structure, a desire for greater artistic unity and coherence. "I am more conscious of my unworthiness and also of my desire of perfection which—from the conditions of the case—is so unattainable."

By November 25, Conrad had a favorable report from Henley via Pawling: that if the rest of *The Nigger* was up to the sample, it would most certainly appear in *The New Review*. In his note to the novel in the Collected Edition many years later, Conrad quoted Henley's comment and called it "the most gratifying recollection of my writer's life!" To be recognized by Henley, as later by *Blackwood's*, was to have been received into the inner sanctum where literature itself was forged. Conrad now worked steadily on *The Nigger*, by November 29 reaching eighty-two pages of manuscript.

Garnett must have commented upon the unpopular subject, for Conrad said it would have to remain, although he felt it was "trivial enough on the surface" to appeal to the man in the street. Conrad's contempt for his audience was constant for the next fifteen years at least, and he gained considerable satisfaction from the fact that the average man would have no idea what he, the author, was striving for. Yet, at the same time, he desperately wanted that average man to buy his book. In this respect, Conrad followed that detestation of the bourgeoisie—who, after all, bought the books—which began with Flaubert and continued into the modernist movement. Conrad always denied he wrote for other writers, but there is little question his ideal audience consisted of Flaubert, Turgenev, James, and others of that level. In later years, even Garnett fell below that ideal.

Interspersed with progress on *The Nigger*, Conrad reports to Unwin that he has received a letter from Roger Casement, his acquaintance from Congo days. Although we have no idea what Casement said—Conrad's reply, if he did indeed reply, is lost—it is very possible that the letter set off in Conrad's mind a chain of circumstances which led him back to his Congo fiasco and spurred him on to another short-story idea, the eventual "Heart of Darkness." In 1903 and 1904, as we have seen, Conrad wrote at least five letters to Casement concerning atrocities in the Congo. Looking ahead from 1896, it is more probable that Casement's attention to Congo atrocities entered into *The Inheritors*, the collaboration of Conrad and Ford completed in 1900. There, the Congo becomes Greenland and Leopold II the Duc de Mersch.

In early December, Conrad heard that Henley wanted some additional pages of *The Nigger*, even though the latter was to take another month before he decided on serialization in his *New Review*. Conrad's work on the manuscript produced "some real bad days" and he planned to take it with him on a Christmas visit to the Kliszczewskis in Cardiff. He had evidently thought vaguely of a trip to Poland, but he tells the Zagórskis five days short of Christmas that no holiday is possible; he must write, and write endlessly. On January 3, 1897, he can tell Unwin that Henley will serialize *The Nigger*, indicating that Unwin may have the other stories plus two new ones on his own terms for a volume of short stories. *The Nigger* had clearly outgrown that collection.

On January 10, Conrad announces to Garnett completion of the short novel, but another letter to Garnett, dated the nineteenth, mentions he has been in bed for two days after finishing *The Nigger*, which points to a January 17 completion date. He called his illness a "cheap price for finishing that story." To further confuse the matter, the wrapper of the manuscript, which he sold to John Quinn many years later, indicates February 7 as the completion date, and the manuscript is itself dated 19 February, 1897. Most probably, Conrad kept updating the manuscript as he worked over details, so that at each stage as he dated it he did consider it complete, complete as far as he had decided to go at that point.

Besides serialization in *The New Review*, the novel would appear under the imprint of Heinemann, with eight copies published in 1897 to secure copyright and the book officially appearing in 1898. As of yet, Conrad did not plan on any accompanying document, what would be the Preface, which would follow serialization in Henley's periodical. As soon as he had finished the novel in draft, Conrad tried to assess it, underplaying his own sense of it as a landmark work for him. Writing to Helen Watson, who would marry Ted Sanderson in 1898, he said: "Candidly, I think it has certain qualities of art that make it a thing apart. I tried to get through the veil of details at the essence of life. But it is a rough story—dealing with rough men and an immense background. I do not ask myself how much I have succeeded; I only dare to hope that it is not a shameful failure." Conrad suggests his triumph will come if a few readers see what he was trying to do: even now, to make them "see" was his aim.

With the completion of *The Nigger*, Conrad, consciously or not, had put behind him the kind of imaginative effort that went into *Almayer* and *Outcast* and prepared to enter different "realms of gold." As he approached forty, he was reaching maturity as a novelist, and even though he had begun very late, he was on schedule as far as his own development was concerned. Physically, he had sufficient energy remaining to see his work through and intellectually he was on the edge of discovering himself. He had made the kind of marriage that would sustain him emotionally and, apparently, sexually; his intellectual and imaginative needs he could supply himself. This latter point many commentators have missed when they speak of his lack of intellectual stimulation; he was a man who needed little—sufficient was an occasional visit with Galsworthy, Garnett, even Ted Sanderson, or Wells and James. The collaboration with Ford also provided both emotional and intellectual stimulation, especially in the area of language and aesthetics. But he was, withal, the man who had chosen the sea, where communication in words is brief and where silences fill the time and space between sentences.

The Nigger demonstrates Conrad's first serious experimentation with novelistic form, although he evidently did not attempt to be consistent. The structure of the book is simple enough; the story is told by an omniscient shipmate on the *Narcissus* who doubles as author-narrator and as participant in the action. But the logic of the storytelling shows that Conrad was lazy in his conception, or at least was indifferent to the logic of the narration. Beginning in the third person as a viewer, the narrator soon passes into the first-person "we" and "us." From there, he fluctuates between viewer and participant. The discrepancy or difficulty arises when as the "we" he participates in events at which he could not logically be present; or when as narrator he describes events and/or conversations from which he is logically removed.

The method suggests Conrad's move toward the use of a participatory central narrator, what he developed more consistently with Marlow in "Youth," "Heart of Darkness," and *Lord Jim. The Nigger*, however, is less a novel of "how" than it is Conrad's demonstration of a representative situation in which an individual moves so far beyond the comprehension of the group, or crew, that he expresses the "other": death itself. Almayer and Willems have become the West Indian Negro James Wait, who was himself based on several seamen, white and black, Conrad had encountered in his seagoing days. Wait's qualities are a distillation of elements Conrad had already explored in his earlier characters, although for them he had not as yet formed quite the correct context for their enervation, exhaustion, and marginality. With Wait's death-in-life and life-in-death, Conrad had found his own voice.

In presenting Almayer and Willems against a jungle background, Conrad lacked the right mix of elements necessary for his kind of imagination, which worked on ironies, tensions, contraries, and opposites. He needed a more suggestive dialectic of forces, perhaps a more mythically charged atmosphere. By moving Wait against an active ship's crew, especially a crew caught in an elemental storm that almost sinks the ship, Conrad discovered the correct tension. An enervated Wait who approaches death, a man feigning death in order to evade work, a crew which must work to survive an almost lethal storm: the play of opposites fed Conrad's view of life and fiction. This mix of forces would recur on far larger scales in his major fiction: as Marlow and Kurtz, Lord Jim and Marlow, Decoud and Nostromo, Razumov and Haldin.

These had been, after all, the staples of his own life: that pendulum swinging back and forth between torpor, enervation, languor, and bursts of activity on ship or, now, at the writing desk. These alternating forces were not simply external circumstances weighing upon the inner man. They were elements apparently deeply entwined with every aspect of his being, and surely attached to those feelings which had led to his suicide attempt at twenty. As he moved closer to his distinctive themes, he moved back toward those conflicts between life and death which had motivated his own attempt at nullification. When Conrad returned to life after having placed a bullet in his chest, he returned from a world he had glimpsed that made him unique. With Wait and the crew, he began to explore the disproportions of that vision, between the movement toward death of Wait and the slow movement of the crew away from Wait toward life. The opening out of the novel has itself the rhythms of a man who, having chosen death one moment, lies in a kind of limbo—as the *Narcissus* lies for days on her side between destruction and recovery—and then slowly turns toward life.

What Conrad had done with *The Nigger of the "Narcissus"* was to bring his fictional material, for the first time, into the paces and beats of his own life. When we say he was beginning to achieve maturity as a novelist, we mean, in Conrad's instance, he had found the correct rhythms in his fiction; and these rhythms fitted his own sense of life from twenty on, as well as from before. That tremendous preponderance of death and suicide in Conrad—fifteen suicides alone—is attached not only, as Dr. Meyer suggests, to the relationship of men and women, but to the perhaps deeper theme in Conrad that actual extinction was the sole way of gaining or understanding life.

A major element in Conrad's insight into his material came in his decision to place a "live" equivalent of the dying Wait in the crew itself, in the shape of Donkin. This was, for Conrad, a move toward the kind of counterpointing his earlier fiction lacked. For Donkin has, in his social and political attitudes, the enervated qualities of Wait, but they are contained in a fully healthy, if emaciated, body. Thus, Donkin becomes the death principle that exists in life, while Wait represents the life principle that wanes as it moves toward death. The relationship between the two, which involves the crew and officers, even the captain, suggests a choreographed movement in which life and death are the dancers. At stake, however, is not only Wait's life, which is, after all, foredoomed because of lung complications, but the *Narcissus* itself: that is to say, Life. Through the name of the ship, we enter a mirroring pattern, in which life and death are reflections of something comparable.

That mirror image was not lost on Conrad, for in a February 13 letter he wrote about James's *Spoils of Poynton*, which had arrived, inscribed, that morning. Conrad's comment is remarkably accurate, and his major image is of a mirror, a double evocation of "here" and "there": "The delicacy and tenuity of the thing are amazing. It is like a great sheet of plate glass—you don't know it's there till you run against it. Of course I do not mean to say it is anything as gross as plate glass. It's only as *pellucid* as clean plate glass."

Such an image descriptive of James and implicit in his own work helps support the mythological dimension and reference of *The Nigger*. Wait is the classic intruder, the Jonah, the marginal figure who jeopardizes all life, who must be accommodated and, ultimately, exorcised. That he is black, blackness personified, is appropriate, for his negritude intensifies what he is—Benito Cereno comes to mind. Yet unlike Melville, Conrad had no political allegory behind his tale. He was, rather, reaching toward an archetypal, unconscious fear residing in the crew, a fear that lies beneath individual death, within survival itself. It was to sound these depths, far back in the racial unconscious, that Conrad jogged his imagination.

Arnold Bennett, who was a remarkable judge of Conrad's work, wrote H. G. Wells that *The Nigger* moved him to enthusiasm. "Where did the man pick up that style, and that *synthetic* way of gathering up a general impression and flinging it at you? Not only his style, but his attitude, affected me deeply. He is consciously an artist. Now Kipling isn't an artist a bit. . . . He is a great writer but not an artist." Bennett goes on, just as perceptively, to indicate that despite Conrad's extraordinary "management of colour" he needed to "curb his voracity for adjectives." So taken was Bennett with Conrad's manner that he noted in his Journal his desire to revise his own Staffordshire novel in that style of presentation.

This, however, is jumping ahead to the publication of the novel, and to the time when Conrad published his Preface, after the final installment in *The*

New Review. The completion of *The Nigger,* and its subsequent revision, did not help Conrad financially; he still needed to write stories to make a livable income. He told Ted Sanderson his life now was "all stories . . . Something preoccupied and shadowy and I think more illusive even than other existences. And so it goes on, from story to story, from fiction to fiction in an unceasing endeavour to express something of the essence of life." He sees himself as an unequipped traveler "stumbling in a desert in pursuit of mirage!"

Conrad's image of a lost man or of a man moving along the drear edges of life was not isolated but was characteristic of his fiction as well as himself. He began "Karain," another story drawing on his Malay experiences, and completed it on April 1; it would be published in *Blackwood's* in November, his first publication in that prestigious magazine. While writing it—it would grow to nearly 15,000 words—he sent a first draft to Garnett for criticism and then became overly jocular about the latter's suggestions for revision. Conrad was also involved, on March 13, in the move to Ivy Walls, near Stanford-le-Hope. The Conrads' near neighbors were the Hopes, but they knew nobody else. Jessie feared that the isolation of the house would be particularly hard on Conrad, since he would not have the company "of men of his own standard of intellect." She called the first year in Ivy Walls (in all they spent nineteen months there) "one of the most difficult in the whole of our married life." Eventually, Sanderson, Garnett, and Galsworthy visited, and Conrad does not appear to have found the isolation enervating. On February 25, if we accept Garnett's dating, Conrad and James lunched in De Vere Gardens; the former looked forward to it, saying, "There is something to live for—at last!"

With the completion of *The Nigger,* Conrad reached a resting point where he could collect his energies; he would work on stories, but had no novel on his writing table. Intellectually, his development seems to have been completed, and his beliefs were meaningful only to the extent they could be shaped into imaginative materials. That is, like a painter with color or a composer with sound, he was thinking in terms of words as they could be grouped into novels and stories. As we shall see, he was intellectually aware of what was around him, but nothing could occur in the larger world that would alter his fixed opinions. Only in his art would he open himself. He continued to inveigh against the liberalizing tendencies in British official life, and he attacked in particular the "languid imbecility" of Salisbury's government. He made fun of Garnett's nihilist friends, the groups who clustered around Constance Garnett because of her translations of Russian novelists and her interest in Russian affairs. Many of these "ideas" would be tested when he began his long correspondence with R. B. Cunninghame Graham later in the year, even though the Scotsman was a social radical of the kind Conrad usually detested.

"Karain" did not engage Conrad intellectually—he personally preferred "The Lagoon," he told Helen Watson—and essentially it was a left-handed venture into his Malay experiences. While writing it, he had already abandoned this scene artistically. His memories, to begin with, had not been abundant, his experiences relatively few. *Almayer's Folly*, and what it represented, had really been the only essential Malay freight Conrad carried around with him. After that, it was a matter of keeping the writing machine going until new ideas and new themes shaped up. With *The Nigger*, he hoped to have found a direction; thus, at a certain point, he could even tell Garnett he would burn the partial manuscript of "Karain" if his friend suggested it. "Karain," to keep the burning image, later becomes that "infernal story" which he cannot finish. It was, despite its relative brevity, falling into the same impasse as *The Rescue*, that other maze of Malayan experiences. There is good reason to believe Conrad's difficulties here led him directly to seek a mirror image, that is, an objective-subjective persona, and Marlow would become his "rescuer" (as Ford would in real life) when *The Rescue* and Malayan matters floundered.

Conrad, meanwhile, expected to see "An Outpost of Progress" in the April-May issue of *Cosmopolis*, but found it postponed to make way for Kipling's "Slaves of the Lamp." It would now appear in June-July, with payment on publication. His monetary exigencies were clear. He was living right on the edge, and he depended on exact scheduling. A delay or postponement was potentially disastrous. Writing to his old friend in Cardiff, Joseph Spiridion (Spiridion Kliszczewski), he asked for a loan of £20, a not inconsiderable sum, until *Cosmopolis* paid. Conrad undercut his embarrassing request by indicating he did not really need it, calling it "more of a diplomatic necessity than anything else." The financial pattern was set—one that continued until the success of *Chance* sixteen years later—in which he borrowed from many of his close friends, including Galsworthy and Ford, and also depended on Pinker's outlays once he had become his agent. Conrad tells Spiridion Jessie knows of none of this, and it is quite likely she never realized how far Conrad fell into temporary and then permanent debt. He handled money matters, giving her an allowance, and she never questioned where the money came from, whether publishers, friends, Pinker, loans based on insurance policies, or bank robberies.

On April 14, Conrad sent the manuscript of "Karain" to Unwin, now titled "Karain: A Memory." He indicates that the cheerful ending is a departure for him. Totaling up words, he says he needs one other story of 5–7,000 words to make up the length of a potential volume. This story, which he already calls "a London story," was to be "The Return," an attempt on Conrad's part to break with both the Malay settings of his early novels and stories and the sea background of *The Nigger*. As we shall see, it gave him tremendous difficulty—it was not completed until September—and it never found magazine publication. As a "city tale" of marriage and infidelity, its genre was unsuited for Conrad's kind of imagination, although it has biographical interest as an oddity within his canon.

By early May, sheets of *The Nigger* were available. Conrad sent some to Ted Sanderson, warning him that before his mother read it, he should screen it for coarseness and then judge whether it was fit for her. Meanwhile, Garnett had evidently praised the novel highly, and Conrad was extremely gratified, both happy and proud; Garnett was still his only active reader. In a late-May letter, he thanks his "reader" for having sent on Pater's *Marius the Epicurean,* over which he is licking his "chops in anticipation." Pater played a much larger role in Conrad's aesthetic development than has generally been granted, so that when the latter came to write his Preface in the summer, he moved familiarly along the line of Pater's ideas, especially his essay "Style."

Yet despite these little bursts of enthusiasm and gratification, Conrad was seriously stalled. Although heartened by proofs of *The Nigger,* he could not resolve the conflicts with Pawling and Heinemann over the manuscript of *The Rescue.* And even though *Blackwood's* offer to publish "Karain" was certainly a boost for his morale, particularly when the magazine met his demand for £40, that was insufficient to compensate for the impasse. He had, at this time, in June of 1897, no long work going except *The Rescue,* and his future was clouded by the possibility of his writing short stories indefinitely to meet weekly expenses. A letter to Garnett on June 2 indicates a lot of action but little result. Conrad conveys a string of disconnected news: Jessie was not well (by now, she was pregnant with Borys); the first part of *Rescue* had been sent to Pawling (who could not place it); he was, meanwhile, writing "The Return" (which dragged on and on); the Bachellor Syndicate bought *The Nigger* for serialization in the United States (nothing came of it); and Appleton was going to publish the American edition (it did not).* It all added up to frustration, at best a holding action.

Still to Garnett, Conrad says he is "writing nothing [on *Rescue*]; often restraining tears; never restraining curses. At times thinking the world *has* come to an end—at others convinced that it has not yet come out of chaos." Defiance and bitterness, he says, even before Stephen Dedalus, are his sole weapons. Writing to Unwin a rare letter about aesthetic matters, Conrad commented on Somerset Maugham's *Liza of Lambeth,* that 1897 novel in which Maugham drew on his experiences as an obstetrician. Conrad wittily calls it a "society novel"—society of a sort—and then mounts an attack upon what the "naturalistic" novel is up to:

---

* Dodd, Mead eventually published *The Nigger* in the United States under the title of *The Children of the Sea, a Tale of the Forecastle.* The American publisher apparently felt the title was unsuitable for its readers, although Conrad's use of "nigger" derives not from how he, but from how the crew of the *Narcissus* refer to James Wait.

> I am not enough of a democrat to perceive all the subtle difference there is between the two ends of a ladder. One may be low and the other high—a matter of pure chance—just as the ladder happens to be stood-up. The principal thing is that the story gets on a rung and stays there; and I can't find it in my heart to praise it because the rung happens to be low. Rungs are artificial things—that's my objection. There is *any amount* of good things in the story and no distinction of any kind.

He asserts that what it offers, a "genre" picture without any atmosphere, is exactly what the general reader prefers; similar to a George du Maurier drawing—"same kind of art exactly, only in another sphere." Of course, part of Conrad's intention here, besides expressing his contempt for this level of art, was to "educate" Unwin into the difference between Maugham's easily accessible fiction and his own, which required another dimension of understanding. Conrad's dislike of Unwin was twofold: connected to the latter's business dealings (niggardly in Conrad's view) and to his inability to grant there were different levels of art, some of which did not find an immediate audience.

On July 18, he wrote Unwin he was willing to enter into an agreement by which *Blackwood's* would have the refusal for serial purposes only of any short story he might write, with the exclusion of "The Return" from this arrangement. He then states he is not likely to write any more short stories, although, in fact, he did begin *Lord Jim* as a story after "The Return" and followed it by "Youth," "Falk," "Amy Foster," and others. Such statements indicate Conrad had little sense of where he was heading in this second half of 1897, another one of those limbo-like periods when he felt himself pulled by forces he could not control The connection at *Blackwood's* was, nevertheless, heartening. Conrad called the magazine and owner "Modern Athens," and he felt so flattered "that for a whole day I walked about with my nose in the air."

Blackwood and his magazine were extremely conservative, far more so than Conrad, whose reactionary politics were always balanced by countering anarchistic tendencies. *Blackwood's*, however, was the Establishment itself: safe, a conserver of tradition, highly aware of its own esteem, very solicitous about bringing good literature to its readers, and most careful about its selections. William Blackwood at the time Conrad came into his circle, and it was very much a select circle of authors and publisher, had been a member of the firm for forty years and editor for fully twenty. He was well aware that the Blackwood imprint conferred credit on his authors, and in turn, he expected loyalty and no nonsense. Given his ingrained sense of traditional values and his conservative literary tastes, his acceptance and publication of "Heart of Darkness" and *Lord Jim*, first in serial, then in book form, were acts of tremendous perspicacity. For these works, seen from the perspective of 1899–1900, were little less than revolutionary, both in content and in their shaping. For an audience accustomed to Barrie or Kipling to come upon the nightmarish "Heart of Darkness" and then the convoluted, intense *Lord Jim* was not an easy experience, and their publication involved courage on the part of a conservative editor. *Blackwood's*—magazine and editor, as well as the assistant editor, David Meldrum—was a perfect prop for Conrad at a time when everything else seemed uncertain. So taken was Conrad with his newly found anchor that he tried to introduce both Galsworthy and Garnett to the magazine, but Blackwood would not accept their work.

By late July, the exhilaration had apparently worn off, and Conrad's true condition returned to him, for he suffered from "fever, gout, sore throat—a regular assortment of ailings," with both feet in flannel and a pillow at his back. July 26 was also the day on which the initial installment of *The Nigger* would appear in *The New Review*, the first of five monthly parts. Meanwhile, "The Return" was stalled, even though Conrad speaks of trying *The Yellow Book* with it. The materials of the story were proving intractable, unadaptable to Conrad's way of thinking, although full of his own personal fury.

August, however, was to be more auspicious. For Conrad was to begin his lifelong friendship with Cunninghame Graham, first by mail, then with occasional meetings; and he was to write his Preface to *The Nigger*, a document of overwhelming personal and aesthetic importance for him. It was, in several ways, his personal summation of the life of the artist up to 1897 and, in a limited sense, a harbinger of the artist to come after 1897. That Conrad could even write it indicates a depth and intensity belying any other stance he might take that treated writing as negligible. First, the connection with Graham brought out the best in Conrad as a correspondent and person. Graham is to us a man of great interest who has passed from view because we consider him a literary man, and his work, unfortunately, despite occasional pieces, is not the best part of him.

When the correspondence began in August, with Graham writing to Conrad about "An Outpost of Progress," the Scotsman was five years older than Conrad, born into a mixed Spanish and Scots background, a "grand seigneur," as Conrad was to call him. Graham's forebears, like Conrad's, were of the aristocracy and landed gentry, and after his father's death he became Liberal M.P. for North Lanarkshire. His aristocratic background did not impede his radical politics, and he became, along with Keir Hardie, a strong supporter of the early development of the Scottish Labour Party (anathema to Conrad) and the Scottish nationalist movement, all the while writing prolifically in every genre and traveling widely in South America and Africa. He was an idealist, a hard-headed politician, an aristocrat, a socialist, and an anarchist, one who subverts order and stirs up trouble. The combination fascinated Conrad, and their sympathy for each other appears to have been cemented by the first letter. They became, in a sense, allies against imperialism and "politics as usual"—an alliance that helped to bridge the chasm that otherwise separated them politically.

Although it is impossible to cite precise influences, it appears evident from Conrad's letters that Graham proved an educational experience for him; and that his own well-hidden anarchistic tendencies, his own sense of rage and chaos carefully buried under the skin, were allowed freer play because of Graham's presence. Put another way, Graham's insistence on forms of anarchy as part of the normal political scene struck a sympathetic note in Conrad, even as he consciously pursued order and shape. His relationship with the turbulent Graham and the writing of the Preface in the same month provide two very different sides of what he would later resolve in his fiction.

Graham had written originally comparing "An Outpost" (favorably) with Kipling's "Slaves of the Lamp," which had appeared in *Cosmopolis* two months before Conrad's story. Conrad was delighted and let loose on Kipling, whose success he both envied and deplored.

> Mr Kipling has the wisdom of the passing generations—and holds it in perfect sincerity. Some of his work is of impeccable form and because of that *little* thing he shall sojourn in Hell only a very short while. He squints with the rest of his excellent sort. It is a beautiful squint; it is an useful squint. And—after all—perhaps he sees around the corner? And suppose Truth is just around the corner like the elusive and useless loafer it is? I can't tell. No one can tell. It is impossible to know. It is impossible to know anything tho' it is possible to believe a thing or two.

Conrad's contempt is hidden in persiflage, and it was the perfect tone to warm Graham's heart. He knew his man, and under the Conradian irony he could sense the baffled idealist; under the persiflage was a man, like himself, seeking moral direction. Conrad continued at his wittiest: "Most of my life has been spent between sky and water and now I live so alone that often I fancy myself clinging stupidly to a derelict planet abandoned by its precious crew. Your voice is not a voice in the wilderness—it seems to come through the clean emptiness of space. If—under the circumstances—I hail back lustily I know You won't count it to me for a crime."

Conrad followed up his Kipling comments with further remarks, which coincided, probably, with his start on the Preface. He says that in the "chaos of printed matter" at present Kipling's sketches "appear by contrast finished and impeccable. I judge the man *in* his time—and space. It is a small space," Conrad adds. As to posterity, it shall be busy "thieving, lying, selling its little soul for sixpence (from the noblest motives) and shall remember no one except perhaps one or two quite too atrocious mountebanks."

This diatribe derives from Conrad's disdain for the democratization of taste, with its resulting loss of aesthetic standards; undeniably, he had in mind the tremendous popular success of quite inferior work which passed for literary effort, Marie Corelli and others of that kind. Graham himself had little interest in high art, and he wrote essays and fiction to present his feelings without strict regard for lasting quality or universality. He was a writer mainly of the moment, although Conrad in reply always insisted on taking the road of high art. As the correspondence and meetings (the first came at the end of November) continued, Conrad began to learn more about his friend. He was particularly taken with Graham's tale of civil disobedience in 1887, when he led a rush on the police during agitation against unemployment (at a time, significantly, that Conrad was having difficulty in finding a maritime berth), and was knocked on the head with a truncheon, charged with assaulting the police, and imprisoned for six weeks for unlawful assembly. That meeting in Trafalgar Square, incidentally, besides Graham, included figures such as William Morris (and his Socialist League), Hyndman (and his Social Democratic Federation), Prince Kropotkin, Bernard Shaw, Mrs. Besant, and others on the left. Further, in ensuing years, Graham campaigned vociferously for universal suffrage, free secular education, abolition of Lords, disestablishmentarianism, a graduated income tax, a free meal for every state school pupil. He opposed England's expansionism and imperialism—a stand that explains his reaction to "An Outpost," an indictment of imperialism—and he spoke out strongly against the clergy. On these two issues, at least, Conrad could join him. That whole side of Conrad which did not spurn Apollo Korzeniowski's idealism would be reawakened by Graham, if not to activism, then to disputatious letters and meetings. Graham was exactly the kind of man with whom Conrad needed to carry on a dialogue.

Meanwhile, he told Garnett (on August 24) that he had written a "short preface to the 'Nigger.' " He says he will not draw one breath "till your Sublime Highness has spoken to the least of his slaves." What he really must know is whether it stands a chance of being printed, and Garnett, to whom *The Nigger* was dedicated, would be final arbiter. In going over the Preface, the Unwin reader deleted one paragraph, as follows:

> It may seem strange if not downright suspicious that so much should be said in introduction to the unimportant tale of the sea which follows. It may also appear the height of conceit or folly since every word of the preface may be brought in judgment against the work it is meant to introduce. But a preface—if anything—is spoken in perfect good faith, as one speaks to friends, and in the hope that the unprovoked confidence shall be treated with scrupulous fairness. And, after all, everyone desires to be understood; We all with mutual indulgence give way to the pressing need of explaining ourselves—the politician, the prophet, the fool, the bricklayer they all do it; and if so then why not the writer of tales who is, as far as I know, no greater criminal than any of these. It is true that the disclosure of the aim otherwise than by the effective effort towards it is a confession of doubt and so far a confession of weakness. Yet in the region of art such an avowal is not so fatal as it would be elsewhere. For in art alone of all the

> enterprises of men there is meaning in endeavour disassociated from success and merit—if any merit there be—is not wholly centered in achievement but may be faintly discerned in the aim.

Garnett's taste was delicate, and he noted how the wordiness of this section upset the pace and rhythm of the whole. In any event, Pawling of Heinemann subsequently refused to publish the Preface with the novel. Conrad then took it to Henley, who placed it following the last installment of the serial. Yet the version Henley published differs in omissions and details from the one Conrad originally wrote, which is the text attached to the collected and all later editions. Further, in 1902, Conrad apparently had printed for private distribution the text of the Preface as he wished it to appear. This text is basically what he originally wrote in 1897, except for the deletion of the paragraph Garnett had objected to. There is, however, the possibility that this 1902 printing was a forgery by Thomas J. Wise, later a collector of Conrad's manuscripts and typescripts, but throughout his career a notorious forger.

The Preface served as a literary anchor for Conrad in this early segment of his career. Yet even as it helped him to sort out his ideas, it did not particularly define his later writing career when he substantially found his métier. The Preface, however, put him at his ease in those early years when he was seeking both an aesthetic and a language. His debt to nineteenth-century French literature and theory is evident, but the influence of Walter Pater and especially Pater's essay on "Style" (published in 1889 as *Appreciations with an Essay on Style*) is of equal importance, though perhaps less apparent. Another clear influence was James's essay "The Art of Fiction," originally published in 1884.

We see, then, feeding into the Preface several overlapping elements: Flaubert, of course; *symboliste* suggestions and doctrines; Pater, with particular reference to "Style"; James, especially "The Art of Fiction"; a strong post-Wagnerian aesthetic, derived from Wagner's "amalgamation" of the arts; an 1890s language and attitude about aesthetic ideals and artistic elitism; and what was unique, that impressionism which both heightened and lessened in order to make the reader "see" with the peculiar intensity which we call Conradian.

Much of the ground Conrad covered had been well explored before. So close in spirit, despite certain differences in execution, are Conrad's Preface and James's "The Art of Fiction," published thirteen years earlier, that one is tempted to compare them in parallel columns. In arguing for heightened realism, James had pleaded for intelligence in the novel and a seriousness of purpose that had often been brought only to poetry and poetic drama. The novel's *raison d'être* for James is no less than to represent life, and the novelist's very calling stimulates, he says, fidelity to a sacred office. Trollope is castigated for his sense of "only making believe"; his betrayal of a great trust is "a terrible crime." James spoke of fiction as producing an illusion of life, a semblance which is the very air of reality. The novel, like music, is united in texture and interwoven; in each part should be found something of other parts—a functioning of Coleridge's secondary imagination which "dissolves, diffuses, dissipates, in order to re-create." The absolute wedding of the parts themselves is stressed by James, as it was by Flaubert before him, Pater after, and by that small army of Wagnerites, including Mallarmé, who had gathered in Paris following the composer's death. There is little question, although we lack specific proof, that Conrad was caught up in the Wagnerian fervor of the 1880s and 1890s.

For the artist, for the novelist, experience is never finite; his imagination is always catching new hints. His subject matter is all ways of seeing and feeling. James's famous dictum: "Try to be one of the people on whom nothing is lost," is a plea for the novelist to expand his horizons, to be devoted to his craft at all times, in all places. The province of art is "all life, all feeling, all observation, all vision." Art, says James, is created by men enjoying the freedom of unlimited experience and the freedom of its re-creation in whatever form that particular experience suggests. The mind of imagination, says James, the mind of genius operating freely, "takes to itself the faintest hints of life," converting "the very pulses of the air into revelations." Experience is "an immense sensibility." James implies that under these conditions of fidelity to art, beauty and truth are sufficient; and that if the intelligence is fine, the art will be fine, while the moral and aesthetic unite into a whole.

When we come to the Preface to *The Nigger*, we cannot ascertain whether Conrad obtained this idea of the alliance of the moral and the aesthetic from James, Flaubert, Pater, or even Keats, or else derived it from his earlier French reading or from the literature of the late 1890s. Conrad speaks of the artist "snatching in a moment of courage . . . a passing phase of life" and bringing to bear upon it an imagination bathed in tenderness and faith; the artist must show life's "vibration, its colour, its form; and through its movement, its form, and its colour, reveal the substance of its truth—disclose its inspiring secret: the stress and passion within the core of each convincing moment." Whoever holds to these convictions, says Conrad, cannot be faithful to any one of the temporary formulas of his craft. All the gods of realism, romanticism, naturalism, and even sentimentalism must abandon the artist on the threshold of his struggle with his own conscience. At that moment the temporary formulas are left behind and only the individual intelligence remains. "In that uneasy solitude," Conrad says, "the supreme cry of Art for Art itself, loses the exciting ring of its apparent immortality. It sounds far off. It has ceased to be a cry, and is heard only as a whisper, often incomprehensible, but at times and faintly encouraging."

Conrad echoes James on the necessity of artistic awareness, remarking that to show intelligence at every moment and to search out the fundamental, the essential, and the enduring are the work of the artist. The artist appeals to what is in us a gift and not an acquisition. All art appeals emotionally, primarily to the senses—to our senses of pity and beauty and pain and mystery. And how, Conrad asks, can art, particularly fiction, catch this air of sensory reality; how, in short, "does it penetrate to the colors of life's complexities?" Art must, he says, in a passage already partially quoted that is reminiscent of Pater,

> strenuously aspire to the plasticity of sculpture, to the colour of painting, and to the magic suggestiveness of music—which is the art of arts. And it is only through complete, unswerving devotion to the perfect blending of form and substance; it is only through an unremitting never-discouraged care for the shape and ring of sentences that an approach can be made to plasticity, to colour, and that the light of magic suggestiveness may be brought to play for an evanescent instant over the commonplace surface of words: of the old, old words, worn thin, defaced by ages of careless usage.*

Conrad then made his now-famous declaration of intention, which repeats James's dictum that the artist should "produce the illusion of life"; Conrad said: "My task which I am trying to achieve is, by the power of the written word, to make you hear, to make you feel—it is, before all, to make you *see.*" It is to catch at rest each passing moment and to reproduce that moment so that it arrests the interest of men; that function, he says, is the aim "reserved only for a very few to achieve." At that moment, the artistic aims of the creator assume a moral importance, achieving a sense of grandeur and of something fully *done* which captures the moral significance of the moment.

As it turned out, the Preface was more a point of demarcation for Conrad in the late 1890s than it was a directive. At this stage, in 1897, as he was, Janus-like, looking both ways, back toward *The Rescue* and forward from

* In Pater, music and prose literature are, in one major sense, compatible. "If music be the ideal of all art whatever, precisely because in music it is impossible to distinguish the form from the substance, the subject from the expression, then, literature, by finding its specific excellence in the absolute correspondence of the term to its import, will be but fulfilling the condition of all artistic quality in things everywhere, of all good art." From Pater, Conrad may have also come across, for the first time, Buffon's famous phrase "The style is the man," and it is also possible that in Pater's essay he gathered up ideas from Flaubert's letters as well as from Maupassant's introduction to the collection of letters Flaubert wrote to George Sand. Flaubert speaks there of the end of art as the beautiful, the end of the physician as healing, and the painter painting. And Maupassant wrote about Flaubert's search for the "one thing, one word to call it by, one adjective to qualify, one verb to animate it." Since we do not know when Conrad read these words in Flaubert and Maupassant, it is quite possible, although unprovable, he first learned of them through Pater, especially the Maupassant introduction. From that, he may have gone to the original.

The Nigger, he needed to define what he was and what he was seeking literarily. The Preface provided that definition, giving him an anchor both in his French past and his Pater-oriented present. Through James and Pater, he had found a way to blend Flaubert, Maupassant, (some) Zola, the Wagnerites, the *symbolistes* (whom he may have known only indirectly), with a further group who seemed not to fit with the first group, that is, Nietzsche, Darwin, Schopenhauer, and Hardy. At the time the Preface appeared in print, in December of 1897, Conrad wrote two of his most splendid letters to Graham, and two passages in particular capture this undertow of unrelenting pessimism—whose only relief, as Schopenhauer had indicated earlier, may come from art and aestheticism:

> There is a—let us say—a machine. It evolved itself (I am severely scientific) out of a chaos of scraps or iron and behold!—it knits. I am horrified at the horrible work and stand appalled. I feel it ought to embroider—but it goes on knitting. You come and say: "this is all right; it's only a question of the right kind of oil. Let us use this—for instance—celestial oil and the machine shall embroider a most beautiful design in purple and gold." Will it? Alas no. You cannot by any special lubrication make embroidery with a knitting machine. And the most withering thought is that the infamous thing has made itself; made itself without thought, without conscience, without foresight, without eyes, without heart. It is a tragic accident—and it has happened. You can't interfere with it. The last drop of bitterness is in the suspicion that you can't even smash it. In virtue of that truth one and immortal which lurks in the force that made it spring into existence it is what it is—and it is indestructible!
>
> It knits us in and it knits us out. It has knitted time, space, pain, death, corruption, despair and all the illusions—and nothing matters. I'll admit however that to look at the remorseless process is sometimes amusing.

And three weeks later, Conrad wrote a variation on the above:

> The mysteries of a universe made of drops of fire and clods of mud do not concern us in the least. The fate of a humanity condemned ultimately to perish from cold is not worth troubling about. If you take it to heart it becomes an unendurable tragedy. If you believe in improvement you must weep, for the attained perfection must end in cold, darkness and silence. In a dispassionate view the ardour for reform, improvement, for virtue, for knowledge, and even for beauty is only a vain sticking up for appearances as though one were anxious about the cut of one's clothes in a community of blind men. Life knows us not and we do not know life—we don't know even our own thoughts. Half the words we use have no meaning whatever and of the other half each man understands each word after the fashion of his own folly and conceit. Faith is a myth and beliefs shift like mists on the shore; thoughts vanish; words, once pronounced, die; and the memory of yesterday is as shadowy as the hope of tomorrow—only the string of my platitudes seems to have no end. As our peasants say: "Pray, brother,

forgive me for the love of God". And we don't know what forgiveness is, nor what is love, nor where God is. Assez.

Conrad could write this way only to Graham, Don Quixote reborn, who fought privilege and sought social justice. Conrad was himself compassionate but disdained men who lost sight of their universal situation while they pursued individual gain, or even hope. Accepting the nineteenth-century scheme of the universe as a machine, yet lacking Victorian religious hope as a way of ameliorating that mechanistic view, he could, like Hardy and the very naturalists whose art he abhorred, only show the universe as malevolent, or at best schemingly neutral.

While the correspondence with Graham and the writing of the Preface called him to empyrean patterns, the present was more prosaic: he had to do something about *The Rescue*, which was sinking him. On August 28, he laid out a proposal for Blackwood to look over the manuscript with an eye toward serialization only, since book publication was promised to Heinemann. Conrad indicates the book will be advanced by November and finished "by the end of Jan^ry^ 1898." Blackwood told him to send it on. *The Rescue* was not, of course, moving along as he had told Blackwood, and "The Return" was also stalled—"worried [he informed the publisher] almost to extinction by a short story I've been trying to write for the last three months."

A good deal of Conrad's difficulty with these stalemated works was, apparently, that he was caught at the conjunction of several literary styles. He was, in effect, trying to put his energies into at least three distinct modes. In *The Rescue* (on September 6, the new title became official) he was writing, as we have noted, in a romantic mode, somewhat characteristic of the style of his two earliest novels, with a setting from the Malay-Borneo area, and a character, Lingard, who fitted only in a lush prose. In "The Return," which grew to novella length, he was moving toward a somewhat leaner, more suggestive prose, away from his "jungle language." His models seemed to be Ibsen (*A Doll's House*) and a modified naturalism. In *The Nigger*, he had turned to a more "natural" style, though without the irony that would become characteristic of his middle career. We can even speak of a fourth style, that of the Preface, with its heavy indebtedness to aestheticism, its post-Wagnerian rhythms, its appeal to the sensuous, the emotional, the intuitive.

His artistic progress was impeded by a lack of clarity of purpose, by a failure to have achieved the correct mode of expression. For a man whose shaping of English depended on accommodating himself to a learned language, the matter of style, as he had recognized, was paramount: style, individual words, idiom, tone, colors, voice, textures. If we borrow the idiom of the structuralists, he had mastered the diachronic or historical flow of the language, but the paradigmatic or synchronic aspect—the full potentiality of sound and meaning—still escaped him. Such matters had to be resolved, and would be, in the years 1899 to 1904. Meanwhile, he wrote to Blackwood his plan for *The Rescue*, a scheme that would have made perfect sense for Conrad at a different stage of his career. The outline is long, but worth repeating:

—The situation "per se" is not new. Consequently all the effect must be produced in the working out—in the manner of telling. This necessity from my point of view is fascinating. I am sure you will understand my feeling though you may differ with me in the view. On the other hand the situation is not prosaic. It is suitable for a romance. The human interest of the tale is in the contact of Lingard the simple, masterful, imaginative adventurer with a type of civilized woman—a complex type. He is a man tenacious of purpose, enthusiastic in undertaking, faithful in friendship. He jeopardizes the success of his plans first to assure her safety and then absolutely sacrifices them to what he believes the necessary condition of her happiness. He is troughout [sic] mistrusted by the whites whom he wishes to save; he is unwillingly forced into a contest with his Malay friends. Then when the rescue, for which he had sacrificed all the interests of his life, is accomplished he has to face his reward—an inevitable separation. This episode of his life lifts him out of himself; I want to convey in the action of the story the stress and exaltation of the man under the influence of a sentiment which he hardly understands and yet which is real enough to make him as he goes on reckless of consequences.

If we break in, we note how close this formulation is to Willems's situation in *An Outcast*, and yet evidently Conrad was striving for something grander and more ambitious. What held him back was not the idea, which even has tragic potentialities implicit within it, but the right frame of reference and the correct tone-language-rhythms, which he could not discover. He continues:

It is only at the very last that he is perfectly enlightened when the work of rescue and destruction is ended and nothing is left to him but to try and pick up as best he may the broken thread of his life. Lingard—not the woman—is the principal personage. That's why all the first part is given up to the presentation of his personality. It illustrates the method I intend to follow. I aim at stimulating vision in the reader. If after reading the *part 1*st you don't *see* my man then I've absolutely failed and must begin again—or leave the thing alone. Of course the paraphernalia of the story are hackneyed. The yacht, the shipwreck, the pirates, the coast—all this has been used times out of number; whether it has been done, that's another question. Be it as it may I think rightly or wrongly I can present it in a fresh way. At any rate as I wish to obtain the effect of reality in my story and also wanted the woman—that kind of woman—there was no other way to bring her there but in the time-honoured yacht. Nothing impossible shall happen.

That final line indicates how sharply Conrad felt he had broken with traditional romantic literature. Yet the very rhythms of *The Rescue* belie the intention; the prose itself points to the high road of rhetorical flourish. Our first introduction to Lingard is not promising for a man with a "tragic flaw," nor is the description of his brig:

> To him she was as full of life as the great world. He felt her live in every motion, in every roll, in every sway of her tapering masts, of those masts whose painted trucks move forever, to a seaman's eye, against the clouds or against the stars. To him she was always precious—like old love; always desirable—like a strange woman; always tender—like a mother; always faithful—like the favourite daughter of a man's heart.

At the time Conrad put the manuscript aside, although he picked at it for years, its conflicting styles and tones discouraged any single line of development. In 1919, as we have seen, he was to revive his hopes for the now-completed novel and write to Pinker that he felt it might catch the eye of the Nobel Prize Committee. It was, he said, "in its concentrated colouring and tone" the "swan song of Romance as a literary art."

Blackwood, as we know, rejected any plan for his magazine to serialize the novel, since its book form was promised to another firm, Heinemann. In a guarded letter to Conrad (on October 28), he praised the first part and advised him to come to some arrangement with Heinemann so that he, Blackwood, would have clear title to it. In return, Conrad indicated he felt a "moral obligation" to Heinemann, although not legally bound to him. Beneath both sides, one hears dissenting voices: Blackwood's, not being overly happy with the manuscript thus far, and Conrad's, seeking a way to break with Heinemann despite that moral commitment.

CHAPTER 18

Holding On

CAUGHT up by two works that did not satisfy him or others, Conrad wrote Garnett in a tone with a subsurface of annoyance. "The fact is my dear fellow your criticism, even when most destructive, is so shamelessly adulatory that I simply *can't* live without it. As a matter of fact it's about all I have to live upon." Meanwhile, the title of the collection of stories was established as *Tales of Unrest*, promised to Unwin, and of course without *The Nigger*. Conrad was still trying to sell "The Return," for which he had a "physical horror" and which "embittered five months" of his life. Withal, he tried to defend the story against Garnett's attack upon it, asserting that "if I have to explain that to you—to you!—then I've egregiously failed." Conrad concluded that his fate was "to be descriptive and descriptive only."

Early in October (the second), he wrote in French a very candid letter to the Baroness Janina de Brunnow, one of the Taube sisters from his Cracow days. Without embellishment, he describes his situation as a writer and an artist:

> I have been married now almost 18 months; and since then I have worked uninterruptedly. I have some reputation—literary—but the future is anything but certain, for I am not a popular author and probably I never will be. That does not sadden me at all, for I have never had the ambition to write for the all-powerful masses. I haven't the taste for democracy—and democracy doesn't have any taste for me. I have gained the appreciation of a few select spirits and I do not doubt I will be able to create for myself a public, limited it is true, but one which will permit me to earn my bread. I do not dream of fortune; besides it is not within an inkwell that one finds it. But I confess to you I dream of peace, a little reputation, and the rest of my life devoted to the service of Art and free from material worries. Now, dear Madame, you have the secret of my life.

The remainder of the letter is a journey through nostalgia. Uncle Tadeusz is mentioned, and then the Baroness's four brothers, all of whom along with Conrad had formed a band, with the latter reputedly in love with Janina. Conrad's long letter, in response to hers, reminds us, as it apparently reminded him, of the bizarre nature of his situation: the Pole, with all his memories of the past, writing in French to a possible "childhood love" of his beginning career as an English novelist seeking an audience whose very tastes he deplored.*

Even in his Note to the Collected Edition of *Tales of Unrest,* Conrad spoke of "The Return" as a "left-handed production," and we recognize how much energy was going into simply remaining afloat. Except for sporadic work on *The Rescue,* Conrad was at an impasse as he moved toward his fortieth birthday. His condition seemed hallucinatory: "I feel like a man who can't move [he wrote Garnett], in a dream. To move is vital—it's salvation—and I can't! . . . It's like being bewitched; it's like being in a cataleptic trance." Garnett was his chief supporter during this time; Conrad depended on him as heavily as he had leaned on Bobrowski earlier and as much as he would on Pinker in later years. Neither principal, however, could know that this impasse and ensuing malaise, a typical "breakdown" for Conrad, was characteristic of his way of working.

In mid-October (the fourteenth), Conrad mentioned to Garnett a luncheon meeting with "P and Crane," Pawling and Stephen Crane. The luncheon was to form the basis for a close and warm friendship between Crane and Conrad, one so sympathetic in fact that after Stephen's death Conrad remained on good terms with Cora, whose relationship with the writer was of the kind Conrad ordinarily deplored. Crane had come to England in the summer of 1897, with *The Red Badge of Courage,* published in England at the end of 1895, having been exceptionally well received. When he arrived,

---

* In 1897, Conrad saw his first translation into Polish, of *An Outcast,* in a Warsaw weekly, and it is quite possible he had himself sent on the manuscript, although there appears to be no direct proof. *Lord Jim,* in 1904, would be his first book-text publication in Poland. This would, in fact, be the beginning of a large-scale polemical reaction to Conrad's work in his native country, his reputation fluctuating between condemnation and admiration, glimmerings of which we noted in the Orzeszkowa-Lutosławski attack and defense. In 1922, with Poland reestablished, the official recognition began with an edition of his selected writings, in which Aniela Zagórska enjoyed a major role. With this, Polish critics turned to serious consideration of Conrad's fiction from a moral and philosophical point of view. However, by the mid-1930s, interest in Conrad fell. During the war years the Nazis banned his work—although the banning had the effect of creating renewed interest. Conrad was, in fact, the almost perfect novelist for people suffering under a foreign occupation. After the war, Jan Kott, who later became known in the United States for his radical interpretation of Shakespeare as "our contemporary," attacked Conrad and his work for being antiprogressive and obstructing the development of a socialist mentality. He accused his "countryman" of loyalty to the laws of slaves, of abetting slave mentality. Conrad's reputation seesawed, until by the late 1950s he was no longer viewed solely as an opponent of the socialist state. By now, the resurrection of his reputation has been completed, with a full translation into Polish, supervised by Zdzisław Najder. (See Stefan Zabierowski, *Conradiana,* VI, 3, pp. 197–209; Adam Gillon, "Conrad and Poland," in *Conrad and Shakespeare,* pp. 211–35.)

he wanted to meet Conrad, whose *Nigge*r was beginning to appear in *The New Review.* S. S. Pawling, of Heinemann, Crane's English publisher and also the owner of the *The New Review,* invited Crane and Conrad to luncheon on October 15. The two hit it off, and after Pawling left they tramped for hours through the London streets, stopping for tea and a late supper, discussing Balzac and the *Comédie humaine*—the sensitive and perceptive, but uneducated, American questioning the sophisticated, well-read European. The two parted without exchanging addresses, but Conrad sent Crane an inscribed *Almayer,* and the latter wrote on the eleventh of November (having received proofs of the novel) to praise *The Nigger* as "simply great" and the death of Wait as "too good, too terrible." The first of Conrad's letters in a sequence of over thirty to Cora and Stephen, together or separately, displays sheer pleasure that another craftsman has understood him. Conrad's comments warrant full quotation:

> If I've hit *you* with the death of Jimmy I don't care if I don't hit another man. I think however that artistically the end of the book is somewhat lame. I mean after the death. All that rigmarolle [sic] about the burial and the ships coming home seems to run away into a rat's tail—thin at the end. Well! It's too late now to bite my thumb and tear my hair. When I feel depressed about it I say to myself "Crane likes the damned thing"—and am greatly consoled. What your appreciation is to me I renounce to explain. The world looks different to me now, since our long pow-wow. It was good. The memory of it is good. And now and then (human nature *is* a vile thing) I ask myself whether you meant half of what you said! You must forgive me. The mistrust is not of you—it is of myself: the drop of poison in the cup of life. I am not more vile than my neighbours but this disbelief in oneself is like a taint that spreads on everything one comes in contact with; on men on things—on the very air one breathes.

Three weeks short of forty, Conrad was speaking to a man just turned twenty-six, and yet he could write to him "as though we had been born together before the beginning of things." This was the kind of interlude that made him rejoice, even in his gloom; but meanwhile, events kept intruding. While Crane praised *The Nigger* and Conrad awaited first copies, he was in a sense dealing with past history. The present was not of triumphs but of rejections. "The Return," as if the title were itself prophetic, came back again; no one wanted it. Also, it was not as though Conrad were preparing himself intellectually for a future foray or waiting to strike; he was not reading in any particular area and apparently not disciplining himself. He was waiting for something to happen. His letters in October and November suggest a holding action—comments on Hallam Tennyson's *Memoir* of his father, a defense of those who seek revolutionary change as the result of a strongly held idea, indications of a beginning friendship with David Meldrum of Blackwood's, cursory remarks to Unwin and Ted Sanderson, glimmers of hope that Blackwood will take *The Rescue* even with the Heinemann book rights still vague.

As noted, eight copies of *The Nigger* had been produced in 1897 to secure the copyright, the book itself not appearing until 1898. Then on November 5, Conrad settled that *The Rescue* would go to Heinemann and, therefore, could not be considered by Blackwood's for serialization. Conrad now had only *Tales of Unrest* to look forward to, and that prospect, dimmed by his need to deal with Unwin, was a dead end. His only hold on a publisher of any consistency was Blackwood's and, vaguely, Heinemann over *The Rescue.* These conditions, almost self-imposed, put Conrad in an uncertain position; and even his connection with Garnett was colored by the latter's plans to leave Unwin and move on elsewhere, going first to Heinemann and then to Gerald Duckworth.

In an early November letter to Unwin, Conrad took a new tack, asking his publisher if he would like an entirely unpublished story ("The Return") for the collection, asserting that he thought "it much too good for any blamed magazine." He says he does not want to throw it away "where the *right people* won't see it." The private estimation of the story as dreadful, the public one as something too good to be thrown away: this was not the kind of thing Conrad normally practiced. He was quite candid about his art, but in this instance he evidently needed some sign of external success to regain confidence, especially since on the same day he more or less closed with Pawling over *The Rescue,* £100 for book, £400 for serial rights—for a book he could not write. Impotent before the blank sheet of paper, he fantasized success. On the same day (to Garnett) he refers to Unwin as the "Patron Jew" and says he is done with him, quite a different tone from that in his letter to Unwin offering him the stories. To Blackwood, Conrad had to write to assure him he was staying with Heinemann not for money but to honor a prior commitment: "It was simply a question of fidelity—if I may so express it." In that letter, Conrad indicates he has in mind a "study of a Scotch seaman," very probably an early sketch of MacWhirr of "Typhoon," a story he would write in 1901.

On November 30, Conrad wrote Henry James at De Vere Gardens that he was sending *The Nigger of the "Narcissus,"** which has, he says, "the virtue of being brief." The remainder of the short letter is depreciatory of the novel: "One cannot communicate the poignant reality of illusions." Conrad adds that destiny calls for the dream to end, the words to vanish, and the book to be forgotten. Then, with profound humility before his "Cher Maître," he bows out of the letter. James himself demonstrated uneven taste in Conrad, admiring the early work and showing little appreciation of the

* With its touching motto from Pepys's *Diary:* "My Lord in his discourse discovered a great deal of love to this ship."

major achievements. He nevertheless gave vital support to a Royal Literary Fund grant for Conrad, who desperately needed both the money (£300) and the show of confidence in his work. At that time, in 1902, James called *The Nigger* in his opinion "the very finest and strongest picture of the sea and sea-life that our language possesses—the masterpiece in a whole great class; and *Lord Jim* runs it very close." James continued, to the Fund:

> When I think that such completeness, such intensity of expression has been arrived at by a man not born to our speech, but who took it up, with singular courage, from necessity and sympathy, and has laboured at it heroically and devotedly, I am equally impressed with the fine persistence and the intrinsic success. Born a Pole and cast upon the waters, he has worked out an English style that is more than correct, that has *quality* and ingenuity. The case seems to me unique and peculiarly worthy of recognition. Unhappily, to be very serious and subtle isn't one of the paths to fortune. Therefore I greatly hope the Royal Literary Fund may be able to do something for him.

Yet when Conrad had developed his artistic powers more completely, in *Nostromo*, *The Secret Agent*, and *Under Western Eyes*, James characterized these works as "impossibilities" and "wastes of desolation that succeeded the two or three final good things of his earlier time." *Chance*, which is not vintage Conrad, he attacked slyly in a well-known review, which we will examine in a later chapter. Very possibly, Conrad's "middle period" disturbed James because the Pole was challenging the American on much his own ground, and in *Chance* James found almost a too close imitation of his own later style. Early in their relationship, James had shown Conrad a draft or scenario of *The Wings of the Dove*, an indication that he was truly interested in Conrad the artist and solicited his advice. Nothing like this would recur later, especially after *Nostromo* began the period of "challenge," when Conrad and James were the two premier novelists working in English, not of course known to the general reading public, but certainly to other craftsmen. Arnold Bennett, one of the shrewdest observers of the literary scene, watched Conrad carefully; as did André Gide, who was beginning to note Conrad's work in his Journals.

The presentation of early copies of *The Nigger* was a pleasant episode, reminding Conrad of the potentialities of his calling and temporarily separating him from the financial scramble. He read Crane's stories, on Garnett's recommendation, and found himself excited by "A Man and Some Others" and "The Open Boat." He wrote Crane that he was a "complete impressionist" from whose hands the illusions of life come out without a flaw. "It is not life—which nobody wants—it is art." Four days later, he repeated his estimation of Crane to Garnett.

> His eye is very individual and his expression satisfies me artistically. He certainly is *the* impressionist and his temperament is curiously

> unique. His thought is concise, connected, never very deep—yet often startling. He is *the only* impressionist and *only* an impressionist. Why is he not immensely popular? With his strength, with his rapidity of action, with that amazing faculty of vision—why is he not? He has outline, he has colour, he has movement, with that he ought to go very far. But—will he? I sometimes think he won't. It is not an opinion—it is a feeling. I could not explain why he disappoints me—why my enthusiasm withers as soon as I close the book. While one reads, of course, he is not to be questioned. He is the master of his reader to the very last line—then—apparently for no reason at all—he seems to let go his hold. It is as if he had gripped you with greased fingers. His grip is strong but while you feel the pressure on your flesh you slip out from his hand—much to your own surprise.

Conrad's characterization of Crane's talent is trenchant. By Crane's "impressionism," a term quite slippery in itself, Conrad probably meant that the American writer attempted to gain his artistic effects through a surface technique. That is, he worked through colors, shapes, proportions, balances, and tones as a way of conveying total meaning; ignoring the broader issues of interpretation, analysis, and resolution. Conrad's criticism is of some interest, since *The Nigger* has superficial resemblances to Crane's work, especially to *The Red Badge of Courage*, similarities not at all lost upon early reviewers. W. L. Courtney, of the *Daily Telegraph*, an extremely influential critic, wrote in his review of *The Nigger:*

> Mr. Joseph Conrad has chosen Mr. Stephen Crane for his example, and has determined to do for the sea and the sailor what his predecessor had done for war and warriors. The style, though a good deal better than Mr. Crane's, has the same jerky and spasmodic quality; while a spirit of faithful and minute description—even to the verge of the wearisome—is common to both. If we open any page to *The Nigger of the "Narcissus"* we are told with infinite detail what each one was doing, what the ship was doing, and what sky and sea were doing.

He continues that Conrad builds "up his scenes piece by piece, never by one large and comprehensive sentence, but through a mass of commas, semicolons, and full-stops, especially when it is his business to depict character or narrate incidents. It is in these that the example of Mr. Crane is most obvious and potent upon him."

Courtney was suggesting an impressionism of method: small elements, often mere suggestions, which hint at the whole, not the whole as deductively leading back to details. We can find such resemblances between *The Nigger* and *The Red Badge* in several places, especially in the kind of contrast each uses to develop a passage. For example, at the beginning of Chapter 2, when the *Narcissus* sails from Bombay, Conrad writes of the smooth water which lay "sparkling like a floor of jewels, and as empty as the sky." The juxtaposition of the splendor of jewels with the vacuity of the sky is typical Conradian impressionism, a way of suggesting the lushness of romantic experience only to undercut it with late-nineteenth-century pessimism. In Crane, such juxtaposition suggests ironic contrast between indifferent nature (Conrad's empty sky) and human aspiration, the moving masses of troops. "The sun [Crane writes] spread disclosing rays, and, one by one, regiments burst into view like armed men just born of the earth." For both writers, that surface impressionism permitted them to assert their paradoxical acceptance of nature's determinism and their fierce defense of human values in the face of a mechanical universe.

To go further, however, and emphasize that Conrad "learned" from Crane is nonsense. Conrad was, in 1897, undergoing the kind of artistic development that Crane had himself experienced two years earlier; and Conrad was to pass through this phase of impressionism, just as Crane might have done had he lived beyond the age of twenty-nine. Both *The Red Badge* and *The Nigger* were significant novels in the respective development of their authors; since Conrad lived for another twenty-seven years, we can see *The Nigger*, apart from its intrinsic value, as a stage in that development. He was to move on from his technique here; whereas Crane, with his foreshortened life, simply did not have the opportunity to mature—if he ever would have. Superficially, we have the parallel development of two writers who touch temporarily and tentatively but are otherwise vastly different.

Even at this early date, Conrad had a great desire "to write a play myself," even though plays themselves seemed "an amazing freak of folly." Crane was to importune Conrad to collaborate,* but the latter had to square his sense of dramatic art with art itself. Writing to Graham, he tried to see past the actors to the art they practiced:

> The actors appear to me like a lot of *wrongheaded* lunatics pretending to be sane. Their malice is stitched with white threads. They are disguised and ugly. To look at them breeds in my melancholy soul thoughts of murder and suicide—such is my anger and my loathing of their transparent pretences. There is a taint of subtle corruption in their blank voices, in

---

* The proposal from Crane was that they collaborate on a play with an American Western background. It was, as Conrad related in his introduction to Thomas Beer's *Stephen Crane*, to be called tentatively "The Predecessor," and its general subject consisted in "a man personating his 'predecessor' (who had died) in the hope of winning a girl's heart. The scenes were to include a ranch at the foot of the Rocky Mountains, I remember, and the action, I fear, would have been frankly melodramatic. Crane insisted that one of the situations should present the man and the girl on a boundless plain standing by their dead ponies after a furious ride (a truly Crane touch). I made some objections. A boundless plain in the light of a sunset could be got into a backcloth, I admitted; but I doubted whether we could induce the management of any London theatre to deposit two stuffed horses on its stage" (*Last Essays*, pp. 168–9).

their blinking eyes, in the grimacing faces, in the false light, in the false passion, in the words that have been learned by heart.

Marionettes, however, are different. "Marionettes are beautiful—especially those of the old kind with wires, thick as my little finger, coming out of the top of the head. Their impassibility in love, in crime, in mirth, in sorrow—is heroic, superhuman, fascinating. Their rigid violence when they fall upon one another to embrace or to fight is simply a joy to behold. I never listen to the text mouthed somewhere out of sight by invisible men who are here to day and rotten tomorrow. I love the marionettes that are without life, that come so near to being immortal!"

Marionettes, we recognize, are like characters in a novel, at the beck and call of the author and not subject to fits of temperament or acts of emotional rebellion beyond what their creator desires. That apart, Conrad's interest, even in jesting, in the idea of a play with Crane, whom he hardly knew, indicates his readiness for support. Ford was to come along less than a year later; he was, like Crane, in his mid-twenties. Conrad's desperate need for support is made clear by his willingness to work with someone fifteen years his junior.

The interest in a play continued into the new year, for writing to Crane on January 12, Conrad showed his usual blend of withdrawal and curiosity. Also, Jessie was at term, and he may have felt the need for a radical effort of some sort to divert him from the nervousness and anxiety, as well as distaste, he felt when his routine was upset. He was afraid, he told Crane, that collaboration would be "cheating or deceiving you." Conrad says he has "no dramatic gift," whereas Crane has terseness, a clear eye, and an "easy imagination." Conrad then draws the contrast more sharply:

> My ideas fade—yours come out sharp cut as cameos—they come all loving out of your brain and bring images—and bring light. Mine bring only mist in which they are born, and die. I would be only a hindrance to you—I am afraid. And it seems presumptuous of me to think of helping you. You want no help. I have a perfect confidence in your power—and why should you share with me what then may be of profit and fame in the accomplished task?

Working with Crane, nevertheless, had its compelling side. The American writer did have ideas, he was facile, and he was an adventurer, a type Conrad knew well. Both had spent years running, and both, having lived tangentially, moved naturally to bizarre situations. Also, a collaboration would give Conrad reason to escape the impending doom of an infant (he was to write Garnett: "I hate babies").

> But I want to know [he wrote Crane]! Your idea is good—I am certain. Perhaps you, yourself, don't know how good it is. I ask you as a friend's

> favour to let me have a sketch of it when you have the time and in a moment of inclination. I shall—if you allow me write you *all* I think of it, about it, around it. Then you shall see how worthless I would be to you. But if by any chance such was not your deliberate opinion—if you should really, honestly, artistically think I could be of some use—then my dear Crane I would be only too glad to work by your side and with your lead. And Quien sabe? Something perhaps would get itself shaped to be mangled by the scorn or the praise of the Philistines.

Like Conrad's earlier whaling schemes, the collaboration came to nothing, although he did not drop the idea, writing the next month to Ted Sanderson: "Stephen Crane is worrying me to write a play with him. He won't believe me when I swear by all the gods and all the muses that I have no dramatic gift. Probably something will be attempted but I would bet nothing shall be done." Crane, apparently, had grandiose plans, for he wrote a friend he was thinking of Oscar Hammerstein as the producer for his play; Hammerstein, he said, understood the popular mind better than anyone except "Willie Hearst."

During this jesting and half-serious affair, Conrad was trying to introduce Crane to the Blackwood "family" and obtain for his American friend some affiliation that would provide income for him, a meeting that took place on March 25 at a dinner party with Meldrum, Crane, and Conrad himself. The idea of collaboration with Crane suggests Conrad was desperate for some way to focus his creative energies. Implicit in his imagination was the still vague need to review the past for literary materials; both *Lord Jim* and "Heart of Darkness" would begin to emerge in the spring. But in the dead months of 1897–98, what must have seemed for him a true "winter's tale," he exhumed nothing but the morbid matter of *The Rescue.*

The novel, by now, had taken on a life of its own, but not a vital one; its life was that of a barely breathing body kept alive by a doctor who recognizes futility. Conrad hung on to bits and pieces of things, whether writing, reading, or living. He praised Constance Garnett's translation of Turgenev's *The Torrents of Spring and Other Stories* (1897), after he was presented with a copy. He paid attention to the reviews of *The Nigger* and was especially hurt by the *Daily Mail*'s characterization of it as a disappointment, a work lacking any plot. As if reveling in his failure, he repeated this remark to many people. He corrected proofs of *Tales of Unrest*, a book that now seemed distant and for a publisher who was part of the past. He fell back on *The Nigger*, answering criticisms of it and trying to explain it to Graham and others. It was a support as he struggled to break out of the miasma. And such is the freakishness and unpredictability of the imagination, he was, unknowingly, preparing himself for a great creative surge, one that could carry him for several years into the mainstream of his finest work.

Marguerite Poradowska, Conrad's cousin by marriage and chief correspondent in the early 1890s

Matadi. 18.6.90

Merci! Merci mille fois
chère Tante pour votre bonne
et charmante lettre, venue
à ma rencontre à Boma.
Il n'y a qu'une petite
Tante chérie pour imagi=
ner des si jolies surprises.
Si ça m'a fait plaisir?!
J'ai bien envie de dire
non pour vous punir
de me l'avoir demandé,
pour avoir eu l'air d'en
douter!

Je pars demain
à pattes. Pas d'âne ici
excepté votre très humble
serviteur. Vingt jours de
caravane. La température
très supportable ici et
santé très bonne.
Aussitôt possible
j'écrirai. A présent
je vous embrasse bien
fort et baise les mains
qui a tracé les mots
qui m'ont rendu très
heureux avant-hier.
Votre neveu très aimant
et serviteur dévoué

Conrad.

A letter to Marguerite Poradowska, dated June 18, 1890, from Matadi, in the Congo

The *Roi des Belges*, the steamer which took Conrad to Stanley Falls in 1890

Roger Casement (left) in the Congo. Casement later sought Conrad's help in documenting Belgian cruelty and genocide in the Congo

285

87.

more than justice! I rang the bell before a mahogany door on the first floor and while I waited he seemed to stare at me out of the polished panel, stare with that wide and immense stare embracing, condemning, loathing all the universe — I seemed to hear the whispered cry "Oh! the horror!"

The dusk was falling. ~~I waited~~ had to wait in a lofty drawing room with three long windows from floor to ceiling that were like three luminous ~~column~~ and be-draped columns. The bent ~~legs~~ gilt legs and backs of the furniture ~~gleamed~~ shone in indistinct curves. The tall white marble ~~mantelpiece~~ ~~mantel~~ fire place had a cold and heavy whiteness. A ~~long~~ grand piano stood ~~heavily~~ massively in a corner ~~gleaming darkly~~ with dark gleams on the flat surfaces like a sombre and polished sarcophagus. A ~~door~~ high door opened — closed. I rose.

She came forward ~~in the dusk~~ all in black with a pale head, floating toward me in the dusk. She was in mourning. It was more than a year since his death

The manuscript of "Heart of Darkness," with Kurtz's cry of "Oh! the horror!"

The *Torrens*, on which Conrad sailed as first mate from 1891 to 1893

Jessie George in 1893, and in 1896, the year of her marriage to Conrad

Conrad's "Woman with Serpent," drawn between 1892 and 1894

This little sketch was done by
Joseph Conrad in his rooms
in Willow Road Victoria in
1896. To show me how the girls
for the ballet were engaged.

Conrad's drawing "The Three Ballet Dancers," 1896

Conrad in 1896, the year of his marriage and the publication of *An Outcast of the Islands*

View of Lannion in Brittany, where the Conrads spent their honeymoon in 1896

To
Henry James.

16 Oct.r 1896.

I address You across a vast space invoking the name of that one of Your children You love the most. I have been intimate with many of them, but it would be an impertinence for me to disclose here the secret of my affection. I am not sure that there is one I love more than the others. Exquisite Shades with live hearts, and clothed in the wonderful garment of Your prose, they have stood, consoling, by my side under many skies. They have lived with me, faithful and serene — with the bright serenity of Immortals. And to You thanks are due for such glorious companionship.

I want to thank You for the charm of Your words, the delight of Your sentences, the beauty of Your pages! And, since the book before You has obtained some commendation, (for men have been good to an erring brother) I trust that You will consent, by accepting this copy, to augment the precious burden of my gratitude.

Jph. Conrad.

Signed letter to Henry James, sent October 27, 1896, with a copy of *An Outcast of the Islands*

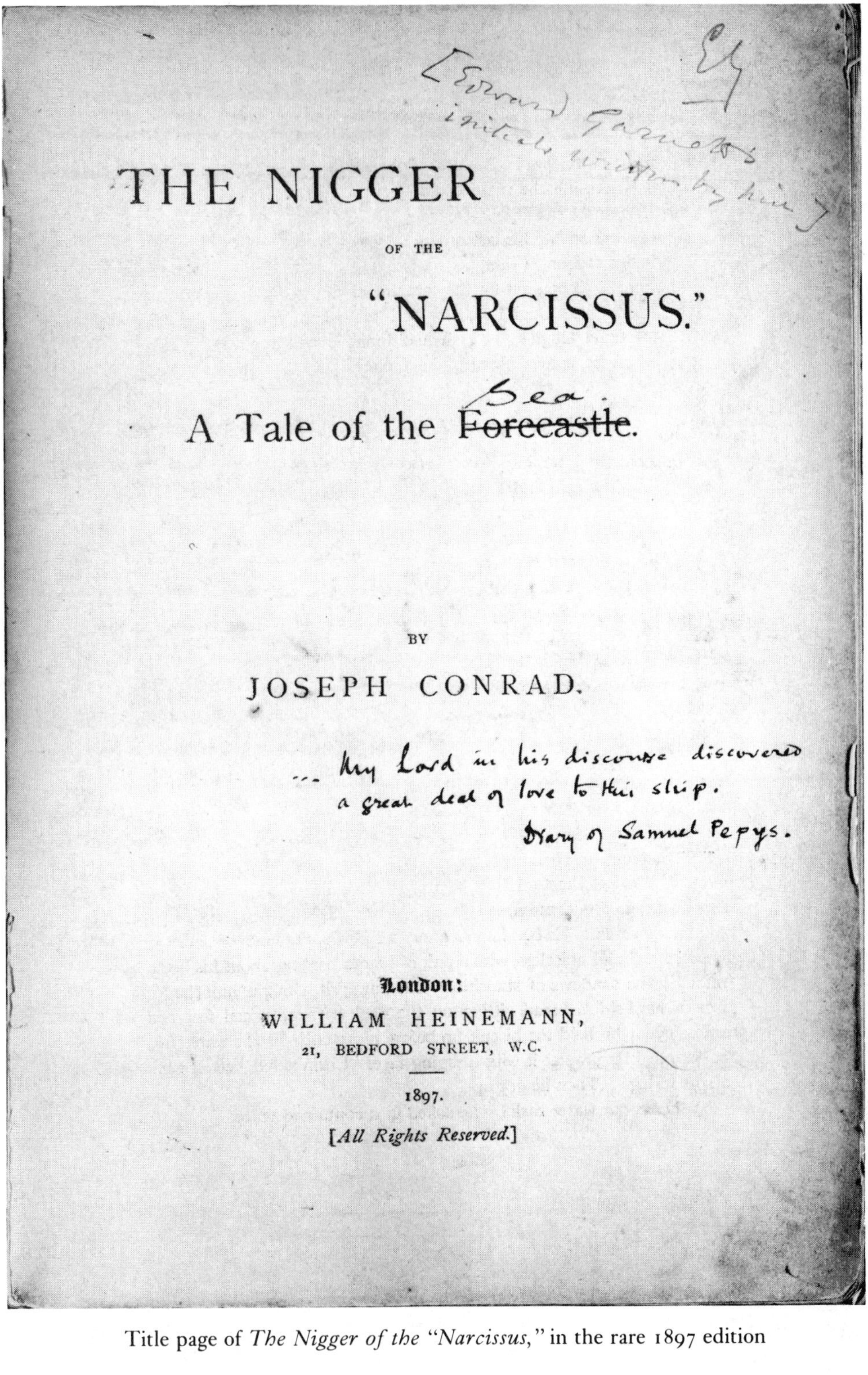

EG

[Edward Garnett's initials written by him]

THE NIGGER

OF THE

"NARCISSUS."

A Tale of the ~~Forecastle~~ Sea.

BY

JOSEPH CONRAD.

... My Lord in his discourse discovered
a great deal of love to this ship.
Diary of Samuel Pepys.

London:

WILLIAM HEINEMANN,

21, BEDFORD STREET, W.C.

1897.

Title page of *The Nigger of the "Narcissus,"* in the rare 1897 edition to our desire of unrest; too seldom to our prejudices, sometimes to our fears, even to our greed — but always to our credulity. And their words are heard with reverence, for their concern is with weighty matters: with the cultivation of our minds and the proper care of our bodies; with the attainment of our ambitions; with the perfection of the means and the glorification of our precious ends. It is otherwise with the artist.

Confronted with the same enigmatical spectacle the artist descends within himself. And in that lonely region of stress and strife if he be deserving and fortunate, he finds the terms of his appeal. His appeal is made to the less obvious capacities, to that part of our nature which because of the warlike conditions of existence is necessarily kept out of sight under the more resisting and hard qualities like the vulnerable body within a steel armour. His appeal is less loud, more profound, less distinct, more stirring — and sooner forgotten. Yet its effect endures for ever. The changing wisdom of successive generations discards ideas, questions facts, demolishes theories. But

A page from the manuscript of the Preface to *The Nigger of the "Narcissus,"* a key document in Conrad's artistic development

At Ravensbrook, Stephen Crane's home, in 1898: Conrad and Jessie in the doorway, Crane holding the black dog, Cora Crane with Borys in her arms

Henry James at Brede Place, in 1899

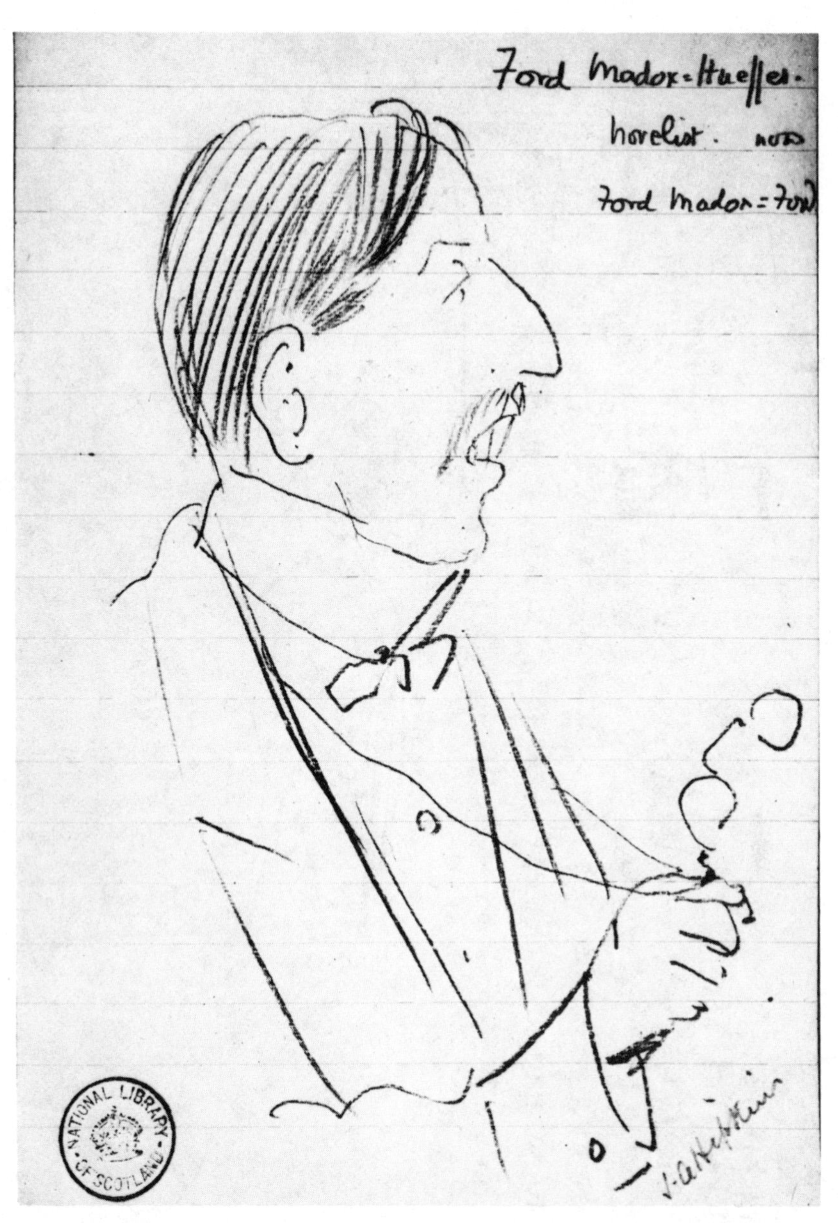

Ford Madox Hueffer (Ford), whom Conrad met in 1898. Sketch by J. A. Hipkins, 1895–96

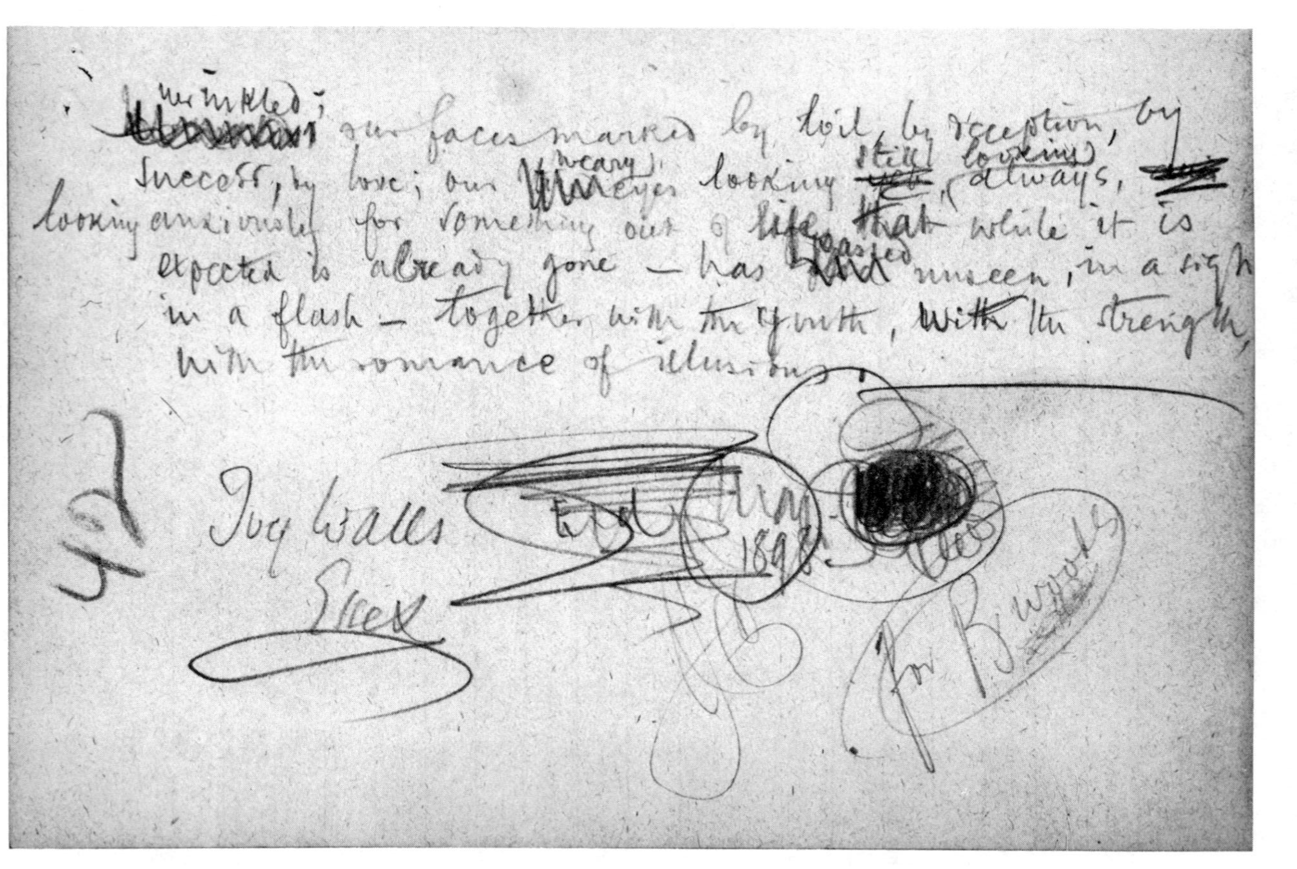

wrinkled; our faces marked by toil, by deception, by success, by love; our weary eyes looking still, looking always, looking anxiously for something out of life, that while it is expected is already gone — has passed unseen, in a sigh, in a flash — together with the youth, with the strength, with the romance of illusions.

Ivy Walls
Essex

End
1898

The final lines of the "Youth" manuscript

335

and cab horse. "I haven't found
a guano island" I said. 'It's
my belief you wouldn't know one
~~if you stood on it for a year~~
~~he riposted swiftly and glared.~~
if you were led up to it' he
riposted quickly. "You got to see
a thing first before you can ~~do~~
~~anything with it~~
~~any good with it~~
make use of it. Got to see it
just its proper size ~~as it is~~ neither more
nor less!" "And make others to see
it too" I said with a marked glance at
the back of the man by
his side. Chester snorted at me. "His eyes
are right enough — don't you worry.
He ain't a puppy." "No" I said. "Come
along captain Robinson" he shouted
deferentially under the rim of the
old man's hat. The holy terror
gave a little jump. They made a
curious pair; Chester
well set up
and portly with a conquering mien
and the other long, wasted, bent and
shuffling his withered shanks desperately,

Manuscript page of *Lord Jim*

near the French border later on. There had been room and to spare for that sort of pike, in the muddy waters, during the last half century. But the waters were clearing, and the good Castro found it safer to seek his impending rope in the Antilles or in Mexico. When inclined for the Grand Manner he would swear that his arm had been cut off at Austerlitz; swear it with a great deal of asseveration, making one see the cuirassiers charging the gunners, being cut down, and his own sword failing suddenly.

Carlos, however, used to declare with affectionate cynicism that the arm had been broken by the cudgel of a peasant while Castro was trying to filch a pig from a stable. . . . "I cut his throat out though," Castro would grumble darkly, "so like that, and it matters very little—it is even an improvement. See, I pull off my hand. See, I transfix you that fly there. . . . See how astonished he was. He did never expect that. . . ." He had actually impaled a crawling cockroach. He spent his days cooking extraordinary messes, crouching for hours over a little charcoal brazier that he lit surreptitiously in the back of his bunk, making substitutes for eternal gaspachos.

All these things, if they deepened the romance of Carlos' career, enhanced also the mystery. I asked him one day, "But why do you go to Jamaica at all if you are bound for Cuba?"

He looked at me smiling gaily.

"Ah, Juan mio," he said, "Spain is not like your England, unchanging and stable. The party who reign to-day do not love me, and they reign in Cuba as in Spain. But in his province my uncle rules alone. There I shall be safe." He was condescending to roll some cigarettes for Tomas, whose wooden hand incommoded him, and he tossed a fragment of tobacco to the wind with a laugh. "In Jamaica there is a merchant, a Don Ramon; I have letters to him, and he shall find me a conveyance to my uncle's town."

He laughed again.

There was certainly some mystery about that town of his uncle's. One night I overheard Carlos say to Castro—

Conrad's proof corrections of *Romance*

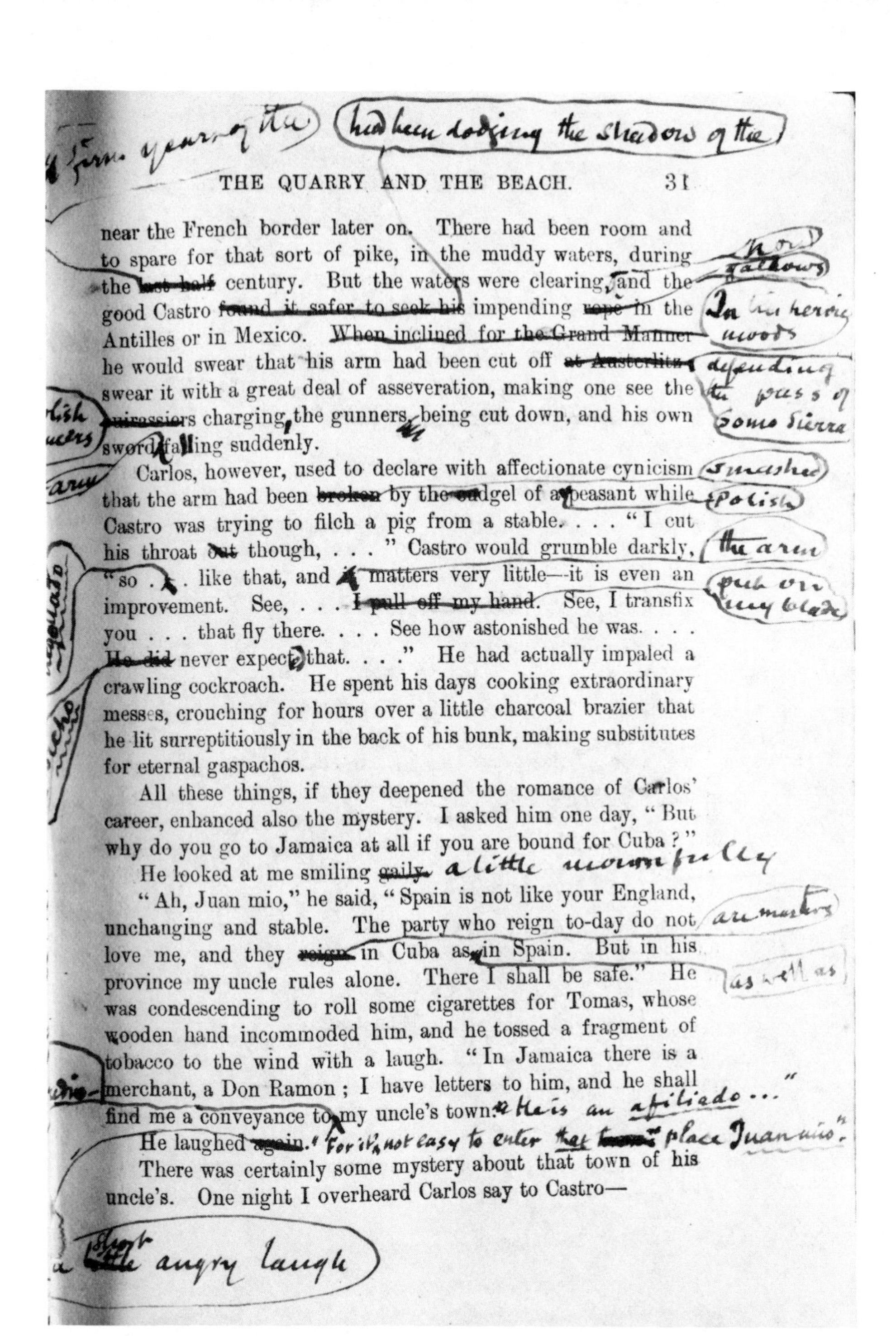

THE QUARRY AND THE BEACH. 31

near the French border later on. There had been room and to spare for that sort of pike, in the muddy waters, during the last half century. But the waters were clearing, and the good Castro found it safer to seek his impending rope in the Antilles or in Mexico. When inclined for the Grand Manner he would swear that his arm had been cut off at Austerlitz, swear it with a great deal of asseveration, making one see the cuirassiers charging, the gunners being cut down, and his own sword falling suddenly.

Carlos, however, used to declare with affectionate cynicism that the arm had been broken by the cudgel of a peasant while Castro was trying to filch a pig from a stable. . . . "I cut his throat out though, . . . " Castro would grumble darkly, "so . . . like that, and it matters very little—it is even an improvement. See, . . . I pull off my hand. See, I transfix you . . . that fly there. . . . See how astonished he was. . . . He did never expect that. . . ." He had actually impaled a crawling cockroach. He spent his days cooking extraordinary messes, crouching for hours over a little charcoal brazier that he lit surreptitiously in the back of his bunk, making substitutes for eternal gaspachos.

All these things, if they deepened the romance of Carlos' career, enhanced also the mystery. I asked him one day, "But why do you go to Jamaica at all if you are bound for Cuba?"

He looked at me smiling gaily.

"Ah, Juan mio," he said, "Spain is not like your England, unchanging and stable. The party who reign to-day do not love me, and they reign in Cuba as in Spain. But in his province my uncle rules alone. There I shall be safe." He was condescending to roll some cigarettes for Tomas, whose wooden hand incommoded him, and he tossed a fragment of tobacco to the wind with a laugh. "In Jamaica there is a merchant, a Don Ramon; I have letters to him, and he shall find me a conveyance to my uncle's town."

He laughed again.

There was certainly some mystery about that town of his uncle's. One night I overheard Carlos say to Castro—

Ford's proof corrections of *Romance*, with many of Conrad's alterations

NOSTROMO.. 1.

Part First
The Silver of the Mine
~~The Isabels~~.

I

Through all the ages of Spanish rule and for many years afterwards the town of Sulaco (the luxuriant beauty of the orange gardens bears witness to its antiquity) had never been anything more important than a coasting port with a petty trade in salt fish and oxhides. The clumsy ~~gets~~ deep sea galleons of the conquerors, that, needing a brisk gale to move at all would lie helplessly becalmed where your modern sailing-

First two pages of the manuscript of *Nostromo*

2

ship built on clipper lines forges ahead on her three-knot way by the mere flapping of her sails, had been barred out of Sulaco by the prevailing calms of its gulf. Some harbours of the earth are made difficult of access by the treachery of sunken rocks and the tempestuous character of their shores: Sulaco seemed to have found an inviolable sanctuary from the temptations of the world in the solemn hush of the deep Golfo Placido as if within an enormous semicircular and unroofed temple open to the ocean, while its walls of lofty mountains remain hidden under the sombre festoonings of

4

now was to avoid a collision with either. Sulaco for him was a railway station, a terminus, workshops, a great accumulation of stores. As against the mob the railway defended its property, but politically the railway was neutral. He was a brave man; and in that spirit of neutrality he had carried proposals of truce to the self appointed chiefs of the popular party the deputies Fuentes and Camacho. Bullets were still flying when he had crossed the plaza on that mission waving above his head a white napkin belonging to the table linen of the Amarilla Club.

He was rather proud of this exploit; and reflecting that the doctor busy all day with the wounded in the patio of the Casa Gould had not had time to hear the news he began a succinct narrative.

...andoned and the Engineer-in-Chief having arranged this truce removed his workmen from the town some hours before.

"I found Fuentes walking up and down a room on the ground floor

4

A heavily revised typescript page of *Nostromo*, Part III

To an unidentified reviewer of *The Nigger*, Conrad wrote one of his rare letters responding directly to a notice; his comments, not unusually, overlap with the Preface, which was being published that month:

> I wrote this short book regardless of any formulas of art, forgetting all the theories of expression. Formulas and theories are dead things, and I wrote straight from the heart—which is alive. I wanted to give a true impression, to present and [sic] undefaced image. And you, who know amongst what illusions and self-deceptions men struggle, work, fail—you will only smile with indulgence if I confess to you that I also wanted to connect the small world of the ship with that larger world carrying perplexities, fears, affections, rebellions, in a loneliness greater than that of the ship at sea.

This part of his task Conrad only obliquely carried out, since mainly we see the *Narcissus* disconnected, except at the very end, from the larger world, a world in miniature that gains its very power from being disconnected. Conrad cannot have it both ways: he cannot insist on the particularity of the work and, at the same time, suggest its symbolical or allegorical quality. Although succeeding works such as "Heart of Darkness" and *Lord Jim* have profound symbolical dimensions, quite consciously so, the very substance of *The Nigger* depends on its rootedness in particulars; and even the presence of Wait, that mythical figure of death, cannot dissipate the individuality of the experience. Conrad continued:

> To you, whose mind will sympathise with my feeling, I wish to disclaim all allegiance to realism, to naturalism and—before all—all leaning towards the ugly. I would not know where to look for it. There is joy and sorrow; there is sunshine and darkness—and all are within the same eternal smile of the inscrutable Maya.

Pursuing an evident attachment to *The Nigger*, intensified surely by his lack of any other creative focus, he answered Graham at length. To his delight, Graham liked the book, but Conrad's joy was brief: "In my mind I picture the book as a stone falling in the water. It's gone and not a trace shall remain." Graham had indicated that Singleton, the semiliterate seaman who is the backbone of the *Narcissus* crew, would be complete if educated. Conrad met this comment with his own view of Graham's social egalitarianism:

> "Singleton with an education." Well-yes. Everything is possible, and most things come to pass (when you don't want them). However I think Singleton with an education is impossible. But first of all—what education? If it is the knowledge how to live my man essentially possessed it. He was in perfect accord with his life. If by education you mean scientific knowledge then the question arises—what knowledge, how much of it—in what direction? Is it to stop at plane trigonometry or at conic sections? Or is he to study Platonism or Pyrrhonism or the philosophy of the gentle

> Emerson? Or do you mean the kind of knowledge which would enable him to scheme, and lie, and intrigue his way to the forefront of a crowd no better than himself? Would you seriously, of malice prepense cultivate in that unconscious man the power to think. Then he would become conscious—and much smaller—and very unhappy. Now he is simple and great like an elemental force. Nothing can touch him but the curse of decay—the eternal decree that will extinguish the sun, the stars one by one, and in another instant shall spread a frozen darkness over the whole universe. Nothing else can touch him—he does not think.

Can you seriously tell such a man to know himself, Conrad asks, when knowing yourself means you will learn "thou art nothing, less than a shadow, more insignificant than a drop of water in the ocean, more fleeting than the illusion of a dream"?

Conrad endeavored to hold on until more profound things began to flow! His pessimism at this time, the period of his letter to Graham characterizing the universe as a gigantic knitting machine, was very possibly tied to Jessie's advanced pregnancy and his realization that, with additional dependents, he had not advanced financially beyond his original starting place. Galsworthy was already laying out small sums to support him, and Graham also offered assistance. None of it was sufficient, and Conrad, during this impasse, was even unable to barter away his future for advances. He continued to seek a command, however halfheartedly he pursued it; and when he solicited Graham's aid here, the Scotsman may have alerted some shipping offices not to offer Conrad a berth for fear he would stop writing if he went to sea. As 1897 closed out and he entered his forty-first year, Conrad pecked away at *The Rescue*, the book looming larger than ever even as its composition became more intractable.

Letters praising *The Nigger* provided momentary gratification, one from Arthur Quiller-Couch sending Conrad in response into an involved analogy between his work and Plato's metaphor of the cave. "It [Quiller-Couch's letter] is a sign that endeavour has come somewhere within sight of achievement, that the thought has cast its shadow upon the wall of the cavern and the discriminating eyes of a fellow captive have seen it pass, wavering and dim, before vanishing for ever." Conrad's years of staring on board ship are repeated in those "wavering and dim" ocular experiences; peering has created its own kind of reality, different in kind and degree from what the layman observes.

Conrad says [to Quiller-Couch] writing in a solitude is almost as great as the solitude of the ship at sea, forgotten by the "great crowd outside." One sails along the margins of existence; then one writes in an isolation almost as intense. The whiteness of sail and blankness of sky become the white sheet, Conrad's equivalent of Mallarmé's "l'Abîme blanchi"—the whitened abyss of "A Throw of the Dice Never Will Abolish Chance," itself a poem about the Artist-Captain who tries to control Death and Fate with his Art. Conrad continues:

> Twenty years of life, six months of scribbling and a lot of fist-gnawing and hair tearing went to the making of that book. If I could afford it I would never write any more—not because I think the book good, but because it is what it is. It does not belong to the writing period of my life. It belongs to the time when I also went in and out of the Channel and got my bread from the sea, when I loved it and cursed it. Odi et amo—what does the fellow [Catullus] say?—I was always a deplorable schoolboy. But I don't hate it now. It has the glamour of lost love, the incomparable perfection of a woman who has been loved and has died—the splendour of youth.

The new year began with an attack upon Unwin. His publisher had given up trying to place "The Return" and was now planning immediate publication of *Tales of Unrest* in order to capitalize on the stir of *The Nigger*, "not caring how he may injure me," Conrad says. "The man is unsafe and I am a fool when dealing with such a type for I can't understand it." Conrad feared that publication of two books at the same time would be fatal; it would confuse the public, throw off the reviewers, and lead to a fatal loss of sales. From Unwin's point of view, Conrad had been a losing proposition, a prestigious item but not a popular one, and his desire to recoup at the expense of Heinemann was clear. Conrad thought Unwin should sit back and wait for sales to materialize; for Unwin, an author was a marketable commodity in a keenly competitive area.

Writing to Garnett about Unwin's impossible behavior, Conrad proposed that the firm of Heinemann, through Pawling, lend him money, with the security of his writing as collateral. He says two parts of *Rescue* are complete, but he will not approach Pawling until the book is half done. He had, by now, somewhat under 30,000 words of a novel he felt would run to 90,000; he would complete another 10–20,000 words before laying out his proposal for borrowing. In reality, he had not one third, but about one sixth, of the completed novel. To Unwin, his objections to early publication of *Tales of Unrest* are in the almost desperate terms of survival:

> . . . my last book the *Nigger* had not as yet its chance. It looks as tho' it would be discussed; and many important reviews have not yet appeared. I had letters about it from various people. I know that even as late as middle Febr^y^ a *causerie* about it shall appear by Quiller Couch in a popular magazine. The book is worth notice as much perhaps by its faults as by its qualities—and I think that *notice* it will get. Now it strikes me that another work of mine launched on its heels, so to speak, won't get its fair value of attention, besides interfering with the sale of the previous work while doing no good, commercially, for itself. I want—and of course you do also—to have the *vol* of short stories, noticed *properly*. They also deserve it. The longer the discussion of the last published book the better

it shall be for its successor. Let the critics have their say about one thing before they begin on another or else they will neglect one of them. Now you may take my word that they won't neglect the *unique* sea tale. They will hate it or praise it—it's all one to me but there will be no conspiracy of silence.

Conrad suggested a late March or early April publication date; Unwin agreed to the latter. In the same letter, Conrad tried to defend "The Return" as not being a "tale for puppy dogs nor for maids of thirteen." "I am not," he said, "in the least ashamed of it." During this mid-winter malaise, Conrad invited Crane to Ivy Walls Farm, saw Galsworthy only infrequently, corresponded with Graham and Garnett. Except for Crane, he remained virtually isolated, using his letters as a means of holding on to the outside world. When he reached such a writing impasse, he did not attempt to dissipate it with socializing, which only further depressed him. He would concentrate, become more nervous and anxious, break down physically, put an emotional burden on Jessie, and then gradually find his way toward some artistic solution. In the spring, he would do just that, starting *Lord Jim* and "Heart of Darkness," writing "Youth," and thus launch himself into a new phase of his career, which ended fifteen years later with the writing and publication of *Victory*.

On the fifteenth of January, Borys, his first son, was born. The birth coincided with, or caused, one of the most depressing periods of Conrad's life. His view of man's role in the universe reached a minimal level; we are, he felt, but flies in the farthest reaches of the cosmos. "Borys" is itself of interest, since the name is surely more Russian than Polish. In a January 21 letter to Mrs. Aniela Zagórska, in Polish, Conrad explained the naming, in the process demonstrating his own discomfort at living under Korzeniowski in an English-speaking country or on English ships. After announcing the birth of Borys on the "17th," he says:

He will be christened in the Chapel of the Cloister of the Carmelites in Southwark (London). [No such record exists.] The principle on which his name was chosen is the following: that the rights of the two nations must be respected. Thus, my wife representing the Anglo-Saxons chose the Saxon name Alfred. I found myself in an embarrassing situation. I wanted to have a purely Slavonic name, but one which could not be distorted either in speech or in writing— and at the same time one which was not too difficult for foreigners (non-Slavonic). I had, therefore, to reject names such as Władysław, Bogusław, Wienczysław, etc., I do not like Bohdan: so I decided on Borys, remembering that my friend Stanisław Zaleski gave this name to his eldest son, so that apparently a Pole may use it. Unless, Aniela dear, you care to suggest a nicer name (and there is still time) please remember that there is a certain Alfred Borys Konrad Korzeniowski, whom I commend to your heart.

By naming his son Borys, Conrad confused the Polish background—since Borys is little used in Poland—and by citing the rest of the name as Konrad Korzeniowski, he both claimed him and disavowed him as a son. Konrad was, of course, Conrad's own baptismal name; but Korzeniowski, which Borys was to become, was no longer Conrad's principal name; he now called himself and signed his books Joseph Conrad. Further, Borys came to call himself a "Conrad"; in a book he wrote late in life, he was Borys Conrad and used this name when he was growing up. Conrad never formally adopted his pen name as his family name (his passport read Korzeniowski), and yet when his second son was born on August 2, 1906, he was named John Alexander Conrad. The second son, by name, was a typical Englishman, whereas the first was caught between national traditions.

As we have observed with Conrad's own names, the act of naming is so intimate, so profoundly personal, it is tempting to scrutinize it as carefully as the subject's sexual profile. The naming of Borys, at its simplest level, indicates the sharp split in Conrad's own mind, the uncertainty as to his own identification as a "Conrad" or a "Korzeniowski," his desire to do the right thing along with a lingering confusion about the past: use of a Russian Christian name and the Polish surname. By the time of John's birth (nicknamed Jack after Galsworthy), Conrad had settled into "Conrad"; his second son was, indeed, English. At a more profound level, his use of names for Borys, we should not forget, was surely attached to his confusion about becoming a father. It was not babies themselves he hated—he turned out to rather like them—but the disruption of his concentration and very likely the loss of Jessie's attention. He had been conditioned by his uncle and other guardians to expect and need adult attention; the birth of Borys led directly to the partial loss of his rights.

CHAPTER 19

"Into the Mouth of Hell"

IN this six-month period, until the appearance of Ford, Conrad demonstrated little hope for himself and even less for mankind. In a letter that, at the very end, would indicate "an infant of male persuasion arrived and made such a row that I could not hear the Postman's whistle," he felt driven to unravel and mock every Graham belief in mankind. The latter had commented on "An Outpost" and on the final scene in particular, where Kayerts's' swollen tongue points at the Managing Director. Conrad tried to defend it as an act of scorn and then questioned whether even scorn matters:

> "Put the tongue out" why not? One ought to really. And the machine will run all the same. The question is, whether the fatigue of the muscular exertion is worth the transient pleasure of indulged scorn. On the other hand one may ask whether scorn, love, or hate are justified in the face of such shadowy illusions. The machine is thinner than air and as evanescent as a flash of lightning. The attitude of cold unconcern is the only reasonable one. Of course reason is hateful—but why? Because it demonstrates (to those who have the courage) that we, living, are out of life—utterly out of it. The mysteries of a universe made of drops of fire and clods of mud do not concern us in the least. The fate of a humanity condemned ultimately to perish from cold is not worth troubling about. If you take it to heart it becomes an unendurable tragedy. If you believe in improvement you must weep, for the attained perfection must end in cold, darkness and silence.

Conrad's final words to Graham are not unlike Tolstoy's "the kingdom of God is within you" and uncannily close to many of his diary entries in his final days of life. On January 21, 1910, as Tolstoy recognized he was dying slowly, he wrote:

> 1. The more definite and decisive one's solutions are to questions about the unknown, about the soul, God, the future life, the more indefinite and indecisive is one's attitude to moral questions, to questions about life.
> 2. There is no more widespread superstition than the notion that man and man's body are something real. Man is only a center of consciousness that receives impressions.

From there, Tolstoy made the leap to faith, to the idea of the soul living also "before life" as well as after death, and on to God; such leaps, whether religious or existential, Conrad could not make. His chief accusation against Graham, in fact, is that the latter has leaped to his ameliorism from a view of man which provides no basis for optimism.

Shortly afterward, on January 23, Conrad once again assaulted Graham's ideas directly, the ferocity (in good humor) of his attack indicating how sharply he felt Graham's position threatened his own. In a sense, he had to resolve Graham's egalitarianism in his own mind before he could undertake that decade of some of the most unrelieved pessimistic fiction ever written, perhaps duplicated only by Kafka's work at a slightly later time, the Pole and Czech moving along parallel lines. Conrad wrote in reference to Graham's article "The Impenitent Thief," which appeared in the January *Social-Democrat* and in which Graham defended an impenitent thief as being more human and dignified than those thieving bankers, solicitors, and confidential agents who after swindling the public seek pardon in the dock.

> You with your ideals of sincerity, courage and truth are strangely out of place in this epoch of material preoccupations. What does it bring? What's the profit? What do we get by it? These questions are at the root of every moral, intellectual or political movement. In the noblest cause men manage to put something of their baseness; and sometimes when I think of You here, quietly You seem to me tragic with your courage, with your beliefs and your hopes. Every cause is tainted: and you reject this one, espouse that other one as if one were evil and the other good while the same evil you hate is in both, but disguised in different words. I am more in sympathy with you than words can express yet if I had a gram of belief left in me I would believe you misguided.

Graham goes wrong, Conrad indicates, in his faith in human nature, that it can be reformed, when even institutions cannot be reformed.

> Your faith will never move that mountain. Not that I think mankind intrinsically bad. It is only silly and cowardly. Now *You* know that in cowardice is every evil—especially that cruelty so characteristic of our civilisation. But without it mankind would vanish. No great matter truly. But will you persuade humanity to throw away sword and shield? Can you persuade even me—who write these words in the fulness of an irresistible conviction? No. I belong to the wretched gang. We all belong to it. We are born initiated, and succeeding generations clutch the inheritance of fear and brutality without a thought, without a doubt, without compunction—in the name of God.

Cowardice as the core of mankind: this paradox (the basis of *Lord Jim*) is at the heart of Conrad's mockery. Neither Calvinist nor Pauline, Conrad disbelieved in everything except that final stage of civilization that rests in each man. How man reaches back to put himself in touch with that civilizing force remains a mystery, *the* mystery. In "Heart of Darkness," whose philosophical superstructure already looms in these remarks to Graham, Conrad speculates that in a mechanical universe—"evolved out of a chaos of scraps of iron"—what is flesh or body, no less soul? The profusion of metallic and mechanical images suggests that resistant objects have superseded softness, flexibility, humanity itself; that, clearly, one is tempted to become an object, tough and durable and unfeeling, in order to survive. If Carlier and Kayerts of "An Outpost" had had more mettle, they would have turned into Kurtz. Yet how does one not become a Kurtz, when, isolated and unsupported, the mechanical universe turns soul and flesh into a metallic object, whether the solidity and color of ivory or, later, the very silver of the mine.

Conrad was to write to Graham, on January 31, that "our refuge is in stupidity, in drunkenness of all kinds, in lies, in beliefs, in murder, thieving, reforming—in negation, in contempt—each man according to the promptings of his particular devil"; if all of these are the pillars on which society must build, what is there left? "There is," Conrad adds, as if Graham may have missed the point, "no morality, no knowledge and no hope; there is only the consciousness of ourselves which drives us about a world that whether seen in a convex or concave mirror is always but a vain and floating appearance." That "consciousness of ourselves"—is this Conrad's mockery of Socrates' "self-knowledge"? These questions are the very ones, of course, he could not answer directly; such responses would come cloaked artistically as Marlow attempts to penetrate the images reflected by concave and convex mirrors. How does Marlow, that good angel, with Conrad hovering over him, create order from the shards of nihilism, negativism, distortion, deception, savagery, and, ultimately, fear and cowardice? While intensified in the Congo, or on board the *Patna*, these are the normal feelings, the "givens," of the world; one does not escape them by withdrawing from the Congo or jumping from the deck of the *Patna*.

The questions haunted Conrad, and he drove relentlessly against Graham's belief that he had the answer in social change, in socialism itself. Conrad could offer only a dubious restraint. Somehow, one must find it within. It is an individual matter, and evidently either one has it or one does not. It is by no means solely a European quality, since Kurtz, that Pan-European, lacks it and the Congolese tribal natives possess it. Restraint, a kind of muscular courage not to do, marks the difference between civilization and capitulation to savagery. Yet where does it come from? How does one obtain it? Does the lack of it always brutalize? Society as constituted means little; only the responsible individual counts. Possibly the individual acquires restraint as the sum total of what he is. Yet, decency, indeed the future of civilized society, hangs in the balance.

In the letter above (for the thirty-first of January), Conrad, with Singleton's fixity of purpose in mind, says that man's consciousness is fatal.

> Egoism is good, and altruism is good, and fidelity to nature would be the best of all, and systems could be built, and rules could be made—if we could only get rid of consciousness. What makes mankind tragic is not that they are the victims of nature, it is that they are conscious of it. To be part of the animal kingdom under the conditions of this earth is very well—but as soon as you know of your slavery the pain, the anger, the strife—the tragedy begins. We can't return to nature, since we can't change our place in it.

Fixed by the Darwinian plan for man and nature, Conrad could not accept any social or societal breakout from determinism and pessimism, except in that inner determination to remain civilized, although one cannot account for its source or predict its application to mankind as a whole.

As though on another planet, Galsworthy, whose attitudes and philosophy were so distant from Conrad's preoccupations, was meanwhile beginning a serious writing career and becoming dependent on his friend to help him make his work marketable. Conrad was caught up by a multitude of trivia. He did not realize how close he was to Grub Street, or how attractive its temporary rewards could be. Forced to respond, he praised Galsworthy's *From the Four Winds* (1897) for its "fidelity to the surface of life—to the surface of events—to the surface of things and ideas. Now this [he continues] is not being shallow. . . . To me you have absolutely touched the bottom and the achievement is as praiseworthy as though you had plumbed the very ocean. It is not your business to invent depths—to invent depths is not art either. Most things and most natures have nothing but a surface." The beauty of this kind of criticism was that Conrad could spin out its opposite just as readily; it is the type of critical prose he developed to deal with writers whom he liked personally but whose work fell outside the (Jamesian) pale.

When we read Conrad's critical response to others' work (whether Galsworthy's, Garnett's, Wells's, even Gide's), we must keep in mind how indifferent he was to anything outside his own concentrated and intensified view of things. As a man Conrad was cordial; as a writer, he was an egomaniac, and he arranged every aspect of his existence so as to maximize the energy he could pump into his own writing. Perhaps this inner timetable was the result of his having come to fiction so late, or it may have been his recognition that his body was declining rapidly and would leave him few opportunities for a leisurely pace.

Before departing from Ivy Walls to spend ten days with the Cranes (beginning February 19), Conrad was disquieted to see a reference to him in

Arthur Symons's notice, in *Saturday Review*, of D'Annunzio's *Trionfo della Morte.* In his comments on Georgina Harding's translation of the D'Annunzio work, Symons commented that the Italian writer, with his background of literature and philosophy, was grounded in the very elements missing in English literature of the present day. He cited Kipling (in *Captains Courageous*) and Conrad (in *The Nigger*) as writers "with great ability of the narrative kind," but lacking in ideas. In an article on Kipling, which he wrote for the *Outlook* (but left unsigned), Conrad attempted to respond to Symons's objections. About all the two books have in common, he would have agreed, was their sea background; philosophically and ideologically, the two novelists were as different as Flaubert and Wells.*

The *Outlook* also printed Conrad's piece on Alphonse Daudet, in the April 9 issue. It was a publication Conrad could only scorn: ". . . its price three pence sterling, its attitude—literary; its policy—Imperialism, tempered by expediency; its mission—to make money for a Jew; its editor Percy Hurd (never heard of him); one of its contributors Joseph Conrad—under the heading of 'Views and Reviews.' " Daudet, nevertheless, had been one of Conrad's favorites, rather inexplicably, and the essay is less an act of criticism than an appreciatory memorial for the author of *Lettres de mon moulin, Fromont jeune et Risler ainé,* and *Sapho,* who had died the previous year. Conrad admits Daudet was not an artist, but, nevertheless, he came "as near the truth as some of the greatest. His creations are *seen.*" Yet interesting as Daudet's creations are, poignant as is their fate, they are "of not the slightest consequence." Conrad refused the last stages of puffery and insisted on his own view: that one's creations must be seen *and* of consequence.

Pawling, meanwhile, was still working to place *The Rescue.* The Heinemann editor tried to find space in *Scribner's Magazine,* but it was full for 1898 and 1899, with Barrie's *Tommy and Grizel* carrying through most of 1900; there was some irony in Barrie blocking Conrad. The latter's view of the marketplace was fully substantiated. As though in another world, Karol Zagórski, Conrad's second cousin once removed, had died on January 19, and Conrad wrote, in Polish. He called Zagórski "the man most akin to me in thought and by blood—after my Uncle, who took the place of my parents." Then, in French, Conrad in real sadness at the passing of an old, almost invisible order wrote: ". . . during painful moments the thought that there

* Symons's remarks on D'Annunzio were, in any event, exaggerated, since the Italian's so-called philosophy was of the most shallow kind and probably tempting to Symons at this time because of his immersion in his symbolist studies. In his dedication to Yeats of this collection of essays, in 1899, Symons referred to Yeats's Irish literary movement as one expression of the symbolist movement; and to Gabriele D'Annunzio as an Italian symbolist. Given this stretching of the term to fit anyone new or different, it is remarkable that Symons failed to see in Conrad a natural heir to this tradition, with *The Nigger* no small representative.

would be a day when I could reveal to him my entire life and be understood—this thought was my greatest consolation. And now this hope—the most precious of all—is extinguished for ever." Conrad indicates how close he feels to Aniela and to her two daughters, Angele and Karola, the former of whom (now seventeen) was to become the chief translator into Polish of this whole early phase of his fiction: *Almayer's Folly*, "Youth," *Lord Jim*.

As the visit to Crane approached, for the nineteenth of February, Conrad's system cranked up: anxiety, unsettled nerves, and general physical ailments. He looked forward to seeing Crane, but he dreaded the interruption; it was as though he were taking a vacation after months of malaise. He writes to Crane he will bring "a lot of paper," apparently for their collaboration on what Crane called "a new kind of play."* He announces to all his friends he is "beastly seedy—nerve trouble—a taste of hell." He tells Graham: "I *suspect* my brain to be yeast and my backbone to be cotton." His description of bodily changes looks forward to his period of "transformation," when he would reshape himself for a new kind of creative life. While his imagination was still sluggish, his body foretold of the changes that would come, however painfully.

A sudden boost was Pawling's news that he had sold the serial rights to *The Rescue* to S. S. McClure, in New York, for £250, with £100 on account. Delivery date was July, when in actuality *The Rescue* would be far from his mind as he worked on *Lord Jim* and "Heart of Darkness." These advances, incidentally, were not small amounts for the time and not at all discouraging for a writer who sold in the hundreds, not the thousands. The sale to McClure involved a purchasing power in current money of about $4,000. Conrad's difficulty was not in the sums he obtained as advances and for serial rights but in the slowness of his production, usually no more than 1,500 to 2,000 words a week.

On March 4, the Conrads returned home, having gone from the Cranes at Ravensbrook, in Surrey, to the Garnetts', a few miles away at the Cearne in Limpsfield. Some further social activity followed, with a London visit for the Meldrum-Crane luncheon, on March 25, and previous to that, a dinner on the nineteenth at Ravensbrook. At that latter event, Crane proposed he and Conrad work on a story called "The Predecessor," a "dead-sure thing," he called it. Nothing came of that, or, as we saw, of Crane's earlier proposal for

* Professor Norman Sherry speculates that Conrad took with him not an idea for a play but notes that he had made for a project based on the Siege and Fall of Paris, 1870–71. Sherry discovered these notes, dated "12th Febr. 1898," during a visit to G. F. W. Hope's grandson, the Reverend Charles Dobree. Conrad's jottings, as Sherry points out, appear to be a summary of his reading in historical accounts of the siege, perhaps in those by Henry Labouchere. Conrad was, of course, alert to a collaboration, whether with Crane or Ford, but it is impossible to be certain what use, if any, he planned to make of these notes (see TLS, 25.6.70).

collaboration on a play; but the shifting interest Conrad demonstrated in taking up with Crane suggests he was ready for a more stable collaborator, who would come along shortly in Ford.

Like so much other social activity, however, this burst was the source more of anxiety than of pleasure. It was as if Conrad's imagination were in his nerve endings alone, bypassing the brain, and those nerves would trigger all kinds of ailments, which would act as transforming agents. On March 29, as he was poised to begin something—anything—he wrote a desperate letter to Garnett, demonstrating possibly a more hopeless state of mind than any since his suicide attempt twenty years earlier. The difficulty was, ostensibly, over the *Rescue* manuscript—"I sit down religiously every morning, I sit down for eight hours every day—and the sitting down is all. In the course of that working day of 8 hours I write 3 sentences which I erase before leaving the table in despair. There's not a single word to send you." Meanwhile, McClure waits—"not to speak of Eternity for which I don't care a damn." The continuing temptation to get into Grub Street journalism and scribbling must have been tremendous, for he had no other resources except these advances and occasional loans from friends, Galsworthy, Graham, Joseph Spiridion, later Ford.

He wonders if he is the victim of the "jettatura," the evil eye.

> I assure you—speaking soberly and on my word of honour—that sometimes it takes all my resolution and power of self control to refrain from butting my head against the wall. I want to howl and foam at the mouth but I daren't do it for fear of waking that baby and alarming my wife. It's no joking matter. After such crises of despair I doze for hours till half conscious that there is that story I am unable to write. Then I wake up, try again—and at last go to bed completely done-up. So the days pass and nothing is done. At night I sleep. In the morning I get up with the horror of that powerlessness I must face through a day of vain efforts.

Conrad then moves to questions of style.

> I seem to have lost all *sense* of style and yet I am haunted, mercilessly haunted by the *necessity* of style. And that story I can't write weaves itself into all I see, into all I speak, into all I think, into the lines of every book I try to read. I haven't read for days. You know how bad it is when one *feels* one's liver, or lungs. Well I feel my brain. I am distinctly conscious of the contents of my head. My story is there in a fluid—in an evading shape. I can't get hold of it. It is all there—to bursting, yet I can't get hold of it no more than you can grasp a handful of water.

Painful as it might be, this dissociation of his observing power from his imaginative function—"I feel my brain"—would foreshadow his creation of Marlow. The latter would, as narrator, stand outside Conrad's direction, and yet, as persona, would be privy to his creator's every wish.

Conrad informed Garnett that, having cut out several paragraphs of *The*

Rescue, he is attempting to incorporate the latter's remarks into his corrections of Part II. But real alterations would not be forthcoming. Meanwhile, he says he has to plug along because whatever the final book looks like, the serial "must go anyhow. I would be thankful to be able to write anything, anything, any trash, any rotten thing—something to earn dishonestly and by false pretences the payment promised by a fool."

Ted Sanderson married Helen Watson at this time, and the couple invited their dear friend to the wedding. Conrad genuinely liked the Sandersons—their hopefulness and courage, their belief in England and themselves, their attempts to lead a normal life and do the right thing, all the questions and issues he was usually so cynical about—but the idea of facing a celebration in his present state was abhorrent. Pleading the "despotism of the baby," his own wretched health, and the needs of his work, he declined the invitation. He added that his "sour face" and his "constitutional melancholy," the visage and soul of the Ancient Mariner, would make him an apposite wedding guest, when "all the omens should speak of unalterable serenity, and peace, and joy."

Conrad began to split into pieces, and one result was the emergence of Charley Marlow, a middle-aged seaman. Conrad's route toward the discovery of Marlow is mysterious; we really do not know precisely how or why he came to depend on this figure. Nevertheless, his next three works all used Marlow in varying degrees of dependency: "Youth," "Heart of Darkness," and *Lord Jim*, with the Marlow of the Congo story a key to the reading and understanding of it. How can we account for Conrad's movement toward a doubling figure as a way out of his impasse and malaise? Part of this question will be answered in the next section, on the development of his imaginative powers; here, we can suggest that with his stress on mirrors, reflections, the *Narcissus* and narcissistic images, he was already moving along, however subconsciously, toward a sense of himself as two. The use of Marlow, further, provided a support, an object beyond the destructive personal process. For even as "The Rescuer" manuscript turned into *The Rescue*, so Conrad was seeking a rescuer, financially and literarily. Lacking a sibling, an intimate, or a wife his intellectual equal, he created a puppet, a Sancho Panza to his Don.

None of this internal transformation appears in his letters before May 18, when he writes Garnett that only a "ridiculously small quantity of the *Rescue* has been done," an indication, very possibly, he had moved to another project. Meanwhile, in April, he wrote a review of Hugh Clifford's *Studies in Brown Humanity*, based on Clifford's experiences as governor of Malaya. The review, published in the *Academy* for April 23, began a friendship and correspondence between Clifford and Conrad that continued for most of the latter's life, despite severe doctrinal and ideological differences between the two men. The review is of interest for Conrad's distinction between a book focusing on literal truth (Clifford's studies) and a book that handles the same material artistically (Conrad's own Malayan "studies"): ". . . to apply artistic standards to this book would be a fundamental error in appreciation. Like faith, enthusiasm, or heroism, art veils part of the truth of life to make the rest appear more splendid, inspiring, or sinister." At the same time, Conrad rejected an offer from the *Academy* that he review Crane's *The Open Boat and Other Stories*, saying the connection between the two had been too close and any words of appreciation from him would be suspect.

On May 28, Conrad suddenly announced a whole new creative life for himself. The inner surge had finally arrived as words on blank sheets of paper. First he indicates he has sold the "sea thing" to Blackwood for £35, by which he means "Youth," written in part by this time and to be completed by June 3. He then moves into the major news, that McClure is anxious to have a volume of short stories from him: "I think *Jim* (20.000) Youth (13.000) A seaman (5.000) Dynamite (5.000) and another story of say 15.000 would make a volume for B here and McC there." *Jim* is, of course, *Lord Jim*, which originated as a short story or novella; "A seaman" has not been identified; and "Dynamite" was apparently an early title for what later became *Chance*. Conrad would refer to it again, as the "Dynamite ship story" in a 1905 letter to Pinker. The burst of activity lays out several years of work for Conrad; at hand the early completion of "Youth" and the beginning of *Lord Jim*, far in the future *Chance*.

The rush of activity was to increase considerably when Conrad decided to collaborate with Ford Madox Hueffer (Ford), whom he probably had already met in mid-May.* The order of composition was probably as follows: a start on *Lord Jim*, as a long story; then, having put it aside, work on "Youth," with rapid progress; sporadic attention to *The Rescue*, which, inexplicably, was promised for the fall; then, sometime in later summer or early fall, beginning of "Heart of Darkness," also promised for the fall. With the collaboration fixed in later fall, Conrad began to think, additionally, of Ford's "Seraphina," which was to become their collaborative effort *Ro-*

* Although a September meeting with Hueffer is usually cited, we find three earlier 1898 Conrad letters with the Pent Farm letterhead on them, for May 17 to Clifford, for June 28 to Galsworthy, and for August 10 to Meldrum. The Pent had been rented to the Hueffers since October 15, 1896. Although the property was let during May 1898—while Ford and Elsie lived at Gracie's Cottage on the High Chart near Limpsfield—it is quite possible the Hueffers returned while Conrad was a guest of the Garnetts at the Cearne. If so, Ford and Conrad met in mid-May. If not, there is the difficulty of accounting for the Pent Farm stationery in Conrad's possession. Jean-Aubry, in his second biography of Conrad, *The Sea Dreamer*, placed the initial meeting in February, at Ravensbrook, when Conrad visited Stephen Crane (p. 232). There is no way to prove or disprove this dating, except that Jean-Aubry's memory, like Conrad's and Jessie's, often played him false.

mance; and then to devote some time to *The Inheritors*, which was mainly Ford's work. The period became a crazy quilt of conflicting styles and modes, of varying kinds of demands on his time. This was apparently the way Conrad worked best—in turmoil, with hysteria close to the end of his pen.

To Meldrum, on June 4, he sent eighteen pages of *Jim*, the beginning of what he thought would eventually be 20–25,000 words, for two numbers of "Maga" (*Blackwood's Magazine*). Then in a June 7 letter to Garnett, Conrad indicates he will stick with *The Rescue*, put aside *Jim* until at least September, and let Blackwood and Meldrum discuss the short stories. *The Rescue*, he repeats, makes him miserable and frightens him: "I have lost all sense of form and I can't see *image*. But what to write I *know*. I have the action only the hand is paralysed when it comes to giving expression to that action." Conrad began to receive payment for *Jim*, £5 on account.

Inexplicably, given his attention to more weighty matters, Conrad wrote a short piece on the novelists Marryat and Cooper for the *Outlook* (June 4 issue). In a sense, he was honoring the early influence of both on his thought and work; he had in mind the Cooper not of Leatherstocking but of his sea tales. Both Marryat and Cooper, he says, had faulty technique, but they were true to their own vision. However, aside from noting their importance in his own development—Marryat's "youthful glamour" and "headlong vitality" and Cooper's "profound sympathy" and artistic insight—he had little to say. Such essays were left-handed productions to earn a few pounds.

Conrad was beginning to work well, and more rapidly. Although he told Garnett he was continuing with *The Rescue*, he was evidently moving along on *Jim*. In a letter to Galsworthy (which we can date as June 28), Conrad indicates: "Jim takes his time to come out but it never stops for long." He had not put *Jim* aside for any length of time; *its* writing now, not *The Rescue*, became the thread holding together his creative life. In that same letter to Galsworthy, Conrad disclosed that "Hueffer has been here inquiring with quite an anxiety," the "here" referring to Pent Farm, where the Conrads would not move until October 26. Not only does this letter pinpoint an earlier meeting date, it also suggests a certain familiarity with Ford; the language does not indicate an initial meeting. If indeed these facts are so, then Conrad's burst of creative energy, which began in May-June, can be attributed partially to his introduction to Ford as early as mid-May and the confidence he gained from the offer of some kind of support. Talk of collaboration would come later.* Stephen Crane, we know, was away in Cuba, and the opportunity for collaboration with him, however uncertain it was at best, had vanished.

---

* Ford's words in *A Personal Remembrance* suggest a lapse of time between the meeting and the actual collaboration: "So the writer left Limpsfield [Gracie's Cottage] and

Even more incredibly, amid this creative vitality,* Conrad was corresponding with Graham about returning to sea. This had been a minor motif in his letters dating back to January 31; but now, at the end of June or in early July, the enterprise was revisited in earnest. Through Graham, Conrad was put into touch with Sir Francis Evans of the Union Line, and, at the same time, he hoped to obtain the recommendation of Sir Donald Currie of the Castle Line, which operated Scottish ships. According to Graham's biographer, A. P. Schiffely, as noted above, Graham called at various Scottish shipping offices "where he told his friends, the directors, that he would soon introduce a certain Polish sea-captain to them, and he asked them on no account to give him employment, for, should they do so, he assured them that a great writer would be lost to the world." This may or may not have occurred, since Graham left for Morocco on September 8. In any event, Conrad went forward to an interview with Evans and wrote Graham:

> I've seen Sir Francis Evans this morning [July 19]. He was full of business with twenty people waiting for an interview, but he received me at once and was kindness itself. The upshot of it is this: It is of course impossible to place me in the Union Line—I said I did not even dream of such a thing but explained that I thought he might have some tramp or good collier. The Company he said owns no tramps or colliers but he might hear of something of the kind and in such a case would let me know." [sic]—He has my card but my address is not on it. Perhaps you

---

returned to the Pent Farm. A complete veil dropped between himself and Conrad. And then suddenly came the letter at whose reading the robin attended. The writer had indeed roared at Limpsfield. Obviously he had told Conrad the story of John Kemp–Aaron Smith ["Seraphina"], for Conrad asked him to consider the idea of a collaboration over that story—which Mr. Garnett had told him was too individual ever to find even a publisher. It would otherwise have been an impertinence on the part of Conrad. And Conrad was never impertinent. His politeness even to his grocer was always Oriental."

---

* So that we do not think Conrad proceeded in linear fashion toward productivity and achievement untroubled by doubts, we need only follow his letters. On June 15, in the midst of his creative surge, he wrote to Graham in French, the language of *Les Philosophes.* The comments are worth repeating. "There are none converted to ideas of honor, justice, compassion, liberty. There are only those who, without knowing, understanding, or feeling, exist on words, repeat them, shout them—without believing in anything but gain, personal advantage, satisfied vanity. And words vanish, and nothing remains, do you understand? Absolutely nothing, of foolish man! Nothing. A moment, a wink of the eye and nothing remains—only a drop of mud, cold mud, dead mud launched in black space, turning around an extinguished sun. Nothing. Neither thought nor sound nor soul. Nothing." There is a good deal of nineteenth-century science or technology in those remarks—the sense of entropy, of a dying universe turning increasingly colder—but the crux of it is Conrad's own cynicism about human nature and the potentialities of reform. He is writing this to Graham, and the intensity of his negativism is explained by the counterintensity of Graham's reforming spirit.

would drop him a line pour l'entretenir dans la bonne voie and mention where I live. —He said he would be "extremely pleased to do anything for a friend of Mr. Cunninghame Graham." Thereupon I salaamed myself out and another man rushed in.

Conrad asked Graham to keep any opportunities in mind, ending this section of his letter: "Now some shadow of possibility to go to sea has been thus presented to me I am frantic with the longing to get away. Absurd!" Possibly, the idea of *Chance*, that "Dynamite ship story," was born here, in the ship captain Anthony, who takes on board his wife, Flora, as Conrad would have taken Jessie.*

Conrad pursued Graham's Scottish connections and traveled to Glasgow in late September to seek a command. He wrote Garnett on September 29: "I got back today. Nothing decisive happened in Glasgow, my impression however is that a command will come out of it sooner or later—most likely later, when the pressing need is past and I had found my way on shore. I do not regret having gone. McIntyre [Graham's friend, Dr. John McIntyre] is a scientific swell who talks art, knows artists of all kinds—looks after their throats, you know."

While in Glasgow, Conrad was well entertained by Dr. McIntyre, one of the first radiologists, who also had literary connections. Through him, Conrad met Neil Munro, a poet and novelist, whose *The Lost Pibroch* he found "wonderful in a way." Conrad was suitably impressed by the demonstration of the X-ray machine, but he could not avoid persiflage in recalling to Garnett the "scientific" explanation behind the waves:

> These things [the fact that different states of consciousness can exist simultaneously] I said to the Dr while Neil Munro stood in front of a Röntgen machine and on the screen behind we contemplated his backbone and his ribs. The rest of that promising youth was too diaphanous to be visible. It was so—said the Doctor—and there is no space, time, matter, mind as vulgarly understood, there is only the eternal something that waves and an eternal force that causes the waves—it's not much—and by the virtue of these two eternities exists that Corot and that Whistler in the diningroom upstairs (we were in a kind of cellar) and Munro's here writ-

* Her comment on this episode is vague, but does suggest the uncertainties of her early married life: "Joseph Conrad made one or two abortive efforts during these months to return to his sea life, even if he was to be accompanied by our small son and his doting mother. The sea called with an insistent voice, and I should never have been surprised to find myself left alone while he made one or two voyages before he finally settled down. I am convinced that what proved the greatest influence against this course was his indifferent health and a certain indolence that had descended upon him in consequence. During those early months I held myself always ready for his decision, and I would never have raised a dissenting voice. I was more or less prepared for him to demand freedom, complete and unrestricted."

> ings and your Nigger and Graham's politics and Paderewski's playing (in the phonograph) and what more do you want?

The literary equivalent of all this, as Conrad almost touched upon it in that sentence, was stream of consciousness or, at least, free association: sensations, emotions, objects, levels of consciousness of differing kinds existing together. As to the object of the visit, a command, nothing came of this. He wrote to Graham on November 9, showing special gratitude, because his friend was himself engaged in a desperate struggle to save the family's estates despite his father's overwhelming debts.*

These activities, however serious they seemed, turned out to be diversions; the real events were the manuscripts at hand and the collaboration to come with Ford. On August 10, Conrad wrote Meldrum that "September *is* safe *quite*" for "Jim," a clear indication he had not put it aside. His contrast between it and *The Rescue* is of interest. After indicating that Blackwood had sufficient for two installments on hand (it would, eventually, run for fourteen installments, October 1899 to November 1900) and possibly three or four, he wrote: "This work isn't like the *Rescue* where I am at purely aesthetic (if I dare so) effects." He adds that nothing bars the way of a happy termination of Jim's troubles; the entire second section, on Patusan, was of course not yet in mind. He then provides a sharp look into his peculiar kind of malaise, in which the imagination is active but the pen will not write:

> The worst is that while I am thus powerless to produce my imagination is extremely active: whole paragraphs, whole pages, whole chapters pass through my mind. Everything is there: descriptions, dialogue, reflexion—everything—everything but the belief, the conviction, the only thing needed to make me put pen to paper. I've thought out a volume in a day till I felt sick in mind and heart and gone to bed, completely done up, without having written a line. The effort I put out should give birth to masterpieces as big as mountains—and it brings forth a ridiculous mouse now and then.

This explains, he adds, why "I must sell my mice as dear as I can."

Yet ten days later he told Garnett he was able to write and he now saw *The Rescue* as a book of some 150,000 words, which is what the completed novel came to. Garnett had apparently found the manuscript visually vivid and gave sufficient encouragement for Conrad to continue, all the while the latter was announcing "Jim" as ready for fall serialization. Conrad indicates the horrors of the previous four months have dissipated, although the fear of

* He had decided at this point to forsake Gartmore (through auction) and to retain Ardoch, in Dunbartonshire. All this was, of course, of interest to Conrad because of their somewhat common background as "landed gentry," the ownership of property being the basis for their class status.

their return makes him shiver. He views himself as a figure blundering in the dark, with all the "doors behind me . . . shut"—an apt image of entrapment, an animal cornered. To Graham, later in August, he continues the atmosphere of entrapment. Clement Shorter, editor of the *Illustrated London News*, had bought *The Rescue* from McClure and decided to put it into the October number. Since Conrad had an advance from McClure, he realized he "must write or burst." Since at least half the book was unwritten, he had about three months in which to write 75–100,000 words.* Much of this was simply talk, for there was absolutely no chance of Conrad's finishing *The Rescue* on time, especially as he was committed to Blackwood and Meldrum for *Jim*. The game was a familiar one: juggle his properties, gain advances so as to live, promise deliveries which he could not possibly make, and, all the while, goad himself through anxiety into some of his best work. He already knew quite well what he was later to write in *Chance:* "Yet it is so true that the germ of destruction lies in wait for us mortals, even at the very source of our strength, that one may die too of too much endurance as well as of too little of it."

Conrad had time to visit the Garnetts at the Cearne, in Surrey, and to write very respectfully to H. G. Wells that since the latter's review, he, Conrad, had lived on "terms of close intimacy with you," by which he meant he had pruned his style and scrutinized his sentences with Wells's criticism in mind. Wells had also commented on the extended ending of "Youth," suggesting it should have concluded at the paragraph describing the men sleeping in the boats. Now, seventeen years after the event, Conrad indulges in some nostalgia about the *Palestine* episode and its captain, Elijah Beard, which becomes in "Youth" the *Judea* under John Beard. Despite Wells's criticism, he apparently felt pleased with his effort, for itself and because it provided a way out of his impasse.

From September 6 through the twenty-ninth, when he wrote both Garnett and Ford, there is a gap in Conrad's correspondence which suggests intense activity. During that period, he was planning to collaborate with Ford and move into Pent Farm, a lovely farmhouse at Postling, near Hythe, in Kent. The house itself, where he lived until 1907, with its wooden porch above the

* To Mrs. Sanderson (Ted's wife), he announced the news in a jaunty, even manic, tone: "This is sprung on me suddenly; I am not ready; the 'artist' is in despair; various Jews are in a rage; McClure weeps; threats of cancelling contracts are in the air—it is an inextricable mess. Dates are knocked over like ninepins; proofs torn to rags; copy rights trampled under foot. The last shred of honour is gone—also the last penny. The baby however is well. He is singing a song now. I don't feel like singing—I assure you. . . . I am like a tight-rope dancer who in the midst of his performances should suddenly discover that he knows nothing about tight-rope dancing. He may appear ridiculous to the spectators but a broken neck is the result of such untimely wisdom."

front door and grapevines growing over it, was to prove a most productive place for Conrad. In a real sense, he made it his command post or captain's bridge, for he left it relatively little and the literary world visited him: Wells, Crane, Galsworthy, Garnett, Gissing, Shaw, James, Hudson, Graham, William Rothenstein, Clifford, even Roger Casement.

The decision to collaborate with Ford was momentous for Conrad. What did they see in each other? Ford, at twenty-four, and his wife, Elsie, at twenty, were virtually children when Conrad met them; they had, in fact, while still children, done adult things, having married when he was twenty and she seventeen. Since Conrad had himself married a woman closer to their age than to his own, he was, in associating with them, moving among two women and a man almost young enough to be his own offspring. In speaking of the collaboration, we should not forget that except for Conrad the youth of the foursome was extreme. What was for Ford at this time a kind of lark or adventure, the self-discovery, apparently, he periodically needed, was for Conrad, at close to forty-one, life and death.

Hueffer (born Ford Hermann Hueffer, later anglicized from the German to Ford Madox Ford),* also known as "Fordy," was, according to Wells's apt description, a "long blond with a drawling manner." He was indeed well over six feet tall and slim. Ford appears to have selected George Moore, the Irish novelist, as his model, for both affected a fey pose, an upper-class manner, a stylishly drooping stature and visage. Even in his mid-twenties, Ford, as befitting his illustrious forebears, was already affecting a high aesthetic tone: he fitted well into the nineties.

His father was Dr. Franz Hueffer (Hüffer), a man of several interests and accomplishments: a philosopher (specializing in Schopenhauer), librettist, and musicologist (he wrote a study of Wagner). In his English years, he started two magazines devoted, respectively, to Schopenhauer and Wagner (*The New Quarterly* and *The Musical World*), and in 1872, he married Catherine Madox Brown, daughter of the painter Ford Madox Brown. Ford's maternal grandfather connected him to Pre-Raphaelite circles, and he was himself to write, by twenty-four, a biography of Brown. Through his mother, the sister-in-law of William Michael Rossetti, he was connected to every level of the artistic world. After his father's death in 1889, Ford spent his later youth in a dwelling in Regent's Park (at 1, St. Edmund's Terrace) that virtually adjoined that of the William Rossettis. His tradition was both artistic and "arty"; he was clearly prepared for the kind of life he would lead, and no small part of his attraction for Conrad was the world he belonged to. Even his extremely youthful marriage fitted well into his circle, in which

* Given Conrad's own shift of names and use of a pseudonym, it is of interest that his collaborator should also in later life assume a different name, for nationalistic reasons—so as to mute his German background.

girls of seventeen were aging brides. His own maternal grandmother, Emma Hill, was fifteen when she married Brown.

Elsie Martindale came from quite a different background, not at all artistic or bohemian; in fact, it was quite middle class and "scientific." Her father was Dr. William Martindale, author of *Extra Pharmacopeia*, the pharmacist's handbook, and a colleague and friend of Joseph Lister, the founder of antiseptic surgery and a baron. The Martindales' expectations for Elsie were quite different from what Ford presented in his lounging, drawling, aesthetic manner. He must have conjured up visions of Oscar Wilde and that raffish world; yet the very qualities that made the Martindales stiffen against him were apparently the elements that charmed their daughter. Theirs was, and would turn out to be, the love of two children who outgrew each other as they became adults.

Ford's career was almost the reverse of Conrad's, at least in its external aspects. Internally, they may have been, as Dr. Meyer has indicated, "secret sharers" of a very complicated, symbiotic kind. Ford had started to write before he had had much experience; and for someone his age he had written voluminously—out of background, reading, and natural "feel" for the literary word. By twenty-four, an age at which Conrad was still feeling his way on English ships and learning the language, Ford was the author of a novel, *The Shifting of the Fire;* a biography of Ford Madox Brown, his maternal grandfather; a volume of poetry; and at least three fairy tales. Although his range had been enormous—poetry, tales, biography, and fiction—the achievement was slight. He was, at the time of the meeting, still learning his craft, very much the apprentice with great expectations but little accomplishment. He lacked weight, pacing, narrative skill, all the elements Conrad had torturously taught himself.

It is impossible to disentangle the extravagant claims made by the Fordians, on one hand, who assert Ford all but taught Conrad how to write English;* and the Conradians, on the other, who have seen his young friend as a

* Not a little encouraged by Ford's own words in *Joseph Conrad: A Personal Remembrance:* "Conrad confessed to the writer that previous to suggesting a collaboration he had consulted a number of men of letters as to its advisability. He said that he had put before them his difficulties with the language, the slowness with which he wrote and the increased fluency that he might acquire in the process of going minutely into words with an acknowledged master of English. The writer imagines that he had actually consulted Mr. Edward Garnett, W. E. Henley and Mr. Marriott Watson. Of these the only one that Conrad mentioned was W. E. Henley. He stated succinctly and carefully that he had said to Henley—Henley had published 'The Nigger of the Narcissus' in his *Review*—'Look here. I write with such difficulty: my intimate, automatic, less expressed thoughts are in Polish; when I express myself with care I do it in French. When I write I think in French and then translate the words of my thoughts into English. This is an impossible process for one desiring to make a living by writing in the English language.' And Henley, according to Conrad on that evening, had said, 'Why don't you ask H. [Hueffer] to col-

parasite eating off the literary body of his more famous collaborator. The unpublished correspondence, while settling nothing, suggests that neither assertion is very close to the truth; that, indeed, each writer had much to gain from the other's ideas and techniques, and each had a good deal to lose from the time expended on their relatively inferior collaborative work.

In discussing any joint work, one must start by assuming that each agent in the collaboration has measured what he himself has to gain and lose. Conrad was entering a desperate period: memory and experience seeking an outlet, but an inability to write steadily; a personal malaise and an impasse with existing manuscripts; a long, complicated novel (*The Rescue*) that would not work; and recognition, perhaps not fully conscious, that he had entered a critical time when he would either leap toward solid land or fall into the destructive element. His immediate work limning the insanity of a Kurtz and the haunted obsessions of a Jim cannot be ignored as providing insights into his own sense of sanity and insanity. Blocked in a situation that offered no resolution, he sought a rescuer, however superficially and externally.

Conrad needed someone who could convince him, as it were, that he was not making a fool of himself when he, son of Polish landed gentry, Frenchman by adoption, Englishman by language, turned to a literary career. Perhaps he was born to be a fool, a Don Quixote. "Fordy" was *there* as a reality, as was Edward Garnett earlier in his role as reader and editor. Also, Conrad felt shaky in his use of language, and Ford, with his background among illustrious Browns, Madoxes, and Rossettis, as well as his precocious literary endeavors before he was twenty-five, knew English idiom much better than Conrad could at this stage, despite his remarkable ear for nuances and rhythms.* It is reasonably certain that Conrad suggested the collaboration, for at the time (October) he wrote a long letter to Henley. His explanation seems reasonable:

---

laborate with you. He is the finest stylist in the English language of today.' " Ford's self-praise and egomania are well documented, and this comment seems to place this relatively unknown youth at the center of Henley's literary world. And yet intermixed with his exaggerations and lies is an element of truth: Conrad's sense of English idiom was shaky.

Whatever the truth of Ford's actual contribution to Conrad's work, and his claims were extensive, he was a substantial prop for many years. As we shall see, Ford may have done some writing on "Heart of Darkness," actually wrote a section of *Nostromo*, helped considerably with *The Mirror of the Sea*—and received a check covering some part of the royalties—but asserted he had "worked over" every one of Conrad's books between "Heart of Darkness" and *Nostromo*.

---

* The *Daily Mail* review of *Tales of Unrest* (on April 12) pointed to Conrad's grammatical weaknesses and may have made him redouble his efforts for support: "It is sufficient testimony to Mr. Conrad's power that we accept and enjoy him as we do, considering the continual weakness of his grammar and the frequent slipshodness of his general method. In this book, for instance, a story of quite ordinary people, moving in quite ordi-

When talking with Hueffer my first thought was that the man there who couldn't find a publisher had some good stuff to use and that if we worked it up together my name, probably, would get a publisher for it. On the other hand I thought that working with him would keep under the particular devil that spoils my work for me as quick as I turn it out (that's why I work so slow and break my word to publishers), and that the material being of the kind that appeals to my imagination and the man being an honest workman we could turn out something tolerable—perhaps; and if not he would be no worse off than before. It struck me the expression he cared for was in verse; he has the faculty; I have not; I reasoned that partnership in prose would not affect any chances he may have to attain distinction—of the real kind—in verse. It seemed to me that a man capable of the higher form could not care very much for the lower. These considerations encouraged me in my idea. It never entered my head I could be dangerous to Hueffer in the way you point out. The affair had a material rather than an artistic aspect for me. It would give—I reflected—more time to Hueffer for tinkering at his verses; for digging, hammering, chiselling or whatever process by which that mysterious thing—a poem—is shaped out of that barren thing—inspiration. As for myself I meant to keep the right to descend into my own private little hell—whenever the spirit moved me to do that foolish thing—and produce alone from time to time—verbiage no doubt—my own—and therefore very dear.

Conrad indicates he is no Dumas who "would eat up Hueffer without compunction. . . . Not being *that* I must navigate cautiously at this juncture lest my battered, ill-ballasted craft should run down a boat with youth at the helm and hope at the prow—pursuing shapes—shapes. . . . It seems to me it would be sinful to sink Hueffer's boat which for all I know may be loaded with splendid gems or delicate robes—and all for my private ends. No. I shall not go mad and bite him—at least not without a fair warning." From the literary point of view, there seems little reason to distrust Conrad's version, especially since the letter outlining his plans coincides with the plans themselves.

From Ford's point of view, the desire for collaboration was more vague, but perhaps less complicated. He was turning twenty-five, married, the father of a small daughter, and missing a father figure since the deaths of his father in 1889 and of his maternal grandfather in 1893. Conrad, at an "old forty," had the solidity of adulthood as well as proven authorship. One significant element in Ford's entire career was his desire, a driving need, to ally himself with the chief literary forces of the day. Later, he was to discover and help as many important writers as was Ezra Pound; and frequently, their

nary London life 'The Return' grips and holds us by sheer force of the author's psychological insight and his unusual ability to see common things in an uncommon way. It is because of this ability that we reconcile ourselves to tolerate laxities of style which would be unpardonable were they less richly redeemed."

careers overlapped. The Conrad of the late 1890s was already picking up a reputation as a new, major writer, although known only to a few. Ford very possibly sensed that his own development depended on association with major figures. If there was expedience in his choice, it was equaled by Conrad's.

At a deeper, personal level, as Dr. Meyer points out, Conrad and Ford shared a common identity, although much of his "evidence" is based on an acceptance of the latter's extravagant stories. "The nature of the personalities of Conrad and Hueffer undoubtedly facilitated such a conception of a common identity, for aside from whatever qualities Conrad might have held with Hueffer's father [both were non-practicing Catholics, both were Europeans with prominent beards, both spoke English with a heavy accent], there were other aspects of his nature which more closely resembled Hueffer himself. Perhaps the most compelling reason for their mutual attraction lay in the sense of isolation shared by both men." Further, each was "evidently seeking for a firm human relationship of a parent-child configuration to compensate for weak, frustrating, and unstable childhood attachments. As a consequence both were attracted to women who were either strikingly older [Hueffer after he left Elsie] or much younger than themselves, toward whom both men engaged in active and passive fantasies of rescue, which theme, incidentally, occupies a conspicuous position both in their separate fictional creations and in the books they wrote together."

Ford was, apparently, a chronic "rescuer" of many varieties and on occasion sought victims. In *Quartet*, a fictionalized account of her relationship to "Fordy" (Heidler, not Hueffer, is his name), Jean Rhys saw him as an insistent rescuer, as much as she was the classic victim. That is, apart from any other aspect of their attachment, this was the dominant note of their arrangement; so that Ford depended on her monetary and emotional need in order to keep the relationship going. If we read back from her account (the affair began at almost exactly the time Ford's book on Conrad was to appear, in November 1924), we can speculate that Ford's personal need of Conrad was as powerful as Conrad's professional (and emotional) need of him.

The correspondence between the two, meanwhile, was concerned almost solely with Conrad's impending move into Pent Farm as a tenant, with Ford as landlord and occasional guest. On October 6, Conrad told him he wanted to come to the Pent for a day, a visit that took place, and it is very possible that the two men discussed the collaboration at that time, although a more formal announcement of the arrangement did not come until later in the month. Conrad wrote Wells he was in a "state of jubilation" at the thought they were going to be nearer neighbors, Wells having settled at Sandgate on the Kentish coast. Conrad's letters demonstrate a considerable pickup in spirit, both the impending move and the upcoming collaboration beginning to appear like a rebirth, an unforeseen circumstance that could improve his manner of working.

Edward Garnett's essay on Conrad appeared in the *Academy*, unsigned, and became the first general (as separate from review) article to appear on him. Conrad in Jamesian prose called it "magnificent" and was immensely gratified to find himself "wrapped in the glamour of your intention—not of what has been done, but of what should be done, what should be tried for, what should be desired—what cannot be attained." Even a single paragraph from Garnett shows how the latter's comprehension of Conrad was very sound, and his criticism, coming in 1898, was quite prescient:

> What is the quality of his art? The quality of Mr. Conrad's art is seen in his faculty of making us perceive men's lives in their natural relation to the seen universe around them; his men are a part of the great world of Nature, and the sea, land and sky around them are not drawn as a mere background, or as something inferior and secondary to the human will, as we have in most artists' work. This faculty of seeing man's life in relation to the seen and unseen forces of Nature it is that gives Mr. Conrad's art its extreme delicacy and its great breadth of vision. It is pre-eminently the poet's gift, and is very rarely conjoined with insight into human nature and a power of conceiving character. When the two gifts come together we have the poetic realism of the great Russian novels. Mr. Conrad's art is truly realism of that high order. *The Nigger of the "Narcissus"* is a masterpiece—not merely because the whole illusion of the sailor's life is reproduced before our eyes . . . but because the ship is seen as a separate thing of life, with a past and a destiny, floating in the midst of the immense mysterious universe around it; and the whole shifting atmosphere of the sea, the horizon, the heavens, is felt by the senses as mysteriously near us, yet mysteriously aloof from the human life battling against it. To reproduce life naturally, in its close fidelity to breathing nature, yet to interpret its significance, and to make us see the great universe around—art cannot go beyond this, except to introduce the illusion of inevitability.

As they moved toward collaboration, Ford could not have missed the import of such an article, or of the kinds of reviews *Tales of Unrest* was gathering. From the other side, Conrad described to Meldrum the Pent as "full of rubbishy relics of Browns and Rossettis. There's Brown's first picture, likewise that of Dante Gabriel; Christina Rossetti's writing table which I intend to profane by my own wretched MSS.—and so on." The raffish air with the vintage background Conrad found immensely satisfactory, as he did Ford—an "exceedingly decent chap who lets me have the thing awfully cheap."

In an October 20 letter to his future collaborator, Conrad details with great precision, as if planning for some great ship to steam out of harbor, the move to the Pent, which would take place on the twenty-sixth.* We note the intense anxiety as he prepares each stage, and in a kind of code ("Mystery! Silence! Codlin's your friend—not Short") indicates their collaboration is firm. Conrad would announce it to Galsworthy eight days later. Intermixed with these momentous decisions—to move in, collaborate, and continue working—were worries about Stephen Crane and incessant importuning from Cora for aid. Crane lacked funds to return to England and she had asked Conrad (the improvident!) for help; further, rumors had sifted back to England that Crane had "eloped" with the wife of General Adna Chaffee, although what Cora wanted Conrad to do about that is uncertain. The rumor was unsubstantiated, and he dismissed it as "what the world calls scandal," which he said did not affect him. In later years, comparable scandal surrounding Ford would very seriously affect him.

During this difficult time for himself, Conrad did attempt to help Crane. He asked the firm of Blackwood for a loan of £75 or £100 and offered as security a bill of sale on the Crane furniture, a future story by Crane, or his own work, a book of short stories on which a royalty arrangement had been made. Conrad expected Meldrum to put this proposal before Blackwood, but Meldrum felt he could not, since he did not believe Crane would produce the required material. Instead, he promised to help Conrad with Crane through his friends, among them John Macqueen, a London publisher, by becoming security himself. As it turned out, Heinemann came up with the £50, which was cabled to Crane for his return, and for security Heinemann accepted Crane's future work.

The collaboration with Ford began almost immediately. The plan was to rework Ford's version of "Seraphina," which they would transform into *Romance*, what they hoped would be a popular piece of romantic literature that could tap the audience for Stevenson, Anthony Hope, and Rider Haggard. Although *The Inheritors* turned out to be their first book together—an attempt here to work along the lines of Wells's new genre of science fiction and political fantasy—they began on "Seraphina." The twin thrust of the collaboration was clear, to reach the audience in two popular areas: hit it high, with a sophisticated science-fiction tale full of political savvy; and hit it fairly low, in the region of pirates, adventure, and romance.

---

* Two months later, on December 18, he wrote Aniela Zagórska about the Pent and his life in it: "Before my window I can see the buildings of the farm, and on leaning out and looking to the right, I see the valley of the Stour, the source of which is so to speak behind the third hedge from the farmyard. Behind the house are the hills (Kentish Downs) which slope in zigzag fashion down to the sea, like the battlements of a big fortress. A road runs along the foot of the hills near the house—a very lonely and straight road, and along which (so it is whispered) old Lord Roxby—he died 80 years ago—rides sometimes at night in a four-in-hand driven by himself. . . . We live like a family of ancho-

To clear the air, Conrad read or reread Ford's early novel, *The Shifting of the Fire* (1892), which he had begun to write before he was twenty. Indicating that he was looking for the "inside" in that book, Conrad says he found it "delightfully young," instead of drearily or morally young. He notes that he appreciated the "movement, the imagination, the conviction of it," and the writing is "wonderfully level." Finally, however, he came to the point: that the effects are lost because the material is not integrated; the idea is not presented adequately. Trying to be gentle, he drives home his argument that Ford does not make the reader *see*. Conrad's work on *Romance*, however obvious and coarse the materials, was to make the reader *see*.

In this same letter (on November 12), Conrad says he gets on "dreamily with the *Rescue*, dreamily dreaming how fine it could be if the thought did not escape, if the expression did not hide underground, if the idea had a substance and words a magic power, if the invisible could be snared into a shape." He invokes the blankness of the page as his fate: "And it is sad to think that even if all this came to pass—even then it could never be so fine to anybody as it is fine to me now, lurking in blank pages, in an intensity of existence without voice, without form—but without blemish."

The "dreamily dreaming" over *The Rescue* must have led to a chain of thought that moved forward in memory from the Malay experiences to those in the Congo two years later, for Conrad, following a line from "An Outpost of Progress" and "Youth," would begin "Heart of Darkness" in mid-December. He would complete it in about a month, all the while asserting that *The Rescue* was to be serialized in the *Illustrated London News*, beginning in April. To Graham's mother, Mrs. Bontine, he announced the certainty of publication with the assurance that everyone would be disappointed—"the idea has the bluish tenuity of dry wood smoke. It is lost in the words, as the smoke is lost in the air. Attempting to tell romantically a love story in which the word love is not to be pronounced seems to be courting disaster deliberately." The assessment of wordiness is trenchant; nearly every passage is overwritten. In "Heart of Darkness," Conrad could afford overwriting because the scale was broad enough to include the burden of excess verbiage; the scale of *The Rescue*, whether by design or unintentionally, was too frail.

Toward the close of 1898, Conrad was preparing himself emotionally and imaginatively to enter the "great period" of his life, for which everything else

---

rites. From time to time a pious pilgrim belonging to la grande fraternité des lettres comes to pay a visit to the celebrated Joseph Conrad—and to obtain his blessing. Sometimes he gets it and sometimes he does not, for the hermit is severe and dyspeptic et n'entend pas la plaisanterie en matière d'Art! At all events, the pilgrim receives an acceptable dinner, a Spartan bed—and he vanishes. I am just expecting one today, the author [Galsworthy] of *Jocelyn*, which is dedicated to me! The novel is not remarkable, but the man is very pleasant and kind—and rich, que diable fait-il dans cette galère—where we are navigating whilst using pens by way of oars—on an ocean of ink—pour n'arriver nulle part, hêlas!"

had been preparatory. Nevertheless, he was still blocked on his long novel, with the even worse prospect of having seen it announced for serialization while he wrote words and not pages; he was at an impasse on *Lord Jim*, which he had apparently put aside; he was raking over Ford's idea of "Seraphina" for a collaborative effort, but putting that aside to work on *The Inheritors* shortly thereafter; he would not yet, evidently, begin to write "Heart of Darkness" until the middle of December, although the idea of it may have occurred earlier; and he had no other stories on the worktable, although he had come upon Marlow, the agent who would get him, eventually, out of his malaise.

At the beginning of December, H. G. Wells sent over a copy of *The Invisible Man*, which Conrad called "uncommonly fine." Although his comments are circumscribed—"If it just misses being tremendous [he wrote Wells] it is because you didn't make it so," a kind of litotes of criticism—the novel evidently alerted him and Ford to the kind of thing that might be worthy of their collaborative efforts. Conrad called Wells a "Realist of the Fantastic," saying he gives over "humanity into the clutches of the Impossible" without forgoing the human elements of flesh, sorrow, and folly. At the same time, Conrad indicates he is eating his heart out over "the rottenest book [*Rescue*] that ever was—or will be."

On December 13, he announced to Blackwood that he would be able to send on "about 30,000 words or perhaps a little less" in January. Shortly after this, Blackwood wrote and asked for a contribution to Maga's thousandth number, which would be the February 1899 issue. Conrad's speed in concluding "Heart of Darkness" can be attributed to that invitation, which delighted him. He responded on December 31: "I expected to be ready in a very few days. It is a narrative after the manner of *youth* [sic] told by the same man dealing with his experiences on a river in Central Africa. The *idea* in it is not as obvious as in *youth*—or at least not so obviously presented. I tell you all this, for tho' I have no doubts as to the *workmanship* I do not know whether the *subject* will commend itself to you for that particular number." He continued: "The title I am thinking of is "*The Heart of Darkness*" but the narrative is not gloomy. The criminality of inefficiency and pure selfishness when tackling the civilizing work in Africa is a justifiable idea. The subject is of our time distincly [sic]—though not topically treated. It is a story as much as the *Outpost of Progress* was but, so to speak 'takes in' more—is a little wider—is less concentrated upon individuals. I destine it for the vol: which is to bear your imprint."

Conrad then says its length will "be under 20,000 words as I see it now." The final version of "Heart of Darkness" was twice that, at just under 40,000 words, and therefore Conrad produced as many words again as he had already written by the time he sent the story in January. On January 16, 1899, the end of the piece seemed imminent, and the actual completion of the draft revision seemed to come shortly after this. "Heart of Darkness," the first of Conrad's mature fictions, appeared in the February number of *Blackwood's* and continued in all for three months. His facility in producing copy for this story, almost 40,000 words of intense work in about a month, indicates a qualitative shift in his imaginative processes, a kind of leap in which his memories had found the right formulas for presentation. Memory, imagination, technical means, the material or subject matter: all of these coalesced, and when they did, the most important thing in the world for Conrad became those moments when he could sit at his desk and produce words, no matter how many or how few.

With "Heart of Darkness," the final days of 1898 flew by. His letters become perfunctory, and he produced only dribbles of *The Rescue.* Even his correspondence with Graham trails off to brief notices, clearly holding actions. He made a sudden visit to Wells on December 23, and found him out, jocularly writing to Wells about "an invisible man" who kept the bell ringing long after Conrad had lifted his finger. His Christmas letter to Aniela Zagórska closes out the year with a review of popular literature, revealing that Conrad had carefully estimated the competition as he prepared for collaboration with Ford. He calls Grant Allen a man of "inferior intelligence" and his *The Woman Who Did* a "livre mort." He says Allen is popular among people who read Marie Corelli and Hall Caine, whose thought is commonplace and whose style lacks distinction. Conrad's venom was reserved for Hall Caine as a man "mad with vanity," a megalomaniac who maintains "that the lower part of his face is like Shakespeare and the upper like Jesus Christ."

He singles out Kipling as a writer who deserves attention, also Barrie, and mentions Meredith and George Moore, whom he cites disdainfully as having Zola for his prophet; he also shows awareness of T. Watts-Dunton, the friend of Swinburne and a novelist. He asserts that Wells's *Invisible Man* would be suitable for her to translate into Polish, and he promises to revise her work if she decides to do it. Then, after all this information, he adds: "I read nothing and I *never* look at the papers, so I know nothing of politics and literature."

With that disclaimer, Conrad leaped into his own kind of darkness, a creative burst that would carry him down not only into memory but into the very chaos and extravagance of the unconscious: ivory, jungle, a sinking ship, a leap, the silver of the mine. His subjects were themselves archetypal images that extended deep into the recesses of mankind itself, denoting riches, power, sexual potency, failure, and achievement. Stalled, depressed, ill, he had touched bottom and had, in his own way, found his subject matter.

VI

The Novelist

1899–1904

A fiery chariot floats on nimble wings
Down to me and I feel myself unbuoyed
To blaze a new trail through the upper air
Into new spheres of energy unalloyed.
Oh this high life, this heavenly rapture! . . .
Nor tremble at that dark pit in which our fancy
Condemns itself to torments of its own framing,
But struggle on and upwards to that passage
At the narrow mouth of which all hell is flaming.
Be calm and take this step, though you should fall
Beyond it into nothing—nothing at all.

GOETHE, *Faust*
(TRANSLATED BY LOUIS MACNEICE)

THE imaginative process, whatever it is and whatever form it takes, may be like dreams: that is, not at all straightforward or predictable, surely not linear, but misleading, deceptive, suggestive of condensation and displacement. Like the dream, an individual's imagination reveals as much as it veils. Whenever we follow a particular thread or line, we may be losing an even more important clue; for we are pursuing something that is essentially irrational, or at least irrational in the light of our present tools to understand it. But as with dreams, the imagination will suggest recurring patterns, schemas, significant statements as well as evasions. It is a coded process which we can pursue at least part of the way.

With a writer such as Conrad, we must be careful not to attribute too many of his ideas to literary sources, for he was intuitive and followed his ganglia as much as he did his reading or the practices of his associates. Such a lonely man had ample time and inclination to work out modes of seeing for himself. And assuredly a man who has spent twenty years staring at the sea has noted how intensity of observation can change an object into new shapes and novel configurations.* Staring for hours at the horizon, at sea and sky, waiting for shifts of wind, watching waves build and recede—these are func-

* In *The Mirror of the Sea*, Conrad saw water as a prehistoric, mythical force, as symbolic of another world entirely beyond man's routine comprehension, like the jungle of the Congo: "If you would know the age of the earth, look upon the sea in a storm. The greyness of the whole immense surface, the wind furrows upon the faces of the waves, the great masses of foam, tossed about and waving, like matted white locks, give to the sea in a gale an appearance of hoary age, lustreless, dull, without gleams, as though it had been created before light itself" (p. 71). Wind, also, whether described in *The Mirror* or in *Typhoon*, has the elemental quality that suggests another time, another place, a world empty of mankind: "Thus there is a certain four o'clock in the morning in the confused roar of a black and white world when coming on deck to take charge of my watch I received the instantaneous impression that the ship could not live for another hour in such a raging sea" (*Mirror*, p. 76).

tions that can transform one into shaman and magician, into the meditative pose not unlike Marlow's "supreme," godlike Buddha position in "Heart of Darkness."*

Since sources of the imagination are infinite and unique, whatever we say is approximate, but such indeterminacy does not mean we can say nothing. Too little has been made of those years at sea which Conrad experienced, years not consumed by reading or shipboard activities but filled with staring and boredom and tediousness, all those hours spent *between* rather than doing. Conrad's metabolism must have become reconstituted to take these long days and nights into account. We are not speaking here of eating or sleeping habits but of the way in which he had to arrange himself for the passage of time on long voyages as opposed to time considerations on land. Whatever internal arrangements Conrad managed, he was, in some sense, preparing himself for an occupation in which time as well as space would take on different dimensions from those in the "real world." Those twenty years at sea were not at all a waste but fell into what Erik Erikson, in a somewhat different context, was to call the *epigenetic principle.* As he explains it, it is a principle derived from the uterine growth of an organism, although Erikson's use of it indicates that "anything that grows has a ground plan, and that out of this ground plan the parts arise, each part having its time of special ascendancy, until all parts have arisen to form a functioning whole."

Those voyages at sea enabled Conrad to integrate himself after the early years in Poland of partial growth and partial stagnation of purpose and/or function. Usually viewed as disconnected episodes on various ships and in various ports, the sea years conditioned Conrad to the disproportion of sea and land, to differing perspectives of time and space, and to the kind of tedious staring that becomes inertness and passivity in his work. The period from 1899 to 1904 is so crucial for Conrad because he was, for the first time, able to get away from the sea and from maritime geography *without* losing those ingredients of preparation he had gained at sea. This is more than a question of his having achieved aesthetic distance, although that element of artistic maturity is surely present as well. It is a question of internal growth, of his facing the unresolvable elements of experience, and, finally, of his attempt to integrate all through impressionism, symbolism, and myth-making. At this point, we reach the frontiers of what we can say; for beyond this the idea blurs, and what we claim for Conrad may become generally true for any serious creative person.

---

* The open sky is always "there" for the seaman. In "Of the Open Sky," Ruskin speaks of the beauty of the sky which is there for all men to enjoy. "Sometimes gentle, sometimes capricious, sometimes awful, never the same for two moments together . . ." the sky presents the artist with a particular challenge, one that Conrad felt it incumbent upon himself to exploit.

Let us follow a parallel but more speculative line of argument. In his study of Mahatma Gandhi, Erik Erikson speaks of Gandhi's antagonism toward his father, expressed in certain actions rather than in words or in consciously hostile behavior. He says: "It is, in fact, rather probable that a highly uncommon man experiences filial conflicts with such mortal intensity just because he already senses in himself early in childhood some kind of originality that seems to point beyond competition with the personal father." In the light of Conrad's concern with fathers and father surrogates in this 1899–1904 period, we might pursue Erikson's line a little and see how this aspect entered deeply into his imaginative processes. Erikson speaks of Gandhi's having possibly felt older than his father because of the "single-mindedness" of his purpose. "Thus he grows up [Erikson writes] almost with an obligation, beset with guilt, to surpass and to create at all cost." Further: "In adolescence this may prolong his identity confusion because he must find the one way in which he (and he alone) can re-enact the past and create a new future in the right medium at the right moment on a sufficiently large scale."

For someone like Gandhi, such concerns take the form of a particular political expression; for Conrad, for whom Erikson's description seems uncanny, the concern takes the shape of a particular cast to his imagination. For a time, his sea career seemed to have the single-mindedness that expressed his conflict and, in a strikingly psychological way, intensified the internal struggle, since the sea expresses a desire for the mother, a desire to be enfolded, embraced, even smothered. The sea career served several imperatives: Conrad's attempt to seek alternatives to his father's type of career as a Polish patriot and man of letters; his wish to meet on a symbolic level with his mother, who had died when he was seven; his need, whether sub- or unconscious, to give himself time for his real career to find its own terms and not strike prematurely. At the right moment, his entire being could express both his conflict and his resolution of it. At that point and at that stage in his development, the conflict and resolution become acts of imagination, become part of the creative process.

Nostromo, coming at the end of this developmental period, has assimilated the entire process. In Gould, that "Rey of Sulaco," Conrad was able to present a father figure whom he could see objectively; for his treatment of Gould is full of irony as well as muted respect. In *Lord of the Four Quarters,* John Weir Perry has written about the mythological representation of the father, a description that is quite appropriate to Conrad's Gould:

> Charged with great potency and awesomeness, that is, with numen, this central position of power [central in the cosmos, that is] took on living form. It found its ceremonial personification in the figure of the sacral king, who was considered to be endowed with its divinity in greater or

> less intensity, and found its mythological personification in the figures of certain King Gods, who represented in the suprahuman plane the several functions of this ruling center. The real, supreme kingship was thought to reside in those kingly deities, which seems perfectly reasonable once we remind ourselves that such gods were the objectification in terms of eternity, of the numinosity of the various ritual processes enacted by the king in the temporal sphere.

For Conrad to have so placed the "king," the father figure, in such perspective is an act of imagination, for it enabled him to work his way through deeply personal ambivalence in order to find literary correlatives of what he sensed in himself. Only by reading back and forth between his sense of himself and the psychological themes in his work can we find such connections and trace them to acts of imagination, to the creative mind working on memory and transforming it in the process. Further, Conrad was able through Gould to examine an almost prototypical father-son relationship, for Gould had seen his own father sink ever deeper because of an idealism he would not compromise. Using his father's idealism as *his* treasure, Gould thinks he has found a way to survive in a situation that maims lesser beings. Conrad's insight here is a true imaginative act, for it does not accept Gould's idealism, no more than he could accept his own father's. He saw that idealism can disguise or screen out forms of gratification based on ego needs, desire for power, the wish to manipulate others. By transforming into myth the figure of Gould, as well as Gould and *his* father, Conrad was able to move beyond the personalized, intimate father-son relationship and turn memory into art.

The treasure is, of course, a way of integrating these personal and objectified elements. Erich Neumann, in pursuing aspects of the Jungian collective unconscious, touches on the need for integration, precisely what the treasure in *Nostromo* affords us: "The world and the collective unconscious in which the individual lives are fundamentally beyond his mastery; the most he can do is to experience and integrate more and more parts of them. But the unintegrated factors are not only a cause for alarm; they are also the source of transformation." Further, the treasure not only integrates elements that would otherwise remain disparate and unresolvable, it also allows for a "solemnization of the secret transpersonal and suprapersonal forces of life and death, which surge up from within to compensate for the materialism dominating the outward picture of our times."

In Conrad's hands, of course, the treasure is somewhat less than transformational in any positive sense, since the silver has disastrous political as well as psychological uses. Nevertheless, it does provide a bridge between past and present, individual and society, human need and historical event. The presence of the silver suggests an act of imagination comparable to the ivory of "Heart of Darkness," the leap into the absurd of Jim. As a treasure, it becomes alive by virtue of its function; yet as inert, passive matter, it supports the Conradian sense of the individual as fated, tied to a mechanical principle which exhausts his will. The silver, then, connects Keats's "realms of gold" with Darwinian destiny; it relates the subjective element which must be transformed to the objective, mechanical element that inevitably destroys whoever touches it.

These tensions dictate Conrad's imaginative thrust. They are suggested by the ivory, gain momentum with Jim's leap, become immobilized with the passivity of Lingard's mixed motives, remain inchoate throughout Kemp's adventures in *Romance,* and resolve themselves in the silver of *Nostromo.* It is as if all Conrad's strivings for correlatives of his imaginative processes had finally been determined. Although an artist's growth may or may not be related to his intellectual or psychological development, we can indeed assume one thing: that he is always aiming to destroy and to dissolve in order to create anew. He "controls the world through his work," as Ernst Kris puts it, or as Conrad implicitly recognized in his Preface to the *Nigger,* ". . . the artist appeals to that part of our being which is not dependent on wisdom; to that in us which is a gift and not an acquisition—and, therefore, more permanently enduring." With uncanny insight for one who denied himself any conscious literary wisdom, Conrad saw the aesthetic appeal of fiction as lying beyond words and conscious endeavor, in that region bordering on the collective unconscious, durational time, involuntary memory, the indeterminacy of the mythical and the magical, even the dream work as narrated by Freud.

The function of the artist, if we follow the lines of this view, is not unlike the shaman's; that is, if, as Mircea Eliade says, the shaman is a specialist in the human soul, then the writer as shaman is concerned with seeing and knowing, almost the same terms Conrad utilizes in his Preface. Further, the shaman enters into mysteries, not to expose or control them, but to demonstrate that experiences beyond the mechanical, destined world exist abundantly and rewardingly. Shamans are separated, as Eliade points out, "from the rest of the community by the intensity of their own religious experience," a distinction that would seem to lie close to Conrad's own sense of art as something impressionistic and antirealistic. We could, in fact, argue that Kurtz, in his relationship to the ivory in "Heart of Darkness," and various figures in *Nostromo,* in their manipulation of the silver, are playing shamanistic roles. Priest, mystic, painter, poet of a kind, musician, Kurtz has taken on a para-colonial role; not simply the exploiter, he is reaching for another level of existence, one based on a demonic, possibly Nietzschean sense of what lies beyond the routinely human. Similarly, in *Nostromo,* both Gould and Nostromo try out the silver for what it can bring them, as if it were a magic elixir whose possession will confer on them powers hitherto lacking.

None of this can be conclusive, of course, but it does indicate the way in which Conrad's imagination was moving in this period: toward an integration of novelistic elements, a means of creating anew. So much of this quest for the whole recalls the *symbolistes* that one is tempted to derive Conrad's attitudes from such literary sources, directly or indirectly conceived, and let it go at that. Surely his sense of destroying the real in order to re-create it as image and symbol is *symboliste* procedure, especially Mallarmé's. Such artful shading intensifies the object until it loses its solidity and achieves another order of being. Yet Conrad did not really need *symboliste* practice before him, since he had assimilated its method and manner in his own way, in the unfolding of his imagination in those years of staring into sea and sky while he sought another dimension of space and time.

We are ready to come full circle. Conrad's Preface to *The Nigger of the "Narcissus"* is usually, and rightly, cited as the basic document in his early artistic development. Without deprecating the importance of this document, or the sophisticated critical explanations of it, we cannot view it as intrinsic to the growth of Conrad's literary imagination in the crucial period from 1899 to 1904. The Preface is a statement of Conrad's bearings in relationship to various late-nineteenth-century critical traditions; chiefly, how he stood outside both realism and naturalism, how he moved close to a personalized brand of impressionism and symbolism. The tortured and twisted rhetoric of the Preface demonstrates how delicately Conrad wanted to thread his way through late-Victorian critical theories, but we must discover his imagination not in single statements but in cumulative data: letters, manuscripts, the finished works.

Conrad's imagination took over, in much the same way Proust allowed involuntary memory to set its own levels. For example: in a letter written during those crucial months when *Nostromo* was still in its rudimentary stages, Conrad was concerned with how an author, caught up in the processes of his own intimate methods, reaches an audience, which by its very nature is unconcerned with anything but what it likes or dislikes. That is, within an author's psyche is the dim awareness that he can never hope to be understood; that his methods and deepest concerns remain outside the comprehension of anyone but himself. The public either likes or dislikes, and so it should. But the public is not a judge: "It cannot pronounce on the question of intellectual work or artistic quality." Conrad adds: "It has no means of knowing." The artist can have "no fellowship with a great multitude whose voice is a shout," and the artist's solitary thought "cannot be imparted to a public which never dies." He concludes that "one writes for oneself," even when one writes for a living.

Conrad was striving for the vision which is uniquely the artist's, essentially a carry-over from the hermetism of French symbolism, and which remains only in the imaginative shape in which it is produced. Conrad had no vocabulary for this kind of effort, nor did he wish to have, since the imagination had to exist for itself, uncommunicable in any form but its own weight. What we are suggesting for Conrad in this period is such an intense immersion in the powers of his own imagination that he left behind all conscious intentions, all statements of motivation, all planned theories of art and his position within it. This former sea captain whose ethical system was based on order, control, discipline, and rejection of anarchic forces in whatever shape gave himself over to a flow and a process he could not consciously control.

Conrad suggested in this period a quality which Wallace Fowlie has ascribed to Mallarmé, a not at all inappropriate parallel. Fowlie says that the French poet, or any like artist, creates his own world and lives within it, calling this quality "angelism." Angelism, in turn, is connected to hermeticism and narcissism, the first indicating the closed system of the artist and the latter the absorption of his self in his work, to the extent that he is himself always the subject of his work, disguised though he may be.

In Conrad's case, the designation is more appropriate than for most writers, for his "angelism" comes by way of Marlow and other surrogate narrators. The four works in which Marlow appears were all begun or completed close to this period: "Youth," "Heart of Darkness," *Lord Jim*, *Chance* (a version referred to as early as 1898). Conrad descends narcissistically into his own world by means of Marlow, who in his turn has already descended into a dark, morbid underworld (whether that of Virgil, Dante, or Faust) and found there a self-sustaining world. Whatever is outside, in phenomena, is inside, in imagination and wish fulfillment. Further, the hermetic aspect of Fowlie's comment on Mallarmé has a twofold application to Conrad: the hallucinatory aspects of the experiences, the mythical quality of ivory, jungle, silver, water; and a related process, the unresolved mysteries of the characters' experiences—the enigmatic nature of Jim's quest for honor in a watery universe, Marlow's for balance in a black jungle, Decoud's for meaning in a "white" cosmos.

The significance lies in all the aspects of the work itself, and the meaning is only what it is. This is symbolistic doctrine, vague and undefined as it was for Conrad. But he grew into manhood in Marseilles, acquired his fluency in French when symbolism was literarily respectable, touched on it in his Preface, and apparently absorbed what he did in his close reading of Flaubert. Conrad hewed to this line even in his fiction of the 1899–1904 period which is not particularly significant: his collaborative efforts with Ford on *The Inheritors* and *Romance* and his own intermittent work on *The Rescue*. Remarkable about this five-year period is the homogeneity of Conrad's vision, even when the fiction is of uneven quality. Critics have tended to consider this time as belonging to the major works only, "Heart of Darkness," *Lord*

Jim, *Nostromo*, but it was as insistently the time of *Romance* and a good deal of *The Rescue*.* The correspondence with Pinker demonstrates that Conrad worked intermittently on *The Rescue* manuscript during these and later years, and its presence is contemporaneous with nearly all of his work. His writing career lasted for twenty-nine years and *The Rescue* can be traced in twenty-three of them.

Even the title *The Mirror of the Sea* fits into Conrad's vision at this time. This collection of essays, which began as a somewhat loose collaboration with Ford, with the latter jogging Conrad's memory and taking notes as Conrad dictated, has true symbolist overtones. The "mirror" of the title suggests the narcissistic component of late symbolist poetry. One thinks primarily of Mallarmé's "Hérodiade," where hair, mirror, and sterility combine to create a vision that is part visible, part invisible. Conrad's use of "mirror" as reflector fits well into his search, among the world's images, for his vision of what he, personally, had seen. The image in the mirror is comparable to the image in one's imagination, not unlike Proust's involuntary memory, Freud's sense of the unconscious, Bergson's conception of *durée*. Mallarmé's Hérodiade tells her nurse to "tiens devant moi ce miroir / O miroir! / Eau froide par l'ennui dans ton cadre gelée / Que de fois et pendant les heures, désolée / Des songes et cherchant mes souvenirs."

None of this would be worth stressing, however, unless Conrad's vision as a whole in this period were not excessively subjective, narcissistic, deeply dependent on memory. Conrad is indeed holding a mirror, not up to nature, but up to himself. We think of essays in the *Mirror* which are deeply personal, such as "The 'Tremolino,' " but it is not so much any particular memory that is mirrored as it is an entire frame of imaginative reference which is at stake. This frame of reference is caught by Fowlie in his comments on Mallarmé:

> When the nurse holds up the mirror before her, Hérodiade's actual words addressed to it are very brief, but their meaning pervades the rest of the poem. Deep in the mirror, as in a black hole, she has searched hours on end for her memories, and appeared to herself as a distant ghost. On certain evenings, when the mirror resembled an implacable fountain (at this point it is obvious that the myth of Hérodiade is joining with the myth of Narcissus), she realized the bareness of the reality of her dream: *J'ai de mon rêve épars connu la nudité?*

The resemblance is extraordinary because Conrad, without, as far as we can determine, knowing Mallarmé's work firsthand, became so absorbed in

* While we must recognize how Conrad depended on certain conventions of the adventure story, we must stress his departure from melodrama and a debased romanticism. His reliance on passivity, inertness, immobility is one of his major achievements in reshaping the romantic sense of adventure. His uniqueness lies in these reshapings.

himself that his Marlow as persona and agent is not far from Mallarmé's Hérodiade holding up a mirror to her own imagination and asking if she—her life's work—is beautiful. The "mirror" of the sea joins with the narcissistic mirror of one's self-image. The reflection, accordingly, is as significant as the reality: the two become indistinguishable. Part of the difficulty Conrad had with *The Rescue* was surely his inability to manipulate reality and its human reflection, what for him became a technical problem that Marlow's presence in other works helped resolve. In *The Mirror of the Sea,* Ford, again uncannily, served as a kind of nurse holding up the mirror to Conrad's memory, letting his imagination pour out, caught as it was between the memory of things past, whether reality or fiction, and the need to transform these events into a mirror language.

That all this should occur while he was writing *Romance, Nostromo,* and *The Rescue* should not surprise us, for if we examine the imaginative process in those books, we see their content as matter shuttling between methods of narration. Conrad is concerned with placement of tellers, narrators, reflections of the material; striking the substance obliquely or refractedly is as important as what is struck. We know Conrad was concerned with a static art, for he had spoken of stopping, arresting, pausing (Conrad's "seeing" is Joyce's "radiance," the scholastic "*quidditas*"), and his art of the next few years is an art of passivity, inertness, longueurs, languor as a metaphysical concept.

A comparative reading of these works shows that although Conrad's vision came in several sizes and shapes, he had a singular imaginative thrust for this period. While he later moved in numerous other directions for *The Secret Agent, Under Western Eyes,* and *Victory,* he did not appreciably develop beyond what his imagination in this period conveyed. The five-year span glowed with virtually everything Conrad was capable of doing. During this time, he borrowed extensively from himself. *Romance* overlapped with whole sections of *Nostromo.* Passages from "Heart of Darkness" and *The Rescue* almost coincide. *Jim* contains paragraphs that are almost repeated in *Romance, The Rescue,* and *Nostromo.** Narrative method, adjectival clusters, descriptive passages as a whole, conception of character (the young Lingard and Nostromo; Jim and Kurtz; Kemp, d'Alcacer and Decoud; Castro and Nostromo), all indicate that Conrad was working imaginatively toward some holistic vision of life.

---

* Although listings are tedious, they do show a remarkable homogeneity. Clearly, there was a Conrad style, modality, even manner that entered into nearly everything he wrote in this busy period. Some analogies are:

1. Mob scenes of *Romance* and *Nostromo,* with some further reference to the clustered native scenes of *Lord Jim* and "Heart of Darkness"; we note a basic shape to his milling groups or mobs.

2. Bay scene of *Romance* and the Gulf scene of *Nostromo,* with further reference to the becalmed yacht in *Rescue* and the drifting *Patna* in *Lord Jim.*

In a letter to William Blackwood, the publisher, before whom he felt profound humility, Conrad at the beginning of this period opened up a little on *Lord Jim:*

> The question of *art* is so endless, so involved and so obscure that one is tempted to turn one's face resolutely away from it. I've certainly an idea—apart from the idea and the subject of the story—which guides me in my writing, but I would be hard put to it if requested to give it out in the shape of a fixed formula. After all in this as in every other human endeavour one is answerable only to one's conscience.
>
> . . . I devote myself exclusively to *Jim.* I find I can't live with more than one story at a time. It's a kind of literary monogamism. You know how desperately slow I work. Scores of notions present themselves—expressions suggest themselves by the dozen, but the inward voice that decides:—this is well—this is right—is not heard sometimes for days together. And meantime one must live!

When a writer as crafty and cunning as Conrad covers his tracks even as he gives his reader glimpses of what he is disguising, the biographer must indeed be careful. Ultimately, after we have considered the letters, the fiction itself, Conrad's own intermittent commentary, and all other supporting material, we must try to develop some psychological bases for Conrad's literary imagination. That is, we must seek beyond his own words and his own work for unifying ideas, for some psychobiographical and historical process which will relate what was in him a pressure to external, possibly mythical, traditions. Pressure and idea needed shape.

In his novels of this period, Conrad worked with objects which he gives certain mythical connotations. That is, he takes fairly common objects and invests them with magical powers which extend beyond the thing itself to a world of totems. In both *Lord Jim* and *The Rescue,* we find a ring (or Seraphina's seal in *Romance*) as the source of great power, both individualized

3. Narrative method: reliance on retrospective technique in "Heart of Darkness," *Lord Jim, Nostromo,* with similarities to the narrative technique of *Rescue,* Narrators overlap: Marlow, Kemp of *Romance,* Mitchell of *Nostromo.* Use of participatory narrator rather than simply impersonal post of observation.

4. Overlapping characters: young Lingard of *Rescue,* Nostromo, Kurtz; Castro of *Romance* and Nostromo; Jörgenson of *Rescue* and Dr. Monygham of *Nostromo;* d'Alcacer of *Rescue* and Decoud of *Nostromo,* with reference, later, to Heyst and Renouard; Mrs. Travers of *Rescue* and Mrs. Gould of *Nostromo;* Seraphina of *Romance* and Antonia Avellanos of *Nostromo;* Shaw of *Rescue,* Morrison of "Typhoon," and Captain Mitchell of *Nostromo;* Kemp and Jim as romantics, with further reference to Kurtz and Nostromo; Jewel of *Jim* and Antonia Avellanos.

5. Jungle background of "Heart of Darkness," *Lord Jim,* and *Rescue;* water of same novels, and in addition, *Nostromo* and *Romance;* fog scenes of *Jim,* "Heart of Darkness," *Nostromo,* and *Romance.*

6. Tensions, action vs. intense inactivity; adventure vs. torpor; need for movement vs. inability to move, passivity; struggle between will to power and need to rest, reflect, self-destruct.

and magical. Whoever has the ring embodies trust, brotherhood, fidelity. At the same time, the possession of the ring obligates the owner to a sharp assessment of himself, for he may not misuse whatever power the ring conveys. Its ownership is a holy obligation, and the ring supposedly sanctifies universal human values. Yet the ring is not freely given to man: like the silver of *Nostromo,* there is a curse attached to its ownership. While it may convey power, the magic also works in unforeseen ways. A symbol of fidelity, it may prove too demanding for its owner, or, as in *Nostromo,* it is attached to a hoard that negates love and destroys the possessor.

We are reminded, of course, of the great musical event during Conrad's younger development in the 1880s and 1890s, that is, Wagner's *Der Ring des Nibelungen,* and we recall Conrad's own comments in his Preface to the *Nigger* which indicate a Wagnerian and Pateresque thrust toward the amalgamation of the arts. To pursue this argument further: in *Nostromo, The Rescue,* and "Heart of Darkness," we note a mythical hoard, the silver of the first, the boat *Emma* of the second with its treasured load below decks, and most clearly, the ivory of the third, a hoard that derives from elephant cemeteries. The three hoards are treasure troves which convey to their owners or temporary possessors great power that extends well beyond the wealth itself. The treasure trove is not unconnected to the idea of the ring, and that, in turn, to death, love, inner depths of will and destruction. Even *Lord Jim* fits into this holistic pattern if we view the *Patna* as a kind of negative treasure: had Jim remained on board, he would have gained the fruits of his romantic sense of self. By deserting the ship just when it could have become a treasure, he lost his chance at power and control. He becomes a marginal man, like all those who in Wagner's cycle miss out on the ring and the hoard.

These examples, closely intertwined as they are with other matters, indicate that Conrad's imagination was dealing with clusters of ideas. Sea and jungle take on further meanings, far removed from their obvious symbolism in *Almayer* and *Outcast.* Sea is particularly meaningful, for (except in "Typhoon") it loses turbulence and becomes placidity, passivity, inertness: a form of inactive nature, indifferent to man's endeavors, an implacable force that has a skew connection to man's will and needs. One thinks of the sea in *Lord Jim,* the Congo River in "Heart of Darkness," the becalmed waters of *The Rescue,* the bay in *Romance,* the Gulf in *Nostromo.* These are not moving waters, even when they are oceans or large seaways, and nothing seems to move through them, although we are aware of sails and oars. Mobility is thwarted; ships and boats are stilled. The sea, acting as receptacle for man's desires, encloses him in passivity. The biographer must stress how lacking in action Conrad really is, this novelist who is associated with sea, adventure, exoticism, the romantic novel. Whenever possible he avoids action, adventure, spatiality in favor of the thwarted move, the inert and the immobile.

One image cluster for this period, like a gigantic glacier, is of various masses of water that remain unstirred. It is an image that dominates *The Rescue* and Lingard's attempts to break away from Mrs. Travers and her party. It appears in both *Romance* and *Nostromo:* in scenes which virtually duplicate each other. In *Romance,* Kemp, Seraphina, and Castro are attempting to find the English ship in a fog that makes their bearings impossible to determine. They move around, in what is typical Conradian fashion, not as characters in an action novel, but as figures unable to connect to action. When Conrad redid this scene in *Nostromo,* he put Nostromo and Decoud on the lighter in the Gulf off Sulaco. The treasure here is silver, whereas earlier it was Seraphina. And the stakes are far higher, more intense; the scene is one of the great fictional scenes of passivity amid the need for action.

In a letter to Ted Sanderson, Conrad intimated this passivity in the writing of *Lord Jim:*

> . . . and the worst is that the menace (in my case) does not seem to come from outside but from within; that the menace and danger or weakness are in me—in myself alone. I fear I have not the capacity and the power to go on—to satisfy the just expectations of those who are dependent on my exertion. I fear! I fear! And sometimes I hope. But it is the fear that abides. . . . I am at it day after day and I want all day, every minute of a day to produce a beggarly tale of words or perhaps produce nothing at all. . . . It is strange. The unreality of it seems to enter one's real life, penetrate into the bones, make the very heart beats pulsate illusions through the arteries. One's will becomes the slave of hallucinations, responds only to shadowy impulses, waits on imagination alone.

Our aim here, however, is not to trace immobility as an isolated phenomenon but to demonstrate how Conrad's artistic imagination was moving along the line of a few glacier-like images. Conrad was rarely a novelist of ideas—not in the way Gide and Mann are considered as such; nor was he a novelist who hung on to a scene or an intimation the way James did. Conrad could not deal simply in glimpses, although he would have liked to. Nor did he, as Arthur Symons claims for him, "have many gifts which Proust never had—all those he enumerated—and besides these a creative genius which was not based on analysis, a wonderful power of evocation, an almost unflagging invention." Conrad's talent was, in fact, not unlike Proust's, and at his best he enters the Proustian world of immobility, static analysis, snail-like movement, retrieval of memory, convolution of time, creation of segregated temporal empires, destruction of spatial elements, passivity of character and observation. Conrad was not inventive, or else the invention was already flagging even by the 1899–1904 period. He felt, himself, that *Lord Jim* lacked sufficient invention for its prolonged size and that *Nostromo* was a failure of imagination.

We note, then, a particular tone to Conrad's creativity in this period: its lack of thrust, its paucity or trivialization of movement, its reliance on a few basic images, its need to retrieve the past and to construct a patchwork present out of disparate historical detail.* If we review Conrad's correspondence with his "realist" friends (Wells, Galsworthy, Bennett), those whom Virginia Woolf much later ridiculed for the tepidity of Edwardian fiction, we see how in terms of movement and passivity he circled outside them even as he wrote sympathetically to them. With all three, Conrad's hesitant attempts to make them see their limitations as realists, and, therefore, their limitations as novelists, were the corollary of his own static art. Unfortunately, during this period we do not have any correspondence between Conrad and an indisputably major novelist. The exchange with James, for example, displays only pleasantries, either because each destroyed the other's more serious letters or because Conrad approached his "cher maître" so shyly his comments are rarely more than deferential.

Yet the thrust toward immobility and inertness is there, even if indirectly. What Conrad did not write to James, he wrote to Galsworthy, about James, while he was working on both "Heart of Darkness" and *Lord Jim.* "Technical perfection," Conrad writes, "unless there is some real glow to illumine and warm it from within must necessarily be cold. I argue that in H.J. there is such a glow and not a dim one either." Conrad continues that, accustomed as we are to "headlong sentiments," the sentiments of James do appear heartless. He distinguishes between a method employed for its own sake and one (James's and surely his own) that carries with it profundity and vividness. Not unusually, Conrad ends the letter with the remark that the "finishing of *H of D* took a lot out of me."

The need throughout this period to find a methodology that would not thwart that "real glow," but would with a Pateresque static art intensify it, characterizes Conrad's imaginative thrust. His memories were immobile phenomena, encapsulated, inert masses, stored away before he had seen any use for them; and he had, by means of his imagination, to turn these dead,

* Rather than invention pure and simple, Conrad had the ability to "defamiliarize" the familiar. This term, "defamiliarization," has gained coinage because of recent interest in literary structuralism and structural analysis, especially the work of the Russian formalists. It was coined by the Russian Victor Shklovsky, and it was used as a response to our seeing with habitual or routine perception; that is, not *seeing* at all. Art, however, allows us to see. It enables us, Shklovsky says, to "recover the sensation of life; it exists to make us feel things. . . . The end of art is to give a sensation of the object as seen, not as recognized."

Thus, art "defamiliarizes" and "makes forms obscure, so as to increase the difficulty and the duration of perception." Shklovsky adds that in art it is not the finished product that counts but "our experience of the process of construction." Conrad's words in his Preface to *The Nigger* were little different, and his techniques in the 1899–1904 period, with their rearrangement of events, time shifts, long spells of passivity juxtaposed to actions retold by a removed narrator, were all attempts to involve us in the construction and to "defamiliarize" the familiar.

historical objects into life. The past is the key presence in Conrad's work, and the retrieval of the past, *that* past, is the chief methodological problem. Conrad's supply of narrators, pieces of information, primary "I" characters and subsidiary "I" characters, his utilization of letters, diaries, journals, his various posts of observation, his commenting choruses of outsiders, his quotes within quotes, the repetition of reportage: all of these methods are part of his imagination in the act of trying to comprehend and retrieve the past.

He is being fully consistent with what Frye calls the "centripetal pattern" of symbolism, in which "elements of direct or verifiable statement are subordinated to the integrity of the pattern." Less conscious an artist than James, who could convert "the very pulse of the air into revelations," Conrad let reverie carry him down deeper and deeper, where he hoped salvation lay in the form of technical methods.

Have we considered reading *Nostromo* as a kind of cautionary tale directed at the artist? The vast treasure is, in this respect, the artist's gift, his storehouse of images, Yeats's *animus mundi.* The treasure must be guarded, for it is clearly all that one may have; it is not renewable, in that an individual has only one chance at it. At the same time, it is treacherous, part of that demonic pact in which one gains its guardianship in exchange for the great danger any treasure carries with it.

As suggested above, it is possible to see that Conrad, perhaps with the Wagnerian legacy in mind—regardless of how he felt personally about Wagner's operas—modeled the San Tomé silver on the Rheingold; or, at least, borrowed some of the Rheingold ideology, which suggests that while the silver is indeed the coin of the realm and does convey power, it also undermines or destroys whoever possesses it. Thus, the treasure has the attraction of a force that destroys, simultaneously with a force that conveys art and imagination, even visionary and prophetic powers. Nostromo's corruption occurs, then, when he switches from the "magic" of silver to its properties as coin, when he goes from spirit to matter.

To argue accordingly is to insist on Conrad's myth-making powers at this time. Surely, if we move to the beginning of the period, we can see that by "Heart of Darkness" and *Lord Jim* Conrad's handling of his material depended on giving it qualities beyond itself. A storm is no longer simply a storm; a failing is not only a failing. Jim's transgression is *the* Fall, the lapse into sin from which only death can rescue him. Similarly, Kurtz's passage is a descent: into Africa, into darkness, into sin, into his own kind of Fall; he, too, lapses. While greed is a factor in his fall, it is only one part of Kurtz's massive transgression against civilization. Likewise, the ever-presence of *The Rescue,* with the Odyssean Lingard unsuccessfully playing godlike roles, is not anomalous. Lingard can "rescue" those who are stranded, but only if Conrad can get beyond his character as a matinee idol and center him more accurately as the savior of all those isolated civilized souls lost on a sandbank where the quality of their life deteriorates. Despite the various weaknesses of the completed novel, there is a consistency of symbolism and myth-making here, with the young Lingard no less a mythical deity than Kurtz is the embodiment of Satan and Lucifer. For Conrad, every element is weighted, is part of that storehouse of treasure his imagination must tap. *The Rescue* is as much myth, saga, epic, and legend as it is novel, and part of Conrad's difficulty with it was that it fell between genres.

In "Heart of Darkness," which Conrad derogated as too symbolic, the sense of human waste that pervades the story is best unfolded in the ivory itself. It is an object for the rich—in decorations, for piano keys and billiard balls, for bibelots—hardly a necessary item for survival, or even for comfortable living. In a way, it is like art, a social luxury, an appurtenance to which we become accustomed; and it is for art, as for appurtenances, that the Congo is plundered and untold numbers slaughtered brutally or casually. This view of art, we may suppose, was part of Conrad's conception; a utilitarian object like copper or iron would have had its own *raison d'être*. Possibly, Kurtz's artistic propensities (he paints, he is a musician, he writes, he collects human heads, he seeks ivory) make him so contemptuous of individual lives; for art and life have traditionally warred.* Beauty for the few is gained with the blood (and sweat) of the many.

Where art rules, artifacts are a form of power. The art object takes on magical significance, becoming a kind of totem, the fairy-tale golden egg or the hoard and treasure of romance and myth. Subconsciously aware of this, like the artist he hopes to become, Kurtz gains his power, indeed his identity and being, from the ivory he covets. In a world of art, the most greedy collector is often supreme; mana, not manner, counts. Aesthetics preempts ethics. One source of Kurtz's fascination for Marlow is the former's will to power, Nietzschean, superhuman, and brutal. Cruelty and sadism are indistinguishable from the vision Kurtz embodies, a vision of power and control which the ivory will provide for him. Ivory is merely a base on which he will grow rich, as mythical kings grew rich on their ability to untangle riddles or to find their way out of labyrinths. Kurtz has risen above the masses by standing on his pile of ivory; later, Nostromo will rise from service to mastery by means of his silver hoard. And Lingard, in *The Rescue*, gains his secret hold over everyone by virtue of the arms stored in the *Emma*. Once the

* Kurtz: death: ivory: art are interconnected. He *is* ivory: "He [Kurtz] looked at least seven feet long. His covering had fallen off, and his body emerged from it pitiful and appalling as from a winding-sheet. I could see the cage of his ribs all astir, the bones of his arm waving. It was as though an animated image of death carved out of old ivory had been shaking its hand with menaces at a motionless crowd of men made of cloth and glittering bronze."

Emma explodes, Lingard's source of power also is exploded, as once Jim leaps from the *Patna, his* source of power is lost.

This equation of art and the power of a treasure, or of imagination and the hoard, has far-reaching ramifications in Conrad's subject matter and language and very possibly accounts for the static quality of his work of this period. We are always caught by the paradox of an "adventure writer" whose work is inert and immobile. "Heart of Darkness," ostensibly, is a journey, Marlow's, to the source of power up the Congo; and yet we recall mainly stagnation. Time and space are stilled in that jungle outpost, and Kurtz, that demon of energy, is ill, passive, awaiting death even while making plans. The scenes of his final hours are images of futility and impotence; and this, too, is surely part of the imaginative process. Conrad's letters themselves lament his sense of artistic impotence, and yet he was able to translate into both tone and theme the very substance of powerlessness.

To Edward Garnett, for example, he wrote of stagnation and impotence at or near the very peak of artistic achievement:

> I've been satanically ambitious, but there's nothing of a devil in me, worse luck. The *Outcast* is a heap of sand, the *Nigger* a splash of water, *Jim* a lump of clay. A stone, I suppose will be my next gift to the impatient mankind—before I get drowned in mud to which even my supreme struggles won't give a simulacrum of life. Poor mankind! Drop a tear for it—but look how infinitely more pathetic I am! This pathos is a kind of triumph no criticism can touch. Like the philosopher who crowed at the Universe I shall know when I am utterly squashed.

In a little-known letter to *The New York Times*'s "Saturday Review" section, Conrad caught the artist's sense of impotence or powerlessness as it combines with the "making" of something, which is art:

> Fiction, at the point of development at which it has arrived, demands from the writer a spirit of scrupulous abnegation. The only legitimate basis of creative work lies in the courageous recognition of all the irreconcilable antagonisms that make our life so enigmatic, so burdensome, so fascinating, so dangerous, so full of hope. They exist! And this is the only fundamental truth of fiction. Its recognition must be critical in its nature, inasmuch that in its character it may be joyous; it may be sad; it may be angry with revolt, or submissive in resignation. The mood does not matter. It is only the writer's self-forgetful fidelity to his sensations that matters. But, whatever light he flashes on it, the fundamental truth remains; *and it is only in its verve that the barren struggle of contradictions assumes the dignity of moral strife—going on ceaselessly to a mysterious end—with our consciousness powerless but concerned sitting enthroned like a melancholy parody of eternal wisdom above the dust of the contest.* (Italics mine.)

We do not ordinarily think of Conrad as caught in that modern idea of still time and restricted space, what we associate more readily with Proust, Kafka, and Beckett. Yet any understanding of his imaginative thrust must take into account his movement toward mythical time and space. In such a formulation, time has qualities of eternity, of rebirth and regeneration, repetition of the cosmogony, escape from history, return to a mythical memory or to a collective archetypal experience. This view of time, not unusually, functions well within a setting in which a treasure or hoard provides a source or base of power. Space itself is usually space denied: the cul-de-sac of Sulaco in *Nostromo*, the stranded yacht in *The Rescue*, the sense of Jim enclosed within his transgression, trapped by memory, Marlow and Kurtz buried deep within a stagnating jungle, Falk sunk in the horror of his cannibalistic act. Space, here, becomes a center, a paralyzed location; it is potentiality and imminence, not where anything is definitely happening, but where anything may indeed happen. Both time and space, as in Proust's novel or in Mann's *Magic Mountain*, take on magical, mythical dimensions, as much beyond reality as within it. They become indistinguishable from what is symbolized by the treasure, a mythical source. "Give me a treasure, and I can control the world," Kurtz, Lingard, Nostromo, Gould, and several others imply.

One reason Conrad was so involved in questions of passivity and in scenic repetition of inert time and immobile space is that his imagination was working toward some deeper understanding of the artistic function as a quarrying power, as having validity only in retrieving the past, not in remaking the present. Further, we can see *Lord Jim*, in some measure, as an allegorical representation of the artist and the artistic life, a more elegant, imaginative, and elusive *New Grub Street.* Although this is by no means the sole way to read the novel, we can view *Lord Jim* as embodying an analogous or metaphorical trip for Conrad. In Jim's indecisions, his desire for adventure, his romanticism about his big opportunity, his nagging sense of failure, his need for integrity, his desire for a good reputation, the novel manifests Conrad's fear that he might fail as artist, possibly as husband, as craftsman in his new calling, as collaborator with Ford, as professional, as someone striking out into fresh territory where adventure is always tempered by reality. It might even recall his failures when he first took the examinations for first mate and captain, but, more surely, his panic that because of a poor reputation he might descend into shabbiness and have to keep running.

His reputation, as we see from his letters to Pinker, was everything for him: "Have you the slightest idea of what I am trying for?" he asked Pinker in a January 8, 1902, letter.

> Of what is my guiding principle which I follow in anxiety, and poverty, and daily and unremitting toil of my very heart. Come my dear fel-

> low, I am not one of your 25-year-old geniuses you have in your pocket, or one of your saleable people who drive three serials abreast. I am another kind of person. If you don't want the bother of my stuff saddled with my other imperfections tell me to go to the devil. . . . Don't address me as if I were a man lost in sloth, ignorance or folly.

Conrad continues concerning a loan of £40 he had requested: "This is the sort of thing one writes to a grub street dipsomaniac to stop his bothering one—not to a man of my value. Am I a confounded boy? . . . I am no sort of airy R. L. Stevenson who considered his art a prostitute and the artist as no better than one."

One hangs on to the sentence: "I am another kind of person." Beneath, as in all men attempting to be artists, is the "other kind" of person. *Lord Jim* is saturated with failures, with Jim's inability once he has achieved something to hold it consistently, *with a "perfect failure" as the other side of a perfect art.* The demands he makes upon himself are always more than what he can achieve; he demands flawlessness, and thus inevitably finds disappointment in what he has gained. Further, failure is implicit in the achievement: as in all works of art, or attempts at it, the flaws are as apparent as the attainment. One may strive for a "seamless art," but it is impossible, except in the dream of one's own mind, what Stein suggests when he speaks of the need to follow the dream.

As we read forward from "Heart of Darkness" and *Lord Jim* through *Nostromo,* we note the ambiguities of Conrad's themes and how these themes, indefinite though they may be, parallel the ambiguities of his imagination. Beneath the energy of the narrative line are opposing conflicts of a basic kind: one's loss of desire and energy at a crucial moment—Jim, Decoud, Lingard; the recognition that external forces negate the personal will—Nostromo, Kurtz; the ability to witness one's own destruction, to be witness at one's own death—Decoud, Jim, d'Alcacer; the ever-present sense of cowardice, the failure to impose oneself because one no longer desires to do so—Jim, Decoud; the reliance on fidelity as a last resort in an absurd universe—Nostromo, Lingard, Castro; the mixed quality of repentance—Jim, Kurtz; the isolation of the individual regardless of which course of actions he follows—nearly all; the futility of power, control, money, treasure, even as one covets it—Kurtz, Jim, Lingard, Gould, Nostromo; the immobility that lies at the heart of movement, an immobility that underlies a fully countering existence—nearly every protagonist.

There are, in addition, the terrible ironies: the cyclical nature of existence for each individual even as he considers himself unique; life as a reflector of the past, so that even while a character feels himself to be escaping, he never escapes; the sense of the world, or universe, as a trap—for hope, desire, will, self itself. All this, we recall, works out against a narrative line moving along on adventure, romance, action.

Drowning figures largely in his fiction of this period, and not simply because Conrad stressed the sea. This emphasis on drowning, on being swallowed up, is indistinguishable from his imaginative processes. The pattern of his imagination appears to be based on dramatic acts of dying or seeking death, and the long periods of passivity which occur in his work are attached to the peculiar thrust of his imagination. Narrative devices constantly retard or still the story line; the apparatus, as we have noted, transforms everything into retrospection. Matter becomes inert; activity is based on a passive mass. The dynamo rusts. Marlow is a Buddha figure in "Heart of Darkness" because he represents stolid passivity, the past, an anchor against movement. The incredible secrecy and withholding that accompany Conrad's manner of narrating, the energy that goes into retrospection, lulls, accounting, the deception and conspiracy implicit in his use of point of view, his focus upon drowning, near-death, suicide, or *dying and becoming reborn through a narrator*—these are clearly, all of them, acts of imagination, part of the very thought and creative processes which account for Conrad in the 1899–1904 period.

Conrad's imaginative processes, as we can chart them in this difficult period, created a tension between Promethean and Orphic elements. The Promethean strain, for Conrad, was attached to the doing, active life which he had lived so elementally in ships and among seamen. Prometheus, traditionally, is the external hero, a rebellious, troublesome, inherently uncontrollable force for change. Defying Zeus, stealing fire, he is a figure of action who brings change from without. His punishment, when it comes, involves vastnesses of space and time, eternal punishment amid valleys and mountaintops, until he is rescued by Hercules, another doer. Prometheus denotes swoops of time and space, a panoramic, picaresque protagonist—not at all at odds with one side of Conrad, who described himself, in *The Arrow of Gold*, as "young Ulysses" and whose protagonists of the 1899–1904 period are "Ulysses figures" of one kind or another: Lingard, Kemp, Nostromo, Jim, even Marlow.

The Orphic side, however, is equally compelling. Orpheus is our hero of internal change, since he is dedicated to transformations of self through meditation and contemplation. Orphism involves self-consciousness, inward-turning, narcissism normally associated with a literary cult of personality, self, inner being. As intensely as Prometheanism is action-oriented, Orphism drives toward a romantic conception of the individual, his desire to will himself imaginatively against an antagonistic world. The Orphic view accommodates quite easily Conrad's temperamental kinship with the Schopenhauerean and Nietzschean ideas that had sifted through his imagination in his formative years.

Whereas Prometheus functions with the ordinary sense of clock and calendar time, Orpheus requires a derangement of the senses, a disruption of proportions and dimensions. Since Orpheus thrives within recesses, his sense of time and space is secretive, subject to different orders of being and arrangement, precisely what Conrad recognized as existing in Proust and coming so close to his own imaginative efforts. To turn all of life as lived into past history, and then to present this past history as eternally present, is to attempt the Orphic derangement of the senses.

The Orphic vision fits myth—of silver, hoards, treasure, cavernous holds—and it sacralizes ordinary spatial and temporal concepts. Besides our definition of Orphism as innerness, we must stress its powers of liberation, its attachment to freedom and the freeing powers of Art even when Orphism moves us close to death images and to death itself.* Conrad plays almost allegorically with the saving graces of Art, even while as a Promethean he cannot fully admit its potential. The Preface to the *Nigger*, after its appearance in *The New Review*, was withheld for so many years possibly because Conrad could not resolve this side of himself, the Orphic element. Orpheus is himself never far from death, but withal, the darkness he penetrates is a freeing process; and temporal and spatial concepts attached to Orpheus, although inner, are dimensions of greater liberation than the apparently more extensive vastitudes of the Promethean myth. This seeming paradox—and we note how akin to drowning and rebirth it is—is resolved if we assume that the inner world is depthless and timeless, literally unmeasurable; the outer world of Prometheus is, ultimately, the temporal and spatial dimension our senses can measure.†

In *Eros and Civilization*, Herbert Marcuse yokes Orpheus and Narcissus, the inner world of regeneration and the self-absorbed, self-loving, inward-turning youth. The juxtaposition is not inappropriate for Conrad, whose utilization of a surrogate narrator or persona for the self, as we have noted, is an act of narcissism. Marcuse enumerates the qualities to which Orpheus and Narcissus are wedded: ". . . the redemption of pleasure, the halt of time, the absorption of death; silence, sleep, night, paradise—the Nir-

* Commenting on Orphic themes in a different setting, Walter Strauss reaches similar conclusions: "The Orphic poet is, once more, at the beginning of a journey, confronted with the task of sacralizing time, space, and language before the Orphic spell can take place. His task is to face the Nothingness, to overcome (abolish) it in order to make poetry once more possible. . . . the Orphic poet seeks to regenerate himself particularly through remembrance and its mandatory self-transformation, followed by return to the world that will become the ground of a vast metamorphosis."

† Not unconnected to these distinctions between inner and outer dimensions is the Jungian conception of the "ancestral soul." According to this, when certain ancestral elements come to the fore in a person, he is thrust into an ancestral role. The idea assumes that deep within the person a spaceless and timeless dimension exists which is immeasurable; that what we see of that person is the tip of an infinitely complicated attachment to the archetypal past, the Orphic element.

vana principle not as death but as life." The point is that Eros, symbolized here by Orpheus and Narcissus, says No (its great refusal) to Prometheus; self-absorption negates an active role. This refusal creates another order of being, a different kind of reality, what we have called the passive strain in Conrad's imagination.

We note that Conrad's stress on historicity (even the distinction he makes in his essay on James between History and Fiction) is an act of narcissism whose intention is to suggest an order of being that conflicts with the active and romantic nature of the Promethean theme. Several critics have theorized that Conrad's literary background was twofold: romantic literature as a whole, and the Polish romantic literature of his youth. Such assessments are valid, and valuable, but literary background suggests one kind of knowledge, the growth of an individual imagination another. We must account for the fact that Conrad resisted those very themes and ideas which would have turned him into a second Anthony Hope and his novels into imitations of *The Prisoner of Zenda*.

We must concern ourselves with the imaginative forces which established passivity and inertness. They illustrate his efforts *not* to be a romantic sea writer, *not* to be simply another 1890s exotic, *not* to follow the romantic Polish literature of his youth, even while influenced and directed by it. We must account for a passage like the following, in which the sea mirrors ourselves and turns our expectations (for adventure? for romance? for Art?) into passive illusions:

> Surely in no other craft [he writes in *Lord Jim*] as in that of the sea do the hearts of those already launched to sink or swim go out so much to the youth on the brink, looking with shining eyes upon that glitter of the vast surface which is only a reflection of his own glances full of fire. There is such magnificent vagueness in the expectations that had driven each of us to sea, such a glorious indefiniteness, such a beautiful greed of adventures that are their own and only reward! What we get—well, we won't talk of that; but can one of us restrain a smile? In no other kind of life is the illusion more wide of reality—in no other is the beginning *all* illusion—the disenchantment more swift—the subjugation more complete.

We are now in a very difficult area, for while we may chart Conrad's performance, we cannot specify the precise reasons he did one thing and not another. Ernst Kris points out how psychoanalytic material can account for the fact that one individual turns to painting, "the other to dancing, writing, or music. . . . However, after all this has been properly taken into account, there remains the question not only of why one is successful and the other is not, but, particularly where science or art is concerned, why one is great while the other barely reaches medium height." Accordingly, although we can account for certain persistent themes in Conrad, especially that conflict between the impulse to adventure and the inert, passive, dying impulse, nevertheless, we cannot predict that he would have turned in such a direction.

The intricacies of *Nostromo* derive from many aspects, but primarily from the fact Conrad had reached a point in his development where he could handle the adventure-passivity tension in all its diversity. After *Nostromo,* he was unable to capture in formal structure the full potential of these conflicting elements, although *Victory* was an ambitious attempt. Erich Neumann speaks of artistic creation as having "magic power; it is experience and perception, insight and differentiation in one." Conrad's line of development in this period illustrates Neumann's thesis, in terms of magical potential, the use of an archetypal hoard or a collective treasure, in the numinosity of the creative situations, a "divine" element usually associated with symbolism.

Not unusually, in *Nostromo,* Conrad flirted with the Faustian archetype. The passivity of that novel, as the inertness of *Jim* and "Heart of Darkness," not to mention *Romance* and *The Rescue,* should alert us to Faustian potentialities. Passivity, as we have stressed throughout, counters activity, heroism, all outward forms, in favor of intense inwardness; it denies one's routine expectations of time and space for stillness, hesitation, stasis. It unmans Conrad's males. Yet, at the same time, passivity has strong associations with romanticism and romantic adventure, for it mythicizes routine experience, has affinities with defiance, with the potential for rebellion. Passivity creates Fausts, *but Fausts of the inner world.* When Nostromo sells himself for silver, he does so secretly, conspiratorily, and the pact he makes gives him no pleasure. It is antisensual, antierotic, antisexual; it is a form of furtive social rebellion against the rich who use the poor and then discard them. It is, whatever else we call it, an internal experience since it never becomes a pleasurable replacement for normal work routines.

Disguised, submerged, concealed, the Faustian experience is present, not only in Nostromo, but in Jim, Kurtz, Lingard, even Decoud. All of them are forced to explore an inner geography, to comprehend an alternate experience. As much as Orpheus has rebelled against matter, these questers (fated to failure and/or destruction by their questing) rebel against the matter of the world, whether it is dull routine, the exploitation of the poor by the rich, or a life experienced without sensual love. All attempt to account for the presence of the divine in man, which in modern fiction means they must throw themselves against the destructive presence of objects. Their heroic stature, which they achieve in some measure despite their passivity and inertness at crucial times, is attained through their rebellion against the grayness of matter itself. In this way, and to this degree, they have entered into the Faustian archetype, as rebels against something that destroys, in favor of something which will also destroy.

Like Orpheus-Faust, they make underground journeys, and like Orpheus, they attempt transformation, mutations of being, adversariness; alternate experiences become potentialities. By so doing, they attempt to turn profane into sacred experience, what we mean by sacralizing or spiritualizing matter. Often, their only weapon is contemplative silence. Once again, we note Conrad's great imaginative achievement, which is, like Proust's, to turn silence (or passivity) into a creative force. Lingard is silent before Mrs. Travers and the nature of his new internal experiences; Marlow is silent before Kurtz, silent before the Russian sailor, silent before Kurtz's fiancée; Nostromo and Decoud experience comparable notions of silence on the lighter and then on the Great Isabel. Nature itself—jungle, river, gulf, island—remains a mute background. We note how appropriate the Orphic analogue is. For Orpheus was himself part Apollo (like Conrad), part Dionysus, and his function was to use disparate elements: to make a timeless, spaceless, seamless element that catches all without becoming true substance itself.

We see that Conrad's creative function in this crucial period was twofold. First, he was developing the fictions that would express his conflicting ways of viewing matter; and second, he was expressing in the latent content of the works themselves the way in which his imagination worked. If we read the novels and stories in terms of large image clusters, as confrontations (often antagonistic) between silence and adventure, as conflicts between memory and present event, as manifestations of inertness and passivity, we can see how Conrad worked with what Kris calls "intuitive insight."

The way in which Conrad's imagination functioned suggests that through conceptualization itself he was testing out the culture. Unlike his Edwardian contemporaries (except for James), he saw seams and crevices, areas of blockage and denial that were as important as doing and moving. Whereas Wells, Bennett, and Galsworthy sensed action as the definition of man, Conrad—closer to Freudian dreams and unconscious—saw the other side of culture, that connected to the inability to move, the very kind of nihilism his conscious mind would have rejected. Among his literary practices, Conrad's denial of time and space is his attempt to move into that world; retrogression of narrative form is a way of suggesting something very profound about life and its manifestations. The idea of a treasure or hoard is by no means antithetical to this creative development.

What Conrad lacked was the equivalent of the Proustian "involuntary memory," which would have allowed the retrieval of the past without the interference of so many narrators and narrative devices. Apparently, he was striving for a "seamless narrative," in which past and present merged with each other to suggest flow, cycle, and process. Yet he could not develop a method or narrative technique which would provide this, although Marlow's tale in "Heart of Darkness" does approach his ideal. What he needed was not only a narrator but a narrator-participant, so that retrogression could be an extension of the present and not simply an episode blocked and cut off in time. Involuntary memory, with its retrieval potentialities, permits access to the pastness of the present, but it does not negate the need for presentness. Time and space, in such a procedure, consist of almost infinite variables, what worked so efficiently for Proust and what would have functioned so well for Conrad in *Lord Jim*, where he desired both a "hard reality" and a blurred sense of inner and outer. This blurring of effects within a solid form was close to his idea of impressionism, although he feared he lacked the ultimate technique to bring it about.

Precisely because he could not discover such correlatives for what his imagination sensed, he foundered on *The Rescue*. Not only was the material changing as his imaginative processes developed, but the method demanded by the material eluded him. Conrad was faced by an insoluble problem, and the impasse on the manuscript was the result. The reason he did not experience blockage on his work contemporaneous with *The Rescue* was that these books did not reach back into his earliest creative phase; consequently, they were not caught up by practices which no longer functioned. This is another way of saying that Conrad's imagination was developing in certain areas, while it remained stagnant and trapped by the past in others, not at all unusual in a novelist whose fictions depend on what has already occurred, rather than on freshly conceived materials.

Yet through it all, in this period, he was conscious of himself as a distinctive creative artist with a unique gift. Writing to the publisher William Blackwood in 1902, Conrad defended not only himself but the very processes of his imaginaton:

> I am long in my development. What of that? Is not Thackeray's penny worth of mediocre fact drowned in an ocean of twaddle? And yet he lives. And Sir Walter, himself, was not the writer of concise anecdotes I fancy. And G. Elliot [sic]—is she as swift as the present public (incapable of fixing its attention for five consecutive minutes) requires us to be at the cost of all honesty, of all truth, and even the most elementary conception of art? But these are great names. I don't compare myself with them. I am *modern*, and I would rather recall Wagner the musician and Rodin the Sculptor who both had to starve a little in their day—and Whistler the painter who made Ruskin the critic foam at the mouth with scorn and indignation. They too have arrived. They had to suffer for being "new." And I too hope to find my place in the rear of my betters. But still—my place. My work shall not be an utter failure because it has the solid basis of a definite intention—first: and next because it is not an endless analysis of affected sentiments but in its essence it is action (strange as this affirmation may sound at the present time) nothing but action—action observed, felt and interpreted with an absolute truth to my sensations (which are the basis of art in literature)—action of human beings that will bleed to a prick, and are moving in a visible world.

VII

The Major Career

1899–1910

There is something else, then, a modification, or a transformation, sudden or not, spontaneous or not, laborious or not, which must necessarily intervene between the thought that produces ideas—that activity and multiplicity of inner questions and solutions—and, on the other hand, that discourse, so different from ordinary speech, which is verse, which is so curiously ordered, which answers no need unless it be the need it must itself create, *which never speaks but of absent things or of things profoundly and secretly felt; strange discourse, as though made by someone* other *than the speaker and addressed to someone* other *than the listener. In short, it is a* language within a language.

VALÉRY,
"Poetry and Abstract Thought"

CHAPTER 20

Racing into Print

THE year 1899 was not only the time of "Heart of Darkness" and *Lord Jim* but the occasion of an atribilious attack upon "Mr. Conrad Korzeniowski" by the Polish novelist Eliza Orzeszkowa. Her bitterness, as we have already seen, was based on Conrad's alleged desertion of Poland. He was part of the exodus which included "engineers and operatic singers," and was, in her words, writing novels that were widely read and bringing in "good profit." Even thinking about this rich Polish exile, growing fat on English pounds, made her sense "something slippery and unpleasant."

Probably unaware of the specifics of this attack, Conrad was, meanwhile, trying to find firm ground on which to stand. He was propped up on all sides: Ford was outside, at his elbow; Marlow, just rising within; Blackwood and Meldrum, as his publisher and editor; Garnett, as his literary conscience; Henley, a believer; Galsworthy, present with small sums of money. The man who had "betrayed" the fortunes of Poland in choosing art over nationalism or propaganda was an exile, a writer going ever deeper into debt. Like Joyce, who would in a very few years choose a similar route, Conrad had made an inner decision—despite the external doubts—and would, as Valéry said, seek a "*language within a language*," which is to say, his own voice.

In a sense, the writing of "Youth," which had come so easily, involved a terrible paradox, perhaps the central paradox of Conrad's three lives. Before Marlow can have his great moment, indeed, a revelation of the East, he must enter the flames, almost literally. The *Judea*, the last thing on earth in the vast Indian Ocean, burns itself out in a final apocalyptic vision.

> She burned furiously; mournful and imposing like a funeral pile kindled in the night, surrounded by the sea, watched over by the stars. A magnificent death had come like a grace, like a gift, like a reward to that old ship at the end of her laborious days. The surrender of her weary ghost to the keeping of stars and sea was stirring like the sight of a glorious triumph. The masts fell just before daybreak, and for a moment there was a burst and turmoil of sparks that seemed to fill with flying fire the night patient and watchful, the vast night lying silent upon the sea. At daylight

> she was only a charred shell, floating still under a cloud of smoke and bearing a glowing mass of coal within.

Like the phoenix, she turns to ash, and from this Marlow will be reborn.

In the tale Conrad discovered a metaphor for his own career. Marlow—"at least I think that is how he spelt his name"—moves rapidly into a story based on memory. As we have observed, he says it all happened twenty-two years ago, when he was twenty; it happened for Conrad in 1882, on the *Palestine,* sixteen years before, when he was not twenty but twenty-four. The general time difference is similar enough. Further, the *Palestine* becomes the *Judea,* so that the archetypal religious-poetical experience remains the same, and there is an Old Testament quality to the ingredients of water, fire, abandonment, and endurance. When the end comes, with the conflagration on board the *Judea,* it involves final things but it is not an end. For Marlow, fire permits his initiation into an experience which becomes the basis of one of the four tales he relates in Conrad. It becomes, then, the foundation for whatever art he controls in his imagination, and the language he discovers in the retelling is a language different from the one he would ordinarily use.

Conrad has touched all his bases, and the revelation which Marlow attains is the revelation Conrad achieves in the period that would see Marlow three times in three different roles. Although he would be a narrator in all three, he narrates from differing points of view; that is, he is a different man each time we see him, as if Conrad were holding his gem up to the light to catch various facets. In Marlow, he had, fortunately, found an embodiment of his own metaphor for existence; and in "Youth," in the burning out and final conflagration, he had found his own sense of his career. When Marlow has that youthful vision of the East "mysterious, resplendent and sombre," he has discovered his "realm of gold." That realm, that Byzantium of golden images achieved through the burning out of the *Judea,* would be Conrad's vision.

With his move to Pent Farm, Conrad lived within a few miles of those who would become his "circle." The Fords settled at nearby Aldington at the end of March, when their lease on Gracie's Cottage at Limpsfield ended. At Rye, of course, was Henry James; Wells lived at Sandgate.* The Cranes were to move to Brede Place, near Rye. Another figure, Rudyard Kipling, lived at Rottingdean; but Conrad and Kipling apparently only exchanged

---

* In his *Experiment in Autobiography,* Wells left a witty description of Conrad, colored, of course, by Wells's rejection of Conrad's "artiness": "At first he impressed me, as he impressed Henry James, as the strangest of creatures. He was rather short and round-shouldered with his head as it were sunken into his body. He had a dark retreating face with a very carefully trimmed and pointed beard, a trouble-wrinkled forehead and very troubled dark eyes, and the gestures of his hands and arms were from the shoulders and very Oriental indeed. He reminded people of Du Maurier's Svengali and, in the nautical trimness of his costume, of Cutliffe Hyne's Captain Kettle. He spoke En-

letters. None of these on Conrad's part has ever turned up, and there is no way of knowing how far the correspondence extended. The most devoted part of the circle visited—Galsworthy, the Hopes, Ford, Graham, Edwin Pugh, Hugh Clifford.

The new year, 1899, began with Conrad asking Meldrum for an advance of £40 (the equivalent of $500–$600) for "Heart of Darkness," which Blackwood sent on. The story was growing "like the geni out of the bottle," a simile Conrad uses in letters to both Ford and Wells. It is an excellent image, for the story as it filled the page also welled out in Conrad's memory. Of less importance than the actual events of his own journey to the Congo, significant as those were, was the way in which his imagination had worked on memory. As we have noted, Conrad was a "silent poet," to use Wordsworth's phrase; which is to say, the imagination was working long before words became the outlet.

The Congo Diary Conrad left indicates personal discomfort and some awareness of human waste, but not the horror which he caught in the story. Except for a few basic details of his own voyage to the African coast and then the journey inland to the Inner Station, Conrad's retelling was indeed like the genie swelling out of the bottle: imagination working on memory to create an ever-expanding presence. By the time he wrote the story, he was interested in a Congo of the mind, and his version seems a greater truth than the actual Congo he had experienced almost ten years earlier. We note the artistic process, of art defining how life can be observed.

By transforming his own experiences into the dramatic content of "Heart of Darkness," Conrad achieved his intention, to make "you see": for several generations of readers, Conrad's Congo *was* Africa, and the Belgian rape *was* colonialism. The story, evidently, was almost fully formed in Conrad's subconscious, for all 38,000 words of it, including revisions, swelled out in less than two months. His letters to Meldrum and to friends indicate a steady progression, with few doubts and no sense of blockage. In a parallel development, the *Academy* "crowned" him and awarded him fifty guineas, an honor he belittled to Garnett but which could not have displeased him, if only for the money. He tells Garnett at the same time he is "turning out some rotten stuff for B.wood's 1000th No"—the depreciation being pro forma rather than what Conrad felt. Even when he wrote to Crane that he had not "a

---

glish strangely. Not badly altogether; he would supplement his vocabulary—especially if he were discussing cultural or political matters—with French words; but with certain oddities. He had learnt to read English long before he spoke it and he had formed wrong sound impressions of many familiar words. . . . He had set himself to be a great writer, an artist in words, and to achieve all the recognition and distinction that he imagined should go with that ambition, he had gone literary with a singleness and intensity of purpose that made the kindred concentration of Henry James seem lax and large and pale."

ghost of a notion" in his head, "a sentence under the pen," he was dissembling what was for him a discovery: that he could produce rapidly.

The true test of how well he was going would come with Graham's opinion. Conrad was already expectant, and hesitant, writing Graham that he was "shy of sending it to you—but have no objection to you looking at it if it should come in your way." "Heart of Darkness" would be Conrad's only work whose political potential would coincide with Graham's ideas. His letter a week later is jubilant that Graham liked "Heart of Darkness" so far. Conrad's words suggest his own high opinion:

> You bless me indeed. Mind you don't curse me by and bye for the very same thing. There are two more instalments in which the idea is so wrapped up in secondary notions that You—even You! may miss it. And also you must remember that I don't start with an abstract notion. I start with definite images and as their rendering is true some little effect is produced. So far the note struck chimes in with your conviction—mais après? There is an après. But I think that if you look a little into the episodes you will find in them the right intention though I fear nothing that is practically effective.

Graham's early reaction to "Heart of Darkness" was particularly encouraging, for Conrad had met difficulty with *The Rescue*, which could not appear in the *Illustrated London News* because it was going to run on too long. So Shorter of the *News* put it—his words rather ironic in the light of Conrad's inability to write it at all. As a consequence, he would have to forgo the *News* and go into the *English Illustrated Magazine*, a periodical far removed from *Blackwood's*. *The Rescue* had now become the "wretched novel which seems to have no end and whose beginning I declare I've forgotten." He adds that the "African nightmare feeling I've tried to put into *H of D* is a mere trifle to it."

In the letter to Graham cited above, Conrad reacts to his friend's invitation to a peace meeting to be held on March 8 by the Social Democrat Federation at St. James's Hall in Piccadilly. Conrad did appear, incredibly, and met several of Graham's friends, including W. H. Hudson, the naturalist and novelist who remained a (distant) friend. That Conrad attended it is remarkable, for his words to Graham indicate his detestation of every aspect of such an international enterprise. First, Conrad's words to Graham:

> As to the peace meeting. If you want me to come I want still more to hear you [Graham was a key speaker]. But—I am not a peace man, nor a democrat (I don't know what the word means really) and if I come I shall go into the body of the hall. I want to hear you—just as I want always to read you. I can't be an accomplice after or before the fact to any sort of fraternity that includes the westerners whom I so dislike. The platform! I pensez-Vous? Il y aura des Russes. Impossible! I can not admit the idea of fraternity not so much because I believe it impracticable, but because its

> propaganda (the only thing really tangible about it) tends to weaken the national sentiment the preservation of which is my concern. When I was in Poland 5 years ago and managed to get in contact with the youth of the university in Warsaw I preached at them and abused them for their social democratic tendencies. L'idée democratique est un trés beau phantôme, and to run after it may be fine sport, but I confess I do not see what evils it is destined to remedy. It confers distinction on Messieurs Jaurès [Jean Jaurès, a radical French deputy, writer and orator, assassinated in 1914], Liebknecht [Wilhelm Liebknecht, member of the Reichstag, founder of the Social Democratic Party, associated with Karl Marx, assassinated in 1919] & C° and your adhesion confers distinction upon it. International fraternity may be an object to strive for and, in sober truth, since it has Your support I will try to think it serious, but that illusion imposes by its size alone. Franchement what would you think of an attempt to promote fraternity amongst people living in the same street. I don't even mention two neighbouring streets. Two ends of the same street. There is already as much fraternity as there can be—and that's very little and that very little is no good. What does fraternity mean. Abnegation—self-sacrifice means something. Fraternity means nothing unless the Cain-Abel business. That's your true fraternity. Assez.

Then in French, Conrad continued his blast against an international brotherhood whose very banner is farcical.

> L'homme est un animal méchant. Sa mechanceté doit être organisée. Le crime est un condition nécéssaire de l'existence organisée. La socíete´ est essentielment criminelle—ou elle n'existerait pas. C'est l'égoisme qui sauve tout—absolument tout—tout ce que nous abhorrons tout ce que nous aimons. Et tout se tient. Voilà pourquoi je respecte les êxtremes anarchistes. —"Je souhaite l'extermination générale"— Très bien. C'est juste et ce qui plus c'est clair. On fait des compromis avec des paroles. Ça n'en finit plus. C'est comme une forêt ou personne ne connait la route. On est perdu pendant que l'on crie—"Je suis sauvé!"*

At the meeting itself, Conrad must have been appalled at what he heard. True, the intention of the meeting was to counter the proposals of the czar's government for a disarmament conference, what became, later, the Hague Conference. The Social Democrat Federation took the position that no peace conference was possible without the active participation of the workers of all civilized countries. The sole hope for world peace derived from an interna-

* Man is a wicked animal. His wickedness must be organized. Crime is a necessary condition of organized existence. Society is fundamentally criminal or else it would not exist. Egoism saves everything—absolutely everything—what we hate, what we love. And all remains. That is why I respect the extreme anarchists. "I hope for general extermination"—very well. It is just and what is more it is clear. We compromise with words. That does not end it. It is like a forest where no one knows the way. One is lost even as one cries "I am saved!"

tional socialism; so that, as Graham said, the industrial classes everywhere should forgo their animosities and combine "upon their worst enemies, the landlords and capitalists at home." What made this argument particularly poignant for Conrad was its similarity to what he had experienced in Poland. Graham's voice, as he spoke of a new order of opposition to landlords and capitalists, as he proclaimed a messianic socialism, was reminiscent of the sentiments of Apollo Korzeniowski, the spokesman of the "Red" position.* Overthrow of the czar was insufficient; Poland must itself be transformed and goods and income redistributed.

Conrad had profound psychological causes for opposing Graham's position, as well as his own reasoned political position, which, as he indicated in "The Crime of Partition," meant opposition to all internationalism. Democratic socialism was not only itself a farce but had created disruption of Poland's nationalism, toward some remote "higher ideal." Graham's March 8 meeting presented an intolerable conflict to Conrad—perhaps explaining why he wrote about it in French, the language of internationalism—for while it would display antagonism to imperial Russia, it would at the same time provide a platform for German speakers such as Liebknecht. As we see in "Autocracy and War," Germany was a *bête noire* almost as ghoulish as the czar; and what Liebknecht represented—anarchists, socialists, Jews, the rank and file of the European slums and ghettos, the tenement crowd—was equally unacceptable. In the face of this threat, Conrad became an aristocrat, an antidemocrat, an elitist, all positions which he eschewed in his fiction or made the source of his irony and mockery. The sores from his early life in Poland were never so painful as when he engaged Graham in political dispute.

Money matters were critical, and no amount of political discussion, however exhilarating such an interlude was, could disguise that Conrad's fortunes were desperate. He had received three messages from Adolf Krieger for money owed him; Conrad does not name him but speaks of him to Meldrum as the man whose business "he [Krieger] started 14 years ago with my

* Yet Graham meant much to Conrad, as we can see in his letter to Blackwood indicating he would like to dedicate the *Youth* volume to his Scottish friend. Blackwood, we recall, was the very arbiter of Tory convictions. Conrad wrote: "Strictly speaking it is a matter between the dedicator and the other person, but in this case—considering the imprint of the House and your own convictions I would prefer to defer to your wishes. I do not dedicate to C. Graham the socialist or to C. Graham the artistocrat (he is both—you know) but to one of the few men I *know*—in the full sense of the word—and knowing cannot but appreciate and respect—abstractedly as human beings. I do not share his political convictions or even all his ideas of art, but we have enough ideas in common to base a strong friendship upon."

money.* In all, Conrad appeared to owe him £180 (about $2,500 today), to which he applied the £50 from the *Academy.* Conrad says he dreads mortgaging his future, but seems to have no choice. His friend Hope is "utterly ruined," and therefore he cannot squeeze any money out of him. What remains is a reluctant request for advance money (£50) from Blackwood for the volume in which "Heart of Darkness" will appear. Conrad indicates it is not for pleasure or for health but for "peace of mind." Blackwood sent the money, and Conrad had entered definitely into that situation he had tried to avoid: mortgaging his future. It would in one way or another be mortgaged for the next fifteen years.

By mid-February Conrad had completed the draft of "Heart of Darkness" and was shifting into his new "story." *Jim*—in manuscript "Tuan Jim: A Sketch." To Blackwood, he indicated he has "Jim" half or one third written—that is, 10,000 words. This story, he thought, was to run to about 25–30,000 words and would form part of a volume to include "Youth" and "Heart of Darkness" (now calculated at 38,000 words, its final length), plus two other stories. One of them, called "First Command," appears to be an early idea for what became *The Shadow-Line;*† the other, what he calls a sketch, "A Seaman," may have become "Typhoon." Beyond the immediate work at hand, besides the ever-present *Rescue,* Conrad was sketching out work for some years to come, with "First Command" reaching deep into his later career. An alternate volume could consist, he says, of "Youth," "Heart of Darkness," and "Jim"; and if that arrangement was considered better, then he would plan to complete the last by April, a deadline he missed by well over a year.

Under such conditions, the size of "Jim" Conrad had in mind for the volume is uncertain, since at 25–30,000 words he would not have even gotten through the *Patna* episode. The "sketch" of the story at Harvard's Houghton Library would appear to indicate notes for more than the *Patna* chapters as they appeared in the book text. Probably, Conrad quite consciously wanted to write a story, even going as far as novella length (30–50,000 words), so that he would have a volume to present to Blackwood to justify the advances he had already received. Yet once he began to work over

---

* A confidential letter from Meldrum to Blackwood (February 9, 1899) provides some background for Krieger's loan, saying that it totaled £150 two or three years before, repayable when Conrad made a name for himself. Meldrum recommended giving Conrad money, saying, "He'll be a feather in *Maga*'s cap yet."

† In his Author's Note to *The Shadow-Line,* the novel written in 1916 and the Note in 1920, Conrad spoke of having the tale "for a long time in my mind, under the title of 'First Command' " (p. viii). The idea of "first command," although not developed until later, could well have been related, in 1899, to Conrad's sense of himself not as a captain on a ship but as a neophyte author, finally setting forth into realms of memory and imagination—but such matters are speculative.

his memory of the *Jeddah* episode as it intertwined with his view of Jim himself, the material determined its own length, regardless of conscious wish. This is another way of suggesting Conrad's imaginative processes had taken over and were establishing their own dictates, which he could not reject short of negating his art altogether.

In *Twilight of the Idols,* Nietzsche speaks of "great men," but his remark is even more appropriate for the creative artist. He says that great men carry within them explosives, a tremendous force stored up: ". . . their precondition is always, historically and physiologically, that for a long time much has been gathered, stored up, saved up, and conserved for them—that there has been no explosion for a long time. Once the tension in the mass has become too great, then the most accidental stimulus suffices to summon into the world the 'genius,' the 'deed,' the great destiny. What does the environment matter then, or the age, or the 'spirit of the age,' or 'public opinion.' "

If we look at a remarkable document in which Conrad sketched out the beginning of *Lord Jim,* we can see how Nietzsche's comment—one struck off the anvil, so to speak—accurately describes Conrad's condition in 1899. This document is called "Tuan Jim: A Sketch," consisting of twenty-eight pages of notes Conrad made for the novel. Of equal importance, however, is the fact that these notes were written in an album which, at one time, was thought to be in the handwriting of Conrad's mother, Ewa. The handwritten matter consists of twenty-five pages of Polish poetry, and the name at the bottom of the title page is that of Teofila Bobrowska, not Conrad's mother, but his maternal grandmother, the Teofila Biberstein-Pilchowska who married Józef Bobrowski. Frequent references to personages in the 1820s make it certain that the Teofila mentioned here was the grandmother and not Conrad's aunt of the same name.

Most compelling about this document, with its handwritten copies of poetry of the period, is that Conrad used blank pages for his notations for "Tuan Jim." One of the poems copied, in fact, was by Józef Korzeniowski, the novelist whose name surfaces in the Orzeszkowa attack upon Conrad. Thus, the document becomes a meeting point of so many historical and personal Conrad-Korzeniowski-Bobrowska matters that one can hardly consider it casual or random. There is, initially, the use of blank pages in a document handed down to Conrad from his maternal grandmother, carrying him deep into his Polish past, to the mother of his mother and of his uncle Tadeusz.

The "mothering" potentiality becomes apparent as Conrad dipped into the past, especially since his "Tuan Jim" lacks a living mother and wanders the East without family ties. Yet the story of Jim was, on Conrad's part, an act of memory, since he used the *Jeddah* episode for the first part and his memories of the East Borneo area for the second. In a curious, imaginative way, he combined his own living memories with those of his maternal grandmother, she who had married a man who opposed Ewa's marriage to Apollo.

Further, these Polish memories crossed with a writer whose very name recalled Conrad to his true name before his alleged "desertion" of Poland; this act of desertion, to use the harshest possible term, which is the subject of the first part of *Lord Jim*, was thrust at Conrad at this very time. It does not matter whether he knew the actual details of the attack—very possibly he did not—because in his way he had associated himself with the idea, if not the substance, of the assault. He could, after all, have afforded to purchase writing paper for a few pages of notes on his new story; but he chose to use a historical document with its handwritten Polish as the basis of his own story of a "desertion."

The conjunction of all these elements, given what we know of Conrad, could not have been happenstance. Besides the intense personal interest of these matters, the document indicates, as Alexander Janta has pointed out, that Conrad had the entire *Lord Jim* in his mind, however dimly. One passage in particular, from the back of page 14 of the document, proves Conrad foresaw the second part on Patusan. This passage contradicts utterly Conrad's own remarks in the Author's Notes in the Collected Edition of the novel, in which he says he thought only of the pilgrim-ship episode. This passage in his grandmother's album is as follows:

> *Afterwards when his (he disappea—*
> *(The Malay) red from a*
> *perception of the intolerable*
> *drove him away from the*
> *haunts of white men, the*
> *Malays of the village where he*
> *(has fancied himself free from*
> *the intolerable) without exercising*
> *his perceptive faculty added (called)*
> *him Tuan Jim—as one (would) might*
> *Lord Jim.*

Conrad suggested to Blackwood a title reminiscent of Flaubert's *Trois Contes:* "Three Tales" by Joseph Conrad. Alternate titles, with something of the subject matter in mind, were *Tales from Memory*, or "Youth and Other Tales." Blackwood wanted the volume for May 1899, which meant Conrad would have to forgo any serialization of *Jim*, a source of considerable income. The latter mentioned to Meldrum he had two more stories in his head besides those above, which would bring the volume to 120,000 words, but they would not be ready until July. Such estimates were overly optimistic by far, since the production of this amount of copy would run months and even years after that. Conrad also told Meldrum he had thought ahead to another volume, which would include "First Command," "the one about a Captain's wife; 'A Seaman' sketch; and 'Equitable Division' (a story of a typhoon)," the eventual "Typhoon."

Conrad was defining a life pattern for himself, although he may not have been fully conscious of it: the writer, excluding nearly all intrusions and diversions, sitting at his desk in Pent Farm, his window overlooking the downs, facing squarely that sheet of white paper, staring at its blankness and trying to fill it with a few hundred words a day. It was a routine Conrad would repeat nearly every day when he was in sufficiently good health for the next twenty-five years. His devotion to that piece of white paper would be as complete as the captain's to his command.

It was all write, drive, push ahead on *Jim,* so as to complete it and not lose serial rights before it became included in the volume of short stories. And yet it is unclear how Conrad could have finished it at story length when, clearly, he foresaw both the *Patna* and Patusan parts implicitly. His mind was full of technique, and he was developing, as he worked, his sense of impressionism, techniques he would work out further with Ford when their collaboration heated up. A February 12 letter to Galsworthy, concerning Henry James's work, demonstrates how much James was in Conrad's mind as he worked on *Jim;* and James repaid the compliment by finding *Lord Jim* a masterpiece.

Galsworthy had reported his cousin's sentiments that James was a cold writer, and Conrad undertook a meticulous, and critically important, distinction between "coldness" and primitive emotions. Himself caught in the need for a technique, he was very careful to demonstrate that technical perfection need not be frigidity. Conrad picked out several works, the stories "The Pupil" and "The Altar of the Dead," for example, as demonstrating James's heart even within his delicacy of handling. We note Conrad attempting to follow through on his remarks in the Preface to *The Nigger,* where he, not unlike James, combined Flaubert and Pater to achieve a blending of form and substance. "I admit he is not forcible," Conrad continued about James, "or, let us say, the only forcible thing in his work is his technique. Now a literary intelligence would be naturally struck by the wonderful technique and that is so wonderful in its way that it dominates the bare expression. The more so that the expression is only of delicate shades. He is never in deep gloom or in violent sunshine. But he feels deeply and vividly every delicate shade."

In this estimation, Conrad has suggested his impressionism, catching glints, slants, intimations, without sinking to the nadir or rising to the zenith, but moving warily in between extremes. He adds that not everyone can be Turgenev, and by that he means the rest of us cannot achieve Turgenev's absolute naturalism of method; we are, the rest, caught in the coils of technique.

Exactly when Conrad and Ford decided to work on *The Inheritors* together is unclear. The novel was not completed until early 1900, and very little of it reflected Conrad's work. The latter wrote to Garnett and others that the conception of the novel as well as the writing of it was Ford's. There are, nevertheless, certain striking elements in *The Inheritors* which appear to be Conrad's.* Chiefly, *The Inheritors* took shape as a political satire, a roman à clef, whose function would be to show the interlinking of political and financial corruption in high places. It was not in any sense a traditional political novel in that it did not attempt to demonstrate the workings of the political process, and its chief character, a writer named Etchingham Granger, is completely an outsider to intrigue and power. It is, rather, a fantasy intermixed with some interesting psychological touches.

Ford and Conrad tried to combine several elements: the arty world as represented by Ford himself, the political world reflected in European interest in the Congo (the exploitation of Greenland in the novel), and the literary interest in science fiction and its derivatives—Wells's *The Time Machine* and *War of the Worlds* and, possibly, Kipling's "An Error in the Fourth Dimension" (1898). The "I" narrator is Etchingham Granger, a writer of impeccable pedigree whose fortunes are none too good and who is forced to take on several disagreeable commercial assignments. Early on, he meets an extremely attractive young lady who is a "Fourth Dimensionist." This tribe of "new people"—there is a dystopian pattern here—lacks feelings and normal or human responses. They, and she, are dedicated to becoming the inheritors of the earth because of their superiority in intellect, control, and deception. In particular, their plan is to undermine public confidence in its institutions, which turns out to be fairly easy given the nature of the men who govern. The political satire lies here: everyone has a price and everyone is self-serving regardless of the seriousness of the issues. There is no "public policy" among public men.

The book provides a cross section of well-known men, all thinly disguised in their fictional roles. They are familiar from Conrad's world—Polehampton is Fisher Unwin; Lea (favorably presented) is Edward Garnett; from Ford's world—the painter Jenkins is Ford Madox Brown, his grandfather. And from the "great" world: Gurnard—Joseph Chamberlain; Churchill (handled sympathetically)—Balfour; the insidious Duc de Mersch—Leopold II of Belgium; Fox—the press lord Northcliffe. Both Gurnard and Fox have or have had connections to the Fourth Dimensionists.

The political aspect is clear: a savage attack on Chamberlain for Boer War

* Ford commented extensively on this collaboration, stressing that in the entire book Conrad's part was no more than "a thousand [words]—certainly there cannot be two—of Conrad's writing." His collaborator's function, he says, was to "give each scene a final tap; these, in a great many cases, brought the whole meaning of the scene to the reader's mind." He says *his* intention had been to create scenes that melted into each other "until the whole book, in the end, came to be nothing but a series of the very vaguest hints." Through this, he hoped to achieve "a sort of silverpoint: a delicacy."

policies; support of Balfour; and a merciless savaging of Leopold II for his exploitation of the Congo—details that Conrad may have provided, although much public evidence had appeared by the late 1890s. It was also, according to Ford, to be an attack upon the younger generation (the Fourth Dimensionists) which lacked all respect for their elders and for social institutions, although their lack of respect in the frame of the novel would appear to be well justified. Probably of more interest, in fictional terms at least, was the nature of the young lady who is the prime representative of the new race. She is, clearly, devastatingly attractive and inaccessible, intent only on her mission, which is to inherit the earth:

> I heard the Dimensionists described; a race clear-sighted, eminently practical, incredible; with no ideals, prejudices, or remorse; with no feeling for art and no reverence for life; free from any ethical tradition; callous to pain, weakness, suffering and death, as if they had been invulnerable and immortal.

The fictional touch—and it may have been Conrad's idea, a carryover from *The Sisters*—was to have the merciless girl pose as Granger's sister. She stresses the sibling function increasingly as he emphasizes his desire for her; so that the roles they play are clearly incestuous. It is uncertain whether her assumption of the sisterly relationship is to keep them apart or to intensify his feeling for her. While there is little enough Adam in Granger, there is a good deal of Eve in the girl: temptress, destroyer of man's peace, an archetypal serpentine figure. She is described, in many respects, as a typical 1890s woman; one thinks of Beardsley's female portraits:

> They had no joy, these people who were to supersede us; their clear-sightedness did nothing more for them than just that enabling them to spread desolation among us and take our places. It had been in her manner all along, she was like Fate; like the abominable Fate that desolates the whole length of our lives; that leaves of our hopes, of our plans, nothing but a hideous jumble of fragments, like those of statues, smashed by hammers; the senseless, inscrutable, joyless Fate that we hate, and that debases us forever and ever.

The hatred of women in this portrait is obvious. While she may seem an extension of Conrad's own Aïssa (in *An Outcast*), the latter was humanized, and was, in a sense, victimized by her own role. Here, however, we have an expression of pure misogyny; and given the nature of future activities, it would appear to be far more Ford's than Conrad's. Ford's instability with women, his need to be worshipped either by much younger or much older women, reflects an infantilism that was connected to a hatred of the sex altogether. It is a harem-and-slave mentality, alternating sadism and masochism, and here the attractive young woman wields, figuratively, the whip.

Granger's pleasure is all masochistic, voyeuristic, self-flagellating; and of course, he succumbs, just as she says he will.

In a March 26, 1900, letter to Garnett, which the latter published, much to Ford's annoyance, Conrad downgraded *The Inheritors* as a lark. "I set myself to look upon the thing as a sort of skit upon the political (?!) novel, fools of the Morley Roberts sort do write. This in my heart of hearts. And poor H was dead in earnest! Oh Lord. How he worked! There is not a chapter I haven't made him write twice—most of them three times over."*

Yet in a letter to the "Saturday Review" section of *The New York Times* (written on August 2, 1901), in response to a review of *The Inheritors*, Conrad became serious. First, he indicated that his own "scruples in the matter of treatment" may have stood as a barrier to Ford's fresher and more individual talent, thus robbing the book of that "private vision" which might have made it more convincing. Then Conrad tried to bend the very slight material to a more serious purpose:

> Therefore it may perhaps be permissible to point out that the story is not directed against "some of the most cherished traditions and achievements of Englishmen." It is rather directed at the self-seeking, at the falsehood that had been (to quote the book) "hiding under the words that for ages had spurred men to noble deeds, to self-sacrifice, and to heroism." And apart from this view, to direct one's little satire at the tradition and the achievements of a race would have been an imbecile futility—something like making a face at the great pyramid.

Conrad continues that tradition and achievement are the very soul not only of a single race but of mankind, "which, without the vast breadth and colossal form of the past would be resolved into a handful of the dying struggling feebly in the darkness under an overwhelming multitude of the dead." Of interest, of course, is how these remarks, ostensibly directed to *The Inheritors*, in which Conrad's role was minimal, feed into his own work, the by now completed *Lord Jim*, the recently published "Heart of Darkness," and the yet to be written *Nostromo*. He says that Granger must come to recognize that no man is permitted " 'to throw away with impunity the treasure of his past—the past of his kind—whence springs the promise of his future.' "

Yet with all its brightness and sprightliness, *The Inheritors* has no center. It is all angles and glare. Ford's method, which both collaborators later devel-

---

* On July 3, 1901, Conrad cast almost his entire letter in terms of the novel: "Am I to understand that, like the hero of the Inheritors, you have fallen amongst the Dimensionists and are about to become an interviewer? Then I must be the Great Callan—who, Pawling says, must be meant for Crockett. . . . But to see you, and to see you here, I am ready to turn myself into a Callan. I believe Fox paid Granger's expenses, so Pawling can't do less than buy you a return ticket for Sandling. But come under any pretence and at whatever cost and help me to inherit the Earth before I die. There is no time to lose."

oped into the *progression d'effet*, was to glance off his subject and substitute obliqueness for center. Nevertheless, the materials of the novel were too diffused. Elements never cohere, nor can they—nor, perhaps, were they intended to. Whatever the purpose, the reader finds no moral center, a confusion that may be cited from the text in which it is uncertain whether blacks or Eskimos inhabit Greenland. At no level is the information rooted sufficiently in real events—no sense of science, geography, or politics—for the satire and parody to operate effectively.

Part of the problem, perhaps the main one, is that neither Conrad nor Ford held any sustained point of view as apart from the desire to ridicule public figures and public events. Yet their ability to parody, the crux of *The Inheritors*, could only have functioned effectively with more detailing of character and event. What was true for their sense of mockery was even more valid of their desire to achieve irony. The effective use of irony, as in "Heart of Darkness," *Lord Jim*, or *The Secret Agent*, or in Ford's *The Good Soldier*, was and would be a derivative of particularization. They were not novelists of sufficient philosophical consistency (or world-view) to be able to move among generalities. When the two of them came to develop their ideas of impressionism, based on the *progression d'effet*, their attempt at oblique, "angular" presentation, they were very careful to base their method on specifics.

Very possibly, Conrad's response to Elsie Hueffer's criticism of "Heart of Darkness" was connected to his awareness of this point. Although we lack her letter, we can assume she attacked the novella and Kurtz for their vagueness, their lack of focus. Conrad responded:

> And, of course, I don't admit the whole of your case. What I distinctly admit is the fault of having made Kurtz too symbolic or rather symbolic at all. But the story being mainly a vehicle for conveying a batch of personal impressions I gave the rein to my mental laziness and took the line of least resistance. This is then the whole Apologia pro Vita Kurtzii—or rather for the tardiness of his vitality.

Referring to their next collaboration, on *Romance*, Conrad chided Ford for failing to give it a sense of "hard reality." "The treatment as it stands [he wrote] is too much in the air—in places. I don't want to bother you now by going into the argument." That phrase "hard reality" recurs in various forms in Conrad's other letters and in his essays. He feared the vague (his antagonism toward Melville), the murky and grandiose (his hatred of Dostoevsky), the shadowy symbolic (his distaste for most poetry)—all of which he rejected as manifestations of confused minds. He, in fact, often misread aspects of the modern movement because he thought it was dreamy, soft, without that hard core of reality which he felt to be the cornerstone of thought.

Ezra Pound once remarked that what Flaubert had done to change French prose, Conrad and Ford did to transform English prose, and he, Pound, was trying to do something similar with English poetry. Conrad's use of *phanopoeia*—the piling up of imagistic details which replaced, in part, a direct narrative—was, said Pound, the way of the imagists. The aim, for both imagists and the collaborators, was to achieve surface tension through oblique reference and slanting approaches or attacks. The goal was to achieve a sense of wholeness by way of a series of break-ups or interruptions. Pound was exactly right, for the break-up of the conventional novel's narratives into small scenes makes the scene function like an image in poetry, in a way like the images in Pound's early poetry. Without any loss of surface solidity, the reader's attention is drawn to sounds, rhythms, nuances.

Writing to Garnett on an auspicious day, Good Friday of 1899, Conrad was himself caught between fears of permanent burial and the desire for resurrection. He was running the manuscript of *Rescue* parallel with that of *Lord Jim*, a tandem operation that suggested a figurative death and burial:

> The more I write the less substance do I see in my work. The scales are falling off my eyes. It is tolerably awful. And I face it, I face it but the fright is growing on me. My fortitude is shaken by the view of the monster. It does not move; its eyes are baleful; it is as still as death itself—and it will devour me. Its stare has eaten into my soul already deep, deep. I am alone with it in a chasm with perpendicular sides of black basalt. Never were sides so perpendicular and smooth, and high. Above, your anxious head against a bit of sky peers down—in vain—in vain. There's no rope long enough for that rescue.

As of May 25, Conrad was still thinking of *Lord Jim* as a story. In a letter to Algernon Methuen, in response to the publisher's request for a manuscript, he indicated his dilemma. He was a year behind in his submission of *The Rescue*, for Heinemann in England and for McClure in the United States. He was "engaged to Mr. Blackwood for a vol. of three stories which is still 80,000 words short"—which would include *Jim*. Conrad suggested that if these publishers became tired of his irregularity, based on a power of production as uncertain as the weather, then he would come to Methuen. But, he added, *Blackwood's* "is the only periodical *always* open to me—and is the only one for which I really care to work."

Conrad's devotion to *Blackwood's* is somewhat ironical, for it was based on a misunderstanding propped up by a good deal of noblesse oblige. There is reason to believe Blackwood hoped Conrad would end up as a writer in the masculine tradition, turning out conservative, solid fictional fare that would support God, country, and empire, the values upon which the firm was founded. Although Blackwood showed considerable courage in publishing "Heart of Darkness" and *Lord Jim*, he was really accustomed to different materials. Conrad's insistence on aesthetic questions, his irregularity in production of copy, his frequent requests for advances, his chronic indebtedness while he edged ever nearer financial disaster—all of these were qualities quite distinct from what Blackwood expected, or was able to deal with. Part of the former's loyalty, if not the whole of it, can be attributed to the presence of David Meldrum, the London literary adviser to the firm and a true friend to Conrad and to his (and Crane's) literary aspirations. It was Meldrum who intervened and supported Conrad, especially at crucial financial impasses; and it was Meldrum who appeared to understand and accept Conrad's artistic intentions.

From mid-spring of 1899 to mid-July of 1900, Conrad was occupied almost exclusively with *Lord Jim.* The novel eventually was to grow to nearly 150,000 words and become the first of Conrad's characteristically convoluted tales: his first entry into what was to become the "modernistic" mode. As he settled in for this long work, with its extreme mental strain—money against words, daily routine against pages, anxieties against chapters—he wrote a touching letter to Helen Sanderson in which he tried to find, for her, something settled and firm. He speaks of the unrest of human thought, which is, comparable to the unrest of the sea, "disturbing and futile." Like Matthew Arnold at Dover Beach, Conrad sees the receding water as indicative of faith: "It seems to me I am looking at the rush and recoil of the waves at the foot of a cliff." He speaks of a church (Helen's Scottish church) as being a rock of certainty in the seas of uncertainty. He attacks the "mad individualism of Nietsche [Nietzsche] the exaggerated altruism of the next man tainted with selfishness and pride." Such values are washed away, whereas faith remains; but it must be a faith that refuses compromise, refuses expedience, or else it becomes "a system a social institution." Only the individual can hold firm. Conrad's "church," located here as "the repository of the highest truth," is really the individual: he is speaking of himself and of Jim, who lacked that rocklike firmness and was doomed by vacillation. Tied to his desk, the pen stuck to his fingers, Conrad sought guidance in the fact of existence, in action; all systems lied and deceived.

CHAPTER 21

Pinker and *Jim*

ON July 31, Conrad wrote Meldrum that *Jim* might turn out longer than "Heart of Darkness," the information accompanied by a request for another £50. We recall Blackwood had wanted the entire "Jim: A Sketch" for the June number. To the owner himself, Conrad wrote how pleased he was at the latter's sympathetic reception of the fragment. Conrad told him *Jim* was turning out more like "Youth" than "Heart of Darkness," which was not, of course, the case. He was anxious to defend the "general reader" and felt *Jim* would not lack such reader interest. If we momentarily look ahead to the reviews *Jim* would receive, we note that several reviewers, even those with most insight, commented on the difficulties of the narrative, its fluctuations and its obstructions. Conrad consoled Blackwood: "The question of *art* is so endless, so involved and so obscure that one is tempted to turn one's face resolutely away from it." Conrad tried to find out from Meldrum exactly where he stood with Blackwood, the man and the firm, since he had several other tales in mind, including what became "The End of the Tether." Also, with the mess he had made of *The Rescue*, he felt he owed Heinemann something. Meldrum encouraged Blackwood to handle Conrad carefully and to advance him the money requested.

At this point, toward the end of August 1899, Conrad was producing copy at a fair rate but his career lacked discipline: that is, his imaginative and creative powers were reaching toward their highest levels of achievement, but his personal affairs were diffuse, uncontrollable, and unresolved. He needed a coordinator, or at least a support. Such supports had come to him regularly at intervals in the past. After his father's death, there was, with Tadeusz Bobrowski, a prop that lasted until Conrad was into his mid-thirties; then Marguerite Poradowska, who offered him literary discussion and aid; followed by Edward Garnett, at the juncture of his sea and writing careers; and now James Brand Pinker, an unlikely figure given Conrad's tastes and predilections.

When Conrad and Pinker first became associated (the initial Conrad letter is dated August 23, 1899), the agent was thirty-six and Conrad was forty-one. Pinker had had a varied career, all commercially oriented, and in areas Conrad usually disdained. Born in England, Jewish, without much formal education, Pinker worked first as a clerk and then as a journalist in Constantinople, for the *Levant Herald.* After marrying a woman well above him in class and money, he returned to England about eight years before he met Conrad. He became assistant editor of *Black & White,* an illustrated weekly which employed quite a reputable staff (Eden Phillpotts, Violet Hunt, M. H. Spielman, W. A. Mackenzie), and its first year of issues included contributions from Hardy, Stevenson, and James. Pinker also read for a publishing house and edited, for a short period, *Pearson's Magazine,* whose function was to play to the very popular audience Conrad so detested. In January 1896, Pinker established himself as a literary agent, in Granville House, Arundel Street. Some of his early clients, besides Conrad, included Wells, Wilde, Crane, James, and Bennett.

From the point of view of Pinker, only newly established as an agent, Conrad was a financial proposition. From Conrad's point of view, the relationship was that between a drowning man and the straw that might save him. The connection to Pinker, following shortly after the beginning of Conrad's collaboration with Ford, was a form of decision. He had, figuratively, entered the valley of the shadow of death, making personal decisions which allowed no retreat. Just as still short of seventeen he had set into motion a twenty-year sea career from which there was no immediate redress, so now, at over forty, a family man, he was entering a new phase. In his own work, he had received fairly generous support from publishers and critics, and his Preface to *The Nigger* indicated he had found sufficient theoretical underpinning to continue. His movement into the world of the publisher Blackwood reflected a seriousness of purpose and dedication to literature far beyond a simple desire to be published. All those aspects of his career mirrored a man setting forth to carry out an intense inner mission.

The personal aspects, however, were far more complicated. Deep within Conrad, if we judge from the works he was engaged in, alternately *Lord Jim* and "Heart of Darkness," he was grappling with terrifying ideas and severe nightmares. Each work was a testing out of personal elements he was uncertain of. The seeming disparity between Marlow's moderation and Kurtz's anarchy is a good objective correlative of divisions Conrad sensed within himself. That persistent image of himself as shards and fragments, as mad, continues to poke through his letters. "My memory is good and sane even if my mind is diseased and on the verge of craziness," he wrote Galsworthy. The yawning chasm or sense of drowning he felt was belied, however, by his social stance: married, the father of a small boy, the friend and companion of respectable writers and editors, the author of three novels and several short stories. All that was outer; within, the opposite beckoned, his own Congo with its strange rites.

Ford and Pinker fitted these opposite aspects of Conrad's personality and need. The collaboration with the former was a plunge into uncertainties, the Grub Street aspect of literary work. Pinker provided a modicum of control, a businessman, a Jew who would make sure profit outbalanced loss. For Conrad, the sea had been certain: tasks were defined, status and roles determined by rank, change shackled by custom and tradition. Literary life, he discovered, had no fixed standards except those posed from within. He sensed the abyss awaiting men like him who had chosen to live with uncertainties and doubts. On the sea, one either survived or not, depending on one's physical endurance and grit. On land, one was never sure; survival was a state of mind, a matter of nerves. There were no traditional values. Ford and Pinker, therefore—until he saw them entire and whole—were ambiguous forces in his life, sustaining and threatening. How he resented his dependence, that sign of his own weakness! From the early letters to both, we sense how close Conrad was to the insanity of a Kurtz, the haunted obsessions of a Jim. To Ford, he said he felt "as if my brain were on the point of boiling over the top of my miserable skull." And a little earlier: "I had in years gone by a certain reputation for courage. Now, no doubt, all this is changed the spirit being crushed out of me by the tyranny of mysterious sensations, yet still a spark, a dim spark exists somewhere—a vestige of the old fire under the tepid ruins."

In this gray, ambiguous, undefined area, the relationship with Pinker commenced and was, for many years, set. Although Pinker would not recognize himself in Conrad's image, the author saw this ultimately very generous man as the enemy; for Pinker demanded that Conrad not for a moment lose sight of his obligation to his craft and his profession. In this respect, Pinker, while making Conrad's continuing career financially more stable, yet, at the same time, caused the writer to appear, in his own eyes, a slave to the demands of his agent. The proud ship captain was, in terms of the relationship, reduced to a common seaman; although he produced the copy, Pinker dictated the terms and controlled the purse. Each stage of Pinker's generosity only intensified Conrad's indebtedness, and each new project of Conrad's put increased strain on Pinker's generosity. Both moved uneasily toward the limits of the other's endurance. Although we lack Pinker's responses to Conrad's (almost 1,200) letters, we can tell from the latter's correspondence that Pinker bridled at unexpected requests for money and at delayed installments of manuscript, especially when Conrad's indebtedness climbed into hundreds of pounds (as high as £1,600 in 1908, about $25,000 in current purchasing power).

The early years of the relationship, as we shall see, were the most difficult, for neither understood what the other really wanted. In addition, Conrad had already entangled himself in prior commitments, which meant he had to bypass Pinker even as he was asking the latter to negotiate for him and financially support his efforts. Further, Conrad had accumulated publishers (Fisher Unwin, for one) who insisted on retaining copyright, which created in his dealings with Pinker numerous difficulties concerning reprint and foreign rights, all sources of potential income for the agent.

Conrad's initial letter begins wittily, and the tone suggests the distance Conrad hoped to keep between the two men. He intended very clearly to remain in command and fought Pinker for every inch of the ship's bridge.

> My method of writing is so unbusiness-like that I don't think you could have any use for such an unsatisfactory person. I generally sell a work before it is begun, get paid when it is half done and don't do the other half till the spirit moves me. I must add that I have no control whatever over the spirit—neither has the man who has paid the money.
>
> The above may appear fanciful to you but it is the sober truth. I live in hopes of reformation and whenever that takes place you and you alone shall have the working of the New Conrad. Meanwhile I must be content to pander to my absurd weaknesses, and hobble along the line of the least resistance.

Since the association began at the time Conrad was writing "Heart of Darkness" (now completed) and *Lord Jim* and these works were already consigned (to Blackwood), his relationship to Pinker was more a matter of fencing than substance. Once past these pieces, however, Conrad began to use the agent for the sale of his collaborative work with Ford, "Seraphina" (*Romance*) and his own "Typhoon." If we move ahead temporarily to that very trying time, we can see from Conrad's letter of January 8, 1902—one already cited and partially quoted—what kind of pressure he was under and how intensely he struggled to keep command. The subject, ostensibly, was "Seraphina." Pinker, apparently, had asked for more prompt work in order to justify his considerable outlay of money, and Conrad responded:

> I fail to apprehend what inspired the extraordinary contents of your letter which I received this morning. All you had to do was to say yes or no. Mine was written fully not to get the easier at your pocket but from another motive—not worth explaining now. But it was never intended to give you an opening for a lecture. It will take more than the delay in delivering *S* to make *me* a failure; neither do I believe it will put you in the B'cy Court. And I am not now in the right frame of mind for the proper appreciation of a lecture. I am working twelve hours in the twenty four with the full knowledge of my ideal and of my risk.

After detailing some of the problems with Ford—illness, his contractual agreement for another work—Conrad moved into the area that was to dominate his side of the correspondence as a counter to Pinker's financial pressure: his own sense of literary worth, the aesthetic ideal he was devoting his middle years to.

> If you don't want the bother of my stuff saddled with my other imperfections tell me to go to the devil. That won't offend me and I'll go as soon as ever you had your money back. But don't address me as if I were a man lost in sloth, ignorance or folly. Were you as rich as Croesus and as omnipotent as all the editors rolled into one I would not let such a tone pass without resenting it in the most outspoken manner. And don't write to me of failure, confound it! because you and I have very different notions of failure.

Conrad closes the letter: "Am I a confounded boy? I have had to look death in the eye once or twice. It was nothing. I had not then a wife and child. It was nothing to what I have to go through now pen in hand before what to *me* spells failure. I am no sort of airy R. L. Stevenson who considered his art a prostitute and the artist as no better than one. I dare say he was punctual—but I don't envy him."

This was in the period just before Conrad began *Nostromo*, and particularly trying was the fact that he was between major projects. His most immediate work, such as "Typhoon" and "To-morrow," as well as other short fiction, must have seemed to him marking time, or else Pinker's comments could not have touched such a nerve or brought forth such a bravura display of self-assertion, of the "artist at work." Whatever the precise reason, Conrad was then, in 1902, in a literary limbo, stalled on "Seraphina" and not yet immersed in a definitive project. The shaky nerves, the wounded ego, the nervous sensibility—all these are indicative of a man anxious to enter into combat but uncertain who or where the enemy is.

All this, however, was later, when Pinker's belief in Conrad would almost daily be put to the test. Back in the fall of 1899, Conrad was immersed in *Lord Jim*, which was mortgaged to Blackwood; stalled on *The Rescue*, which was owed to Heinemann; and living off the future. To Garnett, Conrad caught the moment well: "I am [he said] like a man who has lost his gods." He adds that his efforts seem "unrelated to anything in heaven and everything under heaven is impalpable to the touch like shapes of mist." Plunging downward, confused by mist and fog, touching bottom, sensing the devil himself within his skin, Conrad was able to do his best work. "Every image floats vaguely in a sea of doubt," he told Garnett, and the phrase is directly on target for someone writing *Lord Jim*. His own "swimming in the destructive element" was the precise frame of reference for what his imagination was dredging up; the past, memory, aesthetic ideals—all were, as himself, part of an "unexplored universe of incertitudes."

Writing to Hugh Clifford over his *In a Corner of Asia*, Conrad remarked in almost an aside what was paramount in his own mind as he still intended to complete *Lord Jim* in October.

> You do not leave enough to the imagination. I do not mean as to facts—the facts cannot be too explicitly stated; I am alluding simply to the phrasing. True, a man who knows so much . . . may well spare himself the trouble of meditating over the words, only that words, groups of words, words standing alone, are symbols of life, have the power in their sound or their aspect to present the very thing you wish to hold up before the mental vision of your readers. The things "as they are" exist in words; therefore words should be handled with care lest the picture, the image of truth abiding in facts, should become distorted—or blurred.
>
> These are the considerations for a mere craftsman—you may say; and you may also conceivably say that I have nothing else to trouble my head about. However, the *whole* of the truth lies in the presentation; therefore the expression should be studied in the interest of veracity. This is the only morality of *art* apart from *subject.*

Such considerations were particularly pressing, since the first installment of *Lord Jim* was scheduled to appear in *Blackwood's Magazine* for October 1899, that very month. *Lord Jim* would appear in fourteen installments in all, and Conrad indicated on October 26, to Garnett, that he was not yet finished with the fifth, and final, installment. He had, then, as of mid-October, written four and a half installments and would write not simply another half but ten more, as the novel would run from October 1899 to November 1900. Since Conrad was caught up in the serialization when he was still 100,000 words from completion of the novel, the pressure was immense. And even if he did not foresee the great length of *Jim* (the evidence here is quite ambiguous), nevertheless, his own slow method of working and his insistence on the power of words would point to torturous progress.

Possibly, Conrad had to deceive himself, or else, with the money for the book having already been advanced to him, he could not have faced the long pull. To Ted Sanderson (on October 12), as noted, he says he spends every minute of every day to "produce a beggarly tale of words or perhaps to produce nothing at all." He indicates he had expected to complete it "on the first of this month"—October 1899! He then informs Sanderson that Joseph Conrad's final book will appear in March, a volume of three stories. One of those stories, presumably, would be *Lord Jim,* although how this was to occur we cannot say. No such volume, of course, appeared until 1902, when "Youth" and "Heart of Darkness" were joined by the still unwritten "The End of the Tether," in a volume called *Youth, A Narrative; and Two Other Stories.*

As Conrad recognized, there was an hallucinatory quality to it all. He told Sanderson: "The unreality of it seems to enter one's real life, penetrate into the bones, make the very heart beats pulsate illusions through the arteries. One's will becomes the slave of hallucinations, responds only to shadowy impulses, waits on imagination alone." The "unreality" Conrad speaks of could only have resulted if he felt divided, between imaginative processes which had taken over and bodily functions which had to be ministered to. He speaks in the same letter of being in a land of mist "peopled by shadows" and assures Sanderson they will meet soon, at midnight, as though they were ghosts or ghouls. He compares himself to a "desolate Shade" which haunts "this earth of ours." The imagery here is all oriented toward the unconscious, toward death itself.

One segment of Conrad continued to move among people, but the part attached to *Lord Jim* was haunting the mists of things seen only dimly. Like Proust, he had developed a type of vision in which phenomena could be observed from two points of vantage, from close up and from great distances, whether in the mind's eye or in memory. Conrad's feelings of dissociation, close as they were to complete breakdown, even madness, derived from his sense that he was subsisting on two levels; and the unreality he speaks of is a consequence of his inability to resolve the duality of his kind of existence. Not surprisingly in two months, in February, he would break down. In that condition close to collapse, he seemed to work best.

From a great distance, Ted Sanderson, patriotic and nationalistic, called Conrad's attention to the Boer War. It was an affair on another planet. To Graham, less than two weeks before, Conrad had commented that there "is an appalling fatuity in this business." Conrad would mock Kipling's assertion that the war was undertaken for the cause of democracy: "C'est à crever de rire"—one splits one's sides laughing. Nevertheless, he tells the ferociously antiwar Graham he hopes British successes "will be crushing from the first—on the same principle that if there's murder being done in the next room and you can't stop it you wish the head of the victim to be bashed in forthwith and the whole thing over for the sake of your own feelings."

To Sanderson, however, Conrad responded differently. First, Ted was jingoistic and was preparing to depart for South Africa to fight the Dutch Boers; and second, Ted stood for something—unlike Graham's hatred of the very colonialism and capitalism that had led to the conflict—which Conrad had to settle in his own mind. He would deal with some of Ted's ideas and feelings in the figure of Charles Gould in *Nostromo.* Conrad partially shared his young friend's feeling that the English provided justice and order and therefore their interests must be defended. But he also saw much more widely, and he looked with a jaded eye at the empire and at colonial ventures, even while assuming the English did the thing better than anyone else. He had already suggested this in "Heart of Darkness." Ted's career, outlook, and sensibility had evidently touched something profound in Conrad—there was a good deal of Ted in Jim, of course—and despite the intense pressure of that creative "other world," he felt obliged to answer at length.

Conrad foresaw quite correctly that a war is never "won" in any final sense, that the victory, "unless it is to be thrown away—shall have to be followed by ruthless repression." In that respect, a war should be a final act, "while this war is an initial act." Conrad had the model of Poland and imperial Russia before him. Such an enterprise, with victory followed by repression, Conrad felt, is antithetical to the English character, which relies more on "the expansive force of its enterprise and its morality." English rule in India after the 1857 Sepoy Mutiny was, obviously, an exception to this benign view. Conrad tells Ted that the danger to the empire lies elsewhere, not in South Africa, but in the Near and Far East, and in those areas a war "would have cleared the air—would have been worth the sacrifice."

Conrad's real animosity, however, is extended toward the journalists, "the hysterical transports of some public organs." "Those infernal scribblers," he says, "are rank outsiders."* He also attacks the generals for their strategy. "To a really great general these converging movements in his front would perhaps have given an opportunity. I revel in my imbecility." While inconclusive, these cursory remarks suggest that Conrad, despite other severe pressures, was following the war with some care, as he would later follow the First World War, in which his son Borys served.

On October 27, Conrad told Blackwood the January installment of *Jim* was written and practically ready. The January number would carry the book through Chapters 8 and 9, about one quarter of the novel's final length. These chapters were the crucial ones of revelation in which Jim relates his *Patna* experience to Marlow and must try to make the older man understand what he has done. This section would become the basis for Conrad's later statement that the pilgrim-ship episode "could conceivably colour the whole 'sentiment of existence' in a simple and sensitive character."

Marlow's desire to comprehend Jim's tale is fitted by Conrad into a natural plan, almost a Hardyesque universe: miniaturized man, the immensity of ocean and sky, the darks of the unconscious and the lights of consciousness. Jim's movement into unexpected and confusing color patterns has called into question Marlow's routine relegation of light to sanity and dark to insanity: "He appealed to all sides at once—to the side turned perpetually to the light of day, and to that side of us which, like the other hemisphere of the moon, exists stealthily in perpetual darkness, with only a fearful ashy light falling at times on the edge." Of course, such color patterns suggest the skew arrangement of the entire novel.

Conrad was following his original plan, the pilgrim-ship episode as laid out in the notes for "Tuan Jim," but he still had no idea of the great length of

* One of the most rabid publicity seekers of these journalists was Winston Churchill, who pursued a dual role as soldier and correspondent. Conrad may well have read his inflammatory dispatches in the *Morning Post*.

the finished book. Implicit in Conrad's work thus far, however, is the later career of Jim in the Malay village of Patusan, as well as his running career as water clerk. That is, by October of 1899, still nine months short of completion, he had the basic plan in hand, although matters of pacing, length, and development were still murky. Inexplicably, Conrad told Blackwood he intended to "waylay" him this very year with 2,000 (he meant 20,000) words of a new volume, after *Jim.* Even this deep into the volume, and after the serial had itself begun in "Maga," Conrad was hoping to pull all the diverse elements together, including apparently the Patusan section, within two months or so. Of course, all these so-called promises to his publisher could have been strategies for negotiating his indebtedness, promising more copy than he could supply so as to justify the advances. He existed on just this edge.

Remarkable to us is how still, almost deathlike, the rest of Conrad's life became as *Jim* took over his hours and weeks.* Not until February 1900 would he break his concentration, with a foray to Wells at Sandgate, followed by a visit from Marguerite Poradowska in April. He also found time to see Crane at Dover, in May, before Crane died on June 5 in the Black Forest. In those final months of 1899, Conrad gave himself completely to his work. As he wrote Blackwood, attacking John Buchan and justifying himself:

> To point out to the crowd beauties not manifest to the common eye, to flash the light of one's sympathetic perception upon great, if not obvious, qualities, and even generous failings that hold the promise of better things this is indeed a toil worthy of a man's pen, a task that would repay for the time given up, for the strenght [sic] expended for that sadness that comes of thinking over the sincere endeavour of a soul—for ever debarred from attaining perfection. But the blind distribution of praise or blame, done with a light heart and an empty mind, which is of the very essence of "periodical" criticism seems to me work less useful than skirt-dancing and not quite as honourable as pocket-picking.

He was speaking of the act of criticism, but implicit within it was his own slow and painstaking mode of proceeding.

Conrad was apparently working with Ford, for a November 13 letter to the latter indicates some dissension or misunderstanding of their collaboration. He says he is sorry Elsie feels her husband is wasting his time, and he suggests he had no notion Ford had work of his own to complete. Conrad had

* In *Joseph Conrad As I Knew Him,* Jessie corroborates the desultory nature of this period. She speaks of Galsworthy occasionally coming down, visits from Ford, and their own trips to Winchelsea, where the Fords had a bungalow (pp. 47–8). Jessie also mentions her first sight of Henry James, who came over from Rye. James, it appears, took Borys on his lap, held him for more than half an hour, while the child was awed by the Jamesian presence, and then "released him with a kiss." Jessie's good nature treats the period with a light touch, but it must have been exceptionally lonely and trying.

parts of *Inheritors* before him and found the purely literary side of it superior to any of Ford's previous work. "But beautiful lines do not make a drawing nor splashes of beautiful colour a picture." He indicates he is ready for discussion, out of which may come the conception. He was, in effect, stressing unity and coherence in the manuscript, whereas Ford was striving for angles, colors, and other singular effects. Conrad says the work is all his collaborator's—"I've shared only a little of your worry." He questions whether he is worth anything to his partner: "The proposal [to collaborate] certainly came from me under a false impression of my power for work. I am much weaker than I thought I was but this does not affect you fundamentally." Conrad tells Ford to bring a chapter or two at a time for personal revision.

Jessie describes one of those fairly frequent meetings, when Ford and Elsie came to the Pent. Both Ford and Conrad were gouty, and the onset of an attack, especially for the latter, brought with it extreme apprehension. On this occasion, both men were jumpy, the children peevish, the atmosphere stormy. After lunch, which Conrad barely touched, he stalked through the living room with a request for his gout medicine. This request was accompanied by an announcement that he was retiring to the next room for a nap, demanding that the children be kept quiet. "Totally disregarding his guests, who looked, as they must have felt, uncomfortable [Jessie wrote], he closed one door after the other with considerable violence behind him." Ford then draped himself on the windowseat with books, and Elsie lay on the couch, shoes off. Two hours later, Conrad reappeared and, without comment, became quite agreeable. His sole rebuke was for Jessie, for leaving the room so untidy when he went for a walk. The incident ended; but Jessie had only kind words for her husband and reserved her animosity for Ford, even while granting that Conrad needed the conversation of an equal.

On November 25, 1899, Conrad reassured Meldrum the story "would be finished of course this year," this while he sent on the end of Chapter 13, which carried him through the March installment. Keeping four months ahead of the serialization, Conrad could look forward to smooth going, provided he did not fall ill for any extended length of time. The Hopes, meanwhile, stayed at the Pent for three days, as the shocked Conrad attempted to console them for the murder of their son in the Essex marshes less than a mile from the Conrads' former residence at Ivy Walls Farm. By mid-December, however, Conrad had recovered, the Hopes had left, and he was sitting before the blank sheets of paper that would add to *Jim.* The Boer War continued to intrude; to Graham, he says he wished he could sleep until the African business ended. But to Aniela Zagórska, he is firmer, seeing the Boer War in a more global context. He admits the Boers are struggling in good faith for their independence, but he adds that, like all Dutch and Germans, they have no real sense of liberty. The Dutch are "un peuple essentiellement despotique," and the war is not "so much a war against the Transvaal as a struggle against the doings of German influence." German imperialism, like the old German action against Poland, is the real enemy.

By December 26, he announced, this time to Blackwood himself, that the end of *Jim* was in sight, with only another five days needed to round it off. Clearly he intended to end it with the *Patna* section, even assuring Blackwood that *Lord Jim* would not have the length to stand by itself; and yet the three tales "each being inspired by a similar moral idea . . . will make (in that sense) a homogeneous book."

Just after the new year, on the third, Conrad indicated to Meldrum that more manuscript was coming, to end Chapter 17. The next batch, he says, "should be the last." Conrad adds that *Lord Jim* has given him no pleasure because its extended length has caused severe financial problems for him. He asks Meldrum for an additional £80 or even £100 when the final copy is delivered. Then he will send an additional 20,000 words—"either *A Seaman* or *First Command* or a *Skittish Cargo* ["Typhoon"] or any two of them to make up the number." In this way he can repay advances already spent.

Conrad's dilemma with the development and length of *Lord Jim* was quite different from the frustration he had experienced with *The Rescue.* His situation, in fact, was exactly the opposite of the earlier one when he tried to fit the *Rescue* manuscript into his changing styles. The difficulty with *Jim* derived from its central placement in Conrad's imagination, where its slow, glacial development depended on the maturation of his creative powers.

In this novel, Conrad entertained his most profound theme, which was, to put it in terms of one of his favorite books, to confront the illusionistic, idealistic, dreamlike Don Quixote (Jim) with the realistic, pragmatic, earthy Sancho (the way of the world). *Lord Jim* was, in this regard, a true psychodrama for Conrad, the conflict of opposing ideologies deriving from his Korzeniowski-Bobrowska strains and the tandem elements of his own imaginative powers. Jim aims at heights; he strives after revelations and illusions. Like Camus's Jean-Baptiste, that later Jim, he seeks higher ground so as the better to survey the sordidness beneath him. Yet he is a man who must, but cannot, learn to deal with the lower depths. His experiences wrestle him to the ground, where can cannot escape the base and the iniquitous.

The strain on Conrad to produce a balance of these elements and in addition to find some reason for going on was to tell in nervous ailments and temporary breakdowns. He was, in the fullest sense, being tested, however unconsciously; he would either succumb or come through on the basis of a manuscript whose limits he could not foresee. He speaks, to Graham, of difficulties closing around him, of an "irresistible march of black-beetles" who will devour him. Images of being swallowed up and vanishing dominate, Jim himself being swallowed up by sea and jungle, alternately trying to disappear and to impose himself. "I don't care a damn [Conrad writes] for the best heaven ever invented by Jew or Gentile," by which he means he must invent his own heaven and hell and live in it.*

On January 9, he indicates he is driving hard, with Chapter 19 expected shortly, and then the end; but of course the book was only half completed. This chapter would not even carry him through the May issue and the novel was, eventually, to run through November. Not surprisingly, Conrad wrote Garnett a long letter about his family background, extended remarks that follow upon discussions of Jim. The juxtaposition of family strains and divisions with the career of *Jim* cannot be fortuitous. That is, the writing of *Jim* was bringing into focus those very conflicting elements which derived from Conrad's Polish years and from the family background. The "blessed work" is defective, Conrad tells Garnett, meaning *Lord Jim,* and then launches into a detailed outline of his Korzeniowski-Bobrowska family tree. Among other things, Conrad describes his family seal, Nałęcz, his paternal grandfather, his maternal grandfather, his mother, Ewa, and her siblings, his father, Apollo. We have already pointed to these details of description, but we can see now how Conrad's words and phrases are similar to the way in which he was casting Jim and Marlow.

He stresses the sister cult which existed in his family and mentions how heartened he was by Ewa's correspondence with her brothers and with Apollo before he (Conrad) destroyed her letters. He speaks of Apollo as a man of "exalted and dreamy temperament," juxtaposed to Tadeusz Bobrowski, a "man of powerful intelligence and great force of character . . . a most distinguished man." There is, here, the exalted side of Jim, the more pragmatic nature of Stein. The brief lives of his relatives have the quality of fated beings, and their existence is cast in the terms of inexorable tragedy: the tragedy of their nation, but even more the tragedy of their very being—man's fate in its most unbending sense. Even Conrad's close is grim, although he attempts levity. He says he had always intended to write something like this for Borys's sake, so as to save it all from the abyss. But what, he asks, should Borys really care for any of it? "What's Hecuba to him or he to Hecuba?" Conrad asks. And the lonely answer is "Tempi passati, brother! Tempi passati. Let them go." The words pass beyond sadness, to a profound sense that the waves wash over all of us; and, like Jim, we run and run (or write and write), only to meet the fate dictated ultimately by what we are, who we are.

Not unexpectedly, Conrad fell ill five days later and did not recover until

* He told Graham, that sympathetic repository of his ills, that weeks "disappear into the bottomless pit before I can stretch out my hand. . . . I am one of those condemned to run in a circle." The image is Dantesque, frustration piled upon a circular existence of advances against copy, always behind or delayed.

February 8, including ten days in bed. He recounts he had suffered a severe fit of malaria, followed by bronchitis and an attack of gout, "a debauch of disease," he was to call it. Except for the gout, the other ailments could well have been psychologically induced, although there is no direct evidence to support this. However, in a February 13 letter to Graham, after he had recovered, Conrad speaks of "in reality a breakdown," and adds he remains "under the shadow" with no sense of rebound. This could be the profound depression accompanying an attack of gout or the depression concomitant with a psychological breakdown. In any event, it was not severe, and he could assure Meldrum on February 14 that his head was "full (too full) of Jim's end." Meldrum's support was of tremendous value, since the London editor wrote Blackwood that while the length of Jim did not suit "Maga," nevertheless, "it is a great story now—and in the annals of *Maga* half a century hence it will be one of the honourable things to record of her that she entertained 'Jim.' " Conrad, meanwhile, went to Sandgate to visit Wells for two days. The manuscript of *The Inheritors* was now in Heinemann's hands, and he would soon begin the collaboration on "Seraphina."

On February 20, Conrad once again assured Blackwood that the end of Jim was imminent; and for the first time, we might hear the tone of deception. Although we lack one side of the correspondence, we can infer from Conrad's remarks that Meldrum has conveyed some of "Maga's" dismay at the ever-growing length. Accordingly, Conrad adopted the strategy of assuring the end at any moment, although, in fact, there was still no place for him to finish off Jim or the novel at this stage. The April issue was only at Chapter 15 and Conrad was to write for another three months. He was, in fact, dismayed at the shortness of the April installment, which, he may have suspected, demonstrated some hesitation on Blackwood's part about the entire project. He apologized to Meldrum for "springing on Mr Blackwood such a long affair and for the unfortunate dragging manner of its production," but he adds that "Jim is very near my heart."

He would say the same thing to Garnett: "I am old and sick and in debt—but lately I've found I can still write—*it* comes! *it* comes!—and I am young and healthy and rich." He stresses he has been cutting and slashing whole parts out of *Jim*, the phrasing indicating a struggle to the death, his or Jim's. Inexplicably, he announces to Meldrum that he is thinking of a "*long* book for Mr Blackwood and, if the collaboration stuff [*Inheritors*] goes well, the thing shall be managed sooner than I hoped for. The *R* shall be finished before long—and then we shall see what can be done for the *House.*" The "long book" may have been "Seraphina," which Conrad did submit to Blackwood and which was rejected for publication. The purpose of all these promises was to justify, somehow, the overpayments for *Jim.* On completion of the novel, Conrad wanted an additional £150, which would add to the surplus already accumulated. He promises, still to Meldrum, completion of

Jim by the twelfth installment, which he could not deliver, the novel running to fourteen.

Everything almost literally stopped for Conrad except production of copy. This pattern would recur for almost the rest of his life, where he scooped out his writing time and simply dug in, as though under siege. He hated his desk and the blank pages, and yet they were his salvation. On April 12, still three months short of completion, he wrote Blackwood on the very sensitive issue: would *Jim* ever end?

> I feel the need of telling you that I've done something anyway and to assure you that *Lord Jim has* an end, which last I am afraid you may be beginning to doubt. It has though—and I am now trying to write it out. A dog's life! this writing out, this endlessness of effort and this endless discontent; with remorse, thrown in, for the massacre of so many good intentions.
>
> This by the way. The real object of this letter is to tell you that should you find I'm unconscionably long (for Maga—I mean) I am ready to shorten (what remains) by excision. I am however in such a state of mind about the story—so inextricably mixed up with it in my daily life—that I feel unequal to doing the cutting myself; so, addressing you in your character of Editor of *Maga,* I declare my readiness to make conscientious joints, if the parts that can be taken out are marked for me and the MS with such indications is returned.

Conrad then points out that he and Ford have completed their joint effort and have not offered it to Blackwood since he feels a financial obligation to Heinemann: for payment of half a novel still unwritten, the ubiquitous *Rescue.* He says Mr. Stephen Gwynn, on behalf of McClure, has delivered a favorable judgment. He promises an "adventure story of which the skeleton is set up—with some modelling here and there already worked up." To all this, Blackwood responded very generously that Conrad should not hurry the narrative simply for the sake of cutting down: "The end must now justify the length of the story." He adds he will leave him a free hand with it, but cautions against any further expansion and says he looks forward to receiving the "adventure story" whenever Conrad and Ford complete it.

Marguerite Poradowska visited the Pent in early April, for a week's stay, and Conrad invited Ford and Elsie for lunch on April 4. He told Ford he was "of course anxious very anxious to introduce my 'collaborateur' to the good woman who represents to me so much of my family—she had known so many of them on whom no eye of man'll rest again." He announces, also, the happy outcome of *The Inheritors* with McClure and Heinemann, stressing that the literary quality of the book is all Ford's. Jessie commented on this scene and called Marguerite the "most beautiful woman I had ever seen." More tellingly, she indicates Conrad told his aunt that if she needed assistance in dressing she should only call for Jessie, aid that Marguerite declined with a little speech that Jessie was already busy enough. The story reveals not only Conrad's treatment of Marguerite as a kind of princess but his relegation of Jessie to a social inferior in the face of a member of his family. Early the next month, all this was behind him as he ran down to Dover to see Stephen Crane, who, dying, was on his way to the Black Forest. To Cora, who sought immediate aid, Conrad wrote he was a man without resources: "without connections, without influence and without means." His future, such as it is, he says, was "already pawned," and it was not even within his power to jeopardize his own future to serve Crane.

Conrad's affairs with Blackwood took another turn, as the publisher began to see that *Lord Jim* was already far too long for inclusion in a volume with "Youth" and "Heart of Darkness." He suggested that *Jim* be made into a separate volume to be published in the middle of September. The two stories would remain in limbo until Conrad could add one or two more tales to make up a suitable volume. Conrad's response to all this was unusual. While accepting the inevitability of Blackwood's decision, he still felt *Jim* could make up a volume with the stories. He argued artistic proportion:

> It [*Lord Jim*] has not been planned to stand alone. *H of D* was meant in my mind as a foil, and *Youth* was supposed to give the note. All this is foolishness—no doubt. The public does not care—can not possibly care—for foils and notes. But it cares for stories and *Jim* is as near a story as I will ever get. The title will have to be altered to *Lord Jim. A tale*—instead of *A sketch.* And yet it is a sketch! I would like to put it as *A simple tale A plain tale*—something of the sort—if possible. No matter.

Under the change of a short-story collection into two separate volumes, Conrad tried to renegotiate his arrangement, so as to derive an additional £200 from the firm. His calculations were based on the differing rate for short stories and a novel during serialization. It was a crafty scheme, in which he assumed, for the sake of payment, that a novel was worth ten shillings per thousand words more than a short story. He added he was so weary of the whole thing that Blackwood might print the story or not: "I am so utterly weary of myself (not of my work) that I verily believe I don't care." Three days later, Conrad followed this letter to Meldrum with another, even more complicated. He had, apparently, spent those three days in calculations which put forward his financial situation in the new light. The crux of it was a restatement of his earlier position that *Jim* should be paid for at ten shillings per thousand words, with the additional £200 to be advanced to him against royalties on the book form and £300 more for the serialization. Since he had already received £200, the firm owed him the additional £300. These calculations, which were agreed to, revealed a shrewdness in Conrad that should not be ignored. When his survival depended on it, he knew precisely where his interests lay, and despite his disclaimers of his hatred for the marketplace, he had good business instincts.

Blackwood sent £100 to relieve Conrad's precarious finances, and the latter thanked him, also announcing his grief over Crane's death on June 5, at Badenweiler. If he had not been so intensely preoccupied with the completion of *Jim*, Crane's death would have struck more severely.* He felt so far in arrears with copy, so financially near disaster, that his friend's early death would occupy only the passing moment. Yet it is unlikely he missed seeing in Crane his own earlier career, all speeded up in the American writer: the young man who moves outside traditional or established roles in order to assert his own definition of himself and who, as a consequence, moves along the edges of a society unconcerned at his existence. Crane's death, at twenty-nine, could only have fortified Conrad's pessimism and his allegiance to an indifferent universe.

"Solitary as a mole," as he put it to Davray, French critic and editor, Conrad continued to "dig, to dig without end or truce, without ever arriving at seeing anything clearly." Like those who peered at Jim through mist, he observed *Jim* through a fog. On July 13–14, he announced the "last word of Lord Jim," but he added that he still needed to do some judicious cutting. A few days after that, he described the ending of the novel to Galsworthy in some detail:

> The end of *L.J.* has been pulled off with a steady drag of 21 hours. I sent wife and child out of the house (to London) and sat down at games with a desperate resolve to be done with it. Now and then I took a walk round the house out at one door in at the other. Ten-minute meals. A great hush. Cigarette ends growing into a mound similar to a cairn over a dead hero. Moon rose over the barn looked in at the window and climbed out of sight. Dawn broke, brightened. I put the lamp out and went on, with the morning breeze blowing the sheets of MS all over the room. Sun rose. I wrote the last word and went into the dining room. Six o'clock. . . . Felt very well only sleepy; had a bath at seven and at 8.30 was on my way to London.

To Blackwood, he wrote of important matters in a flurry of activities; for the family was going to join the Fords in Bruges, toward the end of July. Conrad sensed *Lord Jim* as a title was insufficient and there should be some generic subtitle, such as "A Romance." Although he provided no specific reason, he certainly saw the novel as something more than "Jim." His was a novel not of a character but of a situation, a state of mind, a human condition; and therefore, the main character had to be qualified by a context—"romance" or something comparable. Further, Conrad wanted to eliminate

* Even so, to Mrs. Sanderson he wrote: "Sometimes I fancy I am breaking up mentally. I've been much worried this year. First illness; afterwards the death of poor Stephen Crane upset me horribly delaying my work, and all the time Maga's next number hanging over my head. Yet I've written 120,000 words in ten months. . . . I finished in July and felt limp done up, dazed, like a man waking up from a nightmare."

chapter designations. His argument is of interest: "Would it not be better seeing the form of the novel (personal narrative from a third party as it were) to dispense with the word *Chapter* throughout the book, leaving only the Roman numerals. After all, these divisions (some of them very short) are not chapters in the usual sense each carrying the action a step further or embodying a complete episode. I meant them only as pauses—rests for the reader's attention while he is following the development of *one* situation, only *one* really from beginning to end." As he feared, it was too late to make the alteration, but his idea was sound. He saw the novel as a flow, an inner stream of observation that would be obstructed by the usual chapter designations. His desire to leave only numeral divisions was based on "novelty," to escape from established episodes or starts and stops. Of great interest is Conrad's awareness of the "modern flow" or seamlessness, the massing of material without beginning or end. He was, here, moving with the inner direction of his material, attempting to create a measureless, unobstructed stream between inner and outer.

The above technique is connected to what Conrad wrote Blackwood on the following day, an explanation of the final scenes which he presented as almost pure narrative:

> The situation—the problem if you will—of that sensitive nature has been already commented upon, illustrated and contrasted. It is in my opinion that in the working out of the catastrophe psychologic disquisition should have no place. The reader ought to know enough by that time. I enlarge a little upon the new character which is introduced (that of Brown the desperate adventurer) so as to preserve the sense of verisimilitude and for sake of final contrast; but all the rest is nothing but a relation of events—strictly a narrative.

The Conrads left for Bruges immediately after this, a vacation that Jessie wished they had canceled because of the presence of the Fords. In addition to her strong personal dislike of Ford, there is reason to think Jessie was jealous or resentful of Elsie: young, attractive, better educated, and more turned toward literature. In Jessie's eyes, Elsie would appear better suited as the wife of a literary man than she was herself. The foursome began to take on some of the combativeness and inner rage of Ford's later "quartet" in *The Good Soldier*, although most certainly without the covert sexual confrontations. The goal of the vacation was to combine relaxation with collaboration on "Seraphina."

After Bruges, the group moved on to Knocke-sur-Mer, a coastal resort near Ostend. The excursion was, like so many others Conrad took with his family, a period more of consternation, near-disaster, and financial concern than anything approaching relaxation. Borys came down with enteritis and such severe dysentery his life was in danger. Not until August 10, Conrad writes Galsworthy, would he be out of danger, and then he "is a miserable object to behold. . . . I had enough of this holiday." This time it was Borys, later it would be Jessie and her knee, then Borys and John together, and finally Conrad himself, gouty and neuralgic. Attempts at renewal always brought him closer to personal and financial doom, so that it is impossible to escape the fact that he appeared to need these situations, whether holiday-induced or not, as a way of goading himself to creative action.

Conrad described the turmoil of the hotel:

> The whole Hotel was in a commotion; Dutch Belgians and French prowled about the corridor on the lookout for news. Women with babies of their own offered to sit up, and a painter of religious subjects Paulus by name rose up and declared himself ready to do likewise. Elsie Hueffer helped a bit but poor H. did not get much collaboration out of me this tide [sic].

Even Jessie had to admit Ford made exceptional efforts to help:

> At this crisis I have nothing but praise for F.M.H. He earned my gratitude and appreciation by the manner he showed his practical sympathy. He was always at hand to shift my small invalid, fetch the doctor or help with the nursing. It was a nightmarish time, that terrible August we spent in Knocke. Naturally no work was done, and all our nerves were completely frayed long before the child was well enough to be taken home.
>
> Yet she could not resist the final word:
>
> As part of the party had preceded us there, so they made the home journey first. I heaved a sigh of relief, for a week or ten days we could at least rest, and I think my husband had had enough of a double household for a time, at least abroad. The rest of the *Rescue* was written after our return at the Pent [not completed until 1919]. This book I managed to keep clear from collaboration.

As for Conrad, his sole accomplishment for over three weeks' effort was "getting the end of Jim fit for print." Toward the twentieth of August the Conrads returned to the Pent.

Upon settling in, Conrad had several projects to contemplate: the serious collaboration with Ford on "Seraphina"; the completion of the volume of tales for Blackwood's; and the ever-present *Rescue.* It was, nevertheless, a period of treading water—no big novel, no singular project, much "finishing-up" work. Still eighteen months away was the beginning of *Nostromo,* which would occupy him for over two years. After arguing the case of Garnett and Galsworthy to Meldrum for publication of their work by Blackwood, Conrad moved to his own needs: to make a fresh start without further delay. He suggests "First Command" as the tale to fill out the volume of stories under contract. He says that after its completion, and with any success for *Jim,* he will have "a clear road to run after the end of the *Rescue.*"

There is, once again, some fudging of fact or outright dissimulation, in that Conrad was far indeed from completing that novel, not only in terms of hundreds of pages, but even in inclination.

One consolation: Conrad had written about 120,000 words in ten months, and that rapid rate of production convinced him he could, under controlled conditions, turn out more than 10,000 words a month. Of course, he needed not only time to write but time to think of subjects, plan development, dredge up and coordinate appropriate memories. He was still drawing heavily on the past, and his next work, "Typhoon," would be part of his remembrances of things past.* In his Author's Note to the collection in which "Typhoon" appeared, Conrad spoke of MacWhirr, the captain of the *Nan-Shan,* as being "the product of twenty years of life. My own life." Although not based on a particular person, MacWhirr, he says, is "perfectly authentic." Conrad notes that the story of a steamship full of coolies returning from Singapore to northern China through a typhoon had come to him as conversation in the East. Shop talk, as he called it, becomes the matter of fiction. By the time the story reached Conrad's ears, in fact, it was already a fiction; and by the time he wrote it, it was still further removed from whatever had occurred.

Conrad apparently started the story to complete the Blackwood volume, or else he began it simply as a relief from the collaboration with Ford. In any event, it would not end up in *that* volume but would appear later with another set of stories. "The End of the Tether" would complete the Blackwood book. Conrad evidently wrote a good deal of "Typhoon" in late August or in September, for on October 3 he told Meldrum he had not yet finished that story "which is to prolong my wretched existence." He called it that infernal story which he could not bring off. On October 8 he told Pinker firmly he would have "Typhoon" by the fifteenth. He completed it in January 1901. A second story, "Falk," which is "shorter and much more horrible"—its pivotal point is cannibalism—"shall be ready early in November." He completed it in May of 1901. "Typhoon," the first Conrad piece handled by Pinker, was sent to Blackwood's for possible serialization there; but it eventually appeared in *Pall Mall Magazine* for January–March 1902. Conrad did not know it but his connection with *Blackwood's Magazine,* except for the serialization of "Tether" and two papers of *The Mirror of the Sea,* was ending.

Although "Typhoon" is almost top-quality work—and surely more "worked" than Conrad's critics have granted—Conrad's short stories in this period show a certain decline, or else were simply unsuitable for *Black-*

* In Richard Curle's copy, Conrad wrote of the story: "Was meant to be a pendant to the storm in the *Nigger,* the ship in this case being a steamship."

wood's. It was highly improbable that the conservative, traditional old Blackwood would accept a story about cannibalism, even if he did like "Heart of Darkness." Even more than the quality, good or bad, of Conrad's short fiction was the question of "Maga's" dealing with his financial needs and also with his newly acquired agent, Pinker. Conrad had made steady demands on the house that were highly unusual for Blackwood's authors, and he had been consistently late with copy. Furthermore, he had turned potentially story-length fiction into a novel, so that Blackwood was forced to postpone previously accepted material. While the firm is to be highly commended for its support of Conrad in his neediest period, nevertheless, it was not so committed to the life of art that it would continue the relationship when Conrad's short fiction took a different turn.

Meanwhile, Conrad had attempted to place his friends' work with the firm. Garnett and Galsworthy had little success, but Ford published *The Cinque Ports* in 1900 with Blackwood. Writing to the latter, Conrad seemed to contradict everything he and Ford were working toward. "He [Ford] does not stand on his head for the purpose of getting a new and striking view of his subject. Such a method of procedure may be in favour nowadays but I prefer the old way, with the feet on the ground . . . but there is—it seems to me—a good deal of force in his quiet phrasing." He adds that many new theories which jostle us today fall to pieces tomorrow. Apparently this commentary was what Conrad thought Blackwood expected, for his own practice both with Ford and by himself was to take on the colors and tones of those "new theories." Conrad was, in fact, in the midst of becoming new as well as renewing himself.

"Typhoon," not unexpectedly, dragged on. It was, in a sense, a regression for Conrad, for its stress on a simple character, MacWhirr, and the savagery of wind and wave implied a return to *The Nigger* and the values of a Singleton. It was a farewell of a kind, for it lacked the sophistication of Conrad's other longer work during this period. Its very lack of sophistication seems to suggest a desire to escape momentarily from the arty world represented by Ford and to move back to a purer and simpler time. "Typhoon," however, has its own intense interest and comes across as a kind of mutation of *The Nigger* and *Lord Jim.* The chief complexity of the book seems paradoxical, deriving from elemental decisions which, Conrad realized, are never purely finite. MacWhirr is a very uncomplicated man—he had, as Conrad says, "just enough imagination to carry him through each successive day, and no more"—but the choices of a simple man are not themselves necessarily simple. He embodies a view of life which has within it all the complexities we associate with a more sophisticated individual; what is involved is his resolve, and that, in turn, is connected to his ability to enter into the workings of nature. MacWhirr does not believe man is a separate creation but part of the very element which will drown or float him, and man must grapple with that aspect of nature, not try to evade it.

It is not a question of whether MacWhirr was right or wrong in taking the *Nan-Shan* through the typhoon, an action very much against the logic of the situation. The real question is one of man's relationship to the natural universe and whether, by following a running course, he can escape what he is and what his destiny involves. Jim had run; Wait had signified everyman's death; Donkin had refused his place both in man's world and in the natural universe. "Typhoon" becomes a corrective to that. It and *Nostromo* are superficially quite distant from each other; yet both would appear within three years of each other. And both were deeply intertwined in Conrad, part of an evolving philosophy. MacWhirr is hardly a hero of the modern spirit, and yet any literary theory that loses sight of him forgoes a large sense of human aspirations.

Chinese coolies below, ordinary seamen and captain above: the real drama lies in the modulations and transformations of nature, as in the following passage near the beginning of the novella:

> At its setting the sun had a diminished diameter and an expiring brown, rayless glow, as if millions of centuries elapsing since the morning had brought it near its end. A dense bank of cloud became visible to the northward; it had a sinister dark olive tint, and lay low and motionless upon the sea, resembling a solid obstacle in the path of the ship. She went floundering towards it like an exhausted creature driven to its death. The coppery twilight retired slowly, and the darkness brought out overhead a swarm of unsteady big stars, that, as if blown upon, flickered exceedingly and seemed to hang very near the earth.

There is in this passage a sense of entropy, transformation, diminution of man, endless sweeps of space and time, a mythical beginning, and, over all, the wonder of the natural universe. The next sentence places the chief mate, "Jukes," within this universe, and the juxtaposition is ironical: the name was well chosen for its harshness and its lack of fit for his grand role.

Such passages are far more than ornamental descriptions or manifestations of a simple life; they contain all the unspoken mysteries which sweep beyond us in time and space. MacWhirr's "loneliness of command" in this universe has great dimensions; he is first man, this thick Scotsman, first sailor of the seas, and the struggles he wins are landmarks in human aspiration, even if meaningless in man's history. Conrad was striving for a meaningful statement in which words defined ultimate values, those inner areas that the Victorians had explored as compensations for God. Marlow had sought such values in his "first command" and in the Congo; later, he thought he had sighted them in Jim's honest yeoman's face. The question, then, is not whether MacWhirr and the *Nan-Shan* will come through the typhoon, although their lives depend upon it, but whether man has it within him to reach back to his mythical self and exert sufficient energy to keep himself afloat in the vastness of the ocean.

Balzac, whose work Conrad knew well, had asked that same question in "A Passion in the Desert," and his enigmatic conclusion that the desert is "God without mankind," where there is everything and nothing, is Conrad's view of the ocean as "the edge of the world." The *Nan-Shan* "dipped into the hollow straight down, as if going over the edge of the world. The engine-room toppled forward menacingly, like the inside of a tower nodding in an earthquake." Conrad, like Balzac, was striving for a hidden absolute of meaning within the lives of men who live in, not beyond, nature.

The final chapter draws out Conrad's plan. The *Nan-Shan* steams into Fu-chau, and the men now become land creatures, routine and commonplace. They have had their moment. One reason Conrad appealed so strongly to later novelists, Gide, Faulkner, Hemingway, was that they noted the need for great moments in Conrad's characters, moments in which—like the bull-fighter, big-game hunter, or deep-sea fisherman—they move beyond the commonplace into a mythical surrender to an absolute universe. There was in Conrad, as later in Hemingway, some sense of the Nietzschean stress on the *Übermensch*, not as a man in society but as a man who can, even if momentarily, move outside society. Such a man has only moments of greatness, moments of communion; but he connects, nevertheless, to the vastness of the universe, beyond time and beyond measurable space.

CHAPTER 22

Ford and *Romance*

RESPONDING to Garnett's criticism of *Lord Jim*, based on the division of the book into two parts, Conrad commented that he had not "been strong enough to breathe the right sort of life into my clay—the *revealing* life." That sense of life is something that goes well beyond society or social institutions. Conrad was stretching toward infinity. He told Garnett he "stood for a great triumph," but he had only succeeded in falling back into his lump of clay. He had wanted to obtain "a sort of lurid light out [of] the very events," by which he meant some animating power which would have transformed the singular event into universal energy. The one solid thing in his slough of despond was a letter from Henry James, a "draught from the Fountain of Eternal Youth," Conrad called it.

Conrad also lived off his reviews of *Jim*. Except for Courtney's inability (in the *Daily Telegraph*) to adjust to a new talent, the reviews were remarkable for their understanding. The opening of the unsigned notice in *The Manchester Guardian* is not untypical:

> Mr. Joseph Conrad's work has long been known to novel readers who search for their literature, and to them the publication of *Lord Jim* may rank as a memorable event. It is not to be accepted easily, it cannot be read in a half dose, and by the great public which multiplies editions it may remain neglected or unknown. Yet it is of such remarkable originality and merit that one may look for an emphasis of critical opinion which, as in the case of Mr. Meredith, can force a great reputation in the face of popular apathy or distaste.

Citing it as a "great performance," the reviewer says that in the "more intense passages Mr. Conrad has the pregnant brevity of a master of form." The whole gallery of sketches possesses, he says, its own uses; all "are strictly relevant, and they form part of a whole greatly conceived and finely executed."

Similar were the notices in the *Academy* (possibly by Garnett), the *Spectator*, the *Sketch*, the *Daily News*. Remarkable to us is the effort these reviewers made to comprehend a narrative method and style that, admittedly, they found difficult. Characteristic is the unknown reviewer in the *Daily News:* "[*Lord Jim*] is really more of an epic than of a story. It is grandiose, it is poetic, it is thoughtful; in a word, it is masterly, yet it is hardly the sort of thing that will tend much to the butterflies of fiction. The obstructions set in the way of the reader are many, and, moreover, are mainly owing to Mr. Conrad's idiosyncrasies."

One American reviewer, in the *Critic,* placed the novel within a very apt metaphor, as a web, "a marvel of workmanship, built with a foresight and a careless ease that suggests instinct rather than art." Keeping in mind the butterfly-beetle dichotomy of Stein's collection, we can relish the analogy:

> Imagine a fat, furry spider with green head and shining points for eyes, busily at work, some dewy morning, on a marvellous web,—and you have the plot of *Lord Jim.* It spins itself away, out of nothing, with side tracks leading, apparently, nowhere, and cross tracks that start back and begin anew and end once more—sometimes on the verge of nowhere, and sometimes in the center of the plot itself;—and all with an air of irresponsible intentness and a businesslike run at the end that sets the structure trembling on gossamer threads.

While Meldrum was urging Blackwood to print another thousand copies of *Lord Jim* because of excellent notices and because "Conrad is a man whose coming into his own may take very long but is bound to result one day," Conrad himself faced an overwhelming humiliation. Needing two sureties for a loan of £150 on his insurance policy, he came to Blackwood for help; Heinemann or Galsworthy would be the other. Such sureties would guarantee the insurance premium and the interest of 5 percent on the loan and would give him "a chance to breathe for a while." Conrad first approached Meldrum and then Blackwood, who was to become responsible for the transaction. He approached on tiptoe: "No doubt the thing could have been managed in some other way but really my dear Mr Blackwood I am so worried with the thoughts of my work and the pain of my gouty foot that I have not the courage to go 'flying around.' . . . And there is also the fact that I find it easier to put myself under obligation to you than to any other man—a fact not particularly fortunate for you perhaps—but illustrative of my feelings." He closes by saying, "You may imagine how pressing the case must be to prod me into such an appeal."

When no answer was immediately forthcoming, Conrad told Meldrum he was not worried because Heinemann would lend him the amount "without any difficulty." He exerted a slight pressure, that he would take his work to Heinemann, but Blackwood responded on December 18 agreeing to the entire matter and even sending a £50 loan Conrad had requested until the insurance scheme was negotiated. Meldrum was delighted Blackwood had entered into Conrad's plan: "Conrad . . . is an honourable man. I wish I could believe that he would ever be 'popular' in the popular sense, but he is too good for that. On the other hand, it would seem that over 'Lord Jim' he is coming into his own quicker than so 'unfashionable' and clever an author his [has] any right to expect in these days."

Meldrum's comment that Conrad was too good to be popular indicates the rift in reading taste occurring at the turn of the century. For the major Victorian novelists, no such dichotomy between excellence and sales could have been made. Dickens, Eliot, Thackeray, Trollope, among others, were the best as well as popular authors. They may not have been as salable as those lesser novelists who catered directly to a lower level of taste—the writers of romance and adventure—but they were immensely salable in their own right. Only George Meredith comes to mind as a significant novelist lacking a large following, and that would come later. Just before the turn of the century, the best novelists, with Conrad and James in the vanguard, left the audience behind to a different order of writer and moved into realms where the average reader could not follow. All of Conrad's hopes for a wider audience would be dashed by the very elements that made him a writer of the first rank. The demands of the genre as well as the development of a different sensibility, and the differing expectations of a more literate and egalitarian audience, created a sharp division in the arts, and of course most noticeably in fiction, as later in poetry.

Such a change in sensibility and expectation did not occur at any given time, nor was it especially apparent, except to those who were bringing it about: in England, James and Conrad, Ford, then Joyce, Lawrence, and Woolf. While all this was occurring, some of it well out of sight, large numbers of novelists, as in every era, continued as if fiction were static. Most of Conrad's novelist friends, Galsworthy, Wells, and Bennett, continued along basically familiar tracks, working routes and areas laid out by the major Victorians. Conrad's attempts in conversation and correspondence to make them comprehend another order of reality were futile, for their fictional survival depended on their hewing to tradition, while his depended on a very different kind of vision.

Conrad was of course grateful Blackwood had entered into the insurance loan scheme, thanking him on the nineteenth of December and mentioning Galsworthy once again. Blackwood had rejected *A Man of Devon* the first time around, but then accepted it. Conrad's slight exertion of pressure was based on his genuine admiration of Galsworthy, but, very possibly, he could only repay his financial indebtedness by finding his friend a reputable publisher. In the workshop, "Typhoon" would be completed in January, but publication was a whole year off. Particularly worrying for Conrad was the fact that no magazine piece of his would appear in print for nearly two years, from the February–April 1899 serialization of "Heart of Darkness" to the December 1901 publication of "Amy Foster."

He was very much aware of this "stagnation," since for him, experiencing it, there was no way of knowing if it was temporary or permanent. He had passed his forty-third birthday in December 1900 and was only five years younger than Apollo when he died. He saw his future as filled with hurdles, telling Blackwood that his work for "Maga" loomed as big as a mountain, "but now it is more than half scaled at last." By the time of the letter, in May, he had completed "Falk," which would never be serialized, and was working steadily with Ford on "Seraphina." He could joke about the analogy of the mountain: "The simile of hill climbing is not used to hint at the loftiness of my work, but simply as conveying a notion of its arduousness." He brings up the volume of short fiction that Blackwood is holding, awaiting the third story to accompany "Youth" and "Heart of Darkness," and asks if another story of 20,000 words would be sufficient to round it off. He had, as yet, no such story in mind, and when he did write "The End of the Tether" it ran closer to 50,000 words, 12,000 longer than "Darkness."

But that is jumping ahead. With "Typhoon" out of the way, Conrad turned to "Falk," beginning it most probably on January 21. Because of the additional pressures of collaboration,* it would take four months to complete, the story eventually running to over 25,000 words. "Falk" is a spin-off from "Heart of Darkness," in that Conrad attempted his characteristic division of sensibility between those who have faced a primitive, mythical experience and those who remain in a bourgeois routine. This was to become the Conradian archetype, and here, in this story, he had a great potential for a large statement about civilization and the human appetite for survival. As he developed it, however, "Falk" seemed less suitable for the "Heart of Darkness" volume than it did for the "Typhoon" collection, where it in time appeared alongside "Amy Foster" and "To-morrow." This collection was more benign, although on a small scale "Amy Foster" is a savage statement of isolation and marginality. Nevertheless, despite its naturalistic and mythical undertones, "Falk" becomes a romance. Amidst good food, good cheer, and pleasant company, a narrator styled on Marlow (but unidentified) recalls an episode of a different kind of eating, the tale of Falk and his cannibalistic adventure.

Full of portentous trappings, "Falk" finally comes across as a tale of survival in a primitive setting: Crane's "Open Boat" with a more melodramatic setting. The trappings are *there* in abundance: the narrator's friend is captain of a ship called *Diana*—"not of Ephesus but of Bremen"; the captain's niece

---

* Conrad had become so chummy with Ford he asked Pinker if the latter could dispose of Ford's collection of some 300 letters, including those of Burne-Jones, Holman Hunt, William Morris, Rossetti, Millais, Frederick Leighton, and, as he says, "all the preraphaelites." In addition to that, there were letters from Carlyle and Swinburne. He adds that his friend wants to dispose of them abroad, not in England—apparently to disguise the fact he needed the money and did not want to seem to be dumping a family collection for personal use.

is a Valkyrie, a massive young woman who never speaks, but just exists, eternal woman with the "hair of a siren"; Falk himself is a mythical man, a "man-boat"-like creature, whose name suggests a ruthless and cynical manner; there is a metaphorical "rape" scene, when Falk seizes the *Diana;* there is the Wagnerian motif of Siegfried with his Brünnhilde; Falk is compared to Hercules and, at one point, his tale to that of the Flying Dutchman; and there is, finally, the central episode, Falk's great secret (he ate man's flesh in order to survive). The story is almost pure Zola, especially in this passage, which seems to derive from *Germinal:*

> He [Falk] wanted to live. He had always wanted to live. So we all do—but in us the instinct serves a complex conception, and in him this instinct existed alone. There is in such simple development a gigantic force, and like the pathos of a child's naïve and uncontrolled desire. He wanted that girl, and the utmost that can be said for him was that he wanted that particular girl alone. I think I saw then the obscure beginning, the seed germinating in the soil of an unconscious need, the first shoot of that tree bearing now for a mature mankind the flower and the fruit, the infinite gradation in shades and in flavour of our discriminating love. He was a child. He was as frank as a child, too. He was hungry for the girl, terribly hungry, as he had been terribly hungry for food.

Falk's instinct is to live uncomplicated by any other complexity, and we recall Conrad's maternal great-uncle, Nicholas Bobrowski, who in the retreat from Moscow ate dog. Of more interest than basic needs, however, is Conrad's equation of food and sexual longing, of hunger and desire, of the intermixture of Falk's emptiness and his obsessive desire to fill the girl's emptiness sexually. On a far larger scale, this theme was explored and exploited in "Heart of Darkness."

Essentially, Conrad's plan was simple: to contrast the bourgeois reactions of Hermann, the father of the bride, with those of Falk, who must feed his primitive hungers. A potentially large theme, it is dissipated in the conclusion to the cannibalistic episode: "The best man had survived. Both of them had at the beginning just strength enough to stand on their feet, and both had displayed pitiless resolution, endurance, cunning and courage—all the qualities of heroism." This is Jack London territory, watered-down Darwinism, and, for Conrad, left-handed work, a comic interlude, in which the taboo of eating man's flesh never achieves the intensity he is striving for.

Shortly after completing "Falk," Conrad turned to "Amy Foster," a story he completed in June. The subject matter of a Pole washed up on the English shore may have come to him earlier, for on February 14 he wrote a long letter in Polish to his namesake, the historian Józef Korzeniowski (not to be confused with the novelist of the same name who died in 1863). This is Conrad's sole extant Polish letter during a period of almost three years. The subject matter of the letter is Tadeusz Bobrowski's *Memoirs,* which, having been published in two volumes the previous year, had created an uproar for their frankness and intimate gossip. Conrad reaffirms his devotion to the memory of the man who was "uncle, guardian, and benefactor." He mentions Marguerite, who has judged Conrad to be an eminent writer, and he says his chosen profession is not easy; for he is striving "for recognition not by inventing plots but by writing in a style which serves the truth as I see and feel it." Then, accounting for his position as a Pole in England, the subject of "Amy Foster," he justifies his change of name: he cannot bear to hear his Polish name mispronounced. He says it is widely known he is a Pole, and he has not disavowed "either my nationality or the name we share for the sake of success."

These remarks link up with the story of Yanko Goorall. A Pole from the eastern Carpathians in Austria, Goorall is the sole survivor of a ship wrecked off the coast of Kent, a German boat carrying immigrants to America. Despite Conrad's attempts to intensify the size of the story through mythical references and the aura of the incomprehensible, "Amy Foster" works best at its simplest level, which also corresponds to very personal elements in Conrad's own development. At stake in Goorall's attempt at acceptance is the repulsion generated by his person and his foreignness. He is accepted only by a dull-witted peasant girl, but after their marriage she rejects his strange ways and his desire to instruct their child in his native tongue. Chiefly, his rejection comes through language: first his strange tongue, then his unusual way of pronouncing English, finally in his delirious ravings (in Polish, like Conrad on his honeymoon) during his fatal illness—strikingly enough, lung trouble, the disease of Ewa and Apollo.

Goorall may seem unearthly*—he made the most familiar English words sound as if "an unearthly language"—and strikingly, the salient element of the story is the repulsion he causes through his use of language. Only because of this component, so stressed it is inescapable, do we have the right to see the tale as partaking of Conrad's own inner drama. Language unusually used was his heritage from a father who was a poet and translator. Language usage became part of his life when he left Poland; and, of course, language, idiom, vocabulary, tone, sound itself were the components of his literary life. As the narrator says, Yanko "could talk to no one, and had no hope of ever understanding anybody. It was as if these had been the faces of people from the other world—dead people—he used to tell me years afterward."

Conrad possibly picked up the idea of a castaway who eventually had to sleep in a pigsty from Ford, who had mentioned it in his *Cinque Ports*. But whatever the derivation, Conrad made Yanko Goorall his very own, not be-

* "He was different; innocent of heart, and full of good will, which nobody wanted, this castaway, that, like a man transplanted into another planet, was separated by an immense space from his past and by an immense ignorance from his future."

cause of the obvious references to foreignness or because of the hostile female character, but for the linguistic crisis it confronts. Although we lack external evidence of any radical shift in Conrad's mental condition, his stress on the language barrier in "Amy Foster" suggests considerable derangement. For he uses language not as a means of communication but as a bar to communication: language is not only life-giving, not only life-enriching, as we normally see it, but it can create serious barriers between men and even cause disaster.

We have routinely observed Conrad as a man who has mastered English and thus given himself the opportunity to pursue an extremely difficult career as a writer. "Amy Foster," however, raises the question of language beyond what it communicates in daily speech or as fiction. It operates in a binary sense, and it has even a third position, what Humboldt called a "third universe" between empirical phenomena and consciousness itself. As Humboldt recognized, language becomes "all," a universal quality which mediates every aspect of human experience. While we do not make any such pretentious claims for Conrad's story, it is necessary to stress how, by concerning himself with communication itself, he has cast language in a new dimension in his work. For by questioning language in a countryman of his, Conrad has tested out the very precariousness of his own position.

Further under scrutiny in the story is the drama of an exogamous marriage, a continuing aspect of Conrad's work: Almayer and his wife; Willems and his, and then with Aïssa; Kurtz and his African mistress; Jim and Jewel. Through the development of exogamous relationships, Conrad could indulge his theme of individual isolation; that is, despite union, each remains separate. Part of this is a concomitant of language—each speaks a different language, sometimes literally—but also, each invests his own world with a different set of values, a distinct kind of longing. In this arrangement, both men and women move vertically along the lines of their own lives; there is little associational or lateral relationship.

It would be a mistake, I think, to interpret these relationships as misogynic elements or to attribute them to Conrad's inability to understand an equitable distribution of love and friendship. Such observations are beside the point, since the fundamental matter lies elsewhere, in Conrad's larger view, where conflict always exists *because* there can be no understanding, no entering into another's life (until too late); where the bases for a full and solid association are lacking or incomplete. If women "devour" or "burn up" their men, it is a defensive gesture on the woman's part against men who "use" them: these are Conrad's givens.

On June 7, Conrad told Pinker his financial position was disastrous, and he began to work against advances—money for material not yet placed, the beginning of his indebtedness to Pinker, which would last for the next fifteen years. He announced that "Seraphina" was "now complete in MS." He probably meant some sketchy version of it, for the writing continued well past this date. For the next six months, the collaborators would toil on "Seraphina," and Conrad would do nothing else, not until he wrote "To-morrow" toward the beginning of 1902. He was working, now, almost solely for money: short stories for Pinker to place, "Seraphina" itself, and a suitable long tale to complete the Blackwood volume. Conrad's bitterness, especially in his letters to Pinker, reflects his trying position: financial desperation intermixed with no long project, in his forty-fourth year still another dead spot.

The association with Ford sustained him; but like the connection with Pinker, it reminded him of his indebtedness and his commercial orientation. He had had to borrow £100 from his collaborator, presumably on their expectations from "Seraphina," whose publication, incidentally, did not occur until 1903. There seemed to be no way of breaking out of this cycle, unless "Seraphina" had a sudden success. Writing to Ford, Conrad says Meldrum has encouraged him about Blackwood's acceptance of their work. Parts I, II, and IV had gone to Pinker to be transmitted to Edinburgh. Part III, however, needed doing over. This is the section called "Casa Riego," and Conrad felt it lacked a certain "hard *reality.*" "The treatment as it stands [he wrote] is too much in the air—in places. I don't want to bother you now by going into the argument. I shall do the thing myself but of course I would want to speak to you about it. Don't let this interrupt your work on the dear old Harry [Henry VIII, for his *The Fifth Queen*]."

Of great interest to us is the fact that Conrad's contribution to Part III prefigures several elements of *Nostromo.* So that even though he did not formally begin *Nostromo* for at least another eight to nine months, he was thinking in terms of crowd scenes, character groupings, underlying political motives for aberrant behavior, even retrospective narrative and historical detail. Chiefly, for the first time Conrad was handling large groups and indulging his hatred of mob action: "Some of the *Lugareños* carried torches, others had pikes; most of them, however, had nothing but their long knives. They came in a disorderly, shouting mob along the beach, intending this not for an attack, but as a simple demonstration." Conrad adds: "They squeaked like the vermin they were. I [Kemp] brought down the clubbed musket; two went down."

Describing the novel in progress to Blackwood, Conrad enclosed an epitome and explained the basis of the tale and their handling of "romance":

> This tale—which we call a romance—has been grubbed out of the British Museum by Hueffer. All the details of the political feeling in Jamaica (about 1821) are authentic. There was really a perfectly innocent young Englishman who was tried for piracy and escaped the gallows by the merest hair's-breadth. There did exist a nest of pirates about that time on

the coast of Cuba. They were a sorry lot—I admit. O'Brien is our own invention, and he is possible enough—I mean historically possible. Good many Irishmen took refuge in Spain, made careers, and founded families. For the rest you'll see we do not go in for analysis of character seeking rather to present a succession of picturesque scenes and personalities. We try to produce a variation from the usual type of romance our point of view being that the feeling of the romantic in life lies principally in the glamour memory throws over the past and arises from contact with a different race and a different temperament; so that the Spanish girl seems romantic to Kemp while that ordinary good young man seems romantic and even heroic not only to Seraphina but to Sanchez and Don Riego too.

Conrad's explanation of romance seems more of a strategy than a point of view. He and Ford found their way of working leaned toward certain techniques—interweaving of narrative, flashbacks, heavy use of retrospect—at the expense of character. Their collaboration produced its own style, and that style precluded any depth of character; as a consequence, Conrad had to indicate the strongest point possible, which was to stress how their technical means created a different kind of romance.

The Inheritors, meanwhile, was being "worked up" by Heinemann, and Conrad fantasized its potential success:

I've never before heard such talk of anything with my name to it. So hopeful, I mean. There shall be a campaign. Different plans are under consideration. One of them is to start a general discussion on methods of collaboration. Have you noticed in the last *Aca*^{y} a sort of preliminary whisper? That's it. The other hare it seems is to be a philosophical hare. That's what Nietsche's [sic] phil^{phy} leads to—here's your overman—I said. I kept my gravity in the big armchair and with extreme sobriety made suggestions: the authors by the introduction of the *4*th*D* tried to remove their work from the sphere of mere personalities. They attack not individuals but the spirit of the age—the immoral tendencies arising from a purely materialistic view of life which even reach the lower classes (Slingsby, I suppose).

There is a manic quality to Conrad's news, as though in the depths of a creative lull or impasse he needed to hang on to the ridiculous. "Burn this letter [he tells Ford] for fear your young German girl should sell it to a Belgian newspaper and we should stand revealed as the 4th Dim^{ists} ourselves."

A letter to Pinker, dated July 3, suggests the web of deals and counter-deals Conrad could not extricate himself from. He was now entering his mid-forties, coming solidly into the strength of his great creative period, and yet no more secure financially than when he had started *Almayer's Folly*. Far worse, he had a household to support. With his hopes riding on Blackwood's acceptance of "Seraphina," he asked his agent to pay another £40 to Watson, Conrad's banker, offering the still-incomplete manuscript as security. He mentions that "Seraphina" will be finished before he begins another story, which would be the very slight "To-morrow," completed in January. He then opens up his account vis-à-vis McClure, which is complicated by the latter's advance of money for *The Rescue,* dating back to 1898. During that time, he delivered *Jim* to McClure-Doubleday, which he considered some kind of payment for their commitment to the incomplete book. Clearly, he has circled back to his basic need: to "finish the *Rescue.* Much of it [he says] is written and much remains to be done. I don't see how I can set out about it (living as I do from hand to mouth) unless I can get something for it; I mean something more. It is an evident necessity. As to why I went [on] writing Jim and the short stories while it was my evident duty to go on writing the *R* I simply can't explain."

Conrad wanted to assign to McClure (now separated from Doubleday) the copyright of *Jim* and the two volumes of stories (still uncertain) in exchange for a cancellation of the agreement on *The Rescue.* Under those conditions, he felt he would have the peace of mind to continue with it and enter the marketplace with the manuscript. Then Pinker could handle it freely in the States, with Heinemann publishing it in England. All this amounted to a mortgaging not only of the future but of the past; by forgoing his copyrights, Conrad was isolating himself from his own work, selling his efforts outright.

The linchpin of the arrangement was Blackwood's acceptance of "Seraphina." This novel had gone through numerous phases, beginning in 1898, when the collaborators had hoped to complete it the following year. The version Conrad offered to Blackwood on July 4, 1901, was most probably far more Conradian than the earlier version, on which Ford alone had worked. When Conrad informed Pinker on June 7 that "Seraphina" was now complete in manuscript, he may have meant that his rewriting of Ford's effort was settled. For, twelve days later, while staying at Winchelsea with Ford, he said he was going to write another 10,000 words and then run up to London to see Pinker with the manuscript. But "Seraphina," or *Romance,* as it had now become, was far from finished. Conrad held back Part III for further work and Part V does not even appear to have been written. We can gauge a measure of Conrad's financial desperation that in this rather hit-or-miss way he would approach a publisher whom he respected as much as he did Blackwood.

Far from being ended, *Romance* would be strung out until March of 1902, when Conrad was already beginning *Nostromo.* Meldrum wrote to Blackwood that he found the literary quality of the manuscript high, although the fault was a certain split, in its being Ford's story with Conrad's storytelling. The dramatic intensity, he felt, was forced; but he found it capital, told with all "Conrad's wonderfully gleaming and suggestive method." But without waiting for Part III, Blackwood informed Conrad he had come "to an unfavorable decision" regarding the three parts submitted and advised Conrad to send them elsewhere as they are or with the completed third part. Blackwood offered no reason for his decision. We can speculate, however, that he sensed not only an inferior piece of work but a good deal of difficulty in dealing with Conrad over another long manuscript, especially one that remained incomplete. Quite possibly, Conrad lost Blackwood's acceptance by submitting the material in this way, but he was trying to balance all the disparate elements of his own needs.

In his response, Conrad does not even mention *Romance.* This omission so surprised Meldrum that he wrote a memo to Blackwood, not knowing that the firm had rejected the manuscript. Conrad's answer turned not to his own needs but to an allusion in Blackwood's letter to an Admiral Kennedy, author of *Hurrah for the Life of a Sailor: Fifty Years in the Navy.* Conrad says he has read the book, a Blackwood publication, and he rhapsodizes over a maritime experience which, he says, "has a moral value like the acts of faith on which may be built a doctrine of salvation and a rule of life." Conrad then daydreams about life at sea, which he had found much harder and crueler than these reveries suggest:

> . . . the contact of such a genuine personality is like an invigorating bath for one's mind jaded by infinite effort after literary expression, wearied by all the unrealities of a writing life, discouraged by a sunless, starless sort of mental solitude, having lost its reckoning in a grey sea of words, words, words; an unruly choppy sea running crosswise in all the endless shifts of thought. Oh! for a cutter and the Fatshan Creek, or for that wonderful beat-up from Mozambique Channel to Zanzibar!

If he could have dropped everything, health willing, Conrad would have made a run for it.

But his nose was deep in the literary world. *Romance* was still to be completed, Blackwood's rejection had to be faced and assimilated, the collaboration with Ford had to continue, and even Marguerite Poradowska was turning up in correspondence to bring his thoughts back from the sea. Conrad told Ford that Marguerite has been "fascinated by your verse and impressed by your personality"; and Galsworthy "has sung the praise of your art, as shown in the Inh^{tors}. He is really and truly struck." We may suspect Conrad was keeping his partner happy with praise in order to justify his own slow way of working. Also, Blackwood's rejection, on which he commented ambiguously to Ford, must have given him second thoughts about the collaboration. In a letter that comes shortly after Blackwood's rejection, Conrad excused himself for his "inadequate collaboration" and informed his friend that "B with many circumlocutions declines." There are few circumlocutions in Blackwood's letter, simply a very firm response to a manuscript he does not wish to publish. It was, apparently, time to move on, away from a collaboration which was not producing any popular work and from a novel which seemed to absorb time without reflecting genius.

Romance has an uneven quality, which resulted from an incomplete collaboration; that is, the entire manuscript required revision by each, with further rewriting to unify it. Instead, each handled parts, so that the overall narrative lacks coherence, Conrad's desire for intensity and fullness of detail clashing with Ford's need for swiftness, shifting of temporal sequences, and tonal varieties. Except for their use of the *progression d'effet*, or the developing sequence, the two writers were literarily distinct. In a 1923 letter to Ford, when both were trying to sort out what belonged to each of them, Conrad outlined their respective contributions:

> I suppose our recollections agree. Mine, in their simplest forms, are: First part yours; Second part mainly yours, with a little by me, on points of seamanship and suchlike small matters; Third part about 60% mine, with important touches by you; Fourth part mine, with here and there and [sic] important sentence by you; Fifth part practically all yours, including the famous sentence ["Excellency—a few goats. . . ." Kemp's response to a question as to his occupation] at which we both exclaimed "This is genius," (do you remember what it is) with perhaps half a dozen lines by me. I think that, en gros, this is absolutely correct. Intellectually and artistically it is of course right through a *joint production.*

In Richard Curle's copy of *Romance*, Conrad revised his estimate of his own contribution:

> In this book I have done my share of writing. Most of the characters (with the exception of Mrs Williams, Sebright and the seamen) were introduced by Hueffer and developed then in my own way, with, of course, his consent and collaboration. The last part is (like the first) the work of Hueffer, except for a few paragraphs written by me. Part second is actually joint work. Parts three and four are my writing, with here and there a sentence by Hueffer.*

The last part is indeed Ford's, since Conrad was anxious to get on with the idea he had for *Nostromo.* We should not exaggerate Conrad's role in this novel, not because the biographer would like to remove him from a second-rate effort, but because the amount of time he actually spent on the novel free of other obligations was small for something of this length. If we add to that his dilatory production, we cannot make large claims for his contribution.

The collaboration put tremendous strains on the relationship between the two writers and between the couples, not to speak of strains within each marriage. *The Good Soldier*, Ford's 1915 novel, and masterpiece, is one manifestation of the discord, of what must have been intense love-hate relationships. True, Conrad helped Elsie on her Maupassant translations, espe-

* To Pinker, Conrad shifted on the proportions of Part III, calling it "practically my work."

cially in matters of idiom, pacing, and tone. With his own special feel for Maupassant's cadences and tonal varieties, Conrad revised details in Elsie's presentation. Yet despite this, he was getting on Ford's nerves: "I am doing my damnedst [Conrad wrote]. I've been interrupted; I've been upset too; and generally I am not allowed to forget how impossible my position is daily becoming. Anyhow I've worked as hard as I know how."

On another occasion, matters became so strained Conrad had to write a placating letter, indicating he wanted understanding:

> You cannot really suppose that there is anything between us except our mutual regard and our partnership—in crime. "Voyons, Señorita quelle folie." Upon my word I am quite confounded by your letter which my speaking "à coeur ouvert" to Auntie Elsie did not deserve.
>
> I was afraid of taking a course that would seem heartless or offensive to you—especially in your low state of health; and I mistrusted my own nerves which, as you may have perceived, are and were devilishly attuned to the concert pitch of gloom and absurd irritation.
>
> But of any irritation or of any thought about you but of the most affectionate nature I have been utterly unconscious then or now.

The emotional nature of this collaboration cannot be exaggerated, since it involved not only sensitive, high-strung individuals but professional careers which the collaboration was itself frustrating. For Conrad, the older man who sensed the fewness of the years remaining to him, such pressures were overwhelming and would help to explain the aggressive acts he displayed toward Ford: ignoring him after inviting him, delaying his own work on *Romance*, depreciating the novel behind Ford's back, sending abject apologies for hostile behavior.

But such acts could be compensated for by simple moments, such as the occasion when Conrad arranged birthday ceremonies for his son Borys and Christina Hueffer. Baines quotes extensively from the letter, which probably dates from December 14, 1902, but omits the persiflage of the opening:

> It shall be as it must be then; it only emphasizes your goodness, to consent to rush over for such a short time. The thing would be as nothing in our eyes if Xtina failed to appear with her two faithful attendants. But, indeed, its [sic] no lack of hospitable intention but sheer funk that prevents us asking you to come the day (or two) before. First there are the ungovernable passions of the young man which receiving fresh impulse from the proximity of Xtina's charms would make him utterly unmanageable (unless by the help of a leather strap—which is . . . fie!). Then: what would you eat? How would you be attended to? Where could you hide your distracted heads? Already I am warned that on Thursday at lunch time a hunk of bread and cheese shall be thrown out to me at the back door and that I am expected to devour the same in a distant part of the field. Under the circumstances I look to this with a pleasant emotion.

There is peace in the field. Peace! —Vous comprenez? . . . At 3.40 the Young Lady [Christina Hueffer] having had barely time to smooth her plumes shall proceed (attended by the Lady Regent—the Lord Regent is at liberty to swoon for fifty minutes) shall proceed—I say—to the Baronial Kitchen (where the feast is to be engulphed) to receive the guests with the young Cavalier.

Then she takes her arm-chair
at the
High End.

Engulphing by the young princes and princesses of the name of Hopkins, Mills etc etc begins.

The dames Graham and Gates would have come over at two to help. They preside at the flow of tea. The Lady Regent, the Chatelaine and the Chatelain assisted by the Maid of Honour Nellie scout about more or less effectively. But it is *distinctly understood* that the Lady Regent is *not to tire herself out in any way.* What is wanted mostly of her is to shed extra radiance on the glory of her daughter.

Engulphing stops
in the
Natural course of things.
Then
The Young lady
Arises from her armchair

and proceeding up the table on *her* right pulls a cracker with every feaster on that side. The Young Cavalier [Borys Conrad] performs the same rite on *his* right side.

Feasters don caps out of crackers.
A Bell rings cheerfully!
(It is then Five of the clock)

And the open door reveals tree which has been lighted up by the efforts of the Lord Regent (now recovered from the swoon) and the chatelain. . . .

The Young Lady and Cavalier
speeding the parting guests at the door
"The rest is silence"

There was, we should not forget, that aspect of the relationship and the association with the children. Even after Ford left Elsie, Conrad showed concern for Christina and Katherine, the second daughter.

Not until November 7, two and a half months after Blackwood's rejection of "Seraphina," did Conrad respond to his publisher. "Of course I was sorry [he wrote] . . . that you did not see your way to accept Garnett's article [a critical essay intended for "Maga"]; and I will admit the rejection of *Seraphina* had shaken the confidence with which I looked upon that work." Conrad says he has toiled on the book and has not "been exactly lying on the floor and groaning." Instead, he picks up the thread of their association and asserts he intends to send "about 30,000 words for the *Youth Vol*"—this would be "The End of the Tether," which would run to almost 50,000 words and would not be completed until the following October (1902). It would not, in fact, be started for several more months.

While there is still no mention of *Nostromo,* we get glimpses of Conrad's mind working toward some alternative to "Seraphina" and the short stories. To Galsworthy, he tried to convey his sense of irony and ironic attitude toward character and event, warning his friend not to hug his conception of right and wrong too closely. A romance such as the collaborative effort could afford Conrad no such play of mind, since romance generically demanded certain givens. "Seraphina" was, in fact, the old style of picaresque hiding behind a few narrative convolutions. To Galsworthy, Conrad suggested those qualities that would underlie a serious work, the need for skepticism, the scrupulous attention to one's conception of character and event, the attitude of "perfect indifference" toward one's characters, purely intellectual, "more independant [sic], freer, less rigorous." Ostensibly replying to Galsworthy's *Man of Devon,* a Blackwood publication in 1901, Conrad had to remind himself where his own art lay. New Year's Eve of 1901 found him at Ford's, hoping to finish up the last of the collaboration.

The coming of the new year, 1902, saw Conrad with "Seraphina" still hanging about him "like a curse." "There is," he wrote Meldrum, "always something wrong turning up about that story. After M^r^ B'wood's refusal of the same I first dropped it in disgust; then took it up again and have been working very hard at it. It is now a satisfactory piece of work but not quite rearranged and adjusted all through to the changes in action and in the reading of characters which I have introduced. Hueffer was to do all that—instead of which he goes and tries to swallow a chicken bone, gets nearly choked, awfully shaken up, unable to work and so on. I could have wept. Still there was no remedy so I buckled-to again and am still at it driving hard. I had just one days respite—Xmas—that's all—but the book is a new book and really not bad at all this time."

Reviewing the year, Conrad saw it as "disastrous," for he had wasted his time "tinkering here, tinkering there," on *Rescue,* on "that fatal *Seraphina,*" with only three stories finished. He throws out a hint that Blackwood should hire him "permanently take all my stuff as it comes—lock it up in a desk if he likes—publish when he likes, never publish!" "Maga," he says, is his first love, not the *Illustrated London News* or the *Pall Mall Magazine,* where Pinker was placing his copy. He then indicates for the first time his plan to do "some autobiographical matter about Ships, skippers, and an adventure or two"; we have here the early plan of *The Mirror of the Sea,* two of whose sketches did wind up in "Maga." He thought of the sketches as fiction, in the same sense that "Youth" is fiction. Quiller-Couch, he felt, was incorrect in calling the latter a short story. The sketches, then, would be in a twilight zone between fiction and non-fiction, although what Conrad had in mind is difficult to determine. Conrad probably referred to them as stories in order to try to recapture those days when "Maga" published his fiction.

The letter to Meldrum could not avoid the inevitable: the humiliation he now affected in order to request more money, this time £50 on the promise of 5,000 words. This work would be part of an eventual 30,000, he says, what would be "The End of the Tether." Meanwhile, Conrad tried to place "Falk" with *Blackwood's*, for serial publication in two numbers. This story was destined for the Heinemann volume, but its placement with *Blackwood's* as a two-part serial would reduce some of the debt. The story had been kicking around for some time, in Pinker's hands. Setting all this out to George Blackwood (nephew of William), Conrad asked for further money, not on the *Youth* volume, but on the "30,000 words laid up in my cranium." The request was rejected. Also, his attempt to renegotiate the terms of his payment from £2.10 per thousand to £4 per thousand was turned down, since he had agreed to complete the *Youth* volume on the "old conditions." Even more ominously, George Blackwood suggested perhaps two stories for the volume to make it a full one. Conrad's disappointment was intense, and he answered that his hopes were all pinned to Blackwood's: "My ambition had never been to see myself drawn, quartered and illustrated in a Magazine run for the Million by a Millionaire." While he feared the Grub Street aspect of such publication, he nevertheless continued to accept the money.

This situation was bound to blow up in his dealings with Pinker, for underlying Conrad's hatred of the common marketplace was the fact that it was, at least partially, run by Jews to make money for Jews—what he had characterized to Graham as the "shent-per-shent business"—and Pinker was a feed-in of material to that very market. The coming of the new year was not helpful, since it should have meant a fresh start but actually saw Conrad tinkering and finishing old projects. He complains of Ford's inability to work—the chicken bone in his throat that almost strangled him—but behind the complaint is a division of interests. His position was curious: he needed Ford's presence and support for personal reasons and yet disdained the collaboration for professional reasons. The conflict surfaces in his reaction to Pinker's prodding for more work to justify the outlay of money.

> Meantime I am nearly going mad with worry. You may imagine I am hard pushed if I come to you again without a scrap of *MS*. But you must do the best you can for me—and if you can not or are disinclined to make a further advance pray tell me so at once (by return of post *to the Pent*) and I'll see what I can do with B'wood. This life will drive me mad. My ½ years premium on my policies together with int' and paying off instalment of loan is what lies on my mind. I thought the two stories would have done it. Really all these anxieties do drive me to the verge of madness—but death would be the best thing. It would pay off all my debts and there

> would be no question of *MS.* Really if one hadn't wife & child I don't know——There are also some pressing bills. Damn. And with all this my bodily health is excellent it is the brain only that is fogged.—

This was written from Winchelsea, where Conrad was plugging along.

Conrad tried to interest Pinker in *Romance*, and he had to stress the popular aspect, since his agent was trying for money, not aesthetic appeal. Conrad emphasized its easy style—which is not at all the case; plenty of action—for entire chapters, there are only longueurs and dead spots; the romantic atmosphere—which is very slow in developing and only achieves "romanticism" by repeated telling; and a happy ending—after much narrative confusion given the simplicity of the characters and events. He tells Pinker how to describe the novel, every word a mockery of his real interests:

> You may describe and introduce the book (if You do such things in that way) as a straight romantic narrative of adventure where the hero is a Kent youth of good birth, the heroine a Spanish girl, the scene in England, Jamaica, Cuba, and on the sea—the personages involved besides Hero and Heroine smugglers, planters, sailors and authentic pirates—the last of the West Indian pirates; the whole story being founded on a fact carefully looked up in contemporary press and report of trial in Eng.—but by us brought about Romantically—the Romantic feeling being the basis of the book which is *not* a boy's story. You may take my word for it that it is a piece of literature of which we are neither of us at all ashamed.

Curiously, Conrad would describe *The Rescue* in similar terms in 1919, when he thought it might catch the eye of the Nobel Prize Committee. He speaks of *Romance:* ". . . it is a serious attempt at *interesting, animated Romance*, with no more psychology than comes naturally into the action." Yet what self-hatred was involved in Conrad's presentation to Pinker of how he should describe the book; he had entered into the vulgarity of the marketplace. In the same letter, he indicates work on two stories, "To-morrow" and what became "The Brute": the tale of a "barge collision on the Thames and trial in court arising therefrom."

Pinker did not, apparently, enter into the spirit of things and refused further advances. All the misery of his lonely toil surfaced in Conrad's letter, intermixed as it is with his pride as a craftsman and a serious man of letters. From this long letter of January 8, which has already been cited, we could assume the relationship with Pinker was doomed. Conrad denies trying to get at his agent's pocket, asserts that *Romance* is as good as any fifty manuscripts Pinker sells in the year, announces he is "another kind of person" from those the agent is accustomed to, and distinguishes his art from Stevenson's, who considered the artist no better than a prostitute.

By January 16, Conrad had quieted down and returned to business. In the meantime, Wells had seen *Romance* in manuscript and recommended to

Pinker that he offer an advance, which he did. Conrad sent "To-morrow," which he asserted is "by no means a potboiler," although it was adapted to magazine needs. He was inching toward Grub Street. It would appear in *Pall Mall Magazine* for August 1902, and is among Conrad's least memorable short fictions. *Romance* was finally winding down: "Yesterday [he wrote Pinker] had a wire from H. saying Part II is done. There is therefore ready: Pts I. II. III. To part IV a few pages are waiting at the end. To part V. a few need re-writing at the beginning. We divide into five pts to equalize the length. Say 22,000 each." He had made up with Pinker to the extent that he could look forward to the day when his agent would have all his stuff "with no conditions, restrictions and arrears to make up." He mentions *The Rescue*, another loose end, for which he has already exhausted the financial resources. He owed £180 for the serial rights to McClure, which he hoped to pay out of proceeds of a resale, if he ever completed it.

On February 25, after a suitable apology to Pinker, Conrad picked up the torturous history of *Romance* once again. He has had to write another chapter, 9, as a transition to Part V. Thus, we can see that Conrad was really responsible for the overall manuscript, even though the actual writing earlier may have been more evenly divided. The final presentation of the book was his work, his revision, his judgment. The pressing matter of the letter was his desperate financial situation, his inability to pay off money borrowed on his insurance policy, half-yearly payments of £25, from a loan of £250 at 5 percent interest. Conrad proposed a further mortgaging of his future life: if Pinker paid off the loan entirely, about £240 remaining, Conrad would assign to his agent not only his "policy *B* (for £500)" but also every line he planned to write with the exception of the 30,000 words owed to Blackwood. He would repay Pinker by means of the work passing through his hands, although, as the agent discovered, that increased rather than decreased the indebtedness.

Conrad asserted that such an arrangement would benefit Pinker by making his position stronger; Conrad would be needy and Pinker would be assured of copy. With the delivery of the *Rescue* to him for serialization, Pinker would have an "absolutely free hand" for dealing with his material worldwide. Conrad assured his agent he had no weakness or vice, and at his age, he stressed, he was not likely to go wrong suddenly. Also, he had no lingering disabling disease and expected to hang on. "Gouty people do. They also go out suddenly. That's so much the better. I am not worrying about the last scene except in novels." Pinker responded favorably, and the two began to head into another kind of "collaboration," in which Pinker advanced money for which copy was not yet ready, assumed the role of Conrad's banker and financier, and took on the elder counsel's role in relationship to the older man. The arrangement was not unlike that of the patron to the artist which had existed prior to the eighteenth century, before commercial success was possible; or, more recently, between Tadeusz Bobrowski and his nephew. Although Pinker was in no sense a literary man and was quite commercially oriented, he learned how to deal with Conrad, and beginning with the February 28 letter from the latter, their two fortunes began to converge.

Conrad tried to give his agent a legal lien on all his future as well as his past work, except for the *Typhoon* and Blackwood volumes. "Without any mental reservation and in perfect sincerity I do feel (and she does so too) that in case of my early death my wife would be perfectly safe in your hands." Conrad continues: "For the future I only may express my honest conviction that I haven't done my best work yet; and at any rate I've plenty of material to try my hand on." His estimation of his future was certainly valid, and it was Pinker who made possible whatever peace of mind Conrad could obtain from his situation. The conjunction of Pinker and Conrad, almost fortuitously wrought, was of the kind the latter found absolutely necessary. Although he may well have done his work without Pinker's presence, borrowing increasingly from Galsworthy and other friends, he would have found himself under unbearable pressures when he began his longer novels. One may conjecture he could have drifted further into Grub Street work, or he could have forgone some of his longer work or marred it with foreshortened endings or developments. Certainly, works such as *Nostromo* and *Victory*, whose gestation periods drained him physically and mentally, would have been almost impossibly difficult without Pinker's interim support.

By late February of 1902, Conrad had found his pattern for the next thirteen years: he would be engaged in several parallel activities, all going rather badly, so that when he began a new novel (now *Nostromo*), usually misconceived as a long story or novella, he would be in a state of near-panic. In addition to his usual literary anxieties, he would apparently be careless about money, which was never abundant, and thus increase his apprehension about supporting his wife and children. He saw them as adrift, his children orphans, his wife a helpless widow, his own career cut short by early death. His vision was of shipwrecked Korzeniowskis heading, as they did after 1861, toward Scylla and Charybdis, all brought about by his characteristic Quixote-like behavior. He was Ulysses reduced to a fool, lacking even the idealism of the original Quixote.

This accumulation of anxieties, worries, fears, and assorted guilt feelings was connected, evidently, to his way of working and to the functioning of his literary imagination. Apparently, he could not work effectively unless he were close to breakdown, on the edge of psychic disorders, ill in body and mind. Conrad's physical disorders were legion: recurring gout (a hereditary condition), arthritis, delirious fevers, neuralgia, influenza. These, however, were simply the tip. The inner disorder was far greater, and when it was at its most intense, he functioned most effectively artistically. While we cannot pinpoint precisely his most productive days or weeks, we can cite his most substantial periods creatively. These periods, as we trace them in the letters to Pinker, in particular, coincide with his most trying times, when financial, personal, mental, and literary burdens appeared unbearable. With the early work on *Nostromo*, Conrad's greatest achievement, we have a sense of epic labors, the pained and disturbed artist turning out copy at an agonizingly slow rate, while burning within with a raging self-hatred.

CHAPTER 23

Nostromo

ON March 10, Conrad wrote Galsworthy that *Romance* was completed and "gone out of the house she has haunted for this year past. I do really hope it will hit the taste of the street—unless the devil is in it." He rejected McClure's suggestion that he sign *Romance* as the sole author: "Hueffer," he told Pinker, "has done as much and more to the book than I did. I would not *dare* to suggest anything of the sort to him even if I could bring my own conscience to accept such a swindle. . . . The book must be accepted on its merits by the public—as a romantic story not as Conrad's work specifically." But on March 16, when he began the most important phase of his creative life, all other considerations were superseded. Conrad announced to Pinker he hoped to transmit a "considerable batch of *Nostromo*. . . . It is easier for me to make now a story of 75 to 80 thou, which will be I think as easy to place serially and shall make a volume." He indicates that Pinker should be able to get for it £500 (£300 serial, £200 book), which is the amount he received for *Jim*. He assures his agent "most of the MS shall be in your possession by June." All this was accompanied by a severely painful attack of gout, which had afflicted him for the last fourteen days. Having gone through a "little hell," he says that "Nostromo shall be a first rate story." The juxtaposition is apt.

None of this should suggest Conrad had a clear view. As he began the extraordinarily long run on *Nostromo*—it would occupy him for nearly two and a half years—his business interests were a morass. Needing more immediate cash, he wanted to sell Blackwood the copyright to *Lord Jim* as well as to the *Youth* volume not yet completed. Such outright sales would, of course, inconvenience Pinker, who had expected clear rights to these books as part of his overall agreement with Conrad. Outright sale would, additionally, confuse Conrad's attempts later to put together a collected edition, since his work could become scattered among half a dozen publishers.* But the immediate need was preemptory: cash for routine expenses.

* Some of this difficulty became almost immediately apparent. The translator and editor of *Mercure de France*, H. D. Davray, was interested in obtaining French translation rights to *Tales of Unrest* as well as to the volume *Typhoon*, which Heinemann would

Not unexpectedly, in the midst of such mental turmoil, Conrad wrote Ford he missed collaboration "in a most ridiculous manner." "I hope," he adds, "you don't intend dropping me altogether." With the end of *Romance*, "everything in the world seemed to come to an end." In a sense, this world did end, for Conrad traded Ford for Pinker, a literary collaborator for a financial one. Conrad's life moved on several parallel lines at this stage:

1. The dependence on Ford, which was declining as *Romance* headed for publication and Elsie and Ford were moving apart.
2. Early work on *Nostromo*, which began inauspiciously as a short volume and grew to Conrad's longest effort.
3. Increasing dependence on Pinker.
4. Work on "The End of the Tether" for the Blackwood *Youth* volume.
5. Thought, although not actual preparation, of some of the pieces that would become part of *The Mirror of the Sea*.
6. Arrangement for French translation of some of his work, including the stories in the as-yet-unpublished Heinemann *Typhoon* volume.
7. Deepening of financial difficulties.

At the end of April, Conrad wrote Ford a letter that indeed brought them together. Ford had just gone through a most trying time, for on February 2, Elsie's father, the well-known Dr. Martindale, had been discovered dead in his laboratory. Since the cause of death was an overdose of drugs, suicide was suspected. Elsie was herself in poor spirits, and dissension with her husband was growing as he tired of country life. Further, Ford's brother Oliver had suffered financial losses, to the extent that he needed help desperately. The Ford-Conrad foursome was edging toward dissolution. In this atmosphere, Conrad invited him down. Each needed the other:

> Your letters have been touching in their suggestions of your mental state. I am truly impatient and anxious. I say anxious, frankly, because not distrusting you in the least I have from personal experience a rooted mistrust towards our work—yours and mine—which is under the patronage of a Devil. For indeed unless beguiled by a malicious fiend what man would undertake it? What creature would be mad enough to take upon it-

---

publish. *Tales of Unrest*, of course, belonged to Fisher Unwin, with whom Conrad had broken off on less than cordial terms. In a letter to Davray, he refers to Unwin as "L'animal." Furthermore, "An Outpost of Progress" in that collection had already been translated but not published, by Marguerite Poradowska. Not completely happy with that translation, Conrad advised Davray to take the burden on himself. Thus, within only seven years of his beginnings as an author, Conrad was spread over Unwin, Blackwood, and Heinemann. Interestingly enough, the lead story in *Typhoon* would not appear in translation until André Gide undertook it himself, as part of the overall translation of Conrad's work into French. To complicate matters, Davray was also interested in the as-yet-unpublished *Youth* volume, which Blackwood would issue upon the completion of "The End of the Song [Tether]."

> self the task of a creator? It is a thing unlawful. Une chose néfaste, carrying with it its own punishment of toil, unceasing doubt and deception.

Conrad says there is an excitement in braving heaven itself, "in giving form to an idea, in clothing the breath of our life with day. . . . And so the gods encompass our destruction—prius dementat!" Conrad speaks of snatching the forms of art from the forms of "baked clay": "I have no doubt of the breathing of life but the fact remains that without baked clay there is no art, no success, no honesty as you and I understand these terms." Conrad warned his friend not to let his art suffer because his life was undergoing challenges.

Trying to draw together so many disparate elements, Conrad told Pinker a number of contradictory things about his work. First, he reports he has 10,000 words of "The End of the Tether" for the first installment in "Maga." He sees 2,000 words more as providing half the story; another 15,000 would, in actuality, mean half. When he completes the second half, which he says will come more easily, he will turn to the *Rescue* manuscript. Then, two days later, he promises "the first 30 pages of p' III. Nostromo. I see my way clear for the end now; it is only a matter of sitting close." Conrad's misjudgment of the scope and length of this novel was monumental, in fact, inexplicable. Even if we assume he had in mind a short story (20–25,000 words or so) and not the 75–80,000 words he mentioned to Pinker on March 16, it is impossible to see what his plan was for a piece of this truncated length. Yet he built his financial hopes on a quick end, for he told Pinker, "Nostromo ought to put me right."

Conrad began to send copy of "Tether," asking for money along the way, £30 on May 20. His requests for advances from Blackwood would reach a climax at the end of the month, when he asked for an interview with the owner (down from Edinburgh). Though his plan was complicated, it left many financial holes: he would see the copyright of *Jim* and *Youth* for a loan of £300 bearing 5 percent interest and a further advance of £50; he would assign his insurance policy of £400 as security, with Galsworthy as guarantor for the half-yearly premiums. If Conrad died, Blackwood could repay himself from the principal, turning the balance over to Jessie. Conrad would decrease the debt chiefly through sales of books or through outright payments. The weak point, Conrad admitted, was the regular payment of interest, which might have to be worked out with Pinker. Withal, the arrangement proved unacceptable, especially since the firm was already dissatisfied with Conrad's rate of production and his inability to live within fairly reasonable sums of money. On May 31, after the interview, Conrad gave his reactions at length, using the occasion to defend his art and his own life as an artist. The letter is of great length (over 1,000 words), but it warrants extensive quotation since its language is the shield behind which Conrad could work:

I admit that after leaving you I remained for some time under the impression of my "worthlessness"; but I beg to assure you that I've never fostered any illusions as to my value. You may believe me implicitly when I say that I never work in a self satisfied elation, which to my mind is no better than a state of inebriety unworthy of a man who means to achieve something. That—labouring against an anxious tomorrow, under the stress of an uncertain future, I have been at times consoled, re-assured and uplifted by a finished page—I'll not deny. This however is not intoxication: it is the Grace of God that will not pass by even an unsuccessful novelist. For the rest I am conscious of having pursued with pain and labour a calm conception of a definite ideal in a perfect soberness of spirit.

Conrad admits Blackwood's words "carry a considerable weight" with him and that he no longer has "the buoyancy of youth to bear me up through the deep hours of depression. I have nothing but a faith—a little against the world—in my reasoned conviction." He then, rather pathetically, lists those who have praised his work, including a "charming old lady in Winchester," Harriet Capes:

I've rejected the idea of worthlessness and I'll tell you, dear Mr Blackwood, on what ground mainly. It is this:—that, given my talent (which appeals to such widely different personalities as W. H. [E.] Henley and Bernard Shaw—H. G. Wells and professor Yrgö Hirn of the Finland University—to Maurice Greiffenhagen a painter and to the skipper of a Persian Gulf steamer who wrote to the papers of my "Typhoon"—to the Ed of PMM to a charming old lady in Winchester) given my talent, the fundamental and permanent failure could be only the outcome of an inherent worthlessness of character. Now my character is formed: it has been tried by experience. I have looked upon the worst life can do—and I am sure of myself, even against the demoralising effect of straitened circumstances.

George Blackwood, the nephew of William, had found "Tether" lacking in a suitable start: "One can hardly say one has got into the story yet." While "Tether" is not one of Conrad's outstanding efforts, the beginning nevertheless does foreshadow what awaits Whalley. Since the old captain is to go blind, Conrad stresses visual images at the start. What the Blackwood nephew did not know, perhaps, was Conrad's leisurely manner of developing a story, for the original promise of 30,000 words lengthened to nearly 50,000. The remark wounded, in any event, and Conrad found it necessary to range over his entire corpus as defense:

I know exactly what I am doing. Mr George Blackwood's incidental remark in his last letter that the story is not fairly begun yet is in a measure correct but, on a large view, beside the point. For, the writing is as good as I can make it (first duty), and in the light of the final incident, the whole story in all its descriptive detail shall fall into its place—acquire its value and its significance. This is my method based on deliberate conviction.

I've never departed from it. I call your own kind self to witness and I beg to instance Karain—Lord Jim (where the method is fully developed)—the last pages of Heart of Darkness where the interview of the man and the girl locks in—as it were—the whole 30,000 words of narrative description into one suggestive view of a whole phase of life, and makes of that story something quite on another plane than an anecdote of a man who went mad in the Centre of Africa. And *Youth* itself (which I delight to know you like so well) exists only in virtue of my fidelity to the idea and the method.

After a more pronounced defense of "Youth" and his method of reflecting his convictions, Conrad asks Blackwood if he knows why he is revealing so much.

First because I am sure of your sympathy. I hope that this letter will find its place in that memoir which one or two of my young faithfuls have promised to offer to my "manes." It would be good for people to know that in the 20th century in the age of Besants, Authors' Clubs and Literary agents there existed a Publisher to whom not an altogether contemptible author could write safely in that strain. Next because I want to make good my contention that I am not writing "in the air." It is not the haphazard business of a mere temperament. There is in it as much intelligent action guided by a deliberate view of the effect to be attained as in any business enterprise. Therefore I am emboldened to say that ultimate and irretrievable failure is *not* to be my lot. I know that it is not necessary to say to you but I may just as well point out that I must not by any means be taken for a gifted loafer intent on living upon credulous publishers. Pardon this remark—but in a time when Sherlock Holmes looms so big I may be excused my little bit of self-assertion.

Then, reaching for a suitable close, Conrad comes back to art itself. His self-defense is worth repeating. He is different from most other writers in that he is "long in his development." Citing Scott, Thackeray, and Eliot, he asks if their work reads swiftly. Stressing "I am *modern*," and I am "new," he says all artists with a vision must suffer for their art, if not financially, then internally, where art forms. He has *something*, and whether Blackwood buys it or not, he will continue to quarry it: his work is "action . . . nothing but action—action observed, felt and interpreted with an absolute truth to my sensations . . . action of human beings that will bleed to a prick, and are moving in a visible world."

Closing: "This is my creed. Time will show. And this you may say is my overweening conceit. Well, no. I know well enough that I know nothing. I should like to think that some of my casual critics are in the possession of that piece of information about themselves. Starting from that knowledge one may learn to look on with some attention—at least." With that, except for two of the pieces in *The Mirror*, Conrad had finished with the firm of

Blackwood. His work of the next decade would have been unsuitable for "Maga," but even so, Conrad had no reason to be anything but grateful that knotty and difficult work like "Heart of Darkness" and *Lord Jim* had found such a congenial home.

Characteristically, however, he could not let this profound blow to his pride go unpublicized. Writing to Galsworthy, he says that the "old boy [Blackwood] has huffed at my connexion with Pinker" and adds that Blackwood was half tempted to lend him some money in exchange for the two books but intimated Conrad had been a loss to the firm. Yet he misleads Galsworthy into thinking the transaction may still take place, fully knowing it would not, and suggests that Galsworthy back up the premiums of a fresh insurance policy of £450. He asks his friend to guarantee this "if B'wood finally decides to do what I want. If he does not . . ."

Conrad goes still further and indicates Blackwood showed great interest in Galsworthy: ". . . he suddenly expressed such an evidently, unquestionably, genuine appreciation of your person and your work (intelligent too) that I found it in my heart to love him." Creating an interesting triangular arrangement, he offers Galsworthy's finances as bait to Blackwood and suggests Blackwood's publishing resources as bait for Galsworthy. Falk turned to cannibalism when facing extinction; for survival, Conrad had only friends. He requests that Galsworthy write Blackwood saying he will stand behind the guarantee of the insurance loan. In a still further complication, which has humorous overtones, Conrad asks Galsworthy to swap checks with him; he will give him Blackwood's check for £30, take Galsworthy's, and then pay Meldrum with it. "I don't want to put the cheque through my bank and he [Meldrum] wishes to cover up the tracks." From this, we recognize what a true and steady friend Meldrum had proved to be, not only pushing Conrad's work with the firm, but lending him money dependent upon payment from the firm.

Yet on June 5 Conrad wrote Blackwood that he understood the refusal, a rejection Conrad had fully expected from the interview. In the letter, he mentions he expects to complete "Tether" by the last week in June; it would, in fact, drag out to October. Then beginning in July, he indicates he will initiate a number of plans, none of which materialized and none of which made any sense given his increasing concentration upon *Nostromo.*

> From July to Oct: I shall be busy with the last third of my Rescue [it was, perhaps one-third written, about 100,000 words short of completion]. Then at once, I shall begin on a story of about 80,000 words for which I shall allow myself a year [*Nostromo* took over two years more]: thus I have good hopes of being ready in 18 months with another work to try my further luck. It'll be a novel of intrigue with the Mediterranean coast and sea, for the scene.

The description sounds close to what would become *Suspense*, the fragment Conrad wrote near the end of his life.

Fortunately for him, and perhaps for the hard-pressed Blackwood, Conrad received a Royal Literary Fund grant of £200 in July 1902, which relieved some of his most immediate needs. The grant, which was repeated in April 1908, was achieved through a joint effort of several friends and was one of those rescue efforts on which Conrad periodically depended for economic survival. McClure, meanwhile, bought serial and book rights to *Romance* from Pinker, with Conrad and Ford splitting the £130 advance. The collaboration, however, was not over, since for serial publication the beginning had to be shortened. Conrad suggested that Ford tackle it alone, but agreed they could work on it together. Moving along rapidly on "Tether" and holding off Pinker on some version of *Nostromo*, he was not anxious for any other obligations.

"The End of the Tether," the story of an old captain who can no longer perform his maritime functions because of increasing sightlessness, had a symbolic function for Conrad. In its somewhat heavy way, it parallels his conscious sense of himself as a writer and an artist. His letters are all full of loss. Writing to Garnett, for example, he speaks of having lost "utterly all faith in myself, all sense of style, all belief in my power of telling the simplest fact in a simple way. For no other way do I care now. It is an unattainable way. My expression has become utterly worthless." He says he is ashamed of both forthcoming volumes, the Blackwood one as much as the one for Pawling: "I don't believe either in their popularity or in their merit." After saying that his collaborative stuff fills him with least dismay, he adds: "My mind is becoming base, my hand heavy, my tongue thick—as though I had drunk some subtle poison, some slow poison that will make me die, die as it were without an echo." The image "without an echo" is an aural equivalent of Whalley's blindness: the isolation of writer or artist from his sensory surroundings, extinguished without sound or sight. Conrad follows up the "echo" image with an expression of his "mental impotence" and fear of "his hollowness," a sense of weariness with writing and, indirectly, with life.*

To Ford, he presents a view of himself as a flayed martyr, which runs parallel to Whalley's image of self-sacrifice: "I have scrambled through once more [he writes] leaving a few more shreds of my self-respect amongst the thorns. I did not know I had so much left to lose. Be it as it may I stand on

* Or else, Conrad recognized the financial games he was playing with Pinker and friends and saw in Whalley the man who destroys himself because he "cannot cease to be frank with impunity." He continues: "The pathos for me is in this that the concealment of his extremity is as it were forced upon him. Nevertheless it is weakness—it is deterioration."

the other side to draw a breath or two raw from head to foot with the body of my thought in tatters and surveying my dishonourable scars." He enlarges the scope of his own feelings: ". . . in this world—as I have known it—we are made to suffer with the shadow of a reason, of a cause or of guilt." As a Catholic writing to another Catholic, Conrad evokes a scheming God whose ways make us martyrs without seeming cause, a world of stunning indifference: the same Schopenhauerean view he had described to Marguerite in the nineties. In *Romance,* Conrad had recently written of humanity arranged disadvantageously against nature, and the image is not unlike Hardy's use of Tess against the backdrop of Stonehenge:

> It was an awful discovery to make [Kemp's discovery of Manuel's broken body], and the contrast of his anxious and feverish stare with the collapsed posture of his body was full of intolerable suggestions of fate blundering unlawfully, of death itself being conquered by pain. I looked away only to perceive something pitiless, belittling, and cruel in the precipitous immobility of the sheer walls, in the dark funereal green of the foliage, in the falling shadows, in the remoteness of the sky.

Then comes the crucial line, worthy more of *Nostromo* than of *Romance:* "The unconsciousness of matter hinted at a weird and mysterious antagonism." The more Conrad began to probe into his art, with the beginnings of *Nostromo,* the more he noted the isolation not only of himself as a writer but of all men from themselves and from any kind of society. He was slowly sinking ever further into his type of despair, an abysmal mode of life for himself personally, but the sole way in which he could work.

On June 23, a perfect expression of his feelings and of "Tether" itself occurred. Readying the second installment of the story for "Maga" and already three days behind, he discovered that a table lamp had exploded on his study desk (a Madox Brown table) and the whole part had been lost due to flames and charring. Seeking meaning for such an event, as if it were a Job-like trial, he wrote about it successively to Blackwood, Ford, Meldrum, and Galsworthy, and, later, to Garnett. His most dramatic version was aimed at Ford.

> Last night the lamp exploded here and before I could run back into the room the whole round table was in a blaze, books, cigarettes MS—alas. The whole 2d part of End of Tether, ready to go to E'gh. The whole! The fire ran in streams and Jess and I threw blankets and danced around on them; the blaze in the window was remarked in Postling then all was over but the horrid stink. No books of yours have been burnt. The roundtable is charred in one place. The brown carpet damaged by fire and oil. This morning looking at the pile of charred paper—MS and typed copy—my head swam; it seemed to me the earth was turning backwards. I must buckle to. The MS was due in E'gh. I have wired to B'wood. It's a disaster, but the text is fairly fresh in my mind yet. The thing simply *has* to be done.

It was now the end of June, and the first installment of "Tether" was due in the July number, with the burned segment to appear in August. In the next eight days Conrad would have to supply at least 4,000 words, what would be "another dying effort," as he wrote Ford in a second letter on the same day. Caught among styles—*Romance*, the incomplete *Rescue*, "Tether," the start of *Nostromo*, papers for *Mirror*, an idea for *Suspense*—Conrad was intent upon finishing up, not starting out; and loss of copy meant not only effort wasted on commercial enterprise but time devoted to a style he was disdainful of artistically. Through it all, however, Blackwood, who must have wondered how this particular author finished anything, was quite understanding and even sent £25 against the advance. After all his assurances to the firm, Conrad sent off the batch for the July number two weeks later, on July 16, telling Blackwood he would forgo proofs. This was a great sacrifice for him, since he worked and reworked his material in galleys, many of his corrections being in grammar and idiom, which he still felt unsteady about. Yet even his private demon, which insisted on getting things right, was compromised by the prospect of demanding proofs when copy was so overdue. Another 8,000 words was needed in two weeks, when his usual production of copy ran to about 2–3,000 words a week.

How ironic all this was! Captain Whalley, growing blind, needed a pilot fish, his faithful Serang, in order to handle the *Sofala*. Without such aid, he could not function as captain. Similarly, Conrad, in his first efforts after losing Ford as active collaborator—his pilot fish?—sensed the loss of art and self and almost lost the manuscript. Did he feel betrayed? Was the burning of the manuscript attached to the death of a part of himself? Was it even entirely an accident? The Conrads' accidents were often events connected to subconscious needs. Did Conrad need the burning of the second installment as a means of invoking Ford's aid or eliminating the latter's "piloting" entirely? The accident certainly drew in Ford, who asserted he aided Conrad considerably not only during the writing of "Tether" but in the early parts of *Nostromo* and various sections of *The Mirror*.

Ford reports Conrad rented a two-room cottage opposite his in Winchelsea while he worked on "Tether." Trying to recapture the moment, he makes the episode sound like "romance," the romance of their collaboration, in which messages flew back and forth between "ancient Winchelsea and the ancient house of Blackwood in Edinburgh." Ford speaks of the manuscript in terms of "we did this, we did that," climaxing in an all-night sitting over copy calculated to catch the six o'clock mail train. He turns it into a boy's game, this working up of manuscript so as to catch the next installment.

Yet from Conrad's point of view, it was desperate work; it was *his* life, not Ford's. Accordingly, the loss of manuscript copy in the fire, the entire situation that demanded Ford's attention, the falling back upon the firm and upon Galsworthy: all of these have the dependency pattern that seems intrinsic to

Conrad's way of working and surviving. While the fire was unplanned, it nevertheless filled its own kind of need by extending the terms of collaboration. This joint effort, which both principals, unlike their wives, seemed anxious to hold on to, continued during the proofs of *Romance.*

With the finishing of "Tether" in October—"a matter of life and death," he told Garnett, a time of "frenetic idiocy"—Conrad in a sense closed out his "youth" as a writer. Though he was almost forty-five, he had only just completed a phase most other writers reach much younger. The *Youth* volume itself indicated a cycle of existence: the "youth" of the first story, when Marlow is starting out; then the middle-aged Marlow of "Heart of Darkness" recalling his past; finally, Whalley, the older man losing his powers, the name "Whalley," a pun on "a whale of a man." Holding the volume together is not only the three-year period in which the stories were written but the sense of a life cycle they suggest; so that we can note Conrad's own inner timetable telling him he was prepared for a new phase, one he would begin with *Nostromo* and continue through *The Secret Agent, Under Western Eyes, Chance,* and *Victory.* But before he could explore this new sense of himself, he had to wrestle with his inner demon to complete "Tether" and free himself. Like Jacob working off his seven years, he was anxious to reach for the reward.

Conrad applied himself with monastic devotion. He told Garnett in early August he had seen no one except Ford for four or five months when Wells, towing Shaw behind him, dropped in. Conrad was writing not only against a deadline for the installment but for the October publication of the *Youth* volume (which was, inevitably, delayed until November 17). With the completion of "Tether," a task Conrad described as "absolutely nightmarish," he and Jessie went up to London, where they and Borys were the guests of the Galsworthys. Refreshed, he returned after a week and wrote to Pinker about *Romance* and *The Rescue. Nostromo* has disappeared from his correspondence, apparently as it underwent transformation in Conrad's mind from short story or novella to short novel, finally to novel length.

He asks Pinker if he is pleased with *Romance,* now that nearly half the book is gone as a result of revision, the result, he says, of "four days and one whole night" of collaborative work. As for *Rescue,* he says he has been working on it, although not very hard, but nevertheless he expects to complete it by March of next year, news he also transmitted to Ernest Dawson. He told Blackwood something similar on December 4, indicating "a good third is to be written," for which he is "getting up steam . . . slowly, very slowly," with a March completion date expected. Then in what may be a reference to *Nostromo,* Conrad says he has a subject which "may be treated in 30–40 thou: words: the form I like best but which I believe is in no favour with the public." Citing the difficulty of the subject, he admits it may take up most of 1903. That it was *Nostromo* he had in mind for a 30–40,000-word treatment seems possible from a letter Conrad wrote to the editor of the Northern Newspaper Syndicate, who had asked him for a contribution. He indicates he has a subject or two in mind for that length, about the wordage of "Heart of Darkness."

Reviews of *Youth: A Narrative and Two Other Stories** were, with the exception of John Masefield's quibbles, extraordinarily understanding, with "Heart of Darkness" being singled out, by Garnett in the *Academy*, as "the high-water mark of the author's talent." With great insight, he called it a "consummate piece of artistic *diablerie.*" Garnett wrote: "The weirdness, the brilliance, the psychological truth of this masterly analysis of two Continents in conflict, of the abysmal gulf between the white man's system and the black man's comprehension of its results," is conveyed in pages as enthralling as those in *Crime and Punishment.* Apart from Garnett, who was after all writing with *parti pris*, the reviewers tried to instruct their readers how to comprehend "Heart of Darkness," which they saw as needing a different kind of attention from that paid to more routine fiction. Behind the scenes, Meldrum had written to Blackwood that he considered the *Youth* volume "to be the most notable book we have published since George Eliot." He felt that *Lord Jim* and *Youth* would go on selling for twenty years and would probably benefit from a more popular edition, say at 3/6d, or about $2.00 in current money.†

Yet the reviews were only a temporary diversion. Throughout, Conrad must have had *Nostromo* in mind or else he could not have expressed to Ernest Dawson the following strictures on fiction; surely, they cannot apply to *The Rescue:* "In regard of what you say of greatness I doubt if greatness can be attained now in imaginative prose work. When it comes it will be in a new form; in a form for which we are not ripe as yet. Till the hour strikes and the man appears we must plod in the beaten track; we must eternally "rabâcher" [repeat] the old formulas of expression. There is no help and no hope; there is only the duty to try, to try everlastingly with no regard for success."

At the end of the year, the family left for a week or so at Winchelsea, where Conrad hoped to work. He arrived on December 23 and tried to plod along

---

* Dedicated to Jessie, with an epigraph from Grimm's Fairy Tales: ". . . But the Dwarf answered: / No; something human is dearer to / me than the wealth of all the world." The passage referred to Jessie, not the book.

† George Gissing wrote to Edward Clodd about Conrad: "No man at present writing fiction has such imaginative vigour and such wonderful command of language, as Joseph Conrad. I think him a *great* writer—there's no other word." Clodd sent the letter to Conrad, who responded to Gissing, on December 21, basking in his praise, but turning the admiration to irony: "After forty it is easier to spurn away blame than to embrace the fair form of praise. There is a talking spectre, a ghostly voice whispering incessantly in one's ear of the narrow circle circumscribing all efforts, of the shortness of one's vision and of the poverty of one's thought" (Ugo Mursia, ALS).

on *The Rescue*, but little came of that. As a result, on his return to the Pent he mailed the existing manuscript to Ford, for "the only real work of Rescue that will ever be found in its text." We cannot determine at what stage Conrad sent the manuscript, or what Ford did; but we can conjecture that Conrad intended his collaborator to read it through to find a way out of the impasse. Ford's role was possibly to suggest various courses of action rather than to do any actual writing; but it is conceivable that Conrad thought of him as a collaborator in a joint effort to complete the novel. Such an association, while full of disadvantages, would have made sense as a way of giving Conrad's career a certain neatness; that is, in sweeping out the stuffy remains of earlier efforts so as to give him clear going on *Nostromo*. We can so conjecture because in the same letter to Ford indicating the mailing of *Rescue*, Conrad informed him that a "start has been made with Nostromo," although he added he believed it would end "in something silly and saleable."

That Conrad was running *Rescue* and *Nostromo* in tandem is clear from his words to Pinker on January 5, alluded to above. He indicates he has been turning around *Rescue* to do away with retrospect, precisely the opposite of what he was doing with *Nostromo*, which for half its length is in retrospect. He mentions that since "Xmas I've for relief been writing a story called (provisionally) *Nostromo*." He promises half of the manuscript by the fifteenth and the balance at the end of January, about 35,000 words. On that transaction, Conrad hoped to bring in £150, 10 percent of which would be Pinker's fee and £30 of which would be applied against his debt. In his next letter, Conrad reaffirms very strongly the projected length of *Nostromo* as 35–40,000 words.

Although we cannot determine precisely what Conrad had in mind for this version of *Nostromo*, we do know he had found his typical way of working. Not only would he misjudge the length, which was probably necessary for psychological reasons, but he would build a vast edifice on what was a very brief personal experience. Except for his extended journey in the Congo, it is astonishing how sketchy Conrad's knowledge was of those things he claimed as personal experiences; very often, it was merely a glimpse or a bit of hearsay. Discovering his sources, personal and literary, while valuable, only reinforces how intensely he made these materials his own imaginatively and creatively.

He told Wells he was going on as a man cycling over a 14-inch plank spanning a precipice: "If I falter I am lost." The image is an apt one, combining the drive forward with the threat of the fall downward. To Graham, he admitted he was "dying over the curst *Nostromo* thing." Images of death and dying would encourage him; he needed not only the romance of creation but the whiff of extinction. "All my memories of Central America [he tells Graham] seem to slip away. I just had a glimpse 25 years ago—a short glance. That is not enough *pour bâtir un roman dessus.*" And to Richard

Curle, friend and biographer of later years, he wrote cryptically: "As to No. If I ever mentioned 12 hours it must relate to P[orto] Cabello where I was ashore about that time. In La Guayra]sic] as I went up the hill and had a distant view of Caracas I must have been 2½ to 3 days. It's such a long time ago! And there were a few hours in a few other places on that dreary coast of Ven'la."

That glimpse of the coast came in 1876, when the youthful Conrad sailed on the Délestang-owned *Saint-Antoine*, whose first mate was the now legendary Dominic Cervoni. Cervoni was to be one of the models for Nostromo. That West Indies voyage provided some of the local color for Conrad's contribution to *Romance* and perhaps furnished, in addition, some details of illegal activities found in both *Romance* and *Nostromo.* These two novels overlapped in Conrad's mind, for the work on the collaboration very possibly tripped his imagination toward his own West Indies experiences, and that in turn led to Dominic Cervoni as the Nostromo prototype.

In his Author's Note to *Nostromo,* Conrad alludes to his "1875 or '6" contact with the West Indies and the Gulf of Mexico. He says he heard the story of "some man who was supposed to have stolen single-handed a whole lighter-full of silver, somewhere on the Tierra Firme seaboard during the troubles of a revolution." He adds the tale dropped from his mind until "twenty-six or twenty-seven years afterwards I came upon the very thing in a shabby volume picked up outside a second-hand bookshop. It was the life story of an American seaman written by himself with the assistance of a journalist." Through the sleuthing expertise of John Halverson and Professor Ian Watt, this book was tracked down and proved to be *On Many Seas: The Life and Exploits of a Yankee Sailor* by Frederick Benton Williams (pseudonym of Herbert Elliot Hamblen), edited by William Stone Booth (1897). In his Note, Conrad says the lighter exploit was committed by an "unmitigated rascal, a small cheat, stupidly ferocious, morose, of mean appearance, and altogether unworthy of the greatness this opportunity had thrust upon him."

In the book, the thief is named Nicolo, and after murdering the other two crew members of the lighter, he scuttles the boat and then slowly enriches himself from the cargo of silver. This "Nicolo" may have entered not only *Nostromo* but also *Romance,* as the pirate "Nichols, *alias* Nikola el Escoces, *alias* el Demonio, *alias* el Diabletto." In transforming the villain of the Williams story into Nostromo, Conrad was extending his "Lord Jim" theme: that the man who slowly grows rich can be a victim of the silver, not its conqueror; that wealth is not something gained but a trap for those who relinquish, however momentarily, their sense of themselves—as Jim, threatened by a quivering bulkhead, is victimized by his loss of faith. Although the tale of the thief in the Williams volume is extremely brief, Conrad found his theme, which was silver:

> It was only when it dawned upon me that the purloiner of the treasure need not necessarily be a confirmed rogue, that he could be even a man of character, an actor and possibly a victim in the changing scenes of a revolution, it was only then that I had the first vision of a twilight country which was to become the province of Sulaco, with its high shadowy Sierra and its misty Campo for mute witnesses of events flowing from the passions of men short-sighted in good and evil.

Conrad was, of course, dissembling; his sources were far more to the point than he divulged. He actively deceived, saying that for the history of Costaguana he depended on the "History of Fifty Years of Misrule" by the late Don José Avellanos. Conrad's point here is truly Borgean: inventing a book within his own book, he then uses his Author's Note to cite it as one of his principal sources. If he had to divulge anything, he would reveal only what he had borrowed from himself! He had, in fact, most definite sources for names, events, and places.

The factual material was remarkable. For example, from George Frederick Masterman's *Seven Eventful Years in Paraguay* (1869), which he may have heard of from Graham, who used it for his own *Portrait of a Dictator*, Conrad drew the names of many of his chief characters: Decoud, Mitchell, Gould, Fidanza (Nostromo), Corbelan, Barrios, Monygham (whose career was loosely based on that of Masterman himself). These are the major borrowings; minor ones also exist. From Edward B. Eastwick's *Venezuela*, which Conrad may also have heard of from Graham, he borrowed names such as Sotillo, Ribera, Antonia (Ribera, not Avellanos, in Eastwick), Guzman Bento (Guzman Blanco in Eastwick). Further, Conrad found descriptions in *Venezuela* which he applied to the topography of Sulaco, including the gulf, cape, customs house, and lighthouse. As Baines demonstrates, Conrad's port of Sulaco is based on many salient details of Eastwick's Puerto Cabello. And Conrad's conception of Antonia Avellanos, ostensibly influenced by his own "first love," has much in common with Antonia Ribera in *Venezuela*, including appearance and speech mannerisms.

Besides all these details, and they are impressive for the specificity of Conrad's borrowings, he may have picked up a good deal of general lore from Graham, who had traveled extensively in Central and South America.* Also, Graham's point of view as a revolutionary, while rejected by Conrad in a European setting, would prove more sympathetic in a distant one where democracy was almost unknown. Conrad's conservatism was patent for Europe, where he was interested in "conserving" the past and retaining traditional

* For example, Graham's *A Vanished Arcadia* (1901) and *Hernando de Soto* (1903). Conrad also read on his own or learned of through Graham Ramon Páez's *Wild Scenes in South America* (1863), as well as Santiago Pérez Triana's *Down the Orinoco in a Canoe* (with a preface by Graham).

values, but in countries where violence and anarchy were customary, he would not have resisted Graham's insistence on radical change. *Nostromo,* surely, suggests Graham's political orientation, in that material forces, lacking any political ideal, will only inaugurate cycles of dissension, anarchy, and military struggle in which the worst elements will always surface to grab off the goods.

For the biographer, Conrad's disguise of his sources is of great interest. There was, evidently, a compulsion in Conrad, here and elsewhere, to hide his tracks and, masochistically, to make his every situation or condition appear worse than it actually was. Although it is difficult, at times, to draw the line between an obsession and a desire for romanticism, a few distinctions remain. Clearly, Conrad saw himself as a captain who controls the ship under his command from the bridge, a solitary place. He saw his writing in similar terms, in which only that inner world was fruitful, and he tried to discount sources and literary traditions, as if he had himself been freshly conceived and stood fully in command.

Further, furtiveness and secrecy were personal elements since childhood, conditioned as he had been to withholding information and feelings since his earliest days. His parents were conspirators and revolutionaries; survival depended on *not* talking, *not* divulging, *not* giving himself away. Axel Heyst, ten years later, becomes the perfect repository of these attitudes. It was quite in keeping with this conditioning that Conrad remained a sullen youth, a seaman, a writer, and a conspiratorial writer at that. Next, he took upon himself all the responsibility of what he did, and for that, he needed to negate others' influences. Since one of his recurring themes, from Jim and Kurtz through Decoud, Nostromo, Razumov, and Heyst, was responsibility for one's self, he would naturally try to present his experience as monolithic.

A final reason is speculative, since it is associated with a personality type, and types are rarely consistent or coherent. But withholding information or disguising his tracks, as we noted in his refusal to divulge his failures on his chief's and captain's examinations, was connected to his desire to retain whatever he had ingested: he had become a gigantic container of goods, and nothing must be wasted or lost. We see this personality type reflected in his very methods of working. For his way of building through retrospect, manifold narrators, use of memory and past event, overlapping of multiple experiences, compulsive desire not to waste a word, detail, or event—in all these ways, he *retained.* He always felt that the serious writer was a terribly private person: ". . . one writes for oneself even when one writes to live and in the hope of being read by an immortal multitude," he told H. B. Marriott Watson. The author was a lonely being whose "solitary thought cannot be imparted to a public." What could be more natural than for this marginal being to shut off all access, become hermetic, turn back upon himself so that he re-creates himself only in his own work! In *Nostromo*, Decoud would be a failed version of that introspective type.

That was the inner world. The outer one was to be "very low mentally," over the failure of *Romance* to be placed serially (it never was, although McClure had purchased it) and from psychological depletion after the long run on "Tether." Further, Conrad wanted the Blackwood *Typhoon* volume to appear in the spring so as to clear the autumn for *Romance*. He was, he felt, living with a halter around his neck, working slowly on *Nostromo*, while publishers expected him to "shake stuff out of a bag." He hugged his conception of himself, perhaps the sole anchor in an uncertain fate. If silver was to be everyone's destiny in the novel he was writing, then how could he himself avoid the pursuit of a quick return? Harpers in the United States showed interest in a serial of about 85,000 words, with a further advance on book rights. Conrad now saw *Nostromo* as fitting into that scheme if Harpers liked the synopsis. Since it would be a long haul, with uncertainties along the way, he hewed to Ford "to save an instalment or two" should he be suddenly laid out. If necessary, the Conrads would take a cottage in Winchelsea, to prevent staleness and to provide proximity to Ford.

Remaining for him and his collaborator were final touches on *Romance*, which was now like a ghostly presence. Pinker suggested trimming the arrest of Kemp and the Spanish prison scene, which is a good chunk of Part V. Conrad says the notion is too absurd, but the suggestion was a valid one, since this material is among the weakest in the novel: drawn-out, poorly written, obvious in its outcome, and excessively wordy for the pittance of insight it offers. What Conrad really wanted from Pinker was not advice but a subsidy (which he requested formally in a March 17 letter), to the tune of £20 for the next three consecutive months. He hoped to have a large segment of *Nostromo* for showing around.

> There must be a good lot to show the style and the tone of the thing. I promise it won't be long now. The book is sure to come off. Hueffer who is in possession of my innermost mind (and of my notes) on that story is confident of his ability to finish it should something unforeseen occur; and in that case he would *not* expect his name to appear at all. Therefore you will risk but little—unless my reputation is of no value at all.

One year later (on March 29), with *Nostromo* still incomplete and now having expanded to over 150,000 words, Conrad told Pinker that "Galsworthy has been here to see me on Sunday and I have arranged with him to correct for me the MS of Nostromo should I have no time myself." To complete his longest piece of work since *Lord Jim*, he needed propping all around: Pinker financially, Ford for dictation and possible writing of copy, Galsworthy for correction of galleys and for loans, and, of course, Jessie for routine typing. As Conrad isolated himself in Sulaco, that "inviolable sanctuary from the temptations of a trading world in the solemn hush of the deep Golfo Placido," he re-created for himself an external society; in childhood, it had been relatives and friends substituting for parents, and now it was wife and friends giving him the support to continue. In nearly every phase of his life, he would re-create those early years. If he fell ill, he had his wife to nurse him, Ford to continue his work, and Pinker to support him. In the wings was the benevolent and generous Galsworthy, the rich uncle and wealthy patron; and in the great world of publishers and reviewers was Edward Garnett, ever ready with a friendly notice. This "circle," incidentally, would be displaced by another one in later years, with only Jessie and Galsworthy remaining steady. Ford would go, replaced by Curle and Francis Warrington Dawson; Garnett would recede, but there would be the Colvins and then Jean-Aubry and Hugh Walpole. In France, Conrad could rely on the devoted but sorely tested Gide, prepared through translation and general publicity to transmit him to the European literary world. And in Poland, he would have the daughter of his cousin ready to translate him into Polish.

Conrad continued to feel he could complete *Nostromo* within three months; at least he repeated this to Ford on March 23, along with the information that he hoped to finish *Rescue* by December (of 1903, nine months off). For the reader seeking overlapping of character, event, and tone, even verbal mannerisms, the parallelism of activities is of interest: *Nostromo* at various stages, *The Rescue*, some parts of *The Mirror of the Sea*, correction of final proofs for *Romance*, and, a little later, first mention of *Chance*. The famous Humbert swindle of 1902 may have already triggered Conrad's imagination for a novel based on that well-publicized affair. Then, as if he had forgotten where he was in *Nostromo*, he told Meldrum, also on March 23, that he had a story that would grow to "60 or 70 thound words after all," and if the serialization of it could be separated from the book form, he would like to publish the latter with Blackwood. Harpers shortly after this would refuse the still sketchy *Nostromo*, handled in the States by T. D. Watts.

In the midst of this, *Typhoon and Other Stories* was published by Heinemann, with a simple dedication to "R. B. Cunninghame Graham." Conrad explained its "austere simplicity" to his loyal friend as "barrenness and nothing else—the awful lack of words that overcome the thought struggling eagerly towards the lips." Behind the attempt to explain was a good deal of warm feeling, and Conrad knew that Graham, a chronic depressive despite his intense activity, would comprehend the awful gap between intention and execution. The book would appear on April 22, two novellas ("Typhoon" and "Falk") and two stories ("Amy Foster" and "To-morrow"). It was a strange collection, rather incoherent as contrasted with the unity of the Blackwood *Youth* volume and by no means an advance on Conrad's previous work.

Except for a few later efforts such as "Il Conde" and "The Secret Sharer," and, perhaps, "The Planter of Malata," Conrad's shorter fiction was not to be particularly distinguished, especially when compared with the novels he wrote during the next ten years. It becomes clear that with the *Typhoon* volume, his shorter fiction played a different role in his creative life from that enjoyed by the novels; the short stories and novellas ("The Duel," "Freya of the Seven Isles," "Gaspar Ruiz") were work done to fill the seams between the novels and to pluck off an occasional £75 or £100. Conrad may have begun his creative life as equally a short-story writer and a novelist, but, in his own eyes, the shorter fiction became expendable.

The reviews of *Typhoon,* while placing Conrad more firmly as a sea writer than he liked, were extremely favorable and, in some instances, perceptive. An unsigned notice in the *Speaker* caught Conrad not only in this volume but in aspects of his art which were still being developed:

> Mr. Conrad is in the line of our great writers of the romance of the sea, Smollett, Michael Scott [a Scottish author who lived from 1789 to 1835] and Marryat, and he has also introduced something new into our fiction. By no other author have we had the psychology of action so subtly and yet so vividly presented. There are times in reading his work when we think that Stevenson with new experiences has taken up his work when it broke off in his noble fragment *Weir of Hermiston,* and there are others when we think we are reading a translation of a work by Tolstoi or Maxim Görki. But always we realise that Mr. Conrad writes from the fullness of his own experience—passing through a mind that with great and almost painful efforts snatches from it some secret of life and reveals it in the glow of a brilliant imagination.

Quiller-Couch was enthusiastic, but uneven in his tastes, preferring "To-morrow" to the other stories and confessing to a loss at the analytical methods of Conrad and James. Nearly every reviewer yoked Conrad with Kipling, either to cite them as equals or to vaunt Conrad over his contemporary. Similarly, Stevenson's name was evoked, so that in later life Conrad found it almost impossible to separate himself from those two writers with whom he has only the most superficial resemblance. One reviewer (in the *Glasgow Evening News*) felt that because of Conrad's neglect of love, women, human and social relationships, he could not achieve the Olympian heights of the greatest masters; but, with critical acumen, he did focus on Conrad's strength: ". . . that character is for him an essentially individual creation, separate from, comparatively untouched by ordinary human relationship." Comparing him with Zola, the reviewer made a shrewd assessment, given Conrad's own dislike for French naturalism: "While Zola, for example, always tended to make his characters mere social types, representative of great streams of tendency, Mr. Conrad, following rather the old mystics, pushes towards the other extreme of regarding his types as self-pivoted units, though, it is true, always with an aim less directly ethical and more artistic than that of Zola."

This reviewer, like several of the others, had noticed Conrad was different, but could not locate where; and that difference, that movement toward "self-pivoted units," was, of course, connected to Conrad's modernity. "I am Modern," he had trumpeted, himself, and that movement away from the Zolaesque social unit toward the less directly ethical, the less explicit, the more purely aesthetic was a measure of this novelty. If Joyce had been able to publish the fiction he was writing at this time, reviewers and critics would have made similar comments.

The good notices put Conrad in a business frame of mind; that is, he foresaw Heinemann as possible publisher for *Nostromo*, in book form, particularly to keep them in "good humour anent the *Rescue*, which, it can't be denied, is again delayed by this work." From this point on, despite periodic outbursts of depression and curses at an uncaring universe, Conrad would move steadily on *Nostromo*.

Most of Conrad's problems, including his anxieties about money and fear of the writing table, were, as he confessed to Galsworthy, self-induced. He admitted his conditions were "the outcome of my character mainly." Fate had not been particularly cruel to him, and in the next ten years he would have only the normal problems associated with living. True, Jessie would be partially crippled by a bad fall and suffer from lameness for the rest of her life, and Conrad's own ailments would intensify; but they were not extraordinary. His son Borys showed a tendency to catch terrible illnesses, but the second son, John, was healthy. The money that came in was certainly not commensurate with Conrad's worth as an artist, but on the other hand, it could have been sufficient with more careful attention to outlay. His friends were devoted, and most were particularly willing to bear his eccentricities of behavior while remaining loyal. In brief, his life was no better or worse than most, although his complaints, while real enough to him, made him seem marked out as alternately Job or Jonah.

By May, he was ready to discuss his subject with Graham. He had hesitated, perhaps, because of Graham's expertise in Hispanic affairs or, possibly, because he was borrowing freely from materials supplied him in previous conversations. In any event, he excused himself by saying the book was "concerned mostly with Italians," which, except for Nostromo and the Violas, was hardly the case. By June 4, Conrad had definite intimations that *Nostromo* would require far greater development than he had foreseen. Writing Galsworthy that the "pile of pages is bigger certainly by three or four every day," he added that the "story has not yet even begun."

On July 28, 1903, Conrad wrote his first (extant) letter to William Rothenstein, the portraitist and painter, and a friend of Graham's. Rothenstein had evidently asked Conrad to sit for him, and the association began a warm friendship that lasted for the length of Conrad's life. At the time of the association, Rothenstein was fifteen years Conrad's junior but already prominent in the literary and artistic life of London in the 1890s. Having been encouraged by many major artists in Paris—Degas, Pissarro, and Toulouse-Lautrec, among others—he became friendly with Wilde, Beardsley, Beerbohm, Sargent, and was to do portraits of Yeats, T. E. Lawrence, Forster, as well as Conrad. The friendship was never exceptionally close, but it was cordial and supportive for Conrad, financially and otherwise, and suggests the kind of literary-artistic world he might have moved in had he felt so inclined.

By August 22, Conrad had completed 42,000 words of *Nostromo*, which he considered to be half the book and whose writing, he told Galsworthy, had made him feel "half dead and wholly imbecile." To Pinker, he indicated that this wordage formed only the first part, called "The Silver of the Mine," but that, later, it would have to be divided to balance out the other half, consisting of "The Isabels" and "The Lighthouse." The latter two would become, he says, Parts III and IV, while "The Silver of the Mine" would need an additional title. From this, we can see that, still short by a year of completion, Conrad had misjudged only the length, not the basic conception, which would be worked out in the three sections named above. The 42,000 words of "The Silver of the Mine" are the length of the completed section, and what remained for him, although he could not foresee it, were the 150,000 words of the succeeding two parts.

His growing panic derived from his comprehension of what the development of the novel dictated, a juggernaut against which his own desires for a more hasty conclusion were futile. Nevertheless, he knew it was good. "There is no mistake about this. You may take up a strong position [he told Pinker] when you offer it here. It is a very genuine Conrad. At the same time it is more of a novel pure and simple than anything I've done since Almayer's Folly." He indicates the other "half of the book" is well along, some actually written, and suggests a September printing date for the serial would be safe, assuring Pinker that Ford stands in the background in the event of a disaster. Fortunately for Conrad's sanity, the serial, in *T.P.'s Weekly*, would not begin until the end of January 1904, when he was only seven months from the end.

Even by his own standards of complete dedication to the work at hand, Conrad's intense focus upon the manuscript was monastic. Each long work involved the steadiness of the captain threading his way through the eye of a storm. He complained to Galsworthy he was growing into an outcast, "a mental and moral outcast." "I hear of nothing—I think of nothing—I reflect upon nothing—I cut myself off." Proofs of *Romance*, which would be published on October 16, were still undergoing revision, with Conrad rewriting the end, his "conception of the end, which, you'll see [he told Ford], is exactly yours with some alterations." There is a certain defensiveness in Conrad's reasons for making changes. He insists he has done nothing casually and that he has not been "wantonly interfering with quite a remarkable piece of work," comments which suggest Ford considered the novel his and Conrad a trespasser. There is the further suggestion of strain between the two men: those early discords, here about their respective efforts, later over personal matters, which would intensify and lead to the bitter break. Certainly, Ford's insistence on how deeply Conrad depended on him for ideas, dictation, even writing, implies the frame of mind of a man who felt jealousy and envy at the time of the association; or else felt Conrad was reaping all the benefit of the collaboration. Conrad was fully aware, for he would write to Elsie on October 1: "Don't let Ford be angry with me for anything."

This tenseness in the relationship is further revealed in a letter Conrad wrote Ford which concerned something as innocent as the dating of the manuscript of *Romance*. Conrad's annoyance with Ford's dating—"1896–1903"—grew to virtual hysteria at what people would think: two grown men spending six years ("1903" for the publication date) on a single book. "Here my dear boy [he wrote] you've not to deal with my denseness. I understand perfectly the feeling which induced you to put them there." Conrad's fear of attack is complex in its intensity:

> But you have to deal with the stupidity which will never understand that a mere work of fiction may remain six years in the making. Anybody disliking the book would jump at such an unguarded confession. Make no mistake; no one will understand the *feeling;* they will only see the fact and far from taking it as imposing they will seize on it for a sneer. It opens a wide door to disparagement to anybody minded for that game. I don't care for the best criticaster of them all—but I don't want to see their ugly paws sprawling over the book (for which I care) more than is absolutely unavoidable.

Conrad is walking the edge here, hostility at Ford boiling over and yet full of self-pity:

> Sneers at collaboration—sneers at those two men who took six years to write "this very ordinary tale" whereas R.L.S. [Robert Louis Stevenson] single handed produced his masterpieces etc etc. And the so and so can write in a year a romance which is more than *this,* less that, more *'t'other thing.*

To correct Ford's mathematics, Conrad says they began "in Dec. 1900 and finished in July 1902 really." He calls the rest delay, because they could not get themselves "printed sooner. Why intrude our private affairs for the grin of innumerable swine? . . . Even Flaubert was not six years writing Mme Bovary which *was* an epoch making volume." After further polemics, Conrad asserts he would consider putting an explanatory note, to the effect that "this novel written from another point of view by F.M.H.in 1896 under the title of Seraphina—became the subject of collaboration with J. Conrad at the end of 1900 after much preliminary discussion and was finished in its present shape in July 1902." Or else, he added, "put nothing."

If Ford read the letter correctly, he could see it as a veiled attack upon the whole idea of collaboration and time "wasted" on an effort which Conrad would have liked to renounce. The dating suggested by him was merely the occasion; Conrad was revealing his shame at the results, whether of six years' work or two years'. Also, since he was at work on *Nostromo* and recognized the difference between two books which so overlapped in his imagination, he could not help himself; the idea of the earlier book had to be destroyed, even if he destroyed Ford with it. All this is another way of saying Conrad was struggling to protect his own artistic integrity, regardless of the consequences.*

Not unexpectedly, the pressures led to illness: gout and depression. Conrad recognized that "it's good for me to be in a hole," for after reporting to Pinker his ailments, he announced he was thinking of Part III of *Nostromo.* Even with good notices for *Romance,* however, he remained ill and out-of-sorts. His letter to James Barrie of November 23 shows a very shaky hand and reflects a depressed condition. The contents bear this out: sick bed, many complaints, an attack upon the "silly book" he is writing, something "more in the nature of printed matter." He asserts a certain amount of "cheap sincerity" is in it, and some shadow of intention and even an artistic purpose, in all "sheer twaddle." He wrote this, we recall, to Barrie, who was an immensely successful writer, and Conrad's depreciation of himself, when sorted out, would indicate his disdain for Barrie's work.

This same letter, however, contains an interesting hypothetical situation, a response to Barrie, who had told Conrad of a ship's crew that hated an officer to such an extent they put him in a boat to starve, a course of action Conrad felt "somewhat incredible for a lot of average sailors." The idea,

---

* Writing in French to Kazimierz Waliszewski, a Polish historian who had settled in France, Conrad says he regards "*Romance* as something without any importance: I collaborated on it while it was impossible for me to do anything else. It was easy to narrate some events without bothering myself otherwise with the subject." Conrad adds that with all his indifference toward the subject, "within the very style in vogue with the public now," he still believes it is well written. In the same letter, Conrad indicates *Romance* was merely a warming-up exercise for the serious novel he and Ford wanted to write, the picture of an "old and famous painter and the base and perverse intrigues in the following of a great man who had been successful but who—but just because he was a supreme artist—remained misunderstood." For details they planned to use Ford's intimate knowledge of Ford Madox Brown, his maternal grandfather. Conrad requests secrecy and admits the book may never be composed.

Writing one week later to Waliszewski, this time in Polish, Conrad indicates he was having his books sent to the historian, adding it was a "great happiness and honor to return to my home country under your guidance. . . . And if you are prepared to take my word for it and say that during the course of all my travels round the world I never, in mind or heart, separated myself from my country, then I may surely be accepted there as a compatriot, in spite of my writing in English."

which foreshadows the situation in the much later *Mutiny on the Bounty*, "is too inhuman and not enough brutal." Then, in a statement which suggests his own way of using materials, Conrad says: "There is a subtle confusion of motives and action in the anecdote which makes me think that it is invented by a landsman with imagination but without sufficient knowledge of details that cut the ground from under his fundamental assumption. But I am grateful to you for mentioning it since it contains a suggestion for something really credible. A short story will come out of it—when god wills it." Although "The Secret Sharer" was developed somewhat differently and was itself based on the incident aboard the *Cutty Sark* in 1880, there is the germ here of a crew member rising up against an officer and then, in Conrad's version, being struck down by the officer.

The end of November saw a particularly severe attack of gout, the hereditary disease no doubt exacerbated by intense writing sessions and financial worries. He informs H. G. Wells that not only is the "scribbling awfully in arrear but there's no 'spring' in me to grapple with it effectually." He says that formerly, in his sea life, "a difficulty nerved me to the effort," but now he does not feel so. He speaks, once again, of drowning, of "loosing [sic] my footing in deep waters."* Even the success of *Romance*, going into a second edition, is insufficient to buoy him; it is, after all, only a "paper-success." Real writing was something else, a visceral response as opposed to Wells's intellectualization of his creative resources: ". . . writing—*the only possible writing* [he told Wells]—is just simply the conversion of nervous force into phrases. With you, too, I am sure, tho' in your case it is the disciplined intelligence which gives the signal—the impulse. For me it is a matter of chance, stupid chance. But the fact remains that when the nervous force is exhausted the phrases don't come:—and no tension of will can help."

These simple distinctions, expressed in a friendly setting, were to lead eventually to a falling out between Conrad and Wells, as between James and Wells. The latter was to shift from being the literary man interested in countering the sloppy romanticism of the routine popular novel (the very kind of popularity *Romance* attempted to cash in upon) into an oracle with a definite social vision, for whom words were means, not ends. Wells desired social change, and for such a man Conrad's insistent aestheticism was anathema. From Conrad's point of view, Wells—to whom he remained ever grate-

* As befitting a former mariner, Conrad expressed mental states in sea images, his dominant one, as we saw in *Lord Jim*, being drowning. To Galsworthy, his reactions are described typically: "No work done. No spring left to grapple with it. Everything looks black; but I suppose that will wear off, and anyhow, I am trying to keep despair under. Nevertheless I feel myself losing my footing in deep waters. They are lapping about my lips." Drowning here is joined to Tantalus's situation: death combined with anxiety.

ful for the early recognition—was no longer a literary man but a propagandist for everything the former detested: progress, technology, historical discontinuity, support of the newly emerging working and middle classes.

Even as he worked on his most panoramic and expansive novel, Conrad's world moved ever more intensely inward. His work on *Nostromo* is characterized by great stretches of territory suggested by an isolated, encircled, circumscribed Sulaco. Just as Sulaco was isolated from the rest of Costaguana, so Conrad broke off and focused on the solidity of his writing desk, and tried to turn himself into an antenna picking up all the hints and nuances of his subject. To let go would mean to drown, like Decoud, who drops away when he cannot face the quiet of the Golfo Placido, the whiteness or blankness of experience.

On December 1, just short of his forty-sixth birthday, Conrad began a reacquaintanceship and short correspondence with Roger Casement, whom he had first met in Kinshasa, the Belgian Congo. Casement's pursuit of Belgian atrocities was reaching its climax. It would come with his report on Belgian exploitation of African and Indian labor, which would lead to the appointment of a Belgian commission and that, in turn, to a change in the Congo government. Casement's exposure of atrocities and slave trade was, in a sense, the factual basis for what Conrad had projected imaginatively. As we have noted, he very probably saw little of the actual exploitation which he used as a basis for "Heart of Darkness." Working from very few observed details, he created the potential for brutality and cruelty which were, of course, very close to the truth Casement was later to reveal. Jessie Conrad placed Casement's visit to the Pent in 1905, but more likely the visit occurred before that, during the time of the correspondence, between December 1903 and September 1904.

It was fitting, furthermore, that Conrad should have the old memories reopened through his renewed association with Casement; for while writing *Nostromo*, he was putting into it a heavy overlay of the Congo. Behind the Gould concession in Costaguana is the example of Belgian colonialism, which had appeared not only in "Heart of Darkness" but also, satirized, in *The Inheritors*. *Romance*, a lesser example, was not exempt from the colonial idea, with British and Spanish forces, respectively, in Jamaica and Cuba. More specifically, Casement wanted written support from Conrad of his observation of Congo brutalities. He had read "Heart of Darkness" and apparently felt Conrad had noted scenes comparable to the following from his diary:

> . . . the scenes so vividly described seemed to fashion themselves out of the shadows before my eyes. The daily agony of an entire people unrolled itself in all the repulsive terrifying details. I verily believe I *saw* those hunted women clutching their children and flying panic-stricken to the

bush; the blood flowing from those quivering black bodies as the hippopotamus hide whip struck and struck again; the savage soldiery rushing hither and thither among burning villages; the ghastly tally of severed hands.

In his first letter, Conrad invited Casement for the night, making fun of the accommodations and trying to recall the spirit of their previous meetings: "I need not tell you there is no more ceremony than if we called you to step under a tent on the road to Kinchassa. I am glad you've read the Heart of D. tho' of course it's an awful fudge." It is not absolutely certain if Casement visited at this time. Jessie left a description of some visit, when Casement was interested in gaining Conrad's support for his divulgations about the Congo. "Sir Roger Casement, a fanatical Irish protestant, came to see us [she wrote] remaining some two days our guest. He was a very handsome man with a thick dark beard and piercing, restless eyes. His personality impressed me greatly. It was about the time when he was interested in bringing to light certain atrocities which were taking place in the Belgian Congo. Who could foresee his own terrible fate during the war [trial for treason against England and subsequent execution] as he stood in our drawing-room passionately denouncing the cruelties he had seen."

The letters Conrad wrote to Casement are of intense value, since they are almost our sole proof of precisely what Conrad observed in the Congo; the latter's diary is noncommittal, and "Heart of Darkness," while devastating, is an imaginative re-creation of what he felt and sensed. On December 17, Conrad attempted to grapple with Casement's allegations, especially the one that mutilation (severing of the hand) was a common phenomenon:

> During my sojourn in the interior, keeping my eyes and ears well open too, I've never heard of the alleged custom of cutting off hands amongst the natives; and I am convinced that no such custom ever existed along the whole course of the main river to which my experience is limited. Neither in the casual talk of white men nor in the course of definite inquiries as to the tribal customs was ever such a practice hinted at; certainly not amongst the Bangalas who at the time formed the bulk of the State troops. My informants were numerous, of all sorts—and many of them possessed of abundant knowledge.

Conrad's further response, on December 21, is more far-reaching and demonstrates his humanistic feelings, what was already apparent in "Heart of Darkness."

> It is an extraordinary thing that the conscience of Europe which seventy years ago has put down the slave trade on humanitarian grounds tolerates the Congo State today. It is as if the moral clock had been put back many hours. And yet nowadays if I were to overwork my horse so as to destroy its happiness of physical wellbeing I should be hailed before a magistrate. It seems to me that the black man—say, of Upoto—is deserv-

> ing of as much humanitarian regard as any animal since he has nerves, feels pain, can be made physically miserable. But as a matter of fact his happiness and misery are much more complex than the misery or happiness of animals and deserving of greater regard. He shares with us the consciousness of the universe in which we live—no small burden. Barbarism per se is no crime deserving of a heavy visitation: and the Belgians are worse than the seven plagues of Egypt insomuch that in that case it was a punishment sent for a definite transgression; but in this the Upoto man is not aware of any transgression, and therefore can see no end to the infliction. It must appear to him very awful and mysterious; and I confess that it appears so to me too.

Conrad adds that in the old days England "had in her keeping the conscience of Europe." The initiative came from there. Now, he asserts, England is too busy with other things; "too much involved in great affairs to take up cudgels for humanity, decency and justice." He mentions that "that precious pair of African witch-men seem to have cast a spell upon the world of whites—I mean Leopold and Thys [who had given Conrad his short-lived Congo captaincy] of course." This statement of indifference—paralleling Conrad's feeling about the European lack of concern for Poland—feeds into *Nostromo* as well, where the life-and-death struggle over the mine fills twenty minutes a month for the American financier Holroyd.

In his penultimate letter for this series (the final letter, in September 1904, is of little interest), Conrad mentions Graham as a man anxious to see Casement. He says that Graham could be very helpful, since he is fanatical about colonial ventures.

> Do not let his reputation for socialism influence your judgment upon the man. It has never been anything but a form of his hate for all oppression and injustice. His character is upright and unselfish; his talents (with the pen too) are great; he knows everybody worth knowing, and his social relations extend from Dukes to Labour-members. He may be of use to you, if only with his pen; and perhaps in other ways as well. Whatever may be the difference of your political opinions I am sure that you will understand each other perfectly on humanitarian grounds.*

---

* And to Graham, Conrad wrote about Casement: "He's a protestant Irishman, pious too. But so was Pizarro. For the rest I can assure you that he is a limpid personality. There is a touch of the Conquistador in him too; for I've seen him start off into an unspeakable wilderness swinging a crookhandled stick for all weapons, with two bulldogs: Paddy (white) and Biddy (brindle) at his heels and a Loanda boy carrying a bundle for all company. A few months afterwards it so happened that I saw him come out again, a little leaner a little browner, with his stick, dogs, and Loanda boy, and quietly serene as though he had been for a stroll in a park. Then we lost sight of each other. He was I believe Bsh Consul in Beira, and lately seems to have been sent to the Congo again, on some sort of mission, by the Br Gov^{t}. I have always thought that some particle of Las Casas' [the Spanish missionary and historian Bartolomé de las Casas] soul had found refuge in his indefatigable body. The letters [Conrad sent on two] will tell you the rest. I would help him but it is not in me."

With that, Casement passed out of Conrad's purview, until his 1916 trial for treason. Casement's revelations of genocide in the Congo and atrocities in Peru (in his later Putumayo Report) kept him in the public eye—with a vengeance when the British publicized his diaries, with their notations of homosexual acts, as a way of discrediting his activities as an Irish patriot. By then, Conrad, who had felt he could not as "only a wretched novelist" be of much help in the Congo affair, had long since dropped away from such matters. He was a writer, not a reformer.

He slipped back into *Nostromo*. He also fell back into another aspect of his background, the Polish past, as he retold it to Kazimierz Waliszewski on December 5. The letter to Waliszewski is a narrative of Conrad's life from the time his father, Apollo, leased a farm after his marriage, and it is a tale of death and loss. Then Conrad moves into those aspects of his life which are distinctly his; he speaks with considerable pride of his maritime achievements: "I received my first command of a ship at the age of 29, which, you must admit, was not bad for a foreigner without influence." He says he considers himself "to be the last seaman of a sailing vessel," from which we can derive many of his attitudes about technology and materialism, indeed about shore life in general. "I feel that deeply each time I look at the British Channel where nothing but smoking chimneys are to be seen nowadays."

But even the sea was no longer a refuge—the silver of the mine had, so to speak, contaminated it all. Interestingly, Conrad speaks of himself as having the point of view of the English but without being an Englishman: "Homo duplex has in my case more than one meaning." That sense Conrad retained of living in several worlds, duplex here, but even triplex, would reinforce his need for that constant retrieval of the past in his major fiction.

Nostromo had found a periodical for serial purposes: T. P. O'Connor's *T.P.'s Weekly*, a considerable comedown from *Blackwood's Magazine.* O'Connor had given an extraordinarily generous review of *Almayer's Folly* in the *Weekly Sun* eight years previously. Conrad's contempt for his publication in *T.P.'s Weekly* can be found in his willingness to have the novel compressed without insisting on doing it himself and in stipulating that no proofs be sent to him. Since he was usually scrupulous in such matters, he was forgoing the novel for serial purposes so as to "let Mr. O'Connor have an absolutely free hand in making the story acceptable to his large public." Despite all this, an examination of the serial version shows that compressing and tightening of the manuscript proved quite effective.

In all, the serial form was about 7 to 10 percent shorter than the first edition in 1904, although the early parts of the serial are in excess of what the book would contain. That is, had Conrad continued along these lines, the serial would have exceeded its present length by, perhaps, 5–10,000 words, and the first section of the novel, before the revolution, would have overbalanced the second section even more than it now does. These passages, some of which are full of fine and relevant description, demonstrate Conrad's attempts, in the first part, to give density and texture to his narrative, elements unfortunately missing in the later, more hurried sections of the novel. One paragraph that does not appear in the book concerns the possible benefits of the mine as envisaged by Gould:

> . . . skinny, dreadful old hags, ragged men, women with hopeless faces, and then, naked children. . . . Those were the very poor, the starving fringe outside the body of the people that worked in towns and upon the estancias; and the great empty vastness of the landscapes made their existence incredible and their state appear hopeless, for this was not a question of room to live in. Was the remedy for that, too, in the development of material interest? Charles seemed to hug that belief in his taciturn and observing reserve.

That last sentence ironically suggests Gould's fatuous identification of personal gain with social enlightenment, which is the key to his personality. Conrad possibly removed this passage, as he deleted others that were too explicit about Nostromo, so as not to make a fool of either character. We can see that intention from a passage on Nostromo in the serial later cut from the book: "In the still blackness of the gulf obliterating the land and the sea, and even the very memory of events whose weariness still weighed on his [Decoud's] limbs, the overweening vanity of the man [Nostromo], which had many times amused him in their former intercourse, seemed to take a concrete and fateful shape."

Yet despite these and other deletions concerning Dr. Monygham and Hirsch, the book form finally becomes more expansive, so that while Conrad did hold down the verbiage for the serial, he then extended descriptive detail for the book. Beginning about halfway through, he added sentences and even entire paragraphs to flesh out the book. Since he was writing the latter parts of the novel while the serial was running (it began in January, with the book not to be completed until August), he had ample opportunity to keep reshaping later aspects. Unfortunately, the manuscript, only half complete, and the intervening typescript, only fragments, do not make any fully coherent study possible. One must speculate about Conrad's method of working, but with the conclusion of the book coming only six weeks before the serial ended, it is safe to assume Conrad felt uneasy about completion. Since he had to produce copy directly for the serial version, we can see he worked rapidly, with an eye to expansion only when he went into book form. The serial, for example, ends with two pages of material (perhaps eight or ten of regularly printed pages) that takes thirty-six pages to develop in the book. The parts Conrad subsequently developed for the first edition were those concerning Nostromo's interest in the Viola girls and their relationship to the cargador Ramirez; particularly stressed were passages relating to Giselle's love for Nostromo and his preference for her sister, Linda. In the book, then, Conrad tried to emphasize a "new" Nostromo, one who as an accepted member of society develops into a successful businessman and lover.

Conrad appears to have been caught in the middle, trapped between his dilatory methods of working and his artistic intentions. An abrupt ending to the serial would have provided a certain ironic commentary on Nostromo's earlier successes; whereas a fleshed-out ending could have tried to supply a rationale for Nostromo's transformation, that is, given greater credibility to his shift from Tarzan to businessman. In fact, Conrad did neither. The early versions of *Nostromo* suggest, then, that although Conrad conceived the novel in most of its essentials from the first, for some reason, whether psychological, aesthetic, or physical, he was unable to expand the second section to the extent that the detailed early narrative demanded. Both the MS and TS bear out that Conrad worked diligently over his first drafts, particularly in his efforts to integrate natural description and theme, even though his *basic ideas* between the MS and Collected Edition are not appreciably different. Conrad's revisions were made to gain clarity of expression, sharper dramatization of character and scene, and greater fluidity in his use of English idiom.

Those areas that needed *major* revision remained unchanged in the MS, TS, and serial, while in the first edition Conrad was unable to make more than a token effort at expansion and revitalization. The early versions of *Nostromo* reveal that Conrad did not perceive clearly the entire narrative structure and that, as a result, the "split" in the novel was an artistic failing rather than a conscious plan. His efforts to revamp and reorganize the ending of the first edition was a recognition on his part that the novel, despite its considerable attainments, fell somewhat short of his ambitious aims. The hasty final section partially thwarts the effects of the massive rhythms which had carried all before them earlier in the narrative. The novel, like its hero, dies an accidental death.

Ford remarked in later years that Conrad had finished several of his books with contrived endings because of despair and panic; that the grandiose fabrics of *Nostromo*, *Under Western Eyes*, *Chance*, and even *The Secret Agent* are never fully realized in development; and that the unimpressive endings of these novels display an artistic reversal of their earlier parts. For all his commitment to artistic principles, it becomes clear that Conrad could not devote the time and energy to fully fashioned development. Abrupt endings or summary conclusions characterize many of his novels, or else the pacing of the later sections follows a different time sequencing from what the reader has been prepared for in earlier parts. With *Nostromo*, the great length of the manuscript, the more than two years expended upon it, and Conrad's slowness of production could not help but influence the artistic direction of the final version. And even though Conrad apparently realized this fact by the time he went from serial to book form, he could not help himself, since extensive rewriting would have modified his current plans.*

When *Nostromo* was still several months from completion, Conrad was already working on the papers that would make up *The Mirror of the Sea* (which he thought of in the spirit of Turgenev's *Sportsman's Sketches*), planning to finish *The Rescue*, his personal albatross, and looking ahead to *Chance*, however rudimentary his idea of that novel still was. He was, in addition, adapting his story "To-morrow" for the stage.

Writing to Mrs. William Rothenstein and H. G. Wells in early 1904, Conrad made what appeared to be an innocent announcement; to the latter, for example, he said: "Jessie fell in the street and wrenched both her knees. No joke to her and an awful anxiety to me." It was an accident that was to have considerable bearing on their subsequent life. At the beginning of the new year, Conrad decided to take Jessie up to London for examination of and possible treatment for a heart condition. Reassured about this, Jessie did some shopping at Barker's and then in coming out, as she wrote herself, "slipped the cartilage of both knees at once and fell on the pavement, hurting very badly the knee already damaged by an accident I had at the age of sixteen." From this point, she was more or less a cripple for the rest of her life. With Conrad in and out of bed and Jessie only semiactive, the household was more like a hospital than a home.†

---

* A portion of the *Nostromo* manuscript—sixteen pages of Chapter 5 of Part II, most of the April 9, 1904, serial installment—is in Ford's hand, and this fact has led to speculation about his overall contribution to the writing of the novel. Professor John Morey, in a Cornell dissertation, put the matter in proportion, especially by printing a Ford letter addressed to George Keating which described the situation (probably in February of 1904): "Whilst I was living in London with Conrad almost next door and coming in practically every day for meals, he was taken with so violent an attack of gout and nervous depression that he was quite unable to continue his installments of *Nostromo* that was then running as a serial in T.P.'s weekly. I therefore simply wrote enough from time to time to keep the presses going—a job that presented no great difficulties to me. . . . But to argue from that that I had any large share in Conrad's writing would be absurd. . . . I was practically under oath to Conrad not to reveal these facts owing to the misconception that might arise and nothing in the world would have induced me to reveal it now but for the extremely unfortunate sale of these pages." Ford's actual contribution was the brief passage, cited above, and very possibly a revision of the serial proofs.

† Conrad wrote to Meldrum: "My poor wife who has been complaining of not feeling very well ever since last Oct was found to have a valvular defect of the heart. After nearly two months of worry in London (I going on working all the time to stave off utter annihilation) I got her down here. The doctors in consultation have sent her to bed for six weeks both for her heart and her knee. She certainly can't walk and it looks bad; it looks as if she were to be a helpless cripple. The words as I write give a shudder. There is something seriously wrong with the left leg which she had injured in the same way many years before. It is obviously wasting. She has (even in bed) surgical appliances on both. . . . I myself have just gotten over an attack of gout. I stiffen my back but I feel the

Furthermore, equipment—exercisers, special shoes, a new "leg-machine"—plus, of course, a stay of almost two months in London added further financial burdens. As if to cap the new situation, Conrad's bankers, Watson & Co., went under, and his overdraft would now have to be paid up. Conrad immersed himself in work, telling Wells that in addition to moving along on *Nostromo* he has been writing a one-act play based on his story "To-morrow," an idea suggested by Sidney Colvin. Colvin came into Conrad's circle by way of Wells and proved to be a lifelong friend of considerable understanding and loyalty. A literary critic as well as a connoisseur of art, he became Slade Professor of Fine Art at Cambridge, wrote a significant study of Keats, and edited Stevenson's fiction and letters. Of greater significance than the play idea, however, was the fact that Conrad started a series of sea sketches and "sent out P on the hunt to place them. This must *save* me. I've discovered that I can dictate that sort of bosh without effort at the rate of 3,000 words in four hours." For dictation, he used Ford whenever he was available,* but, mainly, Miss Hallowes, who served as secretary, typist, and even nurse for the next twenty years.

The one-acter *One Day More* was one of three plays that Conrad wrote, the others being a dramatization of his story "Because of the Dollars," which became *Laughing Anne* in 1920; and a dramatization, also in 1920, of *The Secret Agent*, which was performed on November 2, 1922, but soon withdrawn. Conrad also played a minimal role in the dramatization of *Victory* by MacDonald Hastings, beginning in 1916. During his career he had shown intermittent interest in working with Crane and other collaborators on a play, and late in life, in doing an original piece that he told Pinker would concern a faked old master and be set in Italy. Further, he indicated he wanted to use the subject of *The Arrow of Gold* as play material; he said he observed dramatic potentialities in the idea, which he planned to keep out of the novel as much too good for a magazine audience.

Yet despite all this sporadic activity, Conrad's attitude toward playwriting, actors, production problems was problematic and even overtly hostile. He never tried his hand at an original play, although his fiction shows he was familiar with Ibsen, and in letters he indicates a knowledge of Scribe and Sardou. Baines quotes from an early Conrad letter to Graham in which he

tension nearing the breaking point. . . . Half the time I feel on the verge of insanity. The difficulties are accumulating around me in a frightful manner."

* Ford suffered from severe depression and probably underwent a nervous breakdown in the early spring of 1904. None of this is surprising, since he was facing terrible personal decisions, including the beginning of the dissolution of his marriage. Nevertheless, forty-three pages of the manuscript of *One Day More* are in his hand, and there is some reason to believe the play was a collaboration. Ford, indeed, wrote to Pinker of the work as being by "self & Conrad." (See below for further details.)

demonstrates such hostility toward dramatic effort that more appears at stake than simply playwriting:

> I haven't seen a play for years; but I have read this one [*Admiral Guinea* by Henley & Stevenson]. And that's all I can say about it. I have no notion of a play. No play grips me on the stage or off. Each of them seems to me an amazing freak of folly. They are all unbelievable and as disillusioning as a bang on the head. I greatly desire to write a play myself. It is my dark and secret ambition. And yet I can't conceive how a sane man can sit down deliberately to write a play and not go mad before he has done. The actors appear to me like a lot of *wrongheaded* lunatics pretending to be sane. Their malice is stitched with white threads. They are disguised and ugly. To look at them breeds in my melancholy soul thoughts of murder and suicide—such is my anger and my loathing of their transparent pretences. There is a taint of subtle corruption in their blank voices, in their blinking eyes, in the grimacing faces, in the false light, in the false passion, in the words that have been learned by heart.

Such words and tone are not isolated. He would tell Garnett that actors have no imagination and he detested the stage; and he would write Richard Curle that he preferred the cinema to the stage. He wrote this as he was preparing to become involved in the production of *The Secret Agent:*

> The Movie is just a silly stunt for silly people—but the theatre is more compromising since it is capable of falsifying the very soul of one's work both on the imaginative and on the intellectual side—besides having some sort of inferior poetics of its own which is bound to play havoc with that imponderable quality of creative literary expression which depends on one's individuality.

Conrad's antagonism was probably based on several factors. As a "masculine" writer, he was surely upset by the so-called feminine aspects of theater: its display of feeling, its responsiveness to sentiment, its lack of concealment. Chiefly, though, it was grounded in pretending, and the actors were themselves voicing someone else's lines, humans turned into puppets. Still further, the theater was a metaphor for aspects of civilization Conrad never fully accepted: a social event, a meeting place of several kinds of talent, an expression of a culture's "artificiality," an unnatural expression of emotions and sentiments. Theater was, for him, a falsification, a demeaning of essential and basic values; and it was all put into the mouths of men and women who would say anything as long as they were paid for it. Essentially, Conrad insisted only on the internal drama of the writer, isolated at his desk, making all the decisions and commanding the performance without further intervention—whether from actor, director, or scenic designer—between himself and his audience. The model was the sea captain in the loneliness of command.

William Ernest Henley had died in 1903 and the Provisional Committee of the Henley Memorial asked Conrad to join his name to the commemoration. His response indicated gratitude at this opportunity to repay an "unexpressed observation." He said, to the committee chairman, that Henley's acceptance of *The Nigger* was the "first event in my writing life which really counted"; Conrad, however, names Henley's periodical as *The National Review*, not *The New Review*, a slip that perhaps suggests antagonism toward Henley's former support as much as his actual words indicate acceptance. But except for the slip, Conrad's sentiment demonstrates that Henley gave him his chance:

> And I don't know when—if ever—there will be another of the same intrinsic value, as encouragement and recognition. The two or three letters I wrote him seem now miserably inadequate as the expression of a very genuine feeling of gratitude. It seemed impossible to tell him on paper that the story he accepted for the Review was written with an eye on him—and yet with no idea whatever that it would ever meet his eye. And that is the strict truth. At the time he was to me but an inaccessible name—so widely did he cast about the spell of his individuality, the beneficent white magic of his masterful temperament working for the truth, vigour, for the right expression and the right thought in literature.

Of course, when Conrad wrote these words he was aesthetically opposed to virtually everything Henley had become: a backer of nationalism and healthiness in literature, a supporter of Stevenson, a cult figure among popular writers. Yet, on the other side, Conrad admired Henley's struggle against adversity and his crippling condition, his doggedness in the face of pain.

As Conrad told Meldrum, what kept him going was work. Toward that end, he completed *One Day More* rapidly—in six days, he wrote Colvin—all the while dictating *Nostromo* to Miss Hallowes and writing papers for *The Mirror.* Ford was around as general handyman, extrapolating the dialogue from the story. His aid, in fact, was such that there was some question as to the authorship of the play, and in a letter to Colvin, Conrad had to stress that the work was his. "The play, as can be shown by the MS, has been written entirely in my own hand; and I wrote it alone in a room lent me by an acquaintance to ensure perfect quiet for the six days it took me to achieve that very small feat. In such matters however one cannot be too scrupulous. I won't say any more. You'll understand a demi-mot." Such closeness of the arrangement, however, lends credence to Ford's later claims for his association with Conrad. The collaboration had not, in fact, wound down, with *The Nature of a Crime* yet to come in 1906.

When he completed *One Day More*, Conrad sent it to Beerbohm Tree in its English original and in a French translation, while indicating he could write "something much more striking in French myself." His aim was to obtain a performance by the Dramatic Society, and *One Day More* was performed more than a year later, by the Stage Society, on June 25, 26, 27, 1905.

While Conrad later felt his work was "murdered," his immediate reaction showed pleasure that Shaw admired it:

> As to the success of the thing I can't say anything. I've heard that some papers praised it and some ran it down. On Tuesday when we went (like the imbeciles we are) there was some clapping but obviously the very smart audience did *not* catch on. And no wonder! On the other hand the celebrated "man of the hour" G. B. Shaw was extatic [sic] and enthusiastic. "Dramatist!" says he. With three plays of his running simultaneously at the lenght [sic] of the season he's entitled to speak. Of course I don't think I am a dramatist. But I believe I've 3 or even 5 acts somewhere in me. At any rate the reception of the play was not such as to encourage me to sacrifice 6 months to the stage. Besides I haven't the six months to throw away.
>
> In the end: loss of time. A thorough unsettling of the writing mood. Added weariness.

The London stay for Conrad, extending into March, kept him close to Ford, and despite Jessie's condition and financial worries, he appeared to get on. He wrote three pieces for the *Daily Mail*, which later became part of *The Mirror* as "The Grip of the Land" and "Overdue and Missing" (originally two pieces). The latter, while ostensibly about shipwrecks or disappearance, seems to have a personal weight: of obstacles which the ship must overcome in order to come through—a "tale of resource, of courage—of helplessness, perhaps." He speaks of the "ghosts of disabled ships, drifting for ever across a ghostly and tempestuous ocean." Waiting for Jessie to recuperate sufficiently to return to the Pent, he possibly saw in the image of a shipwreck a metonymy for his sense of himself.

Letters to Pinker indicate steady progress on all these projects; adversity had, once again, fueled Conrad's imagination and given him the energy and will to continue. Of course, the final portions of *Nostromo* suffered; he was already turning from the novel before he had completed it. On March 3, Jessie left for the Pent, but Conrad stayed in London at 17, Gordon Place, possibly because with Ford in attendance he could work rapidly on multiple projects. He tells Pinker to find some money for these *Mirror* pieces: "Essays—impressions, descriptions, reminiscences, anecdotes and typical traits—of the old sailing fleet which passes away for good with the last century."

At the end of March, he was back at the Pent, with Jessie laid up (knee and heart condition) and himself suffering an attack of influenza; but the dictation went on from bed and couch. Also, the mind was thinking through projects, including a return to the idea of the Mediterranean novel, probably *Suspense*, which he started much later. His schemes, outlined in letters to Pinker, were surely intended to assure his agent of his mental health and to obtain necessary monies for medical expenses and steady secretarial assistance. When he took off forty-eight hours to go to Deal, he told Pinker not to panic, since he needed the relief to get rid of a "certain nervousness." Clearly, the intense literary activity was accompanied by near-breakdown. The race, in a sense, was on: to complete *Nostromo* before he suffered a nervous collapse, to play for working time while his condition deteriorated, like the gamble of a captain deciding whether to steam into the eye of the storm or swing around and avoid it altogether. The first would save time but endanger the ship; the second would lose time but prove safer.

He would describe the situation to Galsworthy and, also, ask for £5: Jessie was groaning with neuralgic pain, her nerves giving way, and "I sit here writing to you at a dressing table with a sort of notion in my head that this is hell. I suppose I am near enough to insanity." Existence is "like a horrible nightmare." The condition, even if exaggerated, is comparable to the early 1890s depression Conrad had described to Marguerite, leading to hydrotherapeutic cures and, to some extent, to his work on *Almayer.* He had come into a similar cycle, only now without time or money for a cure.

He never lost the sense of his own worth. Like many egocentrics, he referred to himself in the third person: ". . . those who know something of Conrad (the individual) shall find it there [in *The Mirror* sketches], and the serialisation being commenced at the right time may help the vogue of Nostromo. Here is Conrad talking of the events and feelings of his own life as he would talk to a friend." On April 25, in a somewhat cursory letter to the very depressed Ford, Conrad indicates "2^d^ part of *N* finished yesterday." It is impossible to know, given the fragmentary manuscript, if that meant Conrad had still to write the entire third part, which in the final version as "The Lighthouse" runs two-fifths of the book's length. More likely, he had completed the second part for serialization and had already sketched out and written a good deal of the third, since he would finish the novel by the end of August.*

Pawling of Heinemann had suggested that Conrad and Graham write a joint article, and Conrad was sufficiently interested to propose a sail and a talk. But, he wrote Pawling, he could not entertain any such idea unless he were certain of publication. The topic was, apparently, to be about the commercial aspect of the port of London, for the *World's Work.* It is unclear what role Graham would have had in the collaboration, for Conrad fails to mention him, stressing rather that he has no knowledge and less interest in such matters. He would, however, be willing to try something between 4 and 5,000 words, for £50 for serial rights in England and America. Nothing came of the proposal.

He hoped, meanwhile, to place the pieces of *The Mirror;* Halkett, the

* In May, he told Pinker he was sending on the first batch of Part III., but indicated it was typescript, meaning manuscript copy was ready in part or full.

editor of *Pall Mall Magazine*, offered to take six at £5.5 per thousand words. Yet the interesting part of Conrad's letter of May 29 to Ford concerned the book version of *Mirror*, whose proceeds were apparently to be prorated between the two collaborators: ". . . a small calculation will fix our proper proportions; for I suppose we can not finish the whole together. Can we?" Ford had indeed become very much part of these sketches, as he had of *Nostromo* (possibly more than the fifteen manuscript pages in his hand would suggest). His role would extend into 1906 with *The Nature of a Crime* and even into *The Secret Agent*, which at one time was listed among Conrad's books as a collaboration with Ford.

In addition, Conrad was financially indebted to his collaborator and trying very hard to pay off at least part of the outlay. His indebtedness now extended to Pinker, Galsworthy, Rothenstein, as well as to Ford and nearly all the local business people. Rothenstein was raising money to support Conrad, the exact sources of which remained hidden from the latter. His comment was wry: "Reverting to the matter of that salvage you are conducting to preserve a rather rotten old hulk (but full of the best intentions)—I think you ought to take charge of my debt in the sense that the policy shall be made over to you and the repayments also shall be made to you. I shall take three years for it—no less. I don't think I could take less unless something very fortunate in the way of book sales were to take place: a contingency not worth reckoning upon. Je n'ai pas le don terrible de la popularité."

Incredibly enough, plans for a new collaborative effort continued throughout the final stages of *Nostromo*. On July 29, 1904, Conrad wrote Ford that if the latter wanted to write something for the Northern Newspaper Syndicate, he, Conrad, would be willing to "put in a few of my jargon phrases and send it on. As I remarked: nothing matters—and we are intimate enough to say anything to each other." It was an opportunity for Ford to earn a few pounds, and Conrad's cooperation was probably intended as a way of repaying his friend.

Nostromo was reaching its conclusion, but not without pain and suffering, both physical (a toothache) and mental. Before he completed it, however, word reached Conrad, via Edmund Gosse, the critic and conduit of much literary gossip, that in the marketplace it was rumored, " 'Pinker deals harshly with Conrad.' " Conrad's defense of his agent is really the beginning of a phase in which the association warmed into friendship, almost another kind of collaboration, here between money and literary effort. Conrad writes:

> He has known me for six years. He has stepped gallantly into the breach left open by the collapse of my bank; and not only gallantly, but successfully as well. He has treated not only my moods but even my fancies with the greatest consideration. I would not dream of wearying you with details and figures; but his action, distinctly, has not been of a mercenary character. He can not take away the weariness of mind which at the

> end of ten years of strain has come upon me; but he has done his utmost to help me to overcome it by relieving the immediate material pressure—and the even more disabling pressure of human stupidity. But let that pass! How much can he expect in return for these services? I don't know. But I fear I am not a "profitable man" for anybody's speculation.

Although a funnel for malicious gossip, Gosse was to prove a friend to Conrad, for in the next year he helped him obtain a £500 grant from Balfour, the Prime Minister.

On August 30, Conrad's longest stretch of writing thus far in his career ended. Not until *Victory*, his final masterwork, would he devote such steady mental and physical effort to a single work. Galsworthy was one of the first recipients of the news, although within the next few days he announced it, as a great victory, to Ford, Rothenstein, Elsie Hueffer, Garnett, even Roger Casement. His words to Galsworthy, intermixing martyrdom with pleasure, are the most compelling. After relating the episode of his toothache, in which the dentist dragged at the "infernal thing" in his gum, Conrad moves to a "swooning":

> I went back to my MS. at six pm. At 11.30 something happened—what it is I don't know. I was writing, and raised my eyes to look at the clock. The next thing I know I was sitting (not lying) sitting on the concrete outside the door. When I crawled in I found it was nearly one. I managed to get upstairs and said to Jessie: We must be off to-morrow. I took 30 drops of chlorodyne—and slept till 7.

Then he was off by car to Hope's house in Stanford in Essex, an adventure in which an old man was knocked down but not badly hurt, fuel ran out, and he felt the exhilarated exhaustion of a man passing into another state of consciousness. His description is of something close to that disordering of the senses we associate with synesthesia:

> Had something to eat—and *tasted it too*, for the first time in 10 days. On crossing the river, began to revive on the ferry. Jessie very good and Borys quite a man watching over Mama's "poor leg" and warning off porters with luggage. At five, in sight of Stanford-le-Hope R^{wy} station, petrol gave out. Man ran on and ran back with a two gallon tin.
>
> That night I slept. Worked all day. In the evening dear Mrs. Hope (who is not used to that sort of thing) gave me four candles and on I went. I finished at 3. Took me another half-hour to check the numbering of the pages, write a letter to P. and so on.
>
> I had not the heart to write to you that same night nor yet the next day. Wasn't sure I would survive. But I have survived extremely well. I feel no elation. The strain has been too great for that. But I am quite recovered and ready for work again. There can be no stoppage till end of November when the Sketches'll be finished. And then, I fancy, something will have to be done to get away.

To Ford, he showed less elation and more discouragement, perhaps in keeping with his friend's severe depression and inability to work: "But I've finished. There's no elation. No relief even. Nothing. Moreover I've got a good fortnight's work for the book form. The miserable rubbish is to shoot out on the muck-heap before this month is out. I'll send you the book. I'm weary! weary!" He reassures Ford, who had lost all faith in his powers, that "without understanding you in the least the man [Pinker, also Ford's literary agent] likes you personally. He also nurses in his mind a by no means irrational idea of your usefulness. You are for him the man who can write anything at any time—and write it well."

Part of Conrad's weariness, besides the financial, personal, and literary problems involved, was very possibly based on the nature of the experience to which he had just subjected himself. The mere writing of a 200,000-word novel would have been sufficient to explain exhaustion and near-breakdown, especially since so much depended on an investment of a huge amount of time. But a further, and perhaps more distressing, factor was Conrad's passage in time into his Polish background, through his re-creation of the political situation in Costaguana. And if that were not enough, he had, with Martin Decoud, tested out his own attitudes: political, social, aesthetic, and, in part, condemned himself by way of condemning Decoud, all the while finding the latter's cynicism and realism an effective antidote to Gould's idealism. Through that nature of the novel, indeed its very strengths, Conrad caught himself in a personal bind. The lot of the Costaguanera was based on Conrad's knowledge of Poland's fortunes, and it does not take much historical imagination to note how dependent he was on his own past for details of Sulacan politics.

> In all these households she [Mrs. Gould] could hear stories of political outrage; friends, relatives, ruined, imprisoned, killed in the battles of senseless civil wars, barbarously executed in ferocious proscriptions, as though the government of the country had been a struggle of lust between bands of absurd devils let loose upon the land with sabres and uniforms and grandiloquent phrases.

It was as if Polish Reds and Whites (Blancos in Costaguana) were at each other's throat, with imperial Russia never distant. The next year, in "Autocracy and War," he was to speak of Russia as a "dreaded and strange apparition, bristling with bayonets, armed with chains, hung over with holy images. . . . partaking of a ravenous ghoul, of a blind Djinn grown up from a cloud."

If we cut back to *Nostromo*, we find:

> We convulsed a continent for our independence only to become the passive prey of a democratic parody, the hopeless victims of scoundrels

> and cut-throats, our institutions a mockery, our laws a farce—a Guzman Bento our master! And we have sunk so low that when a man like you [Don José Avellanos] has awakened our conscience, a stupid barbarian of a Montero—Great Heavens! a Montero!—becomes a deadly danger, and an ignorant, boastful Indio, like Barrios, is our defender.

Decoud adds: " 'We have no political reason; we have political passions—sometimes. What is a conviction? A particular view of our personal advantage either practical or emotional. No one is a patriot for nothing. The word serves us well.' " Decoud was grappling with profound issues: the nature of political commitment, the measurement of ideals against personal gain, the kind of reward one expects from the investment of time and energy. For Conrad, it was a testing out of Apollo Korzeniowski's very being and of his own reaction to his father's career. For Decoud: "Life is not for me a moral romance derived from the tradition of a pretty fairy tale." In "Autocracy and War," Conrad, using Germany as his example, says that "no peace for the earth can be found in the expansion of material interests which she seems to have adopted exclusively as her only aim, ideal, and watchword." The very words moving in and out of Decoud's declarations suggest Conrad's own dualism.

The effort required to investigate two points of view for which there could be no apparent resolution was bound to bring him down; he had, for the sake of his imagination, to follow through the very concepts he wished, as a man, to evade. In the dichotomous association between Nostromo and Decoud, in the talk of separation of Sulaco and Costaguana, in the relationship between Antonia (his first love, or not) and Decoud: in these alignments and counteralignments, Conrad pursued the very ideas that had created both his desire for escape and his defensiveness about having done so.

Nostromo demonstrates the dialectical nature of Conrad's mind, his view of political theory and action as counterthrusting elements. The entire novel, characters as well as scenes and events, is structured on conflicting opposites, which temporarily blend into a synthesis, which itself becomes the new counter in the dialectic. Aesthetic and political needs merge with each other. Decoud's cynicism and skepticism represent something very compelling to Conrad, just as Nostromo's "natural man" does; so, too, does Gould's idealism as well as his courage, and Viola's rocklike steadfastness before the ideal created by Garibaldi. Yet all are insufficient, all typify positions that are somehow irrelevant to the situation at hand, and all except perhaps Viola are motivated by barely disguised self-interest. Nevertheless, they are the political, and, by extension, the moral, process. At one point an emissary of Hernandez, the outlaw turned patriot, asks Charles Gould: " 'Has not the master of the mine any message to send to Hernandez, the master of the Campo?' " It occurs to Gould, who sometimes has Conrad's sensibility and insight, that "they were equals before the lawlessness of the land." Conrad's ability to see that a "close-meshed net of crime and corruption lay upon the whole country" was an insight that lay at the foundation of nearly all his fiction of this decade; it rests at the center of *The Secret Agent*, *Under Western Eyes*, *Chance*, and *Victory*. This, not some theory about democracy, its successes or failures, is Conrad's political base.*

* Various theorists about Conrad's politics—whether those who see him in a Burke-Mill liberal tradition (Fleishman), in the Polish romantic gentry tradition (Najder), or as an antiliberal who argues for the status quo (Howe)—often ignore what the fiction tells us. As a creative artist, Conrad intertwined his politics with matters of tone, texture, irony, all of them indescribable matters. These qualities not only affect his politics, they *are* his politics. In every political act, for Conrad, the entire population is involved; there can be no separation of government or leaders from the people, and therefore, there can be no such thing as a distinct political idea. Conrad was, to use a label, a Hegelian without the character of an Idea or Ideal. Accordingly, every theory of his political ideas is potentially correct as well as incorrect, since he is a dialectician, never an absolutist. None of this argument, of course, obviates a search for Conrad's political sources, whether in Burke, Rousseau, or Polish romanticism. What we must remember, additionally, is that his politics were formed as much by the sea as by ideas, by a community based on endurance and common loyalties.

CHAPTER 24

Nostromo's Epigone

THE book form of *Nostromo* appeared on October 14, published by Harpers in London and New York. With the serial ending a week earlier, Conrad was anxious for his friends to wait and read the novel in its book version, not as fragments. The publication of the book, upon which so much depended, coincided with his journeying up to London with Jessie for an operation upon her knee. Although it was a time when he could work—he wrote a brief essay on Henry James for the *North American Review* and an early version of "Gaspar Ruiz" for the *Strand Magazine* (which refused it)—it was also a period when he hoped for reviews that would lead to greater popularity and a resultant pickup in sales of his books.

One of the first notices, in the *Times Literary Supplement* of October 21, was to dash his hopes. Upset by the narrative convolutions, the reviewer felt that a short-story idea was overwhelmed by the technical machinery. "We do not object [he wrote] to an author's finding his way by first losing it, or at any rate by first trying many others—probably it is the safest means—but we do object to being taken with him on the search. In other words, we think that the publication of this book as it stands is an artistic mistake." Although on October 24 Conrad wrote Rothenstein he had not seen any reviews, he was already suffering from "something resembling asthma . . . a very bad fit of it." By October 31, he had seen enough to tell Pinker: "I am afraid Nostromo had a bad sendoff. . . . I know well enough that the book is no mean feat—but what about the public?"

The narrative difficulties, which cannot be denied, created problems for the reviewers. Rather than seeing that the narrative was part of a larger plan involving history and memory—the attempt to capture cycles of experience and fix the novel in a larger context of human behavior—the reviewers tended to judge the novel by the standards of popular fiction. Typical were remarks attacking the prose, or wishing that Conrad had remained a sea novelist, or citing the storytelling itself as tortuous and non-rewarding. *Black and White*, for example, reported: "Mr. Conrad, however, has hidden what grain of romance or of realism was in him under a multitude of words and lowering paragraphs. Only here and there does he catch anything of the terrible mystery of the sea. Only here and there does he come in touch with the still more terrible mysteries of the human heart. In *The Nigger of the 'Narcissus'* he set afloat a cockleshell of plot on a sea of marvellous descriptive passages. But in *Nostromo,* unfortunately, the descriptive passages themselves are not marvellous."

C. D. O. Barrie in the *British Weekly* took away as much as he gave, indicating that the plot is "not well told," and often it is "difficult to say when or where we are." Yet the reviewer saw that Conrad "had chosen a new way to impart reality"—an insight calculated to attract the littérateur but discourage any potential audience. The *Daily Telegraph* condemned Conrad's lack of a "selective gift":

> While parts of *Nostromo* have an absorbing interest, the impression is not preserved when the book is viewed in its entirety. It has longueurs of a wearisome nature; vital situations hang fire while the author indulges in characteristic digressions; detail absorbs the position of outline, which becomes impossibly blurred; the story which held us by its vigour, its wide human interest, becomes narrowed to some small personal issue; the spell is broken.

Many of the reviewers, including Edward Garnett (in the *Speaker*), while sympathetic and understanding overall, found the latter sections of *Nostromo* weak, more often than not too foreshortened. The *Guardian* reviewer caught the grand plan—"the art of the narrative does at last bring the strange array of characters and figures into significant relation"—but was disturbed about Nostromo's prominence in what becomes "an arbitrary and baffling design." Garnett spoke of Conrad's "*psychology of scene,*" which he shares "with many of the great poets and the great artists." His method of "poetic realism," Garnett feels, aligns him with the great Russian novelists, "but Mr. Conrad, inferior in the psychology of character, has outstripped them in his magical power of creating the whole mirage of Nature." John Buchan, in an unsigned review in the *Spectator,* misunderstood the role of Nostromo in the drama, but did see "the strife of ideals in a sordid warfare" and the "core of seriousness in mock-heroics."

The reviews were nearly all bound to discourage the reader. Buchan's estimation is characteristic: "It is not a book which the casual reader will appreciate. The sequence of events has to be sought painfully through the mazes of irrelevancy with which the author tries to mislead us. But it is a book which will well repay those who give it the close attention which it deserves." Conrad was modern, and modernity, whether of technique or language, would divide the audience. His share was small.

He felt he owed Graham an explanation of the novel, since Graham knew the Hispanic scene; thus, Conrad stressed that Nostromo was not a Spaniard or South American but an Italian, and that would explain his easy way with women. He says he tried to make the Capataz a "romantic mouthpiece of 'the people' "— by which he meant the people's sense of manipulation and exploitation. This distorted reading of his own novel was probably intended to placate Graham. On the personal side, Conrad's life was equally dispiriting. Jessie's operation was becoming a peculiarly Conradian disaster, a medical farce out of Molière, perhaps. Before leaving for London, where they took an apartment at 99b, Addison Road, the impecunious Conrads gave a dinner party for thirty guests. Jessie identifies some of them as E. V. Lucas and his wife, Augustus John, A. J. Dawson, Henry Tonks. Then, once they were settled in London, an examination showed that the knee required no operation. Conrad was relieved, of course, but he was wary, possibly suspicious because of his sense of impending disaster. The doctor in charge, Bruce Clark, did in fact change his mind a few days later.

> She [Jessie] has been a week now in a nursing home near Harley Street [Conrad wrote Ford] with Bruce Clark the joint specialist surgeon, lecturer at Barts. in charge of the case. Various rather horrible things have taken place. The examination under chloroform was made four days ago, and would you imagine?, the mischief was not located—it was not even found. As a matter of fact B. Clark (as good a man as there is, I suppose) took his patient for a pampered silly sort of little woman who was making no end of fuss for a simple stiff joint. You may imagine to what horrible pain he put her acting on that assumption. I daren't trust myself to write of it. Assez!

Clark found and admitted his mistake. The cartilage in Jessie's knee had been displaced for the last fourteen years, since her accident at sixteen, and needed an immediate operation. It was scheduled for November 24. The expense would be immense; Conrad figured it as at least 100 guineas (about $1,250 in current money), and told Elsie Hueffer he was "for the present ruined." Amazingly, he could work: finishing the paper on James, dictating to Miss Hallowes two papers that later went into *The Mirror* ("London's River," which became "The Faithful River," and "Tallness of the Spars," which became "Cobwebs and Gossamer"), and writing, fitfully, "Gaspar Ruiz." Intermixed with all this was the need to extract money from friends and business associates to cover his debts.

Although Conrad's work during this trying period was hardly of major significance, his essay on James does demonstrate his reliance on the dictates of art as a means of enduring. He, in fact, used the James essay as a way of re-expressing his own artistic code, renewing in a sense his 1897 Preface by means of an appreciation of James's work. Nearly every phrase about James reverberates back to Conrad: the need for a symbolic art, the use of art as a way of resisting a short-lived reality, the reliance on form as a means of expressing circumstance and character, the expression of the truth of fiction over the record of history. "All creative art is magic, is evocation of the unseen in forms persuasive, enlightening, familiar and surprising, for the edification of mankind, pinned down by the conditions of its existence to the earnest consideration of the most insignificant tides of reality."

Screwing up his courage, Conrad tried to find what would allow man to endure, writing a passage that not only reverberated through himself and James but would extend to William Faulkner in his Nobel Prize acceptance speech:

> When the last aqueduct shall have crumbled to pieces, the last airship fallen to the ground, the last blade of grass have died upon a dying earth, man, indomitable by his training in resistance to misery and pain, shall set this undiminished light of his eyes against the feeble glow of the sun. The artistic faculty, of which each of us has a minute grain, may find its voice in some individual of that last group, gifted with a power of expression and courageous enough to interpret the ultimate experience of mankind in terms of his temperament, in terms of art.

The entire swarm of life is a precious movement, only temporarily present in the moment, and yet it is the novelist's task to grasp this manifold activity: ". . . by the independent creation of circumstance and character, achieved against all the difficulties of expression, in an imaginative effort finding its inspiration from the reality of forms and sensations." The shaping of discrete, contingent events is our only defense against a reality that otherwise buries us. In "The Faithful River," Conrad found comparable terms. Ships are so formed that they are ready to take on the flow and rhythms of an art form once the wind stirs them. Conrad, of course, refers to sailing vessels, that, when anchored, seem like hopeless prisoners waiting to break free. Ships are indeed faithful creatures, but they are also wild and unruly; the dualism of their existence recalling the career of the artist: wildness controlled by form. He would repeat this theme in the story of "The Brute" (1905), a ship which moves outside the controlled dictates of art and becomes a brutal killer.

All this was, as Conrad recognized, left-handed work. Only a novel was the real thing, and he felt no energy or inclination for the long haul. He and Jessie were, understandably, exhausted. In his first long letter to Marguerite Poradowska since the renewal of the correspondence in 1900, he runs through his miseries. The letter recalls those in the 1890s, when he needed Marguerite to console him; like a schoolboy reporting his trials, he begins the letter with a recital of *his* ills—"five attacks of gout in eleven months"—although it was Jessie who was recuperating. The words become a litany of disaster, including many exaggerations. Conrad speaks of being incapable of work for a year, once again recalling his plaints of depression and enervation of a decade earlier. Yet he had worked well to complete *Nostromo,* adding several thousand words to the serial version for the book form. He mentions, however, that he has miraculously recovered, and he and Jessie plan a vacation in Capri, for four months or so, beginning possibly in a fortnight.

The Conrads left for Capri on January 15, 1905, with Conrad full of hope for good working conditions, recovery for Jessie, and a run of copy that would generate income. The episode, however, was to prove one of the most frustrating in his career, almost risible in its overtones of disaster, poor planning, and calamitous expenditures. If Conrad had courted disaster as a way of activating his imagination, he could not have chosen a richer event. Funding for the venture derived from several sources, chiefly as advances from Pinker, with additional monies from Rothenstein, Galsworthy, and even Ford, although routine loans from the last three are difficult to distinguish from advances for the vacation.

Apparently, Conrad hoped to wrap up *The Rescue* on this trip, or at least get it into shape if Pinker could find someone to serialize it. "More than half is done," he reported.

> And (confidentially) I can get Ford to help me in it a little—block out things and so on. He is here and getting better. However nothing must be allowed to interfere with the new novel [probably *Chance*] which is simmering within me all the time. I'll bring it all complete from Italy I do believe. My mind is freer than it has been for years and a little sunshine will get my steam up—I know.

How he planned to bring back a new novel from Italy "all complete" is baffling. Most probably, he promised Pinker a completed book as a way of gaining travel expenses, although by now his agent must have recognized the symptoms: an enervated Conrad becoming a model author when he needed a sudden advance. In the meantime, he sent on a version of "Gaspar Ruiz," the first part of what would become "a Benavides cycle." This version, which *Strand Magazine* did not publish, is now lost, unless it is the initial section of "Gaspar Ruiz," which Conrad finished in November of 1905. There was, in addition, word from E. V. Lucas, of Methuen, who was interested in a volume of criticism: "No doubt I'll be able to sandwich critical papers [such as the James piece, which appeared in *Notes on Life and Letters*] between the slices of the novel."

Intellectually, however, Conrad was moving on another level, preparing to try out his view of "human imbecility," a phrase he used in a letter to Wells. Commenting on the latter's *A Modern Utopia*, Conrad felt Wells addressed himself too exclusively to a select group—his Samurai, those leaders who would legislate perfection—who were rational and logical in their assumptions about human behavior. By being exclusive, Wells had missed the larger number of people, those outside his net, and therefore he addressed only those already convinced of his ideas for planning and organization.

What he must do, Conrad continues, is to argue with those of all positions: "No one's position is too absurd to be argued with. An *enlightened* egoism is as valid as an *enlightened* altruism. . . . The principle of absolutism did not fail to maintain itself because there is anything absurd in absolutism, but because autocrats had made themselves unbearable through a sheer want of intelligence." Thus, Wells should argue with absolutists as well as with those willing to work for a utopia, or else he is unwilling to take "sufficient account of human imbecility which is cunning and perfidious." This record of human imbecility, recalling *Nostromo,* would be the subject of Conrad's next novel, *The Secret Agent,* which he would dedicate to Wells.

Even before the Conrads left for Capri, tension began to mount, because of the need for money and the complications of a journey with a crippled woman. On January 4 and 10, Conrad tried to work out the discrepancies between what Pinker had already advanced him and what he had spent, preparing his agent for additional outlays to cover the expenses of the trip. The letters detail incredibly fine estimates on Conrad's part, in which he calculates that in three years and ten months he has spent £1,778, or about $25,000 in current money, most of which he figures he has paid back to Pinker in the form of book and serial sales. In the January 4 letter, he indicates a plan for his sea sketches, to make them the first part of a volume called *The Mirror of the Sea,* and to collect his literary papers for the second part, to be called *The Mirror of Life.* That latter segment would eventually become the first half of *Notes on Life and Letters,* published in 1921.

In the January 10 letter, he foresees that his caravan of four (a nurse would accompany them) will add to costs in "a terrific way. . . . I must have carriages at every step. I shudder." He says he will feel easier when he starts to write, a grim irony in the light of ensuing events. Jessie has left a record of their trip: the embarkation at Dover, the arrival and stay in Capri, and the return; but her manner is good-naturedly retrospective, full of humor at her situation, and completely lacking in the intense desperation Conrad could convey. His account of stages of the journey and the stay has qualities of Nostromo's mission with the silver in the lighter episode: it may have seemed the most desperate affair of his life.

Conrad's hope, as he repeated to Wells, was to return with a book. The "caravan" left for Paris as planned on the fifteenth, expecting to spend the night and then depart on a sleeping car for Rome, where they would arrive on Saturday, January 16. At Dover, Jessie almost fell into the water when she embarked in a chair that hovered over "the swirling waters between the ship and the quay," while the man helping her got his hand caught between the chair and the rail of the gangway. They stayed in Paris in the St. Petersburg Hotel, which saved money but which necessitated two large cab fares to go anywhere. Further, Conrad from the beginning of the journey had taken a fierce dislike to Jessie's attendant nurse, a distaste that would continue throughout the trip. Once on the sleeping car to Rome, Jessie had great difficulty in moving around on her crutches—they were new to her and she was no longer slim—and her attempts to negotiate the cars to the dining room created a contretemps with the railway officials. The nurse, meanwhile, baited Conrad, and he became sulky and irritated. At the station in Rome, Jessie was left hanging by her arms to the ledge above the open railway door when her chair was, mistakenly, removed. In Naples, which they had expected to use as a mere stopover, they found bad weather, and the steamship company refused to land Jessie in Capri until the sea calmed. Money was already a problem: unexpected hotel expenses, liberal tips because of Jessie's needs, extraordinary landing costs.

In two letters, one to Galsworthy on the twenty-first of January seeking a loan and the other to Meldrum on the twenty-second, Conrad told his tale of an ill-fated traveling circus. To Galsworthy, while requesting £10, the first of many such sums, he related he had written 1,000 words of a political article ("Autocracy and War"). To Meldrum, he gave a full narrative, and it warrants repeating:

> We arrived in Naples 2½ hours late at 2 o'clock in the morning—snow on the ground and a bitter North wind blowing. The Cook's interpreter waiting for us with the chair and carriers looked the very picture of misery. As to the carriage which was ordered it had gone home simply. Fortunately, we were able to capture the only hotel omnibus in waiting; and the hotel captured us to some purpose—for we had to remain weatherbound in Naples for five solid days. On two of these the boat for Capri never left at all and on the others the weather was still too boisterous to admit of landing an invalid. I thought I had foreseen everything but I had not foreseen that.
>
> . . . At last, taking the first chance, we got landed here yesterday by moonlight the whole population (I should say) of the Marina turning out on the jetty to see the fun. The Captain took his steamer in as close in as he dared and a special big rowing boat came off to do the trans-shipping. The uproar was something awful; but I must say that for all their yelling these Italians did their work extremely well; and though the thing looked (and to my wife must have felt) dangerous I had not a moment uneasiness. The whole affair which had afforded the population of Capri so much innocent enjoyment cost me 40 frcs or so.

Jessie, nevertheless, speaks of Conrad's agitation during the operation. Directly they took over the house, the nurse fell apart, her nerves gone, and she took to bed, requiring nursing herself. For Conrad, the entire venture was to remain a kind of unreal episode in his life. As he wrote Galsworthy, the "whole expedition is a mad thing," not only because of the logistical details, but because its success depended on his ability to write 60,000 words in four months. This rate of production, even under the best of conditions, meant almost 5,000 words a week, two or three times his normal rate. Rightly, he felt "sick with apprehension," and the tension building up in him only made the venture seem more bizarre.*

Withal, the Conrads, Borys, and the nurse settled down at the Villa di Maria. Conrad was to make a number of acquaintances and, in one instance, Norman Douglas, a close friend. Dr. Cerio, who attended both Jessie and her nurse, was a cultivated man, and Conrad utilized his personal library for research on his long-planned Mediterranean novel, what would become *Suspense.* Not far from the Villa di Maria, Count Zygmunt Szembek, an elderly Polish nobleman, lived in part of the Canonicos' villa. "Il Conde" was based on an episode in the count's life, an incident which fitted well into Conrad's own thinking as he worked on anarchy and nihilism in *The Secret Agent.* Finally, the friendship with Norman Douglas proved satisfying to both Conrad and Jessie, and it lasted well beyond the stay in Capri.

The association with Douglas gave Conrad a younger friend at a time when his friendship with Ford had begun to split apart. When they met, in 1905, Conrad was rooting around for some book that would find a market. He would outline to Pinker (on February 23) such a study, treating the struggle for Capri, in 1808, between the French and English. His outline is itself very close to what Douglas was himself to write in his "Materials for a Description of Capri," a nine-part series about the island published from 1904 to 1915. If Conrad was still uncertain of himself, Douglas was fully cast adrift from his familiar moorings. He had divorced his wife (in 1904) for adultery, was in charge of his two small sons, and was undergoing psychological changes that would profoundly affect the rest of his life. Having exhausted his inheritance through extravagance, he was forced to turn to writing for support. Also, following his retirement from the British Foreign Office, he resided in the Bay of Naples area, on Capri, where he could, with less secrecy, indulge the homosexual tastes that were to dominate his personal life.†

In 1905, Douglas (at thirty-seven) was virtually the same age Conrad had been when *he* began to consider a literary vocation. Both men had entered writing from other careers. While Conrad was finishing out his life as a sea-

---

* He tried to explain his plight to Pinker, to justify the latter's advances: "Of course you may say that I ought to disregard all the complications and peg away with my eyes shut to domestic affairs. I know some men are capable of that sort of thing; and with an organized household one could perhaps abstract oneself for six hours per day. It's another matter with me. You understand that my wife was getting pretty helpless and required some attention; the child too. For me to have to lay down my pen ten times in the course of the day is fatal. I wish there had been something of a hack-writer in my composition."

† Appropriately enough, on January 29, from Capri, Conrad wrote the first of eight letters to Robert d'Humières, the author and eventual translator of *The Nigger of the "Narcissus"* into French. Part of Proust's circle in the years before the First World War, d'Humières, to avoid an impending scandal, had himself posted to a Zouave regiment on

man, Douglas had been, from 1893 to 1898, a diplomat, with excellent credentials that included fluency in his native German (he was born in Austria of a Scottish father and a half-Scottish, half-German mother), in French, and in Russian, and he was later to add several Italian dialects. Neither had considered writing as the goal of his life, but in retrospect each could see that he had drifted until he had found himself as a writer. Perhaps the psychological moment was profound, in that both Conrad and Douglas felt outside the main current of conventional thought; and Capri, that unreal island with real flowers and trees, was as well outside conventional history and geography.

In a letter to Ford (May 9), Conrad indicated this feeling of unreality, that extraordinary quality which had marked his entire Capri expedition:

> I've done nothing. And if it were not that Jessie profited so remarkably I would call the whole expedition a disaster. This climate what between tramontana and sirocco has half killed me in a not unpleasant languorous melting way. I am sunk in a vaguely uneasy dream of visions—of innumerable tales that float in an atmosphere of voluptuously aching bones. Comprenez Vous ça? And nothing nothing can do away with that sort of gently active numbness. The scandals of Capri—atrocious, unspeakable, amusing scandals, international, cosmopolitan and biblical flavoured with Yankee twang and the French phrases of the *gens du monde* mingle with the tinkering of guitars in the barber's shops and the rich contralto of the "bona sera Signore" of the big Mrs Morgano as I drag myself in an inwardly fainting condition into the Café to give some chocolate to ma petite famille. All this is a sort of blue nightmare traversed by stinks and perfumes, full of flat roofs, vineyards, vaulted passages, enormous sheer rocks, pergolas, with a mad gallop of German tourists laché a travers tout cela in white Capri shoes over the slippery Capri stones, kodaks, floating veils, strangely waving whiskers, grotesque hats, streaming, tumbling, rushing, ebbing from the top of Monte Solaro (where the clouds hang) to the amazing rocky chasms of the Arco Naturale—where the lager beer bottles go pop. It is a nightmare with the fear of the future thrown in.

In his fiction, Conrad had, with *Nostromo*, entered upon a period of great intensity, a time when he was himself confronting the deepest and potentially most upsetting recesses of his own psyche. Even in his non-fiction, "Autocracy and War," he was forcing himself to acknowledge profound elements of the past and of memory. He was, in brief, dealing with great secrets: of name and name changes, background, ideology, personal philosophy, aspects of dependency. And his knowledge of these secrets, in *The Secret Agent*, *Under Western Eyes*, the stories "The Informer," "An Anarchist,"

---

the front lines in 1915 and charged to his death. Ferdinand Bac referred to him as "one of the Robert de Montesquious of this world." Conrad wrote: "Aimant la France et les Français d'une affection héréditaire et personelle je désire vivement leur être connu. Ce serait un vrai bonheur pour moi que d'être interprété par vous qui avez si bien compris (votre lettre le prouve) la simple âme de ce petit livre."

and "The Secret Sharer," involved the recognition of murder, deceit, betrayal, treachery, amoral obtuseness, sadism, and parasitism. We can only explain the intensity of the vision in this fiction by the fact that Conrad had sensed equivalent feelings in himself, however muffled and controlled they may have been. While such feelings did not emerge in crime or other asocial behavior, they did of course appear in his debilitating illnesses, recurring and hanging on for long stretches.

Conrad's ambivalence toward the family situation, again paralleling Douglas in *his* desperation to break out, appears in his next immediate novel, *The Secret Agent,* begun as soon as he had finished *The Mirror of the Sea.* The family situation turns up, incidentally, for the first time in his serious fiction, and it surfaces not as reflecting warmth or sympathetic dependence but as manifesting desperation. In his psychoanalytic study of Conrad, Dr. Meyer charts the numerous references to biting, eating, even cannibalism in *The Secret Agent,* and shows how the novel can be read at its deepest level as the father killing the "son," which leads, in turn, to the wife's killing of her husband. The psychological situations of this novel, as in those that follow, indicate Conrad's preoccupations. Precisely how much of this he sensed in Douglas we have no evidence to support except the nature of the friendship itself.

To H. G. Wells, Conrad mentioned meeting "a Scot (born in Austria) once in our diplomatic service when he threw up I fancy in sheer intellectual disgust. A man who can not only think but write." From this letter, we understand that Douglas and Conrad had already met at least three times, mainly, we suppose, to discuss literature, writing, and the problems accruing from a literary career. Conrad comments to Wells that he, Douglas, and an American named Jerome had been discussing Wells's *A Modern Utopia,* and all had agreed that "you were the one honest thinker of the day." This sentiment is doubtful, for both Conrad and Douglas were attuned to a different kind of realism and to a considerably different kind of novel from Wells's. The praise was, probably, an attempt to "soften" Wells, whose influence was needed to place Douglas's first efforts.

The result of the association was that Conrad tried to help the young man publish his stuff, not at all an easy task for an essentially coterie author such as Conrad. Finally, when Ford assumed the editorship of *The English Review* in 1908, Douglas had a definite introduction, although Conrad had tried earlier with Garnett, Pinker, and Wells, the difficulties compounded by the fact that Douglas was not himself commercially oriented. Jessie found the former diplomat particularly attractive, especially in comparison with Ford. She described Douglas as a "unique personality, a man of great charm of manner and conversation." There is little question Conrad found him a welcome presence on Capri, for Douglas was a raconteur, a man of considerable knowledge, sophisticated in several cultures, and, overall, an antidote to the difficult home situation. Conrad had come down with his usual ailments; as he tells Pinker on February 23, he has influenza with bronchitis, must remain in bed, suffers from insomnia and nerves, for which he takes medication, and senses the days and weeks slipping away in idleness. It was the old nightmare, uncontrollable, a pattern he had to undergo as a way of indulging the needs of his imagination and unconscious.

Meanwhile, he plugged along on "Autocracy and War," originally to be called "The Concord of Europe," and it reached 4,000 words by February 23. By that time, he had expected to be 15–20,000 words along on his new novel. In late March, there was a brief respite from the debilitating effects of the influenza attack, financial pressures, and overall enervation. It was a respite with a tale attached. William Rothenstein, with much trouble, had been able to obtain for Conrad a grant of £500, via Balfour and King Edward himself, with Henry Newbolt, the barrister and poet, as a co-trustee of the fund. Edmund Gosse, whose connections in the government ran high, had helped Rothenstein arrange for the grant. It was, on the part of all, a sincere effort to help a serious author maintain his equilibrium in the face of reader indifference and was, for the time, a large sum, equal to $6,000–7,500 in current spending power.

Conrad turned it all into drama, grateful for the recognition but horrified that someone should oversee his life and expenditures. He told Gosse, first, that such "moral support [it was financial] or belief is the greatest help a writer can receive in those difficult moments which Baudelaire has defined happily as 'les stérilités des écrivains nerveux.' Quincey too," he continued, "I believe has known that anguished suspension of all power of thought that comes to one often in the midst of a very revel of production like the slave with his *memento mori* at a feast." Conrad followed this letter of gratitude with another on April 11, assuring Gosse of his discretion. Then, on May 16, while the Conrads were staying in Marseilles on their return from Capri, he let go with a blast. Every aspect of his dependency on others, which was so much a part of both his childhood and adult years, rankled and twisted.

> I find it difficult to believe that the Prime Minister intended that or any other curatelle [guardianship or trusteeship] to be established. It seemed to me that the grant was offered without conditions;—else, I feel sure from the most considerate tact invariably manifested in all your communications with me you would have given me a hint beforehand of any such arrangement with all the delicacy displayed in your good works. It is therefore excessively startling to discover that a grant given (in the terms of your own letter announcing the fact) "in recognition of my talents and for my services to literature":—a grant therefore which however beyond one's deserts one could have imagined oneself to have, in a measure, earned—becomes converted into a bounty which has to be begged for; and this not once only but many times as it were: that it is a gift no longer

> conferred upon such merits as I may have but upon two men with power to control, grant and withhold, according to their will and judgment: and that power apparently unlimited in its discretion.

The tone now picks up that of Uncle Tadeusz, the guardian, as he lectured young Conrad:

> The whole affair has assumed an appearance much graver and more distressing than any stress of my material necessities: the appearance of "Conrad having to be saved from himself"—the sort of thing that casts a doubt on a man's sense of responsibility, on his right feeling, on his sense of correct conduct. How it has arisen since your friendly and considerable letter came bringing with it the regret of many imperfections and the comfort of your approving judgment—I can not tell. What indiscreet act or word of mine (or somebody else's) might have given cause for it I cannot tell! All I know is that I haven't been able not only to write a line since but even to think of one worth setting down.

Conrad requested an interview with Gosse to put forward his case: that he could handle the funds without management from above. He also asserted that had he not needed the first check from the grant to cover his travel expenses from Capri, he would not have used it; he is, however, prepared to repay the sum within two weeks of his return, ostensibly with money from Pinker.

In his next letter, on May 19, just after his return to the Pent, Conrad apologized to Gosse,* who had been outraged by the grantee's apparent ingratitude. Indicating he had not known such procedures of governing the fund were usual, not exceptional in his case, Conrad wrote:

> I own to a, not I hope very peculiar, dislike of falling, even by the remotest appearance, into the class of those disorderly talents whose bohemianism, irregularity and general irresponsibility of conduct are neither in my tradition and my training nor in my character. You will in all fairness to me remember that it is through you—and you alone—that I received the only intimation which I could regard as authoritative and official. Granting that I have been unspeakably stupid, to whom else, under my mistaken impression, was it proper for me to appeal for a hearing? It was asked for, in all deference, as a favour. I conclude with a perfectly unaffected regret, that it is refused. But is my readiness to throw

---

* He apparently was appeased, for in 1910, when he outlined a plan to Thomas Hardy for the establishment of an English Academy of Letters, he included Conrad as one of the original thirty members. The academy was modeled after the Académie Française and would eventually grow to forty members. Among the original group, who represented not only literature but history, poetry, and philosophy, were, besides Conrad, Yeats, Hardy, James, Gilbert Murray, Sir Alfred Lyall, A. C. Bradley, Viscount Morley, Robert Bridges, Pinero, Lang, George Trevelyan, and Gosse himself.

> myself unreservedly upon your judgment to be counted a sin so grievous as to reflect on my character?

The apology meant Conrad could accept the money, which he needed desperately to pay current expenses and to hold off Pinker, and at the same time save face. It was a parade of pride swallowed, the self effaced, a last-minute retrieval of fortune.

The Galsworthys visited in Capri, in April, and Conrad must have discussed finances with his generous friend. By mid-April, Conrad had realized the Capri stay was, from the point of view of his career, a disaster. Jessie had benefited from the electricity cure she underwent, but none of this could mitigate the fact that he depended on Pinker for funds to return and he had, except for the article, no copy to send as payment. It was the old bind: money borrowed to buy time, and then time wasted or lost while debts accumulated. He was ready for an attack of gout, and it would come shortly after his return to England. In a desperate move, he reopened to Pinker his plan to collect his sea sketches and literary papers in a single volume, although the collection would not be coherent except as an expression of Conrad's sensibility. He even mentions that the Glasgow *Evening Herald* had asked him for permission to reproduce his Preface to *The Nigger* "as a special article on the Art of Fiction." He gave permission and received three guineas in payment.

The sole copy Conrad was preparing involved the "Dynamite ship" story—*Chance* at story length, and probably only the episode in which Captain Anthony transports dynamite as cargo on the *Ferndale.* The manuscript title of *Chance,* incidentally, is "Explosives." By May 12, Conrad assured Pinker, "Short stories is the watchword now" and "Explosives" ready. And in a May 8 letter to Galsworthy, reviewing his entire Capri disaster, Conrad says he has begun a short story (apparently "Explosives"): ". . . something like 'Youth'—but not at all like it. In the face of my situation it is mere trifling." This early beginning of *Chance,* definitely in mind in some version before *The Secret Agent* and fixed dimly in Conrad's imagination as the "Dynamite ship" in the late 1890s, places the novel well back in the "Youth" and *Lord Jim* period. This fact helps explain the early parts, which focus so intensely on narrators and narrative that the novel moves sluggishly, as though Conrad were fascinated more by technical scaffolding than content. Further, that intricate beginning would appear to be disconnected from the later parts, those devoted to the "Dynamite ship." Thus, the disproportion of various elements and the disconnectedness of the narrative devices reach back far into Conrad's conception of the novel.

Of still greater interest is the early dating of the novel, placing it as overlapping with *The Rescue* and *Nostromo* and running parallel with "Verloc" (*The Secret Agent*) and "Razumov" (*Under Western Eyes*). This interweaving indicates a tightness of conception and creativity far more intense than we had believed, with four long novels in various stages moving in and out of Conrad's mind in this six-to-seven-year period. Conrad's letters to Pinker detailing the progress of *The Secret Agent* also pick up fragments of *Chance*, with the letter of January 25, 1907, indicating he has "done a lot to it."

A full month before leaving Capri, Conrad was already mentally back at the Pent. He planned to stop off on the return to see Marguerite in Marseilles, for only one day, he assures Pinker. Finances, Conrad's Armageddon, were hopeless. He needed Pinker for everything, and the agent had balked at sending funds because of lack of copy. First, Conrad wanted to be rid of the nurse, Miss Jackson, and needed transportation money for her; then, he needed travel money for his family, the cheapest possible way via Marseilles; and third, he had to have expenses, for if he failed to pay up and leave the Villa di Maria by the nineteenth of May he would face "the prospect of being abruptly chucked out (in debt) into the streets in Capri." None of this, he tells Pinker, will get the story done. He informs his agent that if it is his intention to strand the Conrad family on Capri, then he, Conrad, will have to devote all his energies to getting away. "You can my dear fellow put me in a hole but I won't be kept there. In what state of mind do you think I'll be able to approach the work lying before me and to which I shall turn directly this writing is done?"

Added to this near-panic was Conrad's intention to return to attend rehearsals of *One Day More*, which the Stage Society would produce in June. He mentions Granville Barker and George Bernard Shaw as showing interest in his work, surely hoping Pinker will be impressed. Pinker was an agent, however, not a literary man, and he was more impressed by copy turned in on time (such as Arnold Bennett's) than by grand names. If he supported Conrad in the face of his better financial instincts, it was because he believed, finally, in Conrad and not because he thought he was supporting great literature. Conrad said he would sit tight until the twenty-eighth of April, and then if Pinker failed to come through, "I shall consider myself 'left' and what I will do, where I will go and how is a mystery even to myself—and not worth much considering anyhow."

He appeared to revel in the abandonment, repeating the image of a man drowning, of Pinker as rescuer, of himself as deserted. He says he will sit hard and write, assuring Pinker that a "certain amount of pressure may do to bring a drunkard to his bearings but it must fail with my temperament." Money, eventually, was forthcoming, and the Conrads left Capri on May 12, bound for Naples to catch the steamer to Marseilles. With nothing to offer Pinker but a version of "Explosives," Conrad suggested in a May 12 letter that he do a series of short stories based on "extracts from *private* letters of a war correspondent. Imagine him writing to his girl—the inner truth of his feelings—things that *don't* go into his war correspon*dence*—that can't go into it." Nothing came of the idea, and it appears from Conrad's description to be something quite alien to his talent.

After seeing Marguerite and meeting with Robert d'Humières, Conrad returned to the Pent on the seventeenth of May, very tired but in good health. Soon, however, came the inevitable attack of gout, which brought him down after a quick trip to London apparently over *One Day More.* Lying flat on his back, awaiting the relaxation of the attack, Conrad reviewed his prospects. While in London, he had met Henry Newbolt, the barrister who was co-trustee of his grant, and precisely the kind of establishment poet Conrad's art opposed. He was still trying to pry his money away, and he was forced to beg. They met on the twenty-fourth of May and Conrad wrote a summary of his needs on the twenty-fifth. What was dismaying to him was his need to explain his affairs in detail to obtain the first half, £250. The list of his debts, which he totaled for Newbolt, runs into virtually every aspect of his life: an overdraft on his bankers, on which he owed at least £60; arrears on rent for six years, £50; taxes due, £22.10; doctors owed: Hackney—£20, Tebb (who treated Ford and Elsie, as well as Conrad and Jessie)—£10, Cerio in Capri—£18, Batten—£14; local bills around Hythe and Folkestone, £102. The sum came to £298, or about $4,000 in current purchasing power. Conrad says that with the £250 from the grant he can manage if he sits close all next month. He tells Newbolt, in a further demeaning explanation, that he cannot demand the sum from Pinker, because their arrangement is copy against payment; only one friend, apparently Galsworthy, could lend him the funds, but since that friend will not hear of repayment, Conrad says borrowing is out of the question.

The letter closes with several bows of deferential respect: "All these affairs are very miserable; but the point, as I venture to state it with all the deference and gratitude imaginable, is that if I have been judged worthy of that favour there can be no harm of applying it in the way in which its beneficent effect will be most felt. Never perhaps an unexpected help had been more timely. The view also may be taken that more debts being for the *most part* the result of my wife's illness, the grant pays for her cure; which is in fact the feeling I first had when the news reached me. And what greater relief could be given to a man?" He thanks Newbolt for his support and for expressing commendation of his books. He promises to send *The Mirror of the Sea* as soon as it is available, calling it "a pinch of my chaff for your solid grain—but one gives what one has." Conrad's manner is that of an outlaw to the sheriff checking him out for violations.

The above explanation to Newbolt began a series of very lengthy letters, extending through the first half of June, in which Conrad bared his financial dealings. Newbolt luckily thought enough of Conrad's work to retain the letters, although Conrad characteristically destroyed Newbolt's answers.

The former considered the correspondence to be a legal record, enabling Newbolt to justify his actions and Conrad to present his case. Newbolt had suggested that Conrad declare bankruptcy, although not publicly, a step Conrad resisted with dismay. The advice must have sounded to Conrad like Bobrowski's warnings to his improvident nephew. He answered that his dealings with the local tradesmen have been equitable, and for him to declare bankruptcy would mean he would destroy his credit in an area where he has been known for more than six years.

> I ask you [he writes] my dear M[r] Newbolt how would you like such a proposal being made to yourself in relation to your own tradesmen and generally to people who trusted your word? It [is] an expedient for a hopeless situation, a calamitous sort of thing to which in justice to myself as well as to the other parties I cannot consent. There is no sentiment here whatever; I leave that out altogether; but from a practical point of view it would be *bad business*, making my position much worse for the future. I would repel the transaction as unnecessary and practically discrediting; but the true point of my objection lies in this that it is not applicable to my case.

Conrad's argument is that he needs peace of mind in order to work, "serenity of thought necessary for good work," and such actions would upset him for months, as well as incur additional expenses of moving. Conrad retreats to his position of confidence as a maritime captain, of particular significance to Newbolt, who was not only a patriot but a popular writer of sea ballads (particularly "Drake's Drum" in *Admirals All*, 1897). "I am no stranger to business, and know the meaning of things. I've had charge of valuable property and of conflicting interests beyond what falls commonly to the lot of commanders of ships. I look upon a composition with one's creditors as a *most* serious thing, worse than bankruptcy in some respects inasmuch as bankruptcy may be forced on by the stupidity or malevolence of a creditor whereas the other is a confession of absolute inability to meet one's engagements. I hope as long as I can sit a chair and hold a pen to keep it off."

The June 5 letter is especially revealing, since in it Conrad shows how vulnerable he feels himself to be, although he was an established writer with at least three great works behind him. But now he is not the author of "Heart of Darkness," *Lord Jim*, or *Nostromo* but a Polish waif, a foreigner in England squirming at his "differences":

> . . . and as in the case of a writer such as I am, of unconventional origin, everything, literary achievement as well as personal character, may, and probably will be, scrutinised with no friendly eye, I felt bound to explain my position fully and state my arguments "in extenso" with the hope, I own, that some day, perhaps, you, a literary man of undeniable, distinguished and *national* position hearing some harsh opinion would be disposed to say: "It is not so. I knew the man and I know the facts."

Conrad offers his art, in particular *his* way of working, which is absolute: "That I cannot work with the regularity and certitude of an Anthony Trollope is a defect purely temperamental; but that I desire to avoid the most remote appearance of being the XXth century edition of Johnson's Mr Savage you cannot but understand and approve (even if you find my dread exaggerated) knowing as you do the irresponsible judgments passed every day upon the living and the dead alike." He pleads with Newbolt to understand how much he depends on the good opinion of the barrister and Rothenstein, the other trustee: "Pray remember that from the nature of things I cannot count upon the moral support one's family, connections, the opinion of numerous early associates gives one against the hasty judgments of the world. Except for the woman who trusted me and the child not yet old enough—thank God—to understand all the uncertainty of his future, I am so alone that you two stand in virtue of your charge in the positions that only the nearest of blood could occupy with perfect safety to myself."

The June 9 letter, pursuant to the conversation and exchange of correspondence, outlines Conrad's indebtedness in still greater detail. It exceeds the former estimate by £20, the additional sum having gone for furniture purchased since the interview. Conrad has broken down every bill into pounds and shillings, even pence, and we note, in addition to those indicated above, sums owed to the chemist, saddler, stationer, laundryman, as well as several others amounting even to only a few shillings. As he says, they have to be settled "for very shame." Conrad reiterates that if only he had had more copy on hand, he would not appeal to Newbolt for such amounts; but without copy, he cannot go to Pinker. He asks to have the checks made out directly to the people named. When these bills are paid, Conrad will have exhausted £370 of the grant money, with another £100 having been dispatched to Capri to cover expenses there. All this indicates that the Conrads had been living off the cuff for several years, with virtually no hope, barring a miracle, of achieving stability. For even with the unexpected money from the grant—the miracle!—Conrad was, as he tells Newbolt, still in arrears. In thanking Newbolt on the sixteenth of June for having sent the checks, he admits his "position is not made perfectly sound, but short of that for which the only way is steady work . . . you have afforded me the greatest amount of intellectual and moral relief possible under the circumstances."

Yet this was not the end. Pinker had left for the United States on business for Henry James, and Conrad was forced to appeal to Norman Douglas, whose literary efforts he was supporting, to make payment for part of the Villa di Maria bill. While clearing away these debts, some extending back for several years, was helpful, it created the expected condition: severe illness, gout among other things. There was no way in which Conrad could relive years of improvidence, whether earned or not, without repeating the cycle of childhood illness.

By June 22, he had recovered sufficiently, however, to go up to London for rehearsals of *One Day More.* By this time, Ford was separated (temporarily) from Elsie, and Conrad in writing his collaborator extended an invitation first to him and then through him to Elsie. The situation was delicate, for Conrad held a box for four for the June 27 performance, the final one, and invited Ford and Elsie and "no one else." Conrad was apparently fearful Ford would appear with another companion, possibly even with Mary Martindale, Elsie's sister, with whom he was having an affair. As an incentive or as a bit of sardonic humor, Conrad says that three acts by Alma-Tadema (*The Near Felicity*) will precede his play. Conrad's report to Galsworthy of the opening performance on the twenty-fifth is full of scorn. Even his pleasure at Shaw's praise is qualified by his feeling that writing for the theater is not fully adult work. Nevertheless, he is hopeful that a nebulous plan to run *One Day More* as a curtain raiser for Shaw's *Candida* may materialize. So low was he that he pinned his hopes on "Autocracy and War," the article which was appearing in the *Fortnightly,* hoping, as he says, "for a sensation."

The affair of the play ended where it began; whatever interest was shown in it died, and Conrad was left with his writing desk, pen, and white paper. He could barely disguise his depression; he had entered another one of the periodic lulls which characterized even his best years. The second half of 1905 contained several interim works, although he evidently moved along sporadically on *Chance.* Chiefly, though, he settled on stories, which would eventually be collected in *A Set of Six,* and sketches for *The Mirror.* The stories included completion of "Gaspar Ruiz," "The Brute," "The Anarchist," and very possibly "The Informer." The *Mirror* sketches included those that came to be titled "The Nursery of the Craft," "Tremolino," and "The Heroic Age" (about Nelson), the first two being among Conrad's best work for this volume.

Set into this work was a short piece he did for the *Speaker,* called "Books." Ever supportive, Garnett latched on to it as containing all of Conrad's philosophy, which Conrad denied, saying he was ignorant of what his philosophy was. Yet "Books" is one of Conrad's periodic restatements, going back to the Preface to *The Nigger,* and serves as a renewal of his commitment to the craft of fiction. Conrad's "formulas" were simple, but his touchstones were James, Balzac, and Stendhal, and he was quite serious about what art can and cannot do.

> The art of the novelist is simple. At the same time it is the most elusive of all creative arts, the most liable to be obscured by the scruples of its servants and votaries, the one pre-eminently destined to bring trouble to the mind and the heart of the artist. After all, the creation of a world is not a small undertaking except perhaps to the divinely gifted. In truth every novelist must begin by creating for himself a world, great or little, in which he can honestly believe. This world cannot be made otherwise than

> in his own image: it is fated to remain individual and a little mysterious, and yet it must resemble something already familiar to the experience, the thoughts and the sensations of his readers.

The novelist must be free of any restraints—Stendhal, for one, would not have accepted any limitations on his freedom—and yet he cannot indulge in moral nihilism. Conrad was, once again, trying to find that relationship which exists among three elements, all of them apparently at odds with each other: the novelist, his material, and the audience awaiting him. The difficulty is that the author must feel elation to be true to his sensations, and yet that elation cannot lead to a sense of his superiority. He must rise to meet his imagination, but he must not rise so far he loses touch. Outright pessimism for the novelist would be just such a form of superiority or arrogance. The novelist must walk the edge: "To be hopeful in an artistic sense it is not necessary to think that the world is good. It is enough to believe that there is no impossibility of its being made so." In that negation of a negation, Conrad drove his wedge; the "no impossibility" permits the novelist to detect man's "obscure virtues." Word power, as Conrad would be among the first to suggest, is insufficient as a weapon unless the novelist brings understanding to the human condition.

On the eve of beginning *The Secret Agent*, Conrad perhaps had to remind himself that man's virtues did exist, for that novel's irony appeared to give the novelist a devastating authority, even an arrogance. Of the stories written at this time as a spin-off from *Nostromo*, "Gaspar Ruiz" was by far the longest, about half the length of "Heart of Darkness." Conrad indicated that his idea for it came from a book by Captain Basil Hall, *Extracts from a Journal, written on the coasts of Chile, Peru, and Mexico in the years 1820, 1821, 1822*. Conrad found the name "Gaspar Ruiz" in Hall's account of the pirate Benavides, and attached to it a good deal of paraphernalia, so that the story is neither pure action nor philosophical musing but a lackluster hybrid.

Of some interest, however, is the "political play" of the long story, and how its tensions fit into Conrad's work of this period, which is overwhelmingly political. *Nostromo* had opened up the old memories and conflicts, and Conrad faced them. These encounters with the politics of the past would climax with the writing of *Under Western Eyes*. Although "Gaspar Ruiz" is set in a South American country (a carryover from *Nostromo*), the politics are a patchwork from Conrad's Polish past, the archetypal political situation for him. Gaspar Ruiz is a man victimized by all political positions; he is himself a man of the people who is sentenced to death by the Republican forces for desertion. His only salvation lies in his alliance with the Royalists, to whom he is antipathetic; but he is loyal to the Royalist girl who houses and tends him when he escapes from the Republicans. In the next stage of his career, he saves a Republican general from death in an earthquake and rises to a prominent position in the province, only to head an uprising against the Republican government. He is supported by the Royalist girl, now his wife, and he fights to the death against the Republicans, his back being broken when it is used as a support for the gun barrel of a cannon.

Like Nostromo, Ruiz is caught between political elements; Nostromo, we recall, helps to support the very social group which would keep him down, and he fights the mob or "rabble" who represent his own class. He then reverses his sympathies and steals from the rich when he recognizes they have only used him, the exploitation of the working class by the owners. Ruiz is in a similar situation, forced to fight for the Royalists against his own class, then used by his class as he rises to responsibility, only to be done in by Republicans as he struggles for his sense of right.

In another ambiguous political story of this period, "The Informer," Conrad uses the office of *The Torch*,* an anarchist journal, for his central scene, the revelation of Sevrin's activities as a police agent. Information about the Rossetti establishment surely came from Ford, who reports, in *Return to Yesterday*, that he met Prince Kropotkin at the office of *The Torch* in Goodge Street. He says that until his aunt's death, she (the wife of William Rossetti) permitted her children to run an anarchist printing press in the basement of her home. Ford then describes a scene that Conrad would try to capture in "The Informer."

> In any case the world was presented with the extraordinary spectacle of the abode of Her Majesty's Secretary to the Inland Revenue [Michael Rossetti], so beset with English detectives, French police spies and Russian *agents provocateurs* that to go along the sidewalk of that respectable terrace was to feel that one ran the gauntlet of innumerable gimlets. That came to an end.

Conrad's anarchist, however, is really no anarchist at all but a secret-police agent; and his true revolutionary, the interior narrator, is himself a man of extreme polish, "in a sense even exquisite. He was alive and European; he had the manner of good society, wore a coat and hat like mine [the teller of the tale] and had pretty near the same taste in cooking." Yet this paragon of manner and appearance is the "greatest rebel (*revolté*) of modern times," a man who expresses contempt for amateur anarchists and mocks the bourgeoisie, saying that " 'an idle and selfish class loves to see mischief being made, even if it is made at its own expense.' "

These words, coming as they do from a man who hides his anarchism behind an impeccable exterior, a man of polish who advocates terror and violence, demonstrate an amazing political sense in Conrad. Such words if

* Not one to let go of anything, he made use of *The Torch* again as one of the "rousing titles" handled in Verloc's shop in *The Secret Agent*. Evidently, the "rousers" were political as well as sexual.

derived from, say, the professor in *The Secret Agent* (himself foreshadowed, incidentally, in this story as a creature engaged "in perfecting some new detonators"), would stem from his own sense of inferiority. But here, in the mouth of the narrator, the words are not attached to a pathological hatred of mankind. They are a cool assessment of man's folly, and they are particularly applicable to a post-industrial society which creates a class whose ennui consumes their lives. Conrad would pick up this same sense of boredom in "Il Conde," a story of late 1906; the Italian youths there who threaten the old count have no interest in his money or goods, but only in terrorizing someone as a pastime. Yet the insight proves even more profound than that; for it suggests on Conrad's part a cynicism about political movements and ideology that goes well beyond contempt for anarchists or hatred of violence. It suggests that all political action moves beneath layers of motives impossible to penetrate, and surely not linear in their progression or development. Politics are matters of class, assumptions about self, leisure time, power plays, far more than they are matters of ideology. They are not connected to ideas, beliefs, or faith, but are concerned with surfaces, roles, acting out. "The Informer," whose manuscript is dated January 11, 1906, was probably started in late 1905, and was published in *Harper's Magazine* a year later, in December 1906.

This, however, is jumping ahead. Back in September, Conrad was preparing the "*Mediterranean* paper," which is, he tells Pinker, "in the oven and shall be served to you hot in a very few days. Meantime *Chance* simmers slowly on to be ready by the end of the year." The Mediterranean paper was his nostalgic piece on the "*Tremolino*" episode, that Odyssean sequence from his youth when he allegedly smuggled contraband with Dominic Cervoni. The episode, which had attained mythical proportions in Conrad's imagination, would recur, as we have seen, on a somewhat different scale in *The Arrow of Gold.* In his *Mirror* version, Conrad gives us an episode quite in keeping with the "mirror" aspect of his book, as a piece of life decorated with reflections of a bygone heroic age. In the "*Tremolino*," Conrad provides a section not included in *The Arrow*, that concerned with the chase of the balancelle by the coastal craft. At close to fifty, ill, harassed, desperately anxious about his career, Conrad catches the magic of being a teenager and seeing nothing but a pattern of one's own ego extending over the entire universe. The final words flit over that mythical episode, as Dominic, the squat Corsican, takes on the hues and colors of our archetypal Odysseus. Man sails because the sea is *there.*

> It seems to me I can see them [Dominic and Odysseus] side by side in the twilight of an arid land, the unfortunate possessors of the secret lore of the sea, bearing the emblem of their hard calling on their shoulders, surrounded by silent and curious men: even as I, too, having turned my back

> upon the sea, am bearing these few pages in the twilight, with the hope of finding in an inland valley the silent welcome of some patient listener.

At the same time, Conrad completed his piece on Lord Nelson of Trafalgar fame, but since he had no way of grasping Nelson except through the latter's devotion to a maritime tradition, the piece is still-born. To Galsworthy, he called it "a 3,000 words utterance," and his feeling for it may have been contained in that phrasing. The "Nelson" piece was strictly a business proposition; for as he wrote Pinker, he wanted his agent to "squeeze out every penny there is in the book form on this side." In this connection, Conrad thought of contracting with Methuen for three novels under a blanket agreement, a move he would eventually make, and regret.

His parallel literary activities—stories for the eventual *Set of Six*, the *Mirror* papers, work on *Chance*, soon the beginning of *The Secret Agent*—were accompanied by social visits by the Hopes, for four days, and the Galsworthys, also for four days. He mentions to Pinker that Shaw has written urging him to do a play, and he feels "more alive" at the notice. Debts continue to pile up, and although he has £115 remaining from his grant, he prefers to ask Pinker for money to repay local tradesmen. When funds were forthcoming, he sends off £5 to Douglas and assures him his career will come along; he offers Ford as an example of someone whose work was kept off the market for three years and his own as sitting in Pinker's drawer for two. He tells Douglas that since his point of view is "intellectual and uncompromising" it is unpopular. "People don't want intelligence. It worries them—and they demand from their writers as much subservience as from their footmen if not rather more."

The middle and late fall of 1905 was another one of those interludes when Conrad puttered along, writing, as he told Wells, "silly short stories in which there is no pleasure and no permanent profit." He was still attempting to make contact with his distinctive voice. He wrote Pinker that his work rests not on its superiority to other writers but on "that of distinction—or say *distinctiveness*." He insisted on that, and what he grappled for was the Conradian style, which slid away when he undertook trivial projects or wrote ephemeral pieces.

In a revealing letter to Wells, to whom he still felt close, he ran through his loss of control, but he did indicate he was working:

> I stick here fighting with disease and creeping imbecility—like a cornered rat, facing fate with a big stick that is sure to descend and crack my skull before many days are over. If I haven't been to see you (which I admit is beastly and ungrateful) I haven't been to see anyone else—except Ford and, of course, the indispensable Pinker, but that only officially—in his office. As to Ford he is a sort of life-long habit of which I am not ashamed because he is a much better fellow than the world gives him credit for.

> After pulling off with an awful effort the first 15,000 words of a thing which is supposed (for trade purposes) to be a novel [*Secret Agent*] I took an afternoon's rush to Winchelsea and back letting the air blow through me: a silly, perhaps, and expensive restorative but the only one left to me. As to working regularly in a decent and orderly and industrious manner I've given that up from sheer impossibility. The damned stuff comes out only by a kind of mental convulsion lasting two three or more days—up to a fortnight—which leaves me perfectly limp and not very happy, exhausted emotionally to all appearance but secretly irritable to the point of savagery.

The frantic tone foreshadowed that pattern of depression and physical breakdown accompanying a new novel. Intermixed with this was Conrad's near-hysteria that the *Evening Standard* deleted a passage from his "Nelson" paper and thus destroyed the sequence of thought. Writing to the editor, Conrad said that no such thing could have occurred if there had been any standard of editing; even the merest hackwork deserved better treatment. His piece, he says, has been "deeply felt and meditated with care." Why, he wonders, did they even print it? He follows this, on October 24, with further animadversions indicating he would have edited the work himself if he had been asked. He accuses them of mangling, and charges off with the statement that such work is probably the usual practice in journalism. The fury and contempt of Conrad's two letters over a minor deletion are not unconnected to his distaste for his role. He loathed everything the *Evening Standard* and popular journalism stood for, and yet he was forced to help fill their pages.

His own chronic ailments, Jessie's palpitations followed by a "nervous breakdown of a sort," shortly afterward Borys's scarlet fever—all of these suggest very strongly a family going out of control, and only holding itself together by way of its common dependencies. Sickness became endemic, each of the three moving in and out of the other's ailments, so that in some form of symbiosis they could survive, paradoxically, by means of their support of each other. The pattern seems to have been established by Conrad—that cycle of illness which gained attention for him in his childhood—and adopted by Jessie and Borys. Surely, Jessie's means of maintaining some place in Conrad's life, which at this time was moving ever deeper into conflicting areas of his imagination, was to make him grapple with her breakdown. In the middle of this, Jessie was to become pregnant (John was born on August 2, 1906). In purely physical terms, with her heart uncertain, her nerves exhausted, her knees still weak, the financial situation desperate, Borys chronically ill, a pregnancy made little sense. But in terms of their emotional dependency and Conrad's withdrawal into areas she could not hope to follow, the pregnancy realigned the family, so to speak, around the traditional values which made survival possible.

Also, Jessie's ailments, whether knee, heart, or nerves, afforded her the rest she could not otherwise accept. Her condition shifted the family fate to Conrad and gave her a respite. In their symbiotic relationship, such additional pressure on Conrad allowed him to tighten his own screw and work better. Of course, the family situation that he was about to describe in *The Secret Agent* would hardly have been comforting to Jessie had she known what he was doing, or, later, had she applied it to her own family. For in that novel, already begun when Jessie became pregnant, was a perverse shattering of the family situation. Conrad was describing a group that cannibalized itself. With their father dead and their mother becoming senile, Winnie becomes the "mother" of her brother and, at the same time, takes on the father's role of holding the group together.

Every family tie is questioned or undermined, and then murder and suicide destroy all except the senile mother at the almshouse. In a figurative sense, Conrad the novelist has eliminated *his* family, which consisted of a much younger wife (as Winnie is with Verloc) and their young child. By making Stevie retarded, Conrad revealed another aspect of hostility, a measure of retribution for the son who must be supported and cared for.

None of this, obviously, is conclusive. But the succession of novels in this period, beginning with *The Secret Agent*, continuing through *Under Western Eyes* and *Chance*, and ending with *Victory*, cannot be ignored in terms of the family situations they display. In each one, the family is in an antagonistic relationship, leading to destructive consequences, and children are themselves "unrelated" to the people who have borne them: Razumov may or may not know his father and his "half sisters"; Flora de Barral is "exiled" by her swindler father; and Axel Heyst has been tutored by his father to form no attachments, meaning marriage and family.

Conrad planned a London visit as a way of gaining some distance on his work. He told Ada Galsworthy Jessie was a little better, and he alone or the family collectively would drop in. He asks her if Galsworthy has seen his "Autocracy and War" in the *Fortnightly*. "I am greatly moved by the news from Russia. [Following the defeat by Japan, Russia suffered through a revolution in which about one thousand workers were killed by the police on January 22.] Certainly a year ago I never hoped to live to see all that. It's just ½ a century since the Crimean war, forty-two years since the liberation of peasants—a great civic work in which even we Poles were allowed to participate. In the words of my uncle's memoirs this great event opened the way to a general reform of the state. Very few minds saw it at the time. And yet the starting point of orderly rational program in accord with the national spirit was there!"

With that, Conrad went up to London alone, missed Galsworthy, and returned to the Pent with a poisonous attack of gout. He remained in bed. The Conrads would return to London on November 15—so that Jessie could consult with her doctors about her breakdown—staying first at 36, Princess

Square and then at 32, St. Agnes Place in Kensington. The latter address was necessary so that they could be near Borys, who was seriously ill with scarlet fever and isolated at the London Nurses' Association, in Kensington. As Conrad wrote Wells: "This closes the account of the current calamities. What's to come next I can't imagine and don't try to. No doubt it will be bad enough when it does come."

Borys's scarlet fever developed dysenteric complications, and that, in turn, led to slight kidney trouble, but the condition eventually cleared. Conrad then took to his bed in December and, spurred by disaster, churned out a good deal of copy, the aforementioned "Informer" and the final version of "Gaspar Ruiz," as well as the story "An Anarchist." He wrote Galsworthy on December 26 that he would start another short story, which would be "The Informer," with the anarchist story already completed, at least in its first version. Although working well, he told Galsworthy he felt "helplessness with the bitter sense of the lost days that I stand in fear of," what he identified as a powerlessness of body and anguish of mind. As he turned to stories, he had the manuscript of *Chance* unfinished; the manuscript of *The Rescue* unfinished; the manuscript of "Verloc" (*The Secret Agent*) barely begun; a Mediterranean novel in mind, but fading. He was working, it is true, but the main arena went unattended. He closed out 1905 telling Galsworthy (on December 29) that "what cuts me to the quick is the forced deterioration of my work produced hastily, carelessly in a temper of desperation. There is no remedy for that."

"An Anarchist" has the germ of an idea, but lacks the careful development necessary for its realization. It is a hasty, careless piece of work, as Conrad himself observed. Particularly troubling for Conrad in these middle-period stories were his opening pages, in which his struggles to achieve narrative definition could be quite amateurish. Several pages are devoted to establishing the internal story by means of a narrator who is also a lepidopterist, and who is, in turn, surrounded by names and places none of which means anything in the tale. Conrad has all the paraphernalia of an intricately worked piece without the necessary development; when we finally arrive at the anarchist's story, we have futilely struggled upstream.

The so-called anarchist of the tale is an engineer victimized by a ludicrous society. Drunk one day, shouting anarchist slogans, he is arrested, defended by a socialist lawyer who says his client was victimized by society, and the young engineer, a stalwart bourgeois, is sentenced to prison. After his return, he is refused work, falls in with some anarchists, is convicted of bank robbery and sentenced to the penal colony at Cayenne. He escapes and shoots two of the men with whom he had been associated, and now, when the narrator meets him, he is working for a pittance on a cattle farm, tucked away out of sight of all mankind.

Like so many other Conradian attitudes toward political radicals, the views here are ambiguous, full of authorial hesitations and uncertainties. While Conrad's sympathies are with Paul the engineer, he cannot help but find his plight ludicrous. Indeed, Paul is victimized—the story is set in almost purely Zolaesque terms—and yet he is victimized only because of his own foolishness. Although he denies being an anarchist, there is anarchy in him, as in all men. The narrator's conclusion suggests Conrad's dilemma, a dilemma he would catch in *The Secret Agent*, where the police and the radical element derive from the same basket. In "An Anarchist":

> On the whole, my idea is that he was much more of an anarchist than he confessed to me or to himself; and that, the special features of his case apart, he was very much like many other anarchists. Warm heart and weak head—that is the word of the riddle; and it is a fact that the bitterest contradictions and the deadliest conflicts of the world are carried on in every individual breast capable of feeling and passion.

Since the words seem destined for a far more profound story, we can only conclude that Conrad was already full of "Verloc," where the substance of the passage applies.

On January 1, Conrad indicated that the "Informer," now finished, would be handed over on the next day, and he would like it to be entitled "Gestures." He was in the process of delivering Jessie to the Pent, then returning to London for Borys on Wednesday, January 3. Meanwhile, the latter had developed new symptoms, high fever, swollen hands and feet, rapid pulse. Conrad speaks of being put off "the end of my long Anarch. story," meaning "Verloc," whose length he miscalculated as of story size. On February 21, in fact, writing from Montpellier, Conrad indicated that Pinker would be receiving the "balance of *Verloc*" in the course of a week. "Don't imagine," he soothed the hard-pressed agent, "that the story'll be unduly long. It may be longer than the Brute [8,000 words] but not very much so. What has delayed me was just trying to put a *short turn* into it. I think I've got it. I've not done anything to Chance of course." By March 2, Conrad admitted that "Verloc is extending. It's no good fighting against. It would take too much time. Anyway I think the story is good. And you may tell people also that it is authentic enough."

That Conrad began "Verloc" as a short story and then lengthened it out must be seen in the perspective of both his literary and financial needs. Like so many of his other stories that turned into novels, it was aimed at Pinker, who preferred short fiction for rapid sale. Conrad had to hide or disguise his intentions from his agent, simply as a means of survival: to gain money for copy without discouraging Pinker completely. For it is virtually impossible to find a "short story" cut-off point for "Verloc," if we assume Conrad really meant to do that. One of the technical advances of this novel over Conrad's earlier work is, in fact, its seamlessness. By March 5, Conrad was speaking of it as coming to 18,000 words or so, but that length was also improbable.

CHAPTER 25

"The Pit of Babel"

The Secret Agent came to him, he says in his Author's Note, "in the shape of a few words uttered by a friend in a casual conversation about anarchists or rather anarchist activities." Conrad tells us that in the period following the writing of *Nostromo* and the sketches for the *Mirror*, he was peculiarly open to other voices: "It was a period, too, in which my sense of the truth of things was attended by a very intense imagination and emotional readiness which, all genuine and faithful to facts as it was, yet made me feel (the task once done) as if I were left behind, aimless amongst mere husks of sensations and lost in a world of other, of inferior, values."

He had been, in a sense, carried outside himself by the imaginative effort, and we can equate that "ecstasy" to the fact that the novel embodied many of his most intimate sensations and secret beliefs. He continues that his friend (Ford) "recalled the already old story of the attempt to blow up the Greenwich Observatory [the Greenwich Bomb Outrage of February 15, 1894]; a blood-stained inanity of so fatuous a kind that it was impossible to fathom its origin by any reasonable or even unreasonable process of thought . . . so that one remained faced by the fact of a man blown to bits for nothing even more remotely resembling an idea, anarchist or other. As to the outer wall of the Observatory it did not show as much as the faintest crack."

Conrad recalls further that the friend said: " 'Oh, that fellow [Martial Bourdin] was half an idiot.* His sister committed suicide afterwards.' " Following this conversation, Conrad indicates that about a week later he came upon a book "which as far as I know had never attained any prominence, the rather summary recollections of an Assistant Commissioner of Police." This was a reference to Robert Anderson's *Sidelights on the Home Rule Movement;* Anderson had been appointed to his post, Conrad tells us, at the time of the "dynamite outrages in London, away back in the eighties," and not

* Eliot in "Animula" put it more wittily: "Pray for Guiterriez, avid of speed and power, / For Bourdin, blown to pieces, / For this one who made a great fortune, / And that one who went his own way."

unusually some of his activity was connected to Fenian conspiracies against England.

With these "sources" in mind, Conrad evidently planned something of story length concerning only Verloc as a double agent involved in the Greenwich bomb attempt. The piece was, as we know, originally called "Verloc," and Winnie's role assumes larger proportions only as the novel proceeds. Yet once again we are confronted by mysteries. For not only is there no apparent place at which Conrad could have halted for story length, the very materials that he outlines in the Author's Note suggest an extended development. The use Conrad made of the Greenwich incident required a considerable amount of preparation artistically; that is, he could not possibly derive the irony, even the grimly comic overtones of the theme, from the novel without sufficient backgrounding. The irony, which sets the tone from the opening page, depends on a panoply of events and personages. Verloc's attempt with the bomb, for example, is only meaningful in terms of his relationship to Vladimir, the Embassy person,* the relationship of the bombing to the antianarchist conference in Milan, his attachment to Winnie and Stevie, her brother, and, finally, his connection to the anarchists themselves and to the police.

Although Conrad's use of his sources is slight, nevertheless, the Greenwich Bomb Outrage at the heart was a particularly brilliant move. In a sense, it embodied in miniature Conrad's "political sense," his imaginative feel for how political ideas work and are carried out. In actuality, he probably did not need Ford to recall the incident for him, for he was himself in London, at 17, Gillingham Street, working on his first novel, when the bomb attempt was made by Martial Bourdin on February 15. Important details that Conrad later used, reported in the newspapers on February 16, included the mutila-

* Commenting on the completed novel to Graham, Conrad was very pleased his friend liked it: "It had some importance to me as a new departure in *genre* and as a sustained effort in ironical treatment of a melodramatic subject—which was my technical intention." Conrad goes on to provide another source: "Mr Vladimir was suggested to me by that scoundrel Gen: Seliwertsow whom Padlewski shot (in Paris) in the nineties. Perhaps you will remember as there were peculiar circumstances in that case." (Seliwertsow was a Russian agent living in Paris, and it was thought the French police were anxious to protect the assassin, Padlewski, who was either hidden by them or done away with.) Then Conrad zeroes in on what must have been a disclaimer from Graham, who did not satirize revolutionaries and anarchists: "But I don't think that I've been satirizing the revolutionary world. All these people are not revolutionaries—they are shams. And as regards the Professor I did not intend to make him despicable. He is incorruptible at any rate. In making him say 'madness and despair—give me that for a lever and I will move the world' I wanted to give the note of perfect sincerity. At the worst he is a megalomaniac of an extreme type. And every extremist is respectable. I am extremely flattered to have secured your commendation for my Secretary of State and for the revolutionary Toddles. It was very easy there (for me) to go utterly wrong."

tion of the perpetrator (although Bourdin was not instantly killed), the discovery of a container that had held the explosive, with the supposition that the victim had fallen with the bottle in hand, and the physical resemblance between Bourdin and Stevie—both slight and fair.

Conrad would not have remembered these details eleven years later when he began the novel, but he would certainly have recalled the bomb attempt and may have researched the episode in the British Museum. But whatever the nature of the sources, the event was the thing, and its particular significance for Conrad was, surely, its futility. From Conrad's viewpoint, the episode had involved planning, daring, some personal courage, human imbecility, deception, savage indifference to institutions and human life—and they all added up to Babel. As his comment to Graham in 1907 indicates, Conrad was interested in seeing the "world as anarchy," as a gigantic circus given over to acts of futility. His vision was of a nightmare perpetrated by those who wished to effect change. "By jove!" he told Graham, "if I had the necessary talent I would like to go for the true anarchist—which is the millionaire. Then you would see the venom flow. But it's too big a job."

All the world as a place of anarchy—every act as an act of disorder—every attempt at control a move toward chaos: Conrad's intuition of events foreshadowed the destruction of a generation in the First World War. More than Verloc or Winnie, the Professor is Conrad's true creation, a type that lay so deeply encapsulated within his psyche from earliest days that he is a fulfillment of a sort. His "incorruptible" nature—he is the revolutionary ascetic without libidinal ties—makes him the potential ruler of a technological and egalitarian society. Conrad describes him as a man who keeps his fingers around a detonator set deep in his pocket, a creature who gives everyone twenty seconds to change his mind.

We first saw the Professor in "The Informer," in a minor role as an experimenter with explosives who worked in a laboratory at the top of the slightly disguised Rossetti house. In *The Secret Agent,* he has one of the main roles, just beneath Verloc and Winnie, on a par with Heat and the Assistant Commissioner, but well beyond the other anarchists, who remain shadowy and thirdhand. The Professor has founded his significance on people's fear of him because of the detonator he carries in his pocket: " 'I have the means to make myself deadly, but that by itself, you understand, is absolutely nothing in the way of protection. What is effective is the belief those people have in my will to use the means. That's their impression. It is absolute. Therefore I am deadly.' "

The Professor's willingness to kill himself for the sake of his idea, to prove the source of his strength, is quite distinct from, say, Kirilov's suicidal impulse in Dostoevsky's *The Possessed.* While superficially similar, the impulses derive from differing ideologies. Kirilov's "suicide" is based on his desire to be free; if he can end his life whenever he wishes, he is free of all social entanglements, free, indeed, of the restrictions of mortality. The Professor, however, wishes to rule the world, and the perfect detonator, if he could invent it, would be his means. He is, despite his puny appearance, Nietzsche's "*Übermensch*," and he has replaced "inner will" with his control of a deadly weapon. He will, as he recognizes, rule others through their fear of him. Conrad's vision of the future is far more disturbing than Dostoevsky's, since Kirilov is not a threat; he is a lunatic of the inner world, whereas the Professor is a maniac of the outer.

Further, the Professor is a creature of small accomplishment, his inferior position giving him a sense of his superiority. "His struggles, his privations [Conrad writes], his hard work to raise himself in the social scale, had filled him with an exalted conviction of his merits so that it was extremely difficult for the world to treat him with justice." Ordinary, intellectually a nonentity (as Ossipon realizes), the Professor lacks all accomplishment except his one maniacal idea; and this sense of self-aggrandizement is, for Conrad, a profound political force. Not only is the Professor's use of the explosive device a means to political power, but his plan allows him to displace his normally deficient sexual power to an area where it can function effectively. In his pocket, he grasps "lightly the india-rubber ball, the supreme guarantee of his sinister freedom." His politics, in Conrad's prophetic interpretation, are all connected to his personal problems. He is not responding to the world's ills, but to his own. He is, like the rest of mankind, seeking "the peace of soothed vanity, of satisfied appetites, or perhaps of appeased conscience."

His devotion to an idea isolates him, but it also fortifies his sense of superiority. Solitude defines his personal world; he lives in cubbies and holes. But solitude for such a creature is not inhibiting; it is strengthening. ". . . with severe exultation the Professor thought of the refuge of his room with its padlocked cupboard, lost in a wilderness of poor houses, the hermitage of the perfect anarchist." He haunts narrow and dark alleys, dusky streets, gloomy avenues. He is a creature of shadows, an escapee from a Gothic melodrama; and yet he is, not unexpectedly, somewhat like the writer or artist, the man who holds potential destruction in his hand or fist as he pursues his solitudinous occupation, the sole way in which he can control his world. We know that when Conrad suffered from severe gout, he grasped in his fist an oversized pencil, and the image of the Professor grasping that rubber ball which will detonate the explosion is not lost upon us.

Because the Professor moves along these shadows, he upsets that delicate balance which exists between the police and the criminal class. Each, in a normal situation, has an intuitive sense of the other; they share the extremes of society. As Conrad says: "Both recognize the same conventions, and have a working knowledge of each other's methods and of the routine of their respective trades." But the Professor, as Chief Inspector Heat recognizes, does not play that game; he is unpredictable, or else, too predictable. With his

Nietzschean hatred of all middle-class values, he destroys the very idea of the police, whose effectiveness is limited to a criminal class with bourgeois motives.

Yet the Professor is more than a self-serving destroyer of mankind, more than the man who seeks the extermination of the rabble as a form of progress: he is also the voice of an ultimate despair. His feeling for Ossipon is one of "amicable contempt," which is the closest he can come to a feeling or a connection; and yet Conrad cannot dismiss the words he has put into the Professor's mouth. In a somewhat limited sense, the anarchist reflects Conrad's own contempt for the mediocre, for the loss of nerve and vitality, for a world that has become passionless. As we weigh the Professor's most notable speech, we can judge how close it comes to Conrad's own distaste for the modern, the progressive, the new:

> "All passion is lost now. The world is mediocre, limp, without force. And madness and despair are a force. And force is a crime in the eyes of the fools, the weak and the silly who rule the roost. You are mediocre. Verloc, whose affair the police has managed to smother so nicely, was mediocre. And the police murdered him. He was mediocre. Everybody is mediocre. Madness and despair! Give me that for a lever, and I'll move the world. Ossipon, you have my cordial scorn. You are incapable of conceiving even what the fat-fed citizen would call a crime. You have no force."

The depth of passion in *The Secret Agent* can be measured by Conrad's insight into his own feelings. In putting some of his own beliefs into the mouth of a detestable creature, turning all that into irony, and yet insisting on the truth (partial or not) of the utterance, he has confronted those very forces in his own psyche which his early experiences had left. All his conscious contempt for maniacal political activity is there; and yet he can comprehend the impulse that makes the Professor seethe. In a world without passion, craft, or values, mediocrity rules and men like the Professor become prophets.

All this, however, was later. At the beginning of the new year, Conrad was struggling with a rudimentary manuscript entitled "Verloc" (the name retained through the entire manuscript) and a very ill Borys, now back at the Pent with a nurse in attendance. All of this was accompanied by a "desperate fit of gout" right through the end of the old year. Borys's most recent illness, it turned out, resulted from Lysol, which had come in contact with his skin and swelled him up, causing purple blotches to appear all over his body. "Gaspar Ruiz," in the meantime, was sold to *Pall Mall Magazine* for £126, where it would be serialized from July to October 1906. Conrad was, once again, in a publishing lull, except for the occasional sketches of *The Mirror of the Sea.* That book was shaping up not as a series of short pieces but as a continuous book: "My idea [he wrote Pinker] is of a sort of reminiscent discourse running on like this: I. II. III IV etc etc XX XXI and so on, with no titles or blank or half blank pages between; something, in short, like poor Gissing's Ryecroft papers; and only the headings at the top of pages being changed according to the matter created." Conrad's method, which was mainly followed, was exceptionally shrewd as a way of getting around the unmarketability of short pieces or even short stories. A continuous book, even his, stood some chance of sales.

With the *Mirror* to be fixed in final form and with "Verloc" in hand, the Conrads left for Montpellier for the rest of the winter. All three had been seriously ill, and Jessie was, in addition, pregnant. As Conrad told Rothenstein: "I particularly don't want to go to pieces just now." He knew well the balancing act, which he would follow for the rest of his writing career, that interchange between work produced and illness or breakdown. By the thirteenth of February, they were settled in the imposing Riche Hotel and Continental amid a Montpellier scene of carnival and political rioting, a Mediterranean ambiance: "In the same street troops, infantry and cavalry drawn up in front of churches, yells, shrieks, blows—people with broken heads carried into chemist's shops, and through it all bands of costumed and masked revellers pushing with songs and ribald jokes." Conrad would use this or a similar experience for the background in Marseilles, when Monsieur George returns from his failed exploit, in *The Arrow.* Amidst the rioting, Conrad turned in thirteen pages of "Verloc" to Pinker on February 21, assuring his agent that a good deal more existed and he need not fear that the Capri fiasco would be repeated.

The long haul to finish an "unexpected" novel was now on. With Pinker forewarned, Conrad moved to have further debts reduced by his agent. He was clearing his decks, trying to settle down with a reasonably clear mind before Jessie gave birth in August. He tells Pinker: "For all my efforts at economy I find the money goes quicker than I expected," and adds that the sole luxury he has permitted is riding lessons for Borys, a point Conrad could reveal because Pinker was himself an avid horseman. By early March, "Verloc" had grown to 18,000 words. Conrad broke his concentration in mid-March to write a review of Galsworthy's *Man of Property* for *Outlook.** By then, *Mirror* was heading into proofs with Methuen.

* Conrad's attitudes toward the fiction of his friends is of considerable interest, since his methods and theirs were to diverge in this decade from 1900 to 1910. His review of Galsworthy's *Man of Property* was favorable, as expected, but it was aimed at creating market interest in his friend's work, not as a literary analysis. In a long letter to Galsworthy, on April 9, he tried to circumvent that omission, an omission, we suspect, attached to his lack of enthusiasm. He took the high road of flattery: "I reflected that the *quality* of your book was too high to be affected by false admirations." He judges Galsworthy's efforts as an "excellent and faithful unity" which can be compared "in some respects to *Don Quixote* and something that even Balzac did not have." But Conrad admitted he left out such reflections from the article because he chose to be "wise with a worldly and journalistic wisdom."

At the end of March, Conrad was well into harness and predicting the end of "Verloc," at which time he planned to work exclusively on *Chance.* By early April, he began to admit that "Verloc" was a "damnably complicated job." Conrad had great insight into his material, telling Pinker: "It is easy with a subject like this to produce a totally false impression. Moreover the thing has got to be *kept up as a story* with an ironic intention but a dramatic development." He mentions that a "short thing (about a bomb in a hotel) will be ready this month," and he expected to use "Verloc" and that story for a new volume of short fiction: "Gaspar Ruiz," "The Brute" (completed December–January), "An Anarchist," "The Informer," and the two new pieces, with "Verloc," coming to 180,000 words. The "hotel story" does not appear to have been written.

Creeping in was a melancholy note: production of copy was down, as if he were "powerless in an exhaustion of thought and will." Days flitted by without anything: ". . . these days without a line, nay, without a word, the hard, atrocious, agonizing days are simply part of my *method* of work, a decreed necessity of my production." He profoundly questions who and what he is: "I doubt [he told Galsworthy] not only my talent (I was never so sure of that) but my character. Is it indolence—which in my case would be nothing short of baseness—or what? No man has a right to go on as I am doing without producing manifest masterpieces. It seems I've no excuse under heaven or on earth."

Leaving for the Pent on April 16, the Conrads spent three weeks at home and then took over Ford's house in Winchelsea, on May 11. They stayed for two weeks, but according to Jessie's reminiscences of the time there were considerable tensions whenever Ford appeared. Of course, she disliked his bohemianism and indifference to her orderly manner of running the house, but also, he appeared to her a threat: "The two long week-ends that F.M.H. had stipulated he should come down were the longest I have ever known, and a fit punishment for any sins I might have ever committed, or even contemplated." Even allowing for her pregnancy and the delicacy of the Conrad finances, sufficient reasons to make her edgy and poutish, her hostility to Ford seems based on her need to consider Conrad her own, or else to justify her privations by measuring Conrad's dependence on her. Ford unquestionably interceded, leading Conrad from her, and then showing superiority to both. She speaks of Ford's tenacious hold on those he found of interest, and his use of such people as long as they were fascinated with him. Jessie sees this stay, however, as the beginning of the divergences between Conrad and Ford, and she attributes some of this to the introduction of Arthur Marwood, who "usurped a place completely in my husband's regard and esteem."

Marwood properly belongs more to the Ford biography than to Conrad's, especially since only two letters from Conrad to Marwood have turned up. That they saw each other frequently would partially explain the paucity of correspondence, although it is likely some was suppressed. On Ford's part, Marwood ended up as a partial model for Christopher Tietjens in Ford's quartet of novels known as *Parade's End* and, very possibly, served as a measure for Edward Ashburnham in *The Good Soldier*. Nevertheless, he moved sufficiently within Conrad's life that Jessie could write:

> I have used this extract [in which Conrad, in connection with his novel *Victory*, had called Marwood "the real Wise man of the Age"] . . . to show that this friend had a great and beneficial effect upon my husband's whole conception of his work, and that the intimacy between the two men, so widely different in temperament and views, was a stimulus, generally. . . . His reason was always so calm and considered, his understanding so clear, that his companionship could not but help such an artist as Joseph Conrad. Moreover, my husband would always accept his criticism, if not exactly without argument, at least with a reasoned and considered one. I can trace Arthur Marwood's influence in most of the books written during the period of his close friendship.

According to Jessie, Marwood came to know the Conrads just a month before the birth of John, on August 2. Arthur Pierson Marwood came from an English family, in Yorkshire, that could trace its roots back to William the Conqueror's survey of English lands in the Domesday Book. Educated as a mathematician at Trinity College, Marwood possessed a literary as well as a legal intelligence. He became an expert in English Tory law, and in *The English Review*, which he helped to subsidize to the tune of £2,000, he published "Actuarial Scheme for Insuring John Doe against all the Vicissitudes of Life," a plan, incidentally, that prefigured the Douglas Credit Scheme of Ezra Pound. As the title indicates, he had a serene, rather than a nervous, intelligence, and he was in this respect the precise opposite of his two friends, Ford and Conrad. In later years, when *The English Review* was under way and Ford and Violet Hunt had become lovers, Marwood became entangled in the Ford-Hueffer circus; Elsie accused him of making advances. Marwood had, the previous year, in 1908, paid 400 guineas for an operation Elsie underwent, and he was, financially, part owner of the Fords' lives. It was these charges and countercharges, in 1909, three years after Conrad first met Marwood, that led to the final break between Conrad and Ford; in the ensuing melee, Conrad in fact sided with Marwood. How far the claims of Elsie were true and how much they were based on a desire to regain her husband, we cannot say.

In the spring of 1906, Conrad was asked by Methuen to comment on his own work, with *The Mirror of the Sea* in particular in mind. In his response, Conrad tried to avoid self-serving publicity:

> Any definition of one's work must be either very intimate or very superficial. There is only one man [Garnett?] to whom I could open my confi-

dence on that extremely elusive matter without the fear of being misunderstood. The intention of temperamental writing is infinitely complex, and to talk about my work is repugnant to me—beyond anything. And what could I say that would be of use to you? I may say that the book is an imaginative rendering of a reminiscent mood. This is a sort of definition and it is true enough in a way. But the book is also a record of a phase, now nearly vanished, of a certain kind of activity, sympathetic to the inhabitants of this Island.

In June, Conrad made plans to go to London, for two months, from the eleventh of July to the tenth of September, when they would take over the Galsworthys' house in Addison Road for the period of Jessie's confinement and recovery. Conrad had promised the Pent during his absence to Dr. Tebb, the physician for his entire circle, but when Tebb could not take it, he offered it to Rothenstein and his family. In a long letter to Rothenstein, Conrad described the house in some detail and in so doing provided some insight into the routine he and his family followed. Particularly striking about Conrad's presentation of the house is how closely it fitted into what he experienced at sea: a good deal of natural beauty with few comforts or conveniences.

There is within three miles a magnificent aspect of the marsh—the great Romney Marsh: a miracle of colour at times. There are nooks in the folds of the Downs that wait for a "seeing" eye—little lost homesteads, stack-yards around churches and the beautiful lines of the uplands. And within the house there is one well lighted room with a northern exposure where you could set up your easel for indoor work.

The house itself you know. Five bedrooms above, two and the long kitchen below—with everything needful in it except *the bed sheets* which we take up to London. Stove's in good order—water first rate and no possible smells to affect the chicks; with the wooden house (where you worked at my head) for them to play in when they are tired of the fields.

A good-natured ass called Andrews stays in *our* service to clean knives, boots, light kitchen stove in the morning, fetch water from well, give information, and drive the trap which holds four with a kiddy or two thrown in.

I think that with one servant Alice could do but there's plenty of room for two girls. . . .

There would be no difficulty to provision the ship. . . .

The sanitary arrang^{ts} are primitive as you know; and there is no bathroom—but the good natured ass above mentioned is trained to carry hot and cold water upstairs and in due course to empty the sponge baths. There is also a tin bath suitable for baby.

Borys Conrad, in his autobiographical memoir, reminisces about his early days at the Pent, listing the visitors—the Hopes, Galsworthy (Uncle Jack), Edward Garnett, Ford Madox Ford (whom Borys was not fond of),

H. G. Wells, Cunninghame Graham, Henry James, the Dawson brothers (Ernest and A.J., not Francis Warrington), and William Rothenstein. The pace of the house could not have been so desperate as Conrad made it seem, for Borys fills his pages with pleasant memories, such as the following:

> There was one friend in particular whose occasional visits always delighted me—William Rothenstein who, within a few minutes of his arrival, would be squatting on the floor with my box of paints producing the most charming watercolour sketches of my many mechanical toys and of myself operating them. In later years I had several of these framed and hung them on the walls of my bedroom where they remained until they eventually disintegrated.

There was, in addition, great interest in animals—the dog Escamillo (after the character in one of Conrad's favorite operas, *Carmen*), cats, moorhens, stackyard mice, two white owls, a horse—but, most of all, in motorcars, which intrigued both Conrad and his young son. Borys would later become engaged professionally in the motorcar industry, after his discharge from service in the First World War.

On July 10, the Conrads took over the Galsworthy house, with the owners providing every possible comfort for them, including servants. On August 2, John (named after Galsworthy) Alexander Conrad Korzeniowski was born; Conrad described him to Ada Galsworthy as "quiet, unassuming extremely ugly but upon the whole a rather sympathetic young man. . . . Altogether I think already that he will be quite a valuable acquisition for our little circle." And to Marguerite Poradowska, Conrad said he already felt "a good deal of friendship" for the addition to the family. Borys, in his excitement, offered "half his dog" to his new brother, an indication of the "perfect harmony" reigning in the family. Conrad repeated these same sentiments, even the same words, to the Wellses, Norman Douglas, Harriet Capes, the Rothensteins, Elsie Hueffer, and Count Szembek.

But wedged behind the pleasantries was Conrad's "real world," that "trickle of silly fiction" which he was trying to squeeze "out of a dry, sawdusty brain," as he wrote Harriet Capes. To Jane Wells, announcing the birth, Conrad indicated he expected to complete his anarchist story ("Verloc") quickly, "which with two others (short) is to form a special volume," to be dedicated to Wells. But he felt the stories lacked "quality" and were superficial in terms of view and feeling; and therefore, he might postpone the dedication to Wells until *Chance* was finished. Of interest is the fact that "Verloc"—only two months from the beginning of serialization in *Ridgeway's; a Militant Weekly for God and Country*—was still part of a plan to be published in a volume of stories. To the Galsworthys, he wrote of himself as a "caged squirrel in his wheel—tired out in the evening and no progress made." He tells of the desire to retreat from it all: "I feel as if I should like to sit down for a couple of years and meditate in the skyscraping wigwams of the unpainted savages of the grrreat continent"—the reference was to Ford now in America.

Back at the Pent at the beginning of September, Conrad responded to Galsworthy's reading of "Verloc" in manuscript, first discounting it as "but *a tale,*" the whole thing so far superficial. Galsworthy had apparently objected to the ironic mode and to the naturalistic style, what Conrad called "Zola jargon." But Conrad's defense of the first 45,000 words is of interest, turning it into a kind of entertainment:

> I had no idea to consider Anarchism politically—or to treat it seriously in its philosophical aspect: as a manifestation of human nature in its discontent and imbecility. The general reflections whether right or wrong are not meant as bolts. You can't say I *hurl* them in any sense. They come in by the way and are not applicable to particular instances—Russian or Latin. They are—if anything—mere digs at the people in the tale. As to attacking anarchism as a form of humanitarian enthusiasm or intellectual despair or social atheism, that—if it were worth doing—would be the work for a more vigorous hand and for a mind more robust, and perhaps more honest than mine.

This is disingenuous, for Conrad had worked up his materials rather carefully, culling his factual basis from several sources. Writing to Sir Algernon Methuen two months later, while calling *The Secret Agent "purely a work of imagination,"* Conrad said it was "based on the inside knowledge of a certain event in history"—not only the 1894 Greenwich Bomb Outrage but very possibly a pamphlet by David Nicoll written in 1897. Conrad's information, if we are to follow some accounts, was fairly well detailed, including insight into the relationship between Martial Bourdin, the man blown up in the explosion, and his brother-in-law, H. B. Samuels, an editor of an anarchist paper. It is always difficult to determine how much Conrad actually knew of any source—and he was later to deny even this knowledge*—and how much was simply glancing information which he immediately adapted to the needs of his imagination. But in this instance, it seems clear that he had some working knowledge of anarchist activity, whether the result of double agents, Fenian exploits, or his sense of Polish insurrectionists against the Russian occupation. The novel itself, we recall, takes place in 1886, so that Conrad's ambiance is of a period of considerable anarchist activity in Eng-

* To Ambrose Barker, for example, he denied even the most rudimentary information: "As a matter of fact I never knew anything of what was called, if I remember rightly, the 'Greenwich Bomb Outrage.' I was out of England when it happened, and thus I never read what was printed in the newspapers at the time. All I was aware of was the mere fact—my novel being, in intention, the history of Winnie Verloc. I hope you have seen that the purpose of the book was *not* to attack any doctrine, or even the men holding that doctrine. My object, apart from the aim of telling a story, was to hold up the worthlessness of certain individuals and the baseness of some others. It was a matter of great interest to me to see how near actuality I managed to come in a work of imagination."

land and abroad, and he could incorporate into his categories those who were actually anarchists and those, like Ossipon and Michaelis, who are confidence men, swindlers, dreamers, or angels.

Yet Conrad needed to insist on the purely imaginative nature of his work. To Methuen, he wrote that the novel—which, by November 7, when the serial had already begun, he estimates will be 68,000 words—has "no social or philosophical intention." He admits, however, it may have some "moral significance." *The Secret Agent* may have had other aspects as well; that is, beyond its apparent themes of marital disharmony, hostility, intense antagonism, murder, it had intimations of Conrad's sense of his old friendships, hints of a ragtag band of writers, reflected as anarchists and revolutionaries who pull against each other. This is speculative, but *The Secret Agent* and the next novel, *Under Western Eyes*, are so ironical in terms of human relationships and social ties that the reader is encouraged to make some extraliterary associations. The relationship with Ford, despite work on their final collaborative effort, *The Nature of a Crime*, was deteriorating because of the latter's personal life; and the literary relationship with Wells was weakening because of the divergence of their ways. The fact that Conrad elaborately dedicated *The Secret Agent* to Wells in 1907* would indicate a desire to hold on to his early admirer even when he felt otherwise.

By 1906, the correspondence with Wells had diminished significantly, but not because of an increase in personal conversation. Conrad, in fact, appears to have made the chief effort to keep the association going, praising Wells's latest novel, *Kipps*, in extravagant terms, although the novel was not his kind of thing. Both Conrad and Henry James had written Wells about *Kipps*, and it is of some interest to contrast their remarks: Conrad staying within the limits of praise, but James doing the kind of critical ballet that was a masterpiece of disguise. Our reason for focusing on *Kipps* here is literary, not personal. Both Conrad and Wells were writing deeply Dickensian novels at this time; Kipps recalls Pip of *Great Expectations*, and *The Secret Agent* is, in its view of London at least, Conrad's *Bleak House*. First, Conrad, on November 25:

> Upon a mental review of your career, my dear Wells, I am forced to the conclusion that both kinds of your work are strangely and inexplicably underestimated. Praise of course there is in plenty but its quality is not

* It is not simply the fact of the dedication that catches our eye, but the nature of the dedication, an attempt on Conrad's part to recapture their best days—an indication that he recognized the end was near: "To / H. G. Wells / The Chronicler of Mr. Lewisham's Love / The Biographer of Kipps and / The Historian of the Ages to Come / This Simple Tale of the XIX Century / is affectionately inscribed." Conrad continues: "I submit the above to your approval. If it's withheld for some reason, well then, the simple H. G. Wells will do. But pray observe that in this definition I have stated what the perfect novelist should be—Chronicler, Biographer and Historian."

worthy of you. And even the attacks of which one would expect more comprehension do nothing but nibble at the hem of the mantle. The cause of this (setting aside the superiority of your intelligence) it would be curious to investigate and on those lines a fundamental sort of study upon H. G. Wells could be written. I wish I could liberate my tongue-tied soul. But perhaps what I could find to say if it ever came out could be as disappointing to you as it would be to myself.

Coming to the particular case of the latest book I must say here this at least: that the high expectation roused instantaneously as it were by the sight of the 4th or 5th instalment in the P.M.G. [*Pall Mall Gazette*] is fulfilled to every limit of possibility. The book my dear fellow is simply admirable in its justness and its justice in its human and humane quality. Nothing you have written before has approached such perfect proportion or revealed the delicacy of treatment of which you are capable, so well. I would say infinitely more but must end now with most affectionate congratulations.

In brief, vagueness that passes for praise. Conrad returned to laud the book on September 15, 1906, when he received a copy of the completed novel. He speaks of Wells's "harsh and earnest youth" as quite a creation: "in intensity and lucidity a step beyond your other creations. . . . I am as yet under the sheer power of your art—the compulsion of it." But he does have objections, which he says he is too muddle-headed to state, "futile objections" to "matters treated of in this book." James wrote Wells on November 19: "He [Kipps] is not so much a masterpiece as a mere born gem—you having, I know not how, taken a header straight down into mysterious depths of observation and knowledge, I know not which and where, and come up again with this rounded pearl of the diver." James distinguishes Wells from Dickens, who romantically interfered with the lower middle class he handled, a crime, also, of George Eliot; further, Wells has provided a "consistently ironic or satiric novel" in the style of Thackeray, but, once again, without his authorial interference. James skirts the problem of content, of development, and limits his remarks to treatment, his own preoccupation at this date, when *The Golden Bowl* was being published in England (two years after its publication in America).

Wells himself responded only briefly to Conrad, one letter extant in 1906, and that chiefly to tell Conrad that *The Mirror of the Sea* is a "fine book . . . [it places] the sea under my eyes most wonderfully. I shall for all my life be the wiser for it. I see better as I go to and fro. My many thanks." By this time, the two writers were completely divergent in their aims. What could be further from Wells's dream of a utopian society based on a logical machinery supervised by an elite of dedicated "priests" than Conrad's scenes of domestic disenchantment and his presentation of city life as the microcosm of a failing England? Like Dickens's London in *Bleak House*, with its fogs and its streets of death, Conrad's London is filled with broken people who have lost all hope or people whose hopes are founded on conspiracy and deception. Both Wells and Conrad faced social and political disintegration resulting from industrial development, but while Conrad was content to analyze its decadent aspects, Wells conceived of resolutions tied to the purifying powers of an apocalypse.*

Nothing could better illustrate their divergence than to chronicle Wells's activities at this time: a period when he hoped to revitalize the Fabian Society by driving out the established leaders, the Webbs and Shaw, among others, and replace them with new leaders, his own elitist Samurai. This alone would warrant Conrad's irony. Wells wanted to move rapidly, and he thought that the Fabians provided a ready-made organization. Ford, in a whimsical move, tried to help, indicating to Conrad another aspect of his collaborator's instability. They had only recently worked together—Conrad's effort was at most a few pages and a few hundred words—on *The Nature of a Crime*, and that brief novel was in itself an outline of personal problems which led Conrad to put distance between himself and Ford. Meanwhile, Ford had boned up on Fabian materials, and then he and Wells moved in on the old fogies, the "Old Gang," as Ford referred to them. Needless to say, the Webbs and Shaw annihilated the upstarts, and Ford's flirtation with Fabian socialism ended.

From Conrad's point of view, all this was incredible, as behavior and as a waste of valuable time. It was little different from the activities of his anarchists and revolutionaries in *The Secret Agent* and *Under Western Eyes*. If we circle back to that summer collaboration on *Crime* which Conrad later

* Conrad "came back" to Wells in 1908, when he asked the latter for support with the Royal Literary Fund, from which he received a £200 grant. After detailing his own miserable affairs—acute gout, nervous anxiety, infections—he turns to Wells, a Samurai in the fight for a new world: ". . . for who could deny your influence on the thought of the generation most worth influencing, that is the generation that numbers 18 to 20 summers at this date. I have seen and heard enough of it to know it well. You get hold of them by your gentleness, your persuasiveness, by your extraordinary accessibility—and that utter absence of superior prose joined to the warmth of conviction which can be felt. No one *can* be more honest intellectually—and the very young—the workers of our more distant hopes—perceive this at once. And as your grip on every side of the question is very firm—a thing too they require—they repay your high qualities by a sort of mental devotion. It is an enviable fate." Conrad continued, moving to the area of Wells's art, and his well-chosen words indicate how carefully he had to tread: "On the other hand there is your mastery of the art—that side of your writer's genius which contains an infinite possibility. And indeed I need not suffer from divided judgment. For your art—whatever you do—will contain your convictions where they would be seen perhaps in a more perfect light. Your work, like all work that counts, must have its connection with the laborious past and its bearing on the future—that future in which you have willed (and perhaps succeeded) to put the impress of your personality." Without taking anything away from Conrad's gracious words, it is clear that he viewed Wells's art, not as ART, but as a suitable vehicle for his views.

wanted to forget, we find a "joint effort" that was virtually all Ford. It was, both disguised and literally, *his* life that appeared in *The Nature of a Crime* by Baron Ignatz (shades of Korzeniowski) von Aschendorf (the Teutonic "Hueffer"). It would appear in the April and May 1909 numbers of *The English Review.* The collaboration must have occurred between May and July 1906, for in May Ford wrote Elsie about it and in July he told Pinker that Conrad would send the manuscript after he touched it up. We can assume that by July the first draft was completed; and there apparently remained little to do on it, for Conrad returned the manuscript to Ford virtually unrevised. It was, in many ways, a freakish collaboration: a thinly disguised autobiographical memoir by Ford, to which he evidently wanted Conrad to contribute.

The Nature of a Crime is a mixture of "forbidden love" and feelings of suicide; its form is that of a narrator telling the story of another character, which of course foreshadows *The Good Soldier.* Not only was it a prefiguration of aspects of the later novel, it was also an outline of all the problems running through Ford's life: his separation from Elsie, his affair with her sister Mary, his feeling that he was superior to nearly all contemporary literary men, his sense of guilt at his family situation, his desire to hold on to Conrad, and his recognition, implicit in the suicide plan, that things had gotten out of hand. Conrad wanted no part of it and called the project "too fantastic." Whether he read into Ford's desire for collaboration any special psychological meaning we cannot tell.

We do know that when Ford later resurrected the novel, Conrad responded in less than excited terms. Ford not only wanted to publish the novel in the *transatlantic review* (in the first issue, the title was in lower case) he asked Conrad to write a preface for the book form. The latter agreed to the preface, but his response is incredulous:

> *The Nature of a Crime.* I forgot all about it so completely that I mistrusted your statement till I turned up the old E.R.s and discovered it in the first No. of the second Vol. There is also a batch of mixed MS and typescript about the man Burden, of which a very insignificant part, a few pages at most, are in my handwriting right enough. Why on earth did we select a German pseudonym for that? Is it because the stuff is introspective and somewhat redolent of weltschmerz? If you think advisable to dig up this affair, well, I don't see how I can object. I looked at it and it seemed to me somewhat amateurish, which is strange, because that is not *our* failing either separately or together.

After the summer which saw the production of *The Nature of a Crime,* Conrad and Ford fell back into their own lives, until the latter became involved in *The English Review* and interested Conrad in becoming de facto co-editor. Meanwhile, Conrad had still not finished *The Secret Agent,* which was due to be serialized in October. On September 17, he told Pinker he expected to write the "dramatic half of the last chapter," and at about the same time he sent a copy of *The Mirror of the Sea* to Henry James with a long dedicatory note in French.*

The end of the novel became very difficult for Conrad to complete because of an outbreak of enteric fever in the village, which claimed the sister of a small child temporarily staying with them. This was on October 4, two days before the serial was to start in *Ridgeway's;* but more telling than Conrad's difficulty with the end—"It's too important to be dashed off"—is his announcement that the "story will be between 52 and 54 thou: . . ." This is two-thirds of the length of the completed manuscript and resulted from his need to rush the serial. He would add more than 25,000 words to the book form. Conrad followed this up with several letters to Pinker, most of them explaining the difficulty and trying to demonstrate that his artistic intention dictated going slowly. "It's rather a task," he wrote his agent some time in October. "It's the first story of mine dealing with London. And the ironic treatment of the whole matter is not so easy as it looks. And the end is difficult since it just consists in extending that same ironic treatment to the bringing about and the very execution of the final murder (of Verloc by his wife)."

Then Conrad reassures Pinker about his worth:

> If the people who want the story for a serial know my work at all, they must know also that what makes it is not story but quality. And this they can judge of fully without the last half-chap^{er}. On the other hand if the *name* is all they want the last 4–6 thou: words can make no difference. You know that I am not likely to fire off something unsuitable for general reading. You may assure them I am safe.

In the same letter, Conrad mentions having received an "enthusiastic note from Kipling" about *The Mirror of the Sea,* a response which surprised but pleased him. Conrad's answer, or answers, has not survived.

After the first weekly issues, Conrad found *Ridgeway's* a "rag." He called it "awful—and it don't matter in the least," except that their editing of his material upset him. He indicates that he is redoing the knifing scene. On November 8, Conrad wrote Davray that he had "just finished a novel in which there is not a drop of water—except the rain. . . . There are within it a

* Part of it indicates Conrad's obeisance before James: "These sketches were set forth chiefly for my own pleasure. To write for pleasure is a dangerous fantasy. I have gone at it with the risk of provoking some grimaces of boredom or some smiles even more wounding. If within this little preface written for you all alone, I make a confession of it, it is that I am very sure of the friendship with which you honor me. I know that your smile will brighten with a welcome sweetness. Your friendly eye will know how to distinguish within these pages this filial devotion to memory which has guided the groping phrase and an always rebellious pen."

half-dozen anarchists, two women, and an idiot. The rest are all imbeciles." He continued to refer to the novel as his "imbecile story," his characterization of Stevie now applied to the entire book. But even with completion, he had more than a month's work yet to do on it. The inevitable reaction to a long haul set in, and as he told Galsworthy: "I am in a state of such depression as I have not known for years."

Part of the depression can be attributed to his moving along in age, forty-nine the next month, without any commensurate improvement in his financial situation. But the major part can be assigned to his subconscious life, manifested in the very novel he had just completed. He had depicted a family situation that literally blows up: the brother, but really "son figure," destroyed by an "acting father"; that "father figure" murdered by the "mother figure," who is really a wife; and then the latter becomes a suicide. It is a fantasy world of terrible images and terrible motivation, full of resentment, desire for revenge, enervation, and infantilism.

Strikingly, Conrad's next long work, *Under Western Eyes*, concerned itself with a young man who is isolated from everything that would have allowed internal growth; he is the Conradian archetype—Conrad in some guises—cut off by his own doing. The end of *The Secret Agent* touches with its very tip the beginning of *Under Western Eyes*. The first book was about "Verloc," the father and husband figure, who reaches toward "Razumov," the son, who lacks any acknowledged family. An only child, Conrad reproduced only-child situations, whether Stevie as Winnie's "only child," or Razumov, as an isolated child of Russia. The lack of exact symmetry here cannot disguise the similarity of tone and rhythms one finds in both novels; they derive from the same cast of mind, and they focus on the same obsessions. They are both in the most profoundly psychological way Conrad's burden from the past, not only as materials to be sold in book form, but as psychological freight that would overload him with depression and paralysis.

CHAPTER 26

Sailing Close

IN France, "Karain," the first of Conrad's *Blackwood's* publications, appeared in a translation by H. D. Davray. French was, as Conrad said, "the touchstone of expression—or else of thought itself"; and he was especially moved to have his early career filter through, like a memory once lost and now recovered in another form. This double image, as it were, would become more intense and insistent in the years ahead when André Gide undertook the supervision of translating all of Conrad's work into French; but now it was a welcome respite, even if he found that the translation reflected all the faults of the piece.

In this period of late November and early December, Conrad apparently wrote and completed his story "Il Conde," based on an episode in the life of Count Szembek, whom he had met on Capri. There is a two-week gap in Conrad's correspondence, which indicates intensive work; and the manuscript has December 4 at the end. On the eighth, Conrad wrote to Szembek, though without mentioning the story, which did not appear until August 1908. In that same letter to the count, Conrad mentions that Dr. Cerio, who treated Jessie on Capri, had asked him for a letter of introduction to Maxim Gorki, who was in Capri. Conrad says he has never seen Gorki and cannot understand the request; but it is quite possible that Cerio and Conrad had discussed Gorki during Conrad's visit and the doctor received a different impression.

On December 16, the Conrads left for Montpellier, stopping in Paris to see Marguerite Poradowska. To keep logistics to a minimum, Conrad planned to stay at the hotel of the Gare du Nord, meeting Marguerite on the evening of his arrival for dinner, and then Davray and Marguerite for luncheon the following day. Of course, he had business in mind, generally further translations of his work into French for publication in the *Mercure de France*. Specifically, he was thinking of a small volume of selected writings, probably a combination of short fiction, reminiscences, and critical writings, although he did not specify. To Ford, on the eleventh, five days before departure, he complained of all the childhood ills: "Heart thumps, head swims—nervous breakdown? very difficult to keep it away from Jessie."

The trip did take place, however, and the Conrad family settled into the Riche Hotel in Montpellier. From there, he wrote Pinker that he had lunched with Davray and Remy de Gourmont, but principally, that the *Mercure* would publish a volume of his short stories in translation—"Karain," "Outpost," and "Heart of Darkness." He says that Davray intends to find a translator for "Heart," but that was not to occur for several years, when Jean-Aubry and André Ruyters would do both "Youth" and "Heart." The entire *Mercure* project fell through. Conrad also tried to do Pinker a favor by inquiring about a literary agency in London for French writers. He says his scheme is to have Davray and others spot beforehand a work which has some chance of being read in England and then get directly in touch with the author, not the translator. For independent advice, Conrad suggests that Pinker retain Ford, "who anyhow understands French literature thoroughly and is the *coming man* in the literary world. It's my conviction he will become a sort of sublimated Gosse before many years pass over our heads." Conrad's words were prophetic, for Ford and Ezra Pound were to be the great entrepreneurs of modernism in the coming years, although Ford retained his loyalty to late-Victorian writers as well.

As the Conrads settled into Montpellier, it would become, once again, a disastrous attempt at relaxation.* Besides profound personal difficulties, Conrad was uncertain about his writing. He suspected that his fortunes might ride on *Chance*, and he turned to that, telling Pinker in late January that he has "done a lot to it." But he was dissatisfied with *The Secret Agent* and began to add to and rewrite the proofs of that novel, to the tune of 26–28,000 words, an addition amounting to almost a third of the novel's final length. In purely personal terms, his obsession with child and parent figures in the earlier novel overlaps with the father-daughter relationship in *Chance*. How far these preoccupations with perverse family matters were attempts at reconciliation with his own, or signals of profound hostility at his situation, it is impossible to pinpoint. But as if his feelings of grievance required a further cause, Borys would, at the end of January, begin to fall into one of his terribly ill periods. His illness would dominate the remainder of their stay abroad.

At the end of 1906, Conrad wrote Galsworthy and Ada about his sense of drift; instead of sailing close, he had lost direction. After detailing a French volume of his stories, he adds: "But all this is not serious business of the kind that ought to engage the thoughts of a man of 48 with two kids and a wife to

* One of the few positive elements was that he found here the germ of the idea for "The Duel." Besides the setting and his proximity to the Napoleonic world of the First Empire, he engaged in café discussions. Jean-Aubry is more specific and mentions an artillery officer with whom Conrad conversed on military subjects.

leave behind him—un beau jour." He mistook his own age, which was forty-nine, but perhaps he did so because his father had died at forty-nine and it was a fateful number. As he dawdled over *Chance,* he thought of death: "Each day is like a stroke of the inexorable clock to me." The prospect of translation propped him up, as would Gide's work in the 1910s, and he asked Davray about *The Nigger,* believing that Robert d'Humières had abandoned the project. He even composed a dedicatory note to Arthur Balfour that would accompany a presentation copy of *The Mirror of the Sea.* Balfour had been instrumental in Conrad's obtaining a Civil List pension in 1905. And Jessie, amid all her domestic difficulties, managed to turn out a cook book and received an offer of £25 advance for it. Conrad wrote a brief preface to it and indicated to Ernest Dawson that she was so puffed up with pride that nothing "but an epidemic of indigestion setting over all the United Kingdom after publication will subdue her.*

But an occasional jest could not disguise the gloom Conrad continued to feel, even though the sunshine of Montpellier to some extent dissipated the suicidal depression that had forced him to escape the Pent. As he wrote Marguerite on January 5, after admitting to the "laziness common to all Poles": "I prefer to dream a novel rather than write it. For the dream of the work is always much more beautiful than the reality of the printed thing. And English is, too, still a foreign language to me, demanding 'un effort formidable pour être maniée.' "

Chance was indeed far from completion; and *The Secret Agent,* which would appear next September 10, was not yet to his liking, as he shifted the story to Winnie's point of view from its stress on Verloc and anarchists. He began a story called "The Duel," but was far too optimistic when he wrote Pinker on January 25 that he was putting the last touches on it; the story would drag on for several months. He still had his Mediterranean novel in mind, and indicated he was learning Spanish and reading up on Napoleon in

* Conrad was overly optimistic and probably overran the facts in order to encourage Jessie and divert her from their domestic difficulties. Alston Rivers vociferously rejected the idea of such a book, and Jessie's efforts were not published until 1923, by Heinemann, under the title: *A Handbook of Cookery for a Small House.* Conrad's preface was later reprinted in *Last Essays.* Ford has an amusing version of this episode in his *Return to Yesterday* (pp. 239–40). Ford's glee is at the expense of Conrad's impracticality, for the latter felt the cook book could command an advance of £400 (equivalent to $5,000), which was exactly the sum Conrad needed to straighten out his affairs. Conrad himself wrote to Ford (on January 25, 1907) in high spirits: "She's in a state of delightful excitement about it and very grateful to you the 'Onlie begetter' of this work of art like the late lamented Mr H of Shakespeare's sonnets. My preface is a mock serious thing into which I dragged Red Indians and other incongruities. But the little book is not bad. . . . Suggested title: Cooking Precepts for a Little House—or something of that kind—if editors like. Get them to fork out of del: of MS.—in order to make her completely happy. A fur coat for Borys hangs thereby."

Elba at the Town Library. The Spanish lessons were to help him unravel the plots and counterplots surrounding the emperor, who was "menaced by murderers and threatened by revengeful Spaniards and Corsicans." Conrad assures Pinker he is not wasting his time, that he has a distinct theme in mind for a Mediterranean novel "with historical interest, intrigue and adventure." He also missed Ford, or so he wrote him: "I am drunk with colour and would like dearly to have you to lean upon."

In a marginal matter, Sir Humphrey Milford had written Conrad asking him for a preface to an edition of Melville, and Conrad responded with his usual reaction to Melville's work:

> I am greatly flattered by your proposal; but the writing of my own stuff is a matter of so much toil and difficulty that I am only too glad to leave other people's books alone. Years ago I looked into *Typee* and *Omoo*, but as I didn't find there what I was looking for when I open a book I did go no further. Lately I had in my hand *Moby Dick.* It struck me as a rather strained rhapsody with whaling for a subject and not a single sincere line in the 3 vols of it.

Conrad suggested W. H. Hudson, who had shown enthusiasm for *Moby-Dick* and indeed for the whole of Melville's work. As a Flaubertian, a devotee of Turgenev and James, Conrad was dismayed by Melville's turbulence, the same disorder he detested in Dostoevsky; in addition, he found *Moby-Dick* full of "portentous mysticism," perhaps because of its lack of surface concreteness or formal order. For Conrad, a writer with particular insights into disorder, upheaval, and individual anarchy, the surface had to be taut and neatly ordered, only suggesting, not manifesting, the psychological tensions lying beneath.

The important matter now, however, was a domestic crisis, the deterioration of Borys's health, beginning with an attack of adenoids, "if that's how the beastly things are called." At the same time this was discovered, Conrad mislaid his pocketbook or else had his pocket picked, losing 200 francs in the process. The adenoidal condition was followed by measles, and the measles by bronchitis; and the bronchitis was feared to be tuberculosis, for the lungs were affected. Tuberculosis was the Korzeniowski and Bobrowska killer. Conrad's letters become desperate missives, especially since his entire enterprise now rested on Pinker's supply of money, for living expenses, doctors' bills, even possible treatment in Switzerland.

As he moved toward *Under Western Eyes,* worked on "The Duel," rewrote portions of *The Secret Agent,* drifted in and out of *Chance,* and contemplated his Mediterranean novel, Conrad found himself with a sick, even dying, son—now duplicating the depressed and paralyzed Apollo with *his* sick Konrad. Borys's measles precipitated a series of crises: "Borys has got [he told Pinker] a thundering go at measles. That fellow catches whatever is going. I've been nursing him 4 nights now. . . . But you ought not to be surprised if you hear that Baby's got the measles or I, or my wife or Miss Wright or the maid or all of us together. It's the most damnable thing." Mixed in with this anxiety is the need to write *Chance* and Conrad's fear that Pinker may place it too soon: "I can't afford to botch such effects as my writing is able to produce. I want time. . . . I wish to reach a certain point from which I will be able to dictate for a little while."

On March 4, the situation is exacerbated: "I feel I must write to you and yet it seems to me I have hardly the courage to set the thing down on paper. The doctor is just gone. You know how they talk but there is the fact that apparently Borys is menaced in both lungs. . . . The analysis will be made tomorrow. The most terrifying fact in all this for me is that for the last three weeks I myself have had a suspicion of something of the kind." He then tries to evaluate his reaction to events: "I would not give way to it but it has been gnawing at my vitals all that time. And now we shall see. I have a presentiment that if that is it it will not last very long. But of course—as the doctor says—it may be nothing. I confess I have written the above words without conviction. . . . Don't imagine I am utterly knocked over. I feel luckily a good power of resistance within me. Strange fate. Just now when I became conscious of a fresh lease of health and life, when I feel a strengthening of my mental grip on my work this thing must come on."

In the next letter to Pinker (on March 13), Conrad reports the need for a change of climate for Borys and suggests Champel, the hydrotherapeutic establishment where he had himself gone in the 1890s.

> For myself my dear Pinker if it is to be Switzerland for him I much prefer Geneva now than Davos-Platz—later on where the modern Dance of Death goes on in expensive hotels. There's nothing to prevent me writing in Champel (⅓ of my *Outcast* was written there in 1894) and the place is cheap—as such places go. I myself will not be any the worse for a course of water cure after this earthquake sort of shock. Champel has brought me round once and it may give me a fresh lease of mental life again now my health shows signs of general improvement. This 14 months now since my last fit of gout! This is worth following up on the chance of securing permanency.

Intermixed with this news is a complicated plea for money to fund the entire venture and a report on the progress of *Chance*, which he was producing at 500 words per day but would not as yet show to Pinker. "It's no use parting with stuff which may require weeks of correcting work. Moreover when I have it by me a lucky idea occurs and is set down in its place; whereas when the MS is not there it is lost because my brain has no storage room."

The next two important letters to Pinker (now distinctly the "Uncle Tadeusz" in Conrad's life) bring together all the threads: familial chaos, personal depression, an attack of gout, desultory work on a long-term project

(*Chance*), financial pressures, the need to correct galleys, and, through it all, the brain readying itself to churn up a new novel. On May 6, Conrad wrote (on the eve of departing Montpellier for Geneva):

> I was not in a fit state to write you fully last time. I am getting better rapidly tho' I can't use my hand as of yet. It's extremely bothersome. But the hand is getting better and that's the main thing. The weather is horribly wet here and poor Borys has started coughing again. I can hear him now; it's a sound that robs me of my composure in a great measure. . . . Do not doubt for a moment that I will do all I can to get the S.A. ready for the printer soon. If there is hurry I will leave off Chance completely for a fortnight or so. I suppose it will be just as well. My only anxiety was to get Chance forward—you understand. The S.A. however has its importance as a distinctly new departure in my work. And I am anxious to put as much "quality" as I can in that book which will be criticised with some severity no doubt—or *scrutinised* rather I should say. Preconceived notions of Conrad as sea writer will stand in the way of its acceptance.

The May 18 letter is the full cry of anguish: unforeseen expenses, the baby with whooping cough, misconceived plans, inability to work on *Chance*, mangled galleys of *The Secret Agent.*

> I have miscalculated my expenses in Montpellier and must ask you to send frcs *1100* by means of Credit Lyonnais to Mr *Joseph Ducaillar* Riche Hotel Montpellier, in the course of the week. I left that much in his debt. And please don't scold me because I have just now as much as I can bear. Here I am stranded again with baby at its last gasp with whooping cough. It began in Montpellier. We started by medical advice counting on the change of climate to check the disease but it has developed on the road in a most alarming manner. The poor little devil has melted down to half his size. Since yesterday morning he has had a coughing fit every quarter of an hour or so and will not eat anything. We'll have to resort to artificial feeding very soon. . . . Really I haven't got my share of the commonest sort of luck. I suppose *Chance* will have to pay for all this but if you think I ought to come home I will do so as soon as baby can travel and will let my cure go to the devil. Borys of course has whooping cough too but very mildly. Still it isn't good for him. My dear Pinker I feel that all this is almost too much for me.
>
> I am trying to keep a steady mind and not allow myself to dwell too much on the cost of things or I would go distracted.
>
> The proofs of *S.A.* have reached me and I have almost cried at the sight. I thought it was arranged beyond doubt that I was to have *galley slips* for my corrections. Instead of that I get proofs of set pages! Apart from the cost of correction which will be greatly augmented through that there is the material difficulty of correcting clearly and easily on small margins. And upon my word I don't want just now any extra difficulties put in the way of my work.

Trying to pull it all together, Conrad put aside *Chance* to get at *The Secret Agent* proofs, and then (May 25) reported that Borys had "rheumatism" in both ankles, along with whooping cough, while the baby required oxygen. This condition, which eventually improved, continued through the summer, accompanied by Conrad's own attacks of gouty eczema, carrying him almost to the beginning of *Under Western Eyes.*

This was the domestic situation, and it took Conrad from Montpellier to Champel, and then back to the Pent on August 10. In that period of six months, he struggled frantically to concentrate and bring forth a body of work that would justify Pinker's considerable outlay. He promises "The Duel" in mid-February, but did not complete it until April 11. He says he is writing "the famous *Chance,*" which he feels will bring a turn of luck; it did, but more than seven years later. He is confident he will complete it by the end of the year, finished in all details so that he will not have to rewrite it as he is now redoing *The Secret Agent.*

He assures Pinker he will not collapse, that there is sufficient resilience, a power of resistance, in him; but he also senses that most of his hopeful plans are suspended until the outcome of Borys's health is determined. He was surrounded by unfinished or incomplete projects: *Rescue, Chance, The Secret Agent* (being revised, rewritten, added to), "The Duel," the French translation of the stories from *Tales of Unrest.* It was as if he had journeyed back forty years to Cracow, where his father lay among unfinished projects of his own, hopes fading, son ill, the house a kind of limbo populated by ghosts. To Galsworthy, he said: "My dear Jack this is too awful for words." To Borys's "Uncle Jack," he poured out every detail of the diagnosis, the possible cure, the expenses involved.

The plan to take the family to Champel to allow Borys to recuperate would also replay the past for Conrad, his own stays in 1891, 1894, and 1895. These re-views of past events and of former situations may indeed have had much to do with Conrad's choice of a subject for his next novel, the story of Razumov and his relationship to Russia. Conrad was now heading for Geneva, as Razumov would. The way in which the subject worked in and out of Conrad's own most protected feelings would indicate he was writing along the lines of a past now being regurgitated. Such a use of materials would run close to what we have seen repeatedly in Conrad: that flirtation with the very elements that brought him low so as to release energies which he could devote to his work. Here, Borys's illness brought him back forty years, then forward to his early struggles as a writer, when he was working on *Almayer* and *Outcast* at Champel, and then, through that circuitry, to the subject of "Razumov," his young man doomed by his association with imperial Russia.

To Pinker, at the end of March, Conrad sent from Montpellier pages of "The Duel" and copy for *Chance.* He saw "The Duel" as completing a volume of stories, for he now had six fictions, running from the novella-length

"Duel" and "Gaspar Ruiz" to the briefer "Brute," "Anarchist," "Informer," and "Il Conde." After "The Duel" was serialized in *Pall Mall Magazine* in January–May 1908 and "Il Conde" in *Cassell's Magazine* in August 1908, they were collected in *A Set of Six* (1908). D'Humières wrote that he had translated half *The Nigger* and was working on the rest, news which encouraged Conrad. He was hanging on until the end of April, when they would leave for Switzerland.

A new theme, not unusually, poked through: the need to increase sales, the desire to be popular: "I am very possessed [he told Pinker] by the idea of striking a blow for popularity. . . . On the other hand I don't want you to think that I am passing my time in making plans. It is not so. I am steadily hammering at *Chance.* But I want to have something inside of me when that is done—something ready to come out." What came out was an attack of gout in the left hand and wrist, after an interval of eighteen months. Even *The Secret Agent* held out hope: "The *S.A.* approached with a fresh eye does not strike me as bad at all. There is an element of popularity in it. By this I don't mean to say that the thing is likely to be popular. I merely think it shows traces of capacity for that sort of treatment which may make a novel popular." Conrad says he might gain a wider audience by "taking a widely discussed subject for the *text* of the novel," with the more popular subjects being religious problems, questions of war, peace, and labor. Of course he sidestepped treatment, for his kind of narrative, one element that made him distinctive, would guarantee the loss of potential readers.

In the midst of this, *The Rescue,* that twenty-three-year agony on the cross for Conrad, hove into sight, the result of a Heinemann inquiry about the contract. They were, it appears, ready to take it over. Conrad responded that he was very pleased, but the fact remained he planned to complete the novel whoever the publisher was. He needed only the necessary leisure; the "will is there and perhaps the ability to make something tolerable of it too." This sudden interest in *The Rescue,* added to d'Humière's work on the French translation of *The Nigger* and the recent appearance of "Karain" in the *Mercure,* kept the past before him, as though his career were a substance of tremendous elasticity that could be reshaped in infinite ways.

By the end of May, he hoped to turn to *Chance* without interruption, with the rewriting of *The Secret Agent* in page proofs going on unabated throughout April and early May. But by May 3, he saw the impossibility of that and, promising revisions of *The Secret Agent* by the end of June, told Pinker not to worry him. "I must *see* that story. . . . You know it was always understood the book had to be worked upon thoroughly." The desire for popularity was there, but Conrad insisted on his kind of book even if precious time was expended upon revision. To Pinker he wrote of work and further copy, but to Galsworthy he indicated a nervous collapse, the feeling of being "hopeless, spiritless without a single thought in my head." Yet in

December he was to begin a short story called "Razumov," which was to grow into one of the most significant novels of his career.

The comedy had to be played out, however. Conrad made plans to leave for Geneva on May 15, all the while assuring Pinker he would rework the last third of *The Secret Agent* by the end of June. Exceptionally pressing for him was the need to have a book published to bring in additional income, so that while he was still immersed in revisions, he was alerting Pinker to his need for a 1907 novel publication. Besides the revenue, Conrad needed, as we have already seen, that annual or biennial book as assurance his career was functioning. He had not had a novel for three years, not since *Nostromo* in 1904; and although he did have the volume of *The Mirror* in hand, it was a collection of reminiscences—many of the pieces not even "written" but dictated to Ford.

Along the line, Conrad miscalculated his expenses, especially in Montpellier, and he needed additional funds. Also, when the family reached La Roseraie Pension in Champel, the baby, John, having developed whooping cough, the pension would not allow them into their regular rooms. The Conrads camped at the end of a corridor, where the illness reached its crisis. They were then moved to an annex to the hotel, for purposes of isolation, all of these special moves requiring tips and subsidies. Conrad wrote frantically for money, and only Pinker could supply it. This began the worst weeks, when Borys developed what Conrad called rheumatism, by which he probably meant rheumatic fever, to accompany his whooping cough. John was "mere skin and bone," and had trouble breathing. This was followed by Conrad's suffering from "periodical eruptions of gouty eczema," perhaps from his identification with Job. He was, at the beginning of June, anxious to begin his own cure, but he lacked funds for that.

Putting all these tales of disaster in successive letters to Pinker, Conrad also mentioned he had gotten "on so well in planning *Chance* that it is quite possible it may be finished in three months from now"—that is, by the end of August, which is when he expected Methuen to publish *The Secret Agent.* He hedges and suggests it may not be completed until October, but he says Pinker knows how well he works from June to October, as if he planned, like Persephone, to rise from his underworld existence and fructify for the next six months. To Rothenstein, in reporting the events of the last several months, Conrad made his career sound continuous, speaking of a long story completed ("The Duel"), another novel being prepared for the press, and a new novel on which he was working; actually, a false sense of continuity, since in virtually every instance he had miscalculated his time on each project and was far behind whatever schedules he had established.

He indicated to Pinker he wanted to subtitle *The Secret Agent* "A Simple Tale," so that it would not be misunderstood as having "any sort of social or polemical intention," a ridiculous assumption given the nature of the enterprise. What he had in mind, probably, was the desire to focus attention on the Verloc-Winnie association, especially since much of his later revision involved tacking on Winnie's fortunes after she murders Verloc. Equally probable was his desire to mislead, as he would mislead in his next novel, *Under Western Eyes,* in which he denied any conscious animus toward things Russian. "A Simple Tale" as a subtitle meant nothing to the reviewers, nor could it mean anything even to those who comprehended his intention. Through early June, he worked steadily on the novel, mailing segments to Pinker as he completed them.

In the first weeks in June, when his fortunes seemed at their nadir, the worst was actually coming to an end, although the medical prognosis for Borys would not warrant encouragement for some time to come. But, in effect, the family had turned the corner—collectively. Nevertheless, as Conrad labored over proofs and manuscript of a novel he had thought he was finished with, he could not foresee the end, and his frame of mind was quite in keeping with the story he had produced. The bomb which disintegrated Stevie may have been a wish fulfillment for the entire clan. In a June 6 letter to Galsworthy, Conrad presents a dramatic mixture of his own personal life with the domestic situation which leads to Winnie's murder of Verloc:

> From the sound next door (we have three rooms) I know that the pain has roused Borys from his feverish doze. I won't go to him. It's no use. Presently I shall give him his salicylate, take his temperature and shall then go to elaborate a little more the conversation of Mr. Verloc with his wife. It is very important that the conversation of Mr. Verloc with his wife should be elaborated—made more effective, don't you know—more true to the situation and the character of these people.
>
> By Jove I've got to hold myself with both hands not to burst into a laugh which would scare wife, baby and the other invalid—let alone the lady whose room is on the other side of the corridor!
>
> To-day completes the round dozen of years since I finished Almayer's Folly.

Borys seemed a repository of ills. Fifteen days after the rheumatic fever set in, pleurisy symptoms appeared on the right side. Treatment called for puncturing the lung and drawing out the water, but this was delayed because of the build-up of liquid, which reaccumulated rapidly. This was on June 9, and it would appear to go on and on, punishment for some undesignated crime. Through it all, however, Borys's heart remained unaffected, and the treatment now attempted was to be reabsorption of the pleurisy. On top of the pleurisy, bronchitis appeared: hectic fever, rapid emaciation, and a wicked cough. Conrad saw his son's illness in terms of final things. "Dread of going back to the Pent [he wrote Galsworthy]: a sort of feeling that this is the end of things at the end of twelve years' work—all this does not help me much in making Mr & Mrs Verloc effective for the amusement of a public—

which won't be amused by me at all." Upon their return to England, the Conrads did seek another home, in Bedfordshire.

By June 26–27, Borys's fever had broken, and although he was in sorry shape—"a miserable object skin and bone"—he was mending slowly. Conrad's submission of *Secret Agent* material neared an end, and Pinker seemed quite willing to advance money for most of the immediate bills. By the end of July, Borys's convalescence was considered over, as were Conrad's revisions of nearly 30,000 words on his new novel. He also felt something had gone out of him, possibly the realization that a pattern was set for the remainder of his life: "I look forward with dread to an effort which, I fear, from the nature of things, can never any more be adequate." Attached to this sense of an ending was a desire to live closer to London, very possibly to be nearer friends. By the end of July, with revisions still dribbling in to Pinker's office, Conrad felt the novel "as it stands is a work of some mark." He was anxious to get on with *Chance*, but had to clear his mind first of *The Secret Agent.* He tells Pinker that the next twelve months will be crucial, time for a "really heroic effort," in which he will "set to work repairing the disasters of these months." Slowly, he was steeling himself for another long haul, not on *Chance*, but on *Under Western Eyes*, the distillation of his earliest experiences and his current ideas.

Writing to Pinker on July 30 that he figured on four months to wind up *Chance*, Conrad then ran through a very frank appraisal of himself. He was being prophetic, for his sense of himself would be justified, but not for another eight years.

> *Chance* itself will be altogether different in tone and treatment of course, but it will be saleable I believe. By the end of Sept^er you will have a really considerable lot of it to show. Of course it will not be on popular lines. Nothing of mine can be, I fear. But even Meredith ended by getting his sales. Now, I haven't Meredith's delicacy and that's a point in my favour. I reckon I may make certain of the support of the press for the next few years. The young men who are coming in to write criticisms are in my favour so far. I don't get in the way of established reputations. One may read everybody and yet in the end want to read me—for a change if for nothing else. I don't resemble anybody; and yet I am not specialised enough to call up imitators as to matters of style. There is nothing in me but a turn of mind which whether valuable or worthless can not be imitated.

All this was by way of drawing money from Pinker; Conrad needed travel money, which he figured at £80. He also estimated his expenses for the coming year as £664, including house rent of £50 and Borys's private schooling. Added to that, he cited doctors' bills of £126, for a total of £800. He wanted this sum as a guarantee against proceeds, in which he included *Chance* and another novel, all in the next twelve months. The sum of £800 would be about $10–12,000 in current purchasing power, a fairly high amount for rural living. Of that sum, medical expenses were estimated as coming to over $2,000. As it turned out, Conrad's estimate was low.

Conrad now awaited book publication of *The Secret Agent*, for which good reviews were essential to continue the momentum of his career. Pinker came through with various checks for outstanding debts, but drew the line at £600 per year, which would begin on August 10, the day of the Conrads' arrival back at the Pent. Conrad's "payment" would be the production of 80,000 words of copy of novels, not short stories. This was a minimum figure, for Conrad estimated he felt capable of 100,000 words a year, a number not at all far from what he was producing—but that for a combination of stories, novels and sketches. Pinker's estimate held only for novels, which would bring the largest return: from serialization in England and America, and book sales in both countries, with the further possibility of translation into French.

With this loose arrangement, which Conrad broke on several occasions, he entered into an agreement with his agent that would last through *Victory*—so much copy for so much advance money. It was an arrangement, as we shall see, that worked well for Conrad, since it took the daily burden of bills off his mind; yet at the same time it forced him frequently to mislead Pinker about his intentions and production. For we can observe from his correspondence with others that he was quite depressed about his career, even as he told his agent that matters were going well. What all this meant, besides the personal toll, was that Conrad had to, as it were, keep two sets of books, one for himself and one for Pinker; and he was moving ever deeper into secrets and deceptions, so as to disguise his real way of working from the man who was putting out hundreds of pounds on faith and future prospects. For someone like Conrad, brought up on honor and integrity in money matters, such deception, so necessary to *his* sense of his career, must have created its own tensions.

After their return, Conrad did a certain amount of searching for a new home before he settled on one called Someries, two and a half miles from the Luton station, on the Luton Loo estate, and about forty-five minutes from London on the Midland line. In a generally newsy letter to Galsworthy, on August 24, Conrad mentions various illnesses, the fact that Jessie was very tired—she who held the various pieces together in Montpellier—and their preparations for a move. Of interest is Conrad's indication that he has a "very interesting book on Rousseau" for Ada which he plans to send on soon. This information, that he was reading about Rousseau, means very possibly that "Razumov" was coming into his mind; or else he was thinking about locales, and Geneva—close by Champel, that salvation of himself and Borys—

was entering his imagination as the setting for a novel. From Russia to Geneva: Razumov's touchstones had acute meaning for Conrad; doomed in St. Petersburg, he seeks a new identity in Geneva.

Harriet Capes, who would be an encouraging reader and good friend to Conrad through these and later years and to whom he dedicated *A Set of Six*, had urged him to seek a house near Winchester, in her neighborhood, and he had gone looking at a King Charles cottage. But he wanted something inland, as a way of possibly containing his attacks of gout from dampness. He told her considerations of health were paramount, not for the sake of literature, but for the sake of his family—all the while "the sands are running out!" His description to Pinker of the Someries house was favorable enough, but once in it, he found it deplorably uncomfortable: "The house is not big but roomy for its size with a walled garden in front. There is also an excellent kitchen garden with fruit trees, properly fenced and with a door to it which locks—so that one may expect some good from it. The position is excellent 500 ft above sea level on clay and gravel." But he would write Elsie Hueffer on January 1: "I can't help feeling glad we couldn't find anything for you in this neighbourhood. You have no idea of the soul corroding bleakness of earth and sky here when the east wind blows. We had a fiendish ten days of it." The result was, of course, gout, what he called the "refrain of my doleful existence." That was later. At the end of August he was hopeful, and even wrote of having a bathroom installed in the house, the Conrads' first interior bathroom.

On September 10—while he was still touching up "The Duel" for serialization at the beginning of 1908—the Conrads left Pent Farm on their way to Someries, the very day, also, that Methuen published *The Secret Agent.* The time was both a start and a finish. They would take possession on September 12. The move, which was carefully planned, turned out to be disastrous: the workmen still in the house, the water pump broken, one of the vans not arriving. "As usual," Conrad wrote Galsworthy, "Jessie worked while I went about raving and tearing my hair." And to top off his introduction to Someries, he came down with another "bout of gouty eczema," which left him distracted but ambulatory. More revelatory in the letter, however, is a possibly more direct cause of the ailment: a terrible row with Ford, who had apparently put the screws on Conrad for money owed to him, and the abrupt termination of his tenancy of the Pent, rented from Ford.

The precise details are murky, but the argument appears to have been fierce, with Ford accusing Conrad of hiding funds so as to avoid payment of his debt. The latter was frank about it with Galsworthy:

> All he [Ford] may do is to knock me over completely and utterly and even knock me out of house and home, since a clause of the agreement terminates my tenancy in case of bankruptcy or composition with creditors. My past work and my policies are mortgaged up to the hilt to P. anyhow.

Conrad denies his behavior has been base, saying that even when he appeared to be making money he just managed to squeeze through. He admits the Montpellier excursion was a disaster, especially since he had expected to return with three parts of *Chance*. "You may imagine how I raged to feel myself stepping back into the everlasting hole. I've done what work I could but all the same I've come back ruined again for a time. I am too weary for words. . . . I would rather die than be ill again but as a matter of fact I can't afford either. I will have to pump till the handle breaks or the ship goes down under me."

The financial difficulty with Ford exacerbated the relationship between the two collaborators—now only a year after their final joint effort—but nothing more drastic resulted. Conrad could not pay, and Ford retreated; his demand may, in fact, have been his way of keeping in touch. Meanwhile, *The Secret Agent* had appeared, on September 10, and Conrad waited apprehensively for the notices. He had, he recognized, tried something very different from his previous work, and he was naturally worried that the reviewers would fail to observe his departure. For him, each book now had to educate the reviewers so that they would not expect only sea stories or exotica. He had cultivated strange and isolated places as a celebration of his early talent; he was now broadening. One of the first reviewers, A. N. Monkhouse, in *The Manchester Guardian*, noted the difference, as a departure in the genre and as a matter of ironic treatment. Monkhouse understood the novel, and although he was less than overwhelmingly enthusiastic, he pinpointed Conrad's method and manner well. It was a review that any novelist not seeking a popular audience would be proud to receive.

> If it be straining the conception of comedy [Monkhouse wrote] to find it in the idea of madness and despair attempting the renovation of the world, the story that enforces this idea is rich in comic types and details. The Verloc household is a great and original accomplishment, and it does justice to the insatiable curiosity of the artist. Among those queer people, whose comparatively innocent and ostensible means of living is a trade banned by all decent folk, Mr. Conrad moves with senses quite unperturbed. . . . His investigation is coloured with humour and imagination; the obscure and terrible is revealed as comic, but it is not merely comic. Verloc, the mysterious agent, mentioned in important despatches by a symbol, with his husky, confidential voice, changing inopportunely into the booming, oratorical one that has done duty at open-air meetings, turns out to be rather stupid and almost pitiful. . . . We are shown the seamy side of a preposterous world, a festering society that is commonly left to the pathologist or philanthropist. It is all vital and surprising in Mr. Conrad's narrative.

The *Times Literary Supplement* reviewer preferred *The Secret Agent* to *Nostromo*, which he found too crowded; whereas the later novel was "clear throughout." That notice, seeking clarity rather than size or texture, was of little value to Conrad. One reviewer, signed only "Z" (Israel Zangwill?), was hostile to the entire idea, saying that Conrad had blown up a story idea to something ten times its necessary size. He attacked the conception of Verloc, the style of the novel, the failure of Winnie. He even says the character portraits of the Assistant Commissioner, the Inspector of Police, and the Minister (whom he identifies as Sir William Harcourt) were all unnecessary. Interestingly, he attacked the author: "The book might fairly be described as a study of murder by a writer with a personality as egotistical as that of Mr. Bernard Shaw, only lacking in the wit and humour which goes some way to justify the existence of the latter."

What the reviewers, even the more favorable ones, appeared to miss was the peculiar mosaic of characters and events Conrad developed in his fiction in this period. Although neither a prophet nor a seer, he brought a vision to his novels. This vision was not a pretty one, of course, and it offended many readers as being excessively pessimistic and depressing in matter and tone. But Conrad had assimilated into his very bones that sense of Spenglerian final things, the awareness of decline, of entropy, of the last gasp of a civilization heading toward destruction.*

He was, in a manner of speaking, writing his "magic mountain" before the great event of the First World War, not after, as Mann did; and his "magic mountain" involved a vision of Europe and Western civilization that took place over several novels, from *Nostromo* through *Victory* ten years later. When Mann, that voice of European civilization, wrote the preface to the German edition of *The Secret Agent* in 1926, just two years after *The Magic Mountain* was published, he acknowledged how Conrad's political and philosophical ideas threaded in and out of his consciousness and how Conrad's themes both activated and entered into his political awareness. The dialogues between Naphta and Settembrini, although far more learned and textured than anything Conrad could have attempted, involve the very themes Conrad had foreshadowed in his fiction of the prewar decade.

This particular vision of breakdown happened to coincide with a period of English confidence in the future, of relative prosperity, slow gains in democracy and social equality, a reaching after full employment and an egalitarian society. Conrad was the sole novelist of stature and breadth to tell the Eng-

---

* A sizable literature was growing on decline, degeneration, abnormalities of character, and criminal types, although which ones, if any, Conrad knew cannot be determined. He refers to Lombrosan theories in *The Secret Agent*, and he was probably familiar with Max Nordau's *Degeneration*. Of more immediate moment was a 1905 essay by Hans Gross, "Degeneration and Deportation," which recommended deportation of degenerates and criminals to save society. Conrad mocks this racial "wisdom" in *The Secret Agent* when he puts such ideas in the mouth of Ossipon; but he nevertheless saw society as a whole as running toward ultimate destruction.

lish that their goals as well as the texture of their lives were melancholy matters, not reasons for celebration. Like Yeats, he felt that "the nightmare rides upon sleep" and "the night can sweat with terror." In sending a presentation copy of *Agent* to Henry James, Conrad admitted that while the "covers are deep red," what's "inside of them I assure you I haven't the slightest idea. That's where Hazlitt's Indian juggler has the pull over a writer of tales. He at least knows how many balls he is keeping up in the air at the same time." Conrad's "know-nothingness" to James, a display of false modesty, was the other side of his awareness that his vision of life was devastating, made even more brutal and unacceptable by the ironic treatment. And it was fitting he should send the novel to James, for the latter was the "other" novelist touching on all these themes, but lacking the sense of disaster that licks at the edge of every major Conrad novel.

Given the time, energy, and inclination, Conrad could possibly have gathered it all together in a vast novel, perhaps a European novel with the dimensions of *Nostromo.* More likely, however, he saw his work from *Nostromo* onward as the mapping out of a new territory, what he told Graham was his "new departure in genre." The severe irony of tone in all the works of this period, continuing into *Victory,* was a way of putting manner into matter. Curiously enough, it was John Galsworthy, that not at all kindred spirit, who sensed in Conrad what the latter foresaw about humanity and civilization itself. In a lengthy tribute to his friend in the *Fortnightly Review* (for April 1908), Galsworthy put together a remarkable document not only of friendship but of comprehension. He does not follow Conrad all the way—he could not without denying his own talent—but he does sense the Conradian world.

> If man was not disharmonic, there would be no irony of things. We jut out everywhere, and fail to see how we are jutting out. We seek solutions, raise our flags, work our arms and legs loyally in the isolated fields that come within our vision, but having no feeling for the whole, the work we do is departmental. The work of the departments is the game we understand; we spend our lives keeping up the ball and taking down the score. The race of men is a race of partisans feeding their pigeon-holes with contradictory reports of life, and when a fellow comes and lays a summary on the desk, they look at him askance; but the future pays attention, for the impartial is all that it has time for.

Galsworthy speaks of Conrad's ability to force the individual from his singularity into a sense of his relationship to the whole. "There is no other living novelist that so reveals the comfort and the beauty of the mystery in which we live, no other that can make us feel how small and stupid, how unsafe and momentary, solution is. . . . It is the essence of this writer to let in the wind with its wild, mysterious savour." Galsworthy says that for Conrad

"Nature is first, man second. . . . And it is this feeling for, and prepossession with, the manifestations of mysterious forces that gives this writer his unique position among novelists."

Missing from this sensitive appraisal is a full recognition of Conrad's devastating irony and his pervasive pessimism about man's fate. Also, calling nature first, man second is a disservice to Conrad, since nature had for him multiple meanings, not the least of which was the opportunity it gave man for temporary greatness, the way in which it could provide a magical challenge that could take man out of himself. Galsworthy, further, missed Conrad's grand plan: the fact that his novels were mosaically arranged pieces of the whole, including the Far East, South America, London, and once more, Continental Europe. Conrad evidently had in mind a massive scale; if not a "magic mountain," then an entire earth—although for him the magic had already gone out of it.

Even "The Duel"—which McClure published separately in 1908 as "The Point of Honour"—was part of that mosaic, an attempt through the use of the Napoleonic era to suggest a historical challenge, contrast, or conflict with the present age. The two duelists, Feraud and D'Hubert, give meaning and substance to their lives by means of a defense of their honor, no matter how trivial their motivation. Against the backdrop of the "Man of Destiny," they forge their own destinies, based on their periodic duels over a sixteen-year time span, in which France goes from Napoleonic rule to Royalist reaction. Both Napoleon and their own compulsive sense of honor give their lives "magic," and this magic—whether induced from dueling, from charging a fixed battery, or (for Conrad) from coming through a storm—is necessary to keep one alive. Its disappearance or transformation into the comforts of bourgeois life is an indication of man's decline. When the duels end, and D'Hubert finally holds the upper hand, he is struck by his sense of loss, not gain: "He had known moments when, by a marvellous illusion, this love [of a young woman] seemed to be already his, and his threatened life a still more magnificent opportunity of devotion. Now that his life was safe it had suddenly lost its special magnificence. . . . Thus to this man, sobered by the victorious issue of a duel, life appeared robbed of its charm, simply because it was no longer menaced."

In *A Set of Six*, counterpointed to this tale of honor, glory, and individual integrity of a sort, is the modern instance of "Il Conde." Here, in Naples, there is not life but death; not civilization but the end of it; not honor but the traducement of all civilized behavior. While Napoleon brought death and destruction, he also generated a kind of belief, foolhardy and illusive as it may have been. Conrad's interest in Napoleon went further than the relationship between the emperor's France and Polish fortunes, although this was a vital concern. Conrad's fascination involved the whole thrust of his literary intelligence, in that Napoleon provided moments of greatness for ordinary people which were roughly equivalent to those moments of insight granted to the imaginative writer.

In the Author's Note, Conrad suggests that connection between the era and the "moment" for the writer: ". . . that is exactly what I was trying to capture in my small net: the Spirit of the Epoch—never purely militarist in the long clash of arms, youthful, almost childlike in its exaltation of sentiment—naïvely heroic in its faith." These heroic "moments" are contrasted with those of the modern age, the ones experienced by the ill-fated count of the story, who is harassed and terrorized by the bands of young men who want to purify Naples. Their actions, like those of Conrad's revolutionaries and anarchists, stem from boredom, not belief; from ennui, not ideology or a sense of honor. They have no integrity, and, therefore, their deeds are purely solipsistic, without any increment that derives from activities that endanger the self by exposing it.

Napoleon's era allowed men to live in "suspense," at such an edge of terrible excitement that they were willing to forfeit their lives. Conrad's sense of the sea and of maritime life derives from a similar belief. Napoleon was, for Conrad, like some "mythological demi-god" who quickened man's spirit; and he would touch on this Man of Destiny in a further story, "The Warrior's Soul," as well as the era in *The Rover* and *Suspense.*

Like all moments, however, these periods of greatness receded as financial matters took precedence. While Conrad was imagining Napoleon, his creditors were seeking money, and he wrote to Pinker that he had to have a supplemental £60 for each twelve-month period, in addition to the stipulated £600. He begs: "Pray stretch a point. This will clear me completely and make life a different thing altogether. . . . Of course I am ready to disclose all particulars. Anyway you will know how the money is spent." As bait, he offers Methuen's news that *The Secret Agent* is going "very well, very well indeed," and that he has a volume of stories ready even without "The Duel." *Chance* is getting on, he says, even as he begins to move toward the beginning of *Under Western Eyes,* another piece in his European mosaic.

Conrad's association with Edward Garnett had become less intense over the years, with Garnett feeling somewhat neglected as his "protégé" moved on to other friends and achievements of his own. There was no definite break, but correspondence and meetings with Garnett became sparser. Conrad's letter to his old friend about the latter's review, in the *Nation,* of *The Secret Agent* was his first in nearly a year. Like most of his criticisms of Conrad's work, Garnett was acute here, citing Winnie's mother as the "real heroine of the story" because of her effacement of self, and finding in the relationship between Verloc and his wife "a hidden weakness in the springs of impulse," so that they seemed automata. In his response, Conrad readily agreed to the criticisms and seemed ecstatic that Garnett had "spotted my poor old woman. You've got a fiendishly penetrating eye for one's secret intentions." But Conrad's ready agreement disguised an annoyed tone, for he grabbed hold only of Garnett's negative comments, not of the many fine things he also said. After this letter and two others in October, Conrad did not write again until March.

As a favor to Garnett, however, Conrad wrote a fierce denunciation of the censorship of plays, published, after alteration by Garnett and the editors, in the *Daily Mail* for October 12 and later reprinted in *Notes on Life and Letters.* The episode was only a passing one and it produced only an interesting polemic, but it seems to strike a deeper note in Conrad and very possibly called up all his hatred of Russian censorship and restrictions on the Poland of his childhood. Whatever his precise motivation, he recognized the totalitarian mind when he found it. Garnett had suggested that the censor should be a policeman, but Conrad opposed that with "the Censor should *not be at all.*" He asks how such a censor would be selected: who is to be trusted with the power? who is to dismiss him? "Where are you going to find the tact, the wisdom, the breadth of mind, the artistic sense, the philosophical impartiality of thought, the wide intellectual sympathy, the humanistic and brazen self-confidence necessary for such a post for you can't draw a hard and fast line for him." The function calls not for a policeman but for a high functionary: "the supreme judge of form in art, the arbiter of moral intention. No. That function is impossible."

Yet even before he arrives at this argument, which is surely more than Garnett expected, Conrad indicates that his point of view will mean nothing to the public and may even have a negative reaction. For, he says, he has lately been "so cried up . . . as a sort of freak, an amazing bloody foreigner writing in English (every blessed review of *SA* had it—and even yours) that anything I say will be discounted on that ground by the public—that is if the public, that mysterious beast, takes any notice whatever—" Then Conrad moves to his real meaning: that a public fed on a diet by Hall Caine and such ilk are narcoticized. "Most of them have never heard of the Censor of plays and when they hear of his existence they will become at once instinctively his warm partisans. He is an institution, a respectable institution; he is an obvious and orderly fact; he satisfies the common mind and soothes the common cowardice. Andrew Lang will tell them perhaps that he is a historical survival and that'll capture their imaginations."

The conditions were perfect, accordingly, for Conrad to write his denunciation of the censor; he could propose it on ideological grounds, for he hated tyranny, and he could justify it on artistic grounds, the freedom of the artist. But, most importantly, he could attack the reading public, which would embrace a censor—a fact of "national self righteousness," a protector of morality—and not be at all disturbed by the outlawing of certain forms of art.

That is, Conrad had secured the high ground of art and artistic principles, and, once there, like Nietzsche he felt safe to throw his thunderbolts: he would be a martyr to his art, even in denouncing tyranny. The ghost of Apollo Korzeniowski had appeared on the parapet.

The article itself runs to about 1,500 words, and it is superb polemics, tying together Conrad's fierce defense of artistic expression and his hatred of the mentality which, he says, "has come to us by way of Moscow—I suppose." But his anger is chiefly aesthetic, not political. He sees the censor as having the power to kill: "He can kill thought, and incidentally truth, and incidentally beauty, providing they seek to live in dramatic form. He can do it without seeing, without understanding, without feeling anything; out of mere stupid suspicion, as an irresponsible Roman Caesar could kill a senator. . . . I tell you he is the Caesar of the dramatic world." Conrad says that this figure "seems designed in a spirit of bitter comedy to bring out the greatness of a Philistine's conceit and his moral cowardice."

The key passage, however, comes near the end, and in it Conrad summons up the accumulated bitterness of an artist who has toiled for principles that have met only indifference or ignorance.

> He [the censor] must be unconscious. It is one of the qualifications for his magistracy. Other qualifications are equally easy. He must have done nothing, expressed nothing, imagined nothing. He must be obscure, insignificant and mediocre—in thought, act, speech, and sympathy. He must know nothing of art, of life—and of himself. For if he did he would not dare to be what he is. Like that much questioned and mysterious bird, the phoenix, he sits amongst the cold ashes of his predecessor, upon the altar of morality, alone of his kind in the sight of wondering generations.

The writing of this piece must have triggered in Conrad's mind, as he moved inexorably toward fifty, the sense of his own worth; or else, his words alerted him to the dangers facing real art as it attempts to compete in the marketplace with ephemera.* James Joyce was confronting similar distinc-

* In a follow-up to his censor piece, Conrad told Galsworthy he had written an even stronger attack than was printed by the *Daily Mail*, but was dissuaded by Garnett for fear it would provoke a reaction in the censor's favor: "I didn't see the matter in the same light, but I did not discuss the point for fear that Edward (who declares himself Irish) should tell me (as a Slav) I know nothing of the English temper in controversy. To me it seems that if the cause be good the blows should be stout and that if you mean to down a man you don't avoid hitting him under the jaw for fear of 'provoking a reaction.' " Then Conrad gets to those "marketplace favorites," even attacking Ibsen along the way: "I suppose he [the censor] knew what he was doing when he choked off Annunzio that dreary, dreary saltimbanque of passion (out of his original Italian of which I know nothing) and Maeterlin[c]k the farceur who has been hiding an appalling poverty of ideas and hollowness of sentiment in wistful babytalk—two consecrated reputations, not

tions in the words he gives Stephen Dedalus about the marketplace meaning of tragedy and the literary significance of the term, which is far more complex and profound. Conrad's anger remained intense, and he found reason for it in Baron Tauchnitz's request to acquire *The Secret Agent* for his collection of British novels.

> With the exception of my first 2 books I think [he wrote Pinker], the publishing house of Baron Tauchnitz has refrained from publishing any of my work. Meantime it had acquired almost every piece of rubbishy fiction you may think of that fell from the press. Considering the literary value of my work as determined by the consensus of critical opinion in England and the U.S. I have accustomed myself to look upon my exclusion in the light of a distinction.
>
> . . . I can not allow a publishing House so much in the public eye to take two of my early works, then ignore seven as if they were unworthy or unfit to have a place in that great (and undiscriminating) collection—and suddenly offer to include the tenth.
>
> And the books that can't be found in the *Collection of British Authors* under Baron Tauchnitz's imprint include the Nigger, Youth. Lord Jim. Mirror of the Sea the very corner stones of my reputation, the best of seven years of my literary life!

The sum in question was £20 (about $250), but Conrad was insistent, even when he thought Pinker might want the money to reduce the debt: "As a friend you'll understand my feeling. To be excluded from the Tauchnitz Collection *is* a distinction for Joseph Conrad whose place in English literature is made. To come at the call of Baron Tauchnitz after 8 years of neglect is not to be thought of. None of my work shall appear *with my consent* in the Tauchnitz collection unless the head of that eminent firm agrees to include at least four works mentionned [sic] above, which he was ill-advised to neglect."

---

to speak of the sacrosanct Ibsen, of whom like Mrs Verloc of Ossipon, I prefer to say nothing. The refusal to pass Barker's play [Granville-Barker's *Waste*] in the face of the first attack increases my esteem for that imbecile [the censor]. But his office is an ugly anachronism a thing per se unworthy and should be abolished on that ground: not because it stands in the way of Messrs: Annunzio, Maeterlin[c]k and Ibsen or even E. Garnett and G. Barker."

CHAPTER 27

Burrowing In

THE sharpness and bitterness of Conrad's attack on marketplace ideas, and his own defensiveness about his foreignness,* suggest how difficult a time it was for him. His area of maneuverability, in terms of career, was narrow. *He* knew he was attempting different things in his fiction, but he was dropping his books, as it were, into a vast ocean of print, and they were becoming lost. Or else, his early reputation as a sea and exotic writer was interfering with his attempts to demonstrate the other strings on his instrument. He knew that reviewers and readers expected the same tones, and yet his vision of England and Europe was broadening. In a sense, he had to continue writing his own kind of work against what appeared to be his best interests. A few novels and tales in the early Malay idiom could well have solidified for him a popular reputation and large sales, especially when adventurous and romantic novels were the rage. A good deal of his depression and indolence in this period, at the end of 1907, was connected to his recognition that his worth was irremediably lost, whereas lesser figures were reaping the rewards of their accommodation to a fickle audience. The impulse to change his style and manner was overwhelming, and in a long, poignant letter to Galsworthy just after the New Year he defined his malaise even as he offered his original plan for a novel called "Razumov."

> There's nothing more cruel than to be caught between one's impulse, one's art and that question [of salability] which for me simply is a question of life and death. There are moments when the sinking fear sweeps

* In responding to Galsworthy's perceptive article on his work, Conrad read the manuscript or typescript and made very careful corrections of fact, not only of characters' names misspelled by his friend, but of his background. His foreignness was ever there as a wound, or a potential source of ridicule. Galsworthy had spoken of Conrad's family as having belonged to the Polish aristocracy, and he asked for a correction: "The name has never been illustrated by a senatorial dignity which was the only basis of Polish aristocracy. The Equestrian Order is more the thing. Land-tilling gentry is the most precise approach to a definition of my modest origin. As English publications reach far and wide notwithstanding the Censorship, I am anxious not to be suspected of the odious ridicule of passing myself for what I am not."

> my head clean of every thought. It is agonizing—no less. And—you know—that pressure grows from day to day instead of getting less.
>
> But I had to write it. I had to get away from *Chance* with which I was making no serious progress.

His disappointment over *The Secret Agent* was keen:

> The *S.A.* may be pronounced by now an honourable failure. It brought me neither love nor promise of literary success. I own that I am cast down. I suppose I am a fool to have expected anything else. I suppose there is something in me that is unsympathetic to his general public—because the novels of Hardy, for instance, are generally tragic enough and gloomily written too and yet they have sold in their time and are selling to the present day.
>
> Foreignness I suppose.

The example of Hardy is compelling on the surface, since he *is* gloomy, but Hardy's narratives are straightforward and his characters fit the nineteenth-century expectation of stereotypical villains, angels, and saints. Despite his pessimism, Hardy was still a Victorian novelist, that is, moving within recognizable forms of fiction, whereas Conrad by his own admission was "modern" and working technically in areas that were alien and disturbing to his readers. He was, unlike Hardy, forced to educate his readers to the fact that a new and different kind of fiction was arriving; and he and James, his fellow educator, would have to pay the price of being new.

Not only were they facing the traditional punishment meted out to the messengers of bad news, but they would have to deal with the irony of becoming coterie writers when they dreamed of broader success. Unlike Joyce of a slightly later time, Conrad did not have the rarefied sensibility of the completely elitist artist who could conceive of nothing but *his* art, *his* way. He was a more responsible family man than Joyce, more bourgeois in his expectations; and although he may have indeed brought currents of disorder and pessimism into English fiction, he operated within a world of order. Put another way, Joyce was the Happy Warrior of fiction, despite incredible setbacks, while Conrad was the Sad Warrior.

Conrad told Galsworthy he had become a vegetarian. "I eat very little too on purpose. The head is very clear just now but there are moments when I think against my will that I must give up. It's fatal for an imaginative man—this illomened suggestion coming like that from outside as it were. I fight it down of course—while I can." Casting up his accounts at fifty, Conrad finds his finances in complete disarray. Suspecting that he has only a few years remaining, as a man and as an artist, he is frantic.

> Eleven novels. If each had averaged £1000 I would have now 5000 in hand. For counting up all I owe you, other debts, the balance against me with P (1572 to date) and this grant I had together with all I have earned

> it works out at £650 p year in round numbers. Even if I have made a mistake of a 100 a year too little which is improbable (for however carelessly I counted I am not likely to have underestimated all I had by 1200 pounds) this is not outrageously extravagant. And in this there's Jessie's illness, all of my own—(the year wasted when writing Nostromo when I had six fits of gout in eleven months)—and this last fatal year with Borys abroad.

This letter, on January 6, however, jumps ahead. It is, in a sense, the dismal greeting of a new year for Conrad, and it involves the whole play of his life. Meanwhile, before the turn of the year, he was still trying to put out an interim volume, something that would represent him in between novels; and he told Pinker to arrange for a volume of short stories, which would consist of "*Gaspar Ruiz. 3 parts. The Anarchist. The Informer. The Brute. Il Conde.* equivalent to seven short stories—say 57–60 thousand words." When *A Set of Six* appeared on August 6, 1908, under the imprint of Methuen, it included "The Duel," which brought to it an additional 30,000 words. This volume became increasingly important for Conrad as he ran into an impasse on *Chance*, which simply would not come, and there appeared no way to force it. He feared another *Rescue*. "Razumov," begun as a short story, was intended to be an interim work while *Chance* simmered in the background.

"The Duel," which became subtitled "A Military Tale," set off in Conrad's mind, as he told Pinker, the idea for another military story. He probably was thinking of "The Warrior's Soul," which he would not write until 1916, although it contained a broader treatment of the Napoleonic retreat from Moscow touched upon in "The Duel." That episode evidently was in the forefront of Conrad's mind (he was, also, on the edge of his first "Russian" novel) because he resurrected in his reminiscences for Ford's *English Review* the story of his Uncle Nicholas, who ate dog during the retreat from Moscow. These interconnected images—military honor, dueling, paying off debts, the exquisitely complicated shades of his past and early childhood, the figure of Napoleon and of Napoleonic conquest in terms of Russian-Polish interests—were all activated in Conrad's imagination as he prepared himself for a journey into the past. We should not underestimate the psychological tension that was involved as he moved toward the start of "Razumov." Even though it was to be only a short story, it would prove, like Proust's circling return to the purlieus of the Baron de Charlus at the end of his novel, the test of everything he had come to at that stage. "Razumov," in effect, was more than a novel for Conrad; it would become a trial.

Just before December, when he was to announce to Pinker he had in hand "*10* pp. of *Razumov* the first of the two short stories," he suffered from an attack of gout in his foot. He wrote Marguerite on New Year's Day that he was "tired and rejected," and it was very difficult for him to work. "I am one of those who don't sell. And here I am in my fifties!" To Elsie Hueffer, on the same day, he spoke of his "doleful existence." He was definitely cranking up for something significant, although even on January 7 he was still speaking of "Razumov" as a story. He tells Pinker he is "anxious to throw that story off my chest." He adds, possibly to sweeten what he has in store for his agent, "Here is given the very essence of things Russian. Not the mere outward manners and customs but the Russian feeling and thought. You may safely say that. And, I think, the story is effective. Nothing of the sort had been done in English. The subject has long haunted me. Now it must come out."

He even speaks of setting up a volume "for three big machines" like "*Strong Man* ["Gaspar Ruiz"] *the Duel* and *Razumov*," only to conclude that the latter, because of "its sustained intensity," would be more suitable for another volume, presumably of stories. Quite rightly, he saw it as "altogether on another plane." Yet it is impossible to determine what Conrad had in mind when he saw it as a story, unless that was a sweetener for Pinker alone. The reader who scrutinizes the first five or ten thousand words of *Under Western Eyes* finds no cutting point, no apparent seams short of 25–30,000 words. Even more telling, however, is Conrad's description of his plan to Galsworthy, on January 6, one day *before* he wrote to Pinker, to the effect that at first he planned a psychological novel.

> The student Razumov (a natural, son of a Prince K——) gives up secretly to the police his fellow Student Haldin who seeks refuge in his rooms after committing a political crime (supposed to be the murder of de Plehve). First movement is St. Petersburg. (Haldin is hanged of course.) [in margin: "done"]
>
> 2nd in Geneva. The Student Razumov meeting abroad the mother and sister of Haldin falls in love with that last, marries her and after a time confesses to her the part he played in the arrest of Haldin and death of her brother. [in margin: "to do"]
>
> The psychological developments leading to Razumov's betrayal of Haldin, to his confession of the fact to his wife and to the death of these people (brought about mainly by the resemblance of their child to the late Haldin) form the real subject of the story.

Conrad is quite clear about the St. Petersburg and Geneva locales, which would indicate something considerably more ambitious than the short story he was outlining to Pinker. But, in direct contradiction, he also speaks of asking £100 for "Razumov" for serialization, an indication of story length, since he could demand at least £1,000 for a novel. He appeared to be pulling in two directions. Intermixed in the January letters about the novel are some of Conrad's most compelling words about his financial hardships and his refusal to cheapen himself, some of this in response to what he felt was Pinker's prodding.

> It is extraordinary [he wrote Pinker] that people who understand that a carpenter can't make a box if somebody keeps on jogging his elbow will say that no jog of any sort shall matter to a mind. I have no charm, no flow of wit or of facetiousness or mere patter to fill in chinks with. I have only a mind a quite different gift from the gift of the gab. I have no literary tradition even which will help to spin phrases—the chewed up silly phrases. I am not a "sedulous Ape". I wish sometimes I were. Why none of the business men would *sit* as I do with nothing but an inkstand and a pen to make things of. They couldn't. Their health would give way. Mine, rotten as it is, has got to stand it. I have no amusement, no relaxation of any kind—none whatever. I haven't seen a play or listened to a piece of music it seems for years. Jack G's dinner and the day out with Borys yesterday is all I've had since last August. I hate to get away from my table. I've not willingly, on purpose, lost a single minute of my time. It really was hardly worth while to throw a six penny telegram at me. I don't say this as a reproach but as a simple reflection.

These strong words reinforce our contention that romantic martyrdom, intense commitment in the face of adversity, a view of himself as Sisyphus struggling behind the boulder fired Conrad's imagination, not unlike the sea captain moving into the eye of a storm ready to test his ability to neutralize nature itself.

Yet he told Galsworthy that "Razumov" would be "done in a few days." January of 1908 became a crucial month, when the story or novel could have gone in either direction, toward easy resolution or toward the kind of complication of narrative and narrator that Conrad considered to be his special mark. Pressures were everywhere: from Pinker, who understandably wanted his debts reduced; from family, who had special needs—schooling, medical attention, decent living conditions; and, not least, from himself, now fifty and still a struggling writer. He was, financially, in the situation of a man half his age, starting out, and gaining a barely livable income from his art; and yet he was fifty, with nearly a book a year to show for his fourteen years of writing. He was a veteran living on an amateur's income—so it seemed to him. In actuality, he had achieved a large reputation in England; he was considered by reviewers to be one of the major novelists of his generation; and his proceeds, while far below his expectations, were not unreasonable in the light of serious art sales anywhere. With a relatively small reading population, and that readership further reduced by Conrad's difficulties with language and narrative method, it is surprising he sold as well as he did.

The important thing, however, was how he felt about his career. The depression of these years was real, since at the completion of his labors on *Under Western Eyes*, the very end of 1909, he collapsed completely, fought with Pinker and others, and was brought near artistic death. January, then, was the month for decisions, not only about "Razumov," but in terms of his entire career. Still in that month, he told Pinker he was transmitting pp. 51–70 of "Razumov." Since Conrad's holograph was rarely more than 100–150 words per page, we can assume he had written 7–10,000 words of what was still a short story. He then added an ominous note, in terms, possibly, of length: "It has got to be what fate wills but it won't be a mean thing." He assured Pinker, "I am in good working trim. R shall make two inst: of 7000 each. And he who reads the first shall want to read the second." He also mentions *Chance* as not being "wholly neglected," although he had been promising this manuscript for two years and would not deliver it for another four.

Conrad was on the eve of another "collaborative" effort, this time as virtual co-editor of *The English Review*, with Ford as managing editor. It was a curious time, for, personally and aesthetically, Conrad had moved well out of the relationship with Ford; but the attachment, or the memory of good times, apparently remained. Or else, he felt that Ford was a lifeline with the "world of letters," and would serve as buffer between his own self-imposed isolation and a London society he did not want to meet directly. There is, further, the fact that Ford acted as a catalyst on Conrad, offering ideas, stimulating him intellectually, taking dictation, or even turning out some manuscript for him, and the latter needed to be propped up.

January also was a month of incredible financial maneuvering. Pinker had balked at the extraordinary outlays, including unexpected requests, that Conrad made upon him. To Galsworthy, Conrad lamented, the cries of a man shipwrecked and slowly sinking as his strength ebbs. Once again, he tried to gain mental control of his situation by presenting it to Galsworthy, but it included many dubious items. One of them was predicated on his completion of "Razumov" at this time; it would, with other pieces, bring £500 of the £1,500 owed to Pinker. "Razumov" was almost two years off. Pinker wanted Conrad off the payroll for the next five to six months, thus saving himself £3–400. The second assumption was the completion of *Chance*, which Conrad saw as occurring in the summer, which would relieve Pinker of another £900 of the debt, plus outlays until that time. Although Conrad pretended he was always one novel behind in his payments, he was now two novels behind and spending more rapidly than he could make up with copy. Although we lack Pinker's responses, the agent must have recognized that Conrad had moved considerably outside their original calculation, which involved only his subsidization of the novel being brought forward.

Both Pinker and Conrad understandably felt panic: the agent because of Conrad's increasing indebtedness and seeming dawdling; Conrad, for obvious reasons—that he had hatched novel-length ideas when Pinker was pressuring him for salable stories. There was, apparently, a disproportion of expectation, almost the classic confrontation between marketplace and art.

The month of negotiations was so crucial because Conrad was being brought closer to a realization he had avoided for many years: that if he could not produce more rapidly, he would not be permitted to produce his kind of thing at all. In suggesting to Galsworthy a long-term financial arrangement, Conrad saw his position as eschatological. After indicating the end of *Chance* in July, and his fear that something unreasonable might happen to him, he predicted the rest of his career: "I don't allude to the ever present possibility of my demise. I shall fight that tooth and claw. I must leave 20 vols behind me and there are only 11 written—Chance will make the 12th and leave only eight more—a trifle indeed—before I can drop the pen." He feared gout would impede his production; but of interest is his life's goal—to leave twenty volumes. He would, in actuality, leave twenty-seven, plus an additional volume if his dramatic efforts were collected.

By this time, *A Set of Six*, his eleventh volume, was set as presently constituted. "Razumov" was separated from it, to form the nucleus of the next collection. Interestingly, the next collection would include "The Secret Sharer," a story with considerable connection to "Razumov" and, not unusually, written while Conrad was finishing *Under Western Eyes*. By mid-January, he had moved his sights to "nouvelle" length for "Razumov," which for him meant anywhere from 30 to 40,000 words, the length of "Heart of Darkness," "The Duel," or even "The End of the Tether."

With that settled, he went back to Pinker to renegotiate their financial arrangement, although he says he feels as if he were begging. After assuring Pinker he has no vices, neither gambling nor drinking, to lead him astray, he asks for a lump sum of £40 each month. At the same time, he admits he may not count "strictly enough." Pinker had not objected to the original arrangement but to the unexpected requests for money, which were, he felt, the result of poor management. Conrad adds that if necessary he will have to try elsewhere, probably Galsworthy, to get that £40 a month which he needs for minimum living expenses. Pinker did eventually come through, but Conrad found the situation harrowing, like Jim with his hand on the quivering bulkhead of the *Patna*. For neither author nor agent was there any chance of resolution, since Pinker wanted copy and Conrad could not produce it readily. Conrad even tried some explanations based on art, pointing out that, with *Chance* in mind, "a big conception can't be kept going like a shorter work." He adds that the previous year was terribly unsettling: "Not only by what it was then—but also by what it meant for the future. It was a horrid nightmare."

February and March 1908, a time when Conrad was moving professionally toward co-editorship with Ford of *The English Review*, were filled with almost equal amounts of "Razumov," illness (mainly gout and nerves), monetary troubles, worry about professional standing, pride of accomplishment, feelings of extraordinary achievement and inadequacy. It is difficult to pinpoint how much of Conrad's disturbance resulted from his growing involvement with Ford, how much from his own lack of popular recognition, or how much from a sense of futility as he saw everything slipping away. The pessimism of his outlook had to be faced personally, and there was no way in which he could be the exception to what he foresaw for the general run of mankind. All he could hope for, with his mixture of gloom, morbidity, and determinism, was a measure of health to continue his work.

His letters take on a biting, querulous edge, not only to Ford, but also to Galsworthy and Wells. His dealings with Pinker have an adversary quality. Even his long letter of February 5 to Marguerite Poradowska has a listless, subdued tone. In a February 12 letter to Pinker, he speaks of needing a "freer hand with that story. If I can't have a free hand—time—for elaborating my work and freedom from interference I would just as soon stop writing entirely." He says this apparently to keep Pinker from prodding him about a short story for *London Magazine*, which Conrad feels will mangle "Razumov." Or else he knows that no "story length" is there. That short story for *London Magazine*, incidentally, was a revision of "The Black Mate," Conrad's first piece of fictional writing, or else, as Jessie claimed, a different story.

Conrad then defended himself against any charges of indolence, citing thirteen volumes since 1895 and indicating that one-third of his time was lost in illness. In the same letter (to Pinker) he moves to a new tack, mentioning for the first time he may try his hand at writing in French. "I have also proposals [presumably from the *Mercure de France*] for working in French and I don't feel too old to make a fresh start. In the general uncertainty of what is to happen to me the idea doesn't seem so very bizarre. Rather interesting in fact." In another letter in February, he says "the end is in sight" for "Razumov," at a time when he was more than 100,000 words from completion. The letter is itself mainly full of diatribes against Methuen, which was insisting on the literal reading of a contract calling for three novels over 75,000 words. And this gets him into rancor about Methuen's handling of *The Secret Agent:*

> Certainly when signing the special agreement for it I had no idea what I was doing. I was too busy thinking how to make that book—what it is: a distinguished piece of work. I don't think that the book has been made the most of. It has been passed off in the ruck. The others shall too no doubt be treated in the same way. Of course! But I am not satisfied. Far from it. 3 books is a large slice of Conrad's life. I am not a sausage machine that takes rotten scraps on at one end and turns out a marketable sausage at the other. Morally I feel bound to let M. have another novel after *Chance*—and that's all—and morally he has no right to expect more. There is the legal aspect of the case I know. But if I am to go to the devil I'll go in my

> own way—where he certainly will find neither profit nor honours. When one has got an *unique* autor [sic] one had better treat him in a special way.

On another occasion, Conrad warned, "If I write a 65,000 novel he will have to take it. I am not a draper to measure my stuff to the exact yard."

Despite these worries—"Razumov" growing, Methuen refusing to accept *The Secret Agent* under their agreement—Conrad found time to renew his correspondence and friendship with Norman Douglas. His kindness to Douglas, in fact, pokes through on many occasions when he was himself hard-pressed and distracted. Conrad evidently recognized a considerable talent and was, even more, probably taken with Douglas's spirit and intelligence. A good deal of the latter's difficulty in getting placed stemmed from the nature of his material. He was essentially a travel writer, with a trenchant awareness of places, a sharp observant eye, and a sensitive feel for the words with which to capture an image, scene, or impression. *Old Calabria* represents these qualities at their best, as do some of the *Capri* sketches. While all of these characteristics are necessary for the novelist, they are not sufficient; and Douglas's wit and elegance notwithstanding, he could not easily transform his spirit of place into narrative writing. He was tied to the short scene; perhaps this explains Conrad's admiration for a writer so different in temperament from himself.

Conrad's letter of February 29, 1908, comments tactfully on the problem: "Think seriously of writing a novel. Write your fiction in the tone of this very excellent article ["Isle of Typhoeus"] if you like. Place it in S. Italy if that will help. Try to make it a novel of analysis on the basis of some strong situation. A man like you who has seen things and known many people has got only to descend within himself for material. And I promise you that everything I and two or three more can do shall be done to get the novel published with a proper flourish." The asterisk leads to a note in which Conrad urges him not to try to write of Italian peasant life—not as yet, but to place "*European* personalities in Italian frame. European here means an international crowd." Conrad surely had his own *Nostromo* in mind, and also very probably *Under Western Eyes* once he was to move the mise en scène to Geneva. Then follow, in the same letter, several paragraphs of advice about words and phrases, all toward greater precision and visualization of the material. Conrad's corrections are a model of professional writing, in which the master shows his apprentice how to best utilize his talent.

The obvious place for Conrad to seek publication for Douglas was in *The English Review*, whose editorship Ford had assumed in 1908. The four early issues, when Ford had full editorial command of the *Review*, were really Conrad-Ford issues, in that their immediate circle or Ford's "discoveries" took up most of the space. The talent in the *Review* was prodigious, including extensive contributions by Conrad (his reminiscences), also Hardy, Wells (the opening sections of *Tono-Bungay*), James ("A Jolly Corner"), Galsworthy ("A Fisher of Men"), Hudson (a piece on Stonehenge), Constance Garnett's translation of Tolstoy's "The Raid," as well as articles and reviews by Graham, Marwood, W. H. Davies, and Conrad once again. Conrad was successful in placing Douglas's "Isle of Typhoeus" in the third issue of the journal, in February 1909. Douglas's financial position was weak, and he needed considerable propping. Conrad wrote: "It's weary slow work at best this trying to get a footing in the world of scribblers and publishers. Yet it can be done—with patience."

This was a diversion of sorts, perhaps recalling to Conrad his attempts to help the impecunious Crane. Pinker, however, was the key man in Conrad's life, not Douglas. In a letter of March 23, Conrad returned to "Razumov," herein noting (to Pinker) it "may turn out a good thing," growing now to a "serial of 45,000," which is "easier to place than one of 90,000." He says he is ready to write in "a scene of 5000 words" if Fisher Unwin can be induced to take it in book form. At the end of the letter, Conrad mentions his "story deserves a better title than a man's name," although the manuscript at Yale indicates "Razumov" throughout, with "Under Western Eyes" appearing only on the final page. In another March letter, he states categorically that Chapter 4 will be the last and the story will be precisely 43,000 words, which is a little longer than "Heart of Darkness." This leads us to believe Conrad possibly intended to terminate the story with Part I, when Mikulin asks Razumov where he can go, the theme of "Where to?" which runs throughout the completed novel. Yet if this is indeed so, and the Yale manuscript of the novel gives us no further clues, then what happened to Conrad's former plan, outlined to Galsworthy less than three months before, to have Razumov marry Miss Haldin in Geneva and then confess his role to her?

There is a further contradiction. By calling the manuscript "Razumov," Conrad had pointed toward his main character. With that title, the original plan seems closer: that is, the psychological developments leading from Razumov's marriage to Miss Haldin and subsequent confession to her when their child resembles Haldin. That original plan, incidentally, which would flow from a Razumov-oriented manuscript, is more adapted to the distinctly Conradian tone—it recalls *Lord Jim*, in particular*—but very possibly lacked that emotional distancing he needed for a story Russian in nature.

---

* André Gide, in a curious cultural transference, connected *Under Western Eyes* and *Lord Jim* as he planned a novel for himself. Shortly after his Journal indicates he and his wife have been reading *Under Western Eyes* aloud and he was correcting the French proofs of "The End of the Tether," he made a long outline for a new novel. What is remarkable about Gide's outline for *his* novel is how near it is to Conrad's themes for *Western Eyes* and *Jim*. In searching his own mind, Gide touched on the distinctive Conradian note:

In an undated letter, which we can place in May 1908, we have the first firm note of the novel's length. Conrad writes, "I can't let you have 'Razumov' yet. That story must be worked out as it is worth it." He announces that Pinker will "have a volume very soon—or strictly speaking a serial story which for many reasons (subject, manageable length) will be easier to place than a long sea machine." It will be, he hopes, a book which Methuen can publish as part of the contract. In July, Conrad felt himself trapped between the demands of the novel, which was apparently growing, and what he felt was undue prodding from Pinker for a completed project.

> Hall Caine takes two years to write his books. J.C. may be allowed some time. If your idea is that my stuff is unsaleable then all I can say is that I haven't made it so. If I must starve or beg I won't do it *here.* That's all I have to say really. Consider whether it would be a good policy (from a practical point of view) to drive me away. This is nothing but a *statement of the case.* Don't take it in any other spirit. I have no vice to prevent me working and I am willing as soon as practicable to get away into a most economical hole imaginable and write there night and day. I can't believe that my reputation has gone to pieces suddenly.

If we skip ahead to that period: Conrad was running "Razumov" on parallel lines with *Some Reminiscences,* which later became *A Personal Record,* a kind of loosely conceived autobiographical memoir written for *The English Review.* That jogging of memory and that retrieval of the past which

one's loss of desire and energy at a crucial moment, the recognition that external forces vitiate the personal will, the ability to enter into one's own destruction (to be witness, indeed, at one's own death), the ever-present sense of cowardice or the failure to impose oneself in an absurd universe, the mixed quality of repentance even as repentance seems a necessity. Gide's Journal entry follows: "X indulges in a tremendous effort of ingenuity, scheming, and duplicity to succeed in an undertaking that he knows to be reprehensible. He is urged on by his temperament, which has its exigencies, then by the rule of conduct he has built in order to satisfy them. It takes an extreme and hourly application; he expends more resolve, energy, and patience in this than would be needed to succeed in the best. And when eventually the event is prepared to such a point that he has only to let it take its course, the letdown he experiences allows him to reflect; he then realizes that he has ceased to desire greatly that felicity on which he had counted too much. But it is too late now to back out; he is caught in the mechanism he has built and set in motion and, willy-nilly, he must now follow its impetus to its conclusion. The event that he no longer dominates carries him along and it is almost passively that he witnesses his perdition. Unless he suddenly gets out of it by a sort of cowardice; for there are some who lack the courage to pursue their acts to their conclusion, without moreover being any more virtuous for this reason. On the contrary they come out diminished and with less self-esteem. This is why, everything considered, X. will persevere, but without any further desire, without joy and rather through *fidelity.* This is the reason why there is often so little happiness in crime—and what is called 'repentance' is frequently only the exploitation of this." Gide makes us read Conrad a little differently, perhaps more existentially than psychologically, although not to the loss or diminution of Conrad's intense psychological interests.

characterizes his Russian novel fitted perfectly the "remembrance of things past" which he was producing for Ford's journal. By the time he was to begin his reminiscences, he had written 62,000 words of "Razumov," about half the completed novel. In one of those curious parallels, as he was to lead Razumov into destruction in Geneva, he was himself to be reborn in the early pages of his reminiscences. The entire memoir, in fact, was conceived of as a series of births and rebirths: Conrad's various lives, each of which ended, and each of which led into a new one.

However, he did not start the summer of 1908 that easily. It was a struggle to stay alive in order to churn out copy. The pressures were such that almost alone they would help explain Conrad's new connection with Ford, as virtual co-editor of the *Review*. "Razumov" was not coming cleanly, although Conrad was working. In a letter to Davray, he speaks of Razumov—"quiet student—who dies. That is all. One can do something in French. Only the 'great passion' shows at the end. For the rest—analysis—but movement enough all the same—there is the tone of the novel." This came on March 14, and it indicates some kind of interim plan in which Razumov is to die. Conrad may have been following a particular source, the story of a man named Stepniak (S. M. Kravchinsky), whom he knew about from the Garnetts. Stepniak, a combination of Razumov and Haldin in Conrad's handling, had killed a Russian chief of police, fled the country, and been killed in England by a train as he crossed a railway track. It is not certain that Conrad had this source in mind, but the early version of "Razumov" coincides in this matter at least. Once Conrad definitely changed the plan of his novel, he also changed the ending, which was to make it more ironic, if less dramatic. Also, circumstances worked to change the very title. The California novelist Gertrude Atherton published a novel called *Rezánov* (1906), and Conrad feared the titles sounded too similar. At the same time, he felt his story deserved better than a man's name.

In late March, Conrad complained to Wells that since Pinker had partially cut down on him, he needed a Royal Literary Fund grant to carry him through, one of those periodic "miracles" he depended upon. It would be his third grant, and he needed Wells's support in a letter. He says that for a period of three months, only ending in January, he has been laid out by gout, which needed repeated medical attention. As a consequence, he has fallen well behind the promises made to Pinker, and is now twelve months behind schedule. Certainly all plans for finishing "Razumov" and getting back to *Chance* were defeated, although these were not realistic plans to begin with. He received the grant in April, for £200.

The difficulties with Pinker were the early stages of what would lead to a two-year estrangement, after Conrad's collapse upon finishing *Under Western Eyes*. Intermixed with this was his continued exasperation with the Someries house; Conrad told Wells they hoped to "get out of this house" and "creep into some small hole somewhere even more out of sight and hearing than this one." They would move, at the end of 1908, to Aldington, near Hythe, in Kent, remain there until June of 1910, and then again move, to Capel House, which was their residence for almost nine years. Meanwhile, Ford's *Fifth Queen* trilogy had appeared, a very ambitious effort, and Conrad expressed his admiration; but his letter, on March 31, seems strained, especially since Conrad says he is stuck with "Razumov." "Invention's dead."

Out of nowhere, on April 21, Conrad answered Pinker on the "R question." This is evidently a reference to *The Rescue*, for Conrad says he does want "to be positive" about it. This is the first mention of that unfinished manuscript in some time, and we may suppose it arose as a consequence of an impasse on "Razumov." It was followed a few days later (on April 27) by a brief note to Cora Crane, who had sent a memento of Stephen. Within the span of a week, Conrad was thrown back into the 1890s, the time of *The Rescue* and Stephen Crane, even as "Razumov" was thrusting him back into a parallel period, the time when he had been attacked for deserting Poland. Early in the book, he suggests the dualism with which he had to grapple, an English author with Slavic nightmares. The old teacher of languages is attempting to modulate for the Western reader Razumov's sense of his fate:

> It is unthinkable that any young Englishman should find himself in Razumov's situation. This being so it would be a vain enterprise to imagine what he would think. The only safe surmise to make is that he would not think as Mr. Razumov thought at this crisis of his fate. He would not have an hereditary and personal knowledge of the means by which a historical autocracy represses ideas, guards its power, and defends its existence. By an act of mental extravagance he might imagine himself arbitrarily thrown into prison, but it would never occur to him unless he were delirious (and perhaps not even then) that he could be beaten with whips as a practical measure either of investigation or of punishment.

With this, Conrad slipped back still further, to his childhood, to the fate of his parents and other close relatives, to the very bones of his heritage. No wonder, then, that he found the manuscript to be a personal mine field. There is the still further problem, on which we can only speculate, of how closely Nathalie (or Natalia) Haldin is modeled on his dim memories of his mother, Ewa. Nathalie's relationship to her brother, whom she sees as a noble idealist, has a parallel model in Ewa's devotion to Apollo and her entrance into his revolutionary activities. Whatever was in Conrad's mind, however, we can be certain that the very portrait, whether his mother or not, would provide terrible conflicts, since he planned to create a sympathetic young lady whose political fervor is directed toward a cause he detested. All her noble idealism is focused, for Conrad, upon causes and ideas unworthy of her devotion. She seeks human perfectibility in a Russian ambiance which recognizes only cynicism and deception, and she favors a revolutionary process in an atmosphere in which all fervor becomes blunted or even poisoned. At one point, Nathalie and the old teacher exchange views, and Conrad's ambivalence was never more intense. She speaks her noble message, taken from Haldin's letter, that each individual will must be awakened:

> Of course the will must be awakened, inspired, concentrated. . . . That is the true task of real agitators. One has got to give up one's life to it. The degradation of servitude, the absolutist lies must be uprooted and swept out. Reform is impossible. There is nothing to reform. There is no legality, there are no institutions. There are only arbitrary decrees. There is only a handful of cruel—perhaps blind—officials against a nation.

Her point about the individual will seems borrowed from Max Stirner, who argued that rebellion of individuals, not revolution involving a mass, was the sole way of revamping the state. What the state feared, Stirner said, was not mass action but the individual who refuses to be "arranged." Miss Haldin stops short of that truly revolutionary idea, but whatever her exact meaning, the language teacher replies devastatingly, a rejoinder whose cynicism is clearly as much Conrad's as his. Although conceived in 1908–9, its message partially foreshadowed the fate of the Kerensky government in the Russian Revolution of 1917.

> The last thing I want to tell you is this: in a real revolution—not a simple dynastic change or a mere reform of institutions—in a real revolution the best characters do not come to the front. A violent revolution falls into the hands of narrow-minded fanatics and of tyrannical hypocrites at first. Afterwards comes the turn of all the pretentious intellectual failures of the time. Such are the chiefs and the leaders. You will notice that I have left out the mere rogues. The scrupulous and the just, the noble, humane, and devoted natures; the unselfish and the intelligent may begin a movement but it passes away from them. They are not the leaders of a revolution. They are its victims: the victims of disgust, of disenchantment—often of remorse. Hopes grotesquely betrayed, ideals caricatured—that is the definition of revolutionary success.

Had the language teacher presented this countering view to an unsympathetic character, there would have been no conflict in Conrad. But it was directed at someone willing to sacrifice her life for an ideal, regardless of personal safety, and, therefore, someone whose life would be tested by her loyalty to a noble vision. She is, then, a person, like Ewa, whom Conrad admired even as he deplored the misuse of her resources in a hopeless cause.

These were not simply memories; they were psychological moments of terrible intensity. Conrad was, for the sake of his art, harrowing his own form of hell, far more deeply than Proust when he explored memory. For Proust, the consequence was a positive endeavor; for Conrad, it was to reaffirm the impasse of his own devotion. He, too, admired rebellion but detested revolution; rebellion meant individual expression, whereas revolution meant assimilation, a mass movement. And yet rebellion often led directly into revolution for virtually all, and the voracious state, like the "Voreux" in Zola's *Germinal*, swallowed them whole at one end and excreted them at the other. And even as Conrad harrowed his hell, Pinker requested ever more novel copy, as well as stories and sketches, reviews, anything to bring in further revenue.

In April or somewhat later, Conrad wrote Ford about his *Mr. Apollo*, which was to be published in August. Conrad's praise is high, which is unusual, since the Ford novel is of the kind he disliked. It was Ford's attempt to get at issues by way of fantasy, the divinity of "Apollo" contrasted with the rationalism, commercialism, and Fabianism of those around him. Ford's point is that only the divine can lead us from debasement, and for that we need the example of gods and poets. We have no record of how Conrad felt about Apollo—shades of his father—in this role, but he speaks of it as "something impeccable and absolutely above criticism." He sees it not as a startling experience but as a unique one. He adds, for whatever personal reasons: "And if you experience perchance that feeling of intimate secret gratification which visits sometimes an artist, you may take it from me that in this case the moment of 'ivresse divine' is sufficiently justified." Since the whole thing would seem to Conrad a carryover from their *Inheritors* days, with the Fourth Dimensionists as the enemy there, he could not have taken Ford's effort seriously and was surely trying to moderate matters between them as they moved toward the *English Review* co-editorship. It is difficult to prove, but even Ford could not have been serious about such a novel, since his own manifesto for the *Review* would appear to contradict it.

The manifesto, which Ford drew up after considerable consultation with Conrad and Marwood, in sweeping away all ephemera and all modern superficiality, would appear to do away with Ford's own work to that time, except for the *Fifth Queen* trilogy. Since Ford, with Conrad beside him, became a remarkable editor during his brief *English Review* days, the manifesto bears repeating:

> The only qualification for admission to the pages of the Review will be—in the view of the Editors—either distinction of individuality or force of conviction, either literary gifts or earnestness of purpose, whatever the purpose may be—the criterion of inclusion being the clarity of diction, the force of the illuminative value of the views expressed. What will be avoided will be superficiality of the specially modern kind which is the inevitable consequence when nothing but brevity of statement is aimed at. *The English Review* will treat its readers, not as spoiled children who must be amused by a variety of games, but with the respectful consideration due to grown-up minds whose leisure can be interested by something else than the crispness and glitter of popular statement.

This was composed in the fall of 1908, but it expressed Ford's—and Conrad's—point of view, and it certainly could not support a novel such as *Mr. Apollo*. Editorial work probably helped Ford pull his creative talents together, so that his best fiction resulted from the period after he had tried his hand at serious editing. This was an interesting time for the two to come together again, since they were out of phase creatively, although united in their aesthetic demands upon themselves. Ford was still struggling to find the right subject matter for his sense of form, whereas Conrad was still seeking the right form for his assured sense of subject matter. Ford was to push out more firmly into the "modern" movement, in terms of technique, whereas Conrad was to spend this period and the next few years consolidating gains he had already made. The time of the *Review* was one of those overlapping periods, when Victorian and modern, for whatever such terms are worth, crisscrossed or arranged themselves mosaically in the talents brought together.

The feelings of dread continued, however, and Conrad looked forward to leaving Someries, for which he had a "positive horror," and going to Kent for three or four weeks, resting and looking for a new place. Meanwhile, reviews of *A Set of Six* began to come in, the book having appeared on August 6. What was particularly disturbing about two of the reviews, by Robert Lynd in the *Daily News* and W. L. Courtney in the *Daily Telegraph*, was that they questioned his entire career by raising doubts about his use of the English language. Written when he was himself revisiting his Polish memories for "Razumov," these commentaries could not have come at a worse time. They were, in addition, inexplicable, as we can see from Lynd's remarks:

> Had he but written in Polish his stories would assuredly have been translated into English and into the other languages of Europe; and the works of Joseph Conrad translated from the Polish would, I am certain, have been a more precious possession on English shelves than the works of Joseph Conrad in the original English, desirable as these are. What greater contribution has been made to literature in English during the past twenty years than Mrs. Constance Garnett's translations of the novels of Turgénieff? But suppose Turgénieff had tried to write them in English!

To answer this kind of criticism, an author can only hope for wholesale death of all reviewers.

Courtney's notice is more positive, but he uses Conrad's stories as a way of attacking the modern sensibility; it is particularly ironic in that these stories are among Conrad's most conventional. Courtney wrote: "It is a dreary philosophy [stoicism, gloomy resignation] at best, but it is what Mr. Conrad's tales suggest. He, too, belongs to that modern school of violence which, whether in the form of Imperial violence, like that of Mr. Rudyard

Kipling, or psychological violence, like that of our author, appears to be the most popular mode or pose among our writers of today. All the light, all the colours are crude and harsh. There is no softness in the landscape, no healing balm in the atmosphere. The world is an unfriendly place, and most of us, if we begin to think at all, are prisoners."

Conrad's reaction was a compound of amazement and desolation; he could not escape the "foreign" label even though he had been publishing in English for thirteen years and few reviewers were even aware of his full Polish name. As he wrote Galsworthy:

> Courtney did not discompose me much. What does it all matter? There is an [sic] who tells me in Dly News on god knows what provocation that I am a man "without country and language." It is like abusing some poor tongue-tied wretch. For, what can one say? The statement is gross and palpable and the answer that could be made would be incomprehensible to nine tenths of the hearers who would have imagination enough to believe that a complex sentiment can be true. I wonder in what language the Nigger, Youth or the Mirror *could* have been written? But the fellow must be an imbecile anyhow since he goes on falling into raptures over Gaspar Ruiz and comparing that wretched magazine fake with the Lear of the Steppes!!! It's incredible isn't it? Idiocy can no further go! Still a kick from a donkey hurts as much as from a nobler animal and is in a way more humiliating.

Conrad then turns to the rest of the review: that he would have read better in Constance Garnett's English than in his own:

> I don't know why I am telling you all this. My heart has been like a stone and my hand wore lead all day—and I don't know why I should inflict this mood on you. It's indecent. And yet to hold one's tongue is too difficult, at times. To turn out a volume in 10 months is difficult, too—what do you think? The above Dly News genius exclaims that my novels would have been better if translated by Mrs. Garnett. That's an idea. Shall I send her the clean type of Razumov? But why complicate life to that extent? She ought to write them; and then the harmless reviewer could begin something like this: "M[r] Joseph Conrad's latest novel written by Mrs Garnett is a real acquisition for our literature, not like the others previously published which on the whole were rather noxious if amazing phenomena etc etc."*

* To Garnett, on August 21, Conrad continued to vent his anger against Courtney and Lynd. He measures the marketplace value of the remarks: "If I had made money by dealing in diamond shares like my neighbor here, Sir Julius Wernher, of Hamburg, I would be a baronet of the U.K. and provided both with a language and a country." Later in the month (August 28), he defended himself against still further accusations, those by Arthur Symons in a still-unpublished study of Conrad: "At any rate I think I have always written with dignity, with more dignity than the above-alluded-to butterfly ever could command.

Conrad found himself gaining notice, but hardly the kind he desired. Even Garnett's praise of *A Set of Six* took a sinister turn; that is, Garnett supported Conrad's powers by making them into Slavic, not English, strengths: "They [Conrad's stories] are Continental in their literary affinities, Slav in their psychological insight, and Polish in their haunting and melancholy cadence, and in their preference for dwelling on the minor." Further, Garnett speaks of Conrad's humor as "essentially Slav in its ironic acceptance of the pathetic futility of human nature, and quite un-English in its refinement of tender, critical malice." Within the context of his comments, Garnett is basically correct, and his wording is delicate and praiseworthy; yet Conrad, the author of "Amy Foster," was aware of how forcefully he beat against the door of England and how carefully he tried to shape the language so as to be understood by Englishmen.

With his Russian friends, his close associations with anarchists, exiles, socialists, and Russian literature of the fiercest kind (Dostoevsky and Tolstoy), Garnett kept moving Conrad back into everything he had tried to escape. Further, this was occurring just as he was writing "Razumov" and attempting to distance himself from the Russian scene, trying to filter out his hatred and anger by means of an English narrator. Yet all the while he was seeking distance, both technically and psychologically, he was attacking those very anarchists and socialists who sought refuge with the Garnetts at the Cearne. So that even as Garnett protected his former protégé with notices and reviews, Conrad increasingly came to resent the nature of the support. It was a mocking situation, worthy of Conrad's own irony.

Ironically, this attack from the English that he was a Pole in disguise was matched by attacks from Poles that he was an Englishman in disguise. He had to defend himself for not bringing up his sons to speak Polish: they were English. He told Aniela Zagórska a few years later that he felt guilt toward Poles and feared being slighted on his return to Poland. One story is that Spiridion Kliszczewski, his old friend from Cardiff, cooled considerably when he asked Conrad why he did not extol the fame of Poland and the latter replied, raising both arms: "Ah, mon ami, que voulez-vous? I should lose my

. . . The fact is that I have approached things human in a spirit of piety foreign to those lovers of humanity who would like to make of life a sort of Cook's Personally Conducted Tour—from the craddle [sic] to the grave. I have never debased that quasi-religious sentiment by tears and groans and sighs, I have neither grinned nor gnashed my teeth. In a word I have behaved myself decently—which, except in the gross conventional sense is not so easy as it looks. Therefore there are those who reproach me with the pose of brutality with the lack of all heart delicacy, sympathy—sentiment—idealism. There is even one abandonned [sic] creature—who says I am a neo-platonist? What on earth is that?"

Through it all, Garnett supported Conrad's work—despite a certain cooling in their relationship, not the least because of Garnett's Russian associations and continual designation of Conrad as a Slav—and his unsigned review in the *Nation* (August 22, 1908) backed Conrad's claims to greatness.

public." The remark seems inaccurately reported (by way of a Pole named Witold Chwalewik), since Conrad was extremely sensitive to these matters and would not give a "marketplace" response; but whatever the exact answer, his position seemed to him untenable. What is more, his artistic assumptions could be seriously circumscribed by these personal attacks, since he might not feel free to loose his irony at English and foreign matters, for fear his pessimism and gloom would be immediately labeled Slavic or un-English.

Toward the end of August, Conrad began a fairly long correspondence with Arthur Symons, who had written and sent on a study of him. Symons, earlier, in 1898, had commented on *The Nigger* and Kipling's *Captains Courageous*, contrasting them with D'Annunzio's *Trionfo della Morte* and citing them as lacking ideas. The comment had pained Conrad, to such an extent that he wrote an (unsigned) article on Kipling defending him and his own work. Now Symons had returned, with a deeper understanding of Conrad and with a more considerable reputation himself. In the years since his early comments on Conrad, when he was chiefly a literary journalist (contributor to *The Yellow Book* and editor of *The Savoy*), he had published the influential *The Symbolist Movement in Literature* (1899) and had attempted to disseminate Pater's ideas in a more organized fashion. In this respect, he was a figure from the aestheticism of the 1880s and 1890s, the period which helped form Conrad's own ideas for his Preface to *The Nigger*. Further, in Symons's endeavors to define beauty as something that transcended the individual arts, what he referred to as the "universal science of beauty," Conrad could follow.

In his letter of August 20, Conrad expresses his gratification at recognition from "a man like you." His remarks are of considerable interest, since they demonstrate that the symbolic and romantic strains implicit in his Preface of eleven years earlier were hardly forgotten.

> The earth is a temple where there is going on a mystery play, childish and poignant, rediculous [sic] and awful enough, in all conscience. Once in I've tried to behave decently, I have not degraded any quasi-religious sentiment by tears and groans, and if I have been amused or indignant, I've neither grinned nor gnashed my teeth. In other words, I've tried to write with dignity, not out of regard for myself, but for the sake of the spectacle, the play with an obscure beginning and an unfathomable *dénouement*.

Conrad's association with Symons was capped by the latter's little book *Notes on Joseph Conrad*, published the year after Conrad's death. The two finally met in 1911, and Symons became a devotee of what he called somewhat inexplicably a "Dwarf of Genius." Unless Conrad had shrunk considerably by 1911, he was still a man of medium height, and it is difficult to understand why Symons compared his height with Toulouse-Lautrec's, unless Symons were estimating through some synesthesiac vision. Symons, in his early study (rejected for publication), had tried to move Conrad closer to the symbolist tradition, especially to the cruel and sadistic side of it, and toward that end he had cited the novelist as having "a heart of darkness" and an "unlawful soul."

Conrad demurred and said not he but Kurtz possessed such qualities. He tried to dispatch that view of himself and offered instead a bourgeois novelist for Symons's examination: "The fact is that I am really a much simpler person. Death is a fact, and violent death is a fact too. . . . Do you really think that old Flaubert gloated over the deathbed of Emma, or the death march of Matho, or the last moments of Felicie [Felicité]?" Conrad added that he has always approached his task "in the spirit of love for mankind," which indeed may have been his conscious aim. Gratified by Symons's kind words, he thanked him for the "recognition of the work, not the man. Once the last page is written the man does not count. He is nowhere." With that, Conrad recognized the impersonality of the artist, a subject which he had explored eleven years earlier. Like God, he sits above mankind and pares his fingernails, or thumbs his nose.

August was a cruel month, and Conrad was fortunate to get out of it with only disturbing reviews. His health was affected somewhat, but he could continue to work. He had suffered from stomach gout, or so it was diagnosed, and was filled with "depressing drugs." The Someries house had become full of the "horrors," and the Conrads at the end of August went to stay near the Fords, in Aldington. They hoped to find another residence while there and get away from what had become unlivable for them. Not only did the Conrads reestablish contact with the Fords, they also reestablished themselves with the Marwoods, whom they had met two years earlier, just before John was born. It was, for Conrad, a beginning and an end.

CHAPTER 28

The English Review

THE stay in Aldington, while a relief from Someries, played a far more important role in Conrad's life than simply relaxation. It marked the beginning of his renewed collaboration with Ford, on *The English Review,* and it led to Conrad's beginning work on *Some Reminiscences.* This loose autobiographical memoir fitted perfectly into Conrad's life at this time, when he was dredging up memories for "Razumov," and it was once again Ford who provided the impetus. As it would become clear, Ford was a remarkable editor, and his relationship to Conrad over the next year took on the role of editor to author. He had in this sense replaced Edward Garnett, and in creative terms he was far more agile and imaginative than the devoted Edward. Like all good editors, he discovered what he could tease out of Conrad, and his role, besides that of friend, supporter, *Blutsbruder,* was to touch Conrad at the right moment and tap the resources that lay so deep within him.

For Ford, the start of *The English Review* not only led to a kind of reconciliation with Conrad but coincided with another valuable psychological turn of fortune, his long-time liaison with Violet Hunt. Violet Hunt is somewhat peripheral to our study of Conrad, but she does enter into it in some important ways: first, many letters we have from Conrad to Ford are copies which she made before the originals disappeared, and although her copies are inexact and even edited, they are of value. Second, her affair with Ford set up a series of personal circumstances which Conrad could not tolerate. No matter whether he found the relationship morally disreputable—since Ford sought a German divorce from Elsie—or whether he felt his friend was irretrievably lost to him, whatever the reason, the entrance of Violet Hunt was the beginning of the end of his own affair with Ford.

The *English Review* period, as well as being important for Ford and Conrad personally, was a time of great literary excitement. Characteristically, Ford tried to take much credit for beginning it. After denying that he had begun the *Review* in order to publish Hardy's poem "A Sunday Morning Tragedy," which had been rejected by several editors, he went on to say: "It would be more just to say that that was the suggestion of my partner

Arthur Marwood. My own most urgent motive was to provide some money for Conrad by printing the *Personal Record*, and other things which I extracted from him." More likely, Ford felt a gap when he left the *Daily News*, for which he had been writing a weekly article, and needed some focus for his considerable journalistic talents. The immediate literary group to which he belonged, consisting of Wells, Garnett, and Conrad, had already started to speak of a new journal or review, discussions that went back to the early summer or even before. The title was possibly suggested by Conrad, and had indeed been used before by T. W. H. Crosland and Lord Alfred Douglas for a short-lived journal. In fact, when Ford's *Review* began, they tried to collect damages.

Our interest, however, is not in a full history of *The English Review* but only in Conrad's role in that prestigious publication. By early summer of 1908, Ford needed a subeditor and brought in a very young Douglas Goldring, who later became the historian of the *Review* scene. At that point, even before the Conrads went to Aldington at the end of August, Ford may have made his suggestion that Conrad write his reminiscences for the first number in December of that year. Fifteen years later, in 1923, Conrad expressed his gratitude to Ford for his friend's gentle prodding. The latter's role here, no matter how indiscreet his other activities, must have been truly heroic, for Conrad's reticence about divulging his past made any formal autobiography impossible. He wrote:

> I don't think your memory renders me justice as to my attitude to the early E.R. The early E.R. is the only one I ever cared for. The mere fact that it was the occasion of you putting on me that gentle but persistent pressure which extracted, from the depths of my then despondency, the stuff of the Personal Record, would be enough to make its memory dear. My only grievance against the early E.R. is that it didn't last long enough. If I say that I am curious to see what you will make of this venture [the editorship of *Transatlantic Review*] it isn't because I have the slightest doubts of your consistency. You have a perfect right to say that you are "rather unchangeable." Unlike the Serpent (which is Wise) you will die in your original skin. So I have no doubt that the Review will be truly Fordian—at all costs! But it will be interesting to see what men you will find and what you will get out of them in these changed times.

In addition to moving Conrad to write reminiscences for seven issues (December–June 1909, inclusive), Ford also asked him to review Anatole France's *Ile des pingouins* for the first issue. Ford very skillfully went after James, Hardy, Wells, and Bennett, among others. The Hardy poem which Marwood said was so instrumental in causing the start of the *Review* was printed in the first issue. The poem, incidentally, had not run into any great difficulties, although its subject and scorching irony were not quite suitable for most post-Victorian journals, and Hardy was simply holding it back for a further volume of his own poems. The first issue, as we have noted, was splendid, a collection hardly equaled since. Ford not only printed the work of his and Conrad's circle but demonstrated the ability to recognize great talent before it had become clear to others.

Under Ford's direct control, or shortly after he left, with many future issues already set, the array of talent continued and even intensified. Succeeding issues included contributions from D. H. Lawrence (poems and a story), Yeats (three poems), Pound (including "Sestina: Altaforte"), Norman Douglas, Arnold Bennett, and more James (three additional stories), Conrad, Wells (two books serialized), Galsworthy (poems and stories); as well as some lesser figures—C. E. Montague, G. Lowes Dickinson, Rupert Brooke, H. M. Tomlinson. It was, perhaps, the most felicitous accumulation of literary talent ever gathered by a small journal, far outdistancing the taste, scope, and breadth of *Blackwood's* when Conrad felt so devoted to that journal.

If Conrad's idea had been to equal *Blackwood's* with this new journal, he actually helped found and co-edit a review of far greater literary substance. Most of these literary figures appeared in *The English Review* during a period of eighteen months, before Ford's financial mismanagement became obvious and he was eased out. At that point, when with the July 1909 issue the ownership of the *Review* changed, Conrad suddenly ended his reminiscences, and the antagonism he felt toward Ford came to the surface. It was, for all involved, a terrible time, for Ford not only had become notorious because of his open affair with Violet Hunt but had antagonized most of the "circle," and the *Review* began to dissolve.

All that lay ahead, and it helped contribute to Conrad's breakdown in 1910, just after he completed *Under Western Eyes.* On September 25, Conrad announced to Wells he was 60,000 words into "Razumov" and that Ford had persuaded him to produce some reminiscences for the *Review.* Conrad said it was easy material to spin out, calling it "megalomaniac's stuff." But the letter is more than the announcement of news; it demonstrates something very acute in Conrad's mind, which was Wells's influence on the current generation, on whom Conrad had none: ". . . for who could deny your influence on the thought of the generation most worth influencing, that is the generation that numbers 18 to 20 summers at this date."

Such warm sympathies, at his own expense, indicate they must have been meeting rather frequently over *English Review* business and planning. Little could Conrad foresee how much Wells's books of the next few years would reinforce his hold on the young, while Conrad appealed to a much older reader, one devoted not only to ideas but to literature. In *Ann Veronica,* Wells has, indeed, the very phrase that would become the motto of later generations; when Capes speaks to Ann, he says: "Find the thing you want to do most intensely, make sure that's it, and do it with all your might. If you live, well and good; if you die, well and good. Your purpose is done. . . . Well, this is *our* thing."

Conrad could not, of course, compete in this area, even if he wished to. His work during this decade was devoted to providing the opposite of everything Wells asserted so proudly in that statement. Do "*our* thing": that was precisely what Razumov unsuccessfully tried to do. "Your purpose is done": Decoud's purpose is clouded by history, a farce he cannot escape, and even Nostromo, a little Napoleon, is not permitted to steal in peace. "Every human being is a new thing": Conrad agreed with Hardy's "Convergence of the Twain" that an iceberg is forming somewhere to confound man's attempts at self-realization, and that that iceberg may be within or without. Wells would have it melt under the heat of individual desire. Conrad knew only that the iceberg continued to grow until it became the principle of destruction.

As a result, after his "placement" of Wells in the minds and hearts of the young, Conrad moved to the area where he felt deeply, the question of Wells's art, and his well-chosen words indicate how carefully he had to tread.

> On the other hand there is your mastery of the art—that side of your writer's genius which contains an infinite possibility. And indeed I need not suffer from divided judgment. For your art—whatever you do—will contain your convictions where they would be seen perhaps in a more perfect light. Your work, like all work that counts must have its connection with the laborious past and its bearing on the future—that future in which you have willed (and perhaps succeeded) to put the impress of your personality; which you will not see but in which your voice will be heard—till in the ever-increasing distance even that trace of our short day shall be lost.

Wells was appealing to his contemporaries and gaining a popular success because of immediacy; how was Conrad, with his appeal to moral values that had no immediate application, to pick up this audience or one allied to it? Not only that, how could he keep to his views of art when around him nearly all aimed at the marketplace, writing carelessly, or shaping trivial subjects for sensational ends?

As a Middle European of gentry status, Conrad was obsessed with the burden of history, whereas Wells and his contemporaries were interested in shucking off the weight of the past. Apart from their artistic differences, which were growing immense, Conrad had been molded by a class system, whereas Wells, lower-middle-class by background, had scrambled up, never taking class and caste for granted. His theme was the future, not the past, and his future was to contain a different sort of structure, founded on world, not national, states, all governed by a ruling elite of intellectuals. For Wells, the future would eliminate those aspects of the past that humiliated and degraded. In this respect, he was virtually an American: in his belief, well on into his later years, that political idealism was viable, that reasonable men could work out some resolution that would balance the destructive element, and that history could be cast aside in favor of new social forms.

How ironic all that seemed, even as Conrad and Wells warmed to each other for their work on the *Review*. Writing "Razumov," Conrad more than most recognized that the individual does not escape from his past; just as Freud—whose ideas Conrad considered a kind of magic show—instructed generations that the unconscious is part of everyman's baggage and not something to be rationalized and purged. Freud's theory of the unconscious for the individual was roughly analogous to Conrad's sense of history for the race, and for himself. Planning, controls, ruling elites, eugenics, world states: all these may be well and good, but they ignored those more profound aspects of the past which cannot be shuffled off. Whatever our conscious intentions, we introject the world of our fathers, and we can never escape the dosage; like Mithridates, we may become accustomed to it, but the poison has invaded our system. As Conrad had written Graham three years before: "The grave of individual temperament is being dug by GBS and HGW with hopeful industry. Finitá la commedia! Well they may do much but for the saving of the universe I put my faith in the power of folly." We recall that Conrad said this to Graham at the same time he wrote Wells, also from Capri, that he, Norman Douglas, and others had agreed that Wells "was the one honest thinker of the day."

"Faith in the power of folly" is the humanist's final statement of belief—one thinks of Horace's "We are led as a puppet is moved by the strings"; but for the scientist and logician it is a source of dismay. Yet Conrad knew that it was not enough to be, like Wells, life-oriented, or to accept a version of Eros as man's governing libido. Conrad knew that Thanatos, as he would demonstrate in the character of Razumov, was more indicative than Eros of the twentieth century. Wells's was the voice of the new technicians, able, intelligent, logical, rational and reasonable; but such beliefs had nothing to do with the nature of truth or the drift of mankind. And yet popularity and an audience lay where the technicians were heading, not in that nether world of Thanatos which Conrad, Kafka, and Proust were attempting to define.

Ford's apartment at 85, Holland Park Avenue became the office of *The English Review*, and it filled with the literary luminaries of that pre-Pound era: Conrad himself, Hardy, Graham, Hugh Walpole, Violet Hunt, Hudson, Bennett, Perceval Gibbon (a short-story writer), Stephen Reynolds (with whom Conrad had a short but intense correspondence),* and several others.

* In all, Conrad wrote twenty-eight letters to Reynolds, a young, struggling novelist who reminded him of his own earlier career. Conrad gave Reynolds both personal and artistic encouragement, of the kind he had once sought himself from Marguerite Poradowska

It was a heady time. Conrad tried to assure Douglas, in the meanwhile, that the *Review* could become a permanent outlet for his material. For himself, Conrad was now using Miss Hallowes for purposes of dictating his reminiscences and even possibly his novel, "Razumov." For the latter, however, Conrad could not compose rapidly enough to make dictation profitable, even at her low rate of 25 shillings per week. The Conrad house at Someries also served for some of the planning sessions, and they were uproarious. For Jessie, they were a tremendous annoyance, since she disliked Ford intensely under any circumstances. She writes about a time in late October or early November:

> I have wondered many times since where he would have found anyone else so accommodating, and I had almost said foolish, as to allow him to take such complete possession of his home, as Joseph Conrad did on that occasion. Lights blazed from every room downstairs—no expense was spared. To have some four or five strangers quartered on one without more notice than an hour or so was not exactly comfortable. Only the baby and the maids slept that night. Orders, directions, or suggestions were shouted from room to room. It was an uproar all night, and the next day the house was in a chaos. My monthly stock of provisions was soon devoured, and the great trouble was that we had to use lamps and candles. However, that nightmare came to an end at last—and there was that great amount of distinction according to my husband in the first number being edited under our roof.

Conrad later saw it as a time of boyish excitement:

> Do you care to be reminded [he asked Ford] that the editing of the first number was finished in that farmhouse we occupied near Luton? You arrived one evening with your amiable myrmidons and parcels of copy. I shall never forget the cold of that night, the black grates, the guttering candles, the dimmed lamps and the desperate stillness of that house,

and Edward Garnett. When the young man was feeling desperate, Conrad reminded him that a man "is never 'done' till he drops; and an artist should be a man and a half." But Conrad's chief advice came in an October 27, 1910, letter to Reynolds, which is as much about himself as his correspondent. Perhaps *Victory* was dimly in the remote reaches of Conrad's imagination as he told Reynolds: "At moments I am haunted by a lofty (but elusive I own) shape of a great seaboard novel by you with the whole of our civilisation, social and political for a background and with all your ideas and feelings presented to the populace, living, palpitating in a dramatic form. For that you'll have to invent—to come out of yourself in a measure. But all great men have been inventors. This suggestion'll appear to you crude—but any mere suggestion must be that. The first conception of every great enterprise is a raw thing to get hold of. It's about time for a great creative prose work to come out, a fine ringing imaginative utterance drowning the thin, petty babble of fiction. A great *island* novel, with all its life in the setting of the sea and the men nearest to the sea in the foreground—Eh?—the foreground of a really inspiring tale. England, the predestined ground of such comedy-drama may yet produce it." Or perhaps Conrad was thinking of his own valedictory, if he could summon the energy.

> where women and children were innocently sleeping, when you sought me out at 2 a.m. in my dismal study to make me concentrate suddenly on a two-page notice of the "Ile des Péng̃uins" [Pingouins]. A marvellously successful instance of editorial tyranny! I suppose you were justified. The Number One of the E.R. could not have come out with two blank pages in it. It would have been too sensational. I have forgiven you long ago.*

The Conrads were following a crazy pattern themselves, of moving back and forth, until they took a house in Aldington in January of the new year. Their distaste for Someries kept them zigzagging between their own house and a rented cottage in Aldington, returning to Someries in early October until their final move. The desire to move to Aldington may have been motivated by a desire to be near Ford; but the desire to leave Aldington after seventeen months was the reverse: to get away from the mess Ford was making of his personal life and to escape the rumors and impending scandals. When the finances of the *Review* became hopelessly entangled and mismanaged, Ford had to go to outside sources for money, and when he went to a group around David Soskice, his Jewish brother-in-law, Conrad took the opportunity to end his contribution and to break with him. That, however, came later.

---

* Of course, that was long after the event, when Ford's unrealistic management of the *Review* created terrible conflicts with his friends. This history of the *Review*, which is well narrated by Arthur Mizener in his biography, belongs properly to Ford's story; but as the result of several sequences Conrad was ultimately involved. The crux of the matter was that Ford used the *Review* as a way of propping up his own career at a crucial time, especially when his personal life was taking a drastically new turn. As he took over the directorship of the monthly, he saw himself in megalomaniacal terms. Initially, the financing of the *Review* was shaky. Marwood put up, in all, £2,200, and Ford claimed he had himself invested £2,800, but most of the sum was not his. He had borrowed from his family and even from Elsie, whom he planned to leave. He expected to pay his authors on a profit-sharing plan—an idea that made sense to him, but did not assuage either the hard-pressed like Conrad and James or the hard-nosed such as Wells and Bennett. He overpaid his contributors, also, and as a consequence lost three and four hundred pounds on each issue, which he said sold two thousand copies, although he had estimated five thousand. He first had difficulty with Wells, who feared that his *Tono-Bungay* would lose money by being serialized in the *Review* and not elsewhere. He feared, further, that Ford with his loose spending would not be able to pay him at all, which was almost the case when the *Review* went bankrupt. Increasingly, Ford became defensive about the journal, seeing himself as a great patron of the arts, a kind of Maecenas. As Mizener demonstrates, he even created a persona for himself, of a well-off gentleman with a private income from his aunt, Frau Geheimrattin Laura Schmedding, who allowed him to draw sums of money almost at will. Since her first name indicated a kind of "secret fund" or "privy council," Ford may have simply been indulging in a joke. Nevertheless, he dissembled, and one reason was his need to fix a more central literary place for himself. His jealousy of Conrad's reputation among literary people—his own was still quite small—must have goaded him into creating an increasingly larger image of himself. Ford's self-delusions and outright lies appear to have started here in earnest.

During this time, Conrad had to explain his actions to Pinker; that is, he had to justify his use of time which could have been, in Pinker's eyes, better spent on "Razumov," which was definitely growing into a novel that could be serialized for immediate income. He says that a mere casual suggestion "has grown into a very absorbing plan." The plan was "to make Polish life enter English literature," which was "no small ambition to begin with. But I think it can be done. To reveal a very particular state of society, bring forward individuals with very special traditions and touch in a personal way upon such events, for instance, as the liberation of the serfs (which in the number of people affected and in the general humanitarian significance is a greater fact of universal interest than the abolition of Negro Slavery) is a big enterprise." He indicates his task has been eased because of its intimate nature and because of the presence of Tadeusz Bobrowski's two volumes of *Memoirs*, "which I have by me, to refresh my recollections and settle my ideas."

Only someone as intimately connected to Conrad as Ford was, and a person who understood the nature of his talent and imagination so well, could have prodded him into such an intimate examination of his past. For Conrad based his art on an impersonal distancing of the author from his material, and toward that end constructed concentric circles of narrators who act both as a funnel and as a barrier for the reader. One rarely gets close to the nucleus of a Conrad story, but instead penetrates by slow degrees through protective layers of fact, rumor, hearsay, narrative detail, and indirect action. Conrad protected his "secret self" from any true sharers, and his literary method was one with the man.

Conrad recognized he had a rare opportunity for divulgation that might never arise again. He felt the time was right for the success of a personal book, although his reminiscences would not be published as a volume until 1912, as *Some Reminiscences*. "This seems the psychological moment [he told Pinker in explanation]—and the appearance of a new *Review* is a good determining factor. My friendship for the editor (which is known) is a sufficient motive. It is a generally lucky concourse of circumstances. It may be, so to speak, *the* chance of a lifetime—coming neither too soon nor yet too late; for my acceptance as an English writer is an accomplished fact—and the writer is not 'used up,' either in regard to his own mind or in the public estimation of his work." He told his agent that this very letter could serve for negotiations he might enter into with editors. Pinker might tell them that "in the course of development the inner story of my books will come out—a sort of literary confession as to the sources as well as to the aims. I have been even thinking of a little something like: *The Art and the Life*, or *The Pages and the Years*, reminiscences."

He says that if *The English Review* fails after the first four installments, a prescient observation, then another place will be found to continue. The plan was for each installment to run to about 4,000 words, with the first in December to come to 8,000, "to make the beginning full—and anyhow I wanted to give full measure." He indicates his method is dictation and then revision of text, the only method possible to ensure speed of production. In this manner, he hoped to produce 1,500 to 2,000 words per week, all the while working on "Razumov." After that book was completed, he would take up *Chance* once again.*

What is remarkable about Conrad's reminiscences is how clearly he employed fictional techniques worked out with Ford, in particular their notion of the *progression d'effet,* wherein the narrative intensity increases as the story develops. To achieve that, Conrad used a constantly interrupted narrative as a way of unsettling conventional sequences and, thereby, established anticipation of the next episode. Conrad needed a method that permitted intimacy, up to a certain point, and then withdrawal, when he had revealed enough. Just as his parallel work on "Razumov" involved withdrawing from and attacking terrible secrets, so his reminiscences would be matters of attack and retreat.

Conrad's stance was extremely delicate. As he remarked in the "Familiar Preface" to the volume, nobody could expect to find in his book "words of extraordinary potency or accents of irresistible heroism." And yet his early background was full of heroic family acts, and his own career involved considerable moments of heroism to insure survival, all matters of routine at sea. Far more than most writers, he had been close to the very kind of heroism he wanted to mute in his narrative. As a consequence, he devised a strategy based, not on experience alone or pleasure, but on human endurance, endurance of his Polish past, his sea career, and now his profession as writer.

His plan for the early installments was ingenious, founded as it was on a theory of impressionism. He begins: "Books may be written in all sorts of places" and, using that as lever, moves in and around some of the places where he worked on the manuscript of *Almayer's Folly.* That, in turn, brings him to the story of his almost losing the manuscript in Berlin on his way to Poland, which carries him back to early memories, to stories of his family and comments on Napoleon's retreat from Moscow. From that, he moves to speculations about human nature that would make him, a son of the land, choose to go to sea, and from that he can trace his first contact with continuous spoken English at the St. Gotthard Tunnel. The method served Conrad, and it allowed him to become, as his philosophy dictated, a plaything of forces acting upon him as much as he himself acted upon them.

---

* His comment to Pinker (on November 25) that *Reminiscences* need not be more than 80,000 words suggests that he had planned a longer volume than the one he wrote—which is 50,000 words—and that he cut it short because of his trouble with Ford and the *Review.*

He moves in and out of a deterministic, causal universe, not quite accepting it, allowing here and there for chance, but never denying the potentialities of uncontrollable elements which drive us in unforeseen ways. The method of the reminiscences is Conrad's point of view as much as the subject matter. Although he did not really fulfill his words to Pinker that the episodes would reveal "the inner story of my books," the reminiscences do contain the essential Conradian note. They may seem slight upon first reading, but they are essentially a quite clever use of materials, while, admittedly, lacking the more profound reverberations of his major fiction.

Like the meetings over the *Review*, this, too, was heady stuff. But there were other matters, which could not be avoided. On November 3, Conrad wrote Marguerite, the respository of his deepest fears, that "I have ordered my life badly. I have not known how to do any better, for surely I have wanted to do the right thing. But perhaps it was impossible to do otherwise than I have done." This pessimistic assessment would be followed the next month by a "frightful attack of gout." To Wells, he says that the stirring up of his past is not only a "silly enterprise" but a somewhat ghoulish one also, and he should not be suspected of suffering from "incipient softening of the brain." His defensiveness at public display was apparently creating its own kind of tension, especially as the first issue on November 25 became imminent.

His disclaimers to Pinker to the contrary, "Razumov" was bound to suffer from his divided attention. Conrad's physical as well as mental energy were limited, and he could not throw himself wholeheartedly into several projects without loss of concentration and intensity. He recognized that the second part of the novel, when his protagonist goes from St. Petersburg to Geneva, is a letdown. The first section could be considered Conrad's best piece of sustained writing, and it would have been difficult to follow under any circumstances. To Galsworthy, who was reading this later section, Conrad apologized:

> You see, it is all part of the general crookedness of my existence. . . . Good work takes time; to invent an action, a march for the story which could have dispensed with part II[d] as it stands was a matter of meditation, of trying and re-trying for goodness knows how long.

This was a particularly acute insight into his own methods; for essentially in the second section Conrad provided the raw materials of what occurred, whereas in a fully fashioned narrative, he would have utilized these materials for another level of discourse. He continued:

> This I could not afford to do. I went on the obvious lines and on these lines I developed my narrative to give it some sort of verisimilitude. In other words I offered to sell my soul for half a crown—and now I have neither the soul nor the coin—for the novel is not finished yet. A fool's

bargain—no great matter when one is young but at my age such passages embitter and discourage one beyond expression. I have no heart to think of compressing anything, for I have no illusion as to the quality of the stuff. The thing is "bad-in-itself." It should not be there at all.

The professional relationship of Conrad and Ford intensified during this exciting period, but even as it did, personal matters were preparing to turn the renewed friendship into lasting antagonism and animosity. Poor sales, extreme personal anxieties, concern with lack of recognition by a wider public, persistent ill health (and extreme hypochondria even when no illness resulted)—all of these made Conrad begrudge the time spent on the *Review.* To this must be added the tremendous pressures he suffered as he reexamined his past and reentered Apollo's and Ewa's world, however glancingly. Further, Ford's marital difficulties with Elsie and his open relationship with Violet Hunt put the Conrads in a peculiar position; for Jessie had been antagonistic to Ford even when Conrad was close to him, and both had remained sympathetic toward Elsie. In addition, Conrad appears to have been genuinely touched by the two Hueffer daughters, who were caught in the rancor when Ford left his wife, who, as a Catholic, refused to grant him a divorce. Still further, more than most, Conrad disliked all gossip and bickering, which he felt to be distractions from a man's rightful tasks.

In the immediate future, dreadful complications were to develop. Elsie was to accuse Arthur Marwood of making sexual advances toward her. As we have seen, Marwood had put up the money for an operation in 1907, and her helplessness—the traditional helpless female deserted by her husband—may have appealed to his sense of chivalry as well as to his sexual instincts. In a separate action, Violet Hunt had consulted Wells about Ford, an act of some indelicacy, since Hunt and Wells had had an affair of sorts and now Wells and Ford were closely associated on *The English Review,* where *Tono-Bungay* was being serialized. The complications were piling up, and Conrad felt himself siding increasingly with Marwood, who, he felt, was more stable and less egomaniacal.

Just before all these entanglements developed into a storm, Conrad received from Henry James the first six volumes of the New York Edition of his novels and stories. Conrad's response is predictably flattering and obeisant, but it seems heartfelt, an extremely pleasant interlude in the darkening gloom.* He indicates he plans to commune with them "and gloat over the promise of the prefaces." He immediately read the one to *The American,* the first of the James long novels he was acquainted with, from 1891. "Afterward I could not resist the temptation of reading the beautiful and touching last

* James was himself to get drawn into the Ford-Hunt affair, for he had invited them to Lamb House for a weekend, only to rescind the invitation when he was informed that Elsie was planning to sue Ford for divorce. This was Hunt's wishful thinking, for in actuality Elsie later petitioned for restitution of conjugal rights.

ten pages of the story. There is in them a perfection of tone which calmed me; and I sat for a long while with the closed volume in my hand going over the preface in my mind and thinking—that's how it began, that's how it was done!" For Conrad, that preface to *The American* was indeed a renewal, a journey back to his own preface as he read James's words: that "since no 'rendering' of any object and no painting of any picture can take effect without some form of reference and control, so these guarantees could but reside in a high probity of observation." Or: "The real represents to my perception the things we cannot possibly *not* know, sooner or later, in one way or another."*

Back in the society of men and money, Conrad felt his world shrinking even as he hoped it would expand. Ironically, the shrinkage occurred at the very time he expected to gain a financial share in *The English Review*, a participation which he outlined to Pinker on December 17. Conrad was hopeful the *Review* would make some profit, and then he would benefit from Ford's generosity, which, he says, was unasked for. All monies gained from this arrangement would pass through Pinker's hands to reduce the debt. Needless to say, nothing came of this. On the same day, Conrad wrote a very different kind of letter to Ford. It works around to their business dealings over the *Review* and outlines how Conrad must run his accounts through Pinker; but it begins ominously:

> I can't somehow get rid of the idea I have been in some way indiscreet—I can hardly say offensive—vis à vis de vous. I have said something to that effect in a letter to you which has remained unanswered. Perhaps you thought it was not worth answering, the supposition being too silly. If so—good. And indeed it is incredible that you should suspect me of an offensive intention on the ground of some remarks which are not and could not have been of any consequence. And considering our friendship and the confidence you gave me in that particular matter [of his reminiscences] even the charge of mere impertinence could not stand. It was an expression of very great interest which was *not* critical in its intention. But enough of that. I dare say you think I am mad—and truly sometimes I think so myself.†

---

* Conrad would surely have concurred with R. P. Blackmur's gloss on James's prefaces: ". . . that in art what is merely stated is not presented, what is not presented is not vivid, what is vivid is not represented, and what is not represented is not art."

† As if his face were not turned sufficiently to the torturous past with "Razumov," Conrad had to produce documents for Pinker, for purposes of insurance, that authenticated his date of birth. He was, for the time, in the thick of Polish matters. Some of the documents mentioned are: his passport in Russian and German signed by Prince Galitzin stating "*nobleman Korzeniowski travelling with his son Conrad aged 10 years*"—the use of Conrad and not Konrad indicating some confusion of realms; a certificate of baptism in Polish; third, the admission to "citizenship of the town of Cracow of the orphan C.K." Finally, Conrad cites the *Senatorial Gazette*, the official Russian paper, as containing his name when he was released from allegiance to imperial Russia, at thirty-one.

That was the beginning. Mixed in with the Conrad move to Aldington in Kent, in late January or early February of 1909, was the domestic mess Ford had brought about, with Elsie coming to the Conrads with her pleas for aid. It created a considerable conflict, and Conrad had to handle it. We have moved ahead to March 1909, and during that month Conrad had written his friend in sympathy for the failure of a dramatization of *The Fifth Queen.* But after Elsie's visit, a clear sign of desperation on her part, Conrad put the domestic matter in the open. He begins his long letter circuitously, by praising Ford for the latest issue of *The English Review*, probably the April number. He consoles Ford that while the *Review* may have to halt because of finances, it must not fail. He warms to his task by warning Ford: "If you start out crushing people you will discover that they don't 'crush' so easily as all that." Cautioning him that he is ill advised by the people around him, Conrad then comes to the body of his letter:

> Last Monday on her way from the station your wife called here. She informed me that all your differences were happily settled and warned me against the plots and intrigues (vulgo lies) of certain people [Marwood]. I confess I was literally shocked by the nature of her communication the more so that she implied that those darn untruths had, in your opinion, already affeted [sic] my attitude towards you. Against that I oppose an unqualified denial; and as this denial expresses the exact truth I warn you that I demand to be believed without any reservations or doubts whatever. I had heard nothing about you or Elsie except what passes current in ordinary conversation. We, that is Jessie and I had been aware for a week or so that there was some tension the nature of which of course was not our affair and was barely a subject of one or two remarks between us. For the rest I told Elsie with every consideration which is due to her in my house that I could not believe these people were as black as they appeared to her. She seemed to take but little heed of my protest. Later on she proposed that you should come down and stay *with us* for a week. You know that no one is made more welcome under our roof. Let ten years of perfect confidence and intimacy be witnesses to it. But I said at once: no. That can not be. If you are reconciled so completely Ford's place when he is in Aldington is in the cottage.

By now, Conrad had seen Ford as a manipulator of reality, a man who with all his talent and imagination conceived of himself as a Napoleon of letters and, therefore, someone free to maneuver the truth.

> What is the end of such a proposal, what object, what purpose can be served by re-creating an equivocal situation? By such juggling with the realities of life an atmosphere of plots and accusations and suspicions is created. I can't breathe in situations that are not clear. I abhor them. They are neither in my nature nor in my tradition, nor in my experience. I am not fine enough for them. We are a pair of silly innocents.

Conrad says he has been so upset he has not been able to eat or sleep, and that this very evening the Marwoods ("the people in question," who are never named) called at his house. Marwood informed Conrad he had broken off all intimate relations with Ford. Conrad points out that while Marwood was not his, but Ford's, friend, he cannot give him up as a ruffian or a villain. He said Marwood trotted after Ford like a faithful dog, and the latter felt the need to crush him. Then comes the Conradian admonition: a warning Ford failed to heed as he strewed domestic wreckage around him. Perhaps he needed all this to produce *The Good Soldier.*

> I won't believe [Conrad wrote] it's altogether without cause [apparently, Marwood had been importuning Elsie] but it strikes me my dear Ford that of late you have been visiting what might have been faults of tact, or even grave failures of discretion in men who *were* your admiring friends with an Olympian severity. A man who not often takes liberties ventures to ask you now whether it is worth while. Unless words are wind, facts are mist, the confidence you've given me a mere caprice of fancy, and unless an absolute loyalty of thought and act on my part contra mundum gives no privilege I have the right to warn you that you will find yourself at forty with only the wrecks of friendship at your feet. You have always sought to do good to people—that I believe—but don't fail in the other kind of generosity. I've had four most unhappy days but I am afraid you will dismiss it all with a wave of the hand. And indeed I don't know why I should be wretched except from sheer affection.

Conrad saw Ford teetering on the edge, perhaps heading into another nervous collapse. We know Conrad was profoundly disturbed by the situation, for in an April 30 letter to Galsworthy, he presented the circumstances in far more bitter terms.

> We have fallen here [he wrote in a paragraph omitted by Jean-Aubry in his printing of the letter] into a most abominable upset the execution of Marwood by Ford and Elsie. I have seen a man guilliotined [sic] 30 years ago but it hasn't made me feel half as sick as the present operation. For weeks poor Marwood looked as if after a severe illness. My view of M. is that he is a gallant-homme in the fullest sense—absolutely incapable of any black treachery. We couldn't keep the horrid affair off us anyhow—what with E coming with horrible details and revelations (I told her plainly I could not believe what she said—and she only smiled) which it was impossible to silence and the poor M's whom one had to listen to out of common humanity. A beastly affair to be mixed up with even in the role of mere spectators—auditors.

By now, Conrad began to put distance between himself and Ford, so that when the open break came over Conrad's interruption of his reminiscences in the *Review,* the personal matter had already been settled. However, even before that July imbroglio, which was ugly and irremediable, Conrad had another verbal outburst against Ford. Although he was speaking about an incident concerning Willa Cather, his anger at Ford is clear, evidently for his having indiscreetly sent Conrad's note (written to Elsie) about Cather directly to the American authoress.

> What means your letter? It's the first I hear of you having anything to do with this affair. I really don't understand what is (behind what meets the eye) to make you fly out so indignantly. Surely you might have dropped me a line on a p.c. *Dear Conrad I want you to see a Miss C.* etc etc. and of course I would have seen her. Instead of which reproaches for not having guessed at things of which I had no knowledge whatever, are heaped upon me. Frankly I don't like it. . . . *Are you aware* that it is *the first* I hear of Miss C being a particular friend of yours. . . . I don't even remember the name. . . .
>
> But all this is not the question. The question is—what do you mean? What the devil do you mean? . . . Elsie writes to me in the early morning a note asking whether I would see an American lady, apparently her acquaintance, literary editor of McClure's and who wants a story from me. I reply that: *I have no story for McClure*, that this is not the way to do serious business—that the thing looks like an intrusion. I write frankly what I think, being as you know a man who *can't afford* to be disturbed by casual visitors.

Conrad then refers to a (now lost) letter from Ford full of personal matters:

> Then I get your letter like a bolt from the blue throwing at my head a lot of things of which I had no previous inkling—what you never even hinted to me before—as a basis for reproaches! Telling me my attitude is *too bad!!*
>
> This looks like a pretty *coup de chien?* Stop this nonsense with me Ford. It's ugly. I won't have it.
>
> I tell you what is *too bad.* It is to send my letter written with perfect openness to your wife to a third party. And by Jove you good people haven't lost any time over it either. You caught the post all along most neatly. But, since my letters are to be sent about, I consider myself at liberty to forward the copy of all the correspondence: *Elsie's first* note—your extraordinary letter, the material parts of this letter and Elsie's note received this morning to Miss Cather c/o McClure in New York—with my explanation of the episode. As she has my note to Elsie she may as well have the lot.
>
> . . . Look here my dear Ford—this sort of thing I *won't* stand if you had a million dollars in each hand. The proper thing for Miss C was to ask for an interview. She did not because she did not want it. She was clearly coming casually. I am not to be treated like that. Unless I hear from you within the week I will clear up this matter—of which I have my own opinion not to be put on paper here but very much at your service if you will come and talk with me.

Not only was Conrad trying to extricate himself from his role as mediator between the Fords, at the same time he was beginning to undergo all the symptoms of a nervous breakdown: what Meyer calls the "Infection-Exhaustion Psychoses," whereby an acute physical ailment (infection, etc.) is followed by an emotional storm. Meyer indicates that at least part of Conrad's breakdown was the result of Ford's liaison with Violet Hunt, suggesting, strongly, that the two men who had been "secret sharers" were now sundered by an older woman who could play wife and mother to Ford. Without lessening the psychoanalytic context of this interpretation, one can as well seek certain literary reasons for the cooling relationship. Conrad saw that the collaboration had done him little good, either financially or professionally; he watched *The English Review* foundering and passing into "alien" hands. His own career, by 1909, was still—for him—a monstrous joke, and he saw himself, despite fifteen years of intense devotion to craft, slipping away into the bottom of the sea. In a way, he sensed his own death; or he sensed the waning of his creative powers, which for the writer is a whiff of death. The undertow was oceanic.

One can understand Conrad's mind at this time, not only from his letters (to Galsworthy, Graham, Garnett, Douglas, as well as to Ford), but from the psychological situation in the novel he was writing from 1908 to early 1910, *Under Western Eyes.* It is both dangerous and futile to read fiction as autobiography; but it is very fruitful to read fiction for the psychological preoccupations of an author at the time of composition. The Razumov of that novel is all irony and ambiguity; every course he has marked out for himself leaves either death or suicide as a consequence. He is baffled in the labyrinth, whether of Russian bureaucracy or of his own desires for the future. He betrays a man with whom he feels kinship, while he works for forces whose representatives he loathes. He must spend his time and expend his talent with evident frauds. His self-love turns to self-hate. Within this twisted atmosphere, he is all anxiety and nerves, and yet he falls in love. But this one seemingly pure element is unthinkable while he lives amid lies and deceit. Thus, Conrad stages a psychodrama of defeat, frustration, self-loathing, misdirected ambitions, ambiguity, and anonymity: the literary equivalents of a mental breakdown.

In the midst of these doubts and self-doubts consuming Conrad, Ford's mismanagement of the *Review* had become clear. He was losing far too much money, and a new management was called for. Negotiations began with David Soskice, his brother-in-law, who had Russian associates. This came at a particularly unfortunate time since Conrad was barely holding off *his* Russians in "Razumov" by means of the old language teacher. It was all too much for Conrad: the new association of the *Review;* the sensitivity of his own work on "Razumov"; and Garnett, never too far away, with his house full of Russian exiles, anarchists, and socialists—Felix Volkhovsky, Nikolai Chaikovsky, Prince Peter Kropotkin, Prince Cherkesov, and, earlier,

Sergey Stepniak. The break with Ford became not only inevitable but rancorous.

After seven installments of his reminiscences, Conrad halted with the June number, asserting he was too ill to continue. Ill he was, but he wanted to walk away from the *Review* and from Ford. The magazine itself was also sinking, and Conrad had no time for failing ventures. Ford showed his disbelief and published in the *Review* a notice that astonished and angered Conrad: "We regret," Ford said, "that owing to the serious illness of Mr. Joseph Conrad we are compelled to postpone the publication of the next installment of his Reminiscences."* Conrad and Ford exchanged letters, and then Conrad ended the affair with his letter of July 31: not only an end to his association with the *Review*, but the end to his toleration of Ford, to his use of his collaborator and co-editor, and to an entire era that went back to the beginning of his major career.

Before writing that bitter July 31 letter, however, Conrad demonstrated in other ways the early stages of the breakdown that would consume him in 1910. Besides his difficulties with "Razumov," his letters to people quite outside his circle indicate how disarranged he was becoming, even in early 1909. An American critic and admirer, James Gibbons Huneker, had sent his book of "Supermen," as Conrad called it—*Egoists: A Book of Supermen* (1909). Recalled to his beginnings, Conrad reminisced about his "commission with Flaubert," which began with *Salammbô*. Huneker asked if Conrad had ever met the French novelist, and he replied that it would have been possible, but he was at sea in 1879. "It was another life which I remember with misty tenderness, as a transmigrated soul might be supposed by a miracle, to remember its previous envelope." Then he cuts to the very different present, to a virtual stranger: ". . . a sort of horror of pen and ink, a mistrust of the written phrase sits on me like a cold nightmare."

Then to Dr. Mackintosh, who was attending his gout and depression, he wrote about Perceval Gibbon, with whom Conrad would later contemplate doing a play about his African sketches. In the course of his comments, he spoke of the nature of his own art:

> There are so many what I may call be-littling influences waiting upon the life of a literary man—upon the life of *any* man—upon the life of a doctor, of a statesman, of a priest, of a teacher, of a saint. To keep firm hold of reality and yet deal with it in a lofty idealising spirit is so difficult! So dif-

* To Garnett, Conrad pleaded only indisposition for cutting his reminiscences short: "It is a fact I had a most damnable go of gout which absolutely prevented me from getting the 8th inst' of Rems ready in time. But it was neither more nor less serious than other attacks of the kind for the last 15 years. I suppose one of them will finally do for me. All the same I was vexed by that silly editorial note. There was no earthly reason for any note and if he had to do it, *indisposition* was a quite strong enough word for all practical, editorial purposes."

> ficult. And yet truth, expressive, effective truth, the combination of beauty and honesty of outlook can only be conquered by that almost impossible feat.

In a succeeding letter to Huneker, on May 18, Conrad indicated he was on manuscript page 890 of "Razumov," which placed him, after sixteen months, about three-quarters of the way through the final book form. He had another seven months of work to complete it. While the traumatic situation with Ford was ongoing, he was trying to hold it all together, running, as it were, several parallel lives: attempting to pull his sinking finances together with loans, small amounts, pressure on Pinker; writing as steadily as he could on "Razumov," while doubting his ability to produce the very words; and hanging on physically while he was ravaged by gout and neuralgic afflictions. It was, in a sense, that familiar cycle of personal disaster which fed his imagination and goaded him literarily and artistically. But now he was almost fifty-two, and he had tipped the balance. He would start to go under.

Even as late as June 23, when Conrad was too ill to continue this phase of his reminiscences, he planned, as he told E. V. Lucas, to write possibly two volumes of 65,000 words each.

> I don't suppose I could serialise them anywhere, but I am thinking of a volume (or even two short vols of say 65,000 words each) for later on with an interval of a couple of years. I know that the form is unconventional but it is not so unusual as it seems. It has been thought out. I hope still that from the unmethodical narrative a personality can be made to emerge in a sufficiently interesting manner. My case (as before the public) being not only exceptional but even unique I felt I could not proceed in cold blood on the usual lines of an autobiography. However before going on I would value exceedingly your opinion (if you will give it to me) as to the discretion of doing it at all.

Intermixed with this plan is Conrad's sense of "extinction," that death he associated with his inability to write. He calls such "blankness" visitations, whose presence fills him with dread. When he recovers from the blankness, he calls it a "resurrection," which goes on until the next attack. The symbolistic-religious imagery is compelling, that use of nineteenth-century *symboliste* terminology: blankness, death, resurrection, as a way of defining art and the artist. Perhaps in the back of his mind was the figure of Arthur Symons, to whom he wrote on June 24, when Symons was recovering slowly from a breakdown that had seemed total, an act of madness itself.

Then on July 31, sounding like a man at the end of his tether, he wrote angrily to Ford. Conrad felt his installments of reminiscences could stand exactly as they were, this by way of explaining his refusal to publish further episodes. The letter begins rancorously and then becomes self-serving:

> If you think I have discredited you and the Review—why then it must be even so. And as far as the Editor of the *ER* is concerned we will let it go at that—with the proviso that I don't want to hear anything more about it.
>
> But as writing to a man with a fine sense of form and a complete understanding, for years, of the way in which my literary intentions work themselves out I wish to protest against the words—*Ragged condition.*
>
> It is so little *ragged* to my feelings, and in point of literary fact, that in the book (if the book ever appears) the *whole* of the contribution to the *ER* as it stands now without the addition of a single word shall form the Part First.
>
> . . . And actually the very phrase ending the 7th instalment is to my mind an excellent terminal, a perfect pause carrying out the spirit of the work.
>
> All this is not got up ad hoc. I have exposed this view in a letter written to certain publishers in America a fortnight ago. [It was offered to Colonel Harvey of Harpers for serial publication in the *North American Review.*]

Conrad stresses that another installment would "make the thing ragged," and then continues:

> On a dispassionate view I see it so clearly that nothing on earth would induce me to spoil the thing as it now stands by an irrelevant instalment. I will say no more except to add that my contributions were for a *person* not for an *editor*. The ER I hear is no longer your property and there is I believe another circumstance which for purely personal reason (exceptionally personal I mean) make me unwilling to contribute anything more to the *ER*. This reason has of course nothing to do with you you understand. It is not a critical reason. A pure matter of feeling. If I have discredited the R, then I must bear the disgrace.*

An amusing but unsettling follow-up to this break would come, outlined in a detailed letter to Pinker, in August. It is an indictment of Ford that allowed no redress. Conrad, however, was dissembling to his friend when he said his reminiscences had ended naturally. It is true he had told Harpers he would offer the installments for American publication exactly as they had appeared in the *Review*, but we also know he wanted to continue the "personal record." The seventh installment, in contradistinction to Conrad's words, does not end the reminiscences; for as Conrad had set them up, there was no true ending. The ingeniousness of his plan allowed for endless extension, as if he had already read Proust and noted that, once the memory is activated, one can write a memoir or novel of infinite length.

* Whether or not this letter was actually mailed, from Conrad's point of view it represented a final act. With his customary resilience, Ford would have bounced right back into the friendship.

In August, as he told Pinker, Conrad was amazed to discover that Ford had tried to sell the copyright of "*everything* appearing in the Review to Col. Harvey" (of Harpers). Such an action would, of course, bypass Pinker's negotiations to dispose of Conrad's reminiscences by removing copyright from the author and giving it solely to the *Review*. The remainder of the letter is worth quoting, for it describes how friendship has turned to rancor:

> The last rumour about myself reaching *my* knowledge (some 5 weeks ago) was that F.H. was going about saying he has "called Conrad out." The basis of it is a letter I received from him about beginning of May containing 1° An apology which I did not demand. 2° a sort of hint of a challenge being possible. Why? God only knows. 3° A statement that he was on the eve of committing suicide. 4° An invitation in the most pressing terms to come and stay with him at his flat that very night.

Conrad continues:

> I've heard also, since, that I am made responsible for the failure of a negotiation with McClure for the sale of the ER which was he affirms nearly concluded for £2000,—the ground for that phantasy seems to be the fact that I refused to see Miss Cather here. He tried to ram that visit down my throat and charged me with ingratitude for all his efforts to serve me. I told him in effect to go to the devil and warned him that if I heard any more of that nonsense I would take steps to make it perfectly clear that his interference (whatever it was) in my affairs is an unauthorised and impertinent assumption on his part, completely without my knowledge and highly distasteful to me.

He repeats that Ford's conduct has been impossible, that he is a megalomaniac "who imagines he is managing the universe and that everybody treats him with the blackest ingratitude." He feels his former collaborator should undergo medical treatment, Conrad's own fate the next year. He ends by regurgitating every aspect of his resentment: Ford's temperament, the affair with Violet Hunt, the presence of Russian Jews in the *Review:*

> In short he has quarrelled with every decent friend he had; has nearly made mischief between me and some of my best friends, and is, from all accounts, having a most miserable time himself—because he has his lucid intervals. Generally he's behaving like a spoilt kid—and not a nice kid either. I am told that Violet Hunt is mothering him just now and that a Russian Jew refugee (his brother-in-law) has found some unknown person to buy the Review—or something of the kind. At any rate it is to go on apparently with him for editor. I haven't seen him for quite two months and had only two wires from him in that time, which I answered negatively.

CHAPTER 29

"Dreams, Hags, Magic Sleights"

FORD lost control of the *Review*. He quarreled with David Soskice, who represented a political position that was anathema to Ford. He tried to interest Sir Alfred Mond in the *Review;* Mond did buy it, and to Ford's surprise turned the editorship over to Austin Harrison. With that, the history of the collaboration ends. Unlike Conrad's career, which was peaking, Ford's had yet to reach its highest levels. Those terrible conflicts, including his demeaning struggle to break free of Elsie with a German divorce, did not sink him; on the contrary, he revealed an admirable resilience and even as the storms raged never surrendered his belief in himself.

Given these circumstances of the almost murderous conflict between the two collaborators and co-editors, it is necessary to see Conrad's "Secret Sharer," written in November–December, as connected to his personal life. Not only is the story a psychological interpretation of the relationship, it draws directly on the association. We have seen that Conrad's imagination repeatedly worked to transform "real events"—here the *Cutty Sark* incident of 1880—with personal psychological patterns. His literary imagination was often indistinguishable from the ways in which he survived his personal blows.

The house at Aldington, although an improvement over Someries, was proving unsatisfactory; the Conrads would remain only until June 1910 and then move to a permanent residence, Capel House, also in Kent. Aldington was turning out to be too small and intimate, and Conrad could not have that "absolute quiet, complete silence, without which it seems I cannot work to any serious purpose."* To help maintain some stability, he pursued Robert

* Yet his sense of his worth remained. In July, he had written to Harpers proposing serialization in America of *Some Reminiscences*, but his letter remained unacknowledged. Conrad wrote a blistering follow-up: "Be good enough to understand distinctly that I no longer care in what sense your answer is worded nor yet whether you ever publish or not another line of my writing; but from a regard for the dignity of Eng-

d'Humières about the translation of *The Nigger*, which, finally, would appear serialized in the *Correspondant*, in four sections, the final one ending on October 10, 1909. Conrad never tired of speaking about this novel or the period in which he wrote it; it was, for him, the golden age in which he saw himself on the edge of greatness, still young, and with his energies intact. Although he was married then, he was not a family man, and his chances, after recognition from Henley, seemed expansive. If one can imagine Conrad ever grinning, the following passage from his letter to d'Humières was written while its author grinned:

> Quelque illusions qu'un écrivain se fasse sur la puissance de son oeuvre l'idée ne me serait jamais venue que l'histoire de James Wait fût capable d'évoquer les images de la Terreur dans les âmes timorées des lecteurs du Correspondant. Ce serait a proprement parler un miracle d'art. Mais je veux bien y croire et j'en conçois quelque orgueil quoique a fond et par nature je ne suis guère revolutionnaire. J'aime même assez les douairières, que, du reste, je ne pratique pas et dont je me fais conception plutôt idéale.*

Conrad then rakes over his association with Henley, and the magical moment passes.

Parallel with the breakdown of the Ford friendship was the intensification of the one with Norman Douglas. Unquestionably, Douglas filled a gap in Conrad's life at this period, somewhat in the manner of Ford earlier. Conrad tried to place his material and borrowed money; he was the established writer, and he leaned on the friendship while providing literary advice. Douglas visited frequently at Someries, Aldington, and Capel House, until Conrad became disturbed by his homosexual exploits.

When Conrad published *'Twixt Land and Sea* in 1911, he dedicated the volume to Captain C. M. Harris, an archipelago trader, late master and owner of the *Araby Maid*, "in memory of those old days of adventure." "Harris"—which carried into the Collected Edition—was really Captain

---

lish letters in which I occupy a recognized position, I will not let pass what looks like a deliberate slight without calling upon you for such an expression of regret as the least spark of good feeling may prompt you to offer. Failing which I shall leave the merits of the case, with perfect confidence, to the appreciation of all cultured and fair-minded men in the New World and Old." Harpers answered immediately that Colonel Harvey had had a serious accident, apologized profusely, and asked to reconsider Conrad's proposal, which apparently had been misplaced or lost.

---

* Whatever illusions a writer may have about the power of his work, the idea would never have crossed my mind that the story of James Wait could evoke images of the Terror in the fearful souls of the *Correspondant* readers. It would be, properly speaking, to talk of a miracle of art. But I wish to believe it very much and I harbor some pride for it, although at bottom and by nature I am hardly a revolutionary. I even passably like dowagers, whom, moreover, I do not frequent and of whom I have a rather unreal view.

Charles M. Marris, who was based on Penang and married to a local woman. Unexpectedly, he wrote and then visited Conrad at Aldington in October of 1909, and Conrad told Pinker about it:

> . . . I had a visit from a man out of the Malay Seas. It was like the raising of a lot of dead—dead to me, because most of them live out there and even read my books and wonder who [the] devil has been around taking notes. My visitor told me that Joshua Lingard made the guess: "It must have been the fellow who was mate in the *Vidar* with Craig." That's me right enough. And the best of it is that all these men of 22 years ago feel kindly to the Chronicler of their lives and adventures. They shall have some more of the stories they like.

The Marris visit coincided with Conrad's exasperating final work on "Razumov." He still had almost three months until completion, but his mind was turning back to those golden Malay days, and he began to think of stories. While they would not properly be "Malay stories," they were Asian: "The Secret Sharer," "A Smile of Fortune," and "Freya of the Seven Isles." "The Secret Sharer" would, in effect, be his last story of note, and it was triggered as much by the breakup with Ford and his work on "Razumov" as by Captain Marris's visit. Those Malay memories were also stirred by the appearance of the first French translation of one of his novels, *The Nigger*. A little-known fact is that Conrad added to the book proofs of the translation, which d'Humières had arranged to be sent to him. "How could I resist [he asked Rothenstein] the chance of putting something of my real self into the translator's prose?" His "real self," apparently, lay enclosed in an earlier time. And in a letter to Galsworthy in early December, Conrad says *The Nigger* "has been made to look like an original work—almost."

By December 14, Conrad had interrupted "Razumov" in order to work up "The Secret Sharer," a story of some 15,000 words written in less than a month, a testament to Conrad's rapidity when he knew his mind exactly. Of course, by interrupting "Razumov," he brought on a full-blooded revolt from Pinker, who had been waiting almost two years for this novel. "Razumov" was now 15–20,000 words short of completion, and Conrad suggested to Pinker it was so fine he could sell it himself for the price of a postage stamp. "Now I beg you to inform me plainly if with that story in your hands you really mean (as your letter seems to foreshadow) to slam the door on me when I am nearly through for the sake of an odd week." He closes by saying he is "not a confounded hypochondriac in search of sympathy." As if doubting his own response to Pinker's threat to cut off all further advances on copy, Conrad wrote at length to several of his friends about his situation.

His psychological need to share his situation with those close to him is a personal manifestation of what he had just been writing. One can see the reasons why he originally planned to title "The Secret Sharer" either "The Second Self," "The Secret Self," or "The Other Self." He needed these people desperately as props as Pinker seemed prepared, finally, to desert him. We have no way of knowing Pinker's mind, since his letters have not survived, but we can gather some of the tone of his responses from Conrad's desperation. He displayed now his familiar pattern of dependency, seeking supports as he was being deserted, first by Ford, then by Pinker.

Conrad wrote bitterly to Galsworthy, on December 22, and even sent Pinker's letter, a breach of confidence that suggests his psychological unease. What he resented in the Pinker response more than anything else was his agent's treatment of him as "a loafer who wants spurring," his use of a manner one would display to "a dog to make him stand on his hind legs." Not only did Conrad fall back on his pride, he could not bear to hear the tones and accents of Tadeusz Bobrowski. Pinker was coming very close to the censorious uncle chiding his nephew for not making anything of his life, or for wasting his time. We can read back into the agent's letter continual queries about Conrad's use of his time; for repeatedly he must explain that he has lost weeks and months through gout and other ailments.

After raking over his entire situation to Galsworthy—his time for working, his months ill and shaken, his slow production of copy, the fact that he writes long novels—he then moves into high dudgeon about Pinker, whom, elsewhere, he had called "the nourisher of geniuses."

> I have been nearly out of my mind ever since. If he says yes, that was what he meant I wonder if I can restrain myself from throwing the MS in the fire. It's outrageous. Does he think I am the sort of man who wouldn't finish the story in a week if he could? Do you? For what reason. Is it my habit to lie about drunk for days instead of working? I reckon he knows well enough I don't. It's a contemptuous playing with my worry. If he had said No. I will stick to the lot—I wouldn't have been hurt. But this gratuitous ignoring of my sincerity in spirit and also in fact is almost more than I can bear. I who can hardly bear to look at the kids, who without you [Galsworthy laid out the tuition fees] could not have the boy at school even—I wouldn't finish the book in a week if I could—unless a bribe of six pounds is dangled before me!—I sit 12 hours at the table, sleep six, and worry the rest of time, feeling the age creeping on and looking at those I love.

Conrad complains he has been isolated for two years: no human intercourse, no entertainment, no nourishment of any sort. He has depleted himself for the sake of Pinker.The image is of filling and emptying, with Conrad emptying himself out for those who now reject his offers.

> —And he talks of *regular supplies of manuscript* to a man who in these conditions (taking all the time together ill or well) sends him MS at the rate of 7.600 words a month; and he actually writes as if I were a swindler from whom nothing can be got unless he's pinched. Is it a swindle to write a long novel? He had better get some of his clerks to write stuff which he

can sell. But 16 months for a long novel nearly done and some 57000 words of other work is not so bad—even for a man with his mind at ease, with his spirits kept up by prosperity, with his inspiration buoyed by hope. There's nothing of that for me!

Conrad's dependency on Galsworthy's support turns childish and self-serving: " . . . for when people appraise me later on with severity I wish you to be able to say: —I knew him—he was not so bad. By Jove all the moral tortures are not in prison-life. I assure you I feel sometimes as if I could drop everything and beat at the door—you understand." He threatens that if Pinker halts his "miserable pound a day" he will toss the manuscript on the fire. He says he cannot write a line, that he needs a "certain detachment" which lies beyond him. In actuality, Pinker's reluctance to advance money forced Conrad into a rapid conclusion to "Razumov." In January 1910, he wrote Pinker he had final copy in hand, and the typescript of the novel is dated as having been ended on January 22. This would suggest a manuscript conclusion of December 1909, or thereabout.

Even before he collapsed, his nervous system shattered, Conrad was displaying symptoms of a breakdown. He kept going long after he needed rest and medical treatment. He reached out almost helplessly to friends for sympathy and support: to Galsworthy, as we have seen; to Perceval Gibbon and his wife Maisie, not even close friends; to William Rothenstein, Douglas, and even Meldrum after a long hiatus. Some of his comments are malicious, as when he writes to Gibbon that Elsie Hueffer's latest visit is an "evil for which there is no remedy."* His remarks are full of attacks on Ford's veracity and his "carryings on like a spoilt kid." The only ray of light, apparently, was the imminent publication of *The Nigger* by the *Mercure de France* in 1910. In that connection, he wrote to Robert d'Humières and then by way of association circled around to Flaubert, to *Madame Bovary* and *Salammbô*, which he says he read every morning while he wrote *The Nigger*. Conrad

---

* Jessie reports on one scene that she says helped to precipitate Conrad's collapse. Tinged as her description is with present dislike of Elsie, it cannot be taken as completely true. Of course, Elsie was herself under considerable strain with Ford, who was by now well into his new life. Withal, the general effect appears valid, since Ford was to reproduce some of this atmosphere in *The Good Soldier*. Jessie writes: "Apparently her only reason for disturbing Joseph Conrad was to deliver a long tirade against the habits and manners of all literary people. She became greatly excited, warming to her subject and threatening to show up the whole literary world. It was not quite clear to either of us why she inflicted all this upon my husband. I allowed my gaze to wander round the room, and the next moment I was recalled to the present by hearing the name of John Galsworthy. In an instant my husband sprang to his feet wildly excited and stood shaking his finger within an inch or so of the lady's face. 'Don't you say "dat," ' he repeated two or three times. His English had completely deserted him in a moment. He turned aside, grabbed his hat, and almost hurled me through the door [of the Ford cottage]. 'Don't you dare say "dat." ' "

squinted at the past through that ray of light afforded by those magical books. On December 3, he spent his fifty-second birthday at his desk.

The completion of *Under Western Eyes* marked the end of an era. The year 1909–10 was, in a sense, a watershed for Conrad, manifested psychologically by his nervous collapse for four months and demonstrated literarily by his realization of an entire phase of personal writings. After *Under Western Eyes*, he would move back to *Chance*, to lighter short fiction, and to *Victory*, little of which was so markedly personal as the fiction from 1899 to 1910. Only in the father-son relationships of *Victory*, and that in deep narrative retrospect, would Conrad have to face those terrible early years of uncertainty and unexamined hatreds and fears. *Under Western Eyes*, with its direct confrontation of those attitudes, both led into the breakdown and liberated Conrad for other work.

Conrad had, in fact, reached out for what every artist must do or try to do: to dip so deeply into his psyche for what he fears most that he endangers himself; and then, once close to extinction, having discovered what he can do, he either frees himself or cracks up. Only a major artist can perform this way, since the journey into himself must be intense. Not only did Conrad have to confront terrible personal anxieties from his past, he also had to test his very literary tastes. Whereas earlier he had offered up Flaubert as his model, here his model was Dostoevsky. To do what he intended, he had to follow the route laid out by the Russian novelist: Conrad could either follow Dostoevsky or diverge; but the Russian was *there*.

In many ways, Dostoevsky, whose "fierce mouthings" sounded to Conrad like something from "prehistoric ages," carried the Conradian idea to areas to which Conrad himself feared to go, or could not go. Had Conrad been able to maintain the intensity of the first part in the second section of *Under Western Eyes*, he would have been forced to confront Dostoevsky on the latter's ground. Although we have no direct proof Conrad was familiar with the Dostoevsky novel, the first segment of his book does seem closely modeled on *Crime and Punishment*.* Conrad insisted, however, that his ideology was quite different from Dostoevsky's, that he was Western in his outlook and did not at all accept the Russian's Panslavism or immersion in the mystique of land and soul. In these and other respects, Conrad was of the twentieth century, whereas Dostoevsky's ideology was more clearly of the nineteenth.

Once that is said, it is still difficult to believe that Conrad could have written *Under Western Eyes* without the Dostoevsky novel before him as a model. While differing obviously in ideology and political ideas, Conrad and

---

* In addition to the similarities we can deduce in scenes and characters in the two novels, there is the naming of Conrad's Sophia Antonovna. Her manuscript name is, as Hay points out, Sophia Semenovna, which is very close indeed to Sonia's family name in *Crime and Punishment*.

Dostoevsky often meet on common ground: for example, the Mikulin-Razumov and the General-Razumov interviews can be compared to the Porfiry-Raskolnikov interviews in *Crime and Punishment;* Razumov's mental playing with his secret is similar to Raskolnikov's temptation to divulge his crime; the need for spiritual cleansing is common to both "sinners"; the tensions of a pathological condition affect the sanity of both men; and there finally remains the fact, curious in the light of Conrad's hatred for the Russian's ideology, that both Razumov and Raskolnikov consider themselves superior to other men and destined for some calling in which their worth will be realized. Each tries to conduct himself apart from the solidarity of mankind, and each as a result has part of himself destroyed.

That shift in focus between the idea of "Razumov" and the final *Under Western Eyes* is crucial; for once Conrad decided to move Razumov onto a wider stage than marriage and family, he chose to meet Dostoevsky on the latter's favorite ground. Yet with all their similarities, Conrad moderated his materials by observing them through the eyes of a Westerner, the language teacher, thereby restraining his presentation of Slavic "haunted creatures" as well as negating the "fierce mouthings" that would have resulted from direct confrontation with anarchists and socialists. In still another way, through irony, Conrad evoked a different kind of atmosphere from Dostoevsky's. These are matters not only of content but of tone; for Dostoevsky continually moved in and out of his characters, whereas Conrad had already taken a firm position outside them.* He had decided before he wrote that he would reject whatever his characters might say to him, whereas Dostoevsky allowed his characters to gain his sympathies even as he criticized their actions. The Russian showed his love for sinners, while Conrad demonstrated his distaste for nearly all human behavior, caught as it was in a senseless universe. For Dostoevsky, sin, even the worst, was a form of energy and tied one to the workings of the universe; for Conrad, neither crime nor punishment could mitigate the fact that man was strung out in a puppet's existence. Man lived within a world of "Dreams, Hags, Magic Sleights."

In a 1917 essay on Turgenev, which appeared as the introduction to Edward Garnett's study of the Russian novelist, Conrad offered *his* Russia as the more authentic, with Dostoevsky's "convulsed terror-haunted" one as

* *Under Western Eyes* is, to some extent, a roman à clef, although not in the strictest sense. The main incident of Haldin's crime was based, as Conrad indicated to Galsworthy, on Igor Sazonov's assassination of Plehwe and, to some extent, on the 1881 assassination of Alexander II. Sergey Stepniak may have served as a partial model for Razumov. Peter Ivanovich is a composite of many Russians Conrad feared or detested: Prince Kropotkin, Bakunin, even Tolstoy. Councilor Mikulin, as Baines suggests, may be based on Lopuhin, a liberal head of the police, and Nikita seems closely modeled on aspects of the career of Evno Azef (Aseff), a notorious double agent. But behind these shadowy identifications are the more substantial figures —Apollo Korzeniowski in Haldin, Ewa in Nathalie and even Mrs. Haldin, and Conrad himself in aspects of Razumov.

contrast. He said: "All his [Turgenev's] creations, fortunate and unfortunate, oppressed and oppressors are human beings, not strange beasts in a menagerie or damned souls knocking themselves to pieces in the stuffy darkness of mystical contradictions." Conrad of course had a particular theme in this essay; for he saw Turgenev as having been beaten with "almost any stick," and the parallel to his own fortunes in Poland is apparent.

Richard Curle felt, later, that Conrad's antipathy to Dostoevsky was based on his fear that he could not compete on the same ground with the Russian. More likely, Conrad's dislike was founded on a more central motif: the vast difference in their ideologies, his hatred of Russia and Russians, and his immersion in quite another literary tradition. As for Conrad's asymptotic movement toward Dostoevsky's methods, a good deal of that can be explained as a shared Slavic tradition. Secrets, conspiracies, meetings with police and police agents (Conrad's parents, Dostoevsky himself), murderous crimes committed against officials or society—these were not unusual in Slavic fiction, many of whose themes would carry over into the Communist era.

The year 1910 began in the worst possible way: Conrad was incapacitated by a complete breakdown. After his January letter to Pinker indicating the delivery of the final pages of *Under Western Eyes*, his next letter is dated March 3, to Galsworthy, and the one after that on May 3, to Davray. Since he was writing to people who routinely saved his letters, we can assume that because of the fierceness of his collapse he wrote only one letter between January and early May. The breakdown was a compound of attacks of gout and nervous exhaustion. In a curious duplication of Razumov's helplessness and need of Tekla, Conrad became helpless and dependent on Jessie. Her description of his condition indicates that his anger was directed against Pinker and much of it in mutterings that sounded like Polish to her.

> He spoke all the time in Polish, but for a few fierce sentences against poor J. B. Pinker. That day seemed endless. I could get no one to help me but the old maid. I scarcely left his side for he was constantly calling upon me to sit on the side of the bed to make a rest for his back. Hour after hour I sat in that cramped position. Day and Night I watched over him, fearful that if I turned my back he would escape from the room. I slept what little I could on the couch drawn across the only door. More than once I opened my eyes to find him tottering towards me in search of something he had dreamed of. If it had not been for Perceval Gibbon who came often and always, it seemed, in the nick of time, I feel sure I would not have held out.

Conrad, apparently, was in danger of dying: "I felt that my husband was very seriously and critically ill. He seemed to breathe once when he should have done at least a dozen times, a cold heavy sweat came over him, and he lay on his back, faintly murmuring the words of the burial service."

According to Jessie, Conrad chose to hear none of the medical advice offered him, and we are reminded of Razumov's deafness. Jessie's description of Conrad's "deathbed" scene, in fact, recalls Razumov's in *Under Western Eyes*:

> On this plea, they let her [Tekla, the nurse of doomed men] have her way. She sat down calmly, and took his head on her lap; her scared faded eyes avoided looking at his deathlike face. At the corner of a street, on the other side of the town, a stretcher met the car. She followed it to the door of the hospital, where they let her come in and see him laid on a bed. Razumov's new-found relation never shed a tear, but the officials had some difficulty in inducing her to go away.

Writing to David Meldrum, Jessie catches the uncertain situation much better than in her book:

> The novel is finished, but the penalaty [sic] has to be paid. Months of nervous strain have ended in a complete nervous breakdown. Poor Conrad is very ill and Dr Hackney says it will be a long time before he is fit for anything requiring mental exertion. . . . There is the M.S. complete but uncorrected and his fierce refusal to let even I touch it. It lays on a table at the foot of his bed and he lives mixed up in the scenes and holds converse with the characters.
>
> I have been up with him night and day since Sunday week and he, who is usually so depressed by illness, maintains he is not ill, and accuses the D^r and I of trying to put him into an asylum.

The chattering in Polish which Jessie reports carried Conrad deep into his ill childhood, and to his need for ministering servants and relatives. But, also, his use of his native tongue is related to his rebuff by Pinker, who had shamed him by telling him to speak English if he could. The levels of dependency increase, with Polish as both the medium for seeking comfort and the source of his rejection. He was Yanko Goorall once again. Conrad's illness helped him play out sub- or unconsciously what his imagination was projecting artistically. We have here an intense phenomenological occurrence, in which the artistic imagination has delved into the deepest reaches of the writer's psyche, well beyond conscious retrieval, and met there those very elements which would simultaneously feed the art and almost nullify the person. In a play on his speech, Conrad told Pinker on May 23 that he had asked "Robert Garnett [Edward's brother] to be my mouth-piece—at any rate till my speech improves sufficiently to be acceptable." The phrasing is somewhat ambiguous; it may refer ironically to Pinker's rejection of him as a foreigner or else even suggest some impairment as a result of his breakdown.*

---

* The entire passage reads: "As it can't have escaped your recollection that the last time we met you told me that I 'did not speak English' to you I have asked Robert Garnett to be my mouth-piece—at any rate till my speech improves sufficiently to be acceptable. I have asked him to telephone to you re reference to house-agents. I am under notice to

Conrad's recovery was very slow, for the mental damage had been severe. *Under Western Eyes*, of course, remained unrevised, and it must have rankled Pinker even more than Conrad's earlier so-called laxity. While the latter's indebtedness remained huge, close to $25,000 in current money, no work at all was forthcoming. The relationship between author and agent had, in fact, become very formal, and would remain so for the next two years. In still another one of those ironic turns of fate, *Under Western Eyes*, the novel that had created such intense conflicts in Conrad during the writing, would appear in *The English Review* later in the year, when Ford was no longer in charge.

On March 3, in the first letter since his collapse, he told Galsworthy he suffered from abdominal gout, swollen feet, and mental and physical limpness. He says he will attempt to get on with the revision of the manuscript "and discover how far I am capable of sustained mental effort. . . . I am growing desperate with the pain and weariness and the worry of this fatal stoppage of work." Like Persephone awaiting the inner signal to return to the surface, he hopes the "creative power will return—or wake up." At this stage, he was confronted by incomplete items that dominated his imagination: an unrevised *Under Western Eyes*; a fragmentary *Chance*, which was, however, well along; and *The Rescue*, that carryover from fourteen years earlier. He had another volume of stories in mind, also, for which "The Secret Sharer" would be one selection. The sole consolation at this time was the book-form appearance of the French *Nigger*, whose royalties were sufficient to pay Borys's tuition at the Luton school. Even as late as May 3, in a letter to Davray, Conrad spoke of physical weakness, of dragging himself from one room to the other with the aid of a cane. By then, despite complaints, he had to work on revisions of *Under Western Eyes* because Pinker was in the midst of placing it.

The Conrads, meanwhile, were preparing to move in June from what he called "pigging it in 4 rooms in a cottage" to more capacious quarters, at Capel House. Capel House, which Borys later called the "happiest of the Conrad homes," was situated in Orlestone, Kent, five miles from Ashford and only fourteen miles south of Canterbury. The Conrads rented this fairly large establishment with one and a half acres of orchard at the side from Edmund Oliver and remained for almost nine years, when Oliver's son reclaimed it for his own use, in March 1919.

---

quit here on June 24; and I really could *not* do any literary work sitting in a field with my family and furniture about me." After all these years, the letter is addressed "Dear Sir." In a touching passage written much later, on February 19, 1919, Conrad asked that certain harsh letters of his be put aside; for his gratitude to Pinker, he says, "has never been obscured for a moment in my heart, no matter what words might have been written on the spur of the moment."

Conrad's letter on May 17 to Galsworthy indicates the beginning of his return to the living, although still as a painful convalescent.* *Under Western Eyes* had passed on to the negotiating stage, but only after Robert Garnett had agreed to read over and correct the clean final copy. After revision, Conrad told Galsworthy, "There was a good many phrases without grammar and even without sense." The effort left Conrad still crippled and "hardly audible." After praising Borys for his help, Conrad tried to define the quality of his life, as "very much like coming out of one little hell into another." He stresses that he is pleased to have changed one hell for another, that he feels neither helpless nor hopeless, and that any kind of existence is preferable to the "black depression" he experienced. His brain, he says, is still only good for ten-minute snatches. But even so, he feels capable of starting a story about potatoes, what would become "A Smile of Fortune." Financially, he was still wedded to Pinker, with a new agreement, arranged by Robert Garnett, fixing three pounds per thousand words, on delivery of manuscript only. The upcoming move to the new house was a source of hope: a change of venue, regaining of physical strength, and the potential of a reactivated imagination. Conrad sensed the emergence of a new self, however shaky, however uncertain.

Much intelligent sleuthing has been done by scholars and critics into this phase of Conrad's life, most of it attempting to use this breakdown in early 1910 as a way of explaining the decline in his work after his recovery. This line of reasoning is defined best by Dr. Bernard Meyer, and it takes the shape of a psychoanalytic interpretation handled with great sensitivity and considerable literary taste. Meyer identifies Conrad's condition as falling clinically under the term "Infection-Exhaustion Psychoses," in which, as we have seen, a severe physical ailment uncovers an emotional storm, which has been brewing for some time before it explodes. Meyer cites Conrad's strained association with Ford, the result of the latter's relationship to Violet Hunt, as the chief contributory factor in Conrad's breakdown. One could add to Meyer's stress severe financial strains, artistic conflicts, slowness of production, familial discords, and other elements in the collapse.

Following this breakdown, the argument runs, Conrad's fiction took a radically new turn. As Meyer writes:

* By May 11, Conrad felt well enough to write to Laurence Housman, A. E.'s brother, on the subject of women's suffrage. He told Housman that "the shortest road to success for women's suffrage would be in its being made a party question on any ground under heaven except that of justice." This interest in the suffrage question undoubtedly fed into *Chance*, with Conrad's creation of Mrs. Fyne, a militant feminist, a departure for him among female portraits. On June 27, 1910, he followed it up by adding: "I want the women to have the vote and generally their own way in anything and everything under heaven. It will please them and certainly it won't hurt me" (ALS, private collection).

> The most striking manifestation of this change concerns a pronounced shift in the moral and psychological orientation of his stories which is characterized by an exteriorization of the source of suffering. As a consequence the poignant inner mental conflict of the early Conrad was replaced by conflict with the outer world, and doubting, troubled men, like Marlow of "Heart of Darkness," and hapless souls like Jim or Decoud, caught in a neurotic web of their own creation, gave way to simple innocent creatures who, as pawns of fate, struggle with indifferent success against external influence, external accident, and external malevolence.

The explanation may be found in the psychological idea of "projection," which Meyer defines and applies to Conrad's post-1910 body of work:

> The surrender of personal autonomy and the disavowal of personal authorship for the vicissitudes of life implicit in this new orientation is typical of the phenomenon of projection, that psychological device which consists in the attribution to influences or agencies beyond the self of those attitudes, feelings, impulses, and thoughts which reside within the subject's own mind. Carried to an extreme, projection may attain the proportions of paranoid thinking, characterized by delusions and other gross distortions of reality.

One's sense of reality is altered; one loses self-knowledge, so significant to the artist. Even if the artist maintains his stability, it is a precarious stability that disallows searching introspection and audacious flights of imagination. Such an artist, intent on maintaining his balance, must forgo those very elements that fed his art.

As a concomitant of these developments, Meyer feels that Conrad's work declined not because of the usual reasons—ill health, financial pressures, need to dictate his novels, et al.—but "rather by the inevitable consequences of the specific psychological defenses adopted by him after his mental illness. Psychologically it would appear that he could no longer afford those introspective journeys into the self that constitute the greatness of the impressionistic art he created during the years of his close association with Hueffer." Meyer draws the inevitable conclusion:

> Deprived of that mirroring companionship which had sustained him in his earlier bold descent, and terrified by the mad devils leering at him during his illness, Conrad seems to have elected thereafter to confine his art to the surface of life, to become, as it were, a literary Captain MacWhirr. . . . Hemmed in by such self-imposed restrictions it is hardly surprising that his creative artistry declined. Cut off from the dream source of poetic invention and unable to draw on the rich lode of his own well-guarded fancy, he was in time even reduced to picking over the slag of other literary prospectors [i.e., for *Suspense*].

One of the clearest manifestations of Conrad's artistic bewilderment in this post-illness period, according to Meyer, was his reliance on powerful female characters who dominate over the men.

> Beginning with "A Smile of Fortune," written in the latter half of 1910, it is the women who dominate Conrad's fictional stage. Like ballerinas who traditionally comprise the main attraction of the dance, these fictional females perform breathtaking leaps and dazzling turns, while employing their submissive and often seemingly impotent partners as temporarily convenient accessories. With an inexorable consistency, moreover, the choreography turns out to be a dance of death in which the women usually emerge triumphant while their men are systematically unmanned and then destroyed.

Such a view of Conrad's post-1910 "decline" must assume that the work of his last fourteen years is invariably inferior to what came before. It takes over the argument that *Victory* is, as Guerard puts it, "very badly written and very roughly imagined." It also assumes that *Chance* is chiefly the product of the years after 1910 (during the "decline"), and yet the evidence of Conrad's letters to Pinker demonstrates that *Chance* was much further along before 1910 than the decline theorists have granted. Further, these critics agree that Conrad's later work is evenly poor, dismissing besides *Victory* such work as *The Shadow-Line*, "The Planter of Malata," parts of *The Rescue*, *The Rover*, *Chance* altogether. Decline theorists tend to place Conrad in neat categories. Yet even if one admits that his work as a whole for the fourteen years after 1910 is inferior to that of the fourteen years before that date, exceptions to the theory loom quite large. *Victory*—its conception, development, and subject—will be discussed in Chapter 33, but here it is sufficient to say that the novel brings together many important Conradian themes and presents a female figure of considerable depth. The fact that the female characters in Conrad's later fiction seem to dominate does not necessarily signal a weakening of his powers but may point to a deeper recognition of human values and a more complex sense of sexual relationships.

Even Mrs. Fyne of *Chance*, whom Baines characterizes as a "lesbian and feminist,"* represents a step up, not down, in Conrad's conceptual powers and may reflect his greater awareness of women resulting from their agitation to gain the vote. That *Chance* ultimately is unsatisfactory artistically

* Baines's considerable scholarship is diluted whenever he attempts critical statements: "The lesbian and feminist Mrs Fyne [he writes] resents the subordinate position of women and demands that they should compete with men as if they themselves were men. When Flora elopes with Anthony [Mrs. Fyne's brother] she arouses Mrs Fyne's extreme animosity because she has behaved like a woman" (p. 386). He is troubled by his statement, for he follows it with a footnote that despite Mrs. Fyne's being "given all the lesbian's most distinctive characteristics," it is difficult to say whether Conrad intended her to be taken for one.

cannot be traced to the upsurgence of strong female characters but to the fact that like all of Conrad's work which dragged on, it fell victim to varying styles and literary techniques. Conrad began it when his methods called for Marlow, but completed it when he was moving toward a more natural narrative; yet Marlow, Powell, and the primary narrator remained from the earlier conception.

The varieties of argument explaining Conrad's decline after 1910 are ingenious and, in some instances, valid. But all of them *must* assume one point: that *Victory* is an artistic failure, a throwback to Conrad's worst excesses of romanticism, a demonstration of his loss of artistic and imaginative powers. If *Victory* cannot be destroyed, there is no substantive argument—unless one begins the decline *after* 1914. Yet it is possible to view *Victory* as standing with the very best of Conrad's work, with *The Secret Agent* and *Under Western Eyes*, and only a little below "Heart of Darkness," *Lord Jim*, and *Nostromo*, his three acknowledged masterpieces. F. R. Leavis catches the resonances of the novel:

> The characteristic Conradian sensibility is that of the creator of Heyst; that of the writer so intimately experienced in the strains and starvations of the isolated consciousness, and so deeply aware of the sense in which reality is social, something established and sustained in a kind of collaboration ("I have lived too long within myself," says Heyst, "watching the mere shadows and shades of life").

Leavis concludes that even though *Victory* is neither about the Malayan jungle nor about the sea, it nevertheless answers "most nearly to the stock notion of his genius" and, therefore, deserves to represent "his claim to classical standing."

Although no single argument will settle the controversy of the novel's value or the quality of Conrad's decline, the point here is that *Victory* was written by a novelist very much in full control of his powers. As we trace its conception and development, we can see Conrad had not become lax in his use of language, shaping of scene, depiction of character, and management of image and symbol. On the contrary, the manuscript of the novel illuminates how an important book came into being and was brought to completion by an artist struggling to gain the right phrase, the trenchant image, the correct balance of character and social scene.

All this, however, was later. On May 21, 1910, Conrad wrote his first (extant) letter to a new face, that of Francis Warrington Dawson, a young American writer, a Southerner of reactionary social and literary tastes. A good part of the significance of the association would not appear until 1913, when Conrad composed a long response to Dawson's "fourteen points" of his Fresh Air Art Society. Conrad's letter, on June 20, coinciding with some of his most intense work on the manuscript of *Victory*, demonstrates a working aesthetic no less stringent than the points he outlined in the Preface to *The Nigger* sixteen years earlier. Conrad's reply to Dawson suggests that rather than having lost his powers after 1910, he had found ways to renew himself; and that his control of his imagination and shaping powers was complete.

Of little interest as a writer, Dawson has his place in Conrad's biography as one of those props the novelist periodically sought. Dawson, like Curle shortly after, filled the gap left by the loss of Ford and helped out in areas where Galsworthy could not compete. Dawson had been traveling with the Theodore Roosevelt party in Africa when he met Ted Sanderson, who was at that time Town Clerk of Nairobi. When Dawson returned to England, he brought greetings to Conrad from Sanderson; Conrad replied, and Dawson visited Aldington on May 31. It was a crazy pattern, but Conrad was pleased to see anyone who took a sustained interest in him. His recovery throughout the summer was still slow, and his work was going poorly; apparently only "A Smile of Fortune" was going forward.*

His response to the visit was one of amusement, as he wrote Galsworthy after the luncheon ended: "On Sat. a young American writer who has been with Roosevelt in S. Africa arrived for the day. The greatest news is that Mrs. Ted Sanderson has discovered in herself a talent for writing and that the Ex-President has been so struck that he placed three of her E. A. sketches with Scribners Mag. . . . Same young man brought a formal message from the only Teddy. He [Roosevelt] would have invited himself to come and see me only too busy with official festivities. Very safe bunkum that." Despite whatever reservations Conrad may have had about Dawson's manner and attitudes—besides being a literary reactionary, he was a Negrophobe and a "Mama's boy"—the latter provided attention and sympathy, qualities Conrad could well appreciate now.

Also reassuring was the appearance of *The Secret Agent* in a French translation, done by Davray himself. "A Smile of Fortune" was going desultorily, and by June 18 was still not finished. Since the move to Capel House was imminent—possession would take place on the twenty-fourth of June—Jessie sent Conrad away, to the Gibbons' in Trosley, to keep him out of the way. Visitors were coming now that Conrad was recovering: Clifford, back from Ceylon, Marwood (every Thursday afternoon); Conrad invited the Galsworthys, and noted that the Sandersons were returning home from Africa. There was an atmosphere of nostalgia, perhaps intensified by his re-

* That Conrad borrowed extensively from literary sources is evident; but for "A Smile of Fortune" he leaned particularly heavily on Maupassant's "Les Soeurs Rondoli." Very possibly Conrad needed considerable propping at this difficult time, employing both personal experience on the *Otago* and his reading in the familiar Maupassant.

cent illness and by the return, for "A Smile," to the episode on Mauritius during his first command, on the *Otago.*

On June 25, Conrad set foot in Capel House, telling Galsworthy he felt "all of a shake and utterly lost without Jessie." But the theme that runs through this period is, not unusually, *The English Review.* Ironically, Conrad was winding back upon himself, for in trying to help Norman Douglas place his stuff, he was becoming reinvolved in *Review* affairs, although indirectly. Austin Harrison had been installed as editor, and Douglas was to become an assistant editor, but in midsummer of 1910 the whole enterprise seemed to reflect Ford's affairs: a superstructure built on a swamp. Writing to Douglas, Conrad said he should curry favor with Harrison, whom he characterized as the "son of the old Positivist Pope [Frederic Harrison, who, the contemporary of Dickens, died only one year before Conrad]." He writes: "A.H. is worth being civil to as he represents the Mond interest in the world of letters. The Monds bought the ER (I mean the German Jew who has been made a Birthday Baronet this year). They are 'the money' of the Philosophical Radical lot. Lady Mond bosses the ER. You had better come over and fascinate her and so make both our fortunes."

Conrad was struck by the irony of the *Review* serializing *Under Western Eyes* and said snidely that perhaps it was Lady Mond, not the *Review,* who took it. And he could not avoid writing even to Austin Harrison, whose very existence as heir to the Comtist throne he detested on ideological grounds. He wrote tersely that he was "glad my novel stands the test of an informed judgment. Very good of you to mention your opinion." He adds that he wants a double set of proofs, planning to take particular care, as the book publication will be from the text established in the *Review.*

In August, Conrad tried to complete "A Smile," which would come to just under 25,000 words; by August 5, he had done more than half, but even this relatively simple piece did not come easily. He was planning two more stories, one at 7,000 words, which would be "Prince Roman," and the other over 10,000 words, probably "The Partner." "Prince Roman" is part of the material Conrad would have incorporated into his reminiscences if he had not cut them short, for it involved a recollection that fits well into his retrospective material. Strikingly, however, these three stories would not fall into the same volume but would go into three separate collections. "A Smile of Fortune," along with "The Secret Sharer" and "Freya of the Seven Isles," would make up *'Twixt Land and Sea,* published in 1912; "Prince Roman" would be published posthumously in *Tales of Hearsay,* in 1925; and "The Partner" would appear with three as yet unwritten stories in *Within the Tides,* in 1915. Conrad, clearly, was writing stories as a way of working himself into shape and providing ready cash, not because of any unified volume which he had in mind. Until *Victory* began to form in his imagination two years later, the real object was *Chance* or even *The Rescue.* Yet even as he moved along into material for three further collections of stories, Mlle Séligman-Lui was in touch with him over translations of "The Idiots" and "The Lagoon" from his first collection, *Tales of Unrest.*

He appeared to be in one of his holding patterns. By August, his recovery seemed assured, but he still felt shaky and was slow to get back into harness. Then there occurred one of those fortuitous events—the miracle he awaited—which would turn his fortunes: Hugh Clifford met Gordon Bennett of the New York *Herald* in Ceylon late in 1909 and, in truly friendly fashion, tried to get Bennett interested in Conrad's work. By at least August 10, Conrad learned of this development and was already kicking himself that Pinker had thrown away *Under Western Eyes* or else the *Herald,* a mass-circulation newspaper, might have taken it. He felt that "to make use of *Chance* for this opportunity is now impossible. I wouldn't risk it. I have dismissed all thought of it out of my head."

Conrad had, in fact, decided to make a run on *The Rescue,* not on *Chance,* whose narrative convolutions and complicated point of view would have required considerable reacquaintanceship. On August 27, he told Galsworthy that "A Smile of Fortune" was all but completed except for another 2,000 words (it would drag on into late September), and he was attempting to recall *The Rescue.* "I've a hazy recollection of something highly inflated and verbose [he wrote]. But no doubt I can match it well enough out of the rubbish floating in my softened brain." Of course, *The Rescue* was Heinemann's property, Conrad having already received advance money for it, and the deal with the *Herald* would be complicated. Conrad, however, still looked longingly at *Chance* as a way of "parting with P[inker]." Thus he was caught: if he could write *Chance*, he could reduce his indebtedness to his agent and probably break away; whereas *The Rescue* was the easier book, but would keep him entailed. As of this date, his decision was to ask Pinker for the typed copy of *Rescue.* "It will [he told Galsworthy] take me a week to read and think myself into a proper frame of mind."

Besides ease of narration, there may have been more personal reasons in Conrad's choice of *Rescue* over *Chance.* The latter novel involved deeply intimate material, transposed into a different framework from Conrad's own life, but nevertheless full of tensions he carried over from childhood. The relationship between Flora and de Barral, as the young girl is growing up, has many agonizing moments in it, and Conrad very possibly after dealing with such pain as was involved in *Under Western Eyes* did not want another long run on comparable matters. *The Rescue,* on the other hand, involved little personal investment; it was a romantic narrative and, as such, did not require a profound or intimate involvement.

By September 25, Conrad was rethinking the *Herald* offer and told Galsworthy he would ask Clifford, to whom he would dedicate *Chance,* to have the venture reopened in six months' time if Bennett was still serious about it.

By then, he had decided to tinker with *Chance:* to give it a try and see how his health held up. Other matters were running parallel. One happy note was the awarding of a Civil List pension of £100, but a continuing sad note was the deterioration of Jessie's leg, which now faced imminent amputation. Conrad's concern was real, as were his affection for and devotion to his wife. The injured leg was causing pain that put a strain on the entire body and was, as well, damaging the other, already injured knee joint, which was forced to do all the work. Jessie's weight was now considerable. The doctor advised an immediate operation, or else her heart might not stand up to it later.

Jessie was anxious to have the operation and get it over with; but Conrad was horrified by the loss of a limb. The fall of 1910 was a dreary time, heavy with illness and aborted plans. Conrad seemed far older than his fifty-two years. He did write at length to Helen Sanderson, however, offering advice on her story sketches, which Teddy Roosevelt had recommended for publication. Conrad's suggestions fell into his usual pattern, the writer's need to let his mind roam freely while all the while his prose captures sensations and ideas precisely. Conrad found that her writing needed "stringing up," by which he meant a sharpening of visual images as well as a greater economy. He indicates more detail, more angles of observation. We recognize that even in these indifferent comments he was slowly revving up for *Chance.*

By the end of October, *Chance* lay untouched, and Conrad had dawdled his way into a new story, "Prince Roman." Harriet Capes visited, and Conrad also saw Austin Harrison and Frank Harris, who motored up in a "Spyker 30-40." Conrad's fascination with motorcars was already becoming apparent. His account of the meeting is humorous, although full of spite and self-disgust that he should even have to deal with such a person as Harrison:

> They patronised me immensely [he told Galsworthy]. It was funny but not very amusing. I tried to snub the Harrison child [Austin himself] who objected to the title of my novel [*Under Western Eyes*]; but he was so fatuously solemn about it that this rare visitor pity entered my heart and I let him be. I said: Have you considered the gravity of such a step as changing the title? Don't you know that I intend the book to be printed from the text as established in the Review? He surrendered gravely, then, with a sort of deference at which I felt remorseful, because—you know—because I didn't care whether he printed the novel forwards or backwards with a title or without. He meditated a long time, then gently, not to give me too rude a shock, he said: I am afraid that novel won't be very popular. And we nodded at each with immense seriousness.

Conrad, we recognize, was working himself into the disgruntled frame of mind suitable for serious work. Having been depleted by his collapse, he had touched bottom and was now readying himself to surface. His letters to Galsworthy, the repository now of his most intimate thoughts, demonstrate how enraged he became at the market mentality of the journals and their clientele. Perhaps his hatred of the commercial arena was so intense because he felt drawn to it, and had even entered it with some of his short fiction, sketches, and reviews. As his following diatribe indicates, he was aware of how packaging, not true worth, was all.

> A public [he told Galsworthy] is not to be found in a class, caste, clique or type. The public is (or are?) individuals. Le *public introuvable* is only *introuvable* simply because it is all humanity. And no artist can give it what it wants because humanity doesn't know what it wants. But it will swallow anything. It will swallow Hall Caine and John Galsworthy, Victor Hugo and Martin Tupper. It is an ostrich, a clown, a giant, a bottomless sack. It is sublime. It has apparently no eyes and no entrails, like a slug, and yet it can weep and suffer. It has swallowed Christianity, Buddhism, Mahomedanism, and the Gospel of Mrs. Eddy. And it is perfectly capable from the height of its secular stability to look down upon the artist as a mere windlestraw!

Conrad's contempt produced some fine rhetoric. His final lines demonstrate his continued allegiance to the artist as someone magical, a being with mythical connections whose imagination sets him off from a "secular stability." The old anger was there, as it would be when he responded to Dawson's "fourteen points" in 1913, and it demonstrates that he had not sold out to the marketplace, nor had he lost his hold on what he could do. "A Smile of Fortune" was accepted by *London Magazine* and would appear in February 1911, a fact that Conrad derided to Galsworthy. "There's glory for you!" he reported, calling its publication an "exalted destiny." He still had not touched *Chance.* He was, however, writing again, a short story, this time "The Partner," one of his worst. He completed its almost 10,000 words in ten days. Also fitted in were three reviews which would be reprinted in *Notes on Life and Letters:* "A Happy Wanderer" (based on *Quiet Days in Spain* by C. Bogue Luffman), "The Life Beyond" (*Existence After Death Implied by Science* by Jasper B. Hunt), and "The Ascending Effort" (*The Ascending Effort* by George Bourne), all for the *Daily Mail.*

An undated letter from Conrad to Edward Thomas is of considerable interest, even though it may fall somewhat earlier or later. Thomas was planning to write a book on Walter Pater and inscribe it to Conrad, but Conrad felt that the juxtaposition of names was inappropriate. "For the man was a stylist first and last—and I am a vagabond and a stranger in the language." Then he continued in a more personal vein.

> I am now passing through a phase of acute sensitivity as to my own style. It seems the most impossible jargon having the mere merit of being bizarre (if that's a merit) and all your dearest fellows appreciation of it a most amiable, a most precious (to me) form of lunacy. Will not the juxtaposition of these names Pater—Conrad—raise in many readers a doubt of

the sanity of your judgement or the sureness of your literary taste. Pray reflect before you leap.

The caution to Thomas was one Conrad may have felt for himself, as 1910, one of his worst years, slipped by. He had turned fifty-three, and although he had gained a considerable reputation and following among the literati, he was as financially distraught as he had been at forty-three, or thirty-three. Although he did not know it, even intuitively, that casual meeting between Clifford and Bennett halfway around the world in Ceylon was to have a great influence upon his immediate and future career. It would be, in a happier sense, like Hardy's iceberg forming in distant waters and awaiting the *Titanic.*

VIII

Through Victory

1911–1915

SETTEMBRINI:

The duel, my friend, is not an "arrangement," like another. It is the ultimate, the return to a state of nature, slightly mitigated by regulations which are chivalrous in character, but extremely superficial. The essential nature of the thing remains the primitive, the physical struggle; and however civilized a man is, it is his duty to be ready for such a contingency, which may any day arise. Whoever is unable to offer his person, his arm, his blood in the service of the ideal, is unworthy of it; however intellectualized, it is the duty of a man to remain a man.

MANN, *The Magic Mountain*

I don't want a motive for the crime—all I want is an explanation of the criminal. Yes! I mean to lead him into committing a crime gratuitously—into wanting to commit a crime without any motive at all.

GIDE, *Lafcadio's Adventures*

CHAPTER 30

Enter John Quinn and André Gide

FOR the aging writer, as physical and mental energy become increasingly depleted, the imagination must compensate or else the career is over. In 1911, Conrad had to confront precisely that sense of himself and of things in general. If he failed to produce a major effort after the worst effects of his collapse had been dissipated, then his reputation would have to stand on four or five major works since 1899. Yet he sensed a still-incomplete career, if only because two full-length novels still remained unfinished. But even as he sensed this in himself, he was writing "a silly story"—"Freya of the Seven Isles"—which suggested not completion but fragments and pieces. He used this and similar phrases to describe his work to Garnett just after the new year began. "Freya" would fill out the volume that would appear the following year as *'Twixt Land and Sea,* and when Garnett read it the following August, it failed to convince him as something "done."* It was a poor beginning for a man who felt his remaining time was short. "Freya," as we shall see, has a little history of its own, since it created a serious split between Conrad and Garnett.

---

* Part of its failure was Conrad's inability to weld together the factual parts with the invented characters and episodes. The factual part concerned a man named Sutton and a ship called the *Costa Rica,* a story Conrad picked up when he was in Singapore. As he told Garnett: "He [Sutton] died in just that way—but I don't think he died of Slav temperament. He was just about to go home to marry a girl . . . and bring her out there when his ship was run of[f] a reef by the commander of a Dutch gunboat whom he had managed to offend in some way. He haunted the beach in Macassar for months and lies buried in the fort there." Conrad's Jasper Allen ("Sutton") has something of Lingard of *The Rescue* in him, and the story, in fact, recalls that novel, which had reentered Conrad's mind as a possible submission to the *Herald.* Freya, on the other hand, is presented as an agent of Allen's needs, and her own portraiture is unfocused. Bombast, floods of rhetoric, operatics, outrageous acts of villainy interfere with several passages of solid psychological detail. Garnett was quite right in being unconvinced.

At this time, 1910–11, family matters pressed not only in the seriousness of Jessie's condition but with Borys, who was now at the stage of a career decision. Since the English educational system separates those who will be university men from those who will not, Borys by eleven had had to take his Oxford-Cambridge preliminaries, and had failed. He was not cut out for a university career, which is not unlikely given Conrad's lack of interest in formal education and Jessie's indifference to matters beyond the family. Conrad saw his son as a hard worker, but without any academic vocation. The reports from his Luton school all expressed his willingness to work well and steadily. Writing to Harriet Capes, who had taken a special interest in the boy, Conrad said: ". . . good worker and good player tho' he is, he is not brilliant." He felt, nevertheless, that another term at the Luton school would do him good. Conrad finally decided that Borys should pursue some kind of vocational training, and an apprenticeship on board a ship might prepare him for a reputable career.

Toward that end, he wrote Galsworthy, who was first in Borys's regard.

> Meantime I have been on board and had an interview with Wilson-Barker, to whom I could speak openly as a fellow-seaman. He assured me that there were on board a good many boys destined for an engineering career (I don't mean mechanical engineering) and that he thought it was a good preparatory schooling. And I don't know where to look for an authoritative opinion. But I reason like this: The boy is young yet—too young for any technical institute. He would have to put in a couple of years in some school or other—then why not in this one where at any rate they lay themselves out to teach mathematics. I am of course thinking of civil engineering; but I cannot hope for him the possibility of following long studies and getting a degree in C.E.

With that out of the question, Conrad saw Borys as gaining "an apprenticeship to a Rway or some works."

Consumed as he was by his own needs, it is difficult to determine whether Conrad was selling Borys short or had made a shrewd assessment of his older son. Certainly, pursuit of a professional career would have meant an investment of money—special schooling, tutors, expensive books, outfitting—which Conrad felt he could not afford. More likely, he was carrying over attitudes from his own experience, in which he had found little use for formal schooling. His own decision to go to sea so young surely influenced his desire to place Borys vocationally, although it is impossible to judge whether such decisions were founded on common sense or on possible envy of an "educated older son." Typically, Conrad's discussion of Borys bleeds over into his own problems, his pessimism about the future, even about the next day. "But in truth dearest Jack I feel so uncertain of the next day, so completely at the mercy of the first ill wind that may blow that I am not capable of thinking much of the future. I simply dread it; and the only way for me to keep at work (God save the mark) is to forget that there is such a thing as next morning to come."

In a possible display of hostility toward any form of education, he explained to Joseph de Smet, the Belgian critic who wrote the first essay in French on Conrad, that he had never opened an English grammar in his life. "My pronunciation [he explained] is rather defective to this day. Having unluckily no ear, my accentuation is uncertain, especially when in the course of a conversation I become self-conscious. In writing I wrestle painfully with that language which I feel I do not possess but which possesses me—alas!" That was in 1911, after more than twenty years of writing in English.

By mid-February, Conrad could tell Warrington Dawson he was putting the finishing touches to "Freya," which he characterized as "quite good magazine stuff, quite Conradesque (in the easier style)." By "in the easier style," he meant not in the "modern mode," which he saved for his longer work. By March 2, "Freya" was on its way to Pinker, who sold it to both *Metropolitan Magazine* (April 1912) and *London Magazine* (July 1912). Perhaps to keep his critical edge sharp, Conrad corresponded with Galsworthy over the latter's fiction, especially *The Patrician.* Needless to say, his detailed response is enthusiastic,* but of more importance is the nature of the touchstone he applies to his friend's work: Flaubert, especially *Salammbô*, and Turgenev, particularly the figure of Bazarov (of *Fathers and Sons*).

By mid-March, Conrad had made some personal and professional decisions. Jessie was to be operated on in the first week of May, which meant a move up to London for at least three weeks while she remained in a nursing home and Conrad stayed in rooms and looked after John. And, in a parallel decision, he hoped to have enough of *Chance* so that he could begin dictating to Miss Hallowes. By the end of March, he was trying to make "a fresh start" with *Chance,* a fact he indicated in a letter to Ford acknowledging receipt of a volume of stories. Conrad indulges in some moments of nostalgia before groaning at what his own table offers: the "damnable worry of making a start with stuff in which I don't believe and yet must go on spinning out of myself like a disillusioned spider his web in a gale."

This Sisyphean image of the future was in Conrad's mind as he worked on *Chance,* and very probably the potential horror of it gave him some impetus. By May, however, it would all change, as the operation was postponed to give him the opportunity to get on with his novel. It seemed to be a family decision: to delay the operation until August, so as to make Jessie available

---

* To Garnett, two days later, intermixed with comments on Flaubert's works and suggestions for Garnett's own career, Conrad cited Galsworthy's latest novel in quite different terms: "Hint to me something of Jack's novel. I wrote to him about it yesterday but as a matter of fact I feel rather unsettled in my mind. It seems to me all in the air—or is it I who have not (or have lost) the ability to get to the bottom of written things."

for typing and retyping of the manuscript, to keep John out of the London heat, and to give Borys the opportunity to take his vacation in the country. Submerged in all this was some inner voice which was telling Conrad, in its fashion, that in *Chance his* chance lay for financial recovery. Very probably, Bennett's offer appeared a lifeline to survival, for Conrad, despite setbacks of health and wavering determination, kept hammering away at the novel, 12,-000 words in a fortnight after a hiatus "from March 5th to April 29th with not a page."

Even though he felt his courage oozing out of him, words did come, with an additional 30,000 expected by the end of June. The "quantity [of copy] is a record," he told Douglas. "Effects of a sort of dull desperation." He invited Douglas to come to stay in a cottage for the month of July, an invitation which the latter took up upon his return from Italy in August. While at Capel House, he fell violently ill, creating a situation that is quintessential Conrad in its ironic juxtaposition of elements. In his witty and exasperated commentary to Galsworthy, Douglas's host recognized the "appropriateness" of what occurred:

> Providence is looking after me with a vengeance. Last Saturday Norman Douglas . . . came for a week end. But he arrived in a state of high fever and hardly able to stand. We put him to bed and sent for a doctor. On Monday we went for a nurse (after Jessie and I had been up with him for two nights and a day). To day he does not recognise anybody, his temp after most appalling ups and downs has reached 105°. —and here we are.

Conrad's letters and telegrams to Douglas's friend in London and his brother in Scotland brought evasive answers.

> Should he die I shall have to bury him I suppose. But even if he recovers (which we still hope for) it will be a matter of weeks. All my work, all our plans and our little pitiful hopes seem knocked on the head. I have seen and tended white men dying in the Congo but I have never felt so altogether helpless as in this case. As Jessie said last night—this is like a nightmare.

Douglas's recovery was slow. All this occurred, of course, just when Conrad wanted to make a long run at *Chance* so as to have copy on hand before Jessie finally went for her operation in September.

In the two months before Douglas disrupted Capel House, Conrad was facing another period of uncertainties. *Under Western Eyes* would appear in October, and its reviews could possibly build sales, although even he doubted that. Jessie was no longer facing an amputation, but she would need the operation, which involved an expensive recovery as well as a disruptive move to London. Borys's future still had to be considered, since he was thirteen and a half and had few family prospects. *Chance* was itself proving resistant to Conrad's attempts to wrench it into shape, both because of its complexity of narrative and because it was caught among his several styles. Further, it tested out an area in Conrad that was extremely sensitive, a child and her parents: Flora and her father, recalling Conrad and Apollo, and now Borys and *his* father. While the patterns are hardly congruent, they suggested overlapping attitudes and forced Conrad into personally trying situations of past and present history. Although genuinely loving to Borys, Conrad never felt as easy with his older son as he did with John; and as we shall see, when Borys reached adulthood, Conrad acted more in line with his fictional parents toward their children than we would expect from his letters about Borys and his fortunes.

Even a cold caught in June on a short visit to Dymchurch threw him off schedule. The balance was precarious apparently, more acute than ever. By the end of June, Conrad could report about half of *Chance* completed, but his prognosis of a September conclusion date was entirely unrealistic. He continued his covert attack on *The English Review*, telling Galsworthy he was ashamed to see himself in its pages; *Under Western Eyes* would continue through the October issue. Typical is a brief letter to Ford, who had seen the notice in the *Times* (on July 7) of the award of a Civil List pension to Conrad. The latter saw his life as a composite of work, anxiety, little pleasure, sense of doom, with no opening up or out, but, rather, all closing down. He hesitated to leave the shop for even a moment for fear it would all slip away. He even suspects Ford of irony:

> I was touched by your congratulatory telegram and yet it might have been ironic too! That sort of recognition is the consecration of failure, for even talent must be appreciated by the standards of the world we live in. On receiving the gift I glanced back and what I said most clearly then is that there hasn't been a book published for 3 years [since *A Set of Six*, and no novel for four years]! And then I understood how much I deserved the recompense.

Conrad concludes: "I am living in a state of savage exasperation with myself, unfit to talk, unfit to write. And this too you'll maybe understand. I am writing, however, spasmodically, with long intervals of absolute dumbness. *Quel enfer!*"

These seasons in hell for Conrad had always heralded great creative outbursts, and even after 1910 this pattern would not alter. We sense this in a long letter on July 28 to Galsworthy—almost always Galsworthy now!—in which he says he is involved in life as a "dead pull." Happily, Borys's immediate future seemed settled. He was to be apprenticed to the HMS *Worcester*, a nautical school ship in the Thames, where he would study for at least two years in a technical program leading to a certificate. The possibilities after that were of several kinds: entrance into a technical school, employment in an engineering works, or, if he did well, a commission in the navy. In September, Conrad took Borys to join the *Worcester* and wrote Galsworthy a touching description of their last moments together, a wistful view of a father and son relationship:

> Yesterday at 5.30 I went on shore leaving Borys looking after me from the gangway grating of the *Worcester*. The painful part of it was that he had to join in spectacles. Almost at the last minute the medical examination discovered his sight to be defective. . . . I had not warning of any sort, and somehow even the possibility of his becoming short-sighted never occurred to me. . . . Only last Easter a friend of his a Naval cadet came for the day and they amused themselves shooting at tins floating on the moat, and B shot quite as well as the other boy. However, here it is—a deplorable fact [since it would destroy any chance of a naval career]. . . . He is putting on a good face on the matter and I have been chaffing him on his learned appearance in spectacles, but neither of us felt very lighthearted.
>
> . . . I had a long talk with the head-master and liked him very well. He came up on deck with me and was very nice to the boy. Mr May, the Chief Officer promised me to put him through his course of drill and seamanship instruction exactly as if there were nothing the matter with his eyes. Of course he can't expect now to get any of the many prizes given by various shipping companies. Were he ever so proficient it would not be fair to the other boys; but that does not trouble me much as long as he gets a first-class leaving certificate at the end of two or 2½ years.

Then in an image reminiscent of Marlow's final view of Jim diminishing with distance, Conrad tries to gain perspective on his son reduced in size against the ship deck.

> Poor Mons. B looked to me a very small and lonely figure on that enormous deck in that big crowd where he didn't know a single soul. It is an immense change for him. Yes. He did look a small boy. I couldn't make up my mind to leave him and at last I made rather a bolt of it. I can't get him out of my eyes. However there are over twenty new boys and all their hammocks are slung together aft on the port side of the lower deck so he shall have some companions in the first few days of misery. I went ashore in the 14 oared second cutter and I have never seen a nicer boat's-crew. Having more than an hour to wait in Maidstone I wrote a letter to B which I am certain it must have comforted him to receive this morning.

In closing, Conrad asks Galsworthy to drop Borys a line in the next week: "It would be kind, it would be very kind of both [Ada]: or either of you." How profoundly Conrad was reviewing his own very different kind of farewell as he went out into the world, one cannot but speculate upon.

"Freya" was not easy to place, especially since Conrad was himself of two minds about it, looking for publication in *Blackwood's* and yet calling it a "magazine-ish thing." *Scribner's* rejected it on grounds that "its overpowering *gloom* makes it impossible for serialisation." After another rejection, in *Century* magazine, Pinker sent it to Garnett for reconsideration in the same publication; and Conrad, unaware of the history, wrote his friend: "All I can say is that I hope you won't be overpowered by the 'gloom' to the point of swallowing a dose of prussic acid after reading the copy. . . . And do write to me—so that I know you are still alive after the terrific experience which, I understand, has nearly killed the Scribners' man." Five days later, Conrad wrote Garnett he had misgivings about Pinker's sending a story already rejected by the *Century*, as somehow taking advantage of *parti pris*. He also stresses he has resisted "faking a 'sunny' ending" that American magazines might request, saying he rejected "the piffle they print with touching consistency."

Garnett did not die of the gloom—he was, by now, inured to it—but he informed Pinker he had seen the story some "ages ago," very probably the previous April when "Freya" went out to the magazine for which he was now reader. Conrad was enraged, since he would have opposed sending the story back to Garnett after the *Century* had already rejected it. He denied the ancient history of "Freya," and in an angry letter to Pinker offered Marwood and Gibbon as witnesses to the contemporaneity of the story. Part of his anger, however, was a displacement, in which "Freya" served only as the surface of Conrad's annoyance with Garnett, who was being Russianized, and of course with himself for the weakness of his work, his fear that he was sliding toward oblivion.

In the meanwhile, Douglas had recovered, but only after turning Capel House into a hospital. Another development, quite unexpected, added earnings to Conrad's pocket apart from what he could get from Pinker. John Quinn, the American collector, was interested in purchasing manuscripts of both Conrad and Arthur Symons. Through Agnes Tobin, the American poetess intimate with Symons, who was to act as intermediary, Quinn got in touch with Conrad and offered to purchase his manuscripts and, later, typescripts and various drafts.* Quinn offered prices that were, then, quite substantial for a living author: from £40 for a story to between £100 and £150 for longer works. One hundred pounds then was worth about $1,250 in current purchasing power. Quinn hardly fleeced Conrad, who welcomed the new source of income and could have refused the American at any point, or driven up the price if he had chosen to bargain. It was a transaction that worked to the benefit of both: Quinn greatly admired Conrad's work and could indulge his hobby, and Conrad gained several hundred pounds during a period when his earnings were still low.

The initial transaction occurred when Conrad sent off, on August 24, the

---

* *Under Western Eyes* is dedicated to Agnes Tobin, "who brought to our door her genius for friendship from the uttermost shore of the West."

first batch of his manuscripts: *Outcast,* 516 pages, and "Freya," not yet even published, 226 pages. Conrad had intended to send *Almayer's Folly* also, but discovered that the whole of Chapter 9 was missing. As a bonus, he sent the manuscript of the "suppressed preface to the *Nigger of the Narcissus*. . . . The little printed pamphlet I have distributed to a few friends and have enclosed a copy in the envelope containing the 11 pp of MS, which perhaps you may care to join to your collection as a sort of curiosity." Thus, Quinn's collection began to build, and Conrad's correspondence with him became quite voluminous.

The two never met—Conrad rather conspicuously avoided Quinn in later years; and when Conrad bypassed him and began to sell his manuscripts to Thomas Wise, the relationship turned sour. The real split in the association came when Quinn realized over 1,000 percent profit on his Conrad materials in his 1923 auction. The sale of Conradiana, much of which went to A. S. W. Rosenbach, brought Quinn a sum of about $110,000 on purchases of $10,000. And when Quinn was asked to give Conrad some of his gains, he refused outright, attacking F. N. Doubleday for even suggesting it and calling it a "sheeny assault" upon him by Nelson Doubleday's "damned old father." By then, both Quinn and Conrad were dying men.

Back in 1911, the atmosphere was far more pleasant. Recognizing a good thing, Conrad wrote again on September 25, this time about *Under Western Eyes,* a manuscript of 1,300 pages. He indicates that the manuscript contains a great deal more text than has appeared in print and that he has "been cutting down that novel ruthlessly" for first English publication. At the same time, Conrad proposes selling Quinn three recent short stories, which he now sees as forming a distinct volume: "Freya," "Fortune," and "Secret Sharer," for which Conrad requested £40 each. He adds that he hopes Quinn will not feel he has "fallen upon a shark." In every transaction, however, Quinn gave exactly what Conrad requested, and at that time no one else was interested.

This was all a pleasant interlude, but *Under Western Eyes* was about to appear in book form and Conrad's concern was building. By the end of September, he had 60,000 words of *Chance* in hand, but that was less than half of the novel's final length. In addition, he wrote a 300-word preface for his reminiscences, which would appear as "A Familiar Preface" when the book was published in 1912. Although Conrad said he had written 45,000 words since April, the number was probably far less, or else he discarded many earlier pages in order to have only 60,000 of *Chance* by September. He was suffering from another attack of gout and had put the novel aside; but his words indicate he realized *Chance* was his salvation. *The Rescue,* that other incomplete book, had faded.

By September 30, he was ready to send Quinn further manuscripts, and his letter suggests that for the first time he would manage his manuscripts and typescripts so as to provide a maximum of autograph material, since personal handwriting, he knew, drove up the price. After saying he planned to include "Il Conde" and "The Partner," which *Harper's* would publish in November, Conrad apologized for having only dictated typescripts in hand. He does mention *Almayer* again, still incomplete, and "Karain," for which he asks £20, and *The Secret Agent*, £100.

On October 5, *Under Western Eyes* appeared, containing about 30,000 words fewer than the serial text. As the reviews began to filter in, Conrad wrote to Galsworthy that he had revised recklessly, striking out whole pages which he was too ill to reconsider. "The other day I looked at the MS: [for sale to Quinn] 1357 pp averaging about 120 words per page. There are passages which should have remained. I wasn't in a fit state to judge them." Conrad says he has avoided looking at the notices of the novel, but Marwood sent him the one from the *Morning Post*. Conrad's comment upon it is of considerable interest, because the reviewer had struck upon several personal points:

> It was all right [he wrote Galsworthy]; but there was a passage in it which is incomprehensible unless meant as a hint that I, being a Jew, am especially fit to hold the balance between East and West! I believe that some time ago that preposterous Papist Belloc has been connecting me with Father Abraham, whether to hurt me or to serve me, or simply because he's an idiot—I don't know. Anyhow I heard it from somebody a year or more ago. It's an absurd position to be in for I trust I have no contemptible prejudices against any kind of human beings—and yet it isn't pleasant to be taken out of one's own skin, as it were, by an irresponsible chatterer.

The reviewer had said not that Conrad was a Jew but that the narrator with his attempt to balance Russian mysticism and the Western attachment to the earth as it is must be a Jew. The insight is particularly shrewd, and significantly misread by Conrad, since it assumes a certain sympathy on the narrator's part for something which he recognizes as quite different from himself. Conrad's misreading of the passage, in which the narrator, not he, is suggested as a Jew, is connected to his fear that he may have come too close to presenting the Russian character compassionately. Also, the reviewer had poked around in stuffy attics and boarded-up closets, those areas of Conrad's mind which he did not reveal even to himself; and he had come up with divided sympathies, uncertain allegiances, unsure alliances, attempts at balance which were irresolvable.* The remainder of the review is especially percep-

---

* In writing to Garnett only five days later, Conrad revealed this same "open sore." In the *Nation* (for October 21) Garnett had touched on Conrad's hatred of things Russian and yet his affinity for aspects of the Russian character only understood by the great Russian novelists themselves. The comments infuriated Conrad, who was already angry at

tive, calling attention to the similarity between this novel and *Lord Jim* as studies in remorse, "mainly moving from within, but also affected by external forces of personality, according to the psychological theory propounded in the earlier work."

Garnett's notice, to which Conrad had responded, placed the novelist in the company of Russians, ending indeed by comparing his pages to notable passages in Turgenev and Dostoevsky. Garnett found the artistic intensity of the novel not only in its "remarkable drawing of characteristic Russian types" but in the "atmospheric effect of the dark national background." Garnett was quite acute, although his words were wounds to Conrad: "It is, however, in the suggestiveness of the national background of the illusions of frustrated and blighted generations, stretching ominously like a gloomy curtain behind the figures in the drama, that the author's special triumph lies."

Wriggle as he might, Conrad could not withdraw from Garnett's Russian clutches. This frustration carried over into a letter he wrote to Constance Garnett on the same day, October 20, as he wrote to her husband. Mrs. Garnett had criticized the figure of Nathalie Haldin as too wooden, insufficiently in movement, and Conrad offered as explanation that he needed her as a pivot on which to turn the action. He feared that if he made more of her, she would have "killed the artistic purpose" of the book: "the development of a single mood." Then he moves to what worries him. The remarks are worth repeating. "But the fact is [despite her praise of the novel] that I know extremely little of Russians. Practically nothing. In Poland we have nothing to do with them. One knows they are there. And that's disagreeable enough. In exile the contact is even slighter if possible if more unavoidable. . . . I crossed the Russian frontier at the age of ten [actually at four and one half]. Not having been to school then I never knew Russian. I could not tell a Little

---

Garnett's handling of the "Freya" episode. He wrote: "There's just about as much or as little hatred in this book as in the Outcast of the Islands for instance. Subjects lay about for anybody to pick up. I have picked up this one. And that's all there is to it. I don't expect you will believe me. You are so russianized my dear that you don't know the truth when you see it—unless it smells of cabbage-soup when it at once secures your profoundest respect. I suppose one must make allowances for your position of Russian Embassador [sic] to the Republic of Letters. Official pronouncements ought to be taken with a grain of salt and that is how I shall take your article in the Nation which I hope to see tomorrow evening when the carrier comes back from Ashford. But it is hard after lavishing a 'wealth of tenderness' in Tekla and Sophia, to be charged with the rather low trick of putting one's hate into a novel. If you seriously think I have done that then my dear fellow let me tell you that you don't know what the accent of hate is. Is it possible that you haven't seen that in this book I am concerned with nothing but ideas, to the exclusion of everything else, with no arrière pensée of any kind. Or are you like the Italians (and most women) incapable of conceiving that anybody ever should speak with perfect detachment, without some subtle hidden purpose, for the sake of what is said, with no desire of gratifying some small personal spite—or vanity." Conrad adds that Russia, as Bismarck once said, is nothing: "C'est le neant," and anybody "with eyes can see it."

Russian from a Great Russian to save my life. In the book as you must have seen I am exclusively concerned with ideas."

His chief concern in the letter to Mrs. Garnett, however, is not Russia but Poland, and specifically his renewed correspondence with Wincenty Lutosławski. Lutosławski, we recall, was not an unmixed blessing in Conrad's life, since in 1899 he somewhat ironically defended Conrad's "betrayal" of Poland against Eliza Orzeszkowa's attack on those who leave to get rich in the West. Even in 1911, Lutosławski returned to the controversy and asserted that Conrad, despite his work in English and attention to matters unrelated to Poland, was deeply involved in Polish interests. But the defender's arguments were as damning as Orzeszkowa's attacks, for Conrad was made to appear as a man who had grown wealthy in the West, whereas he would have had lean pickings in Poland. Conrad's comment is full of exasperation that they would not leave him alone: "Yes. I had a letter and some books from Mr. Lutosławski. I ought to have written to him before—tho' really and truly I don't know what he wants with me. I don't understand him in the least. His illumination seems to me a very naïve and uninteresting thing. Does he imagine I am likely to become his disciple? He worries and bores me."

This entire correspondence, along with Garnett's *Nation* review, held up before Conrad's eyes that "first life" in all its unpleasantness, he the Korzeniowski who had become Conrad, the Józef who had become Joseph. *Under Western Eyes* had been an obligatory novel for him to write, in a sense, since its development and completion would lead into a major breakdown; so that we can see the novel as coming at the crossroads of his first and final lives. He could either exorcise Apollo or go under. It was a difficult balancing act and created within a veritable explosion of ill feelings; the reviews, then, could not be viewed neutrally. They had to open old wounds, strain still-unclosed sores, and bring to the surface attitudes and feelings Conrad did not wish to admit even to himself.

The review in *The Manchester Guardian*, however, was of another kind, by a young man, as yet unknown, who would enter Conrad's life the next year. He was Richard Curle, who became a true friend and support to Conrad and Jessie, and who wrote the first full-length study of the writer, in 1914. Curle was a constant companion, fulfilling the role in Conrad's later years of Ford, Garnett, Graham, and Galsworthy earlier. He was stable, old-fashioned in his attitudes, very much a preserver of the proprieties, and a steadying force upon Conrad. He and Jean-Aubry were to carry Conrad's reputation through the years after his death when his books went out of print; and only these two faithful friends and biographers were there to help keep his name before the public.

Curle's review of *Under Western Eyes* was by no means adulatory; it was, in fact, quite critical of Conrad's new style. Curle's resistance to Conrad's "modernity" was apparent; he longed for the days of romance, not psychology, a warmer authorial presence, and a more energetic, adventurous narrative. Citing the power and intensity of the new mode, he nevertheless harked back to the "romantic realism" of the earlier fiction which colored "life with an extraordinary vividness." Curle, too, pointed to similarities with Dostoevsky's *Crime and Punishment*, so that Conrad could not evade that issue by tarring the author with Russification, as he had Garnett. Even the reviewer of the *Westminster Gazette* linked Conrad and Turgenev and Dostoevsky, saying he helped us understand them "with greater clearness"; as though Conrad's work existed to explain them. Conrad had Constance Garnett to thank for this explosion of interest in the Russian novelists, for she was making them as familiar to the English audience as Dickens and George Eliot.

When Conrad wrote Norman Douglas on October 27 and asked for a loan of ten pounds, he indicated he had not "written a line all Aug. or Sept. or half Oct." He complained of being in a state of "nervous exasperation," of feeling unfitted for the world, "ill too now and then." That report of inactivity appears exaggerated, for *Chance* was far enough along for Conrad to be able to complete it in five months, in March of 1912, and for the serial to begin in only three, on January 21, in the New York *Herald.* We catch the note of contradiction when he tells Davray that he began *Chance* only last April and has "worked full speed" since then. He adds: "I am enfeebled—but I work always." To Joseph de Smet, he spoke of something very close to himself, the French translation of *Nostromo*, which Conrad was pleased to hear would be done by de Smet himself. The latter, however, did not do it—Philippe Neel translated the novel—but of far greater interest is Conrad's advice on how the book is to appear in French:

> Don't you think [Conrad wrote in French] that this long book could be abridged a little? Not to remove the episodes of action itself—no! but I mean to remove superfluous words. Within this volume there are too many phrases. Phrases of analysis, descriptive phrases, also. It will help the French readers to swallow such a large book. This weeding—pruning, if you wish—must be made by myself and on the English text. If you wish to send me your copy of *Nostromo*, I will get to it, keeping it only eight days and returning it to you marked lightly in crayon.

Of equal interest is the fact that de Smet had already done a translation of *Typhoon*, which Conrad considered, because of its maritime vocabulary, the most difficult of his works to render into French.

But de Smet's translation of *Typhoon* was not to be the one in the standard French edition; it was replaced by André Gide's. Through the auspices of Agnes Tobin, Gide had made a flying visit to see Conrad at Capel House in July; and with that, began to enter Conrad's life at many points, just as Conrad's work, as we shall see, had already entered his. As Conrad's career, with *Chance*, moved toward a broader audience, he was brought increasingly to European readers by Gide's advocacy and by his incredibly dedicated supervision of the translation of Conrad's works into French. Gide's presence became a considerable factor in Conrad's later years.

Even as a shuffling of friends was occurring for Conrad—as Gide, Curle, Dawson, Walpole, and Jean-Aubry had already entered or would shortly enter his life—Ford popped up with a long article on Conrad in *The English Review*. Ford had called his former collaborator "an Elizabethan," a curious analogy which he tried to justify on the basis of Conrad's relationship to a Poland that was romantic, heroic, aristocratic; that is, an atmosphere comparable to England's in the sixteenth and seventeenth centuries. He goes on to cite Webster, Marlowe, Massinger, Kyd, and Heywood as writing material that could fit easily into Conrad's imagination. But the essay becomes an exercise in the Ford ego. He praises Poles for being aristocrats and individuals in "this age of limited companies and democracy." Ford, however, was a political and social reactionary and missed the messianic quality of Polish romanticism, the very basis of Conrad's dualism, as the son of a revolutionary father. He speaks of knowing "very well a writer who collaborated with Conrad in one or two books"—himself, of course—and he uses this method as a means of examining passages from *Romance*, so as to vaunt both writers. But, overall, as with most of Ford's commentary, it is generous. Near the end of his long piece, he says:

> For if our age can have raised up such a conscience in any walk of life, and if our country can have attracted him to live amongst us, our age and our country must have in it something that is good—in its traditions and its teachings. Indeed, when I think that in a light-hearted way I have poked fun at the artistic conscience of this country I feel a little ashamed. For if Conrad has not earned any huge material success, he has secured a recognition even from the more Academic, that few men of his greatness have ever secured in their age and their own day.

Writing to Ford after having read the first part (it was a continuing article, extending into the March issue), Conrad caught the generous note and responded warmly.

> I am infinitely touched by what you say and by the accent you have found to express what may be critically just and true but to a certainty is the speech of a friend. What touches me most is to see that you do not discard our common past. These old days may not have been such very "good old days" as they should have been—but to me my dear Ford they are a very precious possession. In fact I have nothing else that I can call my own. And had you put them aside in your fortunate present I should have felt distinctly poorer for it.

The year 1911 closed with a most significant event, a letter Conrad wrote to Gide, the first (extant) letter since Gide's hurried visit in July. It was an auspicious moment, for it meant Gide's July visit was not a final thing but a beginning. From this would come a further visit by Gide in 1912;* an exchange of at least forty letters (twenty-five from Conrad, fifteen from Gide, and many others now lost); Gide's supervision (along with Jean-Aubry) of the translation into French of Conrad's work; Gide's involvement in every stage of the translation, his ironing out of difficult personal situations and revision of texts when they fell below expectation, himself becoming caught in sharp controversy over *Victory* and *The Arrow of Gold;* Gide's own translation of *Typhoon,* whose difficulty has already been noted, a translation for which Gide had to apprentice himself to English as Conrad had earlier to French. Further, there was the more personal literary association: Gide's use of an epigraph from *Lord Jim* in *Les Caves du Vatican* (at the head of Book V: "Lafcadio"), as follows: "There is only one remedy! One thing alone can cure us from being ourselves! . . ." / "Yes, strictly speaking, the question is not how to get cured, but how to live." (Stein's advice in Chapter 20 is, actually: "One thing alone can us from being ourselves cure!"); the very real possibility that Gide's conception and development of the "acte gratuite" derived from his sense of Conrad and especially from his reading of *Lord Jim,* although many other factors were also involved; Gide's *Voyage au Congo* (1927), which is dedicated "To the Memory of Joseph Conrad"; with Gide's reportage of his visit leaning heavily on Conrad's "Heart of Darkness." Finally, there was Conrad's attempt, unsuccessfully, to see Gide at Cuverville, in Normandy, in late October 1923. As a final gesture, Gide wrote a memorial piece on Conrad in the *NRF* issue "Hommage à Joseph Conrad" (December 1, 1924).

Since Gide was the sole writer of first rank with whom Conrad became this close—the association with James was distant and formal—their strange

---

* Gide very possibly came on this visit with Alexis Saint-Léger Léger, who wrote under the pseudonym of St.-John Perse. Perse was familiar with many of the Conrad circle, especially Jean-Aubry, and in a long letter to Aubry in 1947 mentions a 1911 or 1912 stay with Conrad, most probably the latter date. "I do recall a short stay with Conrad, which you mention. 1911 or 1912 at Ashford, *via* Hamstreet, Kent. The conversations were the least intellectual possible, since I liked in him the man, his clay-colored face, his respect for the most fortuitous human incident, his loyalty in every human relationship, once established, without passing judgments. I do however remember some literary fugues in the course of nocturnal talking (in the room downstairs, at the right of the entrance): Melville, Hudson, and the 'Nonsense Lyrics' ('Jumblies!') which I brought from the children's room (at the top of the stairs, overlooking the courtyard). On the day of my departure, he had thought he ought to invite, 'for a Frenchman,' Arthur Symons, and this was a mistake, touching, between ourselves, for which, humanly, it seemed as if he were apologizing by the expression of his eyes. Do you remember his unexpected taste for Molière and for Zola, the vividness of his reactions against Dostoyevsky, to which he maintained to prefer Turgenev?" (For this episode and the rest of the letter, see Ivo Vidan, *Conradiana,* II, p. 3.) Conrad probably met Valéry Larbaud on the first visit, in 1911, and saw Paul Valéry on another occasion, in October 1922.

relationship bears some scrutiny. The "sharing," if we can call it that, started with Gide, who entered into Conrad's career, especially into *Lord Jim* and the period around that novel. Gide considered *Jim* the apex of Conrad's achievement and a central document in his understanding of Conrad's world. When Gide, in turn, brought Conrad to the attention of the European literary world, he was extracting, really, Conrad's views as seen through that novel. A 1914 Journal entry by Gide reads: "The despair of the man who thinks he is a coward because he yielded to a momentary weakness—when he hoped he was courageous (*Lord Jim*)." Gide must have read the Conrad novel in English—it was not translated into French until 1924, by Philippe Neel—although precisely when we cannot determine. Whenever he read it, however, Gide found in *Jim*, which he called "*mon livre préferé*" among Conrad's works, something very close to his own sense of dualities and opposites. For even before *Lord Jim*, Gide's work had manifested divisions between the romantic self and the need for realistic application, in *Les Cahiers d'André Walter* (1891), *Le Voyage d'Urien* (1893), *Paludes* (1895).

The "Jim" idea obsessed Gide, however, apart from his own attempts to deal with the theme literarily. Much later, after Conrad's death, Gide commented in his Journal on *Under Western Eyes*, saying it is a masterful book, "but one that smells a bit too much of work and application, overconscientiousness (if I may say so) on Conrad's part, in the continuity of outline. . . . Conrad unbends only to become prolix and diffuse. The book is perfectly done, but without ease." Gide's entry on *Under Western Eyes* foreshadows his juxtaposition of that novel with *Lord Jim:* "Much interested by the relationship I discover between *Under Western Eyes* and *Lord Jim.* (I regret not having spoken of this with Conrad.) That *irresponsible act* of the hero, to redeem which his whole life is subsequently engaged. For the thing that leads to the heaviest responsibility is just the *irresponsibilities* in a life. How can one efface that act?"

Gide went right to the heart of Conrad's sense of order and found, lurking beneath, disorder and anarchy. As late as August 2, 1930, he returned to the subject: "Noteworthy that the fatal *irresponsible* acts of Conrad's heroes (I am thinking particularly of *Lord Jim* and *Under Western Eyes*) are involuntary and immediately stand seriously in the way of the one who commits them. A whole lifetime, afterward, is not enough to give them the lie and to efface their mark."

Gide's taste in Conrad was bizarre; he was unable to read *Nostromo*, for example, perhaps because it was ponderous and "un-French." He was a Conradian of the early period, and even included *The Rescue* among his favored books. He took a very personal view of Conrad and was little concerned with overall achievement or even with growth and development. He seized what he wanted or needed in the curiously undefinable way of a writer nourishing his own talent. As for Conrad: his need was to enjoy the admiration of a cosmopolitan writer like Gide, to bask in the esteem of a translation into French by such an important figure, all the time taking care not to make the younger writer regret his profound respect for the older author. Yet Conrad felt little inclination to reciprocate by plunging into Gide's work, often commenting on it no more than politely, or, possibly, not even reading what Gide sent him. Conrad sat back and received admiration, and Gide was simply one of many substitute "sons"—including Curle, Walpole, Jean-Aubry, F. W. Dawson—who gathered at his feet in the 1910s and offered homage.

Conrad's first letter, of December 26, 1911, is tentative, indicating he had read *The Immoralist* and Gide's volume of criticism, *Prétextes,* which may or may not have been true. Of the first twelve letters exchanged between the two—they met perhaps only once more—in the next five years, eleven are from Conrad and only one from Gide. The one-sidedness, however, is deceptive. Conrad was notorious for destroying his correspondence once he answered it, and from internal evidence, we find numerous references to missing letters. Many of the later Gide letters, in fact, thirteen of the extant fifteen, were preserved by Jean-Aubry, and without his interest and care, there is good reason to believe Conrad would have destroyed them as well.

CHAPTER 31

"I fear not death, but dying gives me pause"

THE new year, 1912, began with a flurry of activity, and despite Conrad's gloomy sense of his career, he was hardly lacking in publications. The serial of *Chance* began on January 21, in the New York *Herald;* he had collected sufficient stories for a new volume, *'Twixt Land and Sea,* which would appear in October; and his volume of reminiscences had recently appeared, an inscribed copy of which he sent to John Quinn.* And amid all this, he would soon complete *Chance* and begin a new story, which grew into the novel *Victory.* His life now was devoted completely, and obsessively, to his career; ostensibly to make money, but directed by an inner sense that time was running out for him to make his mark artistically. The two aims, money and reputation, were beginning to merge with each other, but as his letters and manuscripts during this period demonstrate, he was still very much aware of those aesthetic principles which he had outlined fifteen years earlier.

On January 28, he told Quinn he was about one hundred pages from the end of *Chance,* with the understanding that the collector would receive the manuscript in due time. It was a curious procedure, in that Conrad was selling now in four areas, and sometimes even five for stories. First, the manuscript itself would go to Quinn, as well as typescripts; then the work would be serialized, as *Chance* was appearing in the *Herald;* next, the English and American editions, with numerous variants, would appear; and for stories such as "Prince Roman" and "Freya," there would be two magazine publications. Conrad was obviously anxious to finish his work so he could sell the manuscript immediately to Quinn for ready money. There was an additional pressure, then, on his artistic sense, since the very paper on which he was

* The December 1908 section from *The English Review* was first published by Reynolds in 1908, to secure the American copyright, under the title *Some Reminiscences.* In 1912, Nash published the entire text under the same title; and Harpers, in New York, on January 19, 1912, issued it as *A Personal Record.* Until 1916, the book was known in England as *Some Reminiscences* and then changed to the American title.

writing provided immediate cash simply for the asking. Quinn would buy anything, and Conrad was prepared to sell any scrap. How much this determined the quality of his later work is difficult to evaluate; but taken with the fact of dictation, the financial pressure, and that ready market for autograph material and even for corrected typescript, we can see temptations intensifying.

All this activity and productive use of time of course took its toll and Conrad came down with flu. At least, on February 2, he used this ailment as a way of discouraging Ford from coming down to Capel House. Most likely, Conrad suffered from flu with complications arising from an unfinished novel, and he wanted all his time for *Chance.* Nevertheless, he sent Ford a "timid gift" of his volume of reminiscences, a fitting present indeed, since Ford was so instrumental in its even being started. They did meet, however, for Conrad wrote Elsie that her husband—still her husband, although he was trying to force a divorce—did not believe him when he said he would complete *Chance* in another fortnight: "But he knew better. I assure you his knowledge of me is so complete that he didn't believe it for a minute. And it isn't finished. Of course not. As if a novel were ever finished in a fortnight!"*

This was the buildup to another breakdown, from the tension and pressure of finishing a book that was already being serialized. Conrad had sufficient working time, but he lacked leisure for revision with the book already appearing in installments. Quinn, meanwhile, had received assorted shipments, *Almayer's Folly,* the whole manuscript of *The Secret Agent,* and several short pieces. Then on the twenty-fifth of March, at 3 a.m., Conrad finished *Chance.* On that same day, he and Pinker met for lunch, Conrad's antagonism at least partially dissipated by his agent's generosity with further advances. Feeling pleased with himself, he totaled (for Galsworthy) his wordage for the year, an average of 10,000 words per month, with four entire months lost for reasons of health. In a letter to Quinn that day he adjusted his wordage to 140,000 in nine months, a spectacular (for him) 4,000 words a week. He also mentions he has the manuscript of Crane's "Five White Mice," which he would be willing to sell, asserting that he has no proper house for storage and it will most likely get lost while under his care. And very tersely, Conrad wrote Elsie that he was busy revising *Chance* for the press and "must at once start the next novel"—which would be "Berg" or "Dollars," the working titles for *Victory.*

---

* Conrad's cordiality was forced, since he wrote Galsworthy on March 27: "The great F.M.H. who was here shortly after New Year with the somewhat less great V.H. [Violet Hunt] told me you had gone with a breakdown to the Riviera. . . . I did believe you wanted to be quiet. . . . So I kept quiet, too, writing MS for dear life and in a sort of panic as the N.Y.H. began to print on the 15 Jan^y^—of which I heard in a roundabout way from Paris; Pinker having kept the fact from me in order to spare my feelings" (ALS, Birmingham).

Then, in an interesting move if we consider his antipathy toward Harrison and *The English Review*, Conrad wrote the editor suggesting serialization of *Chance* there. Conrad's remarks are particularly compelling because he tried to convince Harrison that the novel was "in its nature simple and biographical" and could be easily followed from month to month. Harrison had objected, apparently, to the difficulties of the narrative method, a point that Henry James was to concur with when he commented on the novel two years later. Conrad says he can rearrange the text to meet Harrison's objections. "I know my business—I mean to say my craft, mon métier—as apart from any quality I may have as a writer of prose—artist if you like. And I am not a superior person. I don't disdain even the lowest side of craftsmanship." Conrad indicates he objects to serial publication, but in the case of *The English Review* his feeling is different, especially since he can arrange the text for serialization so that it will be the final text of the book form. He suggests dividing the text into three parts—he would eventually separate it into only two—and giving each a title, and then the parts into chapters, each having its own heading. All this would provide guidance for the reader and make the narrative more accessible. We recall Conrad was making these changes for readers of *The English Review*, an intellectual journal with a highly educated readership. How he expected the less-favored reader to fare we cannot determine, and the eventual popularity of the novel, Conrad's first popular success, is a source of astonishment.

Conrad's headings and part divisions certainly did cater to his audience, whatever the convolutions of the narrative itself. He used medieval chivalric headings for the two parts: "The Damsel" and "The Knight," and for chapter headings phrases that suggest a more romantic flavor than the novel actually has. Words or phrases such as "Thrift" and "The Governess" and "The Tea-Party" in the first part convey a setting and action rather different from the bitter and ironic tale Conrad actually presented. In order to convince Harrison of the accessibility of *Chance*, Conrad pointed out that in "1899 B'wood's Maga: accepted my *Lord Jim* a much closer knit and more complicated work with a remote psychology—sailors, Malays, and so on—whereas *Chance* is English in personages and locality, much easier to follow and understand. It was a very new form then; and yet old Maga had the audacity to take it up when we all were much less advanced than we are now and Conrad was a practically unknown writer."

That view is true enough, but nothing can mitigate the difficulty of the beginning of *Chance*, with its narrative tucked within narrative, its two Powells, and even its two Charleses—Charles Powell and Charlie Marlow. Further, the first fifty pages or so are all background, with no foreground or moving out into a discernible pattern of action; so that the reader is forced to assimilate detail that apparently has no function or appears to follow no direction. It was all memory, which of course was basic to Conrad's method, but seen from the reader's point of view it is simply blockage or narrative clutter.

Conrad told Harrison time was fleeting: he must have a decision within a week, or else he would be unable to put in the required work once he began a new novel. Harrison had also suggested that Conrad enter into an agreement with the *Review* for a "suite" of his reminiscences, a follow-up of six or seven articles over a period of eighteen months. Conrad found that idea acceptable if Harrison could work it out. Nothing, however, came of this proposal, or of the serialization of *Chance* in *The English Review;* but Conrad's susceptibility to Harrison's suggestions indicates his break with the *Review* stemmed not so much from the new ownership or new editorship, for both of whom he had real disdain, but because of Ford himself.*

In April, Conrad wrote Pinker a fateful letter indicating he had a "short story" in mind, although we know from his other correspondence that he was planning a novel.† Since *Victory*, the eventual product of this "short story" enterprise, is the most controversial of Conrad's novels, its beginnings provide fascinating insights into Conrad's way of approaching his fiction. He wrote Pinker: "In this connection I may tell you that I began the other day a short story (Dollars?). But I have found it difficult to get into the collar especially with that beastly face-ache. Then this Titanic business has disturbed me." By a short story, Conrad meant something in the range of 15,-000 words, forty or fifty printed pages. Also, this "short story" tentatively called "Dollars" is not to be confused with a short story entitled "Because of the Dollars," which he included in *Within the Tides* (1915).

Progress on "Dollars," was not smooth, nor was it uninterrupted. As we shall see, Conrad proceeded by fits and starts, breaking in to write "The Inn of the Two Witches," the above-mentioned "Because of the Dollars," and "The Planter of Malata"—all of which, along with an earlier story, "The Partner," were collected for *Within the Tides.* In addition, Conrad's interest in the sinking of the *Titanic*, apparently related in his mind to the *Patna* in-

---

* Although Ford's affairs after his break with Conrad are tangential to the latter's biography, nevertheless, his life did follow certain patterns which could only have antagonized his former collaborator. In just the period leading up to Elsie's suit against *The Throne*, which called Violet Hunt Mrs. Hueffer—a suit that provided a moment of true scandal—Elsie had petitioned for restitution of conjugal rights, Ford had gone to prison for non-payment of support, and had made plans for a German divorce, on the grounds that he was really a German citizen. Also, he had found time to write *The Simple Life Limited*, which contains a burlesque of a Conrad-like character, and then *The New Humpty-Dumpty*, which savages, among others, Elsie herself, David Soskice, and H. G. Wells, with whom Violet Hunt had once had a brief affair. Nearly every aspect of these activities aimed at Ford's need for self-justification, and his talent lay dormant while he pursued private devils.

† In a presentation copy of *Victory*, Conrad told Curle that the "first idea of this novel occurred to me at the end of the year 1911."

cident in *Lord Jim*, resulted in two articles on the loss, both published in *The English Review* and later reprinted in *Notes on Life and Letters:* "Some Reflections on the Loss of the *Titanic*" (May 1912) and "Certain Aspects of the Admirable Inquiry into the Loss of the *Titanic*" (July 1912).

An even greater interruption, however, came with Conrad's work on *Chance* during the conceptual period of *Victory*. When the early idea of *Victory* moved into his imagination, he was still involved in rewriting parts of *Chance*, fashioning "a fuller ending," as he called it; and this was followed by extensive rewriting of the novel's galleys shortly after the last episodes were serialized in the *Herald* (the final episode appearing on June 30). Since *Chance* goes back to 1905, its start coming only shortly after the completion of *Nostromo*, and that novel in turn points back toward *Romance* and the still-incomplete *Rescue*, we can see a number of overlapping works carrying Conrad from his earliest period right through to *Victory*. For in this sense *Victory* was not a completely new start but a novel in a sequence interrelated with fictions of ten years earlier, and a continuation of an imaginative enterprise that began near the turn of the century and ended only with the First World War.

As if these other considerations and interruptions were not sufficient to create uncertainty, Conrad also had not planned on a long novel when he began "Dollars." On the contrary, he expected his long effort for this period to be his Mediterranean novel, which he envisaged as the great effort of his later career, a parallel to *Nostromo* in this respect. For many years, he had been reading up on the Napoleonic era, his interest in doing a novel about Napoleon on Elba going back to at least 1904. Napoleon was surely a test of many of Conrad's ideas, and even a character like Nostromo, one product of that 1904 interest, can be viewed as "un petit Napoléon." His continuing attention to a "Mediterranean novel" intensified in the period immediately after the serialization of *Chance*, although Conrad was not to settle into this novel until much later, in 1920, and was to leave it as the incomplete *Suspense* (about 75,000 words) at his death in 1924.

As we follow Conrad's progress on "Dollars" or "Berg," we see he lacked the clear-cut working patterns he had developed with his other major efforts, *Nostromo, The Secret Agent, Under Western Eyes*. His development of "Dollars" was becoming increasingly involved with several other strands of his career, e.g., growing reputation in England and America, contractual complications, sale of his manuscripts and typescripts, courtship by a wider circle of friends and admirers. All of this activity was different from patterns in his earlier periods when writing was relatively unencumbered by complex external affairs, and he was engaged mainly in a battle between his creative imagination and his various illnesses. A month after his first mention of the short story "Dollars," Conrad, on May 13, 1912, wrote Pinker that the story was growing but was still of story length:

Would you mind to agree to pay me £10—against each three thousand (3000) words sent in—which would be an advance of £40 for 12,000 w. length or under. That will keep me going without worry. But what if the story grows beyond say 12 or even 15 thou? This is what stumps me. The story now in hand is of that kind which may grow even to 30,000. Short serial. What *can* you do if the story should get beyond the 12 thou. words—in the way of advance against copy? The consideration of pacing such sizes comes in here. I don't want to worry you but on the other hand I feel trammeled in my thinking by such considerations.

In this case (Dollars) the E.R. is safe for serial on this side. I am reading for the novel meantime. It's going to be done round Napoleon in Elba and it may turn out a biggish thing. I am still in doubt about the form. Whether a narrative in the first person or a tale in the third.

Not for another six months, in which Conrad worked on "Dollars" steadily, did he see it as a novel. As we wind in and around his comments to Pinker, we see him struggling with material that seems to grow from within, as though it were controlling him and not he it. On May 30, he wrote: "At last, herewith 3000 words of what I intend to be a story as short as I can make it, for which please send me £10 as I am entirely ruined." On June 6: "Here's some more (3000 w) of the story of Mr G. Berg (Dollars) whom I have painfully built up; and I hope he will run all right now; but it will be nearer 18 than 10 thousand words I fear before he stops. . . . Can't be helped. And I trust you won't mind. I shall make him as saleable as I can." On June 26: "I send you 3000 words of Dollars. I think this thing will be just under 20,000 words, but I shall try to make it shorter on revision. . . . I am reading a lot. I shall begin the novel [*Suspense*] directly this story is done. I feel a bit anxious generally."

The next weeks involved an installment of 3,000 words, for which Pinker dutifully supplied his weekly allowance of £10. Then, on September 3, Conrad wrote:

I've begun formally the novel [*Suspense*]. But that doesn't mean much. Still it will be something to catch on to when this story is finished. Mch or April of next year shall probably see the end of it. [followed now by September 12 comments]. . . . Here's another instalment. I suppose this thing must be allowed to grow. I understand that the E.R. is still keen on having it and it will make a small vol. We must reckon on 40000 w. but no more. Short serial. Meantime the long novel simmers in my head. This is the only possible way to go on, tho' of course it would have been better if I had been able to get away to the Mediterranean for a month of musing and looking at the scene.

Conrad finally accepted that "Dollars" was growing into something he had to call a novel, but he still expected it to come in at under 250 pages, although none of his longer fiction for the last ten years had been this brief. On October 7, he wrote Pinker:

It will be a novel certainly but not long enough to fall under the Methuen agreement [of three novels each over 75,000 words]. When you return [from America] you will find something of mine to negotiate about and I rather think fairly manageable. Meantime should you be asked over there with a view to serialisation you should perhaps tell them something. As, for instance that it has a tropical Malay setting—an unconventional man and a girl on an island under peculiar circumstances to whom enters a gang of three ruffians also of a rather unconventional sort—this intrusion producing certain psychological developments and effects. There is philosophy in it and also drama—lightly treated—meant for cultured people—a piece of literature before everything—and of course fit for general reading. Strictly proper. Nothing to shock the magazine public.

Don't imagine that I have lost sight of the big (or long) novel. I haven't. There is a stack of paper relating to it. It will be done next year in good time.

Two days later, he assured Pinker about the long novel he planned to write: "Next year will be given up to the Elba novel and perhaps 3 stories which with *Prince Roman* and *The Partner* will make a vol I hope. [Norman] Douglas is sending me a whole stack of books about the Mediterranean. If all goes well Harpers will be able to publish the novel just 100 years after Napoleon's exile to that island."

On November 2, Conrad was still speaking of "Dollars" as a "short novel" which he hoped to complete within another two months, if not sooner.

I am now writing this short novel [he told Pinker] and can't lay it aside even for a day. It shall be done before Xmas. Then you will send me the typed copy and I'll go through it during the holiday time and have it ready by the 15th Jan—or earlier if possible. This was my plan all along. Then they may set up and send me the proofs in the usual way, say in March. Marwood has offered to look through them for me as I expect to be very busy with the Elba novel by that time. And then the novel may be published in May. I can't have my books coming out too much in a heap. It won't do for me tho' it may be an advantage to other writers. My reputation doesn't stand on quantity.

A month and a half later, on December 17, he noted "Dollars" had already passed 50,000 words, although on revision he expected to bring it down to 50,000. Yet even with that assurance to Pinker, he turned in another weekly installment of 3,000 words. There was an evident disparity between what he was telling Pinker and what the novel was telling him. For even as he informed Pinker of the end—he now planned on a February terminal date—the novel was growing daily, without any possibility of the end being in sight. The manuscript demonstrates that after 50,000 words Conrad could not possibly finish the novel short of another 40 or 50,000 words. On January 26, 1913, he wrote Pinker once again about the novel, although without any certainty of its completion, and yet, on February 20, he would speak of an imminent conclusion. First, the January 26 letter:

> I suppose you understand that this so-called "Dollars" (I have a mind to call it "The Man in the Moon"—only the public would misunderstand) is nothing second-class. It's a rather queer thing a little savage in parts—but not to be thrown away on D's [Dent's] penny rag unless he forks out something. I could see he would like to get it for six-pence as it were, but I made as if [I] didn't understand. Still considering the stuff is anything but chocolate-cream we may let go for D for, say, eighteen-pence, as long as it can be done without damaging whatever prospect may turn up for serialisation in the US.

Then:

> . . . but still [I] hoped to have the novel finished in Febry. But it has been a bad year for work. Still every artist has his periods of diminished production, and I have done well in the two previous years (nearly 300,000 words in one way or another) so I had to expect a difficult spell.
>
> The *D* novel I hope will be ready end March; and supposing even we can't get free from Methuen it will bring in six hundred certain on book rights. But in a week or two's work on the completed MS. I will put it into shape for serialising; so that you would be able to show it around with a fair chance of netting in some 300 more on the lowest estimate.

Then, on April 13, still fourteen months before completion, Conrad wrote: "The D novel is drawing to an end. It will be more important than ever to have it serialised." It is impossible to determine precisely how long the manuscript was when Conrad made this assured prognosis of completing it, but we can estimate between 65 and 75,000 words, about 600 to 625 pages of the manuscript, at the point when Jones and Ricardo are to arrive at the island. This estimate is based on Conrad's having reached 50,000 words in early December, and then sporadically fulfilling his 3,000-word weekly quota. Allowing for his distractions, we can figure an additional 15 to 25,000 words in the four months from December to April. Also, in an August 21 letter, cited below, Conrad mentioned having reached only 660 manuscript pages, that three full months later. The consideration of length in April is important since it is difficult to understand how Conrad could have in the immediate future completed a novel running to 140,000 words, only about half of which he had written. We can speculate:

1. He was simply feeling his way into the book, still unsure of development and pacing, although the manuscript illustrates considerable control; and/or

2. He had to deceive Pinker, so as not to let his agent know of the morass he had gotten himself into; according to this, his letters have no relationship to his imaginative processes; and/or

3. He was so badly off financially that he was thinking primarily of the weekly quota and payment; and/or

4. He was so personally harassed with internal and external affairs that he honestly did not know where he was, that his creative imagination had taken over from his conscious mind and he was in a region of "unreason."

There is some reason to believe that by April 1913 Conrad may have written even less than we have granted him. He was, after all, to work on the novel for another fourteen months, and the spring of 1913 was for him a time full of *Chance* galleys, which he redid to the tune of 30,000 words. On April 17, 1913, for example, he wrote plaintively to Pinker: "Herewith a miserable 3000. I seem unable to get into a proper swing with this thing. I can do nothing but creep, creep, creep. However—" More tellingly, on May 4 he lamented: "Here's the usual instalment. Will I ever be able to pick up the lost time?—for I have not averaged that much per week since last June. If I had, everything would have been well. As it is.—" Inexplicably, however, after this admission, he could say: "However I may yet be done in a month's time with Mr Berg and his girl and all the rest of them."

That is, however, moving ahead a full year, from April 1912, when Conrad began the novel, to the spring of 1913, when he still did not see what it was becoming. He was a full year away from completion. In the meanwhile, Jessie's care with the old manuscripts led Conrad to discover "Falk," the major part of "Typhoon," pieces of *Lord Jim*, *Romance*, *The Nigger of the "Narcissus,"* and *Nostromo.* He could look forward to publication in the fall of *'Twixt Land and Sea*, which was to be composed of four stories, not three, and from which "The Partner," one of his weakest, was dropped and saved for a subsequent volume. The sales to Quinn continued unabated as rapidly as he could produce copy, and he dispatched parts of *Chance* that went back to 1906, 164 pages of manuscript, including a few in Jessie's handwriting, and an additional 1,089 pages, which made up the rest of the novel. With this, Conrad asked £70 for the lot, which included "Falk"—the neatest, he says, of his manuscripts—and "The Informer." He told Quinn not to read *Chance* in serial form but to wait for the book, in late 1913.

In the spring and summer of 1912, as he awaited publication of *'Twixt Land and Sea* and the final sections of *Chance* in serial, Conrad was entering a period in which frustrated plans were intermixed with sporadic work. He was, more or less, stalled on *Victory*, which hovered between story, novella, and novel length; he was working over *Chance* and planning extensive revisions and reshapings; he was hoping to get on with *Suspense*, his long Mediterranean novel; he had not completely forgotten *The Rescue;* he had plans for further reminiscences, in which Harrison was interested; and he hoped to turn out two or three stories a year both for the immediate income and to keep his name before the public between long novels. His sense of himself, even as he argued that his energy was depleted, was that of a man operating at least mentally at full tilt as he headed into his fifty-fifth year. What clearly abetted his positive frame of mind was the fact of the French translations of his work, which began with Davray and would continue more extensively under Gide and Jean-Aubry.

Gide invited Conrad to spend ten days at the Abbey of Pontigny in Burgundy. The meetings at the abandoned abbey took the form of organized literary discussion groups, and they occurred annually, under the auspices of Paul Desjardins, in the years prior to the First World War. For each ten-day period during the summer months a specific topic was discussed, and to be invited was a considerable honor. It was, however, the kind of affair Conrad would not even consider, first because of his obsessive need to turn out copy, and second because of a constitutional dislike of literary meetings or forums of any kind. He begged off by pleading prior commitments, and then showed, somewhat obligatorily, an interest in Gide's new novel, the still-in-progress *Les Caves du Vatican.* He tells Gide, also, that he will not like *Nostromo;* it is "bien mal fait" and "un foir noir," a black oven, to deal with. He indicates he is going to send on a copy of *The Mirror of the Sea,* which the "harmony of the Universe demands" that Gide possess.

Conrad wrote to all but Pinker that he had been idle for the last ten weeks, although to his agent he continued to indicate production of "Dollars." But not everything was drudgery. There are several family touches which soften Conrad's obsessional drive to produce books. In August, for example, he told Colvin about what his life has been, and it contains some balance. Conrad had acquired a car, which gave him considerable pleasure: "It's a worthy and painstaking one-cylinder puffer which amuses me very much." After his usual dose of the martyr who, like one of Beckett's gladiators, "must go on. Do or die," he turns to family matters: "But at present I have no taste for either alternative. Borys is at home; we go about together. He is a first rate driver. John is learning to read but his forte is geography. He's still the little pagan whom you know but he begins to develop a conscience—I notice. Jessie has been fairly well."

These interludes surely existed, although in most of his letters Conrad presented a far more stoical face. He also developed the habit of giving differing versions of his life and even his work to different people, depending on how strenuously he needed to protect his art. These deceptions, if we can call them even that, were arranged as shields behind which he could work. Typical was a letter to Gide in which he says he is hesitating before "taking up the pen in order to begin another long novel," by which he meant *Victory.* Yet to Pinker, he has spoken only of a *novella-length* work, and insists that his Mediterranean project will be his next long project.

Gide mentioned Conrad's "Future in France," his tentative overture about an overall translation, and indicated a trip to England to see Conrad again. The latter responded that the idea was "good and friendly"—a "meritorious work; an act of charity toward your neighbor"—and adds he will be "very happy" to see Jacques Copeau along with him. Yet he hedges: "But without doubt one must finish this book." It is typical Conradese. He enjoys Gide's attention as long as the French writer's presence becomes no more intrusive than occasional letters; visits were interruptions. And now, as Conrad felt his physical energy running out, he began to tighten the screws and, more than ever, play for working time against the inevitable illnesses and feelings of depletion.*

The very early fall of 1912, with work on "Dollars" going uncertainly, was a meandering period: no clear definition, many projects, a few visits in the area to friends, and an attack of gout in late September which continued into October. The gout was not unexpected, since Conrad was heading into a long work, and that combination of work and anxiety would stimulate his imagination even while it sent him to bed. The attack was accompanied by depression, so that by November 6 he was not well enough to come downstairs, although not actually laid up. There were, however, visitors, whom Conrad may have encouraged to come or not: Huneker, the American critic, arrived for a day; Curle came down in December after being introduced to Conrad by Edward Garnett;† Józef Retinger, a fellow Pole, who wrote a

* Running through this period (from the summer of 1912) is a profusion of letters from Conrad to John Quinn negotiating sales of manuscripts, typescripts, even scraps of stories and novels. The correspondence is large and detailed. For the biographer, while the detail is rich, it is monotonously the same; Conrad maintains the exchanges at the level of business. Withal, there is considerable misunderstanding, with the result that letters go back and forth over a particular arrangement which one or the other has confused. Typical is the confusion over "Typhoon," whose price Conrad had set at £50, and which Quinn had not distinguished from the arrangement over *Chance* and "Falk," whose price together Conrad had set at £70. Quinn considered the "Typhoon" price high and quibbled, and Conrad responded that "Typhoon" was especially valuable to him. But as a sweetener, he offered to throw in some "Heart of Darkness" manuscript pages—as much as he had, about 122 pages, some of them with writing from *Lord Jim* on their verso. A little later, he says he can throw together nearly three hundred pages of *Nostromo*, "Heart of Darkness," and *Jim* manuscript which Quinn can have for an "extra fiver."

These prices, as we have seen, were not unusually low for a living author; the £70 for *Chance* and "Falk," for example, was equivalent to about $1,000. We recall that one could purchase early modern art at comparable or lesser prices. Kenneth Clark mentions in his autobiography that a Modigliani he had his eye on at this time cost £60, an amount he hesitated to spend. And we are of course familiar with the sums Gertrude and Leo Stein paid. The increases came later, as Quinn discovered when he sold his Conrad collection in 1923: "Typhoon" for $5,100; "Falk" at $3,100; *Chance* for $6,600; *Lord Jim* for $3,900; *Victory* for $8,100—the highest prices, as Reid points out, ever paid up to that time for a living author's manuscripts.

† Curle, whose friendship meant so much to Conrad, met the writer for the first time, according to his own account, at the Mont Blanc restaurant, on Gerrard Street. Edward Garnett held Tuesday lunches at the restau-

short book on Conrad; later Bertrand Russell and several others. The visits were friendly in nature, but they were beginning to take on a note of homage: Conrad was slowly emerging as one of the two or three grand old men of English letters, along with James and Hardy, Meredith now being dead. When James died in 1916, Hardy having long since deserted fiction for poetry, Conrad reigned as "king," even as a whole new generation was about to displace him.

The indisposition, gout and depression, was perhaps not unattached to the reviews of *'Twixt Land and Sea,* which appeared on October 14. Conrad's hopes lay in "The Secret Sharer," which he felt caught his distinctive note: "The Secret Sharer [he wrote Garnett], between you and me, is *it.* Eh? No damned tricks with girls there [unlike "Freya"]. Eh? Every word fits and there's not a single uncertain note. Luck my boy. Pure luck. I knew you would spot the thing at sight."

The *Daily News* reviewer, Robert Lynd, immediately went to "The Secret Sharer" as a sign of Conrad's genius, comparable in its mastery to "Typhoon." But even with this evident praise, Lynd had to haunt Conrad with shades of Kipling: "Every sentence has a nerve; that is one of the distinguishing features of his writing. It is not clever writing—at least, not deliberately so. If his genius fails him, he has none of those glittering reserves of cleverness to fall back upon, such as enable Mr. Kipling always to achieve vividness even when he does not achieve life. But in what has been called the sense of life, Mr. Conrad is, within his limits, far richer than Mr. Kipling." Deeming "The Secret Sharer" a masterpiece, Lynd shows considerable insight when he observes that it is the captain, not the fugitive, who "jumps at sudden sounds and at chances of discovery."

John Masefield, who had had trouble with Conrad's modernity before, discovered particular mastery in "The Secret Sharer" and, surprisingly, in "A Smile," and even found Conrad's novella length a "new form" for literary effort in the coming decade. The undisclosed reviewer of the *Standard* singled out "The Secret Sharer" as the "most perfect of all Mr. Conrad's stories." But it is on other grounds that this reviewer's words struck a note that was beginning to sound for Conrad: recognition of his newness. "We may acclaim him [the reviewer writes] perhaps as the first king of a country—that country of story-tellers who will combine the sense of life proclaimed by the great mid-Victorians with the sense of form discovered here in England somewhere about 1890."

---

rant and attracted numerous literary men and artists, including Hudson, Gibbon, Belloc, Muirhead Bone, Stephen Reynolds, Edward Thomas, W. H. Davies, Ford, and occasionally Galsworthy and Conrad. Curle and Conrad met on one of the latter's rare visits, after Curle had written an appreciation of his work in *Rhythm* (November issue), an article Garnett showed to Conrad. Conrad said that all else before Curle's words was "mere verbiage in comparison."

A motor trip to visit the Hopes, about 1900: Conrad, Jessie (partially hidden), Conrad Hope, and Borys

Conrad in 1904

Scene of the "Anarchist Outrage" at Greenwich, February 15, 1894, used in *The Secret Agent.* X marks the spot where Marcel Bourdin blew himself up

Conrad at Someries in 1909, the time of *The English Review*

Edmund Oliver, Borys, and Conrad in 1911, when Borys joined H.M.S. *Worcester*

Conrad in 1913. Inscribed to Alfred A. Knopf, then at Doubleday

TELEGRAMS: CONRAD, HAMSTREET.
STATION: HAMSTREET, S.E.R. & C.RY.

CAPEL HOUSE,
ORLESTONE,
Nr ASHFORD.

13 Sept 1913.

My dear Russell.

Your letter has comforted me greatly. It seems to me that I talked all the time with fatuous egotism. Yet somewhere at the back of my brain I had the conviction that you would understand my unusual talkativeness. Generally I don't know what to say to people. But your personality drew me out. My instinct told me I would not be misread.

Let me thank you most heartily for the pleasure of your visit and for the letter you had the friendly thought to write.

Believe me sincerely yours
Joseph Conrad.

Letter to Bertrand Russell, after the latter's visit

(*opposite*) The garden at Capel House, 1914: Jessie, Borys, Ellen Glasgow, and Conrad

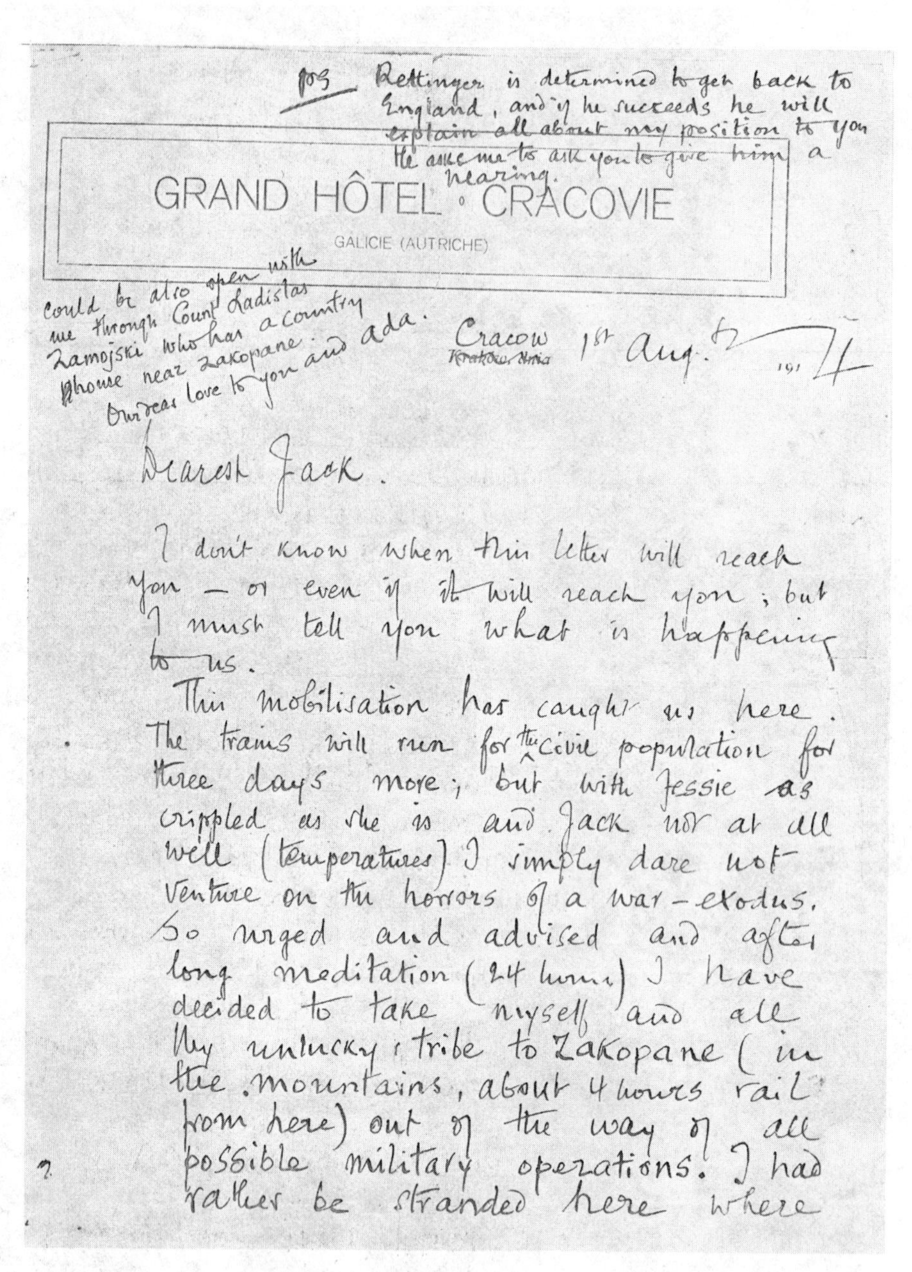

PS Rettinger is determined to get back to England, and if he succeeds he will explain all about my position to you He asks me to ask you to give him a hearing.

GRAND HÔTEL · CRACOVIE

GALICIE (AUTRICHE)

could be also open with me through Count Ladislas Zamojski who has a country house near Zakopane. Our dear love to you and Ada.

Cracow 1st Aug. 1914

Dearest Jack.

I don't know when this letter will reach you — or even if it will reach you; but I must tell you what is happening to us.

This mobilisation has caught us here. The trains will run for the civil population for three days more; but with Jessie as crippled as she is and Jack not at all well (temperatures) I simply dare not venture on the horrors of a war-exodus. So urged and advised and after long meditation (24 hours) I have decided to take myself and all my unlucky tribe to Zakopane (in the mountains, about 4 hours rail from here) out of the way of all possible military operations. I had rather be stranded here where

Conrad's desperate letter to Galsworthy from Cracow when he feared internment for the duration of the war

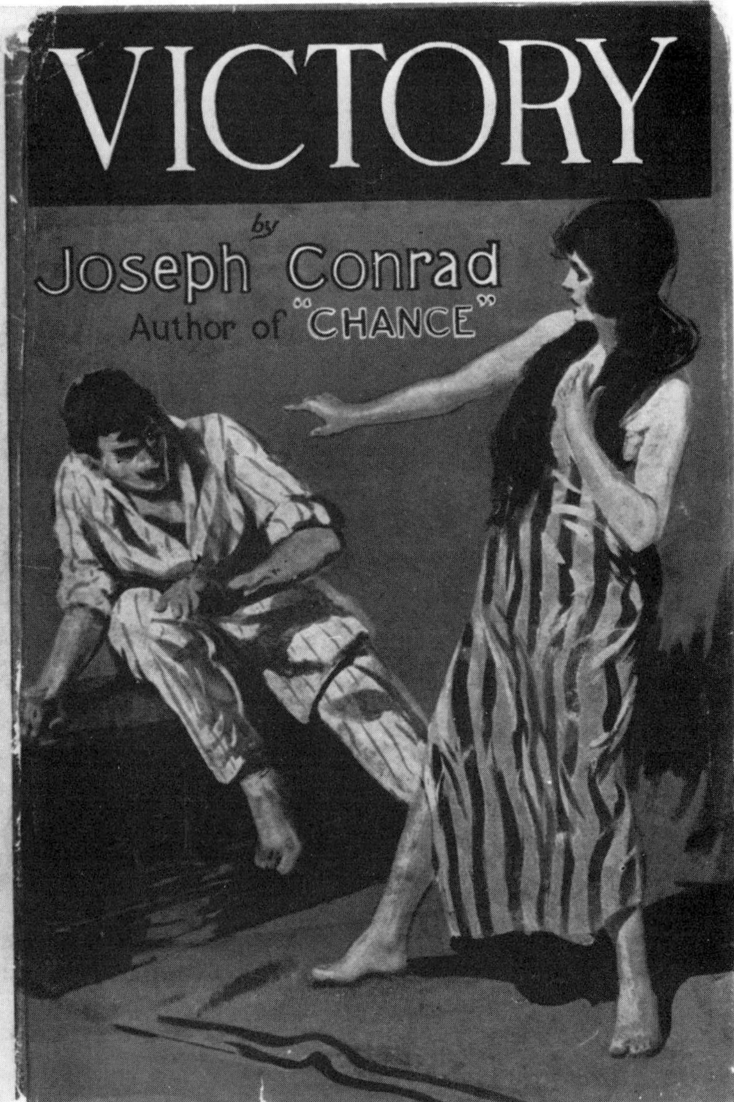

VICTORY
by
Joseph Conrad
Author of "CHANCE"

VICTORY
JOSEPH
CONRAD
In this new story Mr. Conrad returns to the manner of his famous early romance "*An Outcast of the Islands.*" The principal character, a lawless adventurer called "Enchanted Heyst" is one of the great figures in Mr. Conrad's gallery; the scene is laid in and about the tropical island of Samburan; and the theme is love and jealousy.

Jacket for Methuen's edition of *Victory* in 1915

Victory.
An Island Tale.

There is, as every schoolboy knows
in this scientific age a very close
chemical relation between coals and
diamonds. Not being a schoolboy
any longer I have no very clear notion
of its nature. It seems to be — that
if you take coals
and melt, or roast it, or evaporate
it, or destroy it in some such way; in short
you do anything but cook
or warm yourself with them
you may obtain (so they say) out of
a ton of coals (with luck
a diamond rather smaller than the
usual pin-head. It is the reason I
believe why some poetic people allude to coal
as black diamonds. Mankind is prone
to exaggeration of language. Both
commodities represent wealth. But
coals are a much less portable form of pro-

2

perty. There is from that point of
view a deplorable lack of concentration
in coals. Now if a coal mine could
be put into one's waistcoat pocket — but
it can't. At the same time there
is a fascination in coals, the
supreme commodity of the age
we are camped in
like bewildered travellers in a garish, unrestful
hotel. And I suppose those
two considerations, the practical
and the mystical prevented
Berg, Augustus Berg, from
going away. He called himself
Berg but I suspect that
it was not the whole of his name.
I don't mention this surmise to disparage
the man. I suppose he found
it more handy in that form.
More portable — him. Well — Berg.

The Archipelago Coal Syndicate
went into liquidation ... I am truly

The first four pages of the *Victory* manuscript

distressed. I must apologize for the clumsiness of my proceedings. Here I begin as though I were going into chemistry and then I seem to be putting my foot into finance now. Nothing is further from my thoughts than to attract or frighten away my readers by a show of science. But necessity knows no law and I must wear the false mantle of erudition for a little while longer. The world of finance then is a mysterious world in which, incredible as the fact may appear, evaporation precedes liquidation. First the capital evaporates and then the company goes into liquidation. These are very unnatural physics, but they account for the persistent inertia of the body called A. Berg; an inertia at which we "out there" used to laugh amongst ourselves — but

not unkindly inimically. An inert body can do no harm to anyone provokes no hostility is scarcely worth derision. It may indeed be in the way sometimes. But this could not be said of A. Berg. If anybody was ever out of the way it was he. I mean to say that he was out of everybody's way as though he were perched on the highest peak of the Himalayas. and in a sense as conspicuous. Everyone at that time and in that part of the world knew of him dwelling on his little island. An island is but the top of a mountain. But instead of immeasurable space there were only miles of placid shallow sea round him, tepid and unwrinkled, the most passionless offshoot of the great waters which embrace the continents of this globe. His most frequent

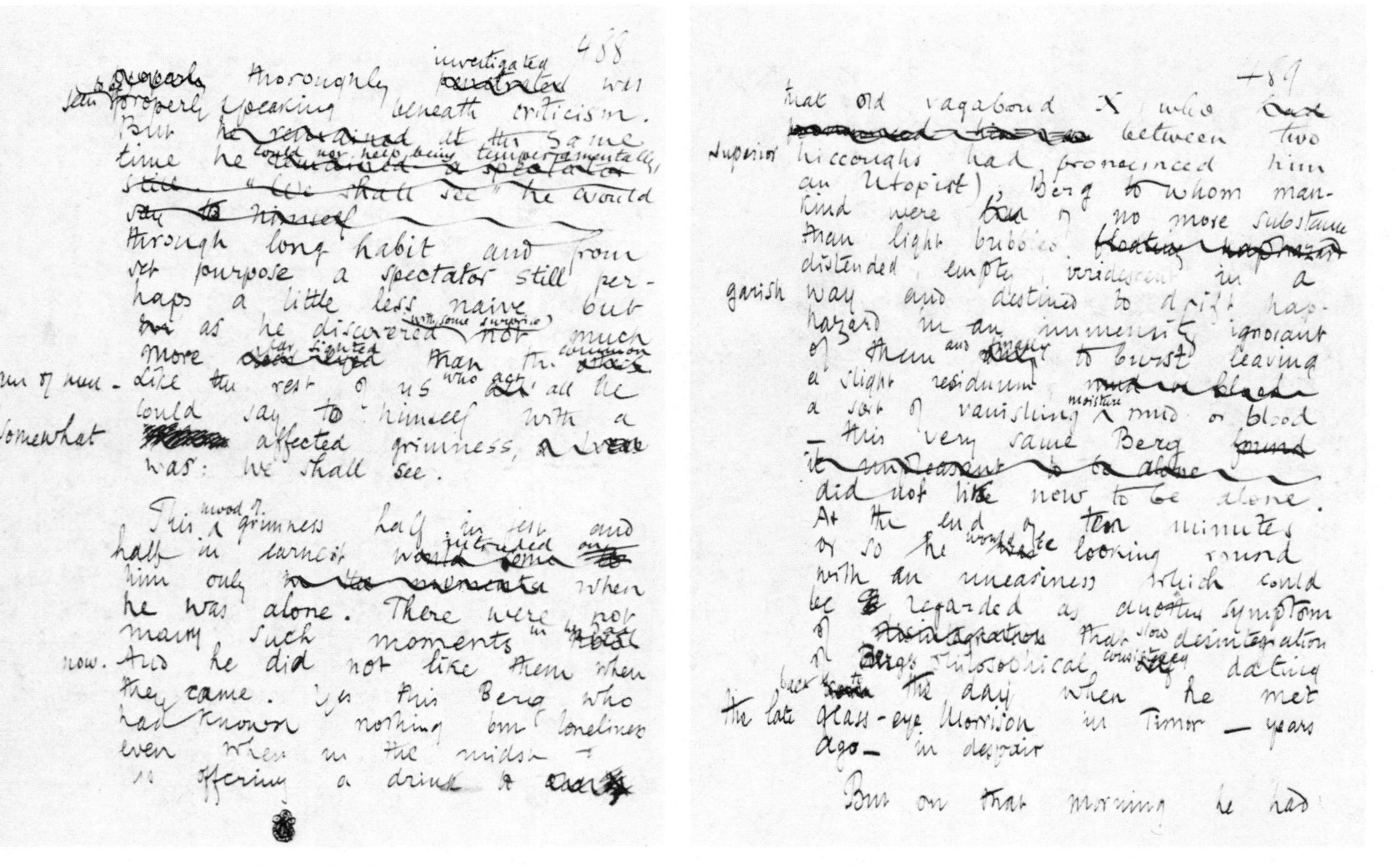

488

thoroughly investigated was properly speaking beneath criticism. But he remained at the same time he could not help being temperamentally still

through long habit and from set purpose a spectator still perhaps a little less naive but as he discovered with some surprise not much more far sighted than the common run of men. Like the rest of us who act all the could say to himself with a somewhat affected grimness, [illegible] was: We shall see.

This mood of grimness half in jest and half in earnest intruded on him only when he was alone. There were not many such moments in his life now. And he did not like them when they came. Yes this Berg who had known nothing but loneliness even when in the midst of [illegible] offering a drink to [illegible]

489

that old vagabond X who [illegible] between two hiccoughs had pronounced him a superior Utopist), Berg to whom mankind were no more substance than light bubbles distended, empty, iridescent in a garish way and destined to drift haphazard in an immensity ignorant of them and finally to burst leaving a slight residuum a sort of vanishing moisture of mud or blood — this very same Berg did not like now to be alone. At the end of ten minutes or so he would be looking round with an uneasiness which could be regarded as another symptom of that slow disintegration of Berg's philosophical consistency dating back to the day when he met the late Glass-eye Morrison in Timor — years ago — in despair

But on that morning he had

A sample of pages from the *Victory* manuscript later deleted from the book text glinting hairs laid out for a frontier. And the worst of it is that at no given moment can one be certain on which side one is standing."

A shade darkened her attentive expectant face. Her half-open lips which seemed to drink his words closed firmly.

"Now you are joking again" she complained

"No. Not now" said Berg looking at her so hard that she blushed averted her face, sighed and feebly as if seeking consolation

"So you really do like my hair" she asked.

"Yes" said Berg. "I am in dead earnest now. I like it immensely. I think a head of such glorious hair a more precious possession than any amount of wisdom if for no other reason than

because it is indisputable. Even a blind man could not deny the glory of which I speak.

"It is glorious then?"

"I believe I have called it so twice just now. But I have no objection to repeating the epithet as many times as you like. How many times shall I? You won't tell me? No? Let me at least say it once more: Glorious! ..."

"Well — it belongs to you now" she said putting a wonderful vibrating seduction into the hidden tenderness of the phrase. Berg made no sound, and there followed a long silence in the dusk — for the sun had set while they were talking.

Between that evening and the day when she came out on to the verandah to join Berg long before the sun risen above the Samburan ridge swept the shadow of the early morning and the remnant of the night's coolness clear off the roof

Conrad in later years

Joseph Conrad (Victory)

TELEGRAMS:- CONRAD, HAMSTREET.
STATION:- HAMSTREET, S.E.R. & C.R.

CAPEL HOUSE,
ORLESTONE,
Nr ASHFORD.

10 Sept 15.

My dear Sir.

I am immensely touched by the kindness of your letter — that apart from the intense satisfaction given me by the approval of an accomplished fellow-craftsman and a true brother in letters — of whose personality and art I have been intensely aware for many years.

A few days before it reached me Perceval Gibbon (a short-story writer and a most distinguished journalist and war corresp:) & I were talking you over endlessly, in the quiet hours of the night. Gibbon who had just returned after 5 months on the Russian front had been taking you in in bulk, soaking himself in your prose. And we admired the vehemence of your strength and the delicacy of your perception with the greatest sympathy and respect.

I havent seen your latest yet. The reviews such as came my way are enthusiastic. The book is in the house but I wait to finish a thing (short) I am writing now before I sit down to read you. It'll be a reward for being a good industrious boy. For it is not easy to write here nowadays. At this very moment there is a heavy burst of gunfire in Dover. I can hear the quick firers and the big guns — and wonder what it is. The night before last a Zep passed over the house (not for the first time) bound west on that raid on London of which you would have read already in your papers. Moreover I've just now a gouty wrist. This explains my clumsy handwriting.

And so no more — this time. Keep me in your kind memory and accept a grateful and cordial handgrasp

Yours sincerely Joseph Conrad.

Reply to Jack London's letter of June 4, 1915, praising *Victory*

Conrad's drawing for the jacket of *The Arrow of Gold*

JOSEPH CONRAD

TYPHON

TRADUIT DE L'ANGLAIS PAR
ANDRÉ GIDE

nrf

PARIS
ÉDITIONS DE LA
NOUVELLE REVUE FRANÇAISE
3, rue de Grenelle, (VIme)

The title page of André Gide's translation of *Typhoon* (1918), limited to 300 copies

Conrad and Jessie in 1919

TELEGRAMS:- CONRAD, BRIDGE.
STATION:- BISHOPSBOURNE, S.E.& C.R.

OSWALDS,
BISHOPSBOURNE,
KENT.

Nov. 30th. 1922.

My dear Mr Squire

I do not like to sign collective tributes, though I admit that Mr Pearsall Smith's text is very nice. I have heard first of Marcel Proust either in 1913 or 1914, and I admire him immensely, but not for reproducing Parisian or French provincial life, which has been done by others admirably before, and, in a certain sense, made Marcel Proust's work understandable to us here; nor yet because he has reproduced for us our own past, for our pasts have been very different and we have felt them differently. I should rather admire him for disclosing to us a past like nobody else's and thus adding something memorable to the general experience of mankind. What compels my admiration for M. Proust's work is that it is great art based on analysis. All his greatness lies in that. Where he is unique and for ever memorable is in this: that he is a prose writer (to put it in French since we all have read him in French) "qui a poussé la force de l'analyse jusqu'au point ou elle devient créatrice." The phrase seems absurd and incredible like the statement of the properties Ether must have to make so much of natural science intelligible in theory. I don't know much about Ether, but phrase about Proust states an obvious fact. All those beings have been created by the force of analysis, of a most minute, penetrating and, as it were, inspired kind. If his Françoise, for instance, (the devoted servant of a middle-class family, which has been done admirably many times before) doesn't live by the mere force of analysis and nothing else, then I am willing, in the words of that other creation, Falstaff, "to have my brains taken out and buttered and given to a dog for a

(*left and right*) Conrad's response to Sir John Collings Squire about Proust, remarks he later repeated to Scott Moncrieff, Proust's translator

PS/ I have sent the signed copy of the message to Mr Pearsall Smith direct.

New Year's gift".

Mr P. S. speaks of beauty in that work. And it is indubitable. But the marvellous thing is that ~~he~~ Proust has attained that beauty "par ~~un~~ procédé tout-a-fait étranger a toute espèce de poètique. Dans cette prose, si pleine de vie, il n'y a ni rêve, ni émotion, ni ironie ni chaleur de conviction, ni même un rythme marqué" -- to charm our fancy. And yet it lives in its tuneless, almost monstrous, greatness. I don't think there is in the whole creative literature an example of the power of analysis such as this; and I feel pretty safe in saying that there will never be another. ~~[illegible]~~

I write you all this because you have, in a manner, asked me what I thought of M. P. You have only yourself to thank for that outbreak. But I know you will bear me no grudge for wasting your time.

That day at the Hudson meeting I could not stay a moment. I was already late for an appointment of some importance — to me. Otherwise I would not have gone away without exchanging if only a bare greeting with you. I hope I am forgiven.

Believe me always, with cordial regard,

Yours
Joseph Conrad.

Conrad, about 1922

(*opposite*) Unwin's 1923 "complete edition" of five Conrad novels

THE ROVER

BY

JOSEPH CONRAD

IN this novel Mr. Joseph Conrad has the Mediterranean, as seen from the French south coast, not for a stage, but for a background, in the depth of which the presence of the English blockading fleet is rather felt than seen throughout the course of events which happen on land in a lonely farm-house. The narrative, intimate in character, deals with the crisis in the lives of two women and some men—the Rover being the central figure—and ends at sea in an episode in which the shapes of the blockading ships and the person of Lord Nelson himself are evoked for a moment. The tale, though in no sense historical, attempts to reflect in part at least the spirit of the period 1802-4, with references to an earlier time, after the evacuation of Toulon, when during the savage excesses of the Republican reaction the Heiress of Escampobar, when still almost a child, passed through experiences which had unsettled her mind.

7s. 6d. net

T. FISHER UNWIN LTD. 1 Adelphi Terrace, London W.C. 2

Uniform Edition of JOSEPH CONRAD'S EARLIER WORKS. Cloth Bound. Gilt Lettered. The Adelphi Edition *3s. 6d. net*

ALMAYER'S FOLLY

Extracts from earlier notices:

"Painful and beautiful — true artistic feeling."
"A realistic transcription of life."
"Skilfully portrayed — excellent workmanship."
"Nothing quite like it."
"Not a single character that one likes."
"The construction of the story is faulty."
"The writer has done a good piece of work."
"Mr. Conrad may go on — and with confidence. He deserves his public and will find his place."

AN OUTCAST OF THE ISLANDS

Extracts from earlier notices:

"Extraordinary force and charm."
"Unresistable note of genius."
"As powerful as it is gloomy."
"Something very like genius."
"Unusual eloquence and power."
"A depressing squalid story."
"Charming romance, powerfully and gracefully written."

T. FISHER UNWIN LTD. 1 Adelphi Terrace, London W.C. 2

Uniform Edition of JOSEPH CONRAD'S EARLIER WORKS. Cloth Bound. Gilt Lettered. The Adelphi Edition *3s. 6d. net*

TALES OF UNREST

Extracts from earlier notices:

"Vivid—but assuredly it is ghastly."
"Marred by a regrettable laxity of style."
"In no way an agreeable book."
"Genuine talent."
"It will not add to the author's reputation."
"Glamour—that is Joseph Conrad."
"Fascinatingly interesting—well written."

Also uniform with the above

THE ARROW OF GOLD

A powerful romance, concerned mainly with the love story of a young sea-captain and a beautiful Spanish girl, Dona Rita, heiress to the fortunes of Henry Alleyne, a strong supporter of Don Carlos de Bourbon, when, in the 'seventies, Don Carlos made his historic attempt for the throne of Spain. The scene of the romance is mainly Marseilles and the Spanish coast. In the character of the heroine, Dona Rita, Mr. Conrad has conceived a singularly fascinating figure, and never, not even in "Victory," has he written a story so direct and so moving.

T. FISHER UNWIN LTD. 1 Adelphi Terrace, London W.C. 2

The greatest living artist in English prose

his arm round the shroud of the mainmast.

The Amelia whose way had carried her past the tartane for nearly half a mile, before sail could be shortened and her yards swung on the other tack, was coming back to take possession of her chase. In the deepening dusk and amongst the foaming seas it was a matter of difficulty to make out the tartane. At the very moment when the master of the man-of-war looking out anxiously from the forecastle-head thought that she might perhaps have filled and gone down, he caught sight of her rolling in the trough of the sea, and so close that she seemed to be at the end of the Amelia's jibboom.

Peyrol sinking back on the deck in another heavy lurch of his craft, saw for an instant the whole of the English corvette swinging up into the clouds as if she meant to fling herself upon his very breast. A blown seatop flicked his face noisily, followed by a smooth interval, a silence of the waters. He beheld in a flash the days of his manhood, of strength and adventure, a sudden superhuman voice like the roar of an angry sea-lion seemed to fill the whole of the empty sky in one mighty and commanding shout: "Steady!"...And with the sound of that English word ringing in his ears Peyrol smiled to his visions and died.

The Amelia, stripped down to her topsails and hove to, rose and fell easily while on her quarter about a cable's length away Peyrol's tartane tumbled like a lifeless corpse amongst the seas.

Typescript page of *The Rover* describing Peyrol's death

1859 PRINCE ROMAN. By Joseph Conrad. In the *Oxford and Cambridge Review* for October 1911. 8vo, wrappers. In a half brown morocco case. London, 1911

The first appearance in print of "Prince Roman." The story has not yet been reproduced in any of its author's collected volumes. It was issued only in a Limited Edition of 25 copies in 1920.

1860 ORIGINAL AUTOGRAPH MANUSCRIPT OF "A SMILE OF FORTUNE." Written on 140 pages, folio. In a crushed brown levant morocco solander case.

THE COMPLETE ORIGINAL MANUSCRIPT of the first of the three stories comprising the book "'Twixt Land and Sea." This, and the two Manuscripts of "The Secret Sharer" and "Freya of the Seven Isles" form the entire volume.

The present manuscript, while containing its customary changes and additions, nevertheless follows the printed version quite closely. On the first page Mr. Conrad has written the caption, with his signature above it, in blue pencil, and at the end he has indicated the period of composition, by writing "*June-August, 1911.*"

Mr. Conrad mentions in a letter to Mr. Quinn that the first title of this story was to have been "A Deal in Potatoes."

A wrapper addressed to Mr. Quinn in Mr. Conrad's hand is included.

"A Smile of Fortune" is based, so far as the story of the potatoes is concerned, on an incident that occurred to the author at Mauritius while in command of a ship loading there.

1861 A SMILE OF FORTUNE. By Joseph Conrad. In the *London Magazine* for Feb. 1911. 8vo, wrappers. In a cloth slip case. London, 1911
The first appearance of "A Smile of Fortune," the first story in "'Twixt Land and Sea."

1862 ORIGINAL AUTOGRAPH MANUSCRIPT OF "UNDER WESTERN EYES." Written on 1351 pages, quarto. In 4 crushed brown levant morocco cases.

THE COMPLETE ORIGINAL MANUSCRIPT of this story, which differs so materially from the printed version as the story progresses, in the arrangement of the chapters, dialogues, paragraphs and phrases, because Mr. Conrad worked over it and deleted many portions before the copy was ready for the printer.

The title of the Manuscript is "Razumov," but the author decided to change it to "Under Western Eyes," upon its completion, as on the margin of the last page he has written: "*Title: Under Western Eyes. A Novel.*" At the foot of this page he has also indicated the date of completion, writing: "*End. 22 Jan. 1910. J. C.*"

22

p. 1 R. 1.

Razumov.

I

To begin with I wish to disclaim the possession of these gifts of imagination and style which would have enabled my pen to create for the reader the personality of the man who called himself, after the Russian custom, Cyril son of Isidor — Kirylo Sidorovitch — Razumov.

If I have ever had these gifts in any sort of living form they have been smothered out of existence a long time ago under a wilderness of words. Words as is well known are

REDUCED FACSIMILE OF THE FIRST PAGE OF "RAZUMOV"—AFTERWARDS CHANGED TO "UNDER WESTERN EYES"—IN THE HANDWRITING OF JOSEPH CONRAD
[1862]

23

The catalogue of John Quinn's sale of his Conrad manuscripts and typescripts at the Anderson Galleries in 1923

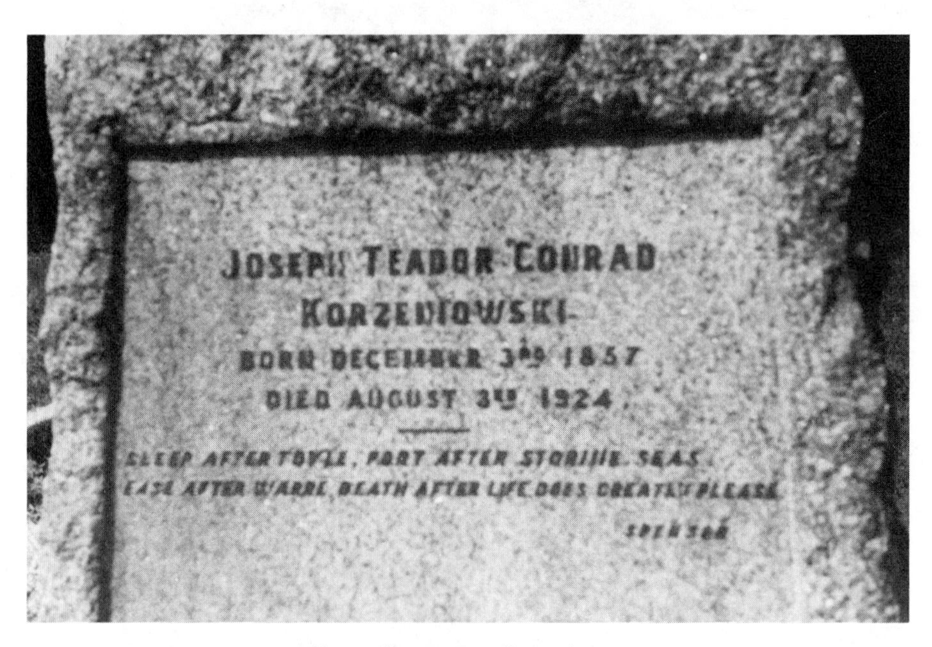

Conrad's grave at Canterbury

The sense of form, however, could be a tricky thing; for the *Spectator* reviewer lamented the influence of Henry James on Conrad. This notice suggested that *The Secret Agent* had lacked the typical Conradian genius because of James's lamentable presence, and the reviewer is pleased to note that Conrad was speaking in his own voice once again with this collection of stories. Not only was Conrad viewed as a representative of something new, he was tarred with the Jamesian brush in the same stroke; so that "newness," while desirable, was also a way of scoring against him. The battle, on a small scale, was on, between the forces of modernity and the late Victorians, and Conrad, quite suitably, was caught in the middle.

When Virginia Woolf gave her now famous speech at Cambridge on "Mr. Bennett and Mrs. Brown" in 1924, her argument was that Wells, Bennett, and Galsworthy provided no direction on how to write a novel, or where fiction was to go. She says that around 1910 or thereabouts "there was no English novelist living from whom they [the writers] could learn their business. Mr. Conrad is a Pole; which sets him apart, and makes him, however admirable, not very helpful. Mr. Hardy has written no novel since 1895." The dismissal of Conrad as one of the new because he is a Pole is curious, since from Woolf's remark one receives the impression that he wrote not in English but in Polish. In fact, Woolf's distinctions about the need for a new system of communication had already been explored, and James and Conrad had done it. Conrad was, indeed, already suffering, by 1912, from the backlash of the new.*

In late November, the Conrads went up to London, but Conrad stayed only one day, rushing home with threatening symptoms of gout. He told Colvin he had two months of enervation, with hardly any work being done. But by mid-December, he informed Pinker that he was producing copy for "Dol-

* Ironically, Arnold Bennett, one of Woolf's traditionalists, had written Conrad praising his mastery, his craftsmanship, and speaking generally of "the *passionate* comprehension which some of us have of your work." Bennett, whose taste in Conrad was excellent, singled out *Nostromo, Under Western Eyes, The Secret Agent,* and "The Secret Sharer." None of his comments suggests he was disturbed by Conrad's being a Pole. The latter was truly overwhelmed: "I am covered with confusion at what you say—and were it all as true as your intense sympathy will have it, its value would still be infinitely increased to me by the generosity of your recognition. It is indeed a rare happiness for a craftsman to evoke such a response in a creative temperament so richly gifted and out of a sincerity so absolutely above suspicion as all your work proclaims you to be. For myself, in my conscience, all I am aware of is a certain tenacity of purpose which has kept me going through these few years under mental and physical conditions of which I'll say nothing, as they were too intimately adverse to bear description. For the rest, I will only say that if the vintage be good the merit of the bottle is slender. It just happened to hold it—that's all." Conrad was particularly pleased at Bennett's response to *Nostromo,* for with the public "it was the blackest possible frost." As for Bennett, he described Conrad's flattery as positively Oriental.

lars." And just the next month, he was to tell Pinker he hoped to bring in the novel by the end of March. None of this was to occur, but he had written steadily since the completion of *Chance* and was by no means as dormant as he indicated to friends. Part of his pose was to discourage invitations and visits, and indisposition appeared a better means than outright refusal.

A rather different person than usual entered Conrad's life by way of Arnold Bennett: Józef Retinger. He appeared in November 1912, not in 1909, as he recounts it in *Conrad and His Contemporaries.* Retinger (or Rettinger, as he was born in Cracow) was trilingual, like Conrad, writing in Polish, French, and English; his first book-length work was a study composed in French of French literature. His political sympathies, however, lay with Poland, and he sought throughout his twelve-year friendship with Conrad to get the latter interested in his projects. One of them, in November 1914, was to propose the formation of a Polish legion in the United States, which would be trained to fight on the side of the Allies. Although Retinger had little practical influence on Conrad, his wife's mother invited the entire Conrad family to Poland, to stay at the family home in Zakopane, an episode that almost resulted in the internment of the Conrads for the duration of the war. Retinger's fervent political activity on behalf of Poland, as we shall see, met with Conrad's often-stated cynicism that Poland would be manipulated according to major power interests, without regard for Polish needs or ethical questions. Retinger's insistent pressure, nevertheless, led Conrad to write his "A Note on the Polish Problem" (in 1916) and, before that, to relate his 1914 visit in "Poland Revisited" (published in the *Daily News* in 1915).

In December, Conrad turned fifty-five. His letters seem dispirited: he did not wish to see new faces, unless they were Conradians, such as Curle or Retinger; but he was working fairly well on "Dollars." He could look forward to a sudden spurt in sales of the American and English editions of *'Twixt Land and Sea.* This increase in sales for the short-story collection seemed to act as a catalyst for Conrad's audience, a large one hovering and waiting for the right moment, and it came with *Chance,* abetted considerably by the efforts of the young Alfred A. Knopf, then an assistant at Doubleday.* Conrad could not, of course, know this in December 1912, but recent reviews of his short-story collection suggested he had arrived; treated as a living classic, he was slowly being pointed toward a broader popularity. The stories, followed

* Knopf very shrewdly laid the groundwork for the success of *Chance* by collecting critical praise from the leading popular writers of the day. Among others, he solicited Robert Service, Rex Beach, Theodore Dreiser, Jack London, Basil King, although William Dean Howells refused to give an opinion for an advertisement. Knopf reached Conrad initially through Galsworthy, and then was instrumental in making Doubleday his chief American publisher. They met for the first time, along with Mrs. Knopf and Curle, at Conrad's home in Bishopsbourne in 1921, and then again in 1923 with Thomas Beer, who wanted Conrad to write an introduction to Beer's *Stephen Crane.*

by *Chance* and then *Victory*, gave him that audience, with the rapid publication of books keeping him before the public. That obsessive need to turn out copy without cessation finally paid off, because the books that made him popular finally were hardly a concession to popular tastes.

Conrad plodded along, seeing his early career turned over in the sale of manuscripts to Quinn and his later career kept continuous by the steady interest in the French translations. The French writer Marcel Prévost was interested in doing "The Secret Sharer," and toward that end asked Edith Wharton to write to Conrad. The latter responded very generously on December 24, rising to Mrs. Wharton's praise of the story and showing great pleasure in the words of a fellow author of "such great and distinctive gifts." Conrad's response is of interest, because in it he says "The Secret Sharer" is so particularly English "in moral atmosphere, in feeling and even in detail" that he hesitates to see it translated unless it were rewritten. Conrad speaks of himself in the third person as having a peculiar diction, a "note personelle."

This sense of himself as a classic, this self-realization of his worth in English letters, comes through very strongly in remarks to Quinn. Conrad and Jessie had discovered in boxes unopened for years the complete manuscript of *The Nigger of the "Narcissus."* Conrad calls it the "story by which, as creative artist, I stand or fall, and which, at any rate, no one else could have written. A landmark in literature, I can safely say, for nothing like it has been ever done before." He asks £80 for it, and indicates that if he had not had a bad year, "no money would have bought it. I would have kept it by me for the sake of old associations and then left it to the MSS Dept of the British Museum. They preserve many less significant MS there."

As Conrad meandered back into the past, he turned those past memories into a golden age of hope and achievement. When Jessie peeped into the box, she cried: " 'Here's the Nigger!' "—her cry reminiscent of "Eureka!" as one strikes a vein of gold. Conrad described the condition of the manuscript as good, and it brought back his early days with Edward Garnett and then his honeymoon in Brittany, landmarks in the development of his literary sensibility. His words are worth repeating, for on *The Nigger* he still placed such value that despite far greater achievement since it had become for him mythical and legendary. How he longed for another "Nigger" that would loosen his imagination and lead to a continuing career, even at fifty-five.

> The pencil notes in the margin [he told Quinn] are by Edward Garnett a very clever critic and an old friend of mine who was then literary adviser to a firm of publishers. I used to send him the MS as I wrote it and the book is dedicated to him; the third written novel and the third published volume of mine. Old, old days! I began writing it in Brittany on our honeymoon and it was finished before we had been twelve months married. I haven't seen the pages for sixteen years and they looked to me strange, as

> if written by some man I used to know in the past and just could remember dimly.

Soon, like Wait, he would be lowered into the sea. Death gave him pause.

Unrelated to any other stirrings in his imagination, Conrad wrote one of his worst stories, "The Inn of the Two Witches," which appeared in March 1913 in *Pall Mall Magazine*, and in May in the *Metropolitan*. He was now writing stories to provide manuscripts for Quinn—that seems certain—and also to try to complete another volume, so as to keep himself before the public. "The Inn" would be collected in *Within the Tides*, in 1915, and help make it one of his weakest volumes, very possibly his worst. As a short-story writer, that is, in the range of under 30,000 words, Conrad would never regain his old form. This collection and the final one, *Tales of Hearsay*, were the very kind of marketplace work he had skirted for the early part of his life.

The real decline, however, was yet to come. By February 9, 1913, Conrad reported that his debts of £2,700 (about $20–25,000 in current monies) had been reduced to £600. He expected to complete "Dollars" shortly, but still unfinished were the extensive revisions of the *Chance* galleys. The installments to Pinker continued, 3,000 words for £10. By March, Conrad had moved on to still another publisher, this time Dent, with whom he signed a contract for three novels. He told Quinn that the idea filled him with terror, for he did not feel three novels remained within him. By the end of March, there were only minor trouble spots, but of the kind that threw Conrad off his concentration. His energies now were so sharply focused and so intense that he had little left for any other activity, whether controversy, friends, or even family life.

The first of the difficulties came in his running argument with Methuen, a publisher with whom he had signed a contract calling for what he thought was three novels of over 75,000 words each. With the delivery of *Chance*, Conrad felt the agreement had been fulfilled on his part. But Methuen claimed the contract called for four novels and had excepted *The Secret Agent* from the arrangement for being too short, which it was not. Conrad was particularly angry because Methuen had rejected *'Twixt Land and Sea*, which had gone to Dent, and had done so without adequate explanation. He asserted his rights as an artist: "I don't shake novels out of my sleeve [he wrote Algernon Methuen]. A novel for Messrs Methuen & Co is after all but an item amongst many on their list; for me it is a considerable fact in my literary activity and a considerable slice of my life. I don't want to 'get away' from my engagements but I object to having them extended for a reason which, properly speaking, is non-existent."

Conrad followed this with a far stronger letter a week later. He suggested he has been deceived, or even tricked. The letter is a fine statement of his position, demonstrating that his instinct for survival has been touched and he will not be brought around by perfunctory praise or slightly higher royalties.

> I protest strongly against your hint at my disappointment. I won't be represented as a discontented person who wishes to wiggle out. You have no right to ascribe to me a disappointment which I have not expressed and have not even felt. But from the last paragraph of your letter it is clear that you have been disappointed with the 2 novels you have published and shall no doubt be disappointed with the third you are going to publish. Why then you should insist on dragging out of me a fourth disappointment to which you are not morally entitled?

Conrad defends his art against those (including Methuen) who cannot distinguish one product from another: "After the confession of your deceived hopes and in view of the fact that the novel I am writing has no more sea in it than the ordinary citizen can enjoy from the end of Brighton pier it could be only for the grim satisfaction of holding by the neck a man who has not given you what you expected for your money, who does not share your view of his writings and of the public's attitude to them, and whose only sin is that he insists on the freedom to dispose of his work to which he now feels morally entitled."

He attacks Methuen's persistence even as the firm feels he has cheated them:

> The apparent perversity of such an attitude is not easy to fathom; but you can not be surprised to hear that after this the mere idea of a work of mine being published by your firm has become extremely distasteful to me. And unless you wish to push a contemptuous disregard for a man's feeling as far as it can go you can't refuse to listen to my offer to relieve you from the necessity of publishing even Chance itself. I am ready to take it over thus terminating at once that connection which has not realised your expectations, returning to you also the fifty pounds paid to me on signature of the contract.

Conrad returns to Methuen's desire for more sea stuff: "I should think that contempt conscious or unconscious for a man's feelings could no further go. . . . There aren't ten thousand words of what you want of 'sea' in the hundred and forty thousand of Chance, nor nearly enough to slake that thirst for salt from which it appears you have been suffering so long." He reiterates his offer to remove *Chance* from their 1913 list and return the £50 advance. Methuen, however, went ahead with its publication.

The other direct disturbance came from Ford, who put pressure on Conrad for the £100 principal and £40 interest owed him, even as Marwood was importuning him (Ford) for his money. Conrad's indebtedness went back to 1901 and included capital as well as rent on Pent Farm. Incidentally, Conrad carried the debt for at least another eight years, long past the time when he could have afforded to pay it. The significant element was, very possibly, reluctance to lose his hold on Ford.

On March 27, in the midst of his imbroglio with Methuen over its contract, Conrad gave Ford a detailed explanation of his finances. Conrad indicates he can see his way to paying only the £40 interest in six or seven months. He says Pinker has closed down on him, except against copy, and will remain obdurate until he, Conrad, settles the debt with *Chance* and his present novel, which he hopes to complete by September. He mentions Marwood, who had almost died of illness, and tells Ford to hold off Marwood, neglecting the intense personal situation between those two as the result of Elsie's charges against the latter. In effect, Conrad gave Ford a firm no about payment at this time, but assured it within twelve months. The letter, rather incredibly, is breezy, the tone friendly, and Conrad closes with " 'Excellency—a few goats,' " Kemp's line from *Romance*, which the collaborators thought was the best thing in the book.

Conrad kept up his friendships with Douglas, who was now assistant editor at *The English Review*, and with Francis Warrington Dawson, who had written an encomium of Conrad for *The New York Times*. Conrad spent long hours over Dawson's manuscripts and placed "The Sin" with Douglas at the *Review*. From the biographical point of view, the relationship with the author of "The Sin" has as its chief interest the June 20, 1913, letter Dawson elicited from Conrad, a letter which illuminates Conrad's frame of mind when he was working most intensely on *Victory*.

Dawson himself represented a particularly virulent stream of literary endeavor, in that he used moral and political strictures as a way of attacking modern art. Modernism, for Dawson, represented that sick and morbid tradition associated with aestheticism and decadence. He opposed to it his "Fresh Air Art Society," which stood for health—in fact, for fourteen points considered the foundations of "reason and sanity in art." The other members of this group, besides Dawson, included John Powell (pianist and composer), the musicians Benno Moisewitsch, Efrem Zimbalist, and Vernon Warner. They were very much influenced by Teddy Roosevelt, and, philosophically, by Max Nordau and his book *Degeneration* (1895, 1913). Nordau praised Conrad, according to Dawson, and this may have created the impression that Conrad was of his party.

Perhaps hoping to be a latter-day Ruskin, Dawson offered opposition to the degeneration and immorality of the modern movement.* His fourteen points are a mishmash of late-Victorian sanctification and, in fact, offer so many semantic difficulties as to make them unintelligible. Some follow: III.

---

* He was certainly reacting to Marinetti's first "Manifesto of Futurism," published in the Paris *Figaro* on February 20, 1909. Marinetti's pre-Fascist manifesto was as much a political as an aesthetic document. It urged the artist to seek inspiration in contemporary life, to be emancipated from traditional forms (museums, libraries, etc.), and to maintain contempt for the prevailing nature of society and its corresponding conception of art. Conrad would find futurism as equally unacceptable as Dawson's Bull Moose heartiness.

"We believe in the Eternity of Art as standing for Life." V. "Before the End [of art] can be conceived, Life must be understood." VI. "Before Life can be understood its responsibilities must be acknowledged." VII. "That the End pursued by Art's means may be true, the Life which Art represents must be true." And XIV. "Wherefore we declare ourselves for the Art as for the Life which rest upon a respect for Nature's laws in the Fresh Air of Health and the clear Light of Truth."

When asked to join, Conrad refused. From his response, which is a defense of art, we see how sadly Dawson misread Conrad's disenchantment with modernism; how completely he failed to see that Conrad's disillusionment with the contemporary scene sustained his sense of conflict, indeed, fed his art and was ultimately translated into individual forms and techniques. While being kind to his new friend, Conrad correctly interpreted this view, the very view that made it difficult for writers like Conrad or James to find an audience, as adolescent, as missing the nature of art altogether.

Conrad began his response by saying that if these points referred to music alone, he would sign the declaration, since music is not representative; but since the manifesto is aimed at all art, he cannot agree. He does not believe in the oneness of life but "in its infinite variety." He says: "And if you tell me that I am a shallow person thinking of forms and not of essence, I will tell you that this is all we have got to hold on to—that form is the artist's (and the scientist's) province, that it is all we can understand (and interpret or represent) and that we can't tell what is behind." Next, Conrad goes after the ambiguities and indefiniteness of the terms; for him, the "Eternity of" something meant nothing. There were only particulars: "As to the Eternity of Art—I don't suppose it is more or less eternal than the earth itself. I can't believe in the eternity of art any more than in the eternity of pain or eternity of love (subjects of art, those) whose emotions art (and of all arts music) brings home to our breasts."

Conrad then winds around to the very points he had already suggested in his Preface, that art is long and life is short: "Art for me *is* an end in itself. Conclusions are not for it. And it is superior to science, in so far that it calls on us with authority to behold! to feel! whereas science at best can only tell us—it seems so!"

Conrad is quick to explain that he does not deny the *fact* of evolution. He insists, however, that the "truth of life" does not lie in evolution. The "truth of life" is, in fact, "too vague an expression to link art's achievement to." And then Conrad comes to the very motif that compels his art: "For me the artist's salvation is in fidelity, in remorseless fidelity to the *truth of his own sensations.* Hors de là, point of salut."

He tries to soften his opposition by agreeing that both he and Dawson aim at sincerity; but he acknowledges that their differences are great. He skirts the ambiguities of sincerity and what it means artistically by returning to his moral imperatives; he repeats that he believes in the "responsibilities of *conduct.*" But it is *his* responsibility, not Life's, which he acknowledges. He insists on the artist's individuation; he rejects general principles. Toward that end, he finds the question of health in Point VIII amusing:

> Unless esoteric one must take it medically. Why insist upon if I may [sic] so the obvious unless for the sake of the street? Sound body (which includes nerves, heart, liver and mind) is just as necessary for the pursuit of burglary or for digging ditches as for the pursuit of art. And let me remind you that almost every new effort of art has morbidity, unhealthiness thrown at it like a brickbat. It is the moral attitude of the Philistines.

With that, we recognize how central Conrad considered himself in the "traditions of the new." For his art, as he recognized, would outrage those who, implicit in Dawson's statement, refused experimentation, sought their models always from the past, and used history and historical models as a way of denying what they found difficult to comprehend.

In the final part of the letter, as he continues this line of argument, Conrad showed familiarity with Robert Buchanan's attack on Rossetti in "The Fleshly School of Poetry" and with Rufus Griswold's memoir of Poe.

> There are millions of perfectly healthy people who are stupid, for whom all art other than oleograph reproduction is morbid. There are sound minds of quite unspeakable meanness of view in matters of art. Creative minds too—or at any rate critical. I am thinking now of a Buchanan barking at certain painters—of an atrocious life of E. A. Poe written by a man professing himself to be his friend. A perfectly sound man in the average cant of the day. *Truth* you say. Well, Truth it is! The soundness of art is not the soundness of a game. Suffering is an attribute almost a condition of greatness, of devotion, of an altogether self-forgetful sacrifice to that remorseless fidelity to the truth of his own sensations at whetever [sic] cost of pain or contumely which for me is the whole Credo of the artist.

Conrad expected to be misunderstood, even reviled. Like D. H. Lawrence in this respect,* he very consciously set himself against the public he hoped to reach and even transform. While his fidelity to the truth of his own sensations was less didactic than Lawrence's predictions of decline and dissolution, the two writers were on a similar course in their recognition that the "modern voice" was the enemy in the eyes of the philistines, and that their own "fidelity," however one interpreted it, could only survive through relentless personal pressure. Conrad's conscious sense of his "mission" and of the nature of his art was as powerful and intense in 1913 as it had been in 1897–98. As he moved into the second half of *Victory,* the final 50–75,000 words, he was not a man losing control over his art but a writer intent upon

* Conrad characterized Lawrence, to Jacob Epstein, as having started well and then gone wrong, as writing "Filth. Nothing but obscenities."

making his art an expression of a distinctive voice. He had found sufficient mental and physical energy to reexpress what was for him the sole note of survival in a world now heading toward a major conflagration: that expression of personal responsibility which, while it might lead to loss of life, nevertheless preserved the integrity of the self.

CHAPTER 32

Craft or Courage, Which?

WITH Alfred Knopf's encouragement, Conrad began to think of a uniform edition of his work, which meant a tremendous amount of consolidation of other copyrights. His publishers in America alone included Appleton; Dodd, Mead; Putnam; Scribner's; Harpers; Macmillan; as well as Doubleday. Even though Doubleday for the time remained vague, Conrad was encouraged that his fourteen volumes could become a kind of treasure trove that would, he told Galsworthy, "leave something for the boys to finish their education with." He fantasized about selling 20,000 sets, with his share ten shillings per set. He felt, however, that Pinker had "no dynamic quality" and would not sufficiently push the idea with Doubleday. "If a thing is put under his nose he will of course get hold of it—but not otherwise." Conrad sensed his salvation lay there, and he asked Galsworthy to jog the memory of the young assistant (Knopf) in Doubleday's firm. He feared that the whole idea was simply Knopf's way of "taking me up" and not a publisher's plan as such.

The latter replied that his idea went further than personal liking, that there was a real chance Doubleday would take Conrad up for an edition. Knopf, in fact, demonstrated his continued support by urging Doubleday to publicize *Chance* so as to push it toward a broader audience. Conrad wrote his new admirer at great length, the old author feeling out the plans of an extremely young man who could so affect his fortunes. Conrad was very defensive, having long felt that publishers underestimated him, and his dealings with Unwin and later Methuen had not encouraged him. He indicated he was attracted by Doubleday's interest, but his books had been available for some time: ". . . the fact remains that Mr. Doubleday might have had all my books up to date in his hands if he had cared. Other people bought them and I haven't heard that they have been ruined by it; though I did not give away my work for ten cents a volume, I can assure you. I am not an amateur who plays at it. It's anything but play to me."

Conrad argues that he has been taken up by publications which cater to popular tastes and that he has received a good American press:

> When it comes to popularity I stand much nearer the public mind than Stevenson who was superliterary, a conscious virtuoso of style; whereas the average mind does not care much for virtuosity. My point of view, which is purely human, my subjects which are not too specialised as to the class of people or kind of events, my style, which may be clumsy here and there, but is perfectly straightforward and tending toward the colloquial, can not possibly stand in the way of a larger public. As to what I have to say—you know that it is never outrageous to mind or feeling. Is it interesting? Well, I have been and am being translated into all the European languages, except Spanish and Italian. They would hardly do that for a bore.

He feels, withal, he is an investment for a publisher. Nevertheless, he dismisses a hit-or-miss association; what he has achieved, he has done without any publisher's efforts. He suspects Doubleday has bought two books and intends to go no further. At this stage of his life, he tells Knopf, he is wary of publishers and yet would like to consolidate his work now sprayed over half a dozen houses. He was willing to cooperate by supplying updated biographical detail and even a portrait, a great concession on his part, as he disliked personal photographs intensely. He informs Knopf that Richard Curle has proposed a short study of his work—exactly what is needed to "educate readers"—and he would like some commitment of interest from Doubleday for such a work. Very clearly, Conrad was shaping his career and managing the new group of young men around him, as he had "used" Marguerite Poradowska and Edward Garnett earlier.

Conrad had still another proposal, and a perceptive one from an exploitive point of view. He asked Doubleday to buy *A Personal Record* from Harpers, who were not doing anything with the book after having sold two thousand copies. Conrad felt it was being wasted, and if Doubleday purchased it, the book could go in a cheap edition for publicity purposes as: *A Personal Record, by J. Conrad. The Story of His First Book and of His First Contact with the Sea.* From that, he says, "people will be able to learn a lot about me." With shrewd business instincts, Conrad agreed to forgo royalties for three years on that book, unless it were to come out as part of the uniform edition. His scheme was clear, to get himself before the public with two "preparatory" works: Curle's critical study and his own autobiographical memoir. After that, as a follow-up, a uniform edition would find its level. This packaging of his career suggests a side of Conrad which he normally disguised. He overtly detested commercialism, and yet he felt, in his neglect, that large numbers of readers simply had not had the opportunity to be exposed to him. In nearly all aspects, his plans took effect. Curle's book, the first full-length analysis, *Joseph Conrad: A Study,* was published by Doubleday in 1914, and gradually, the publisher moved toward a uniform edition.

Conrad followed up this letter with still another one to Knopf, on August 24, publicizing Curle's study as a serious attempt by a serious writer, not simply puffery. "You don't seem to realize that a book about Conrad *will* get published anyhow." He then moves to an interesting issue, his positioning of stories for his volumes, a matter of considerable importance for him now as he moved toward a final arrangement of his career. He felt that the "Falk" volume failed in America because "Typhoon" was removed from the volume as it had appeared in England (*Typhoon and Other Stories*):

> I don't shovel together my stories in a haphazard fashion. "Typhoon" belonged to that volume; on artistic and literary grounds; and its absence ruined the chances of the other stories. The reading of that first story attuned the mind for the reception of the others. And the public by neglecting "Falk" and the others recognized obscurely that the volume had its head off—that it was a corpse which, I fear, you will have some trouble to galvanize into any sort of popularity. There's no harm in trying. But you must be careful not to put people off by forcing on them work of which the quality is not so much on the surface. Later on they will understand me better and recognize the artistic finish of "Falk" and of "Amy Foster"—two of the most highly finished of my stories.

The present, summer of 1913, saw Conrad turning over the galleys of *Chance* for a late-fall publication date, which would be postponed to January 1914. This took most of the month of June, while "Dollars" or *Victory* was stalled. Part of the difficulty with *Chance*, as Conrad told Pinker, rested with the first chapter, which rightfully belonged to another novel, "which will never be written now I guess." That first conception, as we saw, was of a "Dynamite ship" story, tentatively called "Explosives." This split between elements, the part begun in 1905, picked up year by year, and finally reworked intensively in 1911–12, would partially account for the convoluted narrative, the unnecessary doubling of names, the extreme difficulty in moving out of backgrounds into foreground. At the end of June, with *Chance* now off to the publisher, Conrad could turn to *Victory*, for which he had about 70,000 words.

That month, June 1913, was a crucial meeting point of several elements. On numerous occasions, Conrad had had to gather strength for a critical surge, or else succumb to immediate distress, whether physical or psychological. In June of 1913, he was facing in several directions and he could easily have chosen a more relaxing route to follow. He had promised "Dollars" to Dent in mid-August, at the latest. He could have damaged it severely by cutting it short and bringing it in at just over 75,000 words. This would have meant revision of the earlier parts, but that would have taken far less time than the full working out, which consumed another year.

In another way, he sensed a ground swell of interest in him, not only critically in England, France, and America, but popularly as well. Publishers were nibbling at him; and he could have churned out popular romance or adventure. There was still a considerable market for sea stories, as we see from Conrad's angry response to Methuen's request for just this kind of material. Since he was professional enough to throw off fiction that was no longer dependent on memory, he could have played the more popular markets for easy money, or else turned out articles and essays on his past, a more popular follow-up to his reminiscences, vignettes of Poland and France and the like. As a figure of mystery, he commanded interest. As we see, when Bertrand Russell met him in September, Conrad exerted a tremendous personal "mystique," which he could have packaged and sold well.

Further, he retained Pinker, even when more advanced and energetic marketing ideas were turning lesser authors into best sellers who commanded high prices. Personally, he could have moved into society. As his correspondence with Lady Ottoline Morrell suggests, he could have been taken up in high social circles and tried to advance his popularity through personal contacts.* He might also have attached himself to several of the literary subgroups forming in the 1910s, many of which overlapped—Bloomsbury, Ford's circle, those around Pound and Eliot—as D. H. Lawrence moved in and out before rejecting all of them. Through Ford, he had a way in, or through Pound, who knew his work well and later corresponded with Eliot over use of an epigraph from Conrad for *The Waste Land.*

The pressures on Conrad to abandon his distinctive mode of working were considerable. Yet in the name of his own brand of art, he resisted, even when he sensed his powers were failing. The reward for this June crisis was an attack of gout, which he described to Arthur Symons on August 2: enervation, lack of inspiration, languor, and a brain that felt like yeast. John Quinn, who was habitually out of phase with Conrad, took this very poor time to invite him to the United States. Conrad declined "sorrowfully," because of poor health and neglected work. It was the beginning of Quinn's futile eleven-year quest to meet Conrad.

On September 10, Bertrand Russell, through Lady Ottoline Morrell's efforts to bring the two together, took the train down to Capel House to see

* On July 23, for example, he wrote how delighted he would be if she happened to find herself in his part of the country; but he could rest easily—she would not. Even so, he warned her he is not interesting, "a little wearied, a little dulled"—this in the event she wanted to pick him up as something new and exciting. Then he declined her invitation to call on her. "For me going to town c'est toute une affaire. And then I am really very busy all the time . . . the elasticity of youth gone by now and obliged to fall back on dogged application to the task." Nevertheless, sometime during the summer she visited Capel House. Her means of meeting Conrad were by way of Henry James, who reluctantly acted as intermediary. When Bertrand Russell visited Conrad for the first time in September, she very possibly accompanied him.

Conrad. The visit was preceded by a letter, which Conrad answered, telling Russell not to bicycle down but to come via Charing Cross to Hamstreet, with a change in Ashford. This was a different kind of visit altogether from what Conrad usually experienced, for Russell was coming with the expectations of meeting a sage, not simply a novelist. He had himself been involved in his work with Alfred North Whitehead on the *Principia Mathematica*, the three volumes of which were published in 1910, 1912, and 1913. Prior to that, he had published alone *Principles of Mathematics*, in 1903, and several other works, including a study of Leibnitz's philosophy and a series of philosophical essays. His work with Whitehead was to become the cornerstone of mathematical logic, in which he treated logic and mathematics as one and attempted to deduce the whole of pure mathematics from a small number of logical axioms. His work, which is inaccessible to the layman, would appear to be precisely the kind of thing that Conrad, with his hatred of academic thought and dislike of academics, had avoided. Russell at the time was a fellow of the Royal Society and a lecturer at Trinity, where he had excelled in mathematics and obtained a first in philosophy.

But behind the tremendous accomplishment and the confidence of his privileged birth, Russell was a man walking a thin edge. In 1915, two years later, when Russell was forty-three years old, D. H. Lawrence wrote to Lady Ottoline Morrell that what "ails Russell is, in matters of life and emotion, the inexperience of youth. He is, vitally, emotionally, much too inexperienced in personal contact and conflict, for a man of his age and caliber. It isn't that life has been too much for him, but too little. Tell him [Russell and Lady Ottoline were having an affair] he is not to write lachrymose letters to me of disillusion and disappointment and age: that sounds like 19, almost like David Garnett [Edward's son, then twenty-three]. . . . Really, he is too absurdly young in his pessimism, almost juvenile."

Although Lawrence misread Russell, and tried foolishly to "capture" him as Sir Joshua Malleson in *Women in Love*, along with Lady Ottoline as Hermione, he did observe a side of Russell that needed support. Like Mill (his godfather), Russell sensed a gigantic intellect floating free of real purpose, a drift toward nothingness. What he sought in Conrad was some sense of purpose, for he surely did not need intellectual stimulation. Russell wrote about their strange meeting, as though the two men were Platonic halves coming together for the first time.

> My relation to Joseph Conrad was unlike any other that I have ever had. I saw him seldom, and not over a long period of years. In the outworks of our lives, we were almost strangers, but we shared a certain outlook on human life and human destiny, which, from the very first, made a bond of extreme strength. I may perhaps be pardoned for quoting a sentence from a letter that he wrote to me very soon after we had become acquainted. I should feel that modesty forbids the quotation except for the fact that it

expresses so exactly what I felt about him. What he expressed and I equally felt was, in his words, "A deep admiring affection which, if you were never to see me again and forgot my existence tomorrow, would be unalterably yours *usque ad finem.*"

Conrad's use of that "family phrase" *usque ad finem*—the words also of Stein in *Lord Jim*—was, as Russell describes it, incantatory, a form of hypnotism:

> At our very first meeting, we talked with continually increasing intimacy. We seemed to sink through layer after layer of what was superficial, till gradually both reached the central fire. It was an experience unlike any other that I have known. We looked into each other's eyes, half appalled and half intoxicated to find ourselves together in such a region. The emotion was as intense as passionate love, and at the same time all-embracing. I came away bewildered, and hardly able to find my way among ordinary affairs.*

This momentary "sharing" did not, of course, extend into an expansive friendship. It resulted, chiefly, in eleven (extant) letters from Conrad—few from Russell survived. The only significant exchange apparently took place when Conrad responded to Russell's book about China, *The Problem of China*, a letter that dates from October 23, 1922. Conrad used the pretext to voice his views of government and the principles of governing, hope for which Russell placed in international socialism.

> I have never [Conrad wrote] been able to find in any man's book or any man's talk anything convincing enough to stand up for a moment against my deep-seated sense of fatality governing this man-inhabited world. After all it is but a system, not very recondite and not very plausible. As a mere reverie it is not of a very high order and wears a strange resemblance to a hungry man's dream of a gorgeous feast guarded by a lot of beadles in cocked hats. But I know you wouldn't expect me to put faith in *any* system. The only remedy for Chinamen and for the rest of us is the change of hearts, but looking at the history of the last 2000 years there is not much reason to expect that thing, even if man has taken to flying—a great "uplift," no doubt, but no great change.

---

* When I visited the ninety-three-year-old Russell in Penrhyndeudraeth, Wales, in 1965, he spoke warmly of Conrad; his memory seemed clear, although he did draw on what he had already written. The following words are approximately his: "Yes, although we met only a few times, Conrad was a very strange man, as you may know. When he spoke rapidly he became extremely volatile, and his speech was unintelligible. He ranted. He considered himself a raconteur and was amusing, if unpredictable, company. But as I say, we saw very little of each other. I have seven [really eleven] letters from him, but only one or two of real worth. I am including some in my autobiography—I hope you have no objection to that [I was editing the Collected Letters]."

Then, utilizing his image from *Lord Jim* of the beetle, as opposed to the butterfly, Conrad adds: Man "doesn't fly like an eagle, he flies like a beetle. And you must have noticed how ugly, ridiculous and fatuous is the flight of a beetle." Russell commented that Conrad's pessimism was closer to the truth than his own "artificial hopes for a happy issue in China" and that events had so far proven Conrad right. Such pessimistic accounts influenced Russell, but he moved to "solutions," whereas Conrad continued to seek ironies and paradoxes. In "Dollars," Lena may be victorious, but hers is a Pyrrhic victory indeed.

This was an exciting interlude, and Conrad was enthusiastic about Russell's personality and mind; but it was only an interlude. He was turning fifty-six, and his mind was set. Russell was seeking direction and wisdom—his life was less than half over—whereas Conrad had fewer than eleven years remaining. The latter had little chance, even if he wished to do so, to alter his course; he was fixed, compass set, barely able to squeeze out of himself every last word that his vision of things afforded.

Waiting for *Chance*, now postponed to early 1914, Conrad continued to play a numbers game with Pinker about "Dollars." On August 21, he spoke of another quarter of the novel to go, but he mentions he is on page 660. With the final manuscript at 1,199 pages, he was only a little more than half finished. Just two days after the Russell visit, on September 10, he attempted to balance several conflicting elements: another story he wished to write ("Because of the Dollars"); a general malaise which precluded steady work; his desire to get on with the Mediterranean novel—his ultimate salvation; his recognition that "Dollars" was far more ambitious than he had foreseen, although he still felt Pinker should not know this. The latter had written asking for a story for the Christmas number of a magazine:

> I have the original subject of Dollars ["Because of the Dollars"] still unused which would do perhaps. But you understand my hesitation. It isn't laziness that holds me back but the conviction that I am just now unfit to do extra work. And I think the novel is too important to put aside at this particular juncture.

Restating his fretful impatience to get on with the Mediterranean novel, he continues:

> I am gone so stale all over that I can't trust myself to do what I most desperately mean to do. It's the beastly fact. Re your letter of this morning. You know how I am situated with this long novel. It has got to be finished soon—and I've been jammed for six weeks with it, all worry and no work. I think I had better stick to what I have in hand now.

Three days later, Conrad indicated he had corrected all 651 pages of manuscript now in typescript and felt ready for Pinker to show the novel to an interested publisher: Doubleday, through the continuing support of Alfred

Knopf. Yet, as he wrote Bertrand Russell, he felt he had wagered his soul to the devil: "seduced by the tempter's gold, I allowed myself to be drawn into 'fixing' a date for delivery of an unfinished novel—for the first time in my life." He had, in fact, just recently permitted *Chance* to be serialized before the novel was completed and his words suggest real anxiety, for *Victory* was not coming easily. On October 10, however, he qualified this "showing" to include only manuscript pages 100 through 300, which would, he believed, produce the best impression. His promise of "a sensational ending to come" indicated he was close to the conclusion, although even at this date the 651 pages he mentions is more than 500 manuscript pages short of the final version. He goes on to say he has not yet settled on a title, but the subtitle will be: "An Island Story." He asks for the return of 430 pages for final preparation.

> I won't [he told Pinker] mess them up too much. But I must settle the name of my hero. *Berg* won't do and I haven't been able as yet to find another name of the proper sonority ["Berg" remains to the end of the manuscript]. I must also compress the opening. A matter of a week or so.

He assured Pinker that publication in America could begin in monthly installments. It did not occur, in fact, until February of 1915, sixteen months later. Conrad conceded that he would accommodate the manuscript to the requirements of serial publication, such as rearranging certain passages in shorter form to achieve greater swiftness. However, such concessions were suitable only for the serial, which Conrad did not consider representative.

By December 10, Conrad indicated he was ready to sell the novel, a work of 100,000 words, still about 40,000 under the completed text. Writing to I. W. Gilmer of the Authors' Syndicate, he tried to generate interest in "Dollars":

> As to synopsis and all that—well, by this time those that approach Conrad ought to know how he writes and what sort of thing he's likely to give them. I can only say that the subject is not European. Neither is it a sea-tale. It's in the East. There's a man and a girl in it with some rascals and other people round them. The subject will be *An Island Story*. A sight of a portion of the M.S.—say 200 typed pages—could be arranged perhaps and that would be a more genuine test than a synopsis. Large human interest I can guarantee for that *is* my quality.

We recognize how even these few words of description try to provide an opening to popularity: an island setting, a couple, some rascals, when the novel survives on tonal variety, not subject matter.

By now, Conrad had realized "Dollars" for what it was becoming, although he continued to fool either himself or Pinker that he could still pull it off within a few weeks. Having interrupted it once again to write a story called "The Assistant" ("The Planter of Malata"), on January 1, 1914, he told Pinker he hoped to finish "Dollars" within the week. Yet on February 4 he admitted neglect of the novel:

> I feel quite ready to tackle the novel for the last long pull. I think the time is ample, and your audacious handling of this opportunity [a premature sale] has made it worth while to get this thing off with a will. As I have been off the novel for the last 3 months I must ask you to send me the type for a few days. I must glance through it before I start again.

As he went in deeper, however, Conrad found the going harder, not easier. These months of impasse, in which he avoided the novel altogether, indicate clearly that the handling was testing his creative powers. On February 19 he wrote Pinker: "That tale is the very devil to manage. It has too many possibilities. It won't be so with the next novel which I have been thinking out for five years at odd times." He repeats his difficulties in a February 21 letter, implicating even the title:

> This matter of the title for the Dollars story (P.M.M.) has been a worry out of all proportions to its importance. It got into the way of my thinking about the novel—and if ever I wanted uninterrupted concentration it is just now. He [the editor] thinks that the title is clumsy no doubt. But that very fact attracts attention. However he may call the thing simply *The Dollars.* Or if he wants something pretty I would suggest *The Spoiled Smile*, which I myself don't like. It is sufficiently misleading to please (the dear public will think it a woman's of course) and I shall manage to ram a phrase about Davidson's smile (alluded to already at the beginning) into the last part of the story when I get the proof.

By this time, in February of 1914, Conrad's fortunes, like those of Europe, were about to undergo a radical change. By then, the reviews of *Chance* had appeared, and this most unlikely novel proved to be the beginning of Conrad's broader appeal, although its sales, somewhat above 13,000 in the first two years of the English edition, do not define best-sellerdom. Unfortunately, the excellent press notices coincided with Henry James's only published comments on Conrad, in the *Times Literary Supplement* for March 19 and April 2, under the title "The Younger Generation." Even before that, however, Conrad's anxiety about the novel was building as he observed repeated postponement of the publication date, first from 1913, then to January 10 of 1914, finally to January 15. To each of his friends, he nervously announced the delay. His correspondence was hurried and perfunctory—two letters to Bertrand Russell, who made another visit; several to Warrington Dawson, who came down frequently; a curious letter to John Millais, saying they could have a game of chess, if Millais did not mind playing with a man who "has forgotten all the openings he ever knew (not many)." The buildup of worry and apprehension led, as we see from his letter to Graham on January 23, to a "beastly bout of gout," which laid him up for a week. The information is accompanied by a postscript, that he hopes Graham finds "Chance tolerable. I don't."

Although *Chance*, more than most Conrad novels, seems focused on external data—various swindlers who operated in London in the 1890s and the early years of the new century*—the novel is, nevertheless, a familiar part of the Conradian landscape. It is his own story, as much as *Under Western Eyes* was an expression of his own inner drama. The profusion of narrative detail, which James criticized as a "prolonged hovering," was in fact a means of setting up those layers of disguise which Conrad needed before he could unravel the psychological detail of his drama. The core story, once one peels away the layers, is of Flora de Barral, who survives the situation of her childhood experience only because she is too young to comprehend what is occurring to her. "She stood, a frail and passive vessel into which the other [her governess] went on pouring all the accumulated dislike for all her

* Warrington Dawson in his "13 Years—13 Windows" speaks at length of the famous Humbert case of 1902 and 1903 as the basis for de Barral's swindles in *Chance.* Dawson says that by 1911 Conrad already knew a good deal about the case, which was well reported in the Parisian and London press, but still questioned him (Dawson) lengthily about details. Dawson had himself attended the hearings before the Paris Assizes and is quite insistent that Conrad's de Barral is a fusion of the Humbert husband-and-wife team, Frédéric and Thérèse. Dawson's case for these particular models—based on Thérèse's claim to being an heiress and their mutual admission that their safe contained 100,000,000 francs in securities—is strengthened by the presence of a helpless daughter, who was the source of some sympathy in the press.

Conrad, however, was an author who worked by composites and hybrids. He blended, molded, and fitted pieces together according to the needs of his imagination, which Dawson little understood. More likely, he drew on a profusion of sources, although in what degree of each we cannot determine. Certainly, the period from 1895 to 1905 was rich in swindling schemes. Jocelyn Baines and Thomas Moser mention, among others, Jabez Balfour, Horatio Bottomley, and Whitaker Wright. Almer Vallance has an entire book on the subject, *Very Friendly Enterprise, an Anatomy of Fraud and High Finance* (1955), many of whose cases became notorious through press coverage. Conrad purposely kept de Barral's past murky—perhaps suggesting some vague Semitic cast on the French side—so that he seems to have arisen from nowhere with that single "genius," his power drive for money. Professor Moser (*Conradiana*, VII, 3, pp. 209 ff.) makes out a good case for Whitaker Wright, whose story was publicized in the London newspapers in January 1904. Both Wright and de Barral manipulated accounts and balance sheets, drove up stock prices and collected monies long after they knew their securities were worthless. The only difficulty with this patterning of cases is that all large financial swindles contain overlapping elements; they depend on common factors, of price manipulation, doctored balance sheets, and artificially driven-up stock prices. Basically, all swindles and embezzlements work on a few simple ideas, first the creation of trust and then the exploitation of that trust until the bubble bursts. That is why, ingenious as these examples prove to be, Conrad needed little more than some superficial knowledge of financial matters; for the rest his own experience was sufficient.

pupils," for the accumulated frustration of her own existence. The governess had "been living half strangled for years," and her sole outlet, now, was to vent hatred on Flora.

As the youngest and frailest, Flora has no one to pass it on to; she becomes the receptacle of all those errors and wrong turns taken by the adults around her. "Look!" Conrad says. "Even a small child lives, plays and suffers in terms of its conception of its own existence. Imagine, if you can, a fact coming in suddenly with a force capable of shattering that very conception itself. It was only because of the girl being still so much of a child that she escaped mental destruction; that, in other words, she got over it. Could one conceive of her more mature, while still as ignorant as she was, one must conclude that she would have become an idiot on the spot—long before the end of the experience."

Whereas Conrad as a child fell into recurring illnesses which necessitated irregular school attendance and constant home care, Flora has no one close enough to her from whom to elicit that kind of attention. The consequence is that she must deal with the twists of her situation alone, and for that she turns to suicide as a solution, the sole solution for *her*. Thwarted at the very edge of a precipice by Marlow, who comes along unexpectedly, she eventually finds her salvation by going to sea, with Captain Anthony. Her career is to be a sea captain's wife, although she withdraws from sexual contact on their first voyage. Conrad conceives of her not as Antigone but as Iphigenia, the girl-child sacrificed to her father's will to power. Conrad's sympathy here is not only for the child but for the girl; he understands the nature of parental power, even when as in his own instance disaster came along with kindness. Conrad's view of stern fate was Greek: if she is a sacrifice, nevertheless, other fateful forces are already awaiting the father. "Yet it is so true that the germ of destruction lies in wait for us mortals, even at the very source of our strength, that one may die of too much endurance as well as of too little of it."

The essential element for Conrad's purpose was the creation of a man without character, virtually a man without a shadow. De Barral's entire purpose is to be the obverse of his money scheme, that is, not to have any substance of his own. He is a mirror image of a man, a reflection of a person, whose daughter is ironically named Flora. She may later flower, but he is not even a weed. That sense of facelessness which Conrad repeats throughout the novel is a necessary ingredient, for it is the insubstantiality, the conning nature of modern life itself. In that respect, de Barral is a representative man.

The core story, however, is a tale of salvation. Flora herself is first "saved" by the Fynes; she is further saved by Anthony, Mrs. Fyne's brother; she, in turn, saves de Barral, when he is released from prison; and finally, she saves Anthony—and indirectly the Fynes' trust in her—from de Barral when he attempts to poison her husband. The "salvation," such as it is, moves cyclically, and it has that same kind of circular movement we have observed in Conrad's childhood as he "circled" from benefactors to relatives and back. Flora is a human yo-yo, a type of maneuver Conrad understood perfectly. Fittingly, her ultimate salvation from the forces of evil on land occurs on board the *Ferndale,* an Edenesque setting, a Garden where Flora can blossom into maturity. The use of the ship and sea as Eden, where Flora saves Anthony (in the newspaper account of the Humbert case the daughter's name is listed as "Eve"), has within it Conrad's familiar myth: sea as savior, land as bedevilment. The *Ferndale* episode includes an attempt at poisoning—de Barral is the serpentine figure—but the deception is discovered, and Flora swears fidelity to a new master, Anthony, by throwing off the poisoned cloak of her father.

This "victory" of Flora is analogous to Lena's own "victory" in the novel Conrad was writing while he altered the galleys of *Chance.* These triumphs by women with symbolic names—Alma or Lena, or Magdalen; Flora or blossom; plus the presence of Mrs. Fyne, a transparent name—would indicate Conrad's responsiveness to something very positive about women, both socially and fictionally. Rather than calling him a misogynist in this period, that is, by transferring Marlow's statements to him, we find Conrad trying to reflect sympathetically the current conflicts of women, who were then so much in the news as they sought the vote just before the war.

One reason Conrad stayed with such a complicated narrative, even after he revised the manuscript thoroughly, was that he needed disguises. In this era of the "new novel"—Joyce, Lawrence, Woolf hovering expectantly over the scene—the technique was an attempt to find the narrative equivalent of the "secret self." He was solidly in the modern mode: that quest after impersonality which would disguise the intimately personal.* One of the reviewers, in fact, C. E. Montague, of *The Manchester Guardian,* understood Conrad's method far more profoundly than did James in his criticism of the novel. Montague wrote:

> In *Chance* he carries it [the storytelling method] further than ever. He keeps out of sight; he hides behind one man at first and then puts a second

* Although Conrad did not respond directly to Henri Bergson's work, he would surely have had some sense of its impact, which by 1910 was quite intense. In any event, his work on *Chance* indicated he was attempting to grapple with Bergson's warnings, close to his own sense of things, that the logical mind created continuity where none really existed; that this logical mind shaped mechanistic theories of existence because it had no other way of dealing with life; and that, besides this mechanistic impulse, there was another which tried to understand vital phenomena. Conrad's way of handling this discrepancy between the logical and intuitive was by means of a narrative frame (the logical sequencing) which distanced the fragile inner core that palpitates according to a mode of existence unknown to the Powells, Marlows, and Fynes, who hover on the outside.

in front of the first, and perhaps a third in front of the second. Some shadowy figure of a narrator opens the tale and then melts into the dimness behind it and lets the bulk of it come as a tale told by one of the persons whom he has mentioned, and this second narrator, in turn, hands over the job, for a time, to one of his own creatures. So that the core of the story is, in one sense, like a picture within a frame which itself is painted—it is within a frame too, and that frame within another, again. As the story of Flora de Barral draws to an end this coil is unwound; each discarded narrator comes back to his place—in inverse order, of course,—and the shadowy first narrator puts in a last word. It is like one of those algebraical uses of bracket within bracket, even to three or four brackets of various shapes, or like a child's set of concentric boxes, each with its own colour.

We note how Conrad's notices were no longer simply reviews but literary criticism. Montague understood that what Conrad was seeking in narrative technique was some equivalent of the verbal stream of consciousness. Because of his peculiar relationship to the English language, Conrad was incapable of that kind of experimentation which led to the ultimate stream; but, intuitively, he was moving toward the same end that the stream was to serve: that sense of discontinuity between internal feeling and external data which characterizes human consciousness.

When James wrote about *Chance*, he pursued a self-serving thesis, and the Conrad novel fitted his particular need at that moment. In order to call attention to his own novelistic techniques, James attacked an entire generation of writers, new, younger, and otherwise, as having separated matter from method. This was, with suitable differences, a foreshadowing of Virginia Woolf's Cambridge talk on the Wells-Bennett generation. The exception to this thesis, evidently, was Conrad; and James could only prove the validity of his idea by pointing out that Conrad, in his way, overdid it. James's words are very witty in that characteristic manner he had of mocking even as he praised.

It [Conrad's method] places Mr. Conrad absolutely alone as a votary of the way to do a thing that shall make it undergo most doing. The way to do it that shall make it undergo least is the line on which we are mostly now used to see prizes carried off; so that the author of *Chance* gathers up at least two sorts—that of bravery in absolutely reversing the process most accredited, and that, quite separate, we make out, of performing the manoeuvre under salvos of recognition. It is not in these days often given to refinement of design to be recognised, but Mr. Conrad has made his achieve that miracle—save in so far indeed as the miracle has been one thing and the success another.

James continues, now, with his reversal, that the rarity of the Conrad effort is compromised by its being too much "done." We catch James's use of the word "wantonly," which adds a risible dimension to the whole enterprise, as if Conrad were perpetrating some sexual excess.

> What concerns us is that the general effect of "Chance" is arrived at by a pursuance of means to the end in view contrasted with which every other current form of the chase can only affect us as cheap and futile; the carriage of the burden or amount of service required on these lines exceeding surely all other such displayed degrees of energy put together. Nothing could well interest us more than to see the exemplary value of attention, attention given by the author and asked of the reader, attested in a case in which it has had almost unspeakable difficulties to struggle with—since so we are moved to qualify the particular difficulty Mr. Conrad has "elected" to face; the claim for the method in itself, method in this very sense of attention applied, would be somehow less lighted if the difficulties struck us as less consciously, or even call it less wantonly, evoked.

James asserted that Conrad's multiplication of narrators or "producers" made them almost more numerous and "more material than the creatures and the production itself." Rather than losing the agents of the method in the characters, James suggests, the reader pays attention to the agents and loses the characters. James then evokes a telling image for Conrad's plan, in the figure of Marlow in a "prolonged flight of the subjective over the outstretched ground of the case exposed." James continues: "We make out this ground but through the shadow cast by the flight, clarify it though the real author visibly reminds himself again and again that he must—all the more that, as if by some tremendous forecast of future applied science, the upper aeroplane causes another, as we have said, to depend from it and that one still another; these dropping shadow after shadow, to the no small menace of intrinsic colour and form and whatever, upon the passive expanse." The critique itself reads like a parody, and Conrad may have sensed mockery.

Conrad, James adds, has steeped the entire matter in "perfect eventual obscuration as we recall no other artist's consenting to with an equal grace." James now tips his hand: that Conrad having learned his lessons is solidly encamped on Jamesian ground, but overdoing it. James observes that the technique is not imposed from the nature of the materials but forced out from within some "mystic impulse." He then slides Conrad into one of his witty metaphors, of his narrative being handed on as buckets of water needed to extinguish a fire.

> His [Conrad's] genius is what is left over from the other, the compromised and compromising quantities—the Marlows and their determinant inventors and interlocutors, the Powells, the Franklins, the Fynes, the tell-tale little dogs, the successive members of a cue from one to the other of which the sense and the interest of the subject have to be passed on together, in the manner of the buckets of water for the improvised extinc-

> tion of a fire, before reaching our apprehension: all with whatever result, to this apprehension, of a quantity to be allowed for as split by the way.

The spectacle is of an imaginative faculty in search of its materials, a "beautiful and generous mind at play in conditions comparatively thankless."

The long notice by James brought Conrad considerable grief, if we can credit his comments to Quinn fully two years later:

> The only time he did me the honour of speaking of me in print (about 2 years ago) he confined himself to the analysis of method which he rather airily condemned in relation to the method of two young writers. I may say, with scrupulous truth that this was the *only* time a criticism affected me painfully. But in our private relations he has been always warmly appreciative and full of invariable kindness. I had a profound affection for him. He knew of it and he accepted it as if it were something worth having. At any rate that is the impression I have. And he wasn't a man who would pretend.

The immediate notices of *Chance* were of a different kind. No matter how contemptuous or condescending Conrad felt toward the popular press, he could not be indifferent to reviewers who approached him as though he were a deity. Montague, who had been educated to the techniques of the new by precisely such writers as Conrad, ended his notice with the statement that the author of *Chance* was one of the masters. In other reviews, Conrad was repeatedly cited as a gifted and original writer, as a great architect of fiction, as a remarkable author, his novel comparable with *Lord Jim* and *Nostromo*, as coming nearer wizardry than workmanship. The only less than ecstatic notice came from Edward Garnett, writing in the *Nation.* Refusing to be railroaded, Garnett admitted Conrad's ability to spin an "exquisite artistic web" out of bits and pieces, but cited the method of telling the story as "occasionally a trifle artificial." We might note that by this time, Conrad's reviewers were often personal friends: Meldrum (from Blackwood days); Curle, who had just finished his study of Conrad; Sidney Colvin, an intimate; and as ever, Garnett.

Conrad wrote Garnett four days after his review appeared (on January 28) to thank him for identifying his weaknesses. Conrad indicated he was delighted to be so well understood, although it is doubtful if at this pivotal stage in his career he sought anything but support. Arnold Bennett wrote in praise, which he evidently felt, as his Journal entries show considerable envy. Meanwhile, *Munsey's Magazine* bought the serial of *Victory*, on the basis of the 75,000 words written, this by February 17. "The Planter of Malata" was taken up by the *Metropolitan Magazine* for its June-July numbers, and "Because of the Dollars" was accepted by the same journal for September publication. By mid-February, Conrad learned that seven printings of

Chance, about 12,000 copies, had already been sold, what he called "something fabulous."*

He awaited American publication by Doubleday on March 26: "The peace of my future years [he wrote Dawson], the fate of the children hangs in the balance—for I can't write forever and there is not much time left to pursue fortune to follow up a first success!" Lady Ottoline wrote praising *Chance,* using it as a pretext to set up an invitation, but Conrad begged off until April: "I am a slave—the slave of the desk. If I ever do break the unholy spell for a moment I shall most assuredly make for your doorstep." He resisted heroically being added to her collection. A dimmer voice from the past, Elsie Hueffer's, called to Conrad about *Chance;* but, as he had so many times, he put her off gently with his "enormous difficulty" over a very long novel. It was true, but proved a good excuse anyway.

Except for an attack upon Tolstoy's Christian base—"distasteful to me"†—Conrad seemed relatively serene as he settled into the long task of completing *Victory.* He had come up with neither a title nor a name for his major character. For the entire spring of 1914, he devoted himself to the completion of the novel, and he evidently felt secure enough about his renewed abilities that he wrote nothing to Pinker. At the end of May, he foresaw the conclusion, sending on about "half of the rough type of the *Island Story.*"

The rush to finish was according to an inner timetable, as if Conrad sensed a vast upheaval that would knock his "victory" to pieces. As an Eastern European, unlike the English, he knew that world upheavals did not readily sort themselves out. On June 29, he mentioned he expected to do the rest by the fourteenth (of July), and he was evidently speaking of a corrected typescript. For on July 1, still to Pinker, he indicated "Victory" as the title

* Nevertheless, his pleasure was mixed: "How I would have felt about it ten or eight years ago [he wrote Galsworthy] I can't say. Now I can't even pretend I am elated. If I had Nostromo, The Nigger or Lord Jim in my desk or only in my head I would feel differently no doubt. As to the commercial side: Methuen made a ridiculous advertising splash (which was jeered at in the provincial press) and in the sixth week stopped advertising. They confess to 12,500 copies printed . . . but how much of that is sold I don't know." One good sign was that Doubleday would bring out, along with *Chance, The Nigger,* under its proper title, thus removing the ludicrous "Children of the Sea" title of the first American publication. Conrad's gratefulness to Alfred Knopf was repeated in a March 27 letter—"I appreciate infinitely the good will towards my work you express so warmly." From an attitude of indifference or condescension toward America, Conrad was to warm considerably in these and later years, especially when America entered the war.

† He added that Christianity starts from an absurd Oriental fable which irritates him. "Great, improving, softening, compassionate it may be but it has lent itself with amazing facility to cruel distortion and is the only religion which, with its impossible standards, has brought an infinity of anguish to innumerable souls—on this earth."

and said he completed the book on "June 20, about." Within the month he and his family would leave for Hamburg, on their way to Poland, reversing his journey west almost forty years earlier, a trip which unfortunately coincided with the outbreak of the First World War. Conrad's idea for the title, "Victory," was appropriate in 1918, perhaps; but in 1914, when the novel was being completed, it could only be taken ironically: the victor dies with a bullet wound in her breast, and the man for whom she has died turns to ashes.

In February 1915, when Conrad had finally recovered from his Polish misadventure, he wrote Pinker the finale on the *Victory* battle between author and material:

> It has been a long job; and your good opinion justifies my proceeding of never having written a line of it unless I felt quite fit and thoroughly in the mood. And that I could allow myself to pursue that course I owe to you. All the time that novel was being written you have been most patient, you met all my requirements and you ultimately obtained a contract [£1,000 for serial rights, £850 for book rights] before the work was finished, thus enabling me to tackle the last third (or more) in the most favourable frame of mind. And the last third was the most difficult.

But he still possessed some humor, even about such a grim struggle, and he told Pinker: "I think *Victory* may make a libretto for a Puccini opera anyhow."

In the summer of 1914, he was a personage, a figure, a famous author, even a man of letters.* He had reached a peak of sorts just before the new generation was to gain its own foothold. Yet even as James passed from the literary scene, and Conrad had himself gained a precarious grasp on the future, his body of work would be challenged by the ferociously new. Ford was meeting them in literary circles, and aiding their careers, Lawrence and Joyce, among

---

* He evidently was feeling expansive enough, early in 1914, to grant one of his few interviews; what made it even more distinctive was that his interrogator was a Polish journalist, Marian Dąbrowski. In the interview, which appeared in May, in the Warsaw *Illustrated Weekly*, Conrad stressed his Polish background. When Dąbrowski indicated he would like to "discover Poland's immortal genius" in the English writer, Conrad responded: "The English critics—since I am in fact an English writer—when discussing me always note that there is something in me which cannot be understood, nor defined, nor expressed. Only you can grasp this undefinable factor, only you can understand the incomprehensible. It is *polskośc* [what Conrad coined as *polonism*], that *polskośc* which I took into my work from Mickiewicz and Słowacki. . . . Do you know why Słowacki? *Il est l'âme de toute la Pologne, lui.*" Conrad's parting words to the interviewer, to be carried back to Poland, were inspirational: "I am neither a great man, nor a prophet. Yet your immortal fire burns in me too. It is small and insignificant, more in the nature of a *lueur* [gleam], but it is there and it persists. When I think of the present political situation, *c'est affreux!* I am unable to think often of Poland, for this is bitter, painful, bad. I

others. Lady Ottoline Morrell, who moved in both camps, the Bloomsbury circle and the Cambridge-Russell group, could have brought Conrad in, had he wished, but he let literary fashion pass him by. Yet what was to burst around him—Joyce's *Portrait,* Lawrence's *Rainbow* and *Women in Love,* Woolf's first fictional efforts, poetry by Pound, Eliot, and Yeats, vorticism, Marinetti's futurism, Dadaism, surrealism—were not at all fashionable but *the* major shift; and Conrad would himself lose esteem and reputation as a consequence of their efforts, although he would not be extinguished. It was a heady time, a period of upheaval, literarily as well as politically; but Conrad lay back, as he would for the remainder of his life.

He was only fifty-six; but constant illness had made him an old man. The recurring bouts of gout were not only painful but discouraging; for they came like Job's punishment. Whenever he felt well, he knew the condition could not last, and he would, sooner or later, have to sustain another disastrous bout. Seen from a distance, his attacks do not seem so catastrophic; but treatment was primitive and tied to diet, which was only partially helpful, since the condition is hereditary and can only be controlled medicinally.

---

could not live! The English, when taking leave, use the expression *Good luck!* I could not say this to you. Yet, despite of everything, faced with the threat of extermination, we will stay alive." It is quite possible that this interview helped Conrad decide to visit Poland in the late summer.

This episode became the first of several which brought Conrad close to his homeland. The visit itself, the 1914 "Political Memorandum," the 1916 "Note on the Polish Problem," and the 1919 piece on "The Crime of Partition," all discussed above, were not the entire story. In early 1915, a committee to aid war victims in Poland was formed under the direction of Sienkiewicz and Paderewski, the pianist who would become prime minister, and Conrad was asked to join. He refused, and in a telegram sent to Paderewski indicated why. "With every deference to your illustrious personality I cannot join a committee where I understand Russian names [Count D. A. de Benckendorff] will appear. Conrad." His reasoning, which he explained in a 1919 interview with Antoni Czarnecki of the Chicago *Daily News,* was that the presence on the committee of the czarist ambassador to Great Britain made his own contribution impossible. This interview, called "An Evening with Conrad," did not appear until July 31, 1924, in a Polish newspaper published in Toledo, Ohio. In his defense, he said:

> Looking at the Polish problem, I could not with good conscience assist the Committee to bring help to Poland with, at my side, one of the arms of the despot who during the whole past had done everything to crush the Polish nation and destroy its ideals, principles, and aspirations. It was not my business to pass judgment on those who organized this Committee. When I noted that the ambassador of Czarist Russia had accepted the membership, I asked the Polish leaders to excuse me for not being able to cooperate.

The final event in this series of episodes came in 1924, when Conrad attended a reception at the Polish embassy in London. When asked to participate in a Literary Association of Friends of Poland, a kind of lobbying outfit, Conrad offered his name but not his active participation. The association was established to gain publicity for Poland in the West, and Conrad's response was fully consistent with his position: not to contribute to propaganda efforts and to reassert that Poland's spirit had always lived in the West and needed no further resurrection (Morf, p. 112).

Those recurring attacks sustained Conrad's personal philosophy, that every period of well-being was only an interim before a period of ailment. His epigraph for *Nostromo* from Shakespeare's *King John*—"So foul a sky clears not without a storm"—had its personal application as well.

On a more professional note, there were the usual blends of satisfactions and disappointments. Curle's book appeared, and received many poor reviews, some of them questioning a study by a friend of the subject. Himself pleased by the book, Conrad tried to console Curle: "I've told you that you would have brickbats thrown at you. You jostle too many people's idols for my sake. But really with the exception of the . . . (a mere impertinence of no authority) the others, I am delighted to see, all recognise your sincerity, your insight, and every other merit of the book." Then, with his own reviews in mind, Conrad added: "Of course the small dogs yap the most. They would have yapped at an angel from heaven likewise—and I don't suppose you are much disturbed by that noise. After all, that too is recognition." Very possibly, Conrad was thinking of Eliza Orzeszkowa's attack, for on his visit to Poland a few months later he feared disregard or scorn from Polish intellectuals of her stripe. When Aniela Zagórska suggested that he read her novel *Nad Niemnem,* he reacted: "Don't bring me anything by that shrew— You don't know about it, but once she wrote me a letter—"

Borys had reached another critical point in his schooling. He had completed his course of study at the Thames Nautical Training College, H.M.S. *Worcester*, and had done fairly well for himself—third to seventh place in classes containing fourteen to eighteen boys. Captain Barker and the headmaster both felt he had made a distinct place for himself, which, as Conrad says, "for a boy not brilliant in school and not very good at games is rather remarkable." Borys was graduated with a first-class leaving certificate in both school and seamanship. But there was a curious drift, or lack of thought, in the way he was being shaped, or in the manner he was being advised. In a certain sense, Conrad appears to have given up on him even as he placed him with a tutor in Norwood who would prepare Borys for matriculation exams on July 1. Of course, Borys's weak eyes had put an end to Conrad's plan of having him serve in the merchant fleet or the Royal Navy. As Borys wrote later: "The wearing of spectacles was, in those days, an insurmountable bar to either." The result of the *Worcester* training was that he had a good degree in something he could not use, and his education up to this point—he was sixteen—had been narrowly nautical.

The tutor was to prepare Borys for the entrance examination at Sheffield University, where he hoped to pursue a degree in engineering. The tutor, however, was not very demanding and he "learned exactly nothing." On the day of the examination, Conrad accompanied his son to Sheffield and waited out the period. On their last evening, Conrad took Borys to a "Variety Show," which astonished the boy, who says he "had serious misgivings as to the outcome." His description suggests an aspect of Conrad one hardly discerns from his fiction:

> The first turn proved to be a troupe of acrobats which he applauded vigorously—he always appreciated exhibitions of skill. An inferior comedian followed, and was glared at in grim silence. Next came a male singer surrounded by a bevy of scantily clad females. This collection was gazed at with an expression of incredulous disgust. Then came the principal turn of the evening: George Robey. I felt sure this would prove too much for him, but the first few jokes appeared to produce no reaction. Then George got into his stride—he was in very good form that night—and the house rocked with laughter and applause. Weird noises began to emerge from the still figure at my side and I braced myself for the sudden and violent exit which I felt to be imminent. Nothing happened and eventually the audience allowed George to leave the stage, the lights went up and I realized that my Father had, in fact, been convulsed with laughter!

Unfortunately, this pleasant family interlude was shattered by the news, shortly afterward, that Borys had failed the examination. With that, the journey to Poland intervened, and he would have to wait for another try.

A certain symbolic justice took shape in the fact that "The Planter of Malata" would appear (in June-July) on the eve of Conrad's trip to Poland. Conrad was such an intuitive writer that his fiction, even if set in the Far East, wove in and out of his own life in strikingly dramatic ways. The story, his last significant shorter fiction, has much in it of his work on *Victory;* and its chief character, Geoffrey Renouard, recalls Axel Heyst.* Not surprisingly, both stories involve suicides, men who fail their women in one way or another. Renouard's failure, however, is quite different from Heyst's and, given Conrad's projected trip to Poland, potentially more interesting. For on the eve of his journey to his homeland, he is represented in English publications by a man trying to awaken a woman who, pursuing her own futile ideal, refuses to acknowledge his love. The woman, ironically named Felicia Moorsom, is seeking a man wrongly suspected of dishonesty and whom now, she feels, she must find and marry to redress her desertion of him. She is questing after some ideal which she no longer believes in, and rejects Renouard, who believes in her.

The parallels are suggestive. As a detached and isolated person—he owns an experimental silk farm on an island in the Far East near a "great colonial city" (Sydney in the manuscript)—Renouard finds that his life must follow a course of solitude and resignation. He deliberately cultivates his apartness and his ability to forsake the desires of other men. Conrad speaks of him as

---

* The epigraph to *Within the Tides* is Hamlet's advice to the players: "Go, make you ready"—which would have been more appropriate for *Victory* and Heyst. That book, strikingly, contained no epigraph and was dedicated to Perceval and Maisie Gibbon.

being familiar with "wide horizons" and of "holding aloof from these agglomerations of units in which one loses one's importance even to oneself." Looking inward, he can find only self-love—in this respect, he is both narcissistic and idealistic—until he sees Felicia, who "seemed to give new meaning to life." His detachment manifestly lessens as her indifference becomes steadily more evident. For she, unable to believe in any man, seeks her fiancé, Arthur, merely as a salve for her own conceit. Her dream, as Renouard suggests, is to influence a human destiny; a man's happiness is not her goal. Recognizing defeat and incapable of drawing on his own depleted resources, Renouard swims out beyond the confines of life.

The story does not possess sufficient intensity or variety for it to become a precise emblem of Conrad's life as he was poised to return to Poland; but it does embrace enough significant detail to give us a sense of him in his fifty-seventh year. The feeling that is awakened in Renouard is unreciprocated, since Felicia is pursuing her own "ideal," a way of redressing what she senses is her lost honor. Into that quest or process, Renouard cannot enter; for she does not permit him to advance. Yet she is for him a supreme challenge, to the extent that he throws away his life when he is rejected. His drowning fits the precise kind of imagery Conrad used in his letters to characterize his own condition. That Felicia is a "fickle mistress," full of self-love, involved in a hopeless quest for lost honor, and yet the repository of Renouard's love, is suitable as a way of observing Conrad's relationship to his homeland. Interested in her fortunes, anxious about her fate, conscious at all times of how she is Europe's pawn, he also viewed her course as fateful and death-laden. To remain on a sinking ship was a matter of honor; to stay on sinking land was fit only for an idealistic Quixote, someone like Apollo. Rejecting Apollo, Conrad had to be wary not to reject Poland; scorning Apollo's politics, Conrad had to be careful not to lose his humanitarian impulse. When Felicia states on three occasions, "I stand for here!" Conrad is confronting the hard fact of what *he* must stand for. If Felicia represents a kind of "truth," no matter how self-serving, then what does Conrad represent in "drowning himself" over her rejection of him?*

---

* Bernard Meyer's psychoanalytic reading of "The Planter," to the exclusion of aesthetic themes in Conrad's life, leads him to compare it with "A Smile of Fortune," as dual stories of Conrad's unhappy experience with Mlle Eugénie Renouf. Comparing the manuscript and published text of the story, with its many emendations, Meyer cites name changes, concealment of place of origin, and other details. From these data, he conjectures that Conrad's fear of women, and his portrayal of strong females who devastate men, were intrinsic to his way of working and inhibited him as a literary artist. The theory, which is ingenious in its utilization of certain details, avoids others, however; and its most serious evasion is of historical context, of Conrad's unique way of dealing with his own crisis. It assumes he remained fixed in an earlier phase, when, in fact, his "strong women" were a necessary part of his literary development in this period. Put another way: the theory confuses the needs of the person and the needs of the artist; so that it fails to take into account the fact that Conrad would transcend in his art what he perhaps failed to deal with in his life.

He prepared for his journey to Poland as though a man in a dream: "In that town (Cracow) one September day in the year 1874 [he wrote Harriet Capes] I got into the train (Vienna Express) as a man gets into a dream—and here is the dream going on still. Only one is conscious that the moment of awakening is drawing close." On the day of departure, Conrad told Galsworthy: "As to this Polish journey I depart on it with mixed feelings." He preferred, he said, to join Galsworthy in Devon. In any event, he expected to return on September 10. Conrad did not need the European political situation as a backdrop to feel apprehensive. By now, he recognized that his salvation lay at the writing table; whenever he left it, even if temporarily, he found disaster. Vigilance was all. The fact that Poland was his destination of course made his uneasiness all the more intense.

From the perspective of the years, it would appear Conrad should be returning in glory, the hometown boy who has made good. He was an internationally known writer,* his work translated into French and Polish, as well as German; the friend of famous authors on both sides of the Atlantic, the subject, even, of a study devoted entirely to his work. While he was not rich, he had done strikingly well, as a sea captain, a married man, the father of two sons, and now an author returning home. But he was returning as Joseph Conrad, whereas he had left as Konrad Korzeniowski. His books were in English, not Polish. And his reputation in his homeland was mixed, caught as he was between the ultra-nationalists and the more broadly based internationalists. Further, his wife was English, and his two children did not speak Polish, and he had himself been under direct attack. In a certain sense, he was sneaking in, since he was coming as a private person, the guest of Retinger's mother-in-law, and not as a public personage.

The political background was auspicious, made to order for Conrad's sense of things. On June 28, the Austrian Archduke Ferdinand was assassinated by a Serbian nationalist in Sarajevo. When Conrad heard about that, he said he thought Europe was full of archdukes and another one would simply step up and fill the place of the dead one. On July 23, two days before the Conrads departed, Serbia received an ultimatum from Austria-Hungary, the first step leading to war. On July 28, the Austro-Hungarian alliance declared war on Serbia, and then Germany declared a state of war with Russia, followed by an invasion of France on August 2. England was not as yet in the conflict.

* His reputation by 1904–5 had extended to Japan, where Professor Tadaichi Hidaka began to read his works as they appeared. Hidaka later wrote Conrad seeking biographical details, and Conrad replied on July 11, 1911. The Japanese professor forwarded an article on Conrad's work and eleven years later visited Conrad at his Oswalds home, on September 3, 1922.

CHAPTER 33

Fortune, not Wisdom, rules the life of man

CONRAD did not place too much worth on the Archduke's assassination, or so he claimed later in "Poland Revisited," for his uneasiness lay elsewhere. To Galsworthy, that faithful repository of his fears, he describes how he wrestled with *Victory*, an enormous pile of manuscript, he says, with the subject the size of a small apple. He called it "Victory" because the fashion was for short titles. And, then, after flinging it out into Pinker's arms, he became "vacant and supine like an idiot and no doubt went about with my mouth open and glazed eyes." In that state, he prepared for his Polish journey:

> You may remember [he told Galsworthy] being called upon some time ago by a young man of the name of Retinger—a Pole with a very pretty Polish girl for wife. They have been to see us several times. The Mother of Mrs. Retinger has invited all the tribe of us to her house in the country some 16 miles from Cracow but over the Russian border. This caused such an excitement in the household that if I had not accepted instantly I would have been torn to pieces by my own wife and children. So we are going for a month certain and six-weeks possible. And we are going today by the sea-route to Hamburg. Jessie has a fancy to be a little sea-sick apparently, and in the present inflamed state of feminine minds [suffragette agitation for the vote] I don't think it would be prudent for me to argue the point. And indeed I am too limp to argue or do anything at all. I shall travel like a bale or a millionaire, Retinger having taken upon himself the duties of courrier.

The Conrads arrived in Cracow on August 1, only hours after Austria announced mobilization of its forces against Serbia. They stayed in the Grand Hotel, in Cracow, which was in Austrian Poland (Galicia). Four years later, to turn there momentarily, Conrad wrote of his activities when he first arrived in Cracow, the juxtaposition of his movements and the thrust of Europe into war providing a typical Conradian irony: the individual attempting to move along the line of his own interests or development while the world follows a separate course. Even as Germany declared war on Russia, Conrad was invited to visit Jagiellońian University and the library, which he had not seen since 1871, and where, it turned out, a good many of his father's manuscripts were housed. They included letters Apollo had written to friends, with references to Conrad himself. That very afternoon, accompanied by Borys, he saw the bundle of letters which the librarian promised to have copied for him. The name of the librarian was Józef Korzeniowski.

The situation was hallucinatory; for even as Conrad delved into the past for childhood references to himself, the city of Cracow was assimilating the mobilization. He heard it as a vast hush.

> I cannot reproduce the atmosphere of that night, the first night after mobilisation. The shops and the gateways of the houses were of course closed, but all through the dark hours the town hummed with voices; the echoes of distant shouts entered the open windows of our bedroom. Groups of men talking noisily walked in the middle of the roadway escorted by distressed women; men of all callings and of all classes going to report themselves at the fortress. Now and then a military car tooting furiously would whisk through the streets empty of wheeled traffic, like an intensely black shadow under the great flood of electric lights on the grey pavement.

For the people who could not leave or claim foreign nationality, the situation was "the awful desolation of men whose country, torn in three, found itself engaged in the contest with no will of its own and not even the power to assert itself at the cost of life." Conrad speculated: "All the past was gone, and there was no future, whatever happened; no road which did not seem to lead to moral annihilation."

Returning "home," he was thrust into the moral dilemmas facing Apollo. Fifty-one years after the failure of the 1863 Warsaw insurrection, Poles and Poland once more were pawns. It was as though Conrad had returned solely to reexperience in familiar surroundings the very situations he had decided to avoid by leaving Poland forty years before. Yet, ironically, the cycle of experience was little more than a reaffirmation of his own sense of human existence; politics was a centrifugal force that threw off people indifferently.

To Galsworthy, Conrad wrote more frantically, since with only £70 on hand and an uncertain future before him, he needed money. He had to decide on a course of action, given the deteriorating situation: Jessie too crippled to move out on civilian trains, John with a temperature, and the mobilization, which caught them suddenly. He feared "the horrors of a war-exodus" and decided to take the "unlucky tribe" to Zakopane, about sixty-five miles from Cracow, in the Carpathians. There they could stay, for as long as necessary, with Mrs. Aniela Zagórska.

Conrad recognized that with the war taking on a European character he would be cut off from home. He sensed, even as soon as August 1, that England would enter, and he wanted to open a line with the Foreign Office. One of the ironies of the situation is that, as a British subject, he had to handle all business, financial and otherwise, through the name of Konrad Korzeniowski—his passport so stated his name. He was fixed, truly, as a Pole, whereas Jessie was Conrad and his two sons were Conrads, not only English, but living under his assumed name. Conrad wrote very gently of the Austrians, and it is clear from his letter to Galsworthy that, before England's entry into the war, he felt at ease with Austrian occupation. The Austrian "rape" of Poland had never been such a source of agony or oppression to him as had Russia's and Germany's. Further, as a possible aid to Poland's fortunes, Austria was warring on Russia, although, of course, Germany was her ally.*

Barely containing himself at his plight, Conrad wrote Pinker on August 8 from the Villa Konstantnowska in Zakopane. By now, even before England

* We can find further evidence of Conrad's sympathies toward Austria, in Józef Ujejski's Polish life of Conrad, which was translated into French in 1939 (as *Joseph Conrad*). Ujejski cites at least two instances of Conrad's Austrian sympathies, the first in the interview with Marian Dąbrowski, and the second in a (September 1914) document, "Political Memorandum," he left with Dr. Teodor Kosch, but not made available until 1934. Although Conrad's ultimate hope for Poland was a constitutional monarchy—modeled, very clearly, on England's form of government—before the hostilities were established he hoped for a standoff between the opposing powers, with a small German victory but a lessening of German interest in Poland. In the impasse which would be settled at the peace table, he envisaged English support for Poland's fortunes and for Austro-Hungarian interests; he assumed the Austro-Hungarian empire would survive the war. Thus, Germany would be neutralized, or lacking in energy, and Russia, which no longer figured in his reasoning, would be out of the picture, defeated and humiliated, perhaps even siding eventually with Germany.

In other words, because of his interest in Poland, Conrad misread the entire map of Europe. To some extent, he accepted German military might—Germany would control the land masses, while England ruled the seas—and, accordingly, he assumed that the war and subsequent peace would simply perpetuate these existing strengths. As he wrote in that 1914 document, when he seriously underestimated the depth of the issues involved: "It will be, there, in the interest of England to support an Austrian policy towards Poland (even on otherwise unfavourable conditions) and to strengthen the Polish national spirit which is hostile towards the Germans in that Monarchy which in fact can never become dangerous for England, either economically or politically, and as it is one where parliamentary institutions, so highly cherished by the English nation, are better developed than in any other European country." By 1916, when he wrote "A Note on the Polish Problem," under urging from Retinger, he realized the war was of a different kind. At that point, he spoke of a Polish constitutional monarchy based on promises made before the war, and he accepted the reality of the Anglo-Franco-Russian alliance. "An Anglo-French protectorate would be the ideal form of moral and material support. But Russia, as an ally, must take her place in it on such a footing as will allay to the fullest extent her possible apprehensions and satisfy her national sentiment. That necessity will have to be formally recognised."

and Austria were at war, he was extremely worried that he might have to sit out the conflict in Zakopane or some similar location. His situation was beginning to look as desperate as Nostromo's on the lighter. He asks Pinker to send his appeal for help to Walter Hines Page, one of the founders of Doubleday (Page), and at present American ambassador to England. Conrad appealed to him as his former publisher. In addition, he desperately needed money, having asked Pinker previously for £100 and now for £50 in gold. He calls himself a refugee, and says he hopes to get on a train once the Austrian troops have been mobilized on the Russian front. His "escape route," so familiar to refugees in the Second World War, was by way of Switzerland or the South of France, either to Bordeaux or Marseilles, assuming the Calais route was blocked. Conrad reminds Pinker he is "Konrad Korzeniowski."

Then, in one of those extraordinary turnabouts for which he was noted, he indicates he is getting a "mental stimulus out of this affair—I can tell you!" He adds that if it were not for the unavoidable anxiety, he would be deriving considerable benefit from the experience; he expects to put in at least three weeks of work before they can finally move on. This last may have been inserted to justify Pinker's loan, although, as we have observed, Conrad rose to demanding personal occasions with great energy, only to fall back, later, as if extinguished. We have very few details of this period from Conrad's hand, but from those available we note the excitement of a great adventure. The challenge to survive by guile was still there, although here he felt responsible for four, not one.

By September 15, after writing repeatedly to Pinker, he recognizes that all his letters since the twenty-ninth of July have been stopped by the war. Only one has gotten through, to Walter Hines Page, in London. The Conrads, as he presents them, are destitute: with no means, "without warm clothing, and indeed in a very deplorable plight." He lacks the money to get away, which he feels is still possible. The escape route, now, would be through Italy. He worries that their friends will think they have vanished, as indeed they have, and he asks Pinker to get in touch with Galsworthy, Hope, the Colvins, Curle, Gibbon, and others. Conrad pleads complete dependency, as if on his knees before his Uncle Tadeusz, but he tells Pinker that while he cannot apologize for the situation, it has not resulted from any fault of his.

Before all this occurred, as if it were reflecting Conrad's fantasy world of doom and decline, he had moved uneasily but expectantly into the world of his past. He was retracing *his* steps out, even as his family for the first time was entering *into* his early life. In "Poland Revisited," which he published shortly after he returned, Conrad left a record of his feelings and experiences; and fifty-five years later, Borys wrote about his memories of the journey. In 1914, Borys was almost the age Conrad had been when he left Poland, and the entire episode has the quality of a palimpsest. Coming through faintly, however, are those earlier layers, so that we sense slight overlapping, with the past energizing the present.

For Conrad, the journey into memory came with the departure itself, from Harwich, and became ever more intense, a kind of journey into darkness. For him, the German part was indeed comparable to the Congo: "I had no beacons to look for in Germany. I had never lingered in that land which, on the whole, is so singularly barren of memorable manifestations of generous sympathies and magnanimous impulses. . . . Even while yet very young I turned my eyes away from it instinctively as from a threatening phantom. . . . I let myself be carried through Germany as if it were pure space, without sights, without sounds." The center of Europe could have been the heart of Africa.

Conrad always insisted he knew no German, but Borys tells us that in an emergency his father "spoke at considerable length and with great fluency." Under duress, Conrad seemed to activate earlier powers, or earlier needs; he had lived at the edge of survival so long that he had apparently learned all the stratagems for hanging on. His knowledge of German, acquired as a youth in Austrian Cracow, would be in that category, tucked away in areas where his imagination lay; that is, a language not consciously known, but subconsciously hovering, waiting to be used.* If this is even remotely close to the truth, then he perhaps also knew sufficient Russian as well, far more than he ever allowed to get out. Had he needed it, it would possibly have rushed to the surface—while he maintained to Garnett and others that Russian was to him a completely foreign language.

Conrad was now making that round of the past which had so characterized his fiction. It is fitting that in 1915 he would write about his experiences in Poland, only a few years before his native country's fortunes were finally settled by the Great Powers. Retinger accompanied Conrad on his retracing of steps through Cracow, and his account, although perhaps not completely reliable, throws somewhat different glints upon the experience. After Jessie and John retired to bed on that first night, Conrad accompanied by Borys went out to renew his acquaintance with the old city. He attempted to retrace his steps exactly, and to view the Rynek, the central square, from the vantage point of the Florian Gate, under the shadow of the Church of the Holy Virgin. Once there, Conrad explained the call of the bugle, which marked the hours, telling Borys it commemorated the death of a bugler who warned the city of marauding Tartar bands.

---

* Conrad may not have enjoyed active fluency in German, but he had certainly studied it in his youth. In a letter Apollo Korzeniowski wrote to Stefan Buszczyński, on March 17, 1868, he indicates that "Konradek" was studying German so as to attend school in Cracow. How far these lessons went, we cannot judge, but we can speculate that Conrad was gaining at least a working knowledge of the language if Apollo took the trouble to tell his friend. Buszczyński, we recall, was the one to whom Tadeusz Bobrowski revealed Conrad's suicide attempt in 1878.

They then walked through the city's winding streets, as Conrad tried to recall ancient relicts as well as landmarks, speaking to Borys in English and to Retinger in Polish. We have, repeatedly, in Conrad's account, as well as in Borys's and Retinger's, this sense of Conrad's life as he had presented it in his fiction, wherein memory is the central focus of his imagination. He was a man and writer who moved not out but into. In his fiction yet to come, *The Shadow-Line*, *The Arrow of Gold*, as well as the completion of *The Rescue* after twenty-three years, we sense this process at work: the writer standing between past and present, always mediating, making the past the active agent of his artistic powers.

That was the first day in Cracow. The visit to the Florian Gate was indeed rich in memories, and it activated past history in a way perhaps nothing else could. The gate had been the avenue of his walk to school, at eight o'clock "of every morning that God made, sleet or shine." It was the occasion of a "private gnawing worm" of his own, the time of his father's last illness. "Every evening at seven, turning my back on the Florian Gate, I walked all the way to a big old house in a quiet narrow street a good distance beyond the Great Square." There in a large drawing room, under a light made by two candles—like a George de la Tour painting—he did his homework, a door beyond opening into the sick room where Apollo lay tended by two nursing nuns. Those early memories of life in Cracow were foreshadowings also of death, now duplicated by the young Borys accompanying the physically old Conrad. That same Florian Gate recurred in the final episode of this intimate drama, the funeral in which Apollo's death was the occasion of a patriotic display.

> The day of the funeral came in due course and all the generous "Youth of the Schools," the grave Senate of the University, the delegations of the Trade-guilds, might have obtained (if they cared) *de visu* evidence of the callousness of the little wretch. There was nothing in my aching head but a few words, some such stupid sentences as "It's done," or, "It's accomplished" (in Polish it is much shorter), something of the sort, repeating itself endlessly. The long procession moved out of the narrow street, down a long street, past the Gothic front of St. Mary's under its unequal towers, towards the Florian Gate.

We do not know if he visited his father's grave in Rakowicki Cemetery, Cracow, with its inscription that begins: "To Apollo Nałęcz Korzeniowski / Victim of Muscovite Tyranny."

There, as the fifty-six-year-old Conrad concentrated, he recalled the "small boy of that day following a hearse; a space kept clear in which I walked alone, conscious of an enormous following, the clumsy swaying of the tall black machine, the chanting of the surpliced clergy at the head, the flames of tapers passing under the low archway of the gate, the rows of bared heads on the pavement with fixed, serious eyes." This was written in 1915; they were the memories. What the real situation, the real thoughts were, Conrad never tried to tell. We have to search Razumov, Flora de Barral, even the retarded Stevie for hints of that child trying to gain a foothold in life as he was surrounded by illness, death, and personal disaster.

On the following day, Conrad took Jessie to the Wawel, the celebrated hill in Cracow that commemorates Poland's national past. Like the guardian of Cracow's fortunes, it embodied some of the most ancient and famous buildings of Poland: the castle of the Polish kings as well as the most venerable cathedral church; and it was the repository of Polish kings and famous men. Retinger reports that the last time Conrad had seen the royal castle it was in decline, having been used as an army barracks for the Austrian government, while the cathedral church served as a garrison church for the soldiers. Now, he reports, the cathedral had been restored, the castle rebuilt; and Conrad was seeing it in its splendor for the first time. Retinger writes:

> They wandered everywhere, peering into dark crypts where kings, statesmen, and poets are buried; they knelt before the ancient dark crucifix of the Queen Yadwiga. In one of the majestic chapels, all gold and lace-like sculpture, a Mass was being read. Jessie bowed her head and, an indifferent Protestant [Jessie was a Catholic], joined in the prayers of the Catholic religion, overcome with sentiment and emotion.

After a day of wandering through the streets of Cracow, the party returned to the Grand Hotel, only to hear an elderly man cry out (according to Retinger): " 'My little Conrad-Konradku.' " The two stared at each other, and then Conrad recognized Konstantyn Buszczyński, the son of his former guardian, Stefan, and after forty years they fell into each other's arms. The date of the embrace was, ironically, also the day of Austrian mobilization, August 1, and that day would mark the beginning of a four-year struggle, in which nearly everything Conrad believed in was at stake and Borys's life itself would be repeatedly threatened as he fought at the front in the British Army. On the following day, the party visited Konstantyn Buszczyński on his estate of Gorka Narodowa, in the environs of Cracow. With that visit, which brought Conrad so close to Apollo's and his own past, the dip into memories ended. The Conrads had to leave Cracow and settle into Zakopane until events changed, or until they were interned.*

* Conrad took the opportunity to read voraciously in contemporary Polish fiction and to reacquaint himself with the verses of Słowacki. He read Wyspiański's *Warszawianka*, which he said he would like to translate into English. He also went through Żeromski's *Ashes* and *The Works of Sisyphus*, as well as the novels of Bolesław Prus. The Słowacki was *Agamemnon's Tomb*, a verse allegory of Poland's own fate, and Conrad was much affected by the lines.

The family remained in Zakopane, in a pension which they could not afford, cut off from everyone except the American embassy in Vienna, until October 7 (the eighth, according to Aniela Zagórska). On that day, in a snowstorm, at one in the morning, they drove in an open conveyance thirty miles to a small railway station, where they caught a train to Cracow. They had no certainty of escape, but since the Russians were falling back on the front, they hoped that transportation would be available for civilian use. For the fifty-mile journey to Cracow, they sat eighteen hours in a "train smelling of disinfectant and resounding of groans." Obviously, Conrad could not escape this without a severe attack of gout; his ailment was made to order for this kind of strain.

> In Cracow [he later told Galsworthy] we spent untold hours sitting in the restaurant by the railway station, waiting for room in some train bound to Vienna. All the time I suffered exquisite tortures—Ada will understand [Galsworthy's wife also suffered from gout]. We managed to get away at last and our journey to Vienna was at comparatively lightning speed: 26 hours for a distance which in normal conditions is done in five hours and a half. But in Vienna I had to go to bed for five days.

The arrangements for their return to Cracow were not easy to make. Through the intervention of Dr. Teodor Kosch, whom Conrad had helped in Zakopane, a permit was obtained from the military commandant of Cracow which authorized travel that would ultimately land them in Vienna. Even though suffering from gout, Conrad appeared to be a demon of energy, contacting friends, arranging for a fresh water supply on the train trip to Vienna, making sure the travel permit was delivered. Jessie insisted on looking for their luggage, which had been lost in the earlier part of the journey, and with Borys along to speak some French, she went cane in hand to various depots and stations until she found the baggage. But the key element in the Vienna enterprise was to get out: to find either a neutral country or one that would permit their exit. Through the intervention of Frederick C. Penfield, the American ambassador to whom Conrad later dedicated *The Rescue*, the family obtained permission to leave Austria. By October 20, they entered Milan by way of Cormons, the Pontebba route being closed.

Borys has given us a younger person's portrait of his father during this time, in which the excitement of adventure—what Conrad may himself have felt at sixteen—replaced the fear of being interned for the duration of the war. Incidentally, unknown to the Conrads, orders from Berlin were dispatched a week later to have them detained until the end of the war. According to Borys, rather than being in bed for five days while their papers were being prepared, his father tramped the streets of Vienna. On one occasion, he suggested patronizing a shooting gallery, only to discover that the target consisted of movie screens on which kilted Scottish infantry were charging with fixed bayonets. The idea was to fire at them, and if one was hit, the film was stopped and the marksman awarded a prize. Conrad was startled, but told Borys to go through with it so as not to attract attention, "but take care you don't hit any of those fellows." Borys missed his five shots and was relieved, only to discover that he had to fire Conrad's five as well; his father didn't trust himself to miss the target.

The document permitting an exit visa was finally delivered. At the border, however, the Conrads were stopped by Prussians, who had replaced the more easygoing Austrians; and their documents were considered unacceptable, which meant a disastrous return to Vienna. Conrad at this stage spoke what appeared to Borys to be fluent German, to no avail. Then suddenly he pulled out his British passport bearing the German visa that allowed entrance on the journey out. That worked on the official mind, and the family moved on, over the Italian frontier.

At Milan, Conrad cabled Pinker for money, and with that in hand departed for Genoa. On October 25, the rapidly collapsing family caught a Dutch mail steamer homeward bound from Java, with London as a port of call, and arrived back in England on November 9.* Conrad broke down when he arrived at Capel House, too ill even to write Galsworthy. It now struck him how near disastrous their entire enterprise had been, and how his career, under internment, would have come to a halt, because he could not have worked under such duress or changing fortunes. Their escape or rescue could only have been effected through a close network of friends, who also afforded Conrad the opportunity of discussing Poland's future. Unexpectedly, he had become immersed in the Polish question; what had begun as a tourist's reentry into European politics, a superficial glide, became a deadly earnest endeavor to understand the situation so as to escape it. Never had England looked more promising.

In Vienna, with Marian Biliński, the brother of the Austro-Hungarian minister of finance, Conrad had discussed the Polish question both in general and in detail when he still felt England and Austria would be able to settle the issue for themselves. Stanisław Zajączkowski, a businessman, took especially good care of them in Vienna; and, of course, the American ambassador was particularly helpful. Conrad left debts behind him, including one to the American ambassador himself. One of the first letters he wrote on his return was to Walter Hines Page, to thank him for his aid in Vienna through Penfield. The rescue effort intertwined with the political, Americans and English with Poles, as well as Austrians and Germans; and Conrad's dip into the past

---

* The original plan had been torturous: to go via northern Spain; that is, from Milan to Barcelona, then to Bilbao and from there by sea to Falmouth, finally home by train. With Conrad still gouty and Jessie in great pain from a swollen ankle in her good leg, the Dutch boat was great luck.

had, if nothing else, provided further proof that he had been fortunate to leave forty years before.

He was indisposed for a good part of the rest of the year, as well as into January of 1915. At his age, with his temperament, he could not have sustained such a psychic blow without paying for it. Financially, his problems were relieved, or improving rapidly. Pinker sold serial rights to *Victory* for £1,000, or about $12–13,000 in current monies; and the book rights for an additional £850. So that *Victory*, even without sales of a single copy, brought in the equivalent of close to $25,000. Besides, *Chance* continued to sell, and Conrad had another volume of short fiction ready for publication, *Within the Tides*. He was in a good position, but his concentration was sadly broken, and his health followed; he drifted for months.

Early in January 1915, he began *The Shadow-Line*. It was a time when his statement "All creative art is magic" would be more and more difficult to achieve in actuality. As *Victory* faded from his worktable and mind, Conrad moved ever deeper into his own past, for hints, nuances, glints; as he told Curle, he dreamed of his topics, sometimes waking in the night with an intimation. But they were becoming harder to settle upon, and he had in the main exhausted the technical expertise of which he was capable. The war, old age, a general physical breakdown, uncertainties about Borys, lack of financial urgency—all of these were very much there as he found meaningful work increasingly difficult. He had, in effect, given up all effort to achieve contemporary topics; with *The Shadow-Line*, *The Arrow of Gold*, renewed work on *The Rescue*, even *Suspense* and *The Rover*, he dredged his own memories as if the world had suddenly emptied of topics.

The Rescue begins to reenter his letters in 1915; the time for uncompleted business apparently struck Conrad, and a "rescue" was appropriate. The impact of the world war was upon him, for the fortunes of three of his countries were involved, and much of the rest of Europe at war had been part of his world since childhood. His three countries, Poland, France, and England, were doing poorly. Poland seemed lost amid big-power maneuvers; France and England were losing to German advances. But Russia, Austria, and Germany were also part of Conrad's world; he was not an isolated Englishman looking out only for British military successes. He represented, like Kurtz, nearly all of Europe. As he wrote Lady Wedgwood, whose husband, Sir Ralph, was to be co-executor of Conrad's will, two months after his return from Poland: "It seems almost criminal levity to talk at this time of books, stories, publication. This war attends my uneasy pillow like a nightmare. I feel oppressed even in my sleep and the moment of waking brings no relief—on the contrary."

Besides the actual countries involved, the war meant for the historically oriented Conrad the kind of anarchic action in which everything he believed in was disrupted, stained, or destroyed. There was no opportunity for rational thought, no preservation of those ideas which had sustained civilization; Europe had become the arena of savages, in which one hoped that one's own savages would prevail. The European battleground was curiously like the scene Conrad had described in *Victory*, that foreshadowing of the great conflict. Heyst may be the best Europe can produce, and yet whatever he tries to stand for is brutally insufficient; for in addition to his intellectual abilities, he must be prepared to defend his rights. As Settembrini tells Hans in *The Magic Mountain*, no matter how civilized a man is, he must stand ready to fight a duel, that primitive, physical struggle. It was a melancholy thought, and Heyst's plight and fortunes had drained Conrad.

Without dismissing the psychological origins of Conrad's decline in these years, it is equally convincing to see him as a man and an artist who had come to the bottom of what sustained him. With *Victory*, he had reached as deeply into his imagination as he could go; regardless of whether one feels he is successful or not, the book was indeed a culmination. He had scraped it out, and he had found Heyst, the silent son of a silent father, the best Europe could bring forth, insufficient as that was. *Axel* Heyst, that prototypical Axel, Villiers's Axel, who seeks isolation and loneliness as a response to the frantic world, is prototypical European, French and Polish as well as Swedish. Earlier, Kurtz represented a surge of energy, the diabolical artistic energy that almost turned Marlow into an adventurer and outlaw. Now the energy was silent, running secretively, and Heyst is the man of that world. Yet even though he is much finer than Kurtz, he is insufficient, as partially formed as Kurtz. In effect, Conrad had nowhere to go intellectually.

Ironically, much of 1915 was filled with reverberations of "Victory," at least until the novel was published on September 24. "Victory" and "Rescue," those titles representing the halves of his life, would close in and close out his later years. It was a chilling frame. Heyst and Lena, shortly after their escape to the island, and just before they experience their first sexual intimacy together, sit under the picture of the elder Heyst. Heyst explains to her that his father had perhaps thought of the world as a factory and all mankind as workmen in it. He then discovered that the wages were paid in counterfeit money. Heyst says he found the philosophy irresistible. "It was as if that mind were taking me into its confidence, giving me a special insight into its mastery of despair." His interpretation of that despair is that "man on this earth is an unforeseen accident which does not stand close investigation." Believing that, Heyst agrees that he could not take his "soul down into the street to fight there"; he could not face the duel, which is the mark of the man.

Lena assumes that all this is an explanation of why he killed Morrison, whose fate she fears may be her own. " 'You saved a man for fun?' " is her way of putting it. Heyst is trying to explain what it is to be a "victim of the Great Joke," but she can think only of her own fate in his hands, not really listening as he winds down the world into its petty details, its inconsequence. On that island, where Heyst and Lena play at Adam and Eve, Heyst is outmatched by that first man: having given up trying to be Adam, he settles for minimal survival. His need is to justify his existence, not to make anything out of it. It is questionable that with this vision, so important a part of Conrad's mature reflections, the author could have gone on to other fictional triumphs even if the physical elements had held.

Yet an examination of the 1,199-page manuscript of *Victory** and its revisions for book publication supports a view of Conrad as still very much the conscious artist. One way to view this is to recognize that in the manuscript Conrad attempted a far greater degree of realism than he felt was suitable in his final version. The manuscript fills out characters, situations, and scenes which in the book are approached more obliquely and suggestively. Throughout his revisions, after the manuscript was complete, Conrad moved toward a more symbolic presence. This is an extremely important aspect of Conrad's career, for no matter how we feel about the final version, we see Conrad working toward an artistic vision, revising insistently for finer expression and shapelier presentation. He displayed both craft and courage. That trenchant and ironic beginning of the novel† did not come easily; it was hacked out of four pages of manuscript, to create two paragraphs. The manuscript version follows:

> There is as every schoolboy knows in this scientific age a very close chemical relation between coals and diamonds. Not being a schoolboy any longer I have no very clear notion of its nature. It seems to be—that if you take a lot of coals and melt, or roast, or evaporate it, or destroy it in some

* The manuscript seems to run to 1,139 pages, but there are 60 additional pages resulting from renumbering and interleaving, for a total of 1,199; it contains about one-sixth more material than appeared in the book text.

† "There is, as every schoolboy knows in this scientific age, a very close chemical relation between coal and diamonds. It is the reason, I believe, why some people allude to coal as 'black diamonds.' Both these commodities represent wealth; but coal is a much less portable form of property. There is, from that point of view, a deplorable lack of concentration in coal. Now, if a coal-mine could be put into one's waistcoat pocket—but it can't! At the same time, there is a fascination in coal, the supreme commodity of the age in which we are camped like bewildered travellers in a garish, unrestful hotel. And I suppose those two considerations, the practical and the mystical, prevented Heyst—Axel Heyst—from going away.

"The Tropical Belt Coal Company went into liquidation. The world of finance is a mysterious world in which, incredible as the fact may appear, evaporation precedes liquidation. First the capital evaporates, and then the company goes into liquidation. These are very unnatural physics, but they account for the persistent inertia of Heyst, at which we 'out there' used to laugh among ourselves—but not inimically" (p. 3).

such way, if in short you do anything but cook or warm yourself with them you may obtain (so they say) out of a ton of coals (with luck) a diamond rather smaller than the usual pin-head. It is the reason I believe why some pecular [sic] people allude to coal as black diamonds. Mankind is prone to exaggeration of language but the commodities represent wealth. But coals are a much less portable form of property. There is from that point of view a deplorable lack of concentration in coals. Now if a coal mine could be put into one's waistcoat pocket—but it can't. At the same time there is a fascination in coals, the supreme commodity of the age we are camped in like bewildered travellers in a garish, unrestful hotel. And I suppose those two considerations, the practical and the mystical prevent Berg [Heyst], Augustus Berg, from going away. He called himself Berg but I suspect that it was not the whole of his name. I don't mention this surmise [line obliterated] . . . found it more handy in that form. More portable.—hm. Well—Berg.

The Archipelago Coal Syndicate went into liquidation. . . . I am truly distressed. I must apologise for the clumsiness of my proceedings. Here I begin as though I were going into chemistry and then I seem to be putting my foot into finance now. Nothing is further from my thoughts than to either attract or frighten away my readers by a show of science. But necessity knows no law and I must wear the false mantle of erudition for a little while longer. The world of finance then is a mysterious world in which incredible as the fact may appear, evaporation precedes liquidation. First the capital evaporates and then the company goes into liquidation. Those are very unnatural physics, but they account for the persistent inertia of the body called A. Berg; an inertia at which we "out there" used to laugh amongst ourselves—but not inimically. . . .

As we read the manuscript, it becomes clear that Conrad's description of Berg or Heyst often approximates his presentation of Gould in *Nostromo*, another "son" whose father's philosophy hangs like a veil over him. The coal for Berg finds an echo in the silver for Gould. Both try to rationalize private interests by speaking of the general welfare, Berg of "the great stride forward" (Gould of the belief that "a better justice will come afterward"); and both have dissociated themselves from the larger complexities of the world, Berg for coal and island, Gould for his mine.

Further, in revising the manuscript for the book text, Conrad altered not only wordiness but also our view of Berg, transforming him from a retiring idealist interested in human welfare to the ironic Heyst; an achievement accomplished by Conrad's turning from realism and "exclusive meanings" toward indirection and a parodic sense. Many of these changes occur in the first chapter, where Conrad had to establish the tone in which Heyst and the book should be taken. We see he maintained a firm conception even in manuscript; but more intensively for book publication, while the serial was still running, he shaped and reshaped according to his firmest artistic principles.

In another sense, in the expanded manuscript the tonal relationship between Berg and his father is freer and rather less austere than the book text ultimately makes it appear. The conception is firm, the tone less certain. The following passage was later deleted from the book:

> Berg had told him [Davidson, "Davis" in MS] he remembered his father best in a dressing gown for days on end writing and calculating in dark littered rooms, in [?] inventing things that wouldn't work and finding out facts that didn't pay, as far as one could make out. "An amateur scientific crank, I guess" was Davidson's shrewd comment. Lost most of his money and quarreled with his people in Sweden.*

Conrad's usual way of working, as we observed with the galleys of *Under Western Eyes* and *Chance*, was to write in large blocks of material between manuscript and serial and/or first edition, usually between serial and book text. Curle tells us Conrad had little interest in the serial and considered the book the real publication. In this respect, *Victory* appears unique among his longer works, in that the manuscript, even while he disguised his intentions to Pinker, contained all the source material he needed. Further, the fullness of this first version shows Conrad's powers were hardly depleted when he began *Victory;* on the contrary, he was psychologically prepared for a long haul, for a two-year ordeal, comparable to a long sea voyage, at the pace he felt he could maintain. And despite some doubts of modern critics that Conrad was subconsciously incapable of facing his past with the strengths of his earlier imagination, we see him in this novel confronting many very painful aspects of his past and doing so with a fullness of conception he was able to sustain throughout. At no time in this very long manuscript does one feel Conrad hurrying the pace, as he did in *Nostromo*, in order to bring off a long project because he could not afford further expenditure of time and effort.

The problems, if they are considered as such, are those implicit generally in his handling of male-female relationships, whether in Jim-Jewel, Gould-Mrs. Gould, Nostromo-the Viola girls, Razumov-Miss Haldin, not something intrinsically wrong with Heyst-Lena or related to his decline in handling sexuality. The equation of Conrad's difficulty with sexual matters to a

* The stress on Heyst and his father in the manuscript, in large blocks as well as in lesser places, throws Conrad forward as a curious contemporary of Kafka. The son shackled by the physical authority of the father, the son tied to what he feels as overwhelming respect for the older man, the son made impotent by the father's memory, the alternation of deference and resentment: such aspects of the Axel–elder Heyst relationship cut deeply into Kafka's themes. And they indicate, also, that despite Conrad's disclaimer of any sympathy for or even knowledge of Freud, he was very much part of the "new" in the first decade of the century, picking up and assimilating psychological concepts even while rejecting Freud.

loss of imagination or artistic control is a false one; it would be like arguing that Kafka's inability to focus on normal male-female relationships made it impossible for him to function as an artist. Conrad's focus throughout *Victory* is on the immense difficulty of the Heyst-Lena relationship, on demonstrating the essential lack of interest the withdrawn, self-sufficient male has in any attachment and the need the played-out Lena has to define herself through the first man who seems to believe in her.

In a passage of Jamesian banter later deleted from the book text, Heyst plays with the idea of her hair, so that hair in its infinite possibilities both attaches them and suggests their distance. Lena queries Heyst about it:

> "I like it immensely [he says]. I think a head of such glorious hair a more precious possession than any amount of wisdom if for no other reason than because it is indisputable. Even a blind man could not deny the glory of which I speak."
>
> "It is glorious then?"
>
> "I believe I have called it so twice just now. But I have no objection to repeating the epithet as many times as you like. How many times shall I? You won't tell me? No? Let me at least say it once more: Glorious!"
>
> "Well—it belongs to you now" she said putting a wonderful vibrating seduction into the sudden loudness of the phrase.

The occasional flatness of the prose cannot disguise the ironic tone of the word "glorious," followed by the very point Heyst's banter tries to protect him from: that the hair now belongs to him. No matter the glory, he wants nothing; and yet he has praised it, and it is his. Not only the hair, but the seductive voice, Lena herself—they are all his.

Here and elsewhere, Conrad is playing with the very elements of the male-female relationship he is reputedly incapable of confronting. Not only has he faced the difficulties of the relationship, for Heyst, and for any man, but he is trying to find ways in which the divisions can be bridged. The hair, or the physical attraction of Lena, has to be comprehended by Heyst's reason; and he recognizes that what twinges him in the lower half of his body cannot be explained in the upper. The exposed hair, on the head, is also the body hair, the genital hair—and it promises a considerable trophy; but what can the mind make of this?

The manuscript, further, makes very clear that in order to win over Heyst Lena must woo him from his father: what could be more personal and intimate than Conrad's confrontation of this terrible dilemma? The father figure has his eagle-like talons in the son's liver. Even after his first sexual union with Lena, Heyst immerses himself in his father's manuscripts, refusing to recognize that the physical need has taken over from the rational explanation. This is not the failure of a mature relationship on Heyst's part; it is Conrad's attempt to try to understand how a mature relationship is possible in a man who has shunned social contact. It is a point of view, not a deficiency. Conrad had to balance contact and distance, love and hate, body and brain, feeling and dismay, ultimately very tangled life and death forces as they struggle for supremacy in Heyst's psyche.

Implicit throughout, also, is Lena's own recognition that her past experiences as a "soul born in the streets" have in no way prepared her for this present situation. In the manuscript, Lena is a more complicated woman than the victim and martyr of the book. Conrad's aim, evidently, was to stress Lena's own alternating loyalty and alienation at the very moment Heyst was himself incapable of deciding whether he should have fled with the girl. Consequently, when he recognizes her ultimate worth, he is doubly bitter, his manner less tinged by the ironic tone we find in the later version, which may sound more technically correct but is, possibly, less vivid in human terms.

The manuscript of "Dollars," if retained in all its features, would have become a novel of 175,000 words, almost the length of *Nostromo.* Without massive deletions, it would have given the reader fuller explanations of Heyst's background, more material on Lena's past, further insights into Jones and Ricardo, as well as into the Heyst-Lena relationship, even further description of the bestial Pedro. The only area in which the manuscript approximates the book text is in natural description; Conrad apparently felt he had reached a balance between nature and humanity. Although the materials of *Victory* are not so vast as those of *Nostromo,* Conrad had to funnel several extremely difficult elements into a narrative line. The manuscript shows how inexorably he moved along with his basic idea, while at the same time it demonstrates how refinement, indeed purification, of his material was never distant from his mind.

Contemporary reviewers caught many of the novel's tints and nuances. Walter de la Mare, in the *Times Literary Supplement,* although doctrinally indifferent to Conrad's view, granted the power of the vision. We peer, he says, into Conrad's "magic crystal." "And we see this familiar life of ours, heightened and deepened, charged with phantasmal terror, carnal disgust, with a thwarted, venomous, and phantasmal evil; and transfigured with humble dutifulness, self-sacrifice, courage, scorn of pain and of death. And confronted with this miracle—whether of verisimilitude or of transformation—those of us who are not irritated are seduced." The reviewer for the *Daily News,* Robert Lynd, caught a truly Conradian note: ". . . his work is an exaltation of all those beautiful things whose doom is so sure." In the *New Statesman,* the notice captured some of Conrad's peculiar tonal variety: ". . . a rather fatigued air of delicacy, an evasion, a reticence, in the manner, despite the stark horror of the matter."

Although some of the reviews were less than ecstatic, the critics had become educated to Conrad's work and recognized not only what he was attempting but what he had accomplished. He had, in a sense, conditioned them to read him, what any artist must do. He had begun the long process with the Preface to *The Nigger*, and his work since then had been to define for himself that corner of literature where he could work intensely, all the while waiting for his readers to catch up to him. By the time of *Victory*, he had accomplished the educational process, and ironically, so strong was his hold now on his literate public that it continued to praise his work long after it had declined in quality.

The publication and reviews were in September of 1915. When the Conrads returned to England on November 9, 1914, there were still the questions of Borys's future and, of course, of Conrad's illness. It was decided that Borys would make another attempt at Sheffield, and toward that end, which he never achieved, he joined the tutoring establishment of the Reverend Long. Conrad himself made the arrangements, hoping that after six months of hard work his son would move on to an engineering program and a career. Borys, however, began to think along other lines, following to some extent his father's own plans at that age, with military service now serving a function similar to that of Conrad's maritime career.

When just seventeen, Borys obtained his father's permission to enlist, and in September 1915 was gazetted as a second lieutenant. It was Borys's enlistment and subsequent commission that led Conrad to change the title of his next work from "First Command" to the much finer *Shadow-Line.* As he wrote in Richard Curle's copy of the novel: "This story had been in my mind for some years. Originally I used to think of it under the name of *First Command.* When I managed in the second year of war to concentrate my mind sufficiently to begin working I turned to this subject as the easiest. But in consequence of my changed mental attitude to it, it became *The Shadow-Line.*"

The volume was dedicated to "Borys and all others / who like himself have crossed / in early youth the shadow-line / of their generation / With Love." That Conrad called it "an exact autobiography" is not unusual, since that "shadow-line" would help define his own mortality as well as that of Borys and his generation. The book, like his son's action in joining up, seemed to release the past in a torrent of images which Conrad attempted to gather together now in the last ten years of his life: the Malay period of *The Rescue;* his "early love" in *The Arrow of Gold*—dedicated to that other young man, a surrogate son, Richard Curle; the incomplete pages of *Suspense*, with its intense interest in Napoleon, the man whom Poles hoped would help restore their country; and the "rounding off," *The Rover*, carrying Conrad back to the time when he planned mischief with Dominic Cervoni.

These were extremely difficult years. Although he still had several novels left in him, his work came now only in dribbles. Early in the year, he managed to put together his ideas for "Poland Revisited," for the *Daily News*, but that hardly required a "creative" effort. His imagination lay dormant, and his energies—he had no way of knowing—might never return. Gout and general indisposition were strong; the body was winding down, giving little support to the desire to get back into harness. He felt depressed about the course of the war. "But generally [he told Graham] this looks to me a very ugly business from which no satisfaction commensurate with the efforts and sacrifices can be expected. . . . A miserable affair no matter now much newspapers may try to write it up." But he did believe in the men themselves, especially those navy men, "bearded pirates," he called them, who searched for German ships that were sinking English boats. He envied Graham his energy, as his friend at sixty-three was commissioned to buy horses in Uruguay and the Argentine for the cavalry.

Intermittent work on the galleys of *Victory* continued; and Conrad awaited publication of *Within the Tides.* There were still the overlapping aspects of his career, that is, works appearing as the result of backlog; but he had no more short-story ideas for a future volume. By early spring, he had only incomplete projects to contemplate, wrecks of the past and present: the barely started *Shadow-Line*, the still incomplete *Rescue*, the inchoate idea for the Napoleonic novel, even the barely begun *Sisters*, which he still mentioned. In an amusing but ironic exchange with the critic R. A. Scott-James, of the *Daily News*, Conrad pointed out—he did not as yet know the name of the reviewer—that in connection with the *Tide* stories, he was neither "promising" nor "young." Scott-James had so characterized the stories, and Conrad responded, "I am speaking perfectly seriously when I say that they can't but give a great (if unexpected) pleasure to a man who has behind him some nineteen years of pen-work and sixteen volumes in print." He says he values those words, if not intended ironically, as an indication his prose has remained fresh and his wit innocent.

When Scott-James revealed himself, Conrad knew him from previous reviews of his work and insisted in his reply that he did not consider this "little vol. as of any importance in the body of my work. Dent insisted on putting it out." The lassitude into which Conrad sank—and which he also found in Marwood, who would die in May of the following year—was part of that "season of queer sensations." Even the sales figures of *Within the Tides* brought little relief. To Galsworthy, to whom he sent the volume, he expressed how the world rewards its artists:

> The Planter est bien manqué! I had not time to wait for better inspiration. The others—well! You see my dear Jack this vol is not so much art as a financial operation. You have no idea how much these second rate efforts have brought in. The Planter alone earned eight times as much as Youth, six times as much as Heart of Darkness. It makes one sick. However I was stumped with my novel then and it was either sitting doing nothing or writing these stories. It was hardly a choice. I could not afford to sit doing nothing.

This malaise, which might have brought Conrad's career to an end after *Victory* and *Within the Tides*, continued into the spring of 1915. A letter to Violet Hunt, thanking her for *The House of Many Mirrors* (dedicated to Conrad!), brings forth a gloomy greeting to her and Ford set amid an even gloomier assessment of himself: "no work and no ease."* The chronicle of illness becomes Conrad's history: lumbago, gout, depression, irritability, an intellectual and moral enervation. To James, on July 24, he indicates he has not written "10 pages since last Nov^er^." He tries a pun: "Quand je suis ému je deviens muet," which he admits is "absurd for a writing man." But then he calls himself "an absurdity altogether." Deeply hurt as he was by James's handling of *Chance,* he kept the letter very brief.

Beneath all this malaise and enervation, Conrad was building for a final grappling with whatever was left. Like Tennyson's Ulysses, he did not intend to settle in with his success and reputation; he would play the game out and die in unknown, not familiar, waters. His Rover, Peyrol, was his response to those who felt he should stay in port. On August 17, in a long letter to Eugene F. Saxton, his editor at Doubleday† and the designer of a map for the inside cover of *Victory,* he mentions *The Rescue* for the first time in many months. He says it will be finished "when God wills," for now his deepest feelings "are engaged in the momentous events of the time." He also suggests that since his reputation depends on the words he writes, he does not wish to write idly something that may injure that reputation. This consciousness of his worth apart from the marketplace suggests he had not forsaken the role of serious artist, as far as his energy would permit him. Yet he could not help feeling close to that sense of life implied in the lines from Baudelaire attached to Chapter 1 of *The Shadow-Line:* "—D'autres fois, calme plat, grand mirroir / De mon désespoir."

In September, through Graham's intervention, Borys obtained his commission as second lieutenant and was attached to a Mechanical Transport Corps. This coincided with the appearance of *Victory,* on the twenty-fourth, which led to a renewal of correspondence with Ford. Conrad even went up to visit Violet Hunt in mid-October, only to rush home with chill and gout. The gouty condition remained throughout October and made any real work

---

* Writing to Ford on August 12 (addressed quite familiarly as "My dear Hueffer"), he gives his regards to his friend's wife—fully knowing that Ford considered Violet Hunt, not Elsie, to be his wife. Having just published *The Good Soldier,* Ford was off to the wars. On August 30, Conrad could only lament the period, a fated world: "Our world of 15 years ago is gone to pieces; what will come in its place God knows, but I imagine doesn't care." All that survives is: " 'Excellency a few goats' . . . esoteric, symbolic, profound and comic."

† Alfred Knopf by now had left Doubleday to form his own firm.

out of the question. To John Quinn, he indicated that his work for the year 1915 was "about 50,000 words," but it is doubtful if he accomplished that much, certainly not in fiction. "Poland Revisited," written for Edith Wharton's Belgian Fund Sale in Paris and then published in the *Daily News*, alone accounted for more than 10,000 words of that total. Most of the wordage was in connection with sporadic work on *The Shadow-Line.* This book, which Conrad now called "a sort of autobiography" in a letter to Quinn, appears to have been completed in the main by the end of 1915. In the Author's Note, Conrad spoke of writing it "in the last three months of the year 1916," by which he meant 1915. It was probably the writing of *The Shadow-Line* which made him postpone his reading of Ford's great triumph, *The Good Soldier:* "Your cadences [he told his friend] get into my head till I can't hear anything of mine and become paralyzed for days." For the mature Conrad, the year 1915 was one of the worst of his professional career. In 1910, he was stunned by a complete collapse; in 1915, he lacked all will. Visiting Poland had not nourished but depleted him.

IX

Final Things
1916–1924

A gull. Gulls. Far calls. Coming, far! End here. Us then. Finn, again! Take. Bussoftlhee, mememormee! Till thousandsthee. Lps. The keys to. Given! A way a lone a last a loved a long the riverrun, past Eve and Adam's, from swerve of shore to bend of bay, brings us by a commodius vicus of recirculation back to. . . .

JOYCE, *Finnegans Wake*

CHAPTER 34

"This age is broken down, the earth outworn"

AFTER *Victory,* all of Conrad's work was an extension of *A Personal Record:* reminiscences, autobiography, and memoir material. As we sift through those later works, short as well as long, we find Conrad turning back to his own life in a more personal and intimate way than he had done before. The unevenness of this work resulted chiefly from Conrad's inability to turn personal experience into creative materials. Whereas earlier he had utilized mere hints and isolated details as the basis for his fiction, now he strained the past futilely to find imaginative structures for the detail. His work lost that very quality of symbolic overtone which had characterized his struggle not to be realistic; and once that symbolic overlay was lost, his language relinquished its burnish and vitality and he indulged in both flat and "purple" passages.

Two points remain, however, and they serve as corrective to those who see Conrad's decline in these years as monolithic. First, if he had died after *Victory* was written, his work dating from his breakdown in 1910 up to that novel would not have been considered part of a general decline. He would have died, as it were, completely in harness, and there would have been no decline theory; or, if so, a less radical one. That he lived the additional ten years was, so to speak, an accident in terms of his work. Second, despite the evident imperfections of the later work, after 1914, even the least convincing of those fictions contains characters, scenes, and passages which evidence Conrad's most effective phases. Such interludes—even in *The Arrow of Gold* and *The Rescue,* and more apparently in *The Shadow-Line* and *The Rover*—suggest that Conrad had not lost contact with his imagination at its best; but that through general exhaustion and enervation he could not maintain consistency.

The Shadow-Line began the "Viconian recirculation" of Conrad back upon himself. In dedicating that novella (of 45,000 words, his longest short fiction since "The End of the Tether") to Borys, Conrad almost literally curved back upon his own body; for Borys and Conrad were curiously equated in their joint ability to cross the line between youth "care free and fervent, to the more self-conscious and more poignant period of maturer life." The novel leads directly into *The Arrow of Gold*, not only in terms of chronological continuity, but in theme. In Monsieur George of *The Arrow* (Conrad's older son was often referred to as Monsieur Borys), Conrad has gone back to the time when he was his own son's age and, like Borys now in the war, undergoing the test that would take him from youth to maturity.

In *The Shadow-Line*, Conrad says that the matter is personal experience "seen in perspective with the eye of the mind and coloured by that affection one can't help feeling for such events of one's life as one has no reason to be ashamed of." "Worthy of my undying regard," the epigraph to the novel reads, and while Conrad says it applies to the ship's company, it is also a tribute to his own youth. In the symbolic framework of the novel, we have a sick ship—a maritime "magic mountain"—a sick crew, and a captain struggling to save his becalmed empire. It is a tale of "first command," which for Conrad was the first imperative of the world: how one handled oneself in the testing situation; and for the captain, how he handled that "empire" which was his responsibility.

The world was at stake, or at least Europe. The theme struck at the very heart of Conrad's political and social universe. The captain, the untried adventurer, and Ransome, the cook with heart disease, are king and prime minister of that tiny shape pasted onto the water. Coleridge's Life-in-Death and Death-in-Life join on that first command.* Conrad writes of the captain: "I was already the man in command. My sensations could not be like those of any other man on board. In that community I stood, like a king in his country, in a class by myself. I mean an hereditary king, not a mere elected head of a state. I was brought there to rule by an agency as remote from the people and as inscrutable almost to them as the Grace of God." In his assessment of values and responsibilities in a controlled society, Conrad is suggesting, in a fictional representation, his belief in a constitutional monarchy.

For the experience itself, Conrad had returned to his own assumption of the command of the *Otago*. He had, according to his words in the novel, become bored with his assignment, his voyages on the *Vidar* in 1887–88, and had lain around in the Sailors' Home in Singapore. In a 1917 letter to Sidney Colvin, Conrad put the novella in the perspective of his feelings when he returned from Poland in 1914; his dates of composition are inaccurate, but he

* The entire book is indebted to Coleridge's "Ancient Mariner," descriptions as well as situations. "With her anchor at the bow and clothed in canvas to her very trucks [Conrad writes], my command seemed to stand as motionless as a model ship set on the gleams and shadows of polished marble. It was impossible to distinguish land from water in the enigmatical tranquillity of the immense forces of the world."

may have been referring to skimpy beginnings and revision rather than to actual writing.

> The locality doesn't matter; and if it is the Gulf of Siam it's simply because the whole thing is exact autobiography. I always meant to do it, and on our return from Austria, when I had to write something, I discovered that this was what I could write in my then moral and intellectual condition; tho' even *that* cost me an effort which I remember with a shudder. To sit down and invent fairy tales was impossible then. It isn't very possible even now. I was writing that thing in Dec 1914, and Jan to March 1915. The very speeches are (I won't say authentic—they are that absolutely) I believe, verbally accurate. And all this happened in Mch–April 1887. Giles is a Capt. Patterson, a very well known person there. It's the only name I've changed. Mr. Burns' [Born, in actuality] craziness being the pivot is perhaps a little accentuated. My last scene with Ransome is only indicated.

Conrad's intimate feeling for his material made it difficult for him to see it as something "to be tossed to the public's incomprehension, for journalists to gloat over." Such revelations of personal sentiment were almost obscene. "No. It was not an experience to be exhibited 'in the street.' "

Conrad justified his use of autobiographical materials by claiming his experience had been "transformed into spiritual terms—in art a perfectly legitimate thing to do, as long as one preserves the exact truth enshrined therein. That's why I consented to this piece being pub[d] by itself. I did not like the idea of it being associated with fiction in a vol. of stories." This turning back upon himself derived not only from his description of his own layover in Singapore but from the way in which he obtained his command. Even the subsequent voyages of the fictional command and the real *Otago*—three weeks to do the eight hundred miles from Bangkok to Singapore—run parallel. Yet despite this paralleling, Conrad's desire to revive this early period went further. He was trying nothing less than to regain an existence which was passing forever from him. As the captain contemplates his first command, he senses a quickening of the life force itself:

> A sudden passion of anxious impatience rushed through my veins and gave me such a sense of the intensity of existence as I have never felt before or since. I discovered how much of a seaman I was, in heart, in mind, and, as it were, physically—a man exclusively of sea and ships; the sea the only world that counted, and the ships the tests of manliness, of temperament, of courage and fidelity—and of love.

With that, Conrad in 1915–16 had swung back to 1887–88 when he was twenty-nine, a new captain with a new command, and the whole world before him.

As though to complete the recirculation, *The Shadow-Line* was published in *The English Review* (for September 1916–March 1917; in the United

States, in the *Metropolitan*, October 1916). Despite Conrad's abrupt break with it, the *Review* had, after all, published his "Reminiscences," and in this curious way he continued them with the novella. This publication was like the middle act of a continuing drama, and it very possibly led to Conrad's resumption of *The Rescue* and, intertwined with that, to his first thought of the Marseilles period of *The Arrow of Gold.*

In February he worked on what became "The Warrior's Soul," a tale of 7,500 words, and a response to his continued interest in the Napoleonic campaign in Russia. As he told Colvin, he had found hints for it in Philippe de Ségur's *Mémoires*, the story of a French officer and a young Russian. But Conrad did not need a source for this tale; it was continuous with his reading for *Suspense*, his early story "The Duel," the beginning of his reminiscences, and even "Prince Roman," which formed part of the same block of material. It is a mutation of sorts, as so much of Conrad's work now became: patchworks of earlier ideas and worked-out pieces. Given that concession, the tale shows Conrad's descriptive powers unimpaired, as the narrator speaks of the French retreat from Moscow: "I had the intimate sensation of the earth in all its enormous expanse wrapped in snow, with nothing showing on it but trees with their straight stalk-like trunks and their funeral verdure; and in this aspect of general mourning I seemed to hear the sighs of mankind falling to die in the midst of a nature without life." He describes the French trail: "A pathetic multitude of small dark mounds stretching away under the moonlight in a clear, still, and pitiless atmosphere—a sort of horrible peace." This was the Grand Army, Napoleon's legions, those on whom Poland had placed its hopes for liberation.

Even while Conrad was writing "Tomassov," the early title of this story, he asked Quinn to buy the manuscript of it. He admits he needs money badly, and reassures Quinn that if the boat carrying it is sunk or if he dies before completing it, the Estate will make up the difference: "Fact is I am hard up simply because I haven't been able to write of late to any serious amount. I have been affected mentally and physically more profoundly than I thought it possible. Perhaps if I had been able to 'lend a hand' in some way I would have found this war easier to bear. But I can't. I am slowly getting more and more of a cripple—and this too preys on my mind not a little." Later that year, however, in September, he would join a mine sweeper and then make a flight from the Royal Naval Air Station at Yarmouth. The unexpected news is that he still needed money, even after the success of *Chance*, *Victory*, and *Within the Tides.* Curle reported that Conrad earned more than £10,000 in one year, probably at a later time from accumulated royalties. Very possibly, these monies had not yet caught up with him, or else he was simply anxious to gather in as much as he could while the sources remained open.

Fortunately for his morale, he was on the eve of two editions of his work.

The Orlestone Edition to be published by Heinemann was in the contractual stage, although issuance of most of the volumes would not occur until after the war. The plan was to print 1,000 sets (780 were actually printed), at the rate of two volumes a month, with each volume, beginning with *Almayer*, to contain an introduction by the author. By 1921 Heinemann had published eighteen volumes, with two more to appear posthumously. Conrad hoped, he told Quinn, for an American edition of 1,500 sets, given the large population of the United States. Simultaneously with talk of a uniform edition was the actual beginning of Gide's supervision of the French translations. These would, as we shall see, increasingly involve both authors, as Conrad bent Gide to his will, forcing the French author to accept his view of the translations or to forgo them altogether.

The spring of 1916 was one of those "dead" periods for Conrad, coinciding with the devastating casualties at Verdun. It was a time of no work and apparently not even that deep probing that preceded a period of work. He was caught up by his hope for an American edition, and wrote Eugene Saxton of Doubleday about such plans. In an interesting comment on the war—which obviously was engaging his attention, with Borys now at the front*—Conrad speaks of being a true friend of the United States. And yet he hopes that America will remain out of the war. He feels, very possibly with a Polish settlement in mind, that American intrusion would "only introduce an additional complication into the Allied war-command." Quite rightly, he sees America as demanding a "voice in the business in which it takes a part." With that, "there will be the problem of peace, extremely complicated, purely European involving deep seated feelings, aspirations and convictions absolutely foreign to American mentality and even to American emotions." He continues:

> I am afraid, the participation of the US may possibly result in distaste, disappointment, and even animosity on the part of your people, towards what would appear to Am: sentiment the unreasonable attitude of the Allies. No. It is much better as it is—better for the future I mean. The attitude of the US will be of the greatest importance, *after the peace*, to

* On March 29, he informed Galsworthy that since the middle of February Borys had been with the 34th Brigade of heavy guns in the vicinity of Armentières. Conrad's sentiments are proud and apprehensive: "He is in command of the advanced detachment and sees his capt^{n} only once or twice a week. Apart from being always at the call of the gunners for anything unexpected that may have to be done, his work is regular. It consists in running munitions convoys at night while a certain proportion of the day he spends in overalls, grubbing under the cars, as the adv^{ce} detach^{t} must be in a state of absolute efficiency at any instant of night or day. He writes cheerful boyish letters in the same tone as his 'Worcester' correspondence. We send him a tuck-box now and again. It's as if he were still at school."

> the Anti-Teutonic group, and it is most desirable for us to preserve your (mainly friendly) feelings unaffected by the complications that *might* arise in the course of a material collaboration.

Later, when the war seemed to be endless, Conrad, like most Western Europeans, welcomed American intervention.

Fame was accumulating. In the United States, Doubleday published a short study of Conrad's work by Wilson Follett, and in England, the sculptor Jo Davidson was making a bust for exhibition. The Follett study is considerably superior to Curle's book of the previous year, and Conrad was quite pleased with it. He told Doubleday that nothing else written about him "had come anywhere near it, in tone, in discernment, in comprehension." Conrad felt Follett understood unerringly "every line" he had written. Perhaps as he read Follett's excellent study, he was reminded of Matthew Arnold's grim lines: "It is—last stage of all— / When we are frozen up within and quite / The phantom of ourselves, / To hear the world applaud the hollow ghost / Which blamed the living man."

Unable to work properly, Conrad intensified his arrangement of his reputation. Like an undertaker devotedly preparing a body for presentation, Conrad became concerned about details of appearance, matters which ordinarily he would have ignored when the fullness of his imagination was upon him. Two letters on May 19 are characteristic of his immersion in settling his affairs, a concern that became less insistent when he found he could work again. Writing to Doubleday, he reiterated his desire not to be considered a sea writer: "You will gather from it [Pinker's letter] that in the particular design of the edition my inclination is to avoid all reference to the sea. I want the edition to be perfectly distinctive and to bear no specialized symbols or marks. I am something else, and perhaps something more, than a writer of the sea—or even of the tropics. I am not even generally exotic, tho' at first the critics were rather inclined to class me under one of these heads. But this is no longer the case. I am acknowledged to be something, if not bigger, then, at any rate, as something larger."

And yet Conrad's work since *Victory* had been and would continue to be more concerned with the sea than with the land—*The Shadow-Line*, *The Rescue*, *The Rover*, the background of *The Arrow of Gold;* and exotic—the first two novels demonstrated a return to the old Borneo backgrounds. Conrad renewed his acquaintanceship with his past work and past geography, and yet all the while wanted to become recognized as a more broadly based European writer. Ever mocking him was the first attempt at an edition of his work, the "Deep Sea" Edition published by Doubleday in 1914; but the new one planned for 1921, for collectors and large libraries, was to have a special character. Conrad wanted no sea insignia, and suggested the "Sundial Edition." He rejected, absolutely, Doubleday's idea of an "Otago Edition," named after his first command.

Then, on the same day, May 19, as part of his arrangement of his past, he began the long and often quite bitter discussion with Gide over the translation of *Victory* into French. As translator, Gide had selected Isabelle Rivière, sister of the novelist Alain-Fournier and wife of Jacques Rivière,* and as it turned out, the translation of the novel gave Gide almost as much difficulty as the writing of it had given Conrad. Conrad first refers to Gide's own plans, and indicates that the latter's promise to translate "Youth" and "Heart of Darkness" himself "m'a fait un honneur infini devant le monde" and provides him with feelings of intimate joy as very precious proof of Gide's friendship. Conrad then refers to the matter of *Victory:* he fears his idiomatic quality will be lost in the translation: "my style," he says, "is almost constantly altogether idiomatic." Also, as we shall see, Conrad was not pleased with a woman as the translator, to such a degree that Gide had to bring in Philippe Neel to assist Mme Rivière.

Gide caught the edge of Conrad's tone and wrote on June 8, trying to placate the latter by defending the translator. After giving her credentials and pedigree, he said: "Isabelle Rivière est de plus instruite et cultivée, capable d'apprécier votre texte pleinement. Elle sait et sent le Français; et malgré ses résistances, finit toujours par m'écouter quand j'insiste et que j'ai raison d'insister."†

Gide then specifies, for the first time, that he is "plonger dans *Typhoon.*" He says he will not hide that it is an "énorme travail," but his admiration for the author is profound. In a witty postscript, Gide pleads with Conrad not to

* We know T. S. Eliot's interest in Conrad—his plan to attach Kurtz's "horror" as an epigraph for *The Waste Land* and his use of "Mistah Kurtz—he dead" for "The Hollow Men"—but not of Conrad's awareness of Eliot. Their lives, however, almost came together in the career of Gide, for Eliot was tutored by Alain-Fournier. Eliot managed easily in the groups around the *Nouvelle Revue Française* as well as those of the *Action française.* Had Conrad moved at all in literary circles, whether in England or France, he could hardly have avoided meeting Eliot, or Pound, for that matter. Pound, however, was less than taken with Conrad and discouraged Eliot's use of the Kurtz epigraph: "I doubt if Conrad is weighty enough to stand the citation" (December 24, 1921). What is clear, nevertheless, is that all the major writers of the "New"—Joyce, Lawrence, Woolf, Forster, as well as Eliot and Pound—were reading Conrad as he appeared. For many, his was the work that had to be eclipsed. Lytton Strachey is, perhaps, characteristic: ". . . very superb—in fact the *only* superb novelist now [1907], except old Henry James, etc.—and Lord Jim is full of splendid things. The Nigger of the Narcissus is another very wonderful one, and perhaps the best of all is a shortish story called Heart of Darkness in a book called *Youth.*"

† In his Journal, however, Gide "cursed out Isabelle Rivière and her childish theories about how *faithful* a translation must be." And he returned to the subject: "Oh, how poor that translation by Isabelle Rivière is, and how much time I am forced to give to it. . . . Yet since, out of regard for her vanity, which is immense, I am leaving as much as possible of her version, I doubt whether the result can ever be a happy one; I do not think I shall let my name be used on it. Most likely Conrad himself will never know, or ever suspect, the trouble I have got into simply through affection for him, for his book, and for the 'well-done job.' "

address him as "cher Maître," or else he threatens to return the compliment with Conrad. The only other writer addressed as "Dear Master" by Conrad was Henry James, and that in a somewhat different sense: James *had been* one of his masters. Gide's comments indicate his high regard for *Victory*, and he may well have found in Axel Heyst and his disregard for normalcy a prototypical hero of disaffection and ennui, someone curiously akin to his own Lafcadio and Michel, an older version of all those disturbing young men who roam his novels.

Arthur Marwood's death in May 1916 affected Conrad deeply. Marwood had become a special friend, and it is unfortunate we have so little information about their relationship. For years, Marwood made weekly visits to Capel House and talked with Conrad for hours. What they spoke about, what Marwood had to say about literature, how they related their memories of Ford and the *Review*, of Ford's personal life and of Elsie, all of which deeply involved Marwood, we have no way of knowing. Only one Conrad letter to Marwood (and one to his wife) remains extant, probably because they lived near enough to obviate correspondence. Marwood, however, was the one sustained friendship of this mature period in Conrad's life that had no direct relationship to his career; but there is little question that Marwood stood in relationship to him as Ford and Garnett had earlier, and perhaps more intimately, more personally, because the purely literary dimension was missing.

Conrad's boredom was apparent, especially since writing daily was his sole way of filling his hours.* Proper work was impossible; worry about Borys continued unabated, and father and son exchanged long letters. An interesting, but momentary, interlude came in June when Conrad received a letter from a prisoner in Dannemora Prison in upper New York State. The convict, Le Roy Ruhl, had gotten hold of "Karain"—"decrepit and ravaged from much use"—and had so enjoyed it that he asked Conrad for copies of any of his other volumes, however battered, *Lord Jim*, *Chance*, and others. Conrad asked Eugene Saxton to send a complete set of the "Deep Sea" Edition and debit to his account. Boredom would also account for his temporary interest in Jane Anderson, the journalist introduced to Conrad by Lord Northcliffe. Jane Anderson, whom he described as a "yum-yum" young woman from Arizona, caused some tempests in the Conrad home, as we saw earlier. Jessie evidently felt she had stumbled on an intrigue, for she dwelled on aspects of the relationship, such at it was, for nearly ten pages in her *Jo-*

* Conrad's ennui was evidenced in other ways: his willingness to sit for his portrait and for sculpting. Besides Davidson, who sculpted a bust, Rothenstein did a portrait drawing, which Gosse bought with the intention of presenting it to the National Portrait Gallery. Conrad told Quinn he would pose for Augustus John, and later, he sat for what became the strongest of the artistic representations, a bust by Jacob Epstein.

seph Conrad and His Circle. Besides the reappearance of Jane Anderson at Capel House, Lord Northcliffe became a fairly frequent visitor. Northcliffe tried to gain Conrad as a writer for the *Daily Mail,* but his interest seems also to have been personal, although for Conrad he represented the very worst elements of the popular press. As he told Pinker, he found him obtuse, for Northcliffe came and spoke for hours of his mother and of his great affection for her. If Conrad had been able to work seriously, he would not have tolerated such days, but in his boredom and malaise, the attention of the great Northcliffe may have been flattering.

A further relief from boredom came in the form of long, detailed letters to Quinn, many of them narcissistically concerned with Conrad's plans for an American edition of his works. This would be the Doubleday "De Luxe" Edition, which Conrad hoped would be not only a memorial to his name but a source of income for his family. His plan was to have the edition follow the first editions in England, an idea that goes beyond literary preservation and suggests survival itself based on past achievement. Also, Conrad pressed for Pinker's involvement in every aspect of the financial dealings; Quinn had suggested some bypassing of the agent, very possibly because of Pinker's Jewish background.

Conrad's defense of Pinker is splendid: "Our relations are by no means of client and agent. And I will tell you why. It is because those books which, people say, are an asset of English literature owe their existence to Mr Pinker as much as to me." Although he has had his recognition, Pinker was the only man who backed his opinion with money. Conrad adds that his publishers cared very little for his product: Blackwood gave him up as having proved "a not-good enough business," and Doubleday, among others, let his books go out of print. "I can't enter into the detail of these 15 years but if I were to live a hundred years I could not forget them. And that's why our relation is not of business but of intimate friendship in the last instance."

Conrad also wrote at length to his old friend Ted Sanderson, whose son Ian was in the navy and about to be attached to the fleet. He is struck by Ian's naval service, which he tells Sanderson will be infinitely preferable to Borys's position with the guns at the front. Borys had been involved in some of the bitterest, and most futile, fighting, near the Ypres front on the Belgian-French frontier north of Armentières. Conrad understated his apprehension, but it was there: "You will not perhaps think me a soft sort of idiot if I tell you that I miss him more than I can say. Both our hearts go out to you with perfect comprehension."

Conrad corresponded, further, with Henry Irving, over a dramatization of *Victory,* with Macdonald Hastings as the adaptor. This would become a considerable enterprise in 1917 and would even lead Conrad to contemplate a collaboration with Hastings about a faked old master, an idea he had also considered with Ford, about Ford Madox Brown. No matter how antagonistic he felt toward the stage, Conrad could not give up his idea of writing a theatrical work, whether an original play or an adaptation of one of his own works. If nothing else, Hastings's work on the dramatization and Gide's on the translation kept *Victory* before Conrad; both the novel, his last fully fashioned fiction, and the title served as a tonic, if anything could during this low period. To borrow one of Yeats's metaphors, Conrad felt out of phase with himself and his era, at the dark end, where "there's no human life."

From the beginning, he was dissatisfied with Hastings's version; the first act he found altogether unacceptable. But he was interested in the money it might bring, although he balked at being named co-author of the dramatic version.* He felt he was still capable of some good work—"I am not done yet," he told Pinker. After trying to convince his agent that he showed some dramatic ability in his sea things, he said: "I am still impressionable and can adapt my mind to various forms of thought—and, perhaps, of art." Conrad's final attempt at dramatization came with *The Secret Agent*, in 1920, and it proved to be a wasted effort, in terms of art and financial return.

The Hastings-Conrad collaboration and subsequent dramatization produced no masterpiece, but its presence in Conrad's life served a function. It appeared to reactivate him and give him some impetus toward original work. For in the following year, he informed Pinker he was planning a magazine fiction that contained dramatic possibilities, what became *The Arrow of Gold*, the beginning of a whole sequence of interrelated fictions.

As if the present were not sufficiently trying, the past in the form of Roger Casement emerged. Casement had attempted to provision the Irish side with German arms while the English were occupied on the European front, or so he was charged. On April 12, 1916, he had sailed for Ireland in a German submarine, hoping to prevent the Easter Dublin uprising as a futile gesture when he discovered the Germans were unwilling to risk a supportive expedition. British authorities seized the ship accompanying the submarine and found German arms destined for the rebels; when Casement landed in County Kerry, on April 24, he was arrested and taken to London, where he was charged with treason. On July 18, his appeal against conviction was rejected, and he was hanged on August 3. Of course, once Casement tried to undermine the Allied war effort and the British authorities circulated the homosexual diaries, Conrad turned very cold toward Casement's memory.

Conrad repeated to Quinn that his knowledge of Casement was slim. After the initial meeting in the Congo in 1890, he indicates a further meeting

* To Hastings, he was firm: "*Victory* / A Play in Acts [sic] / Adapted by Macdonald Hastings / from a novel by J. Conrad. . . . It must be as above. There can be no question of collaboration. Collaboration implies a close daily intercourse for six weeks or so—which under the circumstances is impossible. It would also mean me having not only my say but also my way in the construction and in the very words of the play. Which is not to be thought of."

in 1896, in London, at the Johnson Society; this led to a long talk well into the morning at the Sports Club, and Casement subsequently returned for the night—this must have been in late 1896. Conrad then skips altogether the 1903 correspondence with Casement and moves to a meeting in 1911, when they saw each other in Surrey Street, Strand. At that time, Casement was British consul in Rio de Janeiro, on home leave for three months. Conrad says that that was their last meeting. He mocks Casement's politics, saying that a Home Ruler who accepts Salisbury's patronage cannot be taken very seriously. Then Conrad moved to his estimation, a devastating one, and worth repeating:

> He was a good companion; but already in Africa I judged that he was a man, properly speaking, of no mind at all. I don't mean stupid. I mean that he was all emotion. By emotional force (Congo report, Putumayo—etc) he made his way, and sheer emotionalism has undone him. A creature of sheer temperament—a truly tragic personality: all but the greatness of which he had not a trace. Only vanity. But in the Congo it was not visible yet.

Writing again to Quinn after Casement had been convicted of treason but before his appeal was rejected, Conrad said he doubted Casement would "swing." He saw the Irishman as a mere pawn in a German game. He felt England could not allow the treasonous action to go unpunished, although he thought Casement had done his work without taking German money. Nevertheless, he foresaw German subsidies as bringing about an Irish rebellion, while in the ensuing bloodbath Germany would let only Irish blood flow. On August 10, Conrad wrote Lady Ottoline Morrell a few further details and indicated the case was closed; Casement had been hanged a week earlier. In the same letter, he rejected another one of her invitations to visit.

Conrad had decided that his American Collected Edition should await the end of the war. Although Pinker had cleared copyrights, planning that went back to 1913, Conrad refused to allow Doubleday to hurry him into something that he felt was not yet right. He feared that the edition would be poured into the "boiling caldron" of the war, where it would sink unnoticed. His argument was unassailable: Doubleday might have thousands of authors on its list, but for him there is only one, himself, whose few books were his life's work. He would wait until the moment was more auspicious for fiction.

That Conrad at this stage of his life, when he expected an early death, could still plan his entire career indicates a desire to hang on, even if no work was forthcoming. He was also forcing his physical energy toward some final movement, even to giving himself some role in the war effort. Borys was at the front. Ford also was at the front—Conrad dropped him a short note on August 15. Sanderson's son was in the navy. Letters and plans for the future could not dissipate the gloom he felt, now with Marwood dead and even

Richard Curle gone, to Africa. Edward Thomas, the poet, would die in October of 1917; an entire generation of young Englishmen was vanishing. Meanwhile, Retinger was busily trying to gain Allied support for a Polish state, and toward this end Conrad himself wrote "A Note on the Polish Problem" (1916), whose chief import was that Poland was a European country, not a Slavic entity. As we have seen, Conrad's interest was in preserving Poland not only as a national state but as a Western European nation with a constitutional monarchy very much along English lines. His words are particularly striking, since they appear to be those of a man dictating the way in which he wants to be saved as his ship sinks under him.

> The Poles, whom superficial or ill-informed theorists are trying to force into the social and psychological formula of Slavonism, are in truth not Slavonic at all. In temperament, in feeling, in mind, and even in unreason, they are Western, with an absolute comprehension of all Western modes of thought, even of those which are remote from their historical experience.
>
> That element of racial unity which may be called Polonism, remained compressed between Prussian Germanism on one side and the Russian Slavonism on the other. For Germanism it feels nothing but hatred. But between Polonism and Slavonism there is not so much hatred as a complete and ineradicable incompatibility.

Conrad's careful distancing of himself from the great Russian writers (except Turgenev) was attached to this view of Poland and of himself as distinctly separate. And yet reviewers, fed now on Constance Garnett's translations, were persistent in pointing to Conrad's powers as having derived from his Slavic background; his very strengths stemmed from the different sources of his experience. In denying Poland's Slavonism, Conrad had to deny his own "incompatibility," the very element which nourished his imagination. Even this late, in 1916, he was maneuvering among cultures and national backgrounds, no more at home than Yanko Goorall in England, Razumov in Geneva, or "Monsieur George" seeking adventure in Marseilles.

This "Note on the Polish Problem" is especially compelling because Conrad was attempting to draw together his political ideas in terms of the three countries that had nourished him: Poland, France, and England. He and Retinger, as though a government in exile, presented the "Note" and their idea to Sir George Russell Clerk (whom Conrad referred to as "Clark") of the Foreign Office, and it was no less than a plea for a tripartite agreement involving Poland, with England and France forming a protectorate. To this Clerk responded: "Let the Poles first make a clearly defined request." This request would have to be supported by important personalities and public figures representative of all political and social elements in Poland. Only then, Clerk insisted, could the Conrad "Note" raise the question of Poland's future.

With this, Conrad advised Retinger to pursue the matter firmly; for Retinger's role now was to gain the agreement of all Polish parties. As Conrad says: "For it is obviously better to receive the gift of national existence from one's friends than from one's enemies. . . . Now, the main thing is to start to live, breathe, and put on flesh. Later on the battle of ideas will develop within the fundamental institutions as it does in every free country." Conrad reports to Curle that as he was leaving Clerk said: " 'Well I never thought I would have this sort of conversation with the author of The Nigger of the Narcissus.' " Conrad did not find it amusing: "Which shows the man to have the sense of contrasts in him, though he looked like a stick of sealing wax and seemed to be made of parchment."* He was, apparently, unused to English officialdom.

Conrad's involvement demonstrates his continuing interest in Poland's fortunes, despite Retinger's assertion that he was lukewarm; and his words indicate further how Conrad intertwined Poland's fortunes with those of his adopted countries, France and England. It is somewhat doubtful, however, that he would have devoted this energy to political problems if he had not been stalled on his fiction or if his imagination were active, a hesitation Retinger may have picked up. Conrad tended to concentrate his powers on the matter at hand, and if that matter had been *Jim* or *Nostromo* or *Victory*, there is some question whether even the war, except for Borys's fortunes, could have intruded. But distracted as he was—even *The Rescue* turns up in a letter—he found himself given over to several matters not normally his direct concern. Shortly after this, he joined the mine sweeper *Brigadier*, which he boarded at Lowestoft, the original entry point for him in England. With a lack of clear direction for the future, he returned to his youth, arranging Poland's fortunes, trying to fight the war, reliving his first days in England at Lowestoft, and holding off a kind of death with a flurry of discrete activities. Until he began *The Arrow of Gold*, he was a man without a profession and even a routine.

Conrad required adventure, just as "Young Ulysses" of *The Arrow of Gold*, his next long venture, needed gunrunning and smuggling to feel alive and alert. When he was asked by the Admiralty to write some articles on the

* To Christopher Sandeman, a young man deeply involved in Poland's fortunes, Conrad tried to deal with Russia's position, still in August 1916, as an ally of France and England: "Poland attached to Russia would end by getting absorbed either by massacre or conciliation or by mere economic pressure or from other hopeless aspects of its future. And I submit that with all possible loyalty to our present engagements it is no part of our duty to work gratuitously for the aggrandizement of Russia, which is big enough in all conscience. And, after all, if Poland owes something to Russia, she owes even more to England and France. Without the Western Powers there would have been the biggest crumpling up in the history of the world: and the Germans would be watering their horses in the Volga to-day."

merchant service, he journeyed up to London on September 5 to see Captain Sir Douglas Brownrigg. By September 14, Conrad was en route to Lowestoft, and his spirits appear to have soared. He wrote immediately to Jessie as "Dear Chica" and signed off, "Ever your lover and servant and devoted husband," more in Polish than English style. Before departing from London, Conrad made last-minute arrangements with Hastings, who was to continue writing the lines agreed on between them, and then went to Jane Anderson's for tea, which turned into dinner. Conrad's relationship with her, as noted earlier, was evidently personal enough for her to divulge intimate matters about her own life, which seemed precarious.

> She talked of you [he wrote Jessie] and the boys a good deal. Rather a lot of herself. Very curious. Very nebulous of course. No facts but a lot about sensations, intelligence and so on. You know what I mean—I fancy she feels her position to be not without danger (of a shake up) and would be perhaps glad to know (or to feel) that you, I mean *you* personally as a woman (as distinct from *us*) would be likely to stand by her. —I was very reserved on these matters generally.

Jane Anderson reappears in Conrad's next letter to Jessie, on September 29, from Glasgow. Before going there, he had made an exciting flight, his first, from the Royal Naval Air Station at Yarmouth, a flight that served no purpose except to make him feel part of the war effort and young enough to stand the rigors of the rudimentary craft. Very possibly, as he moved from the aircraft to the mine sweeper and then to his assignment on the boat that mended torpedo nets, he felt like a companion of Borys and of all those young men who were passing the shadow line.

In that September 29 letter to Jessie—addressed to B.W. (Beautiful Wife or Woman)—he speaks very circuitously of Jane Anderson: "Had a letter from your pair-mate [an unusual phrase to use to Jessie] about N'cliffe. N. obviously cooled down a lot. Letter curiously indefinite but I seem to see that N. has found some new Am^can^ wonder. Just what I expected. But this is strictly between us. The dear Chestnut filly is obviously put out. Am trusting the dearest dark-brown mare [that is, the 200-pound Jessie] to steady that youngster in her traces. See?" Retinger felt that Jane became part of Conrad's conception of Rita in *The Arrow of Gold*,* and very possibly, as

* As Retinger, not the most reliable of men, put it: "Brilliant and beautiful, she turned the heads of many conspicuous and famous men both in Europe and in her own country. Exceptionally gifted, a good newspaperwoman and a short-story writer of more than average talent, she had a marvellous capacity for listening and understanding. After she arrived in London in 1916, and until she left a year or so later, Conrad saw a lot of her. She became part-heroine in one of his last novels *The Arrow of Gold*. She was one of the very rare persons whom Jessie could not stand, as is shown in the latter's memoirs. She also, after the war, caused a certain estrangement between Conrad and myself."

we have seen, Rita was a fantasy figure of Conrad's old age superimposed on his youth, when it was possible for him to indulge the fantasy without retribution.

Conrad, however, demanded greater (or less personally threatening) adventure than Jane afforded, which we note from the melodramatic tone in his letter to Pinker as he started his "service" from Granton Harbor in Edinburgh. He indicates he may never return; a desperate mission, as Nostromo informed Decoud: "I am going—you know on what errand. Should the ship fail to report herself for more than 10 days after the time fixed for her return (by wireless—at night) there will be no use hoping for her return. . . . I have no nearer friend on whom I could lay the painful task. I believe I have your approval; Borys isn't likely to be angry with my memory; Jessie understands and John knows nothing of course. As to these last I know you will do all you can to make their fate as tolerable as it can be made." Although there was danger from German submarines, Conrad intensified his role: ". . . It's no use ignoring the fact that the vessel has made three trips already and she may have been spotted. Also there are spies about. The prospect of an expedition of this sort gives a curious force to the idea of spies. It drives home to one's conviction that they do exist."

Conrad's health never seemed better; he was rejuvenated. He was connecting not only to Borys at the front but to his own youth. In late October or early November, he wrote to Jessie about his activities, her "ever loving man" reporting to his "dearest," and the relationship seems more between son and mother than husband and wife of twenty years.

> We went out to the net defences but before long the ship was fairly washed away and blown off from her station. Her cap" a Lieut: said to me "I don't think we can do any good work today." I said: "For God's sake let's get out of this[.]" And we got out accordingly. I was never so pleased in all my sea-life to get into shelter as I was on Friday at about 5 pm. On Sat: I went out with the Commodore inspecting and gun testing in Firth of Forth. While we were at it 3 divisions of our newest destroyers came in from sea. It was an exceedingly fine sight. The day was fair and cold.

Exhilarated, he tells Jessie he will be joining the HMS *Ready*, going out to her in the commodore's flagship. The *Ready* was commanded by Captain Sutherland, who later wrote a little book about the cruise of the ship in October-November with Conrad aboard. When Sutherland sought Conrad's permission to publish his reminiscences of the cruise, Conrad replied: "What this experience meant to me in its outward sensations and deeper feelings must remain my private possession." To Jessie, Conrad conveyed the adventure, that they were heading out into an unknown: "Pray do not be uneasy if you don't hear from me for some days. She's not likely to communicate. It's safer not to do so." And to Pinker, Conrad sent something like a telegram or communiqué, an admiral reporting to Whitehall:

> *All well.*
> *Been practice-firing in sight of coast.*
> *Weather improved.*
> *Health good.*
> *Hopes of bagging Fritz high.*
> *Have dropped a line to Jessie.*
> *Don't expect to hear from me for 10* days

The Shadow-Line had already begun to appear in *The English Review* in September, and in the United States in October. Conrad's wartime activities as an observer, which ended in late November (he was back at Capel House by at least November 27), paralleled his "first command" now being serialized, just as the narrator of that tale had scooped up his own past on the *Otago.* Conrad was, in a sense, working laterally across his experience and finding parallels between past and present. Meanwhile, the saga of Borys in action with the 40th Siege Battery was ever before him as a representative of all stages of Conrad's life, what he was and what he still hoped to be.

On December 4, at home, Conrad felt low once again, with a new attack of gout building. To Dent, however, he mentioned some vague plans: to use *The Shadow-Line*, for example, as the first story in a volume of short fiction. He mentions, also, *The Rescue*, as not being "very far from its termination," although he cannot prophesy its completion date. Even as he was denying his designation as a "sea writer," he was turning to *The Rescue*, a sea novel in setting and atmosphere, and observing the serialization of his past in *The Shadow-Line*, a sea fiction in every respect. The land brought no sea breeze, however; it, in fact, brought poison, including news that Ford had been gassed at the front. Conrad wrote to him, on December 24, at a Rouen Red Cross Hospital. Conrad was himself one year short of sixty and simply holding on.

The Shadow-Line was appearing in very small portions in *The English Review*, its less than 50,000 words stretched out to seven installments. The story, consequently, seemed unduly harsh, and it was beginning to gain a reputation as being morbid, this description upsetting Conrad considerably. If the story is read at one sitting, of course, it provides sufficient change of pace to dispel morbidity. Conrad felt that Harrison was at fault: "He has been doling it out in drops, as if it were poison. No wonder he spoiled its taste altogether." Conrad stressed that the "nasty rap" for the story disturbs him because it is "exact autobiography," as is "Prince Roman." He was so upset he felt he would "cancel the dedication as I don't want the boy's name to be connected with a work of which some imbecile is likely to say: that it is a 'good enough' sort of story in the Conrad manner but not a work to be put out by itself with all that pomp." For the book text, he created more continuity, omitting the division into two parts and using only roman numerals, not chapter designations. The plan was to encourage a read-through at a single sitting.

The end of 1916 brought with it a change of government, with Lloyd George replacing Asquith on December 6; a shift that Conrad felt was about as meaningful as turning the whole thing over to the Devil. "Nothing short [he told Graham] will put this pretty business we're engaged on right." The war had settled into a malaise based on young men aimlessly murdering each other. All fronts were stalled, and the Allied offensives brought few results to justify the great losses, dead, wounded, and ill. Borys was expected home on January 15, although Conrad feared it would be only a respite before he returned to become cannon fodder.

The "victory" which was not forthcoming on the battlefield or on any of the fronts ironically followed Conrad into 1917 in the form of Hastings's continued attempts to transform *Victory* into a play. In his letters, Conrad offered detailed comments on costumes, place names, modes of addressing people in the archipelago, and even ways of saying things. The dramatization of *Victory*, which was doomed by the intermittent collaboration, nevertheless turned Conrad's mind to the theater, and when he did begin to write again, with *The Arrow of Gold*, it was for its dramatic potential. He planned a story whose dialogue and dramatic sequences could be extracted and turned to stage usage.

Conrad's return to his world of the 1870s was appropriate, for the old world was coming to an end. The first war was a watershed for European politics, and the "end" was seen everywhere. Conrad had foreseen it himself in *The Secret Agent*, "Il Conde," and *Victory*, and it was facing him now in Borys's manner and appearance when he returned from the front. The serenity Conrad tried to capture in Monsieur George in *The Arrow* was very possibly related to Borys's maturity: "What struck me most [he wrote Quinn] was a sort of good-tempered imperturbable serenity in his manner, speech and thoughts—as if nothing in the world could startle or annoy him any more." Although Borys stayed close to his family while on leave, he had passed the shadow line in one direction, whereas Conrad was passing it in the other. For a very short time, their two worlds overlapped.

Conrad's attempt to define the old even while it was passing away came in his four-page preface to Edward Garnett's study of Turgenev. For Conrad, Turgenev was an antidote to the insanity raging outside. He would have liked, in Yeats's words, to "mock Plotinus' thought / And cry in Plato's teeth," but he could only hold the past up to a mirror and seek for human images in the madness of the present. For him, Turgenev was this link with a past no longer functioning; Conrad sought sanity in order to hang on.* He was surely reading his own career into Turgenev when he cited the attacks from both the autocracy and the Revolutionists on the Russian writer. Turgenev represents the best, but now he is under a curse in a world symbolized by the "convulsed terror-haunted Dostoevski."

Conrad was read in the trenches for much the same reason he himself read Turgenev: to reach back into a world of normative values. It was that very quality of moderating values that Conrad stressed as he got older, to the detriment of his "other self," which displayed a ferocious anarchy. To Colvin, for example, in the spring of 1917, he spoke of his work being based on the " 'ideal' values of things, events and people. That and nothing else. The humourous, the pathetic, the passionate, the sentimental *aspect* came in of themselves—mais en vérité c'est les valeurs idéales des faits et gestes humains qui se sont imposés à mon activité artistique." It was in this spirit that Conrad wrote his Author's Notes for the Collected Edition that appeared after the war, notes that stressed the realism and typicality of his work while playing down its bizarre, aberrative aspects. When Jean-Aubry wrote his biography of Conrad in the later 1920s, he also emphasized these normalizing dimensions and by so doing influenced a generation of Conrad readers.

The first part of the Russian Revolution occurred in March, in the form of opposition to a corrupt czarist government. This was the provisional phase, which lasted only until May, when Kerensky took over the government with plans for a socialist transformation of the country. Conrad's reaction to the revolution was predictable; he cared not about what happened to Russia but about what the turmoil would mean to the efficiency of the Alliance. "I don't think it will be of any advantage to us [he wrote Dent]. Political trustworthiness is not born and matured in three days. And as to striking power an upheaval of that sort is bound to affect it adversely for a time at least." To Colvin he wrote essentially the same, although he did see the possibility of a peasant uprising, with "immense bloodletting" as a consequence. The early aspects of the Revolution had dimensions that reflected the Polish uprisings which had consumed Bobrowskis and Korzeniowskis.†

---

* Yet he adamantly refused the definition characterized as the so-called Newbolt Man, or *homo newboltiensis*, wittily named after Sir Henry Newbolt, the poet and barrister who had administered Conrad's Civil List grant. Newbolt represented those old values of the military, loyalty and bravery, and damned those who offered aesthetic, witty, or intellectual solutions to contemporary problems. For Newbolt, Field Marshal Haig, in sending waves of young men to their deaths, showed greater courage than the men who were to die. Lord Northcliffe, who misread Conrad as someone similar to himself in ideology, represented this same "war as games" attitude.

† Conrad's lack of interest at this phase was understandable, since two-thirds of Polish territory, going back to the 1772 frontier, was in German, not Russian, hands. Also, at the beginning the Revolution was not so clearly an overthrow of everything that was

Conrad's entanglements with still other aspects of his past were intensified even as he was poised to start *The Arrow.* This time the Bangkok-Singapore period of his life returned, the result of the publication of *The Shadow-Line.* It came in a letter to W. G. St. Clair, former editor of the *Singapore Free Press,* who had written about Conrad and the Singapore background in the *Ceylon Observer.* Much of St. Clair's article concerned itself with Tom Lingard, whom the editor had known and spoken to, whereas Conrad knew him only by hearsay. Conrad's answer, on March 31, downgraded his actual contacts in the East, although admitting to Captain Patterson as the original of Giles, and the steward: "He was a meagre, wizened creature, always bemoaning his fate, and did try to do me an unfriendly turn for some reason or other." What was remarkable about the exchange, however, was the mention of Lingard at a time when Conrad was thinking of taking up *The Rescue* again.

Hastings was now ready to cast *Victory,* and Catherine Willard tried to obtain the role of Lena. Catherine Willard and her mother, "Mama Grace," were old friends of the Conrads, Mrs. Willard having helped them to furnish and decorate their various homes. In the exchange with Catherine, Conrad demonstrated a knowledge, perhaps surprising, of Congreve's *Love for Love* and *The Way of the World,* although he did not think it quite proper for him to discuss Congreve with a young lady. As his career wobbled among inconsequentials, he entertained demands on his time that once he would have dismissed curtly. W. T. H. Howe, for example, suggested making pictorial groupings of characters and scenes from Conrad's novels, this as part of a charitable enterprise in America. The United States had entered the war on April 6, and Conrad's suspicions of American intervention had now turned to gratitude that their military strength might end the war. He insisted, nevertheless, that his work did not lend itself too well to such dramatic groupings; he suggested as exceptions Linda Viola and her father after he has fired his shot, and Renouard and Felicia against the rocky pinnacle of the island in "The Planter." One could, however, think of several from *Victory, Under Western Eyes, The Secret Agent,* and *Nostromo.* The grouping of Verloc and Winnie, just before she plunges the knife in his chest, would have made quite a dramatic pictorial setting, especially for a war charity.

As the war resisted all solutions, and Borys continued in the thick of

old Russia. In March, in fact, it was possible to see the incipient Revolution as an attempt by the Allied embassies to overthrow the czar so as to prevent a separate peace with Germany. That is, when the czar's Petrograd garrison refused to fire on striking and rioting workers, an action that led to a lack of support for the czar's policies, one could view this action as simply foreign subversion. Not until Lenin made his way through Germany the following month and moved to put the Bolsheviks in power was it possible to see that Russia was undergoing a revolutionary convulsion.

things, Conrad had only himself or his views to concentrate upon. He sank back into himself, deeper and more intensely, not for great works of imagination, but for ways of comprehending the universe. His very political ideas had become meaningless: Russia as an ally of England and France in a war against Germany and Austria; America as a potential savior; the old Europe irretrievably lost in the chaos and slaughter of the war; the fortunes not only of Poland but of England and France as well now threatened. He believed that the Entente would come through, but whatever was saved would be hardly worth preserving. Writing to Colvin, whose generous support was so important to him now, Conrad spoke of the "People" and the "Nation" as being the greatest figures of the times: "For 150 years the French people has been always greater (and better) than its leaders, masters and teachers." The same can be said of the English, although admittedly they have been less sorely tried than the French.

Evidently, his feelings about the people did not extend to the Russians. Even when the Revolution was taking its new form, with Kerensky attempting a socialist government, Conrad felt that "a nation's nature can't be changed" in twenty-four hours. "Russia was an untrustworthy ally before—and it remains so still." Conrad's sole interest was in Russia's ability to engage large numbers of Germans on the eastern front, and now he saw even that capability destroyed. He spoke of those experts who will go to Russia to try to achieve some kind of organization comparable to people "being thrown overboard in a storm to organise the waves of the sea." There is little doubt that Conrad's detestation of even a "new" Russia went further than hatred based on Poland's fortunes. Russia represented to him the very violence and spiritual chaos which undermined his sense of moral values or ethical procedures. Even *Under Western Eyes* had not settled Conrad's ambivalence, for his view of Russia there was finally resolved not in the home country but in Geneva.

Conrad had made a new friend in the New Zealand-born novelist Hugh Walpole, who became one of those adoring young men gathered around the master in the 1910s and 1920s. Walpole had published, in 1916, a short study of Conrad's fiction, treating his work as both lyrical and philosophical. As an attempt to pioneer in Conrad criticism, it was superior to Curle's study, but it moved into dangerous areas by suggesting that *Victory* and other later works lacked the discipline and restraint of his "middle period." Although there was a twenty-seven-year difference between them, Walpole was intelligent and attentive, and Conrad quickly used the younger man as a sounding board for his troubles, someone who would provide solace for the entire family; in fact, both Borys and Jessie kept in touch with him after Conrad's death.

To Walpole, Conrad correlated the various threads of the European situation as they ran into his mind, connections that no one else was likely to make. He saw the European "theatre of operations" as a gigantic drama or a huge scenario for one of his novels. His description below is reminiscent of the forces in *Nostromo*, or the meeting of elements in the more recent *Victory*. After stating that he is "completely out of it" because of age and infirmity, he gets to his chief point, which is the moral quagmire that Europe has become:

> I have been (like a sort of dismal male witch) peering (mentally) into the caldron in which la force des choses has plunged you bodily. What will come out of it? A very subtle poison or some very rough-tested Elixir of Life? Or neither? Just mere kvass so to speak. It's very curious. *I feel startled when I remember that my foster-brother is an Ukrainian peasant* [my italics]. He is probably alive yet. What does he think? I am afraid that what he thinks bodes no good to the boys and girls with whom I used to play and to their children. Are those gracious shades of my memory to turn into blood-stained spectres [Conrad has in mind the Russian Revolution]? C'est possible, vous savez! And those houses where under a soul-crushing oppression so much noble idealism, chivalrous traditions, the sanity and the amenities of western civilisation were so valiantly preserved—are they to vanish into smoke? Cela, aussi est très possible! And at any rate moral destruction is unavoidable. Meantime I have been asked to join into public ecstasies of joy. I begged to be excused. Le monde est bête.

Conrad's mind was reaching toward some novelistic means of capturing this sense of destructive upheaval, this mixture of bravery and insanity, of idealism and amorality; and his work on *Suspense* later was probably his attempt to deal with it imaginatively. Calling up Napoleon and his era, Conrad hoped to create that background of conflicting elements which would be his sense of the European conflict—*the* archetypal conflict of European countries at war with each other and with themselves, where radical change is inevitable, and yet where change is simply another name for reaction, retrogression, and futility.

What Conrad needed, in order to regain his artistic sanity, was that sense of his own life "arranged, combined, coloured" for imaginative purposes. He had not lost subjects so much as he had that "mental and emotional reaction" to his subjects which defined his method of working. His ability to produce little more than fleeting ideas was attached to the way his imagination had always functioned, and had Conrad been a younger or healthier man, very possibly this creative crisis would have led to either a new direction or a strengthening of purpose. There was no reason to assume his present crisis would lead only to decline and breakdown. Intermittent passages and several scenes in his work to come indicate he had not lost contact with his main subject matter or his treatment of it; and a novel such as *The Rover*, while flawed, demonstrates that on a small scale he could still evoke the distinctive Conradian tone.

In a curious way, both Conrad and Gide were undergoing comparable breakdowns or malfunctions, with the novel *Victory* the connective tissue. We are suggesting not any cause and effect, but one of those cultural phenomena that cannot be ignored. In 1916–17, while Gide was immersed in his "*Victory* thing," he was, like Conrad, undergoing tremendous conflicts that brought him close to anomie. Whereas Conrad's condition involved a physical breakdown that had its psychological counterpart in feelings of anomie and will-lessness, Gide was floundering in a religious and personal crisis of equal intensity.

In his "Intimate Journal," Gide spoke of "wallowing in a terrifying intellectual disorder" during this time, and his work, rather than his letters to Conrad, indicates such disorder: *La Porte étroite, Isabelle, Les Caves du Vatican, La Symphonie pastorale*, the beginning of the second part of *Si le grain ne meurt.* The attachment to Conrad and to Conrad's fiction struck Gide somewhere in those nebulous regions where personal conflicts, malaise, and artistic possibilities all struggled for supremacy.

The Conrad psychodrama, though less dramatic, was no less intense and debilitating. He, too, journeyed through the valley of breakdown and death. The decline of personal control found its psychological counterpart in certain sexual ambiguities in his fiction—Monsieur George's passion juxtaposed with Rita's sculptured passionlessness in *The Arrow*, for example—and a personal malaise which appeared to derive as much from Conrad himself as from the misery of the war years. The critical point for him may have been the measuring of himself against a maturing Borys, the man forced by the boy to take account and incapable of handling what he found. His letters, full of the usual illness and apathy, suggest an emotional crisis. His recurring image is of a man on a tightrope, walking forward without a net beneath. The crowd expects to be pleased, but the walker has only one thought: not to fall.

If we jump ahead a few months, to December 30, 1917, Conrad's first extant letter to Gide after eighteen months juxtaposes his own inaction with the latter's celebrity. Conrad mentions a favorable study of Gide in the *Times Literary Supplement*, although, he says, "One cannot say anything grand about André Gide in two columns." Nevertheless, one finds an admiration "which pierces through the lackluster phrases and which renders the article sympathetic as a whole." Following this, Conrad refers to himself: "I do not work [he was starting *The Arrow of Gold*]; I have nearly ceased to think of work. I think of my friends, in truth, but I have nothing to say to them. Once

I put my pen in hand, it is only to recoil, as if from fear." Not only is the moment of contrast striking, the phrasing is especially trenchant: Gide basking in universal praise, while he, Conrad, is fearful of even holding a pen, recoiling from it, a shadow of himself.

This attitude continued into 1918, when Conrad hung on to the translations as though they were a lifeline with reality. Even his work on *The Arrow* seemed to him the efforts of a man playing the lyre while Rome burned. The real showdown between the two, Conrad and Gide, would come over the translation of *The Arrow*, in 1919, when the personal relevance of that novel would meet with a treatment Conrad could not bear to face. By then, Gide's spiritual malaise had passed—he was younger and healthier than Conrad—and he regained contact with his creative talent.

But before the return of his powers, Gide threw himself into the translations, disguising his personal losses while preserving his active role in a central literary tradition. To translate a writer into French who had himself learned to write English after perfecting himself in French was full of those paradoxes which Gide could not as yet work out creatively. With Gide, one must always look directly to his ego needs to interpret his activities. His work on Conrad, and it was truly heroic, was not an abnegation of self but a singular display of self, what was still left to him while his own creative energies were dammed. When the correspondence became inflamed in 1919 over *The Arrow of Gold*, the writers had moved beyond their roles as sharers of sorts; they had become combatants, where intense personal needs lay behind something as apparently superficial as a translation.

None of this could dispel the worry over Borys, which was a continual wound and distraction. It was now midsummer of 1917, and an entire generation of European youth had died on the several fronts. The English officer corps had been particularly hit, and most young officers in the twenty-to-twenty-five range, Borys's slightly older contemporaries, were dead. In eighteen months, he had had only sixteen days of leave, including three days in Paris in July. Retinger had taken him to lunch, and some Americans had been kind to him; one of them, a steel magnate, promising him a position in a motorworks after the war. Conrad's own attitude toward Americans had altered, at least temporarily, from condescension to gratitude. "It strikes me I'll have to be mightily civil to a good many Americans after the war," he told Colvin.

T. S. Eliot, in 1917, published *Prufrock and Other Observations*, with a dedication, from Dante, to his young friend Jean Verdenal, who died at twenty-six in the Dardanelles, Churchill's costly folly. Eliot knew of Conrad, of course, but it is questionable if Conrad had ever heard of the American poet, although Ford or Quinn may have spoken of him. The *Prufrock* volume, inconspicuous in itself during a war—the title poem had appeared separately in *Poetry* in 1915—might seem to someone like Conrad to be a publication on another planet. And yet Eliot was exploring territory that had been Conrad's for some time, especially with *Jim* or "Heart of Darkness," or with protagonists such as Decoud, Heyst, and Renouard. Eliot used an epigraph from the *Inferno* for *Prufrock*, and Conrad had used the Dantesque and Virgilian journey underground for "Heart of Darkness." Eliot's protagonist is effete and asexual, torn by doubts and fears, but when he asserts "I am Lazarus, come from the dead, / Come back to tell you all, I shall tell you all"—he shifts our attention to Conrad's Marlow, to Decoud's vision, to Heyst's sense of self just before he immolates himself.

Prufrock's fear of the real world, with its images of impotence, dryness, desolation, are all aspects of the Conradian sensibility, although only touched upon in the later years. In 1917, Eliot himself underwent a severe psychological impoverishment, a critical period when he lost all active will; but he descended into himself, regained his powers, emerged with a poem that would become *The Waste Land*. When he did surface, he attached to that poem an epigraph from "Heart of Darkness," the line expressing Kurtz's "Horror," and only Pound, his "*miglior fabbro*," could dissuade him from using it.

The new sensibility which had appeared with Eliot (and Pound and Yeats) in poetry and Joyce, Lawrence, and Woolf in fiction meant that Conrad would be designated as an "old master" and, therefore, bypassed as a living force. Since this coincided with his own creative passivity and inability to work regularly, it meant that even as he gained a wider reading public and his sales increased several-fold, he lost standing with younger writers. Woolf was characteristic, in that she wanted to "place" Conrad and then conveniently forget about him, a curious Pole writing in English. Although much of the experimentation that characterized this new sensibility occurred with language, the younger generation failed to see that Conrad had himself explored the potentialities of language and had created a literary language for describing places and people that had not existed as such in literature previously. The "new language," however, meant the re-forming of words, the use of the stream of consciousness, free associative patterns, elision of words and meaning, elimination of routine punctuation; and in these areas, Conrad was of course found lacking. We have, then, a great paradox: that while Conrad had helped to shape the new sensibility, a fact few of the above writers rejected, he was to be bypassed in his own lifetime, viewed as traditional, an "anti" force in literature.

Part of Conrad's frustration in these years, possibly one reason he could not work, was his sense of things as changing not only socially and politically but literarily. Yet even if he were physically removed, and heard about London society through surrogates such as Colvin, he may have stayed more directly in touch through Ford, Norman Douglas, or even John Quinn, who in 1917 had sent Conrad the latest volume of Ezra Pound. This may have been his *Lustra* (1916), which Conrad said he could not read without the kind of concentration he did not possess. If he had read about Pound's Mauberley, he would have recognized familiar territory, although the shifting lines and rearrangement of experience might have discouraged him before he sighted some of his own characters and tones. Mauberley ponders, "What god, man, or hero / Shall I place a tin wreath upon!" and Conrad could have responded that he had heard it all before.

CHAPTER 35

"A little dust, a ghost, a gossip's tale"

TO Pinker, he announced, in August 1917, that he was working on a story with stage possibilities. He planned it as a magazine fiction. It involved putting "a *femme gallante* (not exactly in that character but as an ardent Royalist) and her peasant sister, very hard-headed, very religious and very mercenary, on the stage." This decision to work on the dramatic potentialities of his idea coincided with a plan to collaborate with Hastings on an original play having to do with a faked old master, to be set in Italy.* Conrad may have had in mind a scheme formed many years ago and worked out in some detail in those notes written into Teofila Bobrowska's commonplace book, where he had outlined "Tuan Jim." The notes for a play follow several items: the section on "Tuan Jim," a few sentences of *The Rescue*, a list of some tentative titles, and the names of Lucas, the critic, and Pawling, the publisher. Then comes the outline of a play set in Ferrara, the protagonist one Fabio. There is no clear indication of any forward movement, simply a good deal of Verdi dramatics—a pageant suggested, some anger, a fight looming. The outline does not go much beyond the first act.

It was unlikely, however, that Conrad would dredge up this old idea, mainly because it goes back to a stylistic period which he felt was over. Also, a drama set in the Renaissance would not seem to be quite the right thing for a war audience. There is the further possibility that he had in mind the project he and Ford planned based on Ford Madox Brown, Ford's grandfather, although a "faked old Master" would not fit. In any event, as he became engaged with his other "dramatic venture," *The Arrow of Gold*, he retreated from any further collaborations. The original plan of *The Arrow*, in part at least, was epistolary: to be made up of "Selected Passages from Letters"

* A further collaboration on *Under Western Eyes* was also in the works, but Hastings declined because he thought Conrad's *One Day More* was hopeless from a theatrical standpoint.

written by the protagonist to a woman he had known thirty-five years earlier. The age of the protagonist at the time of the writing was close to Conrad's in the early autumn of 1917, fifty-nine. The canceled opening of the novel, which we can assume he wrote in the late summer–early fall of 1917, speaks of two earlier loves, the second of whom would be the correspondent for the novel.

All this, however, was merely superstructure. The real substance of the novel-to-be was a journey into Conrad's past, when he was approximately Borys's age and engaged in his own great adventure. As he indicated in the Author's Note, the story was not so much a part of his memory as it was "an inherent part" of himself. And in the same Note, he clearly associated his memory of his Marseilles days with those dark hours of the war when the novel was written. It seems certain that Conrad required an "adventure" to parallel the hazards experienced by that younger generation passing through the "shadow line," just as his voyages with the fleet and flight in a plane were attempts to find some useful function in an exploit that needed only younger men. In this respect, we can say that the war helped draw Conrad out of his malaise, in about the same proportions that it had thrown him into it.

Once Conrad began to work, he by no means had clear sailing. That sense of freedom would never come again; and even in the past, it had been fleeting. Too many external affairs now intruded. As he wrote Edith Wharton, he was terribly anxious about Borys, who had just been home, at the end of September; but almost of equal worry was the condition of Jessie's knee, which would require another operation. In the meantime, Conrad had gotten to know Gérard Jean-Aubry, a young writer and music critic, friend of Gide and the Gide circle, and the man who was to bring together Conrad's letters and personal papers for a full-length biography in the later 1920s. The association was a felicitous one for Conrad, for now he was surrounded by young men who were writing favorably about him—Curle and Walpole in a critical sense, Jean-Aubry as the future biographer. Of course, standing beyond them was the "real" literary world, the men and women who were reshaping the course of poetry and fiction in the twentieth century; and some of them, like Pound and Lawrence, were more interested in fulfilling their own visions than in reading critical interpretations.*

Before going up to London for three months, Conrad responded to a letter from H. L. Mencken, who had been celebrating him as one of the great modern masters. Mencken had sent Conrad some of his thoughts about the writer, but for all of Mencken's praise, Conrad was annoyed at several mis-

* Lawrence, for example, who of course read for his own needs, had great respect for Conrad's abilities but thought he was wasting himself on Razumov types and worried that he had become one of those "Writers among the Ruins": "I can't forgive Conrad for being so sad and for giving in."

conceptions. He used his response to review his entire career, but his real response he saved for a letter to George Keating more than four years later. At that time, he spoke of Mencken as possessing a vigor like an electric current. "In all he writes [Conrad told Keating] there is a crackle of blue sparks, like those one sees in a dynamo house amongst revolving masses of metal that give you a sense of enormous hidden power."

Conrad says he is pleased that such a person likes him; otherwise, he feels, he would have been torn limb from limb. "It makes me giddy." Yet despite all this, he is terribly disturbed that Mencken harps on his "Slavonism." He wonders if Mencken has in mind some "primitive natures fashioned by a Byzantine theological conception of life, with an inclination to perverted mysticism?" The description is witty, but underlined by contempt. He suspected that Mencken was trying to make him something unique for his *Smart Set* readers, and the Slavonic aspect suggested Conrad as an exotic bird with rare plumage. "I am a child, not of a savage but of a chivalrous tradition," Conrad insisted to Keating; for Mencken, the savage tradition was preferable.*

Just after the middle of November, the Conrads arrived in London, to stay at Hyde Park Mansions, on Marylebone Road. What was particularly disturbing about this trip is that Jessie expected once again to have her leg amputated at the knee, although the examination by Sir Robert Jones at the end of the month led to a verdict against amputation in favor of further exploratory operations.

The well-known actress Lillah McCarthy was interested in producing *Victory* in her theater, with an eye on the role of Lena for herself. This development coincided with treatment for Jessie's knee, to save the leg. The so-called cure went on and on, and Conrad had no way of knowing how long it would last. He claimed he could not work, but apparently he did, for *The Arrow of Gold,* once he focused exclusively on it, was turned out in less than twelve months, by early June of 1918. Yet he told Ted and Helen Sanderson that although he had been working every morning, "You can imagine what sort of stuff that is. No colour, no relief, no tonality; the thinnest possible

---

* Although Mencken's essay ("Joseph Conrad," in *A Book of Prefaces,* which Knopf published) stressed Conrad's Slavic roots, its criticism is not wide of the mark. Mencken rightfully saw Conrad, in that perennial comparison, as far superior to Kipling, a "first-rate artist" compared to an "adroit artisan." Further, he saw nearly all of Conrad's adventurous elements as having a symbolic import; yet unlike the purely romantic writers, he provided motives and the inner workings of his characters. Mencken brought Conrad together with writers such as Twain, Dreiser, Hardy, and Crane, all of them concerned with man's inability to make the universe intelligible. The Hardy and Crane comparison is apt; the Twain and Dreiser less so. Mencken also pointed out that women count very little in his protagonists' struggles; but this is very much an American, indeed a red-blooded, reading. He is especially pleased that Conrad's heroes are moved very rarely by *amour.* If only they drank German beer!

squeaky babble. And when I've finished with it I shall go out and sell it in the market place for 20 times the money I had for the Nigger—30 times the money I had for the Mirror of the Sea—." Conrad's diagnosis was accurate. The first hundred pages of *The Arrow* are more like the notes for a novel than the novel itself. It is all beginnings; forward movement of any kind is frustrated by long dialogues or scenes which remain static. As he observed, they lack "relief" and "tonality"; and the "setting up" of George and his companions vis-à-vis Rita appears like a still life without sufficient color.

The London stay, however, was not all anxiety and worry. Conrad visited old friends, saw Galsworthy, the Garnetts, Graham's mother, Mrs. Dummett—Graham himself was in Colombia. But for a man who defined himself by his work, it was a bad time. He called himself, like Lear, "chilly, chilly," and found that each day meant a "new, painful start and a calling for help to the gods who are deaf—every morning." And what resulted was "strangely remote." Yet it was based on intimate memories, or fantasies intermixed with memories. In London, as he waited for Jessie's knee to adapt to the heavy metal splint inserted in it to keep it rigid, and as he also awaited Borys on home leave,* he said it felt "like being in jail." He even thought of joining the National Service, possibly to work on the docks, but knew his health was too poor to volunteer.

Conrad looked most wistfully at the navy, in whose service, he felt, one could pursue a "very high idealistic" end. He found the navy thinking "rightly on all questions," by which he did not mean simply like himself. Nevertheless, in this period of moral anarchy and irrationality, he found, he says, that whatever conclusion a "naval officer arrives at, even if distasteful to me, I can't help recognising that he arrives at it on sound grounds, making use of his intelligence and not by way of petty prejudices or ignorant assumptions." Searching for something steady and harmonious, Conrad looked to the ideal here, thinking of himself as a seaman and pondering the men under whom he served. The ideal was a political idea, as well, of a state that depended for its stability not on Lloyd George but on a trustworthy leader. And yet even as Conrad sought this ideal in the naval service, he had rejected it in his fiction, as a fiction.

* The younger son, John, remains on the periphery because of his youth; he was not yet in his teens at this time. His memories of his childhood ("Some Reminiscences of My Father" in *Zywy*) indicate none of the strains which existed between Conrad and his older son. John recounts, chiefly, adventures in the family cars and on sailing expeditions. Conrad was very much a man's man in his handling of his son, stressing an approach based on vigor, endurance, exploits, and honesty, qualities associated with a maritime career. We learn, also, that father and son played chess together on numerous occasions, using Capablanca's book for its games. Conrad would often rout John out of bed late at night for a game. The younger son's less strained relationship with his father surely had to do with the improved fortunes of the family, and to the fact that the younger son usually bears less of the burden of competition with and/or envy of the father.

Polish affairs moved in and out of his life, even as he was writing about Marseilles, his "escape" from Poland. Retinger was in desperate financial condition, and Conrad sent £50. Also, with Walpole's assistance, Conrad planned a luncheon engagement with a Podolian named Sobański, who was, probably, a descendant of the Mrs. Melania Sobańska whose estate in Podolia Apollo Korzeniowski had administered. Sobański was called away suddenly and the luncheon canceled, but the layers of consciousness on which Conrad depended were complex: meeting the descendant of people whose roots extended as far back into Podolia as his own even as he was writing a novel about a young man who had left it all. As he told Walpole: when Sobański apologized for leaving suddenly, the latter pointed out that he and Conrad were "doubly fellow-countrymen" as Poles and Podolians. Conrad commented: "All Podolia's sons are very fond of their romantic province. But I have never seen it and am not likely to, now."

Conrad turned sixty, and the war continued, with no end in sight. For those who lived through it, it could have been a modern version of the Hundred Years War. It would only end when the countries were exhausted and their supply of soldiers depleted. It was as if all of Europe were undergoing a biblical curse, a red flood replacing the customary waters of Noah. Conrad greeted the new year, 1918, by calling it with Coleridgean grimness "like life in death," and he meant a threefold existence: the war outside, his own malaise, and the condition of Jessie's leg. The dramatic version of *Victory* seemed to be acquiring a history, by now, that was an integral part of the general malaise. After all the intense correspondence between Conrad and Hastings, the play was stalled. Originally, Irving had wanted to play Jones, but was troubled by the latter's misogyny, which seemed unmotivated, unless one could say it was constitutional. He then shifted to the role of Heyst, which involved a rewriting on Hastings's part to move the emphasis. As noted above, Lillah McCarthy, hearing *Victory* was available, wanted to produce it and herself play Lena, but dropped the plan; that occurred in the middle of January. Then, Marie Löhr took over the entire project, acquired the rights to produce the play, and both directed it and played the role of Lena. All this would work out during 1918 and early 1919, leading to an opening on March 26, 1919, which Conrad did not attend because of illness. Jessie asserted that Conrad never attended, during neither rehearsals nor the actual run. But according to the director, although Conrad skipped all the rehearsals, he came three times during the run of the play.

Conrad kept up something of a social life. Symons invited him for a chat on January 31, but he was busy with Ted Sanderson, who planned to drop in for a long afternoon's talk. Walpole was invited for later that day or the next. And Edward Garnett was expected on Friday, February 1. By early February, some of the suspense about Jessie's fate had been dissipated, with the operation postponed and the apparatus inserted into her damaged knee.

Announcing this relatively good news to Quinn on the sixth, Conrad inserted an amusing passage on Ezra Pound, whose work Quinn had sent.

> E.P. is certainly a poet but I am afraid I am too old and too wooden-headed to appreciate him as perhaps he deserves. The critics here consider him harmless; but as he has, I believe, a very good opinion of himself I don't suppose he worries his head about the critics very much. Besides he has many women at his feet; which must be immensely comforting.

Quinn tried to engage Conrad in broad political discussions, apparently feeling that his correspondent, as a Middle European living in England, had a political expertise or intuitive sense. Conrad often responded lengthily, as though he felt compelled to instruct the untutored American in European realities. In this same letter, of February 6, Conrad wrote what he felt might be Poland's epitaph: "Have no illusions":

> The great thing is to keep the Russian infection, its decomposing power, from the social organism of the rest of the world. In this Poland will have to play its part on whatever lines her future may have to be laid. And at the same time she will have to resist the immense power of germanism which would be death too, but in another shape. Whether that nation over-run, ruined and shaken to the very foundations of its soul will rise to this awful task I really don't know. What assistance she will be able to get from the Western world nobody can tell. Never was there such a darkness over a people's future, and that, don't forget, coming after more than a century of soul-grinding oppression in which apart from a few choice spirits the Western world took no interest. Fine words have been given to it before. And the finer the words the greater was always the deception.

Conrad then recalls his 1914 visit to Cracow:

> One evening in August in 1914 in a dimly lit, big room I spoke to a small group of Poles belonging to the University and the political life of the town of Cracow. One of the things I said was: "Rest assured that whoever makes peace in six months (that was all the talk then—that the war couldn't last) England will go on for ten years if necessary." But I had also the courage to tell them: "Have no illusions. If anybody has got to be sacrificed in this war it will be you. If there is any salvation to be found it is only in your own breasts, it is only by the force of your inner life that you will be able to resist the rottenness of Russia and the soullessness of Germany. And this will be your fate for ever and ever. For nothing in the world can alter the force of facts."

Conrad's pessimism, his sense of irony and paradox, his recognition that all life is a deadly trap—all of these were never more finely honed than in his outpourings earlier to Graham and later to Quinn: "That is the tragedy—the inner anguish—the bitterness of lost lives, of unsettled consciences and of spiritual perplexities. Courage, endurance, enthusiasm, the hardest idealism itself, have their limits. And beyond those limits what is there? The eternal ignorance of mankind, the fateful darkness in which only vague forms can be seen which themselves may be no more than illusions."

The vision that all is appearance, that all we have is illusions, reverts to Conrad's outlook in "Heart of Darkness" and *Nostromo*, the period when his creative energy was at its highest levels. He concludes: "In this enormous upheaval of Forces and Consciences all Hopes and all Fears are on an equality. Either can lead mankind equally astray. And there is nothing in the world to hold on but the work that has to be done on each succeeding day. Outside that there is nothing to lay hold of but what each man can find in himself." This is not the defeat of an older man trapped in bitterness but a logical consequence of Conrad's progression as a man and an artist. The older he grew, the more baffled he became; his vision at the end was just as fierce and just as intense, although the power to incorporate it into fiction no longer raged.

By mid-February, of 1918, Conrad was moving along on *The Arrow of Gold* (in manuscript known as "The Laugh") sufficiently well so that he could speculate about titles. "The Arrow of Gold" was still not clear to him, and he listed several. One of them, *Two Sisters*, recalls *The Sisters*, the fragment going back to 1896; others include *Mme de Lastaola*, *The Heiress*, even *The Goatherd*. Although Conrad appears to have had a firm grasp of his individual materials, the general outline he provided for a correspondent, S. A. Everitt of Doubleday, suggests a good deal of hollowness, or disconnectedness of parts. He comments on Rita, asserting that the book deals with "her private life; her sense of her own position, her sentiments and her fears." It also deals with an episode "in the general experience of the young narrator"; he stresses that all the interest lies not in backgrounds but in the personages, despite the Southern European coloring. The outline suggests materials running parallel to each other; and it was Conrad's attempts to bring into interrelationship these disparate elements—Rita, George, the background of smuggling and danger, the feuds within the Carlist forces—that proved insurmountable. The difficulty on the personal level, between Rita and George, was manifest on every level,* and only overcome in details or in peripheral matters, such as the dialogue between George and Mrs. Blunt.

On February 26, the Conrads returned from London to Capel House, where they continued to live until March of the following year. The return

---

* In her review of *The Arrow*, Katherine Mansfield felt that it was a novel of Conrad's youth patched up and published later to capitalize on his dazzling reputation. Her reasoning was, in part, connected to his presentation of Doña Rita, who she felt was the fantasy figure of an apprentice writer: ". . . the femme fatale, the woman of all times, the Old Enchantress, the idol before whom no man can do aught but worship the Eternal Feminine, Donna Rita, woman." She did, however, praise *The Rescue* highly in a later review, seeing it as a fully mature work, an opinion shared by Gide and, to a limited extent, by Virginia Woolf.

coincided with Borys's encampment in a heavily shelled area near Saint-Quentin, where the Germans were pressing for an advantage. Conrad felt physically low and, inevitably, depressed, walking the edge of existence, as he put it. Colvin, ever attentive to his needs, invited him to London for a visit near the end of March, but he felt unequal to the effort. Not until late April did Conrad find himself capable of running up to London, and then only when he felt Borys was out of danger, resting for the time being in either Rouen or Le Havre.

On the twenty-seventh of April, he wrote his older son a long letter. It is chatty and affectionate, and particularly solicitous of his safety. We learn that Rothenstein had tried to see Borys near the front, then around Lassigny, but was unsuccessful and returned with only a pencil drawing of Borys for Jessie. Conrad mentions having seen a Rothenstein exhibition of war pictures at the Goupil Gallery, and thanks Borys for his thoughtfulness in having sent Conrad a jar of his favorite olives, which never turned up. On the same day, Conrad told Walpole he expected to come to London with a completed manuscript "of a sort of novel," which meant that his work on *The Arrow* was proceeding rapidly. Despite all his complaints, he had turned out a manuscript of 125,000 words in less than a year.

On May 6 or 7, Conrad went up to London and, under Colvin's sponsorship, became a member of the Atheneum Club. Before the inevitable attack of gout upon his return home, he groped for some sense of life. He wrote to Gide as "Very dear friend" and showed profound gratitude for Gide's plan to issue a small edition of *Typhoon* alone, in his own translation. "Truly, you spoil me. To be spoiled by a friend such as you is very agreeable. I ask myself only what I have been able to do to gain this affectionate friendship which is certainly the 'grand Prix' of my literary life. But to what avail? It is a gift of the gods."

Even more significant than that pleasant news was Conrad's ability to write seriously about art and *his* art. Barrett H. Clark had inquired, apparently, about Conrad's aesthetic principles, and he decided to respond at length. Although we have already mentioned parts of this letter, it is so firm in its artistic principles that it hardly manifests an author at the end of his tether. Conrad first stresses that in terms of career he is not an "Ancient," since his writing life has extended only over twenty-five years. In that time, he feels he has evolved—some critics indeed "have detected three marked periods"—and he insists that the process is ongoing. He emphasizes that he is always himself, completely a formed man, but nevertheless no slave of prejudices and formulas. His attitude, his angle of vision, his methods of composition are not fixed; he is, he says, "always trying for freedom—within my limits." His "limits" do not mean his deficiencies but the boundaries he has set for himself.

Conrad then focuses on Clark's chief question, which was whether he considered himself a realist: he emphasizes that the greater the work of art, the more "it acquires a symbolic character." Art does not limit itself and does not lend itself to a definite conclusion. In this respect, consciously or not, he had aligned himself with the latest in art and literature, even with Pound. By "symbolic" Conrad insists he does not mean the symbolist school of poets or prose writers; theirs was a literary proceeding, whereas he is searching for something broader. All great works, to gain complexity, power, depth, and beauty, must have a symbolic dimension, which is probably what he meant in the Preface to *The Nigger* when he outlined a form of impressionism. He feels there cannot be greater precision.

> I don't think you will quarrel with me on the ground of lack of precision; for as to precision of images and analysis my artistic conscience is at rest. I have given there all the truth that is in me; and all that the critics may say can make my honesty neither more nor less. But as to "final effect" my conscience has nothing to do with that. It is the critic's affair to bring to its contemplation his own honesty, his sensibility and intelligence. The matter for his conscience is just his judgment. If his conscience is busy with petty scruples and trammelled by superficial formulas then his judgment will be superficial and petty. But an artist has no right to quarrel with the inspirations, either lofty or base, of another soul.

With that "position paper" behind him, he intensified the long haul on the novel. He did interrupt it long enough to write to W. H. Chesson, the former reader at Fisher Unwin, and the man who along with Edward Garnett helped to advance Conrad's fortunes as a writer. They had broken off for many years until Chesson wrote that he wanted to prepare a preface for a reprint of *Almayer's Folly*. In responding that he was very pleased to be "confided to your pen," Conrad reviewed the manner in which he had submitted his first manuscript to Fisher Unwin, but makes that great and momentous event for him sound perfunctory and tired. His sole note of urgency comes when he defends his reminiscences as indeed having thrown "some light on my first book." Chesson had shrewdly commented, apparently, that Conrad was being evasive, or had refused to examine the full circumstances of his early years.

On his return from London, Conrad took to his bed for forty-eight hours. He was out of sorts generally, unhappy about his own work, and disturbed by the war and the fate of Borys. His outlook became increasingly resigned; he appeared to stall and falter even over his own givens of responsibility, altruism, individual growth and evolution. He told Garnett that literary satire, Garnett's characteristic mode, seems a "vain use of intelligence" because it assumes there is a revealed truth. There are no such truths—only existence itself—and consequently not only satire but intelligence as well is of little account. If Garnett speaks in terms of right and wrong, which both satire and intelligence assume, he speaks of things "with no connection whatever with the fundamental realities of life." One can, Conrad says, talk only of feelings—which *are*, and "in submitting to them we can avoid neither death nor suffering which are our common lot, but we can bear them in peace."

Even with work on *The Arrow* still incomplete, the Conrads entertained friends rather frequently. Conrad liked to indulge in small dinner groups, or else play host to single friends—Walpole was a frequent guest, the Colvins were others. And toward the end of May, Jean-Aubry, whom Gide had added to the team of translators, paid a call at Capel House. Conrad's way of proceeding on his manuscript was to write or dictate before the arrival of guests, or else to retire after lunch and then work in the evening after they had left. Although his energies were reduced, such visits appeared to enliven rather than exhaust him.

By June 4, *The Arrow of Gold* was complete except for the preliminary and final notes, which made the novel "A Story between Two Notes." As Conrad prepared to write these notes, Borys told him he was doing captain's duty with his battery and living with men, "superiors and inferiors, whom he positively loves and trusts." Conrad commented: ". . . and so, if it must come to, it will be easier to die in their company." Confronting the Conrads, in addition, was another trip to London for the familiar purpose: an operation on Jessie's knee on June 27. They would stay once more at 4, Hyde Park Mansions.

Before leaving, Conrad with apparent delight wrote to Gosse at great length about *Nostromo.* In retelling the story of this fictional Dominic Cervoni, Conrad doubled back upon himself: the fictional Dominic ever in his mind in the shape of Nostromo even as he has just finished writing of the real Dominic in *The Arrow of Gold.* And added to the ironic juxtaposition is, very possibly, Conrad's awareness of how much greater the fictional creation is than the real one. To Gosse, he uses Nostromo to show the world as it is.

> But Nostromo is not a thief. He is a strong man succumbing to a temptation of which mere greed is the smallest possible ingredient. And even while succumbing to the temptation he still remains a strong man. He is not going to succumb to remorse. He will let nothing tear this treasure from his grasp; and at last the treasure gets hold of him and becomes the direct cause of his tragic end. In the very hour of death he is reluctant to disclose his secret to Mrs Gould. Perhaps it is only then that Nostromo secures that recognition of his character for which he had been thirsting all his life, when Mrs Gould, the perfectly sympathetic woman, is obscurely moved to refuse the confession (which she sees it costs him so much to make) with the words: "No, Capataz. Let it be lost for ever."

Deep within Conrad's imagination, this archetypal figure, Nostromo, has taken over his world, and he moves along the line of his character's thought so that it seems his own. And that treasure which Nostromo retains within his grasp is the nub of his power, as of Conrad's, and he will die rather than divulge its source.*

As Jessie's operation drew near, Conrad tried to clear away all encumbrances. He told Hastings to proceed with the long-awaited dramatization of *Victory*, giving him "complete freedom without any reservation or stipulation." Borys arrived home from the front on "compassionate leave" on the Tuesday before the operation, and John, his younger brother, was also brought home from school. The operation proceeded as planned, and Sir Robert Jones, finding the knee septic, removed the kneecap, excised all the cartilage, and made a new socket. The operation was deemed a success, with the expectation that Jessie would have a stiff joint but one free from pain. The expectation was short-lived, however, for in October the Conrads were once again in London for follow-up treatment of the knee.

During the stay in London, in midsummer, Conrad turned to *The Rescue*. As early as July 5, he told Pinker he did not want to start a series of articles so as to keep his head free for work on that novel. By the fifth, he was rereading it, for the twentieth time, he says, and hoped to complete it by the end of the year; that is, within five months. He would, in actuality, take ten, until May of 1919. When he began it, Jessie was facing an undetermined stay in a nursing home, and Borys was preparing to return to the front in Flanders. The title of the novel had, once again, taken on symbolic importance. He felt, he told Helen Sanderson, like a "lost soul" without Jessie.

In August, as it turned out, Borys remained with Conrad at Hyde Park Mansions, both of them ill, the son with influenza, and attended by Dr. Mackintosh. Conrad wrote a series of letters to Jessie, who was still in the nursing home. They reveal that his relationship with Jessie was one of considerable dependence, to the degree that he viewed himself as her son rather than husband, what we glimpsed when he went on "war duty." The letters are signed "Boy" or "Ever your Boy," and they display Conrad's need to gain assurances about his own ailments, like a child with his mother. The letters reveal the maternal side of Jessie, the "son" aspect of Conrad, as if she were the far older one, rather than younger by fifteen years. Conrad suffered from lumbago, which necessitated mustard plasters and nursing. He reports loss of appetite and discomfort, but little other news, except Borys's

* He also tried to place the geography of the novel: "Of course you have seen yourself that Sulaco is a synthetic product. The geographical base is, as you have seen, mainly Venezuela; but there are bits of Mexico in it, and the aspect represented by the mountains appertains in character more to the Chilean seaboard than to any other. The curtain of clouds hangs always over Iquique. The rest of the meteorology belongs to the Gulf of Panama and, generally, to the Western Coast of Mexico as far as Mazatlan. The historical part is an achievement in mosaic too, though, personally it seems to me much more true than any history I ever learned. In the last instance I may say that Sulaco is intended for *all* South America in the seventh decade of the nineteenth century."

progress. The letters sound like hospital reports, although Jessie was herself the one hospitalized. Conrad addresses her: "You are a very dear good, charming plucky, sweet, pretty kitty-faced girl and I love you very much." His devotion is admirable, the words themselves unsettling. He also refers to Borys as "Boy," and so his remarks derive from her "two boys," although John remains John, not "boy." By late August, the Conrads had returned to Capel House, and Borys had gone back to Flanders. In October, the entire saga would repeat itself, with Borys this time returning, severely gassed, for good.

The only work Conrad accomplished during this period of disorientation was to reread *The Rescue* manuscript and turn out a brief article, "Well Done," for the *Daily Chronicle* (August 22–24); earlier, in March, he had written a similar short piece for the *Daily Mail*, "Tradition." These sea pieces, based on his naval trips, were designed to hold up to public view the high level of service of the men who go to sea, and Conrad considered such work a contribution to the war effort. Also, he was building a collection that would in 1921 become *Notes on Life and Letters.* A good deal of the later summer and early fall was spent either in a gouty, bedridden condition, or filled with dread of gout and, therefore, reclusive and quiet. From Conrad's letters to close friends, it is difficult to believe he still had almost three novels in him, one of them *Suspense,* planned as the chef-d'oeuvre of his later years.

With American forces building up on the main front, the war had taken a more hopeful turn, but it was far from over and heavy casualties were still expected. Soldiers were being killed in large numbers even as armistice became common talk. It was, in fact, during an advance of the army that Borys was badly gassed, on October 10, just a month before the Armistice. Partially buried by a salvo of high explosive shells, he was incapacitated not by the explosions but by the gas in several of the shells. This ended his participation in the war and seriously undermined his health for several years thereafter. He was sent to a Red Cross Hospital in Rouen, where he was treated for gas and, later, for shellshock. For the latter condition, he was transferred to a neurological hospital in South London. This combination of events in Borys's life was accompanied by the Conrads' return to London in early October, when Jessie received further treatment for her knee. Since it failed to heal, there were intimations of a new development, a still undiagnosed internal disorder.

Conrad was wretched. The state of England he found incomprehensible: what with strikes at home, a failure to support the war effort fully, and the still-uncertain outcome of the Entente's advance. For this latest bout in London, Conrad planned to stay at the Norfolk, on Surrey Street in the Strand, which was near Pinker's office and the nursing home and Baker Street. Hoping to work, he brought along Miss Hallowes, for dictation. He also asked Pinker if he could use his son Eric's room (Eric was away on war service) as an office for three hours a day. Pinker had suggested some fiction with a possible Polish slant to it, to capitalize on Poland's future now that the Russian Revolution had altered the political situation on the Eastern front. Conrad rejected the idea, however, saying that *The Rescue* was now at the center of his attention and had been for the last six weeks. He indicated, nevertheless, that he would be open to some newspaper contributions of three or four thousand words; but nothing came of that.

It is understandable why Conrad could not write such articles. On Armistice Day he sensed that the end of conflict was not the end of chaos but the inauguration of a new era of anarchy. Yeats's words became an epigraph for the age: ". . . the wick and oil are spent / and frozen are the channels of the blood." Conrad, too, was tired of dreams. The great sacrifice, he said, was consummated, but "I can not confess to an easy mind. Great and blind forces are set catastrophically [he told Walpole] all over the world. This only I know that if we are called upon to restore order in Europe (as it may well be) then we shall be safe at home too. To me the call is already manifest—but it may be declined on idealistic or political grounds. It is a question of courage in the leaders who are never as good as the people." Conrad's "sense of an ending" was apocalyptic: the ones who knew Europe were too weak to take positions of leadership, whereas those who were innocent of European politics, like the American Wilson, would offer dubious solutions and back them with muscle.

In the early part of 1919 he told Clifford: "The intervention of the United States was a great piece of luck for the Western Powers, but luck too has got to be paid for." Although the assistance came late, the price would be a full one. Conrad's immediate anger was directed at the invitation to Lenin's Bolsheviks to attend the peace conference. And yet Wilson, a year earlier, had called for a "united and independent, and autonomous Poland." Then on January 8, 1918, in his thirteenth point, he had spoken, once more, of "an independent Polish state," with free and secure access to the sea.

Maneuvering in this morass was made even more problematic by the fact that the Poles were themselves divided by allegiances. Conservative Poles, fearing the Bolsheviks, wanted to ally themselves with Germany; whereas workers and peasant groups sought an alliance with the new radical forces developing in Russia. Conrad may or may not have been aware of the tremendous schisms that existed in Poland. To Clifford, he depicted the future with typical scorn:

> If the Alliances had been differently combined the Western Powers would have delivered Poland to the German learned pig with as little compunction as they were ready to give it up to the Russian mangy dog. It is a great relief to my feelings to think that no single life has been lost on any of the fronts for the sake of Poland. The load of obligations would have been too great; and certainly, it is better to die than to live under a charge

> of moral bankruptcy, which would have been unfailingly made before many years.

Conrad keeps up his animal metaphor, the German pig, the Russian dog (not bear), the English getting bitten.

> Poland will have to pay the price of some pretty ugly compromise, as you will see. The mangy Russian dog having gone mad is now being invited to sit at the Conference table on British initiative! The thing is inconceivable, but there it is. One asks oneself whether this is idealism, stupidity or hypocrisy? I do not know who are the individuals immediately responsible, but I hope they will get bitten. The whole paltry transaction of conciliating mere crime for fear of obscure political consequences makes one sick. In a class contest there is no room for conciliation. The attacked class cannot save itself by throwing honesty, dignity and convictions overboard. The issue is simply life and death, and if anything can save the situation it is only ruthless courage. And even then I am not certain. One may just as well defy an earthquake.

Conrad then moves into the shrewdest part of his assessment, his awareness that the mechanics of reconciliation were being established even while all the major issues remained unsettled. It is the paradox of the do-gooders acting *because* they have no knowledge of affairs, *because* they wish to have none, a paradigm of the political process.

> There is an awful sense of unreality in all this babel of League of Nations and Reconstruction and production of Commodities and Industrial arrangements, while Fisher prattles solemnly about education and Conciliation Boards are being set up to bring about a union of hearts while the bare conciliation of interests is obviously impossible. It is like people laying out a tennis court on a ground that is already moving under their feet. I ask myself who on earth is being deceived by all these ceremonies? It is really comic, but you know that in human affairs the comic and the tragic jostle each other at every step.

That was in January 1919. Back in October, when these issues were as yet unformed because the war was still on, Conrad was settling in to a somewhat different kind of war. He was preparing to move away from Quinn and sell his manuscripts, for a more favorable return, to Thomas J. Wise, the great collector and, as it turned out, the great forger. By October 2, Conrad had already made his first transaction with Wise, the manuscript of *The Rescue*, by which he meant the segment that dated back to 1896, which is now part of the Wise-Ashley Collection at the British Museum. This manuscript, in Conrad's holograph, was to be distinguished from the several typescripts with alterations that had since intervened in Conrad's composition of the novel. As he pointed out to Wise, the manuscript was unique, in that the final version would be a typed copy with pen-and-ink corrections, but without any pen-and-ink pages. He offered to reserve that version for Wise as well, although he admits that Quinn may have a "moral claim" on it. He suggests that if the two versions, the holograph manuscript and the final typescript, are laid side by side, one will note "a literary curiosity showing the modifications of my judgment, of my taste, and also of my style during the 20 years covering almost the whole writing period of my life." Of course, the manuscript and alterations show no such thing, since Conrad's style from 1896 to 1918–19 did not evolve in a linear fashion. On the contrary, he returned to his early style, and his work on *The Rescue* is homogeneous.

Conrad was already vaunting this novel, however, for, as we have seen, he hoped to win the Nobel Prize with it, or at least catch the eye of the Nobel Committee. Yet even as he recognized that Quinn had a "moral claim," when he wrote to Quinn four days later (on October 6), he made no mention of the manuscript or corrected typescripts. Meanwhile, *The Arrow of Gold* was due to be serialized in *Lloyd's Magazine* beginning in December (and would run on, in small installments, until February 1920). Conrad was able to offer Quinn the first and original typed copy of *The Arrow,* corrected, scored, and interlined in ink. This was, he insisted, the only draft that existed, with the exception of the opening thirty-six pages written by hand. The rest was dictated.*

Thus, while Conrad was offering the far more valuable *Rescue* manuscript to Wise, he mentioned none of this to Quinn and offered him the typescript of *Arrow*—far less valuable because it was not handwritten. Yet, as Conrad knew, Quinn had a claim on all his manuscripts and typescripts as long as he, Quinn, kept them intact as a collection, which he had done. On the other hand, Conrad was indeed free to sell to anyone who offered a better return, although Quinn had always accepted Conrad's own estimation of value. There was, clearly, a gray area here, with the American collector feeling badly used, and Conrad sensing more favorable prices.†

The entire matter of *The Arrow* would surface in the following year, complicated by a contretemps over Conrad's last-minute plan to dedicate the novel to Quinn, after he had already promised it to Curle and allowed Curle's name to stand on Doubleday's first printing of the novel. Further, *The Arrow,* in its French translation, would become the source of considerable conflict between him and Gide, tension that was eased only because of

* Conrad apparently offered the same material to Wise (letter of December 2, 1918), saying that he could get a hundred for it in the States, but would prefer seventy without delay. He says its distinction rests on its being his "first work (novel or story) which may be said to be wholly dictated." Wise snapped it up on December 10.

† By 1918, there was clearly a Conrad market and he came under some attack for not allowing freer competition. He responded to this: "I also wish to say that I regret very much that you and other collectors should deem themselves treated unfairly. I acted in ignorance for which I can hardly be blamed as I am not a collector myself. That particular

Gide's diplomacy. Conrad's involvement in these essentially trivial matters, which became exceptionally important in his eyes, was probably attributable not only to the querulousness of old age or even to illness but to the loss of creative power. With this loss, whether conscious or not, Conrad's narcissistic impulses, which earlier were turned on his memories and then transformed by his imagination, turned upon himself, and he became defensive, protective, urgent about trivialities. Such displaced narcissism is not unusual among writers who sense their powers fading at a relatively early age—Hemingway is a good later example—and their hold upon themselves and objects around them becomes compulsive and distorted. Bad health is, not unusually, also a contributing factor, the poorness of health often disproportionately severe given the age of the writer.

Encroaching old age was rarely far from Conrad's mind. After sixty, as he told Curle, one begins to count the days; and gout, which is faithful, was not a cheerful companion. Conrad saw himself as ending in a wheelchair, but said he hoped to retain his wits: "I don't really mind if I have to end my days in a wheeled chair like Macaulay's Lord Holland. He kept his wits to the end and I have the advantage over him that my wife is not a Lady Holland." Those "wits," while engaged on *The Rescue*, could not grapple imaginatively with the contemporary European situation; for that, he would have needed the powers that went into *Nostromo*, his archetypal political scenario. Implicit in Conrad's warnings and disillusioned comments are the events of the 1920s and 1930s that led into another era of anarchy. He would have agreed with Yeats's "Once more the storm is howling" and people were dancing to a "frenzied drum," while the future would come "out of the murderous innocence of the sea." Conrad could not believe in Wilson's voice, a non-European trying to impose an American ethic and settlement. As he told Sandeman:

> Somehow an air of mystery hangs over the clearest utterances, like a cloud over an open landscape. The force behind these plain words is immense. Immense in every sense. The fact is that the mind uttering these momentous declarations is a non-European mind; and we, old Europeans, with a long and bitter experience behind us of realities and illusions, can't help wondering as to the exact value of words expressing these great intentions.

Conrad says that if his letter turned up fifty years later, perhaps no one would understand its sentiment of wariness and moral defeat. Fifty years later, it sounds like the utterances of the Delphic Oracle.

---

range of emotions is a closed book to me. I never collected anything in my life, not even postage stamps, as so many boys do. This is no doubt regrettable, but I am afraid I am an imperfect being, mentally and morally, in other ways too. Pray forgive my imperfections."

The letter to Sandeman coincided with Conrad's to Borys, now in a hospital in Rouen. Conrad tells of Jessie's worry, but beneath the male stoical façade is gratitude that Borys, while indisposed, is safe. He also mentions that they are seeking a new house, a move they would make in March of the next year, to Spring Grove. When Conrad wrote Borys, however, he had not as yet heard from the War Office, and by the time a telegram finally arrived, he had already assumed Borys had returned to the front and been wounded again.

Meanwhile, Quinn, not suspecting the storm that was building between him and Conrad, was pressing the latter on political matters. On the subject of the Irish, Quinn was of course a patriot, and he sought out Conrad's feelings and advice. Conrad did not feel any great urgency over the Irish question, although he saw some parallel to his own Polish background. He took, finally, the position that England had sincerely tried to make amends for past injustices and that the Irish refused conciliation. "I, who have seen England ever since the early eighties putting on the penitent's shirt in her desire for conciliation, and throwing millions of her money with both hands to Ireland in her remorse for all the old wrongs, and getting nothing in exchange but undying hostility, don't wonder at her weariness." The Irish, he felt, took the money, but went on cursing the oppressor with renewed zest. He attacks their leaders for making their careers in England and then using that connection as a way of undermining the country. "I have seen those things, I, who also spring from an oppressed race where oppression was not a matter of history but a crushing fact in the daily life of all individuals, made still more bitter by declared hatred and contempt." Conrad draws a distinction between Polish oppression by Russia, a living fact, and Irish oppression by England, merely a historical occurrence. He failed to note that to the oppressed the historical occurrence is a living fact.

He says that if Gladstone's Home Bill had passed, England would have had an armed hostile nation across from it, "still nursing the sense of historical wrong as their dearest possession and chumming-up with Germany in sheer lightness of heart and for the sake of a jolly good fight." He assumes they will get their independence in the future, when "President Wilson's Millenium [sic] will reign on earth and even the carrying of walking sticks will be strictly prohibited amongst the members of the League of Nations." Conrad predicts that even after the peace "the Angels on the Central Committee running the League of Nations will have their hands full with the pacification of Ireland. It will be the only state that will be not weary of fighting, on the whole round earth."

Conrad was, of course, correct about Ireland, but he was to be proven wrong about Poland, which achieved independence as a nation in 1920. Not unusually, the Entente's motives in this affair were not ethically but politically and militarily based. Nevertheless, that Poland was unified after the war ended was miraculous whatever the Allied motives, for not only were there political difficulties but the three lands making up Poland were set at different levels of economic and cultural development and possessed different traditions. Parts under Russia and Austria had been devastated by the war; the industrial plant of Congress Poland had been carted off to Russia and Germany. There was widespread unemployment and a lack of raw materials, and the agricultural potential had been destroyed by the exigencies of the war. Class differences had not been settled, and the army was itself composed of various uneven elements: besides Piłsudski's organization, there were units in France, groups formed by the Austrian and German armies, volunteer units from Russia, and several other elements that had been called up in various mobilizations.

In civil and administrative terms, Poland had only the small government from Galicia, newly formed in 1917, in Congress Poland. However, even though the Treaty of Versailles, signed by Dmowski and Paderewski on behalf of Poland on June 28, 1919, granted independence to Poland, it did not settle the frontiers. The borders would, in fact, become a battleground, as Polish forces fought against the Bolshevik Army that, hoping to make contact with German revolutionaries, assumed that the Polish peasantry would rise up and join the Russian advance. Needless to say, this did not occur, and when Piłsudski's forces stopped the Russian incursion, the Allies decided to intervene and Poland's borders were eventually settled.

In discussing the Irish question and introducing his own Polish background as an analogous situation, Conrad was shortsighted. If we assume for the moment that Bolshevik Russia had told Poland that all was forgotten, that Russia now was Poland's friend, and that reparations for past injustices would be forthcoming—roughly what England was attempting with Ireland, at least in Conrad's estimation of the historical situation—it is unlikely that Conrad would have counseled Polish acquiescence. For him, as for the Irish, the historical oppression of the past would have been the living fact of the present.

More immediately, in late October of 1918, *The Rescue* was contracted for, as a serial in *Land and Water*, due to begin at the end of January; and Conrad found himself in an "odious business," attempting to resuscitate the novel, an act "not worth performing even if I do manage it." Trying to regain touch with that novel, at sixty-one, was like seeking to regain a lost paradise or a golden age, a magical time. His youth in fact and feeling gone, he had to rediscover it in his work. Pinker had wanted *The Rescue* for serialization in *Cosmopolitan* and, for that, required a summary or synopsis. Responding to this request, Conrad refused, saying that while he did not expect people to buy a pig in a poke, nevertheless, "buying a Conrad work is not exactly that; and that the style, character and trend of the tale can be sufficiently seen from the M.S. in the state it is in now."

Then, forgetting his comments to friends about what a failure it was, he presented to Pinker a view of the novel as one dealing with shades of psychology, something "sustained by the presentation alone." The subject, he says, seems adventurous, but the tragedy lies in Lingard's feelings; "whatever value there may be in that must depend on the success of the romantic presentation." Conrad insisted on "shades of feeling," or "fine shadowings," as though he were an impressionistic painter, not a novelist. That stress on shades was probably based on his recognition that he could not invent freely any more; and, more significantly, on his desire, as he aged, to seem more Jamesian, less the novelist of sea and adventure. It is also entirely possible that he was responding, as best he could, to the modern note, in which psychological states, adumbrations, and fine lines had replaced narrative drive. Certainly in explaining *The Arrow* to F. N. Doubleday, four months before its American publication, Conrad presented it as an artistic achievement, a human product of great fragility, not as a commercial enterprise.

Doubleday was in London and wanted to see Conrad, but the latter ducked the meeting saying that since Jessie would have to come up for another knee treatment in January they might get together at that time. He then turns to *The Arrow*, and his purpose is to press Doubleday as to why there has been no American serialization of the novel; but Conrad's method is subtle and indirect. He starts by asserting that a novel can come forth from an author "only when it is done at the right time." While he had had the novel in mind for eighteen years, he says, he had felt restrained. Yet when the mood was right, he wrote it rapidly, in about ten months. It is, he adds, a novel that depends on "brush-strokes" and was in a method of presentation which suggested a "new departure in J.C.'s art—if such a thing as J.C.'s personal art exists."

Nevertheless, Conrad insists he has never wanted to be a coterie writer, which he feels is an aristocratic attitude antithetical to his own democratic one. He says he wants to be read by many, and that his writing, whether thought or image, is accessible to all but those of the meanest intelligence. Since that is his feeling, he cannot understand why Doubleday did not arrange for American serialization. He says the "master-quality" of a serial is its "suspended interest," which in turn is attached to the tension generated and may derive from a single adventure rather than from the "mere multiplicity of episodes." While defending his kind of fiction, Conrad is also pointing to its potential popularity. Further, he was dissatisfied with Doubleday's hurrying of the book, for he feels publication will coincide with the public's preoccupation with the settlement of political questions. Doubleday originally intended January publication, but moved it back until April.

Conrad's shaping of his later career is very meticulous, and he had evidently thought out how he wanted to be presented, which we shall see further in his Author's Notes. He hopes, finally, that Doubleday will reach some agreement with Heinemann, to whom he remained ever grateful for its publication of *The Nigger*, so as to give them a certain proportion of the "Limited Edition."

This attention to detail arose in a long letter Conrad wrote to the editor of *Land and Water* about the illustrations for *The Rescue*, forthcoming in the January issue. Conrad found the illustrations by Dudley Hardy to be ludicrous, and he cites Maurice Greiffenhagen, who illustrated "Typhoon," as a man who responded to the text. He says that Hardy has never seen a yacht's gig, or a square-rigged vessel, or the leech of a sail, or even a star-filled tropical sky. He says Greiffenhagen probably had never observed a typhoon, "but had imagination enough to understand the words I had written" and "he tackled his problems like a man." Hardy, however, has overstepped the limits of license. Conrad was wildly angry.

> It almost amounts to gross contempt and I tell you this plainly because I feel it strongly—what does he mean by sticking a fur cap on the head of Lingard? What is it—a joke? Or is it to display a fine independence in a story whose action takes place in the tropics? And what is that face? (Lingard is a man with a beard—I say so)—that face which says nothing, which suggests no type, might belong to a hotel waiter or a stock broker, and with that whole figure which might be that of a burglar, meeting an about 35-year-old guard in some nondescript place that might be in a cellar!

The "cellar" is supposed to be a ship's cabin, brightly lighted and decorated resplendently, white with gold moldings, not the "black hole" of the illustration.

Conrad continues:

> I wonder also why Mr. Hardy didn't dress up Lingard in a Pierrot costume instead of the fur caps. It would have been at least funny, and, in so far better than the duly forcible treatment of that scene; and every bit as truthful—may I ask you whether in your mind these types are settled and are going to be continued right through the story?

Additional illustrators were used in the serial, including Greiffenhagen, and Conrad was appeased. He had, in the meantime, turned toward his sixty-second year, toward *The Rescue.*

The landlord of Capel House, Edmund Oliver, died, and his son decided he wanted to live in the house. The Conrads were given notice terminating their tenancy of the property they had lived in for almost nine years. Conrad had long ago decided that he wanted to remain in Kent, and when his attempts to find another house were unsuccessful, he hoped to rent a temporary dwelling until something permanent could be obtained. A Captain Halsey of the Royal Navy came to their rescue and offered a six-month tenancy of Spring Grove, a large and spacious house located in Wye, a village between Ashford and Canterbury. The Conrads would move in in March and remain until October, but it was to prove one of Conrad's least favorite homes.

Except for the completion of *The Rescue*, whose final words he wrote on May 25, the year 1919 was not a good one. It is perhaps just as well that he lived so much in the past, for the present was filled with doctors, hospitals, and medical treatment. On February 7, he and Jessie dutifully went up to London, expecting a long stay, so that Conrad took rooms at the Durrants Hotel, in Manchester Square, only to have the doctors send Jessie home for another two months, with the possibility that if the knee improved no new operation would be necessary. Conrad suffered from gout, and, in addition, the family had caught bronchitis.

His "escape," if one can label it that, was into memory. Although he was working well on the manuscript of *The Rescue*, he was forced to hurry it because the first episode of the serial had already appeared on January 30. And he was beginning to write his "Author's Notes" for the limited Collected Edition which Doubleday planned to publish now that the war was ended. The Notes he would treat (as always) like short chats or *causeries* with his readers, not at all what Henry James thought of as Notes for his New York Edition. Conrad apparently never conceived of these pieces as serious literary explanations of his work, but rather as a way of establishing rapport with his newly won popular audience. It is not so much that the Author's Notes are trivial as that they are misleading. They were written to catch the eye and mind of those he would have once disdained, and they are part of a relaxation of effort, not an expenditure of it. He appears to have enjoyed writing them—they were, admittedly, a sign of a very hard-won success—and that enjoyment was, for him, a further intimation that the deeper reaches of his imagination lay dormant. In reporting on the writing of the Note for *An Outcast*, he told Pinker: "I wanted to test myself with something I could finish in one go, as it were."

On February 15, Conrad broached with Pinker something that had been on his mind for some time: the real recognition of his worth as a novelist, the Nobel Prize for Literature. If it came, it would coincide, as it does for so many writers, with the depletion of their powers, when their desire for fame has outdistanced their creative ability to achieve it. In Conrad's era, however, this was only partially true, for the Nobel Prize Committee passed over not only those who were depleted but many of the major writers of the 1910s and 1920s—not only Conrad, but also Proust, Kafka, Joyce, Lawrence, and Woolf. Conrad did not wish his name put forward for the Order of Merit, since he did not feel it was appropriate for one who could not "claim English literature as my inheritance" to receive such an honor. The Nobel Prize, however, was an international award and "less in the nature of an honour than of mere reward, [and] we needn't have any scruples about acceptance if it ever comes in our way."

As we have seen, Conrad felt that *The Rescue* might well catch the eye of the committee if it were published more rapidly; with the award announced in July, Conrad felt that Dent should publish in England on termination of the serial and forget serialization and other matters in the United States. Despite the loss of potential revenue, the idea was to have a book afloat in 1919 when the committee met. Conrad assumed he did not have many years left to him. Under his plan, while Doubleday would publish *The Arrow* in 1919 and *The Rescue* in 1920, Dent in England would reverse the procedure, and therefore, the latter book would be available for judgment in 1919, that very year. All these plans were based on the fact that the committee normally awarded the prize only to an author who had published a book in the year of the award, although in 1907, in Kipling's case, this had been disregarded. All of these plans, which came to nothing, were being formulated while Conrad watched fearfully as the installments of *The Rescue* came out "with dreadful regularity," although his own production lagged.*

The dramatization of *Victory* continued to poke through, with Conrad insisting he could not be considered a collaborator, that the play was Hastings's work. It had now become the property of Marie Löhr, and Conrad used the event to make a few amusing remarks at the expense of actors and actresses. After denying any knowledge of the psychology of actresses, he admits to having "a vague recollection of having been fed chocolates by Mme. Modjeska somewhere back in the Middle Ages." He comments that he hopes Hastings has in mind a "couple of men that won't play the clown with the parts of Jones and Ricardo," as he felt Hardy had been doing with his characters in the illustrations of *The Rescue.* Rehearsals were imminent, with the opening on March 26, but Conrad, as we have seen, begged off, claiming he did not feel well enough to spend a night in London.

Apart from his nervousness at seeing the audience reaction—he could not, for example, watch the opening of *The Secret Agent,* which was *his* work—he would be faced by very mixed feelings. The play was based on his novel, and he had given much information to Hastings about setting, costumes,

* Four days later, Conrad agreed that Pinker was right and his own plans unwise. The serialization of *The Rescue* would go on for too long a time to permit book publication in 1919; and in any event, Conrad now said he preferred *The Arrow* to come out first "and leave a clear road for *The Rescue,* the bigger thing of the two." Another twist to this was the fact that Conrad's mind was already working over his Napoleonic material, and very possibly he felt that a novel carved from that would catch the eye of the Nobel Prize Committee.

backgrounds, even the physical nature of the characters, but he had rejected collaboration. He was in it and not, and the situation was, for him, untenable. When he heard about the success of the opening—the play had an unexpected run, into June—he entered into the spirit of things and told Hastings he would run right out and order a Rolls-Royce and buy a house in Surrey commanding an extensive view.* "I will even go so far as to pay my tailor's bill." Many of Conrad's friends attended: Walpole, Pinker, and Colvin, the latter in Conrad's box and amusingly taken for the author himself.

But now, in early spring, Conrad was entering into a period of controversy, some duplicity or edgy dealings, and many ruffled feelings, chiefly with Quinn and Gide, with the battleground defined by the publication of *The Arrow of Gold* in America and the translation in France. On April 10, he asked Quinn to send Doubleday a three-and-a-half-page preface to *Almayer's Folly* which he had written in 1895 but never published. It was to be attached to that volume in the Collected Edition. Conrad also indicated his desire to dedicate *The Arrow* to Quinn:

> . . . the substance of it is so closely related to me personally that it can in fitness be inscribed only to a friend. I hope that after more than eight years' intercourse (though we have not seen each other yet) your kindness has given me that status towards you. The corrected proofs with dedication as above have been already mailed to Garden City so that if you don't want to be compromised by any public association with that unspeakable Conrad you had better telegraph directly to Doubleday and threaten him with legal proceedings in case he disobeys your injunction.

These playful words neglect to mention that the book's dedication had already been promised to Curle, and Doubleday was due to publish *The Arrow* on April 12, as Quinn was to discover.

If Quinn really wanted the dedication, he would have had to attach his name to the second edition, when the first run of 15,000 was exhausted. This would have created a delicate situation and may have seemed to the innocent Curle a traitorous act indeed. Quinn's position was torturous, although he attempted to be witty about it. He wrote Conrad about their being Mormons, with the double dedications of the book comparable to their roles as "plural wives." Even before receiving this heavy-handed attempt at escape from a difficult position, however, Conrad cabled to Quinn that Curle should remain and his Napoleonic novel would be for him.

Conrad followed this up with a cheerful explanation which makes almost no sense.

---

* Hastings had told him on March 29 that the house could expect receipts of over £1,000 for five performances, £1,600 for a week of eight.

> The fact is that the dedication to you was a sudden thought insofar that for a long time I had determined to dedicate to you my Napoleonic novel, which is the next work I am to write after finishing "The Rescue," which now is awaiting its last pages. Then, while passing the first proofs of "Arrow" it occurred to me that I would not keep you waiting and that the "Arrow" was perhaps good enough to be inscribed to you. But in truth it is better as it is, for certainly the Napoleonic novel is bound to be a bigger thing in every way.

As for *The Rescue*, that had been destined ever since 1914 for Frederic Courtland Penfield, the American ambassador who had helped the Conrads escape from Austria.

All this muddle would not have occurred if Conrad, still unknown to Quinn, had not begun to sell manuscripts and typescripts to Wise. Conrad's feelings of guilt about Quinn are manifest in the sudden need to dedicate a work to the American collector even after the book had been promised to Curle. There is, further, the sense that he could do anything he wanted with Curle, since that young man's loyalty was assured. One notes some of that marginal shadiness or indirect dealing which Conrad had always condemned, and it can be attributed to a kind of mental breakdown; not the type of breakdown which incapacitates, but a form that leads to a laxity of behavior, a letting go. The bitter flare-up with Gide takes on the same overtones of loss of control. The extreme desire to keep his name before the public with first-rate work and yet the nagging sense of his decline in quality had driven Conrad into acts of rage and slightly unethical behavior.

The reviews of *The Arrow*, if we can look ahead to them momentarily, were not calculated to cheer. They were not by any means poor—he was by now too much of a literary fixture—but they did not vaunt him as a unique author with his own style and tone. While kind, they intimated a decline in powers, a sense of vagueness that was not the result of hidden strength, a tone of resignation rather than a thrust into unknown areas. *The New Republic*'s Philip Littell found Doña Rita possessed of "too many traits" for Conrad to handle, and suggested that the author had apparently imagined the traits separately rather than in their relationship to each other. The criticism is an excellent one, in fact, for it focuses on Conrad's own lack of clarity in creating Rita, his desire to make her someone extraordinary even while she may have lived only in a twilight zone of his own imagination. Then, as a real blow, the reviewer points out that Conrad's genius "is more apparent in the creation of simpler and more mysterious characters." Such a comment was a suggestion for more sea novels.

The English reviewers, likewise, were full of hesitating pronouncements. To a large extent, they had learned from Conrad how to read him, and now they were drawing on what they had learned to measure him more exactly. In the *Morning Post*, for example, the reviewer wondered just what the story of *The Arrow* was, asserting that in over three hundred pages Conrad had obscured what should be clearer. And if we take that comment at its deepest level, we note that the novel is unclear not as a result of profundity but as a consequence of divided aims. The reviewer runs through the familiar Conrad devices for ambiguity: "His process of elimination, of glosses and glazes, of presenting his characters at double and triple removes in the reflection of other minds, enriching their individualities by innumerable nuances of parallel and contrast also, are too well known." Yet the thrust is that none of these strategies matters in the present novel.

In an immensely long review in the *Times Literary Supplement*, Walter de la Mare presented a detailed précis of the plot, but with conclusions that chilled Conrad.

> Passages abound exemplifying his sense of beauty, his intuition, his grasp of character, his supreme gift of realization. But the colours and shadows of that mystery which veils and yet deepens the ultimate "meaning" of his fiction seem in the progress, and certainly in the conclusion, of his story too thin, and to leave it in a vital degree fragmentary and insecurely told.

Finally, a notice that appeared in the *Nation*, a month after the English publication date on August 6 was devastating in its conclusions:

> Thus, in spite of all the splendours of his style and his wonderful gift of analysis and indirect suggestion, his mystery passes into unreality and his spectral into the grotesque. As the celebrants of the ritual disappear in the smoke of their offering to romance, the observer rubs his eyes in disillusion. Even Ortega and the sinister pietist, Teresa, Rita's sister, who are both horribly well-done and stand out in an incisive terror from the shapes and glooms that surround them, are a tenuous compensation for a book in which genius itself seems to become insubstantial.

The reviewers were only confirming what Conrad suspected, or else he would not have entered into so many controversies over *The Arrow*. The correspondence with Quinn was only beginning to heat up and would take on an even more strident tone when the collector made the unusual suggestion that he would like to try his hand at dramatizing *The Arrow*, a proposal he made to Conrad in a June 19 letter. In the meanwhile, in May, Conrad began negotiations for another move, from Spring Grove, whose location he disliked intensely, to what would be his final residence, Oswalds, at Bishopsbourne. Borys reports that one day, while they were driving in their Cadillac—Conrad had just had a windfall of £3,000 on film options for some of his books—they discovered Oswalds. The house and grounds were pleasing and even luxurious, but the house and village were at the bottom of a deep fold in the downs. Conrad nevertheless entered into negotiations with Tanner, the agent for Colonel Bell, the owner, for £250-a-year rental. The

Conrads would move in October, of 1919, and remain at Oswalds until Conrad's death, although six months or so before his death he was looking for another house, talking of a move to France, and even causing some friends to speculate that he planned to return to Poland. He was, it seems, beginning to entertain ghosts.

CHAPTER 36

A Dubious Rescue

ON May 25, a day which he should have celebrated, Conrad wrote the final words of *The Rescue*, twenty-three years after beginning it. He felt little cheer and, instead, experienced exhaustion and some despair.* The novel had been touched up sporadically over his entire career, so that it suffered from a multiplicity of styles, manners, phrasings. It was not a culmination of craft, as Conrad had hoped, but a potpourri of mannerisms, only some of which he could control. In terms of his career as a whole, he would have done better to let *The Rescue* lie dormant; the novel incomplete might have intrigued rather than dismayed, and suffered the fate of *Suspense*.

Conrad was now a driven man—to produce fresh copy, to keep his name before the public, to capitalize on the increased sales of his books, and, very possibly, to try to write himself back into some kind of control and discipline. These later works, which overall seem so flawed, may have served a multiplicity of purposes, one of which was for Conrad to find his distinctive voice. In *The Rover*, his last completed novel, he did manage his excesses of description and wrote about what he knew well. Peyrol, the exhausted sailor, was his kind of character, an older, more subdued version of Dominic Cervoni, a simple man who is not simplified. *Suspense*, likewise, has fresh elements, although it is difficult to see what Conrad had in mind for what was to be a massively long book. To be an aging writer, he found, was more painful than serving as an apprentice. He might have agreed with the orator Isoc-

* To Garnett, Conrad spoke of finishing *The Rescue* so as to clean up his record before he left this world, hardly a note of triumph in completing something that had hung on him like an albatross for almost his entire writing life. "It was the instinct (not the sense—the instinct) of what you have discerned with your unerring eye that kept me off the R. for 20 years or more. That—and nothing else. My instinct was right. But all the same I cannot say I regret the impulse which made me take it up again. I am settling my affairs in this world and I should not have liked to leave behind me this evidence of having bitten off more than I could chew. A very vulgar vanity. Could anything be more legitimate?" Conrad's words to Garnett suggest his resentment that the latter found such weaknesses in his work. He adds that he never erected his friend into a fetish, and that it was absolute confidence, not "vague dread," that Garnett inspired.

rates: "Now is not the time to do what I can do; and that which it is now time to do, I cannot do."

To Quinn, Conrad stressed how grateful he was for the American collector's patience about the dedication of *The Arrow*. He indicates that Curle was actually to receive the dedication of a new collection of stories, a collection that, incidentally, was expected to contain "The Black Mate," Conrad's 1886 story, and *The Rover*, cast at first as a long story, not a novel. Together, these pieces and others would make up a volume of about 60,000 words. He adds that Curle—a "little eccentric and a little trying," but above suspicion as a friend—did not know of the dedication, as he was in South Africa. To cap his point, he calls Curle "the most devoted of my 'young braves,' " a position that Quinn himself would have liked, but which Conrad always denied to him.

Still hanging over Conrad's head, however, was Quinn's curious suggestion that he dramatize *The Arrow of Gold*, a project he had already discussed at length with his friend Walt Kuhn, the painter. Conrad's awkwardness in responding was connected to Quinn's ignorance, still, that Conrad had started to sell his manuscripts to Wise. Further, Conrad had been negotiating for more general dramatic rights to his novels, and he had in mind his own plan to work them over for the stage. On July 31, he wrote a long, complicated letter to the American collector in response to two of his in arrears. Intermixed with these rather strange negotiations was still another fact: that Quinn had found himself caught as middleman between Conrad and Doubleday over the Collected Edition. The publisher had had some misgivings about the issuance of Conrad's books, and since Quinn was available in New York, he had come to him, turning the collector into a quasi-legal force. Quinn, of course, had no legal right to negotiate for Conrad. Particularly annoying to the latter was Doubleday's idea to issue a special grouping of his books as "sea novels," a suggestion that opened many old wounds.

In one of his letters, Quinn had complained of the demands placed on his time, and Conrad responded that Doubleday had no right to come to the lawyer and further strain the incredibly busy Quinn. Conrad was outraged that the publisher took his private affairs, including royalty matters, to a third party instead of negotiating directly with him and Pinker. He finds it equivalent to "uttering a threat," especially since he feels the royalty matter had been settled. He complains that Wells, a hugely successful best-selling author, has 65 percent on his published price (a highly suspicious figure), while he will obtain only 5 percent. Thanking Quinn for his interest in the matter, Conrad says he does not require a "buffer." He was priming, apparently, for several battles.

Conrad speaks of himself as a man who has achieved his position in letters long before Doubleday approached him; he says, in fact, that he owes nothing to any publisher for either material help or moral support. That came from another quarter, Pinker. Then he comes to the point that really enraged him, of a special set of "sea" books. He unburdens himself here, still not mentioning Quinn's already well-developed plan of dramatizing *The Arrow*.

> How would poor Thackeray have liked a set labelled Mr. Thack's "Society Novels." He lived in society ("The Newcomes" could be described in a sense as a "High-Life" novel). But it would be absurd to brand him as a "Society" writer. The sea is not my subject. Mankind is my subject and "imaginative rendering" of truth is my aim. The *Mirror* certainly is a book of prose inspired directly by the sea. The *Nigger* is a study of seamen with a particular attention to their psychology—not to their adventures. *Youth* has been recognised for what it is too long for me to speak about it. *Typhoon*, it is generally admitted now, conveys much more than mere sea-effects. Those are the only works where the sea is in the foreground. It is often seen in the background of my other books just as "society" (and especially London society) is inevitably present in the foreground or in the background of Thackeray's novels—without making him a "Society" novelist. To be labelled insistently as a sea-writer will repel as many or more readers than it will attract, I fancy. That's why I am not enthusiastic about that scheme.

Conrad finally arrives at Quinn's suggestion. His response has numerous nuances, but Quinn caught on and dropped the idea. First, Conrad says it is a curious thing, but he is presently negotiating about general dramatic rights, and therefore, he must be indefinite about granting Quinn's request. Second, since *The Arrow* contains "shades of intimate emotions," it is not fit for the stage. "It is anything but dramatic in the 'Stage' sense." Conrad had, we recall, originally considered holding several scenes out of the serial so as to preserve them for a stage version. Finally, Conrad answers Kuhn's view of the novel as "melodramatic," passed on by Quinn. "A melodrama [he says] is a play where the motives lack verisimilitude or else are not strong enough to justify a certain violence of action which thus becomes a mere fatuous display of false emotions. Violent action in itself does not make melodrama." Conrad's definition appears valid, but Kuhn's characterization of *The Arrow* as a melodrama also seems well taken, especially the long scene between George and Rita with Ortega raging outside.

In more modern critical terms, Conrad failed to justify the emotions he was trying to elicit; or, more likely, he was confused himself as to what he wanted the reader to sense or feel. He had become, with *The Arrow*, the writer of disparate elements, some of them still fine, others missing the mark. Although he still hoped to use the grotesque or demonic as a way of grasping reality, he now lacked the synthetic ability to bring the pieces together. What would also have been melodrama in his earlier books was restrained by the cohesiveness of Conrad's imagination and by the discipline of his prose.

Now, without that imaginative coherence and control in the prose, his mannered scenes, always perilously close to the edge of artificiality, took on melodramatic dimensions at the very time when such a literary style had become anathema.

Not until two months later did Conrad mention the sale of his materials to Wise. In the meanwhile, he began another line concerning *The Arrow*, sending a copy to André Gide and calling it "un envoi plutôt symbolique," a "rather symbolic package." He designated it as an "offering to the friendship which is precious to me and to this admiration which has become a part of my intimate being." With his dispatch of this novel, Conrad was moving on to new ground with Gide, for the latter assigned *The Arrow* to a female translator, and this news almost destroyed the relationship. The juxtaposition of Conrad and Gide at this time is of considerable interest, since both were writing fiction—Gide, with *La Symphonie pastorale*—which carried an especially heavy personal freight. Because of certain ambiguities in *The Arrow*, Conrad, when he wrote Gide on November 4, was extremely sensitive to its translation. This area, which is deeply personal and revealing, is worth exploring, for we note in Conrad's remarks almost a breakdown, a near-hysterical outburst over relatively small matters.

In both novels, the central characters—Conrad's George and Gide's minister—are involved in ambiguous sexual adventures, often an eroticism disguised or screened. Both novelistic careers had converged toward the symbolic creation of disguised selves or secret lives filtered through a persona. Conrad sufaces partially as George, and his relationship to Rita de Lastaola presents a variety of ambiguous male-female roles.* Further, Rita's transformation by the artist Allègre from a poor shepherdess into the consort of a king finds its curious parallel in Gide's minister transforming the blind, "*sauvage*" Gertrude into a lovely young woman. Both stories, in this respect, fit into variations of what Freud called "Family Romances."† In this "romance," the protagonist imagines himself or herself to be the offspring of someone famous, rich, powerful, or noble, and is transformed in imagination into this new being.

---

* *The Arrow* is not alone in this respect. Lingard and Edith in *The Rescue*, as well as Cosmo Latham and the Countess de Montevesso in *Suspense*, demonstrate young men living through fantasy romances, the women presented as the "women of their dreams." Even old Peyrol in *The Rover* is somewhat transformed by an attachment to Arlette. In fantasizing about youth, his *lost* youth, and competing with Borys in an area where he could not triumph, Conrad created romantic attachments to manifest what he was still unwilling to surrender. As he told Colvin: "The fact is between you and me (and Lady Colvin of course) that I have never been able to read these proofs [of *The Arrow*] in cold blood. Ridiculous! My dear (as D. Rita would have said) there are some of these 42 year old episodes of which I cannot think now without a slight tightness of the chest—un petit serrement de coeur. What a confession!"

† In his study, Meyer makes this point

Both writers used their novels as disguises: Conrad retracing his gunrunning days as a young Carlist when his energies ran freely; and Gide reviewing his entire sexual career in the symbolic terms of the minister's relationship to Gertrude. Aside from the more obvious sexual connotations, the relationship works out several of Gide's emotional problems, especially that conflict between acceptable and forbidden love, between heterosexual love sanctioned by his intense Protestant background and homoerotic love dictated by his personal feelings. Both novels, then, Conrad's and Gide's, serve as symbolic counterparts of deeply felt personal feelings, acting out or showing forth severe inner struggles. For Conrad, the reflection of himself in *The Arrow* was paradigmatic of his later work; and his difficulties in coming to terms with the personal consequences of growing older and useless may help explain the "competition" he felt with Borys. Or else it is impossible to explain why Borys, later, kept his marriage secret from both parents—but pointedly from his father.

We find the first trouble spot when Conrad wrote to Jean-Aubry, on October 10, that Gide told him "une femme vient de s'emparer de *Arrow:* pour de traduire. Je vais protester de toutes mes forces." Conrad's choice of phrase is compelling: "une femme [Madame Maus, the translator] vient de s'emparer"—*a woman has seized upon it.* Even granting his own ambiguities about Rita and her relationship to George, the tone approaches a note of panic, that of a man about to be destroyed by harpies and Amazons, especially since he would repeat the same phrase to Gide three weeks later. The wording suggests an obsessive need to be understood by masculine forces, perhaps because a feminine intelligence would comprehend too well the fantasy aspect of the passion between George and Rita.

His response to Gide, on November 4, is almost hysterical; we must remember he was writing to André Gide, hardly a man who depended on translations for his reputation. He begins by insisting that his writings have a single characteristic, that of virility, in their spirit and expression. And yet, he asserts, you "throw me to the women." Conrad says that if a translation is, as Gide asserted, an interpretation, then he wants to be interpreted by "les esprits masculins." Gide had complained about this (in a letter lost to us),

---

with a number of Conrad's novels and stories, demonstrating how the "family romance" functions in Razumov, Almayer, Willems, Jim, Lena, Alice Jacobus, Cosmo Latham, and several others. *The Arrow of Gold*, however, with its youthful George seeking the love of Don Carlos's mistress, seems the most appropriate, or the most fantastic. The "romance" also has affinities to Ovid's metamorphic reshapings, to mythical transformations, and has as a curious contemporary parallel Kafka's metamorphosed Gregor Samsa, who moves in his own kind of romance. Given the trauma of a world war and the destruction of traditional values, themes based on metamorphosis and transformation would appear to have a solid social foundation.

but Conrad rejects both his argument concerning Madame Maus and his tone. He says that when he expresses something so heartfelt, he does not expect a light response. "Une dame *c'est emparée* du livre(!)" and yet the mighty Gide says he can do nothing. Conrad finds that incredible, and suggests deceit. He repeats the phrase, that a woman has seized upon it. Does he think Gide takes him for a fool! He asks him to respond as a man, yes or no, whether he intends to go on with the translation as it is.

Conrad wanted Jean-Aubry as the translator—he would eventually be—and he wrote his young friend the substance of his comments to Gide. He indicates that if the French writer's slighting manner of reply to his request suggests he wants to drop the translation altogether, Conrad is prepared to let it drop. Three days after running through the problem with Jean-Aubry, Conrad heard from Gide. The latter read Conrad's diatribe "avec stupeur" and says he cannot understand the latter's "courroux," or wrath. He agrees that the translation must go to Jean-Aubry, as Conrad wishes. Gide then tries to placate his "wrathful" friend by indicating his profound sympathy and admiration for both the man and the work. In a follow-up letter, on the twenty-first of November, Gide indicates that Madame Maus is well into *The Arrow* and then protests lightly against Conrad's decision, but he backs off and agrees to insist she step aside. In a mild rejoinder, Gide asks Conrad if he really believes a "masculine translation" is preferable to a feminine one. He says he does not want to displease his friend, but he wonders if they will regret what they are doing.

Conrad was immediately placated. His responses to Gide, on November 24 and December 15, confirm the personal significance of his novel. He stresses that the translator must catch the nuances of his thought. He excuses himself, an old man insisting on what he knows: "Ce livre de ma 60 ème année tient fort au coeur. Vous qui comprenez tant de choses vous saurez peut-être me pardonner cette faiblesse." Rather pointedly, when Gide visited England, chiefly North Wales, the following year, he did not go out of his way to see Conrad.

While the furor with Gide was brewing, Conrad still had Quinn on his mind. The dedication to *The Arrow* had been mishandled badly, and Conrad had rejected Quinn's request for dramatic rights to the novel. Now Quinn wrote with some annoyance. Clement Shorter had told him that Conrad was selling his manuscripts to Thomas J. Wise. Conrad responded with disdain at Shorter's "nosing amongst" Quinn's manuscripts. He admits he sold the typed first draft of *The Arrow* and also the incomplete manuscript of *The Rescue* to Wise, because he needed the money for a specific purpose. Conrad then explains that Quinn has had all his "pen-and-ink MSS" and might not want manuscripts based on a typewritten first draft; further, he felt Quinn might be getting tired of buying his work. Conrad reinforces this line of reasoning by pointing out that Quinn possesses all his prewar productions, Wise his postwar publications. Thus, he says, "your collection, to which I often give a thought, has got a double character of completeness in so far that it is *all* pen-and-ink Conrad and *all* pre-war Conrad." He says he would, if a collector himself, prefer to "have a smaller thing absolutely complete, both in time and kind, than a larger but not complete collection."

He then offers to sell two non-fiction pieces, his political note on Poland and a paper which the Admiralty did not use. These are holograph, and if Quinn wants them, they will insure the completeness of his collection, since Conrad has given up further pen-and-ink work. As a softener, he promises to throw in without cost sixty pages of the "Falk" typescript, with holograph corrections and alterations, which Jessie had discovered. Conrad indicates he does not know if there is a manuscript of the entire "Falk" already in Quinn's collection (there was), but in any event this typescript, although incomplete, has value for its variations and, in places, complete alteration of text. Since Conrad regarded "Falk" very highly, he judged this gift as a salve to his conscience. Then, as though to close off any attempt on Quinn's part to get closer, Conrad asserts he is thinking of dramatizing some of his own work, beginning with *The Secret Agent*, which was staged the following year.

Conrad behaved here strictly within his rights, but his mode of operation was self-deceptive. Quinn had met Conrad's prices, and what the latter really wanted, but could not admit, was a different level of return for his material, a level which Wise rose to. The rest was Conrad's attempt to hold off Quinn's just annoyance. The American had proved to be a loyal friend, helping Conrad when he needed it, interfering in the Doubleday business only to help contractually, and booming Conrad's work in the circles in which he moved as lawyer, collector, and patron of the arts. When Conrad visited Oyster Bay in 1923, he would not see Quinn, no matter how determinedly the lawyer-collector tried to meet Conrad for the first time.

On the very day after this response, in fact, Conrad offered some new materials to Wise: four of his various Author's Notes and four other papers, for £10 each. These were typewritten, of course, but contained handwritten corrections. Conrad indicates that the clean copies, of which no more than two exist, will be destroyed after being set by the printer, giving Wise the only copy. To make them more valuable as collector's items, Conrad signed each on the first and last page, dated it, and noted its history in a line or two of his handwriting. Further, Wise and Shorter began to issue pamphlets of Conrad's Notes, of which Conrad reserved to himself twenty-five copies of the private publication not already issued, and Wise two. This was a whole dimension and new source of revenue missing in the transactions with Quinn. In all, Conrad offered eighty-nine pages of first-draft matter, averaging about 200 words a page, for £80, which Wise paid rapidly. The amount, equivalent to perhaps $750 to $1,000, while not exorbitant for this much material, indicates how Conrad's prices had risen in the last five years. Earlier, he would have sold such a lot to Quinn for half or less.

The bouts with Quinn and then Gide were the actions of an ill man, and Conrad was indeed neurasthenic, subject to uncontrollable outbursts, as well as physically ill. He would not be allowed to grow old gracefully; the family background of early death had not been his fate, but the tradition of frail health touched with extreme nervousness was his lot. Much of it, of course, was self-generated. He carried his fate with his calling. Other aspects of the French translation kept curving back upon him. André Ruyters, who had been involved in the translation of "Heart of Darkness," now inquired about *Lord Jim*. Conrad was sufficiently courteous to say Ruyters's intentions interested him, but then dampened it all by adding: "I feel you'll grow extremely weary of it long before the end. The other day I found that I could not read it myself to the end. It bored me."

Although Conrad's Note to the book, written in June 1917, does make it seem as if he was bored with it, nevertheless his comment to Ruyters derived from a man who must have compared *that* work with his current achievement. The sense of boredom he revealed could only have been a defense against the real matter: the contrast between then and now. Conrad excuses himself by claiming age, his ailing condition, the fact that he has his own English text to revise, and the additional point that he wants time to do nothing—"just do nothing," the note of a man weary beyond his years. Of course, his letter to Ruyters coincided with the English publication of *The Arrow of Gold*, and his apprehension was overwhelming.

To Pinker, he showed bewilderment at Beresford's review in *Everyman* which suggested that Conrad was growing old: "a rather sudden conclusion to arrive at on the evidence of only one book; because as far as I can remember, nobody found traces of senile decay in *Victory* or *Shadow-Line*. However, a beginning of that sort of thing had to be made some time and I quite expected it to come on this occasion." Conrad notes the tone of disappointment in the review and traces it more to the subject and its treatment than to any general perception on the reviewer's part of failing powers in the writer. He explains he is paying the penalty for "having produced something unexpected." He is disturbed that the reviewers keep mentioning *Lord Jim* as a touchstone; and he defends himself: "I only don't see why I should have *Lord Jim* thrown at my head at every turn. I couldn't go on writing *Lord Jim* all my life." The reviewers, of course, were trying to grapple with a writer who had, in their eyes, lost control of prose and situation; they were embarrassed and yet kind, attempting to present Conrad with his entire career, and, like the French translators, turn his career back upon him with *Lord Jim* and "Heart of Darkness." None of this comforted him.

From the distant past, A. Robinson, the second mate of the *Earl of Shaftesbury* in the 1880s, wrote Conrad and renewed memories, sending on a photograph of the *Loch Etive*, which Conrad had served on thirty-nine years before. The latter remembered Robinson as a man he had met in the middle of the eighties, in Penarth Dock, on a cold and dismal afternoon. No matter how depressed he felt, Conrad faithfully answered letters from old seamen who wrote him now that he was famous; many of them read his stories and novels about the waters they had traveled, and Conrad considered all of them friends and equals. The wonder of the sea, and the magic of those years, never left him; those two decades remained the golden age for him, a time out of time.

On August 28, the Conrads went up to London for the next stage in the continuing drama of Jessie's knee. The examination by Sir Robert Jones demonstrated that an operation was in order, and it was scheduled for Sir Robert's facility in Liverpool in December. Conrad had mixed feelings, cheered that they would first have a chance to settle into their new home at Oswalds and depressed by the prospect of spending the holiday season (and his sixty-second birthday) under such forbidding conditions. The nagging quality of the operation is attested to by Conrad's introduction of it into eight or ten letters to different correspondents. Like *The Rescue*, which he had completed but was now revising, it had become one of the leitmotifs of his adult life.

Characteristically, Conrad complained to Warrington Dawson that he suffered from "la sensation du vide," although not completely "le Vide Eternel"; an inner emptiness and loneliness, but not nihilistic. Conrad says he feels like "some strange animal confined within a fence for public view" and rues that he has "missed all along the chances of closer contacts." These remarks are the complement of those he made to Marguerite Poradowska fully twenty-five years earlier, at the beginning of it all, the apprentice writer driven to becoming the "hunger artist" and caught between defying the fates and succumbing to them.*

On October 3, the Conrads began their move into Oswalds and on the sixth spent their first night in the new house. Oswalds was a large, gracious Georgian structure with spacious grounds, a bowling green, three well-tended walled gardens, garage space with chauffeur's quarters above, and its own electric generating plant. Conrad objected that he had no view from his

---

* How would he have felt if he had seen Dawson's letter to John Powell written the next day? "But oh, my dear, have you seen 'An Arrow of Gold'? If not—don't! He did not send it to me. When I first bought it & opened it & saw the dedication to Richard Curle, I thought my beloved Conrad had been ashamed to send it to me on that account [Dawson had written a highly unfavorable review of Curle's *Joseph Conrad: A Study*]. But as I read—I said to myself—that the dedication was all right & there was another reason for not sending it to me! And yet, 'The Shadow Line' was truly worthy of him. I hear, by the way, that the English reviews of the 'Arrow of Gold' have been lengthy & effusive."

study because of the location of the house in the downs, but a ten-minute drive put him within sight of the Thames estuary. The house proved to be a pleasant residence, although Conrad tired of it in his final year. He treated houses like ships; they were good for a time, and then one moved on. Conrad had never been the kind of sailor who keeps signing on and off the same ship; he rarely stayed with one more than a year, unless the voyages were very long, and so he was with his residences. He always rented, never bought.

The move to Oswalds coincided with the storm over *The Arrow* with Gide. The fall of 1919 was, otherwise, desultory, a weeding of his career rather than a seeding or harvesting. In October, he wrote an introduction to Thomas Beer's life of Stephen Crane, but it was little more than puffery. It was published separately in the *London Mercury* in September. However, even such a relatively unimportant piece could be used in several ways: as a magazine publication, as an introduction, as a typescript for sale to Wise, and as an article for inclusion, in 1921, in *Notes on Life and Letters;* in all as four sources of income. Also, by mid-October, while working over his Author's Notes, Conrad began a full-length play based on *The Secret Agent.* But he interrupted this to prepare the book text of *The Rescue*—ever *The Rescue*—which had now been serialized (by July).

For the revision of *The Rescue*, Conrad spent three months working over the serialization, chiefly toward pruning verbal excesses. What he did throughout was to eliminate parallel constructions, long appositive phrases that ran on for twenty or twenty-five words; or else long similes, "as if" phrases of up to 30–40 words. He also cut out entire passages of the kind that had disappeared with the purple writing of the 1890s. Although he was admittedly writing "romance," he recognized that the language of romance was no longer the language of serious fiction. Even if he was not fully responsive to the revolution in literary prose that had been occurring in the 1910s—Ford, of course, had responded to that shift—he realized that literary expression had altered, changes that he had himself tried to bring along at the turn of the century. But *The Rescue* was truly snagged among styles. Cut as he did, he was still left with the kind of prose which deleteriously called attention to itself, quite different from the "romantic" prose of *Nostromo*, which defined as much as it described.

In October, Conrad wrote Dent that he would consider a volume combining his fugitive pieces on literature—he had written essays on Daudet, Maupassant, France, James—and his other articles, what would become the volume *Notes on Life and Letters*. Since it would appear about six months after the book text of *The Rescue*, it would serve to keep his name before both the English and the American public. Although he was uncertain whether to go ahead with the plan, it was appealing chiefly because it provided a volume for him in years when volumes were not easy to produce.

Writing to a producer named Vernon, who was interested in doing *The Secret Agent*, Conrad revealed that he had a narrative plan in mind. He speaks of two kinds of play: that which studies the subject "through mere characterisation of people involved," what we would loosely call the Chekhovian drama; and there is the play where the "story is told in action." In the latter, the bulk of the story is narrated, "not through an arbitrary whim of my own but in the logical development of the plan." Conrad says he sees the first act as a way of establishing visually the characters; Acts 2 and 3 narrated "by people who for various (and I hope perfectly clear) reasons are vitally concerned in what has happened." The fourth act will present, in visual terms, the end of the story "in strict dramatic form of the consequent and final passions and emotions." For the play, the focus, he stresses, will be Winnie, not Verloc. Conrad's plan, still unformed, indicates he was thinking in dramatic terms; unfortunately, he allowed himself to become caught between novel and play. He tried to follow the novel in places and lost the dramatic quality of the play, and he tried to adapt himself to the needs of the stage and lost the irony and tonal variety that made the novel cohere.

The play, however, would not be mounted until November 2, 1922, three years precisely after he had entered into an agreement with Vernon. One cannot help but feel that when Conrad started to work seriously on it, in the fall of 1919, he saw the stage not as something to be achieved but as an escape from malaise and stagnation. With Vernon's encouragement and optimism, which amazed him, he stripped the novel to its sordid essentials, but increasingly saw that the novel had depended on an ironic tone, on the "garment of artistic expression." By returning to those years after *Nostromo* when he had conceived of *The Secret Agent*, he recognized the wellsprings of his imagination: "I confess [he told Pinker] that I myself had no idea of what the story was till I came to grips with it in this process of dramatization. Of course I can't stop now. Neither can I tamper with the truth of my conception by introducing into it any extraneous sentiment. It must remain what it is." Conrad perhaps did not recognize how sordid the tale was in 1906, because the tone of the novel was a piece with his way of thinking; now, in retrospect, with his attitudes having relaxed, he was transported, as it were, into a mind he barely knew.

For Conrad, now, the journey back into time presented few positive elements; as he told Pinker: "There is little chance of salvation." He was speaking of saving the novel on the stage, but his words could apply as well to his sense of himself. These journeys into time, however pleasant or unpleasant, were interrupted by a different kind of journey, first to London and then to Liverpool, where the question of saving Jessie's knee was the issue. The Conrads planned to leave Oswalds on November 27 and then on the thirtieth proceed to Liverpool. Despite the anxiety attendant upon any such move, Conrad made many plans for his short London stay—lunch with Heinemann, a meeting with Vernon over the play, and appointments with Curle and Garnett.

Once in Liverpool, Conrad stayed at 85, Kingsley Road, Princes Park, while Jessie went into the nursing home following the operation. The surgical procedure appeared to be a success, which meant no amputation was necessary, and the prognosis was that she would regain use of her leg. Conrad, in the meantime, came to think very highly of the surgeon, Sir Robert Jones, who invited him to dine, an invitation he declined only because Jean-Aubry was in Liverpool to deliver a lecture. When the Collected Edition was published, Conrad reserved a set for Sir Robert, and only two others, for Garnett and Gide.

By the end of December, Conrad was back at Oswalds, facing proofs of *The Rescue* and a "period of depression," the inevitable depression. On New Year's Day, 1920, he told Garnett he had done nothing for six weeks and was ill with a "beastly complaint (not gout) which prevented me sitting up at the table" and, in fact, made it impossible for him to stir. He was not so incapacitated, however, that he could not work, for he completed the revision of *The Rescue* on February 24, and he was able to turn to the dramatization of *The Secret Agent*. Also, he made plans for his Napoleonic novel, and the following year started, as a short story, an offshoot of that material, *The Rover*. By early January the translation into French of *The Arrow of Gold* had been settled, removed from Madame Maus's hands and put in Jean-Aubry's.

The Conrads had returned to a half-empty Oswalds; furnishing it would proceed slowly. But they had several servants: besides Miss Hallowes, Conrad's secretary, someone to help Jessie, housemaids, an outdoor man and general castabout. Supported by so much external aid, Conrad was able to overcome, in January, a bad cold caught in Liverpool, an attack of gout, as well as depression, and to prune the text of *The Rescue* "with the utmost severity." He spent the month of February in bed cutting away phrases that went back to 1896.

On March 2, Conrad told Quinn that whatever promises had passed between them in 1911–14 were affected, like so many other things, by the war. Conrad pleads that not only, as he had explained, did he need the money for a specific purpose but conditions of communication were so poor that he "went to the man on the spot; and under the prolongations of those same circumstances I went again to the man on the spot." He explains that by coincidence this was also the period when he abandoned handwriting. Thus, he repeats, a point which his correspondent vehemently disputed, that Quinn had everything in pen and ink and his collection in that respect was complete. It was an odd argument, and Conrad's reiteration of it would suggest he felt its hollowness. He emphasizes that there seems a fitness to it: holograph manuscript in America and the rest in England. He then offers some unexpected pages of "An Anarchist," a few pages of *Romance*, in mingled Conrad and Ford handwriting, and promise of the "Falk" fragment, which did not turn up. Conrad quite frankly tells Quinn he will have to pay, as he,

Conrad, has not made his fortune yet. Income taxes, he asserts, take five shillings on the pound, and there are additional war levies.

Conrad then shifted to comments on the Polish situation which we have already noted, stressing the Polish defense of its front against the Bolsheviks as a struggle against "an enormous seething mass of sheer moral corruption generating violence of a more purposeful sort." The bitter irony is there, as it is in his assessment of his physical condition: "The gout clings to me like ivy to a decaying tree." He indicates he has written only a few prefaces for his Collected Edition and worked over the text of *The Rescue.* He admits to having improved it on its artistic side "without interfering in the least with its popular qualities." His mind, he says, has been filled, when filled at all, with ideas for his Mediterranean novel, which he promises to dedicate to Quinn, this after the fiasco of previous attempts at dedication. He adds that it will "be dedicated to you all right if I live long enough to finish it—and even if I don't." Quinn, however, was robbed of his dedication; Conrad died in medias res, as he suspected he might, and Curle saw the work through the press without considering Quinn. Just three days later, as if his sense of fitness were bothering him, Conrad wrote again to mention that Curle was in possession of sets of pamphlets, two series of ten each, of his Notes individually autographed. These he hoped to sell at the top of the market, and he was only mentioning them to Quinn in the event the latter would like to bid.

Conrad had completed the first draft of the dramatization and by the seventeenth would finish the revision. Even as he was completing it, he asked Curle if he could request £100 for the first draft, with about half its 140 pages in pen and ink. At the same time, he noted the sharp appreciation in the value of his pamphlets, with George T. Keating, another collector, upset that $500 was being asked for a complete set. What had occurred in America was that dealers were trying to buy into the booming Conrad market and then selling off at inflated prices, or at prices the market would bear. Quinn purchased the manuscript of Joyce's *Ulysses* for $1,200, paid out over a period of time, beginning in February 1920 and continuing into 1923, and then sold it at his famous auction in 1923–24 to A. S. W. Rosenbach. We recall that at this auction Conrad materials went for $110,000, and the manuscript of "Youth" alone sold for $2,300, to Jerome Kern. "Youth" brought $325 more than *Ulysses!* Relatively minor Conrad items such as "Falk" and "A Smile of Fortune" went, respectively, for $3,100 and $2,300. None of this can be explained except by way of the fluctuations of the market, and the market for the time being belonged to Conrad.

The result of this was, of course, to put pressure on Conrad in 1920 to produce any kind of copy with pen-and-ink corrections or alterations, preferably a holograph manuscript. Then, if he turned this into a typescript, with further handwritten notations, he had two items which were worth hundreds of dollars *regardless of their artistic merit.* Many of the most famous collectors were scrambling over his work—Quinn and Wise, Shorter, now Keating, later Rosenbach, who bought at the height of the market and then held most of the material as the market went even higher. With this in mind, Conrad asked Wise directly for £150 for the first draft of his play, saying that only the copy in Vernon's and Vedrenne's hands existed, although one other copy would have to be made for America. He indicates his reluctance to part with it, his first serious attempt at dramatic effort, but says he needs the money for a specific purpose. The specific purpose was probably the consequence of a sudden change in Jessie's condition. She had been laid up for the past month in a crippled condition, and at the end of March had to go into the nursing home in Canterbury. Once more, she was operated upon, on March 31, by Sir Robert Jones, to relieve congestion in the knee. Conrad wrote Lady Colvin that her pain was relieved and he looked forward to the end of her troubles. Meanwhile, Wise had agreed to the purchase of the play, the equivalent today of about $2,000.

As Conrad awaited publication of *The Rescue*—it would come on June 24—it seemed unlikely that he would be capable of writing anything in a sustained effort. The desultory nature of his working habits, the laxity of his interests, the concentration on purely personal matters, the stress on bringing in ever larger sums of money, and the general loss of control which we sense from his letters: all of these would appear to mitigate against any kind of steady, disciplined work. He would appear, like Whalley, to be at the end of his tether, strung out among various interests and projects, and simply living out the remaining months or years left to him. Except for the internal demons, which ravaged him as much as did the gout and his other physical ailments, he had broken free of all his earlier frustrations and emerged in the promised land: an author of international stature, his work read by a critical and popular audience, a family man living in a large, comfortable house, an income beyond his fantasies, and a circle of devoted friends, of the older kind and the younger generation as well. From that point of view, he had achieved everything he had started out to gain thirty years ago when he wrote those suicidally depressing letters to Marguerite Poradowska about emptiness, malaise, enervation, "*le vide éternel.*"

Yet the personal demons made him miserable. The external rewards were insufficient comfort. His career, seemingly so complete for us when we look back upon it entire, was for him unfinished. He was dissatisfied, of course, with his current work; but he was frustrated in another way, and that in his inability to make the breakthrough, to get beneath a crust or wall which prevented him from making contact with what he suspected was still in him. A good part of it was attached to the Napoleonic novel which he had felt within him for twenty years. He would, in fact, research some of the background at the British Museum in June. But his attitudes went further even than that novel, and that was his desire to reach down toward a prose that seemed no longer there. He told Colvin that he had slaved over *The Rescue.* "That prose!"—he knew it all lay in the prose, and the very sense of language which he had once developed into the Conradian mode or tone was eluding him.

The more certain he became of English idiom, the more easily he slipped into routine expressions and departed from that somewhat unidiomatic prose which was his very strength. His struggle in the last few years of his writing life was to reestablish himself in terms of language; and it was toward that end that he worked so diligently over the revision of *The Rescue.* That novel, then, had begun to take on an importance for him that went even beyond its span of his career; his revisions would be the criterion of his artistic ability.

We recognize how complicated the language question still remained to Conrad when he wrote to Aniela Zagórska, whose sister Karola was staying at Oswalds, about her translations of his work into Polish, an ongoing process contemporary with Gide's supervision of the translations into French. To Aniela, Conrad gave full authority for his Polish translations, as she had already worked assiduously on *Almayer*, which would appear in 1923–24 and then be reissued in 1928 with a preface by Stefan Żeromski. Conrad played on the title, suggesting *Fantazja Almayera*, but pointing out the dual meaning of "Folly" in English, as a building and a madness. He tells her the Polish word *obłęd*—which means insanity—cannot be used in the same sense. He points out that "Almayer's Folly" is a "stupid title which can't exactly be translated into any other language." Aniela at first used "*Fantazja*" and then, in 1928, shifted to "*Szaleństwo,*" another Polish word for insanity or madness but still lacking the duality of the English "folly." He was, at the same time, writing to Gide about his idiomatic use of English, downgrading his "stylistics"; the fight over the translation of *Victory* was, in fact, a struggle over idiom, which he felt Mme Rivière had ignored. As an amusing sidelight, Conrad could not elude female translators, for even as he wrote to Aniela Zagórska, Gide was tenatively suggesting Marthe Duproix for "Youth," and she eventually did the translation.

His concern with prose was appropriate enough, for fiction was itself becoming a "verbal world." Under the insistence of Pound, Eliot, Joyce, Woolf, Stein, the question of language had been transformed from a secondary or functional matter, as it had been for the Edwardians, to one of primacy. Valéry had spoken of poetry as being a language within a language, and we can adapt his remarks to apply as well to fictional prose as it developed in the 1910s and 1920s, as it approximated a "poetic" interior language and became more internalized than poetry itself. Valéry speaks of the poet as possessing no instant repertory of words; he has only the "phonetic and semantic fluctuations of vocabulary." He must work with a mixture of "completely incoherent auditive and psychic stimuli," in which each word "is an instantaneous coupling of a *sound* and a *sense* that have no connection with each other."

As prose came to be composed in the postwar period, this demarcation between forms of expression, prose and poetry, no longer held. If Conrad had been younger, he might have been able to react directly to these revolutionary shifts in the uses of language, and through that in the nature of fiction itself. As an enervated author in his sixties, he could do little; but he was aware that the verbal construct had replaced the narrative line. And further, that all this was occurring almost simultaneously with his publication of *The Rescue*, that swan song of romantic literature which had been sung out even when he first began it twenty-three years earlier.

To Garnett, while reporting that Jessie might need still another operation, Conrad called his now postponed *Rescue* a "patched book." The American publication date was May 21, the English date still indefinite, but then rescheduled for June 24. Jessie's problem was continued infection in the knee joint, which had, however, grown together correctly. The inflammation kept her in constant pain, whose sole relief came from ice packs. Besides Jessie's torture, and she was by no means a complainer, there was the fact of Oswalds as a hospital area: ailments and sickness had become a way of life. On the first of May, Jessie was operated upon again by Sir Robert Jones, but only some of the inflammation could be relieved. Still another operation of a more serious kind was contemplated in the future.

Sales to Wise intensified, to cover costs and other expenses. Conrad now scraped up every fragment. Besides Author's Notes with pen-and-ink corrections, he sold a short introduction to a schoolbook published by Dent and related to "Gaspar Ruiz" and the manuscript of the cable sent to the Polish Government Committee of the State Loan. As he says: "It is hardly literature but, at any rate, it is a public act of mine and very likely to be the only specimen of Conrad's cable style."

Curle left for Burma, to assume the editorship of the *Rangoon Times*, and Conrad felt deserted. As he grew older, he yearned for the in-gathering of friends, that visible support, even though he did not appreciate large groups. When Curle announced his departure for Burma, Conrad spent part of the day—Monday, June 7—with him and Walpole, worked for the afternoon in the British Museum on Napoleonic materials, and then returned to Oswalds to suffer a severe attack of gout, which flattened him. This was also the eve of the publication of *The Rescue*, toward which Conrad looked with terrible misgivings, if we can credit his condition as he reported it to Walpole. He had been on his back in bed with gout, but the more intense ailment seemed to be apprehension, a veritable sinking at the prospect of poor reviews. His depression was complete, the "depth of dumps," and he wondered: "Have dumps any depth?" He compares his state to a Dantesque journey to the infernal regions, from which he has barely returned. "The whole thing was so brutal and unexpected that I feel as if I had been robbed of the last shred of my confidence in the scheme of the Universe. . . . The flatness of this piece of paper on which you read these words is like a mountain compared with the flatness of my spirits." He says he wishes he could have his liver cut out, a Promethean image, "because I believe that nothing but an operation of that sort will do away with this horrible depression." What was, of course, the chief cause of the turmoil was his inability to work.

The condition remained throughout June; on the thirtieth, Conrad responded to an enthusiastic article by the American poet Edwin Markham and indicated a lame wrist which forced dictation of the letter. But it was to Hugh Dent, the publisher, that he suggested the real reason for his state of depression: advance copies of *The Rescue* had arrived, and he feared the reviews with the apprehension of a man who, with few books remaining in him, wanted a favorable farewell. He speaks of how others have predicted success for the novel, while he himself has been so immersed in it he has no clear sense of its quality. He even admits, "All the world *may* be wrong," but he accepts Dent's and Pinker's prognosis for success, by which he means marketability.

The first run of *The Rescue* was 20,000 copies, and everything appeared to go well. The book was attractively produced despite a delay because of a paper shortage, and it was well received. Conrad singled out the unsigned review in the *Times Literary Supplement*, headed "A Disillusioned Romantic," as incorrectly ascribing the misworkings of the novel to his disillusionment. He reacted to the review—it was by Virginia Woolf—by refusing to accept its one final truth, which is that the novel is seriously flawed because of the relationship between Lingard and Mrs. Travers. Mrs. Woolf pinpointed one of the telling faults, Conrad's inability to convince us of Lingard's tragic stature in a situation that goes well beyond the demands of romance. "Simplicity," she writes, "has been undone by sophistication, and fidelity and endurance have not availed. The elements of tragedy are present in abundance. If they fail to strike one unmistakable impression upon us, it is, we think, because Mr. Conrad has attempted a romantic theme and in the middle his belief in romance [because of disillusionment] has failed him."

Mrs. Woolf, however, judged *The Rescue* by way of the earlier novels; her argument seems to derive from the success of *Nostromo* in just this area of romance, or *Lord Jim*, although she recognized that Conrad was trying to attack fictional problems in new ways. She has granted the magnificence of his previous work, and she says that if this novel had not been by Conrad, with all we expect from him, we "should sink all cavil in wonder at the bounty of his gift." Bloomsbury had definitely been reading Conrad—Forster would review *Notes on Life and Letters* and Leonard Woolf *Suspense*—even as it was working out fictional forms that would eclipse him for the next generation.

The most intelligent of the reviews of *The Rescue* was published anonymously in the *Nation*, but the tone seems to be Edward Garnett's. Just before this review appeared, Conrad thanked him for his help in revisions of the latter half of the novel. Conrad acknowledges that he followed all of Garnett's remarks and suggestions in the margins of the *Land and Water* serial text with the exception of one brief change. Conrad shows particular sensitivity to his handling of the Mrs. Travers–Lingard relationship and responds to criticism by suggesting that if he had "hung Mrs Travers for 5 minutes on Lingard's neck" at their last meeting everybody would have been satisfied. He says, however, that he feared heroics: "I cared too much for Mrs Travers to play pranks with her on the line of heroics or tenderness; and being afraid of striking a false note I failed to do her justice—not so much in action, I think, as in expression."

Garnett speaks of the novel as being something of a maze in which the writer is "a great decorator," so that even when we have lost our way we pause "in amazement at his painted world." He singles out Jörgenson, the man of no discernible feeling, as a particularly grotesque but apt portrait, and he sees life itself in the novel as "a dark dream." He attempts to handle the relationship by splitting it into the "dream" part and the realistic part, and suggests that while Mrs. Travers has nobility she lacks fidelity to her heart; while for Lingard, as for Conrad, a woman is an "interlude in the life of men."

An appreciatory letter from the Ranee Margaret of Sarawak about *The Rescue* elicited from Conrad a wide-ranging answer that swept him back to the deepest reaches of his career, to his reading about Rajah James Brooke of Sarawak for *Lord Jim* and *The Rescue.* The ranee was the widow of Sir Charles Brooke, the second white rajah of Sarawak and nephew of Sir James. In 1914, she had sent a copy of her autobiography, *My Life in Sarawak* (1913), to Cunninghame Graham and asked him to pass it on to Conrad. The latter acknowledged receipt in his letter to Graham of January 23, 1914, and the reading of it may well have spurred him to pick up *The Rescue* once the war ended. The ranee was herself a person of considerable charm, courage, and poise, qualities we associate with Mrs. Travers. As the former Margaret de Windt, of mixed French, Dutch, and English blood, she had married, at twenty, Sir Charles Brooke, in 1869, and went with her husband to reign over Sarawak, a small state in northwest Borneo. After bearing Sir Charles seven children within seven years, she left him and returned to England with her three surviving sons. There, she became particularly friendly with Henry James, and then with Morton Fullerton, who later drifted from her to Edith Wharton. Besides James, she knew and corresponded with Gosse, Ford, Wilde, Swinburne, Burne-Jones, Galsworthy, Graham, Pierre Loti, and many others who moved along the contours of Conrad's personal life or just outside of it.

Her autobiography possesses the spirited quality of a woman who is caught in a loveless marriage with a man dedicated to his work. Her experiences in the Malay archipelago and particularly in Sarawak fired Conrad's memory and imagination; for as an alien European, a woman at that, in an exotic landscape, she carried with her some of the experiential quality of Conrad's own period in Borneo. And her confrontation with Malay styles would very possibly have carried over into Mrs. Travers, herself married, lovelessly, we assume, to a man whose compulsion is his work. Furthermore, the prototypical figure of both Jim and Lingard had been Sir James Brooke, her uncle by marriage; and by re-creating the family line in fictional terms, Conrad had been able to redeploy his materials so as to confront the uncle (Lingard) with his fascinating niece by marriage (Mrs. Travers).

Writing to the ranee, Conrad acknowledged his indebtedness to a book she has mentioned, by Captain Rodney Mundy, based on the Journals of James Brooke.* He speaks of taking the figure of Jaffir, the messenger, from that source, and thanks her for his use from her book of the "cage," which Conrad describes as a way of saving Mrs. Travers from mosquitoes on board the *Emma.* In the novel, Conrad invests the "cage" with symbolic value, not only saving the Europeans from mosquitoes, but serving as a prison for Travers and his wife. Only through her association with Lingard can she hope to escape the cage. In a sense, Conrad had read Lady Margaret's autobiography quite well; for he had observed there her dissatisfaction with the "caged" quality of her existence, although he could not foresee her future liberation once she left Sarawak and returned to London.

---

* *Narrative of Events in Borneo and Celebes . . . : from the Journals of James Brooke, Esq.* (2 vols., 1848). Conrad also went back to several books that overlapped with his reading for *Lord Jim,* among them *Brookiana,* Keppel's *Expedition to Borneo,* S. St. John's *The Life of Sir James Brooke,* and others.

CHAPTER 37

"Idle Days Breed Wandering Thoughts"

THESE were only moments, and they did not last. Conrad sensed an early death; although only sixty-two, he felt played out. "There's nothing I dread more," he told Quinn, "than an impotent old age, and I hope the experience will be spared to me." There was little time remaining to him. "Meantime I must keep in at work. But I've had two hard lives—each in its way—physically and mentally and I feel the need of easing down a bit." He hoped to get away in September on a trip to Scotland, with Jessie; but she was not strong enough for the journey. Conrad was being pushed backward—into sea days by the publication of *The Rescue* and a letter from Laurence Holt, managing director of the Ocean Steam Ship Co.—and forward by encroaching illness and uncertainty as an artist. The latest was Jessie's knee again, another operation, on July 24, at Oswalds, with Sir Robert Jones in attendance. She needed an incision to relieve pressure and, with the usual expectation, to start her toward permanent recovery. Conrad himself fell under an attack of gout.

The exchange with Holt is of considerable interest, since Conrad brightened noticeably as soon as the sea entered his life. From his responses, one senses his readiness to throw it all away, at sixty-two, and rush back to those years when the challenge was physical, not elusory. Holt had asked Conrad for suggestions about establishing a training ship for the merchant service, this in connection with the Ocean Steam Ship's plan to build a five-masted barque that would accommodate and train some sixty to eighty cadets. He queried Conrad about the way in which such a training vessel should be operated, as well as about the character of the ship.

Conrad was deeply gratified to be recognized as a seaman, after all these years, by a "House known so long and so highly honored on the wide seas." He says that as soon as he became an officer he tried to do his duty by the boys who served under him, some boys from Conway, Wales, others coming from schools on shore. Although Conrad could not accept a more active role in the planning of the training ship, he did promise to draw up a memorandum for Holt. He followed up his first letter with two more, the second of which indicates a deeply felt attitude about life and education which runs parallel to his views of art. He speaks, first, of the need of an "embodied inheritance of the past." He uses as an analogy the training afforded by a classical education. He says that a public-school man upon graduation has no practical or material use of the classical education he has received. "He cannot slavishly toil in the track of Homer and Virgil or fashion his public life in rigid adherence to the political views of Thucydides or the opportunism of Cicero." Nevertheless, his education can give him something of great value: "What is thought by humanitarianists [sic] is to give him a larger view and what he can expect from it is a deeper sense of his attitude to life and strong inner feeling of that continuity of human thought, effort and achievement which is such an inspiring and at the same time such a steadying element in national existence and in the corporate life of any body of men pursuing a special calling."

Then Conrad comes to his real point, essentially a radical one by this time. He believes in training upon sailing vessels, even though steam had replaced sail well before 1920. His words indicate the artist as much as the seaman. He says:

> A year or a year and a half of training in a seagoing vessel sailing ship I would regard for a boy destined for the sea as a course in classical practice of the sea. What he will actually learn on board that ship he will leave behind him directly he steps on the deck of a modern steamship. But he will have acquired the old lore of the sea, which has fashioned so many generations down to his very fathers and in its essence will remain with the future generations of seamen, even after the day when the last sail and the last oar have vanished from the waters of our globe.*

Such perfection of design that the sailing ship possesses was achieved from 1850 to about 1880, the "golden age" for Conrad. This was the period of the famous clipper ships, when weight and speed were carefully balanced to create one of man's most graceful attainments. After 1880, Conrad indicates, the evolution of the sailing ship ended, for steam was taking over, and a period of artistry, grace, and harmony passed away, with the stress now on carrying ever greater cargoes in the shortest possible time. With 1880, we

---

* In *Last Essays*, Curle included Conrad's lengthy "Memorandum on the scheme for fitting-out a sailing ship for the purpose of perfecting the training of merchant service officers belonging to the port of Liverpool." A good part of the memo is devoted to sailing-ship training, with Conrad recommending a ship of 1,400–1,500 tons, of the kind that were in service between 1880 and 1890, when he himself sailed as seaman, officer, and captain. In *The Rescue*, he had just finished writing at length about Lingard's brig, a ship on whose decks Conrad had tried to recapture an age free of both the machine and machinations.

pass into a commercial era, and the sea becomes contaminated by land values; with steam, a man is part of the machine, whereas with sail he had been part of nature. Waiting for his own death, Conrad saw the death of sail as another kind of end.

These were empty months, with nothing to show for the entire year except work on *The Rescue* revisions earlier and a few Author's Notes, some sporadic corrections of text for the Collected Edition, occasional schemes to put together some money for his estate. On September 21, with the Scotland trip out of the question, the Conrads went to Deal and stayed at the Great Eastern Hotel for three weeks. The vacation was designed chiefly to give Jessie a chance to recover from her latest operation and Conrad the opportunity to clear his head within sight of the sea. Such "local" vacations worked out well for them, whereas the more distant ones, such as the trip to Corsica in January of the next year, proved disastrous, expensive and enervating rather than rehabilitating. By August 18, he could report three chapters of *Suspense*, but considered his work "all very lame and unsatisfactory."

Conrad looked ahead to the stay at Deal, where he planned, among other things, to revise the text of *Notes on Life and Letters.** His younger son, John, was preparing for his Tonbridge examinations, and he had Pinker's second son, Ralph, as guest during the Canterbury "Cricket Week." Conrad motored over to Canterbury and lunched with Lady Northcote at Eastwick Park, where he also met the Duchess of Albany, the daughter-in-law of Queen Victoria, and Lady Gwendolen Cecil, who seemed to impress him with her conversation. Borys was the chauffeur for the occasion. Wise turned up at Oswalds for lunch and charmed Conrad with the "flow of his utterances," as he well might, this mixture of businessman, collector, and forger. Old Dent, the publisher, also turned up with his son Hugh and stayed the night.

---

* He would also work with Pinker over the text of "Gaspar Ruiz" and try to put together a motion-picture scenario. This would prove to be another one of Conrad's aborted collaborations, and one of the strangest. As he told Curle: "I am ashamed to tell you this—but one must live!" The joint effort, which was never produced, resulted from Pinker's having received a good offer for a Conrad scenario. Although "Gaspar Ruiz" was never screened, several other Conrad novels and stories were made into motion pictures, some shortly after his death. Victor Fleming directed *Lord Jim* for Paramount in 1925; Fox made *Nostromo* in 1926; Metro-Goldwyn-Mayer *Romance* in 1927, as *The Road to Romance;* Samuel Goldwyn *The Rescue* in 1928. Also, later: *Victory* (in several versions, two during Conrad's lifetime, two after his death); *The Secret Agent* (as *The Woman Alone*, *Sabotage*, and then *I Married a Murderer*); *Under Western Eyes* (a French production in 1937, called *Razumov*); *An Outcast of the Islands* in 1951; "The Secret Sharer" in 1952; *Lord Jim* again, in 1965; "Laughing Anne"; and "The Duel" as *The Duellists.* Further, the narrative of a film about the Vietnam war, *Apocalypse Now*, is based loosely on "Heart of Darkness," and one hears rumors of remakes of *Victory, Nostromo*, and others.

Despite these moments of entertainment and conviviality, Conrad remained relatively secluded. If he had wished and if his health had permitted, he could have been a social lion of this and many other seasons. Besides his ability to move in the highest literary circles, by means of his own achievements and his connections at every level, he could have been entertained socially among royalty and those who courted royalty. He was in constant demand both in England and in America. Yet when he finally visited America in 1923, it was only because Doubleday made it impossible for him to resist. The fact that Conrad's name is not joined to the younger generation of writers, Bloomsbury as well as those around Pound, Eliot, Joyce, and Lawrence, was a matter of personal choice, not opportunity. Although in the eyes of many, he had outlived his literary maturity, his name still carried a magical aura. Even those who rejected his later work, like Virginia Woolf, saw him as a writer who had achieved something unique. That he would move only on the margins of these several worlds was a decision he had made early in his career, even before his health demanded quiet.

Gout was ever-present, but he rejected Garnett's suggestion that he go to a Kneip establishment for a water cure. He said such places were odious to him, with their "pathetic population" hypnotized to go through with tricks and ceremonies. He saw it all as senseless verbiage put into "healer's literature." One senses that if he had expressed himself at length about Freudian or other analysis, he would have expressed similar contempt, not because he ridiculed the unconscious, but because he rejected the possibility of any part of the human apparatus not being subject to conscious discipline. Despite his flirtation with fate and destiny and the treacheries of nature, Conrad believed halfheartedly in a rational universe, at least as far as the individual was concerned. He was, in this respect, like most late Victorians: caught in the enigmas of existence because of the attacks on rationality and yet unable to forsake completely that rational inner control.

Before leaving for Deal, Conrad visited Pinker, and it was probably then that they discussed the collaboration on "Gaspar Ruiz." By the twenty-ninth of September he was back at Oswalds, preparing for the stay at Deal. His sole work now was connected to his Collected Edition. He was revising galleys and looking for errors, which upset him, whether his own or typos. In going over *The Nigger* text, he recognized that the phonetics of Donkin's speech were wrong; for if he is a Cockney, as Conrad called him, then there should be some uniformity in the dropping of the initial "h." Conrad says it is too late for that, and he excuses himself by saying, to C. S. Evans of Heinemann, that no one really knows what Donkin is.

On the twenty-first, the Conrads returned to Oswalds, the stay at Deal having proven uneventful. Jessie was beginning to walk by herself, although her improvement was always somewhat behind the expectation. Conrad had worked only on the scenario. Even his correspondence trailed off, with only a handful of letters for this period, although his correspondence for 1920 in general was quite heavy. By early October, it was clear that Jessie was involved in another knee complication; it had become a fact of life. In her desire to avoid being a cripple through amputation, she had brought a kind of destiny into their lives. Conrad appeared to enter fully into every aspect of her condition, and her knee complications were usually accompanied by his attacks of gout, seven of them in 1920.

The drift was seemingly complete, and would be until early December, when Conrad began a short story, wrote 5,000 words of it, and then expanded it into a short novel, *The Rover*, the entirety of which he wrote in less than seven months. But now in the fall of 1920, he dallied over the last of his Author's Notes, completing the final one on October 9. He wrote ashamedly to Curle that he was working alone on the "Gaspar Ruiz" project, with occasional assistance from Pinker, a "performance which seems as futile and insecure as walking on a tight rope—and at bottom much less dignified.*

There were, however, some cheering developments. The Collected Edition in the States was fixed at 750 copies and Conrad received an advance against royalties of $12,000. He was pleased that the entire edition was subscribed, and that both print and paper were satisfactory. In another area, Norman McKinnel was planning to take out an option on Conrad's dramatization of *The Secret Agent*, although the actual production would come only after long and protracted negotiations; it was produced by J. Harry Benrimo, in late 1922. Conrad also mentions his plan of taking Jessie to Corsica† for

---

* Because of the interest in his manuscripts, Conrad knew that anything he wrote with pen-and-ink holograph was salable, and therefore even if nothing came of the scenario, he could sell it as Conradiana. In an October letter to Wise, he promises him the manuscript and the first typescript copy of the scenario, telling him not to mention it to anyone because it might not be accepted, although it was being done at the request of the Lasky Company. In a following letter to Wise, on November 1, Conrad describes the physical aspects of the scenario in great detail, as though the collector were his primary market. The manuscript is 175 pages, written in red and blue pencil, with pen and ink as well. Conrad stresses that it is from beginning to end written in his hand. "It is in no sense a collection of notes, but a consecutive development of the story in a series of descriptions, just as the whole thing presented itself to me when I first began to think the subject out in its purely visual aspect." Then after satisfying himself that he could even put together such a novelty, Conrad reports that he dictated a more detailed and final version into a typescript of eighty-one pages, all containing holograph corrections and alterations. Any further copies that will be made, he assures Wise, will be purely clean copies, without any holograph additions or emendations. For both manuscript and typescript of "The Strong Man," what Conrad called probably his last film play, he asked 100 guineas. This would be the equivalent of about $1,500 and would justify his time on it even if nothing else came of the matter. Nothing did.

† After his return, Miss A. S. Kinkead wrote Conrad—he was now the old lion receiving requests for prefaces, contributions, letters, his autograph—asking if he would prepare a series of forewords to photograph catalogues, with Corsica and Ireland as his first assignments. Conrad was amused, asserting that he had little enthusiasm for Corsica, actually preferring it more in Miss Kinkead's photos than in nature. As to Ireland, he says he does not know it at all. He denies being a "literary man apt by temperament and practice to put his emotions and opinions upon

February, March, and April, for the climate and to enable him to soak up atmosphere for his Mediterranean novel, *Suspense.* His mood, as he told Harriet Capes, was not conducive to work; he had been "gouty, seedy, crusty, moody, stupid, perverse, cynical and lame." He was, in his way, in fine fettle to begin *The Rover,* whose Peyrol is crusty, perverse, cynical, but in perfect health. By late November, *Suspense* still did not move, and Conrad was ready to slide away from it.

Suddenly, after several years of no contact at all, Conrad heard from Elsie Hueffer (now Ford, from her husband's change of name). His response was extremely sharp, suggesting a desire to close the door on every aspect of the Ford connection. He says he was under the distinct impression that she no longer wished to maintain any relationship with him, and that had been his impression since 1914, when Jessie had called upon her. Now, six years later, when she says she wants to resume the relationship as before, he is confused: "Without trying to discern your motives, either then or now, we are convinced that no real regard or even mere superficial sympathy could have had possibly anything to do with them—either then or now. Therefore you will not think it strange if I venture to suggest, with all deference, that things should be left as they are." The sharpness of this letter is juxtaposed to one to Gide making peace, in which Conrad says he is reserving one set of the Collected Edition for the French author. It was as if Conrad had to achieve balance in his personal life, expunge the past with Elsie and welcome the present with Gide.

In December or slightly before, Conrad—still thinking of himself as a potential dramatist—turned his short story "Because of the Dollars" (dating back to early 1914) into a two-act play called "Laughing Anne." The memorialization of Conrad was also to begin: the Heinemann Collected Edition, well oversubscribed, started to appear that month; and Jean-Aubry put his plan for a study of Conrad into the hands of Pinker for English and American sale. This book, published in 1927 in two volumes as *Joseph Conrad: Life and Letters,* would remain the standard biography and source of letters until Baines's study in 1960.* The Collected Edition was, of course, the chief sign during Conrad's lifetime that he had become a classic. Furthermore, it in-

anything under heaven on a piece of paper"; he adds he is fit only for creative work. Nevertheless, he promises to send her something, although she should feel free to throw it in the wastepaper basket. He did, in fact, dispatch two brief pages that served as a foreword to her *Landscapes of Corsica and Ireland.*

* Jean-Aubry's second biographical study, *Vie de Conrad,* published in 1947 in Paris, and later in English translation in 1957 as *The Sea Dreamer,* was not a full-scale biography, but served in part as a correction and amplification of the original book. Like the earlier biography, it is unreliable in both details and emphasis.

volved the cooperation of half a dozen publishers, for Conrad's copyrights had been scattered, especially from his first ten years of writing, when he moved among publishers seeking better terms. That such an edition could be brought together was the result of Pinker's devotion to Conrad's work and to the man; by now, they were not only business associates but chums. Pinker was as welcome in the Conrad home as Garnett and Graham earlier. In their association, we have only Conrad's side of the correspondence, but we can remark that in the relationship, if Conrad was a conscious martyr, Pinker was a saint; if Conrad was the artist seeking fulfillment in the only way he knew, Pinker was parental and sustaining. For the writer who needed support at every turn, Pinker was as supportive in the middle and later years as Conrad's Uncle Tadeusz had been in the earlier. The friendship would end only with Pinker's sudden death in 1922.

In December, Conrad wrote Marguerite, the first extant letter in seven years and the final one in the series, that he and Jessie planned to leave for Corsica on the twenty-fourth (really the twenty-third) of January and travel through many of his old haunts: Havre (actually Calais), Rouen, Orléans, Lyons, and Marseilles, on the way to the ship. If they had decided to go to northern Italy, they would have met Karola Zagórska in Milan, but Jessie's condition would permit only limited travel. In a cavalier fashion, Conrad described the journey to Walpole as a kind of safari. They would start out for the conquest of Corsica with two women (Jessie and a nurse), two men (Conrad and Borys, who would accompany them to Rouen, to tour the Somme battlefields), and a motorcar, for which there would be a chauffeur later.

Conrad says that except for fits of depression which are "very worrying to look back upon" he is no worse than usual. In their absence, John Conrad would attend Tonbridge, and on his return from Rouen, Borys would settle into quarters in London and begin a short-term job for a wireless-implement factory. While the Conrads were away, Mrs. Grace Willard would continue to furnish the house at Oswalds. She had been put in charge of decorating, apparently the source of her income, and Conrad periodically sent her large sums of money—£50–£100 amounts are recorded—for her work and the materials.

By writing "Laughing Anne," whether it was produced or not, Conrad generated income from the manuscript. On January 3, he asked Wise for £100 for the typescript, which, he assures him, is much scored, corrected in pen and ink, and interlined. Wise complied with Conrad's asking price, and the amount helped cover some of their expenses in Corsica. Although Conrad still considered himself strapped for money, the family was spending enormously, in the range of £3–5,000 a year, or about $50,000 in current monies. In another area, when the Collected Edition of *The Nigger* appeared, the dedication to Garnett was omitted, an error which appalled

Conrad, especially since their friendship had weakened in later years. Although Heinemann had already mailed many copies to subscribers, Pawling arranged for dedication pages accompanied by an explanatory note to be sent out. After this incident, before leaving for Corsica, Conrad went up to London for dinner at Brown's with Pinker, Jean-Aubry, and Garnett; and Conrad wrote the latter on January 17 that he, Garnett, had been "really Great." He adds: "I am proud of having been discovered by *you* all these years ago." The comment carries the sense of a "rounding off."

On the eve of their departure for what Conrad hoped would be a quiet vacation and a period of good work, he could not shake off his depression. He foresaw disaster in whatever he would achieve. About the play taken for production, he prophesied that the critics would conclude that " 'Conrad can't write a play' " and he already feared he would not get much done in Corsica. He even expected poor weather, when the purpose of the trip was to seek sun.

On the twenty-third (of January), the Conrads left for France, and on the twenty-sixth and twenty-seventh, they were motoring through Orléans. They had spent a day in Rouen, then started south on the twenty-fifth, only to break down on the road between Chartres and Orléans. After a night in Artenay, they made Orléans, and after stops in Moulins, Lyons, Montélimar-Avignon, they reached Marseilles on the thirtieth, staying at the Splendide Hôtel for three days. It was leisurely and nostalgic for Conrad. "Everything looks promising," he wrote Pinker, mainly because the weather was soft and fair. He adds: "Throw care to the winds and come out south with punctuality and dispatch." This letter from Marseilles, Conrad's haunt during his "golden age" of Odyssean journeys, contrasts sharply with a later one from Ajaccio, Corsica, on February 23.

By February 5, they were settled in the Grand-Hôtel d'Ajaccio & Continental in the capital of Corsica, and Conrad realized that exploring the island was a bigger undertaking than he had foreseen. The weather turned miserable, and an unsettled tone intruded in what he had hoped would be idyllic. By February 23, after Pinker's visit, his words are reminiscent of those used on previous vacations abroad. Writing to Jean-Aubry in French, he says that they have not made any excursions because the weather was cold in the afternoon. Besides, the hotel was detestable; he had already described it as beastly in a letter to Eric Pinker. "The Corsicans are charming (I mean the people) but the mountains get on my nerves with their roads which turn, turn in indefinite corniches. One wishes to roar." The vacation had become a self-fulfilling prophecy. Apparently Jessie was enjoying it; only Conrad was seedy and depressed. Miss Hallowes was due to arrive at the beginning of March so that Conrad could dictate, evidently *Suspense*, but he appears to have worked only on background reading. He borrowed extensively from the Ajaccio library, all documentary materials which supplemented another book that provided both details and the base, the memoirs of the Comtesse de Boigne.*

Although Conrad did no real work in Corsica, he soaked up local materials and activated his memories of harbors, sailors, small boats, the entire paraphernalia of *Suspense* and *The Rover.* At the Ajaccio harbor, he spent hours with local skippers and from them moved back in memory to Dominic Cervoni, whose spiritual presence is so apparent in Attilio of *Suspense* and even Peyrol of *The Rover.* Surely, the view from the harbor, thoughts of Napoleon's Elba (which he never visited), memories of Marseilles and Toulon were all forms of "work," even though copy did not immediately result. Like the seaman who existed well before the novelist, Conrad was storing up intimations for the future.

By April 10, the Conrad caravan was back at Oswalds. Before returning, Conrad wrote an introductory note for an anthology of Hugh Walpole's work selected by the author, and then spent a few days in Bastia, on the northeast coast of Corsica, at the end of March. By early April they were on their way home, via the ferry from Ajaccio to Nice. From there, Conrad spent a night in Toulon, in whose environs he would set *The Rover* later in the year. He stopped for a short time in Marseilles and Avignon and then, anxious to get back, beat his way north.

The chief order of business upon his return was to make something of his unfinished manuscript and his notes from his reading; but *Suspense* was to prove intransigent, as unyielding, he feared, as *The Rescue.* Only this time, since he did not have twenty-three years before him, he vowed to shut himself up to make some progress. To Galsworthy he wrote familiar words (Galsworthy could have pickled them in brine): "I can't get my teeth into the novel—I am altogether in the dark as to what it is about—I am depressed and exasperated at the same time and I only wish I could say to myself that I don't care. But I do care. A horrid state." Not unusually, gout followed, in June. With nothing forthcoming, he moved back into the stage world. McKinnel had sent on Conrad's dramatization of *The Secret Agent* to Galsworthy for criticism and suggestions. When Conrad heard of this, he wrote his friend an extraordinarily detailed letter directed at Galsworthy's plans for alterations that went back to the very conception of the play.

Conrad argued that his attitude toward the dramatization was based on his posture toward art in general, which is that it is a subjective thing, containing "as much error as truth and also a certain admixture of completely unreasonable prejudice." For this reason, he decided to write his own play,

---

*Jean-Aubry lists some of the books Conrad borrowed: "Gourgaud's *Sainte-Hélène;* Stendhal's *Napoléon;* Pellet's *Napoléon à l'île d'Elbe;* Gruyer's *Napoléon, roi de l'île d'Elbe,* which he must have read already, in Montpellier in 1907; Rapp's *Mémoires;* Lanzac de Laborie's *Paris sous Napoléon.*"

"a Conrad play, not straining stage conception for the sake of that freedom (possibly in wrong directions) by which no art is ever injured." He says that it would have been relatively easy to write a Grand Guignol, but he preferred to write something whose subject "does not lend itself to exact definition." He insists that the center is *not* the murder of Verloc by his wife, as Galsworthy apparently tried to focus on it, but is a matter of feeling, or else, he insists, Winnie's old mother as a personage would have no place. As an alternative, Conrad indicates Galsworthy might have begun the play with the anarchists sitting in the parlor with Verloc explaining to them the "circumstances which force him to throw a bomb at some building or other." Such a scene, of discussion of ways and means, could end with Verloc dragging Stevie by the scruff of his neck through the door and telling him to carry the explosives, all of them blowing a kiss to Winnie as they go out on their bombing assignment. Conrad says that would be simple to construct, and he would have a "rather pretty Guignol play, with no particular trouble."

He was, however, aiming at something else: no less than the breakdown of all civilized life in a modern city. It was this subject that constrained him to construct scenes which, from the point of view of the action, seem detached and superfluous. He was after a tone, an attitude, a sense of things, qualities he sought as he wrote *Suspense*, or as he completed the revision of *The Rescue*. Conrad in his time was unfairly seen as a novelist of action and adventure; his novels, on the contrary, avoid the big scene, or capture it in retrospect, where he can control the action by feeling and tone. That is why comparisons with Kipling and Stevenson were so inept. Because of this sense of the thing, Conrad looked with trepidation upon the acting version; and he was correct, for the critics found the play almost unworkable. "The mere thought," he told Galsworthy, "of what a perfectly well-meaning actor may make in the way of conventionalised villain of my Professor which I assure you is quite a serious attempt to illustrate a mental and emotional state which had its weight in the affairs of this world, gives me a little shudder."

A current of actual resentment surfaces when, in the same letter, Conrad admits he forgot about the article he had written on Galsworthy in 1906 and, therefore, omitted it from *Notes on Life and Letters* (it was reprinted in *Last Essays*). Conrad argues that he had also forgotten his essays on James (now dead, however) and "Books," as well as other pieces; and he would insist that the Galsworthy article be included in the Collected Edition of *Notes.* It did not appear there, however, although the other omitted pieces did. The oversight may have been connected to Conrad's general depression or else have manifested resentment at Galsworthy's seeming ease in coming to terms with life and art, while he sat, anguished, at his desk, squeezing out every syllable.

In June, while ostensibly busy with his Collected Edition and his *Suspense* manuscript, Conrad stopped everything and completed an English translation of Bruno Winawer's Polish play, *Księga Hioba*, as *The Book of Job.* Winawer, a Polish-Jewish writer, had asked Conrad for ways in which his play could be translated into English and then produced in a London theater. Conrad responded that he was a man with few connections and explained that his fairly wide reputation was confined to his own work. He followed this letter in Polish with another one in August, in English, in which he indicated he had done the translation himself—apparently completed by June 25, according to Jean-Aubry. This began a steady correspondence with Winawer, extending to fifteen letters by Conrad almost to the time of his death, and since it was Conrad's sole attempt at literary translation, it is of some interest. Of course, the story of Job, even in a form such as Winawer's wry comedy, would have interest for him. For any Pole, Job had been a steady and faithful companion in the face of Russian and German adversity.

On August 10, Conrad reported the translation completed and indicated that his work was strictly idiomatic and should be acceptable to a theatrical audience. He mentioned having changed a few speeches, shortening and summarizing, and even altering the phrasing so as to make the play more accessible to both actors and audience. Conrad then showed the play around, a highly unusual procedure for him, but explicable as something he would do for a fellow Pole. Pinker, who saw the work, was agreeable to handling it in England and America, "not only on the ground that it is my translation but on the merits of the play itself." Conrad then suggests that if Winawer shows it around himself, he should do so simply as a translation, without Conrad's name. He says that there can be no question of any financial transaction between them; the translation was a friendly act and that was the end of it. He cautions Winawer that even if he does put it into Pinker's hands, he should have little hope of its being produced, its financial chances much reduced by the fact of its foreignness. Conrad's interest in Winawer's work, and the ensuing correspondence, can be explained by their common country; but it may have extended to the fact that Winawer worked, in his short stories, along semi-scientific lines, in that ambiguous area that Conrad and Ford had explored in *The Inheritors,* although Winawer did not demonstrate any great talent there or elsewhere.

In the meanwhile, Conrad sent Winawer and Aniela Zagórska a copy of his dramatization of *The Secret Agent* for their possible joint effort in translating it into Polish. Another figure from the past also entered this somewhat strange area for Conrad, Mrs. Otolia Retinger, Retinger's first wife, whom Conrad knew from his 1914 visit to Poland. She and Winawer did the translation of the play, and Conrad was quite pleased with many aspects of it, particularly their plans for staging. Winawer reported that it would be performed in Warsaw, which Conrad acknowledged as being very gratifying, but Cracow, not Warsaw, finally saw the production. At the same time,

Conrad kept up his own efforts to have Winawer's *Job* produced by the London Stage Society. Before any of this took place, and we jump ahead to late 1922, *The Secret Agent* was given in London, at the Ambassadors Theatre, on November 2. The play had a highly reputable producer in Benrimo, and accomplished actors: Miriam Lewis as Winnie, H. St. Barbe West as Verloc, and Russell Thorndike as Ossipon. In reporting to Winawer its failure to run more than a week, Conrad suggested some cuts so as to avoid the same errors in the forthcoming Polish production.

Conrad told Winawer he was not strongly affected by the failure of the production, but his words suggest considerable bitterness, surely exacerbated by the fact that he was stalled on *Suspense* and had generated hardly any work for the entire year. How else to explain his attention to Winawer's *Job* and to matters that in better days he would have dismissed sympathetically but firmly!

> I will also tell you that I anticipated what has happened [he wrote] for reasons which are not exclusively connected with the defects and the difficulties of the play itself. The reading of press-cuttings gave me the impression as of being in a parrot-house. Same tones, same words, same noises. Personally I was treated with great consideration; it is a pity that a little more consideration has not been given to the play. If it had been a criminal act it could not have been more severely condemned. There were, however, a few notable exceptions from the first, and afterwards a certain controversy arose upon the manner in which dramatic critics should exercise their function.

The remainder of the correspondence slimmed out, although Winawer sent Conrad a steady stream of his work: plays, newspaper cuttings, letters, articles (including one on Einstein). Conrad felt he had nothing left to give, and his replies are perfunctory, courteous but closed to any further commerce between them. One further note: Conrad sent his novel *The Rover*, as soon as it was published, and Winawer liked it sufficiently so that he offered to prepare a dramatic version of it, in Polish. Conrad's continued interest in the dramatic possibilities of his work led him to encourage Winawer, saying that the great success of the novel in America leads him to feel a dramatic version may be successful. He offers, if Winawer does it in Polish, to work on a translation back into English, "accepting your construction, and whatever spirit your creative instinct will put into it." The production would be designed for America, for Conrad felt that the failure of *The Secret Agent* in England mitigated against any further productions of his work. But who knows? he adds. "I do not think that the Labour Government would forbid the play on the ground that being both Poles we are 'horrid aristocrats' and enemies of the virtuous Bolsheviks." In the sole follow-up letter, Conrad indicates that no one else has asked to dramatize *The Rover*, and he himself begs off doing any further translations of Winawer's work, this in connection with his *R. H. Inżynier* ("R. H. Engineer").

The entire Winawer episode in 1921–22 was, for Conrad, a time in which he played around with literary properties, giving him a sense of being involved while he could not write. There was, of course, the additional factor that he could sell the manuscript to Wise, whatever the value of the translation or the ultimate disposition of the play. On June 21, well before he was finished with it, Conrad offered the original draft and first typescript of *Job* for £100 (or guineas), and the steepness of the amount made Conrad add that he would understand if Wise balked. Wise, however, was prepared to pay whatever Conrad requested. By now, Conrad must have recognized that the collector's presence in his life was a mixed blessing; for there was always the temptation to "create" manuscripts and typescripts rather than literature. He was selling paper, ink, and typed copy now as readily as he had sold stories and novels in the past, and he was being paid at present far more for his handwriting than he had been earlier for his art.

Through the summer of 1921, a time of deadly malaise and inactivity, Conrad puttered around, while Jessie underwent a relapse, becoming crippled and experiencing constant pain. He managed to visit Pinker's home and to get up to London occasionally, but without much enthusiasm. The desire to break out, somehow, lies below the surface of his letters, but the physical energy was lacking and the mental state depressed. One can understand the creation of a novel like *The Rover* and a character such as old Peyrol if one sees Conrad reaching the end of his tether and yet fantasizing a final heroic action that will justify his existence and diminish the debilitation of old age. *The Rover* fits into his work after *The Shadow-Line:* that desire either to rove back into memories and fantasies or to give renewed energy to a seasoned seaman.

His letter of August 5 to André Gide is a tired affair, played out, enervated. *Suspense* moved along at the rate of a few paragraphs and pages at a time, much slower than how even he was accustomed to writing, and what he produced was not to his liking. To Gide, he shows satisfaction that his friend was himself going to edit the translation of *Lord Jim*,* which for the French author was a true labor of love. Gide had also stated that he planned to write a study of Conrad's work, perhaps comparable to his short book on Dostoevsky (a series of six addresses delivered in 1922), but his sole "study" was his memorial item in the *Nouvelle Revue Française* four months after

* Conrad agreed that *Lord Jim* had been excellently translated by Philippe Neel, a particularly happy choice on Gide's part. Neel also translated *Nostromo, Under Western Eyes, Chance,* and "Gaspar Ruiz."

Conrad's death. Conrad mentions having reread Gide's *Les Caves du Vatican,* with its epigraph from *Lord Jim* at the head of Book V, praising it as "truly marvellous, the infinity of things which you have put within this book, where the hand is so light and the thought so profound." Conrad shows interest in Gide's news that he was writing a "long novel," what would become *Les Faux-Monnayeurs.*

Gide responded on October 16, and his letter is concerned almost solely with encomia of *The Rescue,* a somewhat curious focus for a writer deeply committed to his own "long novel" of such different substance. Gide indicates he has spent fifteen days, a difficult time for him, he says, in the company of Travers, Lingard, and Mrs. Travers. Gide found the novel touching "aux points plus sensibles et les plus secrets de l'âme avec une gravité pathétique." He stresses that Conrad has touched upon the "plus étranges problèmes moraux, et il n'est pas de question plus pressantes et plus vitales que celles que vous forcez le lecteur, à travers vos héroes, de se poser." Then Gide makes his central point, one, as we have seen, based on his own sense of moral stresses and tensions which the self can never resolve: that he observes in *The Rescue* the same "noblesse désespérée, la même détresse morale," that he finds in *Lord Jim.*

The key phrase is near the end of the letter, "détresse morale," which in French covers a broad range of "moral anguish," "mental distress," "intellectual or ethical anguish." Reading *The Rescue* through Gide's eyes, we are forced to see, despite its flaws of characterization and language, a greater weight than is usually granted; we notice a certain grandness to Conrad's scheme, from Gide's reading. Of course, Gide's English was imperfect, and he may have passed over the egregiousness of some of the phraseology while seeking out what he wanted in the theme; but, nevertheless, he saw something in Lingard and in the situation that returned him to that early period in Conrad. Like Jim and like Kurtz, Lingard, in Gide's view, is torn between the moral way and the emotional seductiveness of a woman, or power, or loot. Lingard's fatal hesitation between the world of Edith Travers and that of his Malayan friends was roughly equivalent in Gide to his choice between Biskra (release, self-discovery) and Cuverville (discipline, duty), a conflict that lasted well into the 1920s.

The moment was extremely gratifying for Conrad. Sitting tight at Oswalds, writing a perfunctory paragraph, coughing from bronchitis, aching with gout, he was otherwise half dead. To hear the echo of *Lord Jim,* even by way of *The Rescue,* was a form of mental energy. Arthur Symons invited him to Wittersham, but Conrad, pleading illness, could not leave Oswalds. Most of his correspondence was now in English, and took the form of short letters, because he was forced to dictate. If he wrote in Polish or even in French, he had to spell out each word, and so he wrote to Aniela Zagórska in

English, for which he apologized.* As he grew older and even fantasized about returning to Poland, he was unable to communicate in his native language because his wrist was swollen and his secretary, Miss Hallowes, did not know Polish.

Conrad sent the fragment of *Suspense* to Garnett for criticism—shades of *The Sisters* and *The Rescue* twenty-five years before!—and on September 2 thanked him for providing his "unerring judgment." It is unclear how much Conrad had in hand by this time, but it must have been a substantial segment, since Garnett appears to have put in a good deal of time and work on it. The important thing is that Garnett was encouraging, and Conrad felt confident enough to go on. Nevertheless, work on the book proceeded slowly, very possibly because while Conrad had the desire to write a novel he had an insufficient idea. He intended a panoramic novel of Europe in "suspense" while Napoleon was secluded on Elba; but a panorama, as he knew from *Nostromo,* requires some guiding principle or controlling philosophy, and he lacked such intellectual thrust at this time. For *Nostromo,* he not only had silver as a central symbol but a philosophical and political tension between the titular character and Decoud; further, the isolation of the locale gave him the opportunity for concentration and intensity. In *Suspense,* Conrad had no strong counterpoint to his protagonist, Cosmo Latham, and Napoleon necessarily remains offstage, an idea rather than a presence. Besides these structural failings, Conrad's use of the language had deteriorated; though he was still capable of the old tone, he had lost much of his judgment of word and phrase.

Conrad had several times alluded to the fact of his death before the completion of *Suspense,* and so in a sense the novel was doomed even as he worked on it. Intuition of an abrupt end made it difficult for him to develop his ideas, and when he was urged by publishers to put together a volume of short stories gleaned from his magazine publications, he was receptive. The collection, however, lacked one story, actually a novella, and toward the end, Conrad began to write *The Rover.* This collection, incidentally, was to include "The Black Mate," Conrad's first attempt at fiction. When *The Rover* grew to novel length, the collection of stories, such as it was, remained unpublished until after Conrad's death, appearing as *Tales of Hearsay,* with a touching preface by Cunninghame Graham.

---

* Little known is the fact that Conrad supported Karola Zagórska financially in these years, supplying an allowance of £120 a year, which he intended to raise to £200. In his letter to Curle on August 18, 1920, Conrad put it at £130 a year. The various sums meant an outlay of between $1,500 and $2,000 in current monies. In his *Last Twelve Years of Joseph Conrad,* Curle reported that Conrad "sent several thousand pounds to Poland to help his friends" (p. 170). If so, this would partially explain Conrad's chronic shortage of available cash at a time he was earning large sums.

Back in October, just before *The Rover* volume began to take shape, Conrad was genuinely pleased to hear from Bertrand Russell that he planned to visit. Russell had recently returned from China, and when his first son was born, in 1921, he wished to call him John Conrad, "John" the traditional ancestral name and "Conrad" after the novelist. Conrad as the godfather of Russell's son presented him with the cup usual on such occasions, even though there was no formal ceremony. In his October 5 letter, before the "naming" occasion, Conrad indicated he wanted Russell to himself, if he comes, and not with other visitors who would be arriving that week, two old friends, Sydney Cockerell and Hugh Walpole. Russell and Mrs. Russell visited at some time in October, for on November 2 Conrad alludes to his communion with the philosopher, and then refers to that "delightful visit." On November 18 Conrad, always alert to "names" and name usage, responded fully to Russell's request of "Conrad" for his son. After describing the grandeur that comes from paternity and the universality of the experience that ties all men together in fellowship, Conrad speaks of a Russell becoming a Conrad (a Korzeniowski becoming a Conrad could not have been a more wondrous thing):

> Of all the incredible things that come to pass this—that there should one day be a Russell bearing mine for one of his names is surely the most marvellous. Not even my horoscope could have disclosed that for I verily believe that all the sensible stars would have refused to continue in that extravagant manner over my cradle. However it has come to pass (to the surprise of the universe) and all I can say is that I am profoundly touched—more than I can express—that I should have been present to your mind in that way and at such a time.

Russell's "John Conrad" now joined Conrad's own "John Conrad," the English and Polish traditions joining, once again, in the confluence of a name.

The meeting in October was their final face-to-face talk, although the correspondence continued, the final letter on Conrad's part being his long response to Russell's book on China, *The Problem of China* (1922). We have already alluded to Conrad's concern at Russell's suggestion for a "selected council" that would help bring discipline to Chinese society. With post-Versailles cynicism, Conrad attacked any such council, as before he had ridiculed Wells's Samurai, as a collection of power-hungry figures. "But I wouldn't trust a society of that kind even if composed of angels. . . . More! I would not, my dear friend, (to address you in Salvation Army style) trust that society if Bertrand Russell himself was, after 40 days of meditation and fasting, to undertake the selection of the members." He adds that there is not "enough honour, virtue, and selflessness *in the world* to make any such council other than the greatest danger to every kind of moral, mental and political independence." In his essay on Conrad, Russell admitted that the former's view served as a corrective to his own "somewhat artificial hopes for a happy issue in China," although his sense of disciplined councils strikingly became a forerunner of Mao's Communist revision of Chinese society.

Conrad and Jessie spent a few days with Pinker at Bury's Court, in Surrey, at the end of October, where some American producers also came to discuss the film scenario of "Gaspar Ruiz." Conrad then went up to London overnight, while Jessie had her knee examined; he lunched with Doubleday, and left town struggling with an attack of gout. Conrad's letters and activities take on the quality of a holding action; he was waiting for something, as if he had assimilated into his own life the terms of the "suspense" Europe had felt as Napoleon sat at Elba. The sole consolation, in these days of malaise, was that Jessie, however precariously, could walk again and the children seemed settled, Borys in the motor trade and John at Tonbridge. But in a marginal matter, we catch Conrad's terrible anxiety about work, an anxiety that had become an obsession. On November 18, he thanked Wise for his check for £100. The check was payment for a manuscript—of *Suspense,* which was years away from completion. Conrad had sold "future" manuscript and first copy, and Wise had purchased them. The fact of such a sale is as significant as the amount; for £100 was so far less than the amounts Conrad was receiving for novel manuscripts that we can only assume he counted on its being fragmentary, or else he would have billed Wise for several times that sum. Psychologically, a future sale put Conrad in a bind. It provided impetus for completion—he *had* sold it; but completion would mean he had far undersold it.

Miss Kinkead had by now worked up her catalogue of Corsican and Irish landscapes, with a foreword by Conrad, another item for Wise, along with a privately printed copy of *The Secret Agent* dramatization. Major Gordon Gardiner, an amateur writer whom Conrad had known on and off for some years, had sent on some of Bernard Berenson's work to Conrad, who had read the latter's study of Leonardo. His response is one of astonishment: "I had somehow got the notion that Berenson was a noxious old Jew—and now I know better! I know it positively. I am also très flatté, inwardly, by the discovery that I not only can get the hang of but even assimilate sympathetically what old B has to say. Who would have thought it!" But this was marking time, as was Conrad's long response to questions from John Livingston Lowes, who was then working on *The Road to Xanadu,* his study of the imagination in Coleridge. Lowes had inquired about various tales, including that of the Flying Dutchman and the habits of the albatross. Conrad pointed out that Coleridge had invented the albatross business, creating facts of its existence that are not borne up by the facts of nature. He is lavish in praise of Coleridge, however, as he is of Poe's "impressive version of the Flying Dutchman" in "MS Found in a Bottle."

In December, Conrad began *The Rover* as a short story. It was clearly an outgrowth of his stay in Corsica, and his visit to Marseilles and the Toulon roadway. His vacation in Corsica, as we have seen, triggered a whole series of memories and reminiscences about a "seaman's return"; while the historical aspect was clearly part of his research on *Suspense* and a curving back, on his part, to that period when his ancestors enlisted in Napoleon's army in order to join the struggle against Russia. Of greater personal interest is Conrad's use of an old, weary sailor, Peyrol, as his chief character for a story-novel, when at the same time he was using a young man, Cosmo Latham, for his parallel venture into fiction, in *Suspense.* Although Conrad had long ago forsaken an external narrator such as Marlow, he created equivalent narrators in such personae.

The fact of Peyrol's Frenchness—he outsmarts the English and helps the French fleet break out of Toulon and escape Nelson's blockade—suggests that Conrad was still restructuring his own life and capable of trying out alternate roles. With Jean Peyrol, he has a man whose own name is not his but one borrowed from the farmer he once worked for. When he tries to explain about his name, he "didn't know very well how to talk to people, and they must have misunderstood him." Peyrol grows up to go through great adventures as a member of the Brotherhood of the Coast; that is, he has had a span of years lived out of sight of the rest of mankind, as part of a tightly knit "brotherhood," a community set within the larger one. His values have been established by *that* group, and his moral life is one developed by his survival within the brotherhood.

Running parallel to him is another Conrad surrogate or persona, Arlette, the girl whose parents were slaughtered in the anti-Royalist phase of the Reign of Terror. The stress he places on her loss of parents in the revolutionary fervor, and the curving, convoluted method in which he reveals the information piecemeal, suggests that Arlette, like the young Conrad, was a stranger to humanity as a consequence of her experiences. In her early years, she hugged the horror of her memories and, like Peyrol, moved along the margins of humanity: she young, he aged and weary. If he is an outcast among men, even suspected as a deserter once he has done his service, she is a figure unfit to live among other people, as Catherine, her aunt, repeatedly says.

The idea of a "rover," with its ambiguity of a man who, Odysseus-like, strives for experience, had been Conrad's plan in all his major fiction after *The Shadow-Line.* In *The Arrow, The Rescue,* now *The Rover* and *Suspense,* he was exploring what for him was his political, social, and moral world, that society summed up by life on the sea and those who can understand its message. Some of the passages in *The Rover* display Conrad in his best form, and they are, not improbably, passages of the sea. When Peyrol decides to undertake the mission for which Lieutenant Réal had been designated, he sheds his weariness and his hand becomes as steady as that of a young Ulysses. "On that sea ruled by the gods of the Olympus he might have been a pagan mariner subject to Jupiter's caprices; but like a defiant pagan he shook his fist vaguely at space which answered him by a short and threatening mutter." In a sense, Conrad's response to the war and to the cynical attempts at peace at Versailles comes in a novel like *The Rover* and in a character such as Peyrol. In that period of blockade, when the French fleet could not leave the Toulon roadway, Conrad places ultimate political action in the hands of the man who can control the seas; and when Peyrol gives his life in order to deceive the English Captain Vincent, we have Conrad's sense of meaningful life even as it approaches ever closer to death.

The Rover was to be more than a "homecoming" for Conrad, more than "Sleep after toyle, port after stormie seas." It was, in a real sense, a statement about values: connected as it was to the sea as a method of resolving tensions which on land are irresolvable. One must achieve personal mastery, one must demonstrate individual skill, by taking control of the ship oneself and directing the rudder. Conrad expressed a seaman's philosophy in Peyrol, and we are incorrect to think that because it touches on the primitive and elemental it is simplistic. Conrad knew, and in his best work demonstrated, that the same tangle of motives and conflicts which enters into complicated decisions informs more elemental ones. What counts is the way these conflicts are resolved: whether one tries to evade them, as on land, or sails into the teeth of the storm, as at sea. Learned councils, an elitist core of samurai, committees, like government itself, were a means of avoiding on land what could not be evaded at sea.

Once Conrad began *The Rover*, it came easily, apparently, and he finished it in draft by June 1922. Writing to Ford, on December 6, Conrad is very curt and sent £20; Ford had dunned him for a back debt which Conrad claims he does not recall. He complains of no work for two years, and then in a follow-up letter, of December 15, speaks of *Suspense*, his novel of Genoa, and says it goes very slowly. He says nothing of *The Rover*. Flitting through in December was, still, the dramatic version of *The Secret Agent*, which Norman McKinnel planned to produce. Faults were found in the play, however—the third act, for example, was seen as a "blemish"—and McKinnel's partners were afraid to go ahead until a later date. Also, the producers wanted to cut back on the cast and eliminate the character of the Great Lady, so as to save on an actress. While Conrad remained compliant and ready to concede, the affair of the dramatization simply played into his view of the stage: no serious man could do his work there. From this point, the play gradually passed from McKinnel to Benrimo, as Conrad himself passed from sixty-four to sixty-five.

CHAPTER 38

"Sleep after toyle, port after stormie seas"

ON January 3, 1922, Conrad returned from Bury's Court (Pinker's) and Jessie came back from London. Pinker was himself leaving for the States on business, but Conrad was unable to see him off because of "a spasmodic sort of cough." His letter of January 19 explaining his condition also contains his views about inclusion of "The Black Mate" in his Collected Edition. He says its use will, of course, "complicate my literary history in a sort of futile way." But he says there is no need to trumpet its origin, so that *Almayer* may remain as his "first serious work." The immediate thing was whether or not *The Rover* would run long or short; if long, "The Black Mate" was unnecessary to make up a volume; but if short, then the story could be resurrected and included. In any event, Wise was anxious to get hold of it.

The Heinemann edition de luxe of Conrad's works was subscribed and sold out, with its eighteen volumes priced at £20, or about $250 in current monies. But even by publication date, the set had appreciated to nearly double its price, and had Conrad invested his own money, beyond the six sets reserved for him, he could have easily doubled his investment within the year and with a signed copy probably tripled it. On January 27, however, he signed a contract for the publication of an edition which would be unlimited; this was the Dent "Uniform Edition," which would begin to appear in 1923. Sorrowfully, Conrad explained to Aniela Zagórska that he could not send her a set, as he had reserved only two sets for himself, for his two sons.*

Even more sorrowfully, he heard of the death of Pinker, in New York, on February 8, something totally unexpected and a loss of tremendous proportions to Conrad. Not only had Pinker nurtured him in his apprentice years, they had become inseparable friends, true survivors of the publishing wars.

* Actually, of the six sets, one each went to Garnett, Gide, and Sir Robert Jones, to Conrad himself, and to Borys and John. None went to Polish relatives or to Graham, Galsworthy, the Colvins, nor to the newer friends such as Jean-Aubry and Walpole.

Pinker was Conrad's junior by six years, and his death was the first of any close friend. Conrad wrote Eric, Pinker's older son, with a feeling he had reserved for few men in his lifetime—only his Uncle Tadeusz comes to mind.

> Twenty years' friendship and for most of that time in the constant interchange of the most intimate thoughts and feelings created a bond as strong as the nearest relationship. But you know enough to understand the depth of our grief here and our sense of irreparable loss. There are no words of comfort for such a blow. I can only assure you of my affectionate friendship.

Eric took over the firm's business and served as Conrad's literary agent until the latter's death. Sometime after that, Eric went to prison for embezzlement and was followed into the business by his brother Ralph, who was also sentenced to prison for embezzlement.

Conrad told Doubleday, with whom Pinker had been negotiating about the various collected editions,* that during his years of intimacy with his agent, "I learned more and more to appreciate in him qualities which were not perhaps obvious to the world, which looked upon him mainly as a successful man. It is certain that the value of my connection with him cannot be wholly or truly expressed in terms of money." Conrad adds that his sense of loss will always remain with him, no matter how time alleviates his present distress. And to Walpole, fully five months later, Conrad revealed the depth of their affection for each other: "He seemed to think that he had earned the right of laying his innermost thoughts and feelings before me. . . . I feel that we all in this house have lost a personality that counted in our lives for stability and support."

In another sense, Conrad's attitude toward Jews was altered by his association with Pinker. The anti-Semitic assumptions which underlay some of his earliest comments disappeared almost entirely, except for an occasional remark such as Berenson's being a "noxious old Jew." Conrad's anti-Semitism, as noted earlier, was never of the virulent kind, but rather a not very deeply held feeling that came with his birth and class. He took the alleged coarseness and vulgarity of Jews for granted, and he also, to some extent, saw them as part of that radical or revolutionary world he detested. In his nurturing years, he had not observed them as individuals but as men involved in money matters—lending, selling, serving as middlemen—or on the European scene in politically extreme activities. Once he saw them as individuals, Rothenstein, Pinker, Winawer, Knopf, among others, his reactions were

* Pinker's efforts here were heroic, for Fisher Unwin did not easily relinquish his copyrighted material: the three early books as well as *The Arrow of Gold* and, currently, *The Rover*. Unwin, in fact, planned his own "Works of Joseph Conrad," but went no further than five volumes, in 1923. Very possibly, he got hold of *The Rover* as part of an overall agreement with Pinker for the Collected Edition.

directed at the man, not the race. In no way did he enter into the fashionable and often virulent anti-Semitism of many of his contemporaries—Eliot, Lawrence, Pound, Wyndham Lewis, Woolf, Hemingway, or the French writers around Charles Maurras.

With Pinker's death, Conrad's business activities rested in the hands of Eric, who was far less experienced and nowhere near the commanding figure his father had been. But since Conrad's publishing deals had already been set into motion by the elder Pinker, there seemed no reason for change, and out of loyalty he would have remained with the firm anyway. In any event, Conrad had little enough business. On the French front, instead of corresponding at length with Gide, he wrote directly to his translators, especially to Philippe Neel, who had recently completed *Lord Jim* and *Victory.* Both would appear in 1922, the latter under Conrad's recommended title of *La Victoire* (jointly translated by Isabelle Rivière and Neel), serialized in *Le Temps,* and then issued in two volumes by NRF (1923). The French publication of *Victory* was considered a major event, and it received long reviews from, among others, André Maurois and Edmond Jaloux. Conrad's French career was moving formidably along the lines of his major work, at the same time that his English career was stalled or winding down.

Conrad's letters in the winter and spring of 1922 are full of his usual complaints, but he was evidently working sufficiently well to produce *The Rover* by June. It was becoming a fully fashioned novel, and not at all a contemptible effort. While not demonstrating his full powers, it did carry him back to the years of *The Nigger,* with Peyrol reminiscent of Singleton, and one might add, of MacWhirr in "Typhoon." Work on *The Rover* was almost his sole occupation, except for marginal attention to the presentation of his play. Writing to Allan Wade, Conrad showed hesitation about making further changes, such as telescoping the first act, as Wade had suggested, since he felt no one would produce it now that McKinnel had dropped the project. Although he masked his feelings, he looked forward eagerly to a production, saying that McKinnel "might have had a success of curiosity" rather than the "series of three dead failures with which he began his management." In the same letter, Conrad asked Wade to look at Winawer's *Job,* with an eye toward a West European or American production.

Conrad did not let his play drop, for he followed this letter with an even longer one on April 9, also to Wade. The latter had held out some chance that a producer might be found, with Eric Pinker making the arrangements, and used the occasion to praise the dialogue. Conrad was gratified to hear he could write colloquial conversation, saying that even in his novels he did not think he wrote literary dialogue, which is, of course, nonsense. His dialogue is stylized, pointed, and literary to a great degree, except that in its context it appears natural because everything around it is so stylized. One reason

Conrad's stage dialogue failed badly was that he lost the context, and the conversation without support from all the rest of his stratagems sounded bare.

While Conrad was engaged on *The Rover*, he was slowly transforming the way in which he would appear to the public. That is, he was involved in what we now call "packaging," in which an author often denies his greatest strength in order to appear more generally appealing, the aim being to sell books. The occasion for Conrad's "arrangement" of his career came when Curle was preparing an article called "Joseph Conrad in the East." Of course, the whole idea of packaging arose when he became surrounded by young men who had written or were planning to write books about him; what they said, and what he said in his Author's Notes, he felt, would largely determine the kind of audience he would enjoy after his death. He sharply attacked Curle's article (still unpublished) on two grounds: first, that it was too explicit about background materials. Conrad's intense secretiveness was almost conspiratorial in its approach to his past and to his conception of it: "It is a strange fact [he wrote] that everything that I have, of set artistic purpose, laboured to leave indefinite, suggestive, in the penumbra of initial inspiration, should have that light turned on to it and its insignificance (as compared with I might say without megalomania the ampleness of my conception) exposed for any fool to comment upon or even for average minds to be disappointed with." Explicitness, he stresses, is fatal, and he particularly objects to Curle's specifying the landing spot of Marlow in "Youth," a "damned hole" named Muntok. Conrad feels that the lack of charm of the place juxtaposed with the glamour invested in it by Marlow makes his story seem a fake.

Second, and more significantly, he objected ringingly to Curle's presentation of his work as permeated by "gloom, oppression, and tragedy." "You know, my dear, I have suffered from such judgments in the early days; but now the point of view, even in America, has swung in other direction; and truly I don't believe myself that my tales are gloomy, or even very tragic, that is not with pessimistic intention. Anyway that reputation, whether justified or not, has deprived me of innumerable readers." Here, Conrad has turned upon himself; for earlier in his career he had vociferously denied the image of himself as a "sea" or adventure novelist, stressing the moral concerns of his work. Now he was willing to accept the designation of the lighter kind of writer in order to broaden his appeal. He adds that he positively objects to being called a "tragedian."

This remaking of himself, through secretiveness and through a shift of emphasis in his work, was connected to several factors in Conrad's life, and part of it was not deception. He was, in a way, attempting to redress what he had never enjoyed in the way of readership for the first twenty years of his career, when he had had to educate an audience to his distinct tone and method. Possibly, the more significant factor was that he knew he was played out and that the way in which he was presented now did not in any manner or means change the novels and stories he had written. They remained, and the important thing was to have them read. He was not transforming them, although in the Author's Notes he did stress the trivial details of their composition and not their grandness or their difficulty.

Finally, as he declined in physical and mental energy, he was curving back upon himself, like Peyrol, and his weariness took many shapes, one of them being the desire to receive the cheers of the crowd and to give them a less ironic and pathetic view of the world. As he moved closer to death, his vision thinned, the harshness receded, the irony diminished. Artistically, he had become cautious, and naturally, he simplified his sense of his own vision. When he looked deep into the fire and pitch of his imagination, he no longer found the materials of a fated existence lived at the edge of an abyss. In a follow-up letter to Curle, who was quite willing to make changes, Conrad told him that especially in the United States the "average mind shrinks from tragic issues."

By May 24, Conrad could report to Garnett that he was trying to get through a "sort of long short story"; even by this date, he was attempting to fit it into a volume of short fiction. Yet he must have had in hand well over 50,000 words, and *The Rover* was filling out to novel length. Also, the complication of Peyrol's final action required a good deal of preparation and motivation, necessitating a considerable number of explanatory pages Conrad's plan for the novel, once he moved beyond a "sailor's return," required detailed working out, not a quick ending. It was, perhaps, this realization that made him so nervous about the book, telling Garnett that Peyrol "and a lot of other crazy creatures that got into my head have also got on my nerves." He says he has been depressed about work before, but not so exasperated. Another possibility is that he had begun to write the section which would end only with Peyrol's death, not an easy task when the character moves in and out of one's own consciousness. The "memorialization" of Peyrol that occurs at the end of the novel, by Vincent and even Nelson, could be Conrad writing his critical epitaph.

Whatever the subconscious motivation, he was moving Peyrol toward a confrontation with life that would express his final grasp of self. The money Peyrol had acquired, in that vast belt of coins and paper, was insufficient for a man who valued only action, the taste of experience, even violence and death. The money is, finally, hidden at the bottom of a well—was this Conrad's epitaph on the fortune he was making (and spending as rapidly as it came in)? Sitting at Oswalds, barely moving from the house, his wrist almost continuously swollen, dictating to Miss Hallowes, who was his lifeline with the world outside, Conrad imagined the sea, the English blockade of the French fleet, Nelson himself waiting for the enemy to appear and give battle, and an old French seaman with the dual desire to rest and yet make one more effort. If Conrad fantasized himself as Odysseus, he was more the Odysseus of Dante and Tennyson than of Homer, the wanderer who refuses final shelter because of the inner urge to fulfill himself.

Running through these later years is the strange friendship Conrad maintained with Francis Warrington Dawson, that effete American Southerner who gave so many of his qualities to Blunt in *The Arrow of Gold*. Throughout his career, Dawson tried to get started as a novelist, and he pursued Conrad for advice. The latter's patience with Dawson was endless, this with a man who had little enough talent for fiction, although he was an effective journalist. Through Dawson, Conrad met John Powell, a fine pianist and a composer who came to Capel House frequently to play Chopin for the family. Conrad even left his home on occasion to hear Powell at public concerts. Jean-Aubry was also a musicologist, and through these friends Conrad indulged a real love of music, chiefly Chopin and Italian opera. When Jean-Aubry wrote his book *The Music of the Nations*, Conrad acknowledged reading the section on Debussy with the greatest pleasure. Dawson remained a constant in his life and apparently felt that all that came between him and a novelistic career was the right publicity, which he hoped to gain from Conrad. The latter gave Dawson great freedom with his letters, permitting the American to quote from them and reshape them as he wished, so that Dawson created hybrids which praised his work; this he did in the foreword Conrad wrote for his *Adventure in the Night*. This foreword consists of ten sentences Conrad had written on separate occasions, including several so removed from context that their meaning was altered, especially those that made him appear in agreement with Dawson's Negrophobia.

Given this indulgence toward his younger friend, Conrad never revealed to Dawson his true feelings about his work. When Dawson asked for advice on a novel he had worked over since 1909, Conrad avoided specifics and moved to a general philosophy of art. In his letter, of June 2, 1922, written when he was finishing *The Rover* and ill in health and low in mind, he attempted to reformulate his long-held position. He distinguishes between a critical gift, which he says he lacks, and a creative gift, which was the sole thing that qualified him to take a pen in hand. "What I say I can only talk about myself: not because I am a megalomaniac but because I am not sufficiently cultured to talk with authority to the public about other men." He adds: "I dislike writing, I don't believe in my own wisdom, and I shrink from putting forth my opinions to this general public. I am like that. I cannot help it. It is temperamental; and it is closely associated with the unliterary complexion of my mind."

He says that his creative gift has never "been a source of gratification," that, on the contrary, "it has brought me many hours of unhappiness in the doubts and heart searchings it has forced me into at every step." Conrad and

Joyce were perhaps the sole major writers in the early modern period who felt that their expression must come almost solely in creative works; that their creative gifts did not extend to prophetic statements about society or politics. Both spoke mainly through their imaginative work and left few of those incidental writings which most authors pen as their dues to the rest of the world, or, in Lawrence's case, as their effort to change it.

On June 29, Conrad told Curle he would be in London on July 3 or 4 to deliver the completed, but unrevised, draft of *The Rover*. He indicated he was in a terrible state, for the "whole thing came on me at the last as though a broken dam," the result being a month "of constant tension of thought." Eric Pinker's negotiations over *The Secret Agent* were also turning more complicated, and Conrad became increasingly attached to the play as its production seemed even more a will-o'-the-wisp. He feared a summer production because the principal critics would be away, as would most of the intelligent part of the public. He mentions that twenty or thirty of his friends would, as well, be out of town and miss what might well be Conrad's last gasp. Most interesting, however, is his assessment of his work, as juxtaposed to James's:

> The play in itself is not inept—that is, it does not contain the seeds of an obvious failure. It is not a mere exercise in intellect, or in style, or in delicate subtlety, or in over-refined sentiment, as poor Henry James' were who never dealt with a situation but only with the atmosphere of it. On the other hand, in its innermost quality it is as Conradian as anything I ever have written; therefore I may hope for a succès curiosité: say an existence of six to eight weeks, which would satisfy me if associated with a certain amount of recognition as expressed in varied criticism and discussion. (I may of course be the most deluded of mortals in that respect but that is how I feel.) A money success I never dreamt of. For that of course it would be necessary for the same people to come over and over again, and this for a play like "The Secret Agent" can not be expected; unless indeed there was some marvellous acting, on the part of some principals, which would fascinate people.

The combination of arrogance and diffidence is compelling. One of the chief faults of the play *is* that it is caught between styles, and it has a good deal of that Jamesian "sentiment" and "atmosphere" which Conrad dismisses. What started as a lark of sorts, in the dramatization, had now become a cause, and we are surprised to learn that when the play was finally produced in November, Conrad could not bear to attend the opening night. R. L. Mégroz has left an interesting version of that event, which will be picked up later. The more withdrawn Conrad's personal life became, however, the more he insisted on his reputation and publicity in the world beyond. If possible, he would have enjoyed a more direct manipulation of his reputation, while at the same time, as a reserved and secretive man, he clung to his privacy, to his distinctiveness and uniqueness. These conflicting patterns, which had always been present, were now clearer and more torturous because of his inability to control his fate, which is to say, his work and his working habits.

Conrad went up to London on the fourth of July, to deliver *The Rover* as planned and to see Graham, among others, over a particularly distressing episode concerning Borys. The episode involved the payment of a large sum of money, which Conrad agreed to stand for, although he says it would be a "crippling affair" for him. Thanking Graham for his kindness and patience, Conrad indicated that he could raise the money by extra work, but rapid settlement was essential.* Despite the personal worry, he completed the revision of *The Rover* on July 16, and a corrected copy was immediately dispatched to the United States for serialization by Mead, Schaeffer in the *Pictorial Review.* Wise had told Curle he was interested in purchasing the manuscript, but Conrad pointed out that it was only a first-draft typescript, although with many alterations and with twelve pages of manuscript. He asked £150 for it, a low figure because of the small amount of pen-and-ink manuscript. In the same negotiation, Conrad offered the manuscript of the preface he wrote for Curle's book of travels, *Into the East.* Wise, as always, complied, and Conrad was grateful for the money.

The summer of 1922 was a waiting period: for publication and reviews of *The Rover;* for returning energy so as to allow completion of *Suspense;* for visits from admirers on both sides of the Atlantic. Professor Samuel C. Chew was one such visitor, confirming that Conrad had suddenly become an important and suitable "modern." He faced these interviews with trepidation, always assuring the visitor ahead of time that he should expect to be bored. In late July, Borys was offered a position with the Daimler Company, which he took. For some years he had been trying to find a hold in an area of technical manufacturing or with machines. Earlier, he had invested his £400 war gratuity, along with Conrad's £200, in an outfit called the Surrey Scientific Apparatus Co.—a title suggestive of de Barral's enterprises in *Chance*—and

* Although Conrad's letter to Borys for August 16 makes no mention of the problem his son was having with his affairs, he did write about it to Jean-Aubry, on August 9: "Je viens d'arranger cette lourde affaire de B, mais je reste sous le coup d'une amère déception—une espèce de fatigue morale aggravée par le doute, qui subsiste, sur l'avenir. Je ne parle pas de l'embarras materiel que ça m'a causé, qui est serieux; c'est plutôt l'atmosphere de toute cette affaire qui m'opprime. Enfin! Je suis peut-être injuste pour lui. On verra."

The tension was considerable. Yet Borys's memoir of his father for these years indicates a different tone to the relationship, one based on a common interest in motorcars and the entertainment of dinner guests, among other things. On these occasions, Borys was fascinated by Conrad's ability to carry on conversations in three languages, whether Polish with the Zagórskas, French with Jean-Aubry, or English with his manservant, whom he would abuse for his shortcomings as a butler. Borys's enjoyment of Conrad's company seems genuine, and the feeling was, apparently, reciprocated.

lost all when the company went bankrupt. The position with Daimler, at Coventry, paid £400 a year and was welcome for both son and father.

Besides the worry over Borys, Conrad was becoming witness to the death of his contemporaries. First Pinker, then W. H. Hudson (on August 18), and just before (on August 14) Northcliffe, although of course they were not equal in his affections. Hudson had been a sometimes acquaintance, occasionally met in London with Edward Garnett. The latter considered Hudson an outstanding "modern" writer, as did most of his friends. Graham, another member of this close circle, was particularly intimate with that sympathetic but elusive man who had also spent much of his early life in South America. Although Conrad was not intimate with Hudson, he felt something unique about the man. To Garnett, he spoke of his real affection for this author, who was "a nature-production himself and had something of its fascinating mysteriousness." And to Graham, he described him as "Child of Nature," someone they will jointly miss even though the "rare spirit" in Hudson will continue to speak to future generations.

Northcliffe was something else for Conrad, a figure from a Dreiser novel; he admired not the man's ethics but his power and success. Conrad was astonished at the Harmsworths—"it is [he told Graham] as though they had found Aladdin's Lamp." Conrad found the inner man "absolutely genuine," and said that at least his fortune was not made by "sweating the worker" or "robbing the widow and the orphan." As a follow-up on this run of deaths, Conrad was asked by the *Times Book Review* to write a memorial on Hudson, a task he declined on the grounds that he hardly knew him, citing fewer than ten conversations and naming Garnett as the obvious man for the job.

In September, Conrad, Jessie, and John were house guests of Sir Robert Jones in Liverpool. From there, accompanied by Sir Robert, they took a three-day tour of North Wales, the area of forests and parkland, which helped to contribute to a bad cough for Conrad. *The Rover*, meanwhile, was turned down for serialization by Hearst in America, but despite that disappointment—Hearst would have paid well—Conrad planned to try to settle down on *Suspense*, a resolution he made by the end of September. He had no other projects in mind, no other incomplete business. C. K. Scott Moncrieff, the translator of Proust, had sent his version of *Du Côté de chez Swann* for Conrad's perusal, and would later ask him to help suggest a title for Proust's seven-volume opus.

J. Harry Benrimo had by now picked up the dramatization of *The Secret Agent*, and this led Conrad to further speculation about a possible stage version of *The Arrow of Gold*, and even one of *Under Western Eyes*. It was *The Arrow*, however, that caught his imagination; he says that if he felt the thing could be done he would sign an agreement with the Devil himself for the chance. He adds that a woman such as Rita has never been put on the stage and that there are facts only suggested in the book which could be enlarged upon in a dramatic version. Such a play would not be cut from the book, but re-created from the materials that went into the novel. As for *Under Western Eyes*, Conrad says he has already sketched the first and last act in his head; not surprisingly, he skipped the middle of the novel, which has little resonance. He tells Eric Pinker that such an evolution in his life, from novelist to playwright, can be "recognized as a manifestation of creative art," not at all an unusual development in a career as "exceptional" as his.

The last half of October, leading up to the November 2 opening of *The Secret Agent*, gave Conrad a focus for his time: he wrote to Benrimo about the production and he attended several rehearsals. To Benrimo, he spoke of the difficulty of casting for Vladimir and the Professor, although he felt confident about Russell Thorndike as Ossipon and Miriam Lewis as Winnie Verloc. His particular job was to pare the text, cut it to the bone, and think in terms of the stageworthiness of the piece. Conrad feared, however, that too many cuts would alter his points about anarchism and police attitudes, which he felt were essential to the atmosphere of the presentation. At the rehearsals, Conrad was disturbed by the Professor's role. He told Benrimo that tone and expression were essential there, and yet he had seen none of it. He also complained of Heat and even Winnie Verloc. Quite apparently he had the novel in mind when he scrutinized the dramatic version. Intimations of disaster already begin to creep in. To Jean-Aubry, just six days before the opening, he expressed profound depression: "These people will never be able to understand the piece—nor even suitably learn it before Thursday." Conrad went faithfully to rehearsals, coming on Monday, October 30, and working himself into such anxiety that he came close to breakdown.

R. L. Mégroz, a young writer, asked Conrad for an interview, chiefly to explore his personality for a study of the man behind the work. Conrad was, of course, opposed to this, as he felt that the man writing imaginative literature gives only what is in his work; he has, in effect, no other "life." "I don't think [he wrote] that a man who in thirty years has produced twenty-four volumes which are neither philosophy nor sociology, nor anything practical, improving, enlightening or even revealing (except a certain gift for writing prose) can have much to say that would be worth hearing." Nevertheless, Conrad agreed to meet Mégroz on November 2, in the lounge of the Curzon Hotel, where he would be staying for the opening of his play. Conrad did not attend the opening, but spent the time with the young writer, all the while stressing his own indifference and coolness. But Mégroz records that, protestations of coolness aside, Conrad was in a state of intense excitement: "The contrast between his gentle speaking voice and his restless manner was remarkable. From time to time he would leave the smoke-room where we sat and inquire at the office for a message, presumably a message from the Ambassadors Theatre. He at any rate confessed to a splitting headache when excusing himself from eating anything with me about eight o'clock."

Conrad's agitation was clear: if the play was successful, or even promising, he would interrupt his impasse on fiction and turn to the stage, by plundering what he knew best, his own work. He suspected he might be on the frontier of still another career. Yet his intuition was correct.* Both public and press demonstrated little enthusiasm. There was respect for Conrad as a novelist, but no encouragement for him to continue as a playwright. The atmosphere and irony of the novel had made the difference; lacking them, the play seemed all starts and stops. Conrad told Galsworthy of "serene joy," touched by remorse at the injustice of his "past thoughts towards the actors who had a lot of characters . . . thrown at their heads just 20 days before the first performance."

Conrad's friends stood loyally by him, but he had warned them already of the "vulgarization" of the play, as he put it. He also heard from Frank Swinnerton, who sent his appreciation of the drama; and from Henry Arthur Jones, the vastly successful playwright whom Conrad had already met at the Reform Club through Henry James. Jones welcomed Conrad to the theater as the " 'youngest' dramatist." In a follow-up letter to Benrimo, during the short run, Conrad spoke of having received his verdict from the critics, although none called it futile. He also expressed the wish to make one final change, to restore the Professor in the last scene. "I ask you this as man to man and as an artist speaking to another artist . . . my dear Sir you are not presenting a Guignol horror but something which has a larger meaning." By November 11, however, *The Secret Agent* was withdrawn from the Ambassadors Theatre, and Conrad's hopes for a belated career as a dramatist were lost.

As an aftermath, he feared the poor reception of the play in London would affect the chances of a production in Warsaw, and he told Winawer that a failure on the boards by Conrad makes it almost certain that whatever influence he has will be diminished. As we follow the crosscurrents of Conrad's correspondence during and immediately after the closing of the play, we see that, despite his intuition of failure, he had set his course on a dramatic

---

*Just three days before the opening, Conrad wrote at length to Allan Wade, thanking him for his role in putting the play into Benrimo's hands, but at the same time characterizing Benrimo as "*épatant*," amazing, but in a special sense. "I never saw anything of the sort before and when I am talking with him I have often the sensation that he is a person in a tale. An air of unreality, weird unreality, envelops the words, the ideas and the arguments we exchange, the familiar words of the play, the figures of the people; clings to the very walls, permeates the darkness of the fantastic cavern which I can by no means imagine will ever contain anything so real as an audience of men and women—I mean real, not make believe—so that I can't get rid of the feeling that presently I will wake up with a start and find myself with a light by my side and listening to the silence of the night." This letter, incidentally, contains some of Conrad's finest later prose.

career, extending even beyond the transforming of his own novels to collaborative efforts and pressure on the Dramatic Society for the staging of others' plays. As the fictional imagination appeared to diminish, Conrad had moved, already, to another area where he felt that the intensity and drain on his energies would be less. For the theater remained in his mind as a lesser art form, if an art form at all. But the press—whose attacks he characterized to Neel as "Vieille Rome," with its aroma of Christian martyrdom—was the final word, somewhat ironical for a man who had always considered the press parasitical.

With everything else stalled or in ruins, Conrad wrote a short article for *The Manchester Guardian* (December 4) called, then, "Notices to Mariners," and retitled for the American *Bookman* the following year as "Outside Literature." It is a light piece of journalistic fluff, but it does demonstrate Conrad's adherence to his basic distinction between literary effort as based on suggestivity and these "Notices" or pieces of information as based on accuracy. The article was written at the request of David Bone, a ship captain and the brother of the well-known artist Muirhead Bone. On November 12, Conrad entertained Allan Wade and an American portraitist named Walter Tittle, who did an etching of Conrad.

As his other activities lessened in force, his correspondence increased. Although many of his letters in these months are perfunctory, they come with an increasing frequency, and he clearly was seeking the support of his friends and ever-widening circle of admirers. Of course by this time nearly all his letters were being saved, since anything with Conrad's name on it was now valuable. But the increase in volume was more than the result of others' saving his letters; it was clearly his need to repeat a theme that had to be exorcised: that the failure of the play had affected him not at all, that, as he wrote Garnett, "I am myself surprised at my indifference." He speaks of the criticism as the "vocabulary of a hundred learned parrots" who let out a predictable screech when you open the door.

Elbridge Adams, an American writer and editor, wrote Conrad about a number of ways in which he could further his career, strongly recommending that he undertake a lecture tour, and Conrad's response is full of surprising revelations, including a long paragraph on American Prohibition. Conrad said that he was very disappointed that the U.S. Supreme Court upheld the Eighteenth Amendment, which, he felt, "denies the right of a majority to restore a liberty which has been taken away." Indicating interest in the grounds on which the Court decision was based, Conrad adds: "But whatever they may be it only confirms my very early conviction that representative government is but a poor guarantee of liberty."

However, Conrad also remarks: "Yet I don't see what else we could put in the place of it. I am afraid that most human institutions are poor affairs, at best; and that even a Heaven-sent constitution would not be safe from the distorting forces of human passions, prejudices, hasty judgments, emotional impulses, or even from mere plausible noise raised by an active and determined minority." Any chance of a Conradian belief in an "organic community" would appear undermined by his recognition of both majority and minority tyranny, which are endemic to representative government. More realistic was Conrad's lifelong struggle within himself between the self that argues against any individual participation in politics and the self that wants to redress certain national wrongs, a conflict he never resolved.

The major part of Conrad's response, however, is devoted to a far more personal matter, and it is, interestingly, connected to matters of background, name changes, language itself. A Mr. Lee Kendrick had asked Conrad to appear as a lecturer, reading from his own work, something on the order of what Dickens had done so successfully. It would involve an American tour, and given the high regard for Conrad's work and interest in the "mystery man" himself, there was every sign of success, financial and artistic. Conrad's answer directs itself to two points: first, a severe attack of throat gout made it likely that the voice would simply give out in the middle of a lecture; and second, his anxiety about displaying his accent before a large gathering of people prevented public appearances.

Conrad enlarged on that point, as it was one that ran uninterruptedly throughout his life, either as accent itself, or as a matter of mixed nationality, or as part of name changes. Conrad feared that his accent, coming from a man known for his English stylistics, might affect his audience disagreeably, "to my disadvantage. And no man ought to be condemned for shrinking from that kind of risk." He goes on to say: "I will disclose to you that this really is the sorrow of my life; for if it were not for that shrinking I would love nothing better than to give readings from my works, for I know I can read extensively and dramatically and with good effect if it were not for those obstacles to any sort of public appearance." Conrad admits that he certainly wants the money, although he hastily asserts he is not greedy. He points out that he has achieved material prosperity very late in life, and it was further frustrated by the war years.

Remarkable about the letter is that Conrad, at almost sixty-five, felt he had to explain himself. "I don't want [he wrote] to appear before your eyes as careless or negligent of my opportunities, or assuming a pose of disdain or superiority. Neither would I like you to think me unduly timid. But I put it to you that no man can be blamed much by weighing the chances of failure against a possible advantage." Conrad refers to his recent failure on the stage, but insists he is not vexed or cast down by it. Although Adams's proposal for a lecture tour could not be accepted, Conrad acquiesced the following spring to Doubleday's repeated invitations to visit America and help increase sales simply by the publicity of an appearance.

Particularly troubling to Conrad was the fact that a lecture tour, if he had been capable of it, would not have interrupted any serious work; and might, in fact, have acted as impetus for later concentration on *Suspense.* In the fall, he developed incipient asthma, probably what he called throat gout, in which he suffered from bouts of gasping and coughing without any acute symptoms. He tried to settle down, and by late November was at work again on *Suspense,* sufficiently so that he rejected Christopher Sandeman's invitation for a visit. Conrad's reading at this time was, he says, "nothing but Marcel Proust."* He was also selling to Wise, now the "set proofs of the play," with alterations and indications of the cuts. He asked £20 for it, and Wise complied by return mail.

On December 6, Conrad went up to London to lunch with Doubleday, at which time the publisher continued to press his invitation for an American trip. On December 15, Conrad wrote Adams that, his health and state of work permitting, he had been persuaded to go over at the beginning of May as Doubleday's guest for about three weeks. Under those conditions, he might deliver "some semi-private lectures," although neither his health nor his temperament could stand a regular tour with a manager. But he agreed that a few appearances would have a good effect on his book sales. Another reason for the appearances might well have been the desire to contradict H. L. Mencken's repeated praise of him as a Slavic writer who gains his unique insights from his non-Western mentality. While appreciating Mencken's kudos, Conrad objected strenuously to the former's characterization of him, especially in an extraordinary letter he wrote to George Keating, to which we have already alluded. In it, in most forceful language, Conrad speaks of his tradition as Western, denies he even knows any Russian, and associates himself with the liberal traditions of the non-Slavic countries.

Conrad was also having tax trouble with the Inland Revenue Office, which was assessing him for years when he had no direct income, for both regular tax and super-tax; and even the extraordinarily large sum of £10,000 for the De Luxe Edition in 1921 was treated as income and so billed for

* Writing to Sir John Collings Squire after Proust's death on November 18, Conrad agreed to sign a collective tribute to Proust attached to a text by Logan Pearsall Smith, saying that he first heard of the French author in 1913 or 1914 and has since admired him immensely. Conrad indicates his admiration is not based on Proust's reproduction of their past, for he and the Frenchman have experienced a very different kind of past, but, rather, on Proust's power of analysis: ". . . it is great art based on analysis." Conrad asserts that as a prose writer Proust pushed the power of analysis to the point at which it becomes creative. He continues, stressing analysis above stylistics and conviction, even above irony: "But the marvellous thing is that Proust has attained that beauty 'par procedé tout-a-fait étranger a toute espèce de poetique. Dans cette prose, si pleine de vie, il n'y a ni rêve, ni emotion, ni ironie, ni chaleur de conviction, ni même un rythme marqué'—to charm our fancy. And yet it lives in its tuneless almost monstrous greatness. I don't think there is in the whole creative intelligence an example of the power of analysis such as this: and I feel pretty safe in saying that there will never be another."

1922–23. Conrad felt it was ruinous and unjust, and wondered, in a letter to Curle, whether a French residence for nine months in each of the next two years would relieve him of this burden. He would, he says, live in the South of France. He had now been at Oswalds for over three years and was ready for a change. The move to France, incidentally, was one he considered seriously, since John was going to stay in Le Havre for some time the next year, to learn the language and culture.

The name of Proust came up again in late December, when Conrad responded to C. K. Scott Moncrieff's request for a formal tribute to the French novelist. Fifty French writers, including Gide (who had rejected the first volume of *Remembrance* at NRF), had created a volume of tributes for the January issue of the *NRF;* and Scott Moncrieff, now well on in the English translation, conceived of a similar plan for English authors if he could obtain an appreciation from Conrad and George Saintsbury. In his reply, Conrad repeated much of what he had already told Squire and gave the translator carte blanche to alter or revise his words as necessary. In a follow-up letter, Scott Moncrieff asked Conrad to suggest an English title for *A l'ombre des jeunes filles en fleurs* (*Within a Budding Grove*), and according to Jean-Aubry, he suggested *In the Shade of Blossoming Youth* and *In the Shade of Young Girls in Bloom*, tortuous attempts to stay idiomatic in a situation that called for happy invention. Scott Moncrieff, whom Conrad had last met with Northcliffe, came for a day, while spending some time in Canterbury completing this part of his translation of Proust.

Proust and Gide were the two indisputable major writers of the twentieth century with whose work Conrad was familiar, both of them far too late in his career to make any difference. What is interesting is how close Conrad approached the French literary tradition, touching Gide in his underground anarchy and distaste for normal order and Proust in that very power of analysis he had himself cultivated. Seen through a different lens, and if written in French, *Nostromo* becomes Conrad's "Proustian novel," the depiction of a society analyzed and atomized. If Conrad had become a French writer, as he once contemplated, he might have begun like Flaubert and Maupassant, and developed toward Gide or Proust. On this note, of a commemoration of Proust's death, Conrad passed his sixty-fifth birthday and the year 1922.

For the new year, Conrad, who liked to have several prospects before him, had few indeed. He could look forward to the publication of *The Rover*, the serial in September but not the book until the very end of 1923, on December 3. He had his American trip in mind, which would take place on April 21. He had the unfinished *Suspense* before him, but like *The Rescue*, the material appeared intractable. He could look to occasional windfalls, such as Curle's sale of Conrad pamphlets which brought in an unexpected £60. His sons seemed on course: Borys at Daimler and John preparing to live in

France with the Reverend Bost family, friends of Gide. The translations of his work were also appearing, with Aniela Zagórska's of *Almayer* in Polish, and Philippe Neel, among others, working with Conrad's early books, in French. All this was not negligible, but it was not the real thing, either.

He was witness, further, to the flow of publications by a small army of admirers. The Conrad industry was beginning—with books and articles by Walpole, Curle, Jean-Aubry, Ernst Bendz, Elbridge Adams, Mencken, Ruth Stauffer, Ernest Rhys, Sidney Colvin, Hesketh Pearson, Forster, Woolf, Desmond MacCarthy, Henry Seidel Canby, and many others. And yet becoming witness to his memorialization was ironic, the exhausted man listening to the drumbeat of admirers and unable to respond in the sole way he knew how—by producing the materials awaited by these very admirers. Conrad plugged along on *Suspense*, we suspect, in order to convey to himself the semblance of work; but there was no real energy and no flow, or else he surely would not have entertained an American tour in April, with its radical disruption of work patterns and its inevitable effect upon his fragile health.

In February, the vice-chancellor of Cambridge University indicated that the University Senate would offer Conrad an honorary degree. Like the knighthood offered him in 1924 by Ramsay MacDonald, the academic degree was something Conrad would not accept.* In the first draft of his reply written on February 18, he argued that the "inward consistency" of his life compelled him to decline. "An obscure feeling taking its origin, perhaps, in acute consciousness of the inward consistency of a life which at this day may, with truth, be said to have been lived already, compels me to decline an academic degree." On March 15, he sent his formal response to E. P. Pearse and eliminated all personal matters. "With all possible deference I beg to be permitted to decline the offer contained in your letter. I hope you will accept and communicate to the Council of the Senate of your illustrious University my grateful sense of the profered [sic] distinction and the expression of my profound respect."

Conrad's rejection of this highly prestigious offer is fully understandable, connected as it was to his view of himself as a writer moving outside institutions and traditions, intact in his own sphere as a creative person, and not even fully English. He had always insisted on this view of himself, and it is, one may speculate, the reason for his later rejection of the knighthood. His response to awards of this nature was a forerunner of Sartre's rejection of the Nobel Prize in that the acceptance of such distinctions was not consistent

* He informed Doubleday that he had also received offers from "the Universities of Oxford, Edinburgh, Liverpool and Durham" of an honorary degree, and had declined them all. He told Doubleday this not to boast but to forestall any similar offers from American universities on his visit to New York. "Refusing such an honour is the most disagreeable thing in the world, but I am perfectly determined to have nothing to do with any academic distinction."

with what he was and what he had been in his work. He resisted association with such traditional awards because they distracted the reader from what he really was—an author proving himself in the sole way he could, on paper, in the privacy of his own room, working along the lines of what was uniquely his.

His reading continued in Proust, in Valéry's poetry,* in Maupassant. Jean-Aubry introduced him to Laforgue, in a selection of his poetry introduced by Conrad's future biographer. In another area, one of the by-products of Conrad's fame was that the critics by writing about him kept his early successes before him. Ernst Bendz, a Swedish professor, published an acute study of Conrad in English and elicited Conrad's reply that the moral pivot of *Nostromo* was silver, not Nostromo himself. Bendz had also gone over Conrad's prose carefully and pointed out several lapses, which brought the response that the English language had shaped and possessed his mind, so that if he had not written in English he would not have written at all. Conrad's answer indicates that he kept up with the current criticism of his career and, whatever his superficial indifference, insisted on his version of the facts. One fact that he wanted to correct was the belief that he was "literarily a sort of Jack London." He says:

> I sympathised much with the warm and direct talent of Jack London, and was sorry to hear of his death—but, after all, one doesn't like to be taken for what one is not. For one thing, for instance, I am much less of a good humanitarian than Jack London; but I think that I am not taking too much on myself in saying that I am a good European, not exactly in the superficial, cosmopolitan sense, but in the blood and bones as it were, and as the result of a long heredity.

Under conditions of better health or more relative youth, this contact with his early career could well have energized Conrad. As he prepared for still another edition of his work—Dent's 1923 De Luxe Edition—Conrad asked Aniela Zagórska for a drawing of the Nałęcz Korzeniowski coat of arms. He wished to emboss the crest on the cover of each volume of the edition, a memorialization that coincided with the Polish translation of *Almayer* by Aniela, with a preface by Stefan Żeromski. Conrad was in a sense carrying out his father's mission, although literarily and not politically; but he was providing a literary pincer that extended across Europe from Poland to England, with a strong force exerted on France.

---

* Valéry had himself visited Oswalds in October of 1922, although the talk was limited to maritime and other non-literary topics. Valéry wrote Gide of the visit: "J'ai passé le dimanche d'hier chez Conrad qui est tout à fait gentil et presque affectueux. Parlé de toi nécessairement. Je lui dis qu'il devrait écrire *en français* ses souvenirs marins de Marseilles et de Cette. Il parait assez alléché de l'idée, qu'il repousse en même temps . . . *Tibi.*" Gide told Conrad later he was pleased he and one of his oldest friends had finally met.

The past in still another way turned up in the shape of the ghost of Stephen Crane, now resurrected by Thomas Beer in his biography *Stephen Crane: A Study in American Letters.* Beer and Alfred Knopf visited Conrad in Bishopsbourne on March 8 to request a long introduction to the biography, which Conrad reported variously as 30,000 or 3,500 words. Although he told Garnett he did not want to "play the ghoul, feeding on the memory of my friends," he did inform Curle that it was "in truth marvellously good business for me." Conrad composed, in all, three essays on Crane, one that appeared in *Notes on Life and Letters* and that was written in 1919; a second that would appear as the preface to a new edition of *The Red Badge of Courage,* in 1925; and this one, by far the longest, running neither 30,000 nor 3,500 words but closer to 8,500, that served as the introduction to the standard biography. It is a light piece of writing, with reminiscences and nostalgia, a description of their halfhearted attempts at collaboration, all clearly demonstrating Conrad's affection for the doomed young American writer. There is no attempt at literary criticism or serious evaluation, nor could there be, given the occasion of Conrad's essay.

The beginning of this project was intermixed with Conrad's sporadic work on *Suspense*—his lifeline with his real career—which brought the completion of Part III, if his report to Doubleday is accurate. This would carry him to within fifty pages of the point at which he left the novel, and would mean that in the next sixteen months he wrote no more than 15,000 words of the book. Nevertheless, he planned to complete *Suspense* by September or October of 1923; and given the need for *The Rover* to have a year's run in book form, *Suspense* would be issued in the fall of 1924. The "deadline," so to speak, the sailing of the *Tuscania,* on April 21, gave Conrad a date to work against. He expected to finish the Crane introduction in five or six days—it would take until March 25—and then begin work again immediately on the novel, sticking with it until a week before sailing.

The *Tuscania* was to leave from Glasgow and be captained by David Bone, whom Conrad knew well. His first "sailing journey" as a distinguished novelist was, as he recognized, quite different from the sailing adventures of the novice who had just arrived from Poland. Fearing a mob of admirers in New York, in fact, Conrad told Elbridge Adams that he planned to be sneaked into the city; his name was omitted from the passenger list, and he kept the exact date of his arrival dark. Doubleday himself would be at the pier to whisk Conrad away. Nevertheless, as he would see, the newspaper "mob" was there, and he had his usual love-hate relationship with the press.

In an amusing sidelight, Conrad received a letter from the Spanish novelist Blasco-Ibáñez, who had already made an international reputation with his novel of World War I, *The Four Horsemen of the Apocalypse* (1916). Conrad said the letter was written "in the most extraordinary jargon of French I have ever read in my life," and it had been addressed to Grant Richards in London—"apparently the only address in the whole city of London that Ibáñez knows." The Spanish novelist, once Conrad had mastered his language sufficiently, was interested in introducing him to a Spanish audience, under his auspices, and Conrad was quite willing to listen. He told Ibáñez to wait until Pinker returned—Eric was going to America as a parallel trip to Conrad's—and then negotiations, in June, could begin. In the later 1920s, a Barcelona firm, Montaner y Simón, began the Spanish translation of Conrad's major novels, an edition that continued through the Civil War into the 1940s.

As soon as the Crane introduction was completed, Conrad turned to Wise to sell the manuscript, which ran to sixty-two pages and contained nearly 8,500 words. Conrad now had still another dealer interested in buying his manuscripts, Meredith Janvier, who had offered $600, but told Wise he could have it for £110, which was slightly less than Janvier's offer. He adds that besides its worth as a manuscript, it should make some stir, since it relates to an American author whose memory is still alive. Conrad says he needs the sale of the Crane piece to complete his expenses for the journey. He assures Wise, as he assured Graham, Garnett, and others, that he was not leaving on a "dollar hunting expedition." This was no El Dorado exploration. The fact is, if his health had permitted, he could have collected considerable sums for appearances. The lecture circuit for celebrities was a growth industry in these years of American prosperity prior to the market crash.

The invitations had already begun to pour in. A professor of Slavonic languages at Columbia University, Dr. A. Morawski-Nawench, invited Conrad to lecture on Slavonic literature in a formal visit. Conrad refused that, but agreed to meet him and his students in an informal session, saying that he could not lecture on a literature he did not know, or on any other. He accepted only because the professor was the brother-in-law of the president of the Polish Academy of Letters in Cracow, and carried Conrad back to his childhood and through that to Apollo.

There was a temporary revving up of energy and spirits. *The Rover* galleys had proven relatively clean, and Conrad was buoyed by a future book publication. Ellen Glasgow, the Virginia novelist who had come once to Capel House, invited Conrad to visit her in Richmond, but he begged off by saying he felt as though he "were made of brown paper. It is not the sort of thing that gives one much confidence for travelling." He did have the confidence, but feared the loss of energy at vital moments. Critics who have attacked Conrad's later production have failed to recognize what a prematurely aged man he had become; the breakdown in control was clearly as much physical as psychological or creative.

Borys's career seems to have moved along well. He was now acting manager of the Manchester depot of Daimler and earning quite a good salary. But unknown to Conrad, and not divulged to him until after his return from America, Borys had married, not telling even Jessie. By this time, in fact, Borys had been married for several months, dating from before his departure for Coventry. Once at Manchester, Borys kept the secret, and finally told Jessie, who decided to withhold the information from Conrad. Borys's secrecy suggests a sharply hostile attitude toward his father, probably more so than toward his parents together. In his brief book about Conrad, Borys alludes only indirectly to the episode, saying that he had intended, before leaving for Coventry, to tell his parents that he had married some months previously. He adds that he shrank from doing so because "of J.C.'s deep concern for my future welfare which had emerged from our recent talks, and had sharpened my awareness of the shattering effect which my disclosure would have upon him; and I left home taking my secret with me." Jessie, meanwhile, became stuck in the middle of these hostile undercurrents, and she was forced to tell Borys that she could not receive his wife until his father knew of the marriage, a position which her son resented. Once Conrad left for America, Jessie reports that she tried to think of every way she could break the news, although she was certain she "distrusted the idea of the young man undertaking the task himself—and I must confess in spite of my reluctance, I felt that I should be the better person to drop the bombshell."

The explanation of Borys's action and the fear everyone felt about Conrad's finding out is not a simple matter, and despite Meyer's brilliant psychoanalytic work on the relationship between father and son, we cannot rest easily with any single interpretation. Meyer argues Conrad's need to have Jessie all to himself, and, therefore, the writer's antagonism toward Borys as an alien, threatening force in the household. Further, he sees Conrad's attitude toward Borys as his failure to develop into a mature parent, or even a mature husband; so that when he was away he signed his letters to Jessie "Dear Boy" or "Dearest Boy."

All this may have been part of Conrad's attitude, and some of it could be explained by the dislocated quality of his own early life and the loss of his mother at seven. To that extent, he married a woman who would be wife-daughter-mother, an entire family embodied in one person. We find a reflection of that need in *Under Western Eyes*, when Razumov by having Haldin killed "gains" a sister-wife-mother. Another explanation rests elsewhere, and that is in Conrad's disappointment in Borys's development: his poor eyesight, which destroyed the chance of a sea career; his lack of academic drive, which made a university education impossible; his failure to be interested in literature or literary matters; and, of course, intermixed with this, the rivalry of the oldest son with the father. Added to these was the natural hostility that develops from a child growing up in a household which is perennially short of money and centered so intensely on the father. The development of these attitudes must have led to considerable tension and a tremendous degree of mutual resentment, which lay far under the surface of fairly normal relationships.

Years later, when Borys wrote his short book about his father, he stressed family togetherness, common interests, mutual attention to cars and mechanical things. Conrad was made to seem like the father every boy wants to have. There is also the possibility that in the talks between the two, Conrad passed on to Borys the kind of advice his own uncle had given him, which was harsh and judgmental, demonstrating not only apprehension about his career but distaste for what he had done with himself. Conrad had received these very assessments of himself from a distance, by mail, but with his own son, he was informing him directly; and Borys may have felt so belittled by Conrad's evaluation of him and his prospects that he decided to be as secretive about his life as his father himself had once been. His marriage would be his own decision. Secretiveness ran through the family, not at all an unusual course of action for people of mixed Bobrowska-Korzeniowski blood, whose background was a blend of conspiratorial and revolutionary activity.

In any event, Borys's course of action brought to the surface a hidden struggle. The son also may have resented the procession of young men who were passing through Conrad's life, like Curle, Walpole, Jean-Aubry, and others who found more favor than he did himself. There is, further, the essential point of the son reacting adversely to the famous father whose activities have no place in them for the son. To some extent, this had been Conrad's situation vis-à-vis Apollo, and then in relationship to his (otherwise kind) guardians. What we find is a reciprocal action: father turning on son as a way of relieving his own agonies in relationship to his father and father surrogates. None of these explanations, of course, is satisfactory, since no one of Conrad's complex and disruptive background could be consciously mature about all his familial relationships.

In ignorance of this family drama, Conrad made his plans to depart from Glasgow on the twenty-first of April. As the trip approached, Conrad decided to prepare some sketches for a lecture. One that he mentions to Eric Pinker was on distinctions between an art that depends on the literary imagination and one that is based on scenic motion, such as the cinema. Although they both seem superficially similar, Conrad's point is that the artist, while less precise in visual effects, possesses a wider range and is himself a more "subtle and complicated machine" than a camera. Conrad planned to illustrate his theory with readings from *Victory*. When he finally appeared before an invited audience, he made most of the session into a reading from *Victory*.

He was busy on other grounds as well. Through a friend of Jean-Aubry, the well-known hostess Madame Alvar, he was brought together with Maurice Ravel, whom he had already met. He expected to see many other people—Hope, in Colchester, who was recovering from a stroke; Ralph, Eric

Pinker's brother, and Mrs. Pinker; Garnett, of course; Major Gardiner; the Wedgwoods; and Sir Robert Jones. Curle had promised to come to see him off. All this Conrad planned to squeeze in between the sixteenth of April and the twentieth, when he would leave for Glasgow. The burst of activity hardly bespeaks a man languishing in bed or chair.

Conrad wrote guiltily to Aniela Zagórska that he had been neglecting her and attributes some of it to his need to prepare the "30,000 words" of his Crane preface. He also explains that he has been revising the English and American texts of *The Rover*, as well as checking and correcting the first two volumes of the "uniform edition" of his works, now planned for May publication. More generally, he foresaw the build-up of publicity, for David Bone was already stirring up advance notice of the visit. Conrad told Galsworthy he would not be in danger from American newsmen and would leave his revolver at home. "If I have to show them my teeth (artificial) it will only be in an agreeable smile. And as to what may come after I leave it to chance and the inspiration of the moment."

Once Conrad started on his American odyssey, he was "protected" at every stage. Curle went with him to Glasgow, as planned, and there Conrad gave a dinner for Muirhead Bone and A. Munro, the editor of the *Glasgow Evening News.* To Jessie, Conrad gave a detailed account in two letters, including aspects of his health, description of the condition of the ship and his accommodations in first class, plus sailing information—their speed, which engines were running, which stopped. Conrad was clearly the celebrity on board, and he was thick with the captain at his table and on the bridge. It all seemed a lark, except that he suffered occasional pain: lumbago, and gout in finger and wrist. He mentions that he misses John, and indicates, "B. too haunts me rather. I would write to him but there is really nothing to say of actual interest." As the *Tuscania* approached American waters, Conrad received wireless messages from several people, including Owen Wister and Christopher Morley.

He found time to write a short article for the *Glasgow Evening News* (May 15, 1923), "My Hotel in Mid-Atlantic," which became "Ocean Travel" in *Last Essays.* The piece has a certain irony, for in it Conrad contrasts his previous voyages on sailing vessels with his present one on a steam-powered Ritz Hotel. He relives his earlier experience, saying that once sea travel meant a breaking away from shore conditions, when the ship became a new kind of home, whereas now the ship becomes an extension of the shore. The article is slight, but it suggests clearly, once again, that Conrad's "politics" were not founded on political institutions as such but on a tonal reaction to industrialization, modern ease and comfort, the loss of adventure and the unknown. He sought a world in which the adventurer, explorer, and pioneer still had a role. His praise of steam is really a lament for a passing life, for a life past, and all the liberal politics attached to a new or better existence are tainted by this sense of overwhelming loss. Like Wordsworth, he was a "silent poet," serving as witness to a world he could not accept. There is an epitaph in these hastily worded sentiments.

> All this may sound very primitive, but it had a charm and an intimacy of a settled existence no modern steamship with its long barren alleyways swept by the wind and decorated with the name of promenade-decks can give. The modern passenger may be able to walk a good many miles in his ship in the course of the day, but this is the only thing which differentiates him from the bales of goods carried in the hold—this, and the power of swallowing the food which is presented to him at regular intervals. He is carried along swiftly and fed delicately, but the other lived the life of his ship, that sort of life which is not sustained on bread (and *suprême au volaille*) alone, but depends for its interest on enlarged sympathies and awakened perceptions of Nature and men.

On May 1, the *Tuscania* arrived in New York harbor. His welcome was tumultuous. As he wrote Jessie on the fourth:

> I will not attempt to describe to you my landing because it is indescribable. To be aimed at by forty cameras held by forty men is a nerve-shattering experience. Even D'day looked exhausted after we had escaped from that mob—and the other mob of journalists.
>
> Then a Polish deputation—men and women (some of them quite pretty)—rushed me on the wharf and thrust enormous nosegays into my hands. Eric nobly carried two of them. Mrs. D'day took charge of another. I went along like a man in a dream and took refuge in D's car.

Conrad was installed at Effendi Hill, the Doubleday estate in Oyster Bay, Long Island, and from there he had his choice of invitations. On the fifth, there would be a dinner party of notables, including John William Davis, former ambassador to England, and Colonel Edward House, Woodrow Wilson's former confidential adviser. Conrad says the press has been exceptionally friendly, but, withal, he tells Jessie he misses her and is homesick. He had the opportunity to meet Paderewski, the pianist who had become premier of Poland, at lunch at Colonel House's and thought him "extraordinary." He flitted from one hostess to another, and he got around to writing Borys nearly everything he had told Jessie. Fixed on his social calendar was the evening of the tenth at the home of Mrs. Curtiss James, the well-known hostess and society woman.

To Jessie he reported in detail his talk and reading at Mrs. James's. Conrad's account of this and other social evenings somehow conveys the impression of a man out of his element. Nevertheless, he had the requisite manner, the right tone, the slightly haughty bearing which could have made him a social lion; plus, he had the mysteriousness that would have produced a highly desirable dinner guest, especially when he left Jessie at home. After indicating that he felt flat and drained as a reaction to the evening, he wrote:

> I may tell you at once that it was a most brilliant affair, and I would have given anything for you to have been there and seen all the crowd and all that splendour, the very top of the basket of the fashionable and literary circles. All last week there was desperate fighting and plotting in the N. York society to get invitations. I had the lucky inspiration to refuse to accept any payment; and my dear, I had a perfect success. I gave a talk and pieces of reading out of *Victory*. After the applause from the audience, which stood up when I appeared, had ceased I had a moment of positive anguish. Then I took out the watch you had given me and laid it on the table, made one mighty effort and began to speak. The watch was the greatest comfort to me. Something of you. I timed myself by it all along. I began at 9.45 and ended exactly at 11. There was a most attentive silence, some laughs and at the end when I read the chapter of Lena's death, audible snuffling. Then handshaking with 200 people.

"It was," Conrad added, "a great experience."

On May 15, Conrad started on a tour by motorcar that would last ten days, to Boston and other New England points. This would bring him to the twenty-fifth of May, when he would return to rest at Oyster Bay, preparatory to a June 2 departure on the White Star boat for Southampton. The Doubledays decided to accompany him, and to visit Oswalds, a touch that pleased Conrad. As he toured, he saw several correspondents and acquaintances—William Lyon Phelps of Yale, "Mama" Grace and Catherine Willard, John Powell, the Elbridge Adamses; but very pointedly he avoided John Quinn, who tried valiantly to see the man whose manuscripts he had collected for so many years. Quinn had heard, inadvertently, from Jessie that Conrad was coming to New York, and discovered only through inquiry that he was staying in Oyster Bay. Quinn telephoned the Doubleday residence three times, and each time was informed that Conrad's calendar was full, or that he was ready to go on a car tour of New England. The collector was livid, and he wrote Lady Gregory of the episode: "During the time Conrad was here he saw every second rate newspaper man and attended a reception arranged by Mrs. Doubleday and a tuft-hunter named Mrs. James, to which Jew dealers and publishers were invited but they did not invite me."

Ford reported in *It Was the Nightingale* that Conrad felt unhappy about not seeing Quinn, but he was afraid that Quinn might be angry at his action in selling his later manuscripts to Wise. Probably, the explanation, if one can be found, was twofold: Conrad's desire not to have a scene of any kind (Quinn was notoriously short-tempered as well as ill and in pain), and his own awareness that he had acted not quite aboveboard in dealing with the collector.

Conrad, and Doubleday, wanted nothing to mar the perfection of the visit, and it went as ideally as planned. After having written five letters to Jessie,

Conrad heard from her, on the fourteenth, that she had received no mail from him. He quickly mentioned the dates of mailing and added: "Don't imagine my dearest that the delights of this country make me forget my home—which is where you are; and indeed is nothing to me but *you*, and you alone wherever you may be." In the same letter, he told her to plan on putting up the Doubledays for two nights at Oswalds toward the middle of June and to give them the end of the house with the bathroom.

On June 2, he sailed on the *Majestic*, accompanied by the Doubledays. Conrad went directly from Southampton to London, where he met Jessie at the Curzon Hotel. She indicates that she met her husband with some trepidation, fully knowing at the time that Conrad would explode when he heard her great secret about Borys. His first words, in fact, were reproachful that Borys had not met him at the station. Conrad's suspicions at Borys's absence suggest an uneasiness about their relationship, and hardly noticing Jessie, according to her account, he marched upstairs. Their first moments together were like those of strangers because of their older son's absence, and Jessie was filled with anxiety about her message. Finally, after an almost sleepless night, she turned to him with the words "Boy dear," which she used when she wished to be extra friendly, and announced, "Borys is married." At this news, Conrad gripped her arm and said, "Why do you tell me that, why don't you keep such news to yourself?" He added nothing else to this for over an hour and then asked: "I suppose you are certain of what you have told me?" Her attempts at explanation became intermixed with his interruptions that he did not want to know anything more. "I don't want to know anything more about it. It is done and I have been treated like a blamed fool, dam'."

The rest of the scene derives solely from Jessie's description, and its accuracy depends on her point of view. Directly Conrad met the Doubledays for lunch, she overheard him announce that Borys was married and his wife had known all about it. She heard Conrad stress that she should have kept the news to herself, to which Doubleday replied that that could hardly have been possible and he hoped they would be happy. Conrad retorted: "Well, they won't, then. What has he got to keep a wife on? And let me tell you I don't like the way this has been done in secret. I wasn't to know then, why should I now?" After the lunch and for days afterward, Conrad continued to ask if she were sure, if she had any proof. She had, a copy of the certificate of marriage obtained from Robert Garnett and his firm of solicitors.

Conrad's insistence on these details, his anger, his desire for proof, as if Jessie were lying or Borys were involved in deception to get money from him, replayed familiar roles. Earlier he had used illness as a way of manipulating his environment or as a method of making people bend to his will. The illnesses had continued, of course, and they made him the center of a household full of other ailments and complaints: Jessie's knees, her heart, Borys's chronic sicknesses, and then his war service. Now, even as age undermined him, he lost that control. With marriage, Borys had broken away, and he had read Conrad's intentions correctly to the extent that he knew his father did not approve of any action independent of his own wishes and needs. That egocentricity which Conrad needed so desperately for survival as a writer, however, did not work in his personal life as he expected. His sulkiness, his anger, his refusal to accept the fact were, in a broad sense, acts of survival, extensions of his illnesses. If he could deny the whole thing, he could preserve the illusion of omnipotence; if the fact were true, he was being forced toward death.

Borys and his wife finally came for lunch. Before that, Conrad told Eric Pinker that marrying is not a crime, and while he was not anxious to see Borys's wife, he did want to recognize the marriage. He also informed Jessie that he would settle an allowance of £200 a year on Borys, although his son had a good position with Daimler. Conrad insisted on that amount, not a penny more or less—it was not far from what Tadeusz had given him—and demanded they come to lunch on time: he would not wait for his meals. His petulance and dictatorial actions were quite consistent with his attempts at survival. Jessie comments that she felt "years older than the frail figure" lying on his bed, who was played out. These were whimpers, not screams. The young couple arrived for lunch, an hour and a half late; but Conrad controlled himself and remained calm. The blow-up would come later and be translated into illness, so that Jessie would have to pay with renewed attention and devotion. The lunch passed with some tension, and after the couple left, Conrad remarked that he would not have liked the task of finding a wife for Borys. "It had been quite enough to choose his own."

Conrad thanked Aniela Zagórska for sending the Jan Lemański translation into Polish of *The Nigger of the "Narcissus,"* praising it and her own handling of the Preface. In fact, however, he found the novel, done in a romantic or poetic language, "épatant" and wondered where such a fanciful vocabulary came from. As if the translations of his early work were controlling him now, Conrad agreed to write a number of nostalgic pieces, delving into both his early years in Poland and his sea career. The curve of his life was almost complete, all three lives blending with each other. These pieces, furthermore, required no real effort, although they are excellent examples of Conrad's journalism. He did a reminiscence of the *Torrens* for the October 1923 number of *The Blue Peter* called "The *Torrens:* A Personal Tribute." Thirty years after sailing on her "perfect form," Conrad was gratified to hear she had not been broken up and that this lovely ship had found "a merciful end on the shores of the sunlit sea of my boyhood dreams, and that her fine spirit has returned to dwell in the regions of the great winds, the inspirers and the companions of her swift, renowned, sea-tossed life, which I, too, have been permitted to share for a little while."

For the *Daily Mail* (December 24 issue), Conrad wrote "Christmas Day at Sea," which returned him to an episode when he had served on the *Duke of Sutherland* on his first voyage to Australia, in 1879. The third piece from this period is "Geography and Some Explorers," written as an introduction to Hammerton's *Countries of the World* (February 1924) and called then "The Romance of Travel." It was later reprinted in the *National Geographic Magazine* in March 1924 as "Geography . . ." Besides the insight it offers into Conrad's boyhood enthusiasm for geography and exploration, which we traced above, the piece is a touching evocation of his later dreams, of all men who are fascinated by the unknown. Behind it is his sense that the moment is over, not only for him but for all those men who went forth, "each according to his lights and with varied motives, laudable or sinful, but each bearing in his breast a spark of the sacred fire." For Conrad, the frontier between the imagination of such men and the imagination or "sacred fire" of the artist was blurred, perhaps indistinct. He had tempered his whole life in such sacred flames.

Literary imagination, however, was no longer his. He might tell Eric Pinker he was tackling *Suspense*, but he was really doing nothing. In spite of an earlier attempt to broaden his appeal as a "spinner of sea-yarns," he now says his sea life had about as much bearing on his literary existence, "on my quality as a writer, as the enumeration of drawing-rooms which Thackeray frequented could have had on his gift as a great novelist." The analogy is poor, as is the disclaimer. Conrad tried to separate his two careers, when the qualities underlying both are continuous and parallel. At sea, his eye and ear were recording, and that recording occurred in a peculiar context, with its own sounds and sense of things. Such experiences, such echoes cannot, of course, be separated from the kind of writer Conrad turned out to be; and the novels he wrote later, whether directly about the sea or not, were profoundly affected by his almost twenty years aboard ships. As we have observed, he was a man who stared into space and at horizons, and his "frames" or scenes are those large ones which must be filled abundantly or else appear empty. Thackeray, to continue Conrad's analogy, had no such problems, since his frames were intimate and easily filled by familiar objects from our quotidian life. Conrad's sea experience, despite his disclaimers, characterized his uniqueness.

He was also disturbed by Curle's having undertaken to write an article on the Uniform Edition for Bruce Richmond, editor of the *Times Literary Supplement.* Curle's plan had been to give a history of the books, but Conrad disliked the strategy as failing to give the atmosphere of the books in favor of supplying historical detail. One may, he said, provide the bones and destroy all curiosity for the dish. Conrad insisted, as he had done before, that his distinctiveness lay not in the literary treatment of historical materials but in his "unconventional grouping and perspective, which are truly temperamental." He repeats he is neither romantic nor realistic, for his art is fluid, "depending on grouping (sequence) which shifts, and on the changing lights giving varied effects of perspective." These comments arrive like epitaphs. Conrad was leaving behind, with personal critics such as Curle or a future biographer like Jean-Aubry, the way in which he wished to be presented to posterity. If we now view their books critically, especially their hagiographical devotion, we see that Conrad imposed such loyalty and devotion as a given of his cooperation and insisted on his way of seeing himself.*

A reconciliation of sorts occurred with Borys, for the young couple arrived in early August to stay at Oswalds for a few days. But Conrad's testiness remained, since he referred to his son, in a letter to Curle, as Mr. A. B. Conrad, using the "A" or Alfred for the first time and dropping the more familiar "Borys," which was the name his son grew up under. As Conrad well knew, names contained loaded meanings, and his distancing here indicates no small reserve of hostility. By the end of July, he had caught wind of the impending John Quinn sale of Conrad manuscripts, as part of his general unloading of his vast collection of manuscripts, books, and art work. Although Quinn wanted ready cash, his sale of Conrad items may well have been motivated by the latter's neglect on his New York visit. When Conrad heard of the sale, which would occur in November, he wrote Wise that he would like to see his "pieces of paper" pass into Wise's possession. It, of course, turned out quite differently. The collection brought in, for then, the huge sum of $110,000, but became scattered, despite A. S. W. Rosenbach's purchase of about $55,000 of the Conrad items. Toward keeping Wise interested, Conrad instructed Miss Hallowes to append to his letter a detailed listing of his sales to Quinn.

In the later summer, Conrad made some attempt to get on with *Suspense*, or so he noted to Colvin on August 4. He kept close to his room, hoping that he could work, but the physical aftereffects of the American visit remained: a sense of lassitude, lameness attendant upon gout, and a general, wretched enervation. Nevertheless, he hoped to be well enough to take John to Le Havre, where he would live with the Reverend Bost and his family. Jean-Aubry helped in setting up the arrangements, and Conrad planned to leave

*While Curle moved along with his *TLS* article (it appeared on August 30), Conrad followed with detailed suggestions, even recommending an opening to the piece. He thought that some paragraphs should be added, on how authors transform the particularities of their material into the general and thus "appeal to universal emotions by the temperamental handling of personal experience." Then Curle could focus on Conrad himself, adding that the prefaces, now made accessible to the public, give the historical bases for the books, and yet the stories all expand well beyond their limitations of frame. Accordingly, Conrad implies, a tale based on the sea does not end up about the sea but becomes transmuted into something well beyond the original frame. Conrad's approach, even if self-serving, was critically sound, and it foreshadowed the way his work would eventually be analyzed decades after his death.

Oswalds as soon as he completed the *Torrens* article for *The Blue Peter*, which he accomplished at the end of August. The Conrads (Jessie insisted on going) left Oswalds for London on the ninth of September and departed for Le Havre on the eleventh. They expected to return on the fifteenth, with Jean-Aubry. Conrad told Curle he dreaded the idea of having to travel with anybody, even a close friend. John did not remain in France on this particular trip, but met the Bosts in Le Havre and then in October returned to France for the beginning of the school term. This relatively minor excursion became the source of much concern and planning, with Jean-Aubry playing the role of general factotum.* Indisposed as he was, Conrad interrupted the trip to visit Gide's home in Cuverville, but both Gide and Mme Gide were away.

On his return from Le Havre, Conrad took to his bed in a general collapse, although his ailments were still not fatal. He recognized, as he put it, that he manufactured his own troubles, and now possessed a "very high class" cough, which made him feel at his last gasp. Toward the end of September the Conrads went up to the Curzon Hotel for three days when water at the Oswalds was cut off to enable repairs on the main line. Invitations came in unabated, as though Conrad were healthy and receptive. Major Gardiner proposed him for membership in a London club that stipulated the Protestant religion as one of its conditions. Conrad's response to the proposal is both amusing and revealing. He says that his having been born a Roman Catholic immediately makes him ineligible, "and though dogmà sits lightly on me I have never renounced that form of Christian religion. The book of rules is so, I may say, theological that it would be like renouncing the faith of my fathers." He adds that it is not a question of principles "but merely a matter of correct conduct."

He assures the major that he has nothing but great regard and sympathy for the Church of England. Then he muses that he is a lost soul, indeed, someone caught on the prongs of the devil's pitchfork. Many years ago, he

* At this period in his life, Conrad employed the young men around him for general chores and arrangements, as well as for the presentation of his career. An example of how Curle's industry and devotion saved Conrad time and worry arose in the Sir Frank Swettenham affair. After Curle had published his "The History of Mr Conrad's Books" in the *TLS*, Sir Frank, on September 6, responded to Curle and revealed for the first time that Conrad's *Patna* episode in *Lord Jim* was based on an 1880 incident involving the *Jeddah*. Conrad found much in the Swettenham article to disagree with, including the question of the model for Jim, but instead of answering directly had Curle reply on September 13. Swettenham then followed with still another response the next week, and the firm of Alfred Holt contributed the history of the pilgrim ship in the October 11 issue of *TLS*. In his preface, Conrad had not mentioned the *Jeddah* tale, nor did he inform Curle of his source when the latter was writing his article on the history of Conrad's books. Yet without any resentment, Curle took up the fight and handled the several responses to Swettenham, whom Conrad referred to as "an ass rather."

relates, the Duke of Norfolk asked him to join a Roman Catholic association, a complimentary invitation; and Conrad says he exchanged several letters with the duke. When he finally read the articles of the association, he found that members engaged themselves "with all their might and power to work for the restoration of the temporal power of the Pope. Conceive you that imbecility!" Conrad indicates he informed the association's secretary, W. S. Lilly, that this was a political objective and he would not lift a finger to re-establish temporal power. He was then severely lectured. "So you see now [he tells Gardiner] I have got to stand between the two, a prey to the first inferior devil that may come along. My only hope of escaping the eternal fires is my utter insignificance. I shall lie low on the Judgment Day, and will probably be overlooked."

As unlikely as the emergence of a religious connection was the emergence of Ford from the murkiness of the past. Ford was now involved in a number of projects and moving well into the major part of his career, with the Christopher Tietjens quartet of novels which came to be called *Parade's End.* He wrote Conrad about his projected editorship of still another journal, the *Transatlantic Review*, and he wanted to include his former collaborator among the contributors. The *Review* was Ford's opportunity to put together work from the "modern" generation, just as *The English Review* earlier had brought together some of the best of late Victorian and Edwardian writers. The offer from Ford would have given Conrad the opportunity to associate with the generation of novelists and poets who had, in a sense, already displaced him.

Ford's plan was not just grandiose, it was grand; he had a vision, and it was by no means a trivial one. He was a genius at organizing talent, and if we put that together with the fact that he had also begun to produce one of his two masterpieces, we can see he was generating talent outside even as he tapped his own imaginative resources. The *Transatlantic Review*, reflecting Ford's own manic sense of his career, aimed at creating a state of affairs in which there were no distinct national literatures, but only *Literature.* He then attempted to organize talent for this review, talent, incidentally, which had in the main already relegated him to the dustheap. Robert McAlmon said he found it impossible to talk about a place or person without having Ford top the story and appear to know more about that place or person than "anyone else possibly can know. . . . [He] is a Mythomaniac . . . [who] could step into the Moon Mullins cartoons and double for Lord Plushbottom."

Yet this same Ford who suffered such poor treatment from McAlmon and Hemingway, among others, could pry a segment of *Finnegans Wake* from Joyce for the *Review* and propose to call it "Work in Progress," the working title Joyce agreed to. Joyce even acknowledged, to Harriet Weaver, that Ford was the godfather of the book, by virtue of having supplied the working title.

In this atmosphere of literature and literary politics, Ford asked Conrad for a contribution, something along the lines of his reminiscences for *The English Review*. In the same letter, on November 8, he also indicated he wanted to publish in the *Transatlantic* their third and final collaboration, *The Story [Nature] of a Crime*, a slight novella written in 1906 and already published in *The English Review* under the pseudonym Baron Ignatz von Aschendorf. Ford was full of energy, rhapsodizing over their work together in the past, nostalgic about *Romance* and also about the composition of Conrad's *The Mirror of the Sea*, which Ford recalled came from his jogging of his former collaborator's memory.

Conrad's response was a dampener. He refused to buy nostalgia, and he thought their collaboration on *Nature* worthless. He probably suspected that Ford was resurrecting it not because of its literary value, which was negligible, but to put his name before the *Transatlantic* audience and to entice him somehow into the *Review*. Missing altogether that Ford was really a part of the "new," or not caring, Conrad demonstrated, in an insulting passage already quoted, his old annoyance at his friend's manipulation of people and things. Very shrewdly, he noted how outdated the novella was: "somewhat redolent of weltschmerz," he called it.

Conrad followed this with another letter, on November 18, in which he reminisced about the old days of the *Review* and gave Ford full credit for having extracted from the depths of his then-despondency the stuff of *A Personal Record*. His only grievance, he says, is that *The English Review* did not last long enough, and he sincerely, if wanly, wishes Ford well. The new venture will be "truly Fordian—at all costs." But for the matter at hand: "I am afraid the source of the Personal Record fount is dried up. No longer the same man." Conrad adds that although he'd like to do something for the sake of old times he is "not worth having now. . . . My mind is a blank at this moment."

Other arrangements between the two would have to follow, chiefly over how they would allocate royalties for the collaborative books. Conrad arranged to include *The Inheritors* and *Romance* in any English and American edition of his works, Ford as part of any Continental translation. As if gaining strength from the young men around him who disliked and distrusted him, Ford was never more forceful, as impresario and novelist. His first number of the *Transatlantic Review* in December of 1923, amid reminiscences of his own over *Romance*, included contributions from Ezra Pound and E. E. Cummings. Subsequent issues, which involved Hemingway as a quarrelsome sub-editor, featured contributions from Joyce's "Work in Progress" and Gertrude Stein's *The Making of Americans* (which was serialized in nine installments); and then the *Review* veered increasingly toward the Parisian writers, with Ford himself being cut off. Hemingway's influence was squeezing him out, although, when Conrad died, he still had sufficient prestige to organize an entire issue for a man whom he considered one of the four contemporary English novelists "who counted" (the other three being James, Douglas, and—Ford).

Unquestionably, Ford tried to renew old times when he approached Conrad for a contribution to the *Review*, and he further used their past collaborative efforts as a means of reentering Conrad's affections. In his November 8 letter to Conrad requesting the contribution, he made the first issue seem like a "Conrad supplement of appreciation," and he saw the inclusion of *The Nature of a Crime* as a way of throwing a little money (£25) to Conrad. He promised, furthermore, that his analysis of the *Romance* years would not appear without Conrad's perusal and approval. Even more, he says that if the latter's new reminiscences do not flow easily, the two of them could sit in a pub and he, Ford, would jog Conrad's memory, as he once did for *The Mirror* pieces. It was a touching moment, made even more compelling by Ford's recognition that Conrad was played out, no longer capable of writing anything of size or depth.*

Conrad did not return the generosity. In addition to his rejection of a contribution, which he could not have provided even under better conditions, he clearly did not want to renew old times, or even to see Ford. When they did meet, he wrote derisively to Eric Pinker that it was as if they had been familiar every day for ten years, while he, Conrad, asked himself "when would the kink come." The word "kink" is not only cynical but scathing in its denunciatory tone. Conrad's letters continue to describe his annoyance. To Eric, he repeated that Ford wants to be "too friendly," and that his former collaborator feels everyone in the world "has insulted him."

On another occasion, he calls Ford a "swell-headed creature" who imagines he will sweep "all Europe and devastate Great Britain with an eventual edition of his own works." Conrad says that he humors that "strange illusion," simply wishing to have the matter ended. Ford's mention of an edition, while Conrad's work was entering several such editions, suggests a considerable competition, now that Ford was moving well and he, Conrad, was declining. One way Conrad could hang on was to contrast his standing to Ford's in the literary world, even though the latter was producing work and he was not. They were now two old men (Ford was old in the literary wars) battling for position, like chess masters relying on former skills to beat back competition from upstarts with new strategies and tricks.

The renewal of the old friendship, which coincided with another painful episode, the Quinn sale of Conrad manuscripts, brought on a spate of letters from Conrad. He was perfectly willing for Ford to gain his rightful share of

---

* Writing to Edgar Jepson in 1921, Ford said: ". . . to tell you the truth his later work appeals to me so relatively little that I don't want to write any more about it. I mean, it's difficult to do so without appearing, and for all I know, being, ungenerous."

all monies from their collaborative efforts that resulted from sales of the Collected Edition. Ford, however, wanted more; he suggested that his name appear as co-author on those books as issued by Dent, and Dent refused. Through all the negotiations that followed, this point held, although Conrad further agreed to allow Ford to put the collaborative works in any collected edition of his own. What is so disturbing about these letters of Conrad, written through the winter and spring of 1924, is their insistence on financial matters; their work together had now become "properties," matters of negotiation, the bases of quarrels. The past recurred like a nightmare. Conrad's letters are stripped of any adornment, or any token of friendship; and yet after they met in early May of 1924, in London, with Eric Pinker present, Ford was convinced that the friendship had been renewed.

The entire matter became even more exacerbated later in the month when Elsie objected quite strongly to Violet Hunt's use of "Hueffer" in her name and threatened still another lawsuit to claim her own right to her married name. Further, when Elsie heard of the renewed interest in *Romance*, the result of Ford's publicity in the *Transatlantic Review*, she decided to capitalize on it by trying to sell the corrected proofs of the collaboration to Thomas Wise for £400. Wise finally obtained them for £70, a sale that gave Ford considerable anguish, because he prided himself on never having sold anything associated with Conrad. But by this time, his private life had veered out of control: Violet Hunt signing herself as "Hueffer"; Elsie planning a lawsuit and trying to pull something of value from the bitter marriage.

Conrad simply did not want any part of this. He was a dying man, and his letter to Ford on May 22 indicated he would permit Ford to use their joint preface to *The Nature of a Crime* in the *Review*. Ford had speculated that Conrad might not want the association between the two publicized because of his, Ford's, marital difficulties. He had, of course, hit upon some of Conrad's old antagonism to his messy private life. But by now Conrad did not care; he was overwhelmed by other messages of life and death, and he told Ford to go ahead despite his "kind warning" about the "unpleasantness between women." The tattered friendship had a suitable epitaph. Ford, however, refused to be discouraged by Conrad's indifference, or even antagonism. He wrote in *Return to Yesterday* that after Conrad's last words, on May 22, he was "seized with an overwhelming conviction that I should never see Conrad again. I got up and desperately scrawled to him a last letter assuring him of my for ever unchanging affection and admiration for his almost miraculous gifts." Ford sailed for New York on the *Paris*, leaving the *Transatlantic Review* in Hemingway's hands, and that young man proceeded to alter the contents radically. He emptied out the old and brought in the new. Nevertheless, after Conrad's death, Hemingway did not desert him, nor did Ford.

In November of 1923, Conrad's health was so poor that he called in a Dr.

Fox of Ashford for an examination and was told he had a "flabby heart," an organ that was tired and running down. The heart fluttered and missed "about every fourth beat." This was the first diagnosis of an organic defect in Conrad; the rest of his ailments, including the gout, were lifelong conditions that were controllable. Conrad attributed his despondency of his last few years to the "flabby heart." He admits he has been unable to do any work on *Suspense* and thanks Curle for throwing some article writing his way, in this case the general preface on geography for the Hammerton publication.

On November 12, under the auspices of Mitchell Kennerley of the Anderson Galleries, there began one of the most remarkable auctions in the twentieth century, the auctioning of books, drawings, manuscripts, and other items belonging to John Quinn. The number of items ran to over 12,000 (12,096), and the sale was divided into five alphabetical divisions, with A–C run in November, D–H in December, and so on into March. Five catalogues in all were prepared, themselves totaling over 1,200 pages. The catalogues were, in their own way, works of art, with photographs, drawings (by John Butler Yeats), and facsimiles of manuscript pages in the collection. Quinn gave as his reason for selling such treasures the simple fact of moving from larger quarters to smaller ones without sufficient shelf space. That was the public reason; the private one was that he was a very ill man, forced to close out an entire phase of his career. His sale of Conrad items, as we have seen, was also a matter of pique, owing to Conrad's cold-handed treatment on his visit to New York.

The first section of the auction involved Quinn's Conrad materials, and suitably, the catalogue for the November sale had as frontispiece a photograph of Conrad from 1913, inscribed to Quinn. The photograph was a lavish one, in that Conrad is turned full face but with sufficient body to show an elegant suit and a waistcoat, not at all like the impecunious writer he was in fact in 1913. The Conrad items in the first month's catalogue numbered 230, or about one-tenth of the total for the November sale. One item was Jessie's cookbook, *A Handbook of Cookery*, with a brief preface by Conrad, a 1923 publication, and inscribed to Quinn from Jessie.

The Conrad sale indeed turned out to be the high point of the Quinn auction, although that would not be clear until it had run its course in March. Quinn had invested about $10,000 in Conrad and was returned a thousand percent profit. One dealer who benefited enormously from the auction was A. S. W. Rosenbach, who saw that even at those inflated prices for a still living author, the Conrad items would skyrocket in later years, a bit of foresight he also had for Joyce. Some of these items were complete—such as the *Victory* manuscript, which is far lengthier than the published text and which went for $8,100—and some were fragmentary, like the *Nostromo* manuscript, which brought $4,700. Most of the Conrad novels were auctioned in the vicinity of $4–5,000, although we are surprised at "Falk" at $3,100 (whereas *The Secret Agent* went at $3,900) and "A Smile of Fortune" at $2,300.*

Quinn became subjected to considerable criticism for his "killing," even during the auction itself, not least from Frank Doubleday, who felt the collector owed Conrad a percentage. Quinn referred to Doubleday's attack as a "sheeny assault" upon him, an amusing bit of anti-Semitism as directed at Doubleday! Although hardly a lovable man, Quinn had always been absolutely fair with Conrad. Conrad himself never wrote Quinn, nor communicated with him again about any matter. He did read about the prices and the publicity in the London *Times*, and he wrote a wryly amused letter to F. N. Doubleday.

> Was the atmosphere vibrating with excitement, or, on the contrary, still with awe? Did any of the bidders faint? Did the auctioneer's head swell visibly? Did Quinn enjoy his triumph lying low like Brer Rabbit, or did he enjoy his glory in public and give graciously his hand to kiss the multitude of inferior collectors, who never, never, never, dreamt of such a coup? Well, it is a wonderful adventure to happen to a still-living (or at any rate half-alive) author.

Conrad added:

> The reverberations in the press here were very great indeed; and the result is that lots of people, who never heard of me before, now know my name, and thousands of others, who could not have read through a page of mine without falling into convulsions, are proclaiming me a very great author. And there are a good many also whom nothing will persuade that the whole thing was not a put-up job and that I haven't got my share of the plunder.

Conrad rarely went beyond this in his discussion of that "idiotic sale," although Jessie wrote to Quinn on November 18. Since Jessie had been the chief preserver of the manuscripts and typescripts, she felt an active role belonged to her. Her letter was simply to point out that it was indeed a great compliment to a living author to receive such high prices, and she said she hoped Quinn was satisfied with his "great success." She, or Conrad, noticed that the fragmentary manuscript of *The Sisters* had not been listed for sale, and they even wondered if Quinn had it. But Quinn for sentimental reasons

* We need only look at the prices paid for Joyce items to see what the Conrad market meant. The complete manuscript of *Ulysses* had a reserve price of $2,000 on it, and it went to Rosenbach for $1,975. He had a reserve price of $200 on *Exiles*, $75 on the *Egoist* galleys and holograph corrections of *A Portrait*. In all, Quinn realized only $170,000 from his huge auction, and the Conrad items accounted for all but $60,000 of that. It can be estimated that Quinn paid in all about a quarter of a million dollars for the total collection, and if the Conrad items had returned him only what he had paid (that is, about $10,000), his loss would have been over two-thirds of his original investment.

had withdrawn this item as late as September 5 and had held on to it.* That was that. Quinn waited in vain for some sign from Conrad that he even existed.

Conrad had received other messages; and to him they were more significant. The fluttering heart was a signal of one kind of doom.† He also awaited the December 3 publication of *The Rover* and, possibly, the last reviews he would receive. More immediate, however, was a delicate matter with Borys. After discussion with his son about his prospects and finding them fairly good, Conrad agreed to guarantee his account so he could obtain money for living expenses and set up as a married man. Conrad asked Walpole for a curious favor. He did not wish to be known at his bank as the man who was backing Borys, for he, Conrad, was already known there as a weak person who was being exploited. Since he shrinks "from the repetition of the experience," he wonders if Walpole will be good enough to guarantee a £100 overdraft for a year. If necessary, Conrad says he will repay him at once. He closes: "I hope you will neither laugh nor cry but take an indulgent view." The matter remains murky, but it appears Conrad could not himself face the outlay of money to Borys and used the Walpole scheme—Walpole would acquiesce to nearly anything Conrad requested—as a way of giving his son the money without being made to seem a fool in his own eyes.

Conrad did not give up hope of the Nobel Prize, either. When Yeats won it for literature in 1923, Conrad missed Yeats's greatness as a poet and felt he had been given the award chiefly as a "literary recognition of the Irish Free State." He says that if such was the case it does not completely destroy his chance of gaining it within a year or two. Yet while he admits Yeats is good, the fact of his being a poet means that a novelist will be recognized the following year. A novelist was, and a Pole: Reymont, not Conrad.

Before he could receive the Nobel Prize, however, Conrad's latest novel had to receive good notices. And while they were not discouraging, they were not happy reviews. They presaged the inevitable: that he had been exhausting his considerable capital with reviewers who wished him well for past performances but now waited in vain for later proof of accomplishment.

---

* Perhaps he recalled Conrad's words: "I imagine there might be one or two magazine editors who would be eager enough—when I am gone—to publish these few pages as a literary curiosity—and the blessed critics will babble about it. But you mustn't let this be printed till I *am* gone. And only if you like to do so, or think it worthwhile. Will you give me twenty for it?"

† To Curle, however, he presented a more hopeful prognosis: "Fox has been over and we arranged a treatment to be followed for 4 or 6 weeks directly all the acute symptoms are gone. Of course I feel as tho' I had been ill. But as a matter of fact the heart-action is quite normal now, the lungs are clear, pulse and temp have been normal for some time already and my blood-pressure is quite satisfactory. In fact my arteries are younger than my age."

Conrad himself had his doubts about the value of *The Rover*, having failed to show it to Garnett and then jesting that he had neglected to do so because "it is Revolutionary and you are an Aristocrat." Such ideological considerations, which were not true either, were an obvious façade for uneasiness. And to Gide, well before publication, he mentioned the novel in hesitating terms, characterizing it as work that fitted into a year made memorable "pour moi par le four noir de ma pièce."

All the reviewers were struck by the obvious: Conrad, that most indirect of novelists, had become simplified, with Raymond Mortimer in the *New Statesman* stressing that a twelve-year-old could enjoy it. Agreed on simplification, they disagreed radically on whether there were depths beneath. The *Times Literary Supplement* was the kindest; for that publication at least, Conrad had become something of an institution, and their dislike of the experimentally modern meant that they did not attack him in order to praise the new. The reviewer saw *The Rover* as a series of incidents saved from being just a network by "the creative vision in each trait of the land and sea." He found various kinds of beauty in the characters, and very sensitively discovered Conrad's aim, which was to change Arlette from someone close to catatonic to a vital young woman capable of feeling and even love. Many of the other reviewers, however, pictured Arlette as the kind of disastrous creature Conrad drew when he attempted to present women in his fiction.

This was the single independently favorable review. Several in America and Britain praised the novel only because it was simple. The *Herald Tribune* man, Frederic F. Van de Water, found that since Conrad had omitted all the customary disquisitions on ethics and psychology, he could stomach him. Thus, Conrad became better the more he approached Kipling. Many reviews were from the pens of friends, Richard Curle in the *Daily Mail* and David Bone in *The Manchester Guardian.* The general sense of the independent reviewers was surprise that Conrad continued to turn out fiction; he was, in their eyes, already dead.

There was still the past. Garnett sent his edition of Hudson's letters; there were further dealings with Fisher Unwin, Conrad's first publisher, over copyrights still held by that house; Christopher Morley sent his pamphlet called "Conrad and the Reporters," an account of his American trip as reported by journalists. Garnett weighed in with commendation of *The Rover.* Conrad used the occasion of Garnett's praise to write of the novel at length, as though he were speaking to his double, who understood everything. He points out that brevity was his aim, *The Rover* his sole work in which compactness was a conscious aim. And he explains he does not mean "compression," but brevity "in the very conception, in the manner of thinking about the people and the events." One senses here an attempt to redefine his style even at this late date, although his work on *Suspense* was to turn Conrad to the "fuller measure" more characteristic of him.

From the political side, Garnett had objected to Scevola as a so-called revolutionary, and Conrad agreed that he was a "scarecrow of the Revolution," although his extremist qualities and inhumanity were, for Conrad, revolutionary qualities. He says that Scevola is pathological more than anything else, but that admission upsets the balance of the novel, since a pathological case, if so, would require quite a different development of the materials. The tensions are indeed political, since the novel occurs in the period after Napoleon has been proclaimed consul for life. But Conrad recognizes that Scevola's weaknesses are not those of the plan but of the literary treatment. Garnett had raised another interesting point, that someone like Peyrol required real opposition, so that there would be a struggle between evenly matched men. Conrad acknowledges he had thought of that, but it "would have required another canvas," and the mood for that kind of expansion was simply not there. He says he wanted to achieve something of artistic brevity before he died, which led him to reject the potentially "greater thing."

He adds he saw other possibilities as well, such as a more drawn-out relationship between Catherine and Scevola, the old woman who has survived the revolution and the "drinker of blood." He rejected that as being part of a different psychological development, and says he needed the assurance of finishing something. *The Rover* was so brief, in Conrad's terms, because he was stalled on *Suspense* and needed the personal assurance of a book in hand. He stresses that dictation also hampered him; pen and ink, if possible, would have permitted him to "come nearer to expressing myself." These words to Garnett, reminiscent of comments about *Almayer* and *An Outcast*, were virtually the last in which Conrad speculated on presentation of his work, literary treatment, the psychology of his characters or their interactions.

On December 3, he passed his sixty-sixth, and last, birthday. The day was not celebrated, by request, although Borys and John sent letters. On his fiftieth birthday, Conrad had asked for the end to birthday celebrations for himself. With typical thoughtfulness, Doubleday sent Conrad copies of *Victory* and *Lord Jim* in the Conrad Edition, with its Minuteman insignia under the title. Also, Conrad was somewhat encouraged by the *Rover* reviews thus far, which were, at least, benevolent, but most of all by his sense that the "name of the book is, as it were, vibrating in the air."

In an unrelated matter, Muirhead Bone for some time had been pleading with Conrad to permit Jacob Epstein to do a bust of him. For ten years, Epstein had tried to corner Conrad into sitting, but as long as he was working well the latter did not like the idea. But now he agreed, and Bone made the arrangements for Epstein to stay near Oswalds in late March and start work—on what would become the most powerful visual image made of Conrad during his lifetime. With his mind set on illness, Conrad told Graham that "Epstein I believe is going to operate on me now." It would be, in all, a three-week operation. The Christmas season found Conrad in bed, with gout the chief offender and the fluttering heart a secondary villain. The house became, in fact, a hospital, with Jessie suffering from an abscess on the upper part of her leg, in great pain, but trying not to upset Conrad, who was depressed and seedy as well as ill. The faithful Jean-Aubry spent Christmas with them, and proved solicitous and useful. The Muirhead Bones, four strong, came over from Canterbury for the holiday dinner. Borys and his wife were missing.

Conrad's manner now was of weariness, of waiting for the end. He describes himself as captious and "grincheux," grumbling and peevish. He speaks of fighting his "Verdun battle" with his old enemy. Other developments, however, included a semi-asthmatic condition that resulted from spasms in the small bronchial tubes. From a distance, this seems like a nervous condition: the spasmodic state, the cough that results, the asthmatic symptoms. Whatever the reason, Conrad felt pain, and Dr. Fox's recommendation was for periods of prolonged rest without strain. Conrad told Doubleday he felt some stirring of ideas, perhaps broken loose by the physical shaking, but he would not "give them their head" until he felt more confident of recovery. He may have said this, of course, to convince his publisher that he was still active. Sales of *The Rover* made the book a huge financial success, even in the first month of publication.

On the sixteenth of January 1924, Conrad dragged himself up to London so that Jessie could have a consultation with her surgeon over the abscessed leg. On the eleventh, Borys and his wife had had their first child, Philip, a "solid boy," as Conrad described him to Jean-Aubry's father, adding that the young people are joyous. At the end of January, Conrad saw his grandson for the first time, at his son's home, and was reassured by a "quite nice" baby and a seemingly less strained Borys. At about the same time, George Keating informed Conrad of his plans for his "collection," including an expensive illustrated catalogue of Conrad manuscripts, annotated books, typescripts, and autographed first editions. This grouping, which is at the Beinecke Library at Yale University, is one of the choicest Conrad collections.

The texture of Conrad's life had so changed in these last two years or so that he had become like another man, a plutocrat or a man living on his stock dividends. That inner devil which drove him to seek himself outside Poland's boundaries, then to find meaning in a universe of water and sky, and, finally, to explore himself through novels and stories had become exhausted. When E. H. Visiak, the Milton scholar, asked him some questions about his art, to which Conrad responded on the twenty-ninth of January, his answer was like that of a man coming back from another world where such ideas were alien to his existence. We catch a small flash of interest when he tries to explain that a public can understand nothing of what a serious writer truly feels about his creations. Visiak had asked specifically what Conrad felt to be his best work. His reply:

> A man may like one of his works specially on account of some peculiar associations of the time. He may like it because in his conscience he believes that *there* he has come the nearest to his artistic intention, or has conveyed his meaning with the greatest clearness, or has achieved the greatest emotional sincerity, or simply has been able to attain what he thinks his best in plasticity or colouring or atmosphere. And how can those things be made understandable to a public which often fails to perceive the whole point of a composition?

Visiak's query and attempts to penetrate to the "real" Conrad were only one part of the large-scale memorialization that was taking place. He was being pickled for future use even while his body was still warm. He had received several inquiries about his background, his literary tastes, his knowledge of Russian literature, his so-called Polonism, his Slavic tradition, the formative influences upon him; and he gave the same answers, denying his Slavic roots, denying any knowledge of Russian or even of its literature except in translation, stressing that the formative forces on him were purely Western—that is, French and English.

Despite the weariness that undermined all effort, Conrad picked up the manuscript of *Suspense* in early February and tried to see it more clearly, even to the extent of finding thirty pages that he would have to cut. At about this or at a slightly later time, he wrote a very bland preface to a volume of *The Shorter Tales of Joseph Conrad,* which Doubleday planned to publish in America. He was, as he indicates, reluctant to publish such a volume for personal reasons: "frail plants," he calls his cherished illusions, "and fit only for the shade of solitary thought." The private man rebelled against the distinctly commercial character of the enterprise, but the public man acquiesced. Although slipping into an increasing commercial posture, Conrad fought the idea.*

To turn to *Suspense* now was ironical. For much of the public, he feared, had accepted *The Rover* as his big "Napoleonic novel," confusing it with *Suspense.* Yet he promised Eric Pinker that the latter would have "weight and body enough" and satisfy those who found *The Rover* slight. From now to his death, however, Conrad did almost no work on *Suspense;* what he had achieved to this point was what he left, although he did do some revising. The negotiations with Ford over rights to their collaborative efforts contin-

* He told Doubleday that his volumes of stories had a "unity of artistic purpose," each collection possessing a homogeneous texture, a "mood of feeling and expression," all of which a selection disrupts and violates. In addition, besides the homogeneous nature of each book, the volumes were themselves very different from each other. Each expressed his art in a different way, whereas a selection indiscriminately positions a story of one tone "cheek and jowl" with a story from another.

ued throughout the winter and spring, and Conrad settled back to wait.* Galsworthy popped back into Conrad's life; his career was going extremely well—and he would be rewarded with the Nobel Prize for Literature in 1932. His ability to complete work comforted Conrad that some projects could be finished, if not his own "runaway novel," so-called because he had been trying for two years to overtake it. Pleased at Galsworthy's "attack" upon life, he was bitter at his own "chase in a nightmare." "Weird and exhausting" he found his fate, like the doomed creature he described to Marguerite Poradowska in the 1890s.

The narcissism of illness and self-contemplation was somewhat intensified when Epstein arrived in mid-March, took up nearby residence with his wife and daughter, and stayed for three weeks. For Epstein, it was a long-awaited moment, and he put into his effort a sense of Conrad that went well beyond the man who posed, an elderly, sick, declining figure. Epstein, himself of Polish background, identified strongly with the heroic in Conrad, and this aspect characterized his bust. He did not neglect the writer while insisting on the seaman; on the contrary, he presented a particular view of the writer, not as a man sitting at a desk but as a human being trying to meet his fate without flinching. The Conrad of the Epstein bust is the figure of his fictional protagonists challenging their fates, and, if succumbing, then doing so without regret. Very possibly, as an immigrant Jew who had struggled against enormous adversity, Epstein identified personally with the Conradian universe, finding in it sufficient room for several kinds of exile, himself and the Polish Gentile alike. There is in the profile of the bust not a little of that identification, for the Conradian silhouette is classically Hebraic in the structure of the features, although still characteristically "aristocratic."

Personally, the two struck it off well. In his autobiography *Let There Be Sculpture* (1940), Epstein included a sympathetic description of Conrad's many animadversions: his attacks on Melville as being as mystical as his old boots; his mixed feelings about George Meredith; and most interestingly, his view of Lawrence as having started well and then writing nothing but filth and obscenities. Epstein also reports that Conrad was exhausted, the very qualities he tried to avoid in the bust. He describes Conrad as a man who was crotchety, rheumatic, nervous, ill, who spoke of being "finished" with life. He says Conrad pulled a manuscript from a drawer to show he was still active, not beaten, but there "was no triumph in his manner, however." "I am played out," he repeated, while Epstein sculpted on the heroic scale.

Jessie has left an amusing description of the topsy-turvy household. Ep-

* Conrad could barely contain himself over what he took to be Ford's insistence. Writing to Jean-Aubry that Ford can do anything he wants with the translations and that his own contract with Gallimard does not include the collaborated books, Conrad adds he "can not be mixed up in any difficulties with that man." He insists: "I will have nothing more to do with him or the collaborated works."

stein, whom she characterized as "truly Bohemian," ate his meals with Conrad, so as to soak up atmosphere. Borys, his wife and infant also came down to stay at Oswalds, to add to the confusion. Jessie speaks of those three weeks as ones of "steering a big craft through a mine-field." Both artists required careful handling, and she noticed that she was considered a nuisance. The preparation of the plaster-of-Paris cast created such turmoil that Epstein began to get on Conrad's nerves, and an explosion of monumental proportions was only barely avoided, with Jessie the scapegoat for having convinced Conrad to sit in the first place. Yet Conrad was tremendously pleased; he told Curle it was a "marvellously effective piece of sculpture, with even something more than masterly interpretation in it." And he repeated these sentiments to Elbridge Adams, commenting that it was nice to be passed to posterity "in this monumental and impressive rendering."

Adams invited the Conrads to live in a cottage in Massachusetts, as a way of getting some rest, but Conrad declined the offer, saying that they planned to leave Oswalds in September and go into "winter quarters in the South of France." Their chief considerations were those of health, for Jessie might have to remain near her surgeons. She would, in early spring, return to a nursing home for another operation, this time on June 13. By late April, Conrad was certain of this new blow, what he called a "horrible prospect for us both."

Nevertheless, invitations poured in, from Aniela Zagórska to visit abroad, another for a stay in Geneva; and the past intruded in unexpected ways, a visit from Irene Rakowska, whose mother, Maria Ołdakowska, was a frequent referent in Tadeusz Bobrowski's letters to Conrad. Even more intimately from the past, the historian Stefan Pomarański sent Conrad a manuscript of Apollo Korzeniowski's, the poem "The Cinders" and other fragments. When Conrad responded, on June 28, he not only indicated how touched he was but suggested, somewhat vaguely, a possible return to Poland, with the words "Your letter will not remain unanswered." Conrad's precise meaning remains unknown, but Pomarański took it to mean an exile's return. Jessie stated, also vaguely, that Conrad spoke on several occasions of returning to Poland, but she admits it was all a dream and may have been little more than idle talk. "Directly John had embarked upon a successful career we, the old folks, were to divide up what of the home we could not take with us between the boys, and return to his beloved land. It was a dream."

The end of May was notable for three very different events. Jessie, it was decided, would definitely go into a nursing home in Canterbury for another operation. Curle and Graham would come to Oswalds to stay with Conrad, Curle for three days, Graham for a day-long visit. The time was also the occasion of Conrad's final letter to Gide, a kind of valedictory, in which he asks

Gide if this is perhaps the end, a veritable nightmare of illness in which the only consolation derives from the French translations, all of which he owes to Gide. "Et cette consolation c'est à vous que je la dois." Another kind of "final thing" came in the form of an offer of a knighthood from Ramsay MacDonald, the rejection of which we discussed above. MacDonald's letter is dated May 26, and Conrad's refusal the next day; there was no uncertainty or soul-searching. His declining, as we have suggested, was fully consistent with his principles: to accept nothing he had not earned himself, and to refuse any attempt to dislodge him from the two things he knew best, the sea and fiction writing. The argument that he refused the honor because the offer came from a socialist government is nonsense. Conrad heaped ridicule on all government; the institution itself was suspect. He respected the truth of his art, and no government or public knew what that truth was. He refused any other rapprochement and preferred remaining wrapped up in his own mummy's cloth to the dubious rewards of public display. His letters immediately after the offer of the knighthood hardly even mention it, as though he had forgotten MacDonald's letter as soon as it was answered.

Jessie's operation was planned for the thirteenth of June, the first occasion on which Sir Robert Jones was free. Conrad was momentarily cheered by a very perceptive article on *The Rover* by Gilbert Seldes, in the *Dial*, to the extent he felt impelled to write a letter to the editor. Upon reflection, however, he decided that a work of art must speak for itself and that an author who attempts to "explain" exposes himself to a great risk. Yet the opportunity was tempting, since no work of art carried its intention on the face of it. Conrad, on June 2, told Mrs. Doubleday that he had been offered a knighthood, saying that it arrived in an envelope so that he thought it was a "super-tax form." He swears the Doubledays to secrecy, since he does not want to embarrass the government by his refusal.

On June 11, he motored up to London for lunch at the Polish legation and met Curle just before for a drink. On the thirteenth Jessie's operation went well, so Conrad could report the prospect of her having to spend three weeks in all in the nursing home—but not until July 24, nearly five weeks later, was she permitted to return home for convalescence. Conrad's health while Jessie was away seemed to deteriorate, with temperature and severe coughing. His days were a round of discomfort and pain, followed by some relenting, and then a return of the cycle. He was not permitted to move outside freely and, therefore, kept in touch with Jessie by mail.

Conrad felt his concentration wavering, a restlessness and unsteadying quality which he could not explain. He often signed himself "Your own Boy," and his letters are like hospital reports, concerned with bed sheets, fever charts, medicine schedules, signs of discomfort, medical attendance. His dependence on her approval, while she herself was convalescing, was absolute; he calls himself a good patient, as if pleasing his uncle or guardians.

The cough was bronchitis; the pain in the foot was gout; and the restlessness of spirit and mind was the residue of the body running down, the heart beginning to give up. To Curle he said he felt like a rag, and to Ernest Dawson he reported he felt limp, with his spirits standing at about zero. His image for himself is that of a "cornered rat." He felt the house dismal, and his life a matter of desolation: the "vain cry of a man in a bottomless pit. I am the most useless of men," he told the Colvins, "and apparently the most selfish."

In early July, Conrad managed to visit Jessie three times, each visit followed by his return to bed. The idea of work was ludicrous: nothing of real value for over eighteen months. His uselessness, for this driven man, becomes a litany. Through it all, Conrad was, amusingly under different circumstances, fighting to keep *The Nature of a Crime*, his final collaborative effort with Ford, out of his life. With the boom in Conrad, and no new fiction appearing, his every word had become profitable, even words that were Ford's and not his. He refused to sign any copies of *The Nature*, which he called "that idiotic publication," and he refused to allow it to appear in *The Best Stories of 1924*. He was outraged that people were speaking of it as a fresh collaboration, rumors that could have started only with the irrepressible Ford.

On July 24, Jessie came home, to rest in bed for an indefinite convalescence. Before she returned, Conrad evidently felt cheered enough to contemplate writing a 3–6-page preface on "legends"—of sailors, saints, university dons, and others, an essay which he left unfinished. Curle is the witness for the final days, for he arrived for the weekend on Friday, August 1.* Although Conrad had had minor heart attacks on and off and was generally run-down with ailments, there had been none of the major warnings that often accompany death. In his present condition, he seemed capable of months and even years of general decline, with periodic remissions followed by further decline.

Curle and Conrad spent much time talking in Conrad's room on that Friday night. Cheered by Jessie's return, he appeared to Curle to be in good spirits and even well. He revealed to his friend that they would be leaving Oswalds for another house about eight miles away, along the Dover Road. Conrad had seen and liked it, and wanted Curle to have a look at it the next day. From that, he roamed over various matters, bringing up his fragmentary novel *The Sisters* and speculating whether anyone would care to read it now. He mentioned the death of John Quinn earlier that very year. When the evening ended, Curle felt reassured about Conrad's condition.

The next morning just the two of them breakfasted and then went into Conrad's study. He spoke of *Suspense* and of the piece on "legends" he was

---

* He and Sir Ralph Wedgwood would serve as the executors of the Conrad estate.

still working on. He had some plans. He indicated to Curle "about six different lines of treatment" for the novel, and said he hoped to use the "legends" article as part of a volume to succeed *The Mirror of the Sea.* The new volume would deal not with the sea but with the men he had sailed with. It sounded like a solid enough idea and in perfect accord with Conrad's later powers. They then went out by car to see the house he was thinking of renting, when Conrad suffered a sudden pain in his chest. After indicating that it was the same as he had felt a few days earlier, he insisted on going on so that Curle could see the property. Only when they were within a mile and a half of their destination did he agree to turn back. He felt temporary relief, and went to bed when they arrived home. As Curle relates this episode, one is struck by the primitive medical facilities someone as rich and famous as Conrad had provided for himself, especially since he had suffered previous heart attacks. He was, obviously, in general decline, the body simply worn out, but nevertheless he appears to have taken few precautions for emergency treatment, rudimentary as it may have been in the 1920s in a rural area.

Once in bed, Conrad permitted Curle to call his doctor, who came from Ashford. This was Fox, who apparently saw no reason for alarm. He remarked that the shooting pains resembled those of acute indigestion, and with that prescribed a drug (probably a sedative) and gave instructions for a diet. While he was present, Conrad did not undergo the usual paroxysms and breathlessness associated with his attacks, and since his pulse was strong, the doctor left him. That evening Oswalds began to fill with Borys, his wife and son, and John. They had arrived to spend the Bank Holiday at Oswalds, not because of any emergency or special summoning. Meanwhile, Conrad's breathing became more labored and difficult, and a doctor was summoned from nearby Canterbury. This doctor, not Conrad's usual Canterbury adviser, found his pulse normal and took the sole precaution of ordering cylinders of oxygen to be sent from Canterbury.

Neither doctor, then, believed anything serious was wrong. Conrad, they assumed, was simply experiencing the usual heart flutters, difficulty in breathing, and other symptoms of a condition that was hardly terminal. Curle says the atmosphere, nevertheless, was funereal as they all sat together—he, Jessie, Borys and family, John—while Conrad fought for breath in his room. The uneasy night passed into August 3. Toward morning, Conrad insisted on sitting up in his chair, and dozed. At six, he seemed better, or in less difficulty. An hour or so after that, Mrs. Vinten, a trained nurse, took his pulse and found no irregularity. Sometime later there was a cry, and Conrad slipped, dead, onto the floor. He was found at eight-thirty.

The Roman Catholic funeral ceremony took place at St. Thomas's in Canterbury on August 7. The city was decorated for Cricket Week, an annual celebration. All the old friends joined the family—Jean-Aubry and Garnett, of course; Graham, Richard Curle, the Wedgwoods, Ernest Dawson and his brother; representing the Polish minister to England was Count Edward Raczyński. The tombstone in Canterbury cemetery has a misspelling of Teodor and uses Joseph instead of Józef, Conrad instead of Konrad. In some kind of grim irony, which Conrad might or might not have appreciated, he was neither English nor Polish on his tombstone; or, perhaps, he was both, in that intermingling of experiences which had characterized his life.

The final two lines from this passage from *The Faerie Queene* appear on Conrad's tombstone, but the entire passage is fitting. It is spoken by Despair, and counsels suicide:

> *"He there does now enjoy eternall rest*
> *And happy ease, which thou doest want and crave,*
> *And further from it daily wanderest:*
> *What if some little payne the passage have,*
> *That makes frayle flesh to feare the bitter wave?*
> *Is not short payne well borne, that bringes long ease,*
> *And layes the soule to sleep in quiet grave?*
> *Sleepe after toyle, port after stormie seas,*
> *Ease after warre, death after life does greatly please."*

Cunninghame Graham put it differently: "*Inveni Portum:* Joseph Conrad."

Afterword

AFTER Conrad's death, Edward Garnett's career moved in several directions but never found definition, and he died in 1937; as did Marguerite Poradowska, at eighty-nine, having been senile for her last fifteen years. Cunninghame Graham turned his attention increasingly to politics, becoming, in 1928, the first president of the Scottish nationalist movement. He died in 1936. Galsworthy, as we have seen, in 1932 won the Nobel Prize for Literature, which had eluded Conrad, and died the year after. Gosse preceded him, in 1928. Edward Sanderson, never part of the literary inner circle, became headmaster of Elstree and retired in 1935, dying in 1939. Ford wrote some of his finest fiction after Conrad's death, but was pushed aside by young "modernists" and died relatively forgotten, also in 1939. Wells continued to go on to ever greater fame, even as the inner man recognized the futility of his social engineering, and lived to see the morass of the Second World War, dying the year after it ended. Arnold Bennett remained a phenomenal popular success until his death in 1931. William Rothenstein, living until 1945, was knighted in 1931 and became the official British war artist for both world wars. Sir Sidney Colvin outlived Conrad by only three years.

James and Hudson having died earlier, the first circle was completed.

The second circle, of younger men, continued well into our present era. Jean-Aubry, after publishing his *Life and Letters of Joseph Conrad* in 1927, wrote another biography of Conrad in 1947, which was translated into English in 1957 as *The Sea Dreamer.* Richard Curle kept Conrad's memory alive with books, articles, introductions, and reminiscences until his death in 1968. Hugh Walpole, knighted in 1937, enjoyed a dazzling popular success as a novelist until he died in 1941. Francis Warrington Dawson, who remained loyal to Jessie following Conrad's death, never achieved any renown as a creative writer and died in 1962. André Gide achieved an international reputation as a literary figure, won the Nobel Prize for Literature in 1947, and died four years later.

Of the immediate family, Jessie and Borys worked hard to keep Conrad's memory alive in the years when his literary reputation had become somewhat dim. Only John, the younger son, turned to a completely different kind of life, attending architectural school and practicing his profession well into the 1970s. Jessie published two books about her life with Conrad, *Joseph Conrad As I Knew Him*, in 1925, and *Joseph Conrad and His Circle*, in 1935, the year before her death. Chiefly by correspondence, she kept in touch with most of the younger circle who had hovered about Conrad in his later years. In 1970, Borys published a short volume of reminiscences, *My Father: Joseph Conrad.* As of this writing (1978), both Borys and John are alive and well, and Conrad has several grandchildren, only one of whom he ever saw. When I met them all, at Canterbury, in 1974, in a truly international conference on Joseph Conrad, there was little trace of Poland left. They were all very English. At least in his family, Conrad's "third life" had indeed washed away his first.

APPENDIX

Editions of Conrad

DURING and immediately after Conrad's lifetime, the collected editions of his work were not "scholarly" or even accurate. Their primary aim was to provide readable texts of his novels, stories, and non-fiction so as to keep him before the general public. Many of these editions were woefully inadequate, with even the Kent Edition in 1926, one of the more complete, lacking the plays, "The Sisters," and *Last Essays.* Texts of all the editions, including the Heinemann Limited Edition of 1921–27, in twenty volumes, were corrupt. No effort was made to incorporate Conrad's substantial corrections as he went from manuscript to typescript to serial version, then to first English and American editions. For many of his novels and stories, we can follow major revisions in five or more versions, not to speak of the alterations he made for the larger editions themselves.

Since these commemorative editions, most of them in the 1920s, there have been scattered attempts to provide accurate texts, difficult as this is for a writer like Conrad. Paperback editions of "Heart of Darkness" and *Lord Jim* have been moves in this direction, but the main body of Conrad's work has remained untouched in this respect. At present, Cambridge University Press of England has undertaken the publication of a complete Conrad with texts that will contain variants, as necessary, and with editing that will reflect Conrad's changing views of his own texts. One of the first novels that will appear is *The Nigger of the "Narcissus,"* expected in the late 1970s, and other volumes will follow as soon as completed.

A complete edition of Conrad's work into Polish has been supervised by Dr. Zdzisław Najder, the first attempt at a full Polish text. In other languages, Conrad remains only partially translated. Gide's desire to have Conrad appear in the French language fell far short of a complete edition. The project gradually wound down as Gide lost interest and the various translators died or drifted away, although all the major works have appeared in France. In Italy, the firm of Ugo Mursia, in Milan, has been bringing out Italian translations of Conrad's novels and stories based on the Heinemann and Dent texts in their collected editions.

Some works more than others, mainly *Lord Jim* and *Victory*, with "Heart of Darkness" and *Nostromo* not far behind, have enjoyed translation into the major languages of the world. We find *Lord Jim* in French, Spanish, Italian, German, Norwegian, Danish, Swedish, Portuguese, Czech, Polish, Serbo-Croatian, Turkish, Rumanian, Russian, Lithuanian, and Japanese. *Victory* has also appeared in most of these languages.

It is to be hoped that the Cambridge edition will lead to still further translations, themselves based on accurate texts, with accurate editing—and all of this accomplished without discouraging the reader who, uninterested in apparatus, simply wants to read a definitive Conrad text.

Conrad's collected letters will be published in eight or more volumes, the first attempt to bring together his almost four thousand letters to friends and relatives, as well as publishers, agents, collectors and acquaintances. Almost one-third of this total were addressed to his literary agent, J. B. Pinker. The overall editor of this collected edition is Frederick R. Karl, with various co-editors on the different volumes.

Notes

ABBREVIATIONS USED IN THE NOTES

Manuscript Code

AL, ALS—Autograph (holograph) Letter, Signed.
AN, ANS—Autograph Note, Signed.
TL, TLS—Typescript Letter, Signed.
MS.—Manuscript.
n.d.—no date.

Libraries

Alderman, Va.—Alderman Library of the University of Virginia Library.
Berg—The Berg Collection of the New York Public Library, Astor, Lenox & Tilden Foundations.
Birmingham—The University of Birmingham Library, England.
Brotherton—The Brotherton Library, University of Leeds, England.
Colgate—Colgate University Library.
Columbia—Columbia University Special Collections.
Cornell—Cornell University Library.
Dartmouth—Dartmouth College Libraries.
Doucet—Bibliothèque Littéraire Jacques Doucet, Paris.
Duke—Duke University Library.
Fales—The Fales Collection of New York University.
Harvard—Harvard University Houghton Library.
Illinois—University of Illinois Library.
Lilly—Indiana University Lilly Library.
McGregor, Va.—McGregor Library of the University of Virginia Library.
Morgan—The Pierpont Morgan Library, New York.
NYPL—New York Public Library, Manuscript Division.
Rosenbach—The Philip H. & A. S. W. Rosenbach Foundation, Philadelphia.
Rylands—John Rylands University Library of Manchester, England.
Syracuse—Syracuse (New York) University Library.
Texas—The University of Texas Humanities Research Center.
Yale—The Beinecke Rare Book and Manuscript Library.

FOREWORD

p. xiv: "into revelations"—Henry James, "The Art of Fiction," *Partial Portraits* (Ann Arbor, Michigan: University of Michigan Press, 1970). p. 388.

INTRODUCTION

p. 4: "two even remarkable." February 15, 1919; TLS, Berg.

I: THE POLISH YEARS (1857–1874)

p. 10: "*seigneurs* great enough": *Kraj* (*Homeland,* a conservative Polish weekly), April 1899; reprinted in Ludwik Krzyżanowski, ed., *Joseph Conrad: Centennial Essays* (New York: The Polish Institute of Arts and Sciences in America, 1960), pp. 114–15.

p. 11: "like Mme. Orzeszkowa's": Krzyżanowski, p. 115.

p. 12: "his creative activity": *Ibid.*

p. 12: wrote him directly,: The letter has never turned up.

p. 13: "succession of years": *A Personal Record,* p. xvi (Kent Edition). All further references to Conrad's work, unless otherwise stated, will be to this edition.

p. 13: "not to be insensible": *Ibid.*, pp. xx–xxi.

p. 13: "For that spoil!": *Ibid.*, p. 110.

p. 13: "rendered without shame": *Ibid.*, pp. 112–13.

p. 14: "from artistic conviction": *Ibid.*, p. 112.

p. 14: "an eternal rest": MS., Rosenbach.

p. 14: "an undiscovered country": November 1, 1906. Leon Edel, ed., *The Selected Letters of Henry James* (New York: Farrar, Straus and Cudahy, 1955), p. 157.

p. 15: "been recorded before": to C. K. Scott Moncrieff, December 17, 1922; Gerard Jean-Aubry, *Joseph Conrad: Life and Letters* (Garden City, N.Y.: Doubleday, 1927), II, p. 291.

p. 18: "interests of mankind": *Notes on Life and Letters,* p. 100.

p. 18: "he was a Russian": pp. 10–11.

p. 19: "of indistinct ideas": March 29 or April 5, 1894: ALS, Yale. (Translated from the French by F. R. Karl, as will be all future translations from French into English.)

p. 23: business to Jewish elements: January 7, 1898; ALS, Dartmouth.

p. 23: "to various Jews": January 20, 1900; Edward Garnett, ed., *Letters from Joseph Conrad, 1895–1924* (Indianapolis: Bobbs-Merrill, 1928), p. 164.

p. 23: "practical profession": October 28 / November 9, 1891; Zdzisław Najder, *Conrad's Polish Background: Letters to and from Polish Friends* (London: Oxford University Press, 1964), p. 153.

p. 24: "we have a cleavage": July 18 / July 30, 1891; *Ibid.*, pp. 147–48.

p. 25: appears to have been a Bobrowska: In Polish, the "i" at the end of the family name indicates a male, the "a" a female.

p. 27: "to the palate": *A Personal Record,* p. 35.

p. 27: "our imperfect senses": *Ibid.*
p. 28: "not a good citizen": *Ibid.*, pp. 36–7.
p. 31: "degeneration of legality": *Notes on Life and Letters*, p. 101; originally published in the *Fortnightly Review* in 1905.
p. 31: after his death: Adam Gillon (in *Conradiana*, VII, No. 1) provides an excellent survey of the critical reception of Conrad's work during the period 1896–1969. For the Polish reader, *Conrad w Polsce* by Stefan Zabierowski is the source of much of the review. For many aspects of Apollo's literary career, I am indebted to Andrzej Busza's fine study, *Conrad's Polish Literary Background and Some Illustrations of the Influence of Polish Literature on His Work* (Rome: Institutum Historicum Polonicum [ex Antemurale X], 1966).
p. 33: "father and his brothers": Tadeusz Bobrowski, *Memoirs* (Lwów, 1900), I, pp. 363–65; quoted by Gustav Morf, *The Polish Heritage of Joseph Conrad* (London: Sampson, Low, Marston, 1930) pp. 7–9.
p. 35: "great of this world": Bobrowski, I, pp. 361–63; in *ibid.*, pp. 23–26.
p. 36: "limits of decency": *Ibid.*
p. 43: settled Poland's fate: The best sources in English for events in Poland from 1830 on are R. F. Leslie's *Polish Politics and the Revolution of November 1830* (1956; reprinted by the Greenwood Press, Westport, Conn., in 1969) and *Reform and Insurrection in Russian Poland 1856–1865* (1963; reprinted by the Greenwood Press in 1969).
p. 43: "from Russians no doubt": Tuesday, October 1907; Garnett, p. 209.
p. 44: "which Granny? Konrad": (*Kobieta Współczesna*, Lwów, p. 205. 1931, No. 17).
p. 44: "our Mother, is enslaved": Najder, p. 5.
p. 46: "Warsaw demonstrations in 1861": Jocelyn Baines, *Joseph Conrad* (New York: McGraw-Hill, 1960), pp. 11–12. Much of this material was uncovered as the result of research by Zdzisław Najder.
p. 47: "not budge very well": January 6, 1908; ALS, Birmingham.
p. 48: "sword and shield?": Sunday, January 23, 1898; ALS, Dartmouth.
p. 49: "folly and conceit.": Also to Graham, January 14, 1898; ALS, Dartmouth.
p. 49: constrict other men: *Gandhi's Truth* (New York: Norton, 1969), p. 113.
p. 50: "step out of line": *Ibid.*, "He [Freud] was content to demonstrate the unconscious restoration of mastery over our inner complexes by nightly dreaming, but he neglected to dwell on the question of what additional mastery made it possible for him to understand his own dreams."
p. 50: "character of the child": *Ibid.*, pp. 125–26.
p. 50: "developments in later life": *Ibid.*, p. 128.
p. 50: "sufficiently large scale": *Ibid.*, p. 132.
p. 51: The chronicle of their exile: Much of this account derives from Bobrowski, II, pp. 440 ff.
p. 52: "are born to die": June 27, 1862; *Tygodnik Illustrowany*, 1920, No. 4.
p. 52: beyond his conscious memory: According to *A Personal Record*, his memory began to record consciously when he and his mother prepared to return to exile, after a rest at Tadeusz Bobrowski's estate at Kazimierówka, about thirty miles from Zhitomir (pp. 64–5).

p. 53: "6 July 1863—Konrad": Najder, p. 8.

p. 54: "where it is due": February 14, 1901; *Ibid.*, p. 234 (original is in the Warsaw National Library).

p. 54: "writing in English,": November 15, 1903; *Ibid.*, p. 237 (original is in *Ruch Literacki*, 1927, No. 6).

p. 55: "mystic Russian fashion": *Notes on Life and Letters*, pp. 126–27.

p. 58: "down over his eyes": *A Personal Record*, pp. 64–5.

p. 58: "hopes and—well—dog": *Ibid.*, p. 46.

p. 59: "course of his taciturn life": *Ibid.*, pp. 63–4.

p. 60: "midst of all this": Baines, p. 16.

p. 61: "to drink separately": *Ibid.*

p. 63: *Poland and Muscovy: Polska i Moskwa*, which appeared in 1864 anonymously in the émigré newspaper in Leipzig, *Ojczyzna* (*The Fatherland*).

p. 63: "they ended in falsehood": Quoted from Bobrowski's *Memoirs* by Czesław Miłosz, *Mosaic*, [VI 4,] p. 134.

p. 64: "stirrings of a resurrection": *Notes on Life and Letters*, p. 89.

p. 64: "to secure his future": June 10, 1865; Baines, p. 17.

p. 65: "he takes after me": October 31, 1865; *Ibid.*, p. 18.

p. 65: Letter to William Rothenstein: ALS, Harvard.

p. 65: Finally, to Bertrand Russell: ALS, Russell. Lord Russell put these letters at my disposal; they are now in the Bertrand Russell Archives at McMaster University, Hamilton, Ontario, Canada.

p. 66: "its absolute necessity": Busza, p. 131.

p. 67: "well at the age of eight": *A Personal Record*, pp. 71–2.

p. 67: "ship in dry dock": *Ibid.*, p. 72.

p. 67: "and then by fire": *Ibid.*, pp. 72–3.

p. 68: "and some French poets": *Ibid.*, p. 70.

p. 68: "rage in that language": *Ibid.*, p. 71.

p. 68: "for him to sound": February 8, 1924; ALS, Rylands.

p. 69: "object of my affections": January 18, 1866; Baines, p. 19.

p. 69: "we die of hunger": *Ibid.*, p. 20.

p. 69: "of a running sea": *Tales of Hearsay*, pp. 31–2.

p. 70: "been young, rich, beautiful": *Ibid.*, p. 35. The prince could have been Proust's Charlus.

p. 70: "as you did?": November 20 / December 2, 1891; Najder, p. 158. See Najder, p. 9, n. 3, for speculation about possible epilepsy. (The Bobrowski letters to Conrad are in the National Library in Warsaw [sign. MS. 2889].)

p. 72: "that keeps me alive": Baines, pp. 21–2.

p. 72: "Konradek . . . writes well": May 10, 1868: Najder, p. 10; also see Baines, p. 22 *n.*

p. 75: "my father's last illness": *Notes on Life and Letters*, p. 167

p. 76: "she would glide away": *Ibid.*, p. 168.

p. 76: "fear in his heart": *Almayer's Folly*, pp. 199–200.

p. 76: "tip-toe out again": *Notes on Life and Letters*, p. 168.

p. 76: "little wretch on earth": *Ibid.*, pp. 168–69.

p. 77: "could feel and understand": *Ibid.*, p. 169.

p. 77: "but to the Idea": *A Personal Record,* p. x.
p. 77: "University for preservation": *Ibid.*, p. xi.
p. 78: "I broke away early": December 14, 1922; TLS, Yale.
p. 78: "by no means smileless": *A Personal Record,* pp. xi–xii.
p. 80: "of the Georgeon females": *Conrad and His Contemporaries* (London: Minerva Publishing Co., 1941; reprinted by Haskell House, 1973), pp. 21–22. In 1914, Conrad and Retinger collaborated desultorily on a dramatic version of *Nostromo,* in French. See pp. 121 ff.
p. 81: "to me personally": August 3 / 15, 1881; Najder, p. 74.
p. 83: "activity and relationships": *Ibid.*, p. 148.
p. 84: "live in this country": May 18/30, 1881; *Ibid.*, p. 70.
p. 84: "your future destiny": September 8/20, 1869; *Ibid.*, p. 35.
p. 86: "reorientations, the religious": from *Permanence and Change* (quoted by Stanley Edgar Hyman, *The Armed Vision* [New York: Vintage Books, 1955], p. 331).
p. 87: "always busy doing something." Bobrowski, I, p. viii; quoted by Busza, p. 148.
p. 88: "as he needed it": Najder, p. 190.
p. 89: "romance of the world": p. 151.
p. 89: "of the Roman Caesars": p. 152.
p. 89: "constellations of the sky": *Ibid.*
p. 89: "as she could hold": p. 154.
p. 90: did inform others of this fact: "I spent my childhood in the same town of Cracow as he did; went to school to the same *gymnasium* of St Anne's, where he was taught the rudiments of knowledge" (p. 11).
p. 91: "concerned with ideas": October 20, 1911; Garnett, pp. 234–35.
p. 91: "from prehistoric ages": May 27, 1912; ALS, Berg. Commenting on *The Brothers Karamazov,* Conrad called it "an impossible lump of valuable matter. It's terrifically bad and impressive and exasperating." Conrad, however, was careful to praise Constance Garnett's translation.
p. 92: French experience: *The Sea Dreamer* (New York: Doubleday, 1957), p. 46. Jean-Aubry points out that the boy's pro-French sympathies were strengthened.
p. 95: Conrad's Austrian naturalization: Najder, p. 192. In September 1873: "To cover the costs of your naturalization in Austria, I paid a solicitor 20 r. and your equipment cost 70 r." In September 1874, Bobrowski enters another such expense (Najder, p. 193).
p. 96: "antagonism was radical": *Last Essays,* pp. 17–18. Written originally as a preface to *Countries of the World* (February 1924) and entitled "The Romance of Travel." It was reprinted in *National Geographic Magazine,* March 1924. *Last Essays* (London: Dent, 1926) was not part of the Collected Edition, but was a collection edited by Richard Curle of Conrad's fugitive pieces. Had Conrad lived, it might have become a sequel to *Notes on Life and Letters* (1921).
p. 97: "in a loving spirit": *Ibid.*, p. 18.
p. 97: "little way beyond Hospenthal": *A Personal Record,* pp. 37 ff.
p. 98: "painted animals of wood": *Ibid.*, p. 38.

p. 98: "mere amenities of life": *Ibid.*, p. 39. These hardy men were, in their way, explorers of sorts in the eyes of the boy.
p. 98: in 1866 or 1867: *The Sea Dreamer*, p. 52, n. 12.
p. 99: "tone of young ivory": *A Personal Record*, p. 40.
p. 99: a futile gesture: *Ibid.*, p. 41.
p. 99: "and solemn witnesses?" *Ibid.*
p. 100: "for an answer": *Ibid.*, p. 42.
p. 100: "name like a reproach": *Ibid.*, p. 44.
p. 101: She later commented: Najder, p. 13; from information provided by Tadeusz Garczyński.
p. 102: "unanswerable invective": p. xiii–xiv. Morf offers Ofelia Buszczyńska, daughter of Stefan Buszczyński, as a more appropriate model for Antonia. *The Polish Shades and Ghosts of Joseph Conrad* (New York: Astra Books, 1976), pp. 78 and 300. There is little evidence for any clear identification.
p. 102: "of Polish womanhood": pp. 28–29.
p. 103: "took my breath away": p. xiv.
p. 103: In the novel proper: Here, the reference seems more definitely to be Janina Taube (*The Arrow of Gold*, p. 3). Baines (p. 30) reconstructs "facts" where no proof exists.
p. 103: "scarred, almost flayed": MS., Yale, canceled passages.
p. 104: "wholly happy experience": *Ibid.*
p. 104: "awakening draws near": July 25, 1914; ALS, Birmingham.
p. 106: "I shall go *there*": *A Personal Record*, p. 13.
p. 106: "victories can give": *Notes on Life and Letters*, p. 54.
p. 106: "bank of an African river": *Last Essays*, p. 24.
p. 106: "place of darkness' ": *Youth and Two Other Stories*, p. 52.
p. 107: "*its* immense solitudes": *Ibid.*, p. 55.
p. 108: "stories. Go on": p. 311.
p. 108: "regretted his surrender": *Notes on Life and Letters*, p. 57.
p. 108: "my other school-work": *Last Essays*, pp. 16–17.
p. 109: "later to other subjects": *Ibid.*, p. 19.
p. 109: "ages of careless usage": p. xiii.
p. 109: "of land and sea": *Last Essays*, p. 22.
p. 109: "into mere vapouring": *Ibid.*, p. 24.
p. 111: "an Admiral in Japan": September 2/14, 1877; Najder, p. 51. Even as Bobrowski wrote Conrad of foreign nationality, his letter recalls his nephew to his Polish roots—Polish names proliferate as Tadeusz explains his financial deals to pay Conrad's allowance. The money arrangements themselves, in rubles and gulden, called Conrad's attention to his background while he was spending in francs and then pounds.
p. 113: ideas of the movement: *Zywy, The Living Conrad* (London: Świderski, 1957), pp. 285–86.
p. 113: reputation outside of Poland: Busza, pp. 174–75, n. 272.
p. 114: document of considerable prescience: The so-called Political Memorandum, written in Polish, and given to Dr. Teodor Kosch, the Cracow lawyer whom Conrad met at Mme Zagórska's pension, "Willa [Villa]

Konstantynówka, in Zakopane. The English text is printed in Krzyżanowski, pp. 123–24.

p. 118: 3/15 October 1874: Najder, p. 193. Until 1881, Conrad's fixed allowance worked out to about $500 a year; then for the next six years, to about $250. But these figures do not include the extras—for clothing, lost gear, travel expenses, and emergencies. The gulden, or Austrian florin, had a value of about two shillings, or close to fifty cents; the rouble, or ruble, had a comparable value in Russian currency.

p. 119: "of imaginative literature": pp. xviii–xix.

p. 119: "condition of good service": p. xix.

p. 119: "we have to do that": p. xx.

p. 119: "limit of prudent sanity": *Ibid.*

p. 120: "of his own integrity": *Ibid.*

p. 120: "appeal of one's work?": *Ibid.*, "To try to go deeper is not to be insensible," he continues, an attempt to define a hermetic art that is not insensitive to human needs, or lacking in compassion.

p. 120: "strength and maladjustment": *Identity: Youth and Crisis* (New York: Norton, 1968), p. 96.

II: THE FRENCH INTERLUDE (1874–1878)

p. 126: "will regret that conversation": July 28/August 8, 1877; Najder, pp. 47–48.

p. 126: that is not his: *Ibid.*, p. 195.

p. 128: "*métier de chien*": p. 122.

p. 128: "*les mers du sud*": *Ibid.*, p. 122.

p. 129: "dazzlingly white teeth": *Ibid.*, pp. 123–24. One senses, even this early in Conrad's career, the shadowy presence of a figure described in his last years, Peyrol, the old sea pirate turned patriot.

p. 130: "in the Gulf of Mexico": p. 5.

p. 130: related to Mme Déléstang: Information from Hans van Marle.

p. 131: "of the *belle Madame Déléstang*": *A Personal Record*, p. 124.

p. 132: "direction of maritime affairs": *Ibid.*, pp. 124–25.

p. 132: "completely temporal religion": *Ibid.*, p. 125.

p. 132: "of independent assertion": *Arrow*, p. 89.

p. 133: "to my 'honoured uncle' ": *A Personal Record*, pp. 125–26.

p. 133: "danger seemed to me": *Ibid.*, p. 126.

p. 134: "voices inside—nothing more": *Ibid.*, pp. 127–28.

p. 134: "was a stunning experience": *Ibid.*, p. 128.

p. 135: "is translated into solid force": *Ibid.*, p. 129.

p. 135: "austere purity of the light": *Ibid.*, p. 135.

p. 135: "of my very dreams!": *Ibid.*, p. 136.

p. 135: "under my open palm": *Ibid.*, p. 137.

p. 136: "only roof over my head": *Ibid.*, pp. 137–38.

p. 137: "why or the wherefore": pp. 152–53.

p. 138: "sustained by discriminating praise": *Ibid.*, p. 24.

p. 138: "art—which *is* art": *Ibid.*
p. 139: "something looks after it": Najder, p. 37.
p. 139: "to make anything fast": Jean-Aubry, *The Sea Dreamer*, pp. 60–61.
p. 140: "were used for this purpose": *Ibid.*, p. 195.
p. 141: "time and their money": *Arrow*, p. 90.
p. 141: Dominic Cervoni: Born in Luri, Corsica, on May 22, 1834 and, thus, more than old enough to be Conrad's father.
p. 141: "of Corsica, not Ithaca": *Mirror*, p. 163.
p. 142: "extremely experienced soul": *Ibid.*, pp. 162–63.
p. 142: "wisdom and audacity": *Arrow*, p. 89.
p. 143: "amused me considerably": p. 8.
p. 144: "whose names don't matter": p. xii.
p. 144: became the partial model for Don José: One says "partial" because Don José, with his "Fifty Years of Misrule," is deeply rooted in Tadeusz Bobrowski with his *Memoirs*, also a history of "misrule."
p. 145: "he's altogether 'invented' ": June 3, 1917; ALS, Yale.
p. 145: "very misleading circumstance": p. xi.
p. 145: "any damaging admissions": p. xii.
p. 146: "do not even imagine": Najder, p. 37.
p. 146: "was the most in need": *Ibid.*, p. 37.
p. 147: from his friend Henry Grand: Tadeusz Bobrowski to Stefan Buszczyński, March 12/24, 1879; *Ibid.*, p. 178.
p. 147: "of helplessness, perhaps": p. 62.
p. 147: "peace and war upon the sea": p. 81.
p. 147: "always the same": p. 82.
p. 148: "one's self for one's actions": Najder, p. 39 (letter is dated October 14/26).
p. 148: "avoid them in the future": *Ibid.*
p. 149: "as much as to yourself": *Ibid.*
p. 149: "not less than yours?": *Ibid.*, pp. 40–41.
p. 150: "and gratify yourself": *Ibid.*, p. 41.
p. 150: "uncertainty and disquiet": *Ibid.*, pp. 41–42.
p. 150: "any tenderness of heart": *Ibid.*, p. 42.
p. 151: "at your own expense": *Ibid.*, p. 43.
p. 151: "easier way of existence": *Ibid.*
p. 152: "must have been in it?": *Ibid.*, p. 44.
p. 152: "what I have asked you": *Ibid.*
p. 152: "May they be effective!!!": *Ibid.*, p. 45.
p. 153: "voyage round the world": March 12/24, 1879; *Ibid.*, p. 176.
p. 154: "discuss it and write": *Ibid.*, pp. 46–47.
p. 154: in Bobrowski's Document: *Ibid.*, p. 197; the other information from Hans van Marle.
p. 155: "the honour to belong": *Ibid.*, p. 47.
p. 156: "serving on French vessels": *Ibid.*, pp. 176 ff.
p. 158: In the episode: *Mirror*, pp. 157 ff.
p. 158: "set of shipowners": *Ibid.*, p. 160.
p. 159: "sluggish around the corpse": *Ibid.*, p. 179.
p. 159: "eyes on ships and oars": *Ibid.*, p. 183.

p. 161: "or romantic reasons": *Arrow,* p. 8.
p. 162: "for a Sunday afternoon": ALS, Lilly.
p. 162: "you let the boy alone' ": Jessie Conrad, *Joseph Conrad and His Circle* (New York: Dutton, 1935), p. 205.
p. 163: "at least not at present' ": *Ibid.,* p. 206.
p. 163: "to return to town": *Ibid.,* p. 207.
p. 164: "and their charity": p. 421.
p. 164: " 'women of all time' ": *Arrow,* pp. 66–67.
p. 164: "sins of the Borgias": "Leonardo Da Vinci," *The Renaissance* (New York: Modern Library, n.d.), p. 103.
p. 165: "eyelids and the hands": *Ibid.,* pp. 103–4.
p. 165: "to the end of time": *Arrow,* pp. 294–95.
p. 167: "not for me alone": *Ibid.,* p. 106.
p. 168: "to their respective males": *The Romantic Agony* (New York: Meridian Books, 1956 [1933]), p. 205.
p. 168: "century, towards masochism": *Ibid.,* p. 206.
p. 168: early uncompleted novel, *The Sisters:* At one time, Conrad thought of calling *The Arrow of Gold* "Doña Rita," but rejected it as being "unlucky" (Letter to Pinker, August 22, 1918; ALS, Berg).
p. 170: Paula de Somogyi: *The Sea Years of Joseph Conrad* (New York: Doubleday, 1965), pp. 52 ff.
p. 170: Conrad's duel with Blunt: *Ibid.,* pp. 87 ff.
p. 171: running on the *Tremolino: Joseph Conrad,* p. 52.
p. 171: "some kind of contraband!": Najder, p. 176.
p. 173: "He is lucky with people": *Ibid.,* p. 177.
p. 173: "in all 3,009 fr.": *Ibid.,* pp. 196–97.
p. 174: "you leave the ship": *Ibid.,* p. 54.
p. 174: "moderation, morality, and renunciation": *The Psychology of Gambling,* eds. Halliday and Fuller (New York: Harper Colophon Books, 1975), p. 177.
p. 174: "from education and experience": *Ibid.,* pp. 178.
p. 176: "to know his profession well": Najder, p. 177.
p. 176: Bobrowski then moves: *Ibid.,* pp. 178 ff.
p. 177: "did not count in reality": p. 182.
p. 178: "or perish utterly": *Ibid.*

III: THE ENGLISH MARINER (1878–1889)

p. 182: "kicking me downstairs": January 14, 1898; ALS, Dartmouth.
p. 183: "have reached its limit?": June 28 / July 8, 1878; Najder, p. 54.
p. 183: "these difficult circumstances' ": *Ibid.*
p. 183: "fantasies of a hobbledehoy": *Ibid.*
p. 183: uncle reminds him: *Ibid.,* pp. 55–56.
p. 184: command of English improved: Nevertheless, as he told Mégroz, he had been tutored at Boult's Coaching School in London as preparation for his officer examinations, to learn maritime terminology in his adopted language.
p. 185: "Eheu! Fugaces!": February 4, 1898; ALS, Dartmouth.

p. 185: English newspaper, the *Standard:* See letter to Joseph de Smet, January 23, 1911; Jean-Aubry, *Joseph Conrad*, II, p. 124.
p. 185: "smile of affectionate recognition": p. 155.
p. 186: "by his social position": *The English Common Reader* (Chicago: Phoenix Edition, 1963 [1957]), p. 173.
p. 186: "London for the first time": pp. 150–51.
p. 187: "to me off the ground": *Ibid.*, pp. 151–52.
p. 187: "entered was Dickensian too": *Ibid.*, p. 152.
p. 187: "eating-house round the corner": *Ibid.*, pp. 152–53.
p. 188: "about getting a ship' ": *Ibid.*, p. 153.
p. 188: "of the glistening roadway": *Ibid.*, p. 149.
p. 188: "What . . .' ": p. 17.
p. 189: "I wish to produce": I, p. 77.
p. 189: "all now up to you": September 2/14, 1878; Najder, p. 58.
p. 190: "with their crews on shore": pp. 121 ff.
p. 190: "rather intelligent, my man' ": p. 123.
p. 190: "geographical and trading circles": May 18/30, 1879; Najder, pp. 179–80.
p. 191: "with me in Marseilles": *Ibid.*, p. 180.
p. 192: "you will obtain naturalization": October 26 / November 7, 1879; *Ibid.*, p. 59.
p. 193: an "antiauthority" personality: A true descendant of Teodor and Apollo Korzeniowski.
p. 194: "can never put into words": *The Collected Works of C. G. Jung* (Princeton: Princeton University Press, 1966), XV, p. 90.
p. 194: "and not an acquisition": p. xii.
p. 194: "binds men to each other": *Ibid.*
p. 195: "and even your life": Najder, p. 60.
p. 195: during his stay with Ward: Norman Sherry, *Conrad's Western World* (Cambridge, England: Cambridge University Press, 1971), p. 328. Sherry also speculates that Krieger became a partial model for Adolf Verloc in *The Secret Agent*, pp. 328 ff.
p. 196: "to sit for it shortly": Najder, p. 62.
p. 196: "for not having succeeded": *Ibid.*, p. 63.
p. 196: "your work and determination": *Ibid.*, pp. 63 ff.
p. 197: "offered in social roles": Erik Erikson, *Childhood and Society* (New York: Norton, 1950), p. 261.
p. 198: "in terms of eternity": pp. 112 ff.
p. 199: "patronage to support you": June 5/17, 1880; Najder, p. 64.
p. 199: "more good than bad people": *Ibid.*, pp. 64–5.
p. 199: "may God always help you!": *Ibid.*, p. 65.
p. 199: "will astound the whole world!": June 28 (old style), 1880; *Ibid.*, pp. 66 ff.
p. 200: of about $500 annually: After 1881, this was cut in half, but continued for another six years.
p. 200: "over for her speed": p. 39.
p. 200: "only in one's dreams": *Ibid.*, pp. 40 ff.
p. 201: "from the English wool-clipper": *Last Essays*, p. 51.

p. 201: he wrote: ALS, Berg.
p. 202 "conjunction of water and sky": *Mirror*, pp. 137–38.
p. 202: "become a seaman at last": *Ibid.*, pp. 141–42.
p. 204: "than could be expected": May 1/13, 1881; Najder, p. 67.
p. 205: "to a loss of energy": *Ibid.*, p. 69.
p. 205: "giving pleasure to others": June 16/28, 1881; *Ibid.*, pp. 71–2.
p. 206: "as well as we can": August 3/15, 1881; *Ibid.*, pp. 72–3.
p. 206: "no one thinks of the poor": *Ibid.*, p. 75.
p. 206: "got into debt": *Ibid.*, p. 73.
p. 207: "of his craft, and useful": September 11/23, 1881; *Ibid.*, p. 79.
p. 207: "and ends in myself": *Youth*, p. xix.
p. 207: "600 roubles means a lot": Najder, p. 78.
p. 208: "new billet for a fortune": *Youth*, pp. 4–5.
p. 208: "a leak on 24 December 1881": Baines, p. 70.
p. 209: "the sake of a blackguardly profit": January 8/20, 1882; Najder, p. 81.
p. 209: "loafers and dishonest boatmen": *Youth*, p. 16.
p. 209: "and the desire to work": Najder, p. 84.
p. 210: "and a whole society": *Ibid.*
p. 211: "real elements of the people": September 11/23, 1881; *Ibid.*, pp. 79–80.
p. 211: "and possibly something more": *Ibid.*, p. 80.
p. 211: "of their strength": pp. 41–2.
p. 212: "arriving on 22nd March": Norman Sherry, *Conrad's Eastern World* (Cambridge, England: Cambridge University Press, 1966), pp. 297–98.
p. 213: "full of anger and promise' ": p. 41.
p. 213: "ourselves from being burnt' ": p. 20.
p. 213: "wasn't a patch on it' ": p. 15.
p. 214: "and without any glamour": To Richard Curle, April 24, 1922; TLS, Lilly.
p. 214: Bobrowski agreed to lend: Document, Najder, p. 200.
p. 215: forwarded Conrad's allowance: *Ibid.*, p. 199.
p. 215: 6, Dynevor Road, Stoke Newington: Jean-Aubry, *Joseph Conrad*, I, p. 88, n. 1.
p. 215: "citizen of the world": May 24/June 5, 1883; Najder, p. 88.
p. 215: "pleasure for us both": *Ibid.*, p. 90.
p. 216: "no doubt are by now": June 27/July 9, 1883; *Ibid.*, p. 92.
p. 217: "uric acids and salts": *Ibid.*, p. 93.
p. 217: replacement as second officer: For further details, see Geoffrey Ursell.
p. 218: "could tell for certain": *Chance*, p. 31.
"Conrad and the 'Riversdale,' " *TLS*, July 11, 1968.
p. 218: "who embrace it": *Chance*, p. 31.
p. 218: "and the Far East": Jean-Aubry, *Joseph Conrad*, I, pp. 76–7.
p. 219: "of an indirect reflection": *The Philosophy of Literary Form* (New York: Vintage Books, 1957 [1941]), p. 54.
p. 220: "that I left the *Narcissus*": Jean-Aubry, *Joseph Conrad*, I, pp. 77–8.
p. 220: "a loud sigh of wind": *Nigger*, pp. 27–8.
p. 220: be clearly identified: Allen, p. 166; Baines, p. 76.
p. 221: "if he should succeed in passing": Jean-Aubry, *Joseph Conrad*, I, p. 82 (facing).

p. 221: "subject of 'the Day's Work' ": From Hans van Marle.
p. 221: "far from being beautiful": pp. 114 ff.
p. 222: "enough to save them": pp. 116–17.
p. 222: "good luck to serve under": p. 9.
p. 222: "you have a ship, too": *Ibid.*, p. 10.
p. 223: "visited in that way": *Ibid.*
p. 224: "the darkness of oblivion": Copy from the Spiridion (Kliszczewski) family. Jean-Aubry's printing of the letter contains errors of detail and phrase (*Joseph Conrad*, I, p. 80).
p. 224: "Say the 20th": ALS, Berg.
p. 226: "the crashing avalanche?": I, p. 84. Jean-Aubry's printing and my copy from the Spiridion family differ only in minor details. Neither appears more authoritative than the other. My copy has "heard" instead of "herd," and such differences.
p. 227: "necessary—but *love* it": *Ecce Homo*, translated by Walter Kaufmann (New York: Vintage Books, 1969), p. 258.
p. 227: "frenzy of revenge": *Thus Spoke Zarathustra*, 2nd Part, translated by Walter Kaufmann (New York: Viking Portable, 1970), p. 212.
p. 228: "time been bringing me": October 28/November 9; Najder, p. 152.
p. 229: "and affecting the future": *Ibid.*, pp. 153–54.
p. 229: "their family or country": *Ibid.*, p. 154.
p. 230: came on January 6, 1886: The original is at the Lilly Library, in Conrad's holograph.
p. 231: "Sir, as you please": March 24/April 5, 1886; Najder, p. 100.
p. 231: "to secure more orders": *Ibid.*, pp. 101–2.
p. 232: "in sugar and flour": April 12/24, 1886; *Ibid.*, p. 103.
p. 232: He wrote still another,: June 24/July 6, 1886; *Ibid.*, p. 104.
p. 232: "let me know how it went": *Ibid.*, p. 106.
p. 232: master's examination and failed: Information from Hans van Marle.
p. 233: "a very considerable thing indeed": pp. 120–21. By "vindicating himself," Conrad had grown a second skin; he had shed Apollo Korzeniowski's heritage and taken on his own identity as Conrad.
p. 233: "carrying out the Agreement?": October 28/November 9, 1886; Najder, p. 112.
p. 234: "you must do further": November 14/26, 1886; Najder, pp. 114–15.
p. 234: " 'My Experiences as a Sailor' ": Baines, p. 85.
p. 235: "my first serious work": January 19, 1922; TL and ALS, Berg.
p. 235: "it was his first story": In George T. Keating's copy of *Tales of Hearsay: A Conrad Memorial Library*, p. 365.
p. 235: "I shall say so!' ": R. L. Mégroz, *Joseph Conrad's Mind and Method* (New York: Russell & Russell, 1964 [1931]), p. 88.
p. 236: "inland people, aren't you?' ": *A Personal Record*, p. 118.
p. 238: "on barges and schuyts": p. 48.
p. 238: "in the cabin stove": *Ibid.*, pp. 49 ff.
p. 238: "tone of remonstrance or discontent": *Ibid.*, p. 51.
p. 239: "dripping with melting snow": *Ibid.*, p. 52.
p. 239: "till you get it?": *Typhoon*, p. 33.
p. 239: "or by the sea": *Ibid.*, p. 19.

p. 239: "keeping on his feet": p. 53.
p. 239: "along the main deck": *Ibid.*, p. 54.
p. 240: "to see another sunrise": p. 56.
p. 240: "old age comes doubt!": August 8/20, 1887; Najder, p. 117.
p. 240: "line of mine in print": *A Personal Record*, p. 87.
p. 242: "and a Syed at that": pp. 4 ff.
p. 242: "and carried me off" *Ibid.*, p. 5.
p. 242: "which is the art of arts": *Nigger*, p. xiii.
p. 244: "nominal power of Holland": p. 34.
p. 244: hopeful mien, and favorable future: Anyone who delves into this aspect of Conrad's life and work must be grateful for the previous research of Dr. John D. Gordan, Ms. Jerry Allen, and Professor Norman Sherry.
p. 245: "particularly atrocious ghosts": pp. 74–5.
p. 245: Conrad never met him: Sherry, *Conrad's Eastern World*, p. 90.
p. 246: "immobility of a day-dream": pp. 68 ff.
p. 247: "reviewing his own experience": p. 25.
p. 247: born in 1824: See Allen, pp. 209 ff.
p. 247: Sherry shows that: Sherry, *Conrad's Eastern World*, p. 93.
p. 248: as the Brow: *Ibid.*, p. 119.
p. 248: told Jean-Aubry in 1924: Jean-Aubry, *Joseph Conrad*, I, p. 98.
p. 249: "of that fateful event": pp. ix–x.
p. 249: This interplay of wards: See *Conrad's Eastern World*, p. 133. Coming at this material from very different perspectives, Professor Sherry and I have reached similar conclusions.
p. 250: His Malayan reading: See John D. Gordan, *Joseph Conrad: The Making of a Novelist* (Cambridge, Mass.: Harvard University Press, 1941), Chapter II; Baines, p. 254; *Conrad's Eastern World*, Chapter 7.
p. 251: Although it is doubtful: For a differing point of view, see *Conrad's Eastern World*, p. 137.
p. 251: we know that Jim: Allen, p. 228.
p. 252: "truth enshrined therein": ALS, Yale.
p. 254: an account of the voyage: *Last Essays*, pp. 26 ff.
p. 255: "continent on the other": *Ibid.*, p. 28.
p. 255: to chart the route: The chart is part of the Keating Collection at Yale.
p. 255: "under the sinking sun": *Last Essays*, p. 30.
p. 255: "of perfect peace": *Ibid.*, p. 31.
p. 255: Jean-Aubry uncovered: *The Sea Dreamer*, Chapter VII; also, Baines, pp. 95 ff. The original material is in *Essor*, February 15, 1931; and *Radical*, August 7, 1931.
p. 255: Savinien Mérédac: Nom de plume of Auguste Esnouf.
p. 256: "He had vigorous, extremely mobile": I am using Baines's translation, pp. 510 ff.
p. 257: we can believe Jean-Aubry's account: *The Sea Dreamer*, pp. 141 ff. (The fictional presentation comes in "A Smile of Fortune.")
p. 259: "near you in my thoughts": *Ibid.*, p. 145.
p. 259: "A Smile of Fortune": It appeared in *London Magazine* in February 1911, but is more accessible in *'Twixt Land and Sea*.
p. 260: "her indifference was seductive": *'Twixt Land and Sea*, p. 59.

p. 260: "might retire with honor": *Joseph Conrad: A Psychoanalytic Biography* (Princeton: Princeton University Press, 1967), p. 77.
p. 260: "to have roots anywhere": Jean-Aubry, *The Sea Dreamer*, p. 145.
p. 261: "of your future success": *Ibid.*, p. 147.

IV: IN LEOPOLD'S CONGO (1889–1890)

p. 265: "wouldn't even look at me": *Youth*, pp. 51–2.
p. 266: "without fear of men": *A Personal Record*, p. 69.
p. 266: "produced a favourable impression": *Ibid.*, pp. 69 ff.
p. 267: "thinking of the man Almayer": *Ibid.*, pp. 73–4.
p. 268: "by ages of careless usage": *Nigger*, p. xiii.
p. 269: "changed into its absence": *Mallarmé* (Chicago: Phoenix Books, 1962 [1953]), p. 58.
p. 269: "of the Laws of Nature": Letter of June 20, 1913; ALS, Duke. There were, as well, other extensive influences on Conrad when he wrote his Preface: Pater's work, the arguments over naturalism and impressionism (in painting), Maupassant's preface to *Pierre et Jean*, and even, as some critics claim, Brunetière and his essay "Impressionism in the Novel." For the last, see Eloise Knapp Hay, "Joseph Conrad and Impressionism," *The Journal of Aesthetics and Art Criticism*, XXXIV/2 (Winter 1976), pp. 137–44.
p. 270: "admiration full of respect": ALS, Yale.
p. 270: treatment of his Mercenaries: November 11, 1909; ALS, private collection.
p. 270: "made the art of fiction": "Techniques of Fiction," in *The Man of Letters in the Modern World* (London: Meridian Books, 1957), p. 91.
p. 271: "n'a jamais existé!": ALS, Yale.
p. 273: "in the depths of the land": *Youth*, p. 52.
p. 273: In the letter to Thys: November 4, 1889; Jean-Aubry, ed., *Lettres françaises* (Paris: Gallimard, 1929), p. 25.
p. 273: that on September 24 wrote to Thys: See Jean-Aubry, "Joseph Conrad au Congo," *Mercure de France*, CLXXXIII (October 15, 1925), pp. 296–97.
p. 274: "*Mr. Konrad has cost*": Najder, p. 201.
p. 274: sum of four hundred rubles: *Ibid.*
p. 274: Thus, at thirty-one, Conrad was finally on his own: His allowance proper ended at thirty, in 1887; as Bobrowski wrote in his Document: "In view of the fact that in November [Old Style] you will reach the age of thirty, by which time everyone ought to be self-supporting . . . I told you that I must discontinue a regular allowance" (*Ibid.*)
p. 276: "and expense of leaving": *Lettres françaises*, p. 28.
p. 276: "if such was my fancy' ": *Youth*, p. 53.
p. 276: Conrad wrote (on January 16, 1890): Najder, p. 206. (The original letter is at Yale, on paper with Barr, Moering letterhead.)
p. 277: "with you in Cracow": *Ibid.*, p. 207.
p. 277: "perhaps to no avail": January 20, 1890; *Ibid.* (Original at Yale, on Barr, Moering stationery.)

p. 277: on the thirty-first: *Ibid.*, p. 208.
p. 280: "and part simply as friends": July 18/30, 1891; Najder, p. 148.
p. 280: "for a compassionate mother": p. 101. The letter Dr. Meyer quotes from is one Conrad wrote on October 16, 1891 (ALS, Yale).
p. 280: only a month before: September 15,1891; ALS, Yale.
p. 281: "will not go through": ALS, Yale.
p. 282: "concerning my affairs": ALS, Yale.
p. 283: "no end of coin by trade": *Youth*, p. 55.
p. 283: "I passed two whole weeks": May 22, 1890; Najder, p. 211. (French translation of original at Yale, in the Jean-Aubry archives.)
p. 284: "*du calme. Adieu'* ": *Youth*, pp. 58 ff.
p. 284: "centre of the earth' ": *Ibid.*, p. 60.
p. 284: the *Ville de Maceio* on May 6: Information for this comes from two letters Conrad wrote to Maria Tyszkowa (daughter of Kazimierz Bobrowski), May 2, May 6, 1890. (Najder, p. 209, p. 210; originals in *Ruch Literacki*, Warsaw, 1927, No. 5.)
p. 284: "his mind to it": May 15, 1890; ALS, Yale. This is Conrad at his most Hamletic; he was even replacing a Dane!
p. 284: "went *there* too": *A Personal Record*, p. 13.
p. 285: "for this trouble myself": May 22, 1890; Najder, p. 211.
p. 285: "cursing the stones": June 10, 1890; ALS, Yale.
p. 285: "sinister backcloth": *Youth*, p. 61.
p. 286: "Nothing could happen": *Ibid.*, pp. 61–2.
p. 288: "from beyond the seas": *Ibid.*, pp. 66–7.
p. 288: "as much as possible": *Last Essays*, pp. 238–39.
p. 289: "remained on the coast": May 24, 1916; ALS, NYPL (Quinn Collection).
p. 289: "good up to now": *Last Essays*, pp. 239 ff.
p. 289: "Twenty days of caravan": June 18, 1890; ALS, Yale.
p. 290: a wasted landscape of industrial junk: *Youth*, pp. 63 ff.
p. 291: "No birds of prey seen by me": *Last Essays*, pp. 241–43.
p. 291: "Passed a bad night": *Ibid.*, p. 244.
p. 292: "in a Christian country": *Youth*, p. 71.
p. 292: "sick of this fun": *Last Essays*, p. 245.
p. 292: "Sky clouded": *Ibid.*, pp. 247 ff.
p. 292: "in the form of a cross": *Ibid.*, pp. 250 ff.
p. 292: "bullet on coming out": *Ibid.*, p. 253. If the wound is shifted from head to chest, it was not unlike Conrad's own self-inflicted one.
p. 293: "than page by page": p. 19.
p. 293: "turn of the Congo": p. 14. Also, see Gordan, p. 179.
p. 294: "in me for this project": Najder, p. 133.
p. 294: "while he is here": September 26, 1890; ALS, Yale.
p. 295: Norman Sherry ascribes: Sherry, *Conrad's Western World*, pp. 45 ff.
p. 295: derive from the id: Part of what follows is indebted to Sherry's *Conrad's Western World*, Chapter 7.
p. 296: as his Diary shows: This part of the diary is not reproduced in *Last Essays;* it is in the library of Harvard University.
p. 297: "gliding here and there": *Youth*, p. 121.

p. 297: known of him through hearsay: Sherry, *Conrad's Western World*, Chapter 11.
p. 298: "who inhabit it": ALS, Yale.
p. 298: "for a year or longer": September 24, 1890; Najder, p. 213. (Original in *Ruch Literacki*, Warsaw, 1927, No. 5.)
p. 298: "which is being got ready": *Ibid.*, p. 211.
p. 299: "cruel without courage": *Youth*, pp. 87 ff.
p. 300: "to such deadly diseases": Jean-Aubry, *Joseph Conrad*, I, p. 140.

V: THE WRITER (1891–1899)

p. 305: "to it in the future": December 15/27, 1890; Najder, pp. 135 ff.
p. 306: "and look elsewhere": February 1, 1891; ALS, Yale.
p. 307: nor the language: As he admitted later to Hugh Clifford, in a letter on May 17, 1898, in Jean-Aubry, *Joseph Conrad*, I, p. 237.
p. 307: "has gained control over him": "Franz Kafka," *Illuminations* (New York: Schocken Books, 1969 [1955]), p. 126.
p. 307: "to well-made dolls": October 16, 1891; ALS, Yale.
p. 308: "forget their singing": Franz Kafka, *The Complete Stories*, ed. Nahum Glatzer (New York: Schocken Books, 1971), p. 431.
p. 308: it required hydrotherapy: In all, Conrad underwent treatment at Champel on four occasions, in 1891, 1894, 1895, and 1907.
p. 309: "neither more nor *less*": ALS, Yale.
p. 309: he wrote to Graham: ALS, Dartmouth.
p. 310: "and not a human being": Jung, p. 101.
p. 310: "by a suprahuman design": *Ibid.*, pp. 95–6.
p. 311: on February 8, on February 17 (the twenty-seventh): ALS, Yale.
p. 311: From Bobrowski's letter: Of March 12/24, 1891; Najder, p. 143.
p. 311: On March 30, to Marguerite: ALS, Yale.
p. 311: "with the greatest difficulty": Najder, p. 213. (Original in *Ruch Literacki*, Warsaw, 1927, No. 5.)
p. 311: "only nightmares": May 10, 1891; ALS, Yale.
p. 311: "decline and fall": p. 14.
p. 312: "unwise to bother you": ALS, Yale.
p. 312: "more clarity and lucidity": Najder, p. 141.
p. 312: "before having known it": ALS, Yale.
p. 313: "as a girl of sixteen": September 6/18, 1892; Najder, p. 165.
p. 313: "English girl, Jessie George": pp. 109–10.
p. 314: "over your servant": August 26, 1891; ALS, Yale.
p. 314: "of a waterside warehouse": p. 14.
p. 314: "me greatly, my dear lad": Najder, pp. 150–51.
p. 314: "the population of this city": September 15, 1891; ALS, Yale.
p. 315: "(according to Descartes) is impossible": October 16, 1891; ALS, Yale.
p. 315: "your future with equanimity": October 28/November 9, 1891; Najder, pp. 152 ff.
p. 316: Conrad announced to Marguerite: ALS, Yale.
p. 316: "best remedy for pessimism": November 20/December 2, 1891; Najder, p. 157.

p. 317: "boat in heavy weather": *Last Essays*, p. 34.
p. 317: "the greater success": *Ibid.*, p. 39.
p. 317: "has stripped of hope": March 5, 1892; ALS, Yale.
p. 317: suggesting a common epilepsy: *Ibid.*, p. 158, n.1; also see Najder's introduction, p. 9.
p. 318: a letter from Uncle Tadeusz: May 2/14, 1892; Najder, pp. 161 ff.
p. 318: "by false appearances or friends": July 2/14, 1892; *ibid.*, p. 163.
p. 318: "There is nothing to be done!": October 5/17, 1892; *ibid.*, p. 168. Also see letter for September 6/18, 1892; Najder, p. 164.
p. 319: "to call himself a man": September 4, 1892; ALS, Yale.
p. 319: "admit him to be stupid": October 19, 1892; ALS, Yale.
p. 319: In *A Personal Record:* pp. 15 ff.
p. 320: "come off the ship": *Ibid.*, p. 16.
p. 321: "Yes! Perfectly.": *Ibid.*, pp. 17–18.
p. 321: " 'uniform gray' awaiting me": February 3, 1893; ALS, Yale.
p. 321: "Reminiscences of Conrad": This appeared in the issue of *La Nouvelle Revue Française* that memorialized Conrad, and was translated into French by André Maurois.
p. 323: "on which I draw freely": H. V. Marrot, *The Life and Letters of John Galsworthy* (London: Heinemann, 1935), p. 88.
p. 324: letters from Bobrowski: For May 10/22, 1893; also, July 1/13, 1893—the last extant letter from Bobrowski to Conrad, in Najder, pp. 169, 171.
p. 324: "packed in the bag": *A Personal Record*, p. 19.
p. 324: "I were a little child": September 14, 1893; ALS, Yale.
p. 325: "whole idea is very funny": *Ibid.*
p. 325: "Arabs and half castes": p. 9.
p. 325: "I am writing these lines": November 5, 1893; ALS, Yale.
p. 326: "to capture his visions": *A Personal Record*, p. 8.
p. 326: "realities of sea life": *Ibid.*, pp. 9 ff.
p. 326: He wrote Marguerite: December 6, 1893; ALS, Yale.
p. 326: "who knows where else?": December 18, 1893; ALS, Yale.
p. 326: "off the Australian coast": December 20, 1893; ALS, Yale.
p. 327: " 'Almayer's Folly' was begun": *A Personal Record*, p. 3.
p. 327: "setting of light music": *Ibid.*, p. 5.
p. 327: "when I've finished it": ALS, Yale.
p. 327: "succeeded in producing!": February 2, 1894; ALS, Yale.
p. 328: "mon ame avec lui": February 18, 1894; ALS, Yale.
p. 328: "of a piece of bad news": Meyer, p. 103.
p. 328: could not do meaningful work: Albert J. Guerard, *Conrad the Novelist* (Cambridge: Harvard University Press, 1958), p. 11.
p. 329: "but difficult to find": March 2, 1894; ALS, Yale.
p. 330: "encounter of indistinct ideas": ALS, Yale.
p. 330: "in a quarter of an hour": April 16, 1894; ALS, Yale.
p. 330: met Miss Jessie George: Jean-Aubry says Conrad made the acquaintance of Jessie in "October or November, 1893," but he seems to be off by a year. (See *A Sea Dreamer*, p. 212.)
p. 331: In his next two letters: For late April 1894 and May 2, 1894; ALS, Yale.
p. 331: "distinguished critic, Edmund Gosse": May 17, 1894; ALS, Yale.

p. 331: a June letter: June (?), 1894; ALS, Yale.
p. 331: "des romans anonymes": July 12, 1894; ALS, Yale.
p. 332: "divine privilege of thought": July (?) 20, 1894; ALS, Yale.
p. 333: "or the day after": July (?) 25, 1894; ALS, Yale.
p. 333: "for a very long time": ALS, Yale.
p. 333: August 18 letter: ALS, Yale.
p. 333: "K. has collaborated there": August 18, 1894; ALS, Yale.
p. 334: "interesting without any women?": *Ibid.*
p. 334: Garnett's words encouraged him: Unless by "encouraged" Conrad meant he was urged to continue what he had already begun.
p. 335: "either written or typed": September 8, 1894; ALS, Berg.
p. 335: "for several ships": October 2, 1894; ALS, Yale.
p. 335: "competent and charming writer": October 4, 1894; ALS, Rosenbach.
p. 335: "their position as 'under dogs' ": Garnett, p. 2.
p. 336: "a much better check": October 10, 1894; ALS, Yale.
p. 336: "made me an author": Garnett, p. 3.
p. 337: "soon be going to sea' ": *Ibid.*, pp. 3–4.
p. 337: October 10 letter: ALS, Yale.
p. 338: "contempt for Literature itself": From *The Pen and the Book*, quoted by John Gross, *The Rise and Fall of the Man of Letters* (New York: Macmillan, 1969), p. 200.
p. 339: Ford was to draw attention: *Joseph Conrad: A Personal Remembrance* (New York: Octagon Books, 1971 [1924]), p. 97.
p. 339: "to make their acquaintance": Jessie Conrad, *Joseph Conrad: As I Knew Him* (New York: Doubleday, 1926), p. 41.
p. 339: "mutual friend" (Hope): p. 101. Also, see note to page 331 in which Jean-Aubry speaks of a late 1893 meeting.
p. 340: "in some fishing village": Najder, p. 215. (Original is in *Pion*, Warsaw, 1934, No. 50.)
p. 341: "makes me pull out my hair": October 29/November 5, 1894; ALS, Yale.
p. 342: "suicide, still through vanity": *Ibid.*
p. 342: "will be ruined, alas!": November 14 or 21, 1894; ALS, Yale.
p. 343: "who have true courage": December 6 or 13, 1894; ALS, Yale.
p. 343: "that has created them": December 27, 1894; ALS, Yale.
p. 343: he wrote Marguerite: On February 23, 1895; ALS, Yale.
p. 343: his brief letter to Chesson: January (?) 9, 1895; ALS, private collection.
p. 344: "which I do not doubt?!": March 8, 1895; ALS, McGregor, Va.
p. 344: The section in question: *An Outcast of the Islands*, p. 135.
p. 344: "disguises very deep feeling": March 12, 1895; ALS, Yale.
p. 344: "handful of blue earth": March 15, 1895; ALS, Colgate.
p. 345: "paralyze thought and will": April 30, 1895; ALS, Yale.
p. 345: Conrad wrote Garnett: May 1, 1895; ALS, Colgate.
p. 347: in the *Critic:* May 11, 1895.
p. 348: "in their own language": February 14, 1901; Najder, p. 234. (Original in the Warsaw National Library.)
p. 348: "to the voice of my own self' ": *Almayer*, p. 179.
p. 348: "no need for any record": *Ibid.*, p. 190.

p. 349: "both banks of the Pantai": *Ibid.*, p. 131.
p. 350: "with age and dirt": *Ibid.*, pp. 199–200.
p. 350: Writing to Edward Noble: October 28, 1895; ALS, Rosenbach.
p. 351: *Saturday Review:* June 15, 1895.
p. 351: *Weekly Sun:* June 9, 1895.
p. 351: The *Atheneum* critic, the *Daily Chronicle* reviewer, James Ashcroft Noble in the *Academy:* Respectively, May 25; May 11; June 15.
p. 351: he had met the Briquel family: Many of the details which follow derive from Najder's researches.
p. 352: Emilie's diary: Her diary and letters from Conrad are in the possession of her daughter, Mme Françoise Meykiechel. Najder used some of the material in an article called "Conrad in Love," and the letters appeared with some errors in *Les Nouvelles littéraires,* August 6, 1964.
p. 354: "we must help make triumphant": ALS, private collection (Meykiechel).
p. 354: "is not worth the trouble": ALS, private collection (Meykiechel).
p. 354: long letter to Ted Sanderson: I, pp. 176 ff. This important letter, unfortunately, is the sole one of Conrad's 74 to the Sandersons for which no original has turned up. The others are at Yale.
p. 356: writing Emilie Briquel: ALS, private collection (Meykiechel).
p. 357: "light but poisonous lies": ALS, private collection (Meykiechel).
p. 357: "16th inst at 4 p.m.": Garnett, p. 39.
p. 357: "very near my heart": *Outcast,* p. ix.
p. 358: "the end was at hand": Garnett, pp. 8 ff.
p. 358: "in a dismal failure": September 24, 1895; ALS, Berg.
p. 360: Conrad explained to Garnett: *Ibid.*
p. 360: in a letter to Noble: October 28, 1895; ALS, Rosenbach.
p. 361: "close contact by every pore": *Outcast,* p. 140.
p. 361: "an all-pervading discontent": *Ibid.*, p. 56.
p. 362: "is better than strife": *Ibid.*, pp. 80–81.
p. 362: "to witness his slow agony": *Ibid.*, p. 39.
p. 363: "Night already": *Ibid.*, p. 360.
p. 363: "about tropical countries": *Ibid.*, pp. 360–61.
p. 363: He had told Noble: October 28, 1895; ALS, Rosenbach.
p. 363: "dismal lie to me": November 2, 1895; ALS, Rosenbach.
p. 364: Writing to Mlle Briquel: November 14, 1895; ALS, private collection. Conrad mentions in passing: "I find myself now with a law suit on my hands! There is nothing more alien to my tastes and habits!" The episode is unclear, but possibly it was connected to his activities on behalf of Hope's brother-in-law Rorke; or, more likely, the result of a further deal with a man named Maharg and some claims on another reef.
p. 364: the *Bookman:* Vol. LXVI, No. 5. *The Sisters* was reissued by Ugo Mursia in 1968, in Milan, with Ford's introduction. (All references will be to this edition.)
p. 365: "to say the last word": *The Sisters,* p. 34.
p. 365: "immense and tormenting Idea": *Ibid.*, pp. 56 ff.
p. 366: "the most hopeless of all": *Ibid.*, pp. 18 ff.
p. 366: "out of opposed race natures": *Ibid.*, p. 20.

p. 366: by Garnett's adverse criticism: Which we pick up in Conrad's letter to Garnett for March 23, 1896; Garnett, p. 46.

p. 367: "marriage, and family life": p. 115.

p. 368: "idiotic mystery of Heaven": Garnett, p. 46.

p. 369: "In a week—a fortnight?' ": *Joseph Conrad and His Circle*, p. 12.

p. 369: "would not live long": *Ibid.*

p. 370: "no bother at all": April 9, 1896; ALS, Yale.

p. 370: "unworthy even of a curse?": April 13, 1896; ALS, McGregor, Va.

p. 371: *National Observer:* April 18, 1896.

p. 371: *Saturday Review:* May 16, 1896.

p. 373: "such a signal proof": May 18, 1896; ALS, Illinois.

p. 373: "reading your next book": May 11, 1896; Jean-Aubry, ed., *Twenty Letters to Joseph Conrad* (London: First Edition Club, 1926), 8 pamphlets without pagination, numbering, and sequence.

p. 373: "W. Henley—you know": May 22, 1896; ALS, Texas. (In his reprinting of the letter, Garnett [p. 52] has mistakenly dated it May 24.)

p. 374: "to bore you really": May 25, 1896; ALS, Illinois.

p. 375: he was expressing to Garnett: May 22, 1896; ALS, Texas.

p. 376: "stick to the fingers": June 2, 1896; ALS, Colgate.

p. 376: "at that—for two pence": June 6, 1896; Garnett, pp. 56–57.

p. 376: "try some other way": June 10, 1896; ALS, Yale.

p. 376: "harmonize with the drama": These and several other Garnett letters to Conrad are reproduced in *The Garnett Family* by Carolyn G. Heilbrun (New York: Macmillan, 1961).

p. 376: his raving in Polish: *Joseph Conrad and His Circle*, p. 26.

p. 377: "admitted to be necessary": June 19, 1896; Garnett, p. 59.

p. 378: mentioned by Jessie: *Joseph Conrad: As I Knew Him*, p. 27.

p. 378: *Indian Magazine and Review:* For June 1896. This information comes from S. Mario Curreli.

p. 378: "incertitude over every word!" July 22, 1896; ALS, Yale.

p. 378: or at best circumstantial: According to this reasoning, Conrad already had the first pages of *Jim* in hand when Blackwood asked for another submission in the spring of 1898. (See Author's Note to *Lord Jim*, p. viii.) Eloise Knapp Hay argues that Conrad may have made his notes for the novel in Teofila Bobrowska's commonplace book as far back as his honeymoon in 1896. To strengthen her circumstantial argument, Hay cites a brief note for *The Rescue* on the verso of the final page of the "Tuan Jim" sketch. Since *The Rescue* goes back to the summer of 1896, there is some possible connection to an early idea of *Jim* (Hay, *Comparative Literature*, XII [Fall 1960], pp. 289–309).

p. 379: "while I wrote": to Unwin, July 22, 1896; ALS, Yale.

p. 379: "fit only to be stoned": August 5, 1896; Garnett, p. 63.

p. 379: "the persons and feelings": *Ibid.*, p. 64.

p. 379: "I am afraid of it": *Ibid.*

p. 380: Answering Garnett's criticism: August 14, 1896; ALS, Colgate. In this letter, Conrad called his friend "my literary father."

p. 380: "of every artistic endeavour": August 22, 1896; ALS, Berg.

p. 380: Conrad mentions it: To Adolf Krieger, June 28, 1897; private collection; to Unwin, July 2, 1897; ALS, Brotherton.
p. 381: "jerry-built rabbit hutch": Jessie Conrad, *Joseph Conrad and His Circle,* p. 44.
p. 381: very possibly in mid-June: Gordan speculates on June 10 (p. 226).
p. 381: October 19 letter to Unwin: 1896; ALS, Yale.
p. 381: six days later to Garnett: October 25, 1896; Garnett, p. 72.
p. 382: "lived and worked": To Unwin, October 19, 1896; ALS, Yale.
p. 382: "burden of my gratitude": ALS, Texas.
p. 382: Many critics have written: Two excellent descriptions of the relationship are available: in Leon Edel's *Henry James: The Master* 1901–1916, the chapter called "A Master Mariner" (Philadelphia: Lippincott, 1972); Ian Watt's "Conrad, James and *Chance*," in *Imagined Worlds: Essays on Some English Novels and Novelists in Honour of John Butt,* eds. Maynard Mack and Ian Gregor (London: Methuen, 1968).
p. 383: By November 1: In a letter to Garnett, November 1, 1896; Garnett, p. 74.
p. 384: he asked Garnett: November 6, 1896; ALS, Berg.
p. 384: "cannot be called work": Translated by Jacques Barzun (New York: New Directions, 1954), p. 15.
p. 385: "put into a sentence": November 21, 1896; ALS, Yale.
p. 385: "trivial enough on the surface": November 29, 1896; ALS, Colgate.
p. 386: reports to Unwin: December 6, 1896; ALS, Yale.
p. 386: Christmas visit to the Kliszczewskis: The grandson of Joseph Spiridion (Kliszczewski), Dr. Jan Spiridion, told me that, according to his father, Conrad "spent several months writing a part of *The Nigger of the 'Narcissus'* in the family home in Cathedral Road, Cardiff"; this was before his marriage in March 1896. The dating seems unlikely, since Conrad had only a few pages in hand in Brittany on his honeymoon, not the results of several months of application. Possibly, his father had in mind the Christmas of 1896. Much, also, has been written of Conrad's falling out with Joseph Spiridion (see Morf, *Polish Shades,* pp. 90 ff.). According to this, Spiridion had asked Conrad why he did not inform the English about Poland's sufferings, and Conrad is reputed to have replied: "Ah, mon ami, que voulez-vous? I would lose my public!" The falling out, if it did occur, could not have been too severe, because in Conrad's letters supplied to me by the family Conrad was tapping Spiridion for steady loans of £5 to £20.
p. 386: he tells the Zagórskis: Najder, p. 217. (Original in *Droga,* Warsaw, 1928, No. 6.)
p. 386: he can tell Unwin: ALS, Colgate.
p. 387: "not a shameful failure": January 27, 1897; ALS, Yale.
p. 389: "as clean plate glass": To Garnett, February 13, 1897; Garnett, p. 89.
p. 389: "but not an artist": Harris Wilson, ed., *Arnold Bennett & H. G. Wells* (Urbana: University of Illinois Press, 1960), pp. 38–9, dated December 8, 1897.
p. 390: "essence of life": February 2, 1897; ALS, Yale.
p. 390: Jessie feared: *Joseph Conrad and His Circle,* pp. 50 ff.

p. 390: "to live for—at last!": To Garnett, February 19, 1897; ALS, Berg.
p. 390: on his writing table: That is, no novel that he was capable of completing.
p. 391: he told Helen Watson: March 14, 1897; ALS, Yale.
p. 391: he could even tell Garnett: February 28, 1897; Garnett, p. 91.
p. 391: "necessity than anything else": April 5, 1897; ALS, Berg.
p. 391: He indicates that: April 14, 1897; ALS, Brotherton.
p. 392: "chops in anticipation": May 26, 1897; ALS, McGregor, Va.
p. 392: met his demand for £40: Conrad's terms were steep. David Meldrum recommended publication, but Conrad rejected Blackwood's original offer, until his demand for £40 (about $500–$750 in current monies) was met.
p. 392: Garnett on June 2: 1897; ALS, Yale.
p. 393: "no distinction of any kind": June 20, 1897; ALS, Brotherton.
p. 393: he wrote Unwin: July 18, 1897; ALS, Texas.
p. 393: "my nose in the air": To Sanderson, July 19, 1897: ALS, Yale.
p. 394: "a regular assortment of ailings": To Sanderson, July 26, 1897; ALS, Yale.
p. 394: is not the best part of him: I understand that a new biography by C. T. Watts and Laurence Davies, which has not yet appeared, will stress his impact on social history.
p. 395: "believe a thing or two": August 5, 1897; ALS, Dartmouth.
p. 395: with further remarks: August 9, 1897; ALS, Dartmouth.
p. 396: "to the least of his slaves": August 24, 1897; ALS, McGregor, Va.
p. 397: "discerned in the aim": The manuscript of the Preface is at the Rosenbach Library.
p. 397: feeding into the Preface: The Preface was a mix of James, Pater, Flaubert, very possibly Maupassant (his preface to *Pierre et Jean*), and perhaps Brunetière, the critic and editor of *La Revue des Deux Mondes.* For the relationship to Brunetière, see Hay, "Joseph Conrad and Impressionism." With James in mind, it is of some interest that the typescript has the half-erased *The Art of Fiction* on its first leaf. For a detailed description of the typescript, see Neill Joy's "Conrad's 'Preface' to *The Nigger of the 'Narcissus'*: The Lost Typescript Recovered," *Conradiana*, IX, pp. 17–30. Professor Joy also offers ample evidence that the 1902 Hythe pamphlet was not a Wise forgery, although his proof is circumstantial.
p. 398: aesthetic unite into a whole: "The Art of Fiction."
p. 398: When we come to the Preface: The text derives from the Collected Edition of *The Nigger of the "Narcissus."*
p. 399: "of all good art": "Style," in *Appreciations*, 1884. (More accessible in *Literary Criticism*, ed. Lionel Trilling [New York: Holt, Rinehart, 1970], pp. 267–68.)
p. 400: "is sometimes amusing": December 20, 1897; ALS, Dartmouth.
p. 401: "nor where God is. Assez": January 14, 1897; *Ibid.*
p. 401: "for the last three months": September 4, 1897; ALS, National Library of Scotland.
p. 402: "reckless of consequences": September 6, 1897; *Ibid.*
p. 403: "daughter of a man's heart": *The Rescue*, p. 10.
p. 403: In a guarded letter to Conrad: William Blackburn, ed., *Joseph Conrad:*

Letters to William Blackwood and David S. Meldrum (Durham, N.C.: Duke University Press, 1958). p. 13.

p. 403: In return, Conrad indicated: October 30, 1897; ALS, National Library of Scotland.

p. 404: "I have to live upon": September 24, 1897; Garnett, p. 103.

p. 404: "the secret of my life": October 2, 1897; *Lettres françaises*, p. 32. (Original unknown.)

p. 405: "in a cataleptic trance": October 8, 1897; Garnett, pp. 108–9.

p. 405: of abetting slave mentality: Kott's essay, "The Lay Tragic Spirit," appeared in *Creativity* (September 1945), pp. 137–60.

p. 405: Conrad mentioned to Garnett: October 14, 1897; Garnett, p. 115.

p. 406: "too good, too terrible": November 11, 1897; *Two Letters from Stephen Crane to Joseph Conrad* (London: First Editions Club, Carwen Press, 1926).

p. 406: "very air one breathes": November 16, 1897; ALS, Columbia.

p. 407: Conrad took a new tack: November 5, 1897; ALS, Yale.

p. 407: Conrad normally practiced: Possibly this can be traced to his loss of Blackwood for *The Rescue* (to Meldrum, November 5, 1897; ALS, Duke).

p. 407: "Patron Jew": November 11, 1897; Garnett, p. 116.

p. 407: "I may so express it": November 9, 1897; ALS, National Library of Scotland.

p. 407: bows out of the letter: November 30, 1897, in French; ALS, Harvard.

p. 408: "to do something for him": Leon Edel, *Henry James*, p. 53.

p. 408: "of his earlier time": Expressed to Edith Wharton; *Ibid.*, p. 48.

p. 409: "much to your own surprise": December 5, 1897; Garnett, p. 119. (The letter to Crane, dated December 1, is at Columbia.) Ford stressed after Conrad's death that he and his friend, along with Crane and James, were impressionists. Conrad, however, had fought the label, as he fought all labels, and stressed that impressionism as an art form was a surface treatment, lacking solidity—thus, Crane slips from one's grasp. The matter is not a simple one, and my remarks in Part VI will demonstrate how sharply Conrad diverged from the impressionists.

p. 409: "and sea were doing": December 8, 1897.

p. 409: "as empty as the sky": *The Nigger*, p. 27.

p. 410: "just born of the earth": *The Red Badge of Courage* (New York: Norton, 1962), p. 21.

p. 410: "have been learned by heart": December 6, 1897; ALS, Dartmouth.

p. 410: "on its stage": *Last Essays*, pp. 168–69.

p. 411: "in the accomplished task?": January 12, 1898; ALS, Columbia.

p. 412: "nothing shall be done": February 3, 1898; ALS, Yale.

p. 412: he wrote a friend: Stallman and Gilkes, eds. *Stephen Crane: Letters* (New York: New York University Press, 1960), p. 176, n. 22.

p. 412: *Daily Mail's* characterization: December 7, 1897.

p. 413: "of the ship at sea": December 9, 1897; ALS, Rosenbach.

p. 414: "he does not think": December 14, 1897; ALS, Dartmouth.

p. 414: if he went to sea: The opinion of A. F. Schiffely, in his *Don Roberto*

(London: Heinemann, 1937), p. 331; denied by Baines (p. 214 n.), and reexamined by C. T. Watts in *Joseph Conrad's Letters to Cunninghame Graham* (Cambridge, England: Cambridge University Press, 1969), p. 107 n. to lines 25–28.

p. 414: "before vanishing for ever": December 23, 1897; ALS, Foy F. Quiller-Couch.

p. 415: "the splendour of youth": *Ibid.*

p. 415: "I can't understand it": To Galsworthy, January 7 (?), 1898; ALS, Birmingham.

p. 415: Writing to Garnett: January 7, 1898; Garnett, p. 124.

p. 416: "no conspiracy of silence": January 7, 1898; ALS, Berg.

p. 416: "commend to your heart": January 21, 1898; Najder, p. 223. (Original in *Wiadomości Literackie*, Warsaw, 1929, No. 51.)

p. 418: In a letter that: January 14, 1898; ALS, Dartmouth.

p. 418: "that receives impressions": *Last Diaries*, ed. Leon Stilman (New York: Putnam, 1960), p. 45.

p. 419: "in the name of God": Sunday, January 23, 1898; ALS, Dartmouth.

p. 420: "vain and floating appearance": January 31, 1898; ALS, Dartmouth.

p. 421: "nothing but a surface": January 16, 1898; ALS, Birmingham.

p. 422: *Saturday Review:* January 29, 1898.

p. 422: which he wrote for the *Outlook:* April 2, 1898. (Baines [p. 472, n. 88] mistakenly says it was unprinted.)

p. 422: Conrad could only scorn: To Sanderson, February 3, 1898; ALS, Yale.

p. 422: "the slightest consequence": *Notes on Life and Letters*, pp. 20 ff.

p. 422: Conrad wrote, in Polish: To Mrs. Aniela Zagórska, February 6, 1898; Najder, p. 224. (French translation at Yale.)

p. 423: He writes to Crane: February 15, 1898; ALS, Columbia.

p. 423: "my backbone to be cotton": February 16, 1898; ALS, Dartmouth.

p. 423: to make of these notes: The argument *for* a play as the basis for their collaboration comes in a postcard Conrad wrote Crane on Tuesday (February 15, 1898): "I am anxious to know what you have done with your idea for a play. A play to write is no play."

p. 424: "a handful of water": March 29, 1898; Garnett, p. 135.

p. 425: "payment promised by a fool": *Ibid.*, p. 136.

p. 425: "and peace, and joy": To Helen Watson, April 2, 1898; ALS, Yale.

p. 425: "has been done": May 18, 1898; Garnett, p. 137.

p. 426: Conrad suddenly announced: To Garnett, May 28, 1898 (dated "May, 1898" in *ibid.*); ALS, Colgate.

p. 426: Ford and Conrad met in mid-May: For some of my argument here, I am indebted to Professor Eloise Knapp Hay.

p. 427: Then in a June 7 letter: Garnett has listed this as "Tuesday [May 1898]," but it is June 7; ALS, Colgate.

p. 427: "never stops for long": June 28, 1898; ALS, Birmingham. This unpublished letter is a key document in dating the meeting of Conrad and Ford as having occurred before September.

p. 428: "was always Oriental": *A Personal Remembrance*, pp. 10–11.

p. 428: "lost to the world": Schiffely, p. 331. (See p. 708 n.)

p. 428: "nor sound nor soul. Nothing": To Graham, June 15, 1898; ALS, Dartmouth.
p. 429: "another man rushed in": July 19, 1898; ALS, Dartmouth.
p. 429: "their throats, you know": September 29, 1898; Garnett, p. 142.
p. 429: "complete and unrestricted": *Joseph Conrad and His Circle*, pp. 59–60.
p. 430: "what more do you want?": Garnett, pp. 143–44.
p. 430: showing special gratitude: Conrad employs one of his typical drowning metaphors to describe his affairs: "This confounded literature has ruined me entirely. There is a time in the affairs of men when the tide of folly taken at the flood sweeps them to destruction. La mer monte cher ami; la mer monte" (November 9, 1898; ALS, Dartmouth).
p. 430: not yet in mind: That is, not in its present length or scope. Conrad had a few vague notes in the "Tuan Jim" sketch.
p. 430: "mouse now and then": August 10, 1898; ALS, Duke.
p. 430: Yet ten days later: August 20, 1898 (Garnett has only "August"); ALS, Lilly.
p. 431: "of too little of it": *Chance*, p. 310.
p. 431: write very respectfully to H. G. Wells: On September 6, 1898 (ALS, Illinois); "Youth" had just appeared in *Blackwood's*.
p. 431: "of such untimely wisdom": August 31, 1898; ALS, Yale.
p. 434: "English language of to-day": pp. 31–2. Also very useful is Richard J. Herndon, "The Collaboration of Joseph Conrad with Ford Madox Ford," unpublished Stanford University doctoral dissertation, 1957.
p. 435: "and therefore very dear": To Henley, October 18, 1898; ALS, Morgan.
p. 436: "books they wrote together": Meyer, p. 137.
p. 436: move into Pent Farm: In reading *The Good Soldier*, Ford's novel of 1915, we should not forget the symbiotic closeness of this "quartet," extending not only to the collaboration but the "sharing" of a residence.
p. 436: Conrad told him: October 6, 1898; ALS, Yale. Ford is addressed as "Mr. Hueffer." The formality at this stage can be explained by the fact that Conrad was still negotiating his tenancy at Pent Farm.
p. 436: Conrad wrote Wells: October 11, 1898; ALS, Illinois.
p. 437: "what cannot be attained": To Garnett, October 12, 1898; ALS, Colgate. Garnett's essay appeared in *Academy* on October 18, 1898, as *Mr. Joseph Conrad.*
p. 437: "the thing awfully cheap": October 12, 1898; ALS, Duke.
p. 437: to his future collaborator: October 20, 1898; ALS, Yale (dated only "Thursday").
p. 438: on December 18: Najder, pp. 226–7. (French translation at Yale.)
p. 438: importuning from Cora for aid: Conrad's letters to Cora, for October 28, 1898; November 1, 1898; November 3, 1898; all ALS, Columbia.
p. 438: did attempt to help Crane: See Blackburn, pp. 31–33, for Meldrum's attempts to aid Crane without compromising the firm.
p. 439: Indicating that he was looking: To Ford, November 12, 1898; ALS, Yale (dated "Nov. 98, Saturday").
p. 439: "courting disaster deliberately": November 22, 1898; Jean-Aubry, *Joseph Conrad*, I, p. 255.

p. 440: "out of his malaise": My line of argument is that Marlow was the consequence, primarily, of psychological forces in Conrad and only secondarily the result of literary influences. Nevertheless, Andrzej Busza (p. 208) summarizes a Polish "influence" that needs repeating; it by no means contradicts my own stress: "[Wit] Tarnawski suggests that the peculiar narrative technique, involving an intermediary narrator, which Conrad used in 'Youth,' *Lord Jim, Under Western Eyes* [the old language teacher], *Chance* and elsewhere, derives not from Henry James and Sterne as some critics have argued, but from the Polish *gawęda* or 'literary yarn.' The *gawęda* is a loose, informal narrative, told by a speaker in the manner of someone reminiscing. It is often involved and full of digressions. Little attention is paid to chronology. At first, seemingly unimportant details and fragmentary episodes come to the fore, then gradually a coherent picture emerges. By the time the speaker has finished, everything has fallen into place. This form of narration, originating from an oral tradition, first appeared in Polish literature during the romantic period. . . . Tarnawski argues that the *gawęda* style lent itself especially to Conrad, since much of his narrative material was based either on his own memories, or on yarns which he heard from other people."

p. 440: "ever was—or will be": To Wells, December 4, 1898; ALS, Illinois.

p. 440: he announced to Blackwood: December 13,1898; ALS, National Library of Scotland.

p. 440: "to bear your imprint": December 31, 1898; *Ibid.*

p. 441: writing to Wells: December 23, 1898; ALS, Illinois.

p. 441: "of politics and literature": Najder, pp. 228–29. (French translation at Yale.)

VI: THE NOVELIST (1899–1904)

p. 446: "Of the Open Sky": In *Modern Painters,* I.

p. 446: *epigenetic principle: Childhood and Society,* pp. 65 ff.

p. 447: "with the personal father": *Gandhi's Truth,* pp. 132 ff.

p. 448: "in the temporal sphere": *Lord of the Four Quarters: Myths of the Royal Father* (New York: Collier Books, 1966), p. 23.

p. 448: "The source of transformation": *Art and the Creative Unconscious* (Princeton: Princeton University Press, 1959), pp. 178 ff.

p. 449: "more permanently enduring": p. xii.

p. 449: "their own religious experience": Mircea Eliade, *Shamanism: Archaic Techniques of Ecstasy* (Princeton: Princeton University Press, 1964 [1951]), p. 8.

p. 450: "one writes for oneself": To Marriot-Watson, January 23, 1903; ALS, Rosenbach.

p. 452: *"connu la nudité?": Mallarmé,* p. 131.

p. 454: "meantime one must live!": August 22,1899; ALS, National Library of Scotland.

p. 456: "waits on imagination alone": October 12, 1899; ALS, Yale.

p. 456: "an almost unflagging invention": Symons, *Notes on Joseph Conrad* (London: Myers, 1925), p. 30.
p. 457: he wrote to Galsworthy: February 11, 1899; ALS, Birmingham.
p. 457: "not as recognized": Quoted by Robert Scholes, *Structuralism in Literature* (New Haven: Yale University Press, 1974), pp. 83 ff. (The text by Shklovsky, or Chklovski, is *Sur la théorie de la prose.*)
p. 458: "integrity of the pattern": *Anatomy of Criticism* (Princeton: Princeton University Press, 1957), p. 80.
p. 459: "cloth and glittering bronze": *Youth*, p. 134.
p. 460: "I am utterly squashed": November 12, 1900; Garnett, p. 172.
p. 460: "*the dust of the contest*": August 2, 1901. (Original unknown.)
p. 462: "sloth, ignorance or folly": ALS, Berg.
p. 464: "of a vast metamorphosis": *Descent and Return: The Orphic Theme in Modern Literature* (Cambridge: Harvard University Press, 1971), pp. 12–13.
p. 465: "as death but as life": *Eros and Civilization: A Philosophical Inquiry into Freud* (New York: Vintage, 1962 [1955]), p. 149.
p. 465: "the subjugation more complete": *Lord Jim*, p. 129.
p. 465: "barely reaches medium height": *Psychoanalytic Explorations in Art* (New York: Schocken Books, 1964 [1952]), p. 20.
p. 466: "differentiation in one": p. 86.
p. 468: "moving in a visible world": May 31, 1902; ALS, Duke.

VII: THE MAJOR CAREER (1899–1910)

p. 471: specifics of this attack: There is no proof that Conrad read the words of her attack, although he may well have. He certainly was aware of the general contents. He does mention a letter from her, but since it has never turned up, we cannot be sure that its words paralleled her published attack.
p. 472: "glowing mass of coal within": *Youth*, p. 35.
p. 473: he belittled to Garnett: January 13, 1899; ALS, Colgate.
p. 473: Even when he wrote to Crane: January 13, 1899; ALS, Columbia.
p. 473: "seem lax and large and pale": *Experiment in Autobiography* (London: Macmillan, 1934), pp. 615 ff.
p. 474: "should come in your way": February 2, 1899; ALS, Dartmouth.
p. 474: "that is practically effective": February 8, 1899; ALS, Dartmouth.
p. 474: "a mere trifle to it": To Blackwood, February 8, 1899; ALS, National Library of Scotland.
p. 475: "Je suis sauvé!": February 8, 1899; ALS, Dartmouth.
p. 476: "a strong friendship upon": February 12, 1899; ALS, National Library of Scotland.
p. 477: "14 years ago with my money": February 10, 1899; ALS, Duke.
p. 477: "feather in *Maga*'s cap yet": Blackburn, p. 48.
p. 478: "or 'public opinion' ": Walter Kaufman, ed., *The Viking Portable Nietzsche* (New York: Viking, 1954), p. 547.

p. 479: *"as one (would) might Lord Jim":* The document is reproduced by Alexander Janta in *Joseph Conrad: Centennial Essays*, ed. Krzyżanowski, pp. 85–110. Included at the end of the "sketch" are Conrad's brief notes for *The Rescue* and an outline for a play with an Italian setting.

p. 479: Conrad also told Meldrum: February 14, 1899; ALS, Duke.

p. 481: "a sort of silverpoint: a delicacy": pp. 142 ff.

p. 482: "had been invulnerable and immortal": *The Inheritors*, p. 9.

p. 482: "forever and ever": *Ibid.*, p. 205.

p. 483: "three times over": ALS, Colgate.

p. 483: "no time to lose": ALS, Colgate.

p. 484: "tardiness of his vitality": December 3, 1902; ALS, Yale.

p. 484: Conrad chided Ford: Early July 1901; ALS, British Museum.

p. 485: "long enough for that rescue": Garnett, p. 153. In an extremely intimate letter to Ted Sanderson (on October 12, 1899), Conrad repeated similar images of desperation. He says: "I fear I have not the capacity and the power to go on—to satisfy the just expectations of those who are dependent on my exertion. . . . So I turn in this vicious circle and the work itself becomes like the work in a treadmill—a thing without joy—a punishing task" (ALS, Yale).

p. 485: "I really care to work": May 25, 1899; Jean-Aubry, *Joseph Conrad*, I, p. 277.

p. 486: a touching letter to Helen Sanderson: June 22, 1899; ALS, Yale.

p. 487: "resolutely away from it": August 22, 1899; ALS, National Library of Scotland.

p. 488: "on the verge of craziness": April 17, 1899; ALS, Birmingham.

p. 489: "top of my miserable skull": Thursday (n.d.) 1899?–1900?; ALS, Yale.

p. 489: "under the tepid ruins": October 2, 1898; ALS, Yale.

p. 490: "line of the least resistance": August 23, 1899; ALS, Berg.

p. 490: "my ideal and of my risk": ALS, Berg.

p. 491: "who has lost his gods": September 16, 1899; ALS, Lilly.

p. 492: "apart from *subject*": October 9, 1899; Jean-Aubry, *Joseph Conrad*, I, pp. 279–80.

p. 492: appear in fourteen installments in all: As follows: Chaps. I-IV—Oct. 1899; V—Nov.; VI-VII—Dec.; VIII-IX—Jan. 1900; X-XI—Feb.; XII-XIII—March; XIV-XV—April; XVI-XX—May; XXI-XXIII—June; XXIV-XXVII—July; XXVIII-XXX—Aug.; XXXI-XXXV—Sept.; XXXVI-XL—Oct.; XLI-XLV—Nov.

p. 492: "first of this month": ALS, Yale.

p. 493: called Conrad's attention: Conrad's letter for October 26, 1899, to Sanderson; ALS, Yale.

p. 493: "of your own feelings": October 14, 1899; ALS, Dartmouth.

p. 494: "revel in my imbecility": To Sanderson, October 26, 1899; ALS, Yale.

p. 494: "simple and sensitive character": *Lord Jim*, p. viii.

p. 494: "at times on the edge": *Ibid.*, p. 93.

p. 495: "as honourable as pocket-picking": November 8, 1899; ALS, National Library of Scotland.

p. 495: a November 13 letter: Dated "Sunday Nov. 99"; ALS, Yale.
p. 496: Jessie describes one: *Joseph Conrad and His Circle*, pp. 67 ff.
p. 496: "of course this year": ALS, Duke.
p. 497: "doings of German influence": December 25, 1899; Najder, p. 232. (French translation at Yale.)
p. 497: "a homogeneous book": December 26, 1899; ALS, National Library of Scotland.
p. 497: "to make up the number": January 3, 1900; ALS, Duke.
p. 498: "ever invented by Jew or Gentile": January 4, 1900; ALS, Dartmouth.
p. 498: Conrad wrote Garnett: January 20, 1900; Garnett, pp. 164 ff.
p. 498: "to run in a circle": January 19, 1900; ALS, Dartmouth.
p. 499: "that she entertained 'Jim' ": Blackburn, p. 86.
p. 499: "very near my heart": April 3, 1900; ALS, Duke.
p. 499: "healthy and rich": March 26, 1900; ALS, Colgate.
p. 499: he announces to Meldrum: April 3, 1900; ALS, Duke.
p. 500: "such indications is returned": April 12, 1900; ALS, National Library of Scotland.
p. 500: Blackwood responded: April 24, 1900; Blackburn, pp. 91–2.
p. 500: "no eye of man'll rest again": March 31, 1900; ALS, Yale.
p. 500: "I had ever seen": *Joseph Conrad and His Circle*, p. 70.
p. 501: "without influence and without means": May 10, 1900; ALS, Columbia.
p. 501: "if possible. No matter": May 19, 1900, to Meldrum; Blackburn, p. 94. (The original of this letter, which is not at Duke, cannot be traced.)
p. 501: "I don't care": *Ibid.*, p. 96.
p. 501: which were agreed to: *Ibid.*, pp. 96–100.
p. 502: "at seeing anything clearly": In French, June 10, 1900; ALS, Yale.
p. 502: he announced: To Blackwood; ALS, National Library of Scotland.
p. 502: "was on my way to London": July 20, 1900; ALS, Birmingham.
p. 502: "waking up from a nightmare": September 9, 1900; ALS, Yale.
p. 503: "really from beginning to end": July 18, 1900; ALS, National Library of Scotland.
p. 503: "strictly a narrative": July 19, 1900; ALS, National Library of Scotland.
p. 504: "out of me this tide": To Galsworthy, August 11, 1900; ALS, Birmingham.
p. 504: "keep clear from collaboration": *Joseph Conrad and His Circle*, p. 71.
p. 504: Galsworthy to Meldrum: September 1, 1900; ALS, Duke.
p. 505: "My own life": *Typhoon*, p. viii.
p. 505: "and much more horrible": To Pinker, October 8, 1900; ALS, Berg.
p. 506: "in his quiet phrasing": November 7, 1900; ALS, National Library of Scotland.
p. 506: "successive day, and no more": *Typhoon*, p. 4.
p. 507: "very near the earth": *Ibid.*, p. 26.
p. 508: "nodding in an earthquake": *Ibid.*, p. 74.
p. 509: "the *revealing* life": To Garnett, November 12, 1900; Garnett, p. 172.
p. 509: "popular apathy or distaste": October 29, 1900.
p. 510: "Mr. Conrad's idiosyncrasies": December 14, 1900.

p. 510: "trembling on gossamer threads": May 1901.
p. 510: "to result one day": Blackburn, p. 116; Meldrum to Blackwood, December 3, 1900.
p. 510: "into such an appeal": to Blackwood, December 13, 1900; ALS, National Library of Scotland.
p. 511: "to expect in these days": December 19, 1900; Blackburn, p. 122.
p. 511: into the insurance loan scheme: Blackwood wrote Conrad on December 18, 1900; *ibid.*, p. 121.
p. 512: "half scaled at last": May 24, 1901; ALS, National Library of Scotland.
p. 512: four months to complete: The manuscript reads "Winchelsea, May 1901."
p. 512: he asked Pinker: January 18, 1901; ALS, Berg.
p. 513: "terribly hungry for food": *Typhoon*, pp. 223–24.
p. 513: "the qualities of heroism": *Ibid.*, p. 234.
p. 514: "sake of success": February 14, 1901; Najder, p. 234. (Original in the Warsaw National Library.)
p. 514: "tell me years afterward": *Typhoon*, p. 129.
p. 514: "from his future": *Ibid.*, p. 132.
p. 516: "now complete in MS.": June 7, 1901; ALS, Berg.
p. 516: had had to borrow £100: Conrad to Ford, July 19, 1901; ALS, Yale.
p. 516: "on the dear old Harry": June or early July 1901; ALS, British Museum.
p. 516: "as a simple demonstration": *Romance*, p. 217.
p. 516: "two went down": *Ibid.*, p. 223.
p. 517: "Sanchez and Don Riego too": July 4, 1901; ALS, National Library of Scotland.
p. 517: "(Slingsby, I suppose)": To Ford, June or early July 1901; ALS, Yale.
p. 518: "I simply can't explain": July 3, 1901; ALS, Berg.
p. 518: "gleaming and suggestive method": August 5, 1901; Blackburn, p. 131.
p. 518: Blackwood informed Conrad: August 15, 1901; *Ibid.*, p. 132.
p. 519: he wrote a memo: September 6, 1901; *Ibid.*, p. 134.
p. 519: "Channel to Zanzibar!": To William Blackwood, August 26, 1901; ALS, National Library of Scotland.
p. 519: "really and truly struck": July 19, 1901; ALS, Yale.
p. 519: "many circumlocutions declines": To Ford, Wednesday, after August 15, 1901; ALS, Yale. (The letter is not dated.)
p. 520: "through a *joint production*": November 10, 1923; TL, Yale.
p. 520: Conrad helped Elsie: On her *Stories from de Maupassant*, 1903; see his long letter of suggestions, October 28, 1901 [n.d.]; TL, Yale. (Also, October 1902; ALS, Yale.)
p. 520: "practically my work": November 7, 1901; ALS, Berg.
p. 521: "as hard as I know how": June 1901 [n.d.]; ALS, Yale.
p. 521: "unconscious then or now": To Ford [n.d.], from envelope, July 20, 1902; ALS, Yale.
p. 522: "The rest is silence": ALS, Yale.
p. 522: Not until November 7: November 7, 1901; ALS, National Library of Scotland.
p. 523: "freer, less rigorous": November 11, 1901; ALS, Birmingham.

p. 523: "at all this time": January 7, 1902; ALS, Duke.
p. 524: The request was rejected: George Blackwood to Conrad, February 3, 1902; Blackburn, p. 141.
p. 524: "Million by a Millionaire": To George Blackwood, February 5, 1902; ALS, Blackwood, Edinburgh, Scotland.
p. 525: "only that is fogged": January 6, 1902; ALS, Berg.
p. 525: "of us at all ashamed": *Ibid.*
p. 526: "Say 22,000 each": January 16, 1902; ALS, Berg.
p. 526: "last scene except in novels": February 25, 1902; ALS, Berg.
p. 527: "perfectly safe in your hands": February 28, 1902; ALS, Berg.
p. 529: "unless the devil is in it": March 10, 1902; ALS, Birmingham.
p. 529: "not as Conrad's work specifically": February 28, 1902; ALS, Berg.
p. 529: "a first rate story": March 16, 1902; ALS, Berg.
p. 530: Conrad wrote Ford: April 15, 1902; ALS, Yale.
p. 531: "unceasing doubt and deception": April 24, 1902; ALS, Yale.
p. 531: Conrad told Pinker: In letters for May 1 and May 3, 1902; ALS, Berg.
p. 531: On May 31, after the interview: To William Blackwood, May 31, 1902; ALS, Duke.
p. 532: "into the story yet": To Conrad, May 23, 1902; Blackburn, p. 148.
p. 534: Writing to Galsworthy: June 1, 1902; ALS, Birmingham.
p. 534: "and sea, for the scene": June 5, 1902; ALS, Blackwood.
p. 535: "has become utterly worthless": June 10, 1902; ALS, Colgate.
p. 535: "it is deterioration": To Meldrum, Friday, Autumn 1902; ALS, Duke.
p. 536: "my dishonourable scars": June 19, 1902; ALS, Yale.
p. 536: "in the remoteness of the sky": *Romance,* p. 419.
p. 536: "simply *has* to be done": June 24, 1902; ALS, Yale.
p. 538: he told Garnett: October 17, 1902; Garnett, p. 182.
p. 538: He asks Pinker: November 26, 1902; ALS, Berg.
p. 538: "slowly, very slowly": December 4, 1902; ALS, Blackwood.
p. 539: a letter Conrad wrote: November 26, 1902; ALS, Berg.
p. 539: in the *Academy:* December 6, 1902.
p. 539: "since George Eliot": December 19, 1902; Blackburn, p. 172.
p. 539: "there's no other word": November 30, 1902; *Memories* (London: Chapman & Hall, 1916), p. 186.
p. 539: "with no regard for success": December 12, 1902; ALS, Yale.
p. 539: "the poverty of one's thought": December 21, 1902; ALS, private collection.
p. 540: "ever be found in its text": January 2, 1903; ALS, Yale.
p. 540: Conrad reaffirms: To Pinker, January 19, 1903; ALS, Berg.
p. 540: "*un roman dessus*": July 8, 1903; ALS, Dartmouth.
p. 541: "dreary coast of Ven'la": July 22, 1923; ALS, Lilly.
p. 541: "troubles of a revolution": *Nostromo,* pp. vii–viii.
p. 541: "*alias* el Diabletto": Romance, p. 516.
p. 542: "in good and evil": p. ix.
p. 542: As Baines demonstrates: p. 296.
p. 542: his own "first love": pp. xiii–xiv.

p. 542: (with a preface by Graham): See Watts, p. 38, n. 1, and pp. 206 ff. One is also grateful for the research of Edgar Wright, in his London University M.A. thesis on Conrad.

p. 543: "by an immortal multitude": January 28, 1903; ALS, Rosenbach.

p. 544: "be suddenly laid out": To Galsworthy, February 16, 1903; ALS, Birmingham.

p. 544: "no value at all": March 17, 1903; ALS, Berg.

p. 544: "I have no time myself": March 29, 1904; ALS, Berg.

p. 545: on March 23: March 23, 1903; ALS, Yale.

p. 545: "70 thou[nd] words after all": March 23, 1903; ALS, Duke.

p. 545: in the States by T. D. Watts: To Galsworthy, April 12, 1903; ALS, Birmingham.

p. 545: "eagerly towards the lips": To Graham, March 19, 1903; ALS, Dartmouth.

p. 546: in the *Speaker:* June 6, 1903.

p. 546: "than that of Zola": April 30, 1903.

p. 547: "delayed by this work": To Pinker, May 7, 1903; ALS, Berg.

p. 547: "of my character mainly": August 22, 1903; ALS, Birmingham.

p. 547: "concerned mostly with Italians": May 9, 1903; ALS, Dartmouth.

p. 547: "has not yet even begun": June 4, 1903; ALS, Birmingham.

p. 548: To Pinker, he indicated: August 22, 1903; ALS, Berg.

p. 548: "I cut myself off": August 22, 1903; ALS, Birmingham.

p. 549: "remarkable piece of work": ALS, early September 1903; private collection.

p. 549: "with me for anything": October 1, 1903; ALS, Yale.

p. 549: "to put them there": To Ford, n.d. (October? 1902–03); ALS, Yale.

p. 550: letter to James Barrie: ALS, Berg.

p. 550: "otherwise with the subject": November 8, 1903; *Lettres françaises,* p. 54.

p. 550: "of my writing in English": November 15, 1903; Najder, p. 237. (Original in *Ruch Literacki,* 1927, No. 6.)

p. 551: "my footing in deep waters": November 30, 1903; ALS, Illinois.

p. 551: "lapping about my lips": November 30, 1903; ALS, Birmingham.

p. 553: "ghastly tally of severed hands": Quoted by Brian Inglis, *Roger Casement* (New York: Harcourt, 1973), p. 80.

p. 553: "it's an awful fudge": December 1, 1903; ALS, National Library of Ireland.

p. 553: "cruelties he had seen": *Joseph Conrad and His Circle,* pp. 103–4.

p. 553: "possessed of abundant knowledge": December 17, 1903; ALS, National Library of Ireland.

p. 554: "appears so to me too": December 21, 1903; ALS, National Library of Ireland.

p. 554: "perfectly on humanitarian grounds": December 29, 1903; ALS, National Library of Ireland.

p. 554: "it is not in me": December 26, 1903; ALS, Dartmouth.

p. 555: letter to Waliszewski: In Polish, December 5, 1903; Najder, p. 239. (Original in *Ruch Literacki,* 1927, No. 6.)

p. 556: "taciturn and observing reserve": *T.P.'s Weekly,* III (January 29–October 7, 1904), p. 270.
p. 556: "a concrete and fateful shape": *Ibid.*, p. 658.
p. 557: Ford remarked in later years: *Mightier Than the Sword* (London: Allen & Unwin, 1938).
p. 558: "sale of these pages": *Joseph Conrad and Ford Madox Ford* (unpublished dissertation), pp. 120–22. Professor Arthur Mizener provides an excellent summary of the episode from Ford's point of view in his *The Saddest Story: A Biography of Ford Madox Ford* (New York: World, 1971), pp. 89–91.
p. 558: "awful anxiety to me": February 7, 1904; ALS, Illinois.
p. 558: "at the age of sixteen": *Joseph Conrad As I Knew Him*, p. 51.
p. 559: telling Wells: February 7, 1904; ALS, Illinois.
p. 559: "3,000 words in four hours": *Ibid.*
p. 559: "in a frightful manner": April 5, 1904; ALS, Duke.
p. 560: "have been learned by heart": December 6, 1897; ALS, Dartmouth.
p. 560: "depends on one's individuality": August 18, 1904; ALS, Lilly.
p. 561: "right thought in literature": February 17, 1904; ALS, Berg.
p. 561: "understand a demi-mot": April 28, 1905; ALS, Yale.
p. 562: "the writing mood. Added weariness": To Galsworthy, June 30, 1905; ALS, Birmingham.
p. 562: "of helplessness, perhaps": *Mirror*, p. 62.
p. 562: "with the last century": N.d., February–March 1904; ALS, Berg.
p. 563: he told Pinker: March 29, 1904; ALS, Berg.
p. 563: "near enough to insanity": April 5, 1904; ALS, Birmingham.
p. 563: "would talk to a friend": To Pinker, April 18, 1904; ALS, Berg.
p. 563: On April 25: ALS, Yale.
p. 563: he wrote Pawling: May 27, 1904; ALS, Heinemann.
p. 564: "whole together. Can we?": May 29, 1904; ALS, Yale.
p. 564: as a collaboration with Ford: Mizener, p. 114.
p. 564: "don terrible de la popularité": June 27, 1904; ALS, Harvard.
p. 564: "anything to each other": ALS, Yale.
p. 565: "for anybody's speculation": August 19, 1904; ALS, Yale.
p. 565: His words to Galsworthy: September 1, 1904; ALS, Polish Library, London.
p. 566: "I'm weary! weary!": September 5, 1904; ALS, Yale.
p. 566: "uniforms and grandiloquent phrases": *Nostromo*, p. 88.
p. 567: "Barrios, is our defender": *Ibid.*, p. 171.
p. 567: "The word serves us well": *Ibid.*, p. 189.
p. 567: "of a pretty fairy tale": *Ibid.*, p. 218.
p. 567: "aim, ideal, and watchword": *Notes on Life and Letters*, p. 113.
p. 568: "lawlessness of the land": *Nostromo*, pp. 360 ff.
p. 569: "a very bad fit of it": October 24, 1904; ALS, Harvard.
p. 569: "what about the public?": ALS, Berg.
p. 570: "are not marvellous": November 5, 1904.
p. 570: *British Weekly:* November 10, 1904.
p. 570: "the spell is broken": November 9, 1904.

p. 570: (in the *Speaker*): November 12, 1904.
p. 570: "into significant relation": November 2, 1904.
p. 570: "seriousness in mock-heroics": November 19, 1904.
p. 571: intended to placate Graham: October 31, 1904; ALS, Dartmouth. Nostromo, in fact, keeps down the "people" so as to advance his own fortunes as a tool of the silver interests, a Marxist potential to the novel that would have horrified Conrad.
p. 571: Jessie identifies: *Joseph Conrad and His Circle*, p. 89.
p. 571: "to write of it. Assez!": To Ford, November 22, 1904; ALS, Yale.
p. 572: "insignificant tides of reality": *Notes on Life and Letters*, pp. 13 ff.
p. 572: "of forms and sensations": *Ibid.*, p. 15.
p. 572: "gout in eleven months": December 15, 1904; ALS, Yale.
p. 573: "my steam up— I know": December 21, 1904; ALS, Berg.
p. 573: "the slices of the novel": To Pinker, n.d., December 1904; ALS, Berg.
p. 574: "sheer want of intelligence": To Wells, n.d., Wed. to Fri.; ALS, Illinois.
p. 574: On January 4 and 10: To Pinker; ALS, Berg.
p. 574: Jessie has left a record: *Joseph Conrad and His Circle*, pp. 91 ff.
p. 575: "cost me 40 frcs or so": January 22, 1905; ALS, Duke.
p. 575: "is a mad thing": January 21, 1905; ALS, Birmingham.
p. 576: outline to Pinker: ALS, Berg.
p. 576: "hack-writer in my composition": February 5, 1905; ALS, Berg.
p. 577: "of the future thrown in": ALS, British Museum.
p. 577: "de ce petit livre": January 29, 1905; ALS, private collection.
p. 578: "not only think but write": April 25, 1905; ALS, Illinois.
p. 578: "manner and conversation": *Joseph Conrad and His Circle*, p. 97.
p. 579: "*memento mori* at a feast": March 23, 1905; ALS, Yale.
p. 580: "one worth setting down": May 16, 1905; ALS, Yale.
p. 581: "reflect on my character?": May 19, 1905; ALS, Yale.
p. 581: "on the Art of Fiction": April 12–13, 1905; ALS, Berg.
p. 581: By May 12: ALS, Berg.
p. 581: "it is mere trifling": ALS, Birmingham.
p. 582: "this writing is done?": April 24, 1905; ALS, Berg.
p. 582: He appeared to revel: He was tying his hopes, however, to a chimera, the possible success of his play; as he wrote Mrs. William Rothenstein: ". . . the Stage Society offer to perform my little play *Tomorrow* [*One Day More*] in June this year. I think it is really a chance for me; it may lead to the end of all my financial troubles for if the play produces a good impression I may place the 3 acts I've been carrying in my head for the last seven years" (May 1, 1905; ALS, Harvard).
p. 582: suggested in a May 12 letter: ALS, Berg.
p. 583: "could be given to a man?": To Newbolt, May 25, 1905; ALS, private collection.
p. 584: "not applicable to my case": June 1, 1905; ALS, private collection.
p. 584: " 'and I know the facts' ": June 5, 1905; ALS, private collection.
p. 585: The June 9 letter: ALS, private collection.
p. 585: "under the circumstances": June 16, 1905; ALS, private collection.

p. 585: to appeal to Norman Douglas: June 21, 1905; ALS, Texas.
p. 586: invited Ford and Elsie: June 24 (27), 1905; copy at Cornell.
p. 586: report to Galsworthy: June 30, 1905; ALS, Birmingham.
p. 587: "the sensations of his readers": *Notes on Life and Letters*, p. 6.
p. 587: "of its being made so": *Ibid., p. 9.*
p. 588: "That came to an end": Ford, *Return to Yesterday* (New York: Liveright, 1932), p. 112.
p. 588: "same taste in cooking": *A Set of Six*, p. 76.
p. 588: "at its own expense": *Ibid.*, p. 78.
p. 589: "by the end of the year": September 20, 1905; ALS, Berg.
p. 590: "of some patient listener": *Mirror*, p. 183.
p. 590: "a 3,000 words utterance": September 21, 1905; ALS, Birmingham.
p. 590: "book form on this side": October 6, 1905; ALS, Berg.
p. 590: He mentions to Pinker: *Ibid.*
p. 590: "if not rather more": October 18, 1905; ALS, Texas.
p. 590: "and no permanent profit": November 25/27, 1905; ALS, Illinois.
p. 590: "or say *distinctiveness*": October 20, 1905; ALS, Berg.
p. 591: "to the point of savagery": October 20, 1905; ALS, Illinois.
p. 591: "and meditated with care": October 22, 1905; TL, Yale.
p. 591: "nervous breakdown of a sort": To Ada (Mrs. John) Galsworthy, October 31, 1905; ALS, Birmingham.
p. 592: "national spirit was there!": November 2, 1905; ALS, Birmingham.
p. 593: "when it does come": November 25, 1905; ALS, Illinois. Also, to Colvin, December 26, 1905; ALS, Duke.
p. 593: "I stand in fear of": 1905; ALS, Polish Library, London.
p. 593: "no remedy for that": ALS, Birmingham.
p. 594: "of feeling and passion": *A Set of Six*, p. 161.
p. 594: "to Chance of course": ALS, Berg.
p. 594: "it is authentic enough": ALS, Berg.
p. 595: "of other, of inferior, values": p. ix.
p. 595: "as the faintest crack": *Ibid.*, pp. ix–x ff.
p. 596: "my technical intention": October 7, 1907; ALS, Dartmouth.
p. 597: "it's too big a job": *Ibid.*
p. 597: "Therefore I am deadly": *The Secret Agent*, p. 68.
p. 598: "treat him with justice": *Ibid.*, p. 75.
p. 598: "of his sinister freedom": *Ibid.*, p. 81.
p. 598: "perhaps of appeased conscience": *Ibid.*
p. 598: "of the perfect anarchist": *Ibid.*, p. 82.
p. 598: "of their respective trades": *Ibid.*, p. 92.
p. 599: "You have no force' ": *Ibid.*, p. 309.
p. 600: "according to the matter created": January 18, 1906; ALS, Berg.
p. 600: "go to pieces just now": February 7, 1906; ALS, Harvard.
p. 600: "songs and ribald jokes": To Pinker, February 13, 1906; ALS, Berg.
p. 600: "quicker than I expected": March 5, 1906; ALS, Berg.
p. 600: "affected by false admirations": Jean-Aubry, *Joseph Conrad*, II, p. 32.
p. 601: "but a dramatic development": April 4, 1906; ALS, Berg.

p. 601: "heaven or on earth": April 9, 1906; *Ibid.*, p. 33.
p. 601: "committed, or even contemplated": *Joseph Conrad and His Circle*, p. 113.
p. 601: "husband's regard and esteem": *Ibid.*, p. 116.
p. 602: "of his close friendship": *Ibid.*, p. 117.
p. 603: "inhabitants of this Island": May 30, 1906; Jean-Aubry, *Joseph Conrad*, II, p. 34.
p. 603: "bath suitable for baby": Sunday, June 1906; ALS, Harvard.
p. 604: "until they eventually disintegrated": *My Father: Joseph Conrad* (London: Calder & Boyars, 1970), p. 31.
p. 604: "for our little circle": August 2, 1906; ALS, Birmingham.
p. 604: And to Marguerite Poradowska: August 2, 1906; ALS, Yale.
p. 604: "sawdusty brain": August 15, 1906; ALS, Yale.
p. 604: To Jane Wells: August 4, 1906; ALS, Illinois.
p. 605: "of the grrreat continent": August 14–15, 1906; ALS, Birmingham.
p. 605: "more honest than mine": September 12, 1906; ALS, Polish Library, London.
p. 605: "certain event in history": November 7, 1906; Jean-Aubry, *Joseph Conrad*, II, p. 38. See also Sherry's *Conrad's Western World*, p. 229.
p. 605: "in a work of imagination": September 1, 1923; Jean-Aubry, *Joseph Conrad*, II, p. 322.
p. 606: will be 68,000 words: It runs to about 90,000 words.
p. 606: "Biographer and Historian": July 30, 1907; ALS, Illinois.
p. 607: "with most affectionate congratulations": November 25, 1905; ALS, Illinois. (Jean-Aubry has November 28.)
p. 607: "treated of in this book": September 15, 1906; ALS, Illinois.
p. 607: "pearl of the diver": Leon Edel and Gordon N. Ray, eds., *Henry James and H. G. Wells* (Urbana: University of Illinois Press, 1958), pp. 102–3.
p. 607: "My many thanks": *Twenty Letters to Joseph Conrad* (London: First Editions Club, 1926).
p. 608: "the impress of your personality": September 25, 1908; ALS, Illinois.
p. 609: The collaboration must have occurred: Mizener, p. 118.
p. 609: "either separately or together": November 10, 1923; TLS, Yale.
p. 610: is his announcement: To Pinker, October 4, 1906; ALS, Berg.
p. 610: "assure them I am safe": October 1906; ALS, Berg.
p. 610: "matter in the least": October 1906 (Monday); ALS, Berg.
p. 610: "and an always rebellious pen": September or October 1906; *Lettres françaises*, p. 77.
p. 611: "rest are all imbeciles": November 8, 1906, in French; *ibid.*, p. 77.
p. 611: "I have not known for years": November 15, 1906; ALS, Polish Library, London.
p. 612: "of thought itself": To Davray, December 5, 1906; *Lettres françaises*, p. 79.
p. 612: On the eighth: December 8, 1906; *ibid.*, p. 81.
p. 612: small volume of selected writings: To Pinker, December 11, 1906; ALS, Berg.
p. 613: "away from Jessie": December 11, 1906; copy at Cornell.

p. 613: "pass over our heads": December 20, 1906; ALS, Berg.
p. 614: "behind him—un beau jour": December 31, 1906; ALS, Birmingham.
p. 614: "will subdue her": January 3, 1907; ALS, Yale.
p. 614: on January 5: ALS, Yale.
p. 614: "for Borys hangs thereby": ALS, British Museum.
p. 615: "Spaniards and Corsicans": January 25, 1907; ALS, Berg.
p. 615: "have you to lean upon": January 8, 1907; copy at Cornell.
p. 615: "line in the 3 vols of it": January 15, 1907; private collection.
p. 615: "beastly things are called": To Pinker, January 25, 1907; ALS, Berg.
p. 616: "for a little while": February 26, 1907; ALS, Berg.
p. 616: "this thing must come on": March 4, 1907; ALS, Berg.
p. 616: "chance of securing permanency": March 13, 1907; ALS, Berg.
p. 617: "way of its acceptance": May 6, 1907; ALS, Berg.
p. 617: "in the way of my work": May 18, 1907; ALS, Berg.
p. 618: To Galsworthy: March 5, 1907; also, March 9, 1907; ALS, Birmingham.
p. 619: "ready to come out": April 13, 1907; ALS, Berg.
p. 619: "may make a novel popular": May 18, 1907; ALS, Berg.
p. 619: "tolerable of it too": To Heinemann, April 15, 1907; ALS, Heinemann.
p. 619: "to be worked upon thoroughly": May 3, 1907; ALS, Berg.
p. 619: but to Galsworthy: May 6, 1907; ALS, Birmingham.
p. 620: "three months from now": May 25, 1907; ALS, Berg.
p. 620: To Rothenstein: May 28, 1907; ALS, Harvard.
p. 620: He indicated to Pinker: June 1, 1907; ALS, Berg.
p. 621: "I finished Almayer's Folly": June 6, 1907; ALS, Polish Library, London.
p. 622: "be amused by me at all": June 17, 1907; ALS, Birmingham.
p. 622: "any more be adequate": To Galsworthy, July 30, 1907; ALS, Birmingham.
p. 622: "work of some mark": To Pinker, July 27, 1907; ALS, Berg.
p. 622: "can not be imitated": July 30, 1907; ALS, Berg.
p. 623: newsy letter to Galsworthy: August 24, 1907; ALS, Birmingham.
p. 624: "sands are running out!": August 20, 1907; ALS, Yale.
p. 624: "on clay and gravel": August 31, 1907; ALS, Berg.
p. 624: "fiendish ten days of it": ALS, Yale.
p. 624: "and tearing my hair": September 15, 1907; ALS, Birmingham.
p. 624: "to the hilt to P. anyhow": *Ibid.*
p. 625: "in Mr. Conrad's narrative": September 12, 1907. (Norman Sherry identified the reviewer.)
p. 626: "the existence of the latter": *Country Life*, September 21, 1907.
p. 627: "at the same time": September 20, 1907; ALS, Harvard.
p. 628: "it was no longer menaced": *A Set of Six*, p. 259.
p. 629: "heroic in its faith": *Ibid.*, p. xi.
p. 629: "how the money is spent": September 1907; ALS, Berg.
p. 629: in the *Nation:* September 28, 1907.
p. 630: "for one's secret intentions": October 1, 1907; Garnett, p. 207.
p. 630: but Conrad opposed that with: In his letter for October 1907; Garnett, pp. 205 ff.
p. 631: "Caesar of the dramatic world": *Notes on Life and Letters*, pp. 78–9.

p. 631: "sight of wondering generations": *Ibid.*, pp. 79–80.
p. 631: Conrad told Galsworthy: October 24, 1907; ALS, Birmingham.
p. 632: "of my literary life!": October 10, 1907; ALS, Berg.
p. 633: "for what I am not": October 29, 1907; ALS, Polish Library, London.
p. 634: "Foreignness I suppose": January 6, 1908; ALS, Birmingham.
p. 634: Conrad told Galsworthy: *Ibid.*
p. 635: "say 57–60 thousand words": October 1907; ALS, Berg.
p. 635: "I am in my fifties!": ALS, Yale.
p. 636: "Now it must come out": January 7, 1908; ALS, Berg.
p. 636: "real subject of the story": January 6, 1908; ALS, Birmingham. In printing this important letter, Jean-Aubry inexplicably cut more than 500 words.
p. 637: "but as a simple reflection": January 14, 1908; ALS, Berg.
p. 638: "want to read the second": Thursday, January 1908; ALS, Berg.
p. 639: In suggesting to Galsworthy: January 14, 1908; ALS, Birmingham.
p. 639: "It was a horrid nightmare": January 1908; ALS, Berg.
p. 640: "stop writing entirely": ALS, Berg.
p. 640: as Jessie claimed: *Joseph Conrad As I Knew Him*, p. 119.
p. 640: In the same letter: February 12, 1908; ALS, Berg.
p. 641: "in a special way": February 1908; ALS, Berg.
p. 641: "to the exact yard": February 1908; ALS, Berg (a different February letter from the above).
p. 641: "with a proper flourish": ALS, Berg.
p. 641: utilize his talent: We can speculate that Conrad felt he was playing Flaubert to Douglas's Maupassant.
p. 642: "can be done—with patience": Saturday night, 1908; ALS, Colgate.
p. 642: letter of March 23: ALS, Berg.
p. 643: place in May 1908: ALS, Berg, to Pinker.
p. 643: "gone to pieces suddenly": Undated; ALS, Berg.
p. 643: "only the exploitation of this": May 9, 1918; II, p. 230, translated by Justin O'Brien.
p. 644: "the tone of the novel": March 14, 1908; ALS, Texas.
p. 644: from the Garnetts: See David Garnett, *The Golden Echo* (London: Chatto & Windus, 1953), pp. 10 ff.
p. 644: Conrad complained to Wells: March 27, 1908; ALS, Illinois.
p. 645: "than this one": *Ibid.*
p. 645: "Invention's dead": March 31, 1908; copy at Cornell. Conrad adds: "And yet the imagination works dans le vide. It's a most cruel torture."
p. 645: on April 21: ALS, Berg.
p. 645: brief note to Cora: April 27, 1908; ALS, Columbia.
p. 645: "investigation or of punishment": *Under Western Eyes*, p. 25.
p. 645: Nathalie (or Natalia) Haldin: Conrad first introduces her (p. 100) as "Nathalie (caressingly Natalka)," and later refers to her as Natalia.
p. 646: "officials against a nation": *Under Western Eyes*, p. 133.
p. 646: "definition of revolutionary success": *Ibid.*, pp. 134–35.
p. 647: "is sufficiently justified": April? 1908; ALS, Berg.
p. 648: "to write them in English!": August 10, 1908, *Daily News*.

p. 649: "think at all, are prisoners": August 12, 1908, *Daily Telegraph*.
p. 649: "in a way more humiliating": Sunday night, August 1908; ALS, Birmingham.
p. 649: "with a language and a country": Garnett, p. 212.
p. 650: "of tender, critical malice": *Nation*, August 22, 1908.
p. 650: "What on earth is that?": To Garnett, August 28, 1908; ALS, Yale.
p. 651: of a Pole named Witold Chwalewik: "Joseph Conrad in Cardiff," *Ruch Literacki*, VII, No. 8, 1932. Further, even if the remark were accurately reported, matters of tone are crucial. Conrad could have intended irony, or even self-contempt at not having any public to begin with.
p. 651: In his letter of August 20: 1908; copy at Princeton (or August 29, in Jean-Aubry).
p. 652: "He is nowhere": Monday, n.d., August 1908; Jean-Aubry, *Joseph Conrad*, II, p. 73.
p. 653: entrance of Violet Hunt: See Violet Hunt's *The Flurried Years*, Douglas Goldring's *South Lodge*, Mizener's *The Saddest Story*, especially the last, pp. 141 ff.
p. 654: "which I extracted from him": Ford, *Return to Yesterday*, p. 191.
p. 654: "in these changed times": October 13, 1923; TLS, Yale.
p. 655: "summers at this date": September 25, 1908; ALS, Illinois.
p. 656: "Well, this is *our* thing": (New York: Boni and Liveright, 1909), p. 349.
p. 657: "in the power of folly": February 16, 1905; ALS, Dartmouth.
p. 658: "being edited under our roof": *Joseph Conrad and His Circle*, p. 131.
p. 658: "a man and a half": Undated, ALS, Berg.
p. 658: "may yet produce it": ALS, Berg.
p. 659: "I have forgiven you long ago": November 18, 1923; ALS, private collection. (Jean-Aubry has October 23, 1923.)
p. 660: "and settle my ideas": Wednesday, October 1908: ALS, Berg.
p. 660: "*and the Years*, reminiscences": *Ibid.*
p. 661: with Ford and the *Review:* ALS, Berg.
p. 662: "than I have done": November 3, 1908; ALS, Yale.
p. 662: To Wells: November 3, 1908; ALS, Illinois.
p. 662: "for goodness knows how long": November 30, 1908; ALS, Birmingham.
p. 663: He indicates he plans: December 12, 1908; ALS, Harvard.
p. 664: "I think so myself": December 17, 1908, ALS, British Museum.
p. 664: "not represented is not art": *The Art of the Novel* (New York: Scribner's, 1950), p. xi.
p. 664: imperial Russia, at thirty-one: December 29, 1908; ALS, Berg.
p. 665: "a pair of silly innocents": Wednesday evening, March 1909; ALS, Berg. For other aspects from Ford's point of view, see Mizener, pp. 180 ff.
p. 666: "of mere spectators—auditors": 1909; ALS, Birmingham.
p. 667: "disturbed by casual visitors": May 20, 1909; TLS, Berg.
p. 667: "Look here my dear Ford": This paragraph is in Conrad's holograph.
p. 669: "like a cold nightmare": April 16, 1909; ALS, Dartmouth.
p. 669: "practical, editorial purposes": July 19, 1909; ALS, Lilly.
p. 670: "by that almost impossible feat": May 5, 1909; ALS, Colgate.
p. 670: "of doing it at all": June 23, 1909; ALS, Yale.

p. 671: "I must bear the disgrace": July 31, 1909; ALS, British Museum.
p. 672: "highly distasteful to me": Wednesday, August 1909; ALS, Berg.
p. 673: "cannot work to any serious purpose": To Galsworthy, September 7, 1909; ALS, Birmingham.
p. 674: "conception plutôt idéale": October 29, 1909; ALS, private collection.
p. 674: "New World and Old": October 17, 1909; ALS, Colgate.
p. 675: "more of the stories they like": Monday, October 1909; Jean-Aubry, *Joseph Conrad,* II, p. 103.
p. 675: "into the translator's prose?": November 15, 1909; ALS, Harvard.
p. 675: "an original work—almost": ALS, Birmingham.
p. 675: "in search of sympathy": December 20, 1909; ALS, Berg.
p. 676: to Galsworthy, on December 22: ALS, Birmingham.
p. 677: In January 1910: Thursday; ALS, Texas.
p. 677: "there is no remedy": Undated, Sunday night; ALS, Berg.
p. 677: he wrote to Robert d'Humières: December 23, 1909; ALS, private collection.
p. 677: "you dare say "dat" ' ": *Joseph Conrad and His Circle,* p. 140.
p. 678: "prehistoric ages": To Garnett, May 27, 1912; ALS, Berg.
p. 678: family name in *Crime and Punishment: The Political Novels of Joseph Conrad* (Chicago: University of Chicago Press, 1963), p. 282.
p. 679: a notorious double agent: See Baines, pp. 370 ff. and Hay, pp. 268 ff.
p. 680: "darkness of mystical contradictions": *Notes on Life and Letters,* p. 47.
p. 680: "would not have held out": *Joseph Conrad and His Circle,* pp. 143–44.
p. 681: "inducing her to go away": *Under Western Eyes,* p. 371.
p. 681: "put him into an asylum": February 6, 1910; Blackburn, p. 192.
p. 682: "fatal stoppage of work": March 3, 1910; ALS, Birmingham.
p. 682: "family and furniture about me": May 23, 1910; ALS, Berg. (February 19, 1919, also ALS, Berg.)
p. 682: in a letter to Davray: ALS, Texas.
p. 682: "4 rooms in a cottage": To Symons, May 6, 1910; copy at Princeton.
p. 683: "little hell into another": May 17, 1910; ALS, Birmingham.
p. 683: "certainly it won't hurt me": ALS, private collection.
p. 683: three pounds per thousand words: That is, if Conrad wrote at the rate of about 150,000 words a year, he would collect, in current monies, about $110–$125 a week from Pinker. Only Henry James among Conrad's serious contemporaries could point to such paltry earnings.
p. 684: "and external malevolence": *Joseph Conrad,* pp. 221 ff.
p. 684: "close association with Hueffer": *Ibid.,* p. 243.
p. 684: "other literary prospectors": *Ibid.*
p. 685: "unmanned and then destroyed": *Ibid.,* p. 223.
p. 685: "and very roughly imagined": Guerard, p. 255.
p. 686: "shadows and shades of life": *The Great Tradition* (New York: Doubleday Anchor, 1954 [1948]), p. 252.
p. 687: "Very safe bunkum that": May 31, 1910; ALS, Birmingham.
p. 687: in the familiar Maupassant: See Paul Kirschner, *Conrad: The Psychologist as Artist* (Edinburgh: Oliver & Boyd, 1968), pp. 220 ff.
p. 688: "make both our fortunes": July 27, 1910; ALS, Texas.

p. 688: "mention your opinion": July 31, 1910; ALS, Rosenbach.
p. 689: "out of my head": To Galsworthy, September 8, 1910; ALS, Birmingham.
p. 689: "in my softened brain": To Galsworthy, August 27, 1910; ALS, Birmingham.
p. 689: and told Galsworthy: ALS, Birmingham.
p. 690: at length to Helen Sanderson: September 1910; ALS, Yale.
p. 690: "with immense seriousness": To Galsworthy, October 27, 1910; ALS, Birmingham.
p. 691: "as a mere windlestraw!": November 1, 1910; ALS, Birmingham.
p. 691: derided to Galsworthy: November 22, 1910; ALS, Birmingham.
p. 692: "reflect before you leap": Sunday, n.d.; ALS, Chicago Historical Society.

VIII: THROUGH VICTORY (1911–1915)

p. 695: As he told Garnett: January 12, 1911; Garnett, p. 222.
p. 696: "he is not brilliant": December 22, 1910; ALS, Yale.
p. 696: "getting a degree in C.E.": Tuesday evening, n.d.; ALS, Birmingham.
p. 697: "as next morning to come": *Ibid.*
p. 697: explained to Joseph de Smet: January 23, 1911, Jean-Aubry, *Joseph Conrad*, II, p. 125.
p. 697: "(in the easier style)": February 15, 1911; ALS, Duke.
p. 697: Conrad corresponded with Galsworthy: March 10, 1911; ALS, Birmingham.
p. 697: "his web in a gale": March 29, 1911; ALS, Berg.
p. 697: "bottom of written things": March 12, 1911; ALS, Lilly. Garnett omitted this section in his printing of the letter.
p. 698: "with not a page": To Galsworthy, Sunday, n.d.; ALS, Birmingham.
p. 698: "sort of dull desperation": June 2, 1911; ALS, Texas.
p. 698: "like a nightmare": August 18, 1911; ALS, Birmingham.
p. 699: telling Galsworthy he was ashamed: June 26, 1911; ALS, Birmingham.
p. 699: "I deserved the recompense": Friday night, July 1911; copy at Cornell. (Possibly July 3 or 8, neither of which is a Friday.)
p. 699: long letter on July 28: ALS, Birmingham.
p. 700: "to receive this morning": September 23, 1911; ALS, Birmingham.
p. 701: "killed the Scribner's man": July 29 or 30, 1911; ALS, private collection. The letter is undated; Garnett has July 29, but the envelope is postmarked the thirtieth.
p. 701: "with touching consistency": August 4, 1911; ALS, Yale.
p. 702: "as a sort of curiosity": August 24, 1911; ALS, NYPL.
p. 702: wrote again on September 25: ALS, NYPL.
p. 703: "fit state to judge them": October 15, 1911; ALS, Birmingham.
p. 703: "by an irresponsible chatterer": *Ibid.*
p. 704: "propounded in the earlier work": October 12, 1911.
p. 704: "special triumph lies": *Nation*, October 21, 1911.
p. 704: "personal spite—or vanity": October 20, 1911; Garnett, pp. 232–33.
p. 705: "concerned with ideas": *Ibid.*, pp. 234–35.
p. 705: in *The Manchester Guardian:* October 11, 1911.

p. 705: He was stable: Something of a drifter and an adventurer, Curle was stable in his relationship to the Conrads.
p. 706: of the *Westminster Gazette:* October 14, 1911.
p. 706: "ill too now and then": October 27, 1911; ALS, Colgate.
p. 706: "marked lightly in crayon": November 26, 1911; *Lettres françaises*, p.110.
p. 707: "and their own day": *The English Review*, March 1912.
p. 707: "felt distinctly poorer for it": December 21, 1911; ALS, Berg.
p. 709: A 1914 Journal entry: II, p. 63 (translated by Justin O'Brien).
p. 709: "but without ease": III, p. 94.
p. 709: "efface that act?": III, pp. 94–5.
p. 709: "to efface their mark": III, p. 123.
p. 711: he told Quinn: ALS, NYPL.
p. 712: "finished in a fortnight!": February 19, 1912; ALS, British Museum.
p. 712: he totaled (for Galsworthy): March 27, 1912; ALS, Birmingham.
p. 712: Conrad wrote Elsie: March 27, 1912; copy at Cornell.
p. 713: "lowest side of craftsmanship": March 28, 1912; ALS, Berg.
p. 714: Conrad wrote Pinker: Undated, April 1912; ALS, Berg.
p. 716: "or a tale in the third": ALS, Berg. Successive letters on May 30, June 6, June 26 are all at the Berg.
p. 716: "and looking at the scene": ALS, Berg.
p. 717: "next year in good time": ALS, Berg.
p. 717: "exile to that island": ALS, Berg.
p. 717: "doesn't stand on quantity": ALS, Berg.
p. 718: "serialisation in the US": January 26, 1913; ALS, Berg.
p. 718: "more on the lowest estimate": February 20, 1913; ALS, Berg.
p. 718: "to have it serialised": ALS, Berg.
p. 719: "creep, creep. However—": ALS, Berg; also for the May 4 letter.
p. 720: which began with Davray: See letter to Davray, May 10, 1912; *Lettres françaises*, pp. 118–19.
p. 720: "of the Universe demands": June 21, 1912; ALS, Doucet.
p. 720: "Jessie has been fairly well": August 13, 1912; ALS, Duke.
p. 720: a letter to Gide: August 16, 1912; ALS, Doucet.
p. 721: "for an 'extra fiver' ": See August 23, 1912, TLS, NYPL; October 27, 1912, ALS, NYPL.
p. 722: "the thing at sight": November 5, 1912; Garnett, p. 243.
p. 722: "far richer than Mr. Kipling": October 14, 1912.
p. 722: John Masefield: In *The Manchester Guardian*, October 16, 1912.
p. 722: "in England somewhere about 1890": October 25, 1912.
p. 722: "mere verbiage in comparison": To Garnett, October 16, 1912; ALS, McGregor, Va.
p. 723: the *Spectator* reviewer: November 16, 1912.
p. 723: "some of us have of your work": November 22, 1912; *Twenty Letters to Joseph Conrad.*
p. 723: "to hold it—that's all": November 25, 1912; ALS, University College.
p. 724: then an assistant at Doubleday: See "Joseph Conrad: A Footnote to Publishing History," *The Atlantic* (February 1958), pp. 63–7.

p. 725: The latter responded: ALS, Yale.
p. 725: "has been ever done before": December 8, 1912; ALS, NYPL.
p. 726: "just could remember dimly": *Ibid.*
p. 726: Conrad wrote one of his worst stories: In December 1912.
p. 726: Conrad reported that his debts: To Quinn, ALS, NYPL.
p. 726: He told Quinn: March 16, 1913; ALS, NYPL.
p. 726: "properly speaking, is non-existent": March 21, 1913; ALS, Yale.
p. 727: "you are not morally entitled?": March 28, 1913; ALS, Yale.
p. 728: Conrad gave Ford: ALS, British Museum.
p. 728: for *The New York Times:* February 2, 1913.
p. 728: Conrad was of his party: Professor Dale Randall, in his *Joseph Conrad and Warrington Dawson: The Record of a Friendship* (Durham, N.C.: Duke University Press, 1968), provides many of the details.
p. 729: "and the clear Light of Truth": Randall, pp. 70–1.
p. 729: Conrad began his response: June 20, 1913; ALS, Duke.
p. 730: "Nothing but obscenities": Jacob Epstein, *Let There Be Sculpture* (New York: Dutton, 1955), p. 66.
p. 732: "finish their education with": April 12, 1913; ALS, Birmingham.
p. 733: "do that for a bore": July 20, 1913; ALS, Yale (and Jean-Aubry, *Joseph Conrad,* II, p. 146).
p. 734: "highly finished of my stories": August 24, 1913; *ibid.,* p. 149.
p. 734: postponed to January 1914: Some copies were published in 1913 in order to establish copyright.
p. 734: "never be written now I guess": Sunday, June 1, 1913; ALS, Berg. (Jean-Aubry, in error, has June 2.)
p. 735: he described to Arthur Symons: Saturday, n.d. [August 2, 1913]; ALS, Alderman, Va.
p. 735: "dogged application to the task": ALS, Texas.
p. 736: was preceded by a letter: September 4, 1913; ALS, Russell.
p. 736: "in his pessimism, almost juvenile": *The Letters of D. H. Lawrence* (London: Heinemann, 1932), p. 235.
p. 737: "among ordinary affairs": *Portraits from Memory* (New York: Simon & Schuster, 1956), pp. 87, 89.
p. 737: "but no great change": October 23, 1922; TLS, Russell.
p. 738: "at this particular juncture": September 12, 1913; ALS, Berg.
p. 739: "for the first time in my life": February 7, 1914; ALS, Russell.
p. 739: "matter of a week or so": ALS, Berg.
p. 739: "for that *is* my quality": ALS, Berg.
p. 740: "before I start again": ALS, Berg.
p. 740: "five years at odd times": ALS, Berg.
p. 740: "when I get the proof": ALS, Berg.
p. 740: "he ever knew (not many)": Wednesday, n.d., 1913?; ALS, private collection.
p. 741: "Chance tolerable. I don't": ALS, Dartmouth.
p. 741: some sympathy in the press: The entire episode is well related by Randall, pp. 40–46.
p. 742: "half strangled for years": *Chance,* p. 119.

p. 742: "end of the experience": *Ibid.*, p. 117.
p. 742: "too little of it": *Ibid.*, p. 310.
p. 743: of *The Manchester Guardian:* January 15, 1914.
p. 745: within some "mystic impulse": In a letter of October 1916 to Lady Ottoline Morrell, Aldous Huxley said, with *Chance* in mind, that Conrad's presentation of life is like "being under the influence of a drug" (Robert Gathorne-Hardy, ed., *Ottoline at Garsington* [London: Faber and Faber, 1974], p. 155).
p. 746: "a man who would pretend": May 24, 1916; ALS, NYPL.
p. 746: writing in the *Nation:* January 24, 1914.
p. 746: Bennett wrote in praise: On January 18, 1914; the Journal entry is for January 24, 1924.
p. 747: "follow up a first success!": February 17, 1914; ALS, Duke.
p. 747: "make for your doorstep": February 17, 1914; ALS, Texas.
p. 747: "distasteful to me": To Garnett, February 23, 1914; ALS, Berg.
p. 747: "type of the *Island Story*": To Pinker, May 29, 1914; ALS, Berg.
p. 747: "is sold I don't know": March 19, 1914; ALS, Birmingham.
p. 748: "was the most difficult": ALS, Berg.
p. 749: "we will stay alive": Interview reprinted in Mrs. Maria Dąbrowska's *Sketches on Conrad* (Warsaw, Poland: Pańastwowy Instytut Wydawniczy, 1959).
p. 750: "other merit of the book": April 1914; Richard Curle, ed., *Conrad to a Friend, 150 Selected Letters from Joseph Conrad to Richard Curle* (New York: Crosby, Gaige, 1928), p. 19.
p. 750: "once she wrote me a letter—": Quoted by Józef Ujejski, *Joseph Conrad,* translated from Polish into French by Pierre Duméril (Paris: Malfère, 1939), p. 38.
p. 750: "is rather remarkable": To Galsworthy, May 5, 1914; ALS, Birmingham.
p. 750: "bar to either": Borys Conrad, p. 70.
p. 751: "been convulsed with laughter!": *Ibid.*, p. 84.
p. 752: "new meaning to life": *Within the Tides*, p. 35.
p. 753: "is drawing close": July 22, 1914; ALS, Yale.
p. 754: "the duties of courrier": July 25, 1914; ALS, Birmingham.
p. 755: "on the grey pavement": "First News," which appeared in *Reveille* (August 1918), reprinted in *Notes on Life and Letters*, pp. 177–78.
p. 755: "to lead to moral annihilation": *Ibid.*, p. 178.
p. 755: To Galsworthy, Conrad wrote: August 1, 1914; ALS, Polish Library, London.
p. 756: "to be formally recognised": *Notes on Life and Letters*, pp. 138–39.
p. 756: Conrad wrote Pinker: ALS, Berg.
p. 757: In "Poland Revisited": It appeared in four issues of the *Daily News* in 1915: March 29 and 31, April 6 and 9; then was reprinted in *Notes on Life and Letters.* It would also appear in Edith Wharton's *The Book of the Homeless*, 1916, and as a pamphlet printed for private circulation (25 copies only) by Thomas Wise.
p. 758: "without sights, without sounds": *Notes on Life and Letters*, pp. 163–64.
p. 758: "and with great fluency": p. 97.

p. 758: to attend school in Cracow: Polish Academy of Sciences.
p. 759: "beyond the Great Square": *Notes on Life and Letters*, p. 167.
p. 759: "towards the Florian Gate": *Ibid.*, pp. 169 ff.
p. 760: "with sentiment and emotion": p. 133.
p. 760: affected by the lines: See Morf, *The Polish Shades*, pp. 100 ff.
p. 761: "to bed for five days": November 15, 1914; ALS, Polish Library, London.
p. 762: to miss the target: p. 96.
p. 763: "no relief—on the contrary": January 28, 1915: Jean-Aubry, *Joseph Conrad*, II, p. 167.
p. 764: "its mastery of despair": *Victory*, pp. 196 ff.
p. 766: "ourselves—but not inimically": Victory MS., pp. 3–4; Texas MS.
p. 767: "with his people in Sweden": MS., pp. 89–90; *Victory*, p. 33.
p. 768: "loudness of the phrase": MS., pp. 496–97.
p. 769: "not irritated are seduced": September 30, 1915.
p. 769: "whose doom is so sure": September 24, 1915.
p. 769: "horror of the matter": October 2, 1915.
p. 770: Curle's copy of the novel: Curle, *The Last Twelve Years of Joseph Conrad* (London: Sampson, Low, Marston, 1928), p. 94.
p. 771: "try to write it up": February 25, 1915; ALS, Dartmouth.
p. 771: "sixteen volumes in print": March 9, 1915; ALS, Texas.
p. 771: "on putting it out": March 13, 1915; ALS, Texas.
p. 771: "to sit doing nothing": Friday, n.d., mid-1915; ALS, Birmingham.
p. 772: To James, on July 24: ALS, Yale.
p. 772: To Ford on August 12: Copy at Cornell.
p. 772: "momentous events of the time": August 17, 1915; ALS, private collection.
p. 772: "symbolic, profound and comic": ALS, British Museum.
p. 773: To John Quinn: December 24, 1915; ALS, NYPL.
p. 773: "a sort of autobiography": *Ibid.*
p. 773: "become paralyzed for days": Sunday, n.d., 1915?; ALS, Berg.

IX: FINAL THINGS (1916–1924)

p. 778: "period of maturer life": *The Shadow-Line*, p. viii.
p. 778: "to be ashamed of": *Ibid.*, p. ix.
p. 778: "as the Grace of God": *Ibid.*, p. 62.
p. 778: "immense forces of the world": *Ibid.*, p. 76.
p. 779: "Ransome is only indicated": February 27, 1917; ALS, Yale.
p. 779: "fidelity—and of love": *The Shadow-Line*, p. 40.
p. 780: As he told Colvin: April 2, 1917; ALS, Yale.
p. 780: "a nature without life": *Tales of Hearsay*, p. 20.
p. 780: "my mind not a little": February 27, 1916; ALS, NYPL.
p. 780: Curle reported that Conrad: Curle, *Last Twelve Years*, p. 136.
p. 781: "were still at school": ALS, Birmingham.
p. 782: "of a material collaboration": To Saxton, March 18, 1916; ALS, private collection.

p. 782: "in discernment, in comprehension": April 10, 1916; ALS, Alderman, Va.
p. 782: "as something larger": May 19, 1916; TL, NYPL (Quinn Collection).
p. 783: "constantly altogether idiomatic": May 19, 1916; ALS, Doucet.
p. 783: "j'ai raison d'insister": June 8, 1916; Jean-Aubry copy, Yale.
p. 783: "in a book called *Youth*": Michael Holroyd, *Lytton Strachey* (New York: Holt, Rinehart, 1967), I, p. 316.
p. 783: "a translation must be": II, p. 191.
p. 783: "for the 'well-done job' ": II, p. 193 (January 18, 1917).
p. 784: debit to his account: July 4, 1916; ALS, private collection.
p. 784: whom he described: To Curle, August 20, 1916; ALS, Lilly.
p. 785: great affection for her: To Pinker, 1916; ALS, Berg.
p. 785: "as much as to me": July 15, 1916; ALS, NYPL.
p. 785: "with perfect comprehension": July 16, 1916; ALS, Yale.
p. 786: "and, perhaps, of art": Wednesday, n.d., August 16? 1916; ALS, Berg.
p. 786: "to be thought of": Undated; ALS, Colgate.
p. 787: "it was not visible yet": May 24, 1916; ALS, NYPL.
p. 787: one of her invitations to visit: She had also tried to get Conrad to intervene in the Casement affair, but his English patriotism preempted any other considerations. See letters to Quinn, July 15, 1916; ALS, NYPL, and to Lady Ottoline Morrell, August 10, 1916; ALS, Texas.
p. 788: "complete and ineradicable incompatibility": *Notes on Life and Letters*, pp. 135–36.
p. 788: Sir George Russell Clerk: Najder (p. 260, n. 2) corrected Conrad's spelling of "Clark." For this episode, see Conrad's letter, first to Richard Curle, August 20, 1916; ALS, Lilly; then to Retinger, August 21, 1916; Najder, p. 260. The original of the letter to Retinger, in French, is in the Library of the Polish Academy of Sciences in Kórnik.
p. 789: "in the Volga to-day": August 31, 1916; Jean-Aubry, *Joseph Conrad*, II, pp. 174–5. Except for the nine letters to Sandeman printed in Jean-Aubry, this potentially valuable correspondence has not turned up; it was very probably more extensive than nine letters.
p. 790: "in her traces. See?": ALS, Yale.
p. 790: "on these matters generally": September 14, 1916; ALS, Yale.
p. 790: "between Conrad and myself": Busza, pp. 82–3.
p. 791: "that they do exist": October 1916; ALS, Berg.
p. 791: "The day was fair and cold": ALS, Yale.
p. 791: "must remain my private possession": Undated; TLS, Berg.
p. 792: "not to do so": November 1916; ALS, Yale.
p. 792: "from me for 10 days": November 8, 1916; ALS, Berg.
p. 792: To Dent, however: Jean-Aubry, *Joseph Conrad*, II, p. 180.
p. 793: "all that pomp":To Pinker, Sunday, n.d. (early 1917); ALS, Berg.
p. 793: "we're engaged on right": January 3, 1917; ALS, Dartmouth.
p. 793: In his letters: For example, to Hastings, January 22 and January 25, 1917; ALS, Colgate.
p. 793: He planned a story: To Pinker, August 15, 1917; ALS, Berg.
p. 793: "or annoy him any more": February 12, 1917; ALS, NYPL.
p. 794: "mon activité artistique": March 18, 1917; ALS, Yale.

p. 794: " 'war as games' attitude": See Chapter I of Paul Fussell's excellent *The Great War and Modern Memory* (New York & London: Oxford University Press, 1975).
p. 794: "for a time at least": March 19, 1917; ALS, Dent.
p. 795: "for some reason or other": *Malay Mail,* September 2, 1924 (obtained through Norman Sherry).
p. 795: Congreve with a young lady: Easter Monday, 1917; Jean-Aubry, *Joseph Conrad,* II, p. 188.
p. 795: He insisted, nevertheless: To Howe, April 20, 1917; ALS, Berg.
p. 796: "masters and teachers": April 21, 1917; Jean-Aubry, *Joseph Conrad,* II, p. 189.
p. 796: "and it remains so still": To Quinn, May 6, 1917; ALS, NYPL.
p. 797: "Le monde est bête": May 18, 1917; ALS, Texas. (Very poorly reprinted by Jean-Aubry.)
p. 797: "mental and emotional reaction": As described to Alfred Thomas Saunders, June 14, 1917; ALS, Public Library of South Australia. Conrad wrote: "After all I *am* a writer of fiction; and it is not what actually happened, but the manner of presenting it that settles the literary and even the moral value of my work. My little vol. of autobiography of course is absolutely genuine. The rest is a more or less close approximation to facts and suggestions. What I claim as true are my mental and emotional reactions to life, to men, to their affairs and their passions as I have seen them. I have in that sense kept always true to myself."
p. 798: "as if from fear": ALS, Doucet.
p. 799: "Americans after the war": August 9, 1917; ALS, Haverford.
p. 802: "on the stage": August 15, 1917; ALS, Berg.
p. 803: "and for giving in": To Garnett, October 30, 1912; *The Letters of D. H. Lawrence,* p. 66.
p. 804: "of enormous hidden power": December 14, 1922; TLS, Yale.
p. 805: "for the Mirror of the Sea—": December 31, 1917; ALS, Yale.
p. 805: He called himself: To Galsworthy, December 31, 1917; ALS, Birmingham.
p. 805: He found the navy thinking: To Helen Sanderson, n.d., 1917; ALS, Yale.
p. 806: "am not likely to, now": Sunday, n.d., 1917?; ALS, Texas.
p. 807: "which must be immensely comforting": February 6, 1918; TLS, NYPL.
p. 808: "no more than illusions": *Ibid.*
p. 808: outline he provided: February 18, 1918; Jean-Aubry, *Joseph Conrad,* II, p. 200.
p. 808: "Donna Rita, woman": J. Middleton Murry, ed., *Novels and Novelists* (Boston: Beacon Press, 1959), p. 62.
p. 809: On the twenty-seventh of April: ALS, Boston Public Library.
p. 809: Conrad told Walpole: ALS, Texas.
p. 809: "gift of the gods": April 28, 1918; ALS, Doucet.
p. 809: to respond at length: May 4, 1918; Jean-Aubry, *Joseph Conrad,* II, p. 204. Unfortunately, the original of this important letter remains unknown.
p. 810: In responding that he was very pleased: May 6, 1918; TL & ALS, Rosenbach.

p. 810: He told Garnett: May 16, 1918; Garnett, pp. 258–59.
p. 811: "to die in their company": To Walpole, June 7, 1918; TLS, Texas.
p. 811: " 'be lost for ever' ": June 11, 1918; TL & ALS, Syracuse.
p. 812: He told Hastings: June 26, 1918; ALS, Colgate.
p. 812: Conrad wrote a series of letters: They are at Yale.
p. 814: Conrad rejected the idea: September 25, 1918; ALS, Berg.
p. 814: "as good as the people": November 11, 1918; ALS, Texas.
p. 814: "has got to be paid for": January 25, 1919; Jean-Aubry, *Joseph Conrad,* II, p. 216.
p. 816: "writing period of my life": October 2, 1918; ALS, British Museum.
p. 816: "to be wholly dictated": ALS, British Museum.
p. 817: becomes compulsive and distorted: Dickens's obsessive need for an audience he felt slipping away resulted in his physically and psychologically depleting readings; whereas Hemingway offered up his personal exploits, even his life, when he found himself failing on the printed page.
p. 817: "is not a Lady Holland": October 9, 1918; TLS, Lilly.
p. 817: "expressing these great intentions": October 17, 1918; Jean-Aubry, *Joseph Conrad,* II, p. 210.
p. 817: "forgive my imperfections": To Gils, November 25, 1918; TLS, Berg.
p. 818: When Conrad wrote Borys: October 21, 1918; ALS, Boston Public Library.
p. 818: "wonder at her weariness": October 16, 1918; TLS, NYPL.
p. 819: "if I do manage it": To Rothenstein, October 24, 1918; ALS, Harvard.
p. 820: "it is in now": December 31, 1918; TLS, Berg.
p. 820: "personal art exists": December 21, 1918; Jean-Aubry, *Joseph Conrad,* II, pp. 213 ff.
p. 821: Conrad wrote to the editor: December 12, 1918; copy at Yale.
p. 822: he told Pinker: January 30, 1919; ALS, Berg.
p. 823: "parts of Jones and Ricardo": To Hastings, February 27, 1919; ALS, Colgate.
p. 823: "bigger thing of the two": February 19, 1919; ALS, Berg.
p. 824: "pay my tailor's bill": March 29, 1919; ALS, Colgate.
p. 824: "he disobeys your injunction": April 10, 1919; TLS, NYPL.
p. 825: "a bigger thing in every way": May 3, 1919; TLS, NYPL.
p. 825: "and more mysterious characters": May 10, 1919. Theodore G. Ehrsam identified the reviewer.
p. 825: In the *Morning Post:* August 6, 1919.
p. 826: "and insecurely told": August 7, 1919.
p. 826: "to become insubstantial": August 6, 1919.
p. 828: exhaustion and some despair: To Quinn, May 26, 1919; ALS, NYPL.
p. 828: "anything be more legitimate?": July 7, 1919; ALS, private collection.
p. 829: To Quinn, Conrad stressed: May 26, 1919; TLS, NYPL.
p. 830: "enthusiastic about that scheme": July 31, 1919; TLS, NYPL.
p. 831: "a rather symbolic package": August 20, 1919; ALS, Doucet.
p. 831: "What a confession!": Early August 1919; George Keating, *A Conrad Memorial Library* (New York: Doubleday, Doran, 1929), p. 281.
p. 832: Conrad wrote to Jean-Aubry: ALS, Yale.

p. 832: His response to Gide: ALS, Doucet.
p. 833: he wrote his young friend: October 14, 1919; ALS, Yale; and November 7, 1919; TLS, Yale.
p. 833: Conrad heard from Gide: Both Gide letters, for November 10 and 21, are at the Doucet.
p. 833: "pardonner cette faiblesse": ALS, Doucet.
p. 834: "but not complete collection": September 29, 1919; ALS, NYPL.
p. 834: Conrad indicates that the clean copies: September 30, 1919; ALS, British Museum.
p. 835: "It bored me": August 6, 1919; ALS, Yale.
p. 835: "to come on this occasion": August 14, 1919; TL & ALS, Berg.
p. 836: "chances of closer contacts": September 22, 1919; ALS, Duke.
p. 836: "lengthy & effusive": September 23, 1919; Randall, p. 199.
p. 837: Conrad wrote Dent: October 25, 1919; Jean-Aubry, *Joseph Conrad,* II, 230.
p. 837: Writing to a producer named Vernon: November 22, 1919; TLS, Brotherton.
p. 838: "must remain what it is": November 11, 1919; ALS, Berg.
p. 839: "period of depression": To Major Gardiner, December 24, 1919; ALS, Harvard.
p. 839: Conrad told Quinn: TLS, NYPL.
p. 840: Conrad wrote again: March 5, 1920: TLS, NYPL.
p. 841: Conrad asked Wise directly: June 21, 1920; ALS, British Museum.
p. 842: He told Colvin: April 4, 1920; ALS, Hofstra.
p. 842: When he wrote to Aniela Zagórska: April 10, 1920; Najder, p. 261. (Original in *Pion,* 1934, No. 50.)
p. 842: suggesting Marthe Duproix: November 4, 1919; copy at Yale.
p. 842: Valéry had spoken: In his essay "Poetry and Abstract Thought."
p. 843: "patched book": April 27, 1920; ALS, Yale.
p. 843: "of Conrad's cable style": To Wise, May 20, 1920; ALS, British Museum.
p. 843: as he reported it to Walpole: June 14, 1920; ALS, Texas.
p. 844: "world *may* be wrong": June 24, 1920; Jean-Aubry, *Joseph Conrad,* II, p. 241.
p. 844: "has failed him": July 1, 1920.
p. 844: was published anonymously in the *Nation:* July 17, 1920.
p. 845: "I think, as in expression": To Garnett, July 11, 1920; ALS, McGregor, Va.
p. 846: Writing to the Ranee: July 15, 1920; TL & ALS, private collection.
p. 846: *Sir James Brooke,* and others: See John D. Gordan's "The Rajah Brooke and Joseph Conrad," *Studies in Philology,* XXXV, pp. 613–34; also, p. 431, above, for sources of *Lord Jim.*
p. 847: "easing down a bit": July 17, 1920; TLS, NYPL.
p. 847: "on the wide seas": To Holt, July 20, 1920; Jean-Aubry, *Joseph Conrad,* II, p. 244.
p. 848: the second of which: July 25, 1920; TL, Yale. (Jean-Aubry's reprint of the letter is unreliable.)
p. 849: as another kind of end: In his devotion to sailing ships, Conrad was per-

petuating, in his way, his father's romanticism, Apollo's view of the Pole as both individualized and tied to tradition.

p. 849: "very lame and unsatisfactory": To Curle, August 18, 1920; ALS, Lilly.
p. 849: "but one must live!": *Ibid.*
p. 850: "pathetic population" hypnotized: August 26, 1920; ALS, Berg.
p. 850: knows what Donkin is: September 3, 1920; ALS, Yale.
p. 851: "much less dignified": October 9, 1920; ALS, Lilly.
p. 851: of the matter. Nothing did: To Wise, October 1920 (Sunday); ALS, British Museum; and November 1, 1920; ALS, British Museum.
p. 852: "perverse, cynical and lame": November 17, 1920; ALS, Texas.
p. 852: "left as they are": November 29, 1920; copy by Elsie Hueffer at Yale.
p. 852: to one to Gide: December 1, 1920; ALS, Doucet (misdated by Jean-Aubry as February 1, 1920).
p. 852: "on a piece of paper": October 10, 1921; TLS, Texas. (The manuscript of Conrad's little-known foreword is at Yale.)
p. 853: described the journey to Walpole: December 26, 1920; ALS, Texas.
p. 854: "all these years ago": Garnett, p. 276.
p. 854: he prophesied that the critics: To Sandeman, January 17, 1921; Jean-Aubry, *Joseph Conrad*, II, p. 253.
p. 854: "with punctuality and dispatch": January 30, 1921; ALS, Berg.
p. 854: "One wishes to roar": To Jean-Aubry, February 23, 1921; ALS, Yale.
p. 855: "A horrid state": May 10, 1921; ALS, Birmingham.
p. 855: "*Paris sous Napoléon*": *The Sea Dreamer*, pp. 279–80.
p. 856: "with no particular trouble": June 8, 1921; ALS, Birmingham.
p. 856: "gives me a little shudder": *Ibid.*
p. 857: "of the play itself": August 10, 1921; copy at Yale.
p. 857: great talent there or elsewhere: Or else, Conrad grasped at any friendly Polish connection.
p. 857: but Cracow, not Warsaw: Najder, p. 281, n. 4.
p. 858: "should exercise their function": November 23, 1922; copy at Yale.
p. 858: "of the virtuous Bolsheviks": January 31, 1924; Jean-Aubry, *Joseph Conrad*, II, p. 335. (Copy at Yale, but not by Winawer.)
p. 860: "the thought so profound": August 5, 1921; ALS, Doucet.
p. 860: "la même détresse morale": October 16, 1921; copy at Yale.
p. 861: "unerring judgment": ALS, Colgate.
p. 861: to raise to £200: See his September 8, 1921, letter to Tadeusz Marynowski; Najder, pp. 271–72.
p. 862: "and at such a time": November 2, 1921; ALS, Russell.
p. 862: "selection of the members": October 23, 1922; TLS, Russell.
p. 863: he thanked Wise: ALS, British Museum.
p. 863: "Who would have thought it!": November 22, 1921; ALS, Harvard.
p. 863: Conrad pointed out: November 29, 1921; ALS, Harvard.
p. 864: "must have misunderstood him": *The Rover*, pp. 7–8.
p. 865: "short and threatening mutter": *Ibid.*, p. 237.
p. 865: Conrad was very curt: ALS, Yale.
p. 865: of December 15: ALS, Yale.
p. 866: "sort of futile way": January 19, 1922; TL & ALS, Berg.

p. 866: Conrad explained to Aniela Zagórska: January 27, 1922; Najder, p. 277. (Original in *Ruch Literacki*, 1927, No. 5.)
p. 867: "of my affectionate friendship": February 10, 1922; Jean-Aubry, *Joseph Conrad*, II, p. 265.
p. 867: "in terms of money": February 19, 1922; *Ibid.*, p. 266.
p. 867: "stability and support": July 10, 1922; ALS, Texas.
p. 868: "he began his management": April 4, 1922; TLS, Brotherton.
p. 869: "to be disappointed with": April 24, 1922; TLS, Lilly.
p. 870: "shrinks from tragic issues": April 29, 1922; ALS, Lilly.
p. 870: "also got on my nerves": May 24, 1922; TLS, Colgate.
p. 871: to play Chopin for the family: Randall, pp. 59 ff.; also, p. 61, n. 97.
p. 871: Dawson created hybrids: *Ibid.*, p. 108.
p. 871: "into at every step": TLS, Duke.
p. 872: On June 29, Conrad told Curle: ALS, Lilly.
p. 872: "which would fascinate people": June 30, 1922; TL, Berg (incomplete).
p. 873: "crippling affair" for him: To Graham, July 7, 1922; ALS, Dartmouth.
p. 873: Conrad pointed out: To Wise, July 20, 1922; ALS, British Museum.
p. 873: Conrad's letter to Borys: ALS, Keating, Yale.
p. 873: "pour lui. On verra": ALS, Yale.
p. 873: feeling was, apparently, reciprocated: Borys Conrad, pp. 152–54.
p. 874: "of its fascinating mysteriousness": August 22, 1922; ALS, Berg.
p. 874: And to Graham: August 25, 1922; ALS, Ardoch (through C. T. Watts).
p. 874: "the widow and the orphan": *Ibid.*
p. 874: he says that: To Eric Pinker, October 8, 1922; TL & ALS, Berg.
p. 875: To Benrimo, he spoke: October 14, 1922; TLS, private collection.
p. 875: "learn it before Thursday": October 27, 1922; ALS, Yale.
p. 875: "would be worth hearing": October 30, 1922; TLS, Rosenbach.
p. 875: "with me about eight o'clock": Mégroz, p. 25.
p. 876: "before the first performance": Tuesday, n.d.; ALS, Birmingham.
p. 876: Jones welcomed Conrad: See Conrad's letter to Jones, November 3, 1922; ALS, Duke.
p. 876: "which has a larger meaning": November 6, 1922; ALS, Southern Methodist University Library.
p. 876: "the silence of the night": October 30, 1922; TLS, Brotherton.
p. 877: he characterized to Neel: November 8, 1922; *Lettres françaises*, p. 180.
p. 877: did an etching of Conrad: This etching, at the National Portrait Gallery, is on the cover of *Conradiana*, the journal devoted to Conrad studies.
p. 877: as he wrote Garnett: November 17, 1922; Garnett, pp. 288–89.
p. 877: and Conrad's response: November 20, 1922; TLS, Doheny Memorial Library, California.
p. 878: "any sort of public appearance": *Ibid.*
p. 879: "nothing but Marcel Proust": November 21, 1922; Jean-Aubry, *Joseph Conrad*, II, p. 287.
p. 879: Conrad wrote Adams: TLS, Doheny Memorial Library, California.
p. 879: "will never be another": November 30, 1922; ALS, Lilly.
p. 880: in a letter to Curle: December 8, 1922; TLS, Lilly.
p. 880: according to Jean-Aubry: *Joseph Conrad*, II, pp. 292–93, n. 2.

p. 881: "to decline an academic degree": February 18, 1923; ALS, Berg.
p. 881: "of my profound respect": March 15, 1923; ALS, Fitzwilliam, Cambridge.
p. 881: "with any academic distinction": March 13, 1923; Jean-Aubry, *Joseph Conrad*, II, p. 296.
p. 882: which brought the response: March 7, 1923; TLS, private collection.
p. 882: "result of a long heredity": March 7, 1923; TLS, private collection (also in Jean-Aubry, *Joseph Conrad*, II, p. 295).
p. 882: Conrad asked Aniela Zagórska: March 7, 1923; Najder, p. 288. (Original in *Ruch Literacki*, 1927, No. 5.) In the same letter, he thanks her for sending an edition of Słowacki's letters. He adds: "I have not read them yet. I have no time at the moment. My own writing progresses very slowly. I spend all my days sitting at my little table and by the evening I feel so tired that I no longer understand what I am reading."
p. 882: "repousse en même temps . . . *Tib.*": Monday, October 1922.
p. 883: Although he told Garnett: March 10, 1923; Garnett, p. 290.
p. 883: "good business for me": March 12, 1923; Curle, p. 138.
p. 883: if his report to Doubleday: March 13, 1923; Jean-Aubry, *Joseph Conrad*, II, p. 296.
p. 883: Conrad said the letter: To Eric Pinker, March 15, 1923; TLS, Berg.
p. 884: He told Ibáñez: March 21, 1923; TL initialed, Yale (in French). (Ibáñez's letter to Conrad is also at Yale.)
p. 884: and through that to Apollo: See letter to Doubleday, April 2, 1923; Jean-Aubry, *Joseph Conrad*, II, p. 301.
p. 884: "confidence for travelling": April 4, 1923; ALS, Alderman, Va.
p. 885: "taking my secret with me": p. 157.
p. 885: "to drop the bombshell": *Joseph Conrad and His Circle*, p. 250.
p. 886: he mentions to Eric Pinker: April 9, 1923; TLS, Berg.
p. 887: Conrad wrote guiltily: April 11, 1923; Najder, p. 290. (Original in *Pion*, 1934, No. 50.)
p. 887: "inspiration of the moment": April 14, 1923; ALS, Birmingham.
p. 887: Conrad gave a detailed account: April 22–29, 1923; ALS, Yale.
p. 888: "of Nature and men": *Last Essays*, p. 57.
p. 888: "took refuge in D's car": May 4, 1923; Jean-Aubry, *Joseph Conrad*, II, p. 307. See also to Jessie, May 6, 1923; ALS, Yale.
p. 888: to writing Borys: May 6, 1923; ALS, Yale.
p. 889: "handshaking with 200 people": May 11, 1923; AL-TL, Yale.
p. 889: "they did not invite me": B. L. Reid, *The Man from New York* (New York: Oxford University Press, 1968), p. 568.
p. 889: Ford reported: p. 310 (Philadelphia: Lippincott, 1933).
p. 890: "wherever you may be": Undated, May 24, 1923; ALS, Yale.
p. 890: according to her account: *Joseph Conrad and His Circle*, pp. 255 ff.
p. 891: Conrad told Eric Pinker: June 11, 1923; ALS, Berg.
p. 891: Jessie comments: *Joseph Conrad and His Circle*, pp. 260 ff.
p. 891: Conrad thanked Aniela Zagórska: July 3, 1923; Najder, p. 291. (Copy at Yale.)
p. 891: fanciful vocabulary came from: To Winawer, September 9, 1923; *ibid.*, p. 293. See Najder's note 1, p. 293.

p. 891: "to share for a little while": *Last Essays*, pp. 42–43.
p. 892: "a spark of the sacred fire": *Ibid.*, p. 31.
p. 892: "on his gift as a great novelist": To Curle, July 14, 1923; TLS, Lilly.
p. 893: "varied effects of perspective": *Ibid.*
p. 893: in a letter to Curle: July 20, 1923; ALS, Lilly.
p. 893: he wrote Wise: July 31, 1923; ALS, British Museum.
p. 893: so he noted to Colvin: ALS, Yale.
p. 893: decades after his death: July 17, 1923; Curle, p. 152.
p. 894: Conrad's response to the proposal: To Gardiner, October 8, 1923; ALS, Harvard.
p. 894: "an ass rather": To Curle, September 20, 1923; ALS, Lilly.
p. 895: "double for Lord Plushbottom": From McAlmon's *Being Geniuses Together*, quoted by Mizener, p. 331.
p. 896: Conrad's response: November 10, 1923; TLS, Yale. He added: "I looked at it and it seemed to me somewhat amateurish, which is strange, because that is not *our* failing either separately or together."
p. 896: with another letter: 1923; ALS & TL, private collection. Jean-Aubry (*Joseph Conrad*, II, p. 323) has October 23, 1923, but the sequence of Ford-Conrad letters makes November 18 more appropriate.
p. 896: Other arrangements between the two: See Conrad's letters to Ford, April 11, 1924; TL, Yale; and May 2, 1924; TLS, Yale.
p. 897: wrote derisively to Eric Pinker: February 4, 1924; TL, Berg (incomplete).
p. 897: in the world "has insulted him": Letters to Eric Pinker, February 7, 1924; February 17, 1924; May 1, 1924; Berg.
p. 897: "I know, being ungenerous": September 15; Mizener, p. 336.
p. 898: Conrad further agreed: To Ford, May 2, 1924; TLS, Yale.
p. 898: his letter to Ford: May 22, 1924; TLS, Yale.
p. 898: "his almost miraculous gifts": *Return to Yesterday*, p. 201.
p. 899: The heart fluttered: Described to Curle, November 12, 1923; TLS, Lilly.
p. 899: belonging to John Quinn: I am grateful to B. L. Reid's study of John Quinn for several details of the auction, pp. 602 ff.
p. 900: "got my share of the plunder": November 20, 1923; Jean-Aubry, *Joseph Conrad*, II, p. 324.
p. 901: Conrad asked Walpole: November 18, 1923; ALS, Texas.
p. 901: "recognition of the Irish Free State": To Jean-Aubry, November 20, 1923; ALS, Yale.
p. 901: "give me twenty for it?": July 18, 1913; ALS, NYPL.
p. 901: "are younger than my age": December 17, 1923; ALS, Lilly.
p. 902: "you are an Aristocrat": November 21, 1923; ALS, Berg.
p. 902: "four noir de ma pièce": December 28, 1922; ALS, Doucet.
p. 902: in the *New Statesman*: December 15, 1923.
p. 902: "of the land and sea": December 6, 1923.
p. 902: "people and the events": December 4, 1923; TLS, Yale.
p. 903: potentially "greater thing": *Ibid.*
p. 903: "vibrating in the air": To Doubleday, December 6, 1923; Jean-Aubry, *Joseph Conrad*, II, p. 328.
p. 903: Conrad told Graham: December 12, 1923; ALS, Dartmouth.

p. 904: He speaks of fighting: To Bennett, January 2, 1924; ALS, University College, London.
p. 904: Conrad told Doubleday: January 7, 1924; Jean-Aubry, *Joseph Conrad,* II, p. 331.
p. 905: "point of a composition?": January 29, 1924; leaf insert in Visiak's *The Mirror of Conrad* (London: Werner Laurie, 1955).
p. 905: He had received several inquiries: See, for example, his letters to Charles Chassé, Jean-Aubry, *Joseph Conrad,* II, p. 336; to Henry Seidel Canby, *ibid.,* p. 341.
p. 905: "the shade of solitary thought": *Last Essays,* p. 205.
p. 905: he promised Eric Pinker: February 3, 1924; Jean-Aubry, *Joseph Conrad,* II, p. 337.
p. 905: with a story from another: February 7, 1924; *ibid.,* p. 337.
p. 906: "Weird and exhausting": To Galsworthy, February 22, 1924; ALS, Birmingham.
p. 906: filth and obscenities: p. 66.
p. 906: I am played out: p. 91.
p. 906: Jessie has left: *Joseph Conrad and His Circle,* p. 236.
p. 906: "or the collaborated works": April 27, 1924; TLS, Yale.
p. 907: he told Curle: March 25, 1924; ALS, Lilly.
p. 907: to Elbridge Adams: March 26, 1924; Jean-Aubry, *Joseph Conrad,* II, p. 341.
p. 907: When Conrad responded: June 28, 1924; Najder, p. 299. (Original in *Ruch Literacki,* 1926, No. 7.)
p. 907: "It was a dream": *Joseph Conrad and His Circle,* p. 263.
p. 908: "que je la dois": May 30, 1924; ALS, Doucet.
p. 908: told Mrs. Doubleday: Jean-Aubry, *Joseph Conrad,* II, p. 345.
p. 909: "and apparently the most selfish": July 8, 1924; ALS, Yale.
p. 909: Curle is the witness: *The Last Twelve Years,* pp. 197 ff.

Bibliography

CONRAD'S WORKS

(*Magazine publication of short stories is given in parentheses*)

Almayer's Folly, 1895.
An Outcast of the Islands, 1896.
The Nigger of the "Narcissus," 1897. Published in the United States as Children of the Sea: A Tale of the Forecastle.
Tales of Unrest, 1898 (contents: "The Idiots," 1896; "Karain," 1897; "The Lagoon," 1897; "An Outpost of Progress," 1897; "The Return," 1898).
Lord Jim, a Tale, 1900.
The Inheritors, an Extravagant Story, with Ford Madox Hueffer, 1901.
Youth, a Narrative, and Two Other Stories, 1902 (contents: "Youth," 1898; "Heart of Darkness," 1899; "The End of the Tether," 1902).
Typhoon, 1902.
Typhoon and Other Stories, 1903 (contents: "Amy Foster," 1901; "Typhoon," 1902; "To-Morrow," 1902; "Falk," 1903).
Romance, with Ford Madox Hueffer, 1903.
Nostromo, a Tale of the Seaboard, 1904.
The Mirror of the Sea, Memories and Impressions, 1906.
The Secret Agent, a Simple Tale, 1907.
A Set of Six, 1908 (contents: "An Anarchist," 1906; "The Brute," 1906; "Gaspar Ruiz," 1906; "The Informer," 1906; "The Duel," 1908; "Il Conde," 1908).
A Personal Record. Also known as Some Reminiscences, 1908, 1912.
Under Western Eyes, a Novel, 1911.
'Twixt Land and Sea, Tales, 1912 (contents: "The Secret Sharer," 1910; "A Smile of Fortune," 1911; "Freya of the Seven Isles," 1912).
Chance, a Tale in Two Parts, 1913 [1914].
One Day More, a Play in One Act, 1913 (adaptation of "To-Morrow").
Victory, an Island Tale, 1915.
Within the Tides, 1915 (contents: "The Partner," 1911; "The Inn of the Two Witches," 1913; "Because of the Dollars," 1914; "The Planter of Malata," 1914).
The Shadow-Line, a Confession, 1917.
The Arrow of Gold, a Story Between Two Notes, 1919.
The Rescue: A Romance of the Shallows, 1920.

Notes on Life and Letters, 1921.
The Secret Agent, Drama in Four Acts, 1921 (adaptation of the novel).
The Rover, 1923.
Laughing Anne, a Play, 1923 (adaptation of "Because of the Dollars").
The Nature of a Crime, with Ford Madox Hueffer, 1924 (written in 1908).
Suspense, a Napoleonic Novel, 1925 (incomplete).
Tales of Hearsay, 1925 (contents: "The Black Mate," 1908; "Prince Roman," 1911; "The Tale," 1917; "The Warrior's Soul," 1917).
Last Essays, 1926.
The Sisters, 1928 (written in 1896; incomplete).

EDITIONS OF CONRAD'S LETTERS

(*A complete edition is in preparation, to be edited by Frederick R. Karl*)

Five Letters by Joseph Conrad to Edward Noble in 1895. London: Privately printed, 1925.

Joseph Conrad's Letters to his Wife. London: Privately printed, 1927.

Joseph Conrad: Life and Letters. Edited by G. Jean-Aubry. 2 vols. Garden City, New York: Doubleday, 1927.

Conrad to a Friend: 150 Selected Letters from Joseph Conrad to Richard Curle. Edited by Richard Curle. New York: Crosby, Gaige, 1928.

Letters from Joseph Conrad, 1895–1924. Edited by Edward Garnett. Indianapolis: Bobbs-Merrill, 1928.

Lettres Françaises. Edited by G. Jean-Aubry. Paris: Gallimard, 1929.

Letters of Joseph Conrad to Marguerite Poradowska, 1890–1920. Edited by John A. Gee and Paul J. Sturm. New Haven: Yale University Press, 1940. (Published in French in Geneva, Switzerland, by Librairie Droz, René Rapin, ed., 1966.)

Joseph Conrad: Letters to William Blackwood and David S. Meldrum. Edited by William Blackburn. Durham, N.C.: Duke University Press, 1958.

Conrad's Polish Background: Letters to and from Polish Friends. Edited by Zdzisław Najder. London: Oxford University Press, 1964.

Joseph Conrad and Warrington Dawson: The Record of a Friendship. Edited by Dale B. J. Randall. Durham, N.C.: Duke University Press, 1968.

Joseph Conrad's Letters to Cunninghame Graham. Edited by C. T. Watts. Cambridge, England: Cambridge University Press, 1969.

SELECTED WRITINGS ABOUT CONRAD

BOOKS AND ARTICLES

Allen, Jerry. *The Sea Years of Joseph Conrad*. New York: Doubleday, 1965. Some good sleuthing into Conrad's sea career, but with weak interpretations and conclusions.

Baines, Jocelyn. *Joseph Conrad*. New York: McGraw-Hill, 1960. For many years, a standard biography, but with naïve critical interpretations of Conrad's work.

Berman, Jeffrey. *Joseph Conrad: Writing as Rescue.* New York: Astra Books, 1977. An analysis of Conrad's imagination as it derived from his attempt at suicide.

Bradbrook, M. C. *Joseph Conrad: Poland's English Genius.* Cambridge, England: Cambridge University Press, 1941. An early attempt to grapple with his major themes.

Conrad, Jessie (Mrs. Joseph). *Joseph Conrad and His Circle.* New York: Dutton, 1935.

———. *Joseph Conrad: As I Knew Him.* Garden City: Doubleday, 1926.

"Conrad Supplement," *Transatlantic Review,* II (3): 454–65, 570–82, 689–700 (August 1924). Evaluations after Conrad's death.

Crankshaw, Edward. *Joseph Conrad: Some Aspects of the Art of the Novel.* London: John Lane, 1936.

Curle, Richard. *Joseph Conrad and His Characters.* London: Heinemann, 1957.

———. *Joseph Conrad: A Study.* London: Kegan, Paul, Trench, Trubner, 1914. The first book-length study, by a devoted friend.

———. *The Last Twelve Years of Joseph Conrad.* London: Sampson, Low, Marston, 1928.

Dowden, Wilfred S. "*Almayer's Folly and Lord Jim:* A Study in the Development of Conrad's Imagery." *Rice University Studies,* LI: 13–27 (Winter 1965).

———. "The 'Illuminating Quality': Imagery and Theme in *The Secret Agent.*" *Rice Institute Pamphlets,* XLVII: 17–33 (October 1960).

Fleishman, Avrom. *Conrad's Politics: Community and Anarchy in the Fiction of Joseph Conrad.* Baltimore: Johns Hopkins Press, 1967. A study that attempts to place Conrad in the English tradition of Burke and Mill.

Ford, Ford Madox. *Joseph Conrad: A Personal Remembrance.* Boston: Little Brown, 1924. Insights into Conrad's novelistic techniques, intermixed with much unsubstantiated material.

Gillon, Adam. *Conrad and Shakespeare.* New York: Astra Books, 1976. Mainly, Shakespearean influence and language working within Conrad's books; valuable chapter on "Conrad and Poland."

———. *The Eternal Solitary: A Study of Joseph Conrad.* New York: Bookman, 1960. Stress on themes of isolation in Conrad's work.

Gordan, John Dozier. *Joseph Conrad: The Making of a Novelist.* Cambridge, Mass.: Harvard University Press, 1941. A classic of Conrad scholarship, especially for the early novels. Serious Conrad scholarship begins here.

Graver, Lawrence. *Conrad's Short Fiction.* Berkeley: University of California Press, 1969. Argues that Conrad was essentially a short-story writer whose novels slackened beyond a certain point.

Guerard, Albert. *Conrad the Novelist.* Cambridge, Mass.: Harvard University Press, 1958. An important critical study of the major fiction.

———. *Joseph Conrad.* New York: New Directions, 1947.

Guetti, James. " 'Heart of Darkness': The Failure of Imagination." In his *The Limits of Metaphor: A Study of Melville, Conrad, and Faulkner.* Ithaca, N.Y.: Cornell University Press, 1967.

Gurko, Leo. *Joseph Conrad: Giant in Exile.* New York: Macmillan Paperback, 1962. Criticism of Conrad's work, much of it derivative.

Hay, Eloise Knapp. *The Political Novels of Joseph Conrad.* Chicago: University of Chicago Press, 1963. Important analyses of political themes in Conrad's major novels.

Hewitt, Douglas. *Conrad: A Reassessment.* Cambridge, England: Bowes and Bowes, 1952. An influential interpreter of Conrad's "decline" in his last fifteen years.

Howe, Irving. "Conrad: Order and Anarchy." In his *Politics and the Novel.* New York: Horizon Press, 1957. An attack on Conrad's presentation of socialists and anarchists and his political orientation as a whole.

Jean-Aubry, Gerard. *Joseph Conrad: Life and Letters.* 2 vols. Garden City, New York: Doubleday, 1927. The first fleshed-out account of Conrad's life and the source of many important letters; now outdated as to fact and focus. A short, later biography called *The Sea Dreamer* (New York: Doubleday, 1957) adds little to the original study and is equally misleading as to fact and focus.

Johnson, Bruce. *Conrad's Models of Mind.* Minneapolis: University of Minnesota Press, 1971. An examination of Conrad's various models, whether Schopenhauer, Pascal, or others.

Karl, Frederick R. "Conrad and Gide." *Comparative Literature,* XXIX: 148–71 (Spring 1977).

———. "Conrad's Literary Theory." *Criticism,* II: 317–36 (Fall 1960).

———. "Conrad, Wells, and the Two Voices." *PMLA,* LXXXVIII: 1049–66 (October 1973).

———. *A Reader's Guide to Joseph Conrad.* New York: Farrar, Straus & Giroux (Noonday Press), 1960; revised edition, 1969. Discussions of all Conrad's novels and stories.

Kramer, Dale. "Marlow, Myth, and Structure in *Lord Jim.*" *Criticism,* VIII: 263–79 (Summer 1966).

Leavis, F. R. *The Great Tradition.* London: Chatto and Windus, 1948. The placement of Conrad in a tradition that includes Austen, Eliot, James, and Lawrence.

Mégroz, R. L. *Joseph Conrad's Mind and Method: A Study of Personality in Art.* London: Faber and Faber, 1931. Discussions of Conrad's attachments to Poland as manifest in his thought and art.

Meyer, Bernard. *Joseph Conrad: A Psychoanalytic Biography.* Princeton, N.J.: Princeton University Press, 1967. An important Freudian reading of Conrad's life and work, with stress upon mother worship, illness, and fetishes.

Morf, Gustav. *The Polish Heritage of Joseph Conrad.* London: Sampson, Low, Marston, 1930. This and the succeeding book attempt to tie Conrad inextricably to his Polish background; the idea has become increasingly influential.

———. *The Polish Shades and Ghosts of Joseph Conrad.* New York: Astra Books, 1976.

Moser, Thomas. *Joseph Conrad: Achievement and Decline.* Cambridge: Harvard University Press, 1957. An influential book that analyzes Conrad's decline after *Under Western Eyes.*

Najder, Zdzisław. *Conrad's Polish Background: Letters to and from Polish Friends.* London: Oxford University Press, 1964. Important documentation of Conrad's Polish heritage; of particular significance is the translation into English of the Bobrowski "Document."

Nettels, Elsa. *James & Conrad.* Athens, Ga.: University of Georgia Press, 1977. A scholarly analysis of the friendship and literary relationship.

Palmer, John A. *Joseph Conrad's Fiction: A Study in Literary Growth.* Ithaca, N.Y.: Cornell University Press, 1968. The chapter " 'Achievement and Decline': A Bibliographical Note" is of importance.

Perry, John Oliver. "Action, Vision, or Voice: The Moral Dilemmas in Conrad's Tale-Telling." *Modern Fiction Studies,* X: 3–14 (Spring 1964).

Retinger, J. H. *Conrad and His Contemporaries.* London: Minerva Publishing Co., 1941. Some interesting stories, which may or may not be true.

Rosenfield, Claire. *Paradise of Snakes: An Archetypal Analysis of Conrad's Political Novels.* Chicago: University of Chicago Press, 1967. Mainly Jungian analyses of *Nostromo, The Secret Agent,* and *Under Western Eyes.*

Sherry, Norman. *Conrad: The Critical Heritage.* London: Routledge and Kegan Paul, 1973. A valuable collection of reviews and comments on Conrad's works by contemporaries.

———. *Conrad's Eastern World.* Cambridge, England: Cambridge University Press, 1966. Solid documentation of Conrad's early sailing career and its influence on his fiction.

———. *Conrad's Western World.* Cambridge, England: Cambridge University Press, 1971. Some very intelligent sleuthing into the sources of "Heart of Darkness," *Nostromo, The Secret Agent,* and related stories.

Tanner, Tony. "Butterflies and Beetles—Conrad's Two Truths." *Chicago Review,* VI: 123–40 (Winter-Spring 1963).

———. "Nightmare and Complacency: Razumov and the Western Eye." *Critical Quarterly,* IV: 197–214 (Autumn 1962).

Thorburn, David. *Conrad's Romanticism.* New Haven, Conn.: Yale University Press, 1974. Discussions of Conrad in relationship to romantic adventure fiction of the later nineteenth century.

Van Ghent, Dorothy. "On *Lord Jim.*" In her *The English Novel: Form and Function.* New York: Rinehart, 1953.

Warren, Robert Penn. Introduction to *Nostromo.* Modern Library Edition. New York: Random House, 1951. [Reprinted from *Sewanee Review,* LIX: 363–91 (Summer 1951).] An important reading that should be compared with Van Ghent's.

Watt, Ian. "Conrad Criticism and *The Nigger of the 'Narcissus.'* " *Nineteenth-Century Fiction,* XII: 257–83 (March 1958).

———. "Joseph Conrad: Alienation and Commitment." In *The English Mind,* edited by H. S. Davies and George Watson. Cambridge, England: Cambridge University Press, 1964.

Wiley, Paul. *Conrad's Measure of Man.* Madison: University of Wisconsin Press, 1954.

Young, Vernon. "Joseph Conrad: Outline for a Reconsideration." *Hudson Review,* II: 5–19 (Spring 1949).

Zabel, Morton Dauwen. "Conrad." Various essays in *Craft and Character in Modern Fiction.* New York: Viking, 1957. Important studies of Conrad in the revival of interest in his work in the 1940s and 1950s.

COLLECTIONS OF ESSAYS

Karl, Frederick R., ed. *Joseph Conrad: A Collection of Criticism.* New York: McGraw-Hill, 1975. Essays on the major fiction.

Krzyżanowski, Ludwik, ed. *Joseph Conrad: Centennial Essays.* New York: The Polish Institute of Arts and Sciences in America, 1960.

Lehmann, John, ed. *The London Magazine,* IV (11): 21–49 (November 1957).

Mudrick, Marvin, ed. *Conrad: A Collection of Critical Essays.* Englewood Cliffs, N.J.: Prentice-Hall, 1966. A valuable but eccentric presentation of Conrad.

Stallman, Robert Wooster, ed. *The Art of Joseph Conrad: A Critical Symposium.* East Lansing: Michigan State University Press, 1960. A solid and representative selection of criticism.

ANTHOLOGIES

Zabel, Morton Dauwen, ed. (updated by Frederick R. Karl). *The Portable Conrad.* New York: Viking Press, 1947 (1969). Selections from Conrad's work, including novels, stories, letters, and personal writings; with a long introduction, commentary, and bibliography.

Index